Architectural Desktop
and Its Applications

Ron Palma
AEC Solutions Application Specialist, Ideate, Inc.
Owner/Operator, 3D-DZYN
Canby, Oregon

David A. Madsen
Faculty Emeritus, Former Chairperson of Drafting Technology
Autodesk Premier Training Center, Clackamas Community College
Director Emeritus, American Design Drafting Association
Oregon City, Oregon

2007

Publisher
The Goodheart-Willcox Company, Inc.
Tinley Park, Illinois
www.g-w.com

Library of Congress Catalog Card Number 2006050828

ISBN 978-1-59070-796-8

1 2 3 4 5 6 7 8 9—07—11 10 09 08 07

Library of Congress Cataloging-in-Publication Data

Madsen, David A.
    Architectural desktop and its applications 2007/David A. Madsen, Ron M. Palma.
       p. cm.
    ISBN 978-1-59070-796-8
    1. Architectural drawing—Computer-aided design. 2. Autodesk Architectural desktop. 3. AutoCAD. I. Palma, Ron M. II. Title.
    NA2728.M3453 2007
    720.28'40285536—dc22

                                                    2006050828

Autodesk's Architectural Desktop is designed to aid the architect, designer, and drafter through all phases of construction document creation. From the earliest stages of conceptual design, through design development, and finally to the finished set of drawings, Architectural Desktop provides the appropriate tools for getting the job done. Architectural Desktop is a set of architectural tools built into the AutoCAD platform. With standard AutoCAD, you have tools such as lines, arcs, circles, and text to complete your design needs. With the addition of object-oriented tools known as Architecture, Engineering, and Construction (AEC) objects, the design process with Architectural Desktop is moved to a new level. The AEC objects are divided into the three major phases of workflow: conceptual design, design development, and documentation drawings. This text provides you with the real-world knowledge and skills needed to accomplish your architectural drawing needs using Architectural Desktop.

Architectural Desktop and Its Applications is a text providing complete coverage of Architectural Desktop. This text is designed to introduce you to the AEC objects and commands used in Architectural Desktop to complete a set of construction documents. The chapters are arranged in an easy-to-understand format, beginning with basic topics and working toward advanced subjects. This text makes the assumption that you have a basic understanding of AutoCAD, although the most important AutoCAD commands relevant to Architectural Desktop are discussed for beginning AutoCAD users and as a review for trained AutoCAD users. *Architectural Desktop and Its Applications* provides a detailed explanation of the Architectural Desktop tools that aid in producing professional and accurate drawings. This text is intended for anyone who wants to learn how to use Architectural Desktop effectively to create real-world construction documents and drawings and can be used in secondary, postsecondary, and technical schools. *Architectural Desktop and Its Applications* provides the beginning student and the drafting or architectural professional with a complete understanding of Architectural Desktop commands using professional drafting methods and techniques. All software commands are presented in a manner that shows the exact input to be used. This text also contains the following variety of valuable features that help make learning Architectural Desktop easy:

- It is easy to read, use, and understand.
- Learning objectives are provided at the beginning of each chapter to identify what you will learn as a result of completing the chapter.
- Commands are presented in a manner that shows the exact input you should use.
- Notes explain special, alternate, or related applications for using Architectural Desktop.
- Professional Tips provide tricks and tips for using Architectural Desktop.
- Exercises are provided throughout for you to practice as you learn Architectural Desktop.
- Residential and light commercial projects allow you to learn how to use Architectural Desktop in your drafting, engineering, or architectural field.
- Chapter Tests, included on the enclosed Student CD, provide you with the opportunity to review each chapter by answering questions related to the chapter content.

Format of This Text

The format of this text helps you learn how to use Architectural Desktop by example and through complete explanations of each feature. The Student CD also supports your learning. The Exercises allow you to practice while you learn specific content. The Student CD includes Chapter Tests, which provide you with an excellent way to review chapter content.

Accessing Architectural Desktop Commands

In addition to listing available command selection methods, all options are described within the text. For example, the **WALL** command can be accessed by picking **Design** > **Walls** > **Add Wall...** from the pull-down menu, picking the **Wall** tool in the **Design** tool palette, or typing WALLADD. When the command is presented as if it is typed at the keyboard, any available keyboard shortcut is given along with the full command name. One goal of this book is to show you all the methods of using Architectural Desktop commands so you can decide which methods work best for you.

Special Features

Architectural Desktop and Its Applications contains several special features that help you learn and use Architectural Desktop. These features are explained in the following sections.

Learning Objectives

Each chapter leads with learning objectives related to the chapter content. The following is an example of how the objectives are presented.
After completing this book, you will be able to do the following:
- Use Architectural Desktop to prepare drawings for residential and light commercial construction.
- Answer questions related to Architectural Desktop.
- Use Architectural Desktop and drafting-related terminology.
- Do Exercises as you learn Architectural Desktop.
- Use projects to learn Architectural Desktop and create construction documents.

AutoCAD Reviews

Architectural Desktop is a set of architectural tools built into the AutoCAD platform. With standard AutoCAD, you have tools such as lines, arcs, circles, and text to complete your design needs. AutoCAD commands relevant to Architectural Desktop are discussed for beginning AutoCAD users and as a review for trained AutoCAD users. AutoCAD Review features are provided where necessary to help you distinguish AutoCAD instruction from Architectural Desktop content. The more advanced AutoCAD content is found in the general discussion because you might need more than a quick refresher on these topics.

Exercises

An Exercise reference is provided after each Architectural Desktop topic or command lesson, and the Exercises can be found on the enclosed Student CD. The Exercises allow you to practice what you have just learned. Practicing Architectural Desktop applications is one of the most important keys to learning the program effectively. You should complete Exercises at a computer while using Architectural Desktop to reinforce what you have just studied. Some Exercises build on other Exercises, allowing you to develop construction documents as you learn Architectural Desktop. Exercises can be used as only practice or as classroom assignments.

Notes

Notes are another special feature of *Architectural Desktop and Its Applications*. These features are placed throughout the text. Notes provide you with supplemental information related to the current topic and additional instruction about how features work.

Professional Tips

Professional Tips are another special feature of *Architectural Desktop and Its Applications*. These features are placed throughout the text. Professional Tips provide you with professional tips and applications related to the current discussion topic, special features of Architectural Desktop, and advanced applications.

Chapter Projects

Drafting projects are one of the most important ways to complete and solidify your learning and understanding of Architectural Desktop. The projects allow you to put into practice what you have just learned. These drafting projects are different from the Exercises, because the Exercises focus on using the command currently being discussed. The Chapter Projects combine a variety of commands used in the current chapter and past chapters. The projects for every chapter are designed to provide Architectural Desktop practice for residential and light commercial construction. You or your instructor can select the projects relating directly to your specific course objectives. The projects provided in this text are real-world architectural design projects. These projects allow you to finish one complete set or several complete sets of construction documents for a residential or light commercial building as you progress through this text.

Basics through Advanced Coverage

Architectural Desktop and Its Applications covers basic and advanced topics in nearly every chapter. Chapter content begins with basic applications and progresses into advanced topics where appropriate. The basic material generally covers fundamental AutoCAD and Architectural Desktop applications, and the advanced coverage normally involves creating styles and other customization activities.

The content is well rounded for everyone at all levels of learning. The chapters are divided into the types of features used to create architectural drawings. The chapter organization follows the order an architect, a designer, or a drafter commonly uses when creating construction documents in an architectural office.

Students like the idea of having both the basic and advanced material in the same text. This approach benefits those who catch on quickly and want additional challenge. Even if the instructor chooses to cover only the basic material, those students who want to can explore on their own or seek extra credit, if appropriate with course objectives.

Ron Palma
David A. Madsen

About the Authors

Ron Palma is an Autodesk Certified Instructor and the owner and operator of 3D-DZYN in Canby, Oregon. Ron has over 20 years of experience in the architectural industry as a drafter, designer, lead project designer, and most recently, CAD Manager. As a CAD Manager, Ron has been implementing Autodesk Architectural Desktop for Alan Mascord Design Associates in Portland, Oregon, a leading residential design firm. He has also specialized in the professional training of companies and individuals on the Autodesk AEC product line for two Autodesk resellers, as well as an educator at Clackamas Community College and Portland Community College in Portland, Oregon. Ron continues to write professional training manuals and is a coauthor of the Goodheart-Willcox textbook *Architectural Drafting Using AutoCAD*.

David A. Madsen is Faculty Emeritus and a former Chairperson of Drafting Technology at the Autodesk Premier Training Center at Clackamas Community College, in Oregon City, Oregon. David was awarded Director Emeritus of the American Design Drafting Association. His education includes a Bachelor of Science degree in Technology Education and a Master of Education degree in Vocational Administration. During his teaching career, David was an instructor and a department chair at Clackamas Community College for nearly 30 years. In addition to having community college teaching experience, David was a Drafting Technology instructor at Centennial High School in Gresham, Oregon. David also has extensive experience in mechanical drafting, architectural design and drafting, and construction practices. He is a coauthor of several Goodheart-Willcox drafting and design textbooks, including *Architectural Drafting Using AutoCAD* and the *AutoCAD and Its Applications* series, and the author of *Geometric Dimensioning and Tolerancing*.

Acknowledgments

We would like to express our appreciation of professional support from Jon Epley and Alan Mascord; Alan Mascord Design Associates, Inc., www.mascord.com; SERA Architects, www.serapdx.com; and Scott Brown with Quarterpoint Design Group.

Contents in Brief

Table of Contents

Chapter 6
Display Commands

Chapter 7
The Architectural Desktop Display System

Chapter 8
Layer Management

Chapter 9
Architectural Blocks

Chapter 10
Working with Structural Members

Chapter 11
Adding Text and Dimensions

Chapter 21
Space Planning

Chapter 22
Using Schedules

Chapter 23
Creating Custom Schedule Information

Chapter 24
Sheets and Plotting

Chapter 25
Conceptual Design

Student CD Content

Using the Student CD

Textbook Exercises

Chapter Tests

Appendices

     A. Standard Pull-Down Menus
     B. Working with Tools, Tool Palettes, and the Content Browser
     C. Tools and Tool Palette Groups
     D. Typical Sheet-Numbering Conventions
     E. American Institute of Architects (AIA)–Layering Standards
     F. Drawing Name Conventions
     G. Introduction to the Construction Specifications Institute (CSI)
     H. AEC Object Display Representations
     I. Display Sets
     J. Display Configurations and Their Uses
     K. Standard Tables
     L. File Management
     M. AEC Wall Priorities
     N. Using Ceiling Grids
     O. Using Column Grids
     P. Creating Details
     Q. Using Keynotes

Related Web Sites

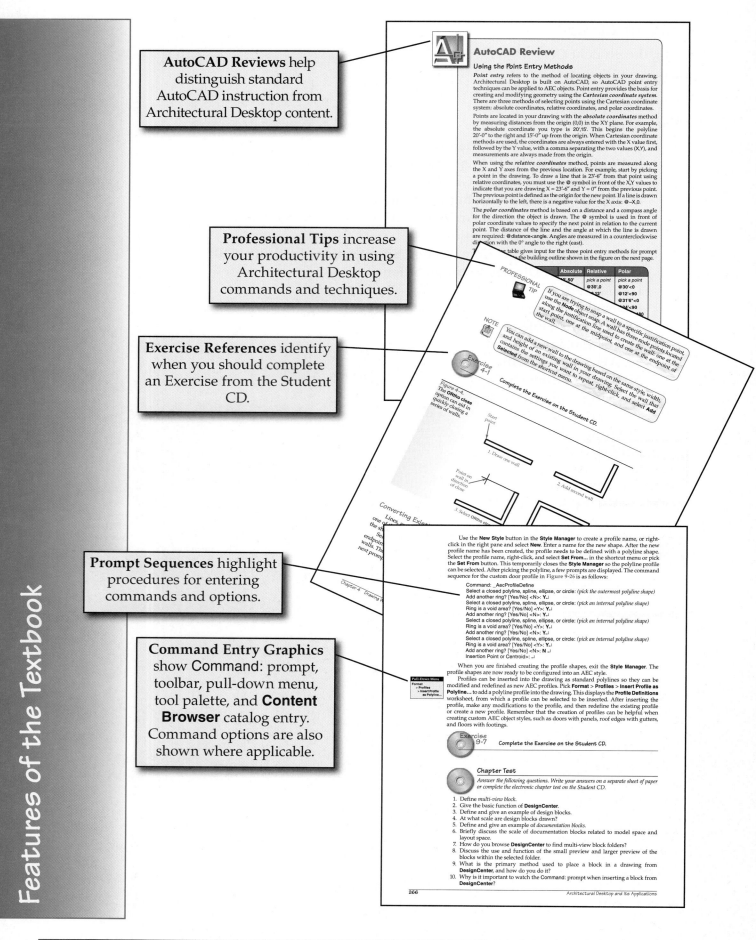

AutoCAD Reviews help distinguish standard AutoCAD instruction from Architectural Desktop content.

Professional Tips increase your productivity in using Architectural Desktop commands and techniques.

Exercise References identify when you should complete an Exercise from the Student CD.

Prompt Sequences highlight procedures for entering commands and options.

Command Entry Graphics show Command: prompt, toolbar, pull-down menu, tool palette, and **Content Browser** catalog entry. Command options are also shown where applicable.

Illustrations, including Architectural Desktop "screen shots" and line art illustrations, make learning easy.

Notes explain important aspects of a topic.

Learning Objectives identify the key items you will learn in the chapter.

Chapter Tests reinforce the knowledge gained while reading the chapter and completing the Exercises.

Chapter Projects require application of chapter concepts and problem-solving techniques.

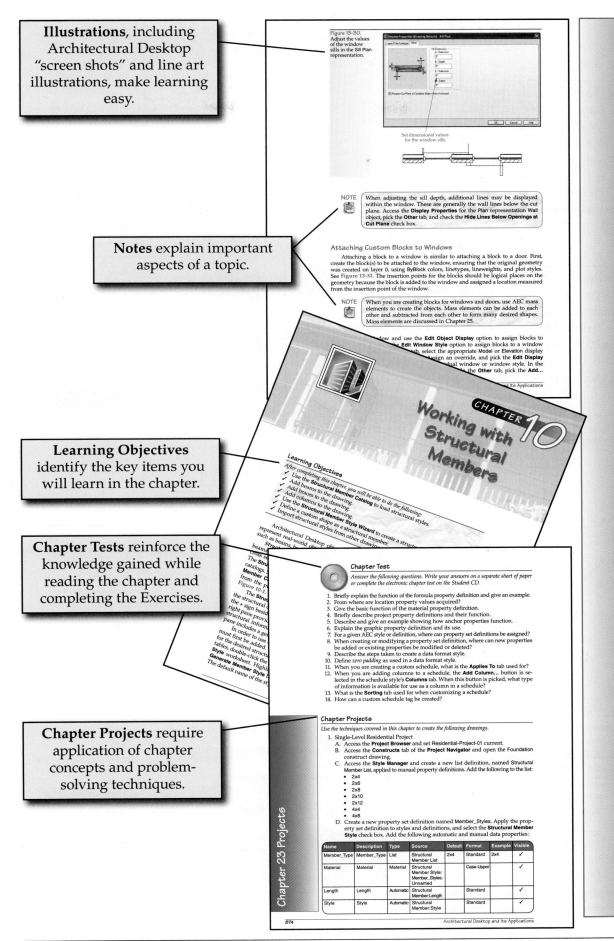

Figure 13-30.
Adjust the values of the window sills in the Sill Plan representation.

Set dimensional values for the window sills

NOTE When adjusting the sill depth, additional lines may be displayed within the window. These are generally the wall lines below the cut plane. Access the **Display Properties** for the Plan representation Wall object, pick the **Other** tab, and check the **Hide Lines Below Openings at Cut Plane** check box.

Attaching Custom Blocks to Windows

Attaching a block to a window is similar to attaching a block to a door. First, create the block(s) to be attached to the window, ensuring that the original geometry was created on layer 0, using ByBlock colors, linetypes, lineweights, and plot styles. See Figure 13-31. The insertion points for the blocks should be logical places on the geometry because the block is added to the window and assigned a location measured from the insertion point of the window.

NOTE When you are creating blocks for windows and doors, use AEC mass elements to create the objects. Mass elements can be added to each other and subtracted from each other to form many desired shapes. Mass elements are discussed in Chapter 25.

CHAPTER 10
Working with Structural Members

Learning Objectives

After completing this chapter, you will be able to do the following:
✓ Use the **Structural Member Catalog** to load structural styles.
✓ Add beams to the drawing.
✓ Add braces to the drawing.
✓ Add columns to the drawing.
✓ Use the **Structural Member Style Wizard** to create a struct...
✓ Define a custom shape as a structural member.
✓ Import structural styles from other drawing...

Chapter Test

Answer the following questions. Write your answers on a separate sheet of paper or complete the electronic chapter test on the Student CD.

1. Briefly explain the function of the formula property definition and give an example.
2. From where are location property values acquired?
3. Give the basic function of the material property definition.
4. Briefly describe project property definitions and their function.
5. Describe and give an example showing how anchor properties function.
6. Explain the graphic property definition and its use.
7. For a given AEC style or definition, where can property set definitions be assigned?
8. When creating or modifying a property set definition, where can new properties be added or existing properties be modified or deleted?
9. Describe the steps taken to create a data format style.
10. Define *zero padding* as used in a data format style.
11. When you are creating a custom schedule, what is the **Applies To** tab used for?
12. When you are adding columns to a schedule, the **Add Column...** button is selected in the schedule style's **Columns** tab. When this button is picked, what type of information is available for use as a column in a schedule?
13. What is the **Sorting** tab used for when customizing a schedule?
14. How can a custom schedule tag be created?

Chapter Projects

Use the techniques covered in this chapter to create the following drawings.

1. Single-Level Residential Project
   A. Access the **Project Browser** and set Residential-Project-01 current.
   B. Access the **Constructs** tab of the **Project Navigator** and open the Foundation construct drawing.
   C. Access the **Style Manager** and create a new list definition, named Structural Member List, applied to manual property definitions. Add the following to the list:
   - 2x4
   - 2x6
   - 2x8
   - 2x10
   - 2x12
   - 4x4
   - 4x8
   D. Create a new property set definition named Member_Styles. Apply the property set definition to styles and definitions, and select the **Structural Member Style** check box. Add the following automatic and manual data properties:

Name	Description	Type	Source	Default	Format	Example	Visible
Member_Type	Member_Type	List	Structural Member List	2x4	Standard	2x4	✓
Material	Material	Material	Structural Member Style: Member_Styles: Unnamed		Case-Upper		✓
Length	Length	Automatic	Structural Member:Length		Standard		✓
Style	Style	Automatic	Structural Member:Style		Standard		✓

Chapter 23 Projects

874　Architectural Desktop and Its Applications

Features of the Textbook

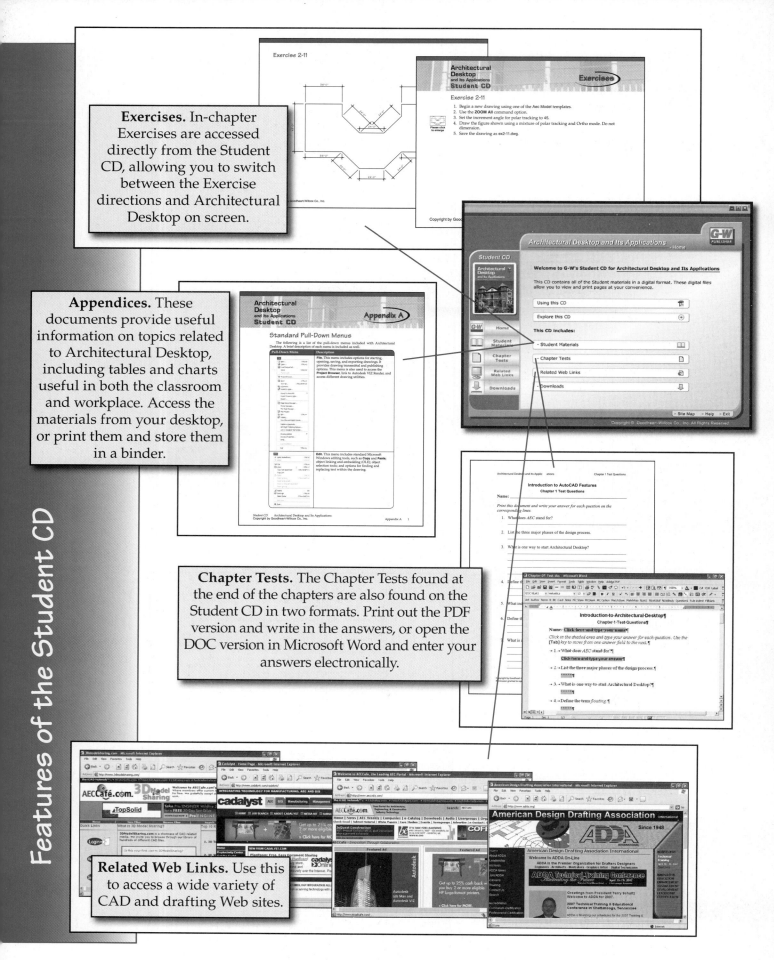

Exercises. In-chapter Exercises are accessed directly from the Student CD, allowing you to switch between the Exercise directions and Architectural Desktop on screen.

Appendices. These documents provide useful information on topics related to Architectural Desktop, including tables and charts useful in both the classroom and workplace. Access the materials from your desktop, or print them and store them in a binder.

Chapter Tests. The Chapter Tests found at the end of the chapters are also found on the Student CD in two formats. Print out the PDF version and write in the answers, or open the DOC version in Microsoft Word and enter your answers electronically.

Related Web Links. Use this to access a wide variety of CAD and drafting Web sites.

Features of the Student CD

CHAPTER 1

Introduction to Architectural Desktop

Learning Objectives

After completing this chapter, you will be able to do the following:
- ✓ Discuss the purpose and function of Architectural Desktop.
- ✓ Compare AutoCAD® and Architectural Desktop.
- ✓ Describe conceptual design.
- ✓ Discuss design development.
- ✓ Describe construction documentation.
- ✓ Identify the features of the Architectural Desktop window.
- ✓ Use Architectural Desktop palettes and menus.
- ✓ Access and use dialog boxes and worksheets.
- ✓ Create user interface workspaces.
- ✓ Use the **Autodesk® Architectural Desktop 2007 Help** window.

Architectural Desktop 2007 is an AutoCAD-based product used to create architectural drawings and models. Architectural Desktop is a stand-alone software package that combines the standard AutoCAD environment and drafting tools with special Architecture, Engineering, and Construction (AEC) objects. AEC objects within a project relate intelligently with each other. For example, a door object knows that it must be inside a wall object and that it must maintain properties about itself such as width, height, and type of material. See **Figure 1-1**.

The AEC objects maintain data and work together throughout the drawing's life cycle. They work with standard AutoCAD commands, allowing you to use your existing AutoCAD knowledge. The AEC objects are useful in both 2D and 3D drafting. You can continue with 2D drafting practices using AEC objects, and 3D representations of these objects are also provided for creating 3D models, **Figure 1-2**.

Figure 1-1.
AEC objects work interactively with each other. A door object understands that it must reside within a wall object.

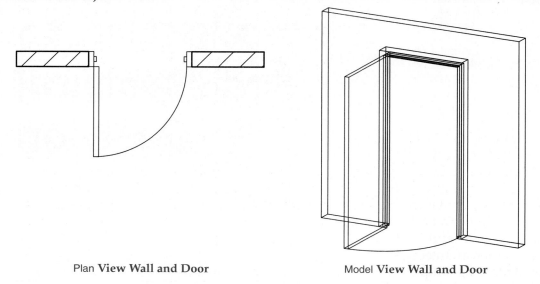

Plan **View Wall and Door**   Model **View Wall and Door**

Figure 1-2.
AEC objects can be displayed as flat 2D geometry in a plan view or as 3D geometry in a model view.

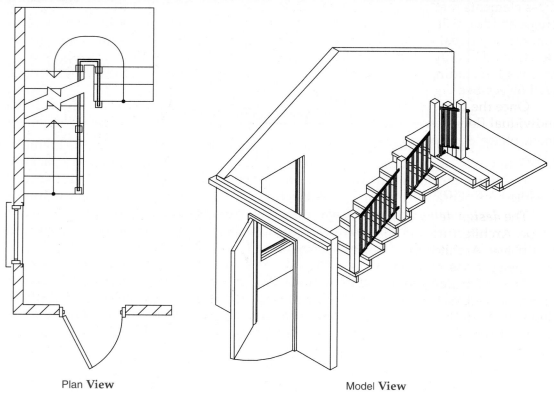

Plan **View**   Model **View**

Architectural Desktop is built on the AutoCAD platform with several significant additions, including AEC objects. The AEC objects are divided into the three major phases that mirror design development: conceptual design, design development, and construction documentation. Similarly, designs have three stages of development to develop, refine, and document the design to complete a set of construction documents.

Conceptual Design

Most architectural projects begin with a phase called *conceptual design*. In traditional design, concepts or ideas often consist of many hand-sketched drawings on paper, from which a design is chosen. Architectural Desktop advances the traditional design process by providing conceptual design tools. Objects known as *mass elements* are 3D shapes that can be brought together to form a massing study. A *massing study* is the study of a building in its general form before detail has been added. This type of study is useful in the early design phase to compare the model to its surroundings. When architects perform massing studies, the immediate surroundings are often created using simple forms to give a sense how the building fits into the surroundings and to demonstrate how the new building interacts and impacts its surrounding environment. However, sometimes only the building is modeled so its overall form can be evaluated for function and aesthetics. A building modeled in this way is called a *mass model*. A mass model is made of a *mass group*, which is made of one or more mass elements that have been combined. These objects are object oriented, so you can create an idea in 3D and a plan in the 2D environment. *Object oriented* refers to tools that represent real world objects such as walls, doors, and windows and have specific functions that only apply to the specific tool. For example, a wall object represents a true wall, including a width and height property that can be adjusted to modify the wall object. See Figure 1-3.

Once the conceptual design has been finalized, the 3D model can be divided into individual floors known as *floor slices*, as shown in Figure 1-4. The design development phase can begin from the floor slices by converting the floor slices into floor plans.

Design Development

The *design development* phase is when the construction documents begin to take shape. Architectural elements such as walls, doors, windows, and stairs are drawn in this phase. Architectural Desktop provides tools and objects to help you create floor plans, elevations, and sections. See Figure 1-5.

The design development phase carries the design from its very early stage through to its final design. As key elements such as walls and columns are created, the building design can go through several alterations before a final design is chosen. Once the final design is selected, additional details such as exact door and window sizes, proper stair locations, and correct wall thickness can be drawn in preparation for the next phase of work.

Figure 1-3.
Mass elements and mass groups are tools that can be used to create conceptual design ideas.

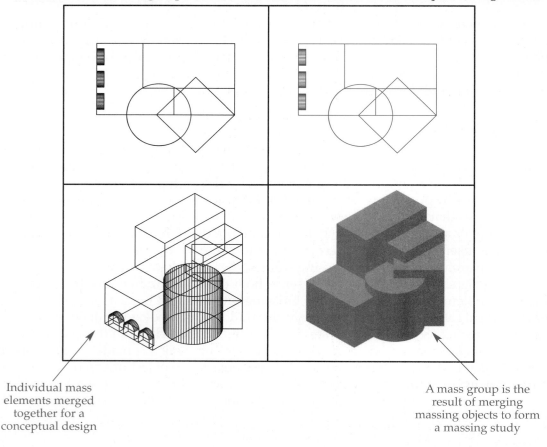

Individual mass
elements merged
together for a
conceptual design

A mass group is the
result of merging
massing objects to form
a massing study

Figure 1-4.
A mass group can be cut into floor slices for development into floor plans.

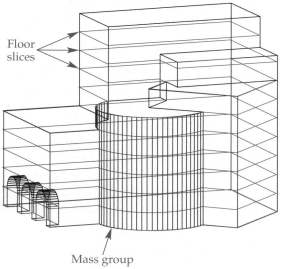

Floor
slices

Mass group

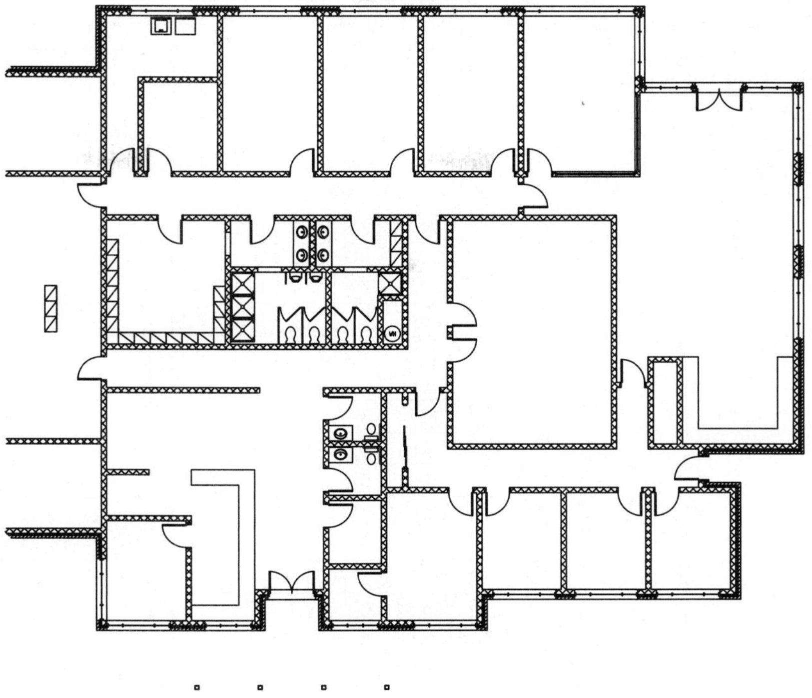

Figure 1-5.
The design development phase is used to develop the layout for the building.

Construction Documentation

After the building design has been fully developed, the construction documents can be completed with the addition of dimensions, detail bubbles, notes, and any other necessary documentation. Architectural Desktop includes many symbols that help you to easily document your drawing. See **Figure 1-6.**

As you add AEC objects to the drawing, you can include information about them that can then be extracted and sorted into schedules and inventories. This information can be updated automatically as the design changes during the creation of the construction documents. A door and frame schedule is shown in **Figure 1-7.**

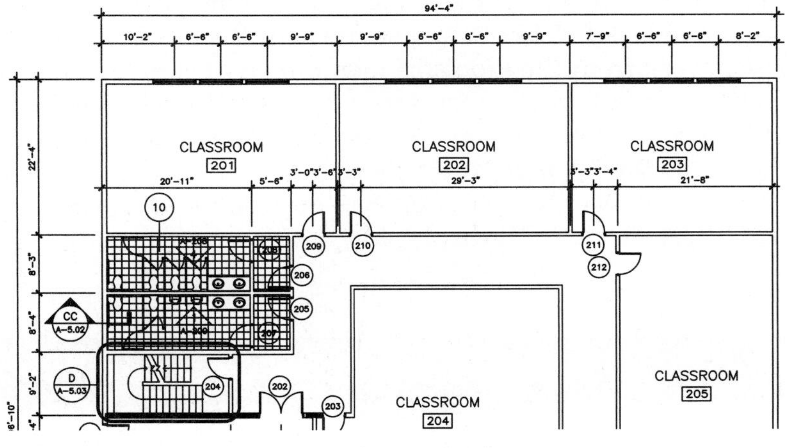

Figure 1-6.
The documentation phase is used to dimension, note, and add detail callouts to the drawing to complete the construction documents.

Figure 1-7.
The documentation
phase includes
creating schedules
that can be
generated from
the objects in the
drawing.

DOOR AND FRAME SCHEDULE

MARK	DOOR SIZE			MATL	FIRE RATING LABEL	NOTES
	WD	HGT	THK			
201	6'-0"	7'-0"	1 3/4"	METAL	2-HR	Double door
202	6'-0"	7'-0"	1 3/4"	METAL	2-HR	Double door
203	3'-0"	7'-0"	1 3/4"		1-HR	
204	3'-0"	7'-0"	1 3/4"		1-HR	
205	3'-0"	7'-0"	1 3/4"		1-HR	
206	3'-0"	7'-0"	1 3/4"		1-HR	
207	3'-0"	7'-0"	1 3/4"			
208	3'-0"	7'-0"	1 3/4"			
209	3'-0"	7'-0"	1 3/4"		1-HR	
210	3'-0"	7'-0"	1 3/4"		1-HR	
211	3'-0"	7'-0"	1 3/4"		1-HR	
212	3'-0"	7'-0"	1 3/4"		1-HR	
213	3'-0"	7'-0"	1 3/4"		1-HR	
214	3'-0"	7'-0"	1 3/4"		1-HR	
215	6'-0"	7'-0"	1 3/4"	METAL	2-HR	Double door

Starting Architectural Desktop

After Architectural Desktop has been installed on your computer, a *desktop icon* for this program is displayed on the Windows desktop. To start Architectural Desktop, double-click the icon with your mouse.

NOTE *Double-click* means to pick the left mouse button twice quickly.

An alternative method of starting Architectural Desktop is to select the Start button on the left side of the Windows taskbar on your desktop. The Windows Start menu is displayed. Select Programs from the Start menu to display the Programs menu. Pick Autodesk from the Programs menu, then pick Autodesk Architectural Desktop 2007 from the Autodesk menu, then select Autodesk Architectural Desktop 2007 or its icon to start the program. If a dialog box asks you to select a workspace, select any workspace and pick the **Do not show again** check box.

Once Architectural Desktop has been launched, the program is loaded, and a default drawing screen is displayed.

The Architectural Desktop Window

The Architectural Desktop window is similar to other Windows-compliant programs in organization and handling. Picking the small control icon in the upper-left corner displays a standard Windows control menu, and the upper-right corner buttons allow you to minimize, maximize, and close Architectural Desktop. Each individual drawing file also includes these three buttons, allowing you to control each of the drawing windows. As in other Windows programs, resizing a window requires that the mouse cursor be moved to the edge of the window until a double-arrow cursor appears indicating the direction the window can be stretched. Pick and hold the left mouse button and move the mouse to stretch the window to the desired size.

Architectural Desktop uses the familiar Windows interface, which includes the use of toolbar buttons, tool palettes, pull-down menus, shortcut menus, and dialog boxes. Common commands such as **New**, **Open**, and **Print** are in the same locations as in other Windows programs. **Figure 1-8** shows the Architectural Desktop window.

The Architectural Desktop Window Layout

The Architectural Desktop window provides a large drawing area with tools arranged around the edges. By default, the drawing window is bordered by *toolbars* at the top edge of the screen, by tool palettes along the left edge, and by the command window at the bottom of the screen.

 NOTE The proportions of the Architectural Desktop window vary depending on the current display resolution. The minimum recommended display resolution is 1024 × 768. A resolution of 1280 × 1024 allows you to see all the toolbars that are initially turned on in Architectural Desktop.

Many of the features within Architectural Desktop are *floating*, which means they can be resized and moved around within the window. A standard Windows border at the top of a feature indicates that the toolbar or dialog box is floating above the drawing screen. The border along the top of the floating feature gives the drawing name, toolbar name, or dialog box name. When the border is highlighted, that feature is considered active. An active drawing window is where drafting takes place. Active toolbars or dialog boxes require buttons or settings to be selected in order to draw.

Figure 1-8.
The Architectural Desktop window uses an organization similar to the standard AutoCAD environment. These features are docked.

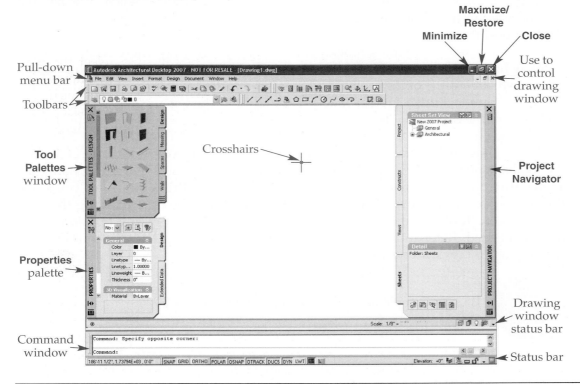

Figure 1-9.
The features in this Architectural Desktop window are floating.

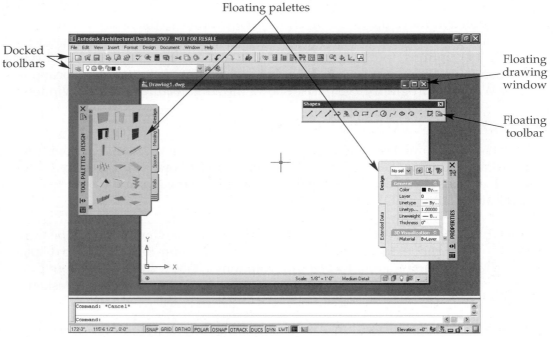

When Architectural Desktop is first started, the Architectural Desktop window is displayed floating on the Windows desktop. The drawing window, which is docked by default, is the smaller window within the Architectural Desktop window. The drawing window can only be adjusted within the Architectural Desktop window. See **Figure 1-9.**

Some features, such as toolbars, can be *docked* in place. Docked toolbars do not display a border or title bar; instead, they display a *grab bar*. A grab bar consists of the two thin bars at the top or left edge of the toolbar. The *title bar* is the bar across the top of the toolbar that gives the name of the toolbar. A docked toolbar has no title bar and is embedded in the program window. To move a toolbar from a docked position to a floating position, double-click the grab bars. This places the toolbar in a floating position on your screen. A floating toolbar can be freely moved anywhere on the drawing window by picking and holding the left mouse button on the title bar. When a toolbar is dragged, an outline of the toolbar is displayed attached to your pointer. An alternative way of undocking a toolbar is to press and hold the left mouse button over the grab bars of the desired toolbar and drag the toolbar away from its docked position.

To dock a toolbar from a floating position, double-click the title bar of a floating toolbar or drag the toolbar to the edge of the screen where you want to dock it. Pick the toolbar's header and move the outline to an edge of the screen until it changes to a long, thin outline and release the left mouse button. The thin outline lets you know that when you release the mouse button, the toolbar will be docked along the edge of the screen. Toolbars and palettes can be moved or docked in any position at any time as needed. Refer to **Figure 1-8** and **Figure 1-9** and your Architectural Desktop window as you review and work with the features.

Exercise 1-1   Complete the Exercise on the Student CD.

Using Pull-Down Menus

Pull-down menus are located on the menu bar across the top of the Architectural Desktop window. The menu bar includes several pull-down menus: **File**, **Edit**, **View**, **Insert**, and **Format**. These include standard AutoCAD commands and some drawing setup commands for Architectural Desktop. The **Window** and **Help** menus are standard Windows menus for arranging drawing windows within Architectural Desktop or for finding help.

Most of the available AutoCAD and Architectural Desktop commands can be found in pull-down menus, shortcut menus, tool palettes, and toolbars; however, some commands are found in only one of these locations. This is why it is very important to familiarize yourself with the layout and tools within Architectural Desktop. Additional pull-down menus included with Architectural Desktop can be loaded by selecting **Window** > **Pulldowns**, which includes the **Design Pulldown**, **Document Pulldown**, **CAD Manager Pulldown**, and **3D Solids Pulldown**. If you select one of these, the corresponding pull-down menu is added to your Architectural Desktop window. The **Design** and **Document** pull-down menus include commands for creating Architectural Desktop objects. Refer to Appendix A on the Student CD for descriptions of the pull-down menus and views of the pull-down menus included with Architectural Desktop.

Exercise 1-2   *Complete the Exercise on the Student CD.*

Using Shortcut Menus

Architectural Desktop makes extensive use of shortcut menus. Shortcut menus accelerate and simplify the process of accessing commands. They are displayed at the cursor location by right-clicking and are context sensitive. *Context sensitive* means that the commands available in the shortcut menu depend on the object or area you picked or right-clicked over.

NOTE   Shortcut menus are discussed where they apply throughout this text. To familiarize yourself with this timesaving feature, try right-clicking at different times and in different areas of the Architectural Desktop window as you are learning how to use the Architectural Desktop commands.

Exercise 1-3   *Complete the Exercise on the Student CD.*

Using Toolbars

When Architectural Desktop is initially started, only a few toolbars are displayed and docked for your drawing needs. Holding the pointer motionless over a button for a moment displays a *tooltip*. The tooltip gives the name of the button in a small box next to the cursor and, in some instances, a keyboard shortcut that can be used to access the command. When a tooltip is displayed, a brief description of the button's function is provided in the status bar at the bottom of the screen. Some buttons include a small black triangle in one corner. These buttons are called *flyouts*. If you pick and hold over a flyout, additional buttons are displayed next to it.

Right-clicking on a toolbar displays a list of toolbars available in Architectural Desktop. A check mark next to a toolbar title in the toolbar list indicates that the toolbar is on and displayed in your Architectural Desktop window. Picking an unchecked toolbar title turns on the selected toolbar. Right-clicking in a blank area of the screen where toolbars are docked displays a list of cascading menus containing toolbars. Select the cascading menu that contains the toolbar you need and pick the toolbar's name to turn it on.

Exercise 1-4   **Complete the Exercise on the Student CD.**

Using Palettes

Palettes are similar to toolbars and dialog boxes, and several palettes are on by default: the **Tool Palettes** window, the **Properties** palette, and the **Project Navigator**. They are docked on the sides of the drawing area. The **Tool Palettes** window is called a palette set, and it contains several tool palettes, the names of which are listed on the tabs shown. These include tool palettes such as the **Design**, **Walls**, and **Doors** palettes, and each tool palette contains related architectural tools for designing and drawing a building. The **Properties** palette controls the different properties of a new or existing object, such as the size or type of door or window. The **Project Navigator** provides tools for organizing and managing several drawings within a project. Any palette set can be turned on and off by selecting the palette set from the **Navigation** toolbar or the **Window** pull-down menu.

All palettes include a title bar along one edge. They can be docked to the right or the left of the drawing screen, and the title bar is always on the side that is along the edge of the screen. **Figure 1-10** shows the different components of the title bar.

Depending on the palette being used, a scroll bar is available next to the palette title bar, which allows you to scroll down to access more tools. The **Auto-hide** button, which allows you to enable or disable auto-hide, is in the palette title bar. Initially auto-hide is disabled. Enabling auto-hide, which is done by picking the **Auto-hide** button, allows the palette to minimize itself when the cursor is not hovering over it. To display the palette with auto-hide enabled, move the cursor over the palette title bar. To hide the palette again, move the cursor away from the palette.

Figure 1-10.
The components of a typical palette title bar and shortcut menu.

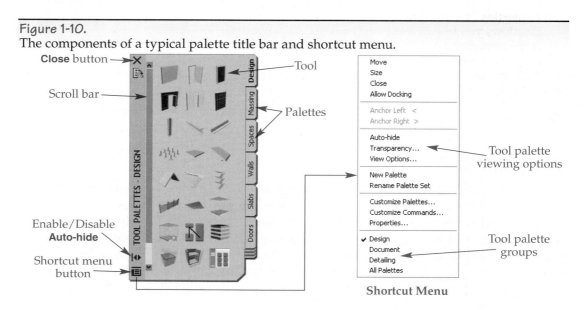

Architectural Desktop and Its Applications

Below the **Auto-hide** button is the palette shortcut menu button. Pick this button to display the palette's shortcut menu. There are many commands available in the shortcut menu, and they vary depending on which palette you are using. These options, which include moving, resizing, closing, docking, and renaming or adding palettes to the palette set, allow you to create a custom palette. Much of the customization can be done using the **Content Browser**, which is covered in Appendix B on the Student CD.

Picking **Transparency...** from the shortcut menu opens the **Transparency** dialog box. This dialog box allows you to make the palette transparent so the drawing behind the palette can be seen when the palette is open. Picking **View Options...**, which is only available in the **Tool Palettes** shortcut menu, opens the **View Options** dialog box. This allows you to control how the tools within a palette are displayed, including the name of a tool and the size of the icon. Other options found in the various palette shortcut menus are explained in the **Autodesk Architectural Desktop 2007 Help** window.

At the bottom of the **Tool Palettes** shortcut menu is a list of tool palette groups. Tool palette groups are individual tool palettes grouped together based on common tasks. For example, the **Design** tool palette group contains tool palettes with tools for designing a building. The **Document** tool palette group contains tool palettes containing tools for documenting your drawings, and the **Detailing** tool palette group contains tool palettes with tools for creating details in your drawings. The **All Palettes** group displays all of the tool palettes and tools loaded into your workspace. Appendix C on the Student CD contains a listing of the tool palettes and tool palette groups in Architectural Desktop by default. To use a tool in one of the tool palettes, pick the desired icon, which initiates the appropriate command so that you can begin drawing.

The **Properties** palette provides an easy way to set and modify the properties of geometry being drawn, such as the wall style, door size, or windowsill height. Existing geometry can be selected in the drawing, and the properties can be modified in the **Properties** palette to reflect a design change. See **Figure 1-11**.

The **Properties** palette includes several properties of the object you are drawing or modifying. The properties are organized into different categories. For example, in the **General** category, properties such as layer color and lineweight are available. Pick the property with the left mouse button to change the value. Different properties become available depending on the object selected or being added. Some of the properties include a drop-down list of options, others require that you enter a value in the text

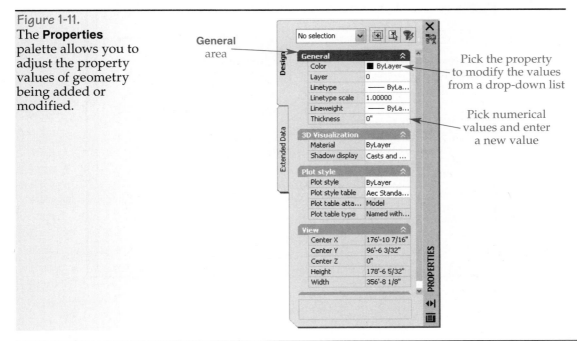

Figure 1-11.
The **Properties** palette allows you to adjust the property values of geometry being added or modified.

box, and others open a worksheet with options or design criteria. Some architectural objects include a diagram and the values affecting the object. Use the scroll bar to access the list of properties. Throughout this text, the **Properties** palette is described as it applies to the specific object being drawn or modified.

Exercise 1-5

Complete the Exercise on the Student CD.

Using Dialog Boxes and Worksheets

Dialog boxes and *worksheets* are used to control settings, to specify properties of objects, and in some cases, to control many aspects of a particular object. Take a few minutes to review the features shown in **Figure 1-12** as you work on Exercise 1-6.

NOTE
Pressing the **Close** (**X**) button on the right side of a dialog box's title bar cancels any changes made in the dialog box. You should always pick the **OK** button in a dialog box so that Architectural Desktop will accept your changes. However, there may be times when an **OK** button is not available. In this case, picking the **Close** button in the dialog box accepts and applies the changes you have made.

Exercise 1-6

Complete the Exercise on the Student CD.

Figure 1-12.
Some features of a dialog box are shown here.

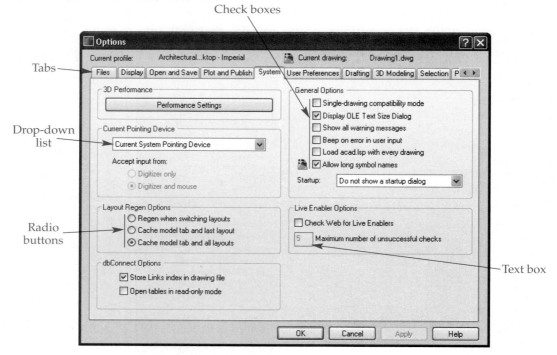

Architectural Desktop and Its Applications

The Command Window

The *command window* is located at the bottom of the drawing screen by default. This window is the line of communication between you and the program. When you activate a command from a toolbar, tool palette, or pull-down menu, the command is entered in the command window at the Command: prompt. You can then enter additional options in the command window using the keyboard. You can also type a command name at the Command: prompt and press the [Enter] key, which tells the Architectural Desktop that you want to execute the entered command. In return, the program prompts you for more information and options.

The command window is not the only place to enter commands. If you type a command, it is shown not only in the command window, but also in the drawing window near your cursor. This feature is called Dynamic Input, and it may be turned on or off using the **DYN** button on the status bar under the command window. Dynamic Input allows you to enter commands and see prompts for other options without needing to look down at the command window. This saves time and allows you to look at your design as you enter options.

The drawing window status bar is located at the bottom of the drawing window and is typically above the command window. This area provides a quick way to display status information about the current drawing.

The application status bar, or simply the status bar, which is found at the bottom of the Architectural Desktop window, contains settings for the entire drawing session. Some settings are only available when working within a project managed through the **Project Navigator**, which is discussed in Chapter 3. You can pick over the buttons or right-click over them and select the appropriate option from the shortcut menu to toggle the functions on and off. The application status bar also contains the status bar tray, which contains several useful options. See **Figure 1-13**.

Figure 1-13.
The status bar at the bottom of the Architectural Desktop window controls settings for the entire drawing session.

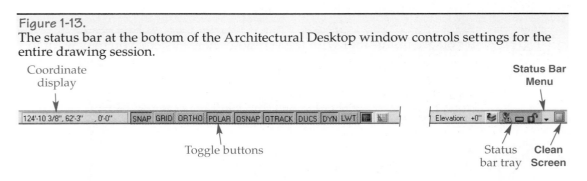

Coordinate display

Status Bar Menu

Toggle buttons

Status bar tray   **Clean Screen**

Creating and Saving Workspaces

Architectural Desktop offers a number of user interface components that can be moved or turned on and off. This means Architectural Desktop offers the flexibility to arrange and combine the different components into a custom, user-defined workspace. The features that can be changed include the visibility of toolbars, pull-down menus, and palettes and the locations of the toolbars and palettes. Once you have these arranged the way you wish, you may want to save your preferences as a named workspace.

To save a workspace, turn on the **Workspaces** toolbar if it is not already visible, **Figure 1-14**. Pick the drop-down list to display a list of workspace names or to save the current arrangement of the workspace. Select the **Save Current As...** option to display the **Save Workspace** dialog box. Enter a name for the workspace you are saving, and then pick the **Save** button. This adds your customized workspace to the drop-down

Figure 1-14.
The **Workspaces** toolbar is used to save and set current workspace arrangements to the user interface.

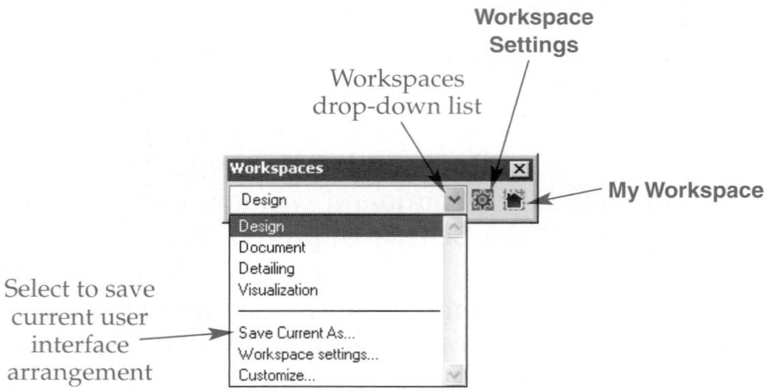

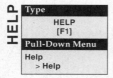

Workspace Settings

Workspaces drop-down list

My Workspace

Select to save current user interface arrangement

list in the **Workspaces** toolbar. You can create as many different workspace arrangements as you need. To set a workspace current, choose the workspace name from the drop-down list in the **Workspaces** toolbar.

Finding Help

HELP

Type
HELP
[F1]

Pull-Down Menu
Help
> Help

If you have trouble understanding how a command works or if you need additional information about a feature within Architectural Desktop, help is easily accessible. To access the **Autodesk Architectural Desktop 2007 Help** window, press [F1] on your keyboard, type HELP, or pick **Help** > **Help**. This window is a powerful online help system, reference tool, and tutorial guide similar to what you are familiar with from your previous AutoCAD training and experience.

NOTE

If you are unfamiliar with the Windows help system, you may want to browse through this help window. Much AutoCAD and Architectural Desktop information can be found that is outside the scope of this textbook.

Exercise 1-7 Complete the Exercise on the Student CD.

Chapter Test

Answer the following questions. Write your answers on a separate sheet of paper or complete the electronic chapter test on the Student CD.

1. What does *AEC* stand for?
2. List the three major phases of the design process.
3. What is one way to start Architectural Desktop?
4. Define the term *floating*.
5. What indicates that a toolbar is floating?
6. Define the term *docked*.
7. What is a grab bar?
8. Explain how to move a toolbar from a docked position to a floating position.

9. Where is the default location of the command window?
10. Explain the function of the command window.
11. What is displayed on the status bar when a pull-down menu item or toolbar button is highlighted?
12. Where are the pull-down menus located?
13. Some commands in a pull-down menu display a small arrow beside them. What does the arrow indicate?
14. What happens when a command with an ellipsis (...) is selected from a pull-down menu or dialog box?
15. What does it mean when shortcut menus are called *context sensitive*?
16. What is a tooltip?
17. What is a flyout?
18. How are toolbars turned on and off?
19. What is the difference between the **Tool Palettes** window and the **Properties** palette?
20. How can a command be accessed from a tool palette?
21. How is a new palette tab created?
22. What is the simplest method for obtaining help?

Chapter Projects

Use the techniques covered in this chapter to create the following drawings.

1. Identify the components of the Architectural Desktop window in the following illustration.

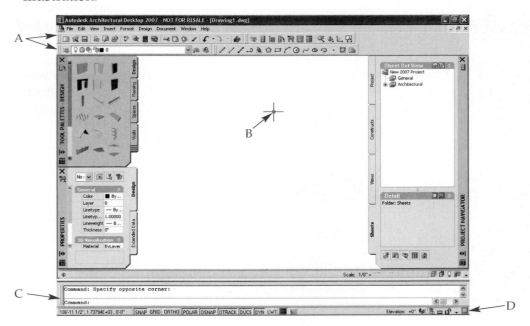

2. Identify the features of the dialog box shown in the following illustration.

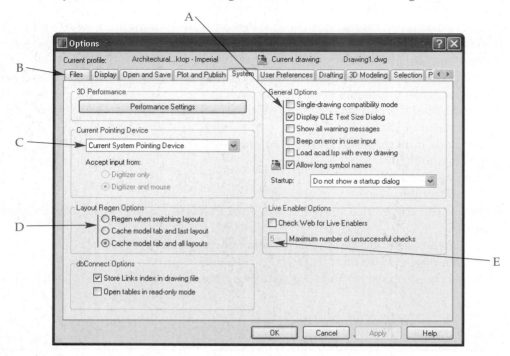

3. Identify the features of the status bar shown in the following illustration.

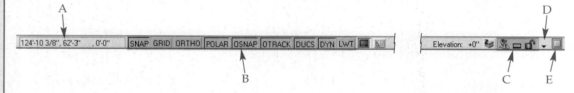

CHAPTER 2

Basic Drafting Techniques

Learning Objectives

After completing this chapter, you will be able to do the following:

✓ Start a new drawing.
✓ Open a drawing.
✓ Save a drawing.
✓ Use model space and layout space.
✓ Set up a drawing.
✓ Establish units.
✓ Set plotting scales.
✓ Establish architectural layers.
✓ Control how default AEC objects appear in a drawing.
✓ Draw polylines.
✓ Draw with Ortho mode on.
✓ Use direct distance entry.
✓ Use tracking and polar tracking.
✓ Print or plot a drawing.

There are a number of AutoCAD and Architectural Desktop commands that once mastered can save you time and simplify the drafting process. This chapter covers a few basic tools that can be used in everyday drawing projects within Architectural Desktop.

Starting a New Drawing

The Architectural Desktop default drawing is known as a template. A ***template*** is a drawing file that is preconfigured with standard settings, allowing you to begin work without having to set up the drawing. Architectural Desktop includes a number of templates that contain preestablished settings for you to quickly begin drawing. The two main types of templates are color table (CTB) and style table (STB) templates. The difference between these templates is the process used to plot the drawings. CTB templates assign a lineweight and grayscale specifically to a color used in the drawing. STB templates are more flexible, assigning lineweights and grayscales to components within objects, layers, and objects themselves regardless of the color used. In addition to the CTB and STB templates, each includes an imperial (feet and inches) and metric template.

Within the two main template types, are three subtypes of templates for different purposes. The three subtypes of templates included are the AEC Model, AEC Sheet, and Structural Model templates. The AEC Model template is used to draw and develop your architectural designs. The AEC Sheet template is used for laying out your sheets for plotting. The Structural Model template is used for the layout of structural drawings. The default template uses the AEC Model (Imperial Stb).dwt file.

To create a new drawing file quickly, pick the **QNEW** button in the **Standard** toolbar. This begins a new drawing using the AEC Model (Imperial Stb) template. If you wish to change the default template, you can do so in the **Options** dialog box. To access this dialog box, pick **Format** > **Options...** from the pull-down menu. In the **Files** tab of the **Options** dialog box, expand Template Settings, and then expand Default Template File for QNEW.

New drawings can also be started by selecting **File** > **New...** from the pull-down menu, by typing NEW, or by pressing [Ctrl]+[N]. This displays the **Select Template** dialog box. See **Figure 2-1**. This dialog box allows you to select one of the templates as the basis for your new drawing. Select the desired template, and then pick the **Open** button. A new drawing based on the selected template is displayed in the application window.

Exercise 2-1

Complete the Exercise on the Student CD.

Figure 2-1.
The **Select Template** dialog box is used to select a template as the basis for your new drawing.

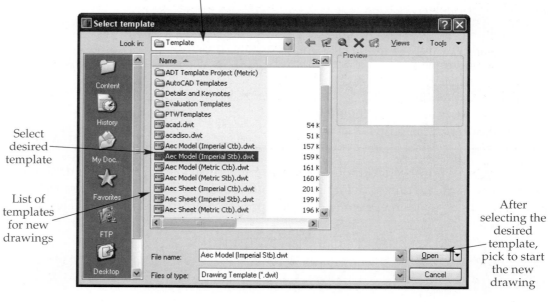

Architectural Desktop and Its Applications

Much drawing time is spent in Architectural Desktop working on existing drawings. This requires you to know how to find and open existing drawings. The **OPEN** command is used to open a drawing that was previously created. To access the command, pick **File** > **Open...** from the pull-down menu, pick the **Open** button in the **Standard** toolbar, type OPEN, or press [Ctrl]+[O]. This displays the **Select File** dialog box. See **Figure 2-2.**

The **Select File** dialog box displays the current directory or folder. You can browse through a list of folders and directories by picking the **Look in:** arrow. A list of files is displayed below the current folder drop-down list. An AutoCAD/Architectural Desktop drawing file is indicated in the list box by a yellow and gray icon. Selecting a drawing file from the list provides a preview of the drawing file in the preview tile. To open the highlighted drawing file, pick the **Open** button in the lower-right corner of the dialog box, or double-click the file name in the list box.

The **Select File** dialog box also contains buttons that may be used to access drawings from different locations, including the Internet. The **FTP** button is used to download drawings from an FTP site. The **Buzzsaw** button accesses folders where drawings may be exchanged with other architects, contractors, or clients. Visit the Autodesk Web site for more information concerning Buzzsaw.

 Exercise 2-2   Complete the Exercise on the Student CD.

Figure 2-2.
The **Select File** dialog box is used to browse through hard drives and network drives to find and open a drawing file.

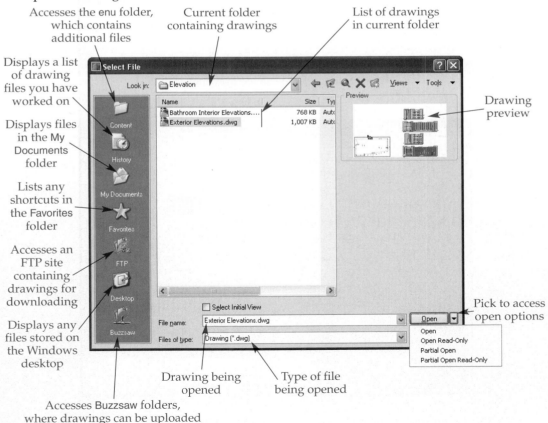

As good practice, you should save a drawing every 10 to 15 minutes. *This is very important!* By saving periodically, you have the latest version of the drawing available in case of a power failure, a severe editing error, or other problems. It is also recommended that you back up your work to a Zip disk, CD, or other media at the end of the day. If anything should happen to your hard drive, your work is saved in the other location.

Architectural Desktop includes the **SAVEAS** and **QSAVE** commands for saving your work. Architectural Desktop displays a warning box if you attempt to close a drawing without saving, giving you the option of saving or discarding the drawing before it is closed.

Using the Saveas Command

The **SAVEAS** command may be used for new drawings that have not been saved. It is also used if the current drawing needs to be renamed, saved in a different location, or saved as a different file type.

When you start a new drawing, the drawing does not have a file name. The title bar of the drawing shows the name Drawing*nn*.dwg, where *nn* represents an assigned sequential number. The **SAVEAS** command allows you to save the drawing with a name of your choosing. You can access this command by selecting **File > Save As...** from the pull-down menu or picking the **Save** button from the **Standard** toolbar if this is the first time you are saving the drawing. The **Save Drawing As** dialog box shown in **Figure 2-3** appears.

By default, drawings are saved in an AutoCAD 2007 drawing format. If you need to save as another type of file, select from the **Files of type:** drop-down list at the bottom of the dialog box. This automatically applies the file extension. Select the location for

Figure 2-3.
The **Save Drawing As** dialog box is used to save a drawing file to a location on a hard drive or a network drive.

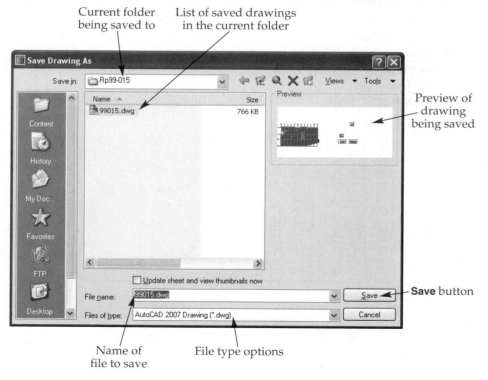

your drawing from the **Save in:** drop-down list. Enter a name for your drawing file in the **File name:** text box above the **Files of type:** drop-down list. Finally, pick the **Save** button. Once a drawing has been saved, the name of the drawing file is displayed in the drawing title bar.

If you try to save a drawing using the same name and location as another drawing file, AutoCAD displays a warning box. You have the option of canceling the save operation or replacing the existing drawing with the current drawing. *Be very careful*—picking the **Yes** button causes the existing drawing to be overwritten with the new drawing information, and the existing drawing is gone forever.

Using the Qsave Command

QSAVE stands for *quick save*. The **QSAVE** command quickly saves a drawing after it has initially been saved with a name. When the **QSAVE** command is used to save a drawing, Architectural Desktop saves the drawing without displaying the **Save Drawing As** dialog box, because the program already knows the drawing has a name and is saved to a specific directory. This command can be accessed by picking the **Save** button from the **Standard** toolbar or by selecting **File** > **Save** from the pull-down menu.

If this is a new drawing that does not have a name, the **Save Drawing As** dialog box is displayed. Select a directory in which to save the drawing, enter a name for the drawing, and specify a drawing format type. After the drawing is named, these options save the drawing without displaying the **Save Drawing As** dialog box.

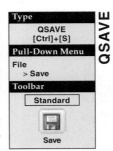

| Type |
| QSAVE [Ctrl]+[S] |
| Pull-Down Menu |
| File > Save |
| Toolbar |
| Standard |
| Save |

Sharing a Drawing with Other Users

Architectural Desktop 2007 is based on the AutoCAD 2007 platform. When you save your Architectural Desktop drawing in the default DWG file format, your drawing can be opened and worked on by other users with Architectural Desktop 2007 or AutoCAD 2007. In order for an AutoCAD user to view your Architectural Desktop objects and work on the drawing, the **PROXYGRAPHICS** variable must be turned on.

The **PROXYGRAPHICS** variable saves an image of proxy objects within the drawing file. A *proxy object* is an object that is a non–AutoCAD-created object, such as the Architectural Desktop objects. When **PROXYGRAPHICS** is set to 1, an image of the Architectural Desktop objects (proxies) is saved in the drawing so AutoCAD users can view the objects. Proxy objects cannot be modified unless they are viewed in the original version of Architectural Desktop in which they were created. When **PROXYGRAPHICS** is set to 0, no proxy images are saved in the drawing.

NOTE
> If you do not intend to share drawings with non–Architectural Desktop 2007 users, you can set the **PROXYGRAPHICS** variable to 0. This decreases the file size of your drawing between 25% and 75%. The **PROXYGRAPHICS** variable is stored within the drawing file.

If your drawing is going to be sent to another AutoCAD 2007 user, you can export the drawing in a 2007 format. Exporting in a 2007 format explodes the Architectural Desktop objects, turning them into standard AutoCAD primitive objects. To use this option, pick the **File** > **Export to AutoCAD** > **2007 Format...** from the pull-down menu. This opens the **Export** *drawing name* dialog box, where you can specify a location and name for the file to be exported. If the user sends the drawing back to you, the geometry is standard AutoCAD geometry and cannot be converted back to Architectural Desktop objects.

| Pull-Down Menu |
| File > Export to AutoCAD > 2007 Format... |

Pull-Down Menu
File
> Export
  to AutoCAD
  > 2004 Format...

Pull-Down Menu
File
> Export
  to AutoCAD

If your drawing is shared with users of AutoCAD 2004, 2005, or 2006, you need to export the drawing in a 2004 format. Pick the **File** > **Export to AutoCAD** > **2004 Format...** from the pull-down menu. This explodes the drawing into AutoCAD objects.

If the drawing is to be sent as a direct exchange format (DXF) file, you must first set the **PROXYGRAPHICS** variable to 1, then export as a 2007, 2004, 2000, or R12 format. These formats are available by picking one of the DXF options after selecting **File** > **Export to AutoCAD** from the pull-down menu.

Exercise
2-3   Complete the Exercise on the Student CD.

Closing a Drawing

The **CLOSE** command is the primary way to exit a drawing file without ending the drawing session. You can close the current drawing file by picking **File** > **Close** from the pull-down menu or typing CLOSE. If you access the **CLOSE** command before saving your work, an alert box gives you another chance to save. Pick **Yes** to save the drawing, or pick **No** if you want to discard changes made to the drawing since the previous save. Pick the **Cancel** button if you decide not to close the drawing and you want to return to the drawing area.

An Introduction to Model Space and Layout Space

Every drawing in Architectural Desktop includes a **Model** tab found at the bottom of the drawing screen. The **Model** tab accesses *model space*, which is the area where your drawing is created. Everything that is drawn in model space is drawn at full scale, 1:1. See **Figure 2-4**.

Depending on the template or drawing file, at least one layout tab is also present. A layout tab, also known as *layout space*, is where the drawing sheet is laid out for plotting. This is the area where your drawing/model is given a scale, the title block is added, and annotation notes are created so the drawing can be plotted. One layout tab can contain many views in your drawing at different scales. For example, a detail sheet can have many views of different parts of the drawing at different scales. A drawing can have only one **Model** tab, but a drawing can include multiple layout tabs, each representing a different sheet in a series of construction documents. See **Figure 2-5**. If the tabs are not present, pick the **Display Layout and Model tabs** check box in the **Display** tab of the **Options** dialog box.

Switching between tabs is done by picking the desired tab from the bottom of the drawing screen. Right-clicking over a tab gives you a menu of options, such as creating new layout tabs, setting up the layout, and plotting the contents of the tab. Layouts and plotting are discussed in greater detail later in the text.

Exercise
2-4   Complete the Exercise on the Student CD.

Figure 2-4.
The **Model** tab is
where full sized
drawings/models are
created.

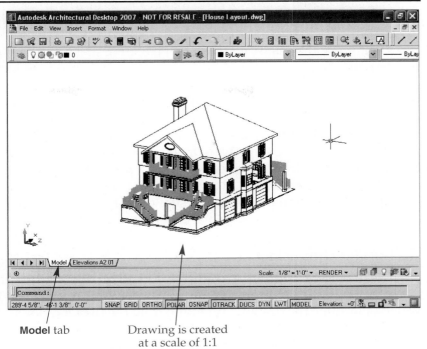

Model tab

Drawing is created
at a scale of 1:1

Figure 2-5.
Layout space is
where the drawing
from model space is
given a scale, a title
block is added, and
views are arranged
on the "paper" for
plotting.

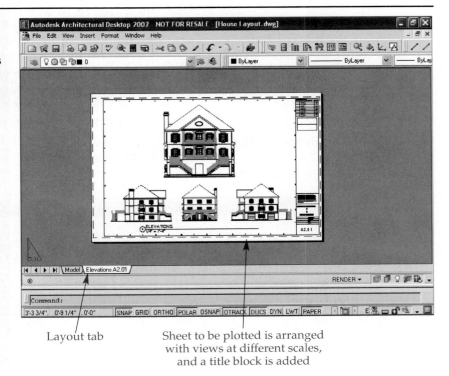

Layout tab

Sheet to be plotted is arranged
with views at different scales,
and a title block is added

Pull-Down Menu
Format
> Drawing
Setup...
Toolbar

Open drawing menu

One of the first steps you should take after starting a new drawing is to set up the drawing. When setting up a drawing in Architectural Desktop, things to consider are the desired drawing units, the scale at which you intend to plot the drawing, how Architectural Desktop objects are placed on layers, and how the objects appear when you draw. The **Drawing Setup** dialog box can be used to set these variables.

To access the **Drawing Setup** dialog box, pick **Format** > **Drawing Setup...** from the pull-down menu or pick the **Open Drawing Menu** icon from the drawing window status bar. Selecting this icon provides you with a menu of options. Select **Drawing Setup...** at the top of the menu.

The **Drawing Setup** dialog box shown in **Figure 2-6** appears. The dialog box is divided into four tabs: **Units**, **Scale**, **Layering**, and **Display**.

Using the Units Tab

Every object drawn in Architectural Desktop is measured in drawing units. For example, one unit can represent 1 inch, 1 foot, or 1 millimeter. The **Units** tab allows you to determine the drawing unit type from the **Drawing Units:** drop-down list. Once the drawing units have been selected, press the **Apply** button. A warning box appears indicating that the drawing units have changed and asks whether you want to scale the existing objects in your drawing to the new settings. See **Figure 2-7**.

The **Inches** option allows you to use architectural units in feet and inches, in which 1 unit is equal to 1″, and 12 units is equal to 12″, or 1′-0″. The other options are **Feet**, **Millimeters**, **Centimeters**, **Decimeters**, and **Meters**. When imperial units are being used, it is most common to choose **Inches** as the drawing units. When inches are being used, the inch symbol (″) is not required to specify inch values. When metric units are being used, it is most common to choose **Millimeters** or **Centimeters** as the drawing units.

Figure 2-6.
The **Drawing Setup** dialog box is used to set up a new drawing.

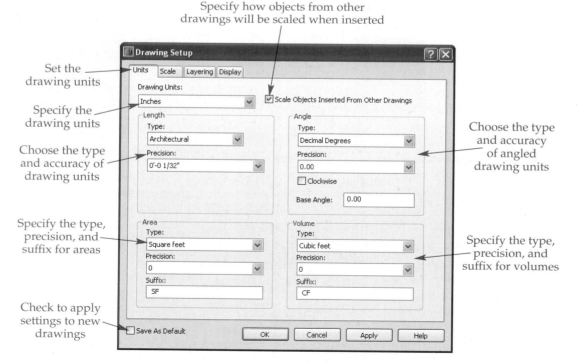

Figure 2-7.
After changing the drawing units, pick the **Apply** button. A warning box is displayed allowing you to scale existing objects in the drawing.

Scales existing objects in the model space drawing to reflect the new drawing units

Scales existing objects in the paper space drawing to reflect the new drawing units

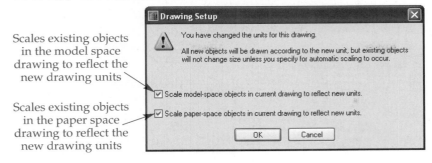

There can be times when you want to copy objects from an existing drawing into your current drawing. The **Scale Objects Inserted From Other Drawings** check box allows you to scale objects from another drawing to the scale of your current drawing. If this option is unchecked, objects from another drawing are inserted at their original drawing scales.

The **Length** area of the **Units** tab includes drop-down lists for the type and precision of length values you enter when creating geometry. The **Type:** drop-down list includes the following options:

- **Architectural.** Examples include 72″, 72, 6′0″, 6′, 12′6, 24′6-1/2″, and 18′3-3/4. A hyphen (-) must be used to separate inch and fractional values. Architectural units are available only when inches are the drawing units.
- **Decimal.** Examples include 144, 24.5, 256.75, 58.015, and 96.50.
- **Engineering.** Examples include 68.5′, 72′-6.5, 54′8.75, and 25′. A hyphen (-) is not required, but one can be used to separate the feet from the decimal-inch value.
- **Fractional.** Examples include 36-1/2 and 24-3/8.
- **Scientific.** Length values are entered as a base number followed by E+ xx, where the xx represents the power of 10 by which the base number is multiplied, such as 10.5E+06 and 25.4E+12.

The **Precision:** drop-down list includes values that change based on the type of units selected. The value you specify determines how length values are rounded off when displayed in the coordinates area at the lower-left corner of the Architectural Desktop window.

The **Angle** area in the **Units** tab specifies how angles are to be entered when angled shapes are drawn or objects are rotated. The following types are available:

- **Degrees.** This system is based on decimal degrees, where 360° equals a complete circle. See **Figure 2-8.** Angular values are entered into Architectural Desktop as decimal values such as 0, 45, 90, 135, 145.5, and 180.
- **Degrees/Minutes/Seconds.** There are 60 minutes (′) in one degree (d), and there are 60 seconds (″) in one minute. Some examples of angular values are 25d39′54″, 274d01′59″, and 359d59′59″.
- **Grads.** *Grads* is an abbreviation of *gradients*. A full circle measured with gradients includes 400 grads. A 90° angle is equal to 100 gradients. Examples of gradient values include 153g, 372g, and 50g.
- **Radian.** The radian type is based on π radians = 180°. Angular values are calculated by multiplying or dividing a number by π and then placing an r after the calculated value. Examples include 3.925r, 1.57r, and 6.28r.
- **Surveyor.** A *bearing* is a direction based on one of the quadrants of a compass. Bearings are measured beginning from north or south, with units in degrees, minutes, and seconds, to the east or west. See **Figure 2-9.** An angle measured from 32°24′33″ from the north toward the east is entered as N32d24′33″E.

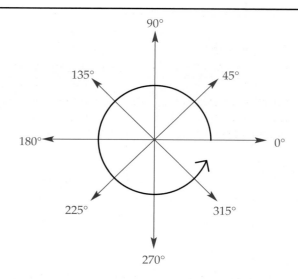

Figure 2-8.
Architectural Desktop measures all angles in a counterclockwise direction beginning with angle 0 to the right.

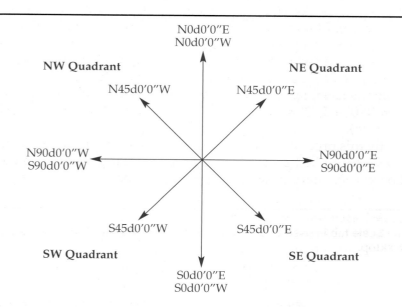

Figure 2-9.
Surveyor units are measured in degrees in the appropriate compass quadrant.

Each angular unit has a different precision value related to the type of angle selected. Selecting a precision determines how the angle is rounded off in the coordinates display in the status bar. Angles can also be measured in a clockwise direction instead of counterclockwise by activating the **Clockwise** check box.

PROFESSIONAL
TIP

It is advisable to always measure angles in a counterclockwise direction, because most AutoCAD users are trained to draw this way. Changing the direction to clockwise moves the 45° angle to the southeast quadrant from the northeast quadrant.

The **Area** section in the **Units** tab controls how areas are measured within Architectural Desktop. The **Type:** drop-down list reflects a squared value based on the drawing units selected. When inches or feet are used, the available area types are **Square Inches**, **Square Feet**, and **Square Yards**. If a metric drawing unit is selected, the available area types include **Square Millimeters**, **Square Centimeters**, **Square**

Decimeters, and **Square Meters**. The **Precision:** drop-down list specifies how areas are rounded off when calculated. The **Suffix:** text box also changes based on the drawing units selected. This allows you to enter a suffix that is displayed after an area is calculated. A *suffix* is a special note or application that is placed behind the value. For example, the word TYPICAL, MAXIMUM, or MINIMUM might be placed after a value.

The **Volume** area of the **Units** tab controls how volumes of objects are calculated. Volumes change based on the type of drawing units selected. After selecting the settings, pick the **Apply** button to apply the settings to your drawing.

Exercise 2-5   *Complete the Exercise on the Student CD.*

Using the Scale Tab

The **Scale** tab of the **Drawing Setup** dialog box is used to set a plotting scale for annotation blocks that are included with Architectural Desktop. See **Figure 2-10**. *Annotation blocks* are symbols that are drawn at the full scale the drawing will be plotted. An example is a detail bubble that has a diameter of 1-1/4″. When the detail bubble is inserted into model space, it is inserted multiplied by a scale factor. When a drawing scale is selected from the **Drawing Scale:** list, the scale factor is entered in the **Custom Scales:** text box. For example, a drawing scale of 1/8″ = 1′-0″ has a scale factor of 96 (1′-0″ ÷ 1/8″ = 96). A drawing scale of 1/4″ = 1′-0″ has a scale factor of 48 (1′-0″ ÷ 1/4″ = 48).

By this process, the detail bubble is scaled by the scale factor. For example, a 1-1/4″ bubble multiplied by a 48 scale factor results in a 2′-6″ scaled bubble. This method allows a standard-sized detail bubble to be used in multiple drawings that have

---

Figure 2-10.
The **Scale** tab is used to determine a plotting scale for the annotation blocks in Architectural Desktop.

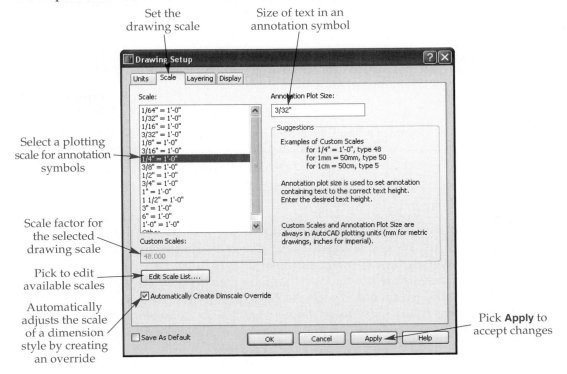

Figure 2-11.
The annotation block is scaled up in the **Model** tab and scaled down to the proper scale in the paper space layout.

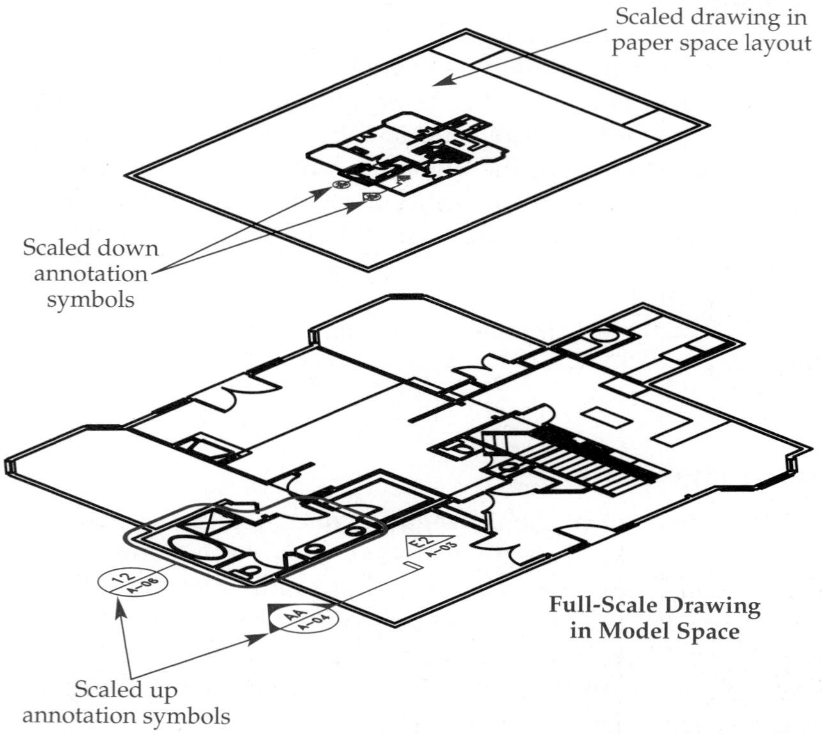

Scaled drawing in paper space layout

Scaled down annotation symbols

Scaled up annotation symbols

Full-Scale Drawing in Model Space

different scales. When the drawing is subsequently plotted, the full-scale drawing and the scaled annotation blocks are scaled down by the scale factor, fitting them on a real-size sheet of paper on a layout tab. See **Figure 2-11.**

Depending on the type of drawing units selected in the **Units** tab, a number of scales are available in the **Scale:** list. Both lists also provide you with an **Other...** option. This option allows you to enter a custom scale factor in the **Custom Scales:** text box.

Below the **Scale:** list is the **Edit Scale List...** button. Pick this button to edit the list of available scales. Custom scales that do not appear in the list can be added. The **Annotation Plot Size:** text box is used to enter a text height for annotation symbols. The default is 3/32". This makes the text in Architectural Desktop annotation blocks 3/32" high when plotting from a layout tab. Any value you enter modifies the height of text in an annotation block when plotted.

Exercise 2-6 Complete the Exercise on the Student CD.

Using the Layering Tab

The **Layering** tab of the **Drawing Setup** dialog box is used to control how Architectural Desktop assigns layers to AEC objects as shown in **Figure 2-12.** There are two parts to layering: layering standards and layer keys. *Layering standards* are a set of rules that determine how a layer name is created. For example, the AIA 3rd Edition layering standard included with Architectural Desktop has rules that create a layer name using the following format: *discipline designator 1 discipline designator 2-major code-minor 1 code-minor 2 code-status code*, for example: AD-Wall-Prht-Dims-D, where AD is Architectural Desktop.

Figure 2-12.
The **Layering** tab is used to set a layer key style current in the drawing. Layer key styles automatically assign Architectural Desktop objects to layers as they are drawn.

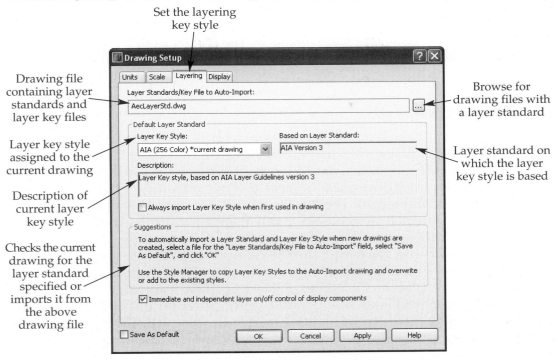

Set the layering key style

Drawing file containing layer standards and layer key files

Layer key style assigned to the current drawing

Description of current layer key style

Checks the current drawing for the layer standard specified or imports it from the above drawing file

Browse for drawing files with a layer standard

Layer standard on which the layer key style is based

The *layer keys* tie the layer standards to AEC objects. For example, the WALL key is assigned to the Wall object. The WALL key uses the layer standard to determine that Wall objects are automatically drawn on a layer named A-Wall. Each AEC object is assigned a layer key that places the object on a layer.

The **Layering** tab is used to assign a layer key style to AEC objects. The **Layer Standards/Key File to Auto-Import:** text box is used to specify a drawing that contains layer standards and layer key styles that are automatically loaded when a new drawing is started. Architectural Desktop is installed with a default layer standard drawing file named AecLayerStd.dwg. This layer standard includes AIA layering standards, British and German layering standards, a generic standard, and associated layer key styles. The ellipsis (...) button can be used to browse other folders for customized layer standards and layer key styles. The AecLayerStd.dwg file can be found in the Layers folder under the **Content** shortcut button after selecting the ellipsis (...) button.

The **Layer Key Style:** drop-down list includes a number of layer key styles: AIA (256 color), BS1192 AUG Version 2 (256 color), BS1192 Descriptive (256 color), BS1192 Cisfb (256 color), DIN 276, Generic Architectural Desktop, and STLB. The AIA (256 color) layer key style is based on the AIA 2nd Edition layering standards. This key style assigns AIA layer names to AEC objects. For example, the WIND key assigns a Window object to the A-Glaz layer. The three types of BS 1192 layer key styles are British layering standards. The DIN 276 and STLB styles assign layer names based on German layering standards. The Generic Architectural Desktop style assigns layers based on the key name. For example, a layer key named DOOR places a Door object on the Door layer.

The **Based on Layer Standard:** text box displays the layer standard that the selected layer key style uses to create layer-naming conventions. The **Description:** text box provides a description for the selected layer key style. Both of these text boxes are grayed out and provide additional information only as you select a layer key style to use. The **Always Import Layer Key Style when first used in a drawing** check box checks the drawing for the most recent key style being specified. If it is not available, the key style is imported from the drawing in the **Layer Standards/Key File to Auto-Import:** text box. Select the **Save As Default** check box to set the key style as the default key style to use for future drawings.

Exercise 2-7

Complete the Exercise on the Student CD.

Using the Display Tab

The **Display** tab of the **Drawing Setup** dialog box is used to control how default AEC objects appear in a drawing when they are first created. See **Figure 2-13.** As previously discussed, every AEC object is assigned to a layer through the use of layer key styles. When an object is placed on a layer, the layer governs properties of the object, such as color, linetype, and lineweight. The **Display** tab allows you to further control how an AEC object displays when viewed from different angles or display configurations.

A *display configuration* allows you to view a drawing in a number of ways. When a template is used, the default display configuration is set to Medium Detail. The Medium Detail display configuration displays a wall as 2D flat when viewed from the Top view, using the colors and linetypes of the layer where it is placed. When the same wall is viewed from an Elevation or Isometric view, the wall is displayed as a 3D wall with colors that reflect the type of building material represented. The Reflected display configuration displays walls with header lines over the doors and windows. A number of display configurations are included with the templates, from which you can select a different configuration at any time while you are drawing.

The information included in the **Display** tab is the first step in controlling how AEC objects appear in your drawings. This step is called *display representations*. Each AEC object in Architectural Desktop has one or more display representations.

Figure 2-13.
The **Display** tab is used to control additional display properties of an AEC object, furthering the display control provided by the use of layers.

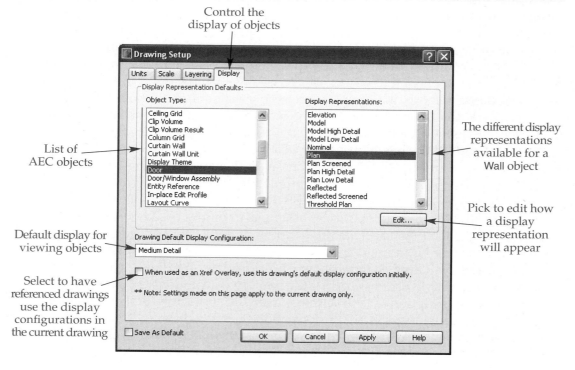

Architectural Desktop and Its Applications

Most of the AEC objects include a Plan (2D) representation and a Model (3D) representation. Many of the symbol blocks have a General representation.

The **Object Type:** list along the left edge of the tab is a list of all the AEC objects included with Architectural Desktop. The scroll bar allows you to scroll through the list of objects in order to view their representations. When an object type is highlighted on the left, the object's representations are listed in the **Display Representations:** list on the right side of the tab, as shown in **Figure 2-13**. A Door object has multiple display representations. For example, a Plan representation for a Door object is displayed when the Door object is seen from a Top view when using the Medium Detail display configuration. The Model representation Door object is displayed when the Door object is seen from an angle other than the Top view when using the Medium Detail display configuration.

Using the Door object as an example, assume you want to change the way a Model (3D) Door is supposed to display in your drawing. First, select the Door object from the **Object Type:** list, and then select the Model display representation from the list at the right. Next, select the **Edit...** button to edit the way the Model-Door is to appear in the drawing. The **Display Properties** dialog box shown in **Figure 2-14** appears. Model view Door objects include five individual components: Door Panel, Frame, Stop, Swing, and Glass. Each of these components is a separate piece of the Door object that can be turned on or off, whose color or linetype can be changed, and whose other properties can be modified. Although these individual properties can be changed, they are all tied together into one object that is similar to a block in AutoCAD.

Object components can be turned on or off, which causes them to display or not display. In **Figure 2-15**, for example, the Swing component for a Door object is turned off. This indicates that if the Model-Door representation is viewed, the Door Swing component is turned off. Yet, if you look at the Plan-Door representation, the Door Swing is turned on. When a component's layer is set to 0, that component is assigned to the layer where the overall object was created, such as the A-Door layer. Layers can be assigned to components, but the component belongs to both the assigned layer and the layer assigned to the overall object. Materials, colors, linetypes, lineweights, and

Figure 2-14.
The **Display Properties** dialog box lists the components of an object that are based on the display representation selected.

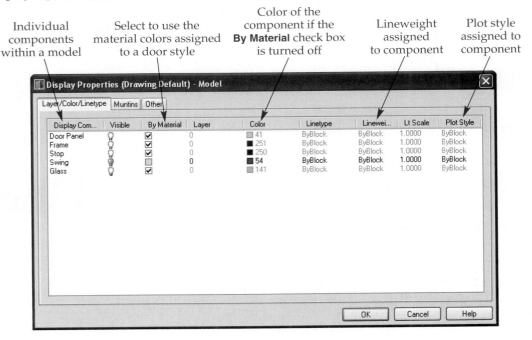

Figure 2-15.
A—The model door does not display the door swing. B—The plan view of the same door displays the door swing.

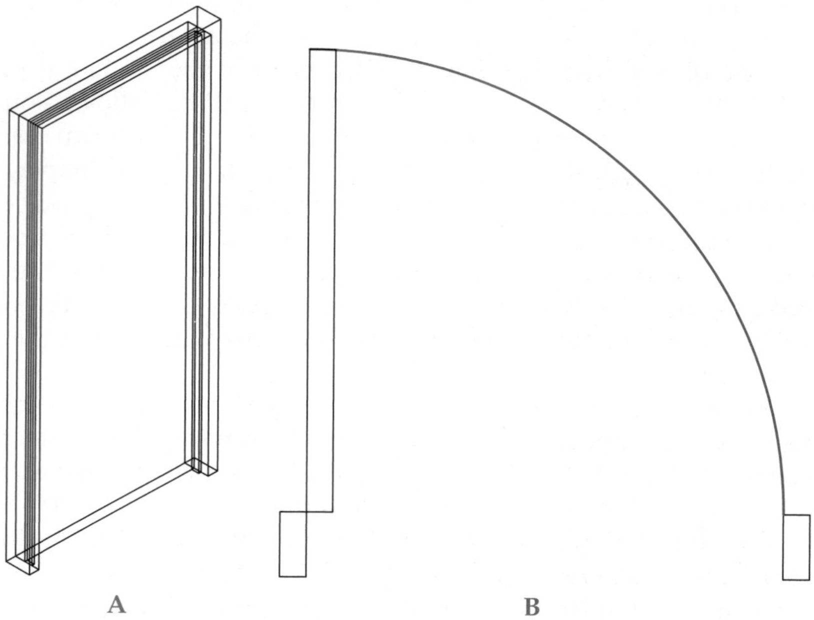

A   B

linetype scales can be assigned to the individual components by picking the appropriate icon or word in the **Display Properties** dialog box. When you are finished assigning properties to components, pick the **OK** button. You are returned to the **Display** tab, where you can configure other default display representations.

NOTE

When first learning Architectural Desktop, you may decide to use the default settings for display representations of AEC objects. As you become more familiar with how the display system works, you may begin to establish color, plotting, and rendering standards for the AEC objects.

Once you are finished setting up the AEC objects' default display settings, you can select the default display configuration to be used in the drawing from the **Drawing Default Display Configuration:** drop-down list at the bottom of the **Display** tab. This sets the default configuration in the drawing and determines what object representations are viewed.

Exercise
2-8

Complete the Exercise on the Student CD.

Drawing Basics

Architectural Desktop uses the AutoCAD *polyline* as an important component in developing drawing objects. Walls, roofs, floor slabs, and railings can be created from polylines. Polylines also generate custom shapes for doors, windows, and caps at the end of walls.

Current AutoCAD users should note that the Architectural Desktop shapes have been developed to enhance current drawing philosophy. You can mix lines, arcs, circles, and polylines with AEC objects to create your construction documents. The polyline enhances the use of many AEC objects.

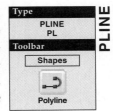

After accessing the **Polyline** button in the **Shapes** toolbar or typing PLINE or PL, AutoCAD prompts you to specify a starting point. Move the cursor to a location in the drawing and pick with the left mouse button to establish the first point of the polyline. See **Figure 2-16A.** As you move the crosshairs around the drawing screen, the rubberband line changes size as it follows the movement of the crosshairs. Generally, a dimension and an angle are displayed from the initial point to the location of the crosshairs. Values can be entered for the length or angle of the segment to be drawn. Use the [Tab] key to toggle to the desired dimension, and then enter a new value using the keyboard. This is called Dynamic Input.

Also notice that the Command: prompt now asks you to specify the next point. Pick a point in the drawing to draw a line segment. See **Figure 2-16B.** Picking more points creates additional line segments. When you are finished drawing line segments, you can right-click for the shortcut menu options, or press [Enter], [Esc], or the spacebar to end the **PLINE** command. Available options that are applicable to Architectural Desktop are discussed later in this chapter.

NOTE
When using Dynamic Input, command options can be accessed by picking the down arrow on the keyboard and then using the arrow keys to move to the desired option within the context menu.

Exercise 2-9   **Complete the Exercise on the Student CD.**

Figure 2-16.
The **PLINE** command is used to create line segments. A—Pick a starting point with the pick button. B—Pick a second point to draw a line between the two points.

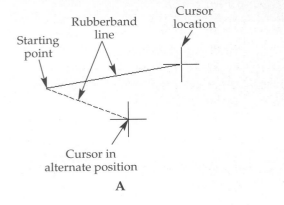
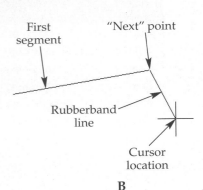

AutoCAD Review

Using the Point Entry Methods

Point entry refers to the method of locating objects in your drawing. Architectural Desktop is built on AutoCAD, so AutoCAD point entry techniques can be applied to AEC objects. Point entry provides the basis for creating and modifying geometry using the *Cartesian coordinate system*. There are three methods of selecting points using the Cartesian coordinate system: absolute coordinates, relative coordinates, and polar coordinates.

Points are located in your drawing with the *absolute coordinates* method by measuring distances from the origin (0,0) in the XY plane. For example, the absolute coordinate you type is 20',15'. This begins the polyline 20'-0" to the right and 15'-0" up from the origin. When Cartesian coordinate methods are used, the coordinates are always entered with the X value first, followed by the Y value, with a comma separating the two values (X,Y), and measurements are always made from the origin.

When using the *relative coordinates* method, points are measured along the X and Y axes from the previous location. For example, start by picking a point in the drawing. To draw a line that is 23'-6" from that point using relative coordinates, you must use the @ symbol in front of the X,Y values to indicate that you are drawing X = 23'-6" and Y = 0" from the previous point. The previous point is defined as the origin for the new point. If a line is drawn horizontally to the left, there is a negative value for the X axis: @–X,0.

The *polar coordinates* method is based on a distance and a compass angle for the direction the object is drawn. The @ symbol is used in front of polar coordinate values to specify the next point in relation to the current point. The distance of the line and the angle at which the line is drawn are required: @distance<angle. Angles are measured in a counterclockwise direction with the 0° angle to the right (east).

The following table gives input for the three point entry methods for prompt sequences to create the building outline shown in the figure on the next page.

Point	Prompt	Absolute	Relative	Polar
Start Point	Specify start point:	40',50'	*pick a point*	*pick a point*
Point 1	Specify next point:	70',50'	@30',0	@30'<0
Point 2	Specify next point:	70',62'	@0,12'	@12'<90
Point 3	Specify next point:	101'6",62'	@31'6",0	@31'6"<0
Point 4	Specify next point:	101'6",86'	@0,24'	@24'<90
Point 5	Specify next point:	40',86'	@-61'6",0	@61'6"<180
Close	Specify next point:	C	C	C

(Continued)

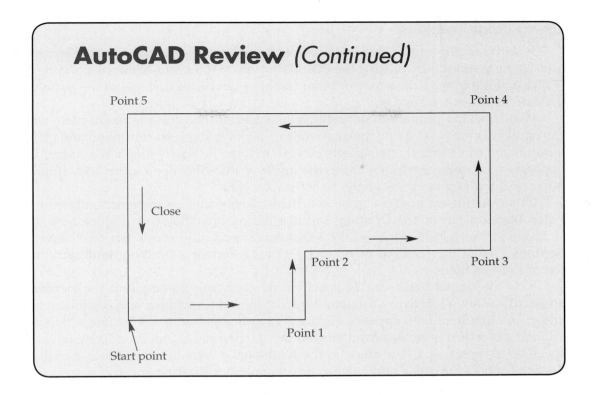

Using Ortho Mode

Ortho mode forces object segments to be drawn horizontally or vertically. This is an advantage when you are creating rectangular shapes because the corners are always square. Ortho mode can be turned on or off by picking the **ORTHO** button in the status bar, by pressing the [F8] key, or by using the [Ctrl]+[L] key combination.

After Ortho mode has been turned on, any new straight polyline segments are limited to horizontal or vertical movement. If an angled line other than horizontal or vertical is desired, relative or polar coordinates can be used to specify the next point.

Exercise 2-10 **Complete the Exercise on the Student CD.**

Using Direct Distance Entry

Direct distance entry is a method of entering point locations to quickly lay out geometry. Direct distance entry can be used after an initial point has been selected, and a rubberband line is displayed. To use this method, drag the rubberband line in the desired direction, enter the length for the line at the Specify next point: prompt, and press [Enter]. This process creates a line segment the correct length and at the correct angle that was specified. See **Figure 2-17.**

PROFESSIONAL TIP

Use direct distance entry in combination with Ortho mode or polar tracking to quickly lay out geometry. This method can be used whenever Architectural Desktop expects a point coordinate value when you are using drawing or editing commands.

Using Polar Tracking

Polar tracking causes the crosshairs to "snap" to a predefined angle increment and can be turned on by picking the **POLAR** button on the status bar or by pressing the [F10] key. Either the Ortho mode or polar tracking can be used. If one of the buttons is picked, the other is turned off.

Polar tracking provides a dotted-line visual aid, called the alignment path, when the crosshairs are moved into the angle. Once you have started a command and picked a point, you can move the crosshairs around to indicate a new angle. If a dotted line appears, your object is drawn along the angle of this line. See **Figure 2-18.** Initially, polar tracking is set to track angles in 30° increments.

Other alignment angles can be specified by choosing an increment angle in the **Polar Tracking** tab of the **Drafting Settings** dialog box shown in **Figure 2-19.** This is accessed by right-clicking on the **POLAR** button in the status bar and choosing **Settings...** from the shortcut menu or by picking **Format** > **Drafting Settings...** from the pull-down menu.

New alignment paths can be specified by changing the angle in the **Increment angle:** drop-down list. Every time the cursor is moved toward the specified increment angle, an alignment path appears. **Figure 2-19** indicates that every 30° angle becomes aligned when the cursor is moved around the starting point. Additional angles can be specified by entering a new angle in the **Additional angles** list box. The use of direct distance entry with polar tracking can greatly enhance drafting speed.

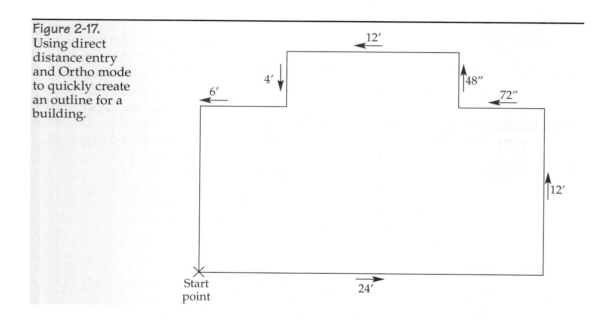

Figure 2-17.
Using direct distance entry and Ortho mode to quickly create an outline for a building.

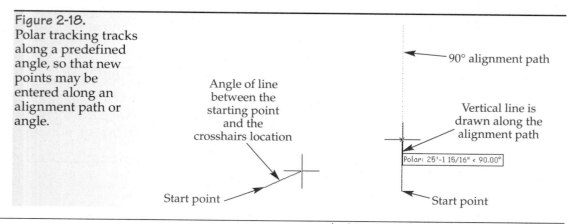

Figure 2-18.
Polar tracking tracks along a predefined angle, so that new points may be entered along an alignment path or angle.

Figure 2-19.
The **Drafting Settings** dialog box allows you to specify a new increment angle for the alignment paths when using polar tracking.

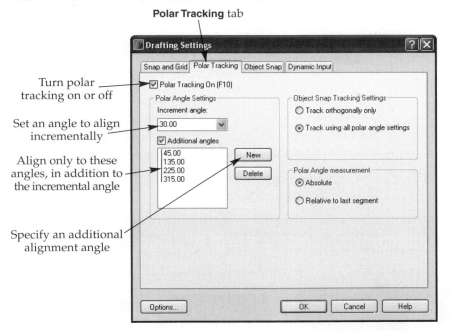

Turn polar tracking on or off

Set an angle to align incrementally

Align only to these angles, in addition to the incremental angle

Specify an additional alignment angle

 **Exercise 2-11**   **Complete the Exercise on the Student CD.**

 PROFESSIONAL TIP

> Try using different point-entry techniques as you draw. Some methods may be better in certain situations than others. Keep in mind that you can use any of the techniques when creating geometry. For example, you may start a polyline using absolute coordinates and then draw it with a mixture of relative and direct distance entry methods.

Using Dynamic Input

Dynamic Input combines the power of direct distance entry with polar tracking. When Dynamic Input is used, dimensions are displayed on-screen to indicate the lengths and angles of the geometry being drawn. Entering values for the dimensions creates the geometry at the desired size and location.

To use Dynamic Input, pick the **DYN** button in the status bar, or press the [F12] key. By default, when Dynamic Input is turned on and a command is used, dimensions are displayed on-screen to indicate the length and angle as the object is drawn, **Figure 2-20.**

You can also type commands or options at the location of the crosshairs. To turn this feature on, right-click over the **DYN** button and select **Settings...** from the shortcut menu. This displays the **Drafting Settings** dialog box. See **Figure 2-21.** Select the **Show command prompting and command input near the crosshairs** check box, so commands can be entered at the crosshairs instead of the Command: prompt. Use the [↓] key to scroll through any available options.

Figure 2-20.
Dynamic Input is used to display dimensions and commands to aid in the creation of geometry.

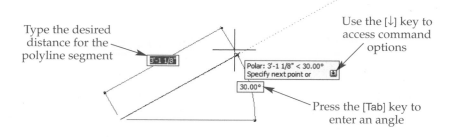

Type the desired distance for the polyline segment

Use the [↓] key to access command options

Polar: 3'-1 1/8" < 30.00°
Specify next point or

30.00°

Press the [Tab] key to enter an angle

Figure 2-21.
The **Drafting Settings** dialog box is used to set options for the Dynamic Input function.

Dynamic Input tab

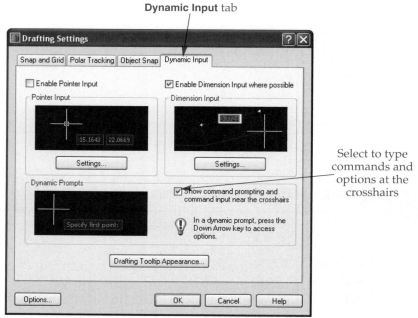

Select to type commands and options at the crosshairs

Using Polyline Options

As discussed earlier in this chapter, polylines are important in Architectural Desktop because they can be used to generate other architectural objects such as walls, roofs, and spaces. When using the **PLINE** command, you are first prompted to specify a starting point, and then options are available, including **Width**, **Arc**, and **Undo**.

The **Width** option allows you to draw wide polylines. The **Width** option requires you to specify a starting and ending width. Specifying the same starting and ending widths creates a polyline with equal width along its length. Specifying two different widths causes the polyline to taper.

The **Arc** option allows you to create polyline arcs. See **Figure 2-22.** Several of the **Arc** suboptions available are similar to the **PLINE** options. The **Angle**, **Center**, and **Radius** suboptions specify those attributes of the arc. The **Direction** suboption specifies the starting direction for the arc. The **Second pt** suboption requires a second and third point to be picked in order to draw the polyline arc. The **Line** suboption resumes drawing straight polyline segments.

The **Undo** option removes a previously drawn line or arc segment. The **Undo** option allows you to "undo" your polyline segments as many times as there are arc or line segments in the polyline. Each time the **Undo** option is used, the last segment is erased.

Figure 2-22.
When the **PLINE Arc** option is used, the arcs are connected to the straight-line segments like other straight-line polylines.

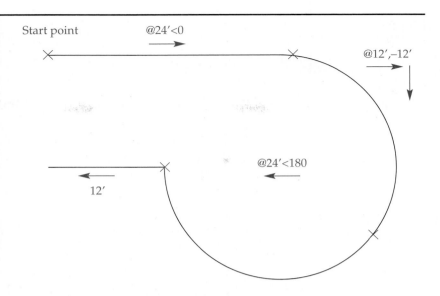

Start point   @24'<0

@12',–12'

@24'<180

12'

Exercise 2-12   **Complete the Exercise on the Student CD.**

Printing and Plotting Basics

As indicated at the beginning of this chapter, model space is the area where your full-scale drawing is created. Layout space is where the title block, border, and scaled drawing are placed. When you have finished creating a drawing, it often needs to be plotted or printed as a *hard copy*, which is the printed version of a computer file. Plotting can be accomplished from the **Model** tab or from a layout tab. This section introduces you to plotting basics from the **Model** tab. Use of layout space is explained in detail later in this text.

To plot a drawing from the **Model** tab, make sure model space is the active drawing area. Select the **Plot** button, type PLOT, press the [Ctrl]+[P] key combination, select **File > Plot...** from the pull-down menu, or right-click the **Model** tab and select **Plot...** from the shortcut menu. The **Plot** dialog box shown in **Figure 2-23** appears.

When the **Plot** dialog box is first accessed, a portion is available. Pick the **More Options** button in the lower-right corner to expand the dialog box. These additional options further refine how the drawing can be plotted.

The first thing to do is assign the plotter to be used. In the **Printer/plotter** area, select from a list of plotters or printers configured on your computer system. All printers or plotters configured to your Windows operating system or in the Architectural Desktop system are available. Selecting a plotter assigns the plotter and also designates the paper sizes available for the specified plotter.

Next, assign the paper size, the area to be plotted, and the scale of the drawing. The **Paper size** area includes a list of paper sizes supported by the chosen plotter. Select a paper size from the drop-down list.

Type
PLOT
[Ctrl]+[P]

Pull-Down Menu
File
> Plot

Toolbar
Standard

Plot

PLOT

AutoCAD Review

Using Object Snap Modes and Object Tracking

Object snaps, also called *osnaps,* are one of the most useful tools in Architectural Desktop. *Object snaps* are drafting aids that "snap" the crosshairs to an exact point or place on an object as you draw. Object snaps increase accuracy and productivity by allowing you to specify exact points when drafting.

To access object snaps while in a drawing command, pick the appropriate button from the **Object Snap** toolbar, select the object snap from the shortcut menu, or type the three-letter abbreviation. The abbreviations are given in the table shown.

Each of the object snap modes includes a marker that indicates the type of object snap that is being referenced. The table shown summarizes the object snap modes. Some of the object snap modes do not work on all objects.

A function known as *running object snap* indicates that object snaps are on and automatically displays symbols as the crosshairs are moved over existing geometry. This function can be turned on and off by pressing the **OSNAP** button in the status bar. To view the available running object snaps, right-click over the **OSNAP** button, and select **Settings...** from the shortcut menu. The **Object Snap** tab is displayed in the **Drafting Settings** dialog box. Checking an object snap mode turns on that object snap.

(Continued)

Figure 2-23.
The **Plot** dialog box is used to assign a plotter, paper size, and scale for the drawing and to plot the drawing.

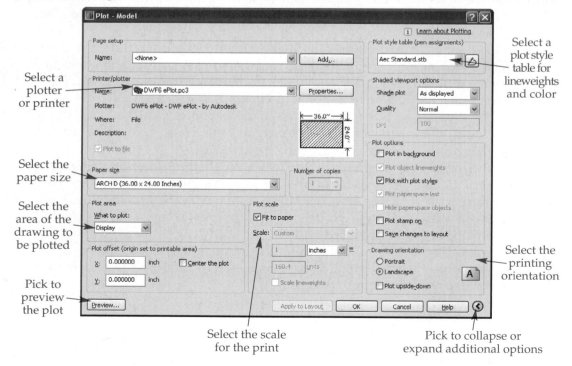

Select a plotter or printer

Select the paper size

Select the area of the drawing to be plotted

Pick to preview the plot

Select the scale for the print

Select a plot style table for lineweights and color

Select the printing orientation

Pick to collapse or expand additional options

AutoCAD Review (Continued)

Tracking can be used by acquiring a point and then moving the crosshairs along either the X or Y coordinate axis of the acquired point to pick a new point along this axis. This mode of tracking is known as *object snap tracking* or *Otrack*. Object snap tracking can be turned on or off by using the **OTRACK** button on the status bar or by pressing the [F11] key. Object snap tracking must always be used in conjunction with running osnaps because the acquired points are referenced from an object snap.

Object Snap Modes			
Mode	**Marker**	**Button**	**Description**
Endpoint (END)			Finds the nearest endpoint of a line, arc, elliptical arc, spline, ray, solid, wall, door, window, stair, railing, or roof.
Midpoint (MID)			Finds the middle point of any object having two endpoints, such as a line, arc, elliptical arc, spline, ray, solid, wall, door, or window.
Center (CEN)			Locates the center point of a curved object, such as circles, arcs, polyline arcs, ellipses, elliptical arcs, and curved walls.
Quadrant (QUA)			Picks the closest of the four quadrant points that can be found on circles, arcs, ellipses, elliptical arcs, and curved walls. (Not all of these objects may have all four quadrants.)
Intersection (INT)			Picks the intersection of two objects.
Apparent Intersection (APP)			Selects a visual intersection between two objects that appear to intersect on screen in the current view but may not actually intersect each other in 3D space.
Extension (EXT)			Finds a point along the imaginary extension of an existing line or arc. (This is used in conjunction with another object snap, such as **Endpoint** or **Midpoint**.)
Insertion (INS)			Finds the insertion point of text, blocks, doors, windows, openings, and window assemblies.
Perpendicular (PER)			Finds a point that is perpendicular to an object from the previously picked point.
Parallel (PAR)			Finds any point along an imaginary line parallel to an existing line or polyline.
Tangent (TAN)			Finds points of tangency between radial and linear objects.
Nearest (NEA)			Locates a point on an object closest to the crosshairs.
Node (NOD)			Picks a point object on a dimension, point object, or most of the Architectural Desktop objects.
None			Turns the running object snap off for the current point to be picked.

The **Plot** area is used to define what will be plotted. The options in this area are described as follows:

- **Limits.** Initially, when a drawing is started, an area known as limits defines a scaled piece of paper in model space. If a drawing is started using one of the AEC templates, the limits are defined by the grid dots displaying in the drawing screen. If you want everything within the limits plotted, then select this option.
- **Extents.** This option plots to the farthest outside edge of the geometry in the drawing.
- **Display.** This option plots what is currently being displayed on screen.
- **View.** If any views are defined in the drawing, a particular view can be selected from the list to be plotted.
- **Window.** Selecting this option returns you to the current space (model or layout) so a windowed area to plot can be specified. Anything within the windowed area is then plotted.

The **Plot scale** area is used to assign a scale to the plotted drawing. A drop-down list with different scales is available. If you want to print without specifying a scale, select the **Fit to paper** check box. This option scales the drawing so it fits within the area of the selected paper.

After specifying the plotter, paper size, plot area, and scale, expand the **More options** button to display additional settings. In the top-right corner of the dialog box, assign a plot style from the **Plot style table (pen assignments)** area. A *plot style table* is used to assign pen weights and printing colors to geometry within your drawing. For example, if Architectural Desktop "sees" red-colored geometry, it can plot that geometry as a red line when using a color table or as a black line if using a monochrome table. Some tables interpret geometry colors and plot them with grayscale colors. Lineweights are preset for many of the colors in Architectural Desktop. These tables can be modified to suit your own needs. This topic is fully discussed later in the text.

After you have selected these settings, you can pick the **Preview...** button to display a preview of the plotted drawing before plotting. It is advisable to preview the plot before plotting because what you see in the preview is what you get when the drawing is plotted. To exit the plot preview, right-click and select **Exit** from the shortcut menu. Make any changes to the settings in the **Plot** dialog box if needed, and check the plot again with the **Preview...** button before plotting. Once the plot is configured as desired, pick the **OK** button to send the plot to the plotter. You also can send the file directly to the plotter from the plot preview by right-clicking and picking the **Plot** option.

Exercise
2-13   **Complete the Exercise on the Student CD.**

Chapter Test

Answer the following questions. Write your answers on a separate sheet of paper or complete the electronic chapter test on the Student CD.

1. What is a *template*?
2. How do you browse through a list of folders in the **Select File** dialog box?
3. Identify the function of the **History** button in the **Select File** dialog box.
4. Why is it important to save the drawing every 10 to 15 minutes?
5. Explain the function of the **SAVEAS** command.
6. Discuss the procedures to use when saving a drawing for the first time.
7. What is the procedure for sending a drawing to an AutoCAD 2004 format user?
8. Explain the function of **QSAVE**.
9. What happens if you use **QSAVE** on a new drawing that does not have a name?
10. Identify the scale used to draw objects in model space.
11. Explain the function of the layout tabs.
12. How many layout tabs can a drawing have?
13. Discuss the function of the **Drawing Setup** dialog box.
14. Identify the most commonly used drawing units when using imperial units.
15. Where does Architectural Desktop begin measuring angles and in what direction by default?
16. What are *annotation blocks*?
17. Calculate the scale factor for a drawing scale of 1/4″=1′-0″.
18. What are layer standards?
19. Give the function of layer keys.
20. Name the two types of display representations that are provided for *most* AEC objects.
21. Identify two ways to access the **PLINE** command.
22. Name the Cartesian coordinate method in which points are located by measurement of a distance and compass angle for the direction an object is drawn.
23. Why is it an advantage to have Ortho mode on when drawing rectangular shapes?
24. Briefly explain how polar tracking functions.
25. Define *alignment path* as related to polar tracking.
26. Define *increment angle* as related to polar tracking.
27. Define *hard copy*.
28. Identify four ways to access the **Plot** dialog box.
29. What is a *plot style table*?
30. Why is it a good idea to preview the drawing before making the print or plot?

Chapter Projects

Use the techniques covered in this chapter to create the following drawings.

1. Draw the figure below, given the following criteria:
   A. Start a drawing using an Aec Model template.
   B. Use the **Drawing Setup** dialog box to ensure architectural units are being specified.
   C. Set the drawing scale to **1/4" = 1'-0"**.
   D. Specify **AIA (256 Color)** in the **Layer Key Style:** drop-down list.
   E. Use polylines, object snaps, and Cartesian coordinates to create the drawing.
   F. Do not dimension.
   G. Save the drawing as P2-1.dwg.

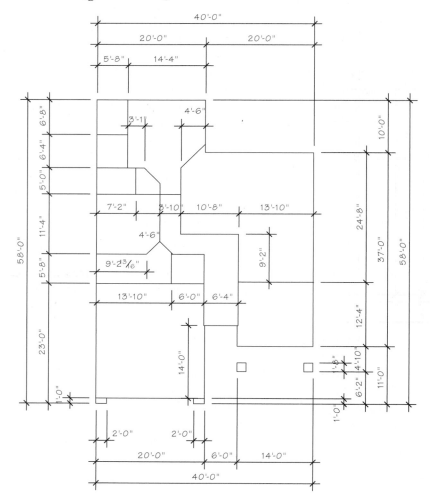

Design Courtesy Alan Mascord Design Associates

2. Draw the figure shown below using the following criteria:
   A. Start a drawing using an Aec Model template.
   B. Use the **Drawing Setup** dialog box to ensure architectural units are being specified.
   C. Set the drawing scale to **1/4″ = 1′-0″**.
   D. Specify **AIA (256 Color)** in the **Layer Key Style:** drop-down list.
   E. Use polylines, object snaps, and Cartesian coordinates to create the drawing.
   F. Do not dimension.
   G. Save the drawing as P2-2.dwg.

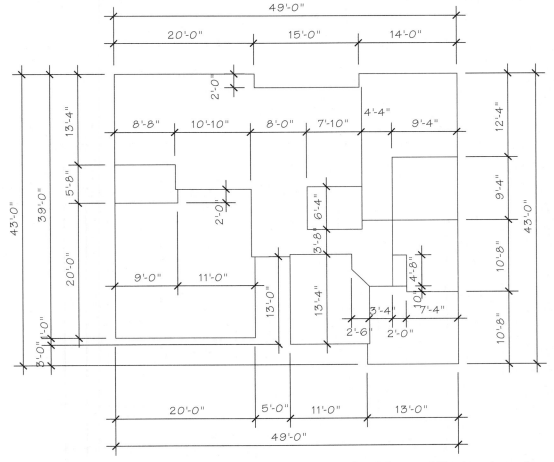

Design Courtesy Alan Mascord Design Associates

3. Draw the figure shown below using the following criteria:
   A. Start a drawing using an Aec Model template.
   B. Use the **Drawing Setup** dialog box to ensure architectural units are being specified.
   C. Set the drawing scale to **1/4" = 1'-0"**.
   D. Specify **AIA (256 Color)** in the **Layer Key Style:** drop-down list.
   E. Use polylines, object snaps, and Cartesian coordinates to create the first and second floors.
   F. Do not dimension.
   G. Save the drawing as P2-3.dwg.

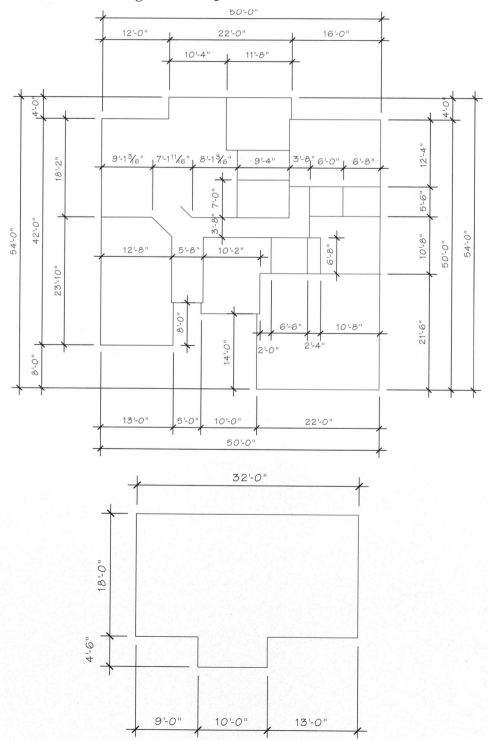

Architectural Desktop and Its Applications

4. Draw the figure shown below using the following criteria:
   A. Start a drawing using an Aec Model template.
   B. Use the **Drawing Setup** dialog box to ensure architectural units are being specified.
   C. Set the drawing scale to **1/4″ = 1′-0″**.
   D. Specify **AIA (256 Color)** in the **Layer Key Style:** drop-down list.
   E. Use polylines, object snaps, and Cartesian coordinates to create the first and second floors.
   F. Do not dimension.
   G. Save the drawing as P2-4.dwg.

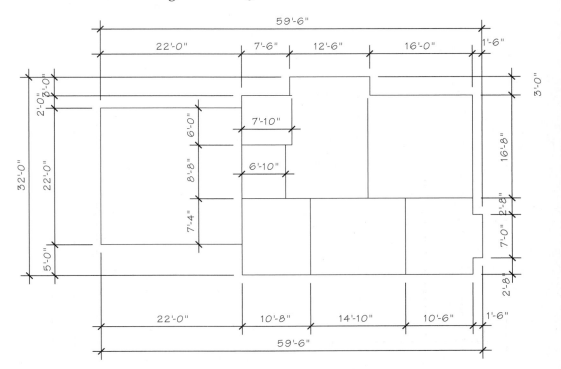

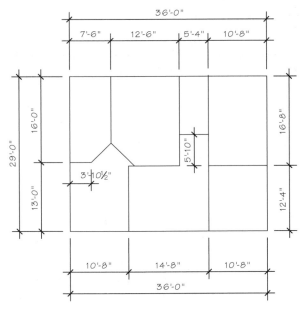

Design Courtesy Alan Mascord Design Associates

5. Draw the figure shown below using the following criteria:
   A. Start a drawing using an Aec Model template.
   B. Use the **Drawing Setup** dialog box to ensure architectural units are being specified.
   C. Set the drawing scale to **1/8″ = 1′-0″**.
   D. Specify **AIA (256 Color)** in the **Layer Key Style:** drop-down list.
   E. Use polylines, object snaps, and Cartesian coordinates to create the drawing.
   F. Do not dimension.
   G. Save the drawing as P2-5.dwg.

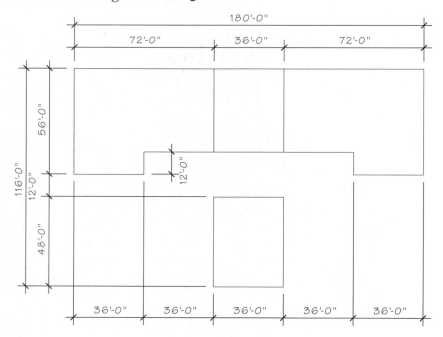

6. Draw the figure shown below using the following criteria:
   A. Start a drawing using an AEC Model template.
   B. Use the **Drawing Setup** dialog box to ensure architectural units are being specified.
   C. Set the drawing scale to **1/8″ = 1′-0″**.
   D. Specify **AIA (256 Color)** in the **Layer Key Style:** drop-down list.
   E. Use polylines, object snaps, and Cartesian coordinates to create the drawing.
   F. Do not dimension.
   G. Save the drawing as P2-6.dwg.

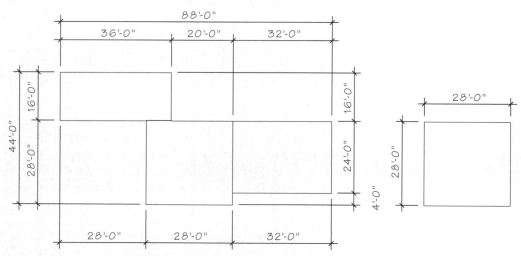

7. Draw the figure shown below using the following criteria:
   A. Start a drawing using an Aec Model template.
   B. Use the **Drawing Setup** dialog box to ensure architectural units are being specified.
   C. Set the drawing scale to **1/8″ = 1′-0″**.
   D. Specify **AIA (256 Color)** in the **Layer Key Style:** drop-down list.
   E. Use polylines, object snaps, and Cartesian coordinates to create the drawing.
   F. Do not dimension.
   G. Save the drawing as P2-7.dwg.

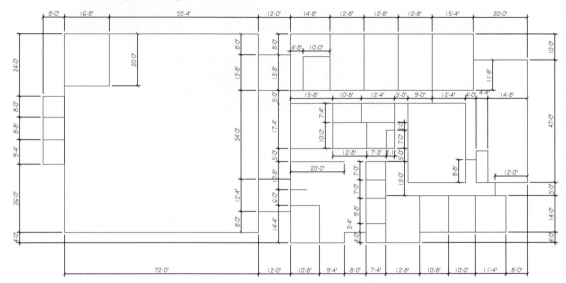

The home page of the Autodesk User Group International Web site is www.augi.com. This Web site offers valuable information about using Autodesk products and peer support from other Architectural Desktop users.

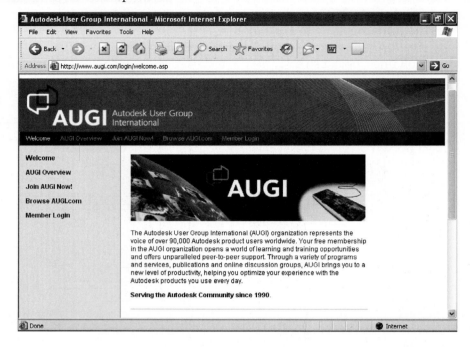

CHAPTER 3

Drawing Management

Learning Objectives

After completing this chapter, you will be able to do the following:
- ✓ Understand the concept and use of constructs.
- ✓ Understand the concept and use of elements.
- ✓ Understand the concept and use of views.
- ✓ Understand the concept and use of sheets.
- ✓ Access the **Project Browser**.
- ✓ Create a new project.
- ✓ Set a project current.
- ✓ Modify a project's properties.
- ✓ Set up levels and divisions within the **Project Navigator**.

This chapter covers a process known as project management. Project management uses the **Project Browser** and **Project Navigator** features to maintain an entire project's drawing and support files.

Drawing Management Concepts

The drawing management system allows you to manage and maintain drawings for different floors, called *levels*, and building wings, called *divisions*, for assembly into a single building information model. The drawings that make up a *building model* are organized into a single project. The building *project* is divided into two main parts: the building model and building reports generated from the model. The building model is composed of two types of building blocks: constructs and elements. The *building reports* are generated from two components: views and sheets. Constructs, elements, views, and sheets are combined to form a building information model. See **Figure 3-1.**

When working through the project management process, different drawings can be referenced together to form new drawings or views. Drawings can also be referenced together to reference locations of different portions of the building, in order to assemble new or revised sections of the building. The process of referencing drawings is referred to as *external reference management*. By using the project management system, external references (xrefs) are automatically updated and maintained.

Figure 3-1.
The graphic on the left shows the structure of an ADT building project. The graphic on the right shows how elements, constructs, views, and sheets collectively are used to create the building information model.

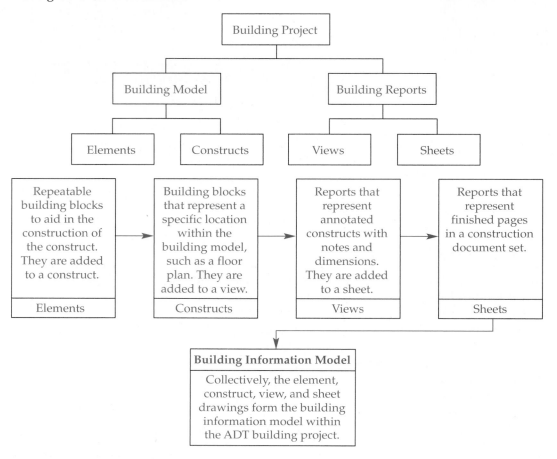

Levels and Divisions

At the heart of the project management system are levels and divisions. Levels divide the building into vertical portions, or elevations, and are most commonly used in the layout of floors, foundations, and floor and ceiling framing components. The number of levels used in a project is unlimited and open to your design criteria. Divisions divide the building into horizontal portions, similar to wings of a building. They are commonly used to lay out different sections of a building and can be used as building options.

Constructs

A *construct* describes a specific elevation section of a building and is assigned to a level and division within the project. Since each construct is assigned to a level and division, constructs are used for floor plans, framing plans, foundations, or roofs. Constructs are drawings in which actual building components, such as walls, doors, and windows, are drawn. See **Figure 3-2.**

As the project management system uses xrefs, constructs can be referenced to aid in the construction of other constructs or tied together to form other drawings. *Element drawings* can also be referenced into a construct to create the construct drawing. Constructs are referenced into *views*, where they are documented with notes and dimensions.

Figure 3-2.
A construct is used
to define a single
level within a
building.

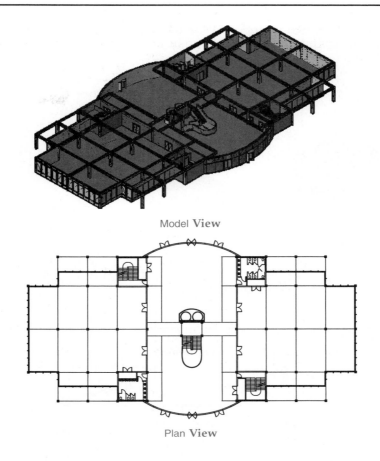

Model **View**

Plan **View**

Some AEC objects, such as curtain walls and stairs, can span the entire height of a building. These are known as *spanning objects*. When these objects are used in a construct, the construct can be assigned to multiple levels and divisions.

Elements

An *element* is used for portions of a building that can be repeated multiple times. Like a construct, an element is a drawing file containing buildable objects, such as stairs, elevators, or generic building blocks. The difference is that a construct represents a specific area of the building and is assigned to an elevation level, while an element is repeatable and is not assigned to a specific elevation level. See **Figure 3-3.**

Being repeatable building blocks, elements are referenced into a construct that is assigned a specific level. Therefore, elements do not adhere to specific elevation levels but gain their elevation location by being referenced into a construct with a level assignment. For example, a bathroom layout can be created within an element drawing and then referenced into the first, third, and fourth floor constructs of a building.

Views

A *view drawing* is used to reference and document constructs. This type of drawing is where individual constructs are placed, noted, and dimensioned. A view drawing can be made up of a single construct or multiple constructs, which can also include elements. After documenting a view, individual named views, which are similar to snapshots or pictures of an area within a construct, can be created for use in laying out a plotting *sheet*. **Figure 3-4** provides an example of a view drawing.

Figure 3-3.
An element is used for repeatable building objects, such as stairs, elevator cores, and bathroom configurations, which can be referenced into constructs.

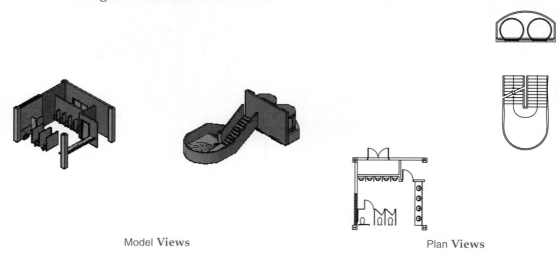

Model **Views**   Plan **Views**

Figure 3-4.
A view drawing is where annotations such as tags, dimensions, notes, and schedules are placed.

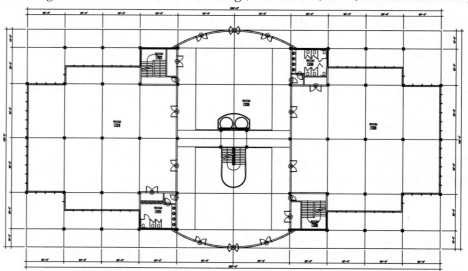

Sheets

A *sheet drawing* is a drawing that includes referenced view drawings or named views, arranged onto a title block for plotting. See **Figure 3-5.** The sheet drawing represents a single final drawing that will be plotted into a set of construction documents. After view drawings and named views have been created, they can be referenced on top of a title block sheet, arranged, and plotted for final output.

Figure 3-5.
A sheet drawing is used to arrange views onto a title block for plotting.

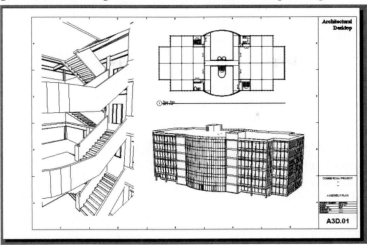

The Project Browser

Before your drawings can be organized into a project, a project must be created. Projects are created through an interface known as the **Project Browser**. To access the **Project Browser**, pick **File** > **Project Browser...** or the **Project Browser...** button in the **Navigation** toolbar. This displays the **Project Browser**, shown in **Figure 3-6**. The **Project Browser** is a cross between a file management window for project files and an Internet browser for viewing a project's home page. The **Project Browser** has four main parts: a project header, navigation bar, selector, and bulletin board.

Type
AECPROJECTBROWSER
Pull-Down Menu
File
> Project Browser...
Toolbar
Navigation

Project Browser...

AECPROJECTBROWSER

Figure 3-6.
The **Project Browser** is used to set a project current, create new projects, browse existing projects, edit project settings, close a project, or refresh a project.

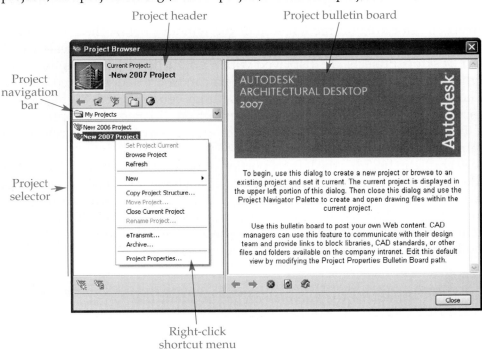

Projects and files created within a project through the **Project Browser** appear as files and folders when viewed in Windows Explorer. As a general rule, do not perform file operations on project files through Windows Explorer, except in cases where a procedure clearly states you should. File operations performed through Windows Explorer are not updated in the **Project Browser** correctly and can cause inconsistencies within the project. In order to manage your project correctly, use the **Project Browser**.

The project header, displayed in the upper-left corner of the browser window, contains the project name and number of the current project. This information is displayed when a new project is created and set current. The project navigation bar is located directly below the project header area and includes toolbar buttons to navigate through the project folder structure. The following buttons are used to navigate through a project:

Button	Description
⇦	Returns to the previously displayed folder.
	Displays the folder structure one level above the current folder.
	Opens the **Project Files** dialog box, where project (.apj) files can be browsed for.
	Displays project (.apj) files in the currently displayed folder.
	Displays a historic list of projects accessed.

Below the navigation buttons is a drop-down list that displays a tree view of folders located on your hard drive, down to the currently displayed folder. This drop-down list can also be used to browse different folders on your hard drive to find a project file.

The project selector area on the left side of the window, below the project navigation bar, displays the folders on your computer system and projects created with Architectural Desktop. Projects are displayed with a unique icon that looks like a roll of paper with a triangle. This area is where a project can be created, renamed, moved, or closed. The project selector area is also where settings can be edited. Right-clicking over a project file displays a shortcut menu where project management options can be selected. Two buttons, below the project selector area, are available to create a new project or refresh a project.

The project bulletin board is the largest portion of the browser window, located on the right side of the window, and displays the project's HyperText Markup Language (HTML) page. When you are setting up a project, the bulletin board can be set to point to your company's Web site or intranet or to a project-specific HTML page. If the HTML page includes additional Web pages, use the standard Web-browsing buttons below the bulletin board to browse through the Web pages.

Exercise 3-1

Complete the Exercise on the Student CD.

Creating a New Project

Architectural Desktop includes three options for creating new projects. A new project can be started from scratch. A project can be created from an existing project, with only its folder structure and settings copied. A new project can also be created from an existing project with all its settings, drawing files, and support files copied.

Creating a Project from Scratch

If you have not created a project in the past, creating a project from scratch is a good place to start. By beginning a new project from scratch, you have the ability to adjust the project settings for specific needs. Later, new projects can be started based on existing projects.

To create a new project from scratch, access the **Project Browser**, right-click an existing project such as the **New 2007 Project**, and pick **New** > **Project...** from the shortcut menu. See **Figure 3-7**. Alternatively, you can pick the **New Project** button below the project selector pane in the **Project Browser**.

This opens the **Add Project** dialog box. See **Figure 3-8**. Each project you create needs a unique identification number. Numerals, alphabetic characters, or a combination of both can be used. Enter the identification number in the **Project number:** text box. This number is placed in the project header of the **Project Browser** when the project is set current.

Next, enter a name for the project. The name of the project is displayed in the project header, is used as the name of the project in the project selector pane, and is the name of the root folder of the project when viewed in Windows Explorer. Enter the name in the **Project Name:** text box.

Below the **Project Name:** text box is the **Project Description:** text box. You can enter a brief description that displays in the project header. Verify that the **Create from template project:** check box is unchecked. This option is used when creating a project based on an existing project.

Picking the **OK** button when you are finished creates the project. By default, the new project is created in the current folder in the project selector drop-down list. Picking the **Close** button in the **Project Browser** displays the **Project Navigator**, where the project can be set up and managed. The **Project Navigator** is discussed later in this chapter.

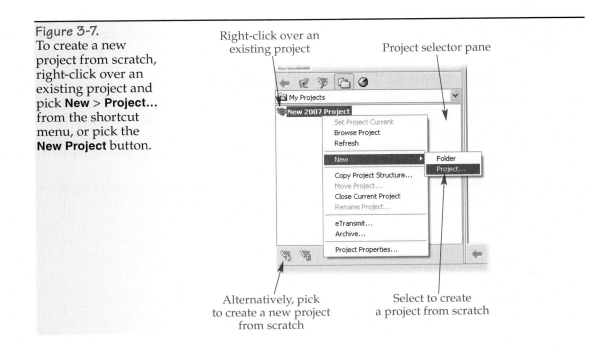

Figure 3-7.
To create a new project from scratch, right-click over an existing project and pick **New** > **Project...** from the shortcut menu, or pick the **New Project** button.

Right-click over an existing project

Project selector pane

Alternatively, pick to create a new project from scratch

Select to create a project from scratch

Figure 3-8.

The **Add Project** dialog box is used to number and name a new project that was started from scratch.

Enter an identification number for the project

Enter a name for the project

Provide a description for the project

Verify that the **Create from template project:** check box is unchecked

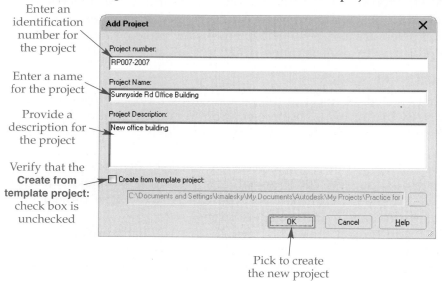

Pick to create the new project

NOTE

Once a project has been created, Architectural Desktop establishes a folder within Windows Explorer with the same name as the project name. Within this root folder is a file that manages settings in the project. The file also has the same name as the project name, with an .apj file extension. Additionally, the Constructs, Elements, Sheets, and Views subfolders are in the project root folder, where the project drawings are stored. Do not use Windows Explorer to move, copy, or rename the project folder or any of its associated files, because this causes undesirable results within the project and can render the project useless.

Exercise 3-2   Complete the Exercise on the Student CD.

Creating a Project Using the Structure of an Existing Project

To create a new project using the folder structure of an existing project, access the **Project Browser**. Use the project selector to locate the folder where the existing project resides. Right-click on the existing project and select the **Copy Project Structure...** option. See **Figure 3-9.** This displays the **Duplicate Project** dialog box shown in **Figure 3-10.**

The **Duplicate Project** dialog box is similar to the **Add Project** dialog box. Enter an identification number for the project in the **Number** text box, a name for the project in the **Name** text box, and a brief description in the **Description** text box. In the **Copy To...** text box, select the text box to display an ellipsis (...) button. Pick the ellipsis (...) button to browse to a location where you want to store the new project. Pick the **OK** button when you are finished, to create the new project.

Exercise 3-3   Complete the Exercise on the Student CD.

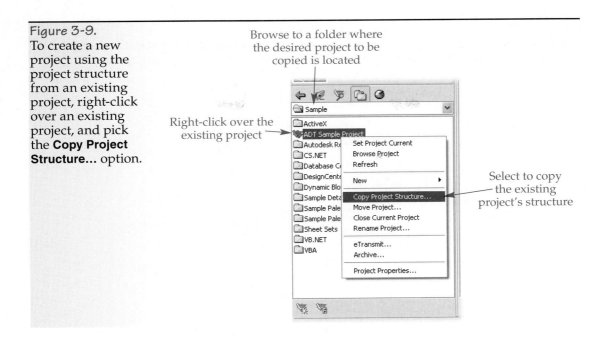

Figure 3-9.
To create a new project using the project structure from an existing project, right-click over an existing project, and pick the **Copy Project Structure...** option.

Browse to a folder where the desired project to be copied is located

Right-click over the existing project

Select to copy the existing project's structure

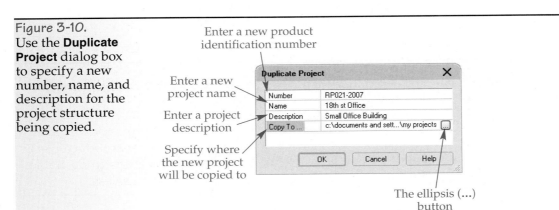

Figure 3-10.
Use the **Duplicate Project** dialog box to specify a new number, name, and description for the project structure being copied.

Enter a new product identification number

Enter a new project name

Enter a project description

Specify where the new project will be copied to

The ellipsis (...) button

Creating a Project Based on a Template or an Existing Project

After a project has been created, new projects can be created based on the existing project's folder structure and on drawings and settings within the existing project. This option is useful if you are creating a building from an existing plan or if an existing project has standard drawing names, a standard folder structure, and standard settings that can be repeated in other projects. Once a project has been set up using standards, a folder structure, and settings that you can use repeatedly, you can use this project as a project template.

To create a project based on an existing project or template, access the **Project Browser**, right-click over a project or the folder where you want to create the new project, and select **New** > **Project...** from the shortcut menu. See **Figure 3-11.** This displays the **Add Project** dialog box shown in **Figure 3-12.** Similar to the way you create a project from scratch, enter an identification number in the **Project number:** text box, a name for the project in the **Project Name:** text box, and a brief description for the project in the **Project Description:** text box.

Figure 3-11.
To create a new project based on an existing project, right-click over a project or folder where the new project will be created and pick **New** > **Project...** from the shortcut menu.

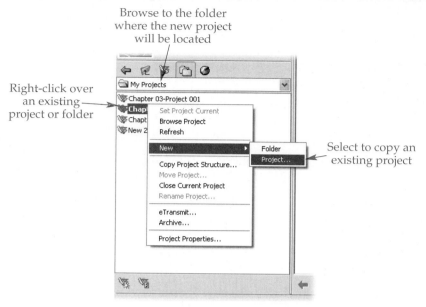

Browse to the folder where the new project will be located

Right-click over an existing project or folder

Select to copy an existing project

Figure 3-12.
Enter a number, name, and description for the new project. Select the **Create from template project:** check box to select an existing project to be copied.

Enter an identification number for the project

Enter a name for the project

Provide a description for the project

Select the **Create from template project:** check box

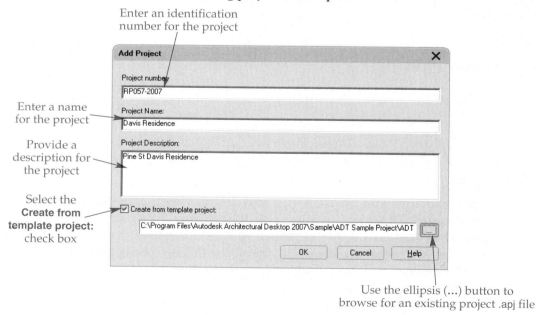

Use the ellipsis (...) button to browse for an existing project .apj file

In order for the new project to use an existing project's folder structure, drawings, and settings, select the **Create from template project:** check box. Pick the ellipsis (...) button to open the **Select Project** dialog box, where you can browse your hard drive for a project .apj file. Select the .apj file, and then pick the **Open** button to select the file. The **Create from template project:** text box now displays the path to the selected .apj file. Pick the **OK** button to create the new project. This option is very useful for creating a new project, especially when an existing project includes a folder structure for organization and standard drawing, view, and sheet names.

Setting a Project Current

In order to work with an Architectural Desktop project, the project must be set current. Only one project can be current at a time. Any project operations you perform, such as adding new element or construct drawings, changing levels, or adjusting sheet drawings, are done within the current project.

When a project is set current, its identification number and name are displayed in the project header of the **Project Browser**. The project's associated HTML file is also displayed in the bulletin board area. Associating an HTML file to a project is described in the adjusting project settings section of this chapter.

To set a project current, access the **Project Browser**, use the project selector to locate the desired project to be set current, right-click over the project, and pick the **Set Project Current** command. Alternatively, you can double-click on top of the project name to set it current. If another project is current at the time, it is closed, and the new project is set current.

Closing a Project

There might be times when you do not wish to work in a project environment within Architectural Desktop. You have the option of closing a project so you do not accidentally make changes to the current project. To close a project, access the **Project Browser**, right-click over the project, and select **Close Current Project** from the shortcut menu. This closes the current project and clears the information from the project header. If you need to work on the previous project or a different project later, find the project in the project selector and set the project current.

NOTE A project must be closed before it can be moved or renamed within the **Project Browser** or deleted from Windows Explorer.

Adjusting Project Settings

After a project has been created and set current, its properties can be defined or changed. For example, a specific HTML file can be assigned to a project for use in the bulletin board area; the location for template drawing files can be assigned; reference file settings can be controlled; and paths for tool palettes, detail libraries, and keynotes can be established. These are considered *general properties*.

To access the general properties for a project, locate the current project in the **Project Browser**. Right-click over the project in the project selector, and pick **Project Properties...** from the shortcut menu. This displays the **Modify Project** worksheet shown in **Figure 3-13**.

The **Modify Project** worksheet contains a number of general properties and their current settings. If a project has been copied in its entirety from an existing project, the original project settings are used here. Some of the properties allow you to pick in the text box and enter a new value, others display an ellipsis (**...**) button when the text box is selected so you can browse for a new path, and other properties display a drop-down list arrow when the text box is selected for a **Yes** or **No** choice. Below the properties table are four buttons to further set up the properties for the project. The properties are described as follows:

Figure 3-13.
The **Modify Project** worksheet is used to adjust the general properties of a project. Project details such as the owner, address, and completion date can be filled out by picking the **Project Details: Edit** button.

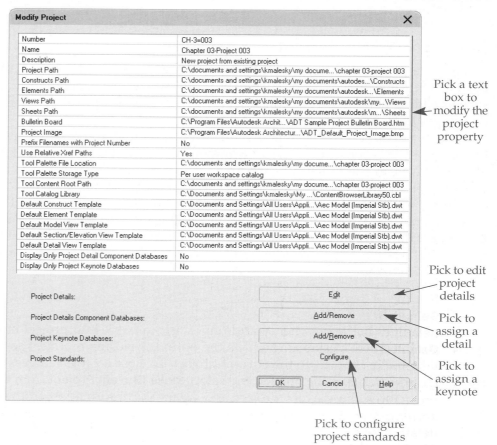

- **Number.** A new number-letter combination can be entered here by picking the text box and entering a new value.
- **Name.** If a new name is entered here, the new name is displayed only in the **Project Browser** and **Project Navigator**. Changing the name of the project here is not recommended.
- **Description.** Pick this text box to enter a new description for the project, which will be displayed in the project header.
- **Constructs Path.** This path is used to specify where the construct drawings for the project can be found. Standard practice is to use the default path set here.
- **Elements Path.** This path is used to specify where the element drawings for the project can be found. Standard practice is to use the default path set here.
- **Views Path.** This path is used to specify where the view drawings for the project can be found. Standard practice is to use the default path set here.
- **Sheets Path.** This path is used to specify where the sheet drawings for the project can be found. Standard practice is to use the default path set here.
- **Bulletin Board.** Selecting this property displays an ellipsis (**...**) button, where an HTML file can be selected for use in the bulletin board area of the **Project Browser**.
- **Project Image.** This property is used to assign a small image to the project displayed in the project header of the **Project Browser**.
- **Prefix Filenames with Project Number.** If **Yes** is selected, drawing file names created within the project are prefixed with the project number. If **No** is selected, the drawings created within the project are named without the prefix.

- **Use Relative Xref Paths.** When **Yes** is selected, xref drawings within the project are inserted with xref paths relative to the project folder. A **No** value creates a permanent path for the reference drawings used in a drawing so Architectural Desktop must always look in that specific path to reload the reference drawing.
- **Tool Palette File Location.** This property is used to associate a tool palette group to the project.
- **Tool Palette Storage Type.** The **Shared workspace catalog** option adds the path found in the **Tool Palette File Location** property to the user's project profile, and the tool catalog is used from the specified location. If the **Per user workspace catalog** option is selected, a folder is created under the \\Documents and Settings*user login name*\ folder, and tool palettes are copied to that folder.
- **Tool Content Root Path.** This property is used to create a root path for the tools used in the project's tool palette group.
- **Tool Catalog Library.** This property is used to specify a content user library (.cbl file) to be displayed when the **Content Browser** is opened from the **Project Navigator**.
- **Default Construct Template.** This property is used to select a default drawing template to be used for construct drawings.
- **Default Element Template.** This property selects a default drawing to be used for element drawings.
- **Default Model View Template.** Use this property to select a default drawing template for use in model view drawings. *Model view drawings* are drawings in which constructs are referenced, documented, and annotated.
- **Default Section/Elevation View Template.** This property is used to specify a default drawing template for section or elevation view drawings.
- **Default Detail View Template.** Use this property to specify a default drawing template for detail drawings.
- **Display Only Project Detail Component Databases.** Selecting **Yes** limits the project to use only specific detail component databases. A *detail component database* contains components that can be assembled to produce large-scale detail drawings. **No** uses the default detail component databases.
- **Display Only Project Keynote Databases.** Selecting **Yes** restricts keynotes added to the drawing to be obtained from a specific database assigned to the project. Selecting **No** causes the project to use the default keynote database.
- **Project Details:.** Selecting the **Edit** button displays the **Project Details** worksheet. See **Figure 3-14.** This worksheet is used to contain project information.
- **Project Details Component Databases:.** Use the **Add/Remove** button to open the **Configure Detail Component Databases** dialog box. This dialog box is used to select .mdb database files that have been created with detail components for use in large-scale detail drawings.
- **Project Keynote Databases:.** Use the **Add/Remove** button to open the **Add/ Remove Keynote Databases** dialog box. This dialog box is used to select .mdb database files that contain keynotes to be used by the project in drawings.
- **Project Standards:.** Selecting the **Configure** button displays the **Configure AEC Project Standards** dialog box, where drawing and object standards can be assigned to the project so drawings generated by the project conform to a standard.

After the properties for a project have been configured, the **Modify Project** worksheet can be closed by selecting the **OK** button. This returns you to the **Project Browser**. Pick the **Close** button to close the **Project Browser**, and open the **Project Navigator**, where work on the project can be started.

Exercise
3-5   Complete the Exercise on the Student CD.

Figure 3-14.
The **Project Details** worksheet is used to enter pertinent information about the project. This information can be recalled at any time into a drawing.

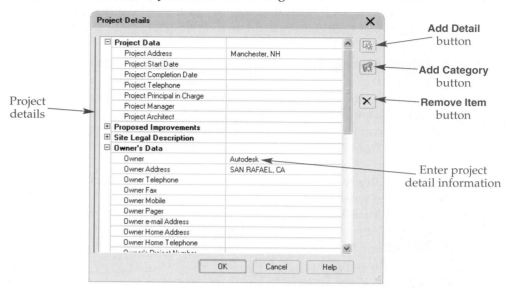

Project details

Add Detail button

Add Category button

Remove Item button

Enter project detail information

The Project Navigator

Type
[Ctrl]+[5]
Pull-Down Menu
Window
> Project Navigator
Palette
Toolbar
Navigation
Project Navigator
Palette

After a project has been set current in the **Project Browser** and the window has been closed, the **Project Navigator** is displayed. See **Figure 3-15.** Occasionally, the **Project Navigator** is not displayed. The **Project Navigator** can be toggled on or off by picking **Window** > **Project Navigator Palette**, picking the **Project Navigator Palette** button in the **Navigation** toolbar, or pressing the [Ctrl]+[5] key combination.

Figure 3-15.
The **Project Navigator** is similar to the **Tool Palettes** window. The **Project Navigator** includes four tabs for adjusting project levels and divisions and creating and managing construct, view, and sheet drawings.

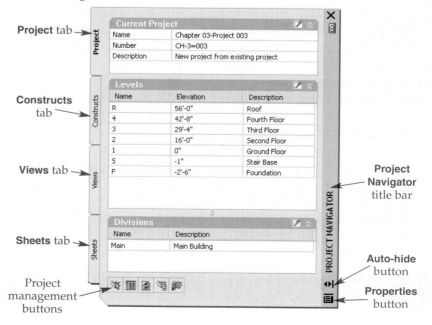

Project tab

Constructs tab

Views tab

Sheets tab

Project management buttons

Project Navigator title bar

Auto-hide button

Properties button

Architectural Desktop and Its Applications

The **Project Navigator** is the main interface for creating, opening, managing, and connecting drawings within a project. This palette includes four tabs: **Project**, **Constructs**, **Views**, and **Sheets**. These tabs are described as follows.

The Project Tab

The **Project** tab is used to add, modify, and delete the levels and divisions used within the project; change the project information; launch the **Project Browser** and **Content Browser**; and refresh the project. At the top of the **Project** tab is information pertaining to the current project. The name, number, and description for the project are displayed under the **Current Project:** header. See **Figure 3-16.** These text fields can be changed by picking the **Edit Project** button in the header, which displays the **Modify Project** worksheet previously described. Changing the number renumbers the project, and changing the name renames the project only within the **Project Browser** and **Project Navigator**.

Buildings are split into horizontal levels and vertical divisions, or segments. Horizontal levels can represent the floors and horizontal framing within the building. Vertical divisions can represent building wings or cores, such as a stairwell or an elevator shaft. Below the **Current Project** section of the **Project** tab is the **Levels** section. This portion of the tab controls the elevation location of each level of a building and the height of the level from floor to floor. See **Figure 3-16.** To add, modify, or delete levels within a project, pick the **Edit Levels** button in the **Levels** section header. This displays the **Levels** worksheet shown in **Figure 3-17.**

Figure 3-16.
The **Project** tab is used to add, delete, and modify the levels and divisions within the project and change project information.

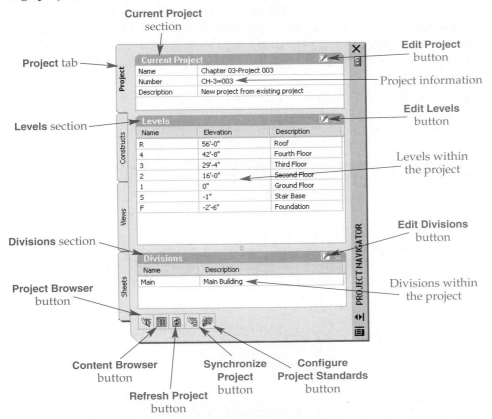

Figure 3-17.
The **Levels** worksheet is used to add, modify, or delete levels within a building project.

Level names can be letters, numbers, or words

Level elevations indicate the height at which each level begins

Level heights from floor to floor control the height of a single level

Level IDs are used in schedules to identify the floor where items belong

Level descriptions

Add Level button

Remove Level button

Name	Floor Elevation	Floor to Floor Height	ID	Description
R	56'-0"	13'-4"	R	Roof
4	42'-8"	13'-4"	4	Fourth Floor
3	29'-4"	13'-4"	3	Third Floor
2	16'-0"	13'-4"	2	Second Floor
1	0"	16'-0"	1	Ground Floor
S	-1"	1"	S	Stair Base
F	-2'-6"	2'-6"	F	Foundation

☑ Auto-Adjust Elevation

OK   Cancel   Help

Select to automatically adjust level elevations

Figure 3-17 displays the **Levels** worksheet with a few levels created. To add a new level, pick the **Add Level** button. This adds a new level above the currently selected level in the table. Pick inside the cells of the new level to configure its settings, such as the name, floor elevation, floor-to-floor height, ID, and description. If the **Auto-Adjust Elevation** check box is selected, the elevations of all levels above or below the new level are automatically adjusted.

New levels can also be created by right-clicking over an existing level. This displays a shortcut menu of options, shown in **Figure 3-18**, which include the following:
- **Add Level Above.** This option adds a new level above the currently selected level.
- **Add Level Below.** Pick this option to add a new level below the currently selected level.
- **Copy Level.** Use this option to copy a level and its settings to the Windows Clipboard.

Figure 3-18.
Right-clicking over an existing level displays a shortcut menu of options for creating and modifying levels.

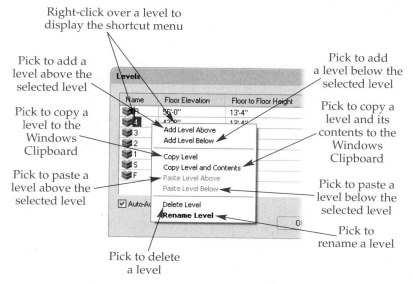

Right-click over a level to display the shortcut menu

Pick to add a level above the selected level

Pick to copy a level to the Windows Clipboard

Pick to paste a level above the selected level

Pick to add a level below the selected level

Pick to copy a level and its contents to the Windows Clipboard

Pick to paste a level below the selected level

Pick to rename a level

Pick to delete a level

- **Copy Level and Contents.** This option is used to copy a level, its settings, and any contents assigned to the level, such as constructs or elements, to the Clipboard.
- **Paste Level Above.** Use this option to paste a level from the Clipboard above the currently selected level.
- **Paste Level Below.** Use this option to paste a level from the Clipboard below the currently selected level.
- **Delete Level.** Pick to delete the currently selected level.
- **Rename Level.** Use this to rename the selected level.

When you are finished adding or modifying levels, pick the **OK** button to exit the **Levels** worksheet.

The last section in the **Project** tab is the **Divisions** section. To add, modify, or delete divisions, pick the **Edit Divisions** button found in the **Divisions** header. This displays the **Divisions** worksheet shown in **Figure 3-19**. This worksheet includes three columns: **Name**, **ID**, and **Description**. To the right of the table are two buttons: **Add Division** and **Delete Division**. The following columns are used to define divisions within a building:

- **Name.** Use this column to enter a name for the selected division.
- **ID.** Similar to the **ID** column for levels, this column is used in schedules to identify which division objects have been placed into.
- **Description.** This column is used to describe a division.

At the bottom of the **Project** tab are five buttons, shown in **Figure 3-20**. They are used to manage your project and are described as follows:

- **Project Browser.** Pick this button to access the **Project Browser**, where project information can be reviewed or another project can be set current.
- **Content Browser.** Pick this button to open the **Content Browser** window, displaying any tool catalogs assigned to the current project.
- **Refresh Project.** This button is used to refresh the view within the **Project Navigator**. When multiple users are working within the same project, the **Project Navigator** does not automatically update the display of new or deleted files within the **Project Navigator**. Pick the **Refresh Project** button to refresh the display of the **Project Navigator**.
- **Synchronize Project.** Use this button to synchronize a project with any standards assigned. Occasionally, standards are updated or modified. In these situations, the project must be synchronized with the standards.
- **Configure Project Standards.** Use this button to open the **Configure AEC Project Standards** dialog box, where standards for a project can be configured.

After you have finished making any adjustments to the project in the **Project** tab, drawings can be created and modified using the other three tabs within the **Project Navigator**.

Figure 3-19.
The **Divisions** worksheet is used to add, modify, or delete divisions within a project.

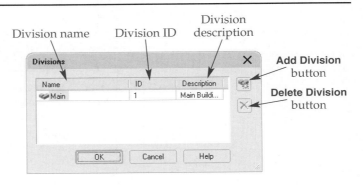

Figure 3-20.
The buttons at the bottom of the **Project** tab are used to manage your project.

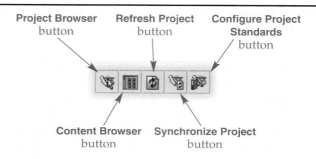

Project Browser button Refresh Project button Configure Project Standards button

Content Browser button Synchronize Project button

Exercise 3-6

Complete the Exercise on the Student CD.

The Constructs Tab

The **Constructs** tab is used to organize, manage, create, and modify construct and element drawings. Within the **Constructs** tab is a Drawing Explorer tree, which contains two main folders, or *categories*: Constructs and Elements. Under each of these folders, new subfolders, or categories; constructs; or elements can be created and organized. See **Figure 3-21.**

Figure 3-21.
The **Constructs** tab is used to organize, manage, create, and modify construct and element drawings.

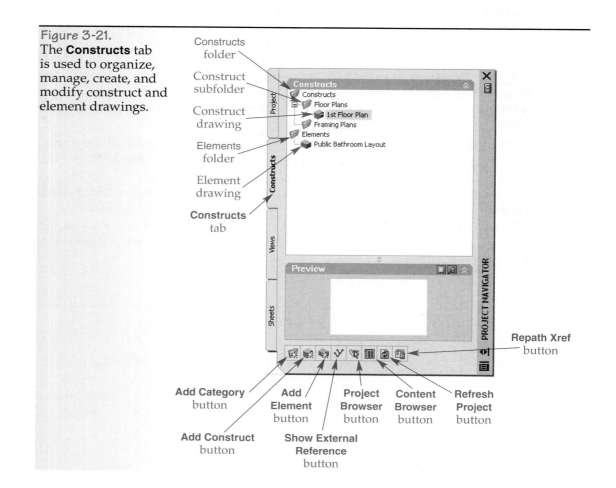

Constructs folder

Construct subfolder

Construct drawing

Elements folder

Element drawing

Constructs tab

Repath Xref button

Add Category button Add Element button Project Browser button Content Browser button Refresh Project button

Add Construct button Show External Reference button

Adding Categories

Categories are used to organize constructs and elements into subgroups for easy identification and arrangement within the project. They can be added to either the Constructs or Elements folder and under new categories you create. To add a category to a folder, select the folder where the new category will be added, and pick the **Add Category** button at the bottom of the **Constructs** tab. See Figure 3-21. A new folder is created under the selected folder. Next, enter a name for the folder. Figure 3-21 shows Floor Plans and Framing Plans categories under the Constructs folder as an example. Alternatively, you can right-click over the folder where you will be adding a category and then pick **New** > **Category** from the shortcut menu. This also adds a new folder that can be named. If a folder was named incorrectly or needs to be renamed, right-click over the folder, select the **Rename** command from the shortcut menu, and enter a new name for the folder. Occasionally, a folder is created under the wrong folder or category. To correct this, drag and drop the folder on top of the desired folder. Categories can also be removed from the project structure by right-clicking over the folder and selecting the **Delete** option from the shortcut menu.

Adding a Construct

To add a construct drawing to the project, select the Constructs folder or a subcategory under the Constructs folder where the construct drawing will be added. Pick the **Add Construct** button at the bottom of the tab or right-click over the folder and pick **New** > **Construct...** from the shortcut menu. This displays the **Add Construct** worksheet shown in Figure 3-22. The **Add Construct** worksheet is used to assign the new construct to a level and division within the project. As you work with the construct, new geometry can be added, and other constructs or elements can be referenced, so new geometry is tied into the building information model. You can open and work on as many construct drawings as needed.

Figure 3-22.
The **Add Construct** worksheet is used to create a new construct drawing and assign it to a level and division.

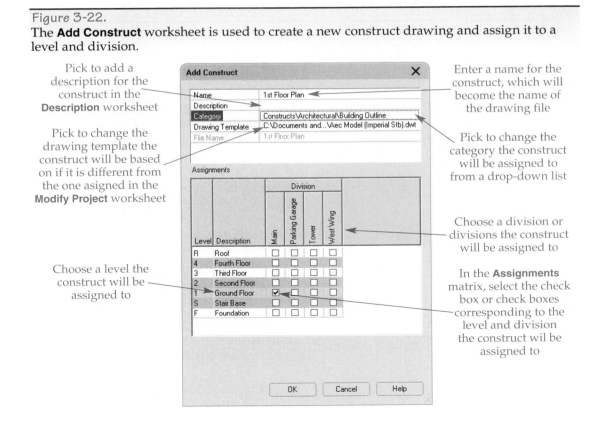

Complete the Exercise on the Student CD.

Copying Constructs to Levels

When creating multistory buildings, you can have several floor levels that maintain a common shape and size. Once an initial construct has been created and geometry has been drawn on the construct, the construct can be copied into several levels. To copy an existing construct into multiple levels, select the construct to copy in the **Project Navigator**, right-click, and select the **Copy Construct to Levels...** command. This opens the **Copy Construct to Levels** worksheet shown in Figure 3-23. Select the levels to which you want the construct copied. The new constructs are named the same as the original construct, but are appended with a consecutive number. Right-click each construct and use the **Rename** command to rename the new copied constructs. Alternatively, right-click over a new construct and select the **Properties** command from the menu. Review the level where the construct is assigned in the **Modify Construct** worksheet, and rename the construct in this worksheet. This is a preferred method, because you can review the assigned level and name the new construct accordingly. When copying a construct to a new level, the contents within the original construct are also copied, making it easy to quickly assemble a multistory building from a single floor.

NOTE The level being copied is automatically selected by default. You cannot check this level.

Exercise 3-8

Complete the Exercise on the Student CD.

Adding an Element

To add an element drawing to the project, select the Elements folder or a subcategory under the Elements folder where the element drawing will be added. Pick the **Add Element** button at the bottom of the **Constructs** tab or right-click over the folder and pick **New > Element...** from the shortcut menu. This displays the **Add Element**

Figure 3-23.
The **Copy Construct to Levels** worksheet is used to copy an existing construct to multiple levels, creating new constructs with geometry copied from the original construct.

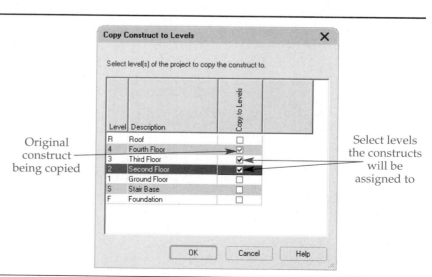

Original construct being copied

Select levels the constructs will be assigned to

Architectural Desktop and Its Applications

Figure 3-24.
The **Add Element** worksheet is used to create a new element drawing within the **Project Navigator**.

Enter a description for the element drawing in the **Description** worksheet

Select a template from the **Drawing Template** dialog box

Enter a name for the element drawing, which will become the name of the drawing file

Pick an Elements category to create the element in by selecting this text box to display a drop-down button

worksheet. See **Figure 3-24.** The **Add Element** worksheet is used to create the new element within the project. This worksheet includes the same settings as the **Add Construct** worksheet. Unlike constructs, however, elements are not assigned to a level, because they can be repeated in different locations throughout the building. To repeat an element drawing within different constructs, you reference the element drawing into a construct.

Exercise 3-9

Complete the Exercise on the Student CD.

Referencing Elements and Constructs

One of the benefits of using the project management system is the use of *reference files.* Referencing drawing files allows you to construct the building by seeing where previously drawn geometry or other building features occur in other drawings. For example, suppose you created a first floor construct containing the shell or outer portions of the building and the elevator core needs to be drawn in a separate element. The elevator core is a repeatable portion of the building that maintains its location and size throughout the building. This allows the element drawing to be created, which can then be referenced into the other floor constructs. Before the element can be referenced into all the floors, you need to reference the first floor construct into the element drawing. This allows you to determine where the elevator core must be drawn, in relation to the building drawn in the construct. See **Figure 3-25.** After drawing the elevator core in the element drawing, the construct drawing is detached, and then the element can be referenced into other constructs.

There are three main methods of referencing element or construct drawings: **Xref Attach**, **Xref Overlay**, and **Insert as Block**. These options are described as follows:

- **Xref Attach.** This option creates a link from the original element or construct into the element, construct, or view drawing to which it is being referenced. The main drawing where other files are being referenced is also known as the *host drawing*. When the host drawing is opened, the linked reference file is displayed. If any changes are made to the original element or construct, the changes are reflected in the host drawing. Attached drawings are carried forward to other host drawings. This is called *nesting*.
- **Xref Overlay.** Similar to **Xref Attach**, this option creates a link from the original element or construct into the host drawing to which it is being referenced. When the host drawing is opened, the overlaid reference file is displayed with the latest changes. Overlaid drawings cannot be carried forward to other host drawings, but they can be overlaid separately into other host drawings.

Figure 3-25.
Referencing element and construct drawings together will aid you in the construction of the building model, by being able to create new geometry in relation to different portions of the building. This will keep drawings in smaller, more manageable pieces, which several people on the project team can work on simultaneously.

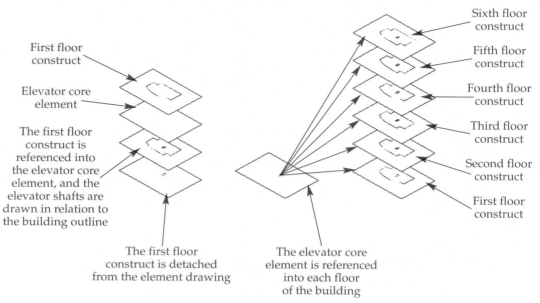

First floor construct

Elevator core element

The first floor construct is referenced into the elevator core element, and the elevator shafts are drawn in relation to the building outline

The first floor construct is detached from the element drawing

The elevator core element is referenced into each floor of the building

Sixth floor construct

Fifth floor construct

Fourth floor construct

Third floor construct

Second floor construct

First floor construct

- **Insert as Block.** This option is similar to both the xref options previously mentioned. The difference is that this option inserts the element or construct fully into the host drawing without creating a link to the original drawing. If changes are made to the original element or construct, they are not updated in the host drawing.

To reference an element drawing or a construct drawing into a host element or construct drawing, drag the drawing to be referenced from the **Project Navigator** onto the drawing window of the host drawing. Depending on the type of file being referenced, the file is referenced into the host drawing as an attached xref or overlaid xref.

When element drawings are dragged and dropped onto a host drawing, whether it is another element drawing or a construct drawing, they are attached to the host drawing. If construct drawings are dragged and dropped onto a host drawing, they are overlaid to the host. Alternatively, right-clicking over the element or construct in the **Constructs** tab of the **Project Navigator** displays a shortcut menu with options to **Xref Attach**, **Xref Overlay**, or **Insert as Block**.

When a drawing contains a reference file, the **Manage Xrefs** icon is displayed in the tray at the right end of the status bar. See **Figure 3-26.** Picking this icon opens the **External References** palette. Alternatively, the **External References** palette can be accessed by picking **Insert > External References...** or typing XR or XREF.

The xref is a permanent part of the drawing, so erasing the xref image removes the image only from the screen, but not from the drawing's memory. Erasing is not a recommended method for removing a reference file. If an xref no longer needs to be referenced, it must be detached through the **External References** palette.

To detach an xref, highlight the xref, right-click, and select the **Detach** option. See **Figure 3-27.** This detaches the reference file from the drawing and removes all layers associated with the xref. The referenced drawing image is also removed from the drawing screen. If the reference file needs to be used later, it must be attached to the drawing again.

XREF

Type
XREF
XR

Pull-Down Menu
Insert
> External References...

Status Bar

Manage Xrefs

Figure 3-26.
Once a drawing has been referenced into a host drawing, the host drawing will display the **Manage Xrefs** icon in the tray at the right end of the status bar. Pick the icon to display the **External References** palette.

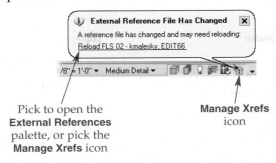

Pick to open the
External References
palette, or pick the
Manage Xrefs icon

Manage Xrefs
icon

Figure 3-27.
The **External References** palette is used to manage reference drawings. To detach a drawing, select the drawing in the palette, right-click, and select the **Detach** option. This will detach the reference file.

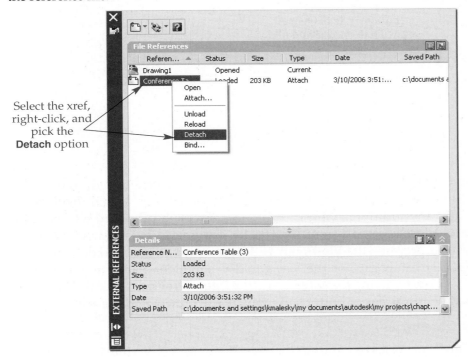

Select the xref,
right-click, and
pick the
Detach option

NOTE

If an xref containing nested xrefs is detached from the drawing, any nested reference files are also removed from the drawing.

Additional Features within the Constructs Tab

Below the Drawing Explorer tree in the **Constructs** tab is a **Detail/Preview** pane. The **Detail/Preview** pane displays the details about the selected drawing or a preview of the drawing selected in the Drawing Explorer tree. Pick either the **Detail** or **Preview** button in the **Detail/Preview** pane to display the appropriate information. Below the **Detail/Preview** pane are eight buttons to manage constructs, elements, standards, and xrefs. See **Figure 3-28.**

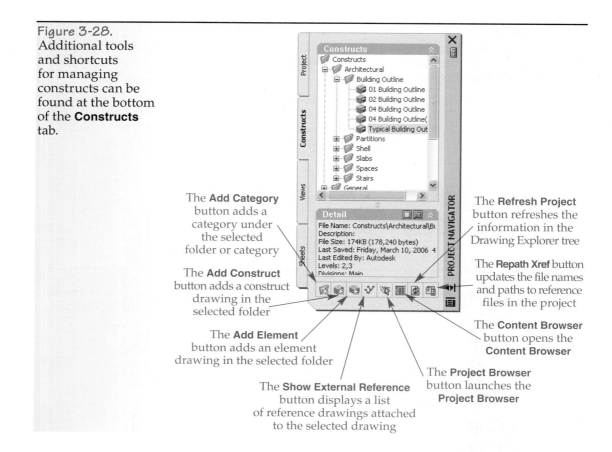

Figure 3-28.
Additional tools
and shortcuts
for managing
constructs can be
found at the bottom
of the **Constructs**
tab.

The **Add Category** button adds a category under the selected folder or category

The **Add Construct** button adds a construct drawing in the selected folder

The **Add Element** button adds an element drawing in the selected folder

The **Show External Reference** button displays a list of reference drawings attached to the selected drawing

The **Refresh Project** button refreshes the information in the Drawing Explorer tree

The **Repath Xref** button updates the file names and paths to reference files in the project

The **Content Browser** button opens the **Content Browser**

The **Project Browser** button launches the **Project Browser**

The Views Tab

The **Views** tab in the **Project Navigator** is used to create view drawings. See Figure 3-29. The **Views** tab consists of a Drawing Explorer tree, which displays the Views category and any additional view category folders or view drawings. Depending on how the project was created—from scratch, by copying a project structure, or by copying an existing project—the **Views** tab will have only the Views folder; the Views folder and subfolder categories; or the Views folder, subfolders, and view drawings; respectively. Below the Drawing Explorer tree is the **Detail/Preview** pane, and below the **Detail/Preview** pane is a series of buttons to manage the project and view drawings.

Adding View Categories

Adding view categories is similar to adding categories to the Constructs and Elements folders. To add a category to a folder, select a folder for the new category, and then pick the **Add Category** button at the bottom of the **Views** tab. See Figure 3-29. A new folder is created under the selected folder. Next, enter a name for the folder. Figure 3-29 shows Floor Plans, Elevations, and Sections categories under the Views folder as examples. Alternatively, you can right-click over the desired folder, and then select **New Category** from the shortcut menu. If a folder was named incorrectly or needs to be renamed, right-click over the folder and select the **Rename** command from the shortcut menu. Enter a new name for the folder. Categories can also be removed from the project structure by right-clicking over the folder and selecting the **Delete** option from the shortcut menu.

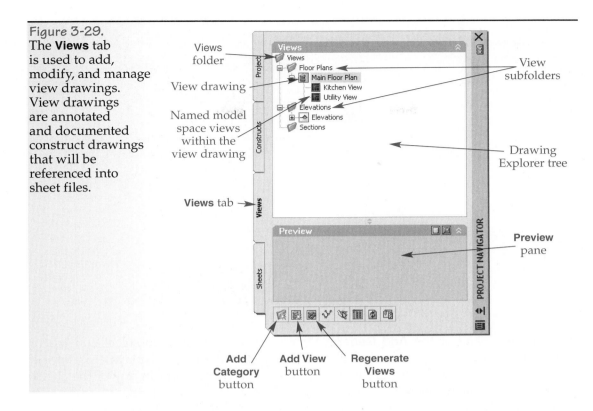

Figure 3-29.
The **Views** tab is used to add, modify, and manage view drawings. View drawings are annotated and documented construct drawings that will be referenced into sheet files.

Views folder

View drawing

Named model space views within the view drawing

Views tab →

View subfolders

Drawing Explorer tree

Preview pane

Add Category button

Add View button

Regenerate Views button

Creating a General View Drawing

A general view contains referenced construct drawings representing a specific view into the building model. If a general view is created, it is based on the template assigned to the **Default Model View Template** property in the project settings. General views are typically used in the creation of documented plan views of the building. Drawings such as floor plans, foundation plans, reflected ceiling plans, plumbing plans, and mechanical plans are created using a general view. General views can also be used to create 3D model views of the building, for use in design review, and renderings. To add a general view drawing to the project, select the Views folder or a subcategory under the Views folder, where the view drawing will be added. Pick the **Add View** button at the bottom of the **Views** tab, as shown in **Figure 3-29.** This displays the **Add View** worksheet shown in **Figure 3-30.** Select the **General View** radio button, and then pick the **OK** button to create a general view. Alternatively, you can right-click over the category where the new view drawing will be created and pick **New View Dwg > General...** from the shortcut menu.

After selecting either the **General View** radio button or **General...** from the shortcut menu, the **Add General View** worksheet is displayed. See **Figure 3-31.** Similar to the way you add construct drawings, enter a name and description for the new general view. Verify which category the view will be placed in and the template drawing being used for the view. When you are finished, pick the **Next** button.

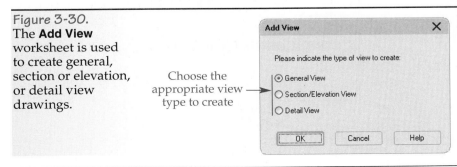

Figure 3-30.
The **Add View** worksheet is used to create general, section or elevation, or detail view drawings.

Choose the appropriate view type to create

Figure 3-31.
The **Add General View** worksheet is used to set up and create a general view drawing.

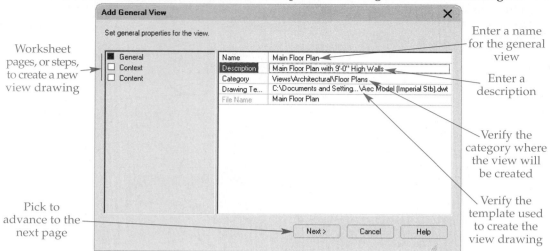

Worksheet pages, or steps, to create a new view drawing

Enter a name for the general view

Enter a description

Verify the category where the view will be created

Verify the template used to create the view drawing

Pick to advance to the next page

The next page of the **Add General View** worksheet is used to select constructs to reference into the view drawing. See Figure 3-32. This page displays a list of the levels and divisions assigned to the project. Placing a check mark in any of the check boxes lets the **Project Navigator** know where to look for specific constructs to be used. For example, in Figure 3-32, the check box at the intersection of the **Main Floor** level and the **Joist Foundation** division indicates to the **Project Navigator** to look for any constructs assigned to the Main Floor level and the Joist Foundation division. When you are finished selecting the levels and divisions, pick the **Next** button to advance to the final page.

NOTE

Typically, if you are creating a general view for a 2D plan view, selecting a single check box for the desired level to be documented is appropriate. If you are creating a 3D model view, checking one or more levels might be desired.

Figure 3-32.
The **Context** page of the **Add General View** worksheet is used to select the levels and divisions where construct drawings to be referenced can be found.

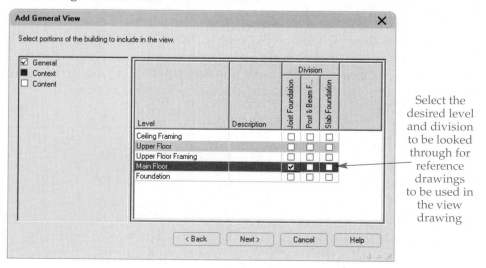

Select the desired level and division to be looked through for reference drawings to be used in the view drawing

Figure 3-33.
The **Content** page of the **Add General View** worksheet is used to select drawings or subcategories of constructs that meet the context criteria and will be referenced into the general view drawing.

Select a category to include all constructs and future constructs within the category to be referenced into the view drawing

Select the desired drawings to be referenced into the view drawing

Pick to create the general view drawing

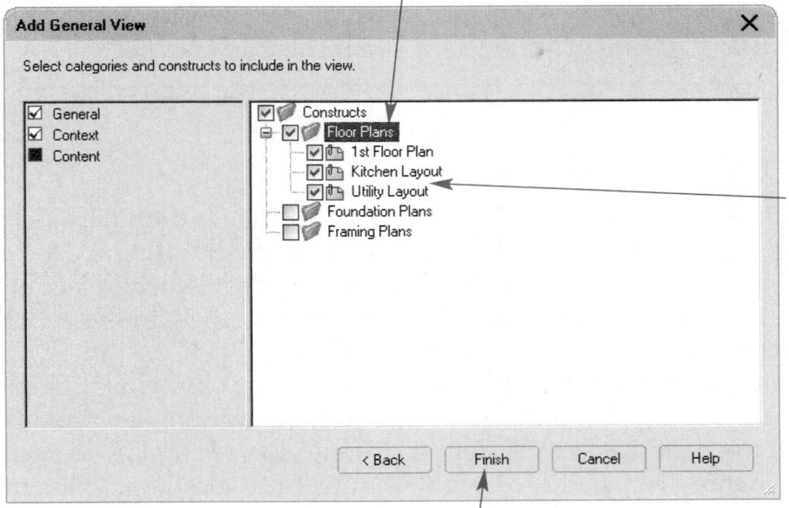

The final page of the **Add General View** worksheet displays a list of constructs that meet the level and division criteria selected on the **Context** page. See **Figure 3-33.** Only construct drawings meeting the levels and divisions selected are displayed. This page displays the Constructs folder and any subfolders, plus any construct drawings meeting the selected level and division context. In **Figure 3-33,** the 1st Floor Plan, Kitchen Layout, and Utility Layout construct drawings are displayed because they are assigned to the Main Floor level and Joist Foundation division.

Select the desired construct drawings to be referenced into the view. If you select a subcategory folder, any drawings within the subcategory are selected. An advantage is that, as new constructs are added under this subcategory and assigned to the Main Floor level and Joist Foundation division, they are automatically referenced into the view drawing. When you are finished selecting the desired drawings and subcategories, pick the **Finish** button to create the general view. Once the view drawing is created, double-click the view in the **Views** tab to open the file. Add any annotations, dimensions, and documentation to complete the view. AEC content for documenting view drawings will be discussed later in the book.

Exercise
3-10   Complete the Exercise on the Student CD.

Creating a Section or an Elevation View Drawing

A section or elevation view drawing contains referenced construct drawings stacked on top of one another to form a 3D building model. From the building model, 2D sections or elevations can be generated using section or elevation tools. Section and elevation view drawings are based on the **Default Section/Elevation View Template** property in the project settings.

The section or elevation view drawing is used to create sections or elevations from the building model, so you might decide to select more than one level and division combination to be included in the view. **Figure 3-34** indicates that all constructs assigned to each level under the **Main** division are available in the **Content** page. You do not have to select all the level and division check boxes. What you want shown in the section or elevation determines how many and which check boxes are selected. When you are finished, pick the **Next** button to advance to the **Content** page.

Exercise
3-11   *Complete the Exercise on the Student CD.*

Creating a Detail View Drawing

A detail view drawing contains referenced construct drawings that display one or more model space views of a defined portion of the building model. Model space views are defined areas of part of the building, such as a kitchen layout or stairwell, derived from a referenced construct. Detail view drawings are based on the **Default Detail View Template** property in the project settings.

These drawings are used in the generation of detail drawings. This type of view can be used in a way similar to the way section and elevation views are used, by using the 3D model to create 2D section details. Detail views can also be used in conjunction with the detail tools included with Architectural Desktop. Once the view with the constructs has been created, section and elevation tools can be used to create the 2D detail drawings from the 3D model. The view can be enhanced with the detailing tools, or new details can be drawn by hand using the detail tools.

To create a detail view, select the category where the new view will be created, and then pick the **Add View** button. This displays the **Add View** worksheet shown in **Figure 3-30**. In the **Add View** worksheet, select the **Detail View** radio button. Picking the **OK** button after selecting the view type displays the **Add Detail View** worksheet. This worksheet is identical to the worksheets for creating the general and section and

Figure 3-34.
When you are creating a section or elevation view drawing, one or more level and division check boxes can be selected. If you are creating partial sections, select only those levels that will be included in the section. Select all the levels if you are creating full elevations.

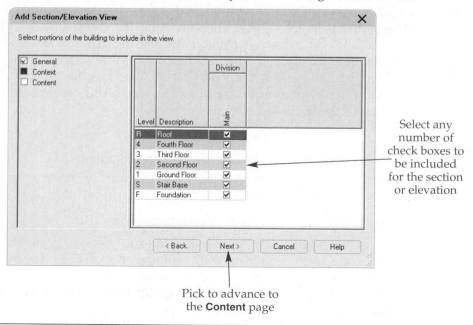

Select any number of check boxes to be included for the section or elevation

Pick to advance to the **Content** page

elevation view drawings. Alternatively, right-click over the category where the new view will be saved and pick **New View Dwg** > **Detail...** from the shortcut menu.

As with the previously discussed views, enter a name and description for the detail view, and verify the category to create the view in and the drawing template to be used. Pick the **Next** button to advance to the **Context** page. In the **Context** page, select any level and division check boxes that will be used to list drawings in the **Content** page and to generate detail drawings. If you are generating details from a 3D model, select any level and division categories that apply. Pick the **Next** button to advance to the **Content** page.

In the **Content** page, select the drawings that will be used to generate details. If you are planning on drawing details by hand, do not select any drawings. If you would like to create a detail by basing it on the 3D model, select any desired drawings that will be included in the detail. When you are finished, select the **Finish** button to generate the view drawing.

 Exercise 3-12 **Complete the Exercise on the Student CD.**

Creating Model Space Views

Model views are specific portions or areas of the building used to establish a viewing area of the building. They are the next step in working with view drawings and the transition to creating sheet drawings. A model view is created within a view drawing and includes its own name, description, and drawing scale. Later, when sheet views are created, model views are dragged and dropped onto a sheet drawing, where they are arranged on a sheet for plotting. Some tools, such as the 2D section and elevation tools, automatically generate model views. If you have created a general view of a floor plan with annotations and dimensions, a model view can be created around the floor plan, annotations, and dimensions, so it can be added to a sheet drawing. To create a model view, first open the view drawing where the model view will be created. In the **Views** tab of the **Project Navigator**, right-click over the opened view drawing and select **New Model Space View...** from the shortcut menu. This displays the **Add Model Space View** worksheet shown in **Figure 3-35**. In the **Add Model Space View** worksheet, enter a name for the model view and a description, and select a scale. Select the **Define View Window** button to return to the drawing, so a window can be established around the desired portion of the view drawing. See **Figure 3-36**. Keep in mind that the model views will be added to a sheet drawing and arranged on a sheet.

Figure 3-35.
The **Add Model Space View** worksheet is used to establish a new model view within a view drawing.

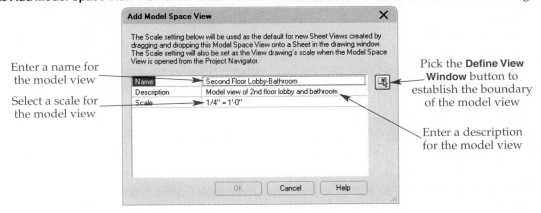

Figure 3-36.
Pick two opposite corners of a rectangle to establish the model view boundary.

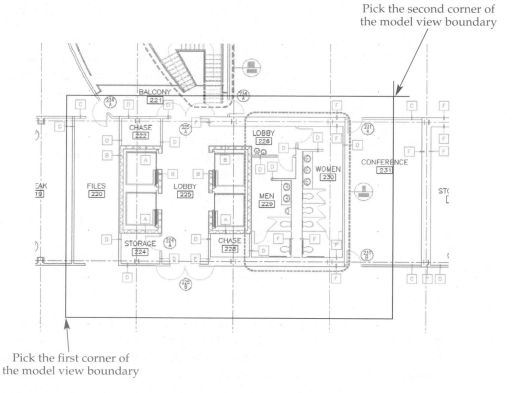

Pick the second corner of
the model view boundary

Pick the first corner of
the model view boundary

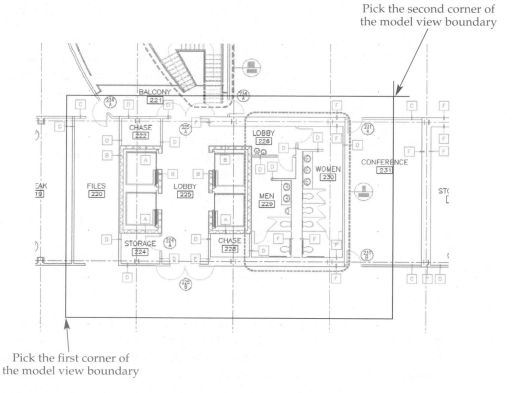

Exercise 3-13

Complete the Exercise on the Student CD.

The Sheets Tab

The final step within a project is to plot, or print, the drawings. Before plotting can be started, sheet drawings must be created, which contain referenced views arranged on different sheets. Sheet drawings are created in the **Sheets** tab of the **Project Navigator**. See **Figure 3-37.** The **Sheets** tab is similar to the **Constructs** and **Views** tabs. The Drawing Explorer tree includes the name of the project and, below that, a listing of subsets, or categories, in which the sheet drawings can be placed. As sheet drawings are created, they are placed under the subset they were assigned to, similar to categories. Depending on whether the project was created from scratch, the folder structure was copied, or the project was copied from an existing project, the subset list can vary. New subsets can be created for sheet organization by right-clicking over the project name or an existing subset in the Drawing Explorer tree and picking **New** > **Subset...** from the shortcut menu. This displays the **Subset Properties** dialog box shown in **Figure 3-38.**

In the **Subset Properties** dialog box, enter a new name for the subset. Below the **Subset name:** text box is a check box to create folders under the Sheets folder, which correspond to the subset names. If you have many sheets for a project, you might want to select this check box so new drawings added to different subsets are also added to a corresponding folder. The **Sheet creation template for subset:** text box displays the default sheet template specified in the project properties. Use the ellipsis (...) button to establish a different template to be used. At the bottom of the worksheet is the **Prompt for template** check box. Select this check box if you want to be prompted for a different template each time a sheet drawing is created. Pick the **OK** button when you are finished, to create the new subset.

Figure 3-37.
The **Sheets** tab is used to create and manage sheet drawings.

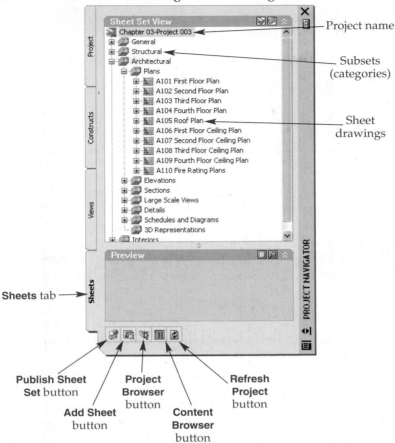

Project name

Subsets (categories)

Sheet drawings

Sheets tab →

Publish Sheet Set button

Add Sheet button

Project Browser button

Content Browser button

Refresh Project button

Figure 3-38.
The **Subset Properties** dialog box is used to create a subset (or category) in which to place sheet drawings.

Enter a name for the new subset

Select to create a corresponding folder for each subset in the project

Select to prompt for a sheet template each time a new sheet is created

Ensure the proper template is being used

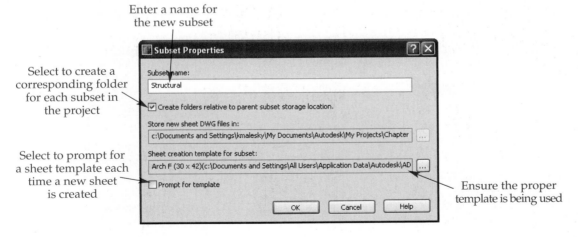

Adding Sheet Drawings

Creating sheet drawings is similar to creating construct or view drawings. First, select the subset where the sheet drawing will be created. Next, pick the **Add Sheet** button at the bottom of the **Sheets** tab, or right-click over the subset and pick **New** > **Sheet...** from the shortcut menu. This displays the **New Sheet** dialog box shown in **Figure 3-39**.

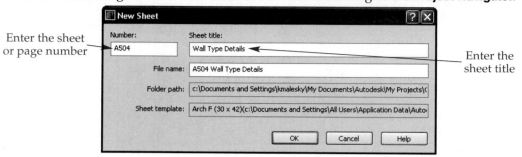

Enter the sheet or page number

Enter the sheet title

In the **New Sheet** dialog box, enter the sheet or page number of the sheet drawing. As you enter the sheet number, it is displayed in the **File name:** text box. A listing of sheet number conventions as suggested by the AIA and National Computer-Aided Design (CAD) Standard is available on the included CD in Appendix D. After entering the sheet number, enter the title of the sheet. As with the sheet number, the sheet title is entered in the **File name:** text box. When you are finished, pick the **OK** button to create the sheet drawing.

Adding Model Views to the Sheet

After a sheet drawing has been created, model views can be dragged and dropped onto the sheet, arranged, and then plotted. To add the model views to the sheet, open the desired sheet drawing. Once the sheet drawing is open, access the **Views** tab. Browse to the desired view drawing, and expand the plus sign beside each view drawing to be accessed to display a list of available model views. Drag the model space view name from the **Project Navigator** onto the sheet. See **Figure 3-40**. The model view dragged from the **Project Navigator** is attached to the crosshairs. The scale of the view is being referenced from the scale specified when creating the model view. If while dragging the model view onto the sheet, you determine that a different scale should be used,

Figure 3-40.
Drag and drop a model view from the **Project Navigator** onto the sheet. After the views have been added, use the **MOVE** command to arrange the views on the sheet as needed.

Drag a view from the **Project Navigator** onto the sheet

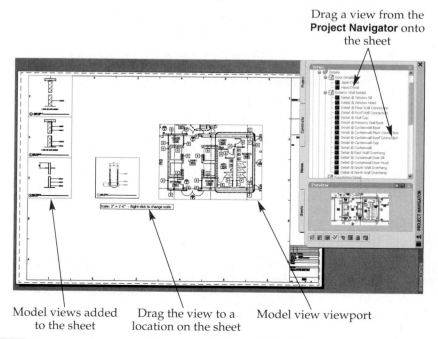

Model views added to the sheet

Drag the view to a location on the sheet

Model view viewport

right-click while the view is still attached to the crosshairs, to choose a different scale. Pick a location on the sheet where you want the view placed. This adds the model view viewport to the sheet.

 Exercise
3-14   Complete the Exercise on the Student CD.

Throughout the remainder of this text, AEC objects and tools are introduced. Each chapter provides a series of exercises that build on one another to create a residence. The use of the **Project Navigator** is the method used to create, organize, and modify the drawings for the residence. Alternatively, new drawings can be created and stored in your own directory system. Xrefs are also used to coordinate different drawings. If you are not planning on using the **Project Navigator**, you should review the **Share Data Between Drawings and Applications** help topic in the **Autodesk Architectural Desktop 2007 Help** window, for information regarding the use of xrefs. Use the following exercise to set up the project for the residence to be created throughout the remainder of this text.

 Exercise
3-15   Complete the Exercise on the Student CD.

 Chapter Test

Answer the following questions. Write your answers on a separate sheet of paper or complete the electronic chapter test on the Student CD.

1. Briefly describe the function of the xref management system.
2. Describe levels.
3. How many levels can be used in a building?
4. Define *divisions*.
5. Give a basic definition of a *construct*.
6. What are spanning objects? Briefly tell how they are used in a construct.
7. Describe and give an example of an element.
8. Explain the difference between constructs and elements.
9. Discuss the function of a view drawing.
10. Discuss the use and content of a sheet drawing.
11. Where are projects created?
12. Describe the function of the project selector and identify how projects are displayed.
13. Briefly explain the function of the project bulletin board.
14. Discuss how you use the **Project Browser** to start a new project from scratch.
15. Explain how you open the **Duplicate Project** dialog box to create a new project using the folder structure of an existing project.
16. Briefly discuss how new projects can be created based on existing projects as templates.
17. How do you access the **Add Project** dialog box when you are creating a project based on an existing project or template?
18. What condition must occur before you can work with an Architectural Desktop project, and how many projects can be set current at one time?
19. Define *general properties*.
20. Give at least two options for toggling the **Project Navigator** on and off.
21. Briefly explain the function of the **Project** tab.
22. Using examples, give a brief explanation of the difference between levels and divisions.
23. Identify the basic function of the **Constructs** tab.

24. How are categories used?
25. How do you copy an existing construct into multiple levels?
26. One of the benefits of using the project management system is the use of reference files. Explain what referencing drawing files allows you to do, and give an example.
27. Briefly discuss the function of the **Xref Attach** option.
28. Give another name for the main drawing that other files are being referenced into.
29. Briefly discuss what happens when you are using the **Xref Attach** option and changes are made to the original element or construct. What is the effect of these changes on attached drawings?
30. Define *nesting*.
31. Explain the function and give an example of using the **Xref Overlay** option.
32. Name the three different types of view drawings.
33. Describe and give an example of a model view.
34. Where are sheet drawings created?
35. After a sheet drawing has been created, how do you add model view viewports to the sheet?

Chapter Projects

Use the techniques covered in this chapter to create the following drawings.

1. Single-Level Residential Project
   A. Access the **Project Browser**.
   B. Use the project selector to browse to the \\Documents and Settings*your user login name*\\My Documents\\Autodesk\\My Projects folder or a folder designated by your instructor or CAD manager.
   C. Pick the **New Project** button to create a new project.
   D. In the **Add Project** dialog box, enter the following:
      a. **Project number:** Res-P01
      b. **Project Name:** Residential-Project-01
      c. **Project Description:** Single-level residential home
      d. Uncheck the **Create from template project:** check box.
      e. Pick the **OK** button when you are finished.
   E. Close the **Project Browser**.
   F. Access the **Project** tab of the **Project Navigator**.
   G. Pick the **Edit Levels** button.
   H. Create the following levels:

Name	Floor Elevation	Floor to Floor Height	ID	Description
Foundation	-2'-8"	2'-6"	F	Foundation
Grade	-8"	8"	G	Finished Grade
Main Floor	0"	8'-0"	M	Main Floor
Roof	0"	25'-0"	R	Roof

   I. Open P2-1.dwg, which was created in Chapter 2.
   J. Access the **Constructs** tab.
   K. Right-click over the Constructs folder and select **Save Current Dwg As Construct...** from the shortcut menu.
   L. Enter the following in the **Add Construct** worksheet:
      a. **Name:** Main Floor
      b. **Description:** Main Floor Plan
      c. **Category: Constructs**
      d. **Assignments: Main Floor**
   M. Drawing P2-1 is now renamed Main Floor.
   N. Save and close the Main Floor construct.

2. Single-Level Residential Project
   A. Access the **Project Browser**.
   B. Use the project selector to browse to the \\Documents and Settings*your user login name*\My Documents\Autodesk\My Projects folder or a folder designated by your instructor or CAD manager.
   C. Pick the **New Project** button to create a new project.
   D. In the **Add Project** dialog box, enter the following:
      a. **Project number:** Res-P02
      b. **Project Name:** Residential-Project-02
      c. **Project Description:** Single-level residential home
      d. Uncheck the **Create from template project:** check box.
      e. Pick the **OK** button when you are finished.
   E. Close the **Project Browser**.
   F. Access the **Project** tab of the **Project Navigator**.
   G. Pick the **Edit Levels** button.
   H. Create the following levels:

Name	Floor Elevation	Floor to Floor Height	ID	Description
Foundation	-2'-8"	2'-6"	F	Foundation
Grade	-1'-8"	8"	G	Finished Grade
Main Floor Framing	-1'-0"	1'-0"	MFF	Main Floor Framing
Main Floor	0"	8'-0"	M	Main Floor
Roof	0"	25'-0"	R	Roof

   I. Open P2-2.dwg, which was created in Chapter 2.
   J. Access the **Constructs** tab.
   K. Right-click over the Constructs folder and select **Save Current Dwg As Construct...** from the shortcut menu.
   L. Enter the following in the **Add Construct** worksheet:
      a. **Name:** Main Floor
      b. **Description:** Main Floor Plan
      c. **Category:** **Constructs**
      d. **Assignments:** **Main Floor**
   M. Drawing P2-2 is now renamed Main Floor.
   N. Save and close the Main Floor construct.

3. Two-Story Residential Project
   A. Access the **Project Browser**.
   B. Use the project selector to browse to the \\Documents and Settings*your user login name*\My Documents\Autodesk\My Projects folder or a folder designated by your instructor or CAD manager.
   C. Pick the **New Project** button to create a new project.
   D. In the **Add Project** dialog box, enter the following:
       a. **Project number:** Res-P03
       b. **Project Name:** Residential-Project-03
       c. **Project Description:** Two-story residential home
       d. Uncheck the **Create from template project:** check box.
       e. Pick the **OK** button when you are finished.
   E. Close the **Project Browser**.
   F. Access the **Project** tab of the **Project Navigator**.
   G. Pick the **Edit Levels** button.
   H. Create the following levels:

Name	Floor Elevation	Floor to Floor Height	ID	Description
Foundation	-2'-8"	2'-6"	F	Foundation
Grade	-8"	8"	G	Finished Grade
Main Floor	0"	9'-0"	M	Main Floor
Roof	0"	32'-0"	R	Roof
Upper Floor Framings	9'-0"	1'-0"	UFF	Upper Floor Framing
Upper Floor	10'-0"	9'-0"	U	Upper Floor

   I. Open P2-3.dwg, which was created in Chapter 2.
   J. Access the **Constructs** tab.
   K. Right-click over the Constructs folder and select **Save Current Dwg As Construct…** from the shortcut menu.
   L. Enter the following in the **Add Construct** worksheet:
       a. **Name**: Main Floor
       b. **Description**: Main Floor Plan
       c. **Category**: **Constructs**
       d. **Assignments**: **Main Floor**
   M. Drawing P2-3 is now renamed Main Floor.
   N. Pick the **Add Construct** button to add a new construct.
   O. Enter the following in the **Add Construct** worksheet:
       a. **Name**: Upper Floor
       b. **Description**: Upper Floor Plan
       c. **Category**: **Constructs**
       d. **Assignments**: **Upper Floor**
   P. Double-click the Main Floor construct from the **Project Navigator** to switch to the drawing.
   Q. Select the lines and polylines used to draw the upper floor layout. Right-click and pick **Clipboard** > **Cut** from the shortcut menu.
   R. Double-click the Upper Floor construct from the **Project Navigator** to switch to the drawing.
   S. Right-click in the drawing area and select **Clipboard** > **Paste to Original Coordinates** from the shortcut menu.
   T. Drag and drop the Main Floor construct into the Upper Floor construct drawing.
   U. Move the upper floor lines so they line up with the main floor building outline.
   V. Detach the Main Floor construct.
   W. Save and close the Main Floor and Upper Floor constructs.

4. Two-Story Residential Project
   A. Access the **Project Browser**.
   B. Use the project selector to browse to the \\Documents and Settings*your user login name*\My Documents\Autodesk\My Projects folder or a folder designated by your instructor or CAD manager.
   C. Pick the **New Project** button to create a new project.
   D. In the **Add Project** dialog box, enter the following:
       a. **Project number:** Res-P04
       b. **Project Name:** Residential-Project-04
       c. **Project Description:** Two-story residential home
       d. Uncheck the **Create from template project:** check box.
       e. Pick the **OK** button when you are finished.
   E. Close the **Project Browser**.
   F. Access the **Project** tab of the **Project Navigator**.
   G. Pick the **Edit Levels** button.
   H. Create the following levels:

Name	Floor Elevation	Floor to Floor Height	ID	Description
Foundation	2'-8"	2'-6"	F	Foundation
Grade	-8"	8"	G	Finished Grade
Main Floor	0"	9'-0"	M	Main Floor
Roof	0"	32'-0"	R	Roof
Upper Floor Framing	9'-0"	1'-0"	UFF	Upper Floor Framing
Upper Floor	10'-0"	8'-0"	U	Upper Floor

   I. Open P2-4.dwg, which was created in Chapter 2.
   J. Access the **Constructs** tab.
   K. Right-click over the Constructs folder and select **Save Current Dwg As Construct...** from the shortcut menu.
   L. Enter the following in the **Add Construct** worksheet:
       a. **Name**: Main Floor
       b. **Description**: Main Floor Plan
       c. **Category**: **Constructs**
       d. **Assignments**: **Main Floor**
   M. Drawing P2-4 is now renamed Main Floor.
   N. Pick the **Add Construct** button to add a new construct.
   O. Enter the following in the **Add Construct** worksheet:
       a. **Name**: Upper Floor
       b. **Description**: Upper Floor Plan
       c. **Category**: **Constructs**
       d. **Assignments**: **Upper Floor**
   P. Double-click the Main Floor construct from the **Project Navigator** to switch to the drawing.
   Q. Select the lines and polylines used to draw the upper floor layout. Right-click and select **Clipboard** > **Cut** from the shortcut menu.
   R. Double-click the Upper Floor construct from the **Project Navigator** to switch to the drawing.
   S. Right-click in the drawing area and select **Clipboard** > **Paste to Original Coordinates** from the shortcut menu.
   T. Drag and drop the Main Floor construct into the Upper Floor construct drawing.
   U. Move the upper floor lines so they line up with the main floor building outline.
   V. Detach the Main Floor construct.
   W. Save and close the Main Floor and Upper Floor constructs.

5. Commercial Store Project
   A. Access the **Project Browser**.
   B. Use the project selector to browse to the \\Documents and Settings*your user login name*\My Documents\Autodesk\My Projects folder or a folder designated by your instructor or CAD manager.
   C. Pick the **New Project** button to create a new project.
   D. In the **Add Project** dialog box, enter the following:
      a. **Project number:** Cmrcl-P05
      b. **Project Name:** Commercial-Project-05
      c. **Project Description:** Single-Level Commercial Store
      d. Uncheck the **Create from template project:** check box.
      e. Pick the **OK** button when you are finished.
   E. Close the **Project Browser**.
   F. Access the **Project** tab of the **Project Navigator**.
   G. Pick the **Edit Levels** button.
   H. Create the following levels:

Name	Floor Elevation	Floor to Floor Height	ID	Description
Grade	-1'-0"	8"	G	Finished Grade
Foundation	-4"	4"	F	Slab Foundation
Main Floor	0"	12'-0"	M	Main Floor
Roof	0"	32'-0"	R	Roof
Ceiling Framing	12'-0"	1'-8"	CF	Ceiling Framing

   I. Open P2-5.dwg, which was created in Chapter 2.
   J. Access the **Constructs** tab.
   K. Right-click over the Constructs folder and select **Save Current Dwg As Construct...** from the shortcut menu.
   L. Enter the following in the **Add Construct** worksheet:
      a. **Name:** Main Floor
      b. **Description:** Main Floor Plan
      c. **Category: Constructs**
      d. **Assignments: Main Floor**
   M. Drawing P2-5 is now renamed Main Floor.
   N. Save and close the Main Floor construct.

6. Commercial Car Maintenance Shop Project
   A. Access the **Project Browser**.
   B. Use the project selector to browse to the \\Documents and Settings*your user login name*\My Documents\Autodesk\My Projects folder or a folder designated by your instructor or CAD manager.
   C. Pick the **New Project** button to create a new project.
   D. In the **Add Project** dialog box, enter the following:
      a. **Project number:** Cmrcl-P06
      b. **Project Name:** Commercial-Project-06
      c. **Project Description:** Two-Story Car Maintenance Shop
      d. Uncheck the **Create from template project:** check box.
      e. Pick the **OK** button when you are finished.
   E. Close the **Project Browser**.
   F. Access the **Project** tab of the **Project Navigator**.
   G. Pick the **Edit Levels** button.
   H. Create the following levels:

Name	Floor Elevation	Floor to Floor Height	ID	Description
Foundation	-9'-0"	8'-0"	F	Foundation
Grade	-4"	4"	G	Finished Grade
Main Floor Framing	-1'-0"	1'-0"	MF	Main Floor Framing
Main Floor	0"	9'-0"	M	Main Floor
Roof	0"	32'-0"	R	Roof
Upper Floor Framing	9'-0"	1'-0"	UF	Upper Floor Framing
Upper Floor	10'-0"	8'-0"	U	Upper Floor

   I. Open P2-6.dwg, which was created in Chapter 2.
   J. Access the **Constructs** tab.
   K. Right-click over the Constructs folder and select **Save Current Dwg As Construct...** from the shortcut menu.
   L. Enter the following in the **Add Construct** worksheet:
      a. **Name**: Main Floor
      b. **Description**: Main Floor Plan
      c. **Category**: **Constructs**
      d. **Assignments**: **Main Floor**
   M. Drawing P2-6 is now renamed Main Floor.
   N. Pick the **Add Construct** button to add a new construct.
   O. Enter the following in the **Add Construct** worksheet:
      a. **Name**: Upper Floor
      b. **Description**: Upper Floor Plan
      c. **Category**: **Constructs**
      d. **Assignments**: **Upper Floor**
   P. Double-click the Main Floor construct from the **Project Navigator** to switch to the drawing.
   Q. Select the lines and polylines used to draw the upper floor layout. Right-click and select **Clipboard** > **Cut** from the shortcut menu.
   R. Double-click the Upper Floor construct from the **Project Navigator** to switch to the drawing.
   S. Right-click in the drawing area and select **Clipboard** > **Paste to Original Coordinates** from the shortcut menu.
   T. Drag and drop the Main Floor construct into the Upper Floor construct drawing.
   U. Move the upper floor lines so they line up with the main floor building outline.
   V. Detach the Main Floor construct.
   W. Save and close the Main Floor and Upper Floor constructs.

7. Governmental Fire Station
   A. Access the **Project Browser**.
   B. Use the project selector to browse to the \\Documents and Settings*your user login name*\My Documents\Autodesk\My Projects folder or a folder designated by your instructor or CAD manager.
   C. Pick the **New Project** button to create a new project.
   D. In the **Add Project** dialog box, enter the following:
      a. **Project number:** Gvrmt-P07
      b. **Project Name:** Gvrmt -Project-07
      c. **Project Description:** Governmental Fire Station
      d. Uncheck the **Create from template project:** check box.
      e. Pick the **OK** button when you are finished.
   E. Close the **Project Browser**.
   F. Access the **Project** tab of the **Project Navigator**.
   G. Pick the **Edit Levels** button.
   H. Create the following levels:

Name	Floor Elevation	Floor to Floor Height	ID	Description
Grade	-1'-0"	8"	G	Finished Grade
Foundation	-4"	4"	F	Slab Foundation
Main Floor	0"	12'-0"	M	Main Floor
Roof	0"	32'-0"	R	Roof
Ceiling Framing	12'-0"	1'-8"	CF	Ceiling Framing

   I. Open P2-7.dwg, which was created in Chapter 2.
   J. Access the **Constructs** tab.
   K. Right-click over the Constructs folder and select **Save Current Dwg As Construct...** from the shortcut menu.
   L. Enter the following in the **Add Construct** worksheet:
      a. **Name**: Main Floor
      b. **Description**: Main Floor Plan
      c. **Category**: **Constructs**
      d. **Assignments**: **Main Floor**
   M. Drawing P2-7 is now renamed Main Floor.
   N. Save and close the Main Floor construct.

Drawing Walls

Learning Objectives

After completing this chapter, you will be able to do the following:
- ✓ Create walls.
- ✓ Convert existing geometry into walls.
- ✓ Modify walls.
- ✓ Clean up walls.
- ✓ Create wall cleanup definition groups.

A typical architectural project is divided into three major phases: conceptual design, design development, and construction documentation. The design development phase is the period during which the construction documents begin to take shape. Architectural Desktop includes tools and objects that aid in the creation of these documents.

AEC objects, such as walls, are representations of real-world building components. The *wall object* is one of the most important features in Architectural Desktop because it provides the basis of the construction documents. The Wall object can be displayed as an architect perceives and draws the wall for a floor plan in a 2D or Top view, while also providing a realistic representation of the wall in 3D for an Elevation or Perspective view. See **Figure 4-1**. A *wall component* is any object used to construct a wall, such as the studs, gypsum, sheathing, siding, brick, or concrete masonry unit (CMU). Walls and other objects, such as doors and windows, are used to provide a comprehensive set of documents that can be used to construct the building.

Adding Walls to Your Drawing

Walls are similar to polyline objects created in standard AutoCAD. Wall objects are single objects that can be quickly modified to reflect changes in the width or height of the wall after it has been drawn. Walls can be drawn by selecting a start point and an endpoint, which is similar to drawing polylines. They can also be converted from AutoCAD linework, or *layout geometry*, such as lines, polylines, arcs, and circles.

Figure 4-1.
The AEC walls and other objects can be displayed as a 2D plan view and as a realistic entity in a 3D view.

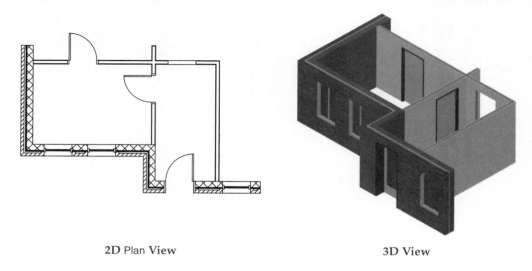

2D Plan View   3D View

Creating Walls

As with many commands in Architectural Desktop, walls can be drawn by selecting the command from a pull-down menu or a tool in a palette. By default, the **Design** palette is displayed. The **Design** palette contains different AEC object commands, including walls. The default pull-down menus, however, do not include a command to add walls.

The **Design** pull-down menu includes several AEC object commands that are duplicated in the **Tool Palettes** window. This pull-down menu can be displayed by picking **Window** > **Pulldowns** > **Design Pulldown**. The **Design** pull-down menu is referred to later, as additional AEC object commands are discussed throughout this text.

To begin drawing walls, pick the **Wall** tool on the **Design** palette, pick **Design** > **Walls** > **Add Wall** from the pull-down menu, or type WALLADD. The start point and endpoint specified are drawn in the current XY plane. These points represent the floor line or bottom of the wall.

Use any Cartesian coordinate method or direct distance entry to specify the length of the wall to get the ending point. Additional walls can be added by picking new ending points. To end the command, right-click and select **Enter**, or press the [Enter] or [Esc] key.

Each time you select an endpoint, that point becomes the start point for the next wall segment. As you draw walls, you can adjust the options for the next segment by changing the value of an option in the **Properties** palette and then selecting the next point for the wall. Walls of varying width, height, and style can be created this way. The **Properties** palette is discussed later in this chapter.

The **Wall** tool from the **Design** palette creates a wall using the Standard wall style. The **Tool Palettes** window also includes a **Walls** palette. See **Figure 4-2.** This palette contains a sampling of some of the wall styles included with Architectural Desktop. Picking a **Wall** tool from this palette begins the wall command specifying the style in the **Properties** palette. As new walls from this palette are added to the drawing, the styles are retained in the drawing and can be used as style property choices in the **Properties** palette. Additional wall styles are included in Architectural Desktop, and new custom styles can be created.

Architectural Desktop and Its Applications

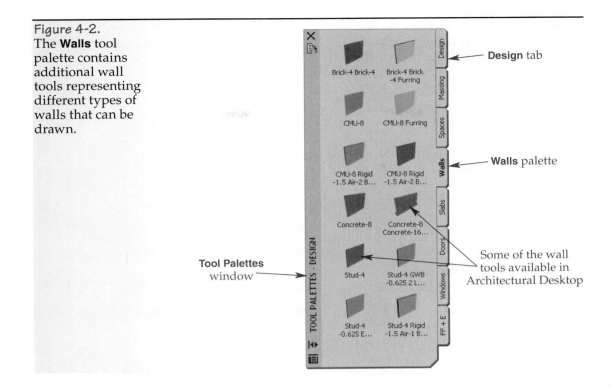

Figure 4-2.
The **Walls** tool palette contains additional wall tools representing different types of walls that can be drawn.

Additional wall tools can be found in the **Design Tool Catalogs** in the **Content Browser**. Refer to Appendix B for information on the **Content Browser** and how to access tools found in the catalogs included with Architectural Desktop. Refer to the online help to create a custom wall style.

The different wall styles available represent real-world building materials such as brick, CMU, concrete, and stud. Some wall styles include a single component, such as CMU or stud components, and others contain multiple components. For example, a stud wall can include insulation and brick.

As these walls are added, they interact with each other based on their building materials. For example, brick cleans up with brick, and CMU cleans up with CMU. However, if a concrete wall crosses a stud wall with brick veneer, the concrete cuts through the stud and brick components. **Figure 4-3** displays an example of different types of walls and how they interact with each other. Experiment with the different wall styles to see how they clean up and interact with each other.

NOTE

> The Standard wall style only cleans up with itself. This wall style cuts through all other wall styles and may not be the best choice when creating a drawing using a variety of wall materials.

The wall styles included in the **Walls** palette contain predefined wall component widths. The name of each style provides a description of the material and its size. For example, the Stud-4 Rigid-1.5 Air-1 Brick-4 wall style includes a stud component 4″ wide with rigid insulation 1-1/2″ wide, then an air space 1″ wide, followed by a brick veneer component that is 4″ wide.

The width property is grayed out and cannot be changed because the wall style includes set widths for the components. Some of the additional wall styles found in the **Design Tool Catalogs** within the **Content Browser** can have their widths adjusted. The naming convention of these variable width walls is similar to the predefined widths previously mentioned. However, if an "X" is in the wall style name, the wall

Figure 4-3.
Wall styles include one or more components. Depending on the building material, the walls may clean up differently with each other.

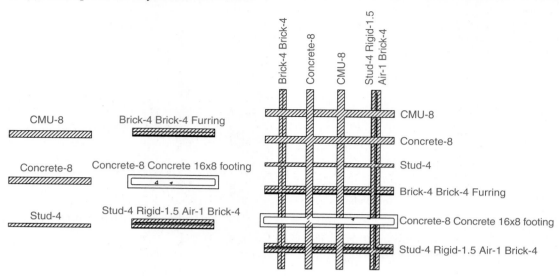

component can have its width adjusted. For example, the CMU-X Air-2 Brick-4 wall style indicates that the CMU component is a variable width and can be adjusted by specifying a width in the **Properties** palette. The air and brick components maintain the width indicated in the style name.

Wall Options

As you begin drawing a wall, its current properties are listed in the **Properties** palette. Properties can be adjusted before drawing the wall by entering values in the appropriate text boxes. Some options are not available in the **Properties** palette. They can be found at the Command: prompt or by pressing the [↓] key when using Dynamic Input. The following options are not available in the **Properties** palette:

- **Match.** The **Match** option allows you to pick an existing wall in the drawing and use its properties as the settings for the new wall being drawn.
- **Undo.** The **Undo** option becomes available as soon as the endpoint of the first wall has been picked, so the wall segment can be undone similar to undoing polyline segments.
- **Close.** If two or more walls are drawn in the same operation, a **Close** option becomes available. The **Close** option adds a wall segment between the endpoint of the last wall segment and the start point of the first wall segment. This is similar to using the **Close** option for the **PLINE** command.
- **ORtho close.** The **ORtho close** option is another option that becomes available when two or more walls are drawn in one operation. This option adds two wall segments between the first and last wall segments. After entering the **ORtho close** option, you are prompted to pick a point in the direction to close. This extends a wall segment from the last wall until it is perpendicular to the edge of the first wall, and then a final wall segment is added, closing the structure. Figure 4-4 shows the steps involved using the **ORtho close** option to create a four-sided building. The **ORtho close** option can be used anywhere two wall segments are desired in order to close the building or room outline.

PROFESSIONAL TIP
If you are trying to snap a wall to a specific justification point, use the **Node** object snap. A wall has three node points located along the justification line used to create the wall: one at the start point, one at the midpoint, and one at the endpoint of the wall.

NOTE
You can add a new wall to the drawing based on the same style, width, and height of an existing wall in your drawing. Select the wall that contains the settings you want to repeat, right-click, and select **Add Selected** from the shortcut menu.

Exercise 4-1   **Complete the Exercise on the Student CD.**

Figure 4-4.
The **ORtho close** option can aid in quickly closing a series of walls.

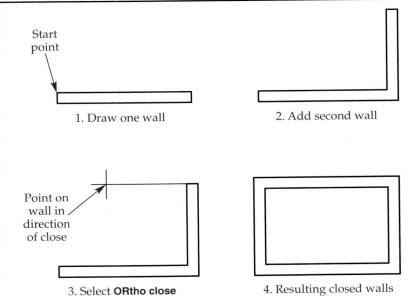

Converting Existing Geometry to Walls

Lines, arcs, circles, and polylines can be converted to walls by right-clicking over one of the **Wall** tools in the **Walls** palette. Pick **Apply Tool Properties to > Linework** in the shortcut menu.

Select the AutoCAD objects you want to convert into walls. The start points and endpoints for the layout geometry are used as the start points and endpoints for the walls. The existing geometry is used as the location edge for the wall justification. The next prompt asks if you want to erase the layout geometry.

NOTE It is usually a good idea to place layout geometry on a "construction" layer that can be turned on/off or frozen/thawed. Then, when you convert the geometry into walls, keep the geometry because it indicates how the justification places the new wall in relation to the existing geometry. When you have finished converting the geometry to walls, you can freeze the layer.

Reversing Wall Endpoints

Occasionally, when you add walls or convert linework to walls, a component of a wall can be on the wrong side of the justification line. In this situation, the endpoints of the wall can be reversed, causing the edge of the wall to flip over or mirror itself. To reverse a wall, select the wall to be reversed, and then right-click. The shortcut menu in **Figure 4-5** is displayed. Select **Reverse** to choose between the **In Place** or **Baseline** options.

Choose the **In Place** option to reverse the wall on top of itself. The left and right edges are maintained, and the wall is reversed. This option can cause the baseline of the wall to be moved if the baseline is not centered on the wall. The start point and endpoint of the wall are reversed, causing the components of a wall to flip to the other side.

The **Baseline** option causes the wall to reverse itself maintaining the baseline location. This option is usually the preferred method of reversing walls if the **Baseline** justification was used to lay out the wall because the start points and endpoints for the baseline specify the length of the wall. The start points and endpoints of the wall are reversed with this method too.

 **Exercise 4-2** Complete the Exercise on the Student CD.

Figure 4-5.
To reverse the endpoints for walls, select the wall, right-click, and select **Reverse** in the shortcut menu.

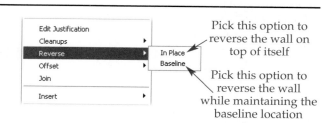

Pick this option to reverse the wall on top of itself

Pick this option to reverse the wall while maintaining the baseline location

Modifying Walls

Standard AutoCAD commands may be used to modify AEC objects. The easiest way to edit AEC objects is to use grips. The **TRIM**, **EXTEND**, and **OFFSET** commands can also be used. These commands are not the only way of modifying AEC objects. For example, you may find that several walls need to have their width, height, or style changed. Rather than erasing the faulted walls, you can use the **Properties** palette to change existing walls to reflect your design needs.

Using the Wall Offset Tool

The **OFFSET** command is an AutoCAD command that can be used on AutoCAD or Architectural Desktop linear or angular geometry. In addition to the standard **OFFSET** command, another offsetting tool specific to walls is included. To use this tool, select the wall to be offset, right-click to display the shortcut menu, and select the **Offset** option. This command includes **Copy**, **Move**, and **Set From** options.

The **Copy** option is similar to the standard **OFFSET** command. The option allows you to specify an offset distance from a specific wall edge or center of a wall component, and the wall is then copied the specified distance.

As the crosshairs are moved across the selected wall, a red line indicates the edge of a wall component that can be picked as the base for the offsetting dimension. For example, if a wall is to be offset from the face of the stud rather than the face of the gypsum board component, move the crosshairs until the red line appears next to the face of the stud component. See **Figure 4-6**. The center of wall components can also be used as a reference point by pressing the [Ctrl] key while moving across each component. The red line is displayed at the center of each component within the wall. Use the pick button to select the desired edge or center to be used as a reference.

As a wall is being offset, a dimension appears between the referenced point specified and the same point in relation to the new wall being offset. Pick a point for the new wall or use direct distance entry to specify the offset distance.

The **Move** option for the wall offset tool works in a similar manner to the **Copy** option, except it moves the wall rather than copying. Finally, the **Set From** option offsets an existing wall a specified distance from an existing point. See **Figure 4-7**.

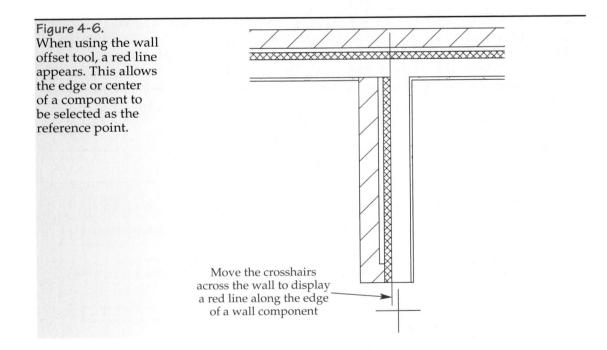

Figure 4-6.
When using the wall offset tool, a red line appears. This allows the edge or center of a component to be selected as the reference point.

Move the crosshairs across the wall to display a red line along the edge of a wall component

AutoCAD Review

Using the Offset, Trim, and Extend Commands

The **OFFSET** command creates a copy of an object set at a specified distance away from the original object. The **OFFSET** command is illustrated as follows:

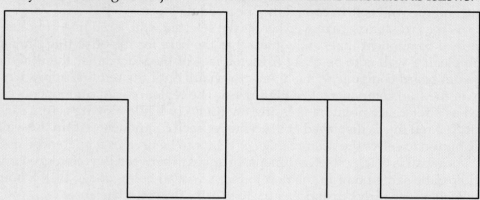

The **OFFSET** command is very useful for laying out floor plans. You can create the desired walls and offset the original walls to lay out room sizes. Measure the offset distance from the justification line of the wall to the justification line of the new wall.

The **TRIM** command is used to trim one object away from another. With the **TRIM** command, an edge is selected as a cutting edge. Then, anything that crosses through the edge can be trimmed. To use the **TRIM** command, select the **Trim** button in the **Modify** toolbar, or type TRIM or TR. After entering the **TRIM** command, you need to select a cutting edge or edges. Several edges can be picked at once to use as cutting edges. If walls are selected, the justification line becomes the cutting edge.

(Continued)

Figure 4-7.
The **Set From** offset option moves a wall to a specified distance set from another point.

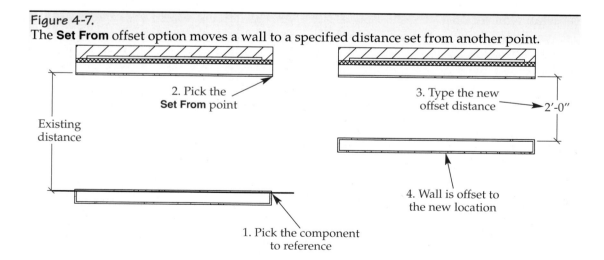

Architectural Desktop and Its Applications

AutoCAD Review (Continued)

The **EXTEND** command extends the end of a wall, a polyline, an arc, or a line to a boundary edge. With the **EXTEND** command, an edge is first selected as a boundary edge. Other objects can then be selected to extend their lengths to the boundary. To access the command, select the **Extend** button in the **Modify** toolbar, or type EXTEND or EX.

When using the **TRIM** or **EXTEND** command, you can select various objects to be edges or to be trimmed or extended. To select all objects as edges, press [Enter] at the Select cutting edges... or Select boundary edges... prompt. To change between the **TRIM** and **EXTEND** command, hold [Shift] while picking.

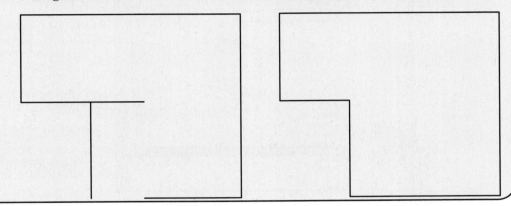

Using the Properties Palette

To quickly modify walls, you can use the **Properties** palette. If it is not already displayed, select the walls you want to change, then right-click, and select **Properties**. Without selecting a wall, you can also pick the **Properties Palette** button in the **Navigation** toolbar; pick **Window** > **Properties Palette** from the pull-down menu; or type PROPERTIES, PROPS, CH, or MO.

The **Properties** palette allows you to change the wall style, width and height of the wall, wall justification, and group. See **Figure 4-8.** Depending on the properties being adjusted, a worksheet, drop-down list, or text box is available. Make any desired changes by picking the different property values and entering new values or picking values from a drop-down list. Modifying the justification for a wall can be helpful, especially after converting walls from existing geometry.

The following properties are available under the **BASIC** header in the **Properties** palette when drawing a wall, as shown in **Figure 4-8**:

- **Description.** This property opens a worksheet where a description of the wall can be entered.
- **Layer.** This property provides a drop-down list of available layers. Layers are discussed in Chapter 8.
- **Style.** This property provides a drop-down list of available wall styles representing different types of walls. By default, the Standard wall style is available. Other styles, such as masonry and stud walls, can be imported into the drawing and used.

Figure 4-8.
The **Properties** palette displays the properties of the wall being drawn. Values can be adjusted before the wall is drawn by selecting the desired property and entering new values.

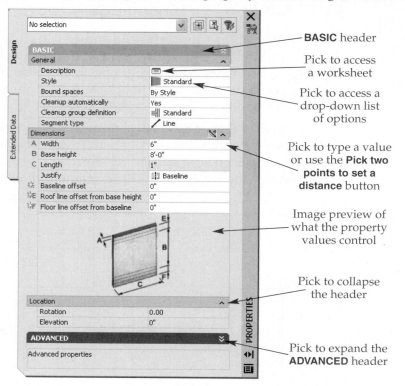

BASIC header

Pick to access a worksheet

Pick to access a drop-down list of options

Pick to type a value or use the **Pick two points to set a distance** button

Image preview of what the property values control

Pick to collapse the header

Pick to expand the **ADVANCED** header

- **Bound spaces.** This property is used to define if the wall is used as a boundary when calculating room space. The options include **Yes**, **No**, and **ByStyle**. The **ByStyle** option looks to the wall style settings to determine if the wall style has been set to be a boundary for space object creation. Spaces are discussed in Chapter 21.

- **Cleanup automatically.** This property also includes a drop-down list with a **Yes** or **No** option. When **Yes** is selected, walls that cross each other or meet at a corner "clean up" without wall lines crossing over each other.

- **Cleanup group definition.** This property displays a drop-down list of cleanup groups. Initially, there is only one cleanup group available named Standard. Walls that belong to the same cleanup group are cleaned up with each other. Walls belonging to different groups do not clean up. Cleanup groups are discussed later in this chapter.

- **Segment type.** This property displays a drop-down list with two options: **Line** and **Arc**. Selecting the **Line** option creates straight wall segments. The **Arc** option draws curved walls.

- **Shadow display.** This property provides a drop-down list with options for casting and receiving shadows. If the property is set to **Casts shadows**, **Receives shadows**, or **Casts and Receives shadows**, the shadows will display after lighting has been created.

- **Width.** This property allows you to enter a value for the width of the wall or pick two points in the drawing to establish a width distance. Some wall styles will not allow you to modify this value.

- **Base height.** This property is used to enter a height for the wall. The base height is considered the height of a wall from bottom plate to top plate. Specifying a height allows the wall to display its height as 3D when viewed from an Elevation or Isometric view only. When viewed from the Top or Plan view, the 3D wall is displayed as a 2D wall.

- **Length.** As a wall is being drawn, the value changes, displaying the current length between the start point of the wall and the location of the crosshairs.
- **Justify.** This property displays a drop-down list of options. The start points and endpoints picked on the screen draw the wall based on one of four wall justification options shown in **Figure 4-9.** In most cases, when using wall styles other than Standard, the **Baseline** justification is usually the best option. The **Baseline** option draws the wall along a logical edge or point in the wall, like the face of a stud or CMU.
- **Baseline offset.** This property allows you to enter a distance value measured from the picked start point for the wall perpendicular to the justification, establishing an offset value. As the start point and endpoint for the wall are picked, the wall is drawn the specified distance from these two points. This property can be seen only as the wall is being drawn.
- **Roof line offset from base height.** This property value sets a distance for the top of the wall. This value measures from the base height or top plate to the actual top of the wall. A value of 0″ creates the top of the wall based on the base height. This option can be used when creating a parapet above the top plate, where the wall extends past the top plate. This property is shown only as the wall is being drawn.
- **Floor line offset from baseline.** This value controls where the actual bottom of the wall is measured. The value measures from the baseline or bottom plate of the wall, extending down. A value of 0″ keeps the bottom of the wall at the locations specified when picking the start point and endpoint. This option can be used when creating a wall that extends down to a footing past the floor line. This property is available only as the wall is being drawn.
- **Rotation.** This value is a read-only property and changes to reflect the current angle of the wall being drawn.
- **Elevation.** This is a read-only property and reflects the current elevation or height of the wall being drawn. A value of 0″ indicates the wall is being drawn on the XY plane. Any other value indicates that the bottom of the wall is being drawn at a different elevation in the Z axis, away from the XY plane.

Exercise
4-3   **Complete the Exercise on the Student CD.**

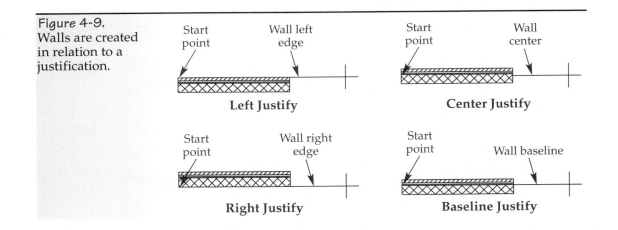

Figure 4-9.
Walls are created in relation to a justification.

Using Wall Grips

Grips on Architectural Desktop objects are placed in strategic locations, but include special grips that control specific functions related to the object. Depending on the type of object selected for editing, different grips appear along the object. **Figure 4-10** shows grips displayed for a 2D and 3D wall.

When stretching the length of a wall, the **Start**, **End**, or either of the **Lengthen** grips can be used. When one of these grips is selected, dimensions appear indicating the length of the wall. As the grip location is stretched, a dimension displays the existing length of wall, the length that is being added or subtracted, and the new total length of wall. If you are using direct distance entry to indicate the new length being modified, a text box appears near the dimension that indicates the length being stretched. See **Figure 4-11**.

When selecting one of the **Width** grips, a tooltip is displayed indicating that the [Ctrl] key can be used to toggle between two different options. See **Figure 4-12**. These options include **Maintain baseline** and **Maintain opposite face**. This indicates that stretching the width of the wall and pressing the [Ctrl] key allows the new stretched width to be added equally to each side of the baseline. This is the **Maintain baseline** option, which maintains the baseline location or adds to the side being stretched. The **Maintain opposite face** option maintains the opposite face of wall location.

Two additional grips in the 2D wall include the **Location** and the **Reverse Direction** grips. Selecting the **Location** grip allows the wall to be moved when in the **Stretch** grip mode. The **Reverse Direction** grip allows the wall to be reversed. Holding the [Crtl] key down when picking this grip maintains the baseline location of the wall, rather than reversing the wall completely on itself.

A 3D wall includes the grips indicated for the 2D wall, in addition to three grips along the top edge of the wall. See **Figure 4-10**. These grips include the **Roof Line Start**,

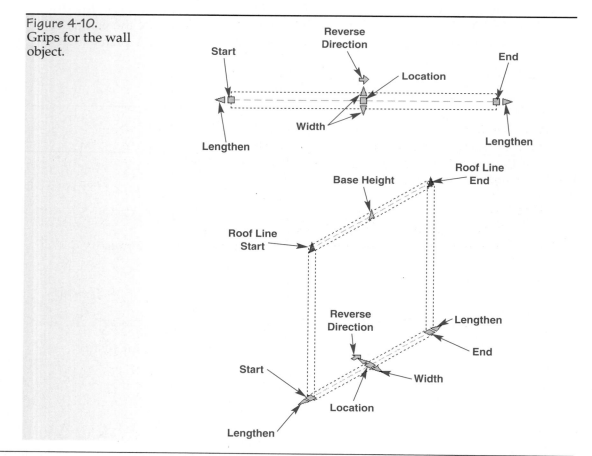

Figure 4-10.
Grips for the wall object.

Figure 4-11.
Dimensions indicate the existing size and modified size of the wall. A text box is displayed when entering numbers using direct distance entry.

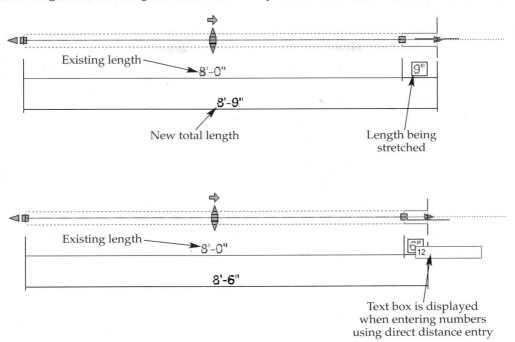

Figure 4-12.
Use the [Ctrl] key to toggle between two options when adjusting the width of a wall.

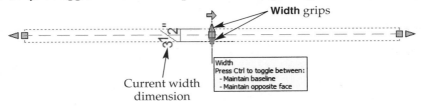

the **Roof Line End**, and the **Base Height**. Picking either of the **Roof Line** grips changes the height of the wall at that end. Selecting the **Base Height** grip changes the overall height of the wall. Three-dimensional aspects of AEC objects are covered in greater depth throughout this text.

Exercise
4-4   **Complete the Exercise on the Student CD.**

AutoCAD Review

Using Grips to Modify Objects

Grips appear on geometry only if the object has been picked without a command active. Grips are typically present at strategic points on an object. *Unselected grips* are blue by default.

When the cursor is moved over the top of a grip symbol, the symbol turns green. This is called a *hover grip*. The hover grips react differently depending on their type of geometry. If the hover grip is displayed over standard AutoCAD geometry, the grip only turns green and displays dimensions. If the hover grip is displayed over an AEC object, dimensions and tooltips can be displayed, showing object sizes or tips explaining what can be done by editing with the grip.

Picking a grip results in a *selected grip*, or *hot grip*. Hot grips are red by default. To select multiple hot grips, press the [Shift] key before picking. Selecting a grip activates the grip-editing feature of AutoCAD. There are five commands that can be used through the grips: **STRETCH, MOVE, ROTATE, SCALE**, and **MIRROR**. Each of these commands also includes a **Copy** option, in which objects can be copied when one of the five commands is performed. Right-click to access the **Copy** option and other options when grips are displayed. With the exception of the **STRETCH** command, all objects with a hot grip are affected by the selected grip mode.

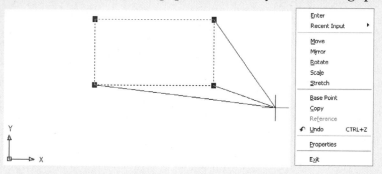

To stretch the selected object, move the cursor around and pick a new location. This relocates the hot grip position, which in turn stretches the object. If a midpoint grip is selected on a wall or line, the object is moved instead of stretched.

If you need to move an object with grips, first select the object, and then pick a grip. The selected grip becomes the base point. You can use an object snap to snap the object to a new location or type coordinates to move the object.

Objects can be rotated with grips. When a grip has been selected, it becomes the base point about which the selected objects are rotated.

An object can also be scaled. The selected grip becomes the base point from which the object is scaled. Move the crosshairs to increase or decrease the size of the object. You can also type the desired scale factor.

You can reverse or create a mirror image of an object or set of objects. Select the objects to be mirrored, and select a grip to be used as the first point of the mirror line. The *mirror line* is the line from which the objects are mirrored. Moving the crosshairs creates a mirror line between the selected grip and the crosshairs. The selected objects are mirrored around the mirror line.

In traditional architectural graphic standards, walls are drawn using two lines defining the width of a wall. When two "walls" cross through each other or meet one another at a corner, the junction is typically "cleaned up" by stopping lines where they meet. This creates a smooth looking plan that is easily readable. ADT walls have a similar function where they automatically clean up with one another. In some instances, due to the way the wall is created or different parameters assigned to the wall, the walls may need to be manually cleaned up.

Working with Wall Cleanups

Occasionally, walls may not clean up properly or as expected and can even display a red defect symbol. Wall cleanups take into consideration the wall components, wall width, and direction the wall was drawn. Each wall includes a wall cleanup radius at the ends of the wall and at any location along the justification line that another wall crosses or contacts. Increasing or decreasing the cleanup radius aids in the cleanup of wall intersections.

By default, the wall styles included in Architectural Desktop are set to a 0" cleanup radius. This requires wall justification lines to touch each other at corners and intersections in order to clean up. In most situations, the 0" wall cleanup radius is sufficient for cleaning up walls. There can be some situations that cause walls to not clean up, such as a thin wall intersecting a wide wall or three or more walls meeting at a common intersection. See **Figure 4-13**. In these cases, the cleanup radius is increased, because the 0" wall cleanup radius has difficulty working properly.

The wall cleanup radius can be set in the **Properties** palette under the **ADVANCED** header. See **Figure 4-14**. This property can be set when first laying out walls, or it can be modified for selected existing walls. Typically, increasing the cleanup radius enough to encompass the width of the wall is sufficient.

NOTE

> In situations where walls do not clean up, use a cleanup radius equal to your most common wall width. This helps reduce wall defect problems. If you still receive the defect symbols when you create walls, try increasing or decreasing the cleanup radius for the defect walls and any walls that touch or cross the defect walls.

Figure 4-13.
The default cleanup radius of 0" results in a defect symbol. With a 12" cleanup radius, the same three walls clean up properly.

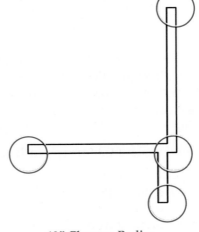

0" Cleanup Radius   12" Cleanup Radius

Figure 4-14.
The wall cleanup radius can be changed by selecting the **Cleanup radius** property under the
ADVANCED header in the **Properties** palette.

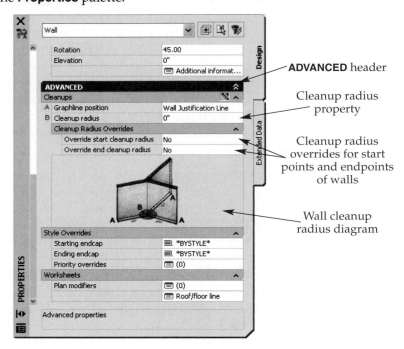

ADVANCED header

Cleanup radius
property

Cleanup radius
overrides for start
points and endpoints
of walls

Wall cleanup
radius diagram

In some instances, a cleanup radius may only be needed at one end of a wall. In **Figure 4-13,** a cleanup radius was assigned globally to each of the walls. This allowed the walls to clean up properly. However, a single cleanup radius can also be assigned to the ends of the three walls where they meet, allowing the other ends of the walls to continue using a 0″ cleanup radius.

There are two methods that can be used to set a cleanup radius for either the start points or endpoints of a wall. The first is to use the **Properties** palette. Under the **ADVANCED** header, select either the **Override start cleanup radius** or the **Override end cleanup radius** property. These properties accept a **Yes** or **No** value. Selecting a **Yes** value displays the **Start cleanup radius** or the **End cleanup radius** property appropriately. Enter the new value for the desired start point or endpoint cleanup radius. See **Figure 4-15.**

NOTE If you forget which end of the wall is the start or end, select the wall to display the grips. The **Reverse Direction** grip indicates where the start and end grips are located.

The other method of applying a cleanup radius to one end of a wall is to select the wall, right-click, and select **Cleanups > Override Cleanup Radius** from the shortcut menu. You are prompted to select a point. Select the end of the wall where you want the cleanup radius applied. The next prompt asks for the new radius. Type in a radius value and press [Enter]. This applies the radius to the selected end.

Viewing the Cleanup Radius

Occasionally, you may want to view the cleanup radii for different walls in your drawing to help determine where wall cleanups are occurring. To view any cleanup radii applied to walls, select a wall, right-click, and select **Cleanups > Toggle Wall Graph Display** from the shortcut menu.

Figure 4-15.
The **Properties** palette can be used to apply a cleanup radius to one end of a wall.

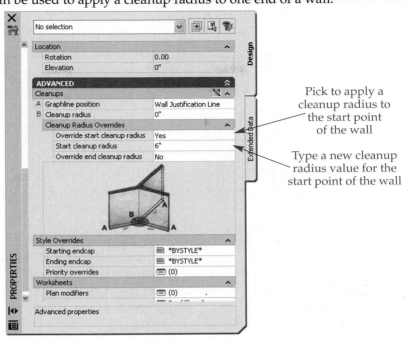

Pick to apply a cleanup radius to the start point of the wall

Type a new cleanup radius value for the start point of the wall

This displays any cleanup radii and the justification lines for the walls that you have overridden and may aid in the proper cleanup of walls. To switch back to a normal display mode, select **Toggle Wall Graph Display** again.

Using the 'L' Cleanup and 'T' Cleanup Options

The **'L' Cleanup** option is used to create an L-shaped intersection between two walls, as shown in **Figure 4-16.** To use this option, select a wall that forms part of the L-shaped intersection, right-click, and select **Cleanups** > **Apply 'L' Cleanup** from the shortcut menu. After the command has been initiated, you are prompted to select the second wall. Pick the other wall that forms the L-shaped intersection. When this option is used, the endpoints of the walls closest to each other are trimmed or extended so their justification lines meet.

Figure 4-16.
The **'L' Cleanup** option creates an L-shaped intersection.

2. Pick the second wall

3. Walls are trimmed or extended to create an L-shaped intersection

1. Select a wall, right-click, and select **Apply 'L' Cleanup**

Figure 4-17.
The **'T' Cleanup** option creates a T-shaped intersection.

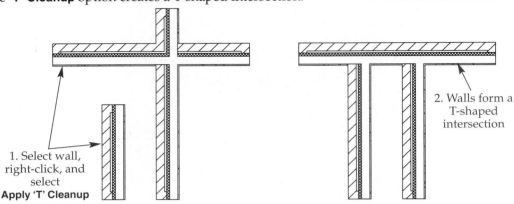

1. Select wall,
right-click, and
select
Apply 'T' Cleanup

2. Walls form a
T-shaped
intersection

The **'T' Cleanup** option is used to create a T-shaped intersection between two walls. See **Figure 4-17.** To access this option, select a wall to be used as the leg of the 'T', right-click, and pick **Cleanups** > **Apply 'T' Cleanup** from the shortcut menu. Once the command is started, you are asked to select the boundary wall. Pick the other wall as the boundary, or top of the T-shaped intersection. The selected walls are trimmed or extended to form a T-shaped intersection.

Merging Walls Together

You may run into the situation where a wall does not clean up, as in **Figure 4-18.** If after trying to adjust the wall justification or the cleanup radius, the walls continue to display a defect symbol or do not clean up, you can add a wall merge condition to clean up the walls.

To access this command, right-click on one of the walls that does not clean up, and pick **Cleanups** > **Add Wall Merge Condition** from the shortcut menu. The option prompts you to select walls to merge with the chosen wall. Select any walls that are touching the first wall selected. This merges the walls together. If a new wall is drawn that intersects a merged wall, you may need to merge the new wall into the existing wall using the same technique.

After walls have been merged, you can remove the merge condition by right-clicking on the initially merged wall and picking **Cleanups** > **Remove All Wall Merge Conditions** from the shortcut menu. This removes any merge conditions and displays the walls as they were originally drawn.

Figure 4-18.
The **Wall Merge** option can be used to merge walls that could not be cleaned up by adjusting the cleanup radius or adjusting the justification line.

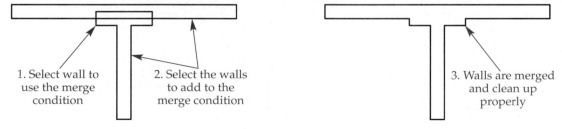

1. Select wall to
use the merge
condition

2. Select the walls
to add to the
merge condition

3. Walls are merged
and clean up
properly

Architectural Desktop and Its Applications

Figure 4-19.
When the Standard cleanup group definition is used on all four walls, defect symbols are displayed. When the smaller outside walls have been assigned to a cleanup group definition that cleans only the outermost two walls, the walls clean up properly. The inner walls still belong to the Standard cleanup group definition.

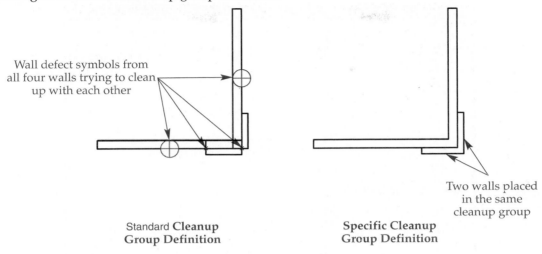

Wall defect symbols from all four walls trying to clean up with each other

Two walls placed in the same cleanup group

Standard **Cleanup Group Definition**

Specific **Cleanup Group Definition**

Creating Wall Cleanup Group Definitions

Occasionally, you may have the desire to create two walls of the same style side by side. Usually, if walls are created side by side, Architectural Desktop tries to clean up both walls, which may cause a wall defect symbol to be displayed. Using *cleanup group definitions* is a method of grouping common types of walls so only walls within the same group clean up with one another. See **Figure 4-19**.

```
Pull-Down Menus
Format
  > Style Manager...
Design
  > Walls
    > Cleanup
      Group
      Definitions...
```

Wall cleanup group definitions can be created by providing a new definition name. Cleanup definitions are created in the **Style Manager**, by picking **Format** > **Style Manager…** from the pull-down menu. This displays the **Style Manager**, shown in **Figure 4-20**. Next, pick the **Wall Cleanup Group Definitions** icon from the Architectural Objects folder. You can also pick **Design** > **Walls** > **Cleanup Group Definitions…** from the pull-down menu.

To create the new definition, select the **New Style** button, or right-click over Wall Cleanup Group Definitions in the tree view in the left pane, and select the **New** option. This creates a new definition in the list box in the right pane. Enter a new name for the definition. The next time a wall is drawn or modified, the new group definition is available in the **Properties** palette for walls under the **Cleanup Group Definition** property.

Walls belonging to the same cleanup group definition can also be made to clean up with walls in an xref drawing that use the same named cleanup group definition. To do this, after creating the wall cleanup group definition, select the cleanup group definition listed in the tree view of the **Style Manager**. The properties for the definition are displayed in the right pane of the **Style Manager**. Select the **Design Rules** tab, and then place a check in the **Allow Wall Cleanup between host and xref drawings** check box. This allows walls using this cleanup group definition to clean up with externally referenced walls using the same cleanup group definition.

NOTE Architectural Desktop includes other wall styles that represent countertops and cabinets. Create a cleanup group definition for these types of wall styles so they do not clean up with structural walls. You do not want countertops and cabinets to clean up with structural walls because you want them to appear independent from the structural walls. Corner trims and quoins can also be created with a wall style. *Quoins* are the corner masonry of a building, typically used decoratively on the exterior.

Figure 4-20.
The **Style Manager** can be used to create a new cleanup group definition.

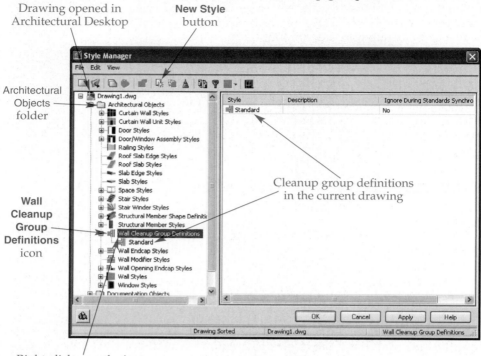

Drawing opened in
Architectural Desktop

New Style
button

Architectural
Objects
folder

Cleanup group definitions
in the current drawing

**Wall
Cleanup
Group
Definitions**
icon

Right-click over the icon
to access a shortcut menu

Exercise
4-5

Complete the Exercise on the Student CD.

Tips for Working with Walls

The following are some tips to aid in the proper cleanup of walls:
- Walls must be created in the same XY drawing plane.
- Wall justification lines must be at the same elevation.
- Walls must be in the same cleanup group.
- When two walls are being cleaned up, the justification points must be within the cleanup radius.
- When three or more walls close together are being cleaned up, the cleanup radius must encompass the justification lines and each side of the walls.
- A cleanup radius that is equal to the wall width is useful.
- When cleaning up short walls, ensure the cleanup radius is not larger than the length of the wall.
- Use the **Toggle Wall Graph Display** command to verify cleanup radii and justification lines are touching.
- Sometimes a combination of changes to the cleanup radius and the wall justification is required to clean up walls.
- If walls cannot be cleaned up through other methods described, try using the tool to merge walls.

Architectural Desktop and Its Applications

Chapter Test

Answer the following questions. Write your answers on a separate sheet of paper or complete the electronic chapter test on the Student CD.

1. Describe the **Baseline** wall justification option.
2. Give the basic function of the **Match** option.
3. What do wall styles represent?
4. Why is it usually a good idea to place layout geometry on a construction layer?
5. What is a cleanup group definition?
6. What is the default Architectural Desktop cleanup radius?
7. What is a recommended cleanup radius to try in situations where walls do not clean up?
8. How do you view cleanup radii?
9. Discuss how the **'L' Cleanup** option and **'T' Cleanup** option function to help in cleanup situations.
10. How does using a merge condition work when you run into the situation where a wall does not clean up?

Use the techniques covered in this chapter to create the following drawings.

1. Single-Level Residential Project
    A. Access the **Project Browser** and set Residential-Project-01 current.
    B. Open the Main Floor construct.
    C. Use the Standard wall style to create your walls.
    D. Convert exterior linework to 6″ wide walls.
    E. Convert interior linework to 4″ wide walls.
    F. Make all walls 8′-0″ high.
    G. Add walls as needed. Draw new walls or copy and offset walls as needed.
    H. Refer to the figure for dimension guidance. Do not dimension.
    I. Save and close the Main Floor drawing.

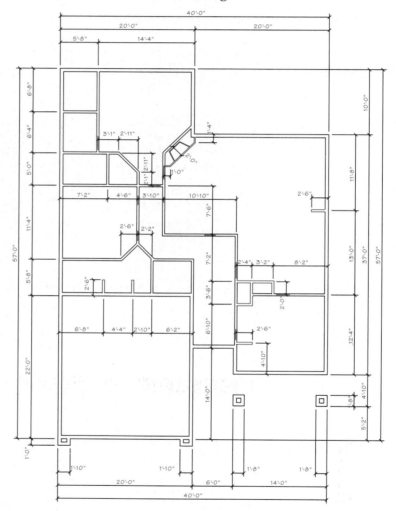

Design Courtesy Alan Mascord Design Associates

2. Single-Level Residential Project
   A. Access the **Project Browser** and set Residential-Project-02 current.
   B. Open the Main Floor construct.
   C. Use the Standard wall style to create your walls.
   D. Convert exterior linework to 6″ wide walls.
   E. Convert interior linework to 4″ wide walls.
   F. Make all walls 8′-0″ high.
   G. Add walls as needed. Draw new walls or copy and offset walls as needed.
   H. Refer to the figure for dimension guidance. Do not dimension.
   I. Create a cleanup group definition named Brick Veneer. Use the Standard wall style to create a 4″ wide by 3′-0″ high "brick veneer" to the front of the building. Place the veneer in the Brick Veneer cleanup group.
   J. Save and close the Main Floor drawing.

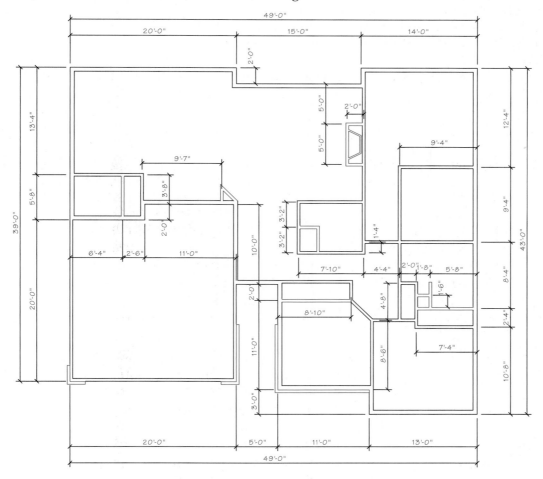

Design Courtesy Alan Mascord Design Associates

3. Two-Story Residential Project
   A. Access the **Project Browser** and set Residential-Project-03 current.
   B. Open the Main Floor construct.
   C. Use the Standard wall style to create your walls.
   D. Convert exterior linework to 6″ wide walls.
   E. Convert interior linework to 4″ wide walls.
   F. Make all walls 9′-0″ high.
   G. Add walls as needed. Draw new walls or copy and offset walls as needed.
   H. Refer to the figure for dimension guidance. Do not dimension.
   I. Create a cleanup group definition named Brick Veneer. Use the Standard wall style to create a 4″ wide by 9′-0″ high "brick veneer" to the front corners of the building. Place the veneer in the Brick Veneer cleanup group.
   J. Save and close the Main Floor drawing.
   K. Open the Upper Floor construct.
   L. Use the Standard wall style to create your walls.
   M. Convert exterior linework to 6″ wide walls.
   N. Make all walls 9′-0″ high.
   O. Save and close the Upper Floor drawing.

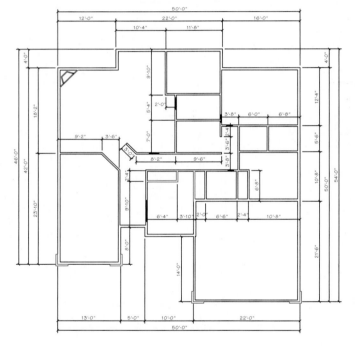

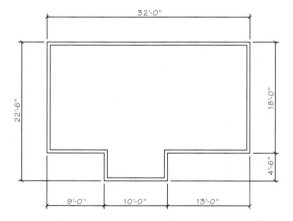

Drawing Courtesy 3D-DZYN

4. Two-Story Residential Project
   A. Access the **Project Browser** and set Residential-Project-04 current.
   B. Open the Main Floor construct.
   C. Use the Standard wall style to create your walls.
   D. Convert exterior linework to 6″ wide walls.
   E. Convert interior linework to 4″ wide walls.
   F. Make the walls 9′-0″ high.
   G. Add walls as needed. Draw new walls or copy and offset walls as needed.
   H. Refer to the figure for dimension guidance. Do not dimension.
   I. Save and close the Main Floor drawing.
   J. Open the Upper Floor construct.
   K. Use the Standard wall style to create your walls.
   L. Convert exterior linework to 6″ wide walls.
   M. Convert interior linework to 4″ wide walls.
   N. Draw the second floor walls 8′-0″ high.
   O. Add walls as needed. Draw new walls or copy and offset walls as needed.
   P. Refer to the figure for dimension guidance. Do not dimension.
   Q. Save and close the Upper Floor drawing.

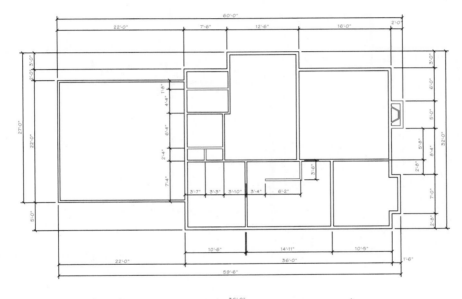

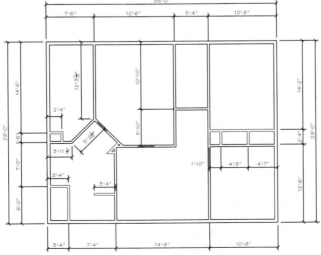

Design Courtesy Alan Mascord Design Associates

Chapter 4 Projects

5. Commercial Store Project
   A. Access the **Project Browser** and set Commercial-Project-05 current.
   B. Open the Main Floor construct.
   C. Convert the exterior linework to walls using the CMU-8 Rigid-1.5 Air-2 Brick-4 wall style with a height of 12'-0". Use a baseline justification for the exterior walls.
   D. Convert the interior linework to walls using the CMU-8 wall style with a height of 9'-0". Use any appropriate justification for interior walls.
   E. Add walls as needed. Draw new walls or copy and offset walls as needed.
   F. Refer to the figure for dimension guidance. Do not dimension.
   G. Save and close the Main Floor drawing.

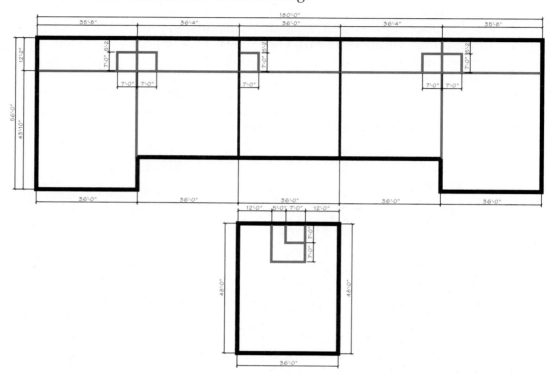

Drawing Courtesy 3D-DZYN

Architectural Desktop and Its Applications

6. Commercial Car Maintenance Shop Project
   A. Access the **Project Browser** and set Commercial-Project-06 current.
   B. Open the Main Floor construct.
   C. Convert the exterior linework to walls using the CMU-8 Rigid-1.5 Air-2 Brick-4 wall style with a height of 12'-0". Use a height of 18'-0" at the garage area.
   D. Convert the interior linework to walls using the CMU-8 wall style with a height of 9'-0". Use any appropriate justification for interior walls.
   E. Add walls as needed. Draw new walls or copy and offset walls as needed.
   F. Refer to the figure for dimension guidance. Do not dimension.
   G. Save and close the Main Floor drawing.
   H. Open the Upper Floor construct.
   I. Convert the exterior linework to walls using the CMU-8 Rigid-1.5 Air-2 Brick-4 wall style with a height of 8'-0". Use a baseline justification for the exterior walls.
   J. Convert the interior linework to walls using the CMU-8 wall style with a height of 8'-0". Use any appropriate justification for interior walls.
   K. Add walls as needed. Draw new walls or copy and offset walls as needed.
   L. Refer to the figure for dimension guidance. Do not dimension.
   M. Save and close the Upper Floor drawing.

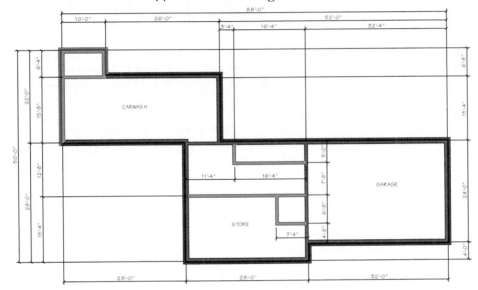

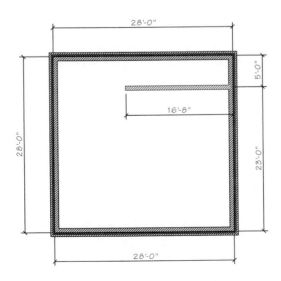

Drawing Courtesy 3D-DZYN

7. Governmental Fire Station
   A. Access the **Project Browser** and set Gvrmt-Project-07 current.
   B. Open the Main Floor construct.
   C. Convert the exterior linework to walls using the CMU-8 Rigid-1.5 Air-2 Brick-4 wall style with a height of 12'-0". Use a height of 16'-0" at the garage area. Use a baseline justification for the exterior walls.
   D. Convert the interior linework to walls using the CMU-8 wall style with a height of 9'-0". Use any appropriate justification for the interior walls.
   E. Add walls as needed. Draw new walls or copy and offset walls as needed.
   F. Refer to the figure for dimension guidance. Do not dimension.
   G. Save and close the Main Floor drawing.

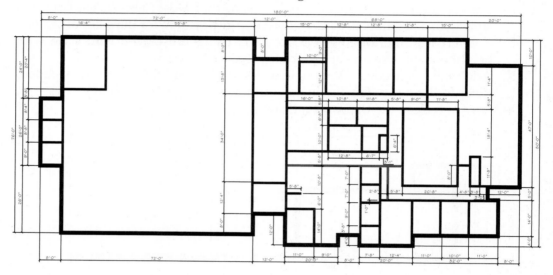

Drawing Courtesy 3D-DZYN

CHAPTER 5

Drawing Doors, Windows, and Openings

Learning Objectives

After completing this chapter, you will be able to do the following:

✓ Add doors to your drawing.
✓ Modify doors.
✓ Add windows to your drawing.
✓ Modify windows.
✓ Add openings to your drawing.
✓ Modify openings.
✓ Add door/window assemblies to your drawing.
✓ Modify door/window assemblies.

Now that you have created Wall objects, the next step in creating your architectural design is to add doors, windows, and openings. You will discover that these objects function intelligently with the Wall objects, allowing the doors, windows, and openings to become part of the wall system in which changes to one automatically affects the other.

Creating Door Objects

Door objects in Architectural Desktop are AEC objects that interact with Wall objects. A door knows that it belongs in a wall. After a door is placed in a wall, it becomes part of the wall system and is affected by any changes made to the wall or the door. When doors are placed inside walls, the opening for the door is cut out of the wall and displayed without a header.

Adding Doors to Your Drawing

There are several ways to add a door to a drawing. Adding a standard door without a specific style is explained first. Standard doors are added to the drawing by selecting the **Door** tool from the **Design** tool palette, by picking **Design** > **Doors** > **Add Door...**, or by typing DOORADD. You can also add a door by selecting a wall, right-clicking, and picking **Insert** > **Door...** from the shortcut menu. Once the door command has been entered, you are prompted to select a wall, space boundary, or grid assembly in which

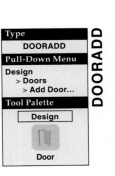

| Type |
| DOORADD |
| Pull-Down Menu |
| Design
  > Doors
    > Add Door... |
| Tool Palette |
| Design |

DOORADD

Door

you want to place the door, or press [Enter]. If you press [Enter] without selecting an object, the door is inserted into the drawing without being inserted into a wall, giving up the interactive nature between a door and a wall. A *space boundary* is an object that can be used when space planning to create boundaries for Space objects. *Space planning* is the design of interior spaces within a building, and *space objects* are the rooms or other features that occupy the space plan. *Grid assemblies* are also known as curtain walls, which are walls made up of a framework and glazing panels. After selecting a wall, the following prompt is displayed at the Command: prompt:

> Insert point or [STyle/WIdth/HEight/HEAd height/Threshold height/Auto/Match/
> CYcle measure to/REference point on]:

Use the crosshairs to move the door around the previously selected walls in the drawing, and then press the pick button to insert the door into a wall. Once a door has been inserted into a wall, you can continue to insert additional doors or end the command.

Another way to insert a door is to select a wall, right-click, and select **Insert > Door...** from the shortcut menu. All the previous options have been to insert a standard door. To insert doors of specific styles, select the desired door tool from the **Doors** tool palette.

During the command, the **Properties** palette can be used to control the properties of the door being added, such as the width, height, and style. See **Figure 5-1.** The following list includes some of the properties available when inserting doors into walls:

- **Description.** Selecting this property opens the **Description** dialog box, where a description for the doors being inserted can be entered.
- **Style.** This property displays a drop-down list of door styles that are used or have been imported into the drawing. Initially, the only style available is the **Standard** door style. Additional door styles can be loaded into the drawing by right-clicking over one of the door tools in the **Doors** tool palette and selecting the **Import** '*xxx - xxx*' **Door Style**, where "*xxx - xxx*" represents the door style name. Then this style is available in the **Style** drop-down list, and it can be selected and added to the drawing.

Figure 5-1.
The **Properties** palette is used to adjust the properties of a door being added to the drawing.

Door size properties

Door position properties

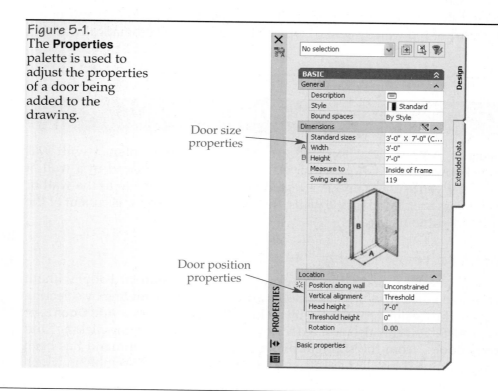

Architectural Desktop and Its Applications

- **Standard sizes.** Some door styles include preconfigured sizes that can be chosen for use from this property. For most door styles, the sizes available represent common door sizes used in industry. Pick the **Standard sizes** drop-down list, and select the size desired for the door being inserted.
- **Width.** This text box property allows you to set a custom width for the door being inserted. Pick the property to enter a new size. When a custom width is added, it becomes the width value of the **Standard sizes** property.
- **Height.** Picking this property allows you to enter a custom value for the door height. Entering a custom height size becomes the height value of the **Standard sizes** property.
- **Measure to.** This property displays a drop-down list with the **Inside of frame** and **Outside of frame** options. This controls how the width property is applied to the Door object. Measuring the width to the inside of the frame means the width is applied only to the door panel. Measuring to the outside of the frame applies the width to the outside edges of the door frame.
- **Swing angle.** This property controls the swing angle of doors with swing. Picking the property allows you to enter a value for the door swing. The value of the door swing angle can be between 0 and 180. A value of 0 closes the door, a value of 90 creates a door half-opened, and a value of 180 opens the door all the way. See the swinging doors in **Figure 5-2.**
- **Opening percent.** This property is available when adding a nonswinging door to the drawing, such as a bifold, pocket, overhead, revolving, or sliding door. The value of the opening percent may be between 0 and 100. A value of 0 closes the door, a value of 50 opens the door halfway, and a value of 100 opens the door completely. See the nonswinging doors in **Figure 5-2.**
- **Position along wall.** This property provides a drop-down list with **Offset/ Center** and **Unconstrained** options. The **Offset/Center** option constrains the door placement to a set distance from the walls' ends or intersections and to the center of walls. When this option is selected, the door may only be placed in these positions. The **Unconstrained** option allows the door to be freely placed anywhere in a wall without being constrained to a specific location.
- **Automatic offset.** This property is available only if the **Offset/Center** option has been selected. The value of this option is the distance from the corner or end of a wall at which doors may be placed when the **Offset/Center** option is selected.

Figure 5-2.
The **Swing angle** property controls how far swinging doors are open. The **Opening percent** property controls how far nonswinging doors are open. Three different types of nonswinging doors are shown here.

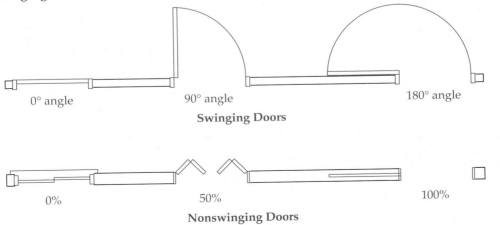

0° angle   90° angle   180° angle

Swinging Doors

0%   50%   100%

Nonswinging Doors

- **Vertical alignment.** This property displays a drop-down list with **Threshold** and **Head** options, controlling the height from which the placement of the door is measured. For example, if **Threshold** is selected, the placement of the door is measured from the bottom of the door up. If **Head** is selected, the placement is measured from the head height location down.
- **Head height.** This property controls the door header location. If the **Head** option in the **Vertical alignment** property is selected, the placement of the top of the door is measured from the value specified here.
- **Threshold height.** This property controls where the bottom of the door is placed vertically within a wall. A value of 0″ places the bottom of the door at the bottom of a wall. Entering a value greater than 0″ moves the door up vertically within the wall.

Once you have changed the properties to the values you wish the new door to have, select a wall in which to place the door. After a wall is selected, the door can still be moved around but only within walls. As the door is moved around to different walls while you are deciding where to place it, dimensions are displayed indicating the size of the door and where it is located in relation to the endpoints of the wall. See **Figure 5-3.** To place the door, move it to the desired location and pick it. The door is placed in that location, and an opening is cut into the wall to accommodate it.

You can accurately place the swing of the door with slight movements of the crosshairs before picking the door location. See **Figure 5-4.** This works best when **Offset/Center** is selected for the **Position along wall** property. As the crosshairs are moved

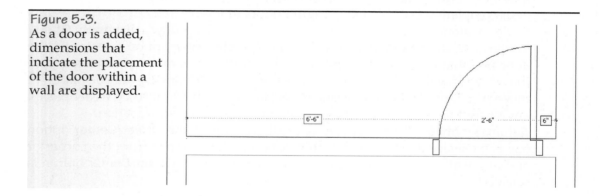

Figure 5-3.
As a door is added, dimensions that indicate the placement of the door within a wall are displayed.

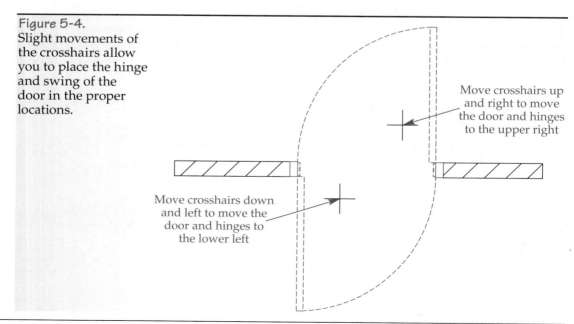

Figure 5-4.
Slight movements of the crosshairs allow you to place the hinge and swing of the door in the proper locations.

Move crosshairs up and right to move the door and hinges to the upper right

Move crosshairs down and left to move the door and hinges to the lower left to a location for the door, the door snaps into the closest place, either offset from the end of a wall or in the center. Move the crosshairs to each side of the wall to see the door's swing change sides. Moving the crosshairs slightly also moves the location of the door's hinges. When you find the desired swing and hinge location, pick to insert the door into the wall. The door can be modified later if its hinges and swing are placed incorrectly.

You can insert as many doors into the drawing as needed. After one door has been inserted, another door is attached to the crosshairs to be inserted next. You can change any of the properties before inserting this next door. When you are finished inserting doors, press [Enter] or right-click and pick **Enter** to exit the command.

Doors can also be added to the drawing based on the properties of an existing door. To do this, select the door with the desired properties, right-click, and pick **Add Selected** from the shortcut menu. The **Properties** palette reflects the appropriate settings from the selected door. Continue to add doors as normal. When you are finished, press [Enter] to exit the command.

Exercise
5-1   Complete the Exercise on the Student CD.

Modifying Doors

Doors can be modified in several ways, which include using standard AutoCAD commands such as **COPY**, **MOVE**, **ROTATE**, **ERASE**, **MIRROR**, and **ARRAY**. Doors can be modified using the **Properties** palette, and doors have grips that can be used for grip editing.

Using Door Grips

Door objects include grip points at important locations on the object, and these grips are different from standard grips. See **Figure 5-5**. Hovering over a door grip displays a tooltip indicating the name of the grip and what the grip controls. For some grips, pressing the [Ctrl] key provides additional options.

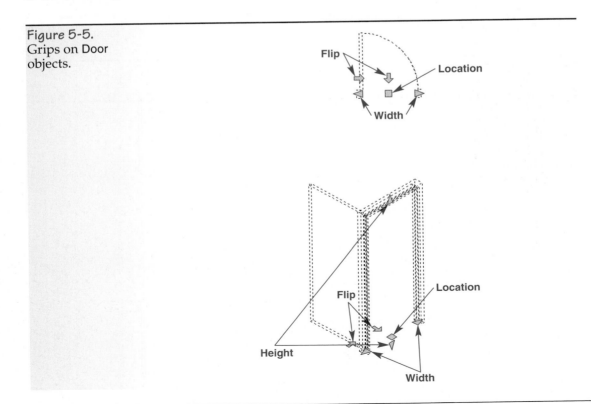

Figure 5-5.
Grips on Door
objects.

The width of doors can be adjusted by selecting and moving one of the **Width** grips on either side of the door, stretching the door, and adjusting the opening in the wall. If the door style includes preconfigured standard sizes, picking one of the width grips displays standard width size markers. Moving the cursor causes the door to snap to the next standard size. See **Figure 5-6.** Pressing the [Ctrl] key while selecting the **Width** grip cycles through the standard size marks that can be used and a custom size door width that can be stretched. When adjusting the width, typing a numerical value and pressing [Enter] sets the door to that size.

The height of the door can also be adjusted by selecting either of the **Height** grips while in a 3D view. If a door style includes standard sizes, tick marks appear for snapping to a different standard size, just as the standard width marks appear. Adjusting the top height grip controls the head height location for the door. Adjusting the bottom height grip controls the threshold location for the door.

Using the **Flip** grips, the door swing can be adjusted after the door is placed. Picking either of these grips changes the hinge position and the direction the door swings. See **Figure 5-7.** To change the side of the door's hinges, pick the **Flip** grip next to the door leaf. This flips the door to the opposite side of the opening. To flip the door to the opposite side of the wall, pick the **Flip** grip in the center of the door.

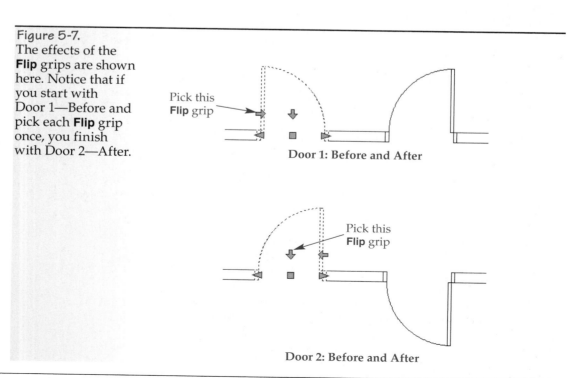

Figure 5-6.
Selecting a door with preset standard sizes displays the standard sizes as hatch marks. Your cursor snaps to these marks as the door is stretched.

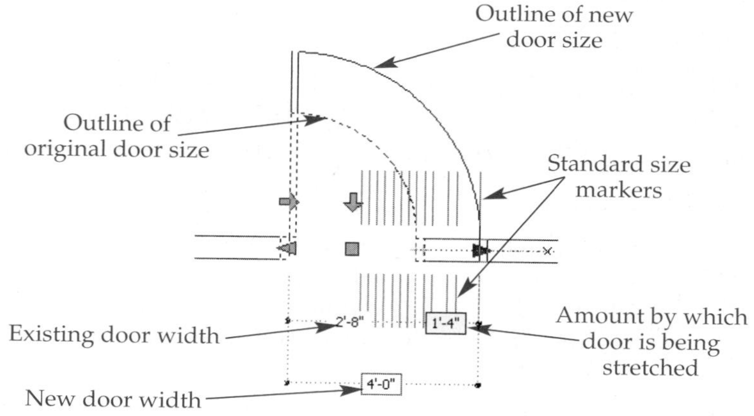

Outline of new door size

Outline of original door size

Standard size markers

Existing door width

2'-8"   1'-4"

Amount by which door is being stretched

New door width

4'-0"

Figure 5-7.
The effects of the **Flip** grips are shown here. Notice that if you start with Door 1—Before and pick each **Flip** grip once, you finish with Door 2—After.

Pick this **Flip** grip

Door 1: Before and After

Pick this **Flip** grip

Door 2: Before and After

Figure 5-8.
After picking the
Location grip,
pressing the [Ctrl]
key allows the
door to be adjusted
within the width of
the wall.

Pick **Location** grip
to move door

Move within width

Press [Ctrl] once to
access this option

Door has been moved
within width

The **Location** grip adjusts the placement of the door, allowing you to adjust or move the door along the wall. When the [Ctrl] key is pressed while using the **Location** grip, you can adjust the door within the width of the wall. See **Figure 5-8**. When the [Ctrl] key is pressed a second time while using the **Location** grip, you can adjust the door vertically within the wall.

Using the Properties Palette

The **Properties** palette is helpful when you are modifying Architectural Desktop objects. Properties such as **Layer**, **Width**, **Height**, and **Style** can be easily changed using the **Properties** palette.

Exercise
5-2   *Complete the Exercise on the Student CD.*

Creating Window Objects

Window objects understand how to interact with Wall objects. Once a window has been inserted into a wall, it becomes constrained to the wall. As with doors, Window objects cut a hole out of the wall, so the header over the window does not display in a plan view.

Adding Window Objects

To add a window to your drawing, pick the **Window** tool from the **Design** tool palette, pick **Design > Windows > Add Window...**, or type WINDOWADD. You can also add a window by selecting a wall, right-clicking, and picking **Insert > Window...** from the shortcut menu. Additional window styles are available by selecting a window type from the **Windows** tool palette in the **Design** tool palette group. After you enter this command, you receive the same prompt you received when inserting a door:

Select wall, space boundary, grid assembly or RETURN:

Type
WINDOWADD
Pull-Down Menu

Design
  > Windows
    > Add Window...

Tool Palette
Design

Window

WINDOWADD

Select the wall, space boundary, or grid assembly in which you wish to place the window, or press [Enter]. If you press [Enter] without selecting an object, the window is inserted into the drawing without being inserted into a wall, giving up the interactive nature between a window and a wall. After you insert the window, you are prompted for a rotation angle. Once you have specified the rotation angle for the new window, it is placed in the drawing independent of a wall.

However, you probably will want to pick a wall in which to place the window. After you do so, as the crosshairs are moved around the drawing, the window is constrained to the wall nearest to the crosshairs. When the window is in the appropriate location, pick to insert the window in the wall. You can continue to pick locations to add additional windows, or you can end the command.

You can change the properties of the window being inserted by adjusting the values in the **Properties** palette. The property values for windows are the same as for doors, except the **Sill height** property for windows replaces the **Threshold height** property for doors. The **Sill height** is measured from the bottom of the wall to the bottom of the window, allowing you to set the bottom of the window a specified height. Adjust any settings prior to picking the location for the new window. The window properties can be modified later if the design changes.

If a new window needs to be added using the same properties as an existing window, select the desired existing window, right-click, and pick **Add Selected**. This adds a window with the same properties as the selected window. You can add as many windows of this type as you need or change the properties in the **Properties** palette. When you are finished, end the command.

Exercise 5-3   Complete the Exercise on the Student CD.

Modifying Windows

AutoCAD commands such as **MOVE**, **COPY**, **MIRROR**, and **ARRAY** all can be used to modify windows. Window objects also have grip editing modes, and the **Properties** palette can be used to modify window properties.

Using Window Grips

Grip editing can be used extensively when modifying windows. See **Figure 5-9.** The grip points located on Window objects are the same as those on Door objects, but the **Height** grip along the bottom of the window controls the sill location of the window.

As with a door, stretching the width of a window that has predefined standard sizes displays tick marks representing the standard sizes. As the width is stretched, the crosshairs snap to the predefined size marks. If a window needs a custom width, press the [Ctrl] key after selecting a width grip. This allows you to freely stretch the size of the window. As the window is being stretched, typing a numerical value establishes that as the new width for the window. The same procedure can be used to adjust the height of the window.

Some designs may call for windows to be grouped together. To do this, insert the windows close to one another, and then use grips to move the windows into place. See **Figure 5-10.** Select a **Width** grip on one of the windows, right-click, and select **Move** from the shortcut menu. Next, use object snap to move the selected window so its frame overlaps or touches the other window frame. If windows are placed too close together, a wall defect symbol may appear because the wall endcap is applied. To fix this problem, change the **Opening endcap** property in the **Properties** palette to the **Standard** style. This allows windows to be placed in close proximity without displaying a wall defect.

Figure 5-9.
Grips for Window objects.

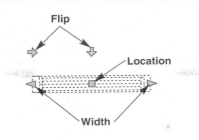

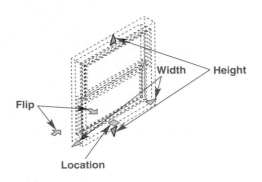

Figure 5-10.
The window frames may be placed so they are overlapping or touching.

Windows placed so window frames are overlapping

Windows placed so window frames are touching

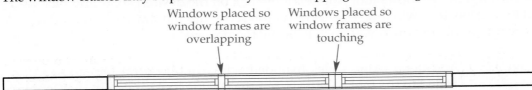

If it is appropriate for the window style, the **Flip** grips can be used to flip the window in the wall or to change the location of the hinges on a hinged window.

Using the Properties Palette

During the design phase of a project, the specifications for windows may change after they have been drawn. Like doors, the **Properties** palette is used to modify windows after placement, and windows include many of the same properties as doors. See **Figure 5-11.**

Some designs may call for windows to be grouped together. To do this, insert the windows close to one another, and then use grips to move the windows into place. See **Figure 5-10.** Select a **Width** grip on one of the windows, right-click, and select **Move** from the shortcut menu. Next, use object snap to move the selected window so its frame overlaps or touches the other window frame. If windows are placed too close together, a wall defect symbol may appear because the wall endcap is applied. To fix this problem, change the **Opening endcap** property in the **Properties** palette to the **Standard** style. This allows windows to be placed in close proximity without displaying a wall defect.

Figure 5-11.
The **Properties** palette is used to make changes to existing windows.

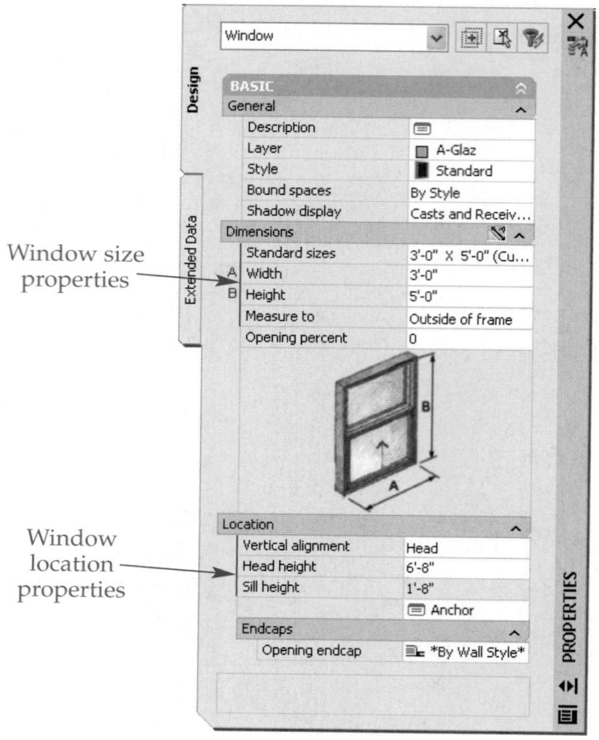

Window size properties

Window location properties

If the design requires that the style of window be changed, picking the **Style** property displays a list of styles loaded into the drawing. If the desired style is not available in the list, you may import the style just as you did with the door styles. You may also look through the **Windows** tool palette, right-click on the desired style, and pick **Apply Tool Properties to > Window**. This imports the style into the drawing and allows you to pick a window to which you wish to apply the new style.

NOTE

Additional AEC styles included with Architectural Desktop can be added to the tool palettes, from the **Design** tool catalog in the **Content Browser**. Refer to Appendix B on the Student CD for more information about accessing these styles.

Exercise 5-4   Complete the Exercise on the Student CD.

Creating an Opening Object

An *opening object* is a hole in a wall similar to a door or window. An opening, however, does not include a frame, leaf, or glazing. Openings can be many shapes and sizes and are represented in a floor plan view with the header lines over the hole.

Architectural Desktop and Its Applications

Adding Openings

To add an opening to your drawing, pick the **Opening** tool from the **Design** tool palette, pick **Design > Openings > Add Opening...**, or type OPENINGADD. You can also add an opening by selecting a wall, right-clicking, and picking **Insert > Opening...** from the shortcut menu.

Openings use a predefined shape, such as a rectangle, arch, or octagon, rather than a style. The list of shapes can be viewed by picking the **Shape** property drop-down list in the **Properties** palette. See **Figure 5-12.**

A custom shape can also be used by selecting **Custom** from the **Shape** drop-down list. This displays the **Profile** property in the **Properties** palette. By default, the only custom shape available is **Standard**. This creates a rectangular opening in the wall. Custom shape types use a shape known as a *profile*. Profiles are closed shapes drawn as polylines and then defined as profiles. Creating profiles is discussed in Chapter 9.

The remaining properties are similar to the Door and Window objects. Specify a width and height for the opening. If the opening is to be placed in the center or a specified distance from a wall, set the **Position along wall** property accordingly. The opening can also be set at a specific head or sill height within the wall.

When you are finished setting the appropriate properties for the openings, pick a wall in which to insert the opening. As with doors and windows, the Opening objects are constrained to walls. When you have finished adding openings to the drawing, end the command.

Type
OPENINGADD
Pull-Down Menu
Design > Openings > Add Opening...
Tool Palette
Design
Opening

OPENINGADD

 Exercise 5-5   Complete the Exercise on the Student CD.

Modifying Openings

Like doors and windows, the width, height, and vertical alignment of openings can be modified through the **Properties** palette. If a different shape is desired, select a new shape from the **Shape** property's drop-down list. Openings can also be modified using AutoCAD commands such as **MOVE**, **COPY**, **ERASE**, and **ARRAY**.

Figure 5-12. Openings use shapes instead of styles to determine the shape of the hole in the wall.

Only available when **Custom** shape is selected in **Shape** property

List of predefined shapes available

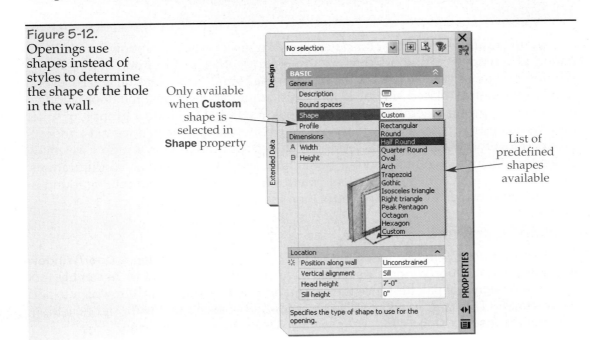

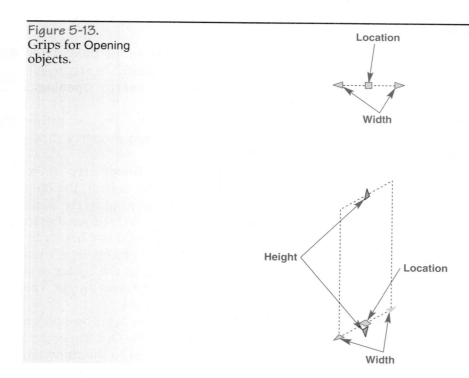

Figure 5-13.
Grips for Opening
objects.

Opening objects include grips similar to those of doors and windows. The **Width** grips can be used to adjust the width of the opening. In a 3D view, adjust the height using the **Height** grips. Openings do not include **Flip** grips. See **Figure 5-13**.

Exercise
5-6

Complete the Exercise on the Student CD.

Creating Door/Window Assembly Objects

Door/window assembly objects are used to insert several windows or a combination of windows and doors that are grouped together to form one object. Door/window assemblies can be used in the creation of a commercial building where several windows are often placed side by side. In residential applications, the door/window assembly can group together a door and sidelight windows, window groups, or other designs as desired. The default door/window assembly tool creates several windows grouped together. Architectural Desktop includes additional door/window assembly styles that include a combination of doors and windows in various configurations. These styles can be added to your tool palettes from the **Design** tool catalog found in the **Content Browser**. Refer to Appendix B on the included CD.

Adding Door/Window Assemblies

To add a door/window assembly to your drawing, pick **Design** > **Door/Window Assembly** > **Add Door/Window Assembly...** or pick the **Door/Window Assembly** tool from the **Design** tool palette. Once the command is active, pick a wall in which to add the assembly. This command can also be accessed by selecting a wall, right-clicking, and picking **Insert** > **Door/Window Assembly...** from the shortcut menu.

Pull-Down Menu
Design
> Door/Window
  Assemblies
> Add Door/
  Window
  Assembly...

Tool Palette

Design

Door/Window
Assembly

As with the other AEC objects, a door/window assembly's properties are controlled through the **Properties** palette. Three properties are included for the door/window assembly that are not properties of the other objects we have covered so far. These are the **Rise**, **Start miter angle**, and **End miter angle** properties, and they are described as follows:

- **Rise.** The **Rise** property is used for nonrectangular assemblies, such as peaked or arched openings. This value is the vertical distance from the top of the assembly to the vertical sides of the frame. See **Figure 5-14.** The default assembly is a rectangular shape.
- **Start miter angle.** This property adds a miter angle to the beginning of the assembly, which is the location where the assembly construction is started. A miter is only visible in a 3D view.
- **End miter angle.** This controls the mitering angle at the end of the assembly, which is the location where the assembly construction is completed.

Once the properties are adjusted, add as many door/window assemblies as you desire, and then end the command.

 Exercise 5-7 **Complete the Exercise on the Student CD.**

Modifying Door/Window Assemblies

Door/window assemblies can also be modified with AutoCAD editing commands and the **Properties** palette, as previously discussed for other openings. It is possible to edit the door of a door/window assembly separate from the windows. This means that for assemblies that include doors, it is important to pick the entire assembly when using the **Properties** palette. You need to select the frame of the door/window assembly carefully, because you may find yourself editing only the door rather than the entire assembly.

The properties that can be modified for the assembly are the same as those used when adding the object. One additional property is the **Opening endcap** property. If a wall defect symbol is displayed after inserting a door/window assembly, you may need to change the **Opening endcap** property to **Standard** to remove the assigned wall endcap that can cause cleanup difficulties.

Figure 5-14.
The **Rise** property of the door/window assemblies is shown here.

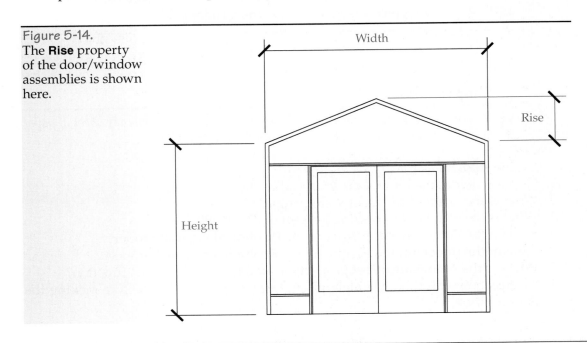

Figure 5-15.
Grips for Door/
Window Assembly
objects.

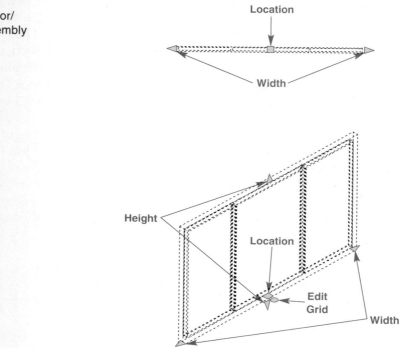

Door/window assemblies include the same standard grips as other Opening objects. See **Figure 5-15.** If you use the **Width** grip, as the assembly is stretched larger, additional windows are added and redistributed equally within the assembly. If the width is made smaller, windows are removed from the assembly, and the mullions are equally redistributed. If an assembly with a door has been used, the swing of the door can be changed using the door **Flip** grips, as previously discussed.

When the assembly is shown using a 3D view, one additional grip is available: the **Edit Grid** grip. When this grip is selected, you are given three options. These options allow you to edit the grid divisions, change the cell infill, or change the frame and mullion assignments. These options are discussed in greater detail in Chapter 16.

Exercise
5-8

Complete the Exercise on the Student CD.

Chapter Test

Answer the following questions. Write your answers on a separate sheet of paper or complete the electronic chapter test on the Student CD.

1. Define *space boundary.*
2. Give another name for *grid assembly* and its definition.
3. What is the effect of a 0° door swing angle? 90°? 180°?
4. What is the effect of an opening percent of 0? 50? 100?
5. Explain the **Offset/Center** setting of the **Position along wall** property.
6. Explain the **Unconstrained** option of the **Position along wall** property.
7. When is the **Automatic offset** property available, and what is its function?
8. Discuss how you can accurately place the swing of the door before picking the door location.

Architectural Desktop and Its Applications

9. How many doors can you insert into the drawing at one time, and can you change door properties before each insertion?
10. How do you stop inserting doors?
11. What do you see when hovering over a door grip, and how do you access additional options?
12. How do you stretch a door, and what is the use of preconfigured standard sizes?
13. What are Opening objects?
14. How do you add a new window with the same properties as an existing window?
15. What are Door/Window Assembly objects?

Chapter Projects

Use the techniques covered in this chapter to create the following drawings.

1. Single-Level Residential Project
   A. Access the **Project Browser** and set Residential-Project-01 current.
   B. Open the Main Floor construct.
   C. Add doors, windows, and openings as indicated in the figure.
   D. Unless noted otherwise, head heights should be set at 6'-8".
   E. Unless dimensioned otherwise, all openings are 6" from a corner or are centered in a wall.
   F. Do not dimension.
   G. Save and close the Main Floor drawing.

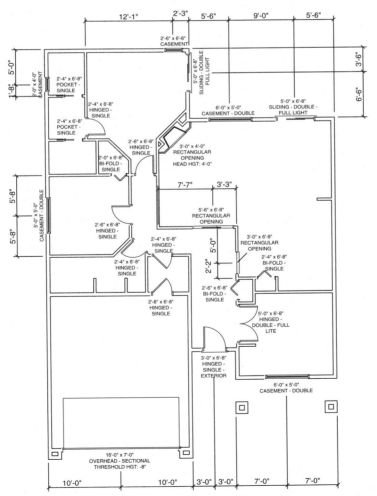

Alan Mascord Design Associates

2. Single-Level Residential Project
   A. Access the **Project Browser** and set Residential-Project-02 current.
   B. Open the Main Floor construct.
   C. Add doors, windows, and openings as indicated in the figure.
   D. Unless noted otherwise, head heights should be set at 6'-8".
   E. Unless dimensioned otherwise, all openings are 6" from a corner or are centered in a wall.
   F. Do not dimension.
   G. Save and close the Main Floor drawing.

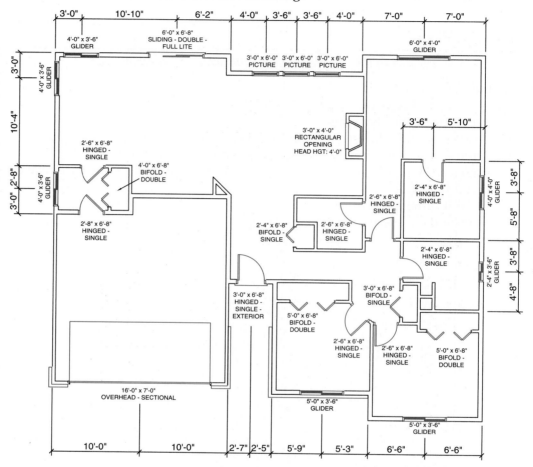

Alan Mascord Design Associates

3. Two-Story Residential Project
   A. Access the **Project Browser** and set Residential-Project-03 current.
   B. Open the Main Floor construct.
   C. Add doors, windows, and openings as indicated in the figure.
   D. Unless noted otherwise, head heights should be set at 7'-0".
   E. Unless dimensioned otherwise, all openings are 6" from a corner or are centered in a wall.
   F. Do not dimension.
   G. Save and close the Main Floor drawing.
   H. Open the Upper Floor construct.
   I. Add doors, windows, and openings as indicated in the figure.
   J. Unless noted otherwise, head heights should be set at 7'-0".
   K. Unless dimensioned otherwise, all openings are 6" from a corner or are centered in a wall.
   L. Do not dimension.
   M. Save and close the Upper Floor drawing.

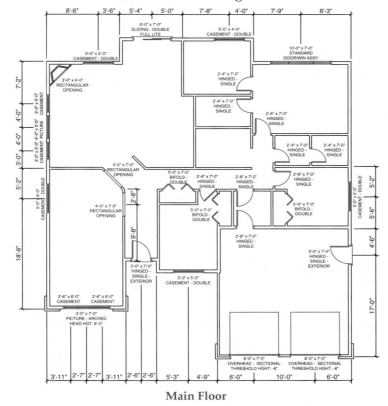

Main Floor

Upper Floor

3D-DZYN

4. Two-Story Residential Project
   A. Access the **Project Browser** and set Residential-Project-04 current.
   B. Open the Main Floor construct.
   C. Add doors, windows, and openings as indicated in the figure.
   D. Unless noted otherwise, head heights should be set at 7'-0".
   E. Unless dimensioned otherwise, all openings are 6" from a corner or are centered in a wall.
   F. Do not dimension.
   G. Save and close the Main Floor drawing.
   H. Open the Upper Floor construct.
   I. Add doors, windows, and openings as indicated in the figure.
   J. Unless noted otherwise, head heights should be set at 7'-0".
   K. Unless dimensioned otherwise, all openings are 6" from a corner or are centered in a wall.
   L. Do not dimension.
   M. Save and close the Upper Floor drawing.

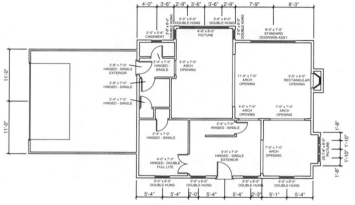

Main Floor

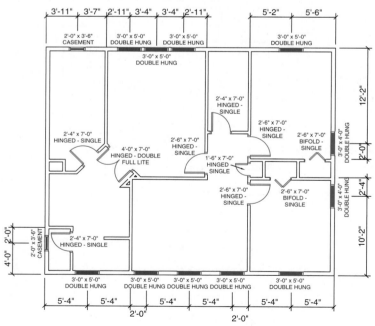

Upper Floor

Alan Mascord Design Associates

5. Commercial Store Project
   A. Access the **Project Browser** and set Commercial-Project-05 current.
   B. Open the Main Floor construct.
   C. Add doors and door/window assemblies as indicated in the figure.
   D. Door head heights should be set at 7′-0″.
   E. Door/window assembly head heights should be set at 9′-0″.
   F. Unless dimensioned otherwise, all openings are 6″ from a corner or are centered in a wall.
   G. Do not dimension.
   H. Save and close the Main Floor drawing.

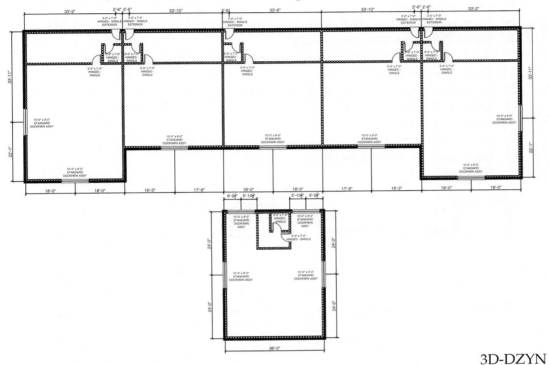

3D-DZYN

6. Commercial Car Maintenance Shop Project
    A. Access the **Project Browser** and set Commercial-Project-06 current.
    B. Open the Main Floor construct.
    C. Add doors and door/window assemblies as indicated in the figure.
    D. Door head heights should be set at 7'-0".
    E. Set the head height for the overhead doors in the car wash area to 9'-0".
    F. Set the head height for the overhead doors in the garage area to 16'-0".
    G. Door/window assembly head heights should be set at 8'-0".
    H. Unless dimensioned otherwise, all openings are 6" from a corner or are centered in a wall.
    I. Do not dimension.
    J. Save and close the Main Floor drawing.
    K. Open the Upper Floor construct.
    L. Add doors and door/window assemblies as indicated in the figure.
    M. Door head heights should be set at 7'-0".
    N. Door/window assembly head heights should be set at 8'-0".
    O. Unless dimensioned otherwise, all openings are 6" from a corner or are centered in a wall.
    P. Do not dimension.
    Q. Save and close the Upper Floor drawing.

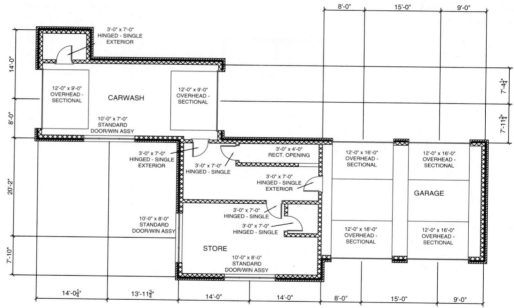

Main Floor

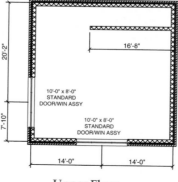

Upper Floor

3D-DZYN

Architectural Desktop and Its Applications

7. Governmental Fire Station
    A. Access the **Project Browser** and set Gvrmt -Project-07 current.
    B. Open the Main Floor construct.
    C. Add doors, openings, and door/window assemblies as indicated in the figure.
    D. Use the schedules for the appropriate sizes and head height locations.
    E. Unless dimensioned otherwise, all openings are 6″ from a corner or are centered in a wall.
    F. Do not dimension.
    G. Save and close the Main Floor drawing.

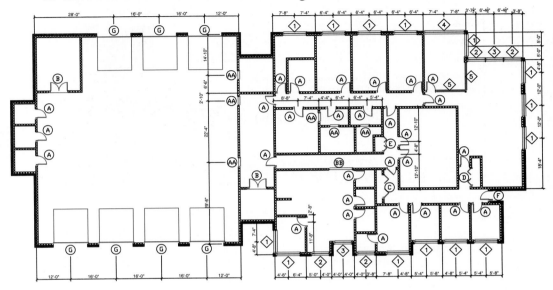

DOOR SCHEDULE					
ID	STYLE	WIDTH	HEIGHT	HEAD HEIGHT	QUANTITY
A	Hinged - Single	3'-0"	7'-0"	7'-0"	29
B	Hinged - Double - Exterior	6'-0"	7'-0"	7'-0"	2
C	Bifold - Double	8'-0"	7'-0"	7'-0"	1
D	Bifold - Double	6'-0"	7'-0"	7'-0"	1
E	Bifold - Double	5'-0"	7'-0"	7'-0"	1
F	Hinged - Single - Full Lite	3'-0"	7'-0"	7'-0"	1
G	Overhead - Sectional	12'-0"	12'-0"	12'-0"	7

OPENING SCHEDULE					
ID	PROFILE SHAPE	WIDTH	HEIGHT	HEAD HEIGHT	QUANTITY
AA	Standard	3'-0"	7'-0"	7'-0"	6
BB	Standard	8'-0"	7'-0"	7'-0"	1

DOOR/WINDOW ASSEMBLY SCHEDULE					
ID	STYLE	WIDTH	HEIGHT	HEAD HEIGHT	QUANTITY
1	Standard	8'-0"	6'-0"	9'-0"	14
2	Standard	6'-0"	6'-0"	9'-0"	4
3	Standard	6'-0"	9'-0"	9'-0"	2
4	Standard	14'-0"	6'-0"	9'-0"	1
5	Standard	10'-0"	9'-0"	9'-0"	2

3D-DZYN

Chapter 5 Projects

CAD User (www.caduser.com) is a free online journal. Articles and CAD news are posted monthly, and CAD users can sign up for a free e-newsletter.

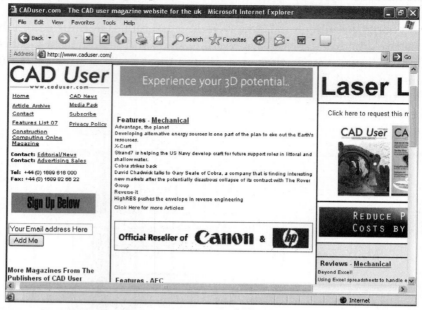

Learning Objectives

After completing this chapter, you will be able to do the following:

✓ Use the **ZOOM** command and its options.
✓ Use the **PAN** command.
✓ Use **3D Orbit** to change views.
✓ Use projection methods, visual styles, and visual aid tools.
✓ Regenerate a drawing.
✓ Create and use view drawings.
✓ Create model views.
✓ Apply preset views.
✓ Use the **Object Viewer**.
✓ Create perspectives and movie files.

When developing a design for a new building or completing construction documents, you may need to view different parts of the drawing from various angles. Architectural Desktop includes tools that let you look closely at a detail, view the entire project at once, and display your project as 2D drawings or 3D models. This chapter covers the visualization tools in Architectural Desktop that allow you to do this.

Using 3D Orbit to Change Your View

The **3D ORBIT** command is used to dynamically change the view or perspective of your drawing. It is very useful when working with 3D models. To access the command, pick **View > 3D Orbit > Constrained Orbit**; pick the **3D Orbit** button in the **Views, 3D Orbit**, or **Navigation** toolbar; or type 3DORBIT or 3DO.

Upon entering the command, the cursor changes shape to indicate that it is in orbit mode. Press and hold the pick button and move the mouse. This twists and rotates the view of the model around the center of the screen. Let go of the pick button, move the cursor to a new location, and repeat the process to continue to spin the model.

Type
3DORBIT
3DO
Pull-Down Menu
View
> 3D Orbit
> Constrained
Orbit
Toolbars
Views
3D Orbit
Navigation
3D Orbit

3DORBIT

AutoCAD Review

Using the Zoom Commands

When taking pictures with a camera, you can *zoom in* for a close-up of the subject or *zoom out* to encompass the entire scene. Similarly, using the **ZOOM** command in Architectural Desktop allows you to zoom in on a small detail or zoom out to view your entire project. Zooming also lets you move around the drawing and display various areas of the design. The **ZOOM** command is a very helpful tool that can be used often as you design a building and complete the construction documents.

There are several options in the **ZOOM** command and on the **Zoom** toolbar. The options on the **Zoom** toolbar can also be found in the **Zoom** flyout on the **Navigation** toolbar. The **ZOOM** command can be accessed by typing Z or ZOOM or by selecting the appropriate button from either the **Zoom** toolbar or the **Zoom** flyout on the **Navigation** toolbar. If you have a wheel mouse, scrolling the wheel allows you to zoom in and out of your drawing. Double-clicking the wheel button performs a **Zoom Extents** of the drawing. If your screen scrolls side-to-side, you may need to turn off horizontal scrolling.

There are several zooming options available, including **All**, **Center**, **Dynamic**, **Extents**, **Previous**, **Scale**, **Window**, **Object**, **Realtime**, **In**, **Out**, and **Aerial View**. To learn more about these options, use **Autodesk Architectural Desktop 2007 Help**.

Zoom Option	Button	Description
All		Zooms to the edge of the drawing limits.
Center		Centers the point you pick.
Dynamic		Used to resize current view or choose new area of the drawing to view.
Extents		Zooms to the outermost geometry in the drawing.
Previous		Restores the previous view or zoom.
Scale		Zooms in or out based on the scale factor you enter.
Window		Displays the portion of the drawing within the window you specify.
Object		Zooms to the outermost geometry of selected object(s).
Realtime		Zooms in or out depending on the movement of the mouse while holding the pick button.
In		Zooms in on drawing by a scale factor of 2X.
Out		Zooms out from the drawing by a scale factor of 0.5X.
Aerial View		Similar to the **Dynamic** option, but with a preview window displayed.

AutoCAD Review

Using the Pan Command

The **PAN** command is used to adjust the drawing display without changing the magnification. It allows you to slide the drawing around the screen. For example, after zooming in on the drawing, some of the geometry you wish to be visible may lie outside the display screen. Use the **PAN** command to adjust the view until the desired portion of the drawing can be seen. To access the command, pick the **Pan Realtime** button found on the **Zoom** toolbar or the **Zoom** flyout, or type PAN or P. Once the command has been entered, the crosshairs change to a hand icon.

Press and hold the pick button and move the mouse to slide the drawing up or down or from side to side. Release the pick button to reposition the cursor for additional panning. Right-clicking displays a shortcut menu from which you can select another zoom function. When you have finished panning, exit the command in the normal way. Note that if you have a wheel mouse, pressing and holding down the wheel while moving the mouse allows you to scroll around the drawing.

If you pan to the edge of the drawing, a bar is displayed on one side of the hand cursor. If this happens, you cannot pan further in that direction until the drawing has been regenerated. You can use the **REGEN** command to do this. The **REGEN** command is discussed later in this chapter.

Projection Methods, Shading, and Visual Aid Tools

The **3D Orbit** command includes many options for controlling how your model appears on the display screen. These options include projection methods such as parallel or perspective, shading and hiding objects, and tools such as a compass and grid. These options can be accessed in the shortcut menu available when the **3D Orbit** command is active, which is shown in **Figure 6-1.**

Some of the **3D Orbit** options are described here:

- **Enable Orbit Auto Target.** This setting allows the orbiting around the model to be centered on the screen or the center of the model. Checking this option will cause the orbit to spin around the center of the model.
- **Parallel.** When choosing parallel mode, the projection of the view causes the sides of the building to be parallel to each other.
- **Perspective.** This option causes the sides of objects to point or project to a vanishing point, producing a more realistic view of the model. **Figure 6-2** shows the difference between the parallel and perspective modes on your model.
- **Reset View.** This option resets the view to the view displayed before the **3D Orbit** command was entered.
- **Preset Views.** This shortcut menu contains a list of preset viewing directions. There are six orthographic views. Four of these views display the front, right, back, and left sides of a building. The top view is used to see the floor plan view. When the top view is selected in Architectural Desktop, the AEC objects revert to 2D objects. There are also four preset isometric views that can be used to display 3D views. Preset views are discussed later in this chapter.

Figure 6-1.
The **3D Orbit** shortcut menu contains many options for controlling how the model is viewed in the display screen.

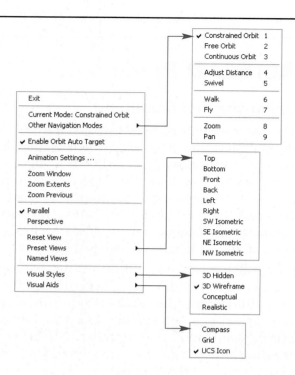

- **Visual Styles.** There are four options available in this shortcut menu: two types of shading that can be applied to your 3D models, a hide mode, and the default wireframe. These shading modes can also be accessed in the **Visual Styles** toolbar. These options are discussed in detail later in this chapter.

- **Visual Aids.** The **Visual Aids** shortcut menu includes three options that assist you in relating the chosen view to the User Coordinate System (UCS) and aid in determining which are the positive and negative Z axes. These visual aids are the following:

    - **Compass.** When this option is selected, a spherical 3D compass is displayed within the arcball. Tick marks and labels indicate the positive X, Y, and Z axes.

    - **Grid.** This option displays a grid that is the same size as the limits, and at the current XY drawing plane, which by default is located at the 0" Z axis. This provides a good "groundline" for visualization but does not print.

    - **UCS Icon.** This option turns on or off the shaded UCS icon. This icon is used to help understand where the positive X, Y, and Z axes are pointing. The X and Y axes determine the drawing plane.

There are additional options that can be used to adjust the view of your model in the shortcut menu. These options can be found in the **Other Navigation Modes** cascading menu. Some of these options include **Adjust Distance** and **Swivel**, which adjust the view in perspective projection. The **Continuous Orbit** is used to spin the model continuously by holding down the pick button, moving the mouse in the direction the model is intended to spin, and releasing the pick button.

Figure 6-2.
With parallel projection, the sides of the building are parallel to one another. With perspective projection, the sides of the building project to a vanishing point.

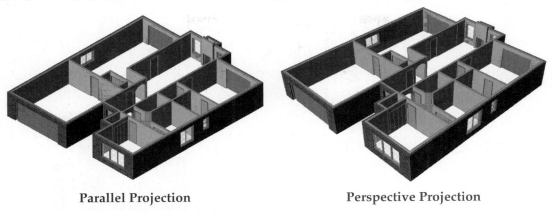

Parallel Projection   **Perspective Projection**

Shading the 3D Model

As indicated in the **3D Orbit** section discussed previously, the model can be viewed using several visual styles. There are five visual styles that can be accessed by selecting the appropriate button in the **Visual Styles** toolbar, selecting the **Visual Styles** flyout in the **Navigation** toolbar, or picking **View** > **Visual Styles** and selecting a style from the cascading menu. See **Figure 6-3.** The visual styles, which are shown in **Figure 6-4,** are as follows:

Figure 6-3.
The shading options can be selected from the **Visual Styles** cascading menu or from the **Visual Styles** toolbar.

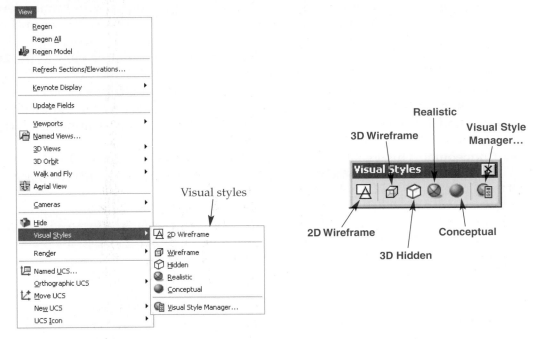

Figure 6-4.
The five different visual styles applied to the same objects.

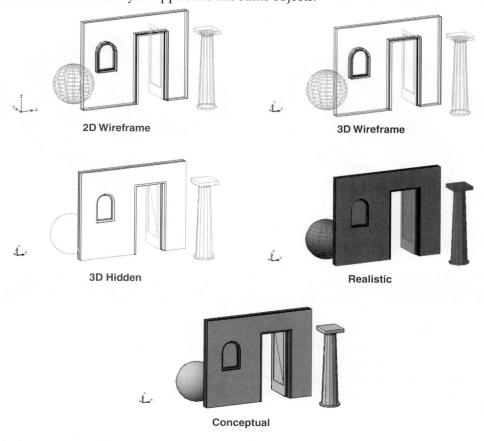

- **2D Wireframe.** This option displays 3D objects as a normal wireframe view. Lines and curves are used to define the edges of the 3D objects. Raster images are visible in this mode, and the UCS is also displayed as a 2D icon.
- **3D Wireframe.** This option displays the same type of wireframe view as the **2D Wireframe**, but the UCS icon is displayed as a colored 3D icon.
- **3D Hidden.** This option hides lines and arcs that are behind a solid object.
- **Realistic.** This visual style shades and smoothes model objects and displays the model geometry using the base color of the material applied to the object.
- **Conceptual.** This visual style also shades and smoothes model objects, but it displays the model geometry using the color of the layer to which the object is assigned.

Regenerating the Display

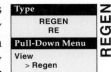

Occasionally, when you are zooming in and out of a drawing, curved objects appear to be segmented. Architectural Desktop uses small line segments to display curves in the drawing because it can redisplay straight-line segments faster than curved objects. If you want Architectural Desktop to redisplay the drawing to show the true curves, you can regenerate the drawing to update the display. The **REGEN** command is used to regenerate the drawing, and it is accessed by selecting **View > Regen** or by typing REGEN or RE. After using the **REGEN** command, curved objects appear curved again.

The **REGEN** command is also used when you can no longer pan to the side or when you have zoomed out so far that zooming no longer has any effect on what you see. This can happen if there is not enough cached memory used by the computer. The **REGEN** command recalculates all drawing objects and their placement in the drawing. If you are working on the drawing while using a visual style other than **2D Wireframe**, you may also notice some discrepancies when editing objects. Use **REGEN** to correct these display problems.

NOTE

When working with layout space viewports, the **REGENALL** command can be used to regenerate all "floating" viewports. This command can be accessed by typing REGENALL or by selecting **View > Regen All**.

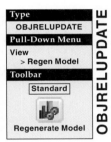

Sometimes, as changes are made to AEC objects, the objects may not display correctly. This is especially the case when cleaning up walls and, after cleaning them up, the defect symbols are not cleared from the walls, or if a change made to the display of an object does not appear after the change has been made. Try using the **Regenerate Model** button to regenerate the objects. If the wall defect symbols are still not removed, continue adjusting the wall cleanup radius or merging the walls, in combination with the **Regenerate Model** button to remove the defect. This command can be accessed by picking **View > Regen Model**, picking the **Regenerate Model** button in the **Standard** toolbar, or typing OBJRELUPDATE.

Using Views in the Drawing

Model space views are similar to photographs. A camera takes a photograph of a subject. This photograph is then displayed on photographic paper or the digital screen, and it is saved to be viewed later. A view in Architectural Desktop is like a photograph, and it is also stored to be used later. With model space views, "photos" are taken of different areas of the drawing, so they can be used later when assembling sheet drawings for the final construction documents.

Before a model space view can be created, you must create a new view drawing. Use the **Project Navigator** to do this. (Chapter 3 covers creating new view drawings using the **Project Navigator**.) After the view drawing is created, double-click on its name in the **Project Navigator** to open the file. Then right-click on its name and pick **New Model Space View...** from the shortcut menu, **Figure 6-5.**

After selecting the **New Model Space View...** command, the **Add Model Space View** worksheet is displayed, **Figure 6-6.** The worksheet includes three properties: **Name**, **Description**, and **Scale**. Enter a name for the model space view that describes the view's contents. The **Description text** property can be used to further describe the model space view name. The **Scale** property allows you to specify a scale to be used when

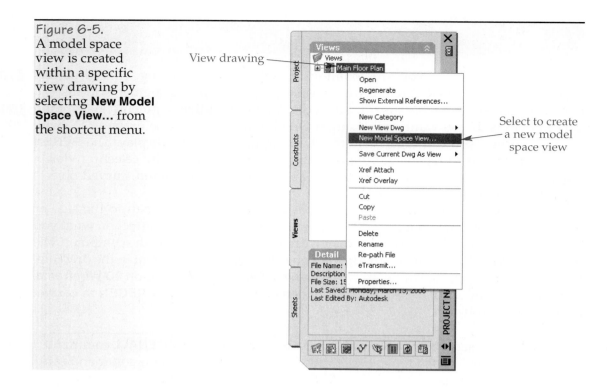

Figure 6-5.
A model space view is created within a specific view drawing by selecting **New Model Space View...** from the shortcut menu.

View drawing

Select to create a new model space view

the model space view is dragged and dropped into a sheet drawing. Finally, select the **Define View Window** button, which allows you to then place a window around the portion of the drawing to be included in the model space view.

After specifying the window that defines the view, the **Add Model Space View** worksheet is returned. Make any necessary adjustments to the model space view, and when you are finished, pick **OK** to create the model space view. Once a model space view is created, the **Project Navigator** displays the named model space view under the view drawing name, Figure 6-7. You can create as many model space views as you wish.

A model space view can be opened by double-clicking on the view's name in the **Project Navigator**. This opens the view drawing and displays the model space view you selected.

If you need to adjust any of the properties of a model space view, right-click on the model space view name in the **Project Navigator**, and select **Properties...** from the shortcut menu. This displays the **Modify** (*view drawing type*) **View** worksheet, where the name, description, scale, and view window can be adjusted. You can delete a named model space view by right-clicking on the name in the **Project Navigator** and selecting **Delete** from the shortcut menu.

NOTE

Model space views can be very helpful when you are working on architectural projects. Architectural drawings are often very large, and to work on small details, you must zoom in on a particular. If you save the view of this area as a model space view, you can restore it quickly after working on another section of the drawing, saving valuable time and effort. It is common in architectural projects for views to be created of parts of the floor plan, a specific area in an elevation, or a particular angle or perspective that is important.

Figure 6-6.
Use the **Add Model Space View** worksheet to create a model space view within the view drawing.

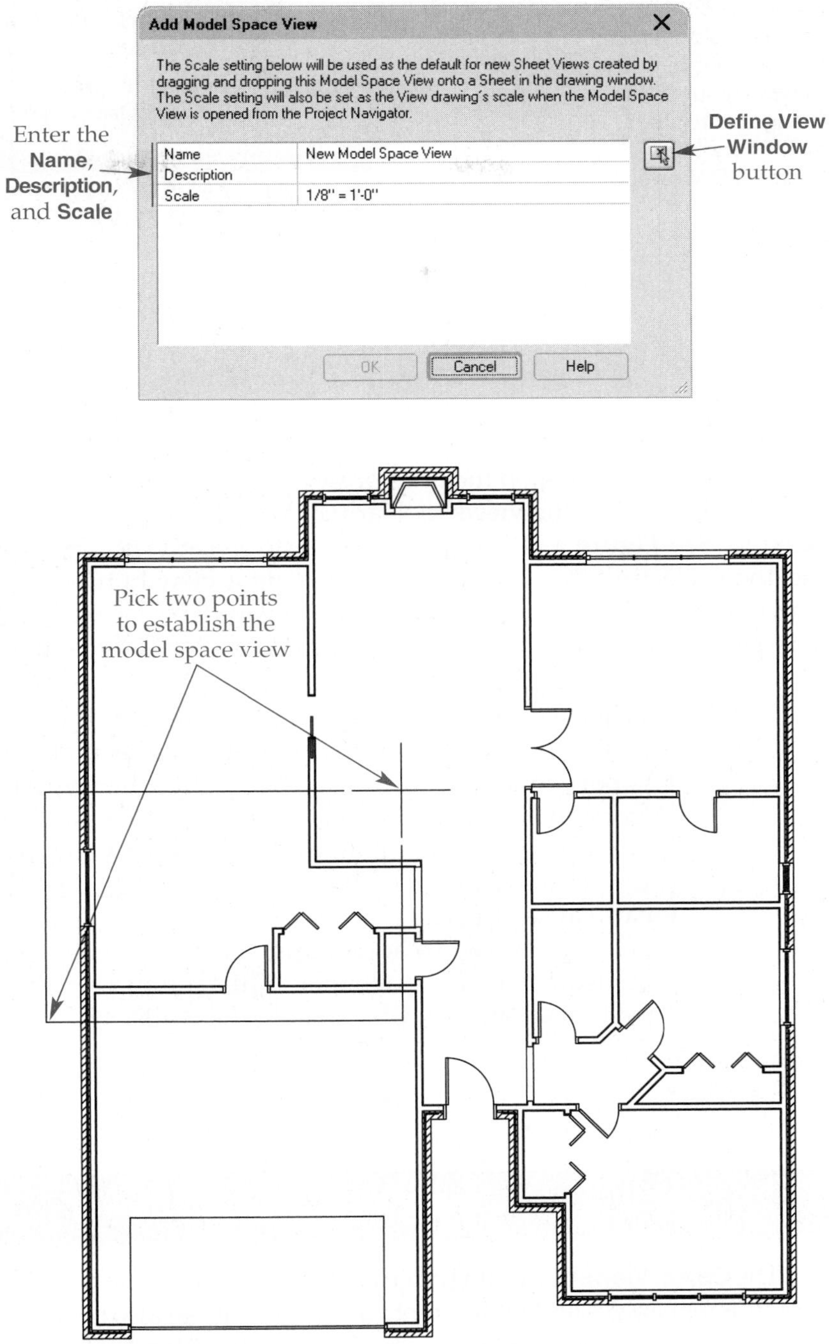

Enter the **Name**, **Description**, and **Scale**

Add Model Space View

The Scale setting below will be used as the default for new Sheet Views created by dragging and dropping this Model Space View onto a Sheet in the drawing window. The Scale setting will also be set as the View drawing's scale when the Model Space View is opened from the Project Navigator.

Name	New Model Space View
Description	
Scale	1/8" = 1'-0"

Define View Window button

OK   Cancel   Help

Pick two points to establish the model space view

Figure 6-7.
After model space views have been created, they appear as named views listed under the view drawing in the **Project Navigator.**

Model space views

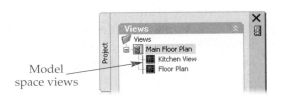

Views
Views
Main Floor Plan
   Kitchen View
   Floor Plan

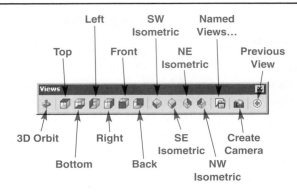

Figure 6-8.
These options are also available in the **Views** flyout in the **Navigator** toolbar and by picking **View** > **3D Views**.

Top   Left   Front   SW Isometric   NE Isometric   Named Views…   Previous View

Views

3D Orbit   Bottom   Right   Back   SE Isometric   NW Isometric   Create Camera

Using Preset Views

Architectural Desktop includes preset views so you can view elevations or isometric views of the model. The **Views** toolbar includes all the preset views within Architectural Desktop. See **Figure 6-8.** You can also select preset views by picking **View** > **3D Views** and then selecting the desired view. Selecting a view button displays that view on the drawing screen. When an elevation view is selected, the UCS adjusts so the drawing plane is perpendicular to your line of sight so you do not have to manually adjust the UCS.

NOTE

When you set an elevation view current, the UCS is rotated so the positive Z axis is pointing out of the screen at you and the XY plane is perpendicular to your line of sight. Changing to an isometric view from an elevation view maintains this UCS configuration. If you need to work on the floor plan in the isometric view, you may be limited to the drawing plane that was established in the elevation view, which can cause difficulty in moving, copying, or drawing objects in the isometric view. To adjust this, set the top view current before setting an isometric view current. This returns to the World Coordinate System where you first created the walls.

Using the Object Viewer

The **Object Viewer** is a dialog box that allows you to view selected portions of your drawing from different angles and in different visual styles. It can also be used to set a view current in the active viewport or drawing screen. To access the **Object Viewer**, first select objects in the drawing that you want to view at different angles. Then right-click and select **Object Viewer...** from the shortcut menu. The **Object Viewer**, shown in **Figure 6-9,** is displayed.

Several buttons are available in the **Object Viewer** for adjusting the view of the objects shown. These buttons are similar to those found in the **3D Orbit**, **Zoom**, and **Visual Style** toolbars. One new button is called **Set View**. Selecting this button sets the view you create in the **Object Viewer** current in the viewport in your drawing screen. This can be helpful when you are creating a perspective view of a drawing.

The **Parallel** and **Perspective** buttons allow you to switch between parallel and perspective views of the objects. The **Lens length** button adjusts an imaginary camera lens. Once a view has been established, pick the **Set View** button to set the view in the drawing window or pick the **Save Image** button to save the view displayed as an image file to be used later. Picking **Save Image** displays the **Save Image File** dialog box. Select the type of file (.png, .jpg, .bmp, or .tif) and enter a name and location for the file.

Figure 6-9.
The **Object Viewer** is similar to **3D Orbit**. The options available within it allow you to view the selected objects from any angle and in several visual styles.

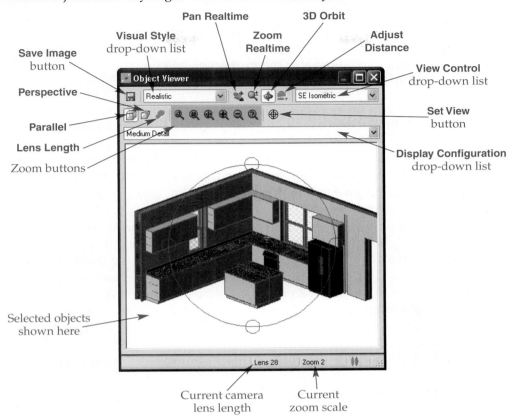

There is a **Visual Style** drop-down list, a **View Control** drop-down list, and a **Display Configuration** drop-down list. These three drop-down lists are available in other locations and have the same options as those lists in the other locations. (The **Display Configuration** menu is covered in Chapter 7.) When you select an option from any of these lists, it updates the **Object Viewer** to reflect the change. When you are finished viewing your design or a portion of your design, pick the **Close** button in the upper-right corner to close the **Object Viewer**.

Creating Perspectives and Movie Files

Architectural Desktop includes additional utilities that make perspective creation even easier than those previously discussed. The use of cameras in Architectural Desktop allows you to specifically identify where the viewer is standing and looking in the drawing. After a camera is placed in the drawing, the camera location and target view can be adjusted until the desired view is attained.

To add a camera into the drawing, pick **View** > **Cameras** > **Add...**, pick the **Camera** tool in the **Massing** tool palette, or type CAMERA. Initially, a camera icon is attached to the crosshairs, and you are prompted to pick a location for the camera. The location you pick represents the spot from which you are looking at the model. After picking the camera location, you are prompted to pick the location for the target. The target location is the spot on which you are focusing the camera.

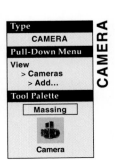

After picking the camera and target locations, you can adjust the name, location, height, target, lens, clipping, and view through the Command: prompt. These values can also be adjusted in the **Properties** palette after the camera has been added.

NOTE
If you use the **Camera** tool from the **Massing** tool palette to add a camera, you are not prompted with the options listed above. Add the camera and adjust it in the **Properties** palette.

After a camera has been added, selecting the camera allows you to modify its properties through the **Properties** palette. The following properties are available when modifying a camera:

- **Name.** This property is used to name the Camera object. By default the first camera added to the drawing is named Camera1, followed by Camera2, and so on. It is useful to give your cameras names that describe their views, such as Front View or Kitchen View.
- **Camera X** (**Y** and **Z**). These three property values indicate the camera location in absolute coordinates. If you want the camera up off the ground, say at the average human eye level, type a value such as 5'-6" in the **Camera Z** property.
- **Target X** (**Y** and **Z**). These three properties control the location the camera is targeting. Adjust the **Target Z** property to adjust the height of the targeted area.
- **Lens length (mm).** The lens length property allows you to zoom in or out on the target. The smaller the zoom value, the farther from the camera the target appears to be.
- **Field of view.** This property controls the width of the viewing angle used by the camera.
- **Roll angle.** This property rotates the camera around the target axis to give the view a tilted viewing angle.
- **Plot.** This **Yes** or **No** value controls whether or not the camera icon is plotted.

If the view was not created when the camera was added to the drawing, it can be displayed at any time. To display the view specified by the camera parameters, first select a Camera object, right-click, and pick the **Set Camera View** command. Camera views can also be created by picking **View > Named Views...** and then setting one of the camera views under the model views section current.

NOTE
When adding cameras to a view drawing, the camera view is saved as a model space view. This view can be restored at anytime by double-clicking on the camera model space view name in the **Project Navigator**.

Adjusting the Camera View

Placing a camera in the drawing is as simple as selecting a zoom length, a height, and a camera position and target point. Adding cameras in the drawing may not always yield the desired perspective. Cameras and their view can be adjusted through the use of the **Adjust Camera Position** dialog box, which is accessed by picking **View > Cameras > Adjust...** from the pull-down menu. See **Figure 6-10**.

If you select a camera in a nonperspective view and then access the **Adjust Camera Position** dialog box, the camera view is displayed in the drawing screen. When you access the **Adjust Camera View** command from the pull-down menu, you are prompted to select a camera or to press the [Enter] key to select a camera from a list. The list is helpful if you are in a perspective view where a camera cannot be selected. Press the [Enter] key to display a list of cameras in the drawing and select a camera. That camera's view is then shown in the drawing screen.

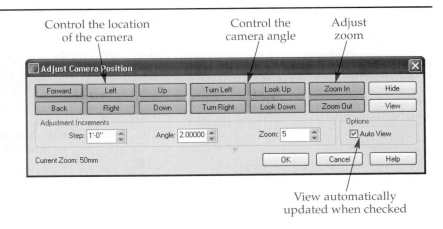

Figure 6-10.
The **Adjust Camera Position** dialog box is used to adjust the camera position and the target and can automatically update in the selected viewport.

Control the location of the camera

Control the camera angle

Adjust zoom

View automatically updated when checked

The **Adjust Camera Position** dialog box contains a number of buttons that can be used to adjust the camera position, angle, and zoom. At the bottom of the dialog box are three text boxes, which are used in conjunction with the buttons. The **Forward**, **Back**, **Left**, **Right**, **Up**, and **Down** buttons control the position of the camera. The **Step:** text box is used to control how large a step is taken when the camera position is adjusted. For example, if 1'-0" is entered in the **Step:** text box, the camera is moved 1'-0" in the direction specified when you pick a button.

The **Turn Left**, **Turn Right**, **Look Up**, and **Look Down** buttons control the angle of the camera. The camera remains in the same location, but it rotates in the direction you specify when you pick these buttons. The **Angle:** text box controls how far the camera turns. The **Zoom In** and **Zoom Out** buttons control the lens length of the camera. The **Zoom:** text box controls how much lens length is applied when zooming in or out of the drawing.

If you pick the **Hide** button, any objects that are positioned behind other objects in the camera's view are hidden from view. When the **Auto View** check box is selected, as you adjust the camera position, angle, and zoom, the drawing screen is automatically updated with the changes to present you with the latest view. If the **Auto View** check box is unchecked, the **View** button can be used to update the current viewpoint with the latest changes made to the camera.

As adjustments are made to the camera through this dialog box, the actual camera is repositioned to reflect your changes. When you are finished adjusting the camera view, pick the **OK** button to close the dialog box. As changes are made, the model space view is updated in the view drawing to reflect the camera view.

The camera can be adjusted with the six grips on the Camera object. One grip on the camera itself moves only the camera. The two flat grips at both of the other corners of the red target triangle control the lens length. The grip in the middle of the triangle moves both the camera and the target. The square grip at the end of the centerline moves only the target location. The triangle grip at the end of the centerline changes the target distance. See **Figure 6-11.**

Creating Movie Files

Architectural Desktop includes a tool that allows you to create a simple *walk-through* of the model using Camera objects and a *walk path*. A camera moves along a walk path to create a walk-through. The walk path represents the path you might take if you were physically in the model walking around it and looking at the building. Before a walk-through can be created, a path needs to be established in the drawing for the Camera object to follow. Paths can be created with a polyline that has been splined to make the walk path smooth. To create the path, use the **PLINE** command to select points that establish the camera's path, as shown in **Figure 6-12.**

Figure 6-11.
The grips on this Camera object can be used to adjust properties such as the camera location, target point, and the field of view (FOV).

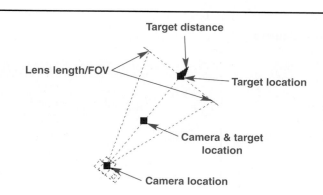

Figure 6-12.
A walk path for the Camera object can be established in the drawing with a polyline.

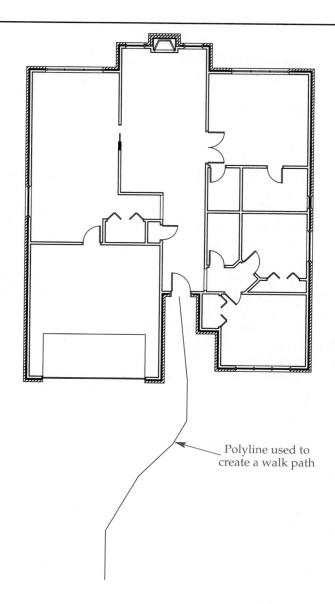

Polyline used to create a walk path

After the path has been drawn with a polyline, it can be edited to create a smooth curve. To do this, select the polyline, right-click, and pick **Polyline Edit**, or type PEDIT. Use the **Spline** option of the **PEDIT** command to smooth the polyline segments. Creating a smooth segment allows the camera to move smoothly along the path.

NOTE   A walk path can also be created with any AutoCAD object such as a line, an arc, or a spline. If a spline is used, the points designated for a spline can be adjusted in the Z axis to allow the camera to move up and down. If a polyline is used, the camera maintains a constant height.

In addition to the walk path, the camera can be focused on a separate path known as a *target path*. The target path determines the location of the target, or where the camera focuses, while the walk path determines the direction the camera moves. When you are creating a walk-through movie, you can focus the camera on one point or along a target path. Because the target path and the walk can be different, you can create the illusion of walking through the model while focusing on a specific area. You can create the target path in the same manner as the walk path using polylines, lines, arcs, or splines. Also, the walk path can be offset and used as the target path.

If the walk path and the target path are drawn on the XY plane, the camera moves and is focused on the ground, not the building. To adjust the paths so that the camera does not show the ground, the walk and target paths are placed at a different height in the Z axis. To do this, select the objects used for the paths. In the **Properties** palette, modify the **Elevation** property to reflect the level at which the walk and target paths should be located.

After the walk path and the target path have been established, the camera can be added to the drawing. Use the **Add Camera** command to add the camera to the desired end of the walk path. When selecting the target location for the camera, select the desired end of the targeting path or the point that the camera is targeting.

To create a simple walk-through of the building, select the camera to be used and pick **View > Camera > Motion Path Animations...** or type ANIPATH. If you do this without selecting a camera and have several cameras in the drawing, you are prompted to select a camera for the video or to press [Enter] for a list of cameras. After you select the camera, the **Motion Path Animation** dialog box is displayed as shown in **Figure 6-13**.

Type	
	ANIPATH
Pull-Down Menu	
View	
> Camera	
> Motion Path	
Animations...	

ANIPATH

The **Motion Path Animation** dialog box contains the following settings:

- **Camera.** This area is used to set the parameters for the camera. Two options are available: **Point** and **Path**. Choose the **Point** option to create a stationary camera. Choose the **Path** option to specify a walk path for the camera. Use the **Select Path** button to choose an entity for use as a walk path. After picking a path object, the **Path Name** dialog box is displayed allowing you to name the object being used as a walk path. This named walk path is displayed in the drop-down list.

- **Target.** This area is used to set the parameters for the target. Similar to the **Camera** area, pick the **Point** option to create a stationary focal/target point. Use the **Select Path** button to pick an entity for use as a target path. After selecting the object, you are prompted to name the target path which is then displayed in the drop-down list.

- **When previewing show camera preview.** Select this option to display a preview of the camera moving along the paths and a preview window looking through the camera to give you an idea of how the camera is moving through the model.

The **Animation settings** area includes options to control the output settings for the animation. These settings include:

- **Frame rate (FPS).** This text box property controls the number of frames per second that are created for the animation. The more frames the animation uses, the smoother the animation.

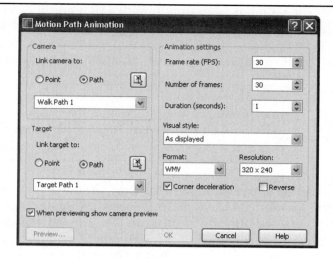

Figure 6-13.
The **Motion Path Animation** dialog box is used to create walk-throughs and video files.

- **Number of frames.** This area controls the number of frames to be used in the movie file. *Frames* are the number of steps to be taken along the path. The total number of frames to be used can be entered in the text box. The more frames, the smoother the walk-through.
- **Duration.** This text box is used to specify the total time for the animation. The frames are spaced evenly throughout the duration time using the specified frame rate.
- **Visual Style.** Choose a visual style to be used in the animation.
- **Format.** This drop-down list includes options for the type of movie file to be created and includes the format options **AVT**, **MOV**, **MPG**, and **WMV**.
- **Resolution.** This drop-down list controls the resolution of the animation file. A larger file size will take longer to create.
- **Corner Deceleration.** This check box slows the camera down while moving around corners.
- **Reverse.** Use this option to reverse the direction of the camera as it travels along the path.

When you are finished selecting the options for the video, pick the **OK** button to create the video. The **Save As** dialog box is displayed, where a location on the hard drive and name for the video file must be entered. Pick **Save** to save the animation file. Architectural Desktop begins compiling each frame in the drawing and compresses it to the animation file. When Architectural Desktop is finished compressing it, the file is ready for viewing.

Chapter Test

Answer the following questions. Write your answers on a separate sheet of paper or complete the electronic chapter test on the Student CD.

1. What is the function of the **ZOOM** command?
2. What is the difference between **Zoom All** and **Zoom Extents**?
3. What do the three rectangles that appear when you use **Zoom Dynamic** represent?
4. How do you use and what is the function of the **ZOOM** command's **Window** option?
5. How does the **ZOOM** command's **Aerial View** option work?
6. What is the function of the **PAN** command, and how is it accessed?
7. What is the basic function of the **3D ORBIT** command?
8. How do you access the **3D ORBIT** command?
9. Give the basic function of the **Visual Aids** option in the shortcut menu accessed while using **3D Orbit**.
10. Identify the basic function of the **3D Orbit** preset viewing options and how they are accessed.
11. When is it helpful to regenerate the drawing?
12. What must be established before a model space view can be created, and how do you access the **Add Model Space View** worksheet?
13. Identify the basic function of the **Object Viewer**.
14. What is the function of cameras in Architectural Desktop?
15. Explain how to add a camera to a drawing.
16. Define *target*.
17. What must be established before a walk-through can be created, and how do you establish this feature?
18. What is the function of a target path?
19. A motion path animation that uses a walk path and a target path is focused on the ground. Why might this be, and how can it be fixed?
20. How does the number of frames affect the quality of a walk-through?

Use the techniques covered in this chapter to create the following drawings.

1. Single-Level Residential Project
    A. Access the **Project Browser** and set Residential-Project-01 current.
    B. Select the **Views** tab of the **Project Navigator** and create a new general view drawing with the following parameters:
        a. **Name**: Design Views
        b. **Description**: Room and model views
        c. **Context**: Select the **Main Floor** level check box in the **Division 1** column.
        d. **Content**: Select the Main Floor construct.
    C. Open the Design Views view drawing.
    D. Create model space views of each of the rooms of the building. Name the views with the room names shown in the figure. Use a scale of 1/4"=1'-0" for each view.
    E. Create a view of the entire floor plan named Floor Plan. Set the scale to **1/4"=1'-0"**.
    F. Create a camera looking at the front of the building. Name the camera Front Camera.
    G. Adjust the camera as needed.
    H. Save and close the drawing.

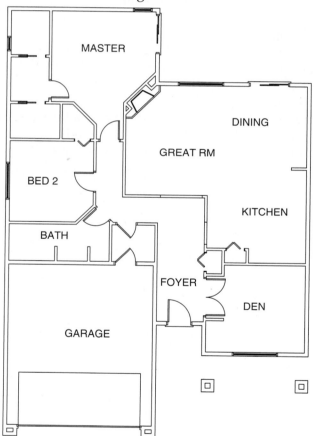

Alan Mascord Design Associates

2. Single-Level Residential Project
    A. Access the **Project Browser** and set Residential-Project-02 current.
    B. Select the **Views** tab of the **Project Navigator** and create a new general view drawing with the following parameters:
        a. **Name**: Design Views
        b. **Description**: Room and model views
        c. **Context**: Select the **Main Floor** level check box in the **Division 1** column.
        d. **Content**: Select the Main Floor construct.
    C. Open the Design Views view drawing.
    D. Create model space views of each of the rooms of the building. Name the views with the room names shown in the figure. Use a scale of 1/4"=1'-0" for each view.
    E. Create a view of the entire floor plan named Floor Plan. Set the scale to **1/4"=1'-0"**.
    F. Create a camera looking at the front of the building. Name the camera Front Camera.
    G. Adjust the camera as needed.
    H. Save and close the drawing.

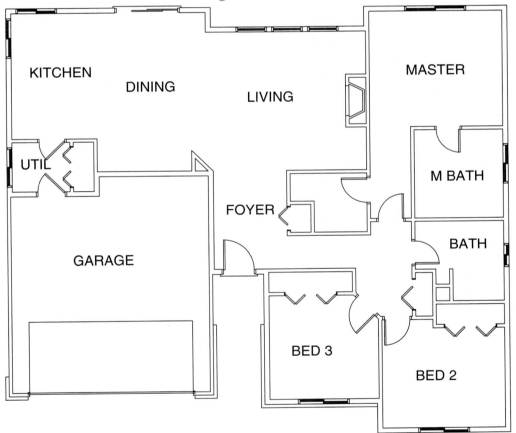

Alan Mascord Design Associates

3. Two-Story Residential Project
   A. Access the **Project Browser** and set Residential-Project-03 current.
   B. Select the **Views** tab of the **Project Navigator** and create a new general view drawing with the following parameters:
      a. **Name**: Design Views.
      b. **Description**: Room and model views.
      c. **Context**: Select the **Main Floor** and **Upper Floor** level check boxes in the **Division 1** column.
      d. **Content**: Select the Main Floor and Upper Floor constructs.
   C. Open the Design Views view drawing.
   D. Create model space views of each of the rooms on the main floor. Name the views with the room name shown in the figure. Use a scale of 1/4"=1'-0" for each view.
   E. Create a camera looking at the front of the building. Name the camera Front Camera.
   F. Adjust the camera as needed. Notice that the upper floor is visible in the appropriate location.
   G. Set the Top view current.
   H. Create a camera looking from the kitchen to the fireplace in the family room. Name the camera Kitchen Camera.
   I. Adjust the camera as needed.
   J. Save and close the drawing.

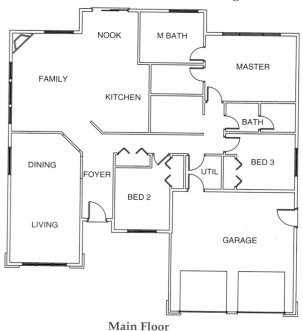

Main Floor

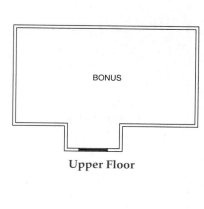

Upper Floor

3D-DZYN

4. Two-Story Residential Project
   A. Access the **Project Browser** and set Residential-Project-04 current.
   B. Select the **Views** tab of the **Project Navigator** and create a new general view drawing with the following parameters:
      a. **Name**: Design Views.
      b. **Description**: Room and model views.
      c. **Context**: Select the **Main Floor** level and **Upper Floor** level check boxes in the **Division 1** column.
      d. **Content**: Select the Main Floor and Upper Floor constructs.
   C. Open the Design Views view drawing.
   D. Create model space views of each of the rooms on the main floor. Name the views with the room name shown in the figure. Use a scale of 1/4″=1′-0″ for each view.
   E. Create a camera looking at the front of the building. Name the camera Front Camera.
   F. Adjust the camera as needed. Notice that the upper floor is visible in the appropriate location.
   G. Set the Top view current.
   H. Create a camera looking from the foyer to the dining room. Name the camera Foyer Camera.
   I. Set the camera view current and then choose one of the visual styles to shade the drawing.
   J. Adjust the camera view as desired.
   K. Save and close the drawing.

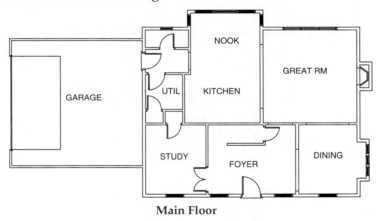

Main Floor

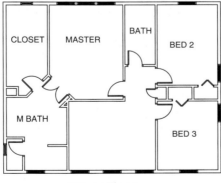

Upper Floor

Alan Mascord Design Associates

5. Commercial Store Project
   A. Access the **Project Browser** and set Commercial-Project-05 current.
   B. Select the **Views** tab of the **Project Navigator** and create a new general view drawing with the following parameters:
      a. **Name**: Design Views
      b. **Description**: Room and model views
      c. **Context**: Select the **Main Floor** level check box in the **Division 1** column.
      d. **Content**: Select the Main Floor construct.
   C. Open the Design Views view drawing.
   D. Create model space views of each of the rooms in the plan. Name the views with the room name shown in the figure. Use a scale of 1/4″=1′-0″ for each view.
   E. Create a view of the entire floor plan named Floor Plan. Assign a scale of **1/8″=1′-0″**.
   F. Create a camera looking from the front right side of the building targeting the middle of Unit 3. Name the camera Front Camera.
   G. Adjust the view as needed.
   H. Save and close the drawing.

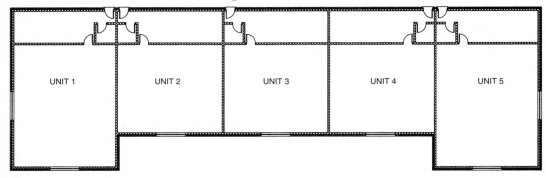

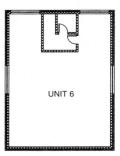

3D-DZYN

6. Commercial Car Maintenance Shop Project
   A. Access the **Project Browser** and set Commercial-Project-06 current.
   B. Select the **Views** tab of the **Project Navigator** and create a new general view drawing with the following parameters:
      a. **Name**: Design Views
      b. **Description**: Room and model views
      c. **Context**: Select the **Main Floor** level and **Upper Floor** level check boxes in the **Division 1** column.
      d. **Content**: Select the Main Floor and Upper Floor constructs.
   C. Open the Design Views view drawing.
   D. Create model space views of each of the rooms on the main floor. Name the views with the room name shown in the figure. Use a scale of 1/4"=1'-0" for each view.
   E. Create a camera looking from the front left side of the building, targeting the storage area. Name the camera Front Camera.
   F. Adjust the camera as needed in the right viewport.
   G. Save and close the drawing.

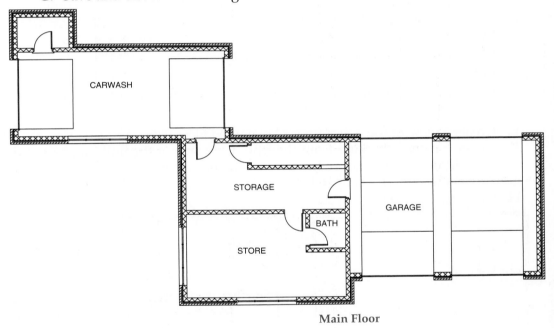

Main Floor

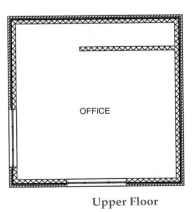

Upper Floor

3D-DZYN

7. Governmental Fire Station
   A. Access the **Project Browser** and set Gvrmt-Project-07 current.
   B. Select the **Views** tab of the **Project Navigator** and create a new general view drawing with the following parameters:
      a. **Name**: Design Views
      b. **Description**: Room and model views
      c. **Context**: Select the **Main Floor** level check box in the **Division 1** column.
      d. **Content**: Select the Main Floor construct.
   C. Open the Design Views view drawing.
   D. Create model space views of the following areas. Use the chart to name the views and choose the rooms included in each view. Use a scale of 1/4"=1'-0" for each view.

View Name	Rooms
Garage Bay	APPARATUS BAY, SHOP, ELEC, COMPR, GEN
Emergency	HOSE RM, TURNOUT, EMT
Living	LNDY, DORMS, EXERCISE
Locker Rooms	LOCKER RM, MEN, WOMEN
Classroom	CLASS RM 1, CLASS RM 2
Dayroom	DAYROOM, DINING, KITCHEN
Offices	OFFICE (x4)
Reception	LOBBY, RECEPTION, OFFICE, STOR, MEN, WMEN

   E. Create a view of the entire floor plan named Floor Plan.
   F. Create a camera looking from the front right side of the building, targeting the middle of the locker room area. Name the camera Front Camera.
   G. Adjust the camera as desired.
   H. Save and close the drawing.

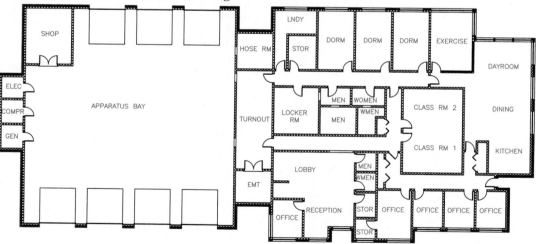

3D-DZYN

CHAPTER 7

The Architectural Desktop Display System

Learning Objectives

After completing this chapter, you will be able to do the following:
- ✓ Use display representations to control the display of individual AEC objects.
- ✓ Group together individual display representations.
- ✓ Edit display representations.
- ✓ Assign a display set to a particular viewing direction.
- ✓ View display representations.
- ✓ Use display configurations.
- ✓ Use custom display settings in other drawings.
- ✓ Apply the display system.
- ✓ Control AEC display by object.

As you have created AEC objects in the drawing, the objects have automatically displayed themselves appropriately based on the viewing direction. For example, a Wall object or a Door object in a Top view is displayed as a 2D object. When the view is changed to an Elevation or Isometric view, the same object is displayed as a 3D object. See Figure 7-1. The method of displaying AEC objects is known as the *display system*.

Figure 7-1.
AEC objects can be displayed in a number of different ways. Top views display objects as 2D representations. Elevation and 3D views display objects as 3D representations.

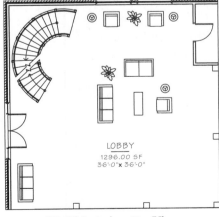

LOBBY
1296.00 SF
36'-0"x 36'-0"

2D Objects in a Top View

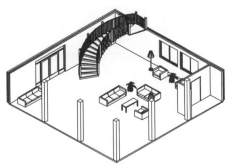

3D Objects in an Isometric View

The display system controls how AEC objects are displayed in model space or in individual floating viewports in layout space. With this system, different displays of AEC objects can be created, such as architectural displays that show floor plans, reflected ceiling plans, details, 3D models, or schematic plans.

The display system is divided into three separate elements that work together to form a particular architectural display. The elements are *display representations*, which control how individual AEC objects are displayed; *display sets*, which group together individual display representations; and *display configurations*, which assign a display set to a particular viewing direction. The display configuration is then applied to model space and individual layout space viewports. Display configurations can include several display sets assigned to different viewing directions, which can include several groups of display representations.

Display Representations

Pull-Down Menu
Format
> Drawing
Setup...
Toolbar
Open drawing menu

The first level of the display system is the display representation, which controls how the individual AEC object parts are displayed. For example, a Wall object includes a Plan representation, which displays the 2D wall, and a Model representation, which displays the 3D wall. Each AEC object includes a varying number of display representations. The display representations for AEC objects can be controlled in the **Drawing Setup** dialog box, shown in Figure 7-2.

The **Display** tab includes different areas for display control. The left side of the tab includes the **Object Type:** list, which lists all the AEC objects within Architectural Desktop. Selecting an object from the **Object Type:** list provides a list of the different representations for the object in the **Display Representations:** list on the right. Figure 7-2 shows the different representations for the Door object. Each representation controls an aspect of the Door object. For example, the Plan representation includes the different components of the Door object in 2D. The Model representation controls how the 3D components for the Door object are displayed in a Model view.

Figure 7-2.
The **Display** tab in the **Drawing Setup** dialog box controls the display of individual representations for each AEC object.

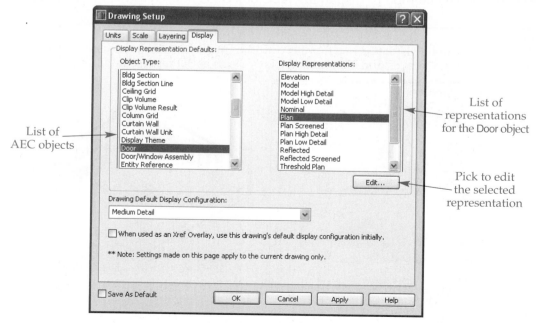

List of AEC objects

List of representations for the Door object

Pick to edit the selected representation

To edit the representations, select a representation from the **Display Representations:** list, and pick the **Edit...** button. The **Display Properties** dialog box, shown in Figure 7-3, is displayed. Depending on the object and the representation selected, the available tabs and list of components vary. Figure 7-3 shows the list of components for the Door object using the Plan representation.

The **Display Properties** dialog box is used to control how the default AEC objects appear when they are created in the drawing. The **Layer/Color/Linetype** tab is used to control how the individual object components appear in the selected representation. In Figure 7-3, the Door-Plan representation components are displayed for modification. The following columns are included in this tab:

- **Display Component.** This column includes a list of the components within the object that are available for the selected representation. This list can vary among Plan, Model, and other representations, depending on the AEC object.
- **Visible.** This column allows you to turn a component on or off in the selected representation. There are situations in which you do not want a particular component to be displayed in a view. For example, if you do not want the door stop to be displayed in a Plan representation, turn off the Stop component in the Plan representation for the Door object. To turn a component on or off, pick the lightbulb icon.
- **By Material.** This property is available in most of the components. Selecting the check box for one of the components assigns the display properties of a material definition to all of the properties within the component. The remaining properties, such as **Layer**, **Color**, and **Linetype**, are grayed out and cannot be assigned. Typically, the assignment of a material to a component controls the color, lineweight, and plot style of the component in the drawing. Assigning the materials to a component is typically done in the Model or other 3D display representations. This causes the 3D geometry to display using the colors of the material assigned to them.

Figure 7-3.
The **Display Properties** dialog box controls the display of components within an object in the selected display representation.

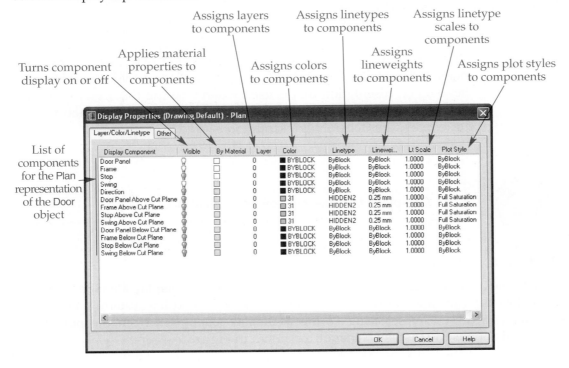

- **Layer.** By default, most of the components in a representation are set up with layer 0 in this column. This allows the components of an object to be placed on the layer on which the object is being inserted or drawn. For example, when a door is inserted into the drawing, it is placed on the A-Door layer. The Plan representation for the Door object has assigned layer 0 to the components, so all the components for a Door object using the Plan representation take on the A-Door layer. To assign a layer to a component, pick the current layer for that component. You can select a layer to assign from a list of layers currently in the drawing. Layers are discussed in Chapter 8.
- **Color.** This column controls the color that is displayed for the component. Select the color swatch to access the **Select Color** dialog box, from which you can select a color and assign it to a component.
- **Linetype.** This column assigns linetypes to components. To change the line-type assigned to a component, pick the current linetype to access the **Select Linetype** dialog box. This dialog box lists any linetypes loaded in the current drawing. Selecting a linetype assigns the linetype to the component.
- **Lineweight.** This column assigns a lineweight to a component. Pick the current lineweight to assign a different lineweight to the component.
- **Lt Scale.** Components can be assigned their own linetype scales. This scale multiplies the value of the current **LTSCALE** in the drawing by the value you enter in this column.
- **Plot Style.** If you are using plot STB tables instead of CTB tables to plot the drawing, a plot style can be assigned to a component. Plotting, plot style tables, and color tables are discussed later in this text.

Depending on the representation selected, different tabs such as the **Other**, **Hatching**, **Contents**, **Cut Plane**, and other tabs become available. Each of these additional tabs includes settings that affect the display of the selected object in the representation that is being modified.

When you are finished setting the values for the selected representation, pick the **OK** button in the **Display Properties** dialog box. You are returned to the **Drawing Setup** dialog box opened to the **Display** tab. You may need to walk through each of the display representations of one type of AEC object in order to set up how the default display settings for the objects should appear.

NOTE

Many of the AEC objects include multiple display representations. The most common representations that are modified for AEC objects include Plan, Model, and Reflected. Door and Window objects include an Elevation representation that is used when viewing the drawing from an Elevation view. Some objects do not include a Plan representation; in these cases, the General representation is used.

Exercise 7-1

Complete the Exercise on the Student CD.

The Display Manager

Pull-Down Menu
Format
> Display
Manager...

Architectural Desktop includes a utility known as the **Display Manager** that can be used to organize and configure all three pieces of the display system. The **Display Manager** is accessed by selecting **Format** > **Display Manager...** from the pull-down menu. This opens the **Display Manager**, as shown in **Figure 7-4**.

Figure 7-4.
The **Display Manager** is used to organize and configure the three parts of the display system.

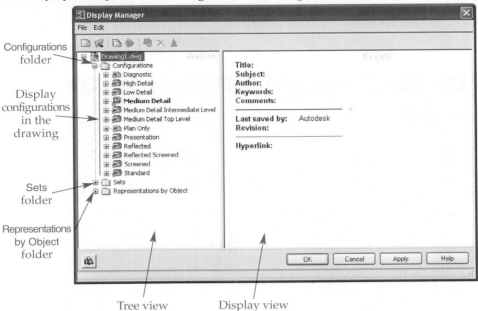

The **Display Manager** is divided into two panes. The left pane contains the tree view. The right pane contains the display view. The tree view displays the three parts of the display system in three different folders. The Configurations folder includes display configurations that are applied to model space or to individual layout space viewports. The Sets folder includes display sets that are assigned to viewing directions within a single display configuration. The last folder, Representations by Object, includes a list of objects with their associated display representations.

Editing Display Representations

To view the individual object display representations, press the + sign to the left of the Representations by Object folder. A list of all the AEC objects within Architectural Desktop is displayed. If you pick the Representations by Object folder, a table is shown in the display pane on the right. See **Figure 7-5**. The table view includes a list of the AEC objects along the left edge and a list of the display representations available within Architectural Desktop along the top. A display representation icon at the intersection of an AEC object and a display representation indicates the representation is available for the object. In **Figure 7-5**, the intersection of the Plan display representation column and the Door object row results in a display representation icon, indicating that the Plan representation is assigned to the Door object.

Moving the cursor over a display representation icon and right-clicking displays a shortcut menu with two main menu items, **Edit...** and **Delete**, and a few options for controlling representations with standards. The **Delete** option allows you to delete a user-defined display representation.

Creating a user-defined display representation is discussed later in this chapter. Selecting the **Edit...** option opens the **Display Properties** dialog box for the representation on which you right-clicked. This is the same **Display Properties** dialog box shown when display representations are edited from the **Drawing Setup** dialog box. See **Figure 7-3**. By right-clicking on the different display representation icons, you can configure the drawing default display representations. Modifying the representations from the **Drawing Setup** dialog box or from the **Display Manager** results in the same configuration.

The **Display Manager** displays a list of AEC objects in the left pane, and a table view of the representations available for each AEC object is displayed in the right pane.

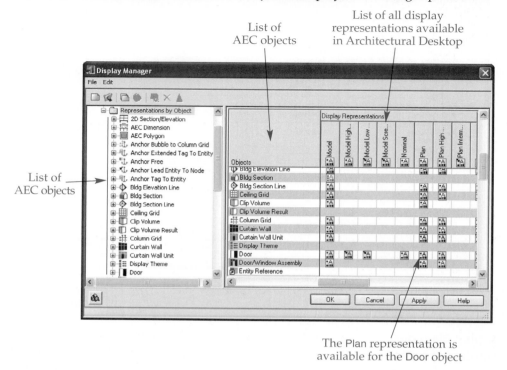

List of AEC objects

List of all display representations available in Architectural Desktop

List of AEC objects

The Plan representation is available for the Door object

Exercise 7-2

Complete the Exercise on the Student CD.

Viewing the Display Representations by Object

If you expand the Representations by Object folder in the tree view of the **Display Manager** and pick an AEC object, a different table is shown in the display pane. See **Figure 7-6.** This table displays the list of representations available for the selected object along the left edge, and a list of the display sets is found at the top of the table. This table indicates which individual display representations belong to a particular display set. **Figure 7-6** shows the representations for a window. A check in a box indicates that the display representation is part of the listed display set.

The intersection of a display representation row and a display set column provides a check box. Picking the check box causes the display representation to be added to the display set. Display sets group together several individual display representations for use in a display configuration. Display sets are discussed in the next section.

Architectural Desktop includes a good selection of display representations for each AEC object; however, there are situations where a custom display representation is required. To create a custom display representation, first select an existing representation to copy, and then right-click on the representation. The shortcut menu is displayed, **Figure 7-7.** Select the **Duplicate** option at the top of the list. This creates a new representation for the object that is listed in the tree view. A new representation is created. Enter a name for the custom representation, and then edit as desired.

Figure 7-6.
Pick an AEC object from the tree view to list the representations available for the selected object and show the display set to which the representations belong.

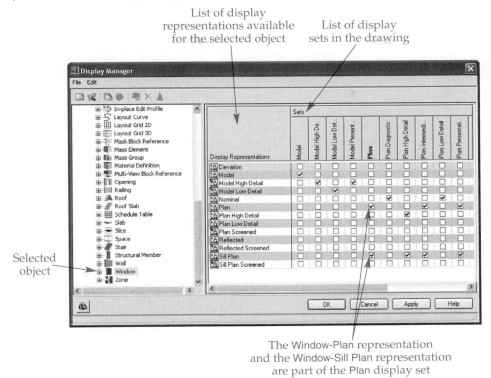

The shortcut menu in **Figure 7-7** also includes the following options for the selected display representation:

- **Delete.** Deletes a custom representation. Default representations cannot be deleted.
- **Rename.** This option is used to rename a custom representation.
- **Synchronize with Project Standards.** This option synchronizes the display representation to a project standard set up in the **CAD Manager** pull-down menu.
- **Update Standards from Drawing.** This option updates the project standards' settings with values set here.
- **Ignore During Synchronization.** This option may be selected to ignore the synchronization of display representation standards when synchronizing a drawing against a master set of standards.
- **Version Representation.** This option adds a date/time stamp to the display representation to indicate the last time the representation was modified.
- **Select All.** Selecting this option places a check in all check boxes of the selected representation. The representation is then added to all the display sets.
- **Clear All.** This clears all the check boxes for the highlighted representation.
- **Edit Drawing Default.** This option opens the **Display Properties** dialog box, where the representation can be configured.

PROFESSIONAL TIP

When you use the existing AEC Model templates, display representations are already configured to display your objects as desired. You may decide that the default representations meet your needs for drafting and plotting; however, this system does allow you to customize what and how objects are displayed in your drawings.

Figure 7-7.
New display
representations
can be created
by right-clicking
over an existing
representation
and selecting the
Duplicate option.

Select
Duplicate
to create a
custom
display
representation

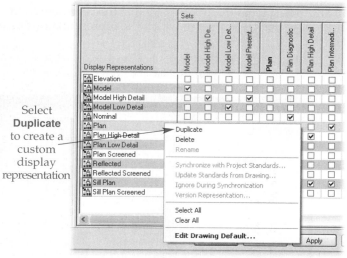

Copying a Representation

Enter a name for the
new representation

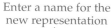

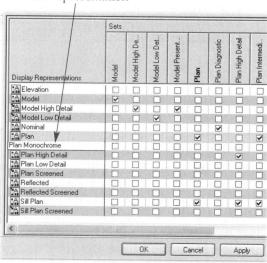

Naming a Representation

Exercise
7-3

Complete the Exercise on the Student CD.

Display Sets

The next level of the display system is the display set. A display set assembles individual display representations into a group or set. Generally, a display set combines similar representations. For example, all the Plan representations for AEC objects can be grouped together into a display set named Plan, and all the Model representations can be grouped together into a display set named Model. Display sets are then used in a display configuration, where the viewing direction is assigned to a display set.

The **Display Manager** is used to create and configure display sets. The Sets folder includes a listing of all the display sets in the drawing. Selecting the Sets folder displays a list of the display sets in the display pane on the right. See **Figure 7-8**. Right-clicking

Figure 7-8.
Select the Sets folder to display a list of display sets in the current drawing. Right-click a
named set to delete or rename the display set.

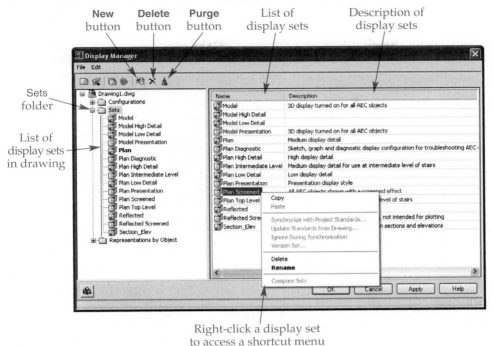

Right-click a display set
to access a shortcut menu

on a display set in the right pane of the **Display Manager** displays a shortcut menu
that can be used to delete or rename a display set. Additionally, this shortcut menu
includes the same project synchronizing and standards tools as mentioned for the
display representations. The **Compare Sets** option is used to compare the settings of
two selected display sets. Press [Ctrl] to highlight two display set icons, and then right-
click and select the **Compare Sets** option.

The toolbar at the top of the **Display Manager** includes buttons. The last three
buttons are used to create or modify display sets and display configurations. These
are described as follows:

- **New.** This button allows you to create a new display set or display
  configuration.
- **Delete.** This button deletes custom display sets or display configurations.
- **Purge.** This button removes unused display sets or display configurations from
  the drawing.

Viewing the Display Sets by Object

Picking the + sign beside the Sets folder provides a tree listing of all the display
sets. When a display set is selected from the tree view, a table is shown in the display
pane. See **Figure 7-9.** The display pane includes four tabs used to configure the display
set: **General**, **Display Representation Control**, **Display Options**, and **Version History**. The
General tab is used to rename the display set and provide a description of what the
set is to be used for. The **Display Representation Control** tab displays a table view in
which display representations can be selected for addition into the display set. The
Display Options tab is used to control how objects cut with a section line appear, and
whether or not the surface hatching is displayed, when using this display set. The
Version History tab is used to indicate when the display set was created or modified
and can be used in managing project standards.

Figure 7-9.
The **Display Representation Control** tab displays a table of display representations assigned to a display set.

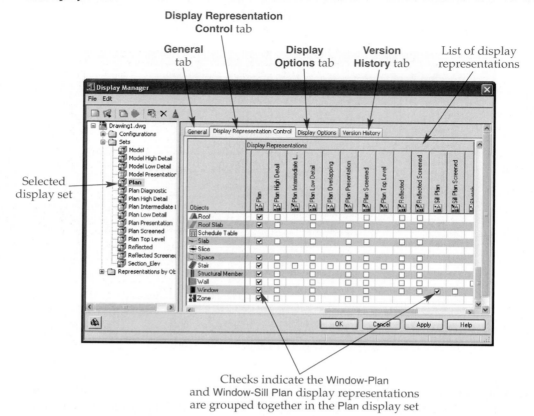

Checks indicate the Window-Plan
and Window-Sill Plan display representations
are grouped together in the Plan display set

When the **Display Representation Control** tab is selected, a table of representations and objects is displayed. See **Figure 7-9**. The display representations in the drawing are listed along the top of the table. The intersection of an AEC object and a display representation produces a check box. The check box indicates the display representation is available for the AEC object. Selecting the check box adds a check mark in the box. A check mark indicates the display representation is grouped into the selected display set.

Typically, common display representations are grouped together into one display set. For example, the display set named Plan includes a check mark in all Plan and Sill Plan representations. This groups together all AEC object Plan and Sill Plan display representations into one group, or display set. Model display representations are grouped together into the Model display set. Reflected ceiling plan display representations are grouped together under the Reflected display set.

Some AEC objects, such as cameras, do not include a Plan, Model, or Reflected display representation. Instead, they may have only one display representation named General because the display of these objects does not change in different views. In these cases, the General display representation can be added to the Plan, Model, or Reflected display sets.

Display sets can be configured to display a mixture of display representations. For example, the Plan Diagnostic display set groups together General, Graph, Logical, Nominal, Plan, and Sketch display representations. Custom display sets can be created by picking the Sets folder and picking the **New** button or by right-clicking on the Sets folder and selecting **New** from the shortcut menu. A new display set is created in the tree view. Enter a name, highlight the new display set, and pick the desired representations to group into the display set. The display set can be renamed by selecting the set from the tree view and right-clicking to display a shortcut menu from which the **Rename** option can be selected. The display set can also be renamed and given a description in the **General** tab.

Exercise 7-4

Complete the Exercise on the Student CD.

Display Configurations

After the display set is created and has been assigned display representations, it is ready to be assigned to a viewing direction within a display configuration. A display configuration assigns a display set to a specific viewing direction. As seen in **Figure 7-1**, different display representations are displayed based on the viewing directions. In a Top view, objects are displayed as 2D objects, and in an Isometric view, the same objects are viewed as 3D representations. It is important to note that display representations and display sets are not dependent on a viewing direction. The display representations control how the individual components appear in a drawing. The display sets then group the display representations together for use in the display configurations. Many display representations are displayed only if you select the appropriate display configuration as you draw or set up the drawing for plotting.

As with display representations and display sets, the **Display Manager** is used to create and configure display configurations. The Configurations folder is used to organize the display configurations. Selecting the Configurations folder displays a table view in the display pane. See **Figure 7-10**. The table view shows the display sets in the current drawing and their assigned display configurations. One of the display configurations appears bold. This is used to indicate the currently active display configuration in the drawing screen.

Cube-shaped view direction symbols with different sides colored indicate the viewing directions the display sets are assigned. A cube with its top shaded indicates the display set is assigned to the Top view. A cube with any of its four sides colored indicates the display set is assigned to the appropriate Left, Front, Right, or Back viewing directions. A cube with all its sides colored indicates the display set is used in all Elevation viewing directions. A cube without color indicates the display set is used in any view other than the standard Top, Bottom, or Elevation views.

Right-clicking on a display configuration displays the shortcut menu shown in **Figure 7-11**. By selecting a display configuration and right-clicking, you can assign the configuration to the current viewport in layout space, assign it as the default configuration in model space, delete it, or rename it. Display configurations included with Architectural Desktop cannot be deleted.

Picking the + sign to the left of the Configurations folder lists all the display configurations in the tree view. Selecting a display configuration from the tree view shows the properties for the configuration in the display pane. See **Figure 7-12**.

Selecting the display configuration from the tree view shows the properties for the selected display configuration in the right pane. The configuration's properties include four tabs used to adjust the display configuration: **General**, **Configuration**, **Cut Plane**, and **Version History**. The **General** tab is used to rename the display configuration and provide a description of its intended use. The **Configuration** tab is used to assign a display set to a viewing direction. The **Cut Plane** tab is used to set cut planes

Figure 7-10.
Select the Configurations folder to display a table view indicating which sets are assigned to a particular display configuration.

List of display configurations in the drawing

List of display sets in the drawing

Select the Configurations folder to display a table in the right pane

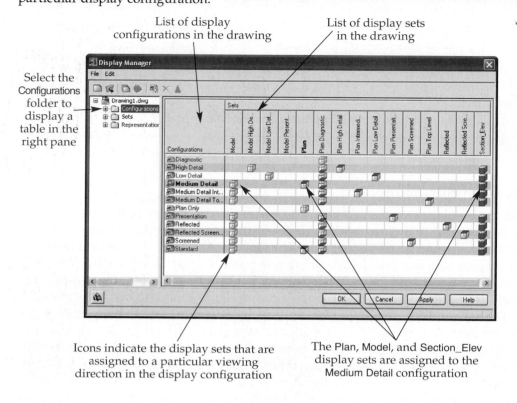

Icons indicate the display sets that are assigned to a particular viewing direction in the display configuration

The Plan, Model, and Section_Elev display sets are assigned to the Medium Detail configuration

Figure 7-11.
Right-click over a display configuration in the table view to display a shortcut menu.

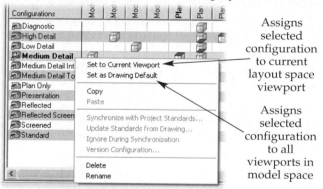

Assigns selected configuration to current layout space viewport

Assigns selected configuration to all viewports in model space

within the drawing that display the model geometry based on where the cut plane cuts through the geometry. The **Version History** tab is used to track the version of the display configuration when synchronizing a project.

When the currently active display configuration is selected and expanded in the tree view, different viewing direction icons are displayed. One of these icons is bold, indicating the current viewing direction and the associated display set that is current in the drawing window.

To create a custom display configuration, highlight the Configurations folder, pick the **New** button or right-click, and select **New** from the shortcut menu. Enter a new name for the display configuration in the **General** tab. After the new display configuration has been created, it can be configured by adjusting values in the different tabs.

Figure 7-12.
Select a display configuration from the tree view to display the configuration properties.

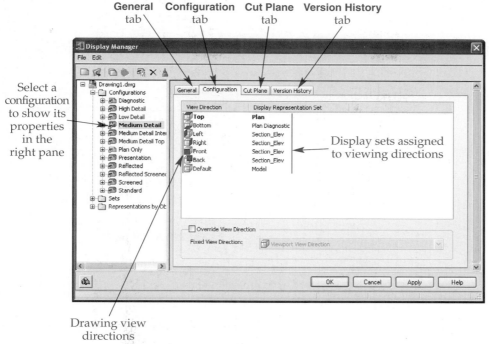

In **Figure 7-12**, the Medium Detail display configuration has been selected. The **Configuration** tab shows a list of standard viewing directions. These include Top, Bottom, Left, Right, Front, and Back. The default view direction indicates any view other than the standard viewing directions. The default viewing direction can be an Isometric view, a Perspective view obtained with a camera, or a view created from the **3DORBIT** command.

Each viewing direction is then assigned a display set. In **Figure 7-12**, the Top view is assigned the Plan display set. This display set provides Plan representations when the drawing is viewed from the Top view. The Elevation views are assigned the Section_Elev display set when the drawing is viewed with an Elevation view. The default viewing direction is assigned the Model display set, which shows Model representations in any view other than the standard views. If a viewing direction is not assigned to a display set, the display set in the default viewing direction is used.

To assign a display set to a viewing direction, pick the area under the **Display Representation Set** column for the appropriate view direction. A drop-down list appears with a list of available display sets. See **Figure 7-13**. Select the desired display set to assign it to the viewing direction.

At the bottom of the **Configuration** tab is a check box labeled **Override View Direction.** Pick this check box to override the display sets assigned to the standard viewing directions and use the display set assigned to the default viewing direction for all viewing directions in the drawing.

The **Cut Plane** tab is used to specify a cut plane for all objects in the drawing when the display configuration is set current. The cut plane cuts all objects at the specified height and displays how the objects appear if the top portions of the objects are removed from the cut plane. The cut plane height is specified by entering a height value in the **Cut Height** text box. See **Figure 7-14.**

A display range can also be set that allows objects above and below the cut plane to be displayed. The cut plane still cuts through the objects and shows the objects as they appear when cut, but items above the cut plane, such as light fixtures, and items below the cut plane, such as footings, are visible and use the display properties for

Figure 7-13.
Select a display set from the list to assign to a view direction.

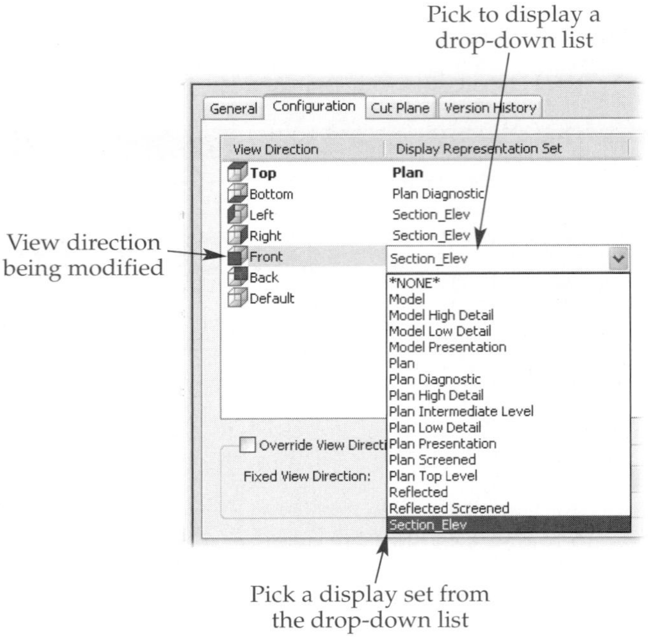

Pick to display a drop-down list

View direction being modified

Pick a display set from the drop-down list

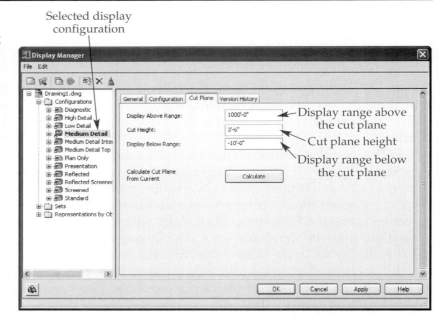

Figure 7-14.
The **Cut Plane** tab sets a global cutting plane that cuts all AEC objects that cross through the plane.

Selected display configuration

Display range above the cut plane

Cut plane height

Display range below the cut plane

above cut plane and below cut plane components. For example, if the cut plane is set to 3'-6", the visible range above the cut plane is set to 14'-0", and the visible range below the cut plane is set at –4'-0", the AEC objects are cut at 3'-6". Objects that lie between 3'-6" and 14'-0", as well as objects that lie between 3'-6" and –4'-0", are also displayed, but with different display properties for above and below the cut plane. Objects that lie outside the display range, such as a transom window that is inserted at 16'-0", are not displayed at all.

NOTE

The cut plane assigned to a display configuration is applied globally to all objects in the viewport using the display configuration, unless an object cut plane is set for individual objects or object styles, in which case the object cut plane is used for those objects.

Exercise 7-5 Complete the Exercise on the Student CD.

Applying the Display System

The fundamental element that is used by the drafter when creating drawings is the display configuration. Display configurations can be assigned globally to all viewports in model space or to individual viewports in layout space.

To set a display configuration current within a floating viewport in a layout tab or within the **Model** tab, pick the appropriate display configuration from the **Display Configuration** menu located in the drawing window status bar. This menu displays the current display configuration for the active viewport. See **Figure 7-15**.

Select a display configuration from the menu to set it current. Display configurations are applied to all tiled viewports in model space or to a single floating viewport in layout space. Applying a display configuration to a floating viewport is discussed in Chapter 24.

The Medium Detail display configuration displays AEC objects as 2D objects in the Top view and as 3D objects in an Elevation or Isometric view. The Reflected display configuration displays the AEC objects in a Top view as they appear in a reflected ceiling plan. In the Reflected display configuration, doors and windows are not displayed, and the header over the wall openings is displayed over the door and window locations. Other display configurations include Low Detail, High Detail, Screened, and Presentation. Each of the display configurations is designed to show the AEC objects only as they should appear based on the type of display configuration chosen.

NOTE   Appendix J, *Display Configurations and Their Uses,* lists the default display configurations included in the templates and provides a description for using each.

Exercise 7-6 Complete the Exercise on the Student CD.

Figure 7-15.
Pick the display configuration pop-up button to display a list of display configurations in the drawing that can be set current in the active viewport.

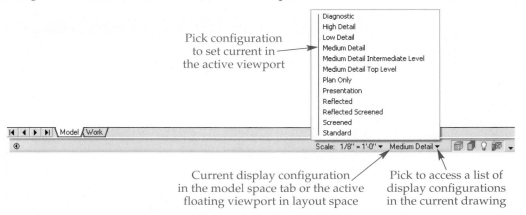

Pick configuration to set current in the active viewport

Diagnostic
High Detail
Low Detail
Medium Detail
Medium Detail Intermediate Level
Medium Detail Top Level
Plan Only
Presentation
Reflected
Reflected Screened
Screened
Standard

Model / Work

Scale: 1/8" = 1'-0"   Medium Detail

Current display configuration in the model space tab or the active floating viewport in layout space

Pick to access a list of display configurations in the current drawing

By using display representations, you have been able to configure how default AEC objects appear when viewed with display configurations. The display representations control only how the default representation for each object appears. AEC object displays can additionally be controlled by the AEC object's style or by the individual AEC object in the drawing.

Every AEC object in Architectural Desktop can have its default representation overridden, so individual objects appear unique. Whenever you select one AEC object and right-click in the drawing, the **Edit Object Display...** option becomes available. See **Figure 7-16**. Picking **Edit Object Display...** from the shortcut menu displays the **Object Display** dialog box shown in **Figure 7-17**.

The **Object Display** dialog box includes three tabs: **Materials**, **Display Properties**, and **General Properties**. Each of these tabs is used to modify the display of the selected object. The **Materials** tab is used to modify the display of materials assigned to the selected object. The **Display Properties** tab is used to adjust the display representations for the selected object. The **General Properties** tab is used to modify AutoCAD properties for the selected object, such as layer, color, and linetype.

Picking the **Materials** tab provides a list of components that belong to the selected object and the materials that are assigned to each component. See **Figure 7-18**. A list of object components is available in the **Components** list. By default, different object styles can have a variety of materials assigned to the different components. Selecting

Figure 7-16.
Selecting an AEC object and then right-clicking displays a shortcut menu with the **Edit Object Display...** option. The partial shortcut menu displayed is specific to wall objects.

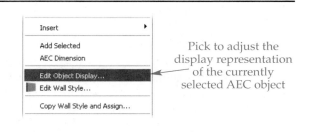

Pick to adjust the display representation of the currently selected AEC object

Figure 7-17.
The **Object Display** dialog box is displayed after selecting the **Edit Object Display...** option from the shortcut menu. This dialog box controls the display representation for the selected object, overriding the default display representations.

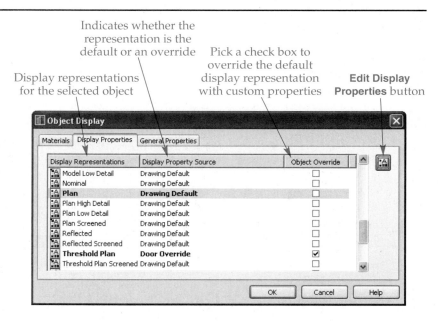

Indicates whether the representation is the default or an override

Display representations for the selected object

Pick a check box to override the default display representation with custom properties

Edit Display Properties button

Figure 7-18.
The **Materials** tab lists the components of the selected object and allows the display of the materials to be modified for the selected object.

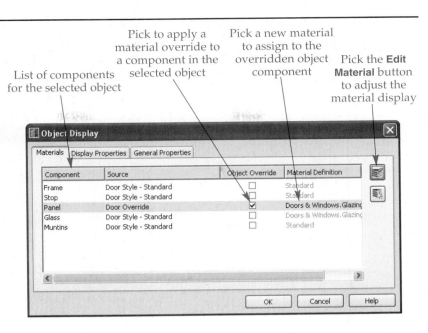

Pick to apply a material override to a component in the selected object

Pick a new material to assign to the overridden object component

Pick the **Edit Material** button to adjust the material display

List of components for the selected object

a check box next to a component applies an object override to the selected component. This allows you to select a different material to assign to the component. Pick the material in the **Material Definition** column to display a list of materials in the drawing. Select the desired material to use an override for the component.

In addition to overriding materials assigned to the components of an object, the display of the materials can be adjusted by selecting a component from the list and picking the **Edit Material** button. This opens the **Material Definition Properties** dialog box, which lists the available display representations for the material. Pick the **Edit Display Properties** button to modify the materials display. The creation and modification of materials and their display properties are discussed in greater detail in Chapter 15.

The **Display Properties** tab includes a list of the display representations assigned to the selected AEC object. Next to the **Display Representations** column is the **Display Property Source** column. This column indicates if the display representations for the selected AEC object uses the default display representations (**Drawing Default**) or if the displays of the representations are being set by the individual object (**Object Override**). The **Object Override** column displays a list of check boxes. A check mark in a box indicates the default display representation is being overridden with new display properties. See **Figure 7-17**.

To modify a default display representation, select a representation from the list, and then pick the **Edit Display Properties** button. This allows the default display representation for all objects to be modified. To apply an override to a display representation for the individually selected AEC object, place a check mark in the check box next to the display representation to be modified or pick the **Edit Display Properties** button. This allows the display representation for the selected AEC object to be modified and does not affect the display of objects using the default display representation.

Once the **Edit Display Properties** button has been selected, the **Display Properties** dialog box for the representation being overridden is opened. See **Figure 7-19**. Any changes made to the display properties here result in the display modification for this object only.

Figure 7-19.

The **Object Properties** dialog box for the door object. Changes made here override the default display representation and are applied to the display of the selected object only.

Make changes to display of components

Pick the **Other** tab to adjust additional display settings

Title bar shows the override is being applied at the object level

Door object components

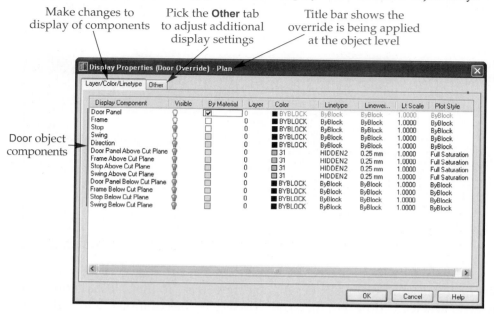

This **Display Properties** dialog box is the same dialog box used to set up the default display representations. The difference is the values you change here affect the display for the object being modified only. Components can be turned on or off or assigned colors, linetypes, lineweights, linetype scale, and plot styles. When you are changing the display for the object, pick the **OK** button to return to the **Object Display** dialog box. Additional overrides to other display representations can be assigned by selecting the appropriate representation from the display representation list and assigning an override or picking the **Edit Display Properties** button.

The **General Properties** tab is the last tab in the **Object Display** dialog box and is used to control the layer, color, and linetype assigned to an object. Although the color and linetype can be modified, the display representation for the object usually overrides these and uses the colors and linetypes assigned to the individual components of the object. The layer on which an object is placed, however, can be reassigned. Layers are discussed in Chapter 8.

Occasionally, when the display of objects is changed, the drawing does not reflect the display changes. This usually means the drawing needs to be regenerated. Use the **REGEN** command, discussed in Chapter 6.

NOTE

When the plan representation for wall objects is edited, a wall style can have up to 20 different boundaries. The boundaries refer to each individual component within a wall. For example, a wall with brick, CMU, and stud components has a total of three boundaries. Each boundary also includes a hatch component. Hatch components can be turned on or off by selecting the appropriate hatch component. For example, Boundary 1 includes the Hatch 1 component. If you want to turn on the hatch pattern for Boundary 1, turn on the lightbulb symbol next to Hatch 1. The hatch can also be edited by selecting the **Hatching** tab and picking the hatch swatch next to the hatch component you want to modify. Modifying the hatch of a wall style is discussed in greater detail later in this text.

Chapter Test

Answer the following questions. Write your answers on a separate sheet of paper or complete the electronic chapter test on the Student CD.

1. Give the basic function of the Architectural Desktop display system.
2. Name and briefly describe the three display system elements.
3. Give the basic purpose of the **Display Manager** and indicate how it is accessed.
4. Name and describe the basic function of each folder in the **Display Manager** tree view.
5. How do you view individual object display representations?
6. What does a display representation icon at the intersection of an AEC object and a display representation indicate?
7. Discuss the basic function of a display set and give an example.
8. Briefly describe the function of a display configuration and give an example.
9. Cube-shaped view direction symbols with different sides colored indicate the viewing directions the display sets are assigned. Identify the representation and meaning of at least three symbols.
10. How do you access the **Object Display** dialog box, so you can override the default representation of an AEC object?

Chapter Projects

Use the techniques covered in this chapter to create the following drawings.

1. Single-Level Residential Project
   A. Access the **Project Browser** and set Residential-Project-01 current.
   B. Select the **Constructs** tab and open the Main Floor construct.
   C. Edit the display properties for the system default Door/Window Assembly objects in the Plan display representation so the Above component is turned off.
   D. Edit the display properties of the system default Door objects in the Model display representation so the doors are closed in a Model view. (*Hint:* Use the **Other** tab in the Model representation's **Display Properties** dialog box. Depending on the door styles used, you may need to use the **Object Display** dialog box to adjust the display that may be set.)
   E. Edit the display properties of the system default Opening objects in the Plan display representation. Change the Length Lines component to the Hidden2 linetype.
   F. Edit the display properties of the system default Window objects in the Sill Plan display representation. Turn off the Sill A and Sill B components.
   G. Edit the display properties of the system default Window objects in the Plan display representation. Turn off the Glass component.
   H. Save and close the drawing.

2. Single-Level Residential Project
   A. Access the **Project Browser** and set Residential-Project-02 current.
   B. Select the **Constructs** tab and open the Main Floor construct.
   C. Select a wall, right-click, and use **Edit Object Display...** to edit the Model display representation. Change the Boundary 1 component to color 254. (*Hint:* You may need to uncheck the **By Material** check box to change the colors.)
   D. Edit the display properties of the system default Door objects in the Model display representation so the doors are closed in a Model view. (*Hint:* Use the **Other** tab in the Model representation's **Display Properties** dialog box. Depending on the door styles used, you may need to use the **Object Display** dialog box to adjust the display that may be set.)
   E. Edit the display properties of the system default Opening objects in the Plan display representation. Change the Length Lines component to the Hidden2 linetype.
   F. Select the front door, right-click, and use **Edit Object Display...** to edit the Threshold Plan display representation. Apply an override for this door, and edit to turn on the Threshold B component. In the **Other** tab, adjust the values for the C-Extension and D-Depth to 2″.
   G. Edit the display properties of the system default Window objects in the Sill Plan display representation. Turn off the Sill A and Sill B components.
   H. Edit the display properties of the system default Window objects in the Plan display representation. Turn off the Glass component.
   I. Save and close the drawing.

Architectural Desktop and Its Applications

3. Two-Story Residential Project
   A. Access the **Project Browser** and set Residential-Project-03 current.
   B. Select the **Constructs** tab and open the Main Floor construct.
   C. Edit the display properties of the system default Door/Window Assembly objects in the Plan display representation so the Above component is turned off.
   D. Edit the display properties of the system default Door objects in the Model display representation so the doors are closed in a Model view. (*Hint:* Use the **Other** tab in the Model representation's **Display Properties** dialog box. Depending on the door styles used, you may need to use the **Object Display** dialog box to adjust the display that may be set.)
   E. Edit the display properties of the system default Opening objects in the Plan display representation. Change the Length Lines component to the Hidden2 linetype.
   F. Select a wall, right-click, and use **Edit Object Display...** to edit the Model display representation. Change the Boundary 1 component to color 254. (*Hint:* You may need to uncheck the **By Material** check box to change the colors.)
   G. Edit the display properties of the system default Window objects in the Sill Plan display representations. Select the **Other** tab and adjust the values for the C-Extension and the D-Depth to 2".
   H. Edit the display properties of the system default Window objects in the Plan display representation. Turn the Glass component off.
   I. Save and close the drawing.
   J. Select the **Constructs** tab and open the Upper Floor construct.
   K. Select a wall, right-click, and use **Edit Object Display...** to edit the Model display representation. Change the Boundary 1 component to color 254. (*Hint:* You may need to uncheck the **By Material** check box to change the colors.)
   L. Edit the display properties of the system default Window objects in the Sill Plan display representations. Select the **Other** tab and adjust the values for the C-Extension and the D-Depth to 2".
   M. Edit the display properties of the system default Window objects in the Plan display representation. Turn the Glass component off.
   N. Save and close the drawing.

4. Two-Story Residential Project
    A. Access the **Project Browser** and set Residential-Project-04 current.
    B. Select the **Constructs** tab and open the Main Floor construct.
    C. Edit the display properties of the system default Door/Window Assembly objects in the Plan display representation so the Above component is turned off.
    D. Edit the display properties of the system default Door objects in the Model display representation so the doors are closed in a Model view. (*Hint:* Use the **Other** tab in the Model representation's **Display Properties** dialog box. Depending on the door styles used, you may need to use the **Object Display** dialog box to adjust the display that may be set.)
    E. Edit the display properties of the system default Opening objects in the Plan display representation. Change the Length Lines component to the Hidden2 linetype.
    F. Edit the display properties of the system default Window objects in the Sill Plan display representations. Turn off the Sill A and Sill B components.
    G. Edit the display properties of the system default Window objects in the Plan display representation. Turn the Glass component off.
    H. Save and close the drawing.
    I. Select the **Constructs** tab and open the Upper Floor construct.
    J. Edit the display properties of the system default Door objects in the Model display representation so the doors are closed in a Model view. (*Hint:* Use the **Other** tab in the Model representation's **Display Properties** dialog box. Depending on the door styles used, you may need to use the **Object Display** dialog box to adjust the display that may be set.)
    K. Edit the display properties of the system default Opening objects in the Plan display representation. Change the Length Lines component to the Hidden2 linetype.
    L. Edit the display properties of the system default Window objects in the Sill Plan display representations. Select the **Other** tab and adjust the values for the C-Extension and the D-Depth to 2".
    M. Edit the display properties of the system default Window objects in the Plan display representation. Turn the Glass component off.
    N. Save and close the drawing.

5. Commercial Store Project
    A. Access the **Project Browser** and set Commercial-Project-05 current.
    B. Select the **Constructs** tab and open the Main Floor construct.
    C. Edit the display properties of the system default Door/Window Assembly objects in the Plan display representation so the Above component is turned off.
    D. Edit the display properties of the system default Door objects in the Model display representation so the doors are closed in a Model view. (*Hint:* Use the **Other** tab in the Model representation's **Display Properties** dialog box. Depending on the door styles used, you may need to use the **Object Display** dialog box to adjust the display that may be set.)
    E. Edit the default display properties of the system default Wall objects in the Plan display representation. Turn off the Hatch 2 and Hatch 3 components.
    F. Save and close the drawing.

6. Commercial Car Maintenance Shop Project
    A. Access the **Project Browser** and set Commercial-Project-06 current.
    B. Select the **Constructs** tab and open the Main Floor construct.
    C. Edit the display properties of the system default Door/Window Assembly objects in the Plan display representation so the Above component is turned off.
    D. Edit the display properties of the system default Door objects in the Model display representation so the doors are closed in a Model view. (*Hint:* Use the **Other** tab in the Model representation's **Display Properties** dialog box. Depending on the door styles used, you may need to use the **Object Display** dialog box to adjust the display that may be set.)
    E. Edit the default display properties of the system default Wall objects in the Plan display representation. Turn off the Hatch 2 and Hatch 3 components.
    F. Use the **Edit Object Display…** dialog box to override the four garage doors in the Plan display representation. Turn off the Swing component.
    G. Save and close the drawing.
    H. Select the **Constructs** tab and open the Upper Floor construct.
    I. Edit the display properties of the system default Door/Window Assembly in the Plan display representation so the Above component is turned off.
    J. Edit the default display properties of the system default Wall objects in the Plan display representation. Turn off the Hatch 2 and Hatch 3 components.
    K. Save and close the drawing.

7. Governmental Fire Station
    A. Access the **Project Browser** and set Gvrmt-Project-07 current.
    B. Select the **Constructs** tab and open the Main Floor construct.
    C. Edit the display properties of the system default Door/Window Assembly objects in the Plan display representation so the Above component is turned off.
    D. Edit the display properties of the system default Door objects in the Model display representation so the doors are closed in a Model view. (*Hint:* Use the **Other** tab in the Model representation's **Display Properties** dialog box. Depending on the door styles used, you may need to use the **Object Display** dialog box to adjust the display that may be set.)
    E. Edit the display properties of the system default Wall objects in the Plan display representation. Turn off the Below Cut Plane component.
    F. Edit the display properties of the system default Opening objects in the Plan display representation. Change the Length Lines component to the Hidden2 linetype.
    G. Save and close the drawing.

The American Design Drafting Association (ADDA) is an international membership organization for design and drafting professionals.

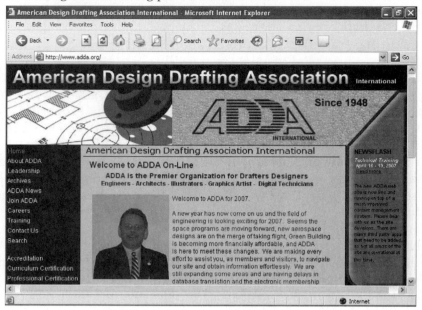

Layer Management

Learning Objectives

After completing this chapter, you will be able to do the following:

✓ Use Architectural Desktop layers in your drawing.
✓ Access and use the **Layer Manager**.
✓ Create and use layer standards.
✓ Establish new layers.
✓ Set a layer current.
✓ Create layer filter groups.
✓ Use snapshots.
✓ Create and use layer keys.
✓ Use layer key overrides.
✓ Import and export layer standards.

Using layers in Architectural Desktop is similar to establishing a group of transparent overlays. Objects that share common properties, such as color, linetype, and lineweight, can be grouped together onto one layer. In architectural drawing, each AEC object is grouped into its own layer. For example, windows can have the same color and linetype and represent real-world windows, so they can be organized in their own layer named Windows or Glazing. Managing multiple objects in the drawing becomes easier by grouping common items together. Color is the most common property of layers. Colors help differentiate the types of information in the drawing. For example, all walls in the drawing can be assigned a specific color on the Wall layer that is different from the color of the objects on the Door layer. Linetypes can also define different types of drafting elements. For example, hidden lines can represent demolition walls, or a gas linetype can represent the gas utilities in the building.

Layers also allow you visibility control over objects in the drawing. Entire groups of objects on different layers can be turned on or off to create many different types of drawings. For example, a drawing given to a client can display only the walls, doors, and windows of a preliminary plan sheet. The same drawing can be given to the contractor, who requires more information, such as display of dimensions, legends, and detail flags. See Figure 8-1. Turning layers on or off and combining sets of layers allows these two different uses to be created from the same drawing file.

In standard AutoCAD, layer names and their properties must be manually created. As objects such as polylines, arcs, text, and dimensions are drawn, layers needs to be created and objects assigned to the appropriate layer. As AEC objects are drawn in

Figure 8-1.
A drawing of a building can have different sets of layers displayed, in order to create two separate plans from one drawing file.

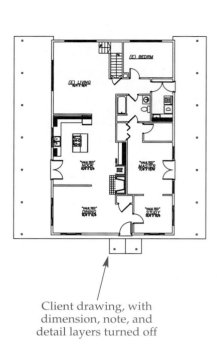

Client drawing, with dimension, note, and detail layers turned off

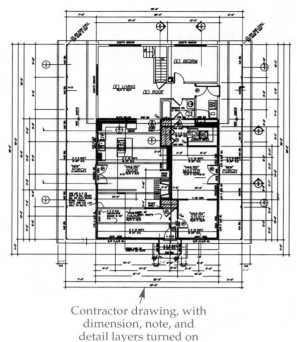

Contractor drawing, with dimension, note, and detail layers turned on

Architectural Desktop, the layer name, color, and linetype are automatically created, and objects are automatically assigned to an appropriate layer.

The Architectural Desktop layering system is built on two main elements: a layer standard and layer keys. A *layer standard* is a set of rules governing how a layer name is created. In Architectural Desktop, layer names are created in accordance with the AIA layering guidelines. See Appendix E for more information on the AIA layer standard. *Layer keys* interpret the layer standard and assign a layer name to AEC objects. When an AEC object is added to the drawing, the layer name and properties assigned to the object are created and added to the drawing, and the object is automatically placed on the layer. This saves layer management time, because layers are created as you draw.

Introduction to the Layer Manager

LAYER

Type
LAYER
LA

Pull-Down Menu
Format
> Layer
Management
> Layer
Manager...

Toolbar
Layer Properties
Layer Manager...

Architectural Desktop includes a utility known as the **Layer Manager**, where layers can be created and their properties are assigned. Within the **Layer Manager**, additional utilities are provided for the management of layers. The **Layer Manager** can be accessed by selecting the **Layer Manager...** button on the **Layer Properties** toolbar, picking **Format** > **Layer Management** > **Layer Manager...**, or typing LAYER or LA. Using one of these options opens the **Layer Manager**. See **Figure 8-2**.

Once activated, the **Layer Manager** provides a list of layers currently in the drawing. The **Layer Manager** is divided into two separate panes. The left pane displays lists of filter groups. Filter groups combine sets of layers together for easy management. Initially, the All layer group and a filter group named All Used Layers are available. The All layer group combines all the layers in the drawing, which are displayed in the right pane. Selecting the All Used Layers filter group displays a list of layers in the right pane that are currently being used in the drawing. Creating filter groups is discussed later in this chapter.

Figure 8-2.
The **Layer Manager** is used to organize and manage layers in the drawing. Additional utilities include creating and sorting layers, as well as establishing a layer standard.

Layer groups list

Layer management utilites

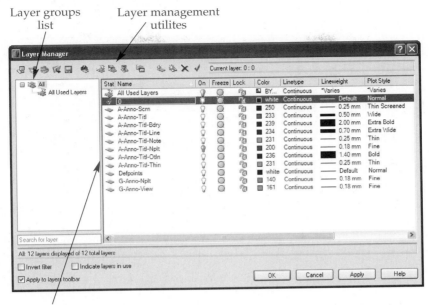

List of layers in the current drawing and their assigned properties

The right pane lists the individual layer names and displays their current properties, such as color, linetype, and status. As AEC objects are created in the drawing, new layers are added to the drawing, and their properties are automatically assembled in the **Layer Manager**. A description of each column in the right pane is described as follows and shown in **Figure 8-3:**

- **Status.** This column displays an icon beside the layer name that indicates the status of the layer, such as if it is the current layer (a green check mark), a filter group (a lightning bolt, hand, or funnel), or a layer that will be deleted (an *X*).
- **Name.** This column provides a list of layers in the drawing by name. The layer names are sorted alphabetically. Layer names can be created with up to 255 characters.
- **On.** This column, represented by a lightbulb, controls the visibility of a layer. Picking the lightbulb symbol beside the desired layer turns the layer on or off. Layers that are turned on are visible in the drawing screen, while layers that are turned off are not visible in the drawing screen. Objects on layers that are turned off are regenerated with the rest of the drawing.
- **Freeze.** This column, represented by a sunshine symbol, also controls the visibility of layers. Picking the sunshine symbol beside the desired layer freezes the layer. Thawed layers are visible in the drawing screen. Frozen layers are not visible in the drawing screen. Freezing layers helps speed up the **ZOOM**, **PAN**, and **3DORBIT** commands. Frozen layers are not regenerated with the rest of the drawing. If there are layers that are not be shown for long periods, the freeze option should be used instead of the off option, to help speed up the performance of Architectural Desktop.
- **Lock.** This column, represented by a padlock, controls the accessibility of the layer. Picking the padlock symbol beside the desired layer locks or unlocks the layer. Unlocked layers allow editing of objects on the layer. Locked layers do not allow objects on the layer to be selected for editing. They lock the objects in place with their current properties.

Figure 8-3.
The right pane includes a list of columns that control the status of different properties for a layer.

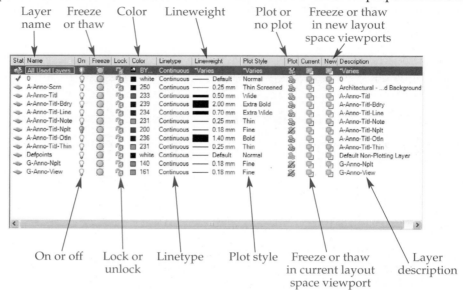

- **Color.** This column is used to assign a color to a layer. The color of the layer is represented in the swatch box with the color name or number beside the swatch. Picking the swatch accesses the **Select Color** dialog box. Pick a color from the dialog box to be used for the layer.

- **Linetype.** This column is used to assign a linetype to a layer. The linetype assigned to the layer is represented by the name of the linetype. Picking the linetype name beside the desired layer accesses the **Select Linetype** dialog box. Selecting a linetype from the list assigns the selected linetype to the layer.

- **Lineweight.** This column is used to assign a lineweight to a layer. Lineweights add width to the objects drawn on the layer. Picking the name or number of the lineweight beside the desired layer accesses the **Lineweight** dialog box. Selecting a lineweight from the list assigns the lineweight to the layer.

- **Plot Style.** This column is used to assign a plot style to a layer. Depending on the drawing template chosen, the plot style column might or might not be grayed out. When a drawing is plotted, pen tables are used to interpret the layer color and translate it into a finished plot. Selecting the name of the plot style associated with the layer name displays the **Select Plot Style** dialog box. Pick a plot style from the list to assign to the layer. When you are beginning a drawing, a template is generally selected to begin as the basis of the drawing. The AEC model templates come in two basic types of pen tables: color tables (.ctb) and style tables (.stb). Choosing an .stb template allows the use of plot styles in the drawing. Pen tables and plotting are discussed in Chapter 24.

- **Plot.** This column is represented by a printer symbol. Picking the printer symbol beside the layer causes the layer to be a plotting or nonplotting layer. When the plot symbol is picked, objects on the layer plot unless they are turned off or frozen. When the no-plot symbol is turned on, objects on the layer are not plotted, regardless of whether or not they are turned on or thawed.

- **Current VP Freeze.** This column, represented by a sunshine with a rectangle, controls the visibility of layers in the active layout space viewport and is available only when a layout space viewport is active. Picking this symbol beside the desired layer causes the layer to be thawed or frozen in the active floating viewport only. Freeze and thaw in the active viewport are different from the standard freeze and thaw options.

- **New VP Freeze.** This column, represented by a sunshine with a rectangle, controls the visibility of layers in newly created layout space viewports and is available only when a layout space viewport is active. Picking this symbol beside the desired layer causes the layer to be thawed or frozen in new layout space viewports. When the sunshine symbol is displayed, the layer is visible when a new viewport is created in layout space, while when the snowflake symbol is displayed, the layer does not appear in new viewports created in layout space.
- **Description.** This column provides a description of the layer. The description is automatically generated when a new layer is created. Depending on the layer standard being used, the description can be quite detailed.

After making any changes to the layer, pick the **Apply** button so the changes are displayed appropriately in the drawing screen. Right-clicking in the right pane of the **Layer Manager** produces a shortcut menu with different options that aid in controlling layers.

> NOTE
>
> When you make a change to a layer, it might not show up immediately. You might need to use the **REGEN**, **REGENALL**, or **OBJRELUPDATE** command to update the layer changes in the drawing. If you need to make several changes to multiple layers, highlight the layers by holding down the [Ctrl] key as you pick on top of the layer names. The selected layers are highlighted, allowing you to make changes to these layers at the same time.

Exercise 8-1   Complete the Exercise on the Student CD.

Using and Creating Layer Standards

Layer standards are used to establish individual, project, or office layer-naming conventions. A layer standard contains a set of rules that determines how a new layer name is to be created. For example, the AIA Version 3 layer standard included with Architectural Desktop contains rules that divide the layer name into five parts, or fields, separated by hyphens: *discipline designator 1 discipline designator 2-major code-minor 1 code-minor 2 code-status code.*

The *discipline designator 1* designates the discipline that created the geometry, such as A for architectural or S for structural. The discipline designator 2 adds a second letter to the first discipline designator to further describe the discipline, such as AF for architectural finishes or AS for architectural sitework. The *major code* designates the type of assembly or construction material being used, such as WALL or DOOR. The *minor 1 code* and *minor 2 code* are used to further describe the major code, such as FULL or DIMS. The *status code* is used to indicate the state of the geometry being drawn, such as D for demolition work or N for new work. Together, these fields create a layer name, such as A-WALL-FULL-DIMS-D. Appendix E explains the AIA layering standard and provides examples of its usage.

New layer names can be created that conform to AIA layer rules or a set of rules that creates a custom layering standard. As AEC objects are added to the drawing, the layer where the objects belong is automatically created, and the objects are assigned to the layer name. AutoCAD objects such as polylines, text, and dimensions must be assigned to a layer manually as they are drawn. To do this, set the desired layer current, and draw the AutoCAD object. Newly drawn AutoCAD objects are assigned to the current layer.

Using Layer Standards

Many architectural offices have adopted the AIA layer guidelines for their CAD drawings. Some offices have their own standards, and some do not use a layer standard. The use of a layer standard can be very helpful in organizing your CAD geometry and can make it easier to change the display of objects in the drawing.

Architectural Desktop includes a few layer standards: AIA 2nd Edition, British Standard (BS)1192-Aug Version2, BS1192 Descriptive, *Deutsche Industrie Normen* (DIN) 276 Format, Generic Architectural Desktop Format, and the *Standardleistungsbuch* (STLB) Format. The AIA Version 3 is the default layer standard when an Architectural Desktop drawing is started from a template and is based on the *AIA Layering Guidelines*, Version 3, published by the AIA. The two BS1192 layer standards are British standards. The Generic Architectural Desktop layering standard is based on European layering guidelines. The DIN and STLB standards are based on German layering standards.

In addition to these layer standards, custom layer standards can be created from scratch or by modifying existing layer standards. Two popular layer standards in residential work replace the discipline code in the AIA layer standard with a floor field, which indicates the floor level of the building. This field can be alphabetic or numeric. For example, M-Window-D can indicate the main floor (M) window that is being demolished (D), and the layer name 3-Door-N indicates the third floor (3) door that is new construction (N). No matter which standard you use, newly created layer names follow the rules set up in the layer standard.

Creating a New Layer Standard

To create a new layer standard, open the **Layer Manager**. Across the top of the dialog box is a set of buttons used to manage layers. The first button is the **Layer Standards** button. Select this button to display the **Layer Standards** dialog box, shown in **Figure 8-4**.

Dialog Box

Layer Manager

Layer Standards

The **Layer Standards** dialog box includes a list of layering standards in the current drawing. Along the right side of the dialog box are buttons to create, edit, purge, and import or export layer standards. To create a new layer standard, pick the **New...** button. This displays the **Create Layer Standard** dialog box.

Enter a new name for the layer standard. If the layer standard is based on an existing standard, select the **Based On:** check box, and choose a standard from the list. The layer standard has to be created from scratch if the new layer standard is not based on an existing standard. If the standard is based on an existing standard, you can edit

Figure 8-4.
The **Layer Standards** dialog box is used to create or modify a layering standard.

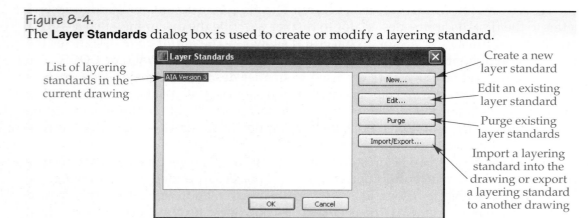

List of layering standards in the current drawing

Create a new layer standard

Edit an existing layer standard

Purge existing layer standards

Import a layering standard into the drawing or export a layering standard to another drawing

the standard to reflect your rules. After a name is entered, pick the **OK** button. The **Layer Standards** dialog box is displayed with the new standard in the list. Next, select the new layer standard from the list and pick the **Edit...** button. The **Layer Standard Properties** dialog box is displayed. This dialog box is used to set up the layer-naming rules for the layer standard. The dialog box includes four tabs, which are described in the following sections.

Using the Component Fields Tab

The **Component Fields** tab is shown by default and is used to set up how a layer name is created. See **Figure 8-5.** The top of the tab displays the current layer standard being modified. The drop-down list includes a list of standards in the current drawing. The main part of the tab is used to list the component fields in a layer name, such as the AIA standard five component fields. The rules governing how the field name is created can be found in this area. At the bottom of the tab are three buttons. The **Delete** button deletes a layer field name. The **Add above the selected item** and **Add below the selected item** buttons control where a new field name is to be created in the list above.

An example of a layer standard created for residential application with a floor field, an object type field, a subobject type field, and a status field is M (main floor), Walls (wall objects), Dims (dimensions), New (new construction). Combining these fields gives this layer standard format: M-Walls-Dims-New.

When a new layer standard is created, the Default value component field is already entered in the layer fields list area. To create a new field, highlight the Default value component field, and pick the **Add above the selected item** button. A new component field is created at the top of the list. Enter the name for the new component field and press [Enter]. In this case, Floor is entered as the component field name in **Figure 8-6.**

Figure 8-5.
The **Component Fields** tab of the **Layer Standard Properties** dialog box is used to create the rules for the layer names.

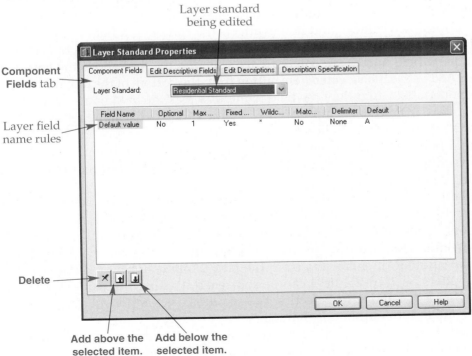

Figure 8-6.
The Residential Standard with the first layer component field named Floor is ready to have rules applied.

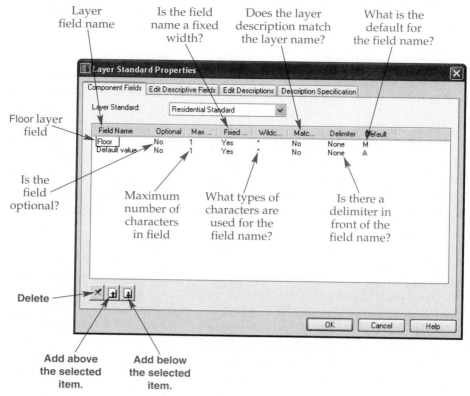

Once the component field name has been created, the rules for the field name can be set up by selecting a value for the field name under each one of the columns. Picking a value displays a shortcut menu with options that can be selected or values that can be entered. Only the **Default** column requires you to enter a value from the keyboard. The following describes each column and how it affects the component field name:

- **Field Name.** This column is used to identify the name of a layer component field. Component field names are entered after selecting the **Add above the selected item** or **Add below the selected item** button from the bottom of the tab. To rename a component field, highlight the field name, and pick the field name again. This places a box around the component field name so the field can be renamed.

- **Optional.** This column indicates whether or not the component field is an optional field. Picking on the value displays a menu containing a **Yes** and a **No**. Selecting **Yes** makes the field an optional field that is not required when creating a new layer name.

- **Max Width.** This column identifies the maximum number of characters that can be used for the component field. Selecting a value displays a menu of several numbers representing the total number of characters to be used.

- **Fixed Width.** This column specifies whether the component field must use the total number of characters from the **Max Width** column or if the number of characters used in the field can be shortened. Picking the value displays a menu with a **Yes** and a **No**. Selecting **Yes** requires the component field name to use the maximum number of characters.

- **Wildcard.** This column specifies the type of characters that can be used in the component field. Selecting the value displays a menu list of options. These options include **Alpha** (alphabetic characters), **Numeric** (number characters), **Any** (letters, numbers, or special characters), and **Other....** The **Other...** wildcard displays a dialog box in which certain characters can be entered separated by commas.

- **Match Description.** This column recognizes the layer component field only if it exactly matches a description. For example, the AIA layering standard dictates that component field names are created in the following order: discipline, major, minor 1, minor 2, and status. The minor 1, minor 2, and status component fields are optional fields, so it is possible to create a layer that includes the discipline, major, and minor component fields or the discipline, major, and status component fields. If the value for **Match Description** is set to **Yes** for the status component field and a layer is to be created with the discipline, major, and status component fields, the status component field descriptions are checked against the descriptions of the minor component field to determine if there are any matches. If there are any matches, the layer name is invalid. This column is most commonly set to **No** to avoid this complication.
- **Delimiter.** This column specifies a character to be placed in front of the layer component field for clarity between the layer field names. Picking the value displays a list of valid delimiters for a layer field name. These options include **$, - (Hyphen)**, **_ (Underscore)**, and **None**. **None** is most commonly used in front of the first layer field, because a delimiter is not necessary.
- **Default.** This column allows you to enter a default field name that appears when layer names are created. These values can be left blank.

Each layer component field in the layer standard is a part of the overall layer name. Picking a value for the component field allows you to control how the layer name can be created. Component field names can be added above or below a selected component field to create the order of a layer component field name. The completed **Component Fields** tab for the sample Residential Standard is shown in **Figure 8-7**.

Exercise
8-2   *Complete the Exercise on the Student CD.*

Figure 8-7.
The Residential Standard has been assigned four layer fields, two of which are optional and all of which have varying rules applied.

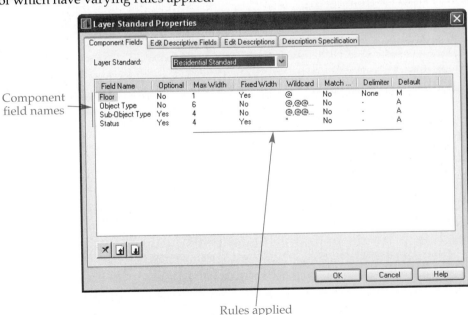

Component field names

Rules applied to fields

Chapter 8   Layer Management

Using the Edit Descriptive Fields Tab

The **Edit Descriptive Fields** tab is used to set up descriptive field names in the layer standard. *Descriptive field names* are different from the component field names created in the **Component Fields** tab. The descriptive fields are used in the **Edit Descriptions** tab, where layer names and descriptions are added to the layer standard. When a descriptive field name is created, a component field from the **Component Fields** tab is assigned to it. This ties the component field to the descriptive field used in the **Edit Descriptions** tab. See **Figure 8-8**.

A descriptive field is added to the **Field Name** column. The descriptive field can be a brief description of what the component field means in a layer name. For example, the Building Floor descriptive field in **Figure 8-8** indicates that the first part of the layer standard uses the Floor component field and designates the floor level in a layer name. Descriptive fields can also match the assigned component field name. For example, the Object Type descriptive field is assigned the Object Type component field.

To create descriptive field names, highlight the Default value descriptive field, and pick the **Add above the selected item** button to add a new descriptive field. Type a name and press [Enter]. After a descriptive field name is created, it needs to be assigned to one of the component fields created in the **Component Fields** tab. Under the column **Component 1**, pick the space that coincides with the descriptive field row you are editing. A list of component field names in the layer standard that can be assigned to the descriptive field is displayed. Select a component field from the list and move to the next descriptive field.

Additional component fields can be added to the same descriptive field by selecting the appropriate space below the **Component 2** column. This is most often done in layering systems where the layer names are hierarchical. Normally, one descriptive field is made for each component field.

Figure 8-8.
The **Edit Descriptive Fields** tab is used to create descriptive field names for use in the **Edit Descriptions** tab. Assign a component field name to a descriptive field name.

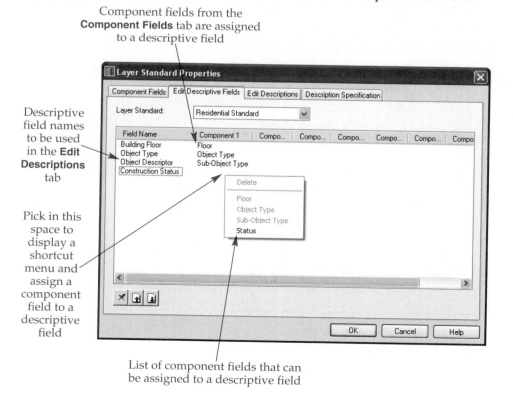

Component fields from the **Component Fields** tab are assigned to a descriptive field

Descriptive field names to be used in the **Edit Descriptions** tab

Pick in this space to display a shortcut menu and assign a component field to a descriptive field

List of component fields that can be assigned to a descriptive field

Architectural Desktop and Its Applications

Using the Edit Descriptions Tab

The **Edit Descriptions** tab is used to assign layer descriptions to each descriptive field. The *layer description* is the actual part of the layer used for the layer name. Each part (description) of the layer is assigned to a component field by means of the descriptive field. For example, the Construction Status descriptive field might have the descriptions New, Demo, Extg, and Phs1, which become a part of the Status component field. When a layer is created, the layer name is made up of descriptions for each component field, such as M-Walls-Demo.

To edit the descriptions, first access the **Edit Descriptions** tab, shown in Figure 8-9. At the top of the tab is the **Layer Standard:** drop-down list. The layer standard currently being modified is listed here. To the right is the **Field to Edit:** drop-down list. This list includes a list of the descriptive fields created in the **Edit Descriptive Fields** tab. Selecting a descriptive field from the list displays the layer component names and their descriptions.

Initially, the only description displayed is the value you entered in the **Default** column in the **Component Fields** tab. A layer component can have as many parts or descriptions as needed for the creation of new layer names. For example, in Figure 8-9, the Floor layer component field (Building Floor descriptive field), has six descriptions representing the six floor levels of a residential building. This allows the creation of M layers, U layers, and F layers, for example.

Figure 8-9.
The **Edit Descriptions** tab allows you to create and manage the parts (layer components) of a layer name and provide a description for each part.

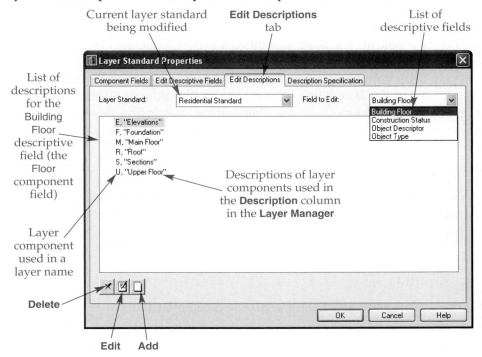

Figure 8-10.
The **Add Description** dialog box is used to enter layer component names and descriptions for each descriptive field.

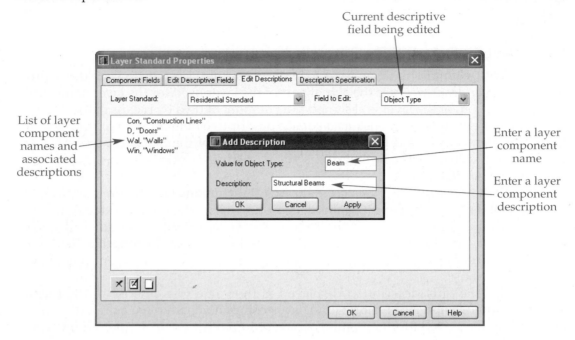

To add your own descriptions, select a descriptive field from the **Field to Edit:** drop-down list, in which to add components and descriptions. Select the **Add** button at the bottom of the tab. The **Add Description** dialog box, shown in **Figure 8-10,** is displayed. Enter a value in the **Value for** *component field***:** text box. This value is used in the creation of the layer name. In the **Description:** text box, enter a description for the layer part name. Pick the **Apply** button to enter the layer component name and the description beside it. Enter as many layer parts as needed when assembling layer names for your standard. When you are finished with one descriptive field, move to the next descriptive field in the **Field to Edit:** drop-down list, and create the layer component names and descriptions for that descriptive field.

When entering layer component field names, you are limited to the total number of characters specified in the **Max Width** column in the **Component Fields** tab. As you refine the layer standard, you can use the **Edit** button to edit the description for a layer component name. Use the **Delete** button to delete layer component names and descriptions.

NOTE

The layer standard is a *living document*. This means that it can continually be edited and updated to reflect your individual, industry, project, or office layering standards. Additional descriptions can be added or deleted as required.

Exercise
8-4   Complete the Exercise on the Student CD.

Using the Description Specification Tab

The **Description Specification** tab is used to configure how descriptions of layer names appear in the **Description** column of the **Layer Manager**. As component names are put together to form a layer name, the corresponding layer descriptions are also assembled and displayed in the **Description** column of the **Layer Manager**. The **Description Specification** tab controls how the descriptions are assembled.

This tab is divided into two columns. The first column, **Prior Text**, indicates a symbol used to separate the parts of a layer description. The **Field** column is used to organize the order in which the descriptions are created. Add a description field by selecting the **Add above the selected item** or **Add below the selected item** button. The first descriptive field is added to the list. Selecting the descriptive field allows you to choose a different descriptive field. In the **Prior Text** column, the word New is entered. When a layer is created, the word New precedes the description. To change this, pick the word New and press the [Backspace] key.

Additional descriptive fields can be entered, and a symbol or other text can precede the description. In **Figure 8-11**, the Building Floor descriptive field does not have a character for the prior text. The Object Type descriptive field has a colon placed in the **Prior Text** column. These settings create a description that displays the Building Floor description, a colon, and then the Object Type description. For example, Main Floor: Walls.

Exercise 8-5   *Complete the Exercise on the Student CD.*

When you are finished creating the layer standard, new layers can be established with the **Layer Manager**. Layer names can also be assigned to AEC objects through the layer key styles. Layer key styles are discussed later in this chapter. Keep in mind that the layer standard is created in the current drawing and is not a system setting. Layer standards can be imported into other drawings or into a template. Importing and exporting layer standards is discussed later in this chapter.

Figure 8-11.
The **Description Specification** tab is used to organize how the descriptions appear in the **Description** column of the **Layer Manager**.

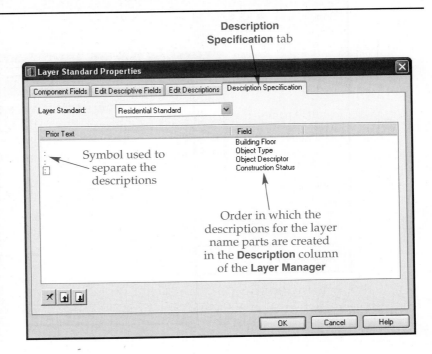

After layer standards are created, new layers can be established through the **Layer Manager** by selecting the **New Layer from Standard** button. See **Figure 8-12.** This displays the **New Layer From Standard** dialog box.

The current layer standard is displayed at the top of the **New Layer From Standard** dialog box. Depending on the layer standard selected, component fields are listed under the **Field** column. The **Value** column displays the default value set up in the **Layer Standard Properties** dialog box's **Default** column. Also included in the **Value** column is a set of ellipsis (...) buttons. There is one ellipsis (...) button for each component field. Selecting an ellipsis (...) button displays the **Choose a Pre-Specified Value** dialog box, shown in **Figure 8-13.**

A list of layer component names and their descriptions from the **Edit Descriptions** tab in the **Layer Standard Properties** dialog box is displayed. Select a description from the list to assemble the new layer name, and pick the **OK** button. This returns you to the **New Layer From Standard** dialog box, where the selected value is displayed in the **Value** column. As values are assembled, the layer name begins to take shape in the **Layer Name:** text box. Below the layer name, the description is also assembled in the **Description:** text box, based on the values selected from the ellipsis (...) buttons. The **Make Current** check box is used to set the newly created layer as the current layer in the drawing. When a layer is set current, new AutoCAD geometry is placed on the layer. This is not true for AEC Objects. AEC Objects are automatically placed on layers when they are created.

Figure 8-12.

The **New Layer From Standard** dialog box is used to create a new layer in the drawing based on layer standard rules.

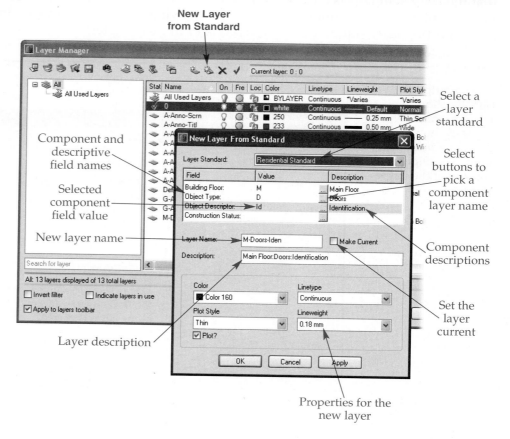

Figure 8-13.
The **Choose a Pre-Specified Value** dialog box displays a list of layer field component names and their descriptions for the ellipsis (...) button selected.

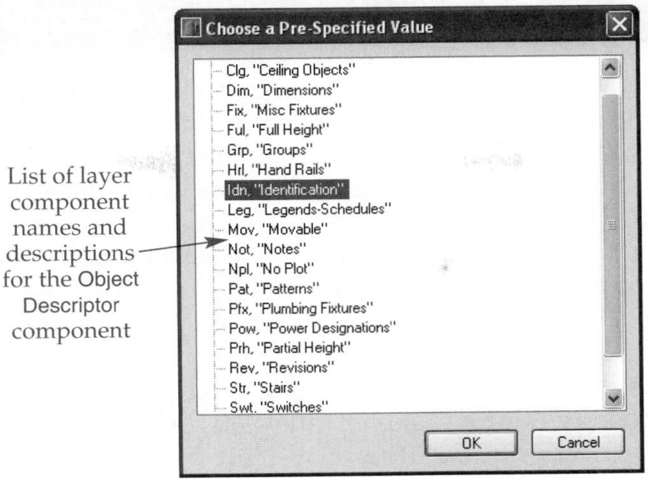

List of layer component names and descriptions for the Object Descriptor component

Choose a Pre-Specified Value

- Clg, "Ceiling Objects"
- Dim, "Dimensions"
- Fix, "Misc Fixtures"
- Ful, "Full Height"
- Grp, "Groups"
- Hrl, "Hand Rails"
- Idn, "Identification"
- Leg, "Legends-Schedules"
- Mov, "Movable"
- Not, "Notes"
- Npl, "No Plot"
- Pat, "Patterns"
- Pfx, "Plumbing Fixtures"
- Pow, "Power Designations"
- Prh, "Partial Height"
- Rev, "Revisions"
- Str, "Stairs"
- Swt, "Switches"

OK   Cancel

NOTE

Generally, new layers are created for geometry that is not an AEC object. As AEC objects are drawn, a predefined layer name is created, and the object is assigned to the layer through layer keys. Layer keys are discussed later in this chapter. In some cases, a new layer needs to be created for an AEC object that is placed on a different layer than desired.

At the bottom of the **New Layer From Standard** dialog box are drop-down lists to control the properties of the new layer. The new layer can be assigned a color, linetype, lineweight, and plot style (if style tables are being used) and can be a plotting or nonplotting layer. Checking the **Plot?** check box indicates that items drawn on the layer will plot. Once the layer name and properties have been specified, pick the **Apply** button to create the layer in the **Layer Manager**.

By default, whenever you start a new drawing, layer 0 is set as the current layer. Any non–AEC object drawn is placed on this layer. All drawn objects should be placed on a layer in your drawing, because this aids in controlling the visibility of objects in the drawing. For example, suppose you draw a few layout polylines. A layer named M-Constr can be used for the layout polylines. To do this, first create the layer, if it is not available. After the layer has been created and is listed in the **Layer Manager**, highlight the layer, right-click, and select the **Set current** option. Alternatively, double-click the layer; or highlight the layer, and then pick the **Set Current (Alt+C)** button in the **Layer Manager**. The layer is set current in Architectural Desktop, so any AutoCAD geometry is now drawn with this layer's properties. If an AEC object is drawn, it is automatically drawn and placed on a preset layer, regardless of the current layer.

Dialog Box
Layer Manager
✓
Set Current (Alt+C)

Exercise
8-6

Complete the Exercise on the Student CD.

A *layer filter group* is a routine that filters layers into groups meeting specific criteria. *Filter groups* can combine layers according to the state of the layer (on or off, frozen or thawed, and locked or unlocked), the layer properties, or the layer names. For example, a filter group can be created that includes all layers in the drawing using the yellow color. This is referred to as a properties filter type of layer filter group.

To create a properties filter group, pick the **New Property Filter (Alt+P)** button. The **Layer Filter Properties** dialog box, shown in Figure 8-14, is displayed. Enter a name for the filter group. Figure 8-14 shows the creation of a properties filter group with the name Color 231 Layers. The table at the top of the dialog box includes headings of properties that can be filtered. By picking in a cell under a property column, a filter criteria can be established. Property columns and how they are configured are described as follows:

- **Status.** Layers can be filtered by their current state. Selecting a cell in the **Status** column displays a drop-down list with two options. See Figure 8-15. This column filters layers based on whether they are used or unused. Select either the used (filled icon) or unused (unfilled icon) status.

- **Name.** This column is used to filter for layers with a particular name or part of a name. To filter for the beginning part of a layer name, enter the part of the layer name being filtered for in the cell in this column, followed by an asterisk (*). An asterisk is also known as a *wildcard character*. The wildcard indicates any additional layer name characters. For example, Figure 8-16 shows filtering for all layer names that begin with M. The wildcard indicates any additional characters after the M. Additionally, the wildcard can be used at the beginning, in the middle, or at the end of the filtered name. Figure 8-16 gives an example of a layer filter that looks for any layer with Anno in the name.

Dialog Box

Layer Manager

New Property
Filter (Alt+P)

Figure 8-14.
The **Layer Filter Properties** dialog box is used to set up a layering filter that looks for specific criteria. This filter is filtering layers assigned the color 231.

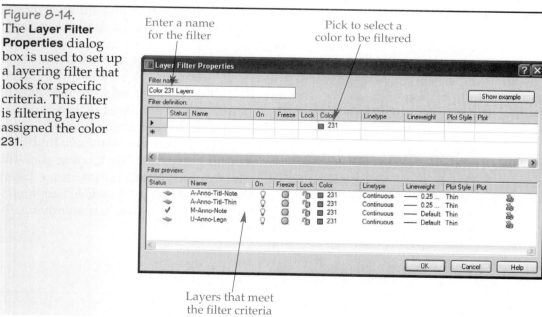

Enter a name for the filter

Pick to select a color to be filtered

Layers that meet the filter criteria

Figure 8-15.
The **Status** column allows you to filter for used or unused layers. Select an icon to add to the filter.

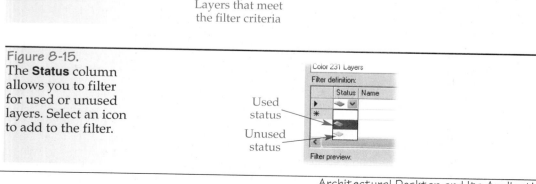

Used status

Unused status

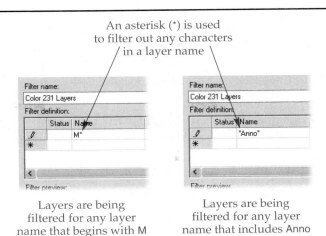

Figure 8-16.
The **Name** column filters for layer names or portions of layer names. The asterisk (*) is used to replace any layer name characters when filtering the layer names.

An asterisk (*) is used to filter out any characters in a layer name

Layers are being filtered for any layer name that begins with M

Layers are being filtered for any layer name that includes Anno

- **On.** This column is used to filter for layers that are either on or off. Picking a cell in the column displays on and off lightbulbs. Select the appropriate icon to filter for layers turned on or off. See **Figure 8-17.**
- **Freeze.** This column is used to filter for either thawed or frozen layers. Picking a cell in this column displays a snowflake and sunshine, representing frozen and thawed. Select the appropriate icon to filter for frozen or thawed layers. See **Figure 8-17.**
- **Lock.** This column is used to filter for either locked or unlocked layers. Picking a cell in this column displays a locked padlock and an unlocked padlock, representing locked and unlocked. Select the appropriate icon to filter for locked or unlocked layers. See **Figure 8-17.**
- **Color.** To filter layers by color, pick a cell in the **Color** column. This displays an ellipsis (...) button. Picking the ellipsis (...) button displays the **Select Color** dialog box. Select any color or enter a color number to be filtered. Pick **OK** after selecting the color to return to the **Layer Filter Properties** dialog box. See **Figure 8-18.**
- **Linetype.** To filter layers by specific linetypes, pick a cell in the **Linetype** column to display an ellipsis (...) button. Picking the ellipsis (...) button shows the **Select Linetype** dialog box. Select any linetype to be filtered. Pick **OK** after selecting the linetype to return to the **Layer Filter Properties** dialog box. See **Figure 8-18.**
- **Lineweight.** To filter layers by specific lineweights, pick a cell in the **Lineweight** column to display an ellipsis (...) button. Picking the ellipsis (...) button displays the **Lineweight** dialog box. Select any lineweight to be filtered. Pick **OK** after selecting the lineweight to return to the **Layer Filter Properties** dialog box. See **Figure 8-18.**

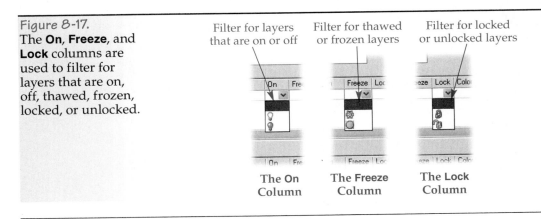

Figure 8-17.
The **On**, **Freeze**, and **Lock** columns are used to filter for layers that are on, off, thawed, frozen, locked, or unlocked.

Filter for layers that are on or off

Filter for thawed or frozen layers

Filter for locked or unlocked layers

The **On** Column

The **Freeze** Column

The **Lock** Column

Figure 8-18.
The **Color**, **Linetype**, **Lineweight**, and **Plot Style** columns are used to filter for layers using specific colors, linetypes, lineweights, and plot styles.

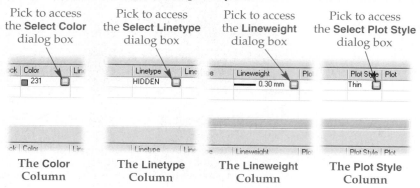

Pick to access the **Select Color** dialog box

Pick to access the **Select Linetype** dialog box

Pick to access the **Lineweight** dialog box

Pick to access the **Select Plot Style** dialog box

The Color Column

The Linetype Column

The Lineweight Column

The Plot Style Column

- **Plot Style.** To filter layers assigned specific plot styles, pick a cell in the **Plot Style** column to display an ellipsis (...) button. Picking the ellipsis (...) button displays the **Select Plot Style** dialog box. Select any plot style to be filtered. Pick **OK** after selecting the plot style to return to the **Layer Filter Properties** dialog box. See **Figure 8-18.**
- **Plot.** This column is used to filter for either plottable or nonplottable layers. Picking a cell in this column displays a printer and a printer with a slash, representing plottable or nonplottable. Select the appropriate icon to filter for layers that are plottable or nonplottable.

After establishing a filter, pick the **OK** button to create the filter group. The filter group name and a symbol are created in the left pane of the **Layer Manager**. See **Figure 8-19.** If the All group is selected, the list of filters also appears in the right pane. If a filter is selected from the list in the left pane, the filtered layers are displayed in the right pane. See **Figure 8-19.**

When the filter groups are displayed in the right pane, the entire group can be turned on or off, frozen or thawed, or locked or unlocked by picking the appropriate symbol in the right pane. Right-clicking a filter group in the left pane also displays a shortcut menu for the filter group. Selecting an option from the menu also allows you to turn on or off, freeze or thaw, or lock or unlock the layers in the filter group.

In addition to creating filters for individual properties, filters can be established by combining different properties. As a filtered property is added to the filter, a new row is added to the table below the previous filtered line, where additional filter criteria can be selected. In this manner, filters can be created for multiple colors; combinations of display properties, such as on and thawed; and combinations of color, linetype, and layer name.

Exercise 8-7

Complete the Exercise on the Student CD.

Figure 8-19.
After the filters are created, the filter group name is displayed in the left pane. Selecting a filter from the left pane displays the list of layers meeting the filter criteria.

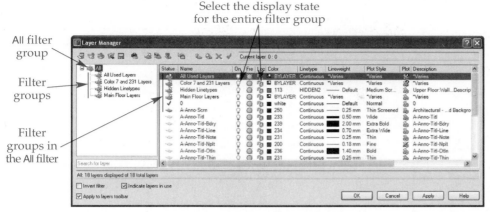

Displaying Filter Groups

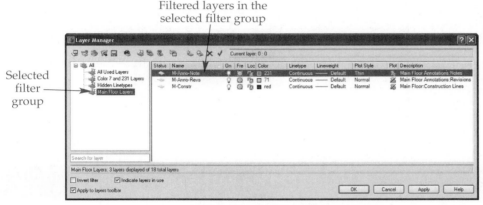

Selecting a Filter Group

Creating Group Filters

In addition to property filter groups, which automatically filter for specific property information, *group filters* can be created, which group together layers of your choice. To create a group filter, select the **New Group Filter (Alt+G)** button. A group filter is added in the left pane, where a name can be entered for the group.

Initially, the new group filter does not contain any layers. Select the All group to see a list of all the layers in the drawing. Highlight the layers to add to the new group filter. With the layers highlighted, drag and drop them from the right pane onto the group filter, and the layers are added to the group filter. See **Figure 8-20.** Pick the group filter in the left pane to display a list of layers in the right pane from the group filter.

Dialog Box
Layer Manager

New Group
Filter (Alt+G)

Figure 8-20.
After creating a new group filter, highlight the layers to be grouped together, and then drag them onto the group filter in the left pane.

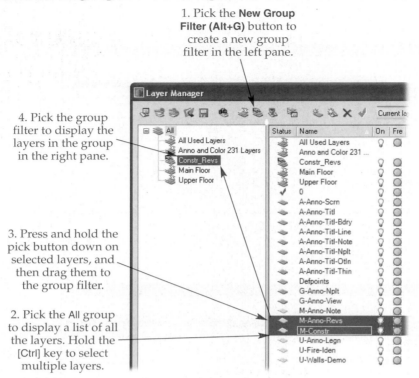

1. Pick the **New Group Filter (Alt+G)** button to create a new group filter in the left pane.

4. Pick the group filter to display the layers in the group in the right pane.

3. Press and hold the pick button down on selected layers, and then drag them to the group filter.

2. Pick the All group to display a list of all the layers. Hold the [Ctrl] key to select multiple layers.

Using Snapshots

A *snapshot* is similar to a photograph of a scene in time. The snapshot remembers the state of the layers at the time it is created, and it is used to reference these layers for other applications. A snapshot can be created within the drawing, with all the desired layers thawed, unlocked, and on, along with the appropriate color, linetype, and line-weight settings. After creating the snapshot, the layer properties can be changed to a single color, and the first floor walls can be frozen, with the exception of the reference layers. Another snapshot can then be created of the current state of the layers. The original layer properties can be restored at any time by selecting the snapshot from the **Snapshots** dialog box.

An example of when to use a snapshot is when you are creating a drawing and you need to reference objects on different layers, in relation to the items being drawn. Suppose you are drawing a second floor plan over the first floor plan as a guide. In this situation, the first floor layers need to be referenced, in order to know where to draw the second floor walls. Typically, all the first floor layers are frozen, except the first floor wall layer. The first floor wall layer is changed to a less distinctive color, locked, and used as a guide for drawing the upper floor walls. When the second floor has been completed, the first floor layers can be thawed, and any colors can be restored to their original properties.

If the design changes, the layers might need to be frozen or locked, and their colors might need to be changed back to a nondistinctive color again, so changes to the second floor can be made. This example is the basic idea behind the use of snap-shot aids in the process of freezing or thawing and changing colors, helping to save time managing the drawing. To create a snapshot, select the **Snapshots** button in the **Layer Manager**, which displays the **Snapshots** dialog box, shown in **Figure 8-21.** The **Snapshots** dialog box contains the following options:

Architectural Desktop and Its Applications

Figure 8-21.
The **Snapshots** dialog box is used to create snapshots of the states of the layers at the time the snapshot is created.

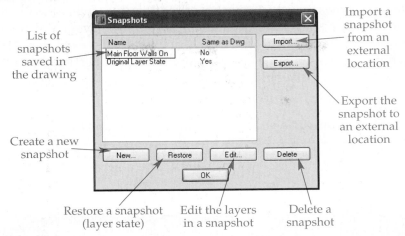

List of snapshots saved in the drawing

Import a snapshot from an external location

Export the snapshot to an external location

Create a new snapshot

Restore a snapshot (layer state)

Edit the layers in a snapshot

Delete a snapshot

- **New....** Enter a name for the new snapshot, and pick the **OK** button. This creates a new snapshot based on the current state of your layers.
- **Restore.** This button restores the state of the layers in a selected snapshot. First select the snapshot from the list, and then pick the **Restore** button.
- **Edit....** Snapshots can be edited after the snapshot has been taken. To do this, first select a snapshot you want to edit, and pick the **Edit...** button. The **Snapshot Edit:** *snapshot name* dialog box, shown in **Figure 8-22,** is displayed. Any property for a layer in this dialog box can be selected to change its state. Modifying any of the properties updates the snapshot. Layers can be added to or deleted from the snapshot by using the buttons in the lower left of the dialog box. This does not add new layers to or delete layers from the drawing.

Dialog Box

Layer Manager

Snapshots

Figure 8-22.
The **Snapshot Edit:** *snapshot name* dialog box is used to modify the properties of layers within a snapshot.

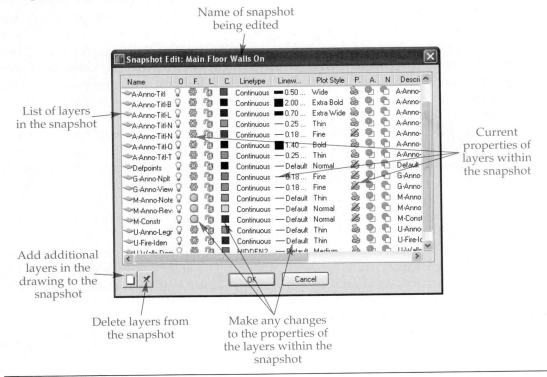

Name of snapshot being edited

List of layers in the snapshot

Current properties of layers within the snapshot

Add additional layers in the drawing to the snapshot

Delete layers from the snapshot

Make any changes to the properties of the layers within the snapshot

- **Delete.** Deletes the highlighted snapshot from the drawing.
- **Export....** Opens the **Create File** dialog box for snapshots. A snapshot and its layer property settings can be saved as an .ssl file for use in another drawing file.
- **Import....** Allows you to import a saved .ssl file created with the **Export...** option. When a snapshot .ssl file is imported, the layers and their properties are imported into the drawing, if they do not already exist there. If the current drawing contains the same layers with different properties, the imported snapshot becomes the current layer state.

Exercise 8-8   Complete the Exercise on the Student CD.

Creating and Using Layer Keys

As AEC objects are added to a drawing, predefined layers are created, and the objects are placed on these layers. This saves you the time of setting different layers current before you draw objects. Every AEC object and symbol included with Architectural Desktop has this automatic layering capability. A feature called *layer keys* is used for this process to work.

A layer key is the map between the layer standard and an AEC object. The layer key interprets the layer standard and assigns a layer to the object. For example, by default, the AIA layer standard and layer key style are used in new drawings started from the AEC model templates. A layer key named WALL is assigned to the wall object. Whenever a wall object is drawn, the layer key looks to the layer standard, creates a layer named A-Wall, and assigns the wall object to this layer.

Layer key styles can be created from scratch or by copying an existing layer key style and modifying it for your needs. They can be created and managed by accessing a layer key style from the **Style Manager**. See **Figure 8-23.** To access the layer key style within the **Style Manager**, pick **Format** > **Layer Management** > **Layer Key Styles...** or the **Layer Key Styles** button in the **Layer Manager**. The **Style Manager**, opened to the Layer Key Styles section, is displayed.

Pull-Down Menu
Format
> Layer
Management
> Layer
Key Styles...
Dialog Box
Layer Manager

Layer Key Styles

New layer key styles can be created by selecting the **New Style** button in the **Style Manager**. A new layer key style, which can be edited, is created in the Layer Key Styles list. Another way of creating a new layer key style is to copy and modify an existing style. This can save a lot of time, because the original layer key style has already been configured, and the copy can be modified very quickly.

To create a new layer key style based on an existing style, highlight Layer Key Styles in the left pane. In the right pane, select the layer key style to be copied and pick the **Copy** button in the **Style Manager**, or right-click and select **Copy**. After copying the existing style, right-click and select **Paste**, or pick the **Paste** button in the **Style Manager**. A new layer key style is created with the same name and the number 2 in parentheses. Right-clicking on the new style and selecting **Rename** from the shortcut menu allows the copied key style to be renamed.

Double-click the new style in the right pane to edit the style or select the style, right-click, and pick **Edit...** from the shortcut menu. The layer key style's properties are listed in the right pane, as shown in **Figure 8-24.** Layer key style properties include three tabs, the **General** tab, **Keys** tab, and **Version History** tab. The **General** tab is used to rename the key style and provide a description, such as the layer standard being referenced. The **Keys** tab includes a list of layer keys that Architectural Desktop uses

Figure 8-23.
The Layer Key Styles section of the **Style Manager** is used to create and manage layer key styles in the drawing.

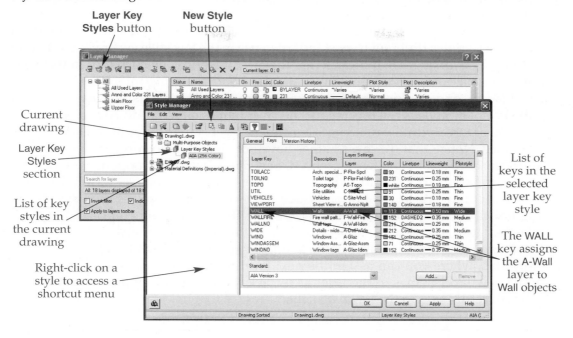

- **Layer Key Styles button**
- **New Style button**
- Current drawing
- Layer Key Styles section
- List of key styles in the current drawing
- Right-click on a style to access a shortcut menu
- List of keys in the selected layer key style
- The WALL key assigns the A-Wall layer to Wall objects

Figure 8-24.
A layer key style's properties include three tabs. The **Keys** tab is used to configure the layer and its properties, which are created automatically for AEC objects.

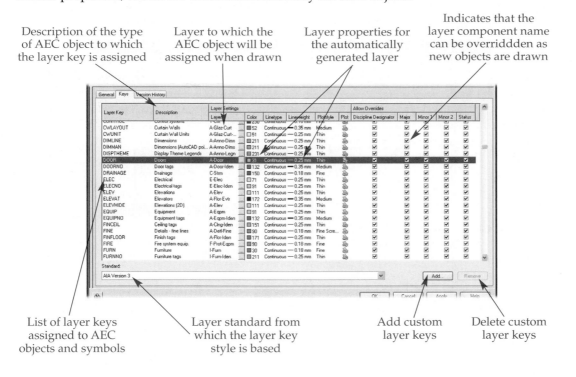

- Description of the type of AEC object to which the layer key is assigned
- Layer to which the AEC object will be assigned when drawn
- Layer properties for the automatically generated layer
- Indicates that the layer component name can be overriddden as new objects are drawn
- List of layer keys assigned to AEC objects and symbols
- Layer standard from which the layer key style is based
- Add custom layer keys
- Delete custom layer keys

for all the AEC objects and symbols and as properties for the automatic layers assigned to AEC objects. The **Version History** tab is used to keep track of different versions of key styles when synchronizing drafting standards.

At the bottom of the **Keys** tab is a drop-down list with the layer standards in the current drawing. The layer standard the layer key style is using is the default standard in the list. Selecting a different layer standard to use in the key style generates a warning dialog box. This dialog box indicates that the layer descriptions currently in the layer key style are based on an existing layer standard and changing might not match the selected layer standard. Pick the **Yes** button to proceed. This resets the layer standard that the layer key style is referencing for the layer names it assigns to AEC objects.

The layer key style now references a different layer standard for the creation of the layer names. Notice that the layer names have not changed; however, in **Figure 8-25**, the Residential Standard is now referenced, and the A-Door layer no longer stands for architectural doors, but for attic doors. To change the layer names for all the AEC objects, select the ellipsis (...) button beside the layer name to access the **Layer Name** dialog box. In the **Layer Name** dialog box, select the appropriate ellipsis (...) buttons beside the layer component name to assemble the new layer name. When you are finished assigning the new layer name to a layer key, pick the **OK** button to return to the **Keys** tab, where you can assign the next layer to the next layer key. After remapping the new layer names to the layer keys, pick the **OK** button in the **Style Manager**, which will return you to the **Layer Manager**.

Figure 8-25.
With the Residential Standard current, begin reassigning the layer names to the layer keys. Use the ellipsis (...) button for each layer to build the layer names.

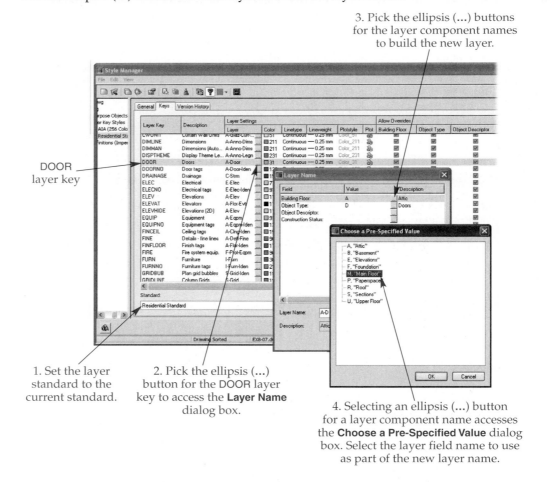

3. Pick the ellipsis (...) buttons for the layer component names to build the new layer.

DOOR layer key

1. Set the layer standard to the current standard.

2. Pick the ellipsis (...) button for the DOOR layer key to access the **Layer Name** dialog box.

4. Selecting an ellipsis (...) button for a layer component name accesses the **Choose a Pre-Specified Value** dialog box. Select the layer field name to use as part of the new layer name.

Architectural Desktop and Its Applications

NOTE Two additional buttons are available in the lower-right corner of the **Keys** tab. The **Add...** button allows the creation of additional layer keys in the key style. Assign new custom layer keys to custom symbols you create. When you are using a custom symbol, such as a lavatory symbol, the symbol can be inserted automatically on a layer using the new layer key. Creating symbols is covered in Chapter 9. Use the **Remove** button to remove custom layer keys that have been created. This button does not remove Architectural Desktop layer keys.

Before drawing new AEC objects, the new layer key style should be set current in the drawing. This is accomplished in the **Layering** tab of the **Drawing Setup** dialog box. See **Figure 8-26**. This dialog box is accessed by picking **Format** > **Drawing Setup...** or the **Open drawing menu** icon in the lower-left corner of the drawing screen to display the shortcut menu and selecting the **Drawing Setup...** command.

Once the **Drawing Setup** dialog box is opened, pick the **Layering** tab and select the appropriate layer key style from the **Layer Key Style:** drop-down list. Any new AEC object created should now be placed on the remapped layer name. When you are drawing items such as polylines, create a new layer for the polylines in the **Layer Manager**, set it current, and draw the polylines. If a layer is set current when you are drawing AEC objects, the layer is ignored, and the AEC object is placed on the layer designated by the layer key style.

NOTE When you are creating a new layer key style using a custom layer standard, it is recommended that a copy of an existing layer key style be created and modified. This saves time, because colors and linetypes have already been assigned, and all you need to do is update the layers assigned to the layer keys to match the desired custom layer standards.

 Exercise 8-9   Complete the Exercise on the Student CD.

Figure 8-26.
Select the layer key style to be used for new AEC objects created.

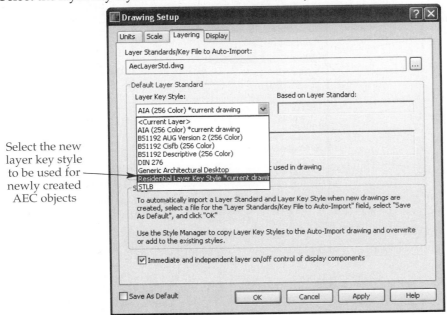

Select the new layer key style to be used for newly created AEC objects

Once a layer standard and layer key style have been created, any new AEC objects are placed on the layers designated by the layer key style. Through the use of *layer key overrides*, the layer on which an AEC object is drawn can be overridden. The preceding section created a layer key style for the Residential Standard. With this layer key style current, new AEC objects are placed on layers beginning with the letter *M*, which indicates the main floor. After you draw main floor walls, if the desire is to create objects using the upper floor (U-) layers, the layer key style needs to be overridden. Overriding the current layer key style allows any part of a layer name to be replaced. In this case, the M- layers are overridden with a U- to create layers such as U-Wall, U-Door, and U-Glaz.

Overriding a layer key can be accomplished by picking **Format** > **Layer Management** > **Layer Key Overrides...** or selecting the **Layer Key Overrides** button in the **Layer Manager**. This opens the **Layer Key Overrides** dialog box. See **Figure 8-27**.

The top of the **Layer Key Overrides** dialog box includes a drop-down list of the layer key styles in the drawing. The current layer key style is the default in this list. The list box in the center of the dialog box includes a list of the component and descriptive field names from the layer standard. The **Override** column includes an ellipsis (...) button for each field. Selecting an ellipsis (...) button for a component field accesses the **Choose a Pre-Specified Value** dialog box. This dialog box contains the descriptions for the selected component. Selecting a value from the list and picking the **OK** button sets the selected value as the override to the layer key style layer names.

Once an override has been selected, any new objects are created with the layer names from the layer key style, using the override substituted for any layer field names. For example, if the Upper Floor value is selected for the Building Floor component, any

Pull-Down Menu

Format
> Layer
Management
> Layer
Key Overrides...

Dialog Box

Layer Manager

Layer Key Overrides

Figure 8-27.
The **Layer Key Overrides** dialog box is used to override the different components of a layer name.

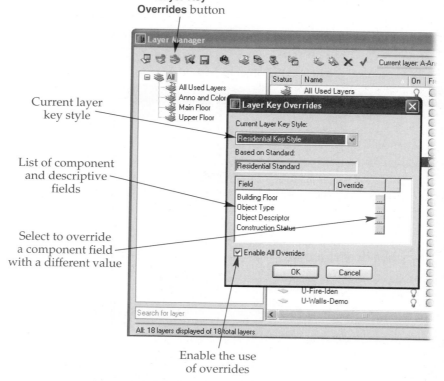

Layer Key
Overrides button

Current layer
key style

List of component
and descriptive
fields

Select to override
a component field
with a different value

Enable the use
of overrides

new objects created now substitute U- for the M- in the layer name. If a layer override has been set, it remains as the overriding value until the value is changed or the layer key overrides are turned off.

 NOTE The layer key style can be adjusted to never use an override for a component—for example, if there is a component field in the layer name that should never be overridden, such as the Object Type field in the Residential Standard. The **Allow Overrides** columns in the layer key style properties **Keys** tab include a check box for each field in a layer name. Unchecking a component field prohibits overrides from being set for the component.

After a layer key override has been set, the override can be turned off so AEC objects generate layers based on the layer key style again. Turning a layer key override off is accomplished by picking **Format** > **Layer Management** > **Overrides On/Off** or the **Layer Key Overrides** button in the **Layer Manager** and unchecking the **Enable All Overrides** check box in the **Layer Key Overrides** dialog box. The override can be turned back on again by selecting the **Overrides On/Off** command or placing the check mark in the box again.

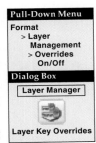

Pull-Down Menu
Format
> Layer
    Management
> Overrides
    On/Off

Dialog Box
Layer Manager

Layer Key Overrides

If objects have accidentally been drawn with an override or the layer key an object uses needs to be changed, the object can be remapped to a different layer key. When an object is remapped to a different layer key, the object takes on the properties, such as color and linetype, that the layer key is assigned in the layer key style. To remap a layer using a different layer key, pick **Format** > **Layer Management** > **Remap Object Layers** or type AECREMAPLAYERS. Once the **AECREMAPLAYERS** command is entered, the Command: prompt asks you to select the objects to re-layer and then to enter a layer key name or use the default layer key assigned to the object.

Type
AECREMAPLAYERS
Pull-Down Menu
Format
> Layer
    Management
> Remap Object
    Layers

AECREMAPLAYERS

The **?** option lists the layer keys available in the drawing. Press the [F2] key to review the list of layer keys in the AutoCAD text window, press [F2] again to return to the drawing screen, and enter the desired key. The **byObject** option can be used to remap an object that was drawn with an override and needs to be placed on the default layer key layer. This command can also be used on standard AutoCAD geometry to assign the geometry to an Architectural Desktop layer key.

 **Exercise 8-10** Complete the Exercise on the Student CD.

Using Layer Standards in Other Drawings

After a standard and key style have been created, you might want to use them in other drawings or future drawings.

Importing and Exporting Layer Standards

A layer standard can be imported into the current drawing by accessing the **Layer Standards** dialog box from the **Layer Manager**, shown in **Figure 8-4**. In the **Layer Standards** dialog box, select the **Import/Export...** button to display the **Import/Export Layer Standards** dialog box, shown in **Figure 8-28**. The left side of the **Import/Export Layer Standards** dialog box includes a list of layer standards in the current drawing. Use the **Open...** button to browse for a drawing that includes the layering standard to import. Once an external

Figure 8-28.
The **Import/Export Layer Standards** dialog box is used to import or export layer standards.

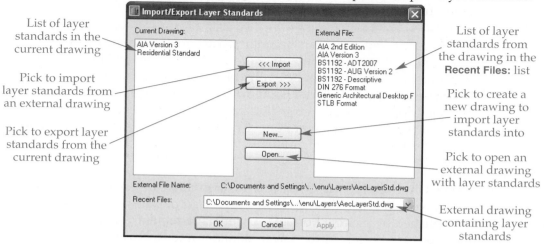

List of layer standards in the current drawing

Pick to import layer standards from an external drawing

Pick to export layer standards from the current drawing

List of layer standards from the drawing in the **Recent Files:** list

Pick to create a new drawing to import layer standards into

Pick to open an external drawing with layer standards

External drawing containing layer standards

drawing has been opened, a list of layer standards included in the external file is listed on the right. Select the layer standard or standards to be imported into the current drawing. Pick the **Import** button to import the standards into the current drawing.

A standard can also be exported to a new or existing drawing file. Select the layer standard or standards to export from the current drawing and pick the **Export** button to export the layer standard. When you are finished importing or exporting layer standards, pick the **OK** button to return to the **Layer Standards** dialog box. Layer standards that are not in use can be purged from the drawing by selecting the layer standard from the list and selecting the **Purge** button in the **Layer Standards** dialog box.

Importing and Exporting Layer Key Styles

Importing a layer standard is important for use in your drawing, but it is not very useful without the layer key style. Layer key styles can also be imported into the current drawing or exported to another drawing by accessing the **Style Manager** for layer keys. See **Figure 8-29.** Use the **Open Drawing** button to browse for the drawing containing the desired layer key style.

The newly opened drawing and the current drawing are listed in the left pane of the **Style Manager.** Expand the layer key styles in both drawings by picking the + symbols. To import or export a layer key style from one drawing to another, select the desired layer key style and drag and drop it to the desired file. In **Figure 8-29,** the Residential Key Style is selected from EX8-07.dwg and then dragged over the Chapter 08.dwg with the left mouse button and dropped. The Residential Key Style is then added to the current drawing. When you are finished importing a layer key style, close the drawing from which you imported the layer key style by right-clicking over the drawing name and selecting the **Close** option. The only thing left to do is set the layer key style current before adding any new AEC objects. Access the **Drawing Setup** dialog box to set the style current to ensure that the new objects are properly placed on the correct layers.

NOTE

> Layer standards, layer key styles, layers, and layer filters can be preset within a template drawing for future drawings. After setting up the drawing as desired, save the drawing as a drawing template file (.dwt). At the bottom of the **Save Drawing As** dialog box is the **Files of type:** drop-down list. Select the **AutoCAD Drawing Template (*.dwt)** option to save the current drawing with the layer settings as a template file that can be used in new drawings, or constructs, and views within a project.

Figure 8-29.
Open a drawing that contains the desired layer key style, and then drag and drop it onto the current drawing.

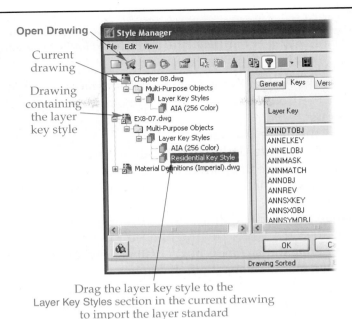

Open Drawing

Current drawing

Drawing containing the layer key style

Drag the layer key style to the
Layer Key Styles section in the current drawing
to import the layer standard

Chapter Test

Answer the following questions. Write your answers on a separate sheet of paper or complete the electronic chapter test on the Student CD.

1. Define, discuss, and give an example of using *layers* in Architectural Desktop.
2. What does it mean to say layers allow you visibility control over objects in the drawing?
3. What is a layer standard?
4. Define and give an advantage of *layer keys*.
5. Compare how layers are created and used in AutoCAD and Architectural Desktop.
6. Define *layer standards*, and give an example using the AIA layer standard.
7. Describe and give an example of an AIA layer standard discipline code.
8. Explain and give an example of an AIA layer standard major code.
9. Describe and give an example of an AIA layer standard minor code.
10. Explain and give an example of an AIA layer standard status code.
11. How are layers assigned to AEC objects as they are added to the drawing?
12. When you are drawing AutoCAD objects such as polylines, text, and dimensions, how are they assigned to layers?
13. What is the difference between descriptive field names and component field names?
14. What is the layer description?
15. Name the default layer when you start a new drawing.
16. How do you set a layer current?
17. Where is AEC geometry placed, regardless of the current layer?
18. Give the function of layer filter groups and give an example.
19. Identify the symbol used as a wildcard and the process to filter for a layer name, and give an example of the beginning parts of a layer name.
20. Give the basic function of group filters.
21. Define *snapshot* and give an example of its use.
22. Define and give an example of a *layer key*.
23. Give the function and an example of using a layer key override.
24. The newly opened drawing and the current drawing are listed in the left pane of the **Style Manager**. How do you expand the layer key styles in both drawings, and how do you import or export a layer key style from one drawing to another?
25. What is the last thing you need to do after importing a layer key style, before you can use it?

Chapter Projects

Use the techniques covered in this chapter to create the following drawings.

1. Single-Level Residential Project
   A. Access the **Project Browser** and set Residential-Project-01 current.
   B. Select the **Constructs** tab of the **Project Navigator** and open the Main Floor construct.
   C. Access the **Layer Manager**.
   D. In the **Snapshots** dialog box, create a new snapshot named Original Colors, and then exit the **Snapshots** dialog box.
   E. Right-click in the right pane of the **Layer Manager** and pick the **Select All** command.
   F. Change the colors of all the layers to a gray color and the linetypes of all the layers to DOT2. Note: You might need to load the DOT2 linetype.
   G. In the **Snapshots** dialog box, create a new snapshot named Overlay Colors, and then exit the **Snapshots** dialog box.
   H. Create a new group filter named Model Layers. Add the following layers to the filter: A-Door, A-Glaz, A-Wall, and A-Wall-Open.
   I. Create a new property filter named A Layers. Set the properties filter to filter for layer names beginning with A-*.
   J. Use the **Snapshots** dialog box to restore the Original Colors snapshot.
   K. Exit the **Layer Manager**. You might need to use the **OBJRELUPDATE** command to regenerate the objects in the drawing.
   L. Save and close the drawing.

2. Single-Level Residential Project
   A. Access the **Project Browser** and set Residential-Project-02 current.
   B. Select the **Constructs** tab of the **Project Navigator** and open the Main Floor construct.
   C. Access the **Layer Manager**.
   D. In the **Snapshots** dialog box, create a new snapshot named Original Colors, and then exit the **Snapshots** dialog box.
   E. Right-click in the right pane of the **Layer Manager** and pick the **Select All** command.
   F. Change the colors of all the layers to a gray color and the linetypes of all the layers to DOT2. Note: You might need to load the DOT2 linetype.
   G. In the **Snapshots** dialog box, create a new snapshot named Overlay Colors, and then exit the **Snapshots** dialog box.
   H. Create a new group filter named Model Layers. Add the following layers to the filter: A-Door, A-Glaz, A-Wall, and A-Wall-Open.
   I. Create a new property filter named A Layers. Set the properties filter to filter for layer names beginning with A-*.
   J. Use the **Snapshots** dialog box to restore the Original Colors snapshot.
   K. Exit the **Layer Manager**. You might need to use the **OBJRELUPDATE** command to regenerate the objects in the drawing.
   L. Save and close the drawing.

3. Two-Story Residential Project
   A. Access the **Project Browser** and set Residential-Project-03 current.
   B. Select the **Constructs** tab of the **Project Navigator** and open the Main Floor construct.
   C. Access the **Layer Manager.**
   D. In the **Snapshots** dialog box, create a new snapshot named Original Colors, and then exit the **Snapshots** dialog box.
   E. Right-click in the right pane of the **Layer Manager** and pick the **Select All** command.
   F. Change the colors of all the layers to a gray color and the linetypes of all the layers to DOT2. Note: You might need to load the DOT2 linetype.
   G. In the **Snapshots** dialog box, create a new snapshot named Overlay Colors, and then exit the **Snapshots** dialog box.
   H. Create a new group filter named Model Layers. Add the following layers to the filter: A-Door, A-Glaz, A-Glaz-Assm, A-Wall, and A-Wall-Open.
   I. Create a new property filter named A Layers. Set the properties filter to filter for layer names beginning with A-*.
   J. Use the **Snapshots** dialog box to restore the Original Colors snapshot.
   K. Exit the **Layer Manager.** You might need to use the **OBJRELUPDATE** command to regenerate the objects in the drawing.
   L. Save and close the drawing.
   M. Select the **Constructs** tab of the **Project Navigator** and open the Upper Floor construct.
   N. Access the **Layer Manager.**
   O. In the **Snapshots** dialog box, create a new snapshot named Original Colors, and then exit the **Snapshots** dialog box.
   P. Right-click in the right pane of the **Layer Manager** and pick the **Select All** command.
   Q. Change the colors of all the layers to a gray color and the linetypes of all the layers to DOT2. Note: You might need to load the DOT2 linetype.
   R. In the **Snapshots** dialog box, create a new snapshot named Overlay Colors, and then exit the **Snapshots** dialog box.
   S. Create a new group filter named Model Layers. Add the following layers to the filter: A-Glaz and A-Wall.
   T. Create a new property filter named A Layers. Set the properties filter to filter for layer names beginning with A-*.
   U. Use the **Snapshots** dialog box to restore the Original Colors snapshot.
   V. Exit the **Layer Manager.** You might need to use the **OBJRELUPDATE** command to regenerate the objects in the drawing.
   W. Save and close the drawing.

4. Two-Story Residential Project
   A. Access the **Project Browser** and set Residential-Project-04 current.
   B. Select the **Constructs** tab of the **Project Navigator** and open the Main Floor construct.
   C. Access the **Layer Manager**.
   D. In the **Snapshots** dialog box, create a new snapshot named Original Colors, and then exit the **Snapshots** dialog box.
   E. Right-click in the right pane of the **Layer Manager** and pick the **Select All** command.
   F. Change the colors of all the layers to a gray color, and the linetypes of all the layers to DOT2. Note: You might need to load the DOT2 linetype.
   G. In the **Snapshots** dialog box, create a new snapshot named Overlay Colors, and then exit the **Snapshots** dialog box.
   H. Create a new group filter named Model Layers. Add the following layers to the filter: A-Door, A-Glaz, A-Glaz-Assm, A-Wall, and A-Wall-Open.
   I. Create a new property filter named A Layers. Set the properties filter to filter for layer names beginning with A-*.
   J. Use the **Snapshots** dialog box to restore the Original Colors snapshot.
   K. Exit the **Layer Manager**. You might need to use the **OBJRELUPDATE** command to regenerate the objects in the drawing.
   L. Save and close the drawing.
   M. Select the **Constructs** tab of the **Project Navigator** and open the Upper Floor construct.
   N. Access the **Layer Manager**.
   O. In the **Snapshots** dialog box, create a new snapshot named Original Colors, and then exit the **Snapshots** dialog box.
   P. Right-click in the right pane of the **Layer Manager** and pick the **Select All** command.
   Q. Change the colors of all the layers to a gray color and the linetypes of all the layers to DOT2. Note: You might need to load the DOT2 linetype.
   R. In the **Snapshots** dialog box, create a new snapshot named Overlay Colors, and then exit the **Snapshots** dialog box.
   S. Create a new group filter named Model Layers. Add the following layers to the filter: A-Door, A-Glaz, and A-Wall.
   T. Create a new property filter named A Layers. Set the properties filter to filter for layer names beginning with A-*.
   U. Use the **Snapshots** dialog box to restore the Original Colors snapshot.
   V. Exit the **Layer Manager**. You might need to use the **OBJRELUPDATE** command to regenerate the objects in the drawing.
   W. Save and close the drawing.

5. Commercial Store Project
   A. Access the **Project Browser** and set Commercial-Project-05 current.
   B. Select the **Constructs** tab of the **Project Navigator** and open the Main Floor construct.
   C. Access the **Layer Manager**.
   D. Create a property filter group named Graphics Layers that filters for layer names beginning with G.
   E. Create a property filter group named Architectural Layers that filters for layer names beginning with A.
   F. Create a new group filter named Model Layers containing the A-Door, A-Glaz-Assm, and A-Wall layers.
   G. Create a snapshot of the current state of the layers and name it Original Layer Settings.
   H. Freeze the G-Anno-Nplt layer.
   I. Save and close the drawing.

6. Commercial Car Maintenance Shop Project
   A. Access the **Project Browser** and set Commercial-Project-06 current.
   B. Select the **Constructs** tab of the **Project Navigator** and open the Main Floor construct.
   C. Access the **Layer Manager.**
   D. Create a properties filter group named Graphics Layers that filters for layers beginning with G.
   E. Create a property filter group named Architectural Layers that filters for layer names beginning with A.
   F. Create a new group filter named Model Layers containing the A-Door, A-Glaz-Assm, A-Wall, and A-Wall-Open layers.
   G. Create a snapshot of the current state of the layers and name it Original Layer Settings.
   H. Freeze the G-Anno-Nplt layer.
   I. Save and close the drawing.
   J. Select the **Constructs** tab of the **Project Navigator** and open the Upper Floor construct.
   K. Access the **Layer Manager.**
   L. Create a property filter group named Graphics Layers that filters for layer names beginning with G.
   M. Create a property filter group named Architectural Layers that filters for layer names beginning with A.
   N. Create a new group filter named Model Layers containing the A-Glaz-Assm and A-Wall layers.
   O. Create a snapshot of the current state of the layers and name it Original Layer Settings.
   P. Freeze the G-Anno-Nplt layer.
   Q. Save and close the drawing.

7. Governmental Fire Station
   A. Access the **Project Browser** and set Gvrmt -Project-07 current.
   B. Select the **Constructs** tab of the **Project Navigator** and open the Main Floor construct.
   C. Access the **Layer Manager.**
   D. Create a property filter group named Graphics Layers that filters for layer names beginning with G.
   E. Create a group filter named Model Layers containing the A-Door, A-Glaz-Assm, A-Wall, and A-Wall-Open layers.
   F. Create a snapshot of the current state of the layers and name it Original Layer Settings.
   G. Freeze the G-Anno-Nplt layer.
   H. Save and close the drawing.

Autodesk is the company that makes Architectural Desktop. The Autodesk Web site (www.autodesk.com) has many resources for using Autodesk products. This site contains information about Autodesk products, ADT discussion groups, product support, and more.

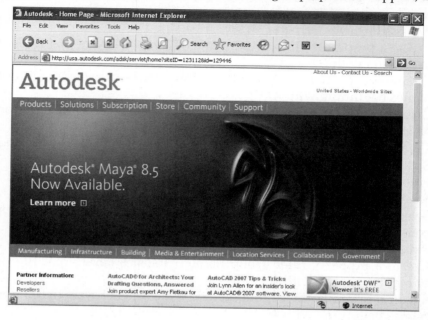

<blockquote><p>CHAPTER 9</p></blockquote>

Architectural Blocks

Learning Objectives

After completing this chapter, you will be able to do the following:

- ✓ Use **DesignCenter**™.
- ✓ Organize design content.
- ✓ Insert documentation blocks.
- ✓ Create standard AutoCAD blocks.
- ✓ Use the **INSERT** command.
- ✓ Create, use, and modify multi-view blocks.
- ✓ Produce mask blocks.
- ✓ Add custom blocks to **DesignCenter**.
- ✓ Add blocks to tool palettes.
- ✓ Create AEC profiles.

Architectural symbols are used to represent various architectural features, such as electrical connections, plumbing fixtures, and doors. Symbols can represent any type of item or feature. In AutoCAD, these symbols can be created as blocks. A *block* is a group of individual lines, arcs, and circles constructed together to form a single object. Once a block is created, it can be stored for further use and inserted as many times as needed into any drawing. For example, blocks that look like a sink and shower can be created and then used repeatedly in drawings.

Architectural Desktop builds on the standard AutoCAD block principle with multi-view blocks, which are made from standard blocks, **Figure 9-1**. A *multi-view block* is an Architectural Desktop block that is comprised of one or more individual blocks and appears different when viewed from different angles. It is similar to an AEC object because it can be displayed as a 2D block in a Top view, as a 2D elevation block in an elevation view, and as a 3D block in a Model view or an isometric view. Architectural Desktop includes many multi-view blocks that can be used in either imperial or metric drawings. **DesignCenter** is used to access these available multi-view blocks.

Figure 9-1.
Multi-view blocks appear differently, depending on the direction from which you view them.

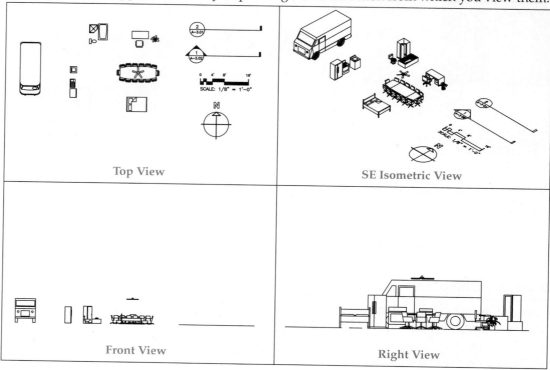

| Top View | SE Isometric View |
| Front View | Right View |

DesignCenter

DesignCenter is a powerful drawing information manager that provides an easy tool for accessing Architectural Desktop multi-view blocks, standard blocks, and content from another drawing and from the Internet. See **Figure 9-2.** Content from **DesignCenter** can be added to a drawing by dragging and dropping it into the drawing.

Using DesignCenter

There are two types of multi-view blocks: design blocks and documentation blocks. *Design blocks* represent real-world architectural objects, such as plumbing fixtures, furniture, and casework. Design blocks are full scale, so a bathtub block inserted into the drawing is displayed at its actual size. *Documentation blocks* are used to document the drawings, such as detail bubbles, revision clouds, and drawing tags. Documentation blocks are scaled to a plotted sheet of paper. When documentation blocks are inserted into model space, they are scaled at the drawing's scale, but if the documentation blocks are inserted into layout space, they are inserted at full scale. Each of these types of blocks can be found in their respective folders within **DesignCenter**.

DesignCenter can be accessed by picking **Insert** > **DesignCenter**, picking the **DesignCenter** button in the **Navigation** toolbar, typing DC or ADC, or pressing [Ctrl]+[2]. By default, **DesignCenter** is opened to the **AEC Content** tab. This tab includes a list of multi-view blocks included with Architectural Desktop; the blocks can be found by browsing through the folders. If other tabs are used, the next time **DesignCenter** is opened, the last tab accessed is the default tab.

DC

| Type |
| DC |
| ADC |
| [Ctrl]+[2] |
| Pull-Down Menu |
| Insert |
| > DesignCenter |
| Toolbar |
| Navigation |
| DesignCenter |

Figure 9-2.
DesignCenter is used to browse for multi-view blocks and other content that can be used in your drawing.

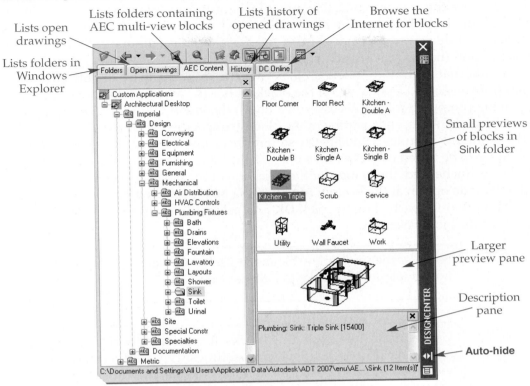

Inserting Design Blocks from DesignCenter

When **DesignCenter** is first accessed, it is displayed in the center of the screen with a title bar along one edge and looks similar to other palettes with which you are familiar. **DesignCenter** and the panes within it can be resized, and as with the other palettes, **DesignCenter** includes the **Auto-hide** feature, which hides the palette when the cursor is not over the palette.

The left pane of **DesignCenter** is used to browse through the folders of multi-view blocks. Pick a folder in the left pane to display a list of blocks in the right pane. Continue picking folders until small previews of the blocks are displayed in the right pane.

Picking one of these preview icons from the preview pane, which is on the top of the right side, displays a larger preview of the block on the lower right side of the palette. This larger preview pane allows you to spin the block around using 3D orbit by moving the mouse into the pane, picking, and moving the cursor. Right-clicking in the larger preview pane displays a shortcut menu from which different visual styles and views can be selected. Below the large preview pane is a description pane. This pane displays a description of the selected block.

NOTE

> The ability to orbit around the large preview and to select different views and visual styles is only available when viewing blocks in the **AEC Content** tab.

When you find the block you want in your drawing, pick the block's small icon in the top right preview pane and, while holding the mouse button, drag and drop the block into the drawing. Release the mouse button to insert, or drop, the block. The **MOVE** command can then be used to place the block in the correct location. You can also select **Insert...** from the shortcut menu in the **AEC Content** tab or **Insert as Block...** from the shortcut menu in the **Folders** tab.

Some of the blocks require that a value, such as a rotation angle, be entered after they have been inserted. Read the Command: prompt to see what type of information Architectural Desktop requests. If you are prompted for a rotation angle, enter the angle or move the cursor to pick the angle. Each multi-view block is assigned to a layer based on the layer key, and the block is inserted on this layer. If the block has been inserted and this layer does not exist in the drawing, it is automatically added to the drawing, and the block is placed on that layer.

An alternative way to insert a block into the drawing is by double-clicking the small preview icon. Depending on the block, either the **Insert** dialog box is displayed, or you are prompted for the necessary values. If the **Insert** dialog box is displayed, the insertion point, scale, and rotation of the block are specified within it, **Figure 9-3.** Each of these options includes a **Specify On-screen** check box. Picking this check box allows the values to be typed or picked on screen as the block is inserted into the drawing. If this box is unchecked, the values for the insertion of the block are set in the dialog box. If the **Explode** option at the bottom of the dialog box is selected, the block is exploded into its individual parts. Finally, pick **OK** and select the point in the drawing where you want the block inserted.

NOTE

Some of the multi-view blocks in **DesignCenter** are 2D blocks that do not appear as 3D blocks in a Model view.

NOTE

Use caution when exploding blocks. If a multi-view block is exploded, it loses its 2D and 3D display capabilities. Typically, a standard multi-view block is composed of standard blocks and other AEC objects. When exploded, these pieces are no longer grouped together. What is left of the block depends on the current view being used when a multi-view block is exploded. The individual block used by the current view is what remains of the multi-view block. For example, if you are viewing the multi-view block in the Top view and it is exploded, the 2D Top view block is the block that remains. If this block is then viewed from an isometric direction, the 2D block is displayed instead of the 3D block.

Figure 9-3.

The **Insert** dialog box is used to insert standard blocks into the drawing.

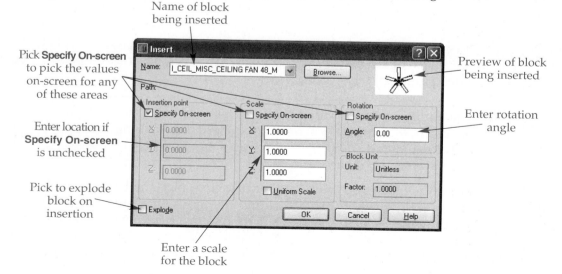

Exercise 9-1 Complete the Exercise on the Student CD.

Inserting Documentation Blocks from DesignCenter

NOTE When you are calculating the scale factor, recall that, for a scale of 1/4″ = 1′-0″,

$$1/4″ \times \text{scale factor} = 1′\text{-}0″, \text{ or}$$
$$1/4″ \times \text{scale factor} = 12″.$$

By dividing both sides by 1/4″, we have

$$\text{scale factor} = 12″ \div 1/4″.$$

Both measurements are in inches, which means the units cancel one another, so

$$\text{scale factor} = 12 \div 1/4.$$

This is the same thing as

$$\text{scale factor} = 12 \times 4, \text{ so}$$
$$\text{scale factor} = 48.$$

As mentioned previously, documentation blocks are inserted into the drawing by the drawing scale. To set the drawing scale, use the **Drawing Setup** dialog box as discussed in Chapter 2. After the scale factor has been determined and applied to the drawing, any documentation blocks you insert are scaled by this scale factor.

NOTE Additional content can be found in the **Documentation Tool Catalog-Imperial** (or **Metric**) within the **Content Browser**. Content from these catalogs can be dragged and dropped to your tool palettes. Refer to Appendix B for information on customizing tool palettes and the **Content Browser**.

Similar to the design blocks, documentation blocks can be added to the drawing by the drag-and-drop technique, by double-clicking the small preview icon in **DesignCenter**, or by right-clicking over the small preview and selecting **Insert...** from the shortcut menu. If documentation blocks are being accessed from the **Annotation** tool palette, the drag-and-drop technique or picking the icon once can be used to insert these blocks. Many of the documentation blocks include a routine for the block. For example, a Title Mark block prompts you to fill out the bubble values and to select points for the line under the title of the drawing. A Revision Cloud block prompts you to select a starting point and an endpoint for the revision cloud. It is very important to read the Command: prompt to see what information Architectural Desktop needs. These blocks are also automatically placed on a layer designated by the layer key style.

Many of the blocks have values that are variable. When inserting a documentation block that prompts you for a value, type the desired value. These values are known as *attributes*. To change the attribute value for a block after it has been inserted, double-click on the block to access the **Enhanced Attribute Editor**, shown in Figure 9-4. This dialog box allows in-depth modification of attributes within blocks, including properties such as the attribute values, the text height, and the color. Use the **Attribute** tab of the **Enhanced Attribute Editor** to modify the value of attributes within the block; select an attribute from the table and enter a new value for it. When you are finished modifying the attribute values, pick **OK** to close the dialog box. The new values are now displayed in the documentation block.

Figure 9-4.
The **Enhanced Attribute Editor** is used to modify the values of attributes in a block. Double-click a block with attributes to access the **Enhanced Attribute Editor** and modify the values.

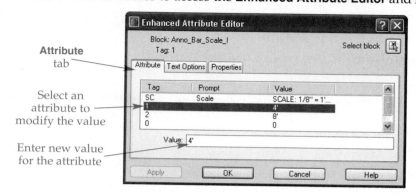

Attribute tab

Select an attribute to modify the value

Enter new value for the attribute

"Smart" documentation blocks known as *callouts* are available in the **Callouts** tab of the **Document** tool palette group and in the **Documentation Tool Catalog – Imperial** (or **Metric**) catalogs. All of the callout blocks include attributes with a gray highlight around the text. This type of attribute is known as a *field*, or automatic text. A field is linked to a construct, view drawing, or sheet drawing, and it changes as the value of that object changes. For example, a detail mark inserted into the drawing contains fields for the detail number and the sheet number. Initially, these values are generic.

Many of the callout tools are followed by a series of prompts for locations or values. Depending on the callout block selected, the **Place Callout** worksheet may be displayed. See **Figure 9-5.** This worksheet is associated with the detail, section, and elevation callout blocks. It is used to establish settings for the creation of sections, partial sections, and elevations. These options are discussed in greater detail in Chapters 19 and 20. If you only want to place a detail, a section, or an elevation mark, pick the **Callout Only** button at the top of the **Place Callout** worksheet. This adds the block to the drawing with fields in the block that are referenced when creating sheet drawings, which is described in Chapter 24.

Figure 9-5.
Callout blocks include automatic fields that link to other drawings. Double-clicking a field value displays the **Enhanced Attribute Editor**, from which you can edit fields.

Pick to add callout without linking it to other drawings

Settings for creating partial sections, building sections, and elevations

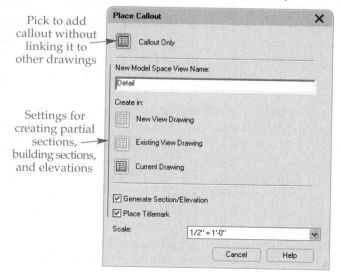

Figure 9-6.

Figure 9-6.
The **Place Callout** worksheet is used to establish settings used by the callout block and begin preliminary linking between the callout and other drawings.

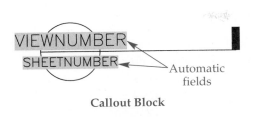

VIEWNUMBER

SHEETNUMBER ← Automatic fields

Callout Block

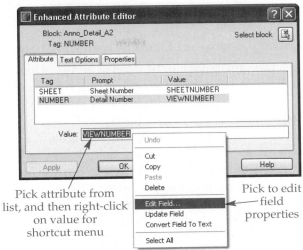

Pick attribute from list, and then right-click on value for shortcut menu

Pick to edit field properties

Double-clicking the field value in a callout block displays the **Enhanced Attribute Editor**, Figure 9-6. Entering a new value for the field being edited disables the automatic text value and breaks the link to other drawings being referenced. Right-clicking over the field value in the **Enhanced Attribute Editor** displays a shortcut menu where the field can be edited.

The advantage of using fields within the documentation blocks is that the field, which may be the detail or section number, the sheet number, or the drawing name, is automatically filled out when dragging model space views onto a sheet. If the model space view name changes or the sheet drawing changes, fields adjust automatically, which means your drawings are always accurate.

PROFESSIONAL TIP

If you are using the **Project Navigator** to manage the drawings within a project, it is highly recommended that you do not manually change the value of automatic fields, because this breaks the links to other drawings and views. Allow the **Project Navigator** to fill in the values as the project is put together. If you are not using the **Project Navigator** to manage the drawings in your project, you need to manually fill in the automatic field values and coordinate the detail and section numbers and title names.

NOTE

Documentation blocks that include text are inserted using the current text style. If a specific type of font is to be used for documentation blocks, create a text style and set it current before adding the blocks. Creating a text style is covered in Chapter 11. The **Text Options** tab in the **Enhanced Attribute Editor** can also be used to change the text style used by the block.

Exercise 9-2   Complete the Exercise on the Student CD.

Using Additional DesignCenter Features

DesignCenter can be used to access other parts of existing drawings besides blocks, and these parts can be added to the current drawing. Items such as layers, layouts, dimension styles, text styles, and linetypes can be brought from existing drawings in other locations, such as a hard drive, network drive, floppy disk, CD, or Zip drive, and placed in the current drawing. Navigate within the tabs of **DesignCenter** to find these other drawings. The tabs are as follows:

- **Folders.** This tab is used to browse for drawings in other drives, Figure 9-7. The left pane is used to browse through folders in a way similar to that of Windows Explorer. Blocks, dimension styles, layers, layouts, linetypes, table styles, text styles, and xrefs from another drawing can all be dragged and dropped into the current drawing.

NOTE

Unlike the Architectural Desktop blocks in the **AEC Content** tab, if blocks are dragged and dropped into the drawing from an existing drawing, the blocks are inserted on the current layer.

AutoCAD hatch and image files can also be viewed and inserted into the drawing from **DesignCenter** using similar methods. Read the Command: prompts to properly insert these types of objects. Hatch files have the file extension .pat. Image files include files with the extensions .bmp, .tga, .jpg, .pcx, .gif, and .tif.

Figure 9-7.
The **Folders** tab allows you to browse through folders to look for a drawing that includes parts of a drawing that you would like to use in the current drawing.

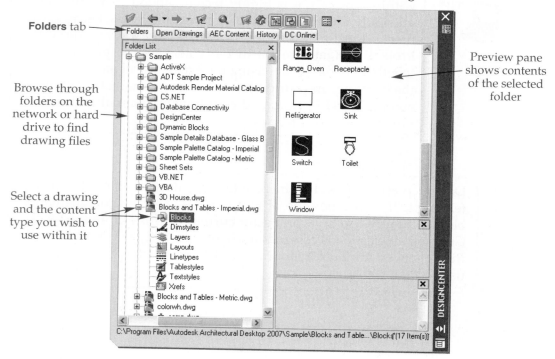

- **Open Drawings.** This tab displays a list of drawings currently open in Architectural Desktop. Objects can be dragged from one open drawing and dropped into the current drawing.
- **AEC Content.** This tab displays a list of the Architectural Desktop multi-view blocks and their organized folders.
- **History.** This tab lists a history of drawings that have been accessed in Architectural Desktop. Double-clicking a drawing from the list displays the **Folders** tab with the drawing file open. Select items from the drawing that you want to use.
- **DC Online.** This tab provides access to 2D and 3D blocks and manufacturers who may have additional content available on the Internet, **Figure 9-8.** Blocks can be added to your drawing by dragging and dropping through i-drop technology. If a Web site contains a block that can be added to the drawing, the i-drop icon, which is a small eyedropper, is displayed over the preview. Dragging and dropping the block into your drawing downloads the block from the Internet and inserts it into the drawing. The **Standard Parts** section contains blocks that can be inserted from the Internet, and the **Manufacturers** section allows you to connect with manufacturers' Web sites, from which you can drag and drop blocks into your drawing.

NOTE

Many of the blocks available are standard blocks, not multi-view blocks. Multi-view blocks can be created from manufacturer's blocks and added to the **Custom** tab library of blocks. Creating a multi-view block and adding it to **DesignCenter** is covered later in this chapter.

Figure 9-8.
The **DC Online** tab provides access to blocks and manufacturer Web sites with content that can be used in your drawings.

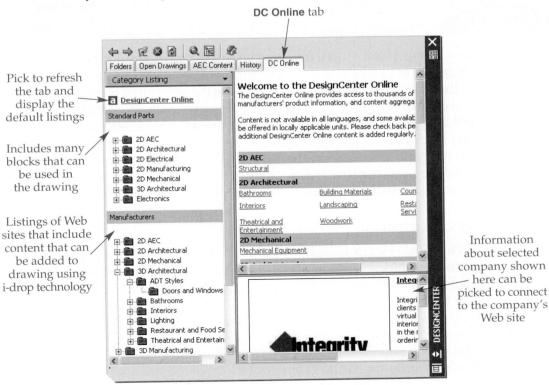

Figure 9-9.
These buttons
provide
management tools
for working with
DesignCenter.

Additional Web sites that contain downloadable blocks may be found through an Internet search for "AutoCAD blocks" or "AutoCAD symbols." Often, these are standard blocks, but they can also be given a multi-block view definition.

In addition to the tabs within **DesignCenter**, a series of buttons is included across the top of the dialog box that is used to help manage the dialog box, **Figure 9-9.** Many of these buttons operate like the similar buttons in Window Explorer. However, there are a few unfamiliar ones. The **Tree View Toggle** button controls the display of the left pane, turning it on and off. The **Preview** button controls the display of the large preview window, toggling it on and off. The **Description** button controls the display of the description pane in a similar way. The **Views** button includes a drop-down list that controls how the icons appear in the small preview pane. The information in this pane can be viewed as large icons, small icons, or a list with or without the details of the content.

NOTE

Remember that blocks inserted from the **AEC Content** button are inserted with an appropriate layer. Documentation blocks inserted from the **AEC Content** tab are also scaled by the drawing scale. Blocks accessed from drawings found in the **Folders** and **DC Online** tabs are inserted on the current layer at the drawn scale.

Creating Standard AutoCAD Blocks

A block is a group of individual objects constructed together to represent a single object. The advantage of blocks is that a single group of objects is drawn once and used many times in the drawing without having to recreate the individual pieces of geometry. Once a block is created, it can be inserted into a drawing with the **INSERT** command or dragged and dropped from **DesignCenter**. There are a few differences between standard AutoCAD blocks and Architectural Desktop blocks. Standard AutoCAD blocks are inserted on the current layer and reflect either 2D or 3D objects, depending on how the original geometry was constructed. Architectural Desktop blocks are inserted onto predefined layers and are displayed as 2D in a Top view and as 3D in a Model view.

Block Creation Criteria

Standard AutoCAD blocks form the basis of an Architectural Desktop multi-view block. The multi-view block is made up of individual 2D and 3D blocks to form the AEC object. Before a multi-view block can be assembled, existing AutoCAD blocks must exist. The following section gives the steps used to make a standard block, and creating a multi-view block is discussed later. Before drawing a block, the following criteria must be determined:

- On which layer should the geometry within the block be created?
- What color should the initial geometry be?
- What linetype should the initial geometry have?
- What lineweight should the initial geometry have?

- What plot style (if .stb tables are being used) should the initial geometry use?

When standard blocks are inserted into a drawing, they are placed on the layer that is current at the time the block is inserted, unless a block is inserted from the **AEC Content** tab in **DesignCenter**. If the initial block geometry was drawn on layer 0, the block is placed on the current layer and is displayed with the color and linetype of the current layer when inserted. If the geometry for the block was created on a layer *other* than 0, the geometry in the block belongs to the current layer *and* to the layer on which the initial geometry was created. To avoid having the geometry attached to two layers, the initial geometry *should* be created on layer 0.

After establishing the initial geometry layer, determine the block color, linetype, lineweight, and plot style. If the block geometry is drawn with a color, linetype, lineweight, or plot style other than **ByLayer** or **ByBlock**, those properties are displayed in the block, overriding the color, linetype, lineweight, and plot style of the layer where the block is inserted. Drawing the initial geometry with a color, linetype, lineweight, and plot style different from the layer 0 properties is least desirable, because most situations rely on the layer to designate the properties for the block. When block geometry is created with a **ByLayer** color, linetype, lineweight, or plot style, it is displayed with the color, linetype, lineweight, and plot style of the layer where the block is inserted. When you are trying to change the color, linetype, lineweight, or plot style of the block, the properties do not change, because the geometry looks for the color, linetype, lineweight, and plot style of the layer where it is inserted. If the **ByLayer** properties are used to construct the block geometry, set the properties current in the **Properties** toolbar. See **Figure 9-10**. This toolbar can be accessed by right-clicking over any existing toolbar to display the toolbars list. Select **Properties** from the menu to display the toolbar.

Another option for block geometry properties is **ByBlock**. When objects are drawn with a **ByBlock** color, linetype, lineweight, or plot style, the block is inserted on the current layer and assumes the properties of the layer, as with the **ByLayer** option, but the color, linetype, lineweight, and plot style of the block can be changed through the **Properties** palette. This is the preferred method of creating blocks for use in Architectural Desktop. The **ByBlock** colors, linetypes, lineweights, and plot styles in a block can be overridden when tying a block into an Architectural Desktop multi-view block. Set the color, linetype, lineweight, and plot style drop-down lists to **ByBlock** before creating geometry for a block.

Creating the Block Components

Prior to drawing the geometry for use in a block, set layer 0 as the current layer and the **ByBlock** color, linetype, lineweight, and plot style current in the drop-down lists. This ensures that the geometry within the block can be used in standard blocks and multi-view blocks. Next, draw the geometry of the block symbol using polylines, arcs, circles, or AEC objects such as walls, doors, or windows.

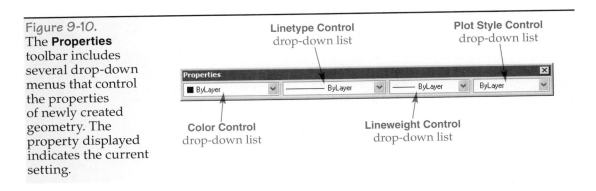

Figure 9-10. The **Properties** toolbar includes several drop-down menus that control the properties of newly created geometry. The property displayed indicates the current setting.

Linetype Control drop-down list

Plot Style Control drop-down list

Color Control drop-down list

Lineweight Control drop-down list

Blocks are inserted into the drawing at the insertion point. When a block is dragged and dropped or inserted, the block is attached to the crosshairs at the insertion point on the block, which is a logical point on the block. The insertion point should be determined before grouping the geometry together and is specified at the time the block is created. **Figure 9-11** displays a few blocks with their insertion points identified. Notice that the insertion point does not need to be drawn and is usually specified using object snaps.

Creating Blocks

Once the geometry for the block has been drawn, a block symbol can be created. The **BLOCK** command can be accessed by picking **Format > Blocks > Block Definition...** or typing BLOCK or B at the Command: prompt. This displays the **Block Definition** dialog box shown in **Figure 9-12.** Use the following steps to create a block:

1. In the **Name:** text box, type a name for the block, such as Corner-Spa. The name cannot exceed 255 characters and can include numbers, letters, spaces, dollar signs, hyphens, and underscores. The block name can be a description of the block or a series of numbers and letters indicating the type of symbol the block represents.

2. The **Base point** area is used to specify the insertion point for the block. Select the **Pick point** button to use the crosshairs to select an insertion point. Remember, this is the point where the block is attached to the crosshairs when inserted in the drawing.

3. The **Objects** area is used to select geometry grouped together in the block definition. Pick the **Select objects** button to return to the drawing screen, and use the crosshairs to select the geometry for the block definition. Press [Enter] when you are finished selecting geometry. The **Block Definition** dialog box reappears, and the number of objects selected is shown in the **Objects** area.

4. The **Objects** area also includes three options for controlling the original geometry selected. The **Retain** radio button retains the original objects on the drawing screen. The **Convert to block** radio button is used to convert the

Figure 9-11.
A few symbols that have been created as blocks are shown. Note that the insertion point has been located.

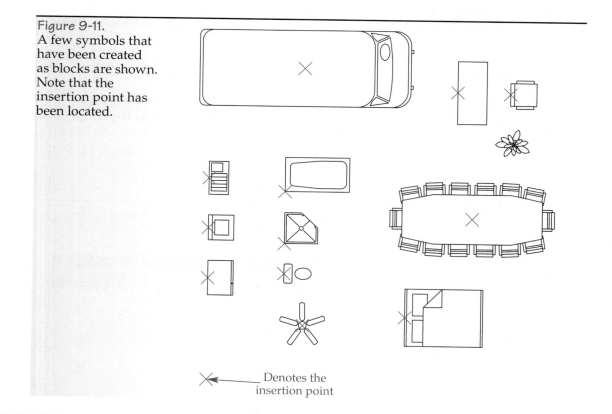

✕⟵ Denotes the
insertion point

Figure 9-12.
The **Block Definition**
dialog box is used
to create a standard
block.

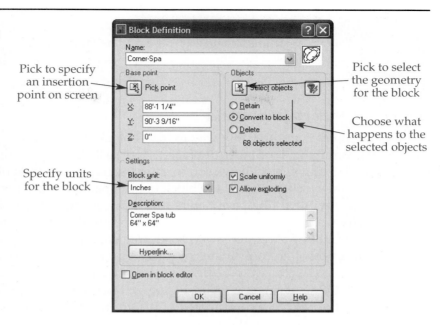

Pick to specify
an insertion
point on screen

Specify units
for the block

Pick to select
the geometry
for the block

Choose what
happens to the
selected objects

selected geometry into a block at the same location. The **Delete** radio button removes the original geometry from the drawing screen. Choose an option for controlling the original geometry.

5. The **Block unit:** drop-down list specifies the type of units **DesignCenter** uses when inserting the block. This option affects standard AutoCAD blocks only and has no effect on blocks inserted from the **AEC Content** tab in **DesignCenter**. Specify the type of units to use.

6. The **Scale uniformly** check box specifies if the block is scaled with the same value in the X, Y, and Z axes. If the box is not selected, it allows the block to be scaled separately in the X, Y, and Z axes. Check the box if you want the block scaled uniformly.

7. The **Allow exploding** check box allows the block to be exploded after insertion in the drawing. Unchecking does not allow the block to be exploded. Check the box if you want to allow the block to be exploded.

8. In the **Description:** text box, type a description to help identify the block for easy reference, such as This is a Corner Spa Tub. The description is displayed when you select a block preview within **DesignCenter**.

NOTE

Blocks can have hyperlinks assigned, such as a manufacturer's specification sheet or marketing material on the Internet, by selecting the **Hyperlink...** button. The **Open in block editor** check box opens the block definition in the **Block Editor**, after picking the **OK** button in the **Block Definition** dialog box. The **Block Definition** dialog box is used to assign behavioral rules to the block. These types of rules cannot be used in blocks that will be turned into a multi-view block.

The block is now ready for use through **DesignCenter**. Locate the block in the **Open Drawings** or **Folders** tab, and drag and drop it into the current drawing. When a block is created, a block definition is generated in the drawing. The block definition resides in the drawing and can be used in other drawings by dragging and dropping the block from **DesignCenter**.

Exercise 9-3   Complete the Exercise on the Student CD.

Using the Insert Command

INSERT

Type
INSERT
I

Pull-Down Menu
Insert
> Block...

DesignCenter is not the only way to insert blocks into a drawing. You can also use the **INSERT** command. Pick **Insert** > **Block...** or type INSERT or I. This displays the **Insert** dialog box. This dialog box allows you to enter the name, insertion point, scale, rotation, and units for the block and to set the block to be exploded when it is inserted.

After specifying all the parameters for the insertion of the block, pick **OK**. If any of the **Specify On-screen** check boxes were selected, read the Command: prompt and enter the information Architectural Desktop needs. To enter a point, you can either enter a point in absolute coordinates or select a point with the crosshairs.

> NOTE   Often, when you are inserting a drawing file into the current drawing, the absolute coordinates of 0,0 are used in order to use the inserted drawing as a reference.

Exercise 9-4   Complete the Exercise on the Student CD.

Multi-View Blocks

The creation of a multi-view block begins with standard AutoCAD blocks. Multi-view blocks use a standard AutoCAD block for each viewing direction. The standard blocks are created first and then tied together in the multi-view block definition. For example, a toilet multi-view block may use five separate standard blocks, each assigned to a different viewing direction, as shown in **Figure 9-13**. When the blocks are combined, the resulting multi-view block displays one of the blocks when it is viewed from a specific direction. Each side of the toilet is drawn and turned into a standard AutoCAD block. The insertion points are also lined up and assembled together, **Figure 9-14**.

Creating a Multi-View Block

The following discussion explains the steps for creating the blocks necessary for a custom multi-view block and then discusses the process of adding the blocks into a multi-view block definition. The example in **Figure 9-15** is a multi-view block representing a cooking range displayed with 2D Top, Front, and side views and a 3D Model view. For this block, the Front view will also be assigned to the Back view, since they look the same.

VPORTS

Type
VPORTS

Pull-Down Menu
View
> Viewports
> New
Viewports...

A new drawing is started using one of the Aec Model templates. After starting a new drawing, the first step in creating a multi-view block is to draw the geometry for the individual standard blocks. Each block needs to be oriented appropriately in 3D space, which is easy to do by dividing the drawing screen into separate tiled viewports within model space. To do this, pick **View** > **Viewports** > **New Viewports...** from the pull-down menu. This opens the **Viewports** dialog box, **Figure 9-16**.

Figure 9-13.
A multi-view block uses several standard blocks. Which one is displayed depends on the viewing direction.

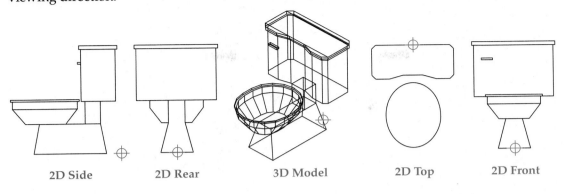

| 2D Side | 2D Rear | 3D Model | 2D Top | 2D Front |

Figure 9-14.
Each block is drawn separately with corresponding insertion points. The blocks are then assembled into a multi-view block, and the individual insertion points line up and become the insertion point of the multi-view block. All five blocks from Figure 9-13 are shown here.

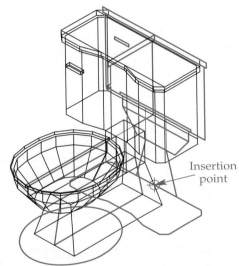

Insertion point

In the **Viewports** dialog box, select **Four: Equal** from the **Standard viewports:** list on the left. This gives a preview of the tiled viewports on the right side of the dialog box. Next, select the **Setup:** drop-down list and pick the **3D** option. This assigns each viewport a different viewing direction. By assigning a different viewing direction to each of the viewports, the drawing place is adjusted in each viewport so the XY place is perpendicular to your view, to aid in the process of creating the elevation-view Top view blocks. The following steps are used to create a multi-view block:

1. The rules for creating multi-view blocks are the same as those for creating blocks. Draw the geometry on layer 0, use ByBlock colors, linetypes, lineweights, and plot styles, unless a part of the block needs to use a specific color, linetype, lineweight, or plot style. The Top view block appears as a rectangle with circles for the burners and another rectangle for a grill. Draw a rectangle 2'-2" × 1'-8". Next, use the **CIRCLE** command to add four burners and the **RECTANGLE** command to add a grill. The first piece for the multi-view block has been created.

Figure 9-15.
Use these specifications to construct the cooking range multi-view block.

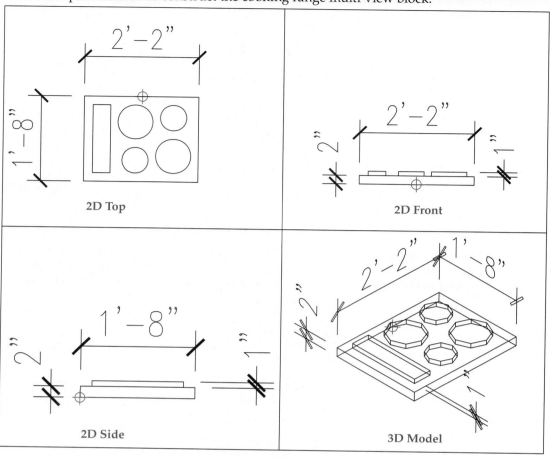

2D Top

2D Front

2D Side

3D Model

Figure 9-16.
Use the **Viewports** dialog box to split the drawing screen into viewports with a preset view assigned to each.

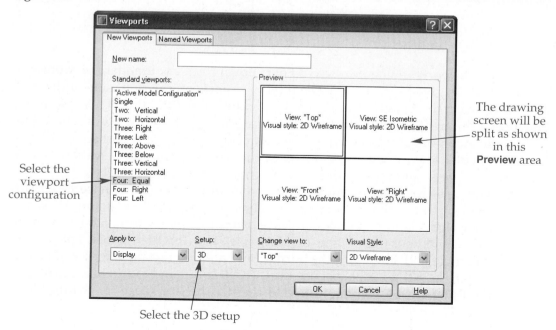

Select the viewport configuration

Select the 3D setup

The drawing screen will be split as shown in this **Preview** area

Architectural Desktop and Its Applications

2. In the Front view viewport, draw a 2'-2" × 2" rectangle. Add polylines representing the front of the grill and the burners raised above the surface of the cooktop. This creates the Front view geometry for the multi-view block. After the Front view geometry has been drawn, pick in the Right view viewport. Draw a 1'-8" × 2" rectangle in this viewport. Add polylines representing the side of the grill. Notice that as the Front view and Right view geometry is drawn, it appears oriented correctly in the isometric viewport.

3. The final piece needing to be drawn is the 3D range. Pick in the isometric viewport to make the viewport active. Copy the geometry used to create the Top view cooktop to the side. Next, select the large cooktop rectangle just copied, right-click, and pick **Convert To** > **Mass Element**. This converts the 2D linework into a 3D massing element. The Command: prompt will show that the **ExtrudeLinework** command has been started and ask you if you would like to erase the selected linework. Type Y to erase the rectangle being converted. You will then be asked to specify the extrusion height. Type 2 for the height of the cooktop. The Command: prompt will let you know that one new mass element has been created.

   The base of the cooktop has been converted to a 3D mass element. Notice that the layer and color have changed and are adjusted when finished. Next, the burners and grill need to be converted to mass elements. When you are converting objects to mass elements, the objects being converted must be closed objects and be the same type of objects. Next, select the four burners, right-click, and pick **Convert To** > **Mass Element**. The Command: prompt will show that the **ExtrudeLinework** command has been started and ask you if you would like to erase the selected linework. Type Y to erase the four circles being converted. You will then be asked to specify the extrusion height. Type 3 for the height of the burners. The Command: prompt will let you know that four new mass elements have been created.

   Repeat the same process for the grill, using an extrusion height of 3. After each of the parts for the 3D cooktop has been created, you can "glue" the pieces together to form a single mass element shape. Select the 3D rectangular cooktop base, right-click, and pick **Boolean** > **Union**. This glues the individual mass elements together into a single part. The Command: prompt will show that the **MassElementUnion** command has been started and ask you to select the objects to union. Pick the grill and four burner mass elements. The Command: prompt will tell you that five objects have been selected and ask you if you would like to select more objects to union. Press [Enter] when you are finished. When you are asked if you want to erase the layout geometry, type Y.

   Now that the 3D mass element has been created, use **Edit Object Display…** to change its properties. Select the mass element, right-click, and pick the **Edit Object Display…** option from the shortcut menu. Pick the **General Properties** tab of the **Object Display** dialog box and change the layer to 0 and the color, linetype, lineweight, and plot style to **ByBlock**. This finishes the geometry for the 3D portion of the cooktop.

4. The final step before creating the multi-view block is to turn the four sets of geometry drawn into separate blocks. While remaining in the isometric view, ensure that the drawing plane is in the world coordinate system by typing UCS at the Command: prompt. The current UCS name will appear, and when you are asked to enter an option, type W.

   Before creating the blocks, you might want to work with a single viewport in the drawing window again. Pick **View** > **Viewports** > **1 Viewport**. The isometric view was the last active viewport, so this is the viewing direction assigned to the single viewport. Next, you might want to move the Front, side, and Top view cooktop geometry closer together. Use the **ZOOM** command to locate the geometry and the **MOVE** command to move the geometry closer together.

Now, the blocks can be defined. When you are naming the blocks for a multi-view block, it is a good idea to create names that reflect the viewing direction of the blocks. For example, the Front view block can be named Cooktop_Front. Insertion points need to be selected for each block so the geometry in the different views line up with each other. Use the **BLOCK** command to create a block for each set of geometry. **Figure 9-17** shows the names and insertion points for each block.

5. Once the blocks have been created, the multi-view block definition can be assembled. To create a multi-view block, pick **Format > Multi-View Blocks > Multi-View Block Definitions...** from the pull-down menu. This displays the **Style Manager** opened to the **Multi-View Block Definitions** section. Pick the **New Style** button, or right-click in the right pane and select **New**, to create a new multi-view block definition. Enter the name Cooktop_Range_MV-Block for the multi-view block.

6. To edit the definition, select the new multi-view block name in the left viewport to display the properties of the new multi-view block in the right pane. See **Figure 9-18**. This area is used to assemble the standard blocks under a display representation for each viewing direction within the multi-view block.

The left side of the properties area lists the display representations used by the multi-view block definition. These include **General, Model, Plan, Plan High Detail, Plan Low Detail,** and **Reflected**. The blocks created for the multi-view block are assigned to one or more of the display representations, in order to be displayed properly.

NOTE

> When you are assigning a Top view block to a display representation, the General or Plan representation can be used. In versions of Architectural Desktop prior to 2007, the Plan representation was not available. If you are creating a multi-view block for use in a version of Architectural Desktop prior to 2007, assign the Top view block to the General display representation. It would not be uncommon to assign the Top view block to both the General and Plan display representations. Review the display sets in the drawing to see what multi-view block representations are used.

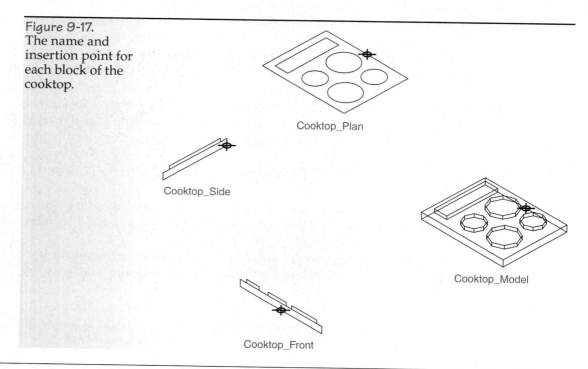

Figure 9-17.
The name and insertion point for each block of the cooktop.

Cooktop_Plan

Cooktop_Side

Cooktop_Model

Cooktop_Front

Figure 9-18.
The **Multi-View Block Definitions** area of the **Style Manager** is used to create and edit multi-view block definitions.

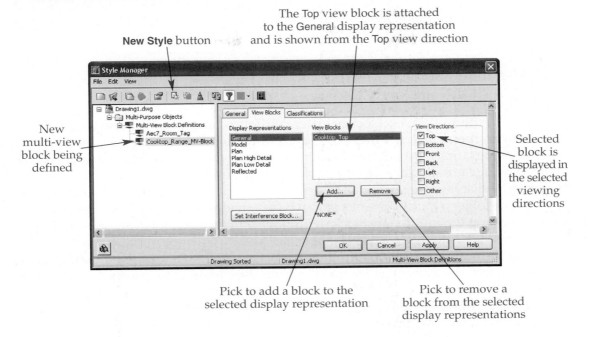

The Top view block is attached
to the General display representation
and is shown from the Top view direction

New Style button

New
multi-view
block being
defined

Selected
block is
displayed in
the selected
viewing
directions

Pick to add a block to the
selected display representation

Pick to remove a
block from the selected
display representations

The Cooktop_Plan block needs to be displayed in a Top view. The General and Plan display representations are used. Highlight the General display representation on the left, and then pick the **Add...** button. The **Select a Block** dialog box is displayed. Pick the Cooktop_Plan block from the list, and then pick the **OK** button. The block is listed in the **View Blocks** area. The next step is to assign a viewing direction to the block. The block is viewed from the top, so select the **Top** check box in the **View Directions** area. For a bottom view, select the **Bottom** check box. Uncheck all the other boxes, because the block is not viewed from those directions.

7. The final step is to finish assigning the remaining blocks to appropriate display representations and viewing directions. The Cooktop_Front and Cooktop_Side blocks are added to the **General** display representation, as the Section_Elev display set uses this display representation. The Cooktop_Front block is assigned to the **Front** and **Back** view directions. The Cooktop_Side block is assigned to the **Left** and **Right** view directions. The Cooktop_Model block is assigned to the **Model** representation using the **Other** view direction. This indicates that if the viewing direction is anything other than a Top, a Bottom, or an elevation view, the model block is displayed. The Cooktop_Plan block is assigned to the **Plan** view direction using the **Top** view direction. This displays the Plan view block when a Top view is shown in display sets where the Plan representation multi-view block is used. If additional detailed Plan view blocks are created, they can be assigned to the **Plan High Detail** and **Plan Low Detail** display representations with the **Top** view direction selected. If a block is to be used in a reflected ceiling plan, it can be assigned to the **Reflected** display representation using the **Top** view direction. When you are finished assigning blocks to display representations and view directions, pick the **OK** button to exit the **Style Manager**.

Adding and Modifying a Multi-View Block

Now that the multi-view block has been configured, it is a definition in the drawing, but it has not been inserted into the current drawing. To use a multi-view block in other drawings, first start another drawing and open the **Style Manager**. The currently open drawings are displayed in the **Style Manager**, and the multi-view block definitions can be displayed by picking the desired drawing from the list and selecting the appropriate folders. Multi-view blocks can be dragged from one drawing into another. To do this, drag the multi-view block definition from the original drawing and drop it into the desired drawing in **Style Manager**.

After the multi-view block definition has been added to the desired drawing, it can be inserted into the drawing. Pick **Insert > Multi-View Block...** to insert the multi-view block into the drawing. If multiple multi-view block definitions exist in the drawing, use the **Properties** palette to specify which definition to use by picking the **Definition** property and selecting the desired multi-view block from the list.

Use the Command: prompt options or the **Properties** palette to specify a scale and rotation angle for the multi-view block. When you are finished specifying the properties, pick the location for the block. If a block is drawn at a 1:1 scale, the multi-view block should be scaled the same when inserting the block. You can create other multi-view blocks where the scale can be adjusted.

Multi-view blocks can also be created for insertion from **DesignCenter**. Adding a multi-view block to **DesignCenter** is discussed later in this chapter.

After a multi-view block has been inserted into the drawing, the scale, rotation angle, and the multi-view block being used can be modified using the **Properties** palette. Enter the appropriate new values in the text boxes for the properties you are changing. A different multi-view block can also be chosen for insertion by selecting a desired multi-view block from the **Definition** drop-down list property.

Exercise
9-5   *Complete the Exercise on the Student CD.*

A *mask block* is an AEC object that is used to cover, or mask, AEC objects. Mask blocks are used similarly to the way correction fluid is used on paper. They can be used to clean up parts of the drawing that cannot be adjusted by other means. Architectural Desktop uses many light fixture blocks as mask blocks to mask out ceiling gridlines in a drawing known as a reflected ceiling plan, which displays the gridlines on a ceiling above the floor plan.

Another use of mask blocks is when an AEC Wall object intersects a wall in an old CAD drawing that uses two lines to represent a wall. The lines do not clean up with Wall objects when they intersect. A mask block can be used to manually clean up the intersection and cover the AEC wall, Figure 9-19.

Mask blocks mask out only AEC objects. They have no effect on standard AutoCAD geometry. They are inserted on the current layer, which can be frozen or set to a nonplotting layer, so that the edges of the mask blocks do not appear on the finished drawing.

Creating a Mask Block

A mask block is created from a closed polyline. To create a mask block, first use the **PLINE** command to draw a closed shape that covers the AEC object you wish to mask. When you are finished drawing the shape, use the command's **Close** option to close the polyline. See Figure 9-20.

After the polyline shape is created, the mask block can be defined. This is done in the **Mask Blocks** section of the **Style Manager**, which can be found by picking **Document** > **Mask Blocks** > **Mask Block Definitions...** from the pull-down menu. (If you do not have the **Document** pull-down menu, pick **Window** > **Pulldowns** > **Document Pulldown**.) The **Style Manager** is displayed, opened to the **Mask Block Definitions** section, Figure 9-21.

Pull-Down Menu
Document
> **Mask Blocks**
> **Mask Block**
Definitions...

Pick the **New Style** button or right-click in the right pane, and select **New** to create a new mask block definition. Type the name of the definition, press [Enter], select the new style in either pane, and pick the **Set From** button or right-click and select **Set From...** in the shortcut menu. The **Style Manager** is closed so you can select the polyline shape to be used as the outline for the mask. The following prompt sequence is used to define a mask block after you have selected **Set From**:

```
Command: _AecMaskDefine
Select a closed polyline, spline, ellipse, or circle: (pick one of these types of objects)
Add another ring? [Yes/No] <N>: Y↵
Select a closed polyline, spline, ellipse, or circle: (pick another one of these types of
    objects)
```

Figure 9-19.
Use a mask block to clean up intersections between AEC Wall objects and standard lines.

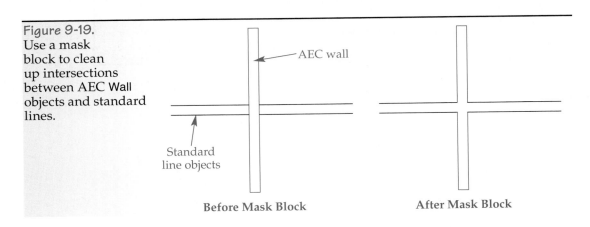

AEC wall

Standard line objects

Before Mask Block

After Mask Block

Figure 9-20.
When creating a mask block, first draw its shape with a polyline.

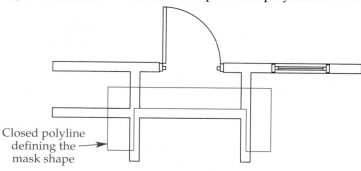

Closed polyline
defining the
mask shape

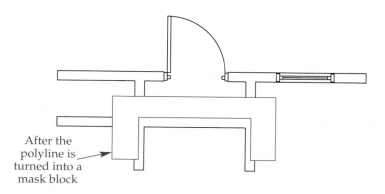

After the
polyline is
turned into a
mask block

Figure 9-21.
The **Mask Block Definitions** section of the **Style Manager** allows you to create new mask blocks, pick the polyline shape to define them, and set several other properties.

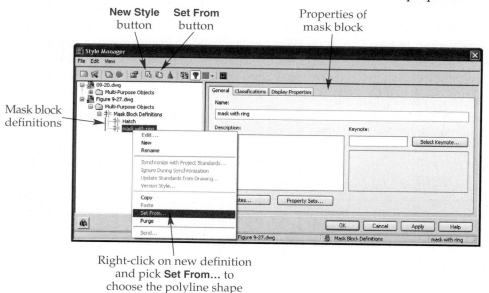

New Style
button

Set From
button

Properties of
mask block

Mask block
definitions

Right-click on new definition
and pick **Set From...** to
choose the polyline shape

Architectural Desktop and Its Applications

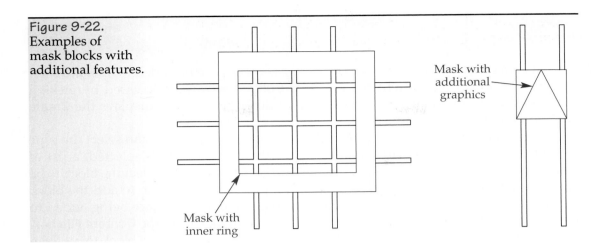

Figure 9-22.
Examples of
mask blocks with
additional features.

Mask with
additional
graphics

Mask with
inner ring

Ring is a void area? [Yes/No] <Yes>: ↵
Insertion base point: *(select an insertion point for the block)*
Select additional graphics: *(pick any additional objects to use on the block or press* [Enter]*)*

The first prompt requires you to select a closed object to be used as the mask block. After you have selected the object, the next prompt asks if you wish to add a ring. A ring is an inner closed polyline shape that does not mask AEC objects if you do not want to cover them. The insertion point is similar to the insertion point for a standard block; this is the point at which the block is attached to the crosshairs at the time of insertion. Finally, additional graphics can be added to the block to enhance it. See **Figure 9-22.**

Once the definition has been created, it can be inserted into the drawing and attached to the AEC objects it is supposed to mask. Pick **Document** > **Mask Blocks** > **Add Mask Block...** to add the mask block to the drawing. Use the **Properties** palette to select the mask block definition to be inserted. Adjust the scale for the mask block in the **Properties** palette by adjusting the **X**, **Y**, and **Z** properties. Then pick an insertion point in the drawing for the mask block.

Pull-Down Menu
Document
  > Mask Blocks
    > Add Mask
       Block...

When the block is first inserted, it does not mask any objects. It must be attached to the AEC objects to be masked. To attach it to AEC objects, select the mask block, right-click, and select **Attach Objects** from the shortcut menu. You are prompted to select the AEC object to be masked. After selecting the object, the **Select Display Representation** dialog box is displayed with a list of the current display representations in use by the object being masked. Pick the desired display representation, and then pick the **OK** button to mask the object.

NOTE

> The mask block can only be applied to one AEC object at a time. You must select the mask block and the **Attach Objects** option for each AEC object to which it is to be attached. AEC objects can also be removed from the mask block by picking the mask block, right-clicking, picking **Detach Objects**, and picking the object to be detached.

Pull-Down Menu
Format
> AEC Content
Wizard...

Custom blocks, multi-view blocks, and mask blocks can be added to **DesignCenter** through the **AEC Content** wizard. The **AEC Content** wizard is accessed by picking **Format** > **AEC Content Wizard...** from the pull-down menu. This displays the **Create AEC Content** dialog box, **Figure 9-23.**

In the **Content Type** section of the first page of the wizard, you can select the type of content to be added to **DesignCenter**. After the content type is selected, a list of blocks in the current drawing appear in the **Current Drawing** box. Select the block to be added to **DesignCenter**. After selecting a block, pick the **Add** button to add the block to the **Content File** box. The **Content File** box lists the blocks that are being added to **DesignCenter**. The **Remove** button is used to remove a block from the **Content File** box. The **Command String** text box is used to enter a command macro for a block to perform when it is inserted. When you are finished selecting the options for the first page, pick the **Next** button.

The second page of the **AEC Content** wizard, **Figure 9-24,** presents several more options. In the **Insert Options** area, you can control how the block is inserted. If you check **Explode On Insert**, the block is exploded when it is inserted. Do not select this option for multi-view blocks or mask blocks because they are no longer "smart" when they are exploded. The **Preset Elevation** is the height along the Z axis at which you want the block inserted. The **Anchor Type** drop-down list includes a number of AEC objects to which the block can be anchored. If an object is selected from this list, the block becomes tied to the AEC object, and if that AEC object is moved, the block moves with it. The **Scale** area allows you to set the scale for the inserted block, either by setting the scales along the axes or by using the **Additional Scaling** options. If the **Enable AEC Unit Scaling** box is checked, the block is scaled to the current drawing units. This is useful if the block was drawn in units other than the current drawing units. The

Figure 9-23.
The first page of the **AEC Content** wizard.

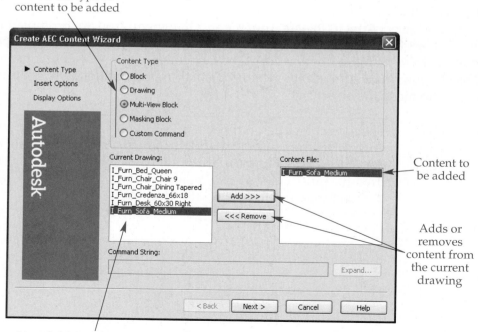

List of objects of the selected
content type in the current drawing

Figure 9-24.
The second page of the **AEC Content** wizard.

General insertion options

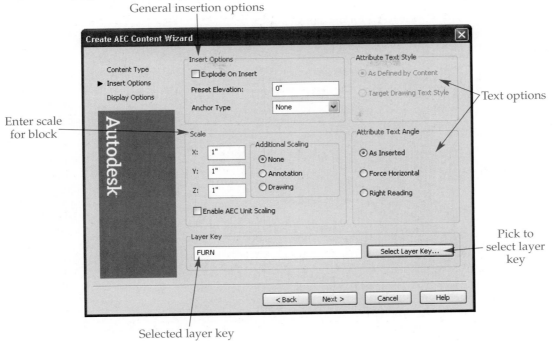

Enter scale for block

Text options

Pick to select layer key

Selected layer key

Attribute Text Style and **Attribute Text Angle** areas control the appearance and display of any attribute text in the block. The **Layer Key** area is used to select a layer key to be assigned to the block content. When you are finished with these settings, pick the **Next** button to move to the final page of the wizard, **Figure 9-25.**

The third page asks you to specify the location and name of the block in the **File Name** area. In order for the custom content to be accessed from the **AEC Content** tab in **DesignCenter** and automatically placed on a layer, the block needs to be saved in the C:\Documents and Settings\All Users\Application Data\Autodesk\ADT 2007\enu\AEC Content folder. A custom folder can be created as long as it is within the AEC Content folder. The **Icon** area shows the preview icon that will be used for this block in **DesignCenter**. Pick the **New Icon...** button to select a .bmp image to use as an icon. Pick the **Default Icon...** button to use the current view in the drawing as the icon for the block. You can enter a description of the block to be displayed in **DesignCenter** in the **Detailed Description** area. The **Save Preview Graphics** check box saves the preview image with the block when it is checked. When you are finished with all the settings for the block, pick the **Finish** button to have Architectural Desktop process the block and add it to **DesignCenter**. Once the block has been processed, it can be accessed and used like any other block from the **AEC Content** tab in **DesignCenter**.

NOTE
Block content from **DesignCenter** can be added to custom tool palettes by dragging and dropping the content from the **AEC Content** tab into a custom palette. Refer to Appendix B for creating and customizing tool palettes.

Exercise 9-6   **Complete the Exercise on the Student CD.**

Figure 9-25.
The third and final page of the **AEC Content** wizard.

Specify location and
file name for the block

Preview icon
of block

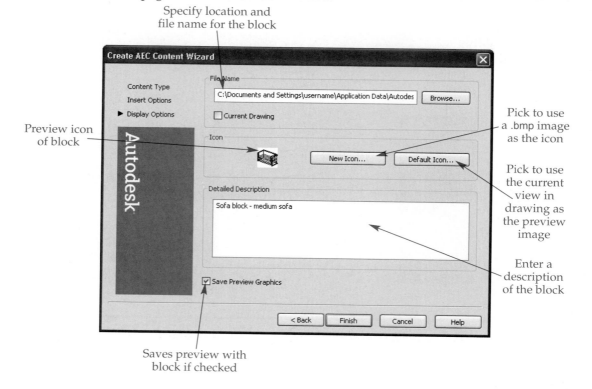

Pick to use
a .bmp image
as the icon

Pick to use
the current
view in
drawing as
the preview
image

Enter a
description
of the block

Saves preview with
block if checked

Creating AEC Profiles

An *AEC profile*, also known as a profile shape, is a predefined shape that can be used in the construction of custom walls, doors, windows, stair railings, fascias and soffits, and mass elements. The AEC objects listed use standard profile shapes but can quickly be modified by using a custom profile shape. A *profile shape* represents the overall shape of a design feature and is created as a closed polyline that is then turned into an AEC profile definition. **Figure 9-26** provides some examples of profile shapes used to create custom AEC objects.

To create an AEC profile, draw the desired shape or design with a polyline, and use the **Close** option to close the polyline. After the shape has been drawn, the AEC profile definition can be created. To turn the polyline into an AEC profile, select the polyline, right-click, and then pick **Convert To > Profile Definition...** from the shortcut menu. The following prompt is displayed:

Insertion point or [Add ring/Centroid]: **C**↵
Profile Definition [New/Existing] <New>: **N**↵

The first prompt requires that you pick an insertion point. For some profiles, you may be able to choose the location of the insertion point on the polyline profile. However, some AEC styles, such as slab and roof edge styles, which will be discussed in later chapters, require that the profile use a specific insertion point. Others, such as door and window styles, use the centroid of the polyline as the insertion point. In most situations, the **Centroid** option can be used when defining AEC profiles. The centroid is the absolute center of the shape and is determined by the program examining the extents of the shape and then finding the center from the edges of the geometry. When the **Centroid** option is selected, the next prompt asks if the profile is a new profile shape

Figure 9-26.
Examples of profile shapes used to create custom AEC objects.

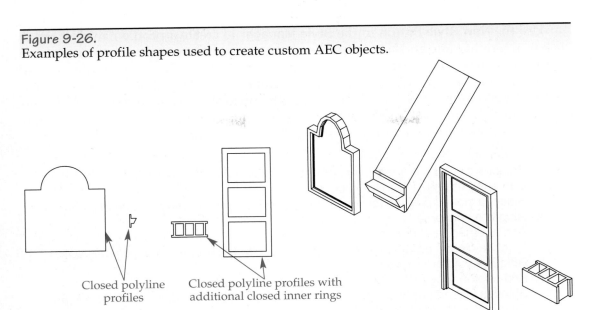

Closed polyline profiles

Closed polyline profiles with additional closed inner rings

Custom window, roof edge, door, and mass element created from the polyline profiles on the left

or an existing profile shape. If you select the **New** option, the **New Profile Definition** worksheet is displayed. Type the name of the profile and pick **OK** to finish creating an AEC profile.

AEC profiles can also be created by picking **Format** > **Profiles** > **Profile Definitions...** from the pull-down menu. This displays the **Style Manager** dialog box opened to the **Profiles** section. See **Figure 9-27**.

Pull-Down Menu

Format
  > Profiles
    > Profile
      Definitions...

Figure 9-27.
The **Profiles** section of the **Style Manager** contains all custom AEC profile definitions in the drawing.

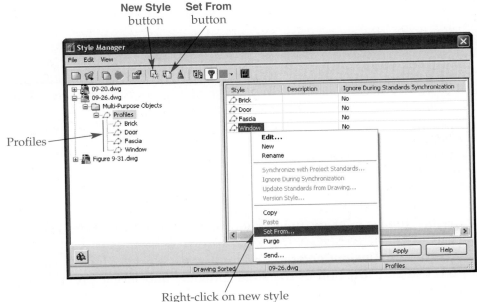

New Style button

Set From button

Profiles

Right-click on new style and select **Set From...** to choose the profile's shape

Use the **New Style** button in the **Style Manager** to create a profile name, or right-click in the right pane and select **New**. Enter a name for the new shape. After the new profile name has been created, the profile needs to be defined with a polyline shape. Select the profile name, right-click, and select **Set From...** in the shortcut menu or pick the **Set From** button. This temporarily closes the **Style Manager** so the polyline profile can be selected. After picking the polyline, a few prompts are displayed. The command sequence for the custom door profile in Figure 9-26 is as follows:

```
Command: _AecProfileDefine
Select a closed polyline, spline, ellipse, or circle: (pick the outermost polyline shape)
Add another ring? [Yes/No] <N>: Y↵
Select a closed polyline, spline, ellipse, or circle: (pick an internal polyline shape)
Ring is a void area? [Yes/No] <Y>: Y↵
Add another ring? [Yes/No] <N>: Y↵
Select a closed polyline, spline, ellipse, or circle: (pick an internal polyline shape)
Ring is a void area? [Yes/No] <Y>: Y↵
Add another ring? [Yes/No] <N>: Y↵
Select a closed polyline, spline, ellipse, or circle: (pick an internal polyline shape)
Ring is a void area? [Yes/No] <Y>: Y↵
Add another ring? [Yes/No] <N>: N ↵
Insertion Point or Centroid>: ↵
```

When you are finished creating the profile shapes, exit the **Style Manager**. The profile shapes are now ready to be configured into an AEC style.

Pull-Down Menu
Format
  > Profiles
    > Insert Profile
      as Polyline...

Profiles can be inserted into the drawing as standard polylines so they can be modified and redefined as new AEC profiles. Pick **Format > Profiles > Insert Profile as Polyline...** to add a polyline profile into the drawing. This displays the **Profile Definitions** worksheet, from which a profile can be selected to be inserted. After inserting the profile, make any modifications to the profile, and then redefine the existing profile or create a new profile. Remember that the creation of profiles can be helpful when creating custom AEC object styles, such as doors with panels, roof edges with gutters, and floors with footings.

Exercise 9-7

Complete the Exercise on the Student CD.

Chapter Test

Answer the following questions. Write your answers on a separate sheet of paper or complete the electronic chapter test on the Student CD.

1. Define *multi-view block*.
2. Give the basic function of **DesignCenter**.
3. Define and give an example of design blocks.
4. At what scale are design blocks drawn?
5. Define and give an example of *documentation blocks*.
6. Briefly discuss the scale of documentation blocks related to model space and layout space.
7. How do you browse **DesignCenter** to find multi-view block folders?
8. Discuss the use and function of the small preview and larger preview of the blocks within the selected folder.
9. What is the primary method used to place a block in a drawing from **DesignCenter**, and how do you do it?
10. Why is it important to watch the Command: prompt when inserting a block from **DesignCenter**?

11. How can you change the location of a block once it is placed in the drawing?
12. How are layers assigned to blocks when you are inserting them from **DesignCenter**?
13. How do you set the drawing scale when inserting a documentation block, and what is the scale factor for the drawing scale 1/8"=1'-0" scale? Show your work.
14. Define *attributes*.
15. How do you change an attribute after a block has been inserted?
16. What are callouts?
17. Name and give the function of the attributes with a gray highlight around the text of callout blocks.
18. Explain how to use the **Folders** tab of **DesignCenter** to locate elements from other drawings that can be dragged and dropped into the current drawing.
19. Discuss the function of i-drop technology.
20. Define and give the advantage of a *block*.
21. What are two ways to insert a block?
22. Briefly discuss the difference between AutoCAD and Architectural Desktop blocks.
23. Why should initial block geometry be created on layer 0?
24. Discuss the function of creating block geometry with a **ByLayer** color, linetype, lineweight, or plot style.
25. Why are **ByBlock** properties preferred in Architectural Desktop?
26. When and how is an insertion point chosen?
27. Briefly explain how the creation of multi-view blocks builds on standard AutoCAD blocks.
28. Describe the function of mask blocks and give at least one application example.
29. Give the basic function of the **AEC Content** wizard.
30. Describe an AEC profile.
31. Define *profile*.

Chapter Projects

Use the techniques covered in this chapter to create the following drawings.

1. Single-Level Residential Project
   A. Access the **Project Browser** and set Residential-Project-01 current.
   B. Access the **Constructs** tab in the **Project Navigator** and create a new construct named Plumbing-Appliances. Assign the Plumbing-Appliances construct to the Main Floor level. Open the Plumbing-Appliances construct.
   C. Drag and drop the Main Floor construct into the Plumbing-Appliances drawing. This externally references the Main Floor drawing into the Plumbing-Appliances drawing as a reference for placing plumbing and appliance blocks.
   D. Add plumbing fixture blocks such as sinks, lavatories, toilets, bathtubs, and a water heater, as displayed in the figure.
   E. Add appliance blocks such as the dishwasher, refrigerator, stove, washer, and dryer, as displayed in the figure.
   F. Detach the Main Floor construct xref.
   G. Save and close the drawing.
   H. Access the **Constructs** tab in the **Project Navigator** and create a new construct named Furniture. Assign the Furniture construct to the Main Floor level. Open the Furniture construct.
   I. Drag and drop the Main Floor and Plumbing-Appliances constructs into the Furniture drawing.
   J. Add blocks for furniture as indicated in the figure.
   K. Detach the Main Floor and Plumbing-Appliances construct xrefs.
   L. Save and close the drawing.
   M. Start a new drawing using one of the Aec Model templates.
   N. Set the drawing scale to **1/4"=1'-0"** in the **Drawing Setup** dialog box.
   O. Use the **INSERT** command to browse to the Constructs folder of Residential-Project-01 and insert the Main Floor drawing.
   P. Insert the drawing at (0,0,0), set the scale to 1 on the X axis, check the **Uniform Scale** check box, and set the rotation angle to 0. This inserts the drawing at the same coordinate as the original floor plan. Check the **Explode** check box and pick the **OK** button.
   Q. Freeze the G-Anno-Nplt layer.
   R. Erase all the doors, windows, and interior walls.
   S. Modify the walls to use the Concrete-8 Concrete-16x8-footing wall style, found in the **Walls** tool palette.
   T. Use the **Properties** palette to modify the base height of the walls to 2'-6" high and change the **Justification** property to Baseline. The walls disappear, but the footings remain in the drawing.
   U. Select **Edit Object Display...** from the shortcut menu to modify the Plan display representation cut plane to 24" high. Note: DO NOT assign an object override. Changes made to the Plan display affect all of the walls of this style, as there is a style override set.
   V. Perform any additional modifications to the walls to reflect the figure.
   W. Access the **Constructs** tab. Right-click on the Constructs folder and pick **Save Current DWG as Construct...** from the shortcut menu. In the **Add Construct** worksheet, set the following:
      a. **Name**: Foundation
      b. **Description**: Foundation.
      c. **Category**: Constructs
      d. Select the **Foundation** level check box in the **Division 1** column.
   X. Save and close the drawing.

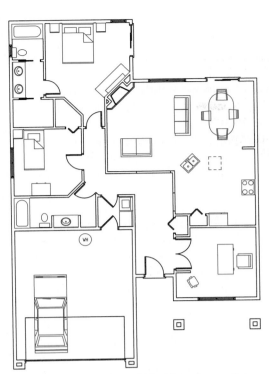

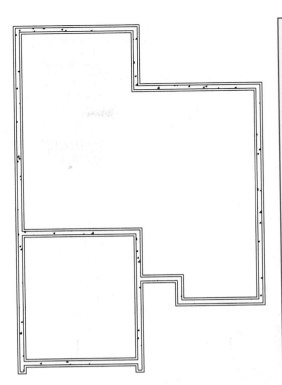

Alan Mascord Design Associates

2. Single-Level Residential Project
   A. Access the **Project Browser** and set Residential-Project-02 current.
   B. Access the **Constructs** tab in the **Project Navigator** and create a new construct named Plumbing-Appliances. Assign the Plumbing-Appliances construct to the Main Floor level. Open the Plumbing-Appliances construct.
   C. Drag and drop the Main Floor construct into the Plumbing-Appliances drawing. This externally references the Main Floor drawing in the Plumbing-Appliances drawing as a reference for placing plumbing and appliance blocks.
   D. Add plumbing fixture blocks such as sinks, lavatories, toilets, bathtubs, and a water heater, as displayed in the figure.
   E. Add appliance blocks such as the dishwasher, refrigerator, stove, washer, and dryer, as displayed in the figure.
   F. Detach the Main Floor construct xref.
   G. Save and close the drawing.
   H. Access the **Constructs** tab and create a new construct named Furniture. Assign the Furniture construct to the Main Floor level. Open the Furniture construct.
   I. Drag and drop the Main Floor and Plumbing-Appliances constructs into the Furniture drawing.
   J. Add blocks for furniture as indicated in the figure.
   K. Detach the Main Floor and Plumbing-Appliances construct xrefs.
   L. Save and close the drawing.
   M. Start a new drawing using one of the Aec Model templates.
   N. Set the drawing scale to **1/4"=1'-0"** in the **Drawing Setup** dialog box.
   O. Use the **INSERT** command to browse to the Constructs folder of Residential-Project-02 and insert the Main Floor drawing.
   P. Insert the drawing at (0,0,0), set the scale to 1 on the X axis, check the **Uniform Scale** check box, and set the rotation angle to 0. This inserts the drawing at the same coordinates as the original floor plan. Check the **Explode** check box and pick the **OK** button.

Q. Freeze the G-Anno-Nplt layer.

R. Erase all the doors, windows, and interior walls.

S. Modify the walls to use the Concrete-8 Concrete-16x8-footing wall style, found in the **Walls** tool palette.

T. Use the **Properties** palette to modify the base height of the walls to 1'-8" high and change the **Justification** property to Baseline. The walls disappear, but the footings remain in the drawing.

U. Select **Edit Object Display...** from the shortcut menu to modify the Plan display representation cut plane to 1'-6" high. Note: DO NOT assign an object override. Changes made to the Plan display will affect all of the walls of this style, as there is a style override set.

V. Modify the brick veneer walls to 1'-8" high.

W. Perform any additional modifications to the walls to reflect the figure.

X. Access the **Constructs** tab in the **Project Navigator**. Right-click on the Constructs folder and pick **Save Current DWG as Construct...** from the shortcut menu. In the **Add Construct** worksheet, set the following:

    a. **Name**: Foundation

    b. **Description**: Foundation.

    c. **Category**: Constructs

    d. Select the **Foundation** level check box in the **Division 1** column.

Y. Save and close the drawing.

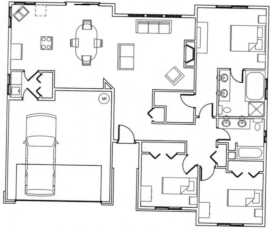
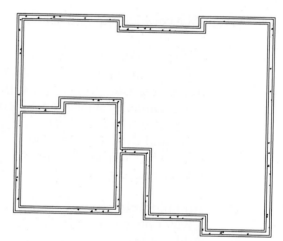

Alan Mascord Design Associates

3. Two-Story Residential Project
   A.   Access the **Project Browser** and set Residential-Project-03 current.
   B.   Access the **Constructs** tab in the **Project Navigator** and create a new construct named Plumbing-Appliances. Assign the Plumbing-Appliances construct to the Main Floor level. Open the Plumbing-Appliances construct.
   C.   Drag and drop the Main Floor construct into the Plumbing-Appliances drawing. This externally references the Main Floor drawing in the Plumbing-Appliances drawing as a reference for placing plumbing and appliance blocks.
   D.   Add plumbing fixture blocks such as sinks, lavatories, toilets, bathtubs, and a water heater, as displayed in the figure.
   E.   Add appliance blocks such as the dishwasher, refrigerator, stove, washer, and dryer, as displayed in the figure.
   F.   Detach the Main Floor construct xref.
   G.   Save and close the drawing.
   H.   Access the **Constructs** tab in the **Project Navigator** and create a new construct named Furniture. Assign the Furniture construct to the Main Floor level. Open the Furniture construct.
   I.   Drag and drop the Main Floor and Plumbing-Appliances constructs into the Furniture drawing.
   J.   Add blocks for furniture as indicated in the figure.
   K.   Detach the Main Floor and Plumbing-Appliances construct xrefs.
   L.   Save and close the drawing.
   M.   Start a new drawing using one of the Aec Model templates.
   N.   Set the drawing scale to **1/4"=1'-0"** in the **Drawing Setup** dialog box.
   O.   Use the **INSERT** command to browse to the Constructs folder of Residential-Project-03 and insert the Main Floor drawing.
   P.   Insert the drawing at (0,0,0), set the scale to 1 on the X axis, check the **Uniform Scale** check box, and set the rotation angle to 0. This inserts the drawing at the same coordinates as the original floor plan. Check the **Explode** check box, and then pick the **OK** button.
   Q.   Freeze the G-Anno-Nplt layer.
   R.   Erase all the doors, windows and interior walls.
   S.   Modify the walls to use the Concrete-8 Concrete-16x8-footing wall style, found in the **Walls** tool palette.
   T.   Use the **Properties** palette to modify the base height of the walls to 2'-6" high and change the **Justification** property to Baseline. The walls disappear, but the footings remain in the drawing.
   U.   Select **Edit Object Display...** from the shortcut menu to modify the Plan display representation cut plane to 2'-0" high. Note: DO NOT assign an object override. Changes made to the Plan display affect all of the walls of this style, as there is a style override set.
   V.   Modify the brick veneer walls to 2'-0" high.
   W.   Perform any additional modifications to the walls to reflect the figure.
   X.   Access the **Constructs** tab in the **Project Navigator**. Right-click on the Constructs folder and pick **Save Current DWG as Construct...** from the shortcut menu. In the **Add Construct** worksheet, set the following:
        a. **Name**: Foundation
        b. **Description**: Foundation.
        c. **Category**: Constructs
        d. Select the **Foundation** level check box in the **Division 1** column.
   Y.   Save and close the drawing.

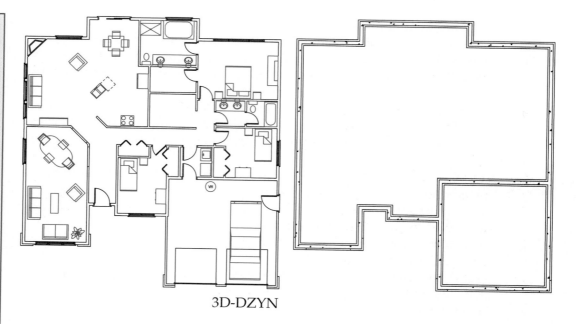

3D-DZYN

4. Two-Story Residential Project
   A. Access the **Project Browser** and set Residential-Project-04 current.
   B. Access the **Constructs** tab in the **Project Navigator** and create a new construct named MainFlr-Plumbing-Appliances. Assign the MainFlr-Plumbing-Appliances construct to the Main Floor level. Open the MainFlr-Plumbing-Appliances construct.
   C. Drag and drop the Main Floor construct into the MainFlr-Plumbing-Appliances drawing. This externally references the Main Floor drawing into the MainFlr-Plumbing-Appliances drawing as a reference for placing plumbing and appliance blocks.
   D. Add plumbing fixture blocks such as sinks, lavatories, toilets, and a water heater, as displayed in the figure.
   E. Add appliance blocks such as the dishwasher, refrigerator, stove, washer, and dryer, as displayed in the figure.
   F. Detach the Main Floor construct xref.
   G. Save and close the drawing.
   H. Access the **Constructs** tab in the **Project Navigator** and create a new construct named MainFlr-Furniture. Assign the MainFlr-Furniture construct to the Main Floor level. Open the MainFlr-Furniture construct.
   I. Drag and drop the Main Floor and MainFlr-Plumbing-Appliances constructs into the MainFlr-Furniture drawing.
   J. Add blocks for furniture as indicated in the figure.
   K. Detach the Main Floor and MainFlr-Plumbing-Appliances construct xrefs.
   L. Save and close the drawing.
   M. Access the **Constructs** tab in the **Project Navigator** and create a new construct named UpperFlr-Plumbing-Appliances. Assign the UpperFlr-Plumbing-Appliances construct to the Upper Floor level. Open the UpperFlr-Plumbing-Appliances construct.
   N. Drag and drop the Upper Floor construct into the UpperFlr-Plumbing-Appliances drawing. This externally references the Upper Floor drawing into the UpperFlr-Plumbing-Appliances drawing as a reference for placing plumbing and appliance blocks.
   O. Add plumbing fixture blocks such as sinks, lavatories, toilets, bathtubs, and a shower, as displayed in the figure.
   P. Detach the Upper Floor construct xref.

Q. Save and close the drawing.

R. Access the **Constructs** tab in the **Project Navigator** and create a new construct named UpperFlr-Furniture. Assign the UpperFlr-Furniture construct to the Upper Floor level. Open the UpperFlr-Furniture construct.

S. Drag and drop the Upper Floor and the UpperFlr-Plumbing-Appliances constructs into the UpperFlr-Furniture drawing.

T. Add blocks for furniture as indicated in the figure.

U. Detach the Upper Floor and UpperFlr-Plumbing-Appliances construct xrefs.

V. Save and close the drawing.

W. Start a new drawing using one of the Aec Model templates.

X. Set the drawing scale to **1/4"=1'-0"** in the **Drawing Setup** dialog box.

Y. Use the **INSERT** command to browse to the Constructs folder of Residential-Project-04 and insert the Main Floor drawing.

Z. Insert the drawing at (0,0,0), set the scale to 1 on the X axis, check the **Uniform Scale** check box, and set the rotation angle to 0. This inserts the drawing to the same coordinates as the original floor plan. Check the **Explode** check box, and then pick the **OK** button.

AA. Freeze the G-Anno-Nplt layer.

BB. Erase all the doors, windows and interior walls.

CC. Change the walls to the Concrete-8 Concrete-16x8-footing wall style, found in the **Walls** tool palette.

DD. Use the **Properties** palette to modify the base height of the walls to 2'-6" high and change the **Justification** property to Baseline. The walls disappear, but the footings remain in the drawing.

EE. Select **Edit Object Display...** from the shortcut menu to modify the Plan display representation cut plane to 2'-0" high. Note: DO NOT assign an object override. Changes made to the Plan display affect all of the walls of this style, as there is a style override set.

FF. Perform any additional modifications to the walls to reflect the figure.

GG. Access the **Constructs** tab in the **Project Navigator**. Right-click on the Constructs folder and pick **Save Current DWG as Construct...** from the shortcut menu. In the **Add Construct** worksheet, set the following:
  a. **Name**: Foundation
  b. **Description**: Foundation.
  c. **Category**: Constructs
  d. Select the **Foundation** level check box in the **Division 1** column.

HH. Save and close the drawing.

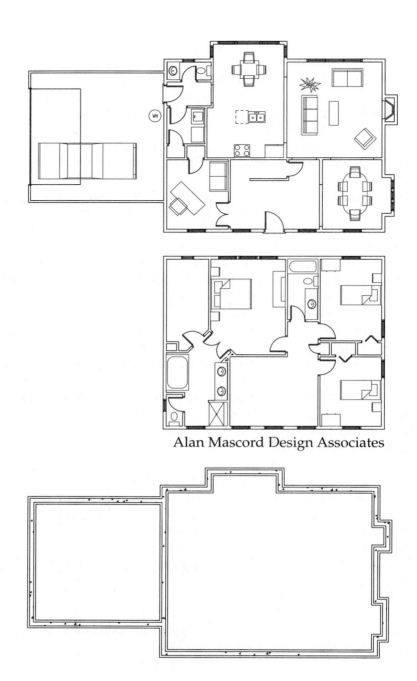

Alan Mascord Design Associates

5. Commercial Store Project
   A. Access the **Project Browser** and set Commercial-Project-05 current.
   B. Access the **Constructs** tab in the **Project Navigator** and create a new construct named Plumbing. Assign the Plumbing construct to the Main Floor level. Open the Plumbing construct.
   C. Drag and drop the Main Floor construct into the Plumbing drawing. This externally references the Main Floor drawing into the Plumbing drawing as a reference for placing plumbing blocks.
   D. Add plumbing fixture blocks such as lavatories and toilets, as displayed in the figure.
   E. Detach the Main Floor construct xref.
   F. Save and close the drawing.

G.	Access the **Constructs** tab in the **Project Navigator** and create a new construct named Furniture. Assign the Furniture construct to the Main Floor level. Open the Furniture construct.

H.	Drag and drop the Main Floor and Plumbing constructs into the Furniture drawing.

I.	Add any furnishing blocks as desired.

J.	Detach the Main Floor and Plumbing construct xrefs.

K.	Save and close the drawing.

L.	Start a new drawing using one of the Aec Model templates.

M.	Use the **INSERT** command to browse to the Constructs folder of Commercial-Project-05 and insert the Main Floor drawing.

N.	Insert the drawing at (0,0,0), set the scale to 1 on the X axis, check the **Uniform Scale** check box, and set the rotation angle to 0. This inserts the drawing to the same coordinates as the original floor plan. Pick the **OK** button to insert the drawing.

O.	Freeze the G-Anno-Nplt layer.

P.	Create a layer named A-Anno-Otln and set current.

Q.	Draw a closed polyline around both buildings.

R.	Erase the floor plan geometry.

S.	Access the **Constructs** tab in the **Project Navigator**. Right-click on the Constructs folder and pick **Save Current DWG as Construct...** from the shortcut menu. In the **Add Construct** worksheet, set the following:

   a.	**Name**: Foundation

   b.	**Description**: Foundation.

   c.	**Category**: Constructs

   d.	Select the **Foundation** level check box in the **Division 1** column.

T.	Save and close the drawing.

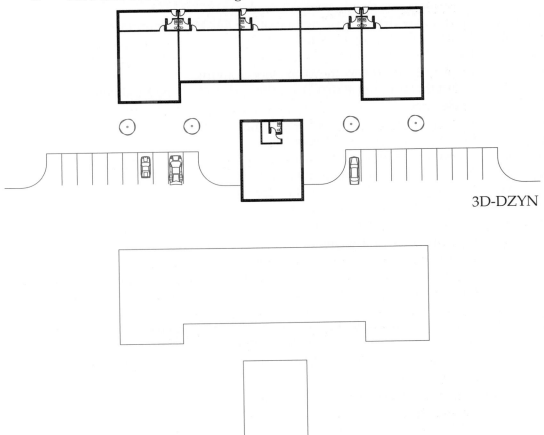

3D-DZYN

6. Commercial Car Maintenance Shop Project
   A.   Access the **Project Browser** and set Commercial-Project-06 current.
   B.   Access the **Constructs** tab in the **Project Navigator** and create a new construct named MainFlr-Plumbing. Assign the MainFlr-Plumbing construct to the Main Floor level. Open the MainFlr-Plumbing construct.
   C.   Drag and drop the Main Floor construct into the MainFlr-Plumbing drawing. This externally references the Main Floor drawing into the MainFlr-Plumbing drawing as a reference for placing plumbing blocks.
   D.   Add plumbing fixture blocks such as a sink, lavatory, and toilet, as displayed in the figure.
   E.   Detach the Main Floor construct xref.
   F.   Save and close the drawing.
   G.   Access the **Constructs** tab in the **Project Navigator** and create a new construct named MainFlr-Furniture. Assign the MainFlr-Furniture construct to the Main Floor level. Open the MainFlr-Furniture construct.
   H.   Drag and drop the Main Floor and MainFlr-Plumbing constructs into the MainFlr-Furniture drawing.
   I.   Add blocks such as vending machines, cars, and furniture, as indicated in the figure.
   J.   Detach the Main Floor and MainFlr-Plumbing construct xrefs.
   K.   Save and close the drawing.
   L.   Access the **Constructs** tab and create a new construct named UpperFlr-Furniture. Assign the UpperFlr-Furniture construct to the Upper Floor level. Open the UpperFlr-Furniture construct.
   M.   Drag and drop the Upper Floor construct into the UpperFlr-Furniture drawing.
   N.   Add blocks for furniture as indicated in the figure.
   O.   Detach the Upper Floor construct xref.
   P.   Save and close the drawing.
   Q.   Start a new drawing using one of the Aec Model templates.
   R.   Set the drawing scale to **1/4"=1'-0"** in the **Drawing Setup** dialog box.
   S.   Use the **INSERT** command to browse to the Constructs folder of Commercial-Project-06 and insert the Main Floor drawing.
   T.   Insert the drawing at (0,0,0), set the scale to 1 on the X axis, check the **Uniform Scale** check box, and set the rotation angle to 0. This inserts the drawing to the same coordinates as the original floor plan. Check the **Explode** check box, and then pick the **OK** button.
   U.   Freeze the G-Anno-Nplt layer.
   V.   Erase all the doors, windows, and interior walls.
   W.   Modify the walls to use the Concrete-8 Concrete-16x8-footing wall style, found in the **Walls** tool palette.
   X.   Use the **Properties** palette to modify the base height of the walls to 8'-0" high and change the **Justification** property to Baseline.
   Y.   Perform any additional modifications to the walls to reflect the figure.
   Z.   Create a layer name A-Anno-Otln with a Hidden2 linetype and set it current. Draw a closed polyline around the carwash area at the back of the building, as shown in the figure. Erase the walls.
   AA.   Access the **Constructs** tab in the **Project Navigator**. Right-click on the Constructs folder and pick **Save Current DWG as Construct...** from the shortcut menu. In the **Add Construct** worksheet, set the following:
       a.   **Name**: Foundation
       b.   **Description**: Foundation.
       c.   **Category**: Constructs
       d.   Select the **Foundation** level check box in the **Division 1** column.
   BB.   Save and close the drawing.

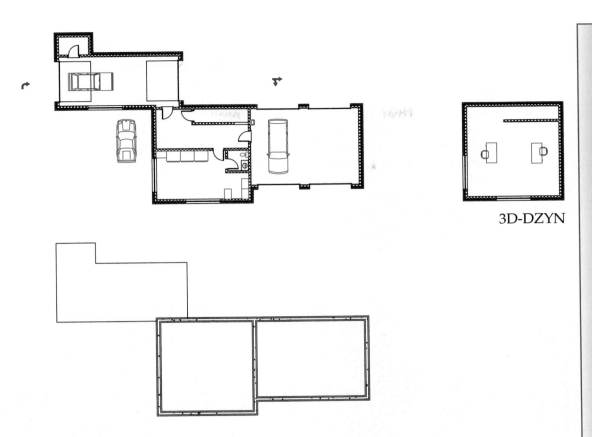

3D-DZYN

7. Governmental Fire Station
   A. Access the **Project Browser** and set Gvrmt-Project-07 current.
   B. Access the **Constructs** tab in the **Project Navigator** and create a new construct named Plumbing-Appliances. Assign the Plumbing-Appliances construct to the Main Floor level. Open the Plumbing-Appliances construct.
   C. Drag and drop the Main Floor construct into the Plumbing-Appliances drawing. This externally references the Main Floor drawing into the Plumbing-Appliances drawing as a reference for placing plumbing blocks.
   D. Add plumbing fixtures as displayed in the figure.
   E. Add appliance blocks as displayed in the figure.
   F. Detach the Main Floor construct xref.
   G. Save and close the drawing.
   H. Access the **Constructs** tab and create a new construct named Furniture. Assign the Furniture construct to the Main Floor level. Open the Furniture construct.
   I. Drag and drop the Main Floor and Plumbing-Appliances constructs into the Furniture drawing.
   J. Add any blocks for furniture as desired.
   K. Use the **DC Online** tab in **DesignCenter** to insert any desired blocks. *Note*: The standard blocks in the **DC Online** tab are typically drawn using the metric system. If the drawing is using feet and inches, scale the blocks after inserting. If the blocks are metric, scale up accordingly.
   L. Refer to the Student CD for additional multi-view blocks that can be inserted into the drawing. These have been processed through the **AEC Content Wizard** and can be saved to a custom folder under the AEC Content folder.

M. Detach the Main Floor and Plumbing-Appliances construct xrefs.

N. Save and close the drawing.

O. Start a new drawing using one of the Aec Model templates.

P. Create a layer named A-Anno-Otln and set it current.

Q. Drag and drop the Main Floor construct into the drawing.

R. Draw a closed polyline around the building.

S. Detach the Main Floor xref.

T. Access the **Constructs** tab. Right-click on the Constructs folder and pick **Save Current DWG as Construct…** from the shortcut menu. In the **Add Construct** worksheet, set the following:

    a. **Name**: Foundation

    b. **Description**: Foundation.

    c. **Category**: Constructs

    d. Select the **Foundation** level check box in the **Division 1** column.

U. Save and close the drawing.

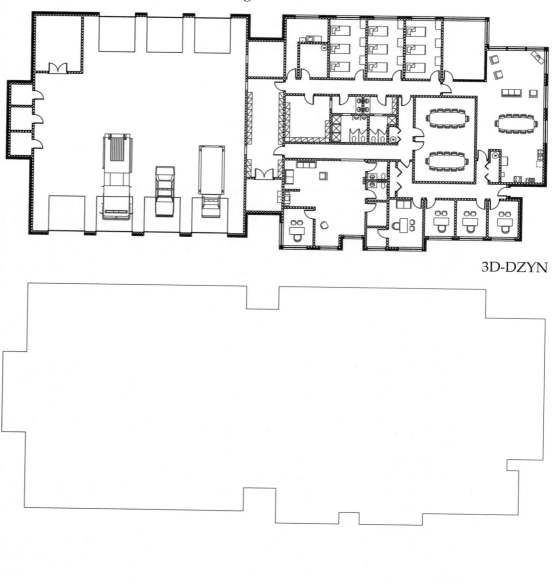

3D-DZYN

CHAPTER 10

Working with Structural Members

Learning Objectives

After completing this chapter, you will be able to do the following:
- ✓ Use the **Structural Member Catalog** to load structural styles.
- ✓ Add beams to the drawing.
- ✓ Add braces to the drawing.
- ✓ Add columns to the drawing.
- ✓ Use the **Structural Member Style Wizard** to create a structural style.
- ✓ Define a custom shape as a structural member.
- ✓ Import structural styles from other drawings.

Architectural Desktop objects such as walls, doors, and windows are used to represent real-world objects. This chapter introduces the use of structural members such as beams, braces, and columns, which are also represented as real objects.

Structural members are objects in Architectural Desktop that are used to create beams, columns, and braces. The shapes are similar to AEC profiles, representing a cross section of the structural member, but are defined through a structural catalog. The **Structural Member Catalog** is organized similarly to industry standard structural catalogs. Structural member shapes include concrete, steel, and timber. The **Structural Member Catalog** is accessed by selecting **Format** > **Structural Members** > **Catalog...** from the pull-down menu. This displays the **Structural Member Catalog** shown in **Figure 10-1.**

> **Pull-Down Menu**
> Format
> > Structural
> > Members
> > Catalog...

The **Structural Member Catalog** is divided into three panes. The left pane includes the structural catalogs for both imperial-unit members and metric members. Pressing the + sign beside the catalog name expands the tree view of each catalog. The lower-right pane provides a list of the structural shapes available for each catalog, along with structural information related to the structural member in a table. The upper-right pane includes a general preview of the structural member selected in the left pane.

In order to use common construction structural members in the drawing, a style must first be added. To create the structural shape style, browse through the catalog for the desired structural member. Once the structural member has been found in the tables, double-click the shape designation in the table to display the **Structural Member Style** worksheet. Highlighting the structural member in the table and picking the **Generate Member Style** button also displays the **Structural Member Style** worksheet. The default name of the style is displayed in the **New Name:** text box of the worksheet.

Figure 10-1.
The **Structural Member Catalog** includes several industry structural catalogs and shapes.

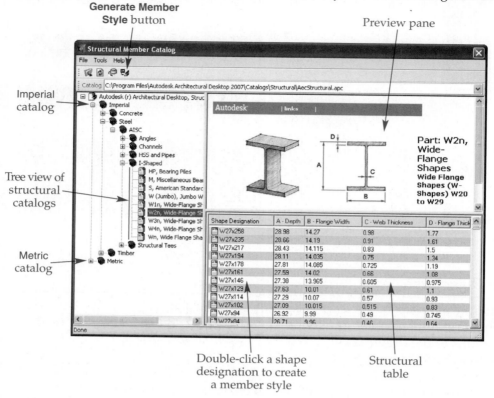

Generate Member
Style button

Preview pane

Imperial
catalog

Tree view of
structural
catalogs

Metric
catalog

Double-click a shape
designation to create
a member style

Structural
table

The style can be given a new name or use the default name from the table. Pick the **OK** button when you are finished, to add the style to the drawing. Special characters, such as: /, $, ', ", and #, cannot be used in a style name.

Add as many structural member styles into the drawing as needed. If a size is not available, or a custom shape needs to be used, it can be created later in this text. When you are finished adding styles, close the **Structural Member Catalog**.

Exercise
10-1

Complete the Exercise on the Student CD.

Using Structural Members

After structural member styles have been created, they can be used to design columns, beams, and braces. Structural members can be drawn by specifying a start point and an endpoint for a structural shape. The distance between the two points is filled with the shape of the structural member style. Structural members can also be created by converting straight, curved, or multi-segmented polylines into a structural member.

Architectural Desktop and Its Applications

Adding a Beam

A *beam* is a horizontal structural member. Beam objects in Architectural Desktop require a start point and an endpoint. Beams are added to the drawing by picking the **Structural Beam** tool in the **Design** palette or by selecting **Design** > **Structural Members** > **Add Beam...** from the pull-down menu.

Pull-Down Menu
Design
> Structural
  Members
  > Add Beam...
Tool Palette
Design
Structural Beam

Once the command has been entered, the properties for the beam can be adjusted before adding it to the drawing. See **Figure 10-2.** The **Properties** palette is used to select the style, offsets, and justification of the beam. A number of properties that are available when creating walls, doors, and windows are available when creating beams.

There are also several properties that are specific to the creation of beams. The **Trim automatically** option is used to automatically trim the ends of new structural members between two existing structural members. The **Start offset** value specifies an offset from the start of the beam. The starting point selected in the drawing indicates where the length of the beam is calculated, but the actual beam can start at an offset distance from the start point. See **Figure 10-3.** The **End offset** specifies an end offset for the beam. See **Figure 10-3.** The **Roll** value rotates the beam along its length. This is the length of the beam between the start point and endpoint and is also referred to as the X axis of the beam.

The **Layout type** property contains the **Edge** option and the **Fill** option. The **Edge** option adds a new structural member along the edge of an object that the crosshairs hover over and highlight. Pressing [Ctrl] while hovering over an object places the structural object over a single edge or around any edges connected to the edge being highlighted. The **Fill** option allows you to add a structural member between the edges of a closed object. Pressing [Ctrl] while hovering over an edge of a closed object toggles between different **Fill** modes.

The **Array** option is available if the **Layout type** property is set to **Fill**. This option is used to array copies of a structural member that is being filled within a closed object. The property is a **Yes** or **No** value. If **Yes** is specified, the **Layout method** property is available. If the **Space evenly** option is chosen, the **Number of bays** property is displayed. This property allows you to specify the total number of divisions to add within the closed object by separating them with the structural member being added.

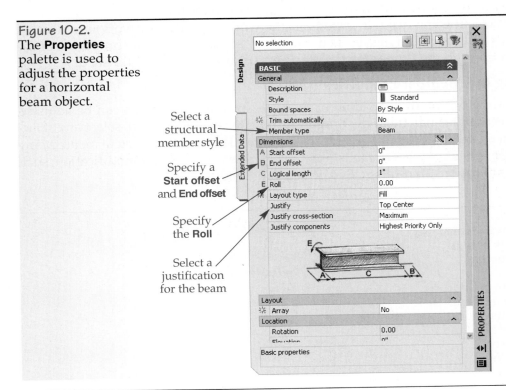

Figure 10-2.
The **Properties** palette is used to adjust the properties for a horizontal beam object.

Select a structural member style

Specify a **Start offset** and **End offset**

Specify the **Roll**

Select a justification for the beam

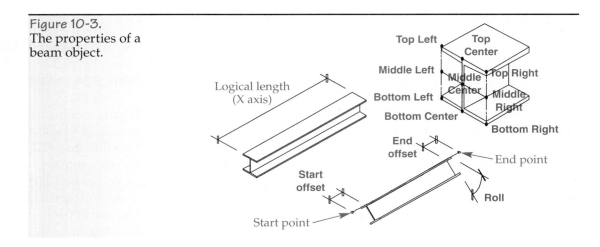

Figure 10-3.
The properties of a beam object.

If the **Layout method** property is set to **Repeat**, you can repeat the insertion of the structural member by specifying a distance between structural members in the **Bay size** property.

Selecting the **Trim planes** property displays the **Beam Trim Planes** worksheet, where the start point and endpoint of the beam can be assigned different mitered or trimmed angles. Trim planes are discussed later in this chapter.

Converting a Polyline to a Beam

Polylines, lines, and arcs can be converted into structural members. To do this, first draw the desired polyline shape, straight, curved, multi-segmented, or a combination of straight and curved. Next, right-click the **Structural Beam** tool in the **Design** palette and select **Apply Tool Properties** > **Linework** from the shortcut menu.

After using the option, select the polylines, lines, or arcs to be converted. When you are finished selecting polylines, press [Enter]. The **Convert to Beam** worksheet is displayed. See **Figure 10-4.** Select the **One Member Per Polyline Segment** to add a structural member along each segment. If you uncheck this option, the entire length of the polyline is converted into a structural member. Select the **Erase Layout Geometry** check box if you no longer need the polyline used to create the structural member.

After selecting the desired options in the worksheet, the linework is converted into a structural beam and highlighted. Make any adjustments to the properties of the new beam through the **Properties** palette. Press [Esc] when you are finished.

Adjusting the Member Properties

The properties of an individual or multiple structural members can be adjusted using the **Properties** palette. If the **Properties** palette is not displayed, select any structural beam member(s), right-click, and select **Properties** from the shortcut menu. Many of the properties used when establishing the beam are available for modification, such as **Roll**, **Justification**, **Start offset**, **End offset**, and **Style**.

Figure 10-4.
The **Convert to Beam** worksheet is used to add the structural member to the entire length or add structural members to each segment of the polyline and to keep or erase the layout polyline.

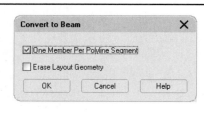

In addition to these properties, several location properties are available for specifying the start or end X, Y, and Z axis points. If the beam is intended to be placed at a specific elevation, use the **Elevation** property to move the beam to the appropriate height.

The **Trim planes** property is used to modify the angle of the beam at the start point and endpoint to create mitered angles. Selecting the property displays the **Beam Trim Planes** worksheet where mitered angles can be added or edited. See **Figure 10-5**.

Use the **Add** button in the worksheet to add a mitered angle. Picking any of the values within the table allows the properties of the angle to be configured. The **From** column allows you to add a mitered angle to the start or the end of the beam. Picking any of the numerical axis values can be used to enter the new value. Positive and negative values can be entered. If additional trim planes are added, the **Copy** button can be used to copy the values of an existing trim plane. If a mitered angle is removed, pick the trim plane, and then select the **Remove** button to delete it. When you are finished adding the mitered angle, pick the **OK** button to return to the drawing.

Trim planes can also be added when a beam intersects with another structural member of an AEC object through the use of the right-click shortcut menu. Select the structural member(s) whose trim planes are adjusted, right-click, and select **Trim Planes** > **Add Trim Plane** from the shortcut menu. You are prompted to select the AEC object the structural member is intersecting. Then, pick a point on the side of the structural member that will be trimmed away.

This adds a trim plane to the structural members and cleans up the intersection of the members. See **Figure 10-6**. After a trim plane has been added, it can be edited by selecting the structural member, right-clicking, and selecting **Trim Planes** > **Edit Trim Planes** from the shortcut menu. A series of grip points is available for editing the rotation and placement of the trim plane within the structural member. If two structural members intersect each other at a corner, you may want to miter their edges. To do this, select one of the structural members, right-click, and select **Trim Planes** > **Miter** from the shortcut menu. You are prompted to select the other structural member to be mitered. Then, pick a point on the side of the structural member that will be trimmed away. The two structural members will be mitered to fit together.

In addition to using the **Properties** palette and trim plane options to modify the beam, standard AutoCAD commands, such as **TRIM** and **EXTEND**, can be used to lengthen or shorten beam lengths. The **ARRAY** and **OFFSET** commands can be used to offset a series of beams that need to be parallel to each other. Grip editing can also be used to modify the beams. **Figure 10-7** shows the grips located along a beam object.

Figure 10-5.
Trimming planes (mitered angles) can be added to either end of a beam.

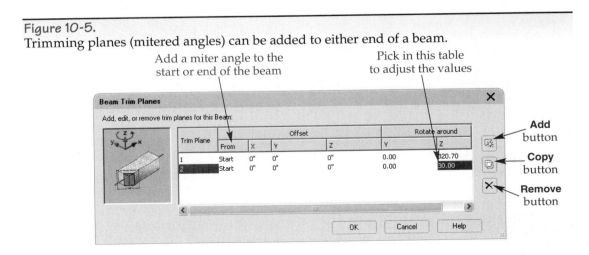

Figure 10-6.
Trim planes can be added to structural members that intersect other AEC objects.

2. Pick the AEC object that is being intersected and will be used to establish the trim plane

3. Pick the side of the structural members to be removed

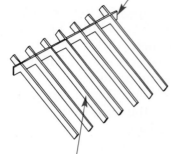
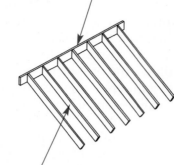

1. Select structural members to add trim planes to

4. Structural members are trimmed against the other AEC object

Figure 10-7.
Beam grips are used to modify the beam object.

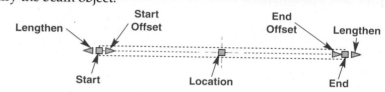

Lengthen

Start Offset

End Offset

Lengthen

Start

Location

End

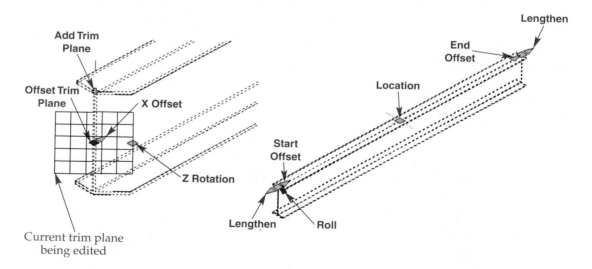

Add Trim Plane

Offset Trim Plane

X Offset

Z Rotation

Current trim plane being edited

End Offset

Lengthen

Location

Start Offset

Lengthen

Roll

Exercise 10-2

Complete the Exercise on the Student CD.

Adding a Brace

A *brace* is a structural element placed at an angle, such as the rafter in a roof or earthquake bracing in a building. To add braces into the drawing, select the **Structural Brace** tool in the **Design** palette, or select **Design** > **Structural Members** > **Add Brace...** from the pull-down menu.

Pull-Down Menu
Design
> Structural
Members
> Add Brace...

Tool Palette
Design

Structural Brace

The properties for structural braces can be specified in the **Properties** palette before adding the brace into the drawing. The **Specify rise on screen** property is specific to structural braces. This property is a **Yes** or **No** value. A value of **Yes** requires you to pick the ending rise height by snapping to a point in the Z axis or by entering a 3D coordinate. A **No** value displays the **Method** property. This controls the angle or rise of the brace when placed against a column and beam. Three options are available for this property. See **Figure 10-8**.

The **Angle** option displays two properties: **Distance along first member** and **Angle from first member**. When adding a brace, select the first structural member and then the second, to establish the brace. The value entered for the **Distance along the first member** is measured from the end of the member to the start of the brace. The value entered for the angle is the angle of the brace measured from the first structural member picked.

The **Distance** option displays two properties: **Distance along first member** and **Distance along second member**. The value entered for the **Distance along the first member** is measured from the end of the first selected member to the start of the brace. The value entered for the **Distance along second member** is measured from the end of the second selected member to the end of the brace.

The **Height** option displays the **Rise** property. You can type an absolute height for the brace as the length of the brace is specified.

Braces can be converted from polylines, lines, or arcs. This technique can be effective for creating a curved, vaulted ceiling. First draw the lines, arcs, or polylines in an elevation view. Next, right-click on the **Structural Brace** tool in the **Design** palette, and select **Apply Tool Properties** > **Linework** from the shortcut menu. You are prompted to select lines, arcs, or open polylines to convert into members. When you are finished selecting linework to be converted, press [Enter]. This displays the **Convert to Brace** worksheet. In the worksheet, decide if a single brace is created or if individual brace objects are created along each segment of the polyline. When you are finished, the new brace is displayed in the drawing. Specify any properties, such as the style or offsets, in the **Properties** palette.

Figure 10-8.
The different rise methods for brace placement.

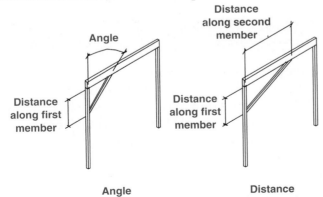
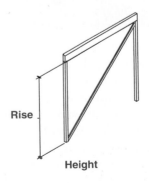

Braces display as hidden lines in elevation and model views. In a Top view, the brace is displayed as a profile along the centerline. This profile is the shape of the brace at the cut plane height. To modify the display of the brace, select a brace object, right-click, and select the **Edit Object Display...** option. Pick the appropriate display representation to modify in the **Object Display** dialog box, and then pick the **Edit Display Properties** button to open the **Display Properties** dialog box.

The components above or below the cut plane can be turned on or off and given different color or linetype properties. The components can also be turned on or off in the **Visible** column to display the profile of brace components. By default, brace objects use the current display configuration's cut plane. To override the cut plane for the brace object, pick the **Other** tab in the **Display Properties** dialog box and select the **Override Display Configuration Cut Plane** check box. This makes the **Cut Plane Elevation** text box available so a new cut plane can be specified.

Adding a Column

Pull-Down Menu

Design
> Structural
  Members
  > Add Column...

Tool Palette

Design

Structural Column

A *column* is a vertical structural member often used as a post to support a beam or brace. Columns can also be used as vertical stud members in a wall. To add a column into the drawing, pick the **Structural Column** tool in the **Design** palette, or select **Design** > **Structural Members** > **Add Column...** from the pull-down menu.

The properties of a column can also be specified through the **Properties** palette. The **Logical length** property for a column refers to the height of the column and is not a read-only value as it is with the other structural members. Although the length property extends up in elevation, it is considered the X axis of the column member. When the **Specify roll on screen** property is set to **Yes**, you can rotate the column after it has been placed in the drawing. If the column is being placed with a preset rotation angle, select **No** in the **Specify roll on screen** prompt and enter the predefined rotation angle in the **Roll** property. After specifying the properties for the column, it can be added to the drawing.

New columns can be created by converting lines, arcs, or polylines into columns. First draw the geometry in an elevation view that defines the shape of the column. Next, right-click the **Structural Column** tool in the **Design** palette, and select **Apply Tool Properties** > **Linework** from the shortcut menu. Select any linework to be converted to columns. Press [Enter] when you are finished to display the **Convert to Column** worksheet. Specify if you want to create a single column object or add columns along each segment of the polyline. Next, decide to erase or keep the layout geometry, and pick **OK** to convert the geometry. After the linework has been converted, use the **Properties** palette to adjust any properties for the new columns.

Using the Structural Member Style Wizard

Pull-Down Menu

Format
> Structural
  Members
  > Wizard...

When browsing through the **Structural Member Catalog**, you may not find an appropriately sized structural member. To overcome this, custom-size structural members can be created by specifying the desired shape from a list of shapes before modifying the size values for the structural shape. The **Structural Member Style Wizard** is used to create custom-size structural members from a list of predefined shapes. To access the wizard, pick **Format** > **Structural Members** > **Wizard...** from the pull-down menu. This displays the **Structural Member Style Wizard** dialog box shown in **Figure 10-9**.

In the **Structural Member Style Wizard**, scroll through the list to locate the desired shape. Pick the shape from the list, and pick the **Next** button. This displays the second page of the wizard. See **Figure 10-10**. A table of sizes is available for the default-size shape. Pick inside of a table value to enter a new size, and pick the **Next** button.

Figure 10-9.
The **Structural Member Style Wizard** is used to create a custom-sized structural member style for use as a beam, brace, or column.

Select the shape to define the structural style

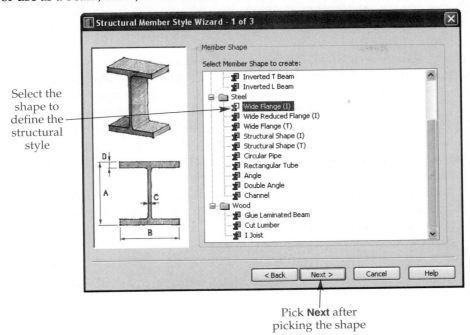

Pick **Next** after picking the shape

Figure 10-10.
Enter new sizes for the custom structural style.

Pick the values in the table to adjust the sizes of the structural member

Preview dimensions match table values

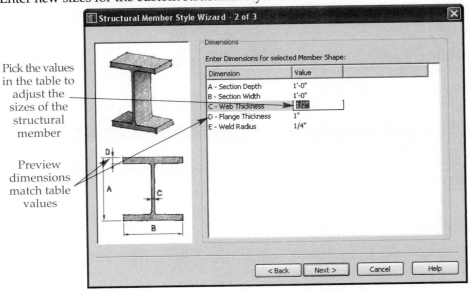

The last page of the wizard is used to enter the name for the style. Any name can be used up to 255 characters, with no special characters. When you are finished specifying the parameters for the custom style, pick the **Finish** button. The style is now ready to be used when creating new or modifying existing structural members.

Although the **Structural Member Catalog** is extensive, there are times when a shape is not available. This section explains how to create a custom shape for use as a structural member.

When a custom shape is defined, the outline of the shape is drawn as a closed polyline. Three separate groups of shapes can be drawn for use in the Low Detail, Medium Detail, and High Detail display configurations. The Plan Low Detail shapes use lines, arcs, and polylines to define the structural shape. The Plan and Plan High Detail shapes must use a closed polyline as the defining shape, and if voids (holes within the shape) are placed in the shape, closed polylines that do not intersect must be drawn inside of the defining shape. See **Figure 10-11.** Once the geometry for the different display representations has been drawn, the shapes can be defined in Architectural Desktop.

To define a shape, pick **Format** > **Structural Members** > **Member Shapes...** from the pull-down menu. This opens the **Style Manager** at the **Structural Member Shape Definitions** section shown in **Figure 10-12.**

Pull-Down Menu

Format
   > **Structural**
      Members
      > **Member**
         Shapes...

Figure 10-11.
Three separate shapes are drawn for the different display configurations when defining a custom shape.

   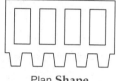   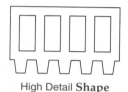

Low Detail **Shape**   Plan **Shape**   High Detail **Shape**

Figure 10-12.
The **Structural Member Shape Definitions** section includes custom defined shapes for use in structural member styles.

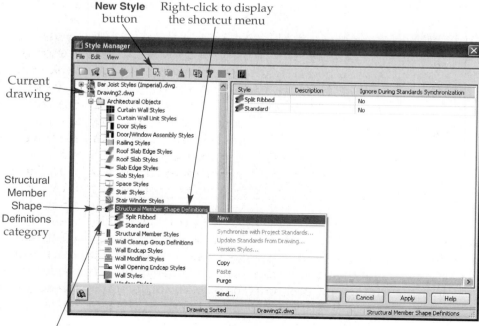

New Style button   Right-click to display the shortcut menu

Current drawing

Structural Member Shape Definitions category

List of custom shape definitions in the current drawing

In the **Style Manager**, pick the **New Style** button to create a new shape definition or right-click on the **Structural Member Shape Definitions** section, right-click, and select **New**. Enter a name for the new shape definition. After the new shape name has been created, select the definition in the left pane of the **Style Manager** to display the definition properties in the right pane. See **Figure 10-13**.

The shape properties include two tabs. The **General** tab is used to rename the shape and provide a description for the shape. The **Design Rules** tab is where the properties for the shape are defined. In the **Design Rules** tab, a preview of the shape is displayed. To the right of the preview is the **Shape Geometry** list box with Low Detail, Medium Detail, and High Detail display configurations available. When one of the display configurations is selected, the appropriate graphics for the display configuration is available in the preview.

Below the **Shape Geometry** list box are two buttons. The first button is different depending on the display configuration option selected in the shape geometry list box. If the **Low Detail** option is selected, this button is used to select linework to be used to display the structural member when a Low Detail display configuration is used. If the **Medium Detail** or **High Detail** option is selected, this button is used to select closed rings to define the shapes for the Medium and High Detail display configurations. Similar to AEC profiles, an outer ring is selected first, and then any internal rings are selected.

To create a Low Detail graphic, select **Low Detail** from the **Shape Geometry** list, and then pick the **Specify elements for Low Detail shape** button. This returns you to the drawing screen where any linework can be selected for the Low Detail shape. You are first prompted to select any graphics that will be used for the Low Detail shape.

Press [Enter] after selecting the geometry for the Low Detail shape. The next prompt asks you to pick an insertion point for the shape. Pick an insertion point that is similar for the Medium and High Detail shapes. Press [Enter] when you are finished. This returns you to the **Style Manager**, where additional geometry can be specified for the Medium and High Detail shapes.

Figure 10-13.
After a **Structural Member Shape Definition** has been created, select the definition in the left pane to display the properties in the right pane of the **Style Manager**.

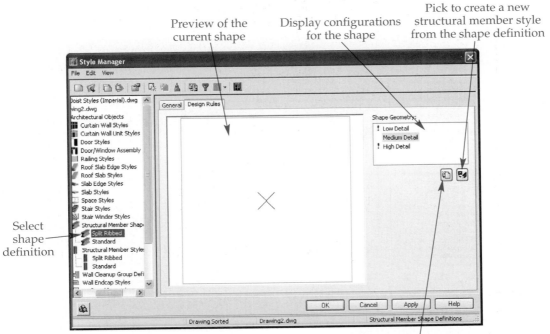

Preview of the current shape

Display configurations for the shape

Pick to create a new structural member style from the shape definition

Select shape definition

Pick to select geometry for the Low Detail shapes or closed rings for the Medium and High Detail shapes

To create the shapes for the Medium and High Detail display configurations, select the **Medium Detail** or **High Detail** option from the list, and pick the **Specify rings for Medium** (or **High**) **Detail shape** button. This returns you to the drawing screen, where the first prompt asks you to select a closed object that defines the outermost boundary of the shape.

After selecting the outer ring, you are prompted to pick an insertion point or to add internal closed rings. Once you are finished defining the geometry for the Medium or High Detail shapes, press [Enter] to return to the **Style Manager**.

The second button is **Create Style**. After a shape has been defined and its geometry has been assigned to the different display configurations, this button can be selected to create a new structural member style from the defined graphics.

If the **Create Style** button is not used to create a new structural member style, a new structural member can be defined in the Structural Member Style section of the **Style Manager**.

Pull-Down Menu
Format
> Structural
Members
> Member
Styles...

To create a new structural member style, select **Format** > **Structural Members** > **Member Styles...** from the pull-down menu. This displays the **Style Manager** at the Structural Member Styles section. Create a new style by selecting the **New Style** button or right-clicking on the Structural Member Styles section and selecting the **New** option. Enter a name for the new style. After naming the style, pick the new style in the left pane to display the properties for the style in the right pane. See **Figure 10-14**.

The dialog box includes five separate tabs for configuring the style. The **General** tab is used to rename and provide a description for the style. The **Design Rules** tab is used to define the rules that make up the structural style. The **Materials** and **Classifications** tabs assign materials and classifications to components within the style. The final tab is the **Display Properties** tab, which controls how the structural member style appears in different display representations.

Figure 10-14.
The **Structural Member Styles** section of the **Style Manager** is used to create and modify structural member styles in the drawing.

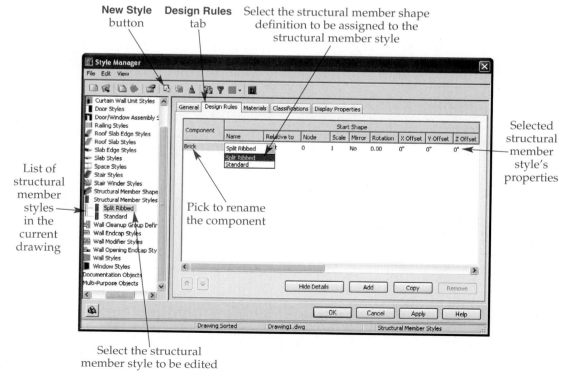

New Style button — Design Rules tab — Select the structural member shape definition to be assigned to the structural member style

List of structural member styles in the current drawing

Pick to rename the component

Selected structural member style's properties

Select the structural member style to be edited

Access the **Design Rules** tab to begin editing. A table is displayed with an unnamed component and the standard shape defined. Pick the unnamed entry to rename the component. See **Figure 10-14.** Next, pick the standard shape name to display a drop-down list of shapes that are loaded in the current drawing. If styles have been added from the **Structural Member Catalog** or the **Structural Member Styles Wizard**, a list of shapes is included in the list. Custom shapes you defined are also in the list. Select the desired shape to be used as a structural style.

When you are finished defining the shape to be used in the style, access the **Display Properties** tab and adjust any display properties for the different display representations. When you are finished, pick the **OK** button to exit the **Style Manager**.

Complex Structural Member Styles

Several individual members can be combined to form complex structural member styles that are referred to as *structural assemblies*. Architectural Desktop also includes some complex structural assemblies that can be used.

To create a complex structural style, select the **Design** > **Structural Members** > **Member Styles...** from the pull-down menu. Create a new structural style, and then select the style in the left pane of the **Style Manager** to access the member's properties. Select the **Design Rules** tab to begin editing the style. See **Figure 10-15.** In the **Design Rules** tab, pick the **Show Details** button. This displays a full table of information for configuring a complex structural style. Pick the values in the table to begin editing.

The columns are used to configure individual structural members in relation to one another in the assembly. The **Component** column displays the name or description of the component. The name does not have to match the actual individual structural member shape or style name being used.

Figure 10-15.
The selected structural member style displays properties in the right pane which are used to create structural assemblies from individual member styles.

Individual structural styles assembled into a complex style

Properties for the starting portion of the individual shape

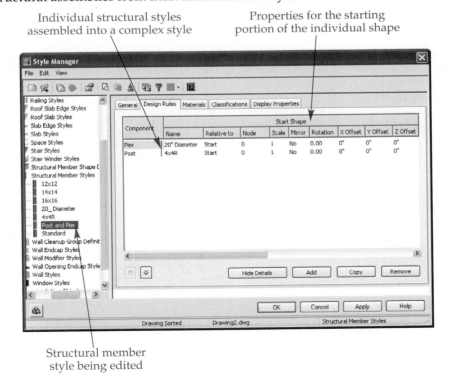

Structural member style being edited

After the **Component** column, the table is divided into **Start Shape** and **End Shape** categories. The start and end shapes can be the same or have two different shapes. The majority of the remaining columns fall under the **Start Shape** and **End Shape** categories, controlling various aspects of the shape at either end. The following columns are found in both categories:

- **Name.** This column refers to the name of the individual structural member shape being used. Selecting the name displays a drop-down list with the individual structural member shapes available in the drawing. Select the desired structural member shape to be added in the assembly. Two different shapes can be used for the start and end shapes to create complex shapes.
- **Relative to.** The column specifies the position of the structural member shape relative to the start point or endpoint of the assembly.
- **Node.** This column places structural member shapes along different points of the assembly known as *nodes*. A single segment within an assembly has two nodes, one at the beginning of the shape and one at the end of the shape. For example, an assembly with three shapes has six nodes, one at each end of the shape that can be assigned an additional shape. The starting point of the first shape in the assembly is known as Node 0. The next point along the assembly is considered Node 2, and so on.
- **Scale.** The column controls the scale of the individual structural member shape.
- **Mirror.** This column mirrors the structural member shape along the length (X) axis.
- **Rotation.** This column rotates the individual structural member shape around the length (X) axis of the assembly.
- **X Offset.** This column offsets the individual structural member shape along the X axis, which is the length of the assembly. **Figure 10-16** is an example of different shapes being placed at different locations in the X axis of the structural member style.

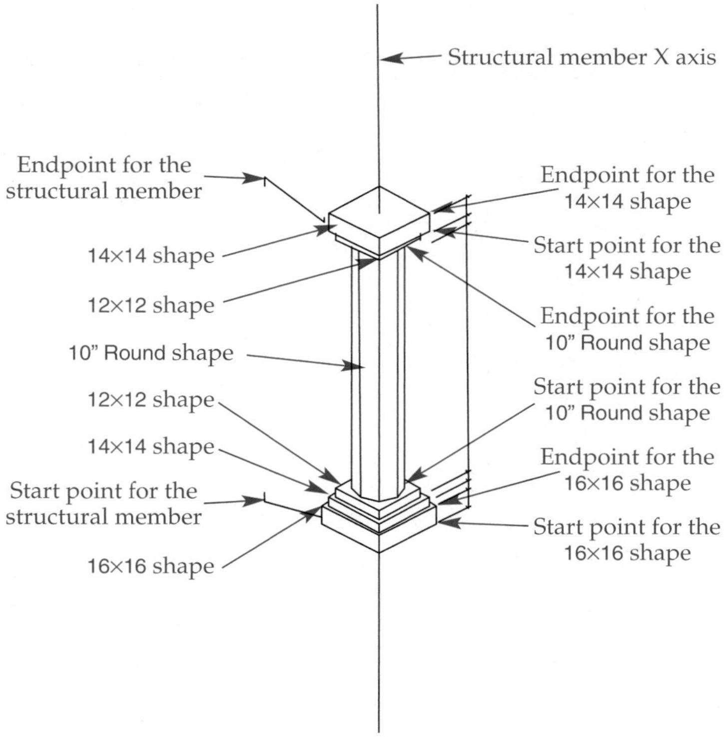

Figure 10-16.
Different shapes can be used for the starting and ending shape of a component within the structural member. Adjust the **X Offset** value to place the component shapes along the X axis of the structural member style.

- **Y Offset.** The values specified in this column offset the structural member shape in the Y direction, perpendicular to the X axis.
- **Z Offset.** This column offsets the structural member shape in the Z direction, perpendicular to the X axis.

The **Priority** column is the final column at the far end of the table. Each individual structural member shape can have a different priority assigned. A high priority is a low number, and a low priority is a high number. Structural shapes that start and end at the same point are mitered based on their assigned priority. A structural component with a high priority overrides a structural component with a low priority where they cross each other.

The buttons beneath the table also affect components. The **Add** button adds another component or individual structural member style to the assembly. The **Copy** button allows you to copy the values of an existing component in the assembly for use as another component in the assembly. The **Remove** button removes individual components from the assembly. The **Hide Details** button hides the table values for the components within the assembly.

Exercise
10-3   **Complete the Exercise on the Student CD.**

Importing Styles

Architectural Desktop includes several preconfigured structural member styles. Some are complex assemblies such as steel bar joists and precast concrete planks, and others are basic structural shapes such as round columns with flared tops and concrete encased steel members. See **Figure 10-17.**

Figure 10-17.
A few additional complex assembly structural members are included with Architectural Desktop.

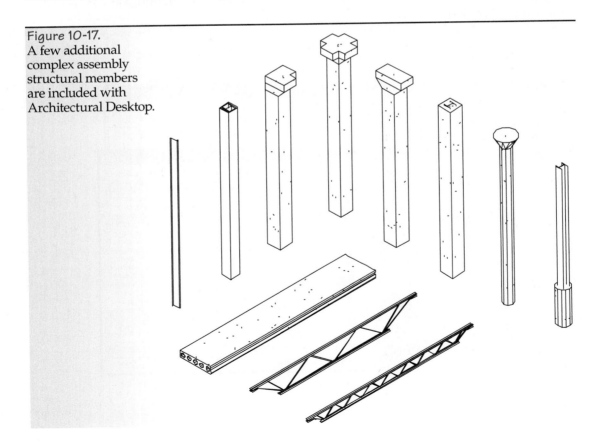

In order to import these styles into the drawing, access the **Member Styles...** option to open the **Style Manager**, and pick the **Open Drawing** button to browse for drawings containing structural styles in the **Open Drawing** dialog box shown in **Figure 10-18**. Pick the **Content** button along the left edge of the dialog box. This opens the enu folder, which includes a list of folders containing extra content included with Architectural Desktop. Double-click the Styles folder, and double-click either the Imperial or Metric folder to access drawings containing different AEC styles.

If you are browsing through the hard drive for the Styles folder that comes with Architectural Desktop, the path is \\Documents and Settings\All Users\Application Data\ Autodesk\ADT 2007\enu. This folder has several folders including the AEC Content folder containing multi-view blocks, the Layers folder that has layering standards, and the Styles folder with the AEC styles. Double-clicking the Styles folder displays the Imperial and Metric folders containing a list of drawings with several different types of styles.

Two drawings containing structural member styles are included within the Imperial folder. These drawings are the Bar Joist Styles (Imperial).dwg and the Member Styles (Imperial).dwg. Select one of the drawings, and pick the **Open** button to return to the **Style Manager** with the new drawing file open. See **Figure 10-18**. To import a style from the new source drawing into your current drawing, expand the Structural Member Styles list in the source drawing, find the desired style, and drag and drop it into your current drawing folder. When you are finished dragging styles from a source drawing, close the drawing by highlighting the drawing icon in the left pane, right-click, and select the **Close** option.

If you are creating a metric scaled drawing, browse through the Metric folder under the Styles folder. This folder includes Member Styles (Metric).dwg containing a few complex structural styles.

Figure 10-18.

The **Open Drawing** button in the **Style Manager** is used to browse for additional AEC content included with Architectural Desktop. Pick the Content icon to browse to the Styles folder for drawings containing additional AEC styles.

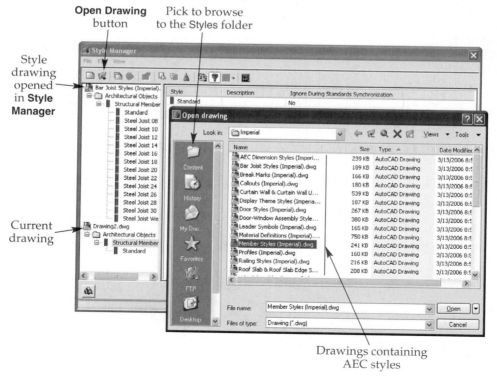

In addition to using the **Style Manager** to browse for and import styles, the **Content Browser** includes several catalogs of AEC Content. The **Design Tool Catalog – Imperial** (or **Metric**) catalog includes the additional structural member styles found in the style drawings. Drag any desired content from a catalog to a tool palette. The tool palette then includes a tool to add the structural member style to your drawing. Refer to Appendix B for additional information on the **Content Browser** and tool palettes.

Two additional sources for free content are available. Visit the Autodesk Web site at *http://usa.autodesk.com*. Different styles are available for download. Once the drawings have been downloaded, use the **Style Manager** to browse for the downloaded drawings and import the styles into your current drawing. Another source for custom styles and content is Autodesk newsgroups. If you have a newsreader, visit the *discussion.autodesk.com* news server. Custom styles are uploaded and available for free to Architectural Desktop users.

The CD included with this book also contains some AEC styles that have been custom created or downloaded from the Internet for your use.

Chapter Test

Answer the following questions. Write your answers on a separate sheet of paper or complete the electronic chapter test on the Student CD.

1. Define and give an example of structural members.
2. Identify the basic function of the **Structural Member Catalog**.
3. Give a very basic definition for a beam.
4. Define and give an example of a brace.
5. Identify two uses for columns.
6. Give the basic function of the **Structural Member Style Wizard**.
7. What are structural assemblies?
8. How many nodes are there in a single segment within an assembly, and where are they located?

Chapter Projects

Use the techniques covered in this chapter to create the following drawings.

1. Single-Level Residential Project
   A. Access the **Project Browser** and set Residential-Project-01 current.
   B. Access the **Constructs** tab and open the Foundation construct.
   C. Create a non-plotting layer named A-Anno-Nplt and set it current.
   D. Draw a closed polyline around the outside edge of the stem wall where the living areas above are located.
   E. Use the **Structural Member Catalog** to add the 4×8R and 4×4R Rough Cut Lumber styles to the drawing.
   F. Use the **Structural Member Wizard** to create a round concrete member that is 18″ in diameter.
   G. Add 4 × 8 beams spaced 4'-0″ apart as shown in the figure. Use a justification of **Top Center**.
   H. Adjust the beams to have a 5″ **Start offset** and a −5″ **End offset**. This will extend the beams 3″ into the foundation stem wall.
   I. Create the Post and Pier structural style as shown in the following tables.

Components	Start Shape								
	Name	Relative to	Node	Scale	Mirror	Rotation	X Offset	Y Offset	Z Offset
Pier	18in Dia Conc	Start	0	1	No	0.00	0″	0″	0″
Post	4×4R	Start	0	1	No	0.00	8″	0″	0″

Components	End Shape								
	Name	Relative to	Node	Scale	Mirror	Rotation	X Offset	Y Offset	Z Offset
Pier	18in Dia Conc	Start	0	1	No	0.00	8″	0″	0″
Post	4×4R	End	0	1	No	0.00	0″	0″	0″

Components	Priority
Pier	100
Post	250

   J. Adjust the display properties for the Post and Pier to display the Below Cut Plane component in the Plan view.
   K. Add the Post and Pier structural members as columns 2'-10″ high along the 4 × 8 beams spaced 8'-0″ apart.
   L. Use the **Properties** palette to adjust the **Elevation** property for the 4 × 8 beams to be 2'-6″.
   M. Use the **Properties** palette to adjust the **Elevation** property for the Post and Pier columns to be −1'-0″.
   N. Save and close the drawing.

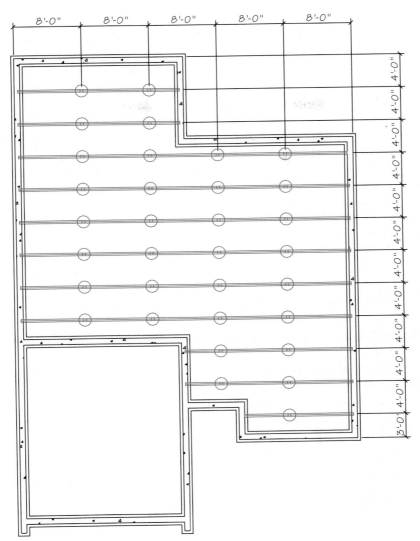

Design Courtesy Alan Mascord Design Associates

2. Single-Level Residential Project
   A. Access the **Project Browser** and set Residential-Project-02 current.
   B. Access the **Constructs** tab and open the Foundation construct.
   C. Create a non-plotting layer named A-Anno-Nplt and set it current.
   D. Draw a closed polyline around the outside edge of the stem wall where the living areas above are located.
   E. Use the **Structural Member Catalog** to add the 4×8R and 4×4R Rough Cut Lumber styles to the drawing. From the Imperial > Concrete > Cast-in-place > Beams catalog, add the 24″×24″ style to the drawing.
   F. Add 4 × 8 beams as shown in the figure. Use a justification of **Top Center**.
   G. Adjust the beams to have a 5″ **Start offset** and a −5″ **End offset**. This will extend the beams 3″ into the foundation stem wall.
   H. Create a Post and Pad structural style similar to the Post and Pier style discussed in this chapter. Use 24″ × 24″ × 8″ high concrete pads instead of the round piers.
   I. Adjust the display properties for the Post and Pad to display the Below Cut Plane component in the Plan view.
   J. Add the Post and Pier structural members as columns 2′-0″ high along the 4 × 8 beams as shown in the figure.
   K. Use the **Properties** palette to adjust the **Elevation** property for the 4 × 8 beams to be 1′-8″.
   L. Use the **Properties** palette to adjust the **Elevation** property for the Post and Pier columns to be −1′-0″.
   M. Save and close the drawing.

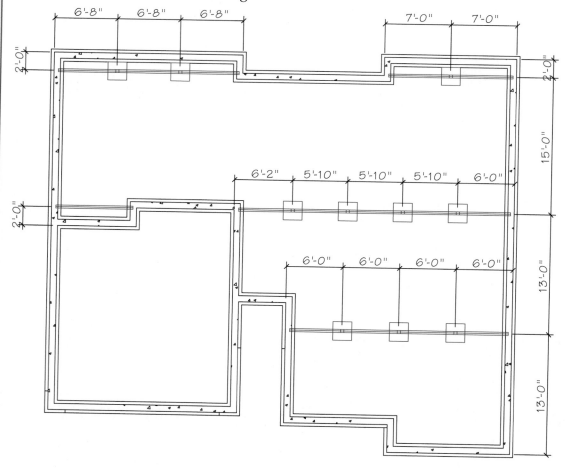

Design Courtesy Alan Mascord Design Associates

3. Two-Story Residential Project
   A. Access the **Project Browser** and set Residential-Project-03 current.
   B. Access the **Constructs** tab and open the Foundation construct.
   C. Create a non-plotting layer named A-Anno-Nplt and set it current.
   D. Draw a closed polyline around the outside edge of the stem wall where the living areas above are located.
   E. Use the **Structural Member Catalog** to add the 4x8R and 4x4R Rough Cut Lumber styles to the drawing.
   F. Use the **Structural Member Wizard** to create a round concrete member that is 18″ in diameter.
   G. Add 4 × 8 beams spaced 4′-0″ apart as shown in the figure. Use a justification of **Top Center**.
   H. Adjust the beams to have a 5″ **Start offset** and a −5″ **End offset**. This will extend the beams 3″ into the foundation stem wall.
   I. Create the Post and Pier structural style discussed in this chapter.
   J. Adjust the display properties for the Post and Pier to display the Below Cut Plane component in the Plan view.
   K. Add the Post and Pier structural members as columns 2′-10″ high along the 4 × 8 beams spaced 8′-0″ apart.
   L. Use the **Properties** palette to adjust the **Elevation** property for the 4 × 8 beams to be 2′-6″.
   M. Use the **Properties** palette to adjust the **Elevation** property for the Post and Pier columns to be −1′-0″.
   N. Save and close the drawing.

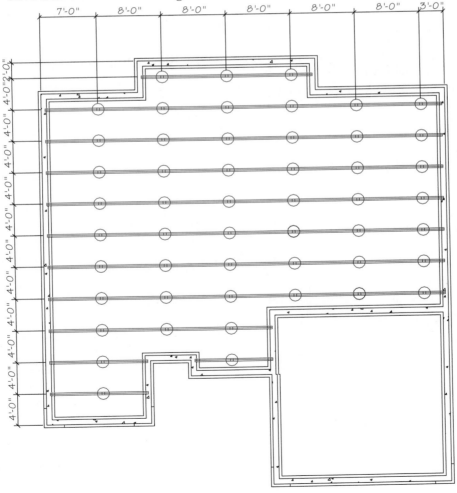

Drawing Courtesy 3D-DZYN

4. Two-Story Residential Project
   A. Access the **Project Browser** and set Residential-Project-04 current.
   B. Access the **Constructs** tab and open the Foundation construct.
   C. Create a non-plotting layer named A-Anno-Nplt and set it current.
   D. Draw a closed polyline around the outside edge of the stem wall where the living areas above are located.
   E. Use the **Structural Member Catalog** to add the 4x8R and 4x4R Rough Cut Lumber styles to the drawing. From the Imperial > Concrete > Cast-in-place > Beams catalog, add the 24"x24" style to the drawing.
   F. Use the **Structural Member Wizard** to create a round concrete member that is 18" in diameter.
   G. Add 4 × 8 beams as shown in the figure. Use a justification of **Top Center**.
   H. Adjust the beams to have a 5" **Start offset** and a –5" **End offset**. This will extend the beams 3" into the foundation stem wall.
   I. Create a Post and Pad structural style similar to the Post and Pier style discussed in this chapter. Use 24" × 24" × 8" high concrete pads instead of the round piers.
   J. Adjust the display properties for the Post and Pad to display the Below Cut Plane component in the Plan view.
   K. Create the Post and Pier structural style discussed in this chapter.
   L. Adjust the display properties for the Post and Pier to display the Below Cut Plane component in the Plan view.
   M. Add the Post and Pier and Post and Pad structural members as columns 2'-10" high along the 4 × 8 beams as shown in the figure.
   N. Use the **Properties** palette to adjust the **Elevation** property for the 4 × 8 beams to be 2'-6".
   O. Use the **Properties** palette to adjust the **Elevation** property for the Post and Pier columns to be –1'-0".
   P. Save and close the drawing.

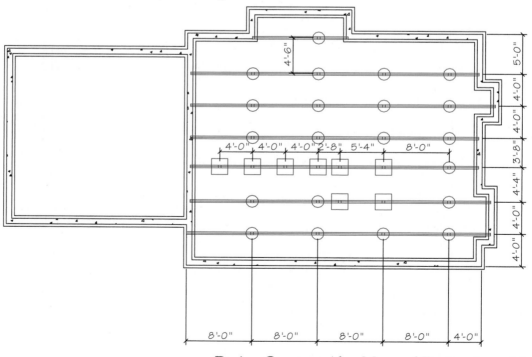

Design Courtesy Alan Mascord Design Associates

5. Commercial Store Project
   A. Access the **Project Browser** and set Commercial-Project-05 current.
   B. Access the **Constructs** tab and create a new construct named Ceiling Framing. Assign the Ceiling Framing construct to the Ceiling Framing level. Open the Ceiling Framing construct.
   C. Drag and drop the Main Floor construct into the Ceiling Framing drawing for use as a reference for the steel framing.
   D. Access the **Member Styles** command, and in the **Style Manager**, open the Bar Joist (Imperial).dwg (found in the \\enu\Styles\Imperial folder). Drag and drop the Steel Joist 20 onto the Ceiling Framing drawing icon in the **Style Manager**.
   E. Place beams using the Steel Joist 20 style 8'-0" apart using a **Top Center** justification. See figure for placement.
   F. Use the **Properties** palette to change the **Elevation** property of the Steel Joist 20 beams to a height of 0".
   G. Use the **Structural Member Catalog** to add two structural members. From the Imperial>Steel>AISC>HSS and Pipes>HSS, Hollow Structural Sections catalog, add the HSS12×4×1/4 style. From the Imperial>Steel>AISC>I-Shaped>W1n, Wide-Flange Shapes catalog, add the W12×16 style.
   H. Add columns using the HSS12×4×1/4 style to the front of the building as indicated in the figure. Make the columns 11'-0" high.
   I. Use the **Properties** palette to adjust the **Elevation** property for the HSS12×4×1/4 columns to −12'-0".
   J. Add beams using the W12×16 with a justification of **Bottom Center** over the columns. See figure for placement.
   K. Use the **Properties** palette to adjust the **Elevation** property for the W12×16 beams to be set at −1'-0".
   L. Detach the Main Floor construct.
   M. Save and close the drawing.

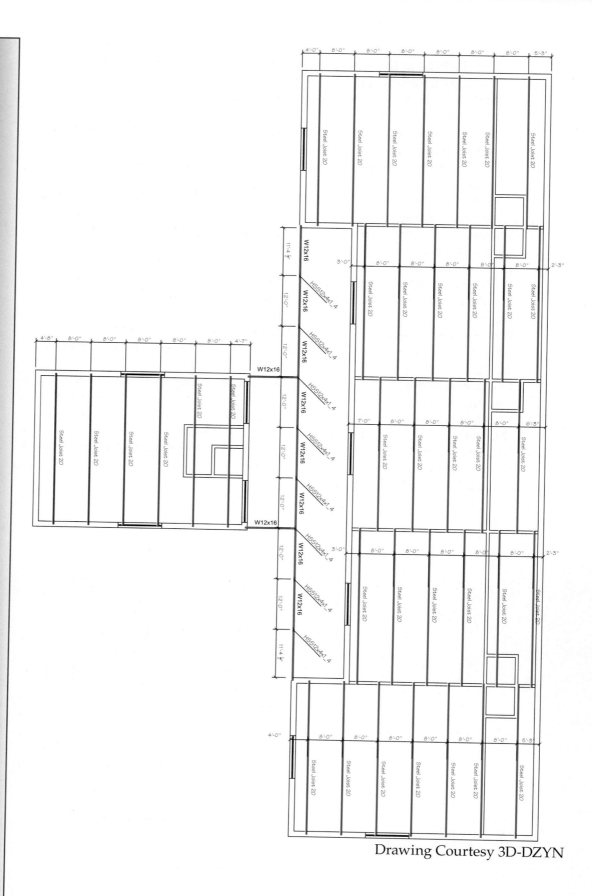

Drawing Courtesy 3D-DZYN

6. Commercial Car Maintenance Shop Project
   A. Access the **Project Browser** and set Commercial-Project-06 current.
   B. Access the **Constructs** tab and open the Foundation construct.
   C. Access the **Structural Member Catalog**.
   D. Load the following styles:
      a. From the Imperial>Steel>AISC>I-Shaped>Wn, Wide-Flange Shapes catalog, load W6×12.
      b. From the Imperial>Steel>AISC>I-Shaped>W1n, Wide-Flange Shapes catalog, load W12×16.
      c. From the Imperial>Steel>AISC>HSS and Pipes>HSS, Small Hollow Structural Sections catalog, load HSS4×3×1/4.
      d. From the Imperial > Concrete > Cast-in-place > Rectangular Columns catalog, load 16″×16″.
   E. Create a Post and Pad style using the 16″×16″ member for the pad and the HSS4×3×1/4 member for the post. Make the 16″×16″ pad 12″ thick and rotated 45°. Adjust the display properties for the style to display the Below Cut Plane component.
   F. Place the W6×12 beams as indicated in the figure using a **Top Center** justification.
   G. Use the **Properties** palette to change the **Elevation** property of the W6×12 beams to 8′-0″.
   H. Add the Post and Pad columns as indicated in the figure at 8′-5 31/32″ high.
   I. Use the **Properties** palette to change the **Elevation** property of the Post and Pad columns to −1′-0″.
   J. Add the W12×16 beams as indicated in the figure using a **Top Center** justification.
   K. Use the **Properties** palette to change the **Elevation** property of the W12×16 beams to 8′-0″.
   L. Save and close the drawing.

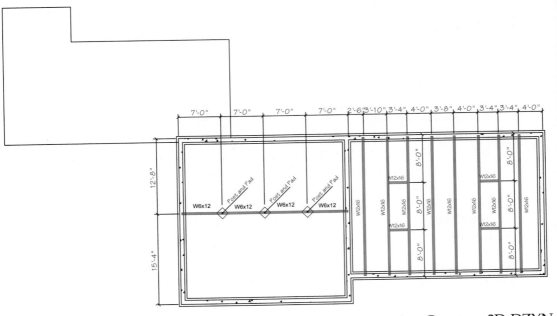

Drawing Courtesy 3D-DZYN

7. Governmental Fire Station
   A. Access the **Project Browser** and set Gvrmt-Project-07 current.
   B. Access the **Constructs** tab and open the Main Floor construct.
   C. In the **Style Manager**, open the Member Styles (Imperial).dwg. Drag and drop the Concrete Encased Steel W8 16D Partial style onto the Ceiling Framing drawing icon in the **Style Manager**.
   D. Access the **Structural Member Catalog**. From the Imperial>Steel>AISC>HSS and Pipes>HSS, Small Hollow Structural Sections (Pipes) catalog, load the HSS4.000×0.220 structural style.
   E. Add the Concrete Encased Steel W8 16D Partial columns in the bay as indicated in the figure. Set the height to 14'-1/2".
   F. Add the HSS4.000×0.220 columns to the front of the building as indicated in the figure. Set the height to 10'-0".
   G. Save and close the drawing.
   H. Access the **Constructs** tab and create a new construct named Ceiling Framing. Assign the Ceiling Framing construct to the Ceiling Framing level. Open the Ceiling Framing construct.
   I. Drag the Main Floor construct into the Ceiling Framing drawing.
   J. Select the Main Floor reference, right-click, and select the **Edit Object Display** option. In the **Xref Display** tab, place a check in the **Override the display configuration set in the host drawing** check box. Select the Screened display configuration from the list below the check box. This will screen the Main Floor xref for clarity and display walls below the Ceiling Framing constructs cut plane, making it easier to add structural members.
   K. Create a non-plotting layer named A-Anno-Nplt and set it current.
   L. Draw a closed polyline around the outside edge of the CMU Wall component in the walls of the Main Floor construct.
   M. In the **Style Manager**, open the Bar Joists (Imperial).dwg. Drag and drop the Steel Joist 24 style onto the Ceiling Framing drawing icon in the **Style Manager**.
   N. Access the **Structural Member Catalog**. Load the following structural styles:
      a. From the Imperial>Steel>AISC>I-Shaped>W2n, Wide-Flange Shapes catalog, load W21×62.
      b. From the Imperial>Timber>Lumber>Nominal Cut Lumber catalog, load 2×12.
   O. Add the W21×62 style as beams in the bay as indicated in the figure. Use a **Bottom Center** justification. Use the **Properties** palette to set the **Elevation** property of the W21×62 beams to 2'-1/2".
   P. Add the Steel Joist 24 style as beams in the bay. Use a **Top Center** justification. Use the **Properties** palette to set the **Elevation** property of the beams to a height of 4'-0".
   Q. Add the 2×12 style throughout the rest of the building at 24" on center. Use a **Top Center** justification. Set the elevation of the 2×12s in the bay to an elevation of 4'-0". Set the elevation of the 2×12s in the main building to an elevation of 0".
   R. Detach the Main Floor construct.
   S. Save and close the drawing.

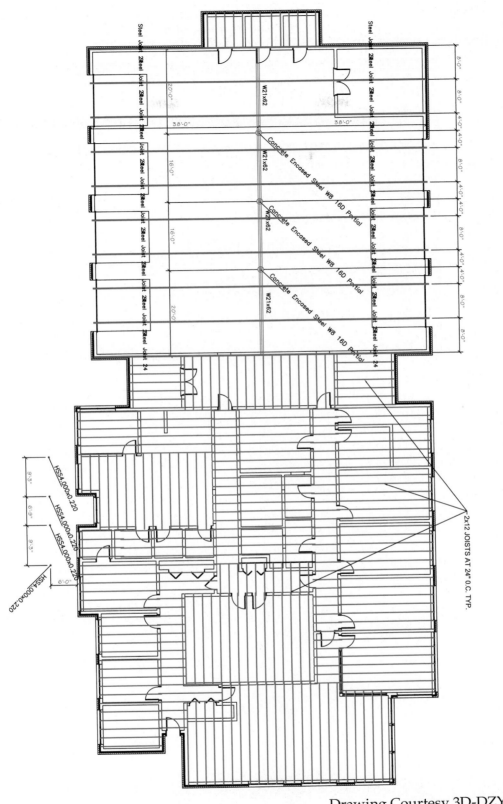

Drawing Courtesy 3D-DZYN

The home page of the Association for Computer Aided Design in Architecture (ACADIA) Web site is www.acadia.org. This Web site offers information about ACADIA, conferences, competitions, awards, publications, resources, and related organizations.

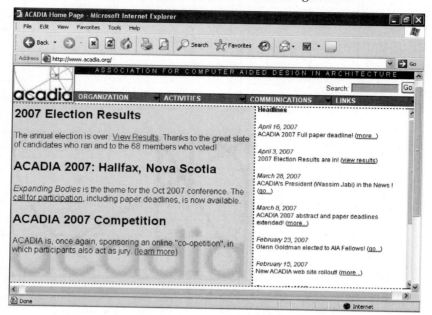

CHAPTER 11

Adding Text and Dimensions

Learning Objectives

After completing this chapter, you will be able to do the following:

- ✓ Create a text style.
- ✓ Add text notes into the drawing.
- ✓ Determine scale factors for text height.
- ✓ Edit text.
- ✓ Use AutoCAD dimensioning commands.
- ✓ Grip edit dimensions.
- ✓ Use AEC dimensions.
- ✓ Edit AEC dimensions.
- ✓ Create AutoCAD dimension styles.
- ✓ Modify dimension styles.
- ✓ Create AEC dimension styles.

Annotations, such as notes and dimensions, are provided in a set of construction drawings to describe how to build a structure. See **Figure 11-1.** This chapter describes how to add notes and dimensions to a drawing.

Figure 11-1.
Notes and dimensions are used to describe how a building is to be constructed. (Designed by Quarterpoint Design Group)

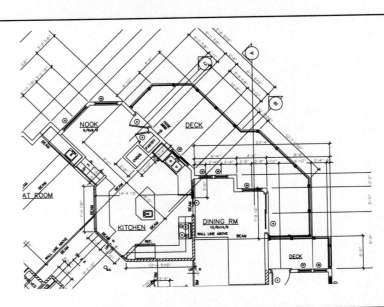

The words and numbers placed on Architectural Desktop drawings are called *text*. The term *annotation* is also commonly used to refer to text. Text can be in the form of notes or dimension values. *Notes* provide written information about the drawing. Two basic types of notes are general and specific notes. *General notes* apply to the entire drawing. They are commonly located together in the *field* of the drawing, which is any space surrounding the drawing and inside the borders of the drawing. Typical locations for general notes are in a corner of the drawing and along the bottom or sides of the drawing. *Specific notes* are notes that apply to a specific feature or item on the drawing. These notes can be placed next to the feature being described or connected to the feature with a leader line. Dimensioning characteristics and leader lines are discussed later in this chapter. AutoCAD provides two systems for creating text. There is line text, for creating single-line text objects, and multiline text, for preparing paragraphs of text. The **TEXT** command is used for creating *single-line text*. Single-line text is typed at the Command: prompt. *Multiline text* is created using the **MTEXT** command and is the most commonly used text application for Architectural Desktop. This text is typed in the text editor, which is discussed later.

Before notes are added to a drawing, a text style should be created with the desired font. A *text style* is a set of text properties controlling settings such as the font, height, width, and oblique angle for notes. Templates included with Architectural Desktop contain a few text styles. The following section describes how to create a text style in the drawing for use when creating notes.

Creating a Text Style

Several text styles can be created with different properties for use with different types of notes, such as general notes, drawing titles, and title block annotations. To create a text style, pick **Format** > **Text Style...**, or type STYLE or ST. This displays the **Text Style** dialog box, shown in **Figure 11-2**.

Figure 11-2.
The **Text Style** dialog box is used to control the properties of text characters using the text style.

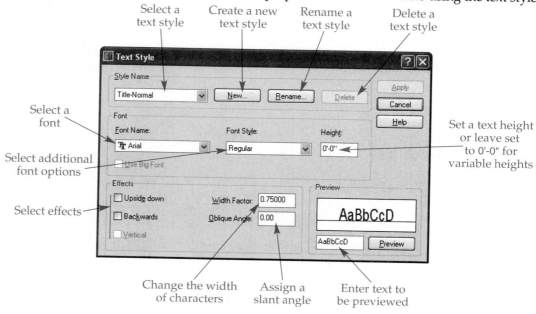

The **Text Style** dialog box is divided into four major areas with different settings. The following describes the settings available to control the text style:

- **Style Name.** This area is used to set an existing text style current by selecting a style from the drop-down list.
  - **New.** This button is used to create a new text style. Picking this button displays the **New Text Style** dialog box, where a new name can be entered. Pick the **OK** button when you are finished entering a new name. The new style becomes the current style in the **Text Style** dialog box.
  - **Rename.** Use this button to rename the style displayed in the drop-down list.
  - **Delete.** This button is used to delete the style in the drop-down list, provided that it is not being used by text in the drawing.
- **Font.** This area is used to assign a font and height to the style.
  - **Font Name.** This drop-down list includes several fonts available on your computer. The list includes Windows True Type (.ttf) fonts and AutoCAD shape fonts (.shx). Choose a font type to assign to the style.
  - **Font Style.** This drop-down list includes additional options for the font selected in the **Font Name:** drop-down list. The shape fonts do not include any additional font styles. Some True Type fonts, however, include different options.
  - **Height.** Use this text box to specify a text height for this style to use. Any notes added to the drawing use this height. The default height is **0'-0"**. A height of 0'-0" allows text in the drawing to use different text heights. If a height other than **0'-0"** is entered, any notes created using this text style always use the specified height. It is often recommended that a height of 0'-0" be used in text styles, because the height can be specified when adding text and does not affect text in dimensions.
- **Use Big Font.** This check box is used in conjunction with shape fonts. When a shape font is selected from the **Font Name:** drop-down list, the **Use Big Font** check box becomes available. Selecting the check box changes the **Font Style:** drop-down list to the **Big Font:** drop-down list. Additional options can be selected for use with the font, similar to the **Font Style:** drop-down list.
- **Effects.** This area provides additional effects that can be applied to the text style.
  - **Upside down.** Selecting this check box creates text drawn upside down.
  - **Backwards.** This check box creates text that displays backwards.
  - **Vertical.** This check box is available only when you are using shape fonts. Selecting this check box causes the letters of words to display vertically, rather than horizontally.
  - **Width Factor.** This text box controls the width of each character in a piece of text, relative to its height. The default value is set to 1.00000. A value less than 1 compresses the characters, and a value greater than 1 widens the characters.
  - **Oblique Angle.** This text box controls the angle, or slant, of the characters in the text. The default value is set to 0.00, which creates characters without a slant. A positive value controls the angle of the characters and slants them to the right. A negative value controls the angle of the characters and slants them to the left.
- **Preview.** This provides a preview of the text with the different properties assigned. Enter any characters in the **Preview** text box, and then pick the **Preview** button to see the characters with the font properties assigned to the style.

When you are finished adjusting the text style, pick the **Apply** button, and then pick the **Close** button. The style listed in the **Style Name** drop-down list becomes the current style, and any text created uses this style.

NOTE

Chapter 9 introduced the addition of documentation blocks to the drawing. Some documentation blocks include text in the block. When a documentation block is inserted, it looks to the current text style and applies the properties of the text style to the text within the block. Before adding documentation blocks, you might want to check the current text style to be sure it matches what you want.

Exercise
11-1   **Complete the Exercise on the Student CD.**

Adding Text to the Drawing

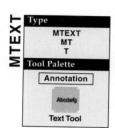

The **MTEXT** command is used to add notes into the drawing. **MTEXT** creates multiple lines of text grouped into a single object. To access this command, select **Text Tool** from the **Annotation** palette in the **Document** tool palette group or type MTEXT, MT, or T. When adding text by picking **Text Tool** from the **Annotation** palette, you are prompted for an insertion point and the text width. This width is the width of the paragraph. After specifying the width, you can begin entering text or press the [Enter] key to access the **Text Formatting** toolbar.

If the text command is accessed by typing MTEXT, MT, or T, you are asked to select the first and second corners for the text boundary. The *text boundary* is a box within which your text is placed. Pick the first corner of the text boundary, pull the cursor to create the size of the boundary, and pick the second point. See **Figure 11-3**. This establishes the size of the text boundary. Text you enter is contained within the left and right boundaries of the box.

After picking the boundaries of the text box, the **Text Formatting** toolbar is displayed with a text editor. See **Figure 11-4**. Enter text in the text editor to create the note. When you are finished, pick the **OK** button on the toolbar to create the text in the drawing.

The **Text Formatting** toolbar and text editor are simple text-editing tools within Architectural Desktop. The text being created or edited can be formatted by highlighting it in the text editor and adjusting the values in the **Text Formatting** toolbar and the tab slider bar in the text editor. Right-clicking within the text editor also provides a shortcut menu of additional formatting options. The following are the tools found in the **Text Formatting** toolbar:

- **Style.** This drop-down list displays a list of text styles in the current drawing. Selecting a style from the list applies the style to all text in the text editor.
- **Font.** This drop-down list displays a list of fonts available on the computer. Picking a font from the list overrides the font the text style uses.

Figure 11-3.
The text boundary is used to contain a text note. The arrow indicates the direction the text will flow as it is created.

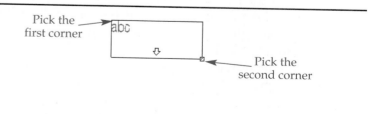

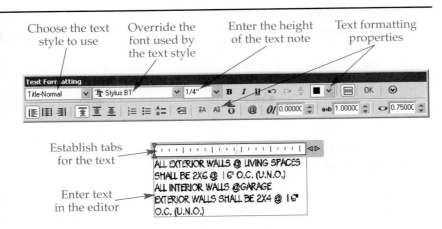

Figure 11-4.
The **Text Formatting** toolbar and text editor window are displayed after defining the text boundary.

Choose the text style to use

Override the font used by the text style

Enter the height of the text note

Text formatting properties

Establish tabs for the text

Enter text in the editor

- **Text Height.** This drop-down list and text box are used to enter the height of the text as it appears in the drawing. Enter the desired text height in the text box or pick from a list of heights used in the drawing. Text entered into the model space drawing is drawn at the desired plotted output height multiplied by the scale factor of the drawing.

  For example, suppose you are creating general notes that are to appear 1/8″ high on the finished plotted drawing. If the text is drawn at an actual 1/8″ height in relation to a 6″ wide wall, the text would be very small when printed. The text in model space needs to be scaled up by the scale factor of the drawing. If the drawing is to be plotted at a scale of 1/4″ = 1′-0″, the scale factor becomes 48 (12″ ÷ 1/4″ = 48). The 1/8″ high text is then multiplied by the scale factor of 48 to create the height of text in model space. The formula is desired plotted text height × scale factor = model space text height. In this example, 1/8″ × 48 = 6″. Appendix K on the Student CD provides a list of common drawing scales and text heights to make it easier to figure out what the text in model space should be. If you are creating the notes in layout space, the text height should be the actual printed text height desired.

- **Bold.** Picking this button creates bold text. This button is not available to all available fonts. Highlight the text in the text editor, and then pick the **Bold** button to make the text bold.

- **Italic.** This button is used to italicize text, but it is not available to all fonts. Highlight the text in the text editor, and then pick the **Italic** button to italicize the text.

- **Underline.** Picking this button creates an underline below any highlighted text in the text editor.

- **Undo.** This button undoes the last formatting applied to text in the text editor.

- **Redo.** Picking this button will redo the undone formatting.

- **Stack.** This button becomes available when you are creating a fraction. If text is entered with a slash separating the text, the text is converted into a stacked fraction. Highlight the fraction and pick the **Stack** button to unstack the fraction and keep the values on a single line.

- **Color.** This drop-down list contains colors that can be applied to highlighted text in the text editor. Setting a color overrides the color of the current layer the text is using.

- **Ruler.** Picking this button turns on or off the indent ruler for the text editor.

- **OK (Ctrl+Enter).** Pick this button when you are finished adding text in the text editor.

- **Options.** Pick this button to display additional options that can be applied to text in the text editor.

- **Left, Center, and Right.** These three buttons on the second row of the **Text Formatting** toolbar control the vertical justification of the text—whether it is left-, right-, or center-justified.
- **Top, Middle, and Bottom.** These buttons control how the text is horizontally justified.
- **Numbering, Bullets, and Uppercase Letters.** These buttons are used to add numbered, bulleted, or lettered indents in the text.
- **Insert Field.** Pick this button to display the **Field** dialog box, where automatic text fields can be added into the text.
- **UPPERCASE and lowercase.** Use these buttons to change highlighted text to uppercase or lowercase text characters.
- **Overline.** Use this button to place an overline above highlighted text.
- **Symbol.** Pick this button to display a shortcut menu of common symbols that can be added to the text. Symbols such as **Degrees**, **Plus/Minus**, **Center Line**, and **Property Line** are available. If you want to add a symbol not included in the list, pick the **Other...** option at the bottom of the list to use the Windows Character Map to insert additional symbols.
- **Oblique Angle.** This text box is used to control the angle, or slant, of text within the paragraph. The entire paragraph or only highlighted portions of text can be assigned an oblique angle.
- **Tracking.** This text box is used to increase or decrease the space between selected characters.
- **Width Factor.** This text box is used to control the width of characters within the text paragraph.

There is also a slider bar for adjusting indents and tabs. Use the slider bar to set up any indents or tabs for the paragraph of notes. Right-clicking over the slider bar displays a menu that can be used to set the indents for the text object.

Text can be entered into the text editor and formatted before and after the text is entered. Highlight any words in the editor to use special formatting, and then adjust their properties. When you are finished adding the text, pick the **OK** button or click outside the text box to exit the text editor and create the text.

All text created with the **Text Tool** is created on the A-Anno-Note layer and adjusts its height based on the **Annotation Plot Size:** and **Scale:** specified in the **Drawing Setup** dialog box. Changing the scale adjusts the height of the text. If the text command is accessed by typing MTEXT, MT, or T, the text is placed on the current layer, and the text height must be set within the **Text Formatting** toolbar. Refer to Appendix K for common text heights at different scales.

Editing Text

After notes have been added to the drawing, they can be edited using commands such as **MOVE**, **COPY**, and **ROTATE**. Selecting the text object produces four grip boxes around the text boundary. These grip boxes can be used to stretch the size of the paragraph of text. The **Properties** palette can also be used to edit properties such as the text style, justification, text height, and line spacing.

In addition to modifying the text properties, the text content can be edited by double-clicking the text object. This displays the **Text Formatting** toolbar and text editor. When you are finished editing the text content, pick the **OK** button in the **Text Formatting** toolbar to return to the drawing.

 Exercise 11-2   *Complete the Exercise on the Student CD.*

AutoCAD has a number of commands that can be used to draw dimensions, found in the **Dimension** toolbar and **DesignCenter**. See **Figure 11-5**. When a drawing is dimensioned using the commands from the toolbar, the dimension object is added to the drawing and placed on the current layer. Additionally, six of the standard AutoCAD dimensioning commands are found in **DesignCenter**. As dimensioning commands are dragged from **DesignCenter** and dropped into the drawing, the dimensions are placed in the drawing and assigned to a dimensioning layer, the A-Anno-Dims layer. These dimensioning commands include **Aligned**, **Angular**, **Baseline**, **Continue**, **Linear**, and **Radius**, and they are the most common AutoCAD dimensioning commands used in architectural drawings. For more information on other AutoCAD dimensioning commands, refer to the **User's Guide** found in **AutoCAD Help** in the **Autodesk Architectural Desktop 2007 Help** window or the *AutoCAD and Its Applications* textbook.

NOTE

Drag and drop is a feature that allows you to perform tasks by moving your cursor over the top of an icon in a folder or menu source. The icon represents a document, a drawing, a folder, or an application, such as a dimensioning command. Press and hold the pick button on your pointing device, drag the cursor to the folder or drawing where you want to drop the content, and release the pick button. The selected content is added to your current drawing or chosen file.

Figure 11-5.
Standard AutoCAD dimensioning commands can be found in the **Dimension** toolbar and **DesignCenter**.

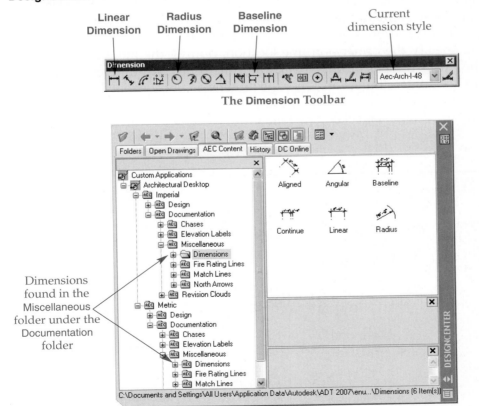

Drawing Linear Dimensions

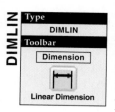

DIMLIN

Type
DIMLIN

Toolbar
Dimension

Linear Dimension

The **Linear Dimension** command creates horizontal, vertical, and rotated dimensions. To create linear dimensions, select the **Linear Dimension** button in the **Dimension** toolbar or type DIMLIN. You can also drag the **Linear** dimension from **DesignCenter** into the drawing by accessing the **AEC Content** tab of **DesignCenter**, selecting the folder icons for Imperial or Metric > Documentation > Miscellaneous > Dimensions, and then picking the **Linear** dimension. When creating a linear dimension, you are prompted for two points. Pick the first point where the first extension line is connected.

Extension lines are thin lines used to show the extent of a dimension, and they generally start a small distance from the feature being dimensioned and extend beyond the last dimension line. *Dimension lines* are thin lines placed between extension lines and are used to indicate a measurement. The dimension numeral is generally placed above an unbroken dimension line in architectural drafting, but it can be placed in a break near the center of the dimension line. Dimension lines are generally terminated by slashes or dots in architectural applications, but arrowheads can also be used where the dimension lines meet the extension lines. Some applications prefer to extend the dimension lines slightly past the extension lines. Extension lines can cross object lines, hidden lines, and centerlines, but they cannot cross dimension lines. *Object lines*, also called visible lines, are thick lines used to show the outline or contour of an object or feature. *Hidden lines*, often called dashed lines, are thin lines drawn as a series of dashes used to represent invisible features of an object. *Centerlines* are thin lines consisting of alternating long and short dashes that locate the center of features. They become extension lines when they are used to show the extent of a dimension. When this is done, there is no space where the centerline joins the extension line.

After the second point has been selected, you are prompted for the dimension line location. Pick the second point for the second extension line. The position picked places the dimension line at that location. When a dimension with an extension line is added to the drawing, a point is placed at the location selected. The point indicates the actual point being dimensioned, and the extension line is offset a distance away from that point. These points are placed onto a layer named Defpoints, which stands for *definition points*. The *defpoints* layer is a non-plotting layer. See **Figure 11-6**.

When you specify the dimension line location, pulling the mouse to the left or right turns the linear dimension into a vertical dimension. Pulling the mouse up or down creates a horizontal dimension. Once the dimension line location has been specified, a dimension object is created with the appropriate text in the dimension. Before the dimension line location is picked, the following options are available for the linear dimension:

Figure 11-6.
The **Linear Dimension** command is used to create horizontal and vertical dimensions in your drawing.

Dimension line location — 6'-3" — Second point
First point
First point
Dimension line location — 4'-3" — Second point

- **Mtext.** Typing M opens the **Text Formatting** toolbar and text editor. The text editor is used to enter dimension text different from the default text. The default text value is displayed, which is the actual length being measured. Highlighting the text and entering a new value overwrites the default size with the one entered. You can also keep the default text and enter additional information or values before or after the default text.
- **Text.** Typing T displays the dimension length in brackets at the Command: prompt. Entering a different value overrides the text and displays the over-ridden text.
- **Angle.** Typing A allows you to adjust the angle of the text between the extension lines.
- **Horizontal.** Typing H creates a horizontal dimension. This overrides the default of moving the mouse up or down to create a horizontal dimension.
- **Vertical.** Typing V creates a vertical dimension.
- **Rotated.** Typing R rotates the angle of the dimension line. Use this option when dimensioning lengths of a building that are not horizontal or vertical. See **Figure 11-7.**

NOTE When you are creating dimensions, use object snaps to snap to the geometry being dimensioned. This ensures accuracy of the dimension.

Drawing Continuous Dimensions

The **Continue Dimension** command builds on an existing linear dimension. Continuous dimensions create one string of dimensions, in which all the dimension lines are lined up. They are created by picking the **Continue Dimension** button in the **Dimension** toolbar or typing DIMCONT. You can also drag the **Continue** dimension from **DesignCenter** into the drawing by accessing the **AEC Content** tab of **DesignCenter**, selecting the folder icons for Imperial or Metric > Documentation > Miscellaneous > Dimensions, and then picking the **Continue** dimension. Continuous dimensions can also be created by first selecting an existing linear dimension, right-clicking, and then picking **Continue** from the list.

If you create a linear dimension prior to entering the **Continue Dimension** command, you are prompted to pick a second extension line point. The command assumes that the last point selected for the previous linear dimension is the first point of the continuous dimension. After you pick the second point to be dimensioned, you are prompted to pick the second point to be dimensioned for the next dimension in the string. You can create as many dimensions as you would like before ending the command. See **Figure 11-8.**

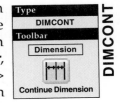

Type	
DIMCONT	
Toolbar	DIMCONT
Dimension	
Continue Dimension	

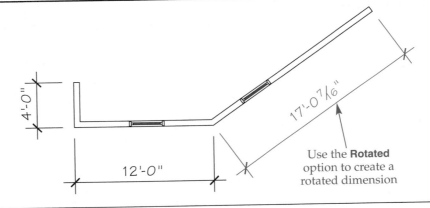

Figure 11-7.
Linear dimensions can be rotated to dimension the length of angled features.

4'-0"

17'-0 7/16"

12'-0"

Use the **Rotated** option to create a rotated dimension

Figure 11-8.
Create a linear dimension before using the **Continue Dimension** command. Pick the second extension point for new continuous dimensions.

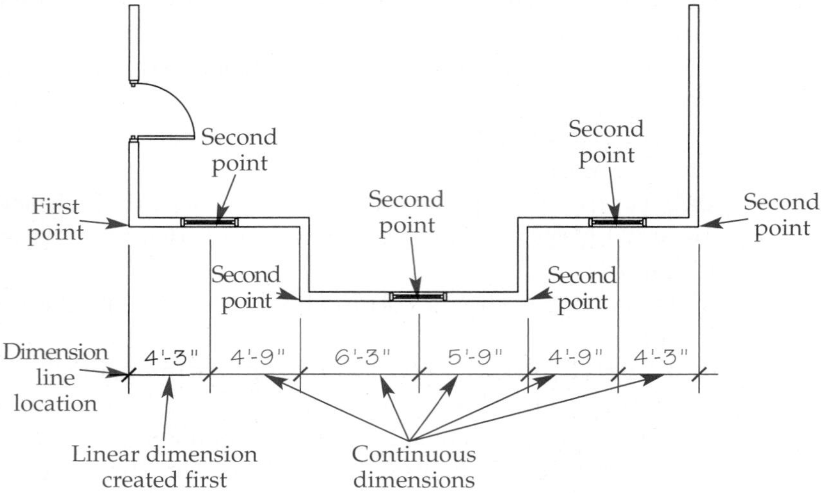

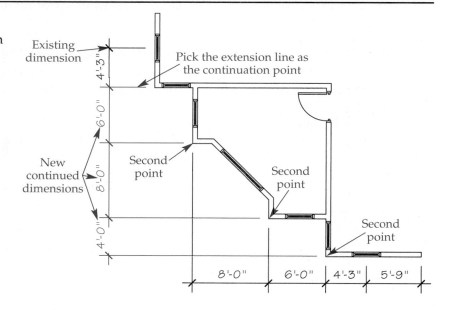

Linear dimensions do not need to be created before you use the **Continue Dimension** command. As long as there is a dimension in the drawing, the **Continue Dimension** command can be used. When first accessing the **Continue Dimension** command, you are prompted to Specify a second extension line origin or [Undo/Select] <Select>. Pressing the [Enter] key or right-clicking allows you to select an existing extension line. This designates it as the first extension line of the new continuous dimension. Once you have selected an extension line to be used as the starting point for the new dimension, begin picking the second extension line locations for the new dimensions. See **Figure 11-9.**

Exercise
11-3   **Complete the Exercise on the Student CD.**

Figure 11-9.
Selecting an extension line on an existing dimension designates the extension line as the first extension line for the new continuous dimension.

Drawing Baseline Dimensions

The term *baseline dimensions* refers to a group of dimensions all starting at the same location. Baseline dimensions are also created in relation to an existing linear dimension. The **Baseline Dimension** command uses the first extension line of the previously created linear dimension as the first extension line for new baseline dimensions. As second extension line points are selected, new dimensions are created and offset from the original or previously created dimension, allowing you to create dimensions on different levels, as shown in **Figure 11-10**.

Baseline dimensions are created by picking the **Baseline Dimension** button in the **Dimension** toolbar or typing DIMBASE. You can also drag and drop the **Baseline** dimension from **DesignCenter** into the drawing by accessing the **AEC Content** tab of **DesignCenter**, selecting the folder icons for Imperial or Metric > Documentation > Miscellaneous > Dimensions, and then picking the **Baseline** dimension. See **Figure 11-11**. To create these dimensions, a linear dimension is created first, and then the **Baseline Dimension** command is used.

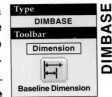

Figure 11-10.
The baseline dimensions use a common extension line as a base point. New dimensions are added offset from the previously created dimension line, with all the first extension line points lining up with each other.

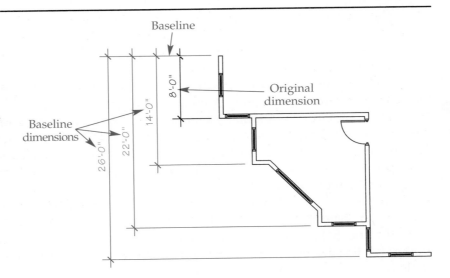

Figure 11-11.
Create a linear dimension first, and then use the **Baseline Dimension** command to create baseline dimensions.

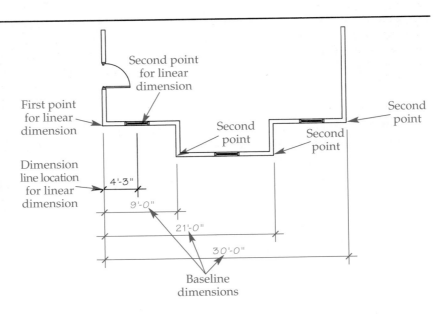

The spacing between the dimension lines is designated in the dimension style under the **Lines** tab of the **Dimension Style Manager**, in the **Baseline spacing** text box. Dimension styles are discussed later in this chapter. An existing extension line can be selected for use as the baseline. At the Specify a second extension line origin or [Undo/Select] <Select>: prompt, press the [Enter] key or right-click to enter the default option, **Select**. Pick an existing extension line for use as the baseline, and then pick the second extension line locations.

 NOTE

> Continuous dimensions are the most commonly used dimension format in architectural drafting, but baseline dimensions are used in some applications. A combination of continuous and baseline dimensions can sometimes be used to lay out the dimensions in the drawing.

 Exercise 11-4

Complete the Exercise on the Student CD.

Drawing Angular Dimensions

DIMANG

Type
DIMANG
Toolbar
Dimension
Angular Dimension

Angular dimensions are used to dimension the angle of a feature. The **Angular Dimension** command is used to create an angular dimension. This command is accessed by picking the **Angular Dimension** button in the **Dimension** toolbar or typing DIMANG. You can also drag and drop the **Angular** dimension from **DesignCenter** into the drawing by accessing the **AEC Content** tab of **DesignCenter**, selecting the folder icons for Imperial or Metric > Documentation > Miscellaneous > Dimensions, and then picking the **Angular** dimension.

After entering the **Angular Dimension** command, you are prompted to Select arc, circle, line, or <specify vertex>. Select one of the objects. You are then prompted to select a second line. Select the next object to establish the angular dimension. Finally, pick a place for the dimension line. Depending on how you move the cursor, one of four angles appears, indicating the sides of the dimensioned objects. See **Figure 11-12**.

You also can specify the vertex point where the two objects cross each other to create an angular dimension. Press [Enter] at the Select arc, circle, line, or <specify vertex>: prompt. Pick the vertex location where the two objects cross each other, and then pick a point designating the extension line location used for the first part of the angle. Next, pick a point designating the second line of the angle. Finally, pick a place for the dimension line. See **Figure 11-13**.

Figure 11-12.
Selecting two objects to be dimensioned with the **Angular Dimension** command.

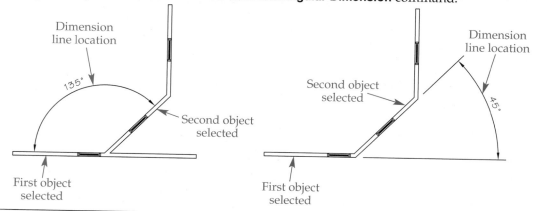

Drawing Radius Dimensions

Radial dimensions are used to dimension the radius of an arc-shaped object. The **Radius Dimension** command is accessed by picking the **Radius Dimension** button in the **Dimension** toolbar or typing DIMRAD. You can also drag and drop the **Radius** dimension from **DesignCenter** into the drawing by accessing the **AEC Content** tab of **DesignCenter**, selecting the folder icons for Imperial or Metric > Documentation > Miscellaneous > Dimensions, and then picking the **Radius** dimension. Once you enter the command, you are prompted to pick an arc or a circle. Pick the arc or circle, and pick the dimension text location. The dimensional radius is displayed with the letter *R*, indicating that the dimension is a radius. If you have a curved wall in the drawing needing to be dimensioned, pick it as you would an arc or a circle. See **Figure 11-14.**

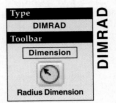

Type
DIMRAD
Toolbar
Dimension

Radius Dimension

DIMRAD

Figure 11-13.
Press [Enter] to select a vertex point. Pick a point to establish the first angle, and then pick a second point for the second angle.

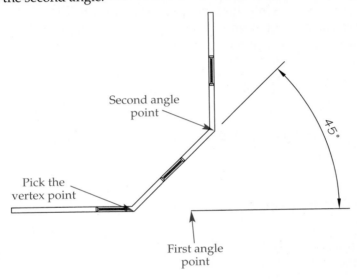

Figure 11-14.
Using the **Radius Dimension** command to dimension the curved wall.

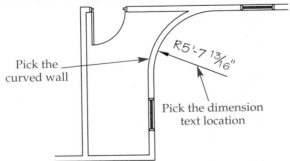

Drawing Aligned Dimensions

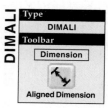

Aligned dimensions are used to align a dimension with an object that is not horizontal or vertical. To create aligned dimensions, pick the **Aligned Dimension** button in the **Dimension** toolbar or type DIMALI. You can also drag and drop the **Aligned** dimension from **DesignCenter** into the drawing by accessing the **AEC Content** tab of **DesignCenter**, selecting the folder icons for Imperial or Metric > Documentation > Miscellaneous > Dimensions, and then picking the **Aligned** dimension. See **Figure 11-15**. You are prompted to specify the first extension line origin. After you pick a point, you are prompted to specify the second extension line origin. Pick a point. You are then prompted for the dimension line location. Pick a location, and repeat the command to create another dimension.

NOTE

> When you are creating a dimension that is not horizontal or vertical, it is often better to use the **Linear Dimension** command, with the **Rotated** option to rotate the dimension line, than to use the **Aligned Dimension** command. Using the **Linear Dimension** command allows you to pick extension line points along a different angle without having the dimension line remain parallel to the imaginary line between the two extension line points.

Exercise 11-5   **Complete the Exercise on the Student CD.**

Using Grips to Modify Dimensions

Grips can be used to speed up the process of modifying a dimension. To do this, first select the dimension to be modified, and then select a grip. Use the grip **STRETCH** mode to adjust the text location, an extension line location, or the dimension line location, as shown in **Figure 11-16**.

Figure 11-15.
Use the **Aligned Dimension** command to create dimensions parallel to the object being dimensioned.

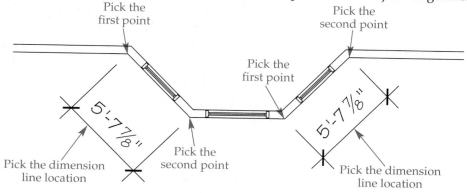

Figure 11-16.
Use grips to modify a
dimension.

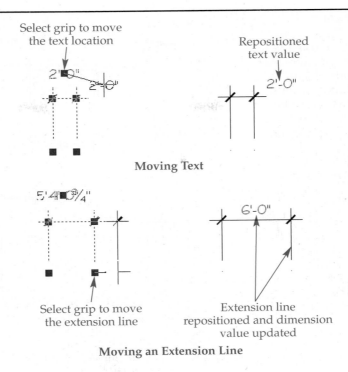

Select grip to move
the text location

Repositioned
text value

Moving Text

Select grip to move
the extension line

Extension line
repositioned and dimension
value updated

Moving an Extension Line

Using AEC Dimensions

The use of standard dimensions gives you the ability to place dimensions where desired, without them having any association to the objects they are dimensioning. If a wall or window moves, the dimensions do not move or update automatically. AEC dimensions, however, are associated to the objects they are dimensioning. For example, if a wall is moved, deleted, or stretched, the AEC dimensions automatically follow the modification and update themselves. AEC dimensions look similar to standard dimensions and use a dimension style for their appearance. The following section describes the use of AEC dimensions.

Adding Automatic AEC Dimensions

AEC dimensions are dimension objects attached to the AEC objects they are dimensioning. If a wall, door, or window with an AEC dimension attached is moved, stretched, or modified, the AEC dimension automatically adjusts to reflect the change. AEC dimensions are also considered AEC objects, so the standard object display rules apply. For example, an AEC dimension can be configured within a display configuration so it does not appear in a model view, but does appear in a top view, if desired. AEC dimensions are added to the drawing by picking one of the three **AEC Dimension** tools in the **Annotation** palette; picking **Document** > **AEC Dimension** > **Add AEC Dimension…**; or selecting an AEC object, right-clicking, and picking the **AEC Dimension** command.

You are prompted to Select Objects or [Pick points]: if the **Add AEC Dimension…** command has been accessed from the tool palette or the pull-down menu. Select the geometry to be dimensioned. If you are adding dimensions to a wall with doors, windows, and other openings, select the wall, and the AEC dimension automatically finds the opening locations. When you are finished selecting the objects to be dimensioned, press [Enter] and pick a location for the dimension line. See **Figure 11-17.** If the wall is selected first and the **AEC Dimension** command is picked from the shortcut menu, all you do is pick the dimension line location.

Pull-Down Menu
Document
> AEC Dimension
> Add AEC
Dimension…

Tool Palette
Annotation

AEC Dimension

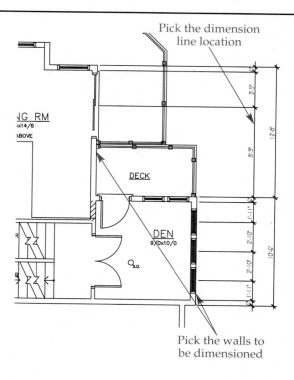

Figure 11-17.
AEC dimensions are similar to the standard AutoCAD dimensions in appearance, but they are attached to the objects they are dimensioning. (Designed by Quarterpoint Design Group)

Pick the dimension line location

Pick the walls to be dimensioned

The **AEC Dimension** tools found on the **Annotation** tool palette are used for dimensioning different portions of your model and use specific AEC dimension styles. *AEC dimension styles* control the number of strings used and how each string dimensions AEC objects. These styles create exterior dimensions measuring to the rough opening of windows and doors, exterior dimensions measuring to the center of doors and windows, and a single string of interior dimensions. Moving, erasing, or modifying a door, window, or wall updates the dimensions and their values automatically. The Aec Model templates include four different AEC dimension styles: 1 Chain, 2 Chain, 3 Chain, and Standard. These dimension styles can be used when picking the **Document** > **AEC Dimension** > **Add AEC Dimension...** command. If one of the AEC dimension tools is used from the **Annotation** tool palette, the styles assigned to the tool are used. Before selecting the dimension line location, the style can be changed in the **Properties** palette. The styles include a one-chain, two-chain, and three-chain style, creating single, double, or triple dimension strings. The creation and modification of AEC dimension styles is covered later in this chapter.

NOTE

By default, the AEC dimensions are displayed in a model view. If you want the dimensions in the top view only and not in the model view, edit the **Model** display set in the **Display Manager**, and remove the AEC dimension's **Plan** display representation from the set. Now, when the view is changed to a model view, the dimensions do not show up. Refer to Chapter 7 for modifying the display of ADT objects.

Adding AEC Dimensions Manually

AEC dimensions can also be added to the drawing manually by picking the extension line origins. When this is done, the AEC dimensions are attached to the ADT geometry they are dimensioning. To add AEC dimensions manually, pick **Document** > **AEC Dimension** > **Add AEC Dimension...** from the pull-down menu. You are prompted to Select Objects or [Pick points]: after entering the command. Type P at the Command:

prompt, or right-click and select the **Pick points** option. Begin selecting points to be dimensioned. When you are finished, press [Enter] to place the dimension line. When placing the dimension line location, you are prompted to Specify insert point or [Style/Rotation/Align]. Pick the side of the wall or object on which to place the dimension line. If AEC dimensions that are dimensioned using manually picked points are moved, stretched, or erased, the manual AEC dimensions will update, as with the standard dimensions.

Exercise
11-6   **Complete the Exercise on the Student CD.**

Modifying AEC Dimensions

When you are creating AEC dimensions automatically, the extension lines initially dimension to each side of the walls intersecting the wall being dimensioned. In some architectural applications, this might not be desired. See **Figure 11-18.** AEC dimensions can be edited by removing or adding extension line points.

Removing Extension Lines

To remove unwanted extension lines, select the AEC dimension object, right-click, and select **Remove Extension Lines** from the shortcut menu. You are prompted to Select extension lines to remove dimension points. Pick any extension lines to be removed. As the extension lines are selected, they turn red to indicate that they are being removed from the AEC dimension object. Press [Enter] when you are finished. The extension lines are removed, and the dimensions are updated. See **Figure 11-19.** The AEC dimension object is still attached to the object it was originally dimensioning. As objects are moved or erased, the AEC dimension object updates to reflect the latest sizes. If new walls, doors, or windows are added to the wall being dimensioned, the AEC dimension updates, and further refinement of the dimensions might need to be done.

Figure 11-18.
AEC dimensions, by default, dimension to each side of the wall.

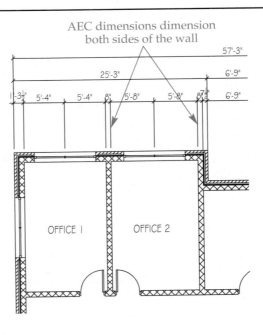

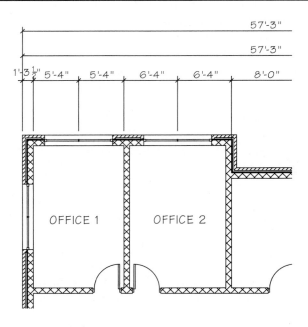

Figure 11-19.
Undesired extension
lines are removed
from the AEC
dimension object.

Adding Extension Lines

New extension lines can be added to points along the object and tied into an existing AEC dimension object. To add new extension lines, select the AEC dimension to have new extension lines added, right-click, and select the **Add Extension Lines** command. You are prompted to pick points: when the command is entered. Begin picking any new points to be dimensioned. When you are finished selecting the new points, press [Enter]. You are next prompted to Select Dimension chain. Select the chain, or string, of dimensions on the AEC object where the new extension lines are to be added.

Using Grips

As with other objects, AEC dimensions can be edited using grips. Initially, when selecting an AEC dimension, a number of grips appear, as in **Figure 11-20**. These grips control the location of the chains within the AEC dimension and allow you to edit the dimensions in place and add or remove extension lines. Selecting the **Move All Chains** grip allows you to grip stretch all the chain locations at the same time.

When an AEC dimension is used on walls drawn in different planes or jogging along the building line, the AEC dimension extension lines can cross over the top of the additional walls. See **Figure 11-20.** To edit the points where the extension lines are measuring from, select the **Edit In Place** grip. This displays additional grips around the AEC dimension object. See **Figure 11-21.** To move the point where the extension lines are measuring from, select the appropriate extension line grip, move it to the new point, and pick the new location. In the case where text is crowded within the extension lines, pick the grip over a piece of dimension text, and then pick the new location. When you are finished editing the AEC dimension, pick the **Exit Edit In Place** grip to return to the standard AEC dimension grips.

Attaching Objects to an AEC Dimension

By default, new objects added to the drawing are not added to the AEC dimension, unless they are added to the wall already being dimensioned. New objects added to the drawing can be attached to an existing AEC dimension object. To do this, first select the AEC dimension to be added to, right-click, and select the **Add Objects** command. You are prompted to Select Building Elements:. Pick any new objects to be attached to the AEC dimension object. Press [Enter] when you are finished. This adds new dimensions and extension lines to the AEC dimension, dimensioning the points of any selected objects.

Figure 11-20.
Pick an AEC dimension to edit using grips.

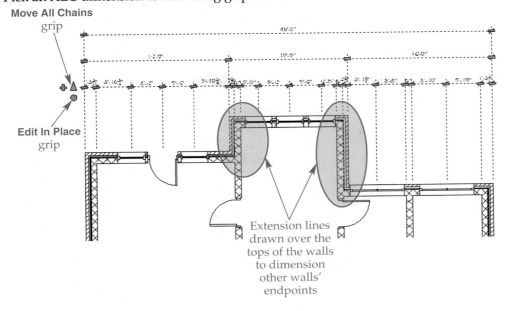

Move All Chains grip

Edit In Place grip

Extension lines drawn over the tops of the walls to dimension other walls' endpoints

Figure 11-21.
After picking the **Edit In Place** grip, grips appear around the AEC dimension object for editing the extension line origins and the text locations. Pick the **Exit Edit In Place** grip when you are finished editing.

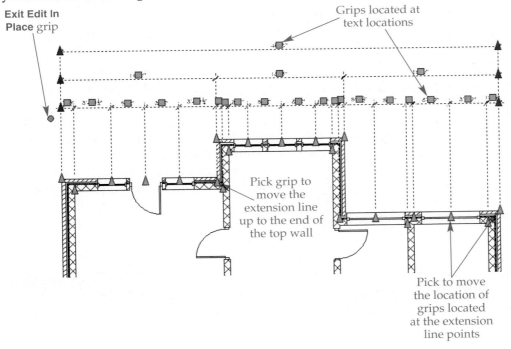

Exit Edit In Place grip

Grips located at text locations

Pick grip to move the extension line up to the end of the top wall

Pick to move the location of grips located at the extension line points

Detaching Objects from an AEC Dimension

In some cases, you might desire to remove objects from an AEC dimension object. First, select the AEC dimension object to have dimensioned objects removed, right-click, and select the **Remove Objects** command. Pick any objects to be removed, and press [Enter]. This removes objects being dimensioned from the AEC dimension object and any associated dimensions and extension lines.

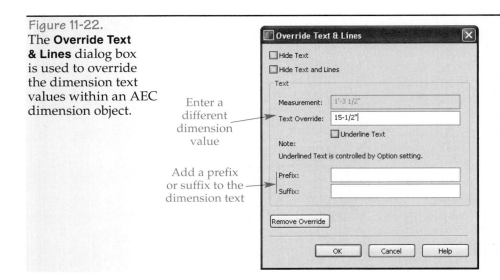

Figure 11-22.
The **Override Text & Lines** dialog box is used to override the dimension text values within an AEC dimension object.

Enter a different dimension value

Add a prefix or suffix to the dimension text

Overriding Text and Lines

When an object is dimensioned using the AEC dimension objects, points and text are automatically calculated and displayed. The dimension text values can be edited to fit your needs. To edit the text values within an AEC dimension, first select the AEC dimension, right-click, and then pick the **Override Text & Lines...** command. You are prompted to Select dimension text to change:. Select the text value on the AEC dimension to be edited. After selecting the text, the **Override Text & Lines** dialog box is displayed. See Figure 11-22.

Two check boxes at the top of the dialog box allow the selected text value or the text and the dimension and extension lines to be hidden. In the **Text** area below the check boxes, the default value is provided as read-only. A new text value can be added in the **Text Override:** text box. If the text is to be underlined, the **Underline Text** check box can also be selected. The **Prefix:** and **Suffix:** text boxes can be used to add additional text before or after the default or overridden text. Values such as TYP, OC, and UNO are typical prefixes or suffixes that can be added to a text dimension. If any of the overrides need to be removed from the edited text, pick the **Remove Override** button.

When you are finished editing the dimension text, pick the **OK** button. The edited text value appears with any changes and an overscore above the text to indicate the value was overridden. The overscore does not plot. If additional text needs to be modified or text overrides need to be removed, select the AEC dimension object, right-click, select the **Override Text and Lines...** command, and edit the text appropriately.

Dimension Styles

Dimension styles control the individual elements used within a single dimension object. A dimension style controls settings such as text height, units, and arrowheads. A drawing can have multiple dimension styles, each with its own specific settings and uses. A dimension style is the saved configuration of these settings.

The use of different dimension styles is required when dimension settings need to reflect a specific appearance for dimensions. For example, a dimension style for site plans might use the romans.shx text font placed between dimension lines and capped with arrowheads, as shown in Figure 11-23. A dimension style for floor plans might use the Stylus BT text font placed above the dimension line, with slashes (tick marks) as dimension line termination, rather than arrowheads. See Figure 11-23.

Figure 11-23.
Different types of dimension styles can be created to produce a unique appearance.

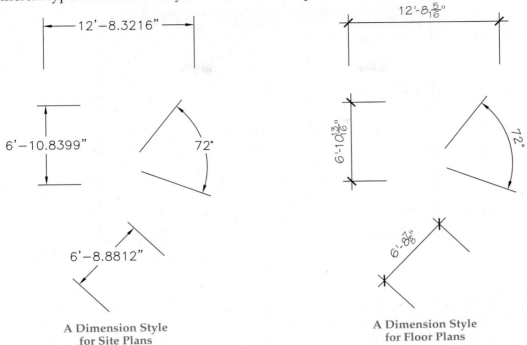

A Dimension Style
for Site Plans

A Dimension Style
for Floor Plans

Dimension styles are included in the Architectural Desktop templates. The AEC model (imperial) templates include three dimension styles for use in different drawing scales: Aec-Arch-I-192 for 1/16″ = 1′-0″ scale, Aec-Arch-I-48 for 1/4″ = 1′-0″ scale, and Aec-Arch-I-96 for 1/8″ = 1′-0″ scale. These dimension styles are configured to meet most architectural office standards. An additional dimension style named Stairs_I is included and used by AEC stair objects. Stair objects and the use of this dimension style are discussed later in this text, where related to specific applications. The AEC model (metric) templates also include three dimension styles for use with metric drawing scales: Aec-Arch-M-100 for 1 mm = 100 mm scale, Aec-Arch-M-200 for 1 mm = 200 mm scale, and Aec-Arch-M-50 for 1 mm = 50 mm scale. A metric stair dimension style is also included.

To create or modify a dimension style, pick **Format** > **Dimension Style...**; select the **Dimension Style...** button in the **Dimension** toolbar; or type DIMSTYLE or D. This displays the **Dimension Style Manager**. See **Figure 11-24**. The **Dimension Style Manager** includes the following properties:

- **Styles.** This list includes all the dimension styles in the current drawing.
- **List.** This drop-down list includes options controlling the styles listed in the **Styles:** list.
- **Don't list styles in Xrefs.** This check box becomes available when referenced drawings are used. If this check box is checked, dimension styles from referenced drawing files are not displayed.
- **Preview of:** *style*. This area provides a preview of the dimensions in the currently selected dimension style in the **Styles:** list.
- **Description.** This area provides a description of the selected dimension style.
- **Set Current.** This button sets the selected dimension style as the current, or active, dimension style in the drawing. The current style is used for any new dimensions created in the drawing and by dimensions that are updated.
- **New.** Select this button to create a new dimension style.
- **Modify.** When this button is picked, the selected dimension style from the **Styles:** list can be modified.

Type
DIMSTYLE
D
Pull-Down Menu
Format
> Dimension
Style...
Toolbar
Dimension
Dimension Style...

DIMSTYLE

Figure 11-24.
The **Dimension Style Manager** is used to manage and create dimension styles.

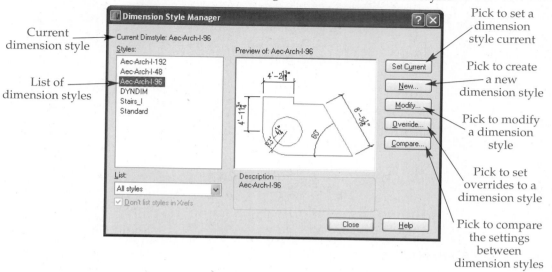

Current dimension style

List of dimension styles

Pick to set a dimension style current

Pick to create a new dimension style

Pick to modify a dimension style

Pick to set overrides to a dimension style

Pick to compare the settings between dimension styles

- **Override.** This button allows the selected dimension style to have overrides attached to one or more of its properties.
- **Compare.** This button compares the property values of two dimension styles.

Whether you use the dimension styles included in the templates or create your own dimensioning style, it is important to understand the parts of the dimension style and how they affect the outcome of dimensions in the drawing. As the style is created or modified, think about how the style is used in the drawing and the types of objects that are dimensioned. Once the dimension style has been configured, it should be used throughout the drawing project to maintain a consistent appearance in the construction documents. Dimension styles are created, modified, and managed using the **Dimension Style Manager**, shown in **Figure 11-24.**

Creating a New Dimension Style

To create a new dimension style, select the **New...** button in the **Dimension Style Manager**. The **Create New Dimension Style** dialog box is displayed as in **Figure 11-25**, with the following options:

- **New Style Name.** This text box is used to enter a new name for the dimension style.
- **Start With.** This drop-down list is used to select an existing dimension style for use as a basis for the new dimension style. The properties from the selected dimension style become the default properties for the new dimension style.
- **Use for.** This drop-down list allows you to select the type of dimensions used with the style. Initially, you must configure a dimension style for **All dimensions** before you can create a style for individual dimension types. These are known as *parent dimensions*. *Parent dimensions* set up the rules for all dimensions. After the parent dimensions have been set up, overrides can be applied to each of the dimension types.

After you finish specifying the parameters in this dialog box, pick the **Continue** button to create and configure the new dimension style.

Figure 11-25.
The **Create New
Dimension Style**
dialog box is used
to create a new
dimension style.

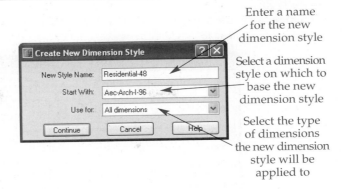

Enter a name
for the new
dimension style

Select a dimension
style on which to
base the new
dimension style

Select the type
of dimensions
the new dimension
style will be
applied to

Configuring a New Dimension Style

Once a dimension style has been created and the **Continue** button has been picked, the **Lines** tab of the **New Dimension Style:** *new style name* dialog box is displayed. See **Figure 11-26**. The tab is divided into two setup areas, plus a preview pane displaying how the dimension style appears. The two areas in the **Lines** tab include **Dimension lines** and **Extension lines**.

Some parameters include text boxes for numerical values, check boxes, and drop-down lists. It is important to note that any numerical value entered should reflect the actual size that can be measured on a finished plotted drawing. For example, if your office standards want all dimension lines to extend 1/8" past the extension lines on the plotted drawing, the **Extend beyond ticks:** size should indicate 1/8". The following describes each area of the **Lines** tab:

- **Dimension lines.** This area is used to control the look and behavior of the dimension lines.
  - **Color.** By default, dimensions are placed on the current layer, which designates the color of the dimension. The dimension line color can be specified here to override the layer's color.
  - **Linetype.** By default, dimensions use the linetype of the layer on which they are drawn. The linetype for the dimension line can be overridden by picking a linetype from the drop-down list.
  - **Lineweight.** By default, dimensions use the lineweight of the layer on which they are drawn. The lineweight for the dimension line can be overridden in this drop-down list.
  - **Extend beyond ticks.** This value specifies the distance a dimension line can extend past an arrowhead or tick mark. Place a 0 here for no extension beyond the extension line. Some offices prefer to have the dimension line extend past the extension lines, and **1/8"** is commonly used.
  - **Baseline spacing.** This value specifies the distance between two dimension strings when the **Baseline Dimension** command is used.
  - **Suppress: Dim line 1.** A check in this box removes the first part of the dimension line. The first and second parts of dimension lines are determined by the first and second points picked to be dimensioned.
  - **Suppress: Dim line 2.** A check in this box suppresses the second part of the dimension line.
- **Extension lines.** This area is used to control how extension lines appear and behave.
  - **Color.** Similar to the dimension line color, a color can be assigned to extension lines to override the specified layer color.
  - **Linetype ext line 1.** The extension line linetype for the first extension line can be controlled by selecting a linetype from the drop-down list.

Figure 11-26.
The **Lines** tab is used to configure the dimension and extension lines.

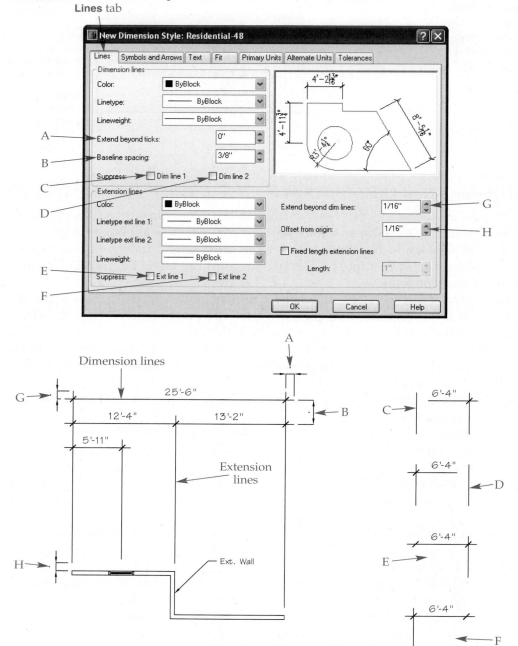

- **Linetype ext line 2.** The extension line linetype for the second extension line can be controlled by selecting a linetype from the drop-down list.
- **Lineweight.** The extension line lineweight can be controlled by selecting a value from the drop-down list.
- **Suppress: Ext line 1.** Checking this box removes the extension line for the first point selected.
- **Suppress: Ext line 2.** Checking this box removes the second extension line for the second point picked.
- **Extend beyond dim lines.** The value entered here controls how far past the dimension line the extension lines will be drawn.

- **Offset from origin.** This is the distance from the actual point being dimensioned to the beginning of the extension line. A **1/16"** distance is common.
- **Fixed length extension lines.** This area is used to restrict extension lines to a specific length, no matter where the dimensioned points have been picked. Selecting this check box allows the **Length:** text box to become available.
- **Length.** When the **Fixed length extension lines** check box is selected, this text box is available to specify the fixed length of an extension line measured from a dimension line.

As changes are made, the preview pane updates and displays a preview of how the values affect the dimensions. When you are finished, move to the next tab, or pick the **OK** button to accept the parameters and return to the **Dimension Style Manager**.

Exercise 11-7   Complete the Exercise on the Student CD.

Modifying a Dimension Style

Once a dimension style has been created and configured, it can be modified at any given time. First access the **Dimension Style Manager**, select the dimension style to be modified, and pick the **Modify...** button. This opens the **Modify Dimension Style:** *style name* dialog box, shown in Figure 11-27. This dialog box is exactly the same as the **New Dimension Style:** *new style name* dialog box. Select the tab with the property needing to be modified and make the desired changes.

The **Symbols and Arrows** tab is used to control the appearance of dimension and leader arrowheads. Figure 11-27 displays the settings and what they control on dimensions. The following are descriptions of the settings:
- **Arrowheads.** This area is used to control the appearance of arrowheads in dimensions and leaders.
  - **First.** This drop-down list includes several arrowheads that can be selected for the arrowhead for the first dimensioned point.
  - **Second.** This drop-down list includes arrowheads for the second dimensioned point. This value is automatically set to the first arrowhead picked, but it can be changed to a different arrowhead.
  - **Leader.** This drop-down list includes arrowheads that can be assigned to leader lines.
  - **Arrow size.** This text box controls the plotted arrowhead size. As with text boxes in the **Lines** tab, enter a value reflecting the actual measured size on a plotted drawing.
- **Center marks.** This area is used to control the display of center marks for curved objects when they are dimensioned with the **Radius Dimension** or **Diameter Dimension** command. A center mark can also be added to a curved object by picking the **Center Mark** command in the **Dimension** toolbar and then picking the curved object.
  - **None.** Selecting this option does not place a center mark for a curved object.
  - **Mark.** Select this option to add a center mark to a curved object.
  - **Line.** Use this option to add a center mark with lines to a curved object.
  - **Size.** This text box controls the size of the center mark, when the **Mark** option is chosen, or the extension length of center mark lines past the curved object, when the **Line** option is chosen.

Figure 11-27.
The **Modify Dimension Style:** *style name* dialog box is exactly like the **New Dimension Style:** *new style name* dialog box, except one is to create new dimension styles, and the other is to modify dimension styles. The **Symbols and Arrows** tab is used to control the display of dimension arrows and symbols within dimensions.

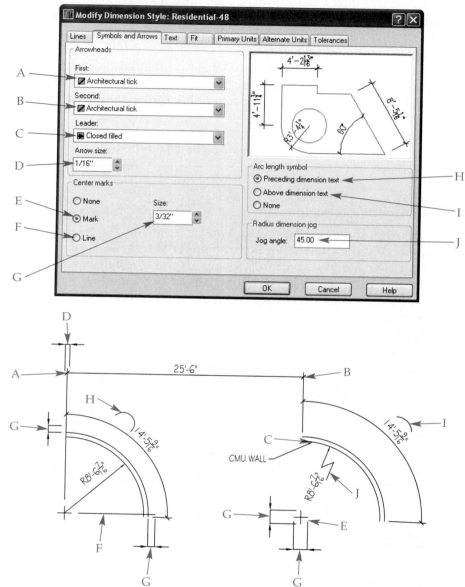

- **Arc length symbol.** This area controls the placement of the arc length symbol on an arc length dimension.
  - **Preceding dimension text.** Select this option to place the arc length symbol in front of the dimension text.
  - **Above dimension text.** Select this option to place the arc length symbol above the dimension text.
  - **None.** Choose this option to not place an arc length symbol in the dimension.
- **Radius dimension jog.** Jogged radius dimensions can be added to arced objects when there is little room for a dimension. Use the **Arc Length Dimension** found in the **Dimension** toolbar for this command.
  - **Jog angle.** Entering a text value here controls the angle of jogged dimensions.

The next tab in the **Modify Dimension Style:** *style name* dialog box (and **New Dimension Style:** *new style name* dialog box) is the **Text** tab. This tab is used to control how the dimension text appears in a dimension. See **Figure 11-28.** The following values can be adjusted to configure the appearance of the dimension text:

- **Text appearance.** This area is used to control the appearance of the text within the dimension object.
  - **Text style.** This drop-down list provides a listing of text styles currently available in the drawing. Select a text style for use in the dimension style. If there are no text styles available, or if a text style needs to be created for the dimensions, use the ellipsis (...) button to create a new text style. This opens the **Text Style** dialog box. Text styles were discussed at the beginning of this chapter.

Figure 11-28.
The **Text** tab is used to control the display of the dimension text within a dimension.

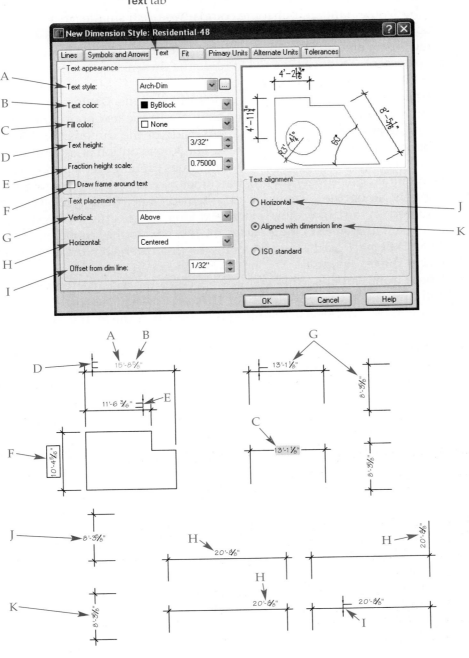

The **Text Style** dialog box includes a **Height:** text box for controlling the height of text objects. If a height greater than 0″ is specified, all text, including text in the dimensions, reflects the height specified in the text style. It is highly recommended that the height in the **Text Style** dialog box be set at 0′-0″ for text styles assigned to dimension styles. This allows the dimension style to control the height of text within dimensions.

- **Text color.** Use this drop-down list to select a color for the dimension text.
- **Fill color.** The fill color is a highlight placed over the dimension text. Use this drop-down list to specify a fill color for dimensions.
- **Text height.** This text box is used to set the height for the text in the dimension string. This should be the actual plotted size, such as **1/8″**.
- **Fraction height scale.** This text box controls the height of the individual numbers in fractions. The fraction numeral height is commonly the same as the whole number, but some companies use a smaller text height for the fraction numerals.
- **Draw frame around text.** Check to draw a box around the dimension text.
- **Text placement.** This area is used to place the dimension text in a location relative to the dimension and extension lines.
  - **Vertical.** This drop-down list includes four options. **Centered** places the text centered on the dimension line. **Above** places the text above the dimension line. **Outside** places the text to the outside of the dimension. **JIS** uses the Japanese Imperial Standard for text. The **Above** option is commonly used in architectural drafting, but some companies prefer other standards.
  - **Horizontal.** This drop-down list includes five options for placing text horizontally along the dimension or extension line. **Centered** places the text centered on the dimension line. **At Ext Line 1** places the text next to the first extension line. **At Ext Line 2** places the text next to the second extension line. **Over Ext Line 1** places the text along the first extension line. **Over Ext Line 2** places the text along the second extension line.
  - **Offset from dim line.** This text box specifies the distance between the text and dimension line. A distance of **1/16″** is typical.
- **Text alignment.** This area is used to specify whether the text is aligned with the dimension line or always horizontal in the drawing.
  - **Horizontal.** This radio button specifies that the dimension text is always horizontal in the drawing, including in vertical dimensions.
  - **Aligned with dimension line.** This radio button aligns the text with the dimension line and places the text in relation to the **Vertical:** placement specified in the **Text placement** area. The **Aligned with dimension line** option is commonly used for architectural drafting.
  - **ISO standard.** This radio button places the text aligned with the dimension line when the text is between the extension lines. If the text is placed outside the extension lines, the text is forced horizontally.

Exercise
11-8

Complete the Exercise on the Student CD.

The next tab in the **Modify Dimension Style:** *style name* dialog box is the **Fit** tab, shown in **Figure 11-29**. This tab is used to control how the dimension text fits in the dimension string and the size of the dimension strings. The following settings are found in the **Fit** tab:

Figure 11-29.
The **Fit** tab is used to control how the dimension text fits in the dimension string.

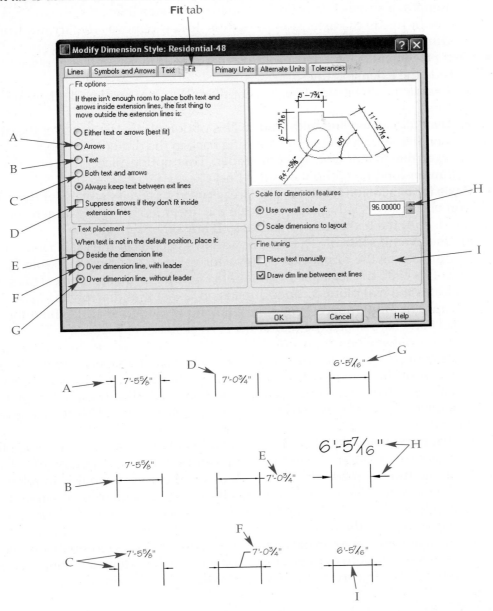

- **Fit options.** This area controls how dimension text and arrowheads are placed in the drawing. When the extension lines for a dimension are too close together, the dimension text and arrowheads for the dimension need to be placed somewhere in the drawing. The following five radio button options and one check box control the placement of the text and arrowheads:
  - **Either text or arrows (best fit).** When this radio button is selected, either the arrowheads or text is moved outside the extension lines. AutoCAD automatically decides how to place text, dimension lines, and arrowheads during tight situations.
  - **Arrows.** When this option is selected, the arrowheads are the first objects to move to the outside of the extension lines in a crowded situation.
  - **Text.** This option moves the text to the outside of the extension lines before moving the arrowheads outside.
  - **Both text and arrows.** This option moves both the text and arrows outside the extension lines when the dimension space is too small.

- **Always keep text between ext lines.** This option always forces the text to be inside the extension lines.
- **Suppress arrows if they don't fit inside extension lines.** If the arrowheads do not fit inside the extension lines, this option removes the arrows from the dimension.
- **Text placement.** This area specifies where the dimension text is placed if it is outside the extension lines.
  - **Beside the dimension line.** This option places the text beside the dimension line.
  - **Over dimension line, with leader.** This option places the text over the dimension line with a leader line pointing back to the dimension line.
  - **Over dimension line, without leader.** This option places the text over the dimension line without a leader line.
- **Scale for dimension features.** This area is used to specify a scale for the dimension objects. This value does not scale the linear length of the dimension, only the sizes of the text and arrowheads and any other set values:
  - **Use overall scale of.** This text box allows you to set the scale factor for the drawing as the dimension scale factor value. If the drawing scale is set to 1/4″ = 1′-0″, the scale factor equals 48. Type 48 in this text box. This setting scales the real plotted paper dimension text size and arrowhead size up 48 times in model space. When the drawing is plotted to scale, the dimension text and arrowheads appear at the correct size.
  - **Scale dimensions to layout.** This option is used when dimensioning the drawing through a floating viewport in layout (paper) space. The scale factor of the viewport is used as a multiplication factor for the dimension objects. Layout space and floating viewports are discussed in Chapter 24.
- **Fine tuning.** This area is used to set two miscellaneous values for the text and dimensions:
  - **Place text manually.** Typically, the placement of a dimension requires three location picks in the drawing. The first and second picks designate the length being dimensioned. The third pick places the dimension line in relation to the extension lines and automatically adds the dimensional value. If this check box is selected, an additional point needs to be picked, designating the location of the text.
  - **Draw dim line between ext lines.** When a dimension is too small and the text or arrows, or both objects, are placed outside the extension lines, this check box forces a line to be drawn between the extension lines.

Exercise 11-9 *Complete the Exercise on the Student CD.*

When you finish configuring the **Fit** values for the placement of text and arrowheads, select the **Primary Units** tab, shown in **Figure 11-30**. This tab is for the type of formatting the dimension text uses. These values are found in the **Primary Units** tab:
- **Linear dimensions.** This area is used to specify the type of units the dimension text uses, as well as to control the appearance of the text in the dimension.
  - **Unit format.** This drop-down list controls the type of units displayed in the dimension text. Options include **Scientific, Decimal, Engineering, Architectural, Fractional,** and **Windows Desktop.**
  - **Precision.** This drop-down list controls how accurately the dimension values are rounded when measuring between two points.

Architectural Desktop and Its Applications

Figure 11-30.
The **Primary Units** tab is used to specify the appearance of the text in the dimension line.

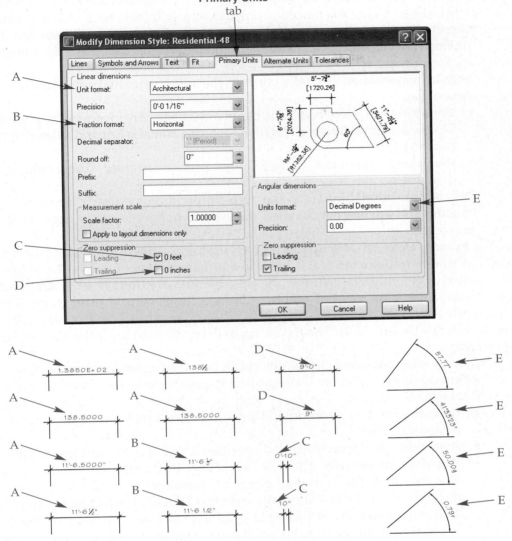

- **Fraction format.** This drop-down list controls how fractions appear when **Architectural** or **Fractional** units are used. The options include **Horizontal**, **Diagonal**, and **Not Stacked**. An unstacked fraction is a fraction appearing along the same line as the main dimension text.
- **Decimal separator.** This option is used with the **Decimal** units. The drop-down list is used to control the separator between the whole number and the decimal number. Options include '.' **(Period)**, ',' **(Comma)**, and ' ' **(Space)**.
- **Round off.** This text box allows the dimension to be rounded up or down.
- **Prefix.** This value is placed in front of the dimension text.
- **Suffix.** This value is placed at the end of the dimension text.
- **Measurement scale.** This area is used to scale the dimension length. For example, a value of 4 makes a 2'-0"–long dimension read as 8'-0". It is important to note that this is not the drawing scale factor and does not scale the text height or arrowhead length. The **Scale factor:** text box is used to enter a scale to be used as the multiplication factor. The **Apply to layout dimensions only** option scales the length of the dimensions when the dimensions are placed in the layout. If you are dimensioning an imperial size drawing using millimeters, type 25.4 in the **Scale factor:** text box, as a conversion of 25.4 mm to 1".

- **Zero suppression.** This area is used to suppress zeros in the dimension text. The **Leading** and **Trailing** check boxes are used for decimal units, and the **0 feet** and **0 inches** check boxes are used for engineering and architectural units. When a check is placed in the **Leading** or **0 feet** check box, any zeros in the whole number or feet column are not displayed on the dimension. If the **Trailing** or **0 inches** check box is checked, the zeros at the end of the dimension are suppressed.
- **Angular dimensions.** This area controls the appearance of the text in an angular dimension.
  - **Units format.** This selects the types of units to display for angular dimensions. Options include **Decimal Degrees**, **Degrees Minutes Seconds**, **Gradians**, and **Radians**.
  - **Precision.** This area controls how precise angular dimension text is displayed.
- **Zero suppression.** Similar to the zero suppression for linear dimensions, the **Leading** and **Trailing** check boxes are used to remove zeros in angular dimension text.

The **Primary Units** tab sets up the primary, or main, dimension text for the dimensions. The **Alternate Units** tab is used to add another element of text in the dimension that is scaled differently. For example, suppose the **Primary Units** is set to **Architectural** units, dimensioning in feet and inches. Alternate units can be used to display the metric equivalent. These units are displayed with squared brackets around the dimensional value. See **Figure 11-31.** The following options are used to set the alternate units, if they are used:

- **Display alternate units.** Select this check box to turn on alternate units.
- **Alternate units.** This area is used to set the parameters for alternate text in the dimension.
  - **Units format.** This drop-down list includes the unit formats for the alternate dimension text.
  - **Precision.** This drop-down list specifies how alternate unit text is rounded.
  - **Multiplier for alt units.** This text box is used as a multiplier for the resulting alternate text. For example, given a dimension of a 12'-0" length and a multiplier of 2, the resulting alternate text is 24'-0". By default, the multiplier 25.4 is used to convert inches to millimeters ($25.4 \times$ inches = millimeters). When this multiplier is used on alternate text, the resulting text is the metric equivalent of the primary units.
  - **Round distances to.** This text box value rounds the alternate unit text to the nearest value specified.
  - **Prefix.** This value is placed in front of the alternate units.
  - **Suffix.** This value is displayed at the end of all alternate units.
- **Zero suppression.** As in the **Primary Units** tab, this area specifies how zeros in a dimension are displayed or suppressed.
- **Placement.** This area includes two options for the placement of the alternate text in the dimension.
  - **After primary value.** This radio button places the alternate unit text beside the primary unit text.
  - **Below primary value.** This radio button places the alternate unit text below the primary unit text.

Exercise
11-10   *Complete the Exercise on the Student CD.*

Architectural Desktop and Its Applications

Figure 11-31.
The **Alternate Units** tab places additional text set to a different scale next to the primary unit text.

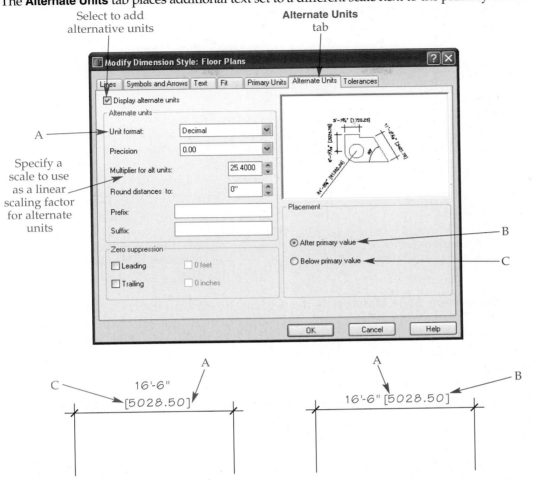

The last tab in the **Modify Dimension Style:** *style name* dialog box is the **Tolerances** tab, which is used to display a tolerance after a dimensional value. Tolerances are used primarily in the mechanical engineering field. For more information regarding tolerances, see the section on **DIMSTYLE** in the **Command Reference** of **AutoCAD Help** in the **Autodesk Architectural Desktop 2007 Help** window or the *AutoCAD and Its Applications* textbook.

Setting Dimension Overrides

Once a dimension style has been set up, the dimension style is used for all types of dimensions in your drawing. For example, if architectural ticks have been specified as the arrowhead choice, linear, angular, radius, and diameter dimensions all use architectural ticks for the arrows. See **Figure 11-32.** You might want to use the **Architectural tick** for linear and diameter dimensions, but **Closed filled** arrows for angular and radius dimensions. Overrides need to be set to specify how a particular type of dimension is displayed. When overrides are applied to different types of dimensions, the dimensions break the rules the parent dimensions set up. Applying the overrides is known as setting up the child dimension styles. *Child dimension styles* are dimension styles that use the initial settings of the main (or parent) dimension style to which they belong. Overriding the main dimension style creates "child" dimension styles, which do not obey the rules of their parent style.

Figure 11-32.
Dimensions using the same dimension style are all formatted similarly. Those with overrides attached might give a more desirable appearance.

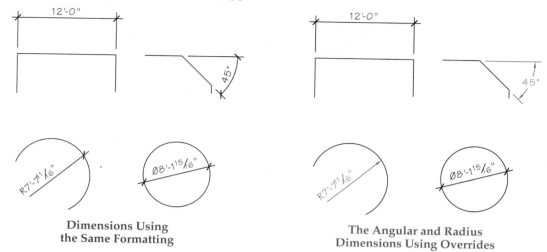

Dimensions Using
the Same Formatting

The Angular and Radius
Dimensions Using Overrides

The **Dimension Style Manager** is used to begin making override settings for the dimensions. To create an override for the radius dimension, select the **New...** button to create a new dimension style. See **Figure 11-32**. In the **Create New Dimension Style** dialog box, select the dimension style being overridden in the **Start With:** drop-down list, shown in **Figure 11-33**. In the **Use for:** drop-down list, select the type of dimension you are overriding. Specifying a dimension type other than **All dimensions** grays out the **New Style Name:** text box. Once the **Continue** button is picked, the **New Dimension Style:** *style name: dimension type* dialog box is displayed.

This procedure is similar to specifying the formatting for all dimensions, except only the values specific to the type of dimension you are overriding are available. The preview pane displays only the type of dimension being overridden. Make the changes desired for the type of dimension you are overriding, and pick the **OK** button. The **Dimension Style Manager** reappears, displaying the parent dimension style with the overriding style beneath, as shown in **Figure 11-34**. Continue adding overrides to dimension types until you have configured all the dimension styles and overrides.

Setting a Dimension Style Current

After a dimension style is created, it must be set current before it can be used for the dimensions. To set a dimension style current, select the style from the **Styles:** list in the **Dimension Style Manager** and pick the **Set Current** button, or select the dimension style from the drop-down list on the **Dimension** toolbar. See **Figure 11-35**.

Figure 11-33.
The **Create New Dimension Style** dialog box for setting overrides to angular dimensions in the Residential-48 parent dimension style.

Parent
dimension style

Type of dimension
being overridden
(child dimension
style)

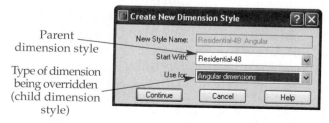

Architectural Desktop and Its Applications

Figure 11-34.
The **Dimension Style Manager** displaying the dimension style with child overriding styles.

Main dimension style (parent style)

Overriding styles (child styles)

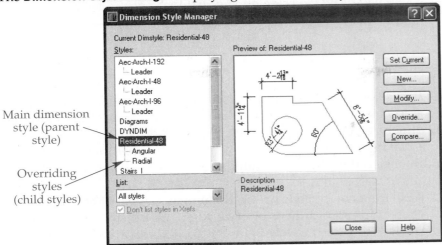

Figure 11-35.
Use the **Dimension Style Manager** or the **Dim Style Control** drop-down list on the **Dimension** toolbar to set a dimension style current.

Current dimension style

Select a style to be current

Pick to set the highlighted style current

Pick to set the highlighted style current

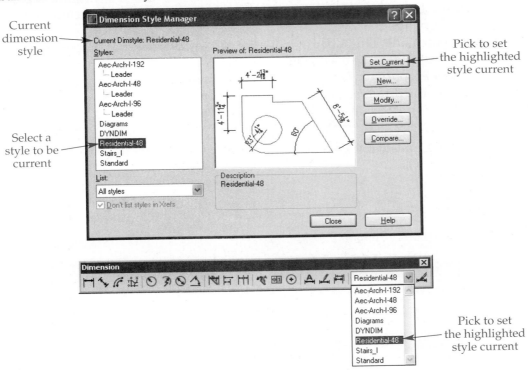

Only parent styles can be set current. Any overrides are automatically assumed to be a part of the parent style. All dimensions added to the drawing are automatically configured to reflect the current dimension settings.

NOTE

When you are using the templates supplied with Architectural Desktop, different dimension styles are available. There are also overrides that have been created within the templates. Save time by using these dimension styles as a basis for creating your dimension standard.

Exercise
11-11   **Complete the Exercise on the Student CD.**

Creating an AEC Dimension Style

The previous discussion explained how to configure dimension styles for use with standard AutoCAD and AEC dimensions. An AEC dimension style is different from an AutoCAD dimension style. For example, in an AEC dimension style, the first string of dimensions can be set to dimension the center of any openings in a wall, the second string can dimension the lengths of walls, and the third string can dimension the overall outer limits of walls.

Pull-Down Menu

Format
  > AEC Dimension
    Styles...
Document
  > AEC Dimension
    > AEC
      Dimension
      Styles...

Pick **Format** > **AEC Dimension Styles...** or **Document** > **AEC Dimension** > **AEC Dimension Styles...** to create an AEC dimension style. Right-click on the **AEC Dimension Styles** icon and select **New**, or pick the **New Style** button, to create a new style. Select the new style from the tree list on the left to display the AEC dimension properties in the right pane. See **Figure 11-36.** The following tabs are available for the AEC dimension style properties:

- **General.** This tab is used to rename and provide a description of the AEC dimension style.
- **Chains.** This tab is used to specify the number of dimension strings (chains) to be assigned to the style.
- **Classifications.** This tab provides a list of named properties that can be assigned to the object for use in schedules.
- **Display Properties.** This tab is used to set up the appearance of the AEC dimensions in the different display representations.

Figure 11-36.
Create a new AEC dimension style, and then edit the properties for the style.

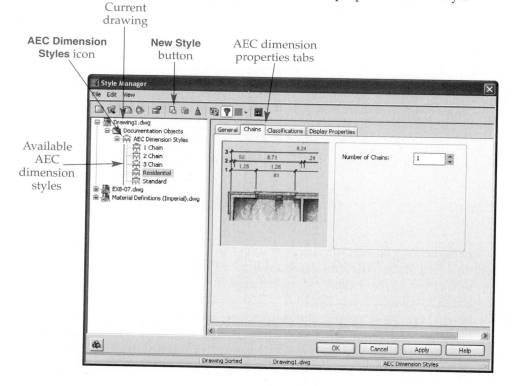

Determine the number of strings, or chains, to use for the AEC dimension style in the **Chains** tab. In the **Display Properties** tab, select the display representation to be adjusted, and place a check mark in the **Style Override** column to have display changes assigned to the style. This opens the **Display Properties** (*display property source*) - *display representation* dialog box for the AEC dimensions. See **Figure 11-37**. The following tabs are available:

- **Layer/Color/Linetype.** This tab controls the visibility and appearance of the AEC dimension. Turn or off the different components, and assign any additional display properties.
- **Contents.** This tab displays the number of chains the style uses, the types of objects that can be dimensioned, and how they are dimensioned.
- **Other.** This tab contains options to control what AutoCAD dimension style to reference and how the AEC dimensions are created.

The **Contents** tab is divided into three areas. The **Apply to:** area lists the different AEC objects associated with the AEC dimensions. The **Other** icon is used for AEC objects not specified in the list. Below the **Apply to:** area is a list of the number of chains in the style. To use this option, first highlight a chain, and then select an object from the list above to assign how the object should be dimensioned for that string. The area to the right provides a list of options for each AEC object in the **Apply to:** list. Select the check boxes desired to configure what will be dimensioned for each string.

When you are finished in the **Contents** tab, select the **Other** tab to control additional display settings. See **Figure 11-38**. The AEC dimension styles use the properties of an existing AutoCAD dimension style. Select the style to use as the basis for the AEC dimensions. Once the AEC dimension style has been configured, new AEC dimensions can be created in the drawing using the style.

 NOTE

The use of AEC dimensions can be helpful during the design phase. Use AEC dimensions when laying out walls and openings. As you modify walls and openings, the dimensions automatically update so you can keep track of measurements. AEC dimensions can also be used alongside standard AutoCAD dimensions to aid in preparation of the finished construction documents.

Figure 11-37.
The **Display Properties** (*display property source*) - *display representation* dialog box for AEC dimensions. The **Contents** tab is used to control what is dimensioned and how an object is dimensioned in the AEC dimension.

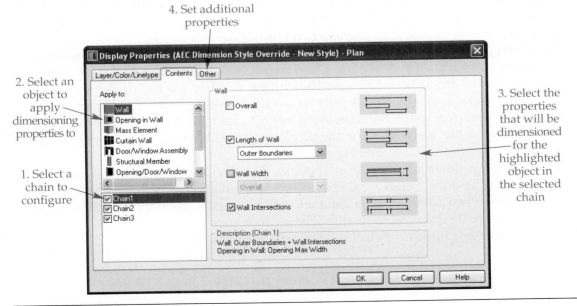

4. Set additional properties

2. Select an object to apply dimensioning properties to

3. Select the properties that will be dimensioned for the highlighted object in the selected chain

1. Select a chain to configure

Figure 11-38.

The **Other** tab sets additional properties for the AEC dimension style.

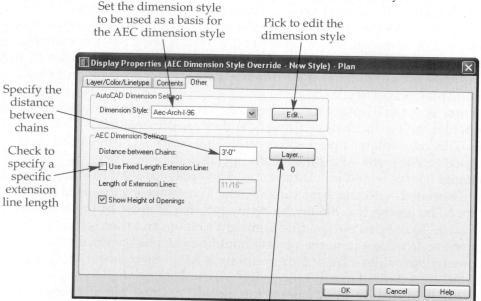

Set the dimension style to be used as a basis for the AEC dimension style

Pick to edit the dimension style

Specify the distance between chains

Check to specify a specific extension line length

Specify the layer for the AEC dimensions. If set to 0, the current layer key will be used to set the layer for the object.

Using the Properties Palette

When dimensions are created from the **Dimension** toolbar, the dimensions are placed on the current layer. In proper drafting management, dimensions should be placed on their own specific layer. For example, when the dimension commands from **DesignCenter** are used, the dimensions are placed on the A-Anno-Dims layer. Also, as you draw, objects can be placed on the wrong layer, or you might want to change other properties of an object, such as color, linetype, or location. The **Properties** palette can be used to modify the layer, additional properties of individual dimension objects, and the properties of all AutoCAD and Architectural Desktop objects.

Initially, the **Properties** palette is docked on the left side of the drawing screen. The **Properties** palette remains on the drawing screen as you work in Architectural Desktop. While the **Properties** palette is displayed, you can continue to enter commands and work on the drawing. Pick the **X** in the title bar to close the palette or select the **Auto-hide** button to hide the palette when it is not needed.

When you display the **Properties** palette without first selecting an object, **No selection** is displayed in the top drop-down list. The **General, 3D Visualization, Plot style, View,** and **Misc** categories are available, listing the current settings for the drawing, as shown in **Figure 11-39.** Under each category is a list of object properties. For example, in **Figure 11-39,** the current color is set to ByLayer. To change a property, pick the property or its current value. Depending on the property selected, one of the following methods is used to change the value. See **Figure 11-40:**

- A drop-down arrow button appears. Pick the drop-down arrow to display a list of options. Select a value available to change the property value.
- A **Pick two points to set a distance** button appears, allowing you to pick a location in the drawing to specify a new coordinate location.
- A text box appears. Select the text box to enter a new value.

Figure 11-39.
The **Properties** palette lists the properties of the selected object and allows you to modify the properties.

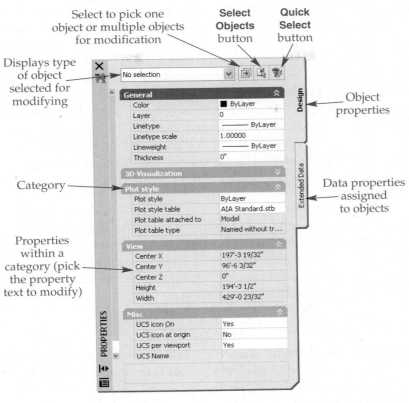

Figure 11-40.
Different methods of changing the properties for dimensions. A drop-down arrow contains a list of options. The **Pick Point** button allows you to pick a coordinate location. A text box allows you to enter a new value.

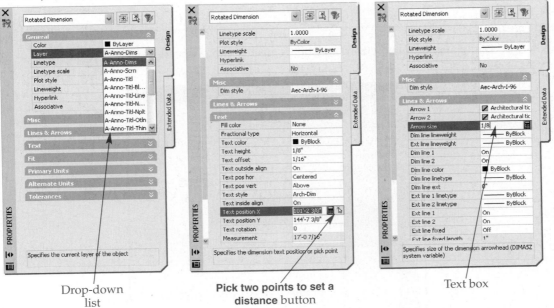

As properties to be modified are selected, a description of what that property controls is shown at the bottom of the **Properties** palette. The upper-right portion of the **Properties** palette includes the following three buttons:

- **Toggle value of PICKADD Sysvar.** Selecting this button allows you to pick only one object at a time. The default allows multiple objects to be modified.
- **Select Objects.** This button allows you to pick objects to be modified.
- **Quick Select.** This button opens the **Quick Select** dialog box, which allows you to filter for objects meeting specific criteria. The selected objects can then be modified in the **Properties** palette.

Once an object has been selected for modification, the properties specific to the type of object are displayed in the **Properties** palette. The drop-down list at the top of the window indicates the type and number of objects being modified. For example, in **Figure 11-40**, a **Rotated Dimension** linear dimension has been selected. The properties of the selected dimension can be modified to override the properties set in the dimension style.

If many different objects are selected, the drop-down list displays the word **All** with the number of objects selected in parentheses. The only properties available are the properties common to all the selected objects. The drop-down list at the top of the window displays all the objects that have been selected and the total number of each type of object. Selecting an object type from the drop-down list allows the properties available for that type of object to be modified.

Using the AEC Dimension Display Wizard

Pull-Down Menu
Format
> AEC DImension
Style
Wizard...

The **AEC Dimension Display Wizard** is used to configure different properties of existing AEC dimension styles. Pick **Format** > **AEC Dimension Style Wizard...** to access the wizard. The first page of the wizard is displayed. See **Figure 11-41**.

On the **Select Style** page, select the AEC dimension style to be modified. Pick **Next** to advance to the **Lines and Arrows** page. This page of the wizard is used to adjust the arrowheads, dimension lines, and extension lines in a selected display representation. See **Figure 11-42**. Make any adjustments, and then pick **Next** to advance to the **Text** page.

The **Text** page is used to control properties of AEC dimension text in the selected

Figure 11-41.
The **AEC Dimension Display Wizard** is used to modify the properties of existing AEC dimension styles.

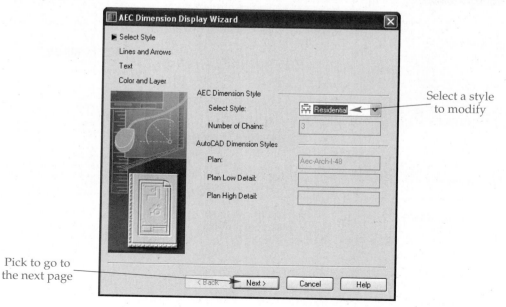

Select a style to modify

Pick to go to the next page

Figure 11-42.
The **Lines and Arrows** page is used to configure the arrowheads, dimension lines, and extension lines in a selected display representation.

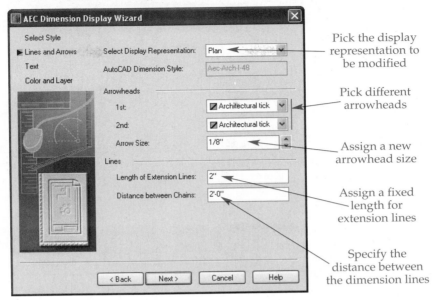

Pick the display representation to be modified

Pick different arrowheads

Assign a new arrowhead size

Assign a fixed length for extension lines

Specify the distance between the dimension lines

display representation. See **Figure 11-43.** Select a display representation to be modified, and then specify the text style, text height, and round off for the AEC dimension text. Pick **Next** to advance to the **Color and Layer** page.

The last page of the wizard controls the colors and assigned layer the AEC dimension uses. See **Figure 11-44.** Select the display representation to be modified, and pick colors for the different parts of the AEC dimension. Pick the **Layer...** button to assign a layer for the AEC dimension to use. When you are finished, pick the **Finish** button. If additional changes need to be made to other display representations this style uses, reenter the wizard and make the adjustments to the appropriate display representation.

Figure 11-43.
The **Text** page is used to control the properties of the AEC dimension text.

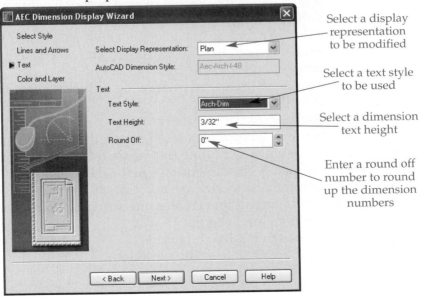

Select a display representation to be modified

Select a text style to be used

Select a dimension text height

Enter a round off number to round up the dimension numbers

Figure 11-44.
The last page of the wizard is used to control colors used in the selected display representation.

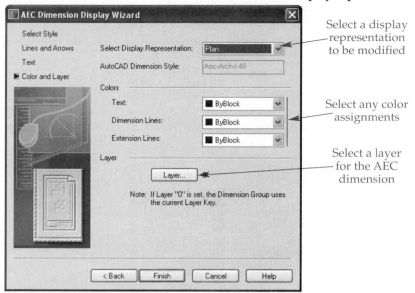

Select a display representation to be modified

Select any color assignments

Select a layer for the AEC dimension

Chapter Test

Answer the following questions. Write your answers on a separate sheet of paper or complete the electronic chapter test on the Student CD.

1. Name the command used in Architectural Desktop to create notes.
2. Define *text style* and identify at least two places where different text styles can be used in a drawing.
3. What are you allowed to do when you enter a text style height equal to 0'-0"?
4. What happens when you draw text using a text style with a height other than 0'-0"?
5. When adding text by picking **Text Tool** from the **Annotation** palette, you are prompted for an insertion point and the text width. What does this text width signify?
6. Describe a text boundary and how it is accessed and used.
7. Give an example of the following statement: Text entered into the model space drawing is drawn at the desired plotted output height multiplied by the scale factor of the drawing.
8. Identify the layer and height adjustment for text created with the **Text Tool.**
9. Identify the layer and height adjustment for text created with the **MTEXT, MT,** or **T** command.
10. Identify the layer used when a drawing is dimensioned using the commands from the toolbar.
11. Identify the layer used when a drawing is dimensioned by dragging the dimensioning commands from **DesignCenter** and dropping them into the drawing.
12. Describe the effect of pulling the mouse to the left, to the right, up, or down when you specify the dimension line location.
13. Name the command used to create horizontal, vertical, and rotated dimensions.
14. Name the command that creates one string of dimensions, in which all the dimension lines are lined up.
15. Identify the use of radial dimensions.
16. Identify the use of aligned dimensions.

17. What does it mean to say that AEC dimensions are dimension objects attached to the AEC objects they are dimensioning, and how does this affect the editing of these AEC objects?
18. Define *dimension styles*.
19. Describe a parent dimension and identify when it has to be set in a dimension style.
20. Define *child dimensions*.

Chapter Projects

Use the techniques covered in this chapter to create the following drawings.

1. Single-Level Residential Project
   A. Access the **Project Browser** and set Residential-Project-01 current.
   B. Access the **Views** tab of the **Project Navigator** and create a new general view with the following settings:
      a. **Name**: Main Floor Plan
      b. **Context**: **Main Floor** level
      c. **Content**: Select the Main Floor and Plumbing-Appliances constructs.
   C. Open the Main Floor Plan view drawing.
   D. Set the Aec-Arch-I-48 dimension style current.
   E. Ensure the drawing scale is set to **1/4" = 1'-0"**.
   F. Use any method of dimensioning to add dimensions to the drawing, as seen in the figure. Use grip editing or AEC dimension editing as needed. Ensure that the dimensions are placed on the A-Anno-Dims layer.
   G. Create a text style for room titles and set it current.
   H. Add room titles into the drawing as shown in the figure. Ensure that the text is placed on the A-Anno-Note layer.
   I. Save and close the drawing.

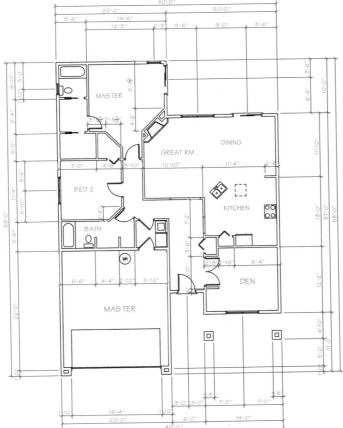

Design Courtesy Alan Mascord Design Associates

2. Single-Level Residential Project
   A. Access the **Project Browser** and set Residential-Project-02 current.
   B. Access the **Views** tab of the **Project Navigator** and create a new general view with the following settings:
      a. **Name**: Main Floor Plan
      b. **Context**: **Main Floor** level
      c. **Content**: Select the Main Floor and Plumbing-Appliances constructs.
   C. Open the Main Floor Plan view drawing.
   D. Set the Aec-Arch-I-48 dimension style current.
   E. Ensure the drawing scale is set to **1/4″ = 1′-0″**.
   F. Use any method of dimensioning to add dimensions to the drawing, as seen in the figure. Use grip editing or AEC dimension editing as needed. Ensure that the dimensions are placed on the A-Anno-Dims layer.
   G. Create a text style for room titles and set it current.
   H. Add room titles into the drawing as shown in the figure. Ensure that the text is placed on the A-Anno-Note layer.
   I. Save and close the drawing.

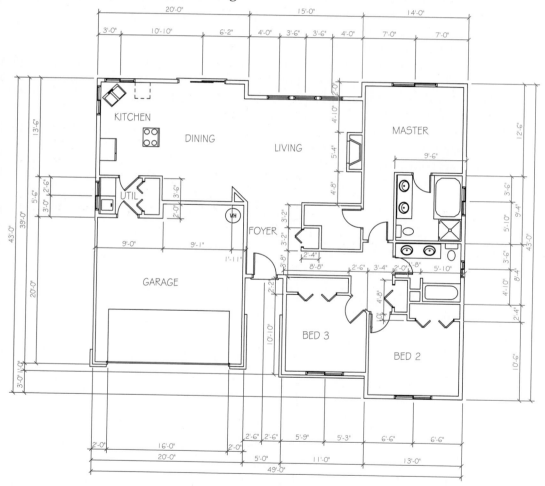

Design Courtesy Alan Mascord Design Associates

3. Two-Story Residential Project
    A. Access the **Project Browser** and set Residential-Project-03 current.
    B. Access the **Views** tab of the **Project Navigator** and create a new general view with the following settings:
        a. **Name**: Main Floor Plan
        b. **Context**: **Main Floor** level
        c. **Content**: Select the Main Floor and Plumbing-Appliances constructs.
    C. Open the Main Floor Plan view drawing.
    D. Set the Aec-Arch-I-48 dimension style current.
    E. Ensure the drawing scale is set to **1/4″ = 1′-0″**.
    F. Use any method of dimensioning to add dimensions to the drawing, as seen in the figure. Use grip editing or AEC dimension editing as needed. Ensure that the dimensions are placed on the A-Anno-Dims layer.
    G. Create a text style for room titles and set it current.
    H. Add room titles into the drawing as shown in the figure. Ensure that the text is placed on the A-Anno-Note layer.
    I. Save and close the drawing.
    J. Access the **Views** tab of the **Project Navigator** and create a new general view with the following settings:
        a. **Name**: Upper Floor Plan
        b. **Context**: **Upper Floor** level
        c. **Content**: Select the Upper Floor construct.
    K. Open the Upper Floor Plan view drawing.
    L. Set the Aec-Arch-I-48 dimension style current.
    M. Ensure the drawing scale is set to **1/4″ = 1′-0″**.
    N. Use any method of dimensioning to add dimensions to the drawing, as seen in the figure. Use grip editing or AEC dimension editing as needed. Ensure that the dimensions are placed on the A-Anno-Dims layer.
    O. Create a text style for room titles and set it current.
    P. Add room titles into the drawing as shown in the figure. Ensure that the text is placed on the A-Anno-Note layer.
    Q. Save and close the drawing.

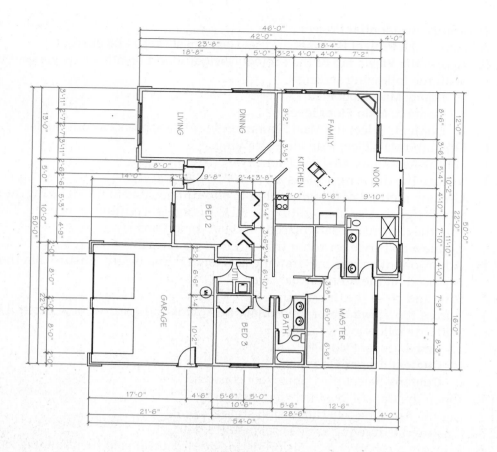

Drawing Courtesy 3D-DZYN

4. Two-Story Residential Project
   A. Access the **Project Browser** and set Residential-Project-04 current.
   B. Access the **Views** tab of the **Project Navigator** and create a new general view with the following settings:
      a. **Name**: Main Floor Plan
      b. **Context**: **Main Floor** level
      c. **Content**: Select the Main Floor and MainFlr-Plumbing-Appliances constructs.
   C. Open the Main Floor Plan view drawing.
   D. Set the Aec-Arch-I-48 dimension style current.
   E. Ensure the drawing scale is set to **1/4″ = 1′-0″**.
   F. Use any method of dimensioning to add dimensions to the drawing, as seen in the figure. Use grip editing or AEC dimension editing as needed. Ensure that the dimensions are placed on the A-Anno-Dims layer.
   G. Create a text style for room titles and set it current.
   H. Add room titles into the drawing as shown in the figure. Ensure that the text is placed on the A-Anno-Note layer.
   I. Save and close the drawing.
   J. Access the **Views** tab of the **Project Navigator** and create a new general view with the following settings:
      a. **Name**: Upper Floor Plan
      b. **Context**: **Upper Floor** level
      c. **Content**: Select the Upper Floor and UpperFlr-Plumbing-Appliances constructs.
   K. Open the Upper Floor Plan view drawing.
   L. Set the Aec-Arch-I-48 dimension style current.
   M. Ensure the drawing scale is set to **1/4″ = 1′-0″**.
   N. Use any method of dimensioning to add dimensions to the drawing, as seen in the figure. Use grip editing or AEC dimension editing as needed. Ensure that the dimensions are placed on the A-Anno-Dims layer.
   O. Create a text style for room titles and set it current.
   P. Add room titles into the drawing as shown in the figure. Ensure that the text is placed on the A-Anno-Note layer.
   Q. Save and close the drawing.

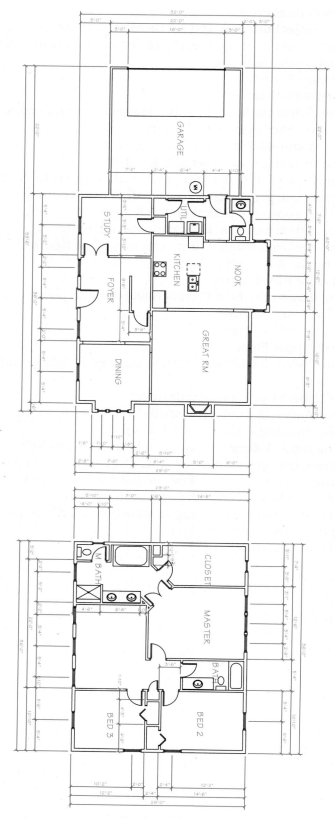

Design Courtesy Alan Mascord Design Associates

5. Commercial Store Project
   A. Access the **Project Browser** and set Commercial-Project-05 current.
   B. Access the **Views** tab of the **Project Navigator** and create a new general view with the following settings:
      a. **Name**: Main Floor Plan
      b. **Context**: **Main Floor** level
      c. **Content**: Select the Main Floor and Plumbing constructs.
   C. Open the Main Floor Plan view drawing.
   D. Set the Aec-Arch-I-96 dimension style current.
   E. Ensure the drawing scale is set to **1/8″ = 1′-0″** in the **Drawing Setup** dialog box.
   F. Use any method of dimensioning to add dimensions to the drawing, as seen in the figure. Use grip editing or AEC dimension editing as needed.
   G. Create a text style for room titles and set it current.
   H. Add room titles into the drawing as shown in the figure.
   I. Save and close the drawing.

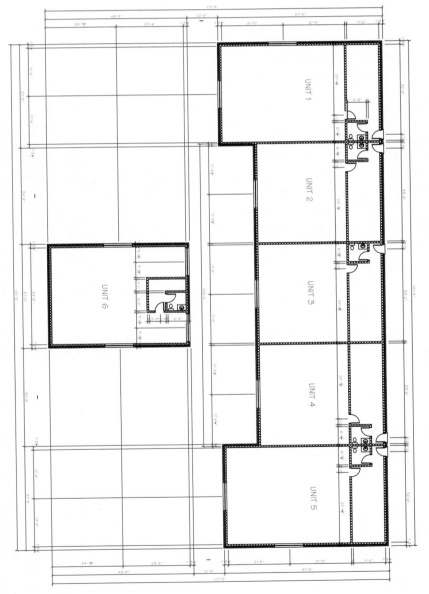

Drawing Courtesy 3D-DZYN

6. Commercial Car Maintenance Shop Project
    A. Access the **Project Browser** and set Commercial-Project-06 current.
    B. Access the **Views** tab of the **Project Navigator** and create a new general view with the following settings:
        a. **Name**: Main Floor Plan
        b. **Context**: **Main Floor** level
        c. **Content**: Select the Main Floor and MainFlr-Plumbing constructs.
    C. Open the Main Floor Plan view drawing.
    D. Set the Aec-Arch-I-96 dimension style current.
    E. Ensure the drawing scale is set to **1/8″ = 1′-0″** in the **Drawing Setup** dialog box.
    F. Use any method of dimensioning to add dimensions to the drawing, as seen in the figure. Use grip editing or AEC dimension editing as needed.
    G. Create a text style for room titles and set it current.
    H. Add room titles into the drawing as shown in the figure.
    I. Save and close the drawing.
    J. Access the **Views** tab of the **Project Navigator** and create a new general view with the following settings:
        a. **Name**: Upper Floor Plan
        b. **Context**: **Upper Floor** level
        c. **Content**: Select the Upper Floor construct.
    K. Open the Upper Floor Plan view drawing.
    L. Set the Aec-Arch-I-96 dimension style current.
    M. Ensure the drawing scale is set to **1/8″ = 1′-0″** in the **Drawing Setup** dialog box.
    N. Use any method of dimensioning to add dimensions to the drawing, as seen in the figure. Use grip editing or AEC dimension editing as needed.
    O. Create a text style for room titles and set it current.
    P. Add room titles into the drawing as shown in the figure.
    Q. Save and close the drawing.

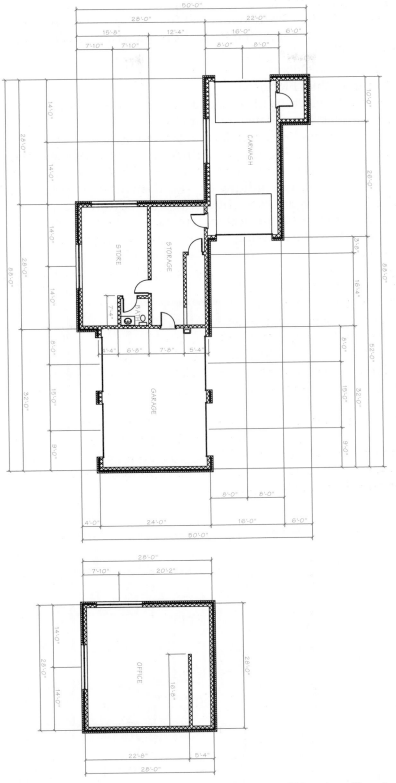

Drawing Courtesy 3D-DZYN

7. Governmental Fire Station
   A. Access the **Project Browser** and set Gvrmt -Project-07 current.
   B. Access the **Views** tab of the **Project Navigator** and create a new general view with the following settings:
      a. **Name**: Main Floor Plan
      b. **Context**: **Main Floor** level
      c. **Content**: Select the Main Floor and Plumbing-Appliances constructs.
   C. Open the Main Floor Plan view drawing.
   D. Set the Aec-Arch-I-96 dimension style current.
   E. Ensure the drawing scale is set to **1/8″ = 1′-0″** in the **Drawing Setup** dialog box.
   F. Use any method of dimensioning to add dimensions to the drawing, as seen in the figure. Use grip editing or AEC dimension editing as needed.
   G. Create a text style for room titles and set it current.
   H. Add room titles into the drawing as shown in the figure.
   I. Save and close the drawing.

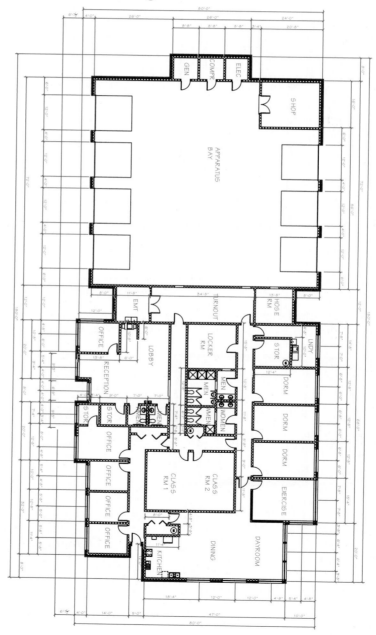

Drawing Courtesy 3D-DZYN

Editing and Modifying Walls

Learning Objectives

After completing this chapter, you will be able to do the following:
- ✓ Use wall object display.
- ✓ Create wall interferences.
- ✓ Use wall modifiers.
- ✓ Create wall sweeps.
- ✓ Adjust the floor lines and rooflines of a wall.
- ✓ Add an object to a wall.
- ✓ Use the **Properties** palette to modify walls.
- ✓ Join and merge walls.

There are many ways to enhance a model's walls and construction documents. As you know, the **Properties** palette is used to make minor adjustments to walls, such as their size or style. However, there are additional ways to improve the appearance of Wall objects in Plan and Model representations. You can add or subtract shapes, columns, or pilasters; modify the shape of a wall; and control additional display properties of a wall. This chapter explains how to use tools for wall modeling and tools for improving the use and appearance of walls in construction documents.

Using Wall Object Display

There are three main display representations commonly used to control how walls appear in the drawing: Plan, Model, and Reflected. Display representations can be set globally, by style, or by individual wall. To change the display of an individual wall, select the wall to be modified, right-click, and select **Edit Object Display...** from the shortcut menu to open the **Object Display** dialog box shown in Figure 12-1. Display representations control how the object is displayed in different viewing directions and display configurations. Modifying a wall's display representation gives you greater control of how your walls display and print.

In the **Display Properties** tab, select the appropriate display representation to be modified from the list of display representations. The **Display Property Source** column displays the level of display control, either the drawing default, wall style override, or

Figure 12-1.
The **Object Display** dialog box for Wall objects.

Indicates when an object
override is applied

List of display
representations
for the Wall
objects

This display
representation
has been
modified

Edit Display
Properties
button

Pick to
override
the object
display

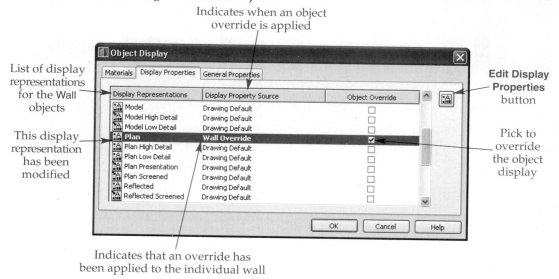

Indicates that an override has
been applied to the individual wall

wall override. Pick the **Object Override** check box beside the desired display representation if you want to attach a display override to the individual wall. This opens the
Display Properties dialog box shown in **Figure 12-2**.

 NOTE

If the **Object Override** box is checked beside the display representation
you wish to modify, highlight the display representation and pick the
Edit Display Properties button to access the **Display Properties** dialog box.

Depending on the display representation chosen for modification, the number of
tabs available for display control can vary. If you are modifying the Plan and Reflected
display representations, the four tabs shown in **Figure 12-2** are available. If the Model
display representation is selected, only the **Layer/Color/Linetype** and **Other** tabs are
available. The four tabs are **Layer/Color/Linetype**, **Hatching**, **Cut Plane**, and **Other**.

Figure 12-2.
The **Display Properties** dialog box for the individual Wall object.

Turns
components
on or off

Displays properties
of the material
when checked

Pick the value of the property
for the component you wish to
change to modify these properties

Wall
components

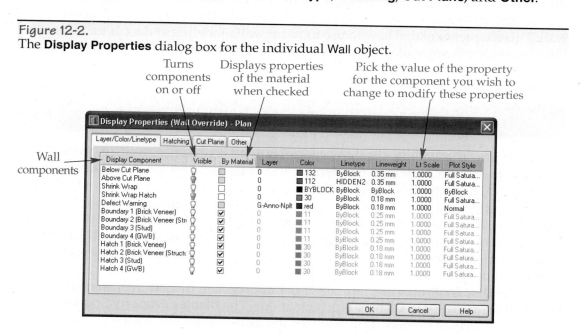

The **Layer/Color/Linetype** tab lists the components of a Wall object. Plan and Reflected wall components can be set differently from Model wall components. Settings including component visibility, layer, color, and linetype are controlled in this tab. To adjust a setting, pick the word or symbol next to the component to be modified. Each component within a wall can have its own display setting to include linetype and lineweight. The following are the components included for Wall objects:

- **Below Cut Plane.** This component is used to control the display of items below the cut plane. The *cut plane*, also referred to as *cutting plane*, is where Architectural Desktop cuts through Wall objects for display in the Top view. By default, Architectural Desktop cuts Wall objects 3'-6" from the bottom of the wall for display in the Top view.
- **Above Cut Plane.** This component is used to control the display of items above the cut plane.
- **Shrink Wrap.** *Shrink wrap* is a component applied to the outermost edges of the walls that allows the outside lines of a multicomponent wall to use a different color and lineweight for plotting purposes. See **Figure 12-3**.
- **Shrink Wrap Hatch.** *Shrink wrap hatch* applies a hatch pattern inside the shrink wrap component of a wall, as shown in **Figure 12-3**.
- **Defect Warning.** This component controls the display of the defect warning symbol in a wall when there is a problem with the wall. This is often assigned to a nonplotting layer.
- **Boundaries.** A wall style can include up to 20 individual boundaries. A *wall style boundary* is an individual component or object contained within the wall style, such as the Stud or Brick Veneer. If you are modifying the wall style or an individual wall display, the number of boundaries within the wall style is given. If you are controlling the display of drawing default walls, all 20 boundaries are available for modification. Each boundary is listed with a number. If you are modifying a specific wall style, the name of the boundary is displayed in parentheses.
- **Hatches.** Each boundary component is assigned a hatch component that can be displayed in a Plan or Reflected view. A *hatch* is a pattern that is used to fill in an area. Each hatch component is assigned a number. The number coincides with the boundary to which it is assigned. For example, the Hatch 2 component is the hatch component assigned to the Boundary 2 component. If the wall boundaries are named, the name of the associated wall boundary is displayed in parentheses beside the hatch component number.

The **Hatching** tab controls the hatches used by the hatch components in the **Layer/Color/Linetype** tab. See **Figure 12-4**. The hatch components are listed in the **Display Component** column. The hatch pattern, scale, rotation angle, and orientation can be controlled for each hatch component. As in the **Layer/Color/Linetype** tab, picking a

Figure 12-3.
Shrink wrap is applied to the outside of a wall. Use a wide linetype for the Shrink Wrap component. Unlike the boundary hatch, the shrink wrap hatch is applied between the two outside lines of a wall.

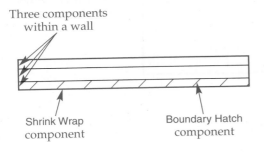
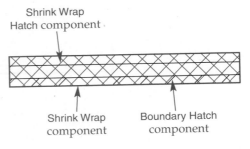

Figure 12-4.

The **Hatching** tab controls how hatch patterns are displayed in a Wall object.

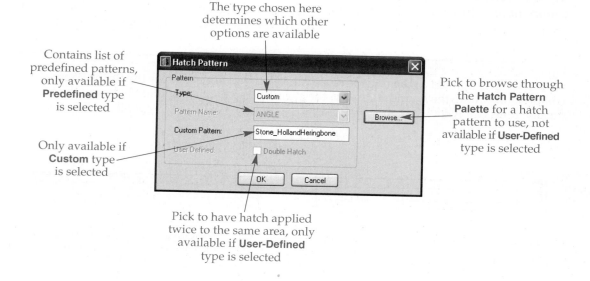

Pick to assign a hatch pattern

Pick to change the scale of the hatch

Pick to adjust the rotation angle of the hatch

Toggles orientation between **global** and **object**

Change value to offset hatch along the X or Y axis

Hatch components in Wall object

symbol or word in each column presents you with options for controlling how the hatch component is displayed. The following columns are available for modification:

- **Pattern.** Pick the swatch next to the desired hatch component to select a hatch pattern other than the default diagonal lines. The **Hatch Pattern** worksheet is shown in **Figure 12-5.** The **Type:** drop-down list includes options for the type of hatch pattern to use. When the **Predefined** type is selected, the **Pattern Name:** drop-down list becomes available with a list of AutoCAD hatch patterns that can be applied to the hatch component. Picking the **Browse...** button opens the **Hatch Pattern Palette** dialog box, which displays a preview of the hatches available. Other types of hatches include Custom, User-defined, and Solid fill. Use the **Browse...** button to preview and select predefined and custom hatch patterns included with Architectural Desktop.

- **Scale/Spacing.** Pick a scale for the selected hatch pattern. The scale controls the spacing of the lines within the hatch.

Figure 12-5.

The **Hatch Pattern** worksheet is used to pick the hatch pattern to be assigned to the Hatch component.

The type chosen here determines which other options are available

Contains list of predefined patterns, only available if **Predefined** type is selected

Pick to browse through the **Hatch Pattern Palette** for a hatch pattern to use, not available if **User-Defined** type is selected

Only available if **Custom** type is selected

Pick to have hatch applied twice to the same area, only available if **User-Defined** type is selected

- **Angle.** Select the angle value to enter a new rotation angle for the hatch pattern.
- **Orientation.** There are two options for the orientation of a hatch pattern: **Object** or **Global**. The **Object** option rotates the hatch relative to the angle of the wall. The **Global** option ensures the hatch always remains at the same rotation angle, regardless of the angle of the wall. See **Figure 12-6.**

The **Cut Plane** tab establishes the cutting plane for wall objects. See **Figure 12-7.** The cut plane establishes where the display of the shrink wrap, component boundaries, and hatching take effect. In addition to the cut plane, additional cut planes can be established that cut through other components within a wall. The tab includes the following four areas for display control:

- **Override Display Configuration Cut Plane.** By default, the current display configuration sets the cutting plane of objects in the drawing. Unchecking this check box allows the cutting plane for the individual wall or wall style to be set in the **Cut Plane Height** text box. Checking this option allows you to set the cut plane for the wall style or individual wall.
- **Cut Plane Height.** This is the main cut plane height. By default, it is set to 3'-6" above the baseline of the wall. The cut plane establishes the components of the wall that will be cut and how the shrink wrap is applied to the wall components. Hatch patterns are also displayed if the cut plane cuts through the boundary where the hatch component has been assigned.

Figure 12-6.
Hatches can be applied with either **global** orientation or **object** orientation.

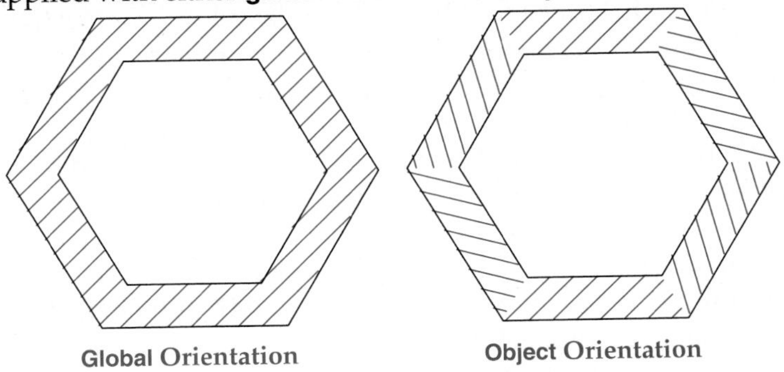

Global Orientation   Object Orientation

Figure 12-7.
The **Cut Plane** tab is used to control the location of the cut plane for Wall objects.

Pick to display objects above and below cut plane if Above Cut Plane and Below Cut Plane components are visible

Enter new cut plane height if overriding the display configuration cut plane

Select to establish additional cut planes manually

Pick to add or remove cut planes

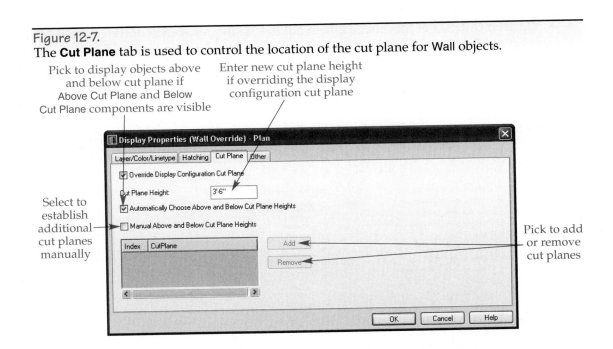

- **Automatically Choose Above and Below Cut Plane heights.** This check box, when checked on, determines where the **Above** and **Below Cut Plane** components are located in the wall. If the **Above Cut Plane** and the **Below Cut Plane** components have been turned on in the **Layer/Color/Linetype** tab, the components display the objects where the cut plane is located.
- **Manual Above and Below Cut Plane heights.** Check this box to establish additional cut planes in a wall. This makes the **Add** and **Remove** buttons available so additional cut planes can be established. Pick the **Add** button to add another cut plane. The table in the lower-left corner is used to establish the heights of additional cut planes. If the additional cut plane is placed lower than the cut plane height, the wall components are displayed using the properties established in the **Below Cut Plane** component in the **Layer/Color/Linetype** tab. If the additional cut plane is placed higher than the cut plane height, the wall components are displayed using the properties established in the **Above Cut Plane** component in the **Layer/Color/Linetype** tab.

The **Other** tab controls additional display properties for wall components, **Figure 12-8.** It contains the following options:

- **Display Inner Lines Above.** This check box turns on any component lines above the cut plane through an opening in a wall.
- **Display Inner Lines Below.** This check box turns on any component lines below the cut plane through an opening in a wall.
- **Hide Lines Below Openings at Cut Plane.** Selecting this check box will hide component lines cut by the cut plane below any openings in the wall.
- **Hide Lines Below Openings Above Cut Plane.** This check box will hide component lines above the cut plane that are displayed in an opening.
- **Display Endcaps.** This check box turns on the endcaps at the ends of walls and openings. An *endcap* is a special shape to describe how the wall is to be built. Endcaps are discussed in Chapter 13.
- **Cut Door Frames.** This check box adjusts the shrink wrap of the wall to include door frames instead of stopping the shrink wrap outside of the door frame (see **Figure 12-9**).
- **Cut Window Frames.** This check mark adjusts the shrink wrap of the wall to include the window sash instead of stopping the shrink wrap outside the window frame (see **Figure 12-9**).
- **Component Draw Order by Priority.** Check this box if one wall component is to be plotted over another wall component.
- **Do True Cut.** Select this check box to cut the 3D model at each of the defined cut planes. This feature is helpful when you are using wall sweeps and wall modifiers, as the Plan view is accurately displayed. Wall sweeps and wall modifiers are described later in this chapter.

Figure 12-8.
The **Other** tab is used to control additional display settings for wall components.

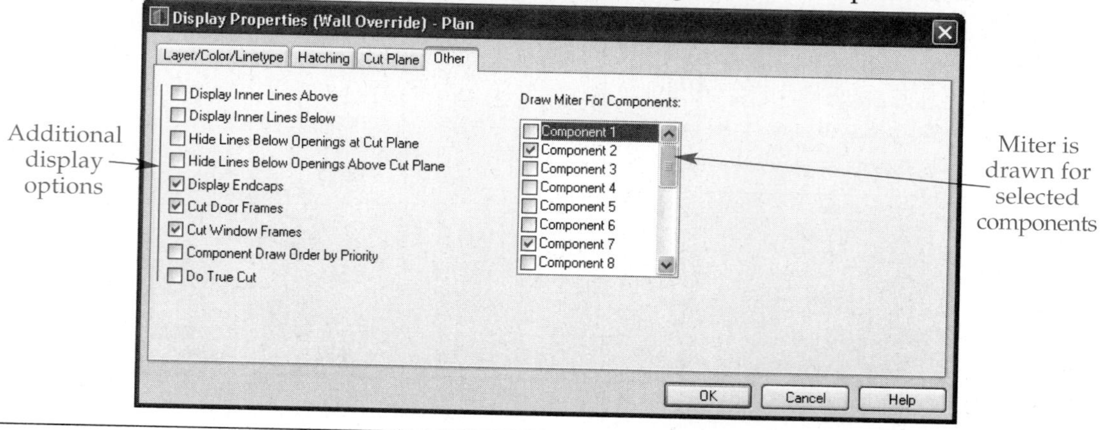

Additional display options

Miter is drawn for selected components

Figure 12-9.
The shrink wrap can be adjusted to only cover the walls or to cover the door and window frames as well.

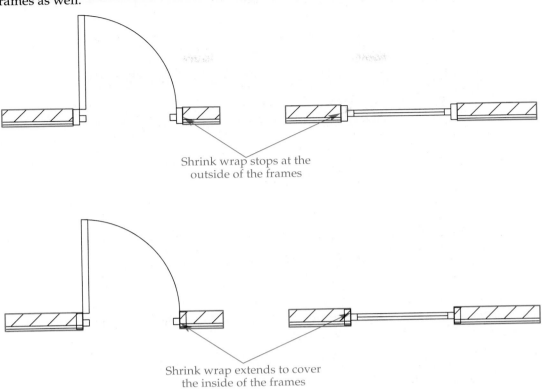

Shrink wrap stops at the
outside of the frames

Shrink wrap extends to cover
the inside of the frames

- **Draw Miter for Components.** This list box displays all the possible boundaries in a Wall object. Select the component(s) to have a miter line drawn where two walls cross each other or join at a corner.

Once you have finished configuring the display for the wall style or individual wall, pick the **OK** button to make the changes appear in the drawing. If the changes do not appear, try picking the **Regenerate Model** button in the **Standard** toolbar to update the display.

Modifying the Material Display

By default, Wall objects in Architectural Desktop include materials assigned to the wall components. The **Materials** tab in the **Object Display** dialog box controls the display of the materials assigned to the Wall object, **Figure 12-10.** When the display properties for the components are modified, the display properties in many of the included wall styles are governed by their material assignments. A check mark in the **By Material** column of the **Display Properties** dialog box indicates that the wall component is looking to the material assignment for its display properties.

To modify the material display control for an individual wall, select the wall, right-click, and pick **Edit Object Display...** from the shortcut menu. Then, pick the **Materials** tab in the **Object Display** dialog box. The **Materials** tab lists the wall components within the selected wall, how the materials are assigned to the components (by the wall style or a wall override), any overrides applied to the components, and the material assigned to each wall component.

Depending on the wall's style, one or more materials may be assigned to different wall components. If you wish to override the material assigned to a wall component, place a check in the **Object Override** check box associated with a wall component. Next, pick **Material Definition** beside the **Object Override** check box to assign a different material to the component. A drop-down list becomes available in the **Material Definition**

Figure 12-10.

The **Materials** tab in the **Object Display** dialog box is used to modify the material display in the selected object.

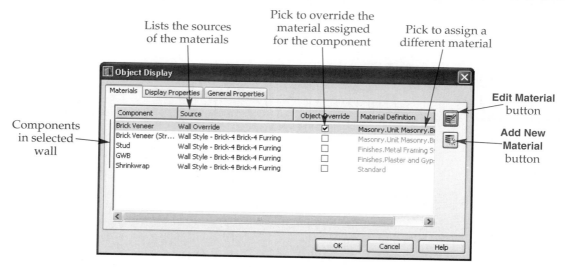

column that displays a list of materials in the drawing that can be assigned to the components. Sometimes the material itself needs to be modified. The next section covers what to do in these situations.

Modifying the Material Definition's Display

When a material assigned to a component needs to be modified, select the material to be modified from the list in the **Materials** tab of the **Object Display** dialog box, and then pick the **Edit Material** button. This displays the **Material Definition Properties** dialog box, **Figure 12-11.** Similar to other AEC objects, an individual material includes several display representations that are used in different display configurations. Select the display representation you wish to modify, apply an override, and then pick the **Edit Display Properties** button. This opens the **Display Properties** dialog box, **Figure 12-12.** This dialog box is similar to the **Display Properties** dialog box for the Wall object.

Figure 12-11.

The **Material Definition Properties** dialog box lists the display representations for the material selected in the **Materials** tab of the **Object Display** dialog box.

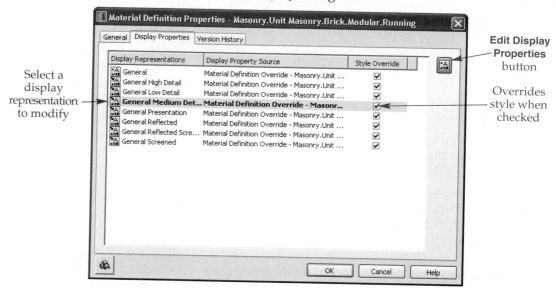

Figure 12-12.
The **Display Properties** dialog box for the material being modified.

Adjust these properties
to modify a component

Components
of the
material

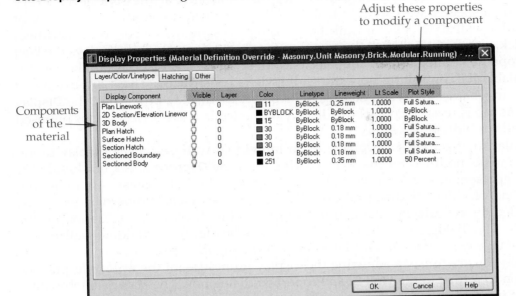

The **Layer/Color/Linetype** tab includes the components of the material that can be displayed in the selected display representation. The Plan Linework component controls the display properties of the Plan view material applied to the Plan view wall component. The Plan Hatch component controls the display of the hatch applied to a Plan wall component. The 3D Body component controls the display properties of the Model wall component. The Surface Hatch component controls the display of the surface hatching applied to the surface of the Model wall component. Additional components are available and used when creating sections or elevations. The **Hatching** tab, similar to the **Hatching** tab for walls, controls the hatch assigned to the hatch components for the material.

The **Other** tab, shown in **Figure 12-13**, is different from the **Other** tab in the **Display Properties** dialog box for Wall objects. This tab controls which sides of the object the material hatch is applied to and the rendering material to be displayed when shading or sectioning the drawing. Creating a material definition and establishing its display properties are discussed in greater detail in Chapter 15.

Figure 12-13.
The **Other** tab controls additional display properties for the material applied to the Wall object.

Pick the
sides of the
object to
display
the hatch

Select a
material to
be displayed
when model
is rendered

Select a
material to
be displayed
when
sectioning
the model

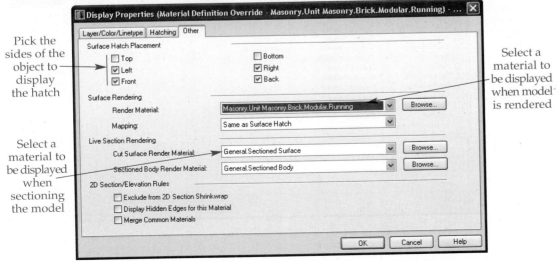

Modifying the Wall Style Display

Generally, the display control for a wall is controlled at the style level. Every wall using a specific wall style is displayed the same way. To modify the display of a particular wall style, select a wall that is using the style that needs to be modified, right-click, and select **Edit Wall Style...** from the shortcut menu. This displays the **Wall Style Properties** dialog box for the selected wall style, **Figure 12-14.** A number of tabs are available for controlling how the wall style is constructed. These are discussed in detail in Chapter 15. When editing the wall style's display properties, the **Display Properties** tab is used to control the display of the walls at the style level, as opposed to all walls or individual walls.

Similar to attaching an override to an individual wall, select the display representation to be modified for the style. Picking the **Style Override** check box beside the display representation allows the wall style to control the wall display. After entering an override, pick the **Edit Display Properties** button. The **Display Properties** dialog box is provided for any display changes to be made to the display representation for the wall style. The dialog box is the same as the dialog box for the individual wall, except changes made here affect the display of all walls using this style.

When you are finished adjusting the display properties for the wall style, pick the **OK** button to return to the **Wall Style Properties** dialog box. The **Materials** tab within the **Wall Style Properties** dialog box controls the display of the materials applied to the wall components within the wall style.

When you are finished making the changes to the wall style, pick **OK** to return to the drawing. Any walls using this style should update to the new display settings. If the walls do not update, use the **Regenerate Model** button in the **Standard** toolbar to update the display of the walls.

NOTE Make the colors that you choose for Plan and Reflected display representations different from the colors of the Model display representation. Doing this gives you more control over how the drawing appears when plotted.

Figure 12-14.
The **Display Properties** tab in the **Wall Style Properties** dialog box is used to modify the wall style's display representations.

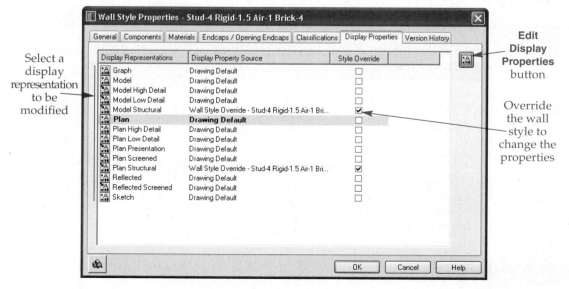

Architectural Desktop and Its Applications

Often, when a floor plan is created, part of the design can include columns within a wall, pilasters applied to the side of a wall, or a niche carved out of a wall. These can be drawn in Architectural Desktop by using *interference conditions*, Figure 12-15. AEC objects can interact with the Wall object by having the shrink wrap go around the AEC object that is interfering with the wall or by having the AEC object subtract part of the wall. Interference conditions are often used to apply the wall shrink wrap around other objects within the wall to enhance specific features of the plan.

Although any AEC object can be used, usually columns and mass elements are used as interference conditions. To create an interference condition, a wall and an AEC object to be used as the interference condition must be present in the drawing. Once the AEC object has been placed in the wall, three different options are available to control how the shrink wrap interacts with the AEC object. If the object is added to the wall, the shrink wrap includes both the wall and the AEC object. If the object is subtracted from the wall, the shrink wrap goes around the wall but not the object. The shrink wrap can also be ignored.

To add an interference condition to a wall, type WALLINTERFERENCEADD or select the wall, right-click, and pick **Interference Condition** > **Add**. This accesses the **WALLINTERFERENCEADD** command. You are then prompted for the wall or, if you used the shortcut menu, for the object to add to the wall. Select any objects you wish to add and press [Enter]. You then must enter how you want the shrink wrap to be displayed.

Sometimes, an interference condition intersects two walls. For example, it may be placed in a corner where two walls meet. If the interference is being added, it must be applied to the two walls individually. For one wall, use the **Additive** option, and for the other wall, use the **Ignore** option. If the interference is being subtracted, it can be applied to both walls at the same time. To do this, select both walls, then access the **WALLINTERFERENCEADD** command, and select the **Subtractive** option when prompted.

The **Remove** option in the **Interference Condition** cascading menu is used to remove an interference condition from a wall. To do this, select the wall with the interference condition to be removed, right-click, and pick **Interference Condition** > **Remove**. You are prompted to select the AEC object to be removed. Select the object and press [Enter] to exit the command.

Figure 12-15.
Three AEC objects placed in the wall are shown before and after interference conditions are added. Note that the behavior of the shrink-wrap depends on the option selected for each AEC object.

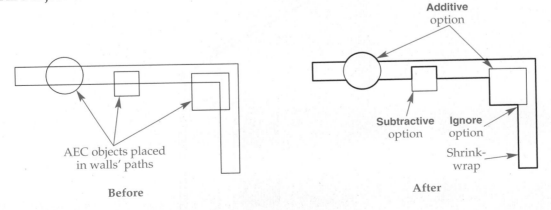

Exercise 12-1

Complete the Exercise on the Student CD.

Using Wall Modifiers

Wall modifiers, which are also called *plan modifiers,* are custom shapes that can be added to the surface of a Wall object to enhance the design or appearance of the wall. Wall modifiers can be used to create a wide footing in a foundation wall or can be applied to an interior wall to represent a custom shelf or decorative feature. Once a wall modifier has been created, it can be added to either side of a wall and at any location, as shown in **Figure 12-16.**

Wall modifiers are similar to interference conditions because they are added to a wall to enhance the appearance. A wall modifier begins with a polyline shape that is turned into a wall modifier style, which is then added to the wall. Typically, the wall modifier is a vertical element that is added to the drawing. Architectural Desktop

Figure 12-16.
Some examples of wall modifiers are shown here.

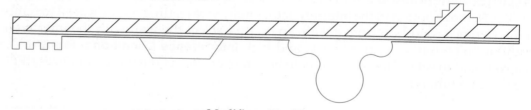

Modifiers–Plan **View**

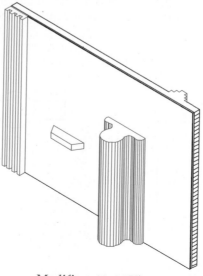

Modifiers–Model **View**

includes a simple, square wall modifier style that can be added to a wall. This default wall modifier style is named Standard.

Adding Wall Modifiers

To add a modifier to a wall, select the wall, right-click, and pick **Plan Modifiers > Add...** or type WALLMODIFIERADD. Once you enter the command, you are prompted for the start point and endpoint, the side of the wall on which to place the modifier, and the modifier's depth, Figure 12-17. Once these have been entered, the **Add Wall Modifier** worksheet is displayed, Figure 12-18. This worksheet is used to select a modifier to be assigned to a wall component and to specify the height of the modifier.

Removing a Wall Modifier

Wall modifiers can be removed from a wall if the design changes. To remove a modifier, select the wall containing the modifier to be removed, right-click, and pick **Plan Modifiers > Remove** or type WALLMODIFIERREMOVE. You are then prompted to select the modifier to be removed. Finally, you are asked if you wish to convert the modifier to a polyline. Entering **Yes** converts the modifier to a polyline, which can be modified and used again as a modifier. Entering **No** removes the modifier completely.

Wall Modifier Styles

Custom wall modifiers can be created from polyline shapes. To create a custom wall modifier style, first draw the shape using a polyline. The start point and endpoint form an imaginary line, and this line establishes how the modifier is placed along the wall, Figure 12-19.

Figure 12-17.
A modifier can be added anywhere along the length of the wall, and the size and shape can be determined as the modifier is added.

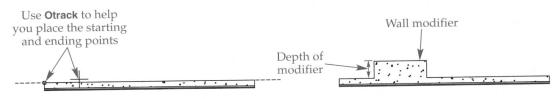

Figure 12-18.
The **Add Wall Modifier** worksheet.

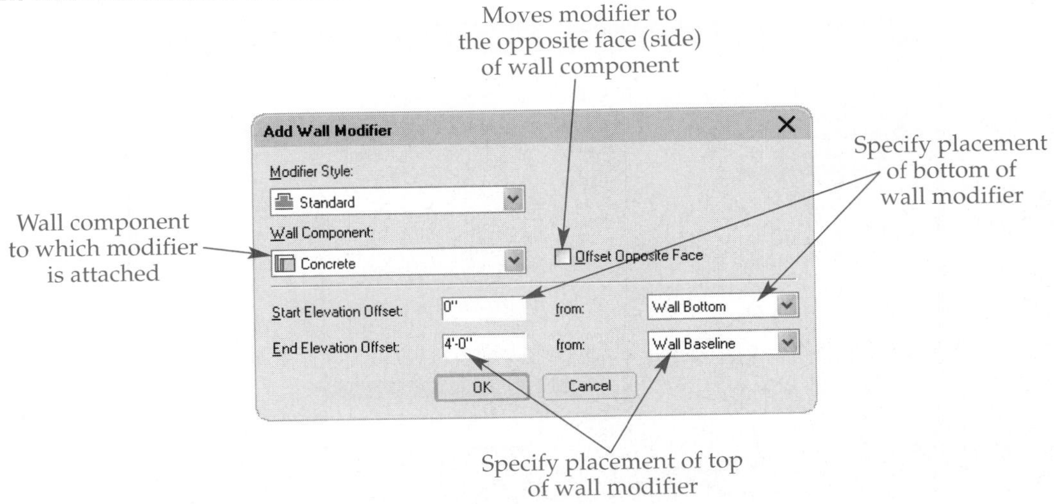

Figure 12-19.
The imaginary lines between the start points and endpoints of these polylines form planes that represent the edge of the wall on which the polyline can be placed as a modifier.

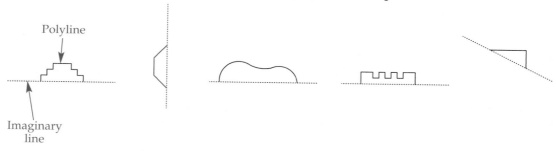

Polyline

Imaginary line

After drawing the polyline shape, the polyline can be turned into a modifier. Pick **Design > Walls > Wall Modifier Styles...** to create a custom modifier shape. This displays the **Style Manager** opened to the **Wall Modifier Styles** section, as shown in **Figure 12-20.**

To create a new style, pick the **New Style** button in the **Style Manager**, or right-click on the section icon and select **New**. Type a name for the modifier and press the [Enter] key to create the named style. Next, pick the new style name, and select the **Set From** button or right-click and select **Set From...** from the shortcut menu. This returns you to the drawing screen, where the polyline that is to define the modifier can be selected. Once the polyline has been picked, the **Style Manager** is displayed again. The wall modifier style is created, and it can be selected from the **Add Wall Modifier** worksheet and applied to a wall.

Converting a Polyline into a Wall Modifier

Another way to create a wall modifier style and apply it to a wall is to convert a polyline into a modifier. In order to convert a polyline into a wall modifier, first draw the polyline shape along the wall where the modifier will be attached, **Figure 12-21.** Next, select the wall that will have the modifier, right-click, and pick **Plan Modifiers > Convert Polyline to Wall Modifier...** or type WALLMODIFIERCONVERT. You are prompted to select the polyline and asked whether to erase the polyline when the wall modifier is

Figure 12-20.
The **Wall Modifier Styles** section is used to create and manage modifier styles.

New Style   Set From

Current drawing

Wall modifier styles in the current drawing

Right-click on style to pick **Set From...** from this shortcut menu

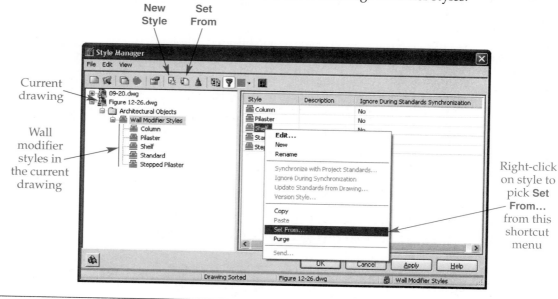

Figure 12-21.
The process for adding a wall modifier from a polyline and the finished modifier are shown here.

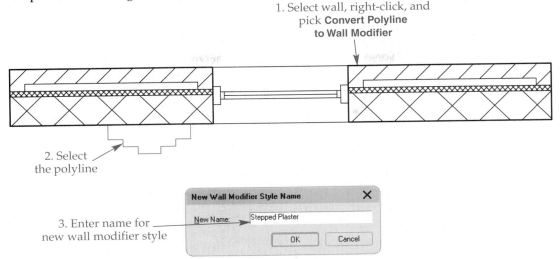

1. Select wall, right-click, and pick **Convert Polyline to Wall Modifier**

2. Select the polyline

3. Enter name for new wall modifier style

Adding a Wall Modifier

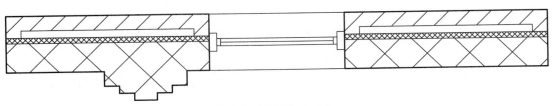

Finished Wall Modifier

created. Type Y to erase it or N to keep it. The **New Wall Modifier Style Name** dialog box is then displayed. Type the name of your wall modifier style in the text box. Finally, adjust the height of the modifier.

Changing a Wall Modifier

A wall modifier can be adjusted using the **Wall Modifiers** worksheet. The **Wall Modifiers** worksheet can be found in the **Worksheets** section of the **Properties** palette when a wall is selected. To display the **Wall Modifiers** worksheet, **Figure 12-22,** select the **Plan modifiers** property.

At the top of the worksheet is a list of the wall modifiers on the selected wall and their properties. Select the wall modifier to be changed from the list. Its settings can then be adjusted in the bottom part of the worksheet. The following settings are some of those available in the **Wall Modifiers** worksheet:

- **Modifier Style.** This drop-down list includes a list of wall modifier styles in the drawing from which you can select a new style for the modifier.
- **Component Name.** This drop-down list includes the wall components in the selected wall. Use it to change the wall component to which the modifier is attached.
- **Apply To.** This drop-down list allows you to change the side of the wall component to which the modifier is attached. The options are **Left Face**, **Right Face**, and **Both Faces**.
- **Start Position Offset.** This section includes a text box and drop-down list. Use the drop-down list to control if the modifier is offset from the start point, endpoint, or center of the wall.

Figure 12-22.
The **Wall Modifiers** worksheet is used to control and adjust the wall modifiers attached to a wall.

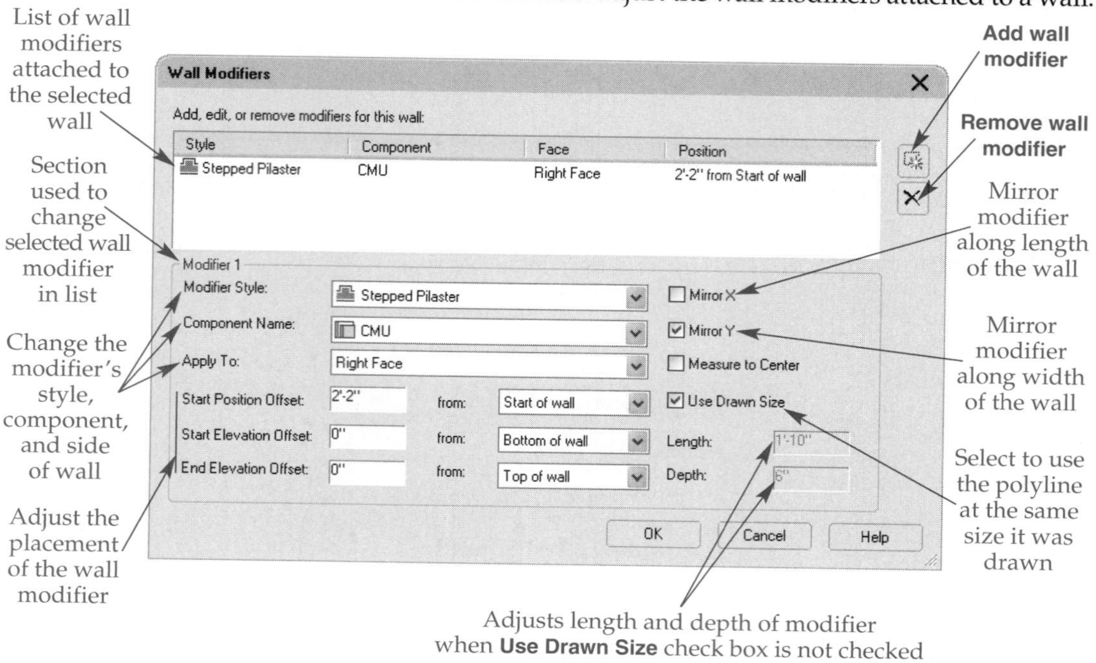

List of wall modifiers attached to the selected wall

Section used to change selected wall modifier in list

Change the modifier's style, component, and side of wall

Adjust the placement of the wall modifier

Add wall modifier

Remove wall modifier

Mirror modifier along length of the wall

Mirror modifier along width of the wall

Select to use the polyline at the same size it was drawn

Adjusts length and depth of modifier when **Use Drawn Size** check box is not checked

- **Start Elevation Offset.** This section also includes a text box and drop-down list. Specify a value in the text box that determines the distance the bottom of the modifier is offset vertically. Use the drop-down list to control if the modifier is offset from the wall bottom, baseline, base height, or wall top.
- **End Elevation Offset.** This is similar to the **Start Elevation Offset** section. This option specifies where the top of the modifier is offset from the wall bottom, baseline, base height, or wall top.
- **Mirror X.** Selecting this check box mirrors the wall modifier about the X direction of the wall (length). The X direction of any AEC object is determined from the start point and endpoint of the object. For example, a wall object's X axis is determined from the start point to the endpoint. The positive X direction is measured from the start point to the endpoint. This would be helpful to mirror the modifier to the other side of the wall.
- **Mirror Y.** Selecting this check box mirrors the wall modifier about the Y direction of the wall (width). The Y direction of an object is 90° from the X direction. This is typically the width of the object.
- **Measure to Center.** Selecting this check box measures the **Start Position Offset** to the center of the wall modifier instead of to the starting edge of the modifier.

Use the **Wall Modifiers** worksheet to manage any wall modifiers you have placed in the drawing. It is often easier to draw the polyline where the modifier needs to be placed, convert it to a wall modifier, and then use the **Wall Modifiers** worksheet to make any necessary adjustments, rather than assigning wall modifiers through the **Wall Modifiers** worksheet.

Editing Wall Modifiers in Place

In addition to changing the wall modifier through the **Wall Modifiers** worksheet, wall modifiers can be edited directly on the Wall object. To edit a wall modifier in place, select the wall with the modifier you want to change, right-click, and pick **Plan Modifiers > Edit In Place** from the shortcut menu. This displays the **In-Place Edit** toolbar shown in **Figure 12-23**. Also, the last drawn or added wall modifier is highlighted with grips displayed along the shape edge.

Figure 12-23.
Use in-place editing to change the modifier directly on the wall.

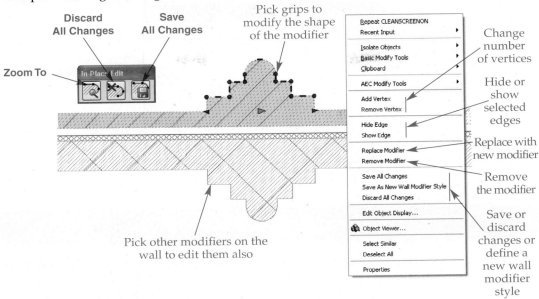

There are three buttons on the **In-Place Edit** toolbar. The **Zoom To** button zooms in to the last added wall modifier so it can be edited. Select the modifier's edge to display the grips again and begin editing. The **Discard All Changes** button discards any changes made to the modifier, restoring the modifier to its original shape prior to editing. The **Save All Changes** button saves any changes made to the modifier.

To edit the wall modifier, you can use grip editing or the shortcut menu, which is specific to in-place editing. Pick any of the grips and use them as you have for other AEC objects to adjust the wall modifier. Right-click to display the shortcut menu shown in Figure 12-23. This shortcut menu can be used to add and remove vertices, hide and show edges, or save the changes as a new modifier style. When you are finished editing the wall modifier, pick the **Save All Changes** button on the **In-Place Edit** toolbar to save the changes you made. While you are editing in place, other modifiers attached to the same wall can be selected, modified, and saved.

Insert Modifier as a Polyline

If you have created several wall modifier styles, the shape used to define them can be inserted into the drawing as a polyline, modified, and turned into new modifier styles. This is helpful when a current wall modifier shape is similar to the new shape needed, and you can use the outline of an existing shape to create a new one. When the polyline is modified, the wall modifier style needs to be redefined, or a new wall modifier can be created. Pick **Design** > **Walls** > **Insert Modifier Style as Polyline...** to insert a wall modifier as a polyline.

Pull-Down Menu
Design   > **Walls**   > **Insert Modifier**   **Style as**   **Polyline...**

The **Modifier Styles** dialog box is displayed as shown in Figure 12-24. Select a modifier to insert and pick the **OK** button. Pick a location in the drawing to insert the modifier as a polyline. Change the polyline to your new specifications, and then use the **Wall Modifier Styles** command to redefine an existing modifier or create a new one using the modified polyline.

Exercise
12-2   **Complete the Exercise on the Student CD.**

Figure 12-24.
The **Modifier Styles** dialog box is used to insert a modifier style into the drawing as a polyline.

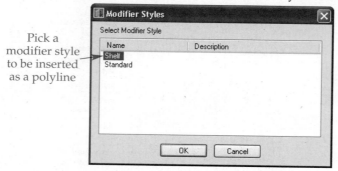

Pick a
modifier style
to be inserted
as a polyline

Creating Wall Sweeps

Wall modifiers are primarily used to add vertical shapes to a wall. A *wall sweep* is used to create horizontal shapes along the length of a wall. For example, a piece of wainscot or molding can be added using the wall sweep feature. Another use for wall sweeps is to create rounded horizontal edges that cannot be created in a wall style, such as the walls of a log home. The curved shapes of the logs can be swept horizontally along the walls, **Figure 12-25**. A custom AEC profile, the cross-sectional shape of the logs, can be applied to a wall component, creating the wall sweep. Multiple AEC profiles can be swept along a multicomponent wall, with the profiles being swept along one component at a time. AEC profiles are covered in Chapter 9.

When an AEC profile is swept along a wall, the profile is inserted at the bottom inside corner of the component that is being swept and is swept from the start point to the endpoint of the wall. See **Figure 12-26**. When the profile is swept along the wall, the wall component maintains the original profile shape and size and is essentially converted to the shape of the AEC profile.

Figure 12-25.
Some examples of wall sweeps are shown here. The AEC profile used for the sweep is shown next to each wall.

AEC profile swept
along wall components

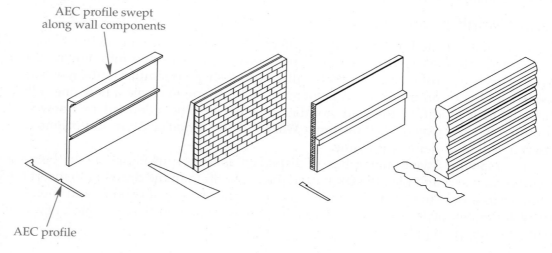

AEC profile

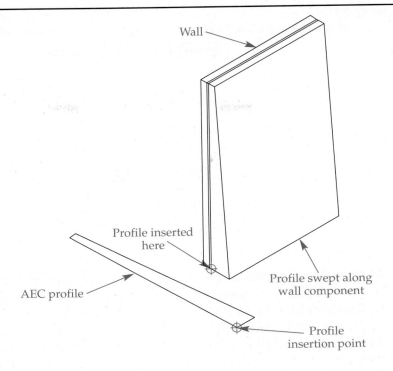

Figure 12-26.
The lower-left corner of the profile is attached to the lower-left corner of a wall component. The profile is then swept from the start point to the endpoint of the wall.

Wall

Profile inserted here

AEC profile

Profile swept along wall component

Profile insertion point

NOTE When you are creating a polyline for conversion to an AEC profile, it is important to draw the polyline at the size and shape that is to be swept along a wall component. It is also critical to establish an insertion point for the profile at the lower-left corner of the polyline in order for the profile to appear correctly. The insertion point for the polyline is then inserted at the lower inside corner of the wall component.

Once an AEC profile has been created, it can be swept along a wall. Select the wall, right-click, and pick **Sweeps** > **Add...** to add a wall sweep. This displays the **Add Wall Sweep** worksheet shown in **Figure 12-27**. This worksheet is used to apply a profile to a wall component within the selected wall. When you are finished, apply sweeps to different wall components within the wall and exit the worksheet. Several walls can be swept at the same time, as long as they are the same style. Select the walls to have the same profile swept along the same component, and then add the sweep. The following components are available in the **Add Wall Sweep** worksheet:

- **Wall Component.** This drop-down list includes a list of wall components included in the selected wall(s). Select the wall component that will have a sweep applied.
- **Profile Definition.** Select the profile to be swept along the selected wall component from this drop-down list of profiles in the drawing. Pick **Start from scratch...** to create a new profile shape. Once the shape has been defined and saved, the profile is swept along the wall.
- **New Profile Name.** This text box is available only when the **Start from scratch...** profile is selected. Enter a name for the new profile here. If an existing profile is selected, this text box is grayed out.
- **Apply Roof/Floor Lines to Sweeps.** When this check box is selected, the wall sweep is applied to the wall component using the shape of the wall at the roofline or floor line of the wall. Rooflines and floor lines are explained in the next section.

Figure 12-27.
Use the **Add Wall Sweep** worksheet to sweep a profile along a wall component.

Select the wall component to have sweep attached

Select profile to use as sweep

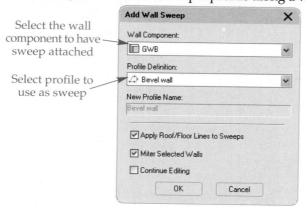

- **Miter Selected Walls.** If selected, a miter is applied to walls that touch each other at their intersection, allowing the walls to clean up.
- **Continue Editing.** Pick this check box to perform an in-place edit of an existing profile that is being applied to the wall component.

As with wall modifiers, the profile of the swept wall can be edited in place. To edit the profile in place, select the wall to be modified, right-click, and pick **Sweeps > Edit Profile In Place.** You are prompted to choose a location on the wall to edit. Select a point along the swept wall where the profile will be edited. This opens the **In-Place Edit** toolbar and a profile within the wall that can be edited. See **Figure 12-28.** Pick the profile to display grip boxes that can be used to modify the shape of the profile.

Right-clicking while editing the profile in place displays a shortcut menu that can be used to add or remove vertices along the profile, add another internal closed polyline as a ring in the profile, replace a ring with a different closed polyline, and save the changes made to the profile. When you are finished editing the profile, pick the **Save All Changes** button in the **In-Place Edit** toolbar.

Figure 12-28.
Use the grips and the shortcut menu to edit the profile.

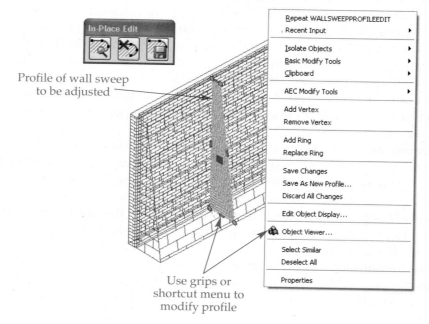

Profile of wall sweep to be adjusted

Use grips or shortcut menu to modify profile

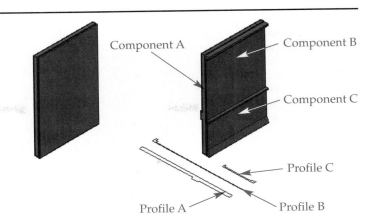

Figure 12-29.
Multiple profiles
may be swept
along different
components of the
same wall. The
profiles on the left
are each swept
along the wall on
the right.

Component A   Component B

Component C

Profile C

Profile A   Profile B

As indicated earlier, multiple profiles can be swept along a wall with more than one component. Each profile must be swept individually and assigned to a different component using the **Add Wall Sweep** worksheet. It is important to remember that only one profile can be assigned to each component of a wall. If a different profile is swept along a component that is already assigned to a profile, the new profile is used along the wall component, replacing the previous one. **Figure 12-29** provides an example of three separate profiles being swept along three different wall components.

If walls that have been swept separately intersect each other, they do not clean up with each other. For separately swept walls to clean up, their ends must be mitered. *Mitering* walls with wall sweeps will extend and join together the ends of the wall where the two walls meet at the corner. To miter two walls, select the walls, right-click, and pick **Sweeps > Miter**. This miters both walls and causes both walls to clean up.

The **Properties** palette can be used to remove wall sweeps. First, select the walls from which you want to remove the sweeps, and then access the **Properties** palette. Scroll to the **Worksheets** section, which is toward the bottom of the palette and contains the **Sweeps** property. Select the **Sweeps** property value to display the **Sweeps** worksheet. Any sweeps applied to the wall components are listed in the worksheet. Select a profile and pick the **Remove sweep** button to remove the sweep from the wall component.

Exercise
12-3   Complete the Exercise on the Student CD.

Adjusting the Floor Line and Roofline of a Wall

As you gain more experience with the modeling aspects of Architectural Desktop, you may find situations in which the top of a wall needs to be projected up to the underside of a roof, or the bottom of a wall needs to be projected down to a sloping site. Architectural Desktop includes two tools to help in these situations: **Modify Roof Line** and **Modify Floor Line**. They project the top or bottom of a wall to a polyline or an AEC object. The effects of these tools are shown in **Figure 12-30**.

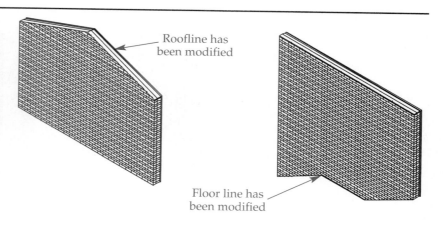

Figure 12-30.
The top or bottom of a wall can be projected to match the shape of a polyline or AEC object to modify the roofline or floor line of the wall.

Roofline has been modified

Floor line has been modified

Modifying the Top of a Wall

When a wall is drawn and a gable roof is added over the wall, the **Modify Roof Line** command can be used to make the wall meet the underside of the Roof object. The following discussion concentrates on projecting the top of the wall to the underside of a polyline because Roof objects have not been discussed yet. Roofs are discussed in Chapter 18.

Before you can project a wall, you must have an AEC object or a polyline to which the wall will be projected. Projecting walls to a polyline works best if the polyline is drawn in a plane that is parallel to the plane of the walls being projected. Use the preset elevation views to establish the drawing plane that is parallel to the walls. When you have the correct plane, you will be looking at the wall perpendicularly, and the polyline should be drawn in this plane. You can verify that your polyline and walls are parallel by viewing them in the Top view. They should appear parallel in this view. See Figure 12-31.

NOTE

After an elevation view is selected, the drawing plane changes to the plane being viewed perpendicularly in that view. If an isometric view is established after an elevation view, the drawing plane remains in the last plane that was established before changing to an isometric view. Any new objects drawn are placed in the current drawing plane. To change the drawing plane back to the "floor," change to the Top view, and the drawing plane changes to a standard flat drawing plane.

To adjust the roofline, draw a polyline above the walls that are to be projected. The polyline can be drawn in any shape using polyline line segments, arced segments, or a combination of the two.

Once the polyline has been drawn, walls that are parallel to the polyline can be projected up to the polyline. To do this, select the wall to be projected, right-click, and pick **Roof/Floor Line** > **Modify Roof Line** or type ROOFLINE.

After accessing the command, you are prompted with several options used to adjust the roofline of the wall. Choose the **Project to polyline** option, and then pick the polyline.

There are additional options offered. The **Offset** option offsets the current shape of the roofline of a wall up a specified distance. The **Generate polyline** option creates a polyline from the current shape of the roofline of a wall. The new polyline can be moved around the drawing and made parallel to other walls so other walls can be projected to the same shape. The **Auto project** option projects the roofline of a wall to the underside of an AEC object such as a roof, stair, mass element, slab, or another wall. The **Reset** option resets the roofline of the wall back to the flat-topped roof using the base height of the original wall.

Figure 12-31.
Access an elevation view to set the appropriate drawing plane current so that a parallel polyline can be drawn above a wall to be projected.

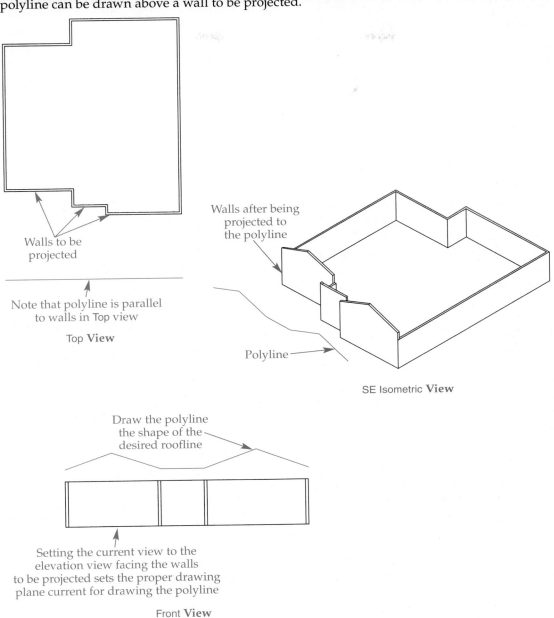

Walls to be projected

Note that polyline is parallel to walls in Top view

Top **View**

Walls after being projected to the polyline

Polyline

SE Isometric **View**

Draw the polyline the shape of the desired roofline

Setting the current view to the elevation view facing the walls to be projected sets the proper drawing plane current for drawing the polyline

Front **View**

Modifying the Bottom of a Wall

Modify Floor Line is similar to **Modify Roof Line**, except it affects the bottom of a wall. The process for modifying the floor line is the same as it is for the roofline. First, create a polyline that is parallel to and below a wall, and then project the wall down to the polyline. After drawing the polyline, pick the wall to be projected, right-click, and select the **Roof/Floor Line** > **Modify Floor Line** or type FLOORLINE. The options and prompts are the same as they were for the **Modify Roof Line** command. The difference is that the bottom of the wall projects down.

Editing in Place

Similar to the wall modifiers and wall sweeps, rooflines and floor lines can be edited in place. To adjust the roofline or floor line directly on the wall, select the wall, right-click, and pick **Roof/Floor Line** > **Edit In Place**. This displays the **In-Place Edit** toolbar and grips along the projected edge, Figure 12-32. Use the grips to modify the projected edge of the wall. Right-click to display a shortcut menu related to roofline/floor line editing. Make any adjustments to the projected edges and save the changes with the **Save All Changes** button in the **In-Place Edit** toolbar.

Roof and Floor Line Worksheet

The **Roof and Floor Line** worksheet controls how the top and bottom of a selected wall appear in elevation. This worksheet can be accessed through the **Properties** palette. Select a wall that includes projected edges, and then scroll toward the bottom of the **Properties** palette, where the **Worksheets** section is located. A **Roof/floor line** property is available. Select the property value to display the **Roof and Floor Line** worksheet, Figure 12-33. The worksheet displays a table that provides numerical information for each vertex of the projected edge and the elevation preview of the selected wall. As new vertices are added to, deleted from, and modified in the wall, this table updates to display the location information for the vertex points. Picking a point from the table highlights the point in the elevation preview of the wall.

At the bottom of the worksheet are two radio buttons: **Edit Roof Line** and **Edit Floor Line**. Selecting the appropriate button allows you to modify the points along either the top or the bottom of the wall. The preview window places vertex point boxes at all the vertex locations. The filled box indicates the vertex point that is being modified. Use the mouse to select a vertex point to be modified.

The buttons in this worksheet have the following functions related to modifying or adding vertex points:

- **Add Gable.** This button adds a vertex point at the top middle or bottom middle of the wall and projects it up or down, depending on whether the roofline or floor line points are being modified. This button is available if the starting vertex point is highlighted.
- **Add Step.** This button adds a step in the wall either up or down, depending on whether the roofline or the floor line is being edited.

Figure 12-32.
Projected edges can be edited in place using the **In-Place Edit** toolbar, grips, or the shortcut menu.

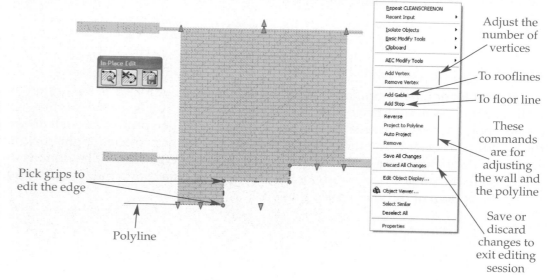

Figure 12-33.
The **Roof and Floor Line** worksheet is used to control and adjust the rooflines or floor lines of the selected wall.

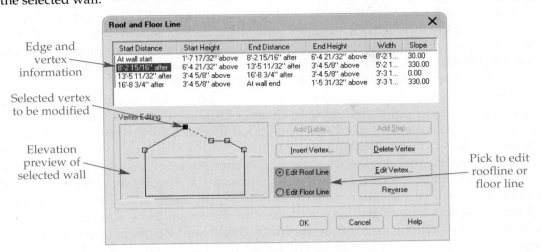

- **Insert Vertex.** This button adds a vertex point to the wall. When this button is selected, the **Wall Roof/Floor Line Vertex** dialog box appears. See **Figure 12-34.** This dialog box allows you to specify horizontally where the new point is placed, in relation to an existing point on the wall, and where the point is placed vertically in the wall, in relation to the wall base height, the next point, the previous point, or the baseline.
- **Delete Vertex.** This button deletes the highlighted vertex point in the preview window.
- **Edit Vertex.** Pick a vertex to modify before selecting this button. When the button is picked, the **Wall Roof/Floor Line Vertex** dialog box appears, allowing you to readjust the horizontal and vertical positioning of the vertex, as shown in **Figure 12-34.**
- **Reverse.** This button reverses the start point and endpoint of the wall, mirroring your edited vertex points.

Exercise 12-4   Complete the Exercise on the Student CD.

Figure 12-34.
Use the **Wall Roof/Floor Line Vertex** dialog box to place a new vertex in a wall.

Objects that have any mass can be added to a wall. AutoCAD 3D solid objects and Architectural Desktop mass elements include mass. Both of these types of objects can be added to a wall without interfering with the wall. For more information on creating an AutoCAD solid object, look up Create 3D Solids and Surfaces in the **AutoCAD Help** book in the **Autodesk Architectural Desktop 2007 Help** window.

Mass elements, which were introduced in Chapter 1, are Architectural Desktop solids. They are thoroughly discussed in Chapter 25. For the purposes of this explanation, a simple mass element is created and added to a wall. To create a mass element, pick a shape tool from the **Massing** tool palette.

After selecting the massing element, the **Properties** palette is used to control the size of the 3D shape. When adding a mass element, the **Specify on screen** property, by default, allows you to enter sizes by answering prompts. Selecting this property and changing its value to **No**, allows the size of the shape to be determined within the **Properties** palette by modifying the **Width**, **Depth**, and **Height** properties. The size properties that become available in the **Properties** palette vary, depending on the shape of the massing element selected. Enter the desired values for the selected shape, and then pick a location for the mass in the drawing. After the mass element has been added to the drawing, the element's rotation angle needs to be specified.

To add the mass element to a wall, the wall should be drawn first, and then the mass element(s) should be added along the wall where desired. **Figure 12-35** shows three different mass elements within a wall. After the mass elements have been added along a wall at the correct positions, the object(s) can be included as part of the wall. When an object with mass is added to a wall, the function to add it to the wall is called a *body modifier*. Select the wall, right-click, and pick **Body Modifiers** > **Add...** to add the body modifier. You are prompted to select objects to apply as body modifiers. Select any massing objects that will be added to the wall and press [Enter]. This displays the **Add Body Modifier** dialog box. See **Figure 12-36.**

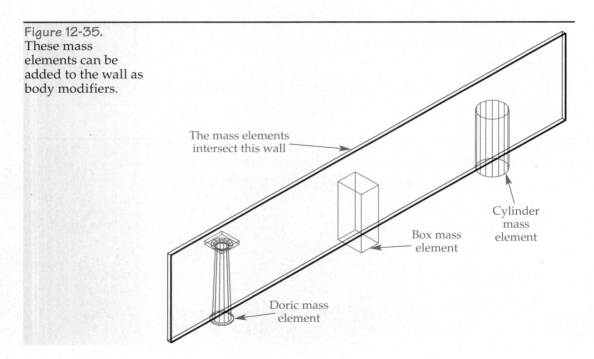

Figure 12-35.
These mass elements can be added to the wall as body modifiers.

The mass elements intersect this wall

Cylinder mass element

Box mass element

Doric mass element

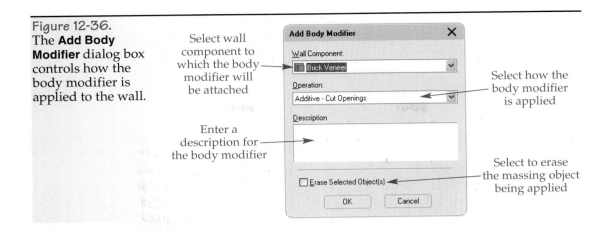

Figure 12-36.
The **Add Body Modifier** dialog box controls how the body modifier is applied to the wall.

Select wall component to which the body modifier will be attached

Select how the body modifier is applied

Enter a description for the body modifier

Select to erase the massing object being applied

The **Add Body Modifier** dialog box controls how the body modifier is applied to the wall. In the **Wall Component** drop-down list, which lists the wall components within the selected wall, choose the component to which the body modifier is to be applied. A body modifier is applied to a single component within a wall. The **Operation** drop-down list includes four options: **Additive-Cut Openings**, **Additive**, **Subtractive**, and **Replace**, Figure 12-37:

- **Additive-Cut Openings.** This option is used when a body modifier will be added to a wall where an opening is already located. This option cuts the opening through the body modifier.
- **Additive.** This option adds a body modifier to a wall component in a similar way to adding a wall modifier.
- **Subtractive.** This option removes the area of the selected wall component that intersects with the body modifier.
- **Replace.** This option replaces the wall component and wall with the shape of the body modifier. Additional walls can be drawn to intersect the body modifier wall, but they will need to be cleaned up by merging the walls.

The **Description** text box allows you to add a description of the body modifier. This description can be useful later, such as when editing the body modifier through the **Properties** palette. The **Erase Selected Object(s)** check box, when checked, erases the original body modifier when it is finished applying the modifier to the wall. When you are finished setting these properties, pick the **OK** button. The body modifier is applied to the wall component assigned, and the modified wall is displayed.

Restoring a Wall

Once a body modifier has been added to a wall component, it becomes a part of the wall. If the design changes and the body modifier needs to be removed, the wall can be restored to its original shape. To restore the wall and remove the body modifier, select the wall, right-click, and pick **Body Modifiers > Restore**. You are asked if you want to remove the body modifiers. Type Y to remove the body modifier and restore the wall. The original wall and original object used to create the body modifier are recreated in the drawing.

Another way a body modifier can be removed, and one way to adjust body modifiers, is through the **Body Modifiers** worksheet. This worksheet is in the **Worksheets** section of the **Properties** palette. Pick the **Body Modifiers** property value to display the worksheet. The worksheet lists any wall components to which body modifiers are applied. You can change the wall component to which the body modifier is assigned to a different component within the same wall. The operation of the body modifier can also be changed. Body modifiers can be removed by selecting the body modifier from the list and picking the **Remove body modifier** button.

Figure 12-37.
Mass elements or AutoCAD 3D solids can be added to or subtracted from a wall component or can replace that component.

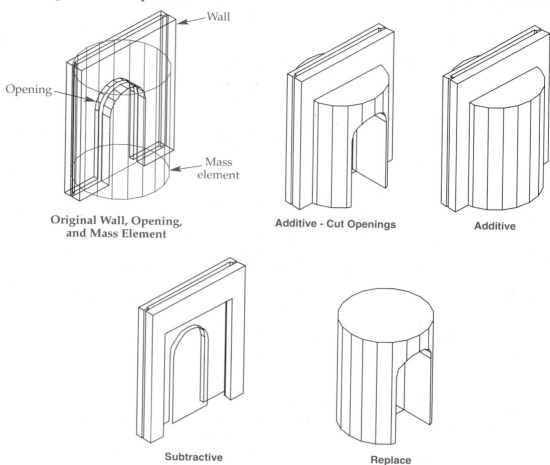

Original Wall, Opening, and Mass Element

Additive - Cut Openings

Additive

Subtractive

Replace

Editing the Body Modifier

As with the wall modifiers, interference conditions, and the roofline/floor line edges, the shape of the body modifier can be edited in place. Select the wall, right-click, and pick **Body Modifiers > Edit In Place** from the shortcut menu. This displays the **In-Place Edit** toolbar and grips around the body modifier shape. See **Figure 12-38.** Use the grips to adjust the shape of the body modifier or use the shortcut menu for additional editing options. If the object being used as a body modifier is a massing element, the **Properties** palette can be used to change the shape and size of the mass element. When you are finished editing the body modifier, pick the **Save All Changes** button to save the changes to the wall.

NOTE

> A single mass element, a solid, or another AEC object can be applied as a body modifier to multiple walls. For example, an expanded foundation footing placed in the corner of two walls may be applied to both walls individually as body modifiers.

Exercise 12-5   Complete the Exercise on the Student CD.

Figure 12-38.
In-place editing can be used to edit a body modifier's size and shape.

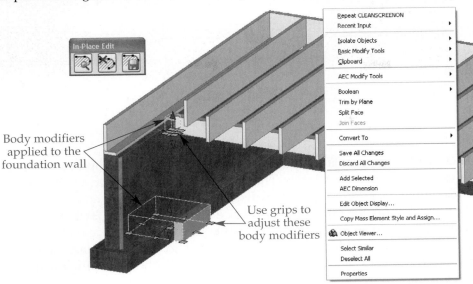

Body modifiers applied to the foundation wall

Use grips to adjust these body modifiers

Using the Properties Palette for Walls

Single or multiple walls can be selected to be modified by the **Properties** palette. If more than one wall is selected, the options available in the palette are limited. Refer to Chapter 4 for more on the basic options for Wall objects in the **Properties** palette.

From the **BASIC** header, pick the **Additional information** property to display the **Location** worksheet. See **Figure 12-39**. This worksheet is used to identify the location of the selected wall(s), relative to a user coordinate system. Two options at the top indicate the wall location relative to the world coordinate system (the standard drawing plane) or the current user coordinate system. When the world coordinate system is used, the Z-axis value indicates where the bottom of the wall is located. If there are walls that need to be adjusted to a different height, adjust the Z-axis value in the world coordinate system. Entering a positive value places the wall up in elevation.

Figure 12-39.
The **Location** worksheet allows you to set the bottom start point of the wall.

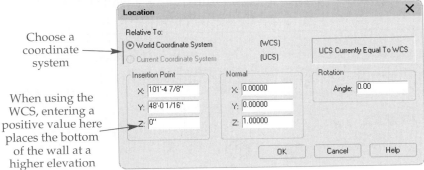

Choose a coordinate system

When using the WCS, entering a positive value here places the bottom of the wall at a higher elevation

Figure 12-40.
Different endcaps can be assigned to the ends of walls.

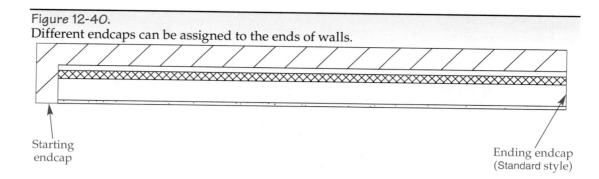

Starting
endcap

Ending endcap
(Standard style)

The **Style Overrides** category in the **ADVANCED** header includes properties for overriding settings established by the wall style. These properties are described as follows:

- **Starting endcap.** Picking this property displays a list of available endcaps that can be applied to the starting point of the wall. See **Figure 12-40**. The **BYSTYLE** option indicates the endcap assigned to the wall style. The styles that are included with Architectural Desktop have an endcap assigned to both the start point and endpoint of the walls. If a wall problem exists in a wall where openings are placed close together, changing the endcap to the **Standard** style will often fix the problem. Custom endcap styles can also be created and are discussed in Chapter 13.

- **Ending endcap.** This property is similar to the **Starting** endcap property, except that it controls the endcap at the endpoint of the wall. See **Figure 12-40**.

- **Priority overrides.** Selecting this property displays the **Priority Overrides** worksheet. See **Figure 12-41**. Each component within a wall is assigned a priority. Wall components with the same priority clean up with each other. A component with a higher priority "cuts through" a wall component with a low priority. See **Figure 12-42**. The highest priority a wall can have is 1. Wall components that represent different types of building materials are assigned priorities that provide the desired display. The example in **Figure 12-42** uses a stud wall with a brick veneer. The stud wall is assigned a higher priority than the brick veneer, so the Stud component cuts through the Brick Veneer component at the intersection of the two walls. If a component within a wall needs to have its priority adjusted so it cleans up with a different wall component, assign the new priority in the **Priority Overrides** worksheet. Pick the **Add priority override** button to add a new priority. After a new override is established, pick the component whose priority will be overridden, the end of the wall at which the override is applied, and the priority value to be used as the override. Wall priorities and how they are assigned within a wall style are discussed in Chapter 15. Appendix M on the CD includes a list of priorities in use by the different wall styles.

Figure 12-41.
Priority overrides are added to wall components using the **Priority Overrides** worksheet.

Component

Location
for override

Add priority
override

Remove
priority
override

Override
priority
value

Priority Overrides

Add, edit, or remove the priority overrides for components of this wall:

Component	Override	Priority
[2] Brick Veneer	At start of wall	650

OK   Cancel   Help

Architectural Desktop and Its Applications

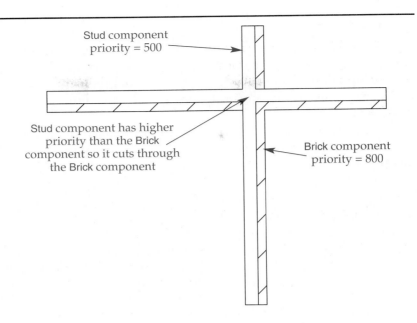

Figure 12-42.
A wall component with a higher priority cuts through a component with a lower priority.

Stud component priority = 500

Stud component has higher priority than the Brick component so it cuts through the Brick component

Brick component priority = 800

Additional Wall Modifying Commands

Additional commands can be used to control walls created in the drawing. Multiple walls can be joined to form a single wall; walls that do not clean up correctly can be fixed; and objects such as doors, windows, door/window assemblies, and openings independent of walls can be anchored to a wall. Descriptions of joining and merging walls are provided next. Descriptions of anchoring doors and windows to walls are provided in Chapter 13.

Joining Walls

Occasionally, you may want to join two walls to form one wall. The **WALLJOIN** command is used to do this. When two walls are joined together, any modifications made to one wall are transferred to the other wall. For example, wall modifiers placed in one of the walls before joining to another wall maintain their location and are added within the new single wall.

In order for two walls to be joined together, the following rules must be followed:

- Straight wall segments must have justification lines that are collinear, and the walls must touch at one endpoint.
- Arced walls must have the same center point and radius, and they must also touch at one endpoint.
- Walls must use the same wall style and width, and they must be in the same wall cleanup group.

To join two walls together, select one of the walls, right-click, and pick **Join** from the shortcut menu or type WALLJOIN. You are then prompted to select the second wall. Pick the wall you want to join to the first wall. Once you do this, the walls are joined and form a single wall.

Merge Walls

The ability to merge walls is designed to provide a means to clean up walls when adjusting the wall cleanup radius fails to do so properly. To do this, a wall merge condition is applied to the walls. Merging walls should be used as a last resort because any walls that cross through or intersect a wall with a merge condition must be merged into that wall.

To merge walls together, select a wall to be used in the merge, right-click, and pick **Cleanups > Add Wall Merge Condition**. You are prompted to select walls you want to merge. Select any walls you want to be merged with the wall you originally selected. If any new walls drawn later intersect a wall with a merge condition assigned, the walls do not clean up. These new walls need to have the wall merge condition applied to them in order to be cleaned up properly. You can use this procedure to add new walls to the existing set of merged walls.

Wall merge conditions can be removed from a set of merged walls. Pick a wall with a merge condition, right-click, and pick **Cleanups > Remove All Wall Merge Conditions**. This removes any wall merges applied to the selected wall.

Chapter Test

Answer the following questions. Write your answers on a separate sheet of paper or complete the electronic chapter test on the Student CD.

1. Define *cut plane* and provide the cut plane default location.
2. Define *shrink wrap.*
3. What is a wall style boundary?
4. Define *hatch.*
5. Explain an interference condition.
6. What are wall modifiers?
7. What does it mean to edit in place?
8. Describe a wall sweep and give at least one example of when a wall sweep is useful.
9. Define *miter.*
10. A(n) _____ is an object with mass that is added to a wall.

Chapter Projects

Use the techniques covered in this chapter to create the following drawings.

1. Single-Level Residential Project
   A. Access the **Project Browser** and set Residential-Project-01 current.
   B. Access the **Constructs** tab of the **Project Navigator** and open the Main Floor construct.
   C. Add wall modifiers to each side of the fireplace, similar to Exercise 12-2. Draw any shape desired. Set the starting height to 0″ from the baseline. Set the ending height to 4′-0″ from the baseline.
   D. Add a wall modifier as a mantle above the fireplace. Set the starting height to 4′-0″ from the baseline and the end height to 4′-2″ from the baseline. The fireplace should look similar to the figure below.
   E. Save and close the drawing.
   F. Access the **Constructs** tab of the **Project Navigator** and open the Foundation construct.
   G. Add box-shaped mass elements 4″ × 6″ × 8″ high to each end of the foundation beams, similar to Exercise 12-5.
   H. Use the **Properties** palette to change the elevation of the mass elements to 1′-10″. This aligns the top of the mass element with the top of the beam.
   I. Add the mass elements to the foundation walls as a body modifier. Use the following settings:
      a. **Wall component**: Concrete.
      b. **Operation**: Subtractive.
      c. **Description**: Beam Pocket.
      d. **Erase Selected Object**: Checked.
   J. Save and close the drawing.

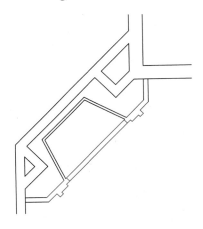

Alan Mascord Design Associates

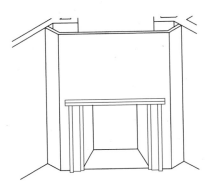

Chapter 12 Projects

2. Single-Level Residential Project
   A. Access the **Project Browser** and set Residential-Project-02 current.
   B. Access the **Constructs** tab of the **Project Navigator** and open the Main Floor construct.
   C. Add wall modifiers to each side of the fireplace, similar to Exercise 12-2. Draw any shape desired. Set the starting height to 0″ from the baseline. Set the ending height to 4′-0″ from the baseline.
   D. Add a wall modifier as a mantle above the fireplace. Set the starting height to 4′-0″ from the baseline and the end height to 4′-2″ from the baseline. The fireplace should look similar to the figure below.
   E. Save and close the drawing.
   F. Access the **Constructs** tab of the **Project Navigator** and open the Foundation construct.
   G. Add box-shaped mass elements 4″ × 6″ × 8″ high to each end of the foundation beams, similar to Exercise 12-5.
   H. Use the **Properties** palette to change the elevation of the mass elements to 1′-0″. This aligns the top of the mass element with the top of the beam.
   I. Add the mass elements to the foundation walls as body modifiers. Use the following settings:
      a. **Wall component**: Concrete.
      b. **Operation**: Subtractive.
      c. **Description**: Beam Pocket.
      d. **Erase Selected Object**: Checked.
   J. Save and close the drawing.

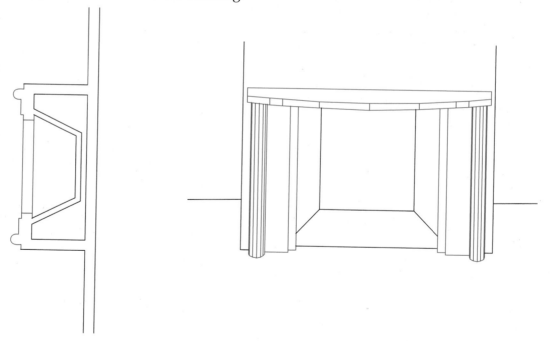

Alan Mascord Design Associates

3. Two-Story Residential Project
    A. Access the **Project Browser** and set Residential-Project-03 current.
    B. Access the **Constructs** tab of the **Project Navigator** and open the Main Floor construct.
    C. Add wall modifiers to each side of the fireplace, similar to Exercise 12-2. Draw any shape desired. Set the starting height to be 0″ from the baseline. Set the ending height to be 4′-0″ from the baseline.
    D. Add a wall modifier as a mantle above the fireplace. Set the starting height to be 4′-0″ from the baseline and the end height to be 4′-2″ from the baseline. The fireplace should look similar to the figure below.
    E. Save and close the drawing.
    F. Access the **Constructs** tab of the **Project Navigator** and open the Foundation construct.
    G. Add box-shaped mass elements 4″ × 6″ × 8″ high to each end of the foundation beams, similar to Exercise 12-5.
    H. Use the **Properties** palette to change the elevation of the mass elements to 1′-10″. This aligns the top of the mass element with the top of the beam.
    I. Add the mass elements to the foundation walls as body modifiers. Use the following settings:
        a. **Wall component**: Concrete.
        b. **Operation**: Subtractive.
        c. **Description**: Beam Pocket.
        d. **Erase Selected Object**: Checked.
    J. Save and close the drawing.

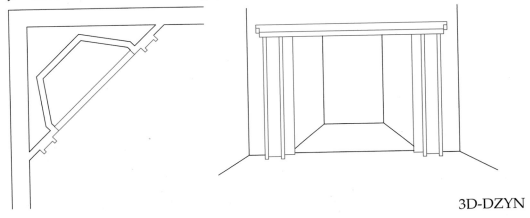

3D-DZYN

4. Two-Story Residential Project
   A. Access the **Project Browser** and set Residential-Project-04 current.
   B. Access the **Constructs** tab of the **Project Navigator** and open the Main Floor construct.
   C. Add wall modifiers to each side of the fireplace, similar to Exercise 12-2. Draw any shape desired. Set the starting height to be 0″ from the baseline. Set the ending height to be 4′-0″ from the baseline.
   D. Add a wall modifier as a mantle above the fireplace. Set the starting height to be 4′-0″ from the baseline and the end height to be 4′-2″ from the baseline. The fireplace should look similar to the figure below.
   E. Save and close the drawing.
   F. Access the **Constructs** tab of the **Project Navigator** and open the Foundation construct.
   G. Add box-shaped mass elements 4″ × 6″ × 8″ high to each end of the foundation beams, similar to Exercise 12-5.
   H. Use the **Properties** palette to change the elevation of the mass elements to 1′-10″. This aligns the top of the mass element with the top of the beam.
   I. Add the mass elements to the foundation walls as body modifiers. Use the following settings:
      a. **Wall component**: Concrete.
      b. **Operation**: Subtractive.
      c. **Description**: Beam Pocket.
      d. **Erase Selected Object**: Checked.
   J. Save and close the drawing.

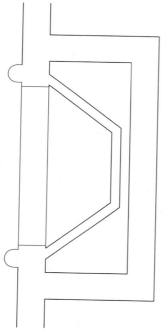
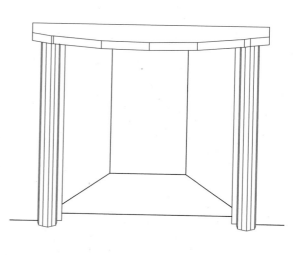

Alan Mascord Design Associates

5. Commercial Store Project
   A. Access the **Project Browser** and set Commercial-Project-05 current.
   B. Access the **Constructs** tab of the **Project Navigator** and open the Main Floor construct.
   C. Create a profile using the sizes shown in the figure.
   D. Use the bottom midpoint of the polyline as the insertion point for the profile.
   E. Name the profile Exterior Brick.
   F. Change the viewing direction to one of the isometric views.
   G. Sweep the profile along all of the exterior walls, assigning the profile to the Brick wall component.
   H. In the **Add Wall Sweep** worksheet, check the **Apply Roof/Floor Lines to Sweeps** and the **Miter Selected Walls** check boxes. Pick **OK** when you are finished.
   I. Note that, after the sweeps have been applied, the brick hatch pattern will not display correctly. To fix this, perform the following:
      a. Select one of the exterior walls, right-click, and select **Edit Wall Style...** from the shortcut menu.
      b. In the **Wall Style Properties** dialog box, pick the **Materials** tab, select the Brick component, and then pick the **Edit Material** button. This will display the **Material Definition Properties** dialog box.
      c. Select the General Medium Detail display representation, and then pick **Edit Display Properties** to display the **Display Properties** dialog box.
      d. Select the **Other** tab. Place a check mark in the **Top** and **Bottom** check boxes. Pick **OK** to exit out of all dialog boxes.
      e. The brick material should display correctly now.
   J. Save and close the drawing.

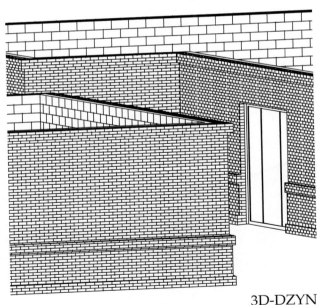
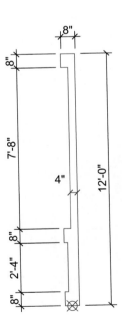

3D-DZYN

6. Commercial Car Maintenance Shop Project
  A. Access the **Project Browser** and set Commercial-Project-06 current.
  B. Access the **Constructs** tab of the **Project Navigator** and open the Main Floor construct.
  C. Create two profiles, as shown in the figure. Use the sizes given.
  D. Name the 12'-0" high profile Exterior Brick 12ft.
  E. Name the 18'-0" high profile Exterior Brick 18ft.
  F. Change the viewing direction to one of the isometric views.
  G. Sweep the Exterior Brick 12ft profile along all of the 12'-0" high exterior walls. In the **Add Wall Sweep** worksheet, check the **Apply Roof/Floor Lines to Sweeps** and the **Miter Selected Walls** check boxes. Pick **OK** when you are finished.
  H. Sweep the Exterior Brick 18ft profile along all of the 18'-0" high exterior walls at the garage area. In the **Add Wall Sweep** worksheet, check the **Apply Roof/Floor Lines to Sweeps** and the **Miter Selected Walls** check boxes. Pick **OK** when you are finished.
  I. Miter any additional walls as needed.
  J. Note that, after the sweeps have been applied, the brick hatch pattern will not display correctly. To fix this, perform the following:
    a. Select one of the exterior walls, right-click, and pick **Edit Wall Style...** from the shortcut menu.
    b. In the **Wall Style Properties** dialog box, pick the **Materials** tab, select the Brick component, and then pick the **Edit Material** button. This displays the **Material Definition Properties** dialog box.
    c. Select the General Medium Detail display representation, and then pick the **Edit Display Properties** to display the **Display Properties** dialog box.
    d. Select the **Other** tab. Place a check mark in the **Top** and **Bottom** check boxes. Pick **OK** to exit out of all dialog boxes.
    e. The brick material should display correctly now.
  K. Save and close the drawing.

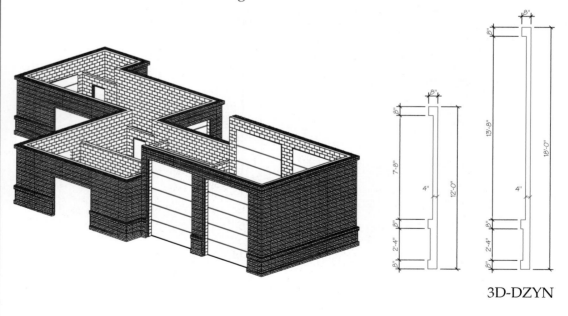

3D-DZYN

7. Governmental Fire Station
   A. Access the **Project Browser** and set Gvrmt-Project-07 current.
   B. Access the **Constructs** tab of the **Project Navigator** and open the Main Floor construct.
   C. Change the viewing direction to the Front view.
   D. Draw polylines as indicated in the figure for the front elevation.
   E. Change the viewing direction to the Right view.
   F. Draw polylines as indicated in the figure for the side elevation.
   G. Change the viewing direction to the Top view. Review the locations of the polylines.
   H. Change the viewing direction to one of the isometric views.
   I. Project the roofline of all front and rear exterior walls to the front polylines.
   J. Project the roofline of all left and right exterior garage walls to the upper side polyline.
   K. Project the roofline of all left and right exterior main building walls to the lower side polyline.
   L. Save and close the drawing.

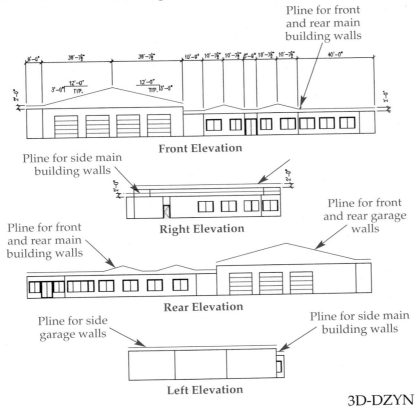

Pline for front and rear main building walls

Front Elevation

Pline for side main building walls

Right Elevation

Pline for front and rear main building walls

Pline for front and rear garage walls

Rear Elevation

Pline for side garage walls

Pline for side main building walls

Left Elevation

3D-DZYN

Realworld Imagery (www.realworldimagery.com) can help make your ADT drawings more realistic. This company offers images of plants, textures, and people that can be added to your drawings to help clients visualize the design.

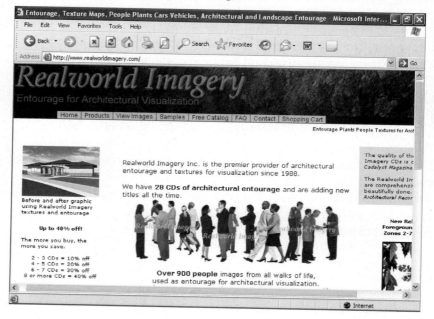

CHAPTER 13

Editing and Modifying Doors, Windows, and Openings

Learning Objectives

After completing this chapter, you will be able to do the following:

✓ Control, attach custom blocks to, edit the profile shape of, and anchor Door objects.
✓ Control, attach custom blocks to, edit the profile shape of, and anchor Window objects.
✓ Control, attach custom blocks to, edit the profile shape of, and anchor Opening objects.
✓ Use door/window assembly tools.

Architectural Desktop includes a number of tools that can be used to enhance the appearance of doors, windows, door/window assemblies, and AEC openings and prepare them for use in construction documents or in the building information model. This chapter covers object displays available for modifying doors, windows, openings, and door/window assemblies. The addition of custom shapes to enhance appearance and the control of properties for Opening objects are also discussed.

Controlling Door Objects

Commands for adding and modifying a Door object provide the basic information for controlling how a door appears in a drawing. For example, when a door is added, the size, style, and opening percentage are specified, controlling the look of the Door object. If the door needs to be adjusted or changed, the **Properties** palette can be used to adjust the size, style, and opening percentage of the door. The **Properties** palette is discussed in Chapter 5. Grips can also be used to control where the door leaf and swing are placed in relation to the Wall object. Architectural Desktop includes additional tools to control many properties of a door to configure the appearance of the object. The following discussion provides many ways of controlling how doors display in the drawing.

Door Object Display

The object display for any AEC object is very important for processing how an object is to appear in a particular view. Doors include their own display settings that can be managed and controlled through the **Object Display** dialog box. Chapter 7 discussed the use of the Architectural Desktop display system, described what a display representation is, and explained how to modify it at the drawing default level. To change the display of a door, select the door to be modified, right-click, and select **Edit Object Display...** from the shortcut menu. The **Object Display** dialog box for the individual door is opened. Select the **Display Properties** tab to adjust the display properties for the selected door, as shown in **Figure 13-1**. Determine in which display representation the door needs to be adjusted. Select the representation from the list in the **Display Representations** column.

The **Display Property Source** column lists the level of display currently applied to the door. The **Drawing Default** level controls the display of doors for each door globally, unless the doors have an override applied. The **Door Style Override** level controls the display of doors based on the door style assigned to the selected door. The **Door Override** level controls the display of the single selected door. To override the display of the selected door, place a check mark in the associated box in the **Object Override** column. This attaches an override to the individual door. **Figure 13-1** displays an override set for a Door object in the Plan High Detail display representation. Pick the **Edit Display Properties** button to adjust the display of the door. The **Display Properties** dialog box is displayed. See **Figure 13-2**.

Depending on the display representation being adjusted, the **Display Properties** dialog box contains different options. Each of the **Display Properties** dialog boxes includes the **Layer/Color/Linetype** tab shown in **Figure 13-2**. This tab controls how the components for a Door object are displayed in the selected display representation. Doors typically include Door Panel, Frame, Stop, and Swing components.

Many of the display representations also include a tab named **Other**. Depending on the representation selected, the **Other** tab displays different options. See **Figure 13-3**. The **Other** tab for the Threshold Plan representation, displayed in **Figure 13-3**, is used to add custom blocks to the Door object. The **Other** tab for the Plan representation, displayed in **Figure 13-3**, is used to adjust door threshold sizes. These topics are discussed later in this section.

Figure 13-1.

The **Object Display** dialog box for Door objects is similar for other AEC objects. Pick the **Display Properties** tab to modify the look of a selected door.

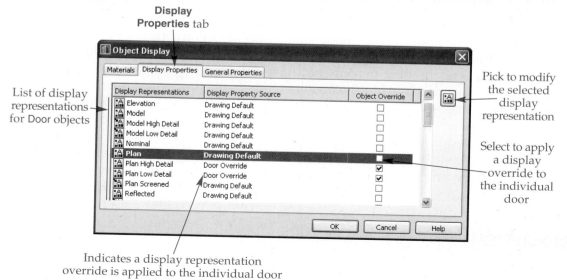

Display **Properties** tab

List of display representations for Door objects

Pick to modify the selected display representation

Select to apply a display override to the individual door

Indicates a display representation override is applied to the individual door

Figure 13-2.
The **Display Properties** dialog box is used to control the display of the components within Door objects.

Controls the layer, color, and linetype properties for door components

Controls the additional display properties for a door

Door components

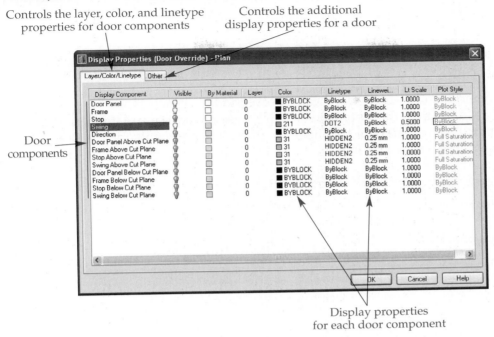

Display properties for each door component

When you have finished adjusting the display properties for Door objects, pick the **OK** button to return to the **Object Display** dialog box, where you can select another display representation and set an override. Pick the **Edit Display Properties** button to adjust the display properties of newly selected display representations to edit them.

When selecting a display representation, notice that there are a few different representations available for doors that are not available for walls. Two of these representations are the Elevation and the Threshold Plan. The *Elevation representation* controls how the door appears in an elevation view. In an elevation view, Door objects are generally displayed closed. The display representation for a door in an elevation view can be modified so the door is closed in Elevation and remains open in the Plan view. To close the door, select the Elevation representation in the **Object Display** dialog box, set the level of override, and then pick the **Edit Display Properties** button. Select the **Other** tab in the **Display Properties** dialog box. Notice that the last option in the tab overrides the opening percentage of the door. If the value is set to 0, the door appears closed in the representation being modified and open in a Plan view.

Threshold Plan Representation

The *Threshold Plan representation* allows you to add an inside door threshold, an outside door threshold, or both in a Plan view. The Plan representation and the Threshold Plan representation can be displayed at the same time for a door while looking in a Top view. To display a door with a threshold, first adjust the display in the Plan representation for the door, and adjust the Threshold Plan display representation.

The Threshold Plan representation includes two main components: Threshold A and Threshold B. The Threshold A component is a threshold that is added to the swing side of the door. Threshold B is added to the opposite side of the door, as shown in **Figure 13-4**. Either or both thresholds can be turned on or off for an individual Plan view Door object.

The Threshold Plan representation also includes an **Other** tab. This tab controls the size of the thresholds on Plan view Door objects. Values A and B control the size of Threshold A. The values C and D control the sizes for Threshold B.

Thresholds are visible only in a Top view. When assigning thresholds, it is usually a good idea to set the override for an individual door. If you have a door style that represents an exterior door, you may want to set the threshold by style.

Overriding the Door Material

The material for a single door can be overridden. When modifying the object display of a single door, the **Materials** tab can be used to assign a material to the door. See **Figure 13-5**. The **Materials** tab includes a list of components for the Door object. The **Source** column indicates how the current material is assigned to the door (**Door**

Figure 13-3.

The **Other** tab for most of the door display representations is shown on top. The **Other** tab used for the door Threshold display representations is shown on bottom.

Add custom blocks to a Plan
representation or Model representation

Use the cut
plane set
by the Wall
object for
the door
cut plane

Adjust the
display of
the Swing
component

Open or close the door
in the display representation

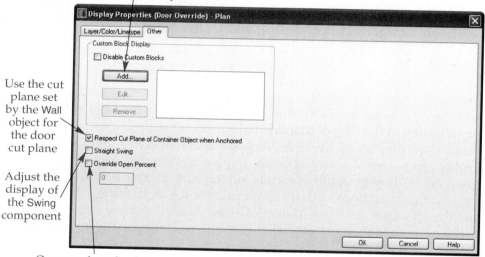

Plan

Preview of
the values
being
controlled

Change the
values for
the
threshold
added to a
Plan view
Door object

Use the cut plane set by the Wall
object for the door cut plane

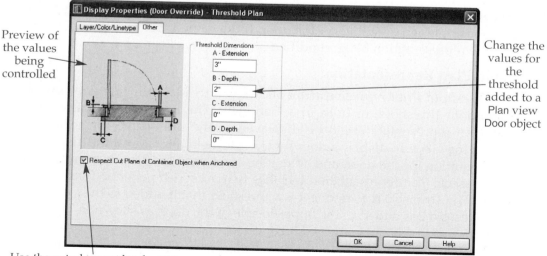

Threshold Plan

Style or **Door Override**). Attaching an override assigns a material to the single Door object being modified. If an override is present, a new material can be chosen from the **Material Definition** column by picking on the current material and choosing a new material.

Figure 13-4.
The Threshold Plan representation includes threshold components that can be viewed in a Top view.

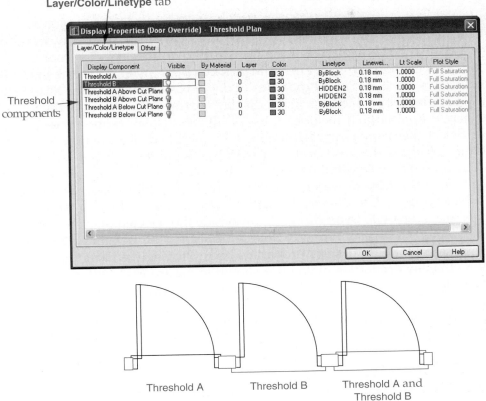

Figure 13-5.
The **Materials** tab is used to assign a material to the individual door.

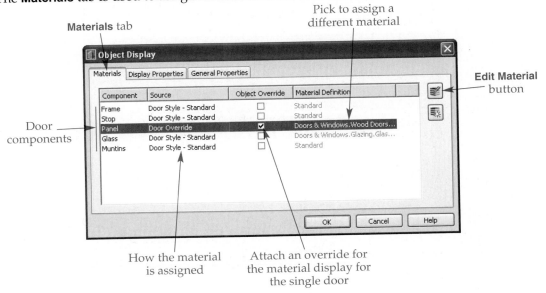

If further modification needs to be made to the material, such as the display color, pick the **Edit Material** button to edit the material display. This opens the **Material Definition Properties** dialog box. Select a display representation in which the material is to be modified, and pick the **Edit Display Properties** button to begin editing. When you are finished making changes, pick the **OK** button to return to the **Object Display** dialog box.

Setting the Display for a Door Style

Typically, the doors on the **Doors** tool palette have been configured to have their display settings controlled through each door style. Occasionally, you may want to change how a door style is displayed in the drawing. To do this, select a door representing the style to be modified, right-click, and pick **Edit Door Style...** from the shortcut menu. This displays the **Door Style Properties** dialog box shown in **Figure 13-6**. Pick the **Display Properties** tab to display a list of display representations for the door.

The **Display Properties** tab includes a list of all the display representations for a door style. Select the display representation to be modified. The **Display Property Source** column indicates the level at which the object display is controlled for the door style. The options are **Drawing Default**, which is controlled through the **Drawing Setup** dialog box, or **Door Style Override**, which sets a display for the door style and is controlled by selecting the **Edit Display Properties** button. To set a display override for the door style, select the **Style Override** check box beside the selected display representation. This changes the **Display Property Source** from **Drawing Default** to **Door Style Override**. Next, select the **Edit Display Properties** button to begin editing the display. This opens the **Display Properties** dialog box shown in **Figure 13-7**. Different display representations for a door have different components that can be adjusted. Make any required display changes.

If material display controls are to be used in a component, turn on the **By Material** check box beside the Door object's component. The materials assigned to the Door

Figure 13-6.
The **Door Style Properties** dialog box is used to configure how the door style will display in the drawing.

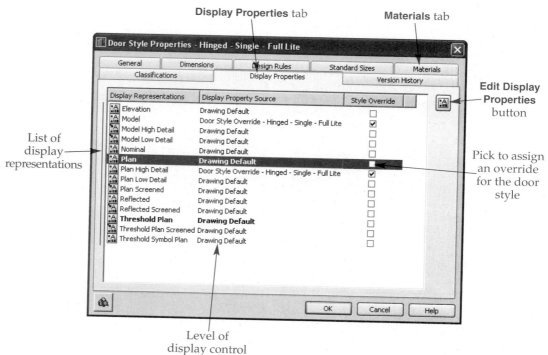

Architectural Desktop and Its Applications

Figure 13-7.
The **Display Properties** dialog box for a door style.

Turn components
on or off

Additional
display settings

Display
components
in the
selected
display
representation

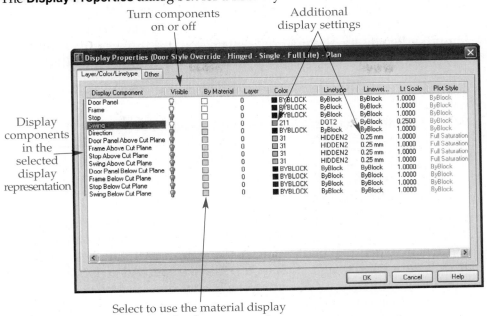

Select to use the material display
settings for the component

object's components can also be set up for the door style. In the **Door Style Properties** dialog box, select the **Materials** tab. See **Figure 13-8**. This displays a list of components and the materials that are assigned to the door style. Pick a material from the **Material Definition** column for the corresponding component. This provides a drop-down list of materials that can be assigned to the different components. Initially, the only materials available are the materials that come with the styles that are in the drawing. Additional materials can be configured and assigned.

Figure 13-8.
Materials can be assigned to the components within a door style. Select the material by picking the current material in the **Material Definitions** column.

Materials tab

Edit Material
button

List of door
components

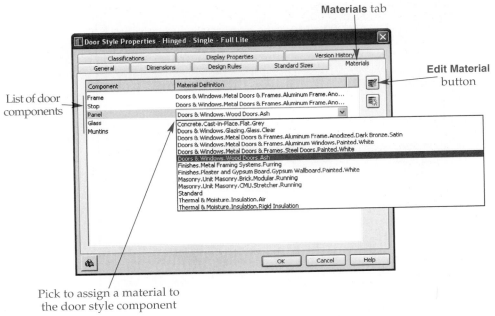

Pick to assign a material to
the door style component

If the display of the materials, such as the color or linetype, needs to be adjusted, select the component with the material to be adjusted, and then pick the **Edit Material** button. This displays the **Material Definition Properties** dialog box. Select the display representation for the material to be modified, pick the **Edit Display Properties** button, and then change the display for the material. When you are finished, pick **OK** until you return to the drawing. Any changes made to the style are updated to all doors of the modified style.

Exercise 13-1

Complete the Exercise on the Student CD.

Attaching Custom Blocks to a Door

Custom blocks can be attached to a door representation through the **Display Properties** dialog box. All the door representations except the Threshold Plan representation can have a custom block attached to the door by style or individual door. Custom blocks can include a door handle or custom molding in a Model and an elevation view, or a dashed line through the door representing the header lines in Plan view.

The first step in attaching a block to a door is to have a block definition in the drawing. The block needs to be created on layer 0, using ByBlock colors, linetypes, lineweights, and plot styles. See Chapter 9 for creating blocks. Once the block is created, it can be attached to the door. If you are creating blocks for use in a Model view, the blocks should be 3D. Blocks attached to an Elevation or Plan representation can be drawn in 2D.

Creating a Door Handle Block

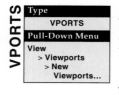

This section walks you through the creation of a simple 3D door handle that can be attached to a door. Start a new drawing and split the screen into four equal viewports by selecting **View** > **Viewports** > **New Viewports...** from the pull-down menu. In the **Viewports** dialog box, shown in **Figure 13-9**, change the **Setup:** to **3D** to provide

Figure 13-9.
Use the **Viewports** dialog box to split the drawing screen into multiple viewports when working on 3D objects.

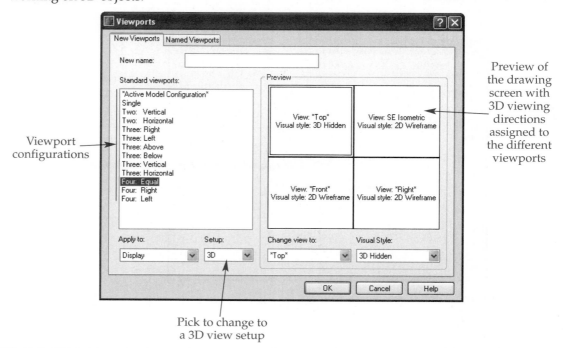

you with a Top, Front, Right, and SE Isometric view. You can also assign the visual style, which controls the way a 3D model is displayed. Pick **OK** to split the drawing screen into four viewports, each with a different viewing direction assigned.

Pick inside the Front viewport (the lower-left viewport, by default) to make the viewport active. Draw a circle 1" in diameter. Select the circle, right-click, and select **Convert To > Mass Element** from the shortcut menu. You are prompted to erase selected linework and given choices of Yes or No. Press [Enter] to accept the default value of No. The next prompt asks you to specify the extrusion height. The *extrusion height* is the length of the closed object as it is being converted into a 3D object. When you are finished, the circle has been extruded into a cylindrical mass element.

The shaft for the door handle is created. Click into each viewport and perform the **ZOOM Extents** command to zoom in on the new cylinder. See **Figure 13-10**. The next step is to create the handle. Change to the isometric viewport (the upper-right viewport, by default). Change the UCS orientation to a front orthographic orientation. Pick **View > Orthographic UCS > Front** from the pull-down menu. This changes the orientation of the crosshairs to be parallel with the end of the cylinder.

Use a mass element to create a sphere and place it at the "front" of the cylinder. The **Sphere** mass element is accessed by picking the **Sphere** tool from the **Massing** palette in the **Design** tool palette group, picking **Design > Massing > Sphere** from the pull-down menu, or typing MASSELEMENTADD.

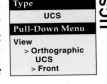

Figure 13-10.
Convert a 1" diameter circle into a mass element cylinder.

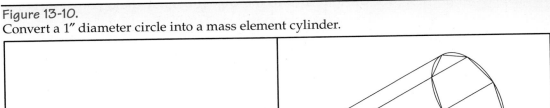

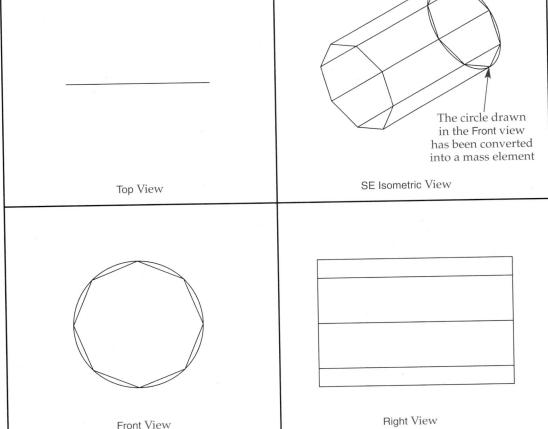

The circle drawn in the Front view has been converted into a mass element

Top View

SE Isometric View

Front View

Right View

After entering the command, you are prompted for the insert point or shape. If you typed the command, type SPHERE. Then, use a **Node** object snap to select the center end of the cylinder. The next prompt asks for a radius or shape. Enter the radius for the door handle. The final prompt asks for the rotation or shape. Enter the rotation angle for the sphere. After adding the sphere, you have the opportunity to add additional spheres.

After adding the sphere, pick the right-side viewport (bottom-right viewport by default). Use the **MOVE** command to move the sphere toward the cylinder to remove any gaps between the two mass elements. The sphere for the door handle is created as shown in **Figure 13-11.**

The final step is to join the two pieces together to form one object. Use a Boolean mass element option to do this. This command is accessed by selecting one of the mass elements, right-clicking, and selecting **Boolean > Union** from the shortcut menu. Select the objects to union and press [Enter]. Decide whether or not to erase the layout geometry, and then end the command.

The next step is to ensure the door handle is on layer 0 and using ByBlock colors, linetypes, lineweights, and plot styles. Pick the door handle shape, and select **Edit Object Display...** from the shortcut menu. Select the **Display Properties** tab, pick the Model display representation, and then pick the **Edit Display Properties** button to change the drawing default display settings. Change the layer to 0 and the color, linetype, lineweight, and plot style to ByBlock. Pick **OK** when you are finished. After changing the display properties, pick **OK** to return to the **Object Display** dialog box. Select the

Figure 13-11.
The sphere mass element is used to create a door handle at the end of the mass element cylinder.

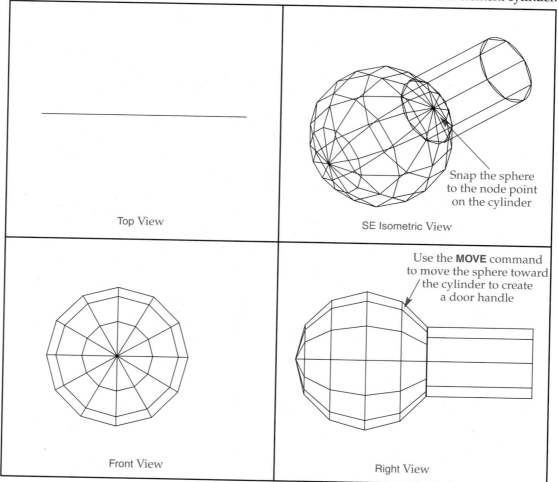

Top View

SE Isometric View

Snap the sphere to the node point on the cylinder

Front View

Right View

Use the **MOVE** command to move the sphere toward the cylinder to create a door handle

General Properties tab. Change the layer to 0 and the color, linetype, lineweight, and plot style to ByBlock. Pick **OK** when you are finished.

The final step is to turn the handle into a block. Use the **BLOCK** command to turn the mass element into a door handle block. When you are creating a block to be attached to a door, set the orientation of the crosshairs parallel to the floor. In the top-right viewport, change the view to the SE Isometric view. Pick **View** > **Orthographic UCS** > **Top** from the pull-down menu. The crosshairs are oriented correctly for selecting the insertion point of the block.

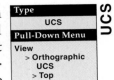

The insertion point for the block should be located at the end of the cylinder opposite the end that includes the sphere, as shown in **Figure 13-12**. Use the **Center** object snap to snap to the center of the original circle. Once the block is created in this drawing, it can be dragged and dropped into other drawings using **DesignCenter**.

 NOTE
3D blocks can be constructed from AutoCAD solids or surface objects. 3D blocks also can be constructed from AEC mass elements. The blocks do not have to be created in a different drawing file, but they can be created in the drawing where they will be used. Additionally, knowing how to manipulate the UCS can be a great help in creating 3D blocks for use in an AEC object.

Adding the Door Handle to a Door

Once the door handle block has been defined in the drawing where it will be used, it can be added to a single door or to a door style through the **Display Properties** dialog box. This section discusses how to attach the door handle to the door style. To do this, select a door representing the style to which the door handle will be added, right-click, and select **Edit Door Style...** before picking the **Display Properties** tab. Select the Model representation, and set the override by style. Pick the **Edit Display Properties** button to modify the Model view Door object. Select the **Other** tab to add the block to the door style. Selecting the **Add...** button displays the **Custom Block** dialog box, shown in **Figure 13-13**.

The dialog box is divided into two parts: the left side controls how the block is inserted, and the right side provides a preview of how the block appears. If you are adding blocks to a Model representation, you may want to select an isometric view angle from the drop-down list in the upper-right corner of the dialog box.

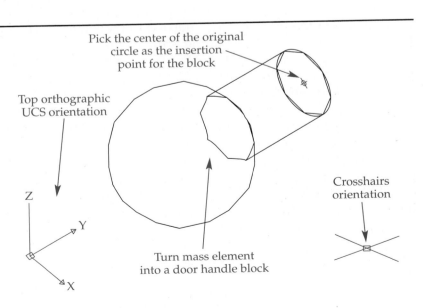

Figure 13-12. Change the UCS in the **SE Isometric** viewport to a Top orthographic orientation. Use the **Center** object snap to select the center point of the original circle as the insertion point for the block.

Pick the center of the original circle as the insertion point for the block

Top orthographic UCS orientation

Crosshairs orientation

Turn mass element into a door handle block

Figure 13-13.

In the **Other** tab for the Model or Elevation display properties, pick the **Add** button to open the **Custom Block** dialog box. The **Custom Block** dialog box is used to add custom blocks to a door.

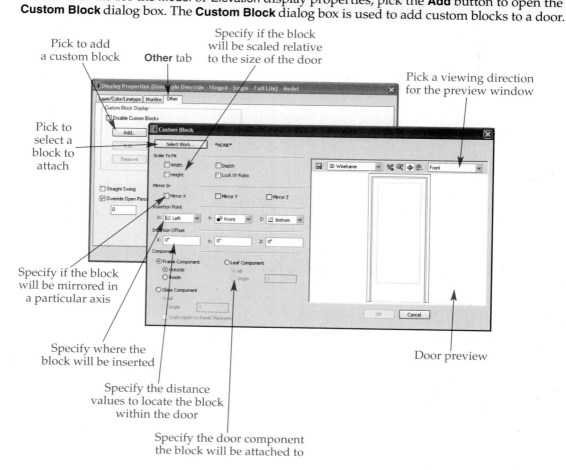

Pick to add a custom block

Other tab

Specify if the block will be scaled relative to the size of the door

Pick a viewing direction for the preview window

Pick to select a block to attach

Specify if the block will be mirrored in a particular axis

Specify where the block will be inserted

Door preview

Specify the distance values to locate the block within the door

Specify the door component the block will be attached to

To add the block, pick the **Select Block...** button to select the door handle block. Once the door handle block is selected, it is inserted at the bottom on the left side of the framing component. This is the X= 0, Y= 0, Z = 0 point for the individual door. Each AEC object includes its own coordinate locating system. Typically, the starting point of the object establishes the 0,0,0 point for the object. See **Figure 13-14**.

The block can be attached to one of three door components. At the bottom of the dialog box, the block can be attached to the Frame, Leaf, or Glass component. See **Figure 13-13**. As you are attaching a door handle, select the **Leaf Component** radio button. This places the block on the Door Leaf component in the preview. Use the **Insertion Point** drop-down lists to position the block along the component's X, Y, and Z axes. The **Insertion Offset** text boxes are used to offset the insertion point of the block in relation to the insertion point for the component. Adjust the values until the door handle appears correctly in the preview window. The values specified for attaching the door handle to the door style are shown in **Figure 13-13**.

When you have finished, pick the **OK** button to return to the **Display Properties** dialog box, where you can attach additional blocks to the door. If a door handle is to be attached to both sides of the door leaf, add two blocks and adjust their values accordingly. Use different viewing directions in the preview pane to adjust the location of the block within the door.

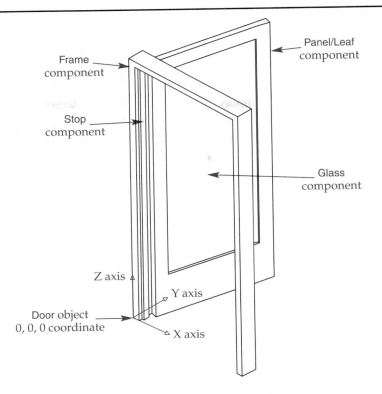

Figure 13-14.
Every AEC object has an X axis (object length), Y axis (object width), and Z axis (object height). The X = 0, Y = 0, Z = 0 point is located at the starting point of the objects.

Frame component

Stop component

Panel/Leaf component

Glass component

Z axis

Y axis

Door object
0, 0, 0 coordinate

X axis

NOTE Occasionally, the preview pane within the **Custom Block** dialog box does not show the block properly to reflect the insertion settings assigned. You may need to accept the insertion settings by picking the **OK** button, which returns you to the **Display Properties** dialog box. Select the block from the list in the **Other** tab, and then pick the **Edit** button. Adjust the insertion settings for the block as needed. Additionally, use the **View Control** drop-down list in the preview pane to view the block from all sides to aid in the placement of the block.

When blocks are added to an AEC object, they become components of the door, and their display can be controlled in the **Layer/Color/Linetype** tab. This is why it is important to create the original block with ByBlock properties on layer 0.

**Exercise
13-2**   *Complete the Exercise on the Student CD.*

Editing the Door in Place

The previous chapter introduced you to the ability to edit the shape of modifiers applied to a wall. This similar practice can be applied to a door. The shape of a door can be based on a profile, similar to a modifier shape. See **Figure 13-15.** The profile shape of a door can be modified, and additional rings or holes can be added to the door to allow for glazing. You may also add door panel blocks.

The application of a profile shape to create a custom door style is discussed in Chapter 9. For now, the existing shape of the door will be modified. When you are editing a door shape in place, the changes made to the profile affect all doors using the profile. Unless a door style includes glazing or panel blocks, the door does not use an AEC

Figure 13-15.
Profile shapes are
used to create the
shape of the door.

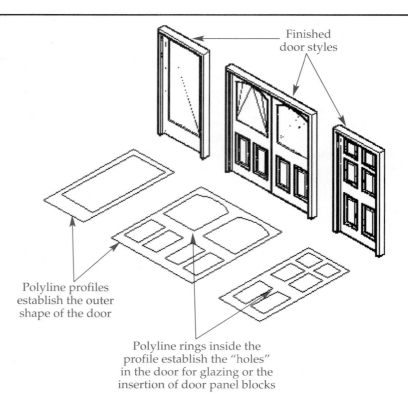

Finished
door styles

Polyline profiles
establish the outer
shape of the door

Polyline rings inside the
profile establish the "holes"
in the door for glazing or the
insertion of door panel blocks

profile. A new shape can be defined and edited to create a new shape. Before editing the shape of the door, you may want to establish an isometric or elevation view of the door. To edit the shape of a typical rectangular door, select the door, right-click, and pick the **Add Profile...** option. The **Add Door Profile** worksheet is displayed. See **Figure 13-16**.

The **Add Door Profile** worksheet includes a **Profile Definition** drop-down list. If there are existing profiles created, a profile can be assigned to the door style. If no profiles are available, the **Start from scratch...** option is available. If you are using the **Start from scratch...** option, enter a name for the new profile in the **New Profile Name** text box, and pick **OK** to begin editing.

The **In-Place Edit** toolbar is displayed along with the profile shape of the door with grip boxes. See **Figure 13-17**. Use the grip boxes to modify the shape of the door. New internal closed polylines can be drawn on the face of the door and then turned into rings within the profile. After drawing any rings, select the profile hatch, right-click, and select the **Add Ring** command. You are prompted to select a closed polyline, spline, ellipse, or circle. After selecting, type Y to erase the layout shape or N to keep the shape. As new rings are added to the profile, the profile shape updates to indicate rings being added. See **Figure 13-18**. Use the shortcut menu to perform additional functions, such as replacing an existing ring with a different shape or adding and removing vertices.

Figure 13-16.
The **Add Door Profile** worksheet is used to assign or create a profile for the selected door style.

Choose an existing
profile or create
a new one

Enter a name
for the new profile

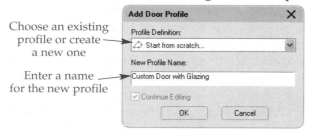

Figure 13-17.
The new profile shape is displayed and ready for editing. Use the shortcut menu to add rings or vertices to the profile shape.

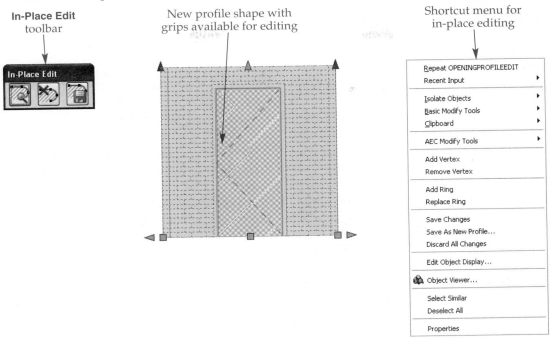

In-Place Edit toolbar

New profile shape with grips available for editing

Shortcut menu for in-place editing

Figure 13-18.
Draw internal polyline shapes to be used as rings in the profile. Use the shortcut menu to add the rings to the profile.

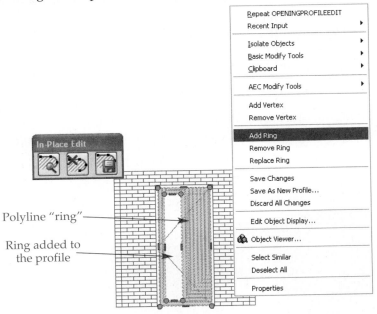

Polyline "ring"

Ring added to the profile

When you are finished editing the new profile, pick the **Save All Changes** button in the **In-Place Edit** toolbar. The door is updated with the new profile shape, and any other doors using the style are also updated.

If a door is already using a profile, selecting the door and right-clicking provides you with the **Edit Profile In Place...** option. Select this option to edit the profile in place. Instead of the **Add Door Profile** worksheet, the profile shape of the door with grips and the **In-Place Edit** toolbar are displayed. Perform any editing as previously described. Remember to save your changes when you are finished.

Exercise 13-3 *Complete the Exercise on the Student CD.*

Adding Muntins to Doors

When you are editing the door in place, rings can be added to create rings or glazing panels within the door. Once a door profile has a ring, the ring automatically becomes the Glass component. Materials and blocks can be assigned to the Glass component to enhance the look of the door. In addition to these features, muntins can be applied within each Glass component. See **Figure 13-19**.

Like blocks, muntins can be added to an individual door or to a door style. A *muntin* is a vertical, horizontal, or angled piece between two panels or glass panes. To add muntins to the door style, select the door that is using the style to be modified, right-click, and select the **Edit Door Style...** option. Pick the **Display Properties** tab, select the Model representation, and apply a style override. Pick the **Edit Display Properties** button to begin editing. In the **Display Properties** dialog box, select the **Muntins** tab. This tab looks similar to the **Other** tab, but it is used to apply muntins. See **Figure 13-20**. Pick the **Add...** button to begin adding muntins. This opens the **Muntins Block** dialog box in **Figure 13-21**.

A name can be specified for the muntin configuration in the **Name:** text box. This can be helpful if applying different muntin patterns to different Glass components within the same door. The **Glass Component** section allows the muntins to be applied to all of the Glass components in a door or to a single Glass component. Each ring in a profile is assigned a number, so if you are assigning the muntins to a single Glass component, enter the number in the **Single** text box.

The **Muntin** area is used to assign the width and depth of the muntin components. In addition to the sizes, two options are available. The **Clean Up Joints** option cleans up the intersection of the muntins, and the **Convert to Body** option is used to create 3D muntins in the Glass component.

The **Lights** area is used to assign the muntin pattern. Six different options are available: **Rectangular, Diamond, Starburst, Sunburst, Prairie - 9 Lights**, and **Prairie - 12 Lights**. Selecting a pattern provides different options below the **Pattern:** drop-down

Figure 13-19.
Muntins can be added to the Glass component within a door.

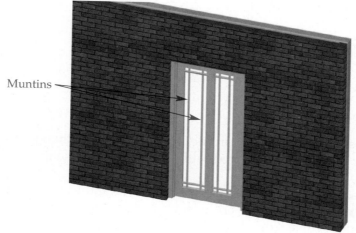

Muntins

Architectural Desktop and Its Applications

Figure 13-20.
The **Muntins** tab is used to add and manage muntins within a door.

Pick to add a new muntin configuration

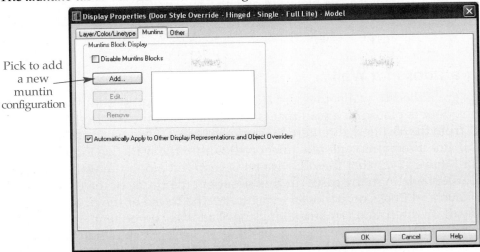

Figure 13-21.
The **Muntins Block** dialog box is used to configure muntins applied to the Glass components.

Name of the muntin configuration

Apply to all Glass components or to a single Glass component

Control the size of the muntins

Check to turn into a 3D component for a Model view

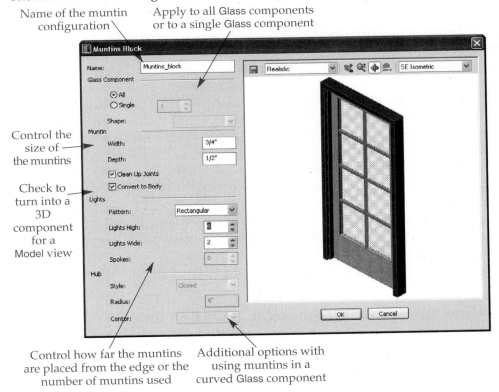

Control how far the muntins are placed from the edge or the number of muntins used

Additional options with using muntins in a curved Glass component

list. The options may require you to specify the number of lights (Glass components between muntins) or how far from the edge the muntins are created.

The **Hub** area is used if the glass panels are curved and a **Starburst** or **Sunburst** pattern is used. This controls the "hub" at the center of the curved glass panel.

When you are finished configuring the muntins, pick the **OK** button to return to the **Display Properties** tab. Add any additional muntins to Glass components, or pick **OK** to return to the **Door Style Properties** dialog box. After adding muntins, you may want to check the material assigned to the muntins in the **Materials** tab. When you are finished editing the door style, pick **OK** to return to the drawing.

Anchoring a Door in a Wall

As doors are added to walls, they are *anchored* to a position within the wall. For example, if the door is placed in a wall that is 12″ from a wall intersection, the door is anchored 12″ from the corner and centered within the wall. The door can still be moved along the wall, but it remains centered (anchored) within the wall. See **Figure 13-22.**

Notice in **Figure 13-22** that the door frame is centered along the wall centerline. This may be acceptable in many cases. In this situation, the frame of the door extends between the Stud and Brick components. In actuality, the frame of the door should be inset in the wall so the frame remains along the Stud Wall component. To adjust the door within the wall, first pick the door, right-click, and select **Reposition Within Wall.** After selecting the command, a red line is displayed within the door. As the mouse is moved, the line snaps to each side of the door frame and the door center. You are also prompted to select position on the opening. This allows you to select the point on the door that lines up with a component within the wall.

After selecting the position on the door, you are prompted to select a reference point. Moving the mouse displays a dimension from the door position to where the crosshairs are located. Enter a distance to move the door or pick the edge of a component of a Wall object. After picking the reference point, you are prompted to enter the new distance between the selected points. You can also press [Enter] to accept the default and place the door position next to the selected wall's component. See **Figure 13-23.**

Another anchor option is to reposition a door along a wall. This option allows you to offset the door a specified distance along the face of the wall. To use this command, select the door, right-click, and select **Reposition Along Wall.** Select a position on the door. A red line is displayed, snapping to each inside edge of the frame or the center of the door. After picking the position, select a reference location. Pick a point on the wall or door to use as a reference, and then enter the distance the door is to be moved.

NOTE
> The **Reposition Along Wall** option is rarely used, since the **MOVE** command can easily be used to reposition (move) the door a specified distance.

Additional anchoring commands can be accessed by selecting the door, right-clicking, and selecting **Wall Anchor.** A shortcut menu with the following series of options for controlling how a door is anchored within a wall is displayed.

- **Set Wall.** This option allows you to move a door into a different wall. Pick the wall to where the door needs to be moved, and the door is anchored to the new wall.

Figure 13-22.
When doors are first placed in a wall, they are anchored to the center of the wall.

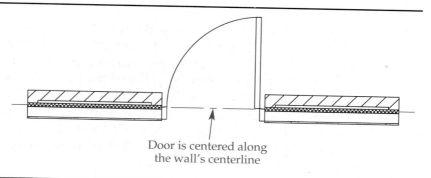

Door is centered along
the wall's centerline

Figure 13-23.
The **Reposition Within Wall** command adjusts the position of the door within the wall.

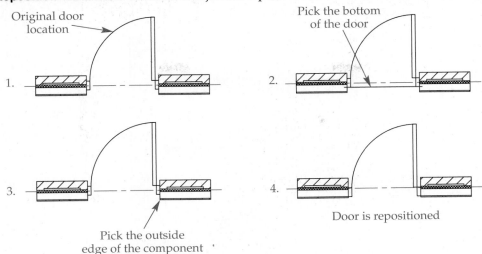

Original door location

Pick the bottom of the door

1.

2.

3.

4.

Pick the outside edge of the component

Door is repositioned

- **Release.** This option releases a door from a wall and fills in the opening within the wall. Once a door is released, it can be anchored to a wall by right-clicking and selecting the **Anchor to Wall** option. Select a wall in which to anchor the door.
- **Flip X.** This option flips the hinge side of the door.
- **Flip Y.** This option flips the swing side of the door.

Changing Door Properties

Door objects can be manipulated in a number of ways, yet there are some things that cannot be controlled with the options mentioned earlier. The **Properties** palette can be used to round out all the modifying options available to you for adding and modifying doors. When a door is selected, the **Properties** palette displays the properties of the door. See **Figure 13-24.** Chapter 5 discusses the properties available with Door objects thoroughly.

The **Location** category includes properties for controlling how the door is placed in the wall and for controlling wall endcaps applied to each side of the doors. These properties are described below:

- **Anchor.** Picking this property displays the **Anchor** worksheet. See **Figure 13-25.** The worksheet controls the placement of the door in a wall. The tab is divided into four areas. Each of the areas adjusts the door within the Wall object's X, Y, and Z axes.
- **Position Along (X).** This area controls the placement of the door along the X axis of a wall. The positive X axis of a wall is designated from the starting point of the wall to the ending point of the wall. The following settings control the door placement along the wall:
  - **From.** This drop-down list specifies where placement of the door is measured along the wall. Options include **Start of wall, Midpoint of wall,** and **End of wall.**
  - **Distance.** Enter a distance from one of the points selected in the **From:** drop-down list to a point on the door.
  - **To.** This drop-down list specifies what point on the door the distance value is measured to. Options include **Start edge of object, Center of object,** and **End edge of object.**
- **Position Within (Y).** This area controls the placement of the door within the wall.
  - **From.** This drop-down list specifies where the placement of the door is measured from within the wall. Options include **Left edge of wall width, Center of wall width,** and **Right edge of wall width.**

Figure 13-24.
The **Properties** palette is used to control the properties of the selected door(s).

Selected object

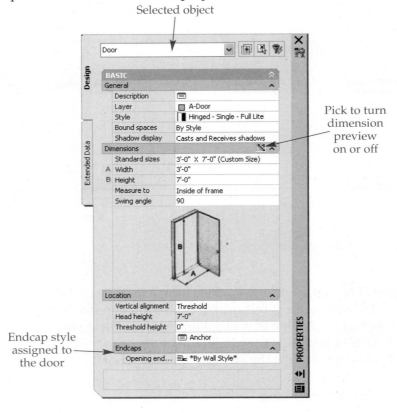

Pick to turn
dimension
preview
on or off

Endcap style
assigned to
the door

Figure 13-25.
The **Anchor** worksheet is used to anchor the door in a wall at a specific position.

Position the
door along the
length of
the wall

Position the
door within
the width of
the wall

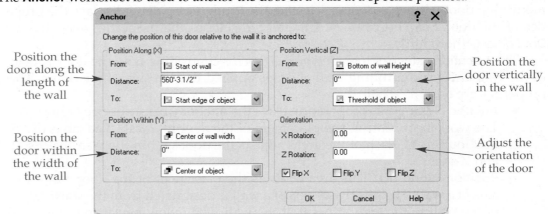

Position the
door vertically
in the wall

Adjust the
orientation
of the door

- **Distance.** Enter a distance from one of the points selected in the **From:** drop-down list to a point on the door.
- **To.** This drop-down list specifies what point on the door the distance value is measured to. Options include **Front of object**, **Center of object**, and **Back of object**.
- **Position Vertical (Z).** This area is used to place the door vertically within the wall.
  - **From.** This drop-down list specifies where the placement of the door is measured from vertically within the wall. Options include **Bottom of wall height**, **Center of wall height**, and **Top of wall height**.
  - **Distance.** Enter a distance from one of the points selected in the **From:** drop-down list to a point on the door.

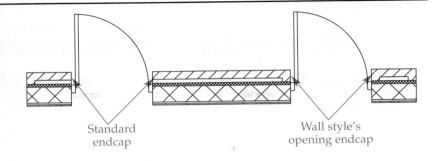

Figure 13-26.
The door on the left is using the Standard endcap style to cap the ends of the wall through which the door is. The door on the right is using an endcap style that wraps the Brick component of the wall around the Stud component.

Standard endcap

Wall style's opening endcap

- **To.** This drop-down list specifies what point on the door the distance value is measured to. Options include **Head of object**, **Center of object**, and **Threshold of object**.
- **Orientation.** This area controls the direction of the door in the wall.
  - **X Rotation.** Entering a value in this text box rotates the door in the wall's X axis, which produces an angled door.
  - **Z Rotation.** Entering a value in this text box rotates the door along the wall's Z axis.
  - **Flip X.** This check box mirrors the door in the wall's X axis.
  - **Flip Y.** This check box mirrors the hinge/swing of the door in the wall's Y axis.
  - **Flip Z.** This check box mirrors the door in the wall's Z axis, producing an upside-down door.
- **Opening endcap.** Picking this property displays a list of wall endcaps that are placed on all sides of the door. The *endcap* controls how the wall appears around the door when a door has been inserted into a wall. See **Figure 13-26**.

Exercise
13-5   *Complete the Exercise on the Student CD.*

Controlling Window Objects

Window objects, like Door and Wall objects, include a number of tools that can be used to enhance their behavior in the construction documents, as well as in the CAD model. Many of the tools are similar to the tools used for Door objects. This section explains the tools used to manipulate the look and behavior of Window objects.

Window Object Display

The individual window display can be controlled through the use of object display much like doors are controlled. To access the object display for a window, first select the window, right-click, and pick **Edit Object Display...** before selecting the **Display Properties** tab. Select a representation that needs to have its display adjusted, and then assign an override. After the override has been set, pick the **Edit Display Properties** button to adjust the window display. **Figure 13-27** shows the components for a Plan representation Window object.

Figure 13-27.
The Plan display representation window includes Frame, Sash, and Glass components.

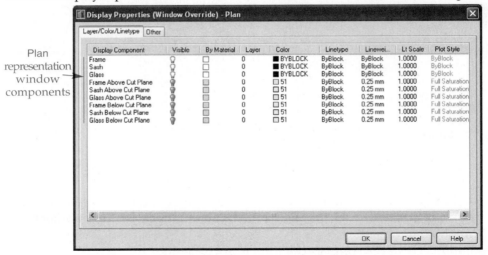

Plan
representation
window
components

Window objects also include an Elevation display representation and a Sill Plan representation. The Elevation display representation controls how the window appears in an elevation view. The Sill Plan display representation controls the display of window sills, similar to door thresholds.

The **Other** tab is used to add custom blocks to a window. Adding custom blocks to windows is discussed later in this chapter.

NOTE

In some instances, a short window may not display in a Plan view Wall object. This usually occurs when the window is above the display configuration cut plane. To adjust for this, the Wall object's Plan display cut plane should be adjusted so it cuts through the window.

Setting the Display for a Window Style

In addition to adjusting the display of a single window, the object display can be set for a window style. To adjust the window style display, select a window that represents the style that will be modified, right-click, and pick the **Edit Window Style...** option. This displays the **Window Style Properties** dialog box in Figure 13-28. Pick the **Display Properties** tab to adjust the display of a window representation.

After accessing the **Display Properties** tab, select a display representation to modify, add a style override, and then pick the **Edit Display Properties** button to make changes to the window display. If materials will be assigned to the window style, use the **Materials** tab to adjust the materials assigned to the window components.

Sill Plan Representation

The Sill Plan representation creates an inside and outside window sill and is used in conjunction with the Window Plan representation. The Sill Plan representation includes two components, the inside sill and the outside sill. See Figure 13-29. The inside of a window is determined by the location of the **Flip** grip that is set off the wall when the window is selected. The Sill A component is considered to be the inside sill, and the Sill B component is the outside component. One, both, or neither of these sills can be turned on for the Top view.

The **Other** tab in the Sill Plan representation includes the dimensional values for the inside and outside sills. Values A and B control the dimensions for Sill A (inside sill), and values C and D control the dimensions for Sill B (outside sill). See Figure 13-30.

Figure 13-28.
The **Window Style Properties** dialog box controls the settings for the window style.

Display Properties tab   Materials tab

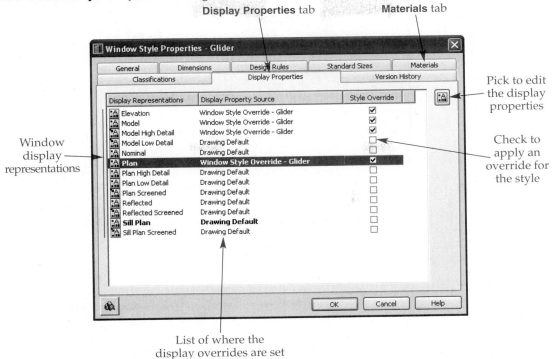

Window display representations

Pick to edit the display properties

Check to apply an override for the style

List of where the display overrides are set

Figure 13-29.
The **Layer/Color/Linetype** tab for the window Sill Plan representation is used to control the graphical display of a window sill in a Plan representation.

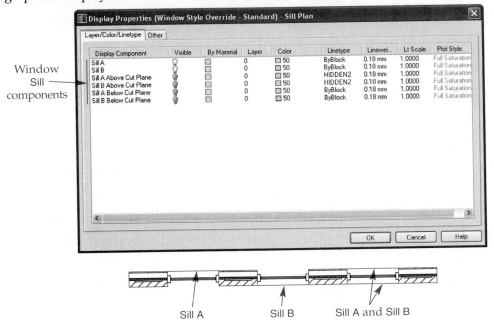

Window Sill components

Sill A   Sill B   Sill A and Sill B

Figure 13-30.
Adjust the values
of the window
sills in the Sill Plan
representation.

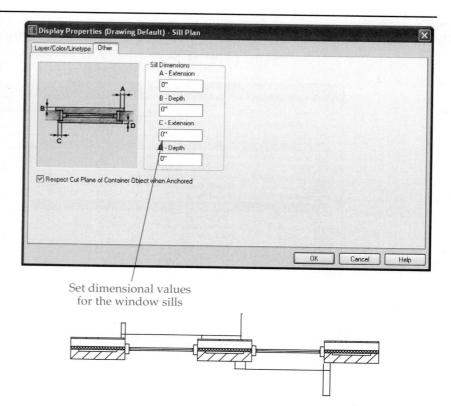

Set dimensional values
for the window sills

 NOTE When adjusting the sill depth, additional lines may be displayed within the window. These are generally the wall lines below the cut plane. Access the **Display Properties** for the Plan representation Wall object, pick the **Other** tab, and check the **Hide Lines Below Openings at Cut Plane** check box.

Attaching Custom Blocks to Windows

Attaching a block to a window is similar to attaching a block to a door. First, create the block(s) to be attached to the window, ensuring that the original geometry was created on layer 0, using ByBlock colors, linetypes, lineweights, and plot styles. See **Figure 13-31**. The insertion points for the blocks should be logical places on the geometry because the block is added to the window and assigned a location measured from the insertion point of the window.

 NOTE When you are creating blocks for windows and doors, use AEC mass elements to create the objects. Mass elements can be added to each other and subtracted from each other to form many desired shapes. Mass elements are discussed in Chapter 25.

Select the window and use the **Edit Object Display** option to assign blocks to individual windows or the **Edit Window Style** option to assign blocks to a window style. In the **Display Properties** tab, select the appropriate Model or Elevation display representation to attach the block to. Assign an override, and pick the **Edit Display Properties** button to begin editing the individual window or window style. In the **Display Properties** dialog box, pick the **Other** tab. In the **Other** tab, pick the **Add...**

Architectural Desktop and Its Applications

Figure 13-31.
Four blocks have been created for attachment to a window. Note the insertion point locations are located in logical positions for easy placement onto the window.

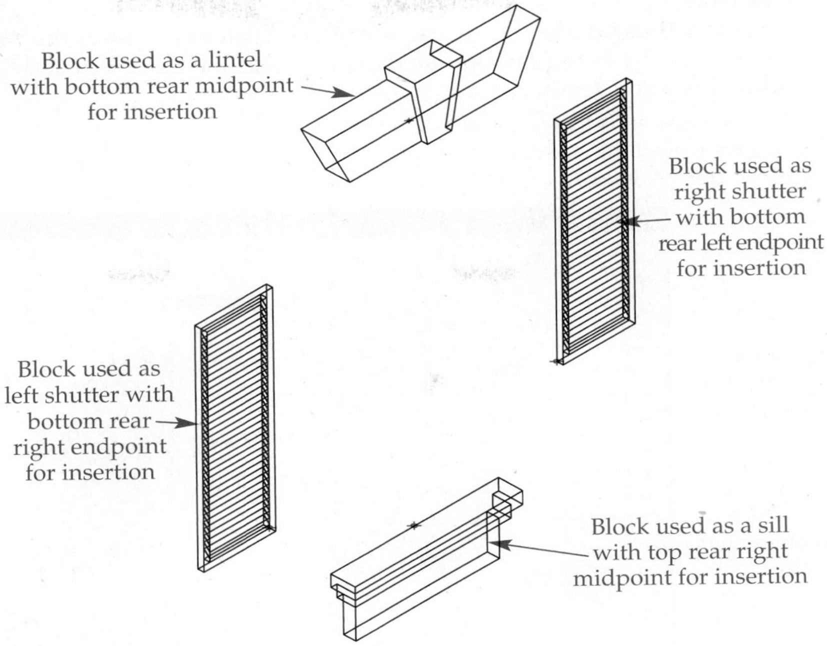

Block used as a lintel with bottom rear midpoint for insertion

Block used as right shutter with bottom rear left endpoint for insertion

Block used as left shutter with bottom rear right endpoint for insertion

Block used as a sill with top rear right midpoint for insertion

button to add a block to the window. The **Custom Block** dialog box for Window objects is displayed. See **Figure 13-32.** The following settings are available to control the addition of a block to a window:

- **Select Block.** Pick this button to choose the block to be attached to the window.
- **Scale To Fit.** This area includes options for scaling the inserted block. The **Width**, **Height**, and **Depth** of the block can be scaled to fit the size of the window. The **Lock XY Ratio** check box locks the scale of the **Width** and **Depth** options.
- **Mirror In.** This area controls whether the block is mirrored in the window's X, Y, or Z axis of the Window object.
- **Insertion Point.** This area is used to specify where the block is inserted in relation to the selected window component. The **X:** drop-down list places the block along the component's left, center, or right edge. The **Y:** drop-down list adjusts the block to the front, center, or back edge of the component. The **Z:** drop-down list adjusts the block to the top, center, or bottom of the component's edge.
- **Insertion Offset.** This area allows you to specify an offset distance for the insertion of the block, relative to the points specified in the insertion point area above.
- **Component.** Blocks that are placed in a window are placed relative to the **Frame Component** or to the **Window Component**. The window component is measured from the edge of the sash to the opposite edge of the sash.

Many blocks can be added to a window at the style or individual window level. As each block is attached, it is added to the component list in the **Layer/Color/Linetype** tab, where display controls can be applied. You can have custom blocks that are drawn at different sizes so when the window is added to a wall, the **Display Properties** dialog box can be used to turn the appropriately sized block component on or off.

NOTE It is a good idea to attach blocks at the style level since the window can be used many times throughout the drawing with the custom blocks applied. If the blocks are not to be shown on a section of the building, simply turn off the block components for that one window.

Figure 13-32.

The **Custom Block** dialog box is used to attach custom blocks to the Window object. The sill block is currently being manipulated. Note where the block is inserted in relation to the window insertion point.

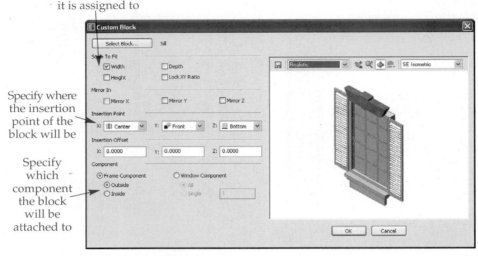

Specify how the block will be scaled against the component it is assigned to

Specify where the insertion point of the block will be

Specify which component the block will be attached to

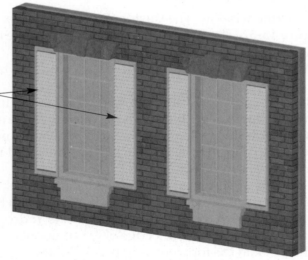

Finished windows after all blocks have been assigned to the window style

Editing the Window Profile

As with the Door object, the profile of the window can be modified to a different shape. By default, all of the windows available in the **Windows** tool palette are not assigned a profile. With the exception of the Picture-Arched window style, all of the window styles use a rectangular shape to define the window. Different shapes can be applied when a window style is first defined.

Custom AEC profile shapes defined in the drawing can be applied to any of the window styles in the drawing to create a custom window shape. When an AEC profile is defined, additional internal rings can be defined within the profile to create holes in the profile. You did this when modifying a door, which resulted in the holes becoming glazing within the door. If a profile with rings is used in a window, the rings become holes in the glass. When you are creating a profile shape for a window, do not add rings unless there is to be a hole cut in the glass. AEC profiles also require an insertion point. When specifying an insertion point for the profile, use the centroid of the profile shape as the insertion for the profile. See **Figure 13-33.**

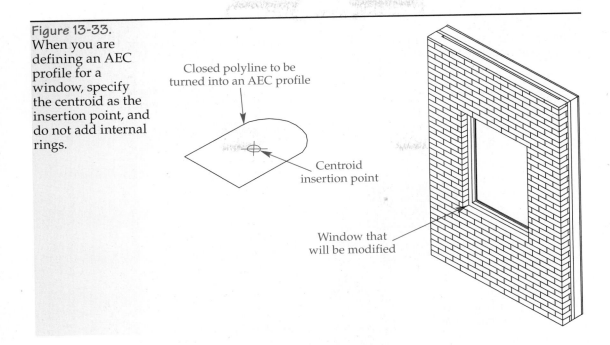

Figure 13-33.
When you are defining an AEC profile for a window, specify the centroid as the insertion point, and do not add internal rings.

Closed polyline to be turned into an AEC profile

Centroid insertion point

Window that will be modified

After the profile shape has been defined, the window style can be modified to use the profile shape. Select the window representing the style that will use the new shape. Right-click and select the **Add Profile...** option. This opens the **Add Window Profile** worksheet, shown in **Figure 13-34.** In the **Profile Definition** drop-down list, select the profile to be applied to the window.

The **Start from scratch...** option allows you to modify the existing shape of the window to create a new profile. The **New Profile Name:** text box is available if the **Start from scratch...** option is selected and is used to provide a name for the new profile.

The **Continue Editing** check box is used for editing the profile in place on the window. Pick the **OK** button when you are finished. The profile is applied to the window, and if you are also editing the profile, the profile is displayed with grip boxes that can be stretched.

After a profile is assigned to a window style, it can be edited in place to modify its shape. To edit the profile, select the window, right-click, and select the **Edit Profile In Place** option. This displays the **In-Place Edit** toolbar and a shaded profile around the window with grip boxes that can be adjusted. Use the grips to adjust the shape or right-click to display the shortcut menu for additional editing, **Figure 13-35.** When you are finished editing the profile, pick the **Save All Changes** button on the **In-Place Edit** toolbar.

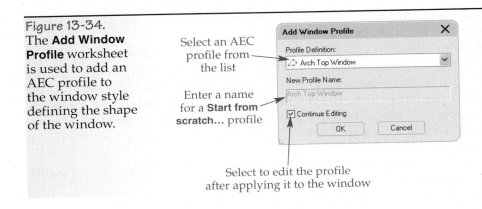

Figure 13-34.
The **Add Window Profile** worksheet is used to add an AEC profile to the window style defining the shape of the window.

Select an AEC profile from the list

Enter a name for a **Start from scratch...** profile

Select to edit the profile after applying it to the window

Figure 13-35.
When editing a window in place, use the grips to adjust the profile shape and the shortcut
menu to add/delete vertices.

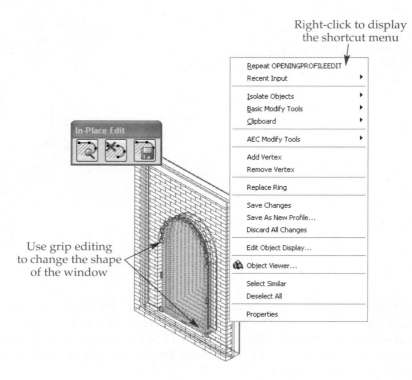

Right-click to display
the shortcut menu

Use grip editing
to change the shape
of the window

Adding Muntins to Windows

Many residential and some commercial buildings include muntins in the windows
as part of the design. Preconfigured muntins such as diamond or rectangular grid
patterns can be added to the Glazing component of a window. The Elevation and Model
representations include a tab named **Muntins**, as shown in **Figure 13-36.** This tab is
used to place muntin configurations within an individual window or window style.

To add muntins to a window style, select the window representative of the window
style to be changed, right-click, and pick the **Edit Window Style...** option. In the **Window
Style Properties** dialog box, pick the **Display Properties** tab, select the Model or Elevation
display representation, attach an override, and then pick the **Edit Display Properties**
button. This opens the **Display Properties** dialog box. Select the **Muntins** tab, and then
pick the **Add...** button to add a muntin configuration. The **Muntins Block** dialog box,
shown in **Figure 13-37,** is displayed. The following settings are available in this dialog box:

- **Name.** Enter a name for the muntin configuration. This name appears as a
  window component in the **Layer/Color/Linetype** tab, where display properties
  can be set.
- **Window Pane.** This area specifies where the muntins are added.
  - **Top.** This radio button adds the muntins to the top glazing pane.
  - **Other.** This radio button provides two options. The **All** option adds muntins
    to all the glazing panels. The **Single** option places the muntin on a specific
    glazing panel. Enter a number to add the muntins to a specific window-
    pane. Generally, for a window with multiple panes, number 1 is the bottom
    pane, and number 2 is the top pane.
- **Muntin.** This area controls the size of the muntins, how the grids clean up, and
  whether the muntin is a 2D or 3D object.
  - **Width.** This text box controls the width size of an individual muntin.
  - **Depth.** This text box controls the depth size of an individual muntin.

Figure 13-36.
The **Muntins** tab is used to place grid patterns within windows.

Muntins tab

Pick to add muntins

Pick to edit muntins

Pick to remove muntins

Muntin blocks applied to a window

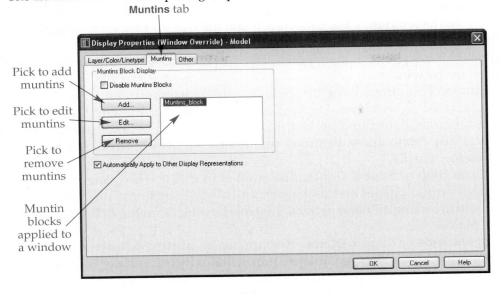

Different muntin patterns added to different types of windows

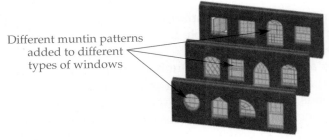

Figure 13-37.
The **Muntins Block** dialog box is used to add muntin configurations to windows.

Specify a name for the muntin block

Specify where the muntin will be added

Control the size of the muntins

Clean up the grid intersections and convert them to 3D

Specify the number of glass panels or distance from the sash

Use for half-round windows

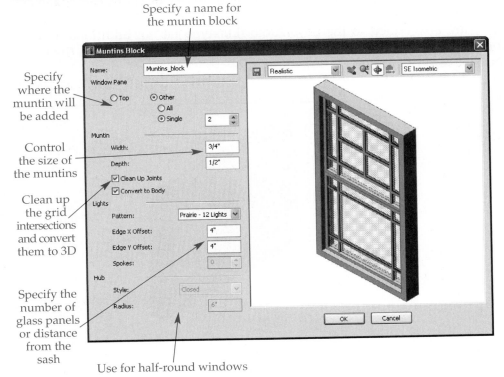

- **Clean Up Joints.** This option cleans up the joints between individual muntins.
- **Convert to Body.** This option converts the muntins into a 3D object embedded within the window. Check this box if you are using a rendering program to render the model.
- **Lights.** This area controls the muntin pattern and the number of lights (windowpanes) in the window.
  - **Pattern.** This drop-down list includes different muntin patterns that can be applied to windows. Depending on the shape of the window, such as rectangular, half-round, or Gothic, different muntin patterns are available. Typically, **Rectangular**, **Diamond**, and **Prairie** patterns are available for most window shapes.
  - **Lights High** or **Edge X Offset.** The number in this text box determines how many windowpanes are created vertically by adding horizontal muntins, or if you are using a **Prairie** pattern, controls how far from the sides the muntin is placed.
  - **Lights Wide** or **Edge Y Offset.** The number in this text box determines how many windowpanes are created horizontally by adding vertical muntins, or if using a **Prairie** pattern, controls how far from the top and bottom the muntin is placed.
  - **Spokes.** This option is available if a **Starburst** or **Sunburst** muntin pattern is added. These two patterns are available for half-round or quarter-round shaped windows only.
- **Hub.** This area becomes available when the **Sunburst** muntin pattern is used. The *hub* is where arched muntins begin. See **Figure 13-38**.
  - **Style.** This option opens or closes the hub in the muntin pattern.
  - **Radius.** This option specifies the inside radius of the **Sunburst** pattern.
- **Preview.** This area allows you to preview the muntin patterns added to the selected window.

After adding a muntin, pick the **OK** button to return to the **Muntins** tab. You can add additional muntin configurations by picking the **Add...** button again. If a window has multiple windowpanes, such as a double-hung or glider window, each pane can have its own muntin pattern applied. As the muntin configurations are added to the window, they are also added to the **Layer/Color/Linetype** tab for additional display control. You may want to make the muntin components the same color as the frame and sash or pick your own color.

Figure 13-38.
The hub of a half-round window using the **Sunburst** muntin pattern.

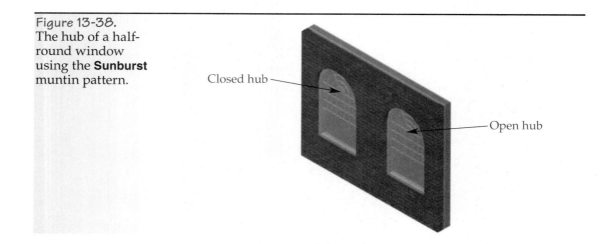

Closed hub

Open hub

Muntins cannot be added to window assemblies; however, if a door/ window assembly includes AEC windows, the AEC windows can have muntins applied.

You may want to add custom muntin configurations to the window objects that are not included in the **Muntins** tab. To do this, create 3D objects in the pattern desired, turn them into a block, and attach the block to the window through the **Other** tab.

Exercise 13-6   Complete the Exercise on the Student CD.

Anchoring a Window in a Wall

The same commands used to control where the door is in relation to a wall are available for windows. To reposition the window within the wall, select the window, right-click, and pick **Reposition Within Wall**.

After entering the option, you are prompted to select a position on the opening. You are then prompted to select a reference point. Pick the point on the wall component where the window is aligned. After picking the two points, you are prompted to enter the new distance between the selected points. You can also press [Enter] to place the window point on the point in the wall chosen.

Windows can also be repositioned along a wall using the **Reposition Along Wall** option. Select the window to be moved, right-click, and pick the **Reposition Along Wall** option. You are prompted to select the position on the opening. Pick the left, right, or center point of the window. You are then prompted to pick a point on the wall to be used as a reference point. After picking the two points, you are prompted to enter the new distance between the selected points. Type the distance between the two points where the window should be measured. As with Door objects, this function can also be performed by moving the window the specified distance to a new location.

Changing Window Properties

The **Properties** palette is used to control additional properties for a single window. When a window is selected, the **Properties** palette displays the properties available for modifying the window. See Figure 13-39. Refer to Chapter 5 to see details of properties available for Window objects.

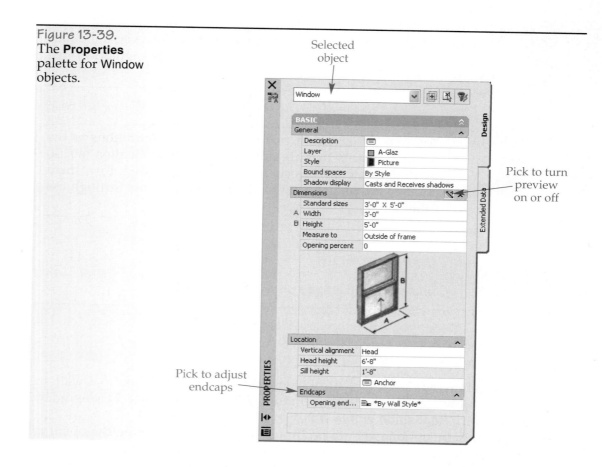

Figure 13-39.
The **Properties** palette for Window objects.

Selected object

Pick to turn preview on or off

Pick to adjust endcaps

Controlling Opening Objects

In addition to modifying an opening, there are a few tools that can be used to improve the appearance of Opening objects. Opening objects have properties similar to those of doors and windows and behave in a similar manner. The following discussion explains the tools available for modifying an AEC Opening object.

Opening Object Display

When an opening is added to a wall, it cuts a hole in a wall, similar to a door or window. The Opening object displays two lines through the hole in a Plan view to indicate that it is a void in the wall and is not filled with a door or window. The Model view opening displays an edge at the center of the hole. See **Figure 13-40.**

The display properties for Opening objects are controlled through the **Object Display** dialog box. To access the **Object Display** for AEC Opening objects, select the opening, right-click, and select **Edit Object Display...** from the shortcut menu. The **Object Display** dialog box shown in **Figure 13-41** is displayed. As you did for the Door and Window objects, select the **Display Properties** tab to modify the display properties.

AEC Opening objects include fewer display representations than doors or windows. To adjust an opening's display representation, select it from the display representation's drop-down list. See **Figure 13-41.** Openings can be controlled at the drawing default level or at the individual opening level only. Attach an override, and then select the **Edit Display Properties** button to modify the display properties. This opens the **Display Properties** dialog box shown in **Figure 13-42.** Depending on the display representation selected, a varying number of components are available in the **Layer/Color/Linetype** tab. In some offices, an Opening object in a Plan view is displayed as two hidden lines

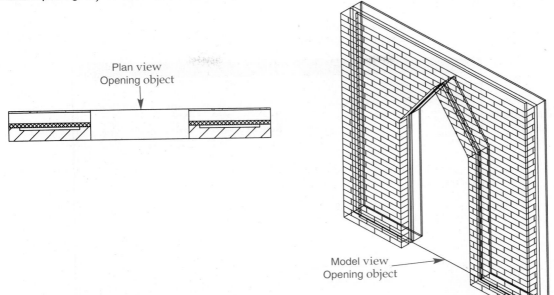

Figure 13-40.
AEC Opening objects in a Plan and Model view.

Plan view
Opening object

Model view
Opening object

Figure 13-41.
The **Object Display** dialog box is used to control the display properties of an Opening object.

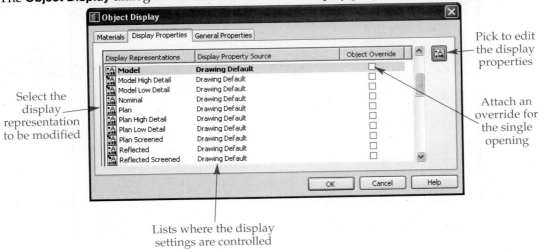

Select the display representation to be modified

Lists where the display settings are controlled

Pick to edit the display properties

Attach an override for the single opening

on each side of the wall. This is the Length Lines component in the Plan display representation. Change the linetype of the Length Lines component to a Hidden linetype.

The Plan display representation also includes a **Fill type** tab. See **Figure 13-43.** This tab controls how a Plan view Opening object appears in the drawing.

Attaching Custom Blocks to Openings

Openings can have custom blocks attached. The block must be attached at the system default level or at the individual object level. The Model and Plan representations include the **Other** tab, which is used to attach custom blocks.

An example of where blocks can be added to an opening is the mantle and firebox blocks illustrated in **Figure 13-44.** Make sure that the blocks are created on layer 0 using ByBlock colors, linetypes, lineweights, and plot styles. Then set the insertion

Figure 13-42.

The **Display Properties** dialog box for a Plan representation opening. Adjust the linetype of the openings if desired.

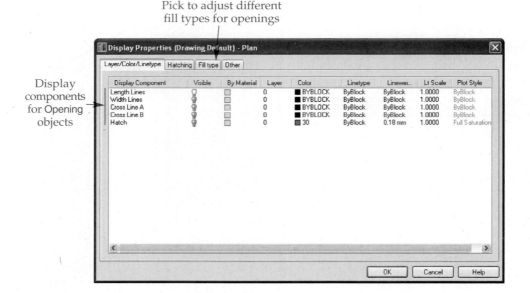

Figure 13-43.

Use the **Fill type** tab to adjust how the openings in a Plan view display.

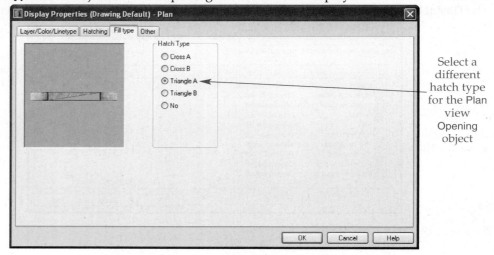

points appropriately. In **Figure 13-44**, 3D blocks and a 2D firebox block have been created. The 2D block is attached to the Plan display representation, and the 3D blocks are attached to the Model display representation.

To attach blocks to a single opening, select the Opening object, right-click, and pick the **Edit Object Display...** option. In the **Object Display** dialog box, pick the display representation to have blocks attached, assign an override, and then pick the **Edit Display Properties** button. This opens the **Display Properties** dialog box for the individual opening. Select the **Other** tab and then the **Add...** button to add a block. This displays the **Custom Block** dialog box shown in **Figure 13-45**. This dialog box is similar to the **Custom Block** dialog box for windows and doors. The difference is that blocks are attached only to the component. Add as many blocks as desired in as many display representations as needed. For the fireplace opening, blocks are attached to the Model and Plan representations.

Figure 13-44.
Blocks can be attached to a single Opening object or to all Opening objects.

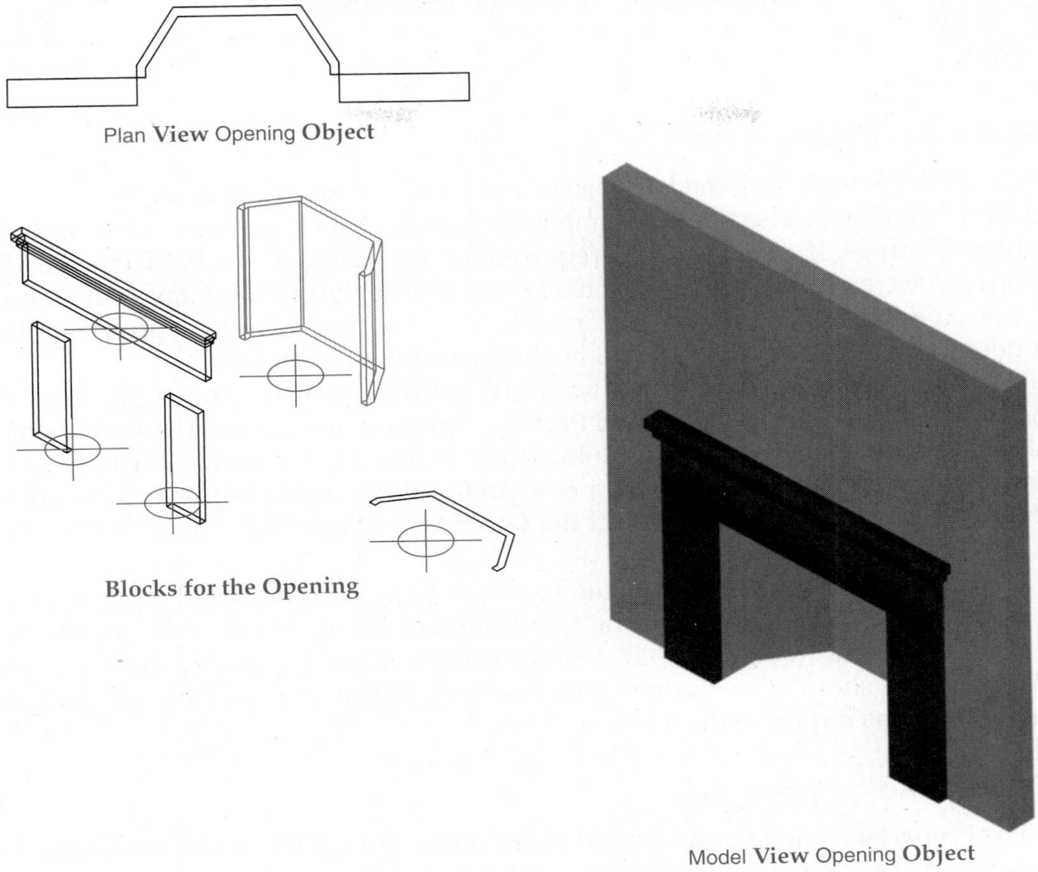

Plan **View** Opening **Object**

Blocks for the Opening

Model **View** Opening **Object**

Figure 13-45.
The **Custom Block** dialog box is used to attach custom blocks to Opening objects.

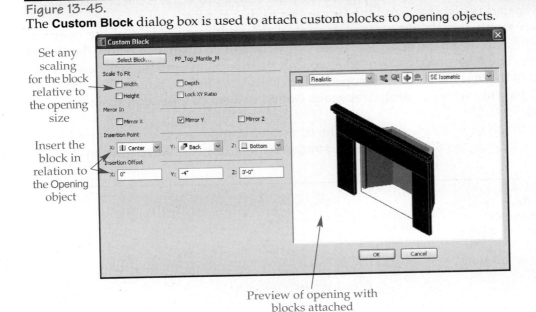

Set any scaling for the block relative to the opening size

Insert the block in relation to the Opening object

Preview of opening with blocks attached

Editing the Opening Profile

As with the Door and Window objects, the profile of an opening can be modified to a different shape. There are a number of default shapes available when initially creating openings. If a shape that is required for the design is not available, an AEC profile can be created and applied to an opening. Create the profile shape with a closed polyline, and then define it as an AEC profile. The insertion point for a profile applied to a door, window, or opening should be the centroid of the profile.

After defining the profile shape, it can be applied to an existing opening. Select the opening, right-click, and pick the **Add Profile...** option. This displays the **Add Opening Profile** worksheet shown in Figure 13-46. Select an AEC profile from the list or use the **Start from scratch...** option to create a new profile shape. If the profile is to be edited after applying it to the opening, select the **Continue Editing** check box. Pick **OK** when you are finished.

If a custom profile has been applied to an opening, it can be edited in place. Select the opening, right-click, and pick the **Edit Profile In Place** option. This displays the **In-Place Edit** toolbar in Figure 13-47. Use the grips to adjust the profile shape or right-click to use the shortcut menu for further editing. When you are finished, pick the **Save All Changes** button in the toolbar.

Using Opening Properties

The **Properties** palette provides additional tools for modifying AEC openings. See Figure 13-48. The **Shape** property assigns the selected opening(s) a different shape. If the **Custom** shape is selected, an AEC profile can be used by selecting the profile name from the **Profile** property that appears below the **Shape** property. A list of custom AEC profile shapes is displayed and can be applied to the opening.

This **Width** and **Height** properties control the width and height of the opening. Depending on the shape selected, a **Rise** property will be displayed below the **Height** property. The **Rise** property is used to control the rise of an opening, measured from the end of the vertical sides of the opening up to the top of the opening. This property is available only when an **Arch**, **Trapezoid**, **Gothic**, or **Peaked Pentagon** shape has been selected.

An illustration displaying what the dimension properties control is provided in this area. Picking the **Show/Hide the Illustration** button turns the illustration on or off.

Figure 13-46.
Use the **Add Opening Profile** worksheet to apply a custom AEC profile shape to an opening.

Select an AEC profile for use in the opening

Pick to continue editing after the profile is applied

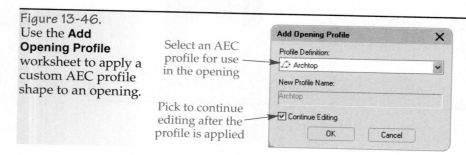

Figure 13-47.
Use the **Edit Profile In Place** option to edit the shape of an opening.

Right-click for additional editing options

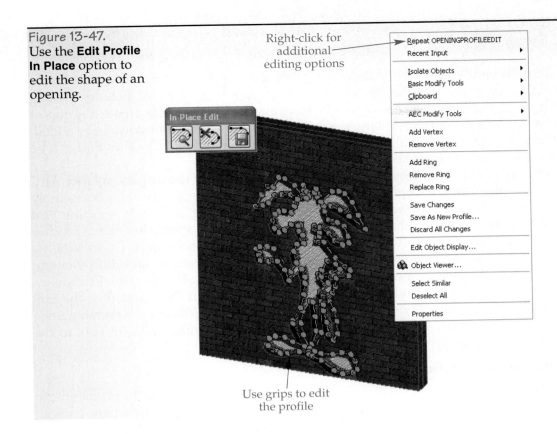

Use grips to edit the profile

Figure 13-48.
The **Properties** palette is used to modify the properties of an Opening object.

Object being modified

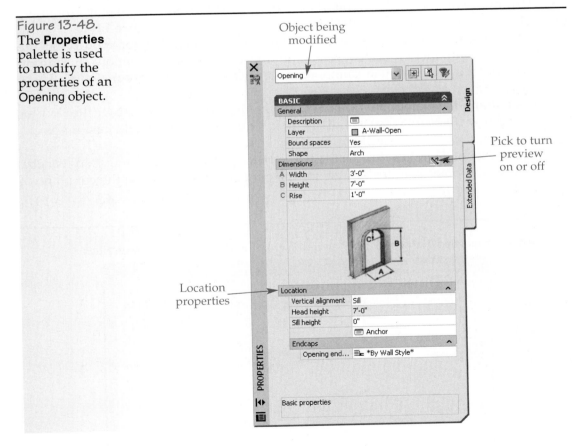

Pick to turn preview on or off

Location properties

Door/window assemblies contain a group of windows, or windows and doors, that act as one object. The Aec Model templates include one style that includes glazing panels only. The Standard door/window assembly is configured to create a group of windows that, when stretched larger, automatically cause more windows to be added. Additional window assemblies are included with Architectural Desktop and can be found in the **Content Browser**.

The display of door/window assemblies is controlled as the display of other AEC objects is controlled. The **Object Display** dialog box can be accessed for a single assembly by first selecting the door/window assembly, right-clicking, and then selecting **Edit Object Display...** from the shortcut menu. Select the **Display Properties** tab to modify the display properties for the selected Door/Window Assembly object. Door/window assemblies do not include an Elevation representation. Instead, an elevation viewing direction uses the Model representation. If you are modifying the display of the door/window assembly at the style level, pick the assembly, right-click, and pick the **Edit Door/Window Assembly Style...** option. This opens the **Door/Window Assembly Style Properties** dialog box. Pick the **Display Properties** tab to make adjustments to the display for the assembly style.

Adjusting the Plan Representation

There are a number of different Plan representations that can be used within different display configurations. The Plan display representations include many components that can be turned on or off. Select the Plan representation that is to be modified, attach the override, and pick the **Edit Display Properties** button. The **Display Properties** dialog box for the Plan representation is displayed, as shown in Figure 13-49.

A **Layer/Color/Linetype** tab and **Hatching** tab are included for modifying the display of the components and hatches within the door/window assembly. In addition to these two tabs, **Custom Plan Components** and **Cut Plane** tabs are included. These tabs are described as follows:

- **Custom Plan Components.** This tab is similar to the **Other** tab in the door or window **Display Properties** dialog box. This allows you to add custom blocks to infills, frames, or mullions in a Plan view.
- **Cut Plane.** This tab designates the cutting plane for Plan view Door/Window Assembly objects. Enter a value for the cut plane height or use the cut plane of the containing object.

Figure 13-49.
The **Display Properties** dialog box for Plan representation door/window assemblies.

Components for a Plan representation Door/Window Assembly object

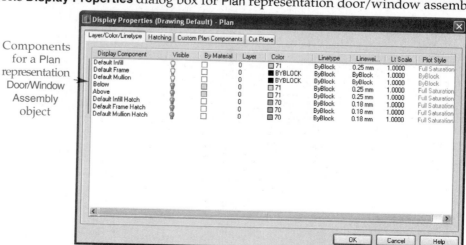

The Model representation is similar, but it includes fewer components and has only the **Layer/Color/ Linetype** and **Custom Model Components** tabs. The **Materials** tab in either the **Door/Window Assembly Style Properties** dialog box or the **Object Display** dialog box can be used to assign materials to the assembly components. The Standard door/window assembly, by default, does not assign materials to these components. You may decide to add materials to the components after inserting windows with materials into the drawing.

Exercise 13-8   *Complete the Exercise on the Student CD.*

Anchoring a Door/Window Assembly in a Wall

Anchors are another tool that can be used to control door/window assembly behavior. Door/Window Assembly objects contain anchoring tools for repositioning the assembly within the wall or along the wall, similar to the anchoring tools for doors or windows. Select a door/window assembly and right-click to access the **Reposition Within Wall** and the **Reposition Along Wall** options. Use these anchor tools to reposition the door/window assembly.

Select a door/window assembly, right-click, and pick **Wall Anchor** from the shortcut menu. Use this cascading menu's options to set the door/window assembly to a new wall. You can also remove the anchor between the assembly and the wall to make the door/window assembly an independent object. The **Flip X** and **Flip Y** options are used to flip the direction of the assembly within the wall.

Chapter 5 describes how to add doors, windows, door/window assemblies, and openings independent of walls. During the insertion process for one of these objects, instead of selecting a wall in which to insert the object, pressing [Enter] adds the object without attaching it to the wall. If you have added any of these objects without attaching it to a wall, you have the option to anchor the independent object to a wall. This is done by picking **Design > Walls > Anchor to Wall**.

> **Pull-Down Menu**
> Design
> > Walls
> > > Anchor to Wall

Once you have entered the command, you must enter whether you are attaching an object to a wall or freeing an object from a wall. Entering the **Attach object** option anchors the AEC object to the wall. Entering the **Free object** option releases the AEC object from the wall, making it an independent object.

PROFESSIONAL TIP

> Sometimes lines are used instead of Wall objects to represent walls. If a line is converted into an AEC wall, this **Anchor to Wall** option can be used to attach doors or windows to the newly converted wall.

Editing Cells

As indicated earlier, a door/window assembly is an object that represents windows, or windows and doors, that are grouped together to form one object. For example, when the Standard door/window assembly is first inserted into a wall, it contains a series of glazing panels. As the door/window assembly is made wider, through the **Properties** palette or by stretching the width grips, additional glazing panels (infill panels) are automatically added to the assembly, as shown in **Figure 13-50**.

Figure 13-50.
The Standard door/window assembly divides the object into a series of infill panels. As the object is stretched larger, additional infills are added to the assembly.

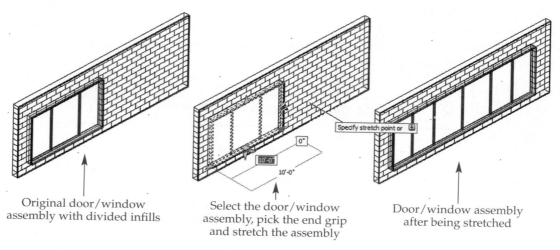

Original door/window assembly with divided infills

Select the door/window assembly, pick the end grip and stretch the assembly

Door/window assembly after being stretched

The infill panels are also called cells. An *infill panel* is the component of a curtain wall or door/window assembly that defines the "fill" between frames and mullions. A *mullion* is the vertical member of a sash, window, or door frame between openings in a multiple opening frame. These fills can be glazing (as in a door/window assembly), or glazing and spandrel components for an office building curtain wall. *Spandrels* are wall panels filling the space between the top of a window in one story and the sill of a window in the story above. A *curtain wall* is an exterior wall that provides no structural support. The cells of a door/window assembly can be modified to reflect a custom door/window assembly. Cells can be merged or filled with a different type of infill panel, such as a door or window. To modify the cells within a door/window assembly, the cell marker needs to be turned on.

A *cell marker* is a symbol that identifies an individual cell within a door/window assembly. To turn on the cell markers, select the door/window assembly, right-click, and pick **Infill** > **Show Markers** from the shortcut menu to turn on all the markers within the door/window assembly. This turns on a series of markers within each cell. Two cells can be merged together by applying an override. Pick the door/window assembly to highlight it, right-click, and select **Infill** > **Merge** from the shortcut menu. You are prompted to select cell **A**. Select the first cell marker to be merged, and then select the next cell marker to be added. This merges the two cells, forming one cell. See **Figure 13-51.**

Additional editing to a door/window assembly can be accomplished by substituting an infill panel, such as a door infill panel for a glazing panel infill, or changing the frame and mullion cross section shape to a custom profile shape. These editing operations are discussed in the next section.

To turn off the cell markers, select the door/window assembly, right-click, and pick **Infill** > **Hide Markers** from the shortcut menu. This turns off the editing cell markers.

Editing the Door/Window Assembly Profile

The shape of door/window assemblies can be modified with an AEC profile. As with the profiles used for Window and Opening objects, the profile shape should not include any internal rings unless a hole is to be placed in the door/window assembly. Also, use the centroid as the insertion point for the AEC profile shape. After the profile has been created, it can be applied to the door/window assembly. Select the Door/Window Assembly object, right-click, and pick the **Add Profile...** option from the shortcut

Figure 13-51.
Door/window assembly cells can be merged using the **Merge** option in the **Infill** shortcut menu.

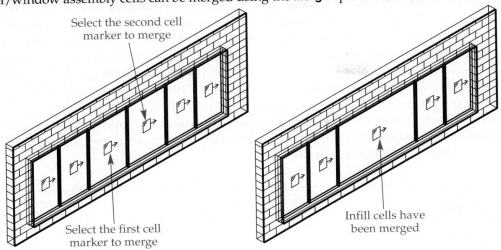

Select the second cell marker to merge

Select the first cell marker to merge

Infill cells have been merged

menu. This displays the **Add Door/Window Assembly Profile** worksheet. Select the profile from the **Profile Definition** drop-down list to apply the shape to the assembly. When you are finished, pick the **OK** button to have the shape applied.

If a profile has been applied to an assembly, the shape can be modified in place. Select the door/window assembly, right-click, and pick the **Edit Profile In Place** option. This displays the **In-Place Edit** toolbar and a profile shape with grip boxes. See **Figure 13-52.** Use the grips to modify the shape of the profile. Right-clicking with the profile selected displays a shortcut menu with additional editing options. When you are finished editing the profile, pick the **Save All Changes** button in the **In-Place Edit** toolbar to apply the changes.

Figure 13-52.
Use in-place editing to adjust the profile of a door/window assembly.

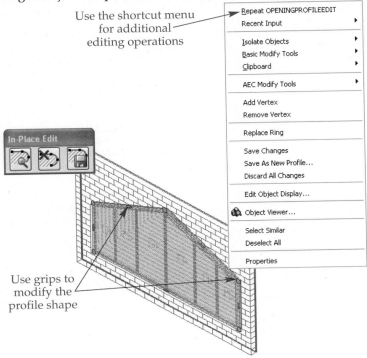

Use the shortcut menu for additional editing operations

Use grips to modify the profile shape

Door/Window Assembly Properties

When a door/window assembly is selected, the **Properties** palette displays the properties of the door/window assembly. See **Figure 13-53**. The properties in the **ADVANCED** header are available if any overrides to the door/window assembly have been made, such as merging infill panels, substituting infill panels, or changing the shape of a frame or mullion. Within this section is the **Overrides** property. Selecting the property displays the **Overrides** worksheet. See **Figure 13-54**. This worksheet indicates any overrides that have been applied to the selected door/window assembly. Overrides can be removed from the door/window assembly by right-clicking in the worksheet table and selecting **Remove** from the menu or by selecting the override and picking the **Remove** button in the worksheet.

Figure 13-53.
The **Properties** palette is used to manage the door/window assembly properties.

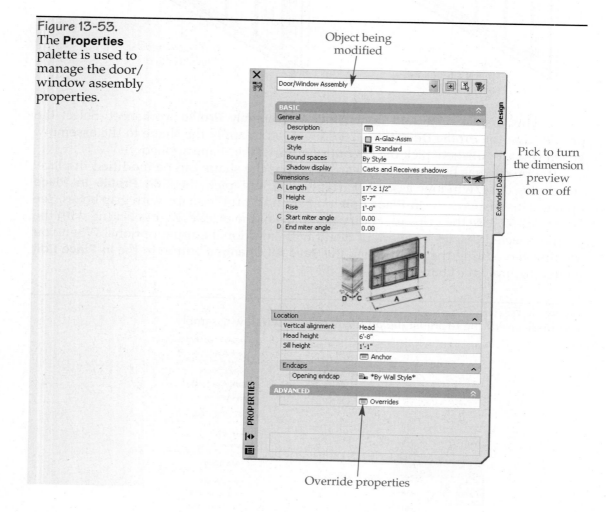

Object being modified

Pick to turn the dimension preview on or off

Override properties

Figure 13-54.
The **Overrides** worksheet displays any overrides applied to a door/window assembly.

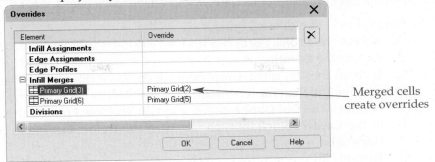

Merged cells
create overrides

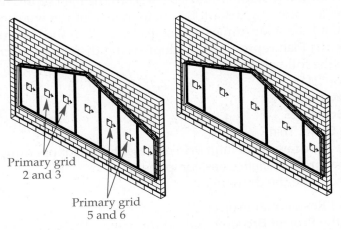

Primary grid
2 and 3

Primary grid
5 and 6

Chapter Test

Answer the following questions. Write your answers on a separate sheet of paper or complete the electronic chapter test on the Student CD.

1. Give the function of the Elevation representation for a Door object.
2. What does the Threshold Plan representation allow you to do?
3. Define *extrusion height*.
4. What happens to doors as they are added to walls?
5. What does the Sill Plan display representation control?
6. Name the components found in the Sill Plan representation.
7. Define *muntin*.
8. Define *hub*.
9. Briefly explain how windows are added automatically, as door/window assemblies are stretched.
10. Where are a number of additional door/window assemblies found in Architectural Desktop?
11. What is an *infill panel*?
12. Define *spandrels*.
13. Define *curtain wall*.
14. Give another name for infill panels.
15. What is a *cell marker*?

Chapter Projects

Use the techniques covered in this chapter to create the following drawings.

1. Single-Level Residential Project
   A. Access the **Project Browser** and set Residential-Project-01 current.
   B. Access the **Constructs** tab and open the Main Floor construct.
   C. Turn on the Threshold component for the front door in the Plan representation.
   D. Change the Plan representation for the wall at the style level. In the **Other** tab, uncheck the **Cut Door Frames** and **Cut Window Frames** check boxes.
   E. In the **Layer/Color/Linetype** tab, turn the **Below Cut Plane** component off for the walls.
   F. Turn off all the window frames by style in the Plan representation.
   G. Turn off the drawing default Sill components for the windows.
   H. Turn off all the door frames and stops by style in the Plan representation.
   I. Change the Plan representation door swing display properties for each door style to the following:
      a. **Color**: 211
      b. **Linetype**: Dot 2
      c. **LT Scale**: .25
      d. **Plot Style**: Thin
   J. Change the drawing default Plan representation for openings to use a Hidden2 linetype for the Length Lines component.
   K. Save and close the drawing.

2. Single-Level Residential Project
   A. Access the **Project Browser** and set Residential-Project-02 current.
   B. Access the **Constructs** tab and open the Main Floor construct.
   C. Turn on the Threshold component for the front door in the Plan representation.
   D. Change the Plan representation for the wall at the style level. In the **Other** tab, uncheck the **Cut Door Frames** and **Cut Window Frames** check boxes.
   E. In the **Layer/Color/Linetype** tab, turn the **Below Cut Plane** component off for the walls.
   F. Turn off all the drawing default window frames in the Plan representation.
   G. Turn off the drawing default Sill components for the windows.
   H. Add muntins to the window Model and Elevation representations.
   I. Turn off all the drawing default door frames and stops in the Plan representation.
   J. Change the Plan representation door swing display properties for each door style to the following:
      a. **Color**: 211
      b. **Linetype**: Dot 2
      c. **LT Scale**: .25
      d. **Plot Style**: Thin
   K. Change the drawing default Plan representation for openings to use a Hidden2 linetype for the Length Lines component.
   L. Save and close the drawing.

3. Two-Story Residential Project
   A. Access the **Project Browser** and set Residential-Project-03 current.
   B. Access the **Constructs** tab and open the Main Floor construct.
   C. Turn on the threshold for all exterior doors.
   D. Change the Plan representation door swing display properties at the default drawing level to the following:
      a. **Color**: 211
      b. **Linetype**: Dot 2
      c. **LT Scale**: .25
      d. **Plot Style**: Thin
   E. Modify the openings to display hidden length lines.
   F. Add **Prairie** muntins to all of the front windows in the Model and Elevation representations.
   G. Save and close the drawing.
   H. Access the **Project Browser** and set the Residential-Project-03 current.
   I. Access the **Constructs** tab and open the Upper Floor construct.
   J. Add **Prairie** muntins to the front windows in the Model and Elevation representations.
   K. Save and close the drawing.

4. Two-Story Residential Project
   A. Access the **Project Browser** and set Residential-Project-04 current.
   B. Access the **Constructs** tab and open the Main Floor construct.
   C. Change the default drawing wall Plan representation. In the **Other** tab, un-check the **Cut Door Frames** and **Cut Window Frames** check boxes.
   D. Turn off the drawing default window frames in the Plan representation.
   E. Turn off the drawing default door frames in the Plan representation.
   F. Change the default drawing Plan representation door swing display properties to the following:
      a. **Color**: 211
      b. **Linetype**: Dot 2
      c. **LT Scale**: .25
      d. **Plot Style**: Thin
   G. Add **Rectangular** muntins to all of the window Model and Elevation representations.
   H. Save and close the drawing.
   I. Access the **Project Browser** and set the Residential-Project-04 current.
   J. Access the **Constructs** tab and open the Upper Floor construct.
   K. Change the default drawing wall Plan representation. In the **Other** tab, un-check the **Cut Door Frames** and **Cut Window Frames** check boxes.
   L. Turn off the drawing default window frames in the Plan representation.
   M. Turn off the drawing default door frames in the Plan representation.
   N. Change the default drawing Plan representation door swing display proper-ties to the following:
      a. **Color**: 211
      b. **Linetype**: Dot 2
      c. **LT Scale**: .25
      d. **Plot Style**: Thin
   O. Add **Rectangular** muntins to all of the window Model and Elevation representations.
   P. Save and close the drawing.

5. Commercial Store Project
   A. Access the **Project Browser** and set Commercial-Project-05 current.
   B. Access the **Constructs** tab and open the Main Floor construct.
   C. Adjust the placement of the rear doors to be centered on the CMU component.
   D. Turn off the Stop component in all doors.
   E. Change the door endcaps to the Standard style.
   F. Adjust the placement of the door/window assemblies to be centered on the CMU component.
   G. Change the door/window assembly endcaps to Standard.
   H. Save and close the drawing.

6. Commercial Car Maintenance Shop Project
   A. Access the **Project Browser** and set Commercial-Project-06 current.
   B. Access the **Constructs** tab and open the Main Floor construct.
   C. Adjust the door/window assemblies to be centered on the CMU component.
   D. Change the endcaps for the door/window assemblies to the Standard endcap.
   E. Change the default drawing Plan representation door swing display properties to the following:
      a. **Color**: 211
      b. **Linetype**: Dot 2
      c. **LT Scale**: .25
      d. **Plot Style**: Thin
   F. Save and close the drawing.
   G. Access the **Project Browser** and set the Commercial-Project-06 current.
   H. Access the **Constructs** tab and open the Upper Floor construct.
   I. Adjust the door/window assemblies to be centered on the CMU component.
   J. Change the endcaps for the door/window assemblies to the Standard endcap.
   K. Save and close the drawing.

7. Governmental Fire Station
   A. Access the **Project Browser** and set Gvrmt-Project-07 current.
   B. Access the **Constructs** tab and open the Main Floor construct.
   C. Adjust the door/window assemblies to be centered on the CMU component.
   D. Change the endcaps for the door/window assemblies to the Standard endcap.
   E. Turn off the Swing component for the Model and Elevation representation garage doors.
   F. Create the profile in the figure. Add the profile to the garage door style.
   G. Change the default drawing Plan representation door swing display properties to the following:
      a. **Color**: 211
      b. **Linetype**: Dot 2
      c. **LT Scale**: .25
      d. **Plot Style**: Thin
   H. Save and close the drawing.

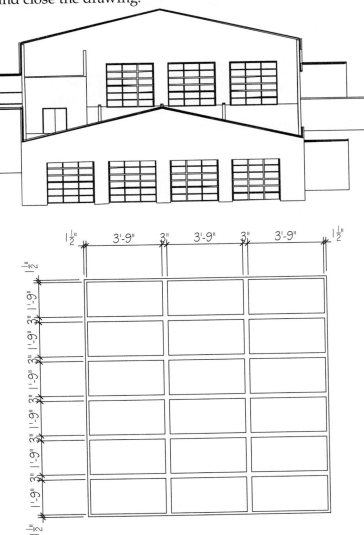

Drawing Courtesy 3D-DZYN

The home page of the Autodesk Student Engineering & Design Community Web site is www.students.autodesk.com. This Web site offers valuable information about industry and educational trends in the fields of architecture and design. This site allows students to network with other students and community experts. Students can also download free student editions of Autodesk software, take self-paced tutorials on the software, and search for jobs.

Creating Stairs and Railings

Learning Objectives

After completing this chapter, you will be able to do the following:
- ✓ Create and modify Stair objects.
- ✓ Adjust the edges of stairs.
- ✓ Change the stair display.
- ✓ Modify stair properties.
- ✓ Create and use stair styles.
- ✓ Create and modify Railing objects.
- ✓ Control the railing display.
- ✓ Modify railing properties.
- ✓ Create and modify railing styles.

An important object in the creation of a floor plan is the stair. The addition of a staircase is very important for any building with more than one floor. The addition of stairs also normally requires the use of railings. *Railings* are AEC objects that represent handrails or guardrails. This chapter covers Stair and Railing objects included in Architectural Desktop.

Creating Stair Objects

The Stair object in Architectural Desktop can be used to create several different types of stairs. Straight, *U*-shaped, *L*-shaped, angled, and curved stairs are all stair design options. The addition of stairs requires two basic sizes: the width of the stair runs and the floor-to-floor height. The floor-to-floor height determines the number of riser and treads used in the Stair object. The *riser* is the vertical portion of the stair between steps. Stair types and components are displayed in Figure 14-1.

Figure 14-1.
A sampling of the
stairs that can be
created using the
Stair object.

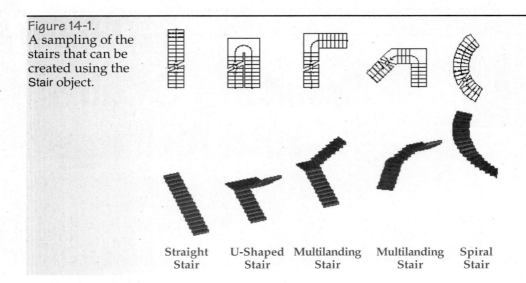

| Straight Stair | U-Shaped Stair | Multilanding Stair | Multilanding Stair | Spiral Stair |

Using Basic Stair Properties

Pull-Down Menu
Design
> Stairs
> Add Stair...
Tool Palette
Design
Stair

Stairs are displayed as 2D objects in a Top view and as 3D objects in a Model view. They can be added by picking the **Stair** tool in the **Design** tool palette or **Design** > **Stairs** > **Add Stair...** from the pull-down menu. Once the command has been entered, use the **Properties** palette to control the properties of the new stair. The **Properties** palette includes two sections to control the different properties of the new stair: **BASIC** and **ADVANCED**. See Figure 14-2. The **BASIC** section is divided into three categories: **General**, **Dimensions**, and **Location**. Depending on the shape of stair being created, different basic properties are available. The following basic properties are common for each stair shape. Additional shape-specific properties are described throughout the chapter.

Figure 14-2.
The **Properties** palette is used to set property values for new stairs.

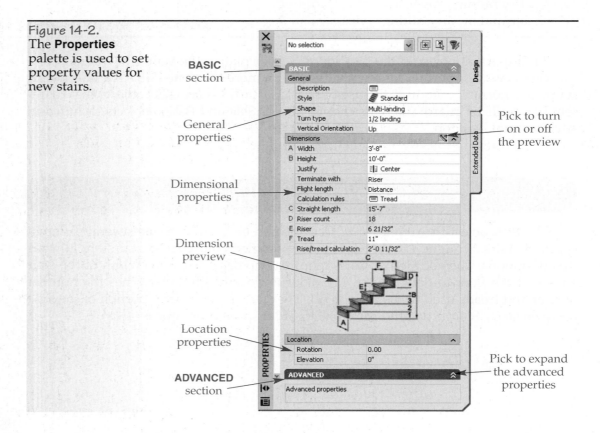

The General Category

The **General** category includes general properties for new stairs. Depending on the shape of stair selected, different properties are displayed here for editing. The properties available for all stair shapes are as follows:

- **Description.** Picking this property displays the **Description** worksheet. This worksheet can be used to provide a description of the new stair.
- **Style.** Selecting this property displays a list of stair styles available in the drawing. By default, only one style is available—Standard. Additional styles can be created or imported into the drawing from the **Content Browser.** This is discussed later in this chapter.
- **Shape.** The **Shape** property includes four different shapes of stairs that can be created: **U-shaped, Multi-landing, Spiral,** and **Straight.** Each shape includes its own set of properties. As a shape is selected, the **Properties** palette displays the properties applicable to the selected shape.
- **Vertical Orientation.** This property controls whether the stair is created up or down in elevation. When the **Up** option is selected, the first point picked for the stair determines the bottom starting riser. When the **Down** option is selected, the first point picked for the stair determines the last top riser.

The Dimensions Category

The **Dimensions** category includes dimensional properties for new stairs. Depending on the shape of stair selected, different properties are displayed here for editing. The properties common to all four shapes are described below:

- **Width.** Picking this property allows you to enter a value that controls the width of a stair run.
- **Height.** Enter a value in the text box for the overall height of the stair. This value reflects the floor-to-floor height and calculates the total number of risers needed to create the stairs.
- **Justify.** Selecting this property displays a drop-down list of three options: **Left, Center,** and **Right.** As a stair is drawn, points are selected to define the length of a stair run. These options control the side of the stair being drawn.
- **Terminate with.** Pick this property to display a list of options for controlling how the end of the stair is created. The options include **Riser, Tread,** and **Landing.** Selecting one of these options terminates the stair with one of the components. When you terminate a stair with a riser, the overall height of the stair is one tread thickness shorter than the height specified.
- **Calculation rules.** Selecting this property displays the **Calculation Rules** dialog box shown in **Figure 14-3.** The dialog box includes four different property values that can be adjusted. Depending on the combination of buttons selected along the right edge of the dialog box beside each property value, different property text boxes become available for editing. A button with a lightning bolt indicates the property is an automatic property. A button with an arrow indicates a user-defined property. When a property is available in the dialog box, it also becomes available in the **Properties** palette.
- **Straight length.** This property becomes available if the **Straight Length:** property is set to a user-defined value in the **Calculation Rules** dialog box. The **Straight length** property indicates the overall linear length of the stair. If the property is automatic, the calculated length of the stair is displayed based on code rules.
- **Riser count.** This property is available when the **Riser Count:** property is set to a user-defined value in the **Calculation Rules** dialog box. Based on code rules applied to the stair style and the overall height of the stair, the total number of risers required is entered here. The riser count can be changed, but if the number of risers does not meet the code rules, a warning box is displayed, indicating that the construction of the stair falls outside of the stair limits.

Figure 14-3.
The **Calculation Rules** dialog box is used to configure different settings for treads and risers within stairs.

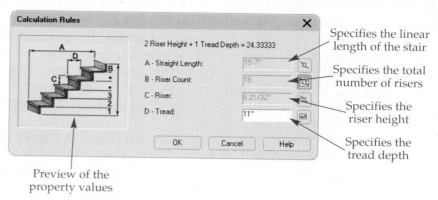

Specifies the linear length of the stair

Specifies the total number of risers

Specifies the riser height

Specifies the tread depth

Preview of the property values

- **Riser.** This property sets the height of the individual risers in the stair. The height and the code rules applied automatically calculate the height of the risers. The property can be made available by picking the button indicating that the **Riser:** property is user defined in the **Calculation Rules** dialog box.
- **Tread.** The **Tread** property is available, by default, for modification. Entering a value controls the depth of the treads in a stair. The tread depths are calculated through the code rules and the length of the stair run. The **Tread:** property can be set to an automatic property by changing the user-defined property to an automatic property in the **Calculation Rules** dialog box.
- **Rise/tread calculation.** This property is a read-only property and indicates the total height of two risers plus one tread depth.

The Location Category

The **Location** category includes location properties for new stairs. Both of the available properties are read-only values when you are initially creating a Stair object. The properties available for all stair shapes are as follows:

- **Rotation.** This property indicates the initial rotation angle of the stair in the Top view.
- **Elevation.** This property indicates the elevation at which the first riser of the stair is placed.

Once the stair properties have been determined, pick a point in the drawing where the first riser is to be located. After the first point has been picked, an outline of the stair is displayed, as shown in Figure 14-4. This outline indicates where the left and right boundaries of the stair will be placed in the drawing, as well as where the last riser will be placed. The last riser location varies, depending on the height specified. If a straight run of risers is being added to the drawing, pick an endpoint past the end of the outline. The stair is then displayed in the drawing. A riser count is also displayed beside the crosshairs. The numbers indicate the number of risers created, out of how many are required. After the first riser location has been picked, moving the crosshairs increases the number of risers being created. Once the total number of risers has been added, the last location picked with the crosshairs might indicate the end of the landing, if the **Terminate with** property was set to **Landing,** or the last riser or tread. After creating a Stair object, additional stairs can be placed in the drawing as necessary. Press [Enter] to end the command.

Figure 14-4.
To add a stair, select the first riser location, and then pick a point past the outline to add the stair.

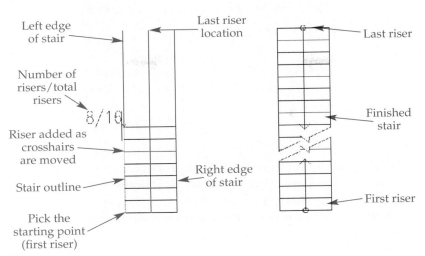

Creating a Straight Staircase

A straight staircase can be created by selecting the **Straight** option from the **Shape** property in the **Properties** palette. If different stair styles are loaded in the drawing, select a style from the **Style** property. Enter a width and height in the appropriate property text boxes. Decide if you want the stair to be created up or down, and enter your choice in the **Vertical Orientation** property. If the stair is created in the **Up** vertical orientation, decide how the stair will terminate in the **Terminate with** property.

Finally, decide the justification to be used when drawing the stair. The left justification allows you to choose the placement of the left edge of the staircase. The center justification allows you to choose the placement of the center of the staircase, and the right justification allows you to choose the placement of the right edge of the staircase. See **Figure 14-5**.

Once you are finished adjusting the properties for the straight staircase, pick a point in the drawing to establish the first riser location. The total number of risers required is displayed next to the crosshairs. As the crosshairs are stretched along the length of the stair, new risers are added to the stair and indicated in the riser numbers

Figure 14-5.
Selecting a justification determines the side of the stair used when selecting start points and endpoints for the stair.

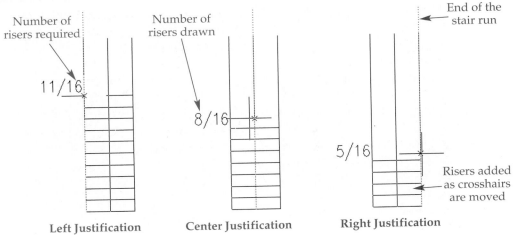

beside the crosshairs. Move the mouse beyond the last riser location in the stair outline and pick a point in the drawing. This picks the last point for the stair and creates the Stair object. Additional Stair objects can be created, or the command can be exited by pressing the [Enter] key.

Exercise 14-1

Complete the Exercise on the Student CD.

Creating a U-Shaped Staircase

Select the **U-shaped** option from the **Shape** property. Selecting this option displays two additional properties. These properties are as follows:

- **Turn type.** Picking this property displays a drop-down list of two options: **1/2 landing** and **1/2 turn**. The **1/2 landing** option places a landing between the two stair runs. The **1/2 turn** option does not add a landing; instead, the risers wind around the corner of the staircase. See **Figure 14-6**. When the **1/2 turn** option is selected, an additional property, known as the **Winder Style**, is available. The **Winder Style** property allows you to apply a style controlling how the risers wrap around the corner of the U-shaped stair. Winder styles are discussed later in the chapter. The default winder style is **Balanced**.
- **Horizontal Orientation.** Selecting this property displays two options: **Counterclockwise** and **Clockwise**. These options control the direction of the risers as the stair goes up or down in elevation.

The justification chosen, along with the **Clockwise** or **Counterclockwise** setting, affects how the stairs are drawn, as shown in **Figure 14-7**. The starting riser location is selected first, and then the ending riser location is selected. Architectural Desktop

Figure 14-6.
The U-shaped stair includes two types of turns: **1/2 landing** and **1/2 turn**. The **Counterclockwise** and **Clockwise** options of the **Horizontal Orientation** property control the direction the risers move up the stair.

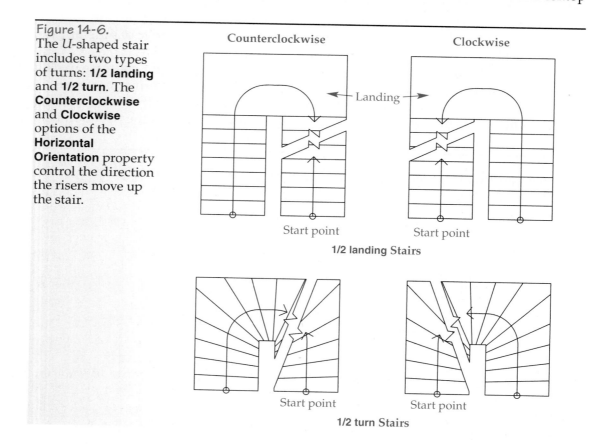

Architectural Desktop and Its Applications

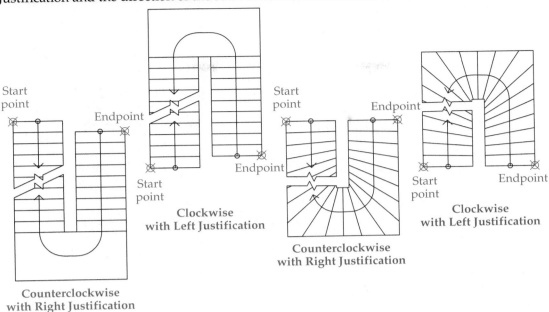

Start
point

Endpoint

Counterclockwise
with Right Justification

Start
point

Endpoint

Endpoint

Start
point

Clockwise
with Left Justification

Start
point

Endpoint

Endpoint

Counterclockwise
with Right Justification

Endpoint

Start
point

Clockwise
with Left Justification

determines how the rest of the stair is added. The height specified determines the number of risers. Architectural Desktop divides the total number of risers in half and creates two runs of stairs, side by side. If you specify the stair from the outside edge, be sure the endpoint selected allows enough room for both stair runs, plus a gap between the two runs. If you are creating the stair from the inside edge, make sure there is a gap between the starting and ending edges of the stair runs.

NOTE

> If the stair runs overlap each other, the stair is invalid. Architectural Desktop displays invalid stairs with a red circle and a slash.

Exercise
14-2   **Complete the Exercise on the Student CD.**

Creating a Multilanding Staircase

The multilanding stair is the most flexible of the stair shapes. Multilanding stairs can be used to create *L*-shaped stairs, *U*-shaped stairs, *S*-shaped stairs, straight stairs with landings, and angled stairs. See **Figure 14-8**. To draw a multilanding stair, select the **Multi-landing** option from the **Shape** property. Multilanding stairs include four options in the **Turn type** property: **1/2 landing**, **1/2 turn**, **1/4 landing**, and **1/4 turn**. The **1/2 landing** and **1/4 landing** options create a landing between stair runs. The **1/2 turn** and **1/4 turn** options create risers that wind around a corner of a stair.

When a multilanding stair is created, the first point picked establishes the first riser location. Once the first point has been selected, the stair outline appears, indicating where the last riser location is placed if a point is picked past the last riser. If a point is selected before the last riser outline, that point becomes the last point of the current stair run and the first point of a landing. Additional points picked create more stair runs and landings, as in **Figure 14-9**.

Figure 14-8.

A few examples of multilanding stairs. Note the difference between the **1/4 landing** and the **1/2 landing** options.

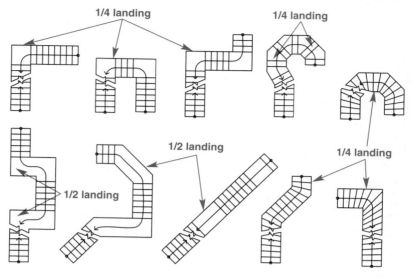

Figure 14-9.

Selecting points before the end of the stair outline establishes landings and new stair runs.

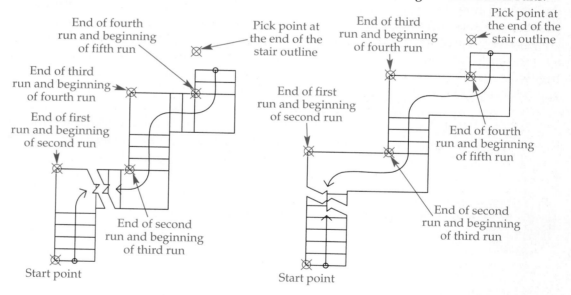

As points are picked for a multilanding stair, the stair outline constantly readjusts to reflect the new ending riser point. As long as points are selected before the outline of the last riser, new runs and landings are created. Selecting a point past the last riser outline creates the staircase.

After the start point has been selected, the next point establishes where the next run turns. Depending on how the crosshairs are moved and the stair justification, the landing adjusts by either adding or subtracting risers from the previous run. See **Figure 14-10.**

NOTE

If a point is selected that causes two runs or landings to overlap each other, the stair might be created with the defect symbol. Erase the stair and draw a new stair with new points. To create a straight stair with landings between the runs, use the **1/2 landing** option, selecting all the points defining flight start points and endpoints along the same line.

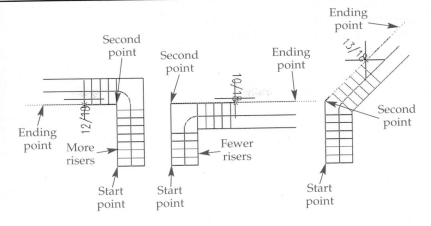

Figure 14-10. Establishing the next stair run. Depending on the location of the crosshairs when the next point is picked, risers are added or subtracted from the previous run.

Exercise 14-3   Complete the Exercise on the Student CD.

Creating a Curved Staircase

Select the **Spiral** option from the **Shape** property to create a curved staircase. When you are using the **Spiral** shape stair, new properties become available in the **Properties** palette. The **Arc constraint** property is located under the **Dimensions** subcategory and includes three options: **Free**, **Total degrees**, and **Degrees per tread**. Depending on the option chosen, additional properties become available under the **Dimensions** subcategory. The types of arc constraints are described as follows:

- The **Free** arc constraint uses the **Radius** text box property to create the curved stair. The radius for the curved stair is measured from the curve center point to the justification point, as shown in **Figure 14-11**. To create the curved stair using the **Free** arc constraint, pick a point in the drawing as the center point of the curve, and then pick a location for the starting riser. The **Clockwise** and **Counterclockwise** options determine the side of the run on which the starting riser is placed. If you would rather specify the radius of the curve directly in the drawing, the **Specify on screen** property can be set to **Yes**. Move the crosshairs from the center point of the stair to the justified edge of the stair to create the radius for the stair.
- The **Total degrees** arc constraint uses the **Arc angle** property. The angle specified establishes the total staircase size in degrees, measured from the starting riser to the ending riser, as shown in **Figure 14-11**. Select the center point for the stair and then the starting riser location.
- The **Degrees per tread** arc constraint also uses the **Arc angle** text box. The value entered in the text box becomes the total number of degrees for a single tread on the staircase. To add this type of constrained stair, pick the center point location in the drawing and then the starting location for the first riser. See **Figure 14-11**.

Exercise 14-4   Complete the Exercise on the Student CD.

Figure 14-11.
The **Spiral** stair shape creates curved staircases in the drawing. Three different arc constraints can be used to aid in the curved stair layout process.

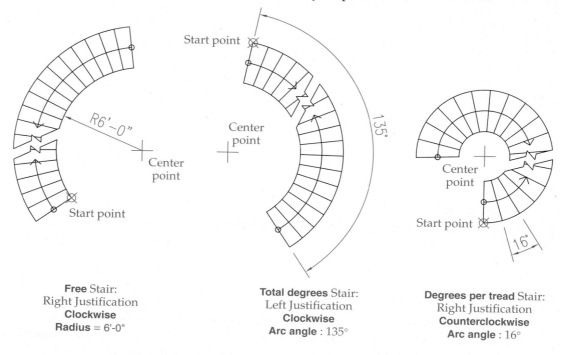

Free Stair:
Right Justification
Clockwise
Radius = 6'-0"

Total degrees Stair:
Left Justification
Clockwise
Arc angle : 135°

Degrees per tread Stair:
Right Justification
Counterclockwise
Arc angle : 16°

Adjusting the Edges of Stairs

The creation of stairs in Architectural Desktop provides you with some common types of stairs found in many buildings. The edges of standard stairs can also be modified in order to create a unique staircase. Stairs can be simply modified by stretching grip locations around the stair or modifying their edges to reflect a custom-shaped edge. See **Figure 14-12.**

Figure 14-12.
Grips can be used to adjust the stair runs and landings. Edges of stairs can also be projected to reflect a custom stair edge.

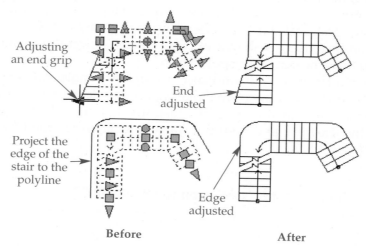

Adjusting an end grip

End adjusted

Project the edge of the stair to the polyline

Edge adjusted

Before

After

Using Grips to Adjust Stairs

When an AEC object is selected in a drawing without a command active, the object is highlighted with a series of colored symbols located at different vertex and midpoint locations. These boxes are known as grips, which are also discussed in Chapter 4 for use on Wall objects. When a staircase is selected, a number of grip points become available. See **Figure 14-13**. Depending on the type of stair created, different grip points are available for the stair.

Hovering over a grip point displays the name of the grip. Different grip points modify different parts of the stair. When a grip point is picked, that point allows stretching or repositioning, as shown in **Figure 14-14**.

Each type of stair includes some common grip points: **Graphics Path Location**, **Construction Line Location**, and **Edit Edges**. The **Graphics Path Location** grip adjusts the position of the walk path arrow within the stair. The *walk path* is a line with an arrow pointing up or down, showing the direction of the stairs. These lines are also called *path lines*. The **Construction Line Location** grip can be used with winder stairs to adjust the tread depth at the narrow portion of a tread. Picking the round, gray **Edit Edges** grips displays additional grips around the stairs, allowing you to modify the edges of the stairs. See **Figure 14-14**.

Pick any of the grips along the edges of the stair to modify the edges of the stair. Some of these grips include different options after the grip is selected. Use the [Ctrl] key to change the grip option. These grips can be identified when you are hovering over a grip and the tooltip indicates that the grip can be adjusted with the use of the [Ctrl] key. When you are finished editing the edges of a stair, pick the **Exit Edit Edges** grip in the center of the stair. This returns the stair to the initial grip boxes for additional editing.

Figure 14-13.
Picking a stair will yield grip boxes. Pick a grip box to edit the stair. Pick the **Edit Edges** grips to edit the edges of the stair.

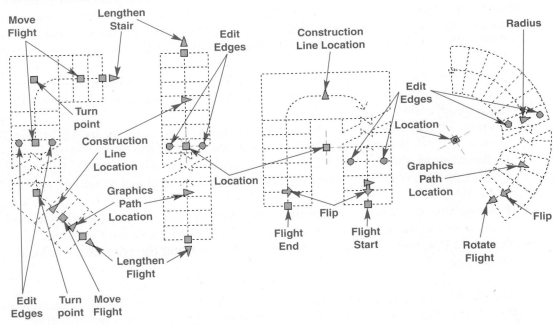

Chapter 14   Creating Stairs and Railings

Figure 14-14.
After picking the **Edit Edges** grip on a stair, additional grips are located around the edges of the stair to modify how the edges of a stair appear. Pick the **Exit Edit Edges** grip to return to the initial grip settings.

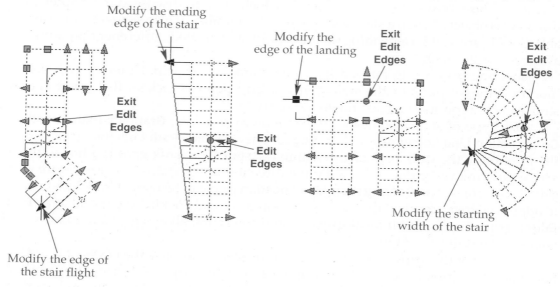

Projecting Stair Edges

In addition to grip editing, the edges of stairs can be adjusted by offsetting the stair edge or projecting the edge of the stair (the right or left side) to a polyline or another AEC object. To edit the edge of a stair, select the stair, right-click, and pick the **Customize Edge** shortcut menu. The shortcut menu includes five options: **Edit**, **Offset**, **Project**, **Remove Customization**, and **Generate Polyline**.

Pick an option to modify the edge of the stair. After an option has been entered, you are prompted to select the edge of a stair. Select the edge to be modified and follow the remaining prompts. The following options are available for modifying stair edges:

- **Edit.** Pick this option to display the edge grips around the stair for modifying the stair edges.
- **Offset.** This option offsets the selected edge the distance specified. A positive value offsets the stair edge away from the stair, and a negative value offsets the edge into the stair.
- **Project.** This option projects the selected edge to a polyline or an AEC object, such as a wall. Before projecting the edge, ensure that the geometry is drawn to the desired shape and in the correct location. See **Figure 14-15**. Enter the **Project** option, select the stair edge, and then pick the object to which you are projecting.
- **Remove Customization.** This option removes any edge or point modifications performed on the stair and returns the stair edges to the default settings.
- **Generate Polyline.** This option creates a polyline along the edge of the selected stair edge.

NOTE When the edge of a stair is projected, if the edges being projected intersect, the stair yields a default symbol. Remove the customization, adjust the object you are projecting to, and try projecting the edge again.

Figure 14-15.
Stair edges can
be projected to a
polyline or another
AEC object.

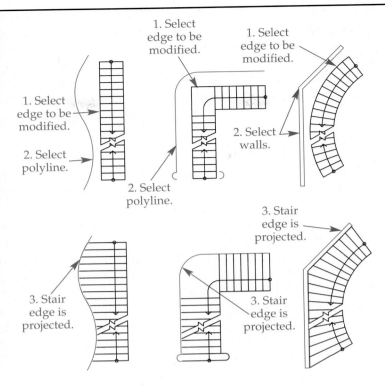

1. Select edge to be modified.

2. Select polyline.

1. Select edge to be modified.

2. Select polyline.

1. Select edge to be modified.

2. Select walls.

3. Stair edge is projected.

3. Stair edge is projected.

3. Stair edge is projected.

3. Stair edge is projected.

Exercise
14-5   **Complete the Exercise on the Student CD.**

Controlling the Stair Display

Throughout this text, display properties have been used to modify how Plan view objects appear, compared with the Model view objects. Stair objects also react to display property settings. Plan view stairs display a break line dividing the stair into a flight going up and a flight coming down. When the same stair is viewed in a Model view, the full stair is displayed as in **Figure 14-16**.

Figure 14-16.
The Plan view stair compared to the Model view stair.

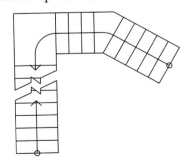

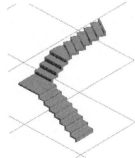

Plan **Representation Stair**   Model **Representation Stair**

To change the display of a single stair, select the Stair object, right-click, and pick **Edit Object Display...** from the shortcut menu. Stairs include a Model and Plan representation. Select a display representation to modify, apply the override, and select the **Edit Display Properties** button to make the modifications. If the display for the stair is to be set by the stair style, select the stair, right-click, pick the **Edit Stair Style...** option, and then pick the **Display Properties** tab. Pick a display representation to be modified, apply the style override, and then select the **Edit Display Properties** button to begin editing.

Adjusting Plan View Stairs

The **Display Properties (Stair Override) - Plan** dialog box includes three tabs: **Layer/Color/Linetype**, **Other**, and **Riser Numbering**. The **Layer/Color/Linetype** tab includes a list of components displayed when the stair is viewed in a Top view, as in Figure 14-17. Typical components include Riser, Nosing, Path, Outline, and Riser Numbers. These are represented as components going up and coming down the stair. The properties of these components can be readjusted as desired by picking the symbol or text associated in each column. For example, if you do not need to see the components coming down the stair, turn off all the down components.

The **Other** tab includes options for adjusting additional display options. See Figure 14-18. The **Cut Plane** area is used to specify the elevation at which the break line cuts through the stair, the distance between the break lines, and the angle of the break line.

Figure 14-17.
The **Layer/Color/Linetype** tab for Plan view stairs controls the display of the stair when viewed in a Top view.

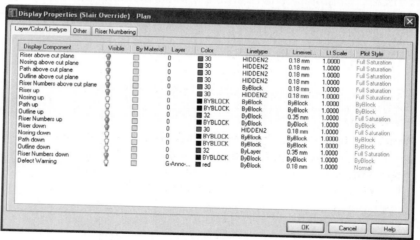

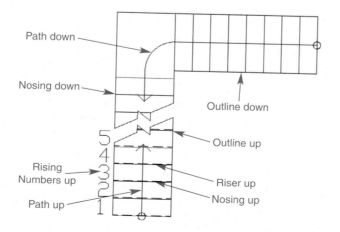

Figure 14-18.
The **Other** tab for Plan representation stairs contains additional options for controlling the display of Plan view stairs.

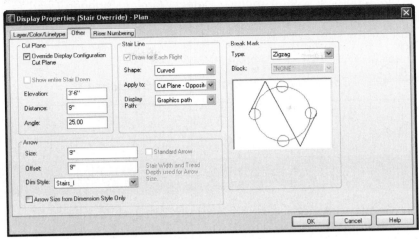

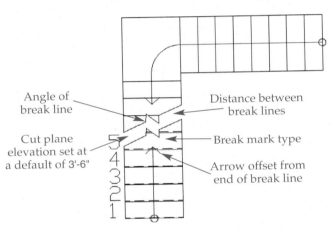

The **Stair Line** area controls how the path lines appear on the selected stair or stair style. The **Shape:** drop-down list creates a curved or straight path when the path line crosses over a landing. The **Apply to:** drop-down list applies the path in one of three ways. The **Entire Stair** option applies the path to the entire stair, which includes the stair flights on each side of the break line. The **Cut Plane - Parallel** option places a walk path in the "up" direction anywhere a flight of stairs appears in the stair. The **Cut Plane - Opposite** is the default, which places walk paths going up and coming down the flight of stairs.

The **Arrow** area controls how the arrowhead appears on the walk path. The size of the area and offset from the break line are controlled in this area. The **Dim Style:** drop-down list specifies the type of dimension style the walk path uses for display of the arrowheads. This defaults to the Stairs_I style, if you are using an Imperial template, and the AEC_Stair_M style, if you are using a Metric template. The **Break Mark** area specifies the type of break line used for the stairs. Custom blocks can be used for a break mark.

The **Riser Numbering** tab controls the display of riser numbers. If the riser numbers have been turned on in the **Layer/Color/Linetype** tab, numbers are placed beside each riser in the stair going up or coming down. The **Style** area controls the text style, alignment, orientation, and height used for the numbers, in model space units. The **Location** area is used to control the justification of the numbers to the left, center, or right side of the stair; where the numbers are placed along the length of the stair (**X Offset:**); and where the numbers are placed perpendicular to the stair (**Y Offset:**). The **First Riser Number:** text box is used to enter the number to be used for the first riser in the stair. If the last riser is to be numbered, select the **Number Final Riser** check box.

Adjusting Model View Stairs

The Model representation for stairs includes only the **Layer/Color/Linetype** tab. Components of a Model view stair include Defect Warning, Stringer, Tread, Landing, Riser, and Clearance. The properties can be set for each component and affect how the Model representation for the stair appears.

Exercise 14-6   Complete the Exercise on the Student CD.

Using Advanced Stair Properties

The stair display properties provide many options for controlling how stairs appear in the drawing. In addition to these commands, the **Properties** palette can be used to control individual settings and sizes for a selected stair. When you are editing an existing stair, properties such as the **Width**, **Height**, and **Style** can be modified, but properties such as the **Shape** and **Turn type** cannot be changed. The following discusses additional properties that can be modified to adjust a Stair object. These properties fall under the **ADVANCED** section in the **Properties** palette.

When a stair is first created or an existing stair is modified, the properties for the stair are divided into **BASIC** and **ADVANCED** properties. The **ADVANCED** properties section includes four categories: **Floor Settings**, **Flight Height**, **Interference**, and **Worksheets**. These categories are described in the following sections.

NOTE   Changing the width of the stair removes any edge customization on the Stair object. Altering the justification of the stair has no visual effect on the stair. Any future width changes are, however, measured from the new justification point.

The Floor Settings Category

The **Floor Settings** category includes dimensional properties to control how the stair works with the floor at the start point and endpoint of the stair run. The header includes a **Show/Hide the Illustration** button, which turns on or off the corresponding preview. See **Figure 14-19**.

- **Top offset.** This text box property is used to specify the thickness of the finished floor at the top floor of the stair.
- **Bottom offset.** Enter a value in the text box to specify the thickness of the finished floor at the bottom of the stair.

The Flight Height Category

Flight Height is used to change the limits for a run of stairs. A stair run can have no constraints applied as the default; or it can have limits applied, such as a minimum or maximum height or number of risers before a landing is added. The properties included in this area are as follows:

- **Minimum Limit type.** Initially this option is set to ***NONE***. This does not add a minimum limit to the stair. Picking the property offers three options: ***NONE***, **Risers**, and **Height**. If the **Risers** option is selected, the **Minimum risers** property is displayed in the **Properties** palette. If the **Height** option is selected, the **Minimum height** property becomes available.

Architectural Desktop and Its Applications

Figure 14-19.
The **ADVANCED** properties for a Stair object.

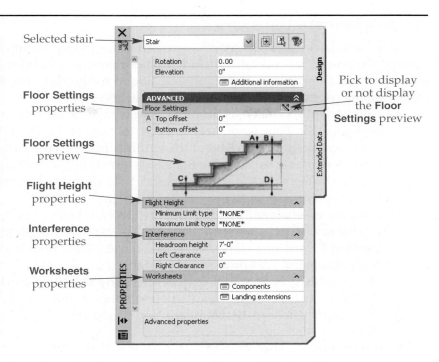

Selected stair

Floor Settings properties

Floor Settings preview

Flight Height properties

Interference properties

Worksheets properties

Pick to display or not display the **Floor Settings** preview

- **Minimum risers.** This property is available if **Risers** is selected in the **Minimum Limit type** property. Enter the minimum number of risers to be created before a landing is added to the stair.
- **Minimum height.** This property is displayed if **Height** is specified in the **Minimum Limit type** property. Enter a minimum height to be attained before a landing is added.
- **Maximum Limit type.** This property is set to ***NONE*** by default. Pick the property to display a drop-down list of three options: ***NONE***, **Risers**, and **Height**. If the **Risers** option is selected, the **Maximum risers** property is displayed in the **Properties** palette. If the **Height** option is selected, the **Maximum height** property becomes available.
  - **Maximum risers.** This property controls the maximum number of risers to be created before a landing is added.
  - **Maximum height.** Enter a height to be used as the maximum height a stair run can be before a landing is created.

The Interference Category

The **Interference** area allows the Stair object to become an interference condition when it crosses through a Wall or Slab object. Wall interferences were discussed in Chapter 12 of this text. When interfering a stair with a wall, use the subtract shrink-wrap option to cut a hole in the wall based on the stair interference properties applied. The properties available in this area control an invisible box around the stair used to cut a hole in a Wall or Slab object, as the stair crosses through the object.

- **Headroom height.** This text box property indicates a head clearance height from the top of the treads. Once the height crosses through an interfering object, the stair can be interfered with the object.
- **Left clearance.** This property controls any additional width to the left side of the stair that is cut out of the interfering object.
- **Right clearance.** This property controls any additional width to the right side of the stair that is cut out of the interfering object.

The Worksheets Category

This area includes worksheets containing additional parameters for a stair. By default, the properties available include **Components** and **Landing extensions**. If body modifiers and interference conditions are added to the stair, the **Body Modifiers** and **Interferences** properties are included in the section.

- **Components.** When this property is selected, the **Stair Components** worksheet is displayed. This worksheet is used to control the dimensions of the tread, riser, nosing, and thickness of the landing. Initially, the values in the worksheet are not available because the Standard stair style does not allow the values to be changed. The values in this worksheet are discussed in greater detail later in this chapter.

- **Landing extensions.** Picking this property displays the **Landing Extensions** worksheet. This worksheet controls dimensions applied to landings. The **Landing Extensions** worksheet is also not available with the Standard stair style.

- **Body Modifiers.** This property is available if a stair has body modifiers attached. Picking this property will display the **Body Modifiers** worksheet, where body modifiers can be detached or their operation and the stair component they are assigned to can be changed. Body modifiers are discussed later in this chapter.

- **Interferences.** This property is available if the Stair object includes interference conditions. Picking the property will display the **Interference Conditions** worksheet, where interference objects can be removed. Interference conditions are discussed later in this chapter.

Converting Linework into Stairs

In addition to creating stairs with the **Stair** tool and then modifying their grips and properties to create complex stairs, Stair objects can be created by converting 2D linework into a stair. To do this, first draw the desired shape of the stair and the layout of the risers using a series of polylines, lines, and arcs. See **Figure 14-20**.

After the stair has been laid out with 2D linework, right-click over the **Stair** tool on the **Design** tool palette and pick **Apply Tool Properties to > Linework**. This begins the conversion routine. When you are asked to pick the left and right sides, pick all the linework defining the edges of the stair. The edges can be a continuous polyline along one edge or a series of lines and arcs. When you are finished, press [Enter]. You will be asked to select user-defined left, right, and center stringer paths. Select the left side,

Figure 14-20.
Use polylines, lines, and arcs to lay out the shape of the stair and the risers for the stair.

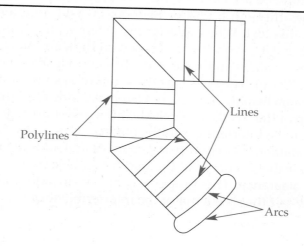

Polylines

Lines

Arcs

right side, and center stringer path of the stair for use as stair stringers or press [Enter]. When you are asked to select the first tread at the current level, select a polyline, a line, or an arc representing the first riser or tread. You will then be asked to select the remaining treads. Select the remaining polylines, lines, or arcs representing risers and treads.

After selecting the last tread, press the [Enter] key to end the selection process. This displays the **Convert to Stair** dialog shown in **Figure 14-21**. This dialog includes the following properties:

- **Stair Style.** Choose a stair style to be applied to the converted linework. Depending on the shape of the stair, you might get defect symbols on the converted stair. You can get the best results using the Standard stair style.
- **Height.** Specify the total (floor-to-floor) height for the stair.
- **Vertical Orientation.** This drop-down list allows you to specify whether the stair is created going up or down.
- **Terminate with.** Use this drop-down list to specify how the end of the stair is terminated. Options include **Riser**, **Tread**, and **Landing**.
- **Erase Layout Geometry.** Place a check mark in this box to erase the layout geometry.

When you are finished specifying the parameters, pick the **OK** button to finish the command. The final converted stair is displayed, as in **Figure 14-22**. Note that converted stairs have fewer properties that can be modified and include their own customizing commands.

Figure 14-21.
The **Convert to Stair** dialog is the final step in converting linework into a stair.

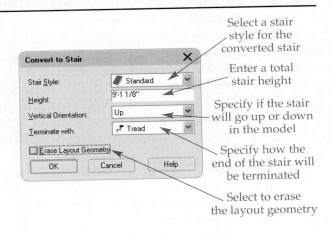

Select a stair style for the converted stair

Enter a total stair height

Specify if the stair will go up or down in the model

Specify how the end of the stair will be terminated

Select to erase the layout geometry

Figure 14-22.
The finished custom stair.

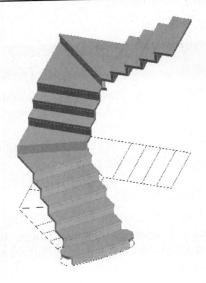

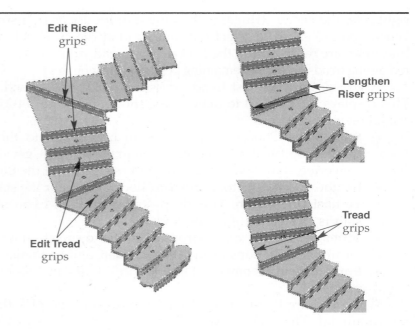

Figure 14-23.
The **Edit Tread/Riser** option is used to edit the individual treads and risers in a custom stair.

Edit Riser grips

Lengthen Riser grips

Tread grips

Edit Tread grips

Modifying Custom Stairs

Once a custom stair has been created, four modifying options are present in the shortcut menu: **Edit Tread/Riser**, **Match Tread/Riser**, **Toggle Tread/Landing**, and **Replace Stringer Path**. These options can be accessed by picking a custom Stair object, right-clicking, and picking the **Modify Custom Stair** shortcut menu. They are explained as follows:

- **Edit Tread/Riser.** Pick this option to turn on grips on the face of each riser and tread. Picking either the **Edit Tread** or **Edit Riser** grip displays grips that can be used to adjust the edges of the tread or riser. See **Figure 14-23**. Note that the **Edit Riser** grip is available only when you are editing a custom stair in a 3D modeling view.
- **Match Tread/Riser.** This option is used to match the shape of one of the existing treads or risers to another tread or riser in the custom stair.
- **Toggle Tread/Landing.** Pick this option to change a tread into a landing or a landing into a tread.
- **Replace Stringer Path.** This option is used to replace the stringer path line with a different path line.

Enhancing Stairs

Similar to Wall objects, Stair objects also can have interferences and body modifiers applied to enhance their look. For example, customizing the edge of a stair or converting linework into a stair might not create the desired shape, as in **Figure 14-24**. In situations such as customizing the beginning set of treads in a stair, a body modifier or interference might need to be applied.

Adding Body Modifiers

Stair objects, like Wall objects, can have other AEC objects applied to create custom shapes for the stair risers, treads, landings, and stringers. Most commonly, mass elements are used to model the desired "attachment" to the stair. Mass elements are discussed in Chapter 25. These elements are created by drawing them relative to their locations on the Stair object.

Architectural Desktop and Its Applications

Figure 14-24.

Body modifiers can
be applied to stairs to
create custom riser,
tread, landing, and
stringer shapes.

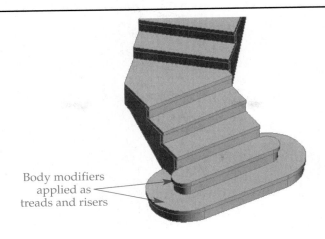

Body modifiers
applied as
treads and risers

After creating the 3D objects for use in the stair, select the Stair object, right-click, and pick **Body Modifiers** > **Add...** from the shortcut menu. Once the command has been entered, you are prompted to select the objects to apply as body modifiers. Select the objects to be added to the stair.

When you are selecting objects as the body modifiers, pick common items to be added as Tread, Riser, Landing, or Stringer components. For example, if you have multiple objects to be added to the stair as risers and treads, pick all the objects for the risers or treads. After selecting the items, press the [Enter] key. This displays the **Add Body Modifier** dialog box, shown in Figure 14-25. This dialog box includes the following settings:

- **Stair Component.** This drop-down menu includes three options: **Stringer**, **Tread**, and **Riser**. Select the type of object to convert.
- **Operation.** This drop-down list includes three options: **Additive**, **Subtractive**, and **Replace**. If the objects are to be added to the stair, select the **Additive** option. If you are subtracting the objects from the stair, select the **Subtractive** option. If the stair component selected is to be replaced, select the **Replace** option.
- **Description.** Use this area to enter a description for the objects being added as body modifiers.
- **Erase Selected Object(s).** Select this check box to erase the original objects being added as body modifiers.

NOTE

After adding objects that make up one type of stair component, use the command to add additional objects for other stair components.

Figure 14-25.
The **Add Body Modifier** dialog box is used to add body modifiers to a Stair object.

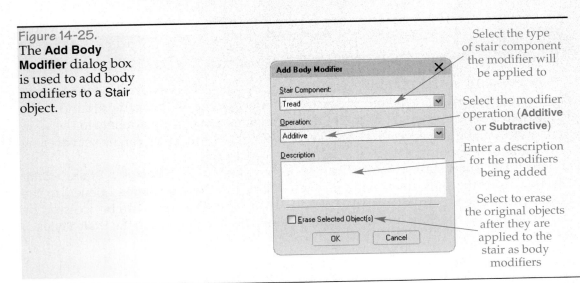

Select the type of stair component the modifier will be applied to

Select the modifier operation (**Additive** or **Subtractive**)

Enter a description for the modifiers being added

Select to erase the original objects after they are applied to the stair as body modifiers

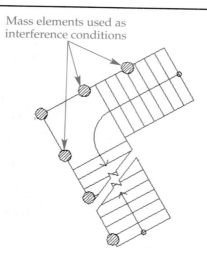

Figure 14-26.
Select a stair,
right-click, and
pick **Interference
Condition** > **Add** to
add interferences to
a stair.

Mass elements used as
interference conditions

Once body modifiers have been added to a stair, they can be edited in place. The body modifiers can also be removed from the stair, restoring the stair to the original shape. To edit the body modifiers in place, select the stair, right-click, and pick **Body Modifiers** > **Edit In Place**.

This displays the **In-Place Edit** toolbar. The original body modifier objects are also displayed, ready for modification. Use the grips around the object to make changes to the body modifier. Right-clicking with the body modifiers highlighted also displays a shortcut menu with editing options. When you are finished editing the body modifier, pick the **Save All Changes** button on the **In-Place Edit** toolbar to save the changes to the stair. To remove a body modifier and restore the stair shape, select the stair, right-click, and pick **Body Modifiers** > **Restore**.

Adding Interference Conditions

As with walls, objects can also be applied to a stair as interference conditions. Use any AEC object as an interference object. After drawing the object in the desired position in relation to the stair, select the stair, right-click, and pick **Interference Condition** > **Add**. You are prompted to select the AEC object to add. Select any AEC object to be added as an interference to the Stair object.

After selecting the objects, press the [Enter] key. This will subtract the objects from the stair. See Figure 14-26. If you need to remove the interfering objects, select the stair, right-click, and pick **Interference Condition** > **Remove**.

Creating and Modifying Stair Styles

When stairs are added to the drawing, one of the options available is the type or style of stair to be used. The stair style directly affects some of the settings found in the **Properties** palette and might or might not allow you to make adjustments to the stair. Stair styles can be customized in Architectural Desktop, and rules can be set covering how stair components are created.

To create a new stair style or edit an existing stair style, pick **Design** > **Stairs** > **Stair Styles...** from the pull-down menu. This displays the **Style Manager**, opened to the Stair Styles section, as in Figure 14-27. Alternatively, the stair styles can be accessed by right-clicking on the **Stair** tool in the **Design** tool palette and picking the **Stair Styles...** option.

Pull-Down Menu

Design
  > Stairs
    > Stair Styles...

The **Style Manager** is divided into two windowpanes. The left pane displays any drawings open in AutoCAD. The open folder icon in the left pane notes the current drawing. When you are accessing the **Stair Styles...** option, the Architectural Objects folder is opened to the Stair Styles section. An icon representing stair styles is displayed, as in Figure 14-27. Pick on top of this icon to display a list of stair styles in the right pane, or pick the + symbol beside the Stair Styles section icon to list the styles in the drawing in a tree view in the left pane. If only the Standard stair style is present, there is no + symbol available. When a style is selected in the left pane, the properties for the style are listed under tabs in the right pane.

New stair styles can be created by selecting the **New Style** button or highlighting the Stair Styles section icon, right-clicking, and then selecting **New** from the shortcut menu. Enter a new name for the stair style and press the [Enter] key. When a stair style is highlighted in the left pane, property tabs for the style can be accessed in the right pane to adjust different properties for the stair style. See Figure 14-27. The following eight tabs are available for creating the stair style:

- **General.** This tab is used to rename the style name and provide a description for the style. The **Notes...** button can be used to add design notes and specs or to attach an external file, such as a text document or spreadsheet, to the style. The **Property Sets...** button is used to attach a property set definition to the style. *Property set definitions* are data about an object that can be placed into a schedule. The creation and use of property set definitions is discussed in Chapter 23.

- **Design Rules.** This tab is used to establish rules governing riser and tread sizes for a stair. See Figure 14-28. The **Code Limits** area allows you to set maximum riser and tread dimensions for stairs at different slopes. The *slope* of the stairs is the total rise divided by the total run. The *total rise* of the stairs is the height between floors (or landings). The *total run* of the stairs is the horizontal distance from the first riser to the last riser. The length drawn and the total stair height specified when adding a stair to the drawing determine the slope of a stair. Architectural Desktop automatically determines the riser and tread sizes, based on the rules established in the **Code Limits** area. When a stair is modified through the **Properties** palette, the values set in this tab determine some settings, such as the number of risers, riser heights, and tread depths.

Figure 14-27.
The **Style Manager** opened to the Stair Styles section.

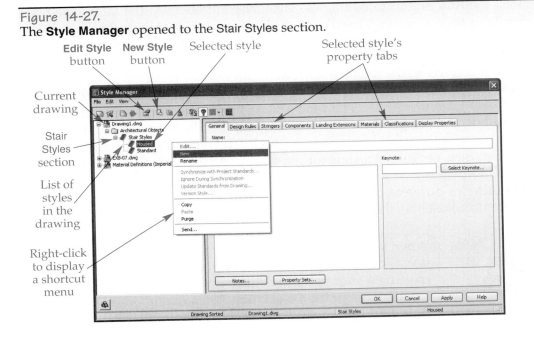

Figure 14-28.
The **Design Rules** tab establishes rules for riser and tread sizes.

The **Code Limits** area
specifies maximum heights and
depths at different stair slopes

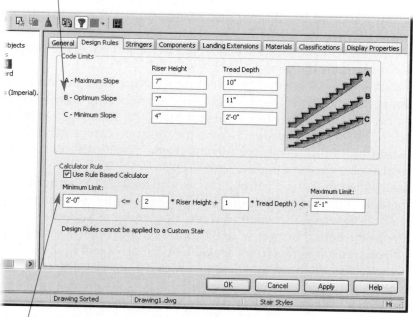

The **Calculator Rule** applies a
constraint to the stair slopes

The **Calculator Rule** area can be used to set constraints for the calculations required to create the proper number of risers as close as possible to the **Optimum Slope.** These rules can be adjusted as needed. In many cases, this calculator can be turned off for the style, which causes Architectural Desktop to create a stair based on the **Code Limits** area only.

- **Stringers.** This tab is used to construct a stair with stringers (as in a wood or metal stair), with a slab (as in a concrete stair), or as a ramp. See Figure 14-29. Pick the **Add** button to add a new stringer component to the table. The table includes several settings used to control how the stringer is created in the stair style. Picking values within the table makes different text boxes and drop-down lists available for modification.

As changes to the style are made in the **Stringers** tab, use the **Floating Viewer** button to display the **Viewer,** which displays the style as you are editing the different table properties. The **Type** and **Alignment** columns are used to determine how the stringers act under the risers and treads. After adding a stringer to the stair, pick the value for the stringer under the **Type** column to create Saddled, Housed, Slab, or Ramp stringers for the stair. Use the **Viewer** to review the differences. Depending on the type of stringer being added to the stair, the **Alignment** tab includes different positions for the stringer type. Pick any additional table values to adjust how the Stringer component looks in the stair style.

PROFESSIONAL TIP

When you are creating a Ramp style, set the **Design Rules** to use a low riser height and long tread depth. When you are creating a stair using the Ramp style, set the **Tread:** property to automatic in the **Calculation Rules** dialog box to avoid the stair defect symbol.

Architectural Desktop and Its Applications

Figure 14-29.

The **Stringers** tab creates a stair with stringers or as a slab or ramp.

Stringer components
in the stringer table

Viewer preview
window

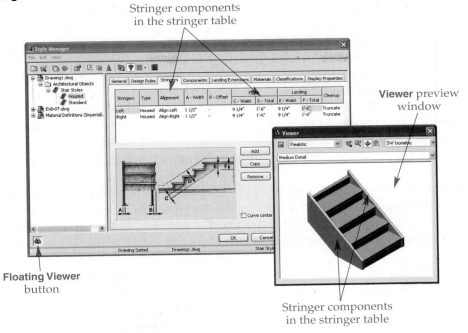

Floating Viewer
button

Stringer components
in the stringer table

- **Components.** This tab is used to specify sizes for risers and treads in a stair. See Figure 14-30. The **Allow Each Stair to Vary** check box in the upper-left corner allows you to adjust these same properties for an individual stair through the **Properties** palette. Use this tab to create treads and risers and adjust their sizes. Use the floating **Viewer** to check on the progress of the stair style.

Figure 14-30.
Use the **Components** tab to adjust the riser and tread sizes.

Select to be able to modify
the stair through the **Properties**
palette worksheets

Select to create
treads and risers

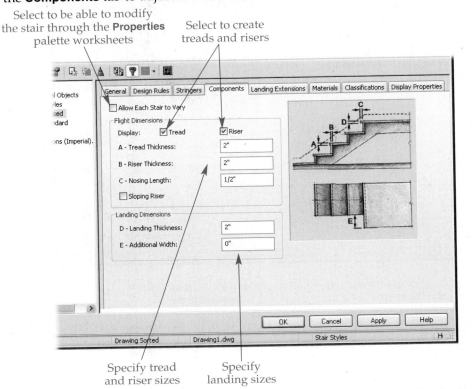

Specify tread
and riser sizes

Specify
landing sizes

- **Landing Extensions.** This tab includes the **Allow Each Stair to Vary** check box. Check this to be able to adjust landing extensions for individual stairs through the **Properties** palette. The **Extension Distances** area is used to control distances from the beginning of the landing to the last or first riser in a flight of stairs. The **Stringer Resolution** area includes a check box that merges stair flight stringers with stringers under a landing. See **Figure 14-31.**

  The **Extend Landings to Prevent Risers and Treads Sitting under Landings** option adjusts the landings when a riser or tread intersects the landing. Keep the value unchecked to create a flush landing. The other two text boxes, **Landing Length:** and **Landing Location:**, are used when creating an automatic landing, such as in a *U*-shaped or multilanding stair. The **Landing Length:** controls the size of the landing, and the **Landing Location:** controls the placement of the landing.

- **Materials.** This tab is used to apply materials to treads, risers, landings, and any Stringer components added in the **Stringers** tab. Select the component to have a material assigned, and then pick a material to assign from the **Material Definition** column. See **Figure 14-32.** The creation of materials is discussed in Chapter 15.

- **Classifications.** This tab is used to assign a classification definition to the stair style. *Classification definitions* are groups of named properties that can be assigned to an AEC object style. Classifications allow you to track objects by construction status, project phase, building element, vendor, or other criteria for use in schedules and legends.

Figure 14-31.

The **Landing Extensions** tab is used to control the placement of the riser in relation to a landing.

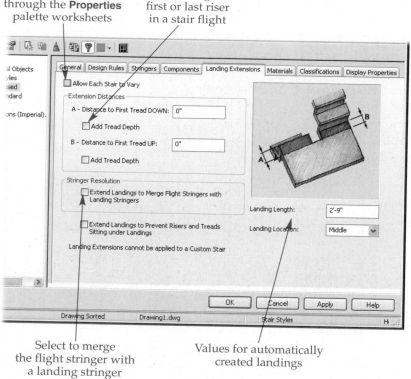

Architectural Desktop and Its Applications

Figure 14-32.
The **Materials** tab is used to assign a material to the different components within the stair style.

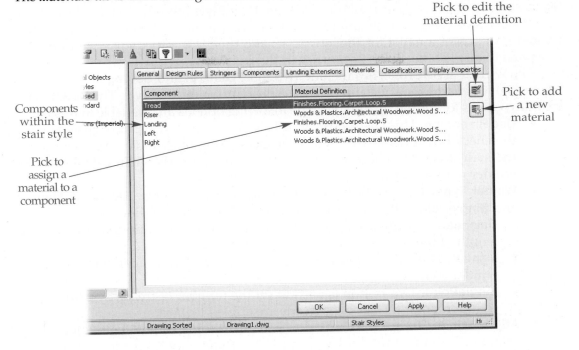

Pick to edit the
material definition

Components
within the
stair style

Pick to add
a new
material

Pick to
assign a
material to a
component

- **Display Properties.** This tab is used to control the display of the stair. Select the representation to be adjusted for the style, attach a **Style Override**, and then pick the **Edit Display Properties** button to open the **Display Properties** (*display property source*) - *display representation* dialog box. Make any adjustments to the display of Plan view, Model view, and Reflected view stairs. If the display settings are to be applied to all stairs of varying styles, do not apply a **Style Override**, as the drawing default display controls all stair displays globally, unless a style or object override has been applied.

When you have finished setting the rules and configuring the components of the stair, pick the **OK** button to accept the modifications to the style and return to the **Style Manager**. Pick the **OK** button to exit and accept the changes to the style. The new stair style is now ready for use in the drawing. Additional stair styles are included in Architectural Desktop and can be accessed from the **Content Browser** catalogs. Refer to Appendix B for accessing the **Content Browser** and additional tools and styles.

Exercise 14-7   Complete the Exercise on the Student CD.

Working with Winder Stairs

The 1/4-turn and 1/2-turn stair types create risers that wind around the corner of a stair. When you are creating winder stairs, a winder style is applied to the stair, in addition to the stair style. The winder style controls how the winders are created at a corner of the stair. By default, when a winder stair is first created, the Balanced winder stair is available. This style causes the winders to turn continuously along the length of a stair. Additional winder styles can be created and applied to winder stairs.

To create additional winder styles, pick **Design** > **Stairs** > **Stair Winder Styles...** from the pull-down menu. This displays the **Style Manager**, opened to the Stair Winder Styles section, shown in **Figure 14-33**. Pick the **New Style** button, or right-click on the Stair Winder Styles section icon and select **New** from the shortcut menu to create a new winder style. Enter a name for the new style, and then select the new style in the left tree pane to display the style's properties in the right pane.

The winder style properties include two tabs: **General** and **Settings**. The **General** tab is used to rename the style and provide a description for the style. The **Settings** tab includes options for setting up the style. The following options are available in this tab:

- **Use Riser Line.** This check box controls how the tread turns are adjusted. Select the check box if risers are used when calculating the winder within a turn of the stair. Keep the check box unchecked to use treads when calculating the winder within a turn.
- **Winder Type.** This drop-down list includes three options: **Balanced, Manual,** and **SinglePoint**. These options are further described as follows:
  - **Balanced.** Use this option if the treads will turn continuously along the length of the stair.
  - **Manual.** This option allows you to control each tread separately within the winder stair.
  - **SinglePoint.** This option is used to set the number of treads in a turn and a common point the risers or treads are angled toward.
- **Adjust Winder Turn.** This check box is available only if the **SinglePoint** type is selected. Selecting this check box causes the **Number of Treads in Turn:** text box to become available.
- **Number of Treads in Turn.** This text box allows you to specify the number of treads to be created in a stair turn.

Figure 14-33.
The Stair Winder Styles section is used to create winder styles.

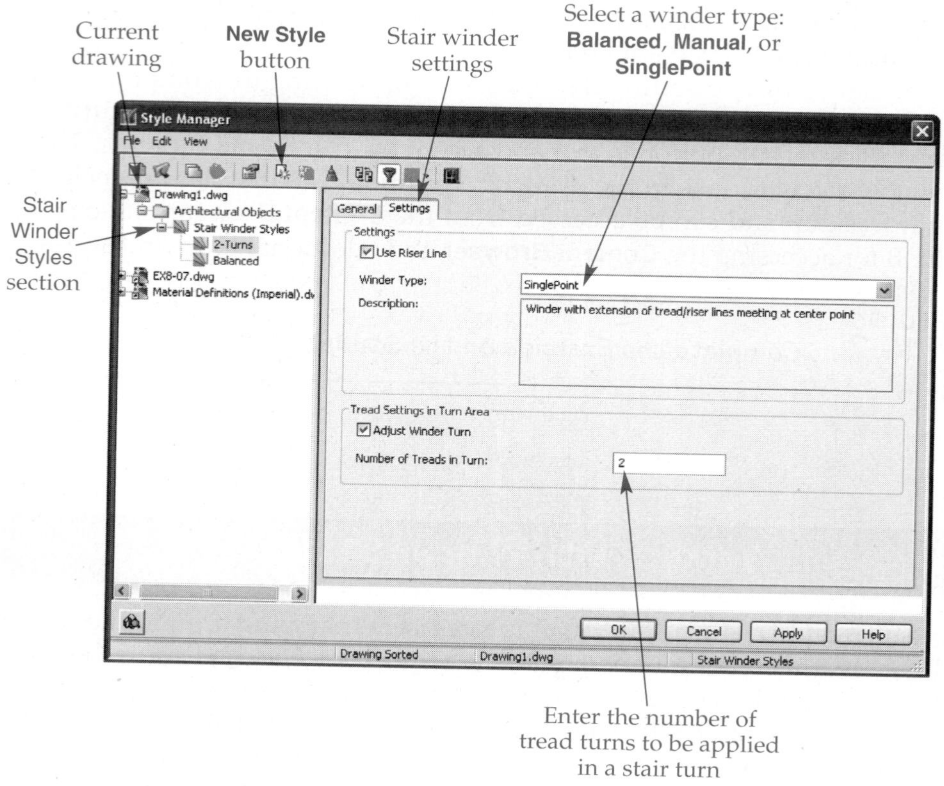

Current drawing

New Style button

Stair winder settings

Select a winder type: **Balanced, Manual,** or **SinglePoint**

Stair Winder Styles section

Enter the number of tread turns to be applied in a stair turn

You might decide to create one of each type of winder style or a few different **SinglePoint** styles with a different number of treads in the turn. After the winder styles are created, they can be applied to existing 1/4-turn or 1/2-turn stairs through the **Properties** palette or assigned to new turn-type stairs added to the drawing.

Creating Railing Objects

As you learned earlier, railings are AEC objects that represent handrails or guardrails. Railings can be freestanding around balconies or decks, added to a flight of stairs, or added to all the flights and landings of a Stair object. They can be added to the drawing by picking the **Railing** tool in the **Design** tool palette; picking **Design** > **Railings** > **Add Railing...** from the pull-down menu; or selecting a stair, right-clicking, and picking the **Add Railing** option. Once the option is entered, the **Properties** palette can be used to specify how the railing will be created.

As with the Stair object, the **Properties** palette includes properties for configuring how the Railing object will be constructed. The **Properties** palette for railings includes a **BASIC** properties section with three categories. See **Figure 14-34**. The railing properties in the following sections are used to configure new Railing objects.

Pull-Down Menu
Design
  > Railings
    > Add Railing...
Tool Palette
  Design

Railing

The General Category

The **General** category includes general properties for new railings. There are two properties available for railing creation: **Description** and **Style**. Picking the **Description** property displays the **Description** worksheet. This worksheet is used to provide a description of the new railing. Selecting the **Style** property displays a list of railing styles available in the drawing. By default, only one style is available—Standard. Additional railing styles can be created or imported into the drawing. This is discussed later in this chapter.

Figure 14-34.
The **Properties** palette for railing styles includes a few **BASIC** railing properties.

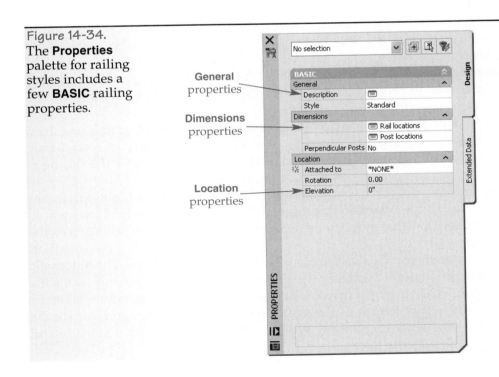

The Dimensions Category

The **Dimensions** category includes three properties for new railings: **Rail locations**, **Post locations**, and **Perpendicular Posts**. Picking the **Rail locations** property displays the **Rail Locations** worksheet. By default, the worksheet properties are not available with the Standard style. The properties in the worksheet are set by the railing style and can be modified in the style. This is discussed later in the chapter. Picking the **Post locations** property displays the **Post Locations** worksheet. Similar to the **Railing Locations** worksheet, the properties are grayed out, as they are set by the Standard style. These properties can be turned on by modifying the railing style. This is discussed later in the chapter. The **Perpendicular Posts** property is a **Yes** or **No** value and controls whether posts along a stair are perpendicular to the slope of the stair run or not.

The Location Category

The **Location** category includes properties controlling where railings are located. The **Attached to** property determines whether the railing is a stand-alone rail or if it is attached to a stair. Depending on the option selected, additional properties are available for controlling the railing location.

- **Attached to.** Picking this property provides a drop-down list of three options: ***NONE***, **Stair**, and **Stair flight**.
  - ***NONE*.** This option allows you to draw a railing on a flat surface for use as a deck or balcony railing. When this option is selected, the **Rotation** and **Elevation** properties are available for configuration. Pick points in the drawing to designate the start point of the railing, and then pick additional points for the turns and endpoint of the railing.
  - **Stair.** This option attaches the railing to the full length of a stair. When a landing is encountered, the railing is run along the landing edge and then up the next stair flight. When this property is selected, the **Side offset** and **Automatic placement** properties are available. To add the rail to a stair, pick the side of the stair where the railing will be added.
  - **Stair flight.** This option is similar to the **Stair** option, except it attaches a railing to a single flight or run within a stair. The railing is not added around a landing, as with the **Stair** option. Picking this property also displays the **Side offset** property.
- **Rotation.** This property is displayed when the ***NONE*** option has been selected in the **Attached to** property. After the railing is created, this property can be modified to rotate the railing orientation.
- **Elevation.** This property is also available when the ***NONE*** option has been selected in the **Attached to** property. The **Elevation** property is a read-only value, as the railing is initially drawn in the 0″ elevation. After the railing is drawn, the elevation can be modified through this property.
- **Side offset.** This property is available when the **Stair** or **Stair flight** option has been selected in the **Attached to** property. Picking this property allows you to enter a numerical value that determines a distance to offset the railing from the edge of the stair.
- **Automatic placement.** This property includes **Yes** and **No** options. The **Automatic placement** property is available when you are attaching a railing using the **Stair** option. When a side of the stair has been selected, the **Yes** option adds the railing to the entire length of the stair. The **No** option allows you to pick the side of the stair where the railing will be added and then pick a starting and ending location for the railing.

Figure 14-35.
The ***NONE*** option is used to create a free-standing Railing object for use around balconies and decks. The **Stair** and **Stair Flight** options are used to add railings to an entire stair or a flight of stairs.

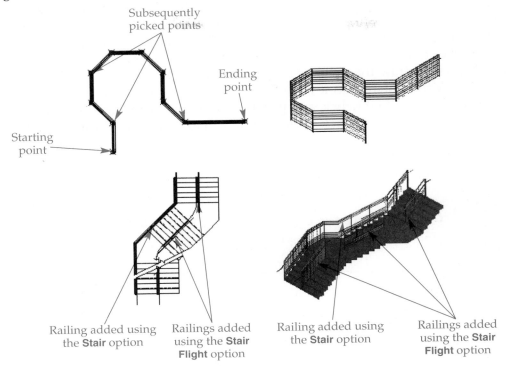

Subsequently picked points

Ending point

Starting point

Railing added using the **Stair** option   Railings added using the **Stair Flight** option   Railing added using the **Stair** option   Railings added using the **Stair Flight** option

Once the options have been selected, the railing can be added to the drawing. If the ***NONE*** option has been selected from the **Attached to** property drop-down list, the railing can be added to the drawing as a freestanding railing. Pick a location for the start point of the railing. As more points are picked, the railing is added to the drawing. Once the endpoint of the railing has been selected, press the [Enter] key to end the command. See **Figure 14-35.**

If a railing is to be added to a stair, use the **Stair** or **Stair Flight** options in the **Attached to** property. Once the railing values have been set, you are prompted to select a stair. Select the side of the stair where you want to place the railing. See **Figure 14-35.**

Polylines also can be converted into railings. The polyline can be composed of straight segments, curved segments, or both. This is the only way to create a curved railing, except for railings attached to a spiral stair or a stair that has had its edge modified. First, draw the polyline in the desired shape. Next, right-click over the **Railing** tool in the **Design** tool palette and pick **Apply Tool Properties to > Polyline**. You are prompted to Select polylines. Pick the polyline to be converted into a Railing object. After picking the polyline, you are asked if you want to Erase layout geometry? [Yes/No]. Type Y to erase the polyline or N to retain the original polyline. After answering this prompt, the polyline shape is converted into a Railing object.

Anchoring Railing Objects

There might be instances when a nonlinear railing is required for the design that must be attached to a stair or other AEC object, such as a slanted wall. By default, when a railing is attached to a stair, it follows the outer edge or path of the stair. If a custom-shaped railing is desired, the railing can be converted from a polyline shape and then anchored to the stair.

In a Plan view, draw the polyline shape along the stair where the railing will be placed. Convert the polyline to a railing. This creates a freestanding railing. Next, select the Railing object, right-click, and pick **Railing Anchor** > **Anchor To Stair**. You are then prompted to Select Stair. Pick the stair to which to anchor the railing. The railing retains its shape and is attached to the stair, as in Figure 14-36. The **Railing Anchor** shortcut menu also includes an **Anchor To Object** command. Using this option, the Railing object can be anchored to other AEC objects, such as slabs, walls, and spaces.

Exercise
14-8   **Complete the Exercise on the Student CD.**

Figure 14-36.
Stand-alone Railing objects can be anchored to a Stair object.

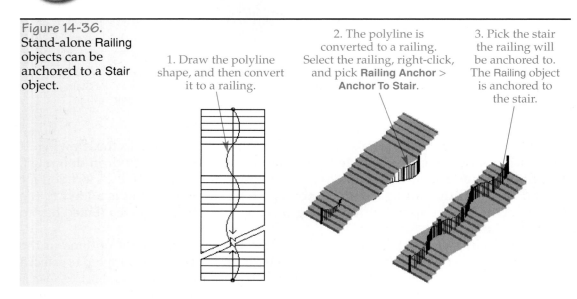

1. Draw the polyline shape, and then convert it to a railing.

2. The polyline is converted to a railing. Select the railing, right-click, and pick **Railing Anchor** > **Anchor To Stair**.

3. Pick the stair the railing will be anchored to. The Railing object is anchored to the stair.

Modifying Railings

Railing objects include grips that can be used to modify the shape of a freestanding rail or post location. When a railing is selected, grip points are located at the corners and ends of the railing. Selecting one of these grips allows you to reposition the post, edge, or vertex location for the railing. Pick a new point to reposition the fixed post position, edge, or vertex. *Fixed posts* are located at the start, the end, and any corners of the railing. If a railing is placed along a stair, adjusting the grip points on the railing repositions the fixed post, but not the guard or handrail.

In addition to using grips to modify the location of fixed posts or the vertices of a freestanding rail, a shortcut menu is available to modify the placement of posts along the railing. First, pick the Railing object to be modified, right-click, and pick the **Post Placement** shortcut menu. The shortcut menu includes five options, which are described as follows:

- **Add.** This option is used to place new posts along the length of a Railing object. New posts can be added to freestanding or attached Railing objects.
- **Remove.** Selecting this option removes manually placed posts added with the **Add** option or the fixed end posts along a rail. When a fixed post is removed, all the automatically placed posts are also removed.
- **Hide.** Use this option to hide manually placed and fixed posts at the end of the Railing object.
- **Show.** This option is used to display, or show, any hidden posts.
- **Redistribute.** Pick this option to evenly redistribute posts along a Railing object after modifying the length, vertices, or edges of a railing.

The components within the railing (Posts, Handrails, and Balusters) use profiles to define their shapes. *Balusters* are the small posts that support the upper railing. Each of these components can have its profile edited in place and assigned a new profile. To add a new profile shape to a railing component, pick the railing to be modified, right-click, and pick the **Add Profile...** option. You are prompted to Select a railing component to add profile. Pick a component on the railing to be modified. This displays the **Add** *component* (**Post**, **Hand Rail**, or **Baluster**) **Profile** worksheet. See **Figure 14-37.**

Select an AEC profile from the **Profile Definition:** drop-down list, or pick the **Start from scratch...** option to create a new profile. If the **Start from scratch...** option is selected, the **New Profile Name:** text box becomes available, so a new profile name can be entered. Pick the **Continue Editing** check box if you want to edit the profile after assigning it to the railing component.

If a railing component has a profile already assigned that needs to be modified, the profile can be edited in place. Select the Railing object, right-click, and pick the **Edit Profile In Place** option. You are prompted to Select a railing component to add profile. Pick the railing component to be modified. The **In-Place Edit** toolbar is displayed, along with grip boxes around the AEC profile's vertices. See **Figure 14-38.** Use the grips to modify the shape and size of the profile; or right-click and use the shortcut menu to add or remove vertices, add or replace profile rings, or save the changes as a new profile. When you are finished editing the profile, pick the **Save All Changes** button in the **In-Place Edit** toolbar. Each component within the railing can be assigned to a different AEC profile. **Figure 14-38** displays a railing with new profiles assigned and examples of profiles that can be used for a railing.

When a new railing is created, the **Properties** palette is used to specify some of the properties controlling the construction of the railing and to modify the railing. Some of the properties vary between freestanding and attached railings. Many of the same properties used to add the railing are available when modifying, such as the properties in the **General** and **Dimensions** subcategories. The following is a list of properties available in either freestanding or attached railings:

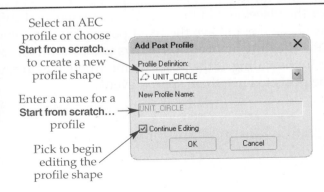

Figure 14-37.
The **Add** *component* **Profile** worksheet is used to add a profile shape to a Railing component. This figure displays the **Add Post Profile** worksheet.

Select an AEC profile or choose **Start from scratch...** to create a new profile shape

Enter a name for a **Start from scratch...** profile

Pick to begin editing the profile shape

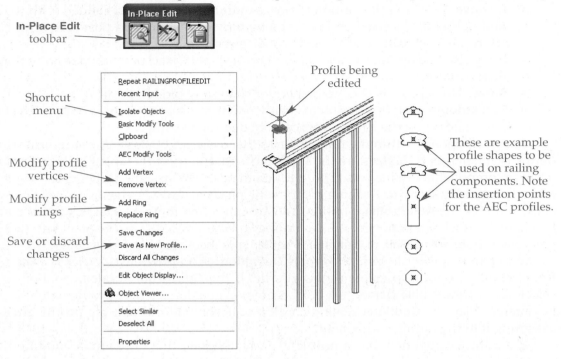

- **Railing Extensions.** This property is found under the **Dimension** subcategory when an attached railing is selected for modification. Picking this property displays the **Railing Extensions** worksheet. This worksheet is used to specify a railing's extension into a landing at the top and bottom of a stair. The **Railing Extensions** worksheet is initially grayed out, because the Standard railing style sets the rail extension properties. To make this property available for modification, the railing style needs to be edited. This is discussed in the next section.
- **Automatic cleanup.** This property is used to control the cleanup of posts with the handrail in an attached railing. The **Automatic cleanup** property includes a drop-down list with **Yes** and **No** options.
- **Anchor.** This property is available to railings that are attached to the stair or a stair flight. Selecting the property opens the **Anchor** worksheet, shown in **Figure 14-39.** The anchor controls where the railing is located on the stair. The **Justify to Stair** drop-down list controls the side of the stair where the railing is placed and works with the **Side Offset** property. The **Side** property controls the distance the railing is offset from the edge of the stair. The **Placement** area is used for the placement of the first and last fixed posts of the railing. Use the **Automatic** check box to have the fixed posts placed automatically on the stair. Unchecking the **Automatic** option allows you to manually specify the start and end posts in the railing. If the posts are modified, you might also want to redistribute the posts to have them spaced evenly.

Figure 14-39.
The **Anchor** worksheet is used to specify anchoring criteria for a rail when the rail is attached to a stair.

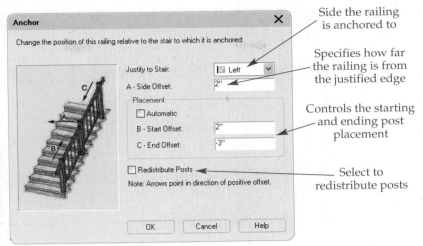

Side the railing is anchored to

Specifies how far the railing is from the justified edge

Controls the starting and ending post placement

Select to redistribute posts

Controlling the Railing Display

Plan view railings can be configured to display a handrail without posts in a Plan representation (Top view) and spindled balusters in a Model representation. The display properties can be assigned to a single Railing object or railing style. To assign the display properties to a single railing, select the railing, right-click, and pick the **Edit Object Display...** option to open the **Object Display** dialog box. To edit the display of the railing style, pick the Railing object representing the style to be modified, right-click, and select the **Edit Railing Style...** option to open the **Railing Styles -** *style* dialog box. In both the **Object Display** and **Railing Styles-** *style* dialog boxes, pick the **Display Properties** tab to begin editing the display properties. In the **Display Properties** tab, select the display representation to be modified, attach an override as appropriate, and then pick the **Edit Display Properties** button. This opens the **Display Properties (***display property source***) -** *display representation* dialog box.

Adjusting Plan View Railings

The **Display Properties (***display property source***) - Plan** dialog box includes two tabs. The **Layer/Color/Linetype** tab includes railing components going up and coming down a stair. If a freestanding railing has been selected, the "up" components are used. Make any display changes to the components for the Plan view railings.

The **Other** tab is used to apply an AEC profile to the different components of the railing in a Plan view. Profiles added to a Plan representation are used in addition to the profile shape assigned to the railing component. Select the **Add...** button in the **Other** tab to add a profile. The **Custom Profile** dialog box is displayed, as shown in **Figure 14-40.**

Select an AEC profile by picking the **Select Profile...** button. Place a check in a component box to use the custom profile, and specify insertion criteria. Use the **Attach to** area to specify where the profile is attached along the railing. When you have finished, pick the **OK** button to return to the **Display Properties (***display property source***) - Plan** dialog box. Any custom profiles added to Plan view railings appear as components in the **Layer/Color/Linetype** tab.

Figure 14-40.
Use the **Custom Profile** dialog box to attach an AEC profile to the components of a railing in a Plan representation.

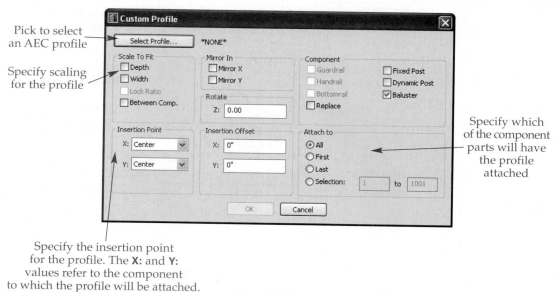

Pick to select an AEC profile

Specify scaling for the profile

Specify the insertion point for the profile. The **X:** and **Y:** values refer to the component to which the profile will be attached.

Specify which of the component parts will have the profile attached

Adjusting Model View Railings

The **Display Properties** (*display property source*) **- Model** dialog box also has the **Layer/Color/Linetype** tab, which is used to make display adjustments to the Model view stair components. These components include balusters, posts, guardrails, handrails, and bottom rails. The **Other** tab is used to add custom blocks to the railing.

This tab can be useful if you are attaching a custom post or baluster block to the railing for modeling or detailing purposes. First, create the desired 3D geometry. Create the geometry on layer 0, using ByBlock colors, linetypes, lineweights, and plot styles. Next, turn the geometry into a block. Access either the **Object Display** or **Railing Styles - *style*** dialog box, and pick the **Display Properties** tab. Select the Model representation, attach a style or object override, and then pick the **Edit Display Properties** button.

To attach the block, select the **Other** tab, and pick the **Add...** button. The **Custom Block** dialog box is displayed, as shown in **Figure 14-41**. Select a block using the **Select Block...** button. In the **Component** area, select the railing components to which to attach the block. Adjust scaling factors or insertion point locations, and pick the **OK** button when you have finished. In the **Layer/Color/Linetype** tab, make adjustments to the new block components.

Creating and Modifying Railing Styles

Styles play a big part in the design of an architectural project. Wall styles representing brick, concrete, and wood have their own display properties. Door and window styles create specific types of openings in a wall. Stair styles are used to represent wood, steel, and concrete stairs. Railings also use styles. Many of the styles included with Architectural Desktop represent commercial and industrial railing types. Custom railings can be created, existing railings can be modified, and additional railings can be imported from catalogs found in the **Content Browser**.

Figure 14-41.
Use the **Custom Block** dialog box to add or edit blocks attached to railing components.

Select a custom block

Set scaling for the custom block

Specify insertion criteria for the block

Select the components that will use the custom block

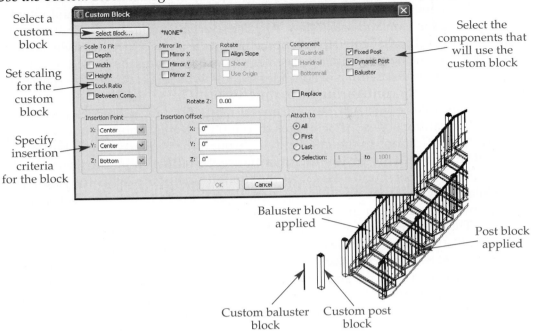

Baluster block applied

Post block applied

Custom baluster block

Custom post block

The **Railing Styles** option can be accessed by picking **Design > Railings > Railing Styles...** or right-clicking over the **Railing** tool in the **Design** tool palette and picking the **Railing Styles...** option. This displays the **Style Manager**, opened to the Railing Styles section. See **Figure 14-42**.

The **Style Manager** is divided into two panes: the tree view on the left and the list or preview pane on the right. Select the Railing Styles section icon to display a list of styles in the right pane. Pick the + symbol beside the Railing Styles section icon to display a list of railing styles in the drawing. There is no + symbol if the Standard style

Pull-Down Menu

Design
> Railings
> Railing
Styles...

Figure 14-42.
The **Style Manager** opened to the Railing Styles section.

Edit Style button

New Style button

Current drawing icon

Railing Styles section icon

List of railing styles

Viewer with a railing preview

Pick to display the **Viewer**

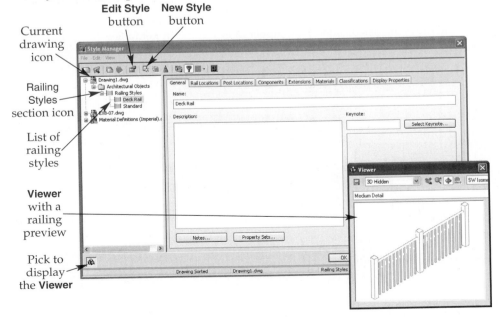

is the only railing style in the drawing. If a style is selected in the tree view, the properties for the railing style are displayed in the right pane.

To create a new railing style, pick the **New Style** button, or right-click on top of the Railing Styles section icon and select **New** from the shortcut menu. Type a new name for the railing style, and press [Enter] to accept the new style name. Once the style has been created, highlight the new style in the tree view to begin editing the style. The selected railing style's properties are displayed under the following eight tabs in the right pane, which are available for configuring the railing style:

- **General.** Like other AEC style **General** tabs, this tab is used to describe or rename railing styles. Attach notes through the **Notes...** button, and add property set definitions to the railing style through the **Property Sets...** button.
- **Rail Locations.** This tab is used to configure the railing components used in the railing style. See **Figure 14-43**. At the top left side of the tab is the **Allow Each Railing to Vary** check box. Placing a check in this box makes the **Rail locations** property available in the **Properties** palette.

  The **Upper Rails** area is used to add guardrails, handrails, or both to the railing style. Place a check in the appropriate check boxes to add desired upper rails. The **Horizontal Height** and **Sloping Height** columns are used to specify the heights of the rails measured from the ground or the slope of a stair. The **Offset from Post** column is used to place the rails a specified distance from a post. A value of 0 places the rails centered on the posts. The **Side for Offset** column is used to specify the side of the posts where the upper railings are placed, if a value greater than 0 is entered in the **Offset from Post** column. The **Auto** option automatically places the railing toward the center of a stair, if the offset value is positive. If the railing is freestanding, the **Auto** option places the rails on the right side of the railing.

  The bottom part of this tab controls the addition of a bottom rail. Check the **Bottomrail** check box to add a bottom rail to the style. Set the heights in the **Horizontal Height** and **Sloping Height** text boxes. If more than one bottom rail is added, enter the total number of bottom rails in the **Number of Rails:** text box. When more than one bottom rail is created, the **Spacing of Rails:** text box is used to specify the spacing between the rails. Use the floating **Viewer** to check the design progress for the railing.

Figure 14-43.
The **Rail Locations** tab is used to configure railings in a railing style.

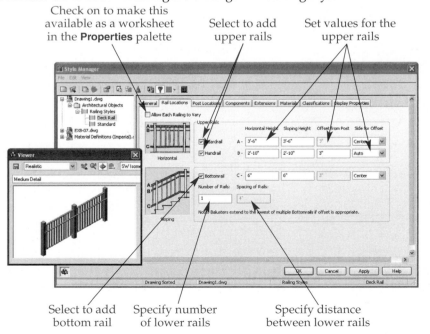

Check on to make this available as a worksheet in the **Properties** palette

Select to add upper rails

Set values for the upper rails

Select to add bottom rail

Specify number of lower rails

Specify distance between lower rails

Figure 14-44.
The **Post Locations** tab is used to configure posts and balusters in the railing style.

Select to make the **Post Locations** worksheet available in the **Properties** palette

Check to add dynamic posts

Check to add fixed posts

Specify the distance between the top of the post and the top of the top rail

Specify where the post is placed in relation to the floor or tread

Specify maximum distance between posts

Specify maximum distance between balusters

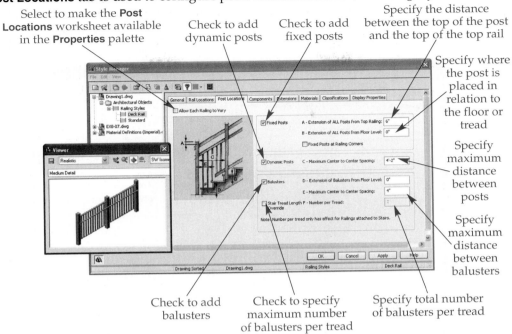

Check to add balusters

Check to specify maximum number of balusters per tread

Specify total number of balusters per tread

- **Post Locations.** This tab is used to specify the addition and configuration of posts in the railing style, as shown in **Figure 14-44**. Place a check in the **Allow Each Railing to Vary** check box to make the **Post locations** property available in the **Properties** palette. The tab has the following three areas:
  - **Fixed Posts.** This area controls the addition of fixed posts.
  - **Dynamic Posts.** This area is used to specify the addition of *dynamic posts*, which are added between fixed posts and spaced evenly along the railing. Specify the maximum distance between dynamic posts.
  - **Balusters.** This area is used to configure balusters in the railing. Specify the extension of the baluster from the floor level and the maximum center-to-center spacing between balusters here. The **Stair Tread Length Override** is used to specify a specific number of balusters per stair tread.
- **Components.** This tab is used to control the shape and size of the individual components of the railing. See **Figure 14-45**. Select the **Profile Name** column to assign an AEC profile to a component to give it a shape. When the profile text is selected, a drop-down list appears with a list of AEC profiles in the drawing. Select values in the **Width**, **Depth**, and **Rotation** columns to size the components.
- **Extensions.** This tab is used to control guardrail and handrail extensions at the top and bottom of stairs or landings, as shown in **Figure 14-46**. Enter the appropriate values for the railing extensions in the text boxes. If building codes dictate that the railing needs to extend a distance plus the tread depth, check the appropriate **+T** check boxes. Place a check in the **Allow Each Railing to Vary** check box to make the **Railing Extensions** worksheet available from the **Properties** palette.
- **Materials.** This tab is used to assign materials to each component within the railing style. See **Figure 14-47**. Pick a material in the **Material Definition** column next to the railing component to have the material assigned. The **Add New Material** button can be used to add a new material definition name. Use the **Edit Material** button to edit the display properties for a material. The creation of new materials is discussed in Chapter 15.

Figure 14-45.
The **Components** tab is used to control the shape and size of the railing components.

Pick to assign a different AEC profile to use as a component shape

Select to specify scaling sizes for the component

Pick to specify sizes for the components

Pick to specify justification of the AEC profile

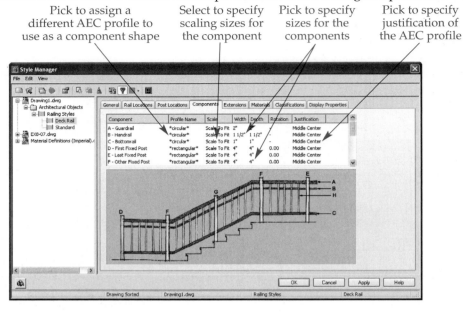

Figure 14-46.
The **Extensions** tab is used to control the extension of upper rails past the ends of stairs.

Select to make the worksheet available in the **Properties** palette

Uncheck to specify extension distances for the railing

Specify extension distance for handrails and guardrails

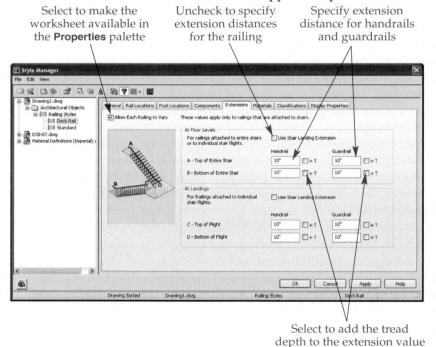

Select to add the tread depth to the extension value

- **Classifications.** By default, this tab does not include anything. This tab is used to assign named properties or characteristics to the style, such as the construction status, the project phase, the building element, the vendor, or other criteria. The creation of classifications is discussed in Chapter 15.
- **Display Properties.** This tab is used to control the display properties of the railing style. Select the appropriate representation to modify, attach an override for the style, and select the **Edit Display Properties** button to modify the display for the style.

Figure 14-47.
Use the **Materials** tab to assign material definitions to the railing components.

Railing
components

Pick to assign a
material to a
railing component

Edit Material
button

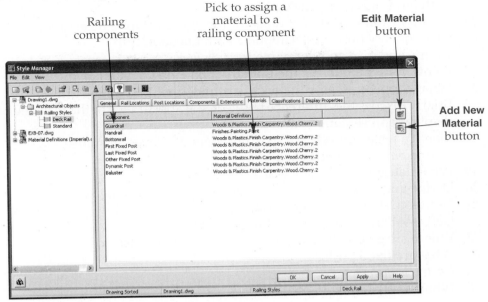

Add New
Material
button

When you are finished editing the style, pick the **OK** button to exit the **Style Manager**, and create a railing with the new style.

PROFESSIONAL
TIP

Most of the default railing styles do not have the **Allow Each Railing to Vary** check box selected. This makes it difficult to modify the railing style through the **Properties** palette. Edit the railing styles so each railing can be edited individually for more control of the railings in the drawing.

Exercise
14-9   Complete the Exercise on the Student CD.

Chapter Test

Answer the following questions. Write your answers on a separate sheet of paper or complete the electronic chapter test on the Student CD.

1. Name at least four types of stairs that can be designed using Architectural Desktop.
2. What does the **Height** property represent?
3. Describe what happens when you terminate a stair with a riser.
4. What does a button with a lightning bolt indicate in the **Calculation Rules** dialog box?
5. What does a button with an arrow indicate in the **Calculation Rules** dialog box?
6. How is the height of risers automatically calculated?
7. Describe the procedures used to place a stair in your drawing, once the stair properties have been determined.
8. Briefly explain what you get with the different stair justification options.
9. Discuss the difference between the **1/2 landing** and **1/2 turn** options.

10. Name the stair shape style that is the most flexible of the stair shapes, allowing you to create *L*-shaped stairs, *U*-shaped stairs, *S*-shaped stairs, straight stairs with landings, and angled stairs.
11. Identify from where the radius for the curved stair is measured.
12. Give the function of the **Graphics Path Location** grip.
13. Define and give another name for *path lines*.
14. Identify the function of the **Construction Line Location** grip.
15. What happens when you pick the round, gray **Edit Edges** grips?
16. Briefly discuss the difference between the appearance of the Plan and Model view display representations of stairs.
17. Identify what controls the riser numbers displayed in stairs.
18. Define *property set definitions*.
19. What determines the slope of a stair?
20. Define and explain the function of *classification definitions*.
21. Describe a Balanced winder stair style.
22. Define *railings* and give the three rail options.
23. Where are grip points located when a railing is selected?
24. What are fixed posts?
25. Define *balusters*.
26. What are dynamic posts?

Chapter Projects

Use the techniques covered in this chapter to create the following drawings.

1. Single-Level Residential Project
   A. Access the **Project Browser** and set Residential-Project-01 current.
   B. Access the **Constructs** tab of the **Project Navigator** and create a new construct with the following properties:
      a. **Name**: Exterior Stair
      b. **Level**: Grade
   C. Open the Exterior Stair construct. Drag the Main Floor construct into the drawing.
   D. Access the **Stair Styles…** option from the **Design** pull-down menu. Select the Standard stair style.
   E. In the **Design Rules** tab of the **Style Manager**, uncheck the **Use Rule Based Calculator** check box.
   F. In the **Stringers** tab, add a stringer. Set the stringer type to **Slab** with an alignment of **Full Width**. Pick **OK** to return to the drawing.
   G. Add a straight stair to the entry of the house, as displayed in the figure. Use the following property settings:
      a. **Shape: Straight**
      b. **Vertical Orientation: Up**
      c. **Width**: 6'-0"
      d. **Height**: 8"
      e. **Terminate with**: **Landing**
   H. Add stairs to the rear doors at the back of the house with the same settings.
   I. Use the **Properties** palette to change the rear stairs to 10'-0" wide.
   J. Use the **MOVE** command as needed to adjust the placement of the stairs.
   K. After positioning the stairs, select all three stairs and ensure that the **Elevation** property is set to 0".
   L. Detach the Main Floor construct.
   M. Save and close the drawing.

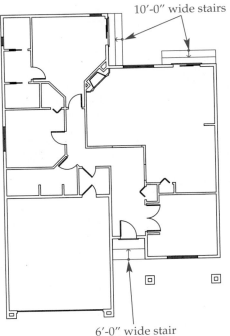

10'-0" wide stairs

6'-0" wide stair

Design Courtesy Alan Mascord Design Associates

2. Single-Level Residential Project
    A. Access the **Project Browser** and set Residential-Project-02 current.
    B. Access the **Constructs** tab of the **Project Navigator** and create a new construct with the following properties:
        a. **Name**: Exterior Stair
        b. **Level**: **Grade**
    C. Open the Exterior Stair construct. Drag the Main Floor construct into the drawing.
    D. Access the **Stair Styles...** option from the **Design** pull-down menu. Select the Standard stair style.
    E. In the **Design Rules** tab of the **Style Manager**, uncheck the **Use Rule Based Calculator** check box.
    F. In the **Stringers** tab, add a stringer. Set the stringer type to **Slab** with an alignment of **Full Width**. Pick **OK** to return to the drawing.
    G. Add a straight stair to the entry of the house, as displayed in the figure. Use the following property settings:
        a. **Shape**: **Straight**
        b. **Vertical Orientation**: **Up**
        c. **Width**: 5'-0"
        d. **Height**: 1'-8"
        e. **Terminate with**: **Landing**
    H. Add a straight stair to the rear door at the back of the house with the same settings.
    I. Use the **Properties** palette to change the rear stair to 10'-0" wide.
    J. Use the **MOVE** command as needed to adjust the placement of the stairs.
    K. After positioning the stairs, select the stairs and ensure that the **Elevation** property is set to 0".
    L. Detach the Main Floor construct.
    M. Save and close the drawing.

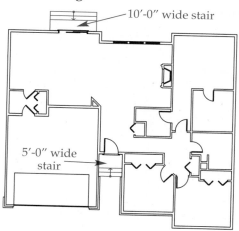

Design Courtesy Alan Mascord Design Associates

3. Two-Story Residential Project
   A. Access the **Project Browser** and set Residential-Project-03 current.
   B. Access the **Constructs** tab of the **Project Navigator** and create a new construct with the following properties:
      a. **Name**: Interior Stair
      b. **Level**: **Main Floor** and **Upper Floor** (This will allow the stair to span two levels, placing the stair at the lowest level—the Main Floor level.)
   C. Open the Interior Stair construct. Drag the Main Floor construct into the drawing.
   D. Access the **Stair Styles...** option from the **Design** pull-down menu. Select the Standard stair style.
   E. In the **Design Rules** tab of the **Style Manager**, adjust the **Riser Height** for the **Maximum Slope** and **Optimum Slope** to 7 1/2" and the **Tread Depth** for the **Maximum Slope** and **Optimum Slope** to 10". Turn off the rule-based calculator.
   F. In the **Display Properties** tab, assign a style override to the Plan representation. Adjust the stair cut plane height to 7'-0".
   G. In the **Display Properties** tab, assign a style override to the Plan High Detail representation. Turn off the Riser up and Riser down components.
   H. Add a stair to the area, using the following properties, as shown:
      a. **Style**: **Standard**
      b. **Shape**: **U-shaped**
      c. **Turn type**: **1/2 landing**
      d. **Horizontal Orientation**: **Clockwise**
      e. **Vertical Orientation**: **Up**
      f. **Width**: 3'-2"
      g. **Height**: 10'-0"
      h. **Justify**: **Outside**
      i. **Terminate with**: **Riser**
      j. **Tread**: 10"
   I. Create a new railing style using only a handrail and balusters.
   J. Add the railing to the inside of the stair.
   K. Detach the Main Floor construct.
   L. Save and close the drawing.

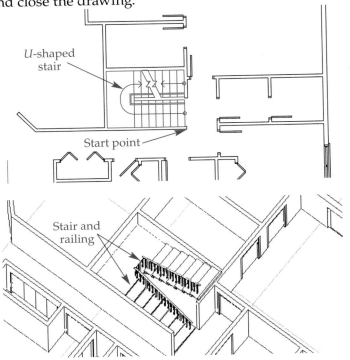

U-shaped stair

Start point

Stair and railing

Drawing Courtesy 3D-DZYN

4. Two-Story Residential Project
   A. Access the **Project Browser** and set Residential-Project-04 current.
   B. Access the **Constructs** tab of the **Project Navigator** and create a new construct with the following properties:
      a. **Name**: Interior Stair
      b. **Level**: **Main Floor** and **Upper Floor** (This will allow the stair to span two levels, placing the stair at the lowest level—the Main Floor level.)
   C. Open the Interior Stair construct. Drag the Main Floor construct into the drawing.
   D. Access the **Stair Styles...** option from the **Design** pull-down menu. Select the Standard stair style.
   E. In the **Design Rules** tab of the **Style Manager**, adjust the **Riser Height** for the **Maximum Slope** and **Optimum Slope** to 7 1/2″ and the **Tread Depth** for the **Maximum Slope** and **Optimum Slope** to 10″. Turn off the rule-based calculator.
   F. In the **Stringers** tab, add a stringer. Set the **Type** to **Housed** and the **Alignment** to **Align Left**.
   G. In the **Display Properties** tab, assign a style override to the Plan representation. Turn off the Stringer up and Stringer down components. Adjust the stair cut plane height to 7′-0″.
   H. In the **Display Properties** tab, assign a style override to the Plan High Detail representation. Turn off the Stringer up, Stringer down, Riser up, and Riser down components.
   I. Add a stair to the area, using the following properties, as shown:
      a. **Style: Standard**
      b. **Shape: U-shaped**
      c. **Turn type: 1/2 landing**
      d. **Horizontal Orientation: Clockwise**
      e. **Vertical Orientation: Up**
      f. **Width**: 3′-2″
      g. **Height**: 10′-0″
      h. **Justify: Inside**
      i. **Terminate with**: Riser
      j. **Tread**: 10″
   J. After adding the stair, use the **MOVE** command as needed to place the stair in the correct location.
   K. Create a new railing style using only a handrail and balusters.
   L. Add the railing to each side of the stair.
   M. Detach the Main Floor construct.
   N. Save and close the drawing.

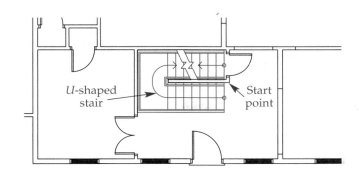

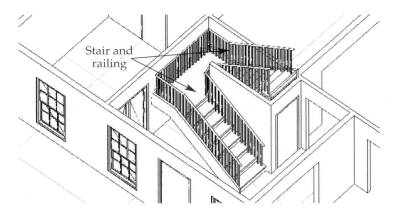

Design Courtesy Alan Mascord Design Associates

5. Commercial Store Project
   A. Access the **Project Browser** and set Commercial-Project-05 current.
   B. Access the **Constructs** tab of the **Project Navigator** and create a new construct with the following properties:
      a. **Name**: Exterior Stair
      b. **Level**: **Grade**
   C. Open the Exterior Stair construct. Drag the Main Floor construct into the drawing.
   D. Access the **Stair Styles...** option from the **Design** pull-down menu and create a new style named Ramp. Select this style.
   E. In the **Design Rules** tab of the **Style Manager**, adjust the **Riser Height** for the **Maximum Slope** and **Optimum Slope** to 1" and the **Tread Depth** for the **Maximum Slope** and **Optimum Slope** to 1'-3". Turn off the rule-based calculator. For the **Minimum Slope**, set the **Riser Height** to 15/16" and the **Tread Depth** to 1'-8".
   F. In the **Stringers** tab, add a stringer. Set the **Type** to **Ramp** and the **Alignment** to **Full Width**.
   G. In the **Components** tab, turn off the **Tread** and **Riser** check boxes.
   H. In the **Landing Extensions** tab, turn on the **Extend Landings to Merge Flight Stringers with Landing Stringers** check box.
   I. Add ramps to the rear of the building, as shown in the figure, using the following properties:
      a. **Style: Ramp**
      b. **Shape: Straight**
      c. **Vertical Orientation: Up**
      d. **Width**: 4'-0"
      e. **Height**: 1'-0"
      f. **Terminate with: Landing**
      g. **Tread**: 1'-8"
   J. Use the **MOVE** command as required to adjust the ramps' locations.

K. Use the **Properties** palette to change the elevation of the ramps to 0″.
L. Access the **Railing Styles...** option from the **Design** pull-down menu. Create a new style named Pipe Rail. Select this style.
M. In the **Rail Locations** tab, uncheck **Handrail** and check **Guardrail**. Turn on the **Bottomrail** check box, and set the **Number of Rails:** to 6 and the **Spacing of Rails:** to 6″.
N. In the **Post Locations** tab, set the **C - Maximum Center to Center Spacing:** for the **Dynamic Posts** to 6′-0″. Uncheck the **Balusters** check box.
O. In the **Components** tab, change the Fixed Post and Dynamic Post components to use the ***circular*** profile name.
P. Add the Pipe Rail railing to the outside of each ramp.
Q. Detach the Main Floor construct.
R. Save and close the drawing.

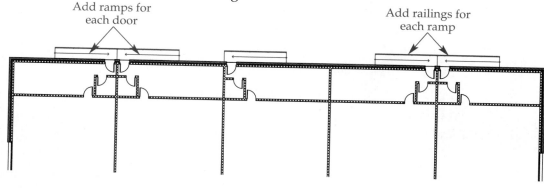

Add ramps for each door   Add railings for each ramp

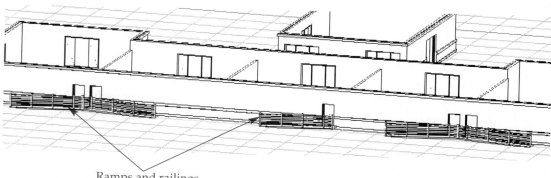

Ramps and railings

Drawing Courtesy 3D-DZYN

6. Commercial Car Maintenance Shop Project
   A. Access the **Project Browser** and set Commercial-Project-06 current.
   B. Access the **Constructs** tab of the **Project Navigator** and create a new construct with the following properties:
      a. **Name:** Interior Stair
      b. **Level: Main Floor** and **Upper Floor** (This will allow the stair to span two levels, placing the stair at the lowest level—the Main Floor level.)
   C. Open the Interior Stair construct. Drag the Main Floor construct into the drawing.
   D. Access the **Stair Styles...** option from the **Design** pull-down menu and create a new style named Stair Saddle.
   E. In the **Design Rules** tab of the **Style Manager**, adjust the **Tread Depth** for the **Maximum Slope** and **Optimum Slope** to 10″. Turn off the rule-based calculator.
   F. In the **Stringers** tab, add a stringer. Set the **Type** to **Saddled**, the **Alignment** to **Align Left**, and the **Width** to 2″. Add another stringer. Set the **Type** to **Saddled**, the **Alignment** to **Align Right**, and the **Width** to 2″.

G. In the **Display Properties** tab, assign a style override to the Plan representation. Turn off the Stringer up component and all the down components. Adjust the stair cut plane height to 9'-0".

H. In the **Display Properties** tab, assign a style override to the Plan High Detail representation. Turn off the Stringer down component and all the up components.

I. Add a stair to the area using the Stair Saddle stair style for a **Multi-landing** stair with a **1/4 landing**, as shown in the figure. Set the **Width** to 4'-0" and the **Height** to 13'-0". Terminate the stair with a **Riser**. In the **Flight Height** subsection of the **Properties** palette, set the **Minimum Limit type** property to **Risers**. In the **Minimum risers** property, type a value of 2.

J. Access the **Railing Styles…** option from the **Design** pull-down menu and create a new railing named Railing Only. Select this style.

K. In the **Post Locations** tab of the **Style Manager**, uncheck the **Balusters**, **Dynamic Posts**, and **Fixed Posts** check boxes.

L. In the **Display Properties** tab, assign a style override to the Plan representation. Turn off all the down components.

M. In the **Display Properties** tab, assign a style override to the Plan High Detail representation. Turn off all the up components.

N. Add the railing to each side of the stair.

O. Save and close the drawing.

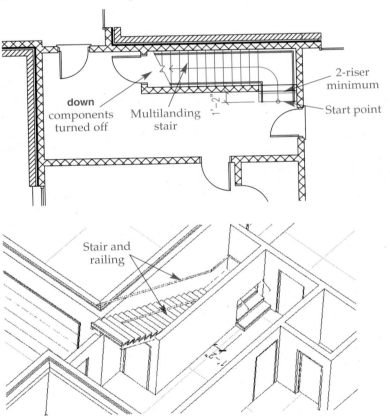

Drawing Courtesy 3D-DZYN

7. Governmental Fire Station
   A. Access the **Project Browser** and set Gvrmt -Project-07 current.
   B. Access the **Constructs** tab of the **Project Navigator** and open the Main Floor construct.
   C. Access the **Railing Styles...** option from the **Design** pull-down menu and create a new railing style named Pipe Guardrail. Select this style.
   D. Edit the Pipe Guardrail by picking the **Rail Locations** tab. Turn on the **Guardrail** check box, turn off the **Handrail** check box, and turn on the **Bottomrail** check box.
   E. In the **Post Locations** tab, change the **A - Extension of ALL Posts from Top Railing:** property for the **Fixed Posts** to 0". Set the **C - Maximum Center to Center Spacing:** property for the **Dynamic Posts** to 5'-0".
   F. In the **Components** tab, set the Guardrail, Bottomrail, Fixed Post, and Dynamic Post components to use the ***circular*** profile name and the **Width** and **Depth** properties to 3". Set the Baluster component to use the ***circular*** profile name.
   G. Add a railing to the front of the building, as shown in the figure.
   H. Save and close the drawing.

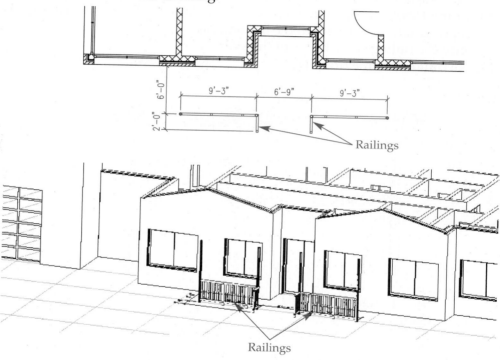

Drawing Courtesy 3D-DZYN

CHAPTER 15

Creating Styles

Learning Objectives

After completing this chapter, you will be able to do the following:

✓ Use the **Style Manager** to manage and create styles.
✓ Import and export styles.
✓ Purge styles.
✓ Use the **Content Browser**.
✓ Use material and classification styles.
✓ Use standard wall, door, and window styles.
✓ Create custom wall, door, and window styles.

The AEC objects included with Architectural Desktop have many types of different styles that represent real-world objects. Most of the styles available are ready to use in your construction documents. For specific types of styles, existing object styles can be modified, or new styles can be created. The **Style Manager** is used to organize all the styles in a drawing and import and export styles to and from your drawing. The **Style Manager** can also be used to purge unused styles from the drawing, reducing the size of the drawing file.

Previous chapters introduced you to the **Style Manager** and showed how to create and access some object styles. This chapter builds on that knowledge and shows how the **Style Manager** can be used to manage your styles. This chapter also explains how to create material and classification definitions, a custom wall and wall endcap style, and unique custom door and window styles that can be used in many of your future drawings.

Working with the Style Manager

The **Style Manager** provides a central location for the management of styles within many drawings, templates, and the current drawing. The **Style Manager** can be used to view, create, edit, and purge object styles in drawings and send drawings to a consultant.

The **Style Manager** can be accessed in a couple of ways. Most commonly, it is accessed from AEC object style commands, such as the **STAIRSTYLE** or **MEMBERSTYLE** command. Accessing the **Style Manager** this way produces a condensed version. When the **Style Manager** is accessed from an object's style command, it filters out the styles not being referenced; however, the **Style Manager** is used to manage all object styles in a drawing.

AECSTYLEMANAGER

Type
AECSTYLEMANAGER
Pull-Down Menu
Format
> Style
Manager...

In addition to being accessed from a particular AEC object style command, the **Style Manager** can be accessed from its own command. Select the **Format** > **Style Manager...** pull-down menu or type AECSTYLEMANAGER. This displays the **Style Manager**, which is shown in **Figure 15-1**.

Across the top of the **Style Manager** is a menu bar of pull-down menus used to access different commands that can be executed. The toolbar buttons are also used to access different **Style Manager** options. The **Style Manager** is divided into two resizable window panes.

The left pane organizes styles in any open drawings into three separate folders: Architectural Objects, Documentation Objects, and Multi-Purpose Objects. The Architectural Objects folder includes architectural styles for Wall, Door, and Window objects. The Documentation Objects folder includes documentation styles for AEC dimensions, schedules, and elevation or section styles. The Multi-Purpose Objects folder includes styles for AEC profiles, multi-view block definitions, layer key styles, and material definitions.

As AEC styles are created, they are organized into the appropriate folders. Picking the + sign beside a folder expands the list of styles under the folder and displays the different section icons. When new styles are defined, the styles are then placed under the appropriate styles section. Selecting the + sign beside a style section icon displays a list of styles for the section. See **Figure 15-1**.

The right pane displays different information, depending on the icon selected in the tree view. If a drawing icon is selected, the right pane displays drawing property information, such as who last saved the drawing, the name of the drawing, comments, and hyperlinks in the drawing. If a folder icon is selected in the left pane, a list of style icons is displayed in the right pane. If a style section icon is selected in the tree view, a list of object styles for that section is listed. If an object style icon from the tree view is selected, a window containing a list of properties for the style is displayed on the right, allowing you to edit the object style.

In addition to accessing the options in the toolbar or the pull-down menu area, right-clicking on different icons provides you with a shortcut menu of available options that can be selected to perform an action.

Figure 15-1.
The **Style Manager** can display all the AEC styles in a drawing.

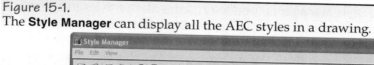

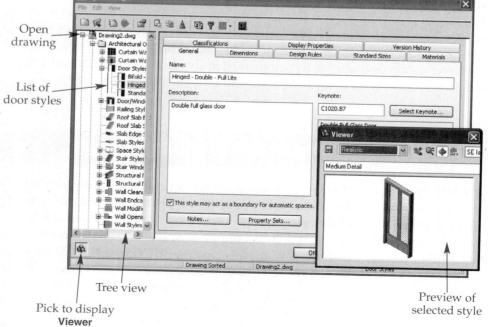

Using Style Manager Toolbar Buttons

The following toolbar options, located along the top of the **Style Manager**, perform a number of functions related to managing object styles in the **Style Manager**. See Figure 15-2.

- **New Drawing.** This button creates a new drawing icon in the **Style Manager**. The new drawing can be accessed later and have object styles added to and pulled from it for use in the current drawing.
- **Open Drawing.** This button is used to open other existing drawings so object styles can be accessed and dragged into the current drawing. Use this button to access drawings included with Architectural Desktop that contain AEC styles. These drawings can be found by picking the **Open Drawing** button, picking the **Content** button on the left in the **Open Drawing** dialog box, and then browsing through the Styles folder. Drawings opened using this method are open in the **Style Manager** only. When you are finished using the styles from these drawings, right-click over the drawing icon in the tree view, and select **Close** to close these drawings.
- **Copy.** This button is used to copy styles from one drawing folder in the tree view to another.
- **Paste.** This button adds object styles copied from one drawing folder to another.
- **Edit Style.** This button becomes available when an object style has been selected from either the right or the left panes in the **Style Manager**. It is used to edit an existing style or a newly created style.
- **New Style.** This button is used to create a new object style. First, select an object style section icon from the tree view, and then pick the **New Style** button to create the new style.
- **Set From.** This button is used for endcap styles, masking block definitions, profile definitions, and wall modifier styles. When one of these styles is highlighted in the left or right panes and this button is picked, the drawing window reappears, allowing you to select a polyline for use as one of these types of styles.
- **Purge Styles.** This button is used to purge the drawing of unused or unwanted object styles. Only styles that are not being used can be purged from the drawing.
- **Toggle View.** This button is used to toggle the left pane from viewing the drawing folder icons with the styles beneath to viewing the object style icons with the drawing folders they belong to under each style icon.
- **Filter Style Type.** This button is used to look at styles of one type. For example, suppose you wanted to view only the wall styles available in a drawing folder icon, instead of all the styles in the folder. Select the Wall Styles icon, and then pick the **Filter Style Type** button to display the wall styles in each of the drawing folder icons.
- **Details.** Use this button to toggle among small icons, large icons, the list view, and the details view. The object style icons appear different, depending on the view selected.

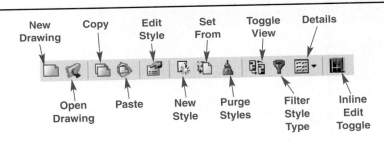

Figure 15-2.
The toolbar buttons in the **Style Manager** are used to create, modify, and manage AEC styles.

- **Inline Edit Toggle.** When an AEC style is selected and displaying the properties of the style, use this button to toggle between the style's list of properties and the **Viewer**.

Importing and Exporting Styles

Object styles can be imported and exported between drawings directly in the **Style Manager**. First, open any drawings containing styles you want to use in another drawing.

To import object styles, you must drag the selected style to another drawing icon, folder, or style section icon. You can drag individual styles from the right pane to another folder or style section icon in the tree view or from one folder in the tree view to another. See **Figure 15-3.** Styles cannot be dragged from the **Style Manager** to the drawing screen.

Multiple styles can be selected using standard Windows selection options with [Shift] and [Ctrl] keys. Styles may be transferred by dragging and dropping, or you may copy and paste them. First, select the desired styles, and then use the **Copy** button to copy the styles. Next, select the drawing icon to which the copied styles are to be transferred, and pick the **Paste** button.

Occasionally, as you copy styles between drawings, you may encounter a situation in which a style already exists in the receiving drawing. In this case, the **Style Manager** displays a warning that the drawing already includes a style with a duplicate name. See **Figure 15-4.** This dialog box contains the following three options for dealing with the duplicate style being imported:

- **Leave Existing.** Use this radio button to leave the existing style in the receiving drawing and discard the style being transferred.
- **Overwrite Existing.** Use this radio button to overwrite the existing style in the receiving drawing with the style being transferred.
- **Rename to Unique.** Use this radio button to rename the incoming style with a number after the style name. Typically, if the style name already exists in the receiving drawing, the newly imported drawing has the number (1) appended to its name. Additional importing of the same style continues to sequentially number the style names.

Figure 15-3.
Different methods of dragging styles from one drawing to another icon.

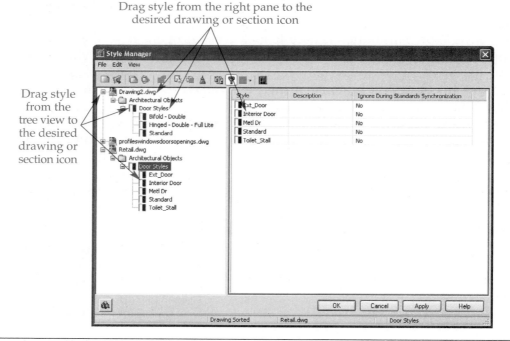

Architectural Desktop and Its Applications

Figure 15-4.
The Import/Export - Duplicate Names Found dialog box is displayed when you try to import a style that already exists in the receiving drawing.

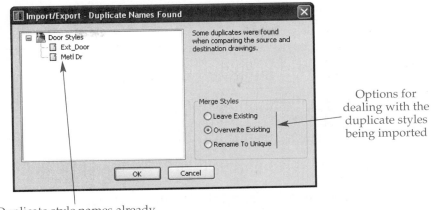

Duplicate style names already exist in the receiving drawing

Options for dealing with the duplicate styles being imported

NOTE

Architectural Desktop includes a number of imperial and metric drawings with several AEC styles that can be imported into your drawings. To access these drawings, pick the **Open Drawing** button and navigate to the Styles folder. Double-click the Styles folder to display the Imperial and the Metric folders. Double-click the desired folder to access the different style drawings. Open a style drawing and drag and drop the desired styles into your current project.

Purging Styles

If there are styles not being used in the drawing, they can be purged from the drawing. Purging unused object styles from the drawing reduces the size of the drawing file.

Object styles can be purged from the drawing globally or individually. When you purge styles globally, all the unused styles in the drawing are purged. When you purge object styles individually, specific unused object styles are removed.

To purge styles globally, select the drawing icon containing the styles to be purged, and then select the **Purge Styles** button. See Figure 15-5. You can also right-click over the drawing icon and select **Purge** from the shortcut menu to display the **Select Style Types** dialog box, shown in Figure 15-5. The list of items in this dialog box includes all the object style types available. A check in the box beside the style type indicates that any unused styles of that type are purged from the drawing. Pick the **OK** button to purge all unused styles from the drawing globally.

To purge styles individually, select the style type icon from the list in the **Style Manager**, and then pick the **Purge Styles** button or right-click and select **Purge**. The **Select** (*current object type*) **Styles** dialog box is displayed. Depending on the style type selected, the name of the style appears in the title bar of this dialog box. See Figure 15-6.

A list of individual styles for the selected style type is listed in the dialog box. A check mark beside the style name indicates that the style will be purged. When you have finished purging object styles, exit the **Style Manager** and save the drawing. Depending on the number of styles used and purged, the drawing file can be significantly reduced in size.

Figure 15-5.
Select the drawing icon to be purged, pick the **Purge Styles** button, and then choose the object style types to be purged.

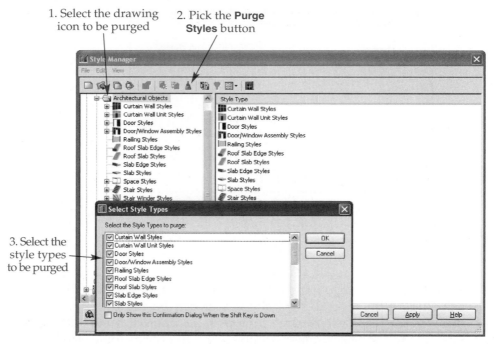

1. Select the drawing icon to be purged

2. Pick the **Purge Styles** button

3. Select the style types to be purged

Figure 15-6.
Highlight a style section icon, and then press the **Purge Styles** button to display the **Select** *(current object type)* **Styles** dialog box. Select the styles in the list to be purged.

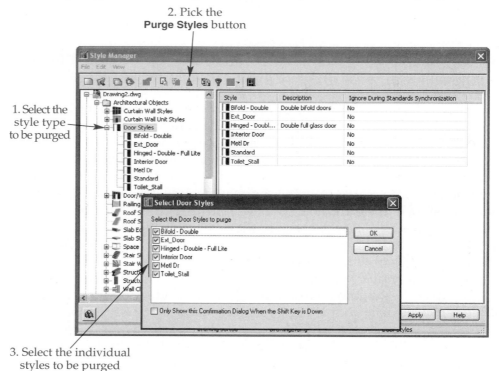

2. Pick the **Purge Styles** button

1. Select the style type to be purged

3. Select the individual styles to be purged

Exercise
15-1   Complete the Exercise on the Student CD.

Working with the Content Browser

Included with Architectural Desktop are drawings with a number of additional styles that can be imported into the drawing and used in the development of your model. The **Content Browser** is another tool that provides access to AEC styles, design content, and tool palettes.

The **Content Browser** is a customizable tool that allows you to create catalogs of tool palettes, styles, commands, and blocks that can be added to the drawing or palettes within the **Tool Palettes** window. This command can be accessed by selecting **Window > Content Browser** from the pull-down menu, by selecting the **Content Browser** button in the **Navigation** toolbar, by pressing the [Ctrl]+[4] key combination, or by typing CONTENTBROWSER. This opens the **Content Browser**, which is shown in **Figure 15-7**.

Figure 15-7.
The **Content Browser** provides access to several catalogs of tools, styles, and design content that can be added to tool palettes or imported into the drawing.

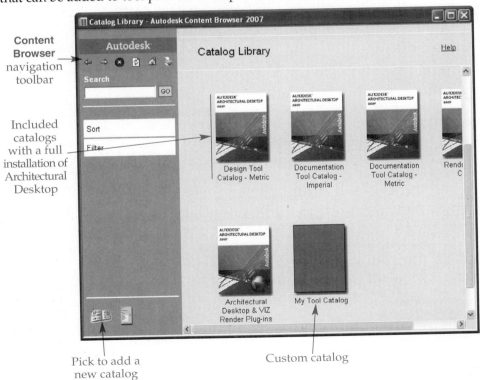

Content Browser navigation toolbar

Included catalogs with a full installation of Architectural Desktop

Pick to add a new catalog

Custom catalog

The **Content Browser** includes several catalogs that vary in number, depending on how you installed the program. **Figure 15-7** includes all the catalogs included when a full installation is performed. Catalogs including tools ranging from stock and sample tools to design, documentation, and render material tools are included in both imperial and metric units. My Tool Catalog, which is a blank catalog ready for customizing, is also available.

The upper, left side of the window includes some standard browser navigation buttons that allow you to browse through the different catalogs. In the bottom-left corner of the window is a button used to create new catalogs. By default, the **Content Browser** remains at the front of your screen. This can be helpful if you are importing styles or content into the drawing or onto a tool palette, or if you are customizing a catalog. There are occasions, however, where you may not want the window at the front of the screen. Right-clicking on the title bar displays a shortcut menu with several options, including the **Always on Top** option. Uncheck this option to give the window the ability to move to the front or back of other windows opened in the computer.

NOTE   Use the **Content Browser** to import wall styles or door styles or to create custom tool palettes of styles for future use.

Accessing Content

Catalogs include several different types of content. Picking a catalog from a window displays the contents of the catalog. In **Figure 15-8**, the Design Tool Catalog – Imperial catalog has been picked. This catalog initially provides you with a title page explaining the catalog use. Along the left edge below the navigation tools, a **Search** text box is available for you to perform searches of content.

Figure 15-8.
Picking most catalogs will display a title sheet explaining what the catalog includes.

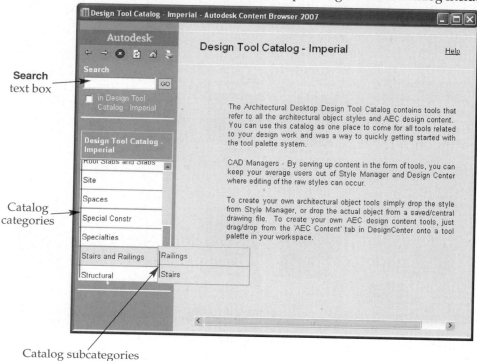

Search text box

Catalog categories

Catalog subcategories

Architectural Desktop and Its Applications

Below the **Search** text box is a list of categories within the catalog that include content. Moving the mouse over a category displays a subcategory of additional content found within the main category. Select a category or subcategory from the list to display content that can be added to the drawing or a tool palette. This displays a page of content associated with the category you selected. See **Figure 15-9**. All the content within the catalogs can be inserted into the drawing through i-drop technology. *I-drop* allows you to drag 2D symbols, 3D objects, and models from a Web page to a virtual environment.

All the styles or multi-view blocks included with Architectural Desktop can be found within each category window. To add content from the window into your drawing, select a piece of content to display the i-drop cursor, and then drag and drop the content into the drawing. This adds the style or the multi-view block to the drawing. If an object style is being added, the process used to add the AEC object is initiated. Perform the function before additional content can be added. If a multi-view block is added, the block is inserted into the drawing. In both cases, the style or definition is added to the drawing for additional use.

The Design Tool Catalog and the Documentation Catalog include all the styles, multi-view blocks, and content included with Architectural Desktop. The Stock Tool Catalog includes all the tools included within the **Tool Palettes** window. In addition to these tools and palettes, custom catalogs and palettes can be created for your use.

PROFESSIONAL TIP

Create your own custom catalogs of content that can be used in other projects. Content from the **Content Browser** can be added and organized in the **Tool Palettes** window. Review Appendix B on the included CD for information for customizing tool palettes.

Figure 15-9.
Railings category content page.

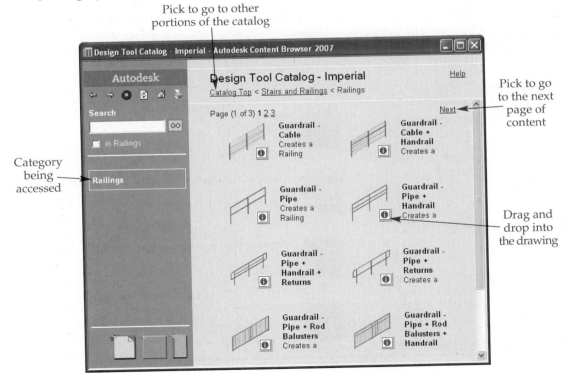

Creating Material Definitions

In many of the design tool styles, such as the stairs and railings, materials can be added to enhance the look of the model when using a shademode. Materials can also control the display of the design tool styles by specifying a color or hatch pattern displayed in a Plan, Model, elevation, or section view.

Before a material definition can be completely created, a render material needs to be added to the drawing. A *render material* is an electronic picture that can be assigned or mapped to surfaces in your model. The **Content Browser** includes a catalog of sample render materials. Access the Render Material catalog to browse for render materials. The catalog is divided into several material categories, ranging from concrete to furnishings to wood materials. Select a material category to browse through any subcategories of materials. Once a material has been found that you want to turn into a material definition, drag and drop the material into the drawing window. See **Figure 15-10**.

After dragging a material into the drawing, the **Create AEC Material** worksheet is displayed. See **Figure 15-11**. This worksheet is used to create a new material definition in the drawing from the **Content Browser**. If the material's display properties are based on an existing material in the drawing, choose the material from the **AEC Material to use as a Template** drop-down list. By default, the name of the VizRender material is used as the material name. Enter a new name if desired. When you are finished, pick the **OK** button to add the new material to the drawing.

Figure 15-10.
Use the Render Material catalog to drag and drop render material bitmaps into the drawing.

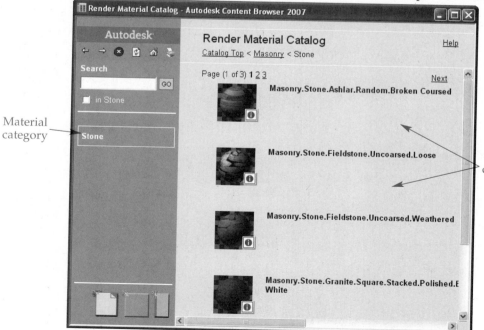

Material category

Render materials that can be dragged and dropped into the drawing

Figure 15-11.

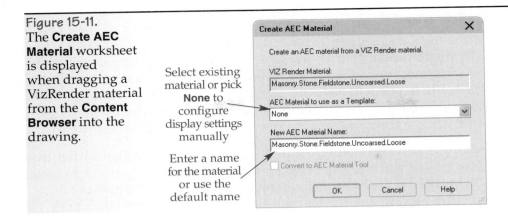

Figure 15-11.
The **Create AEC Material** worksheet is displayed when dragging a VizRender material from the **Content Browser** into the drawing.

Select existing material or pick **None** to configure display settings manually

Enter a name for the material or use the default name

Once the render material has been dropped into the drawing, a material definition is created in the drawing, which in turn, can be assigned to an AEC style or an individual AEC object. To create or modify a material definition, pick **Format** > **Material Definitions...** from the pull-down menu, or type MATERIALDEFINE. This displays the **Style Manager** opened to the Material Definitions section under the Multi-Purpose Objects folder. See **Figure 15-12**.

Preconfigured material definitions, with their display properties already set up for use in AEC object styles, can be imported into your drawing. In the **Style Manager**, pick the **Open Drawing** button. This displays the **Open Drawing** dialog box. Pick the Content folder icon on the left side of the dialog box, and then pick the Styles folder. Pick either the Imperial or Metric folder, and then select the Material Definitions.dwg file. This opens the Material Definitions drawing in the **Style Manager**. Drag and drop any desired material definitions from this drawing onto your drawing icon within the **Style Manager**.

<table>
<tr><td>Type</td></tr>
<tr><td>**MATERIALDEFINE**</td></tr>
<tr><td>Pull-Down Menu</td></tr>
<tr><td>Format
> Material
Definitions...</td></tr>
</table>

MATERIALDEFINE

Figure 15-12.
The **Style Manager** can be used to create, import, and modify material definitions under the Material Definitions section.

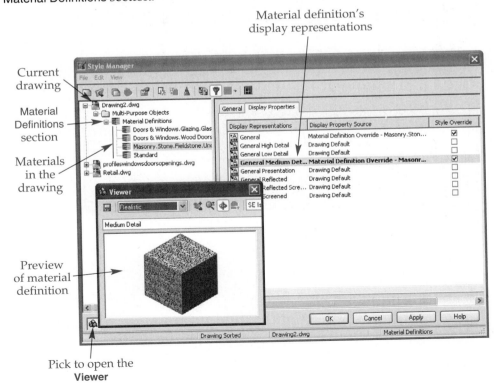

Material definition's display representations

Current drawing

Material Definitions section

Materials in the drawing

Preview of material definition

Pick to open the **Viewer**

Editing Material Definitions

To begin editing a material definition, highlight the new definition in the tree view. This displays tabs containing properties for material definition in the right pane. See **Figure 15-12**. Material definitions include **General** and **Display Properties** tabs.

The **General** tab is used to rename the material definition and provide a material description. Notes, such as material construction or installation, can be applied to the definition in this tab through the **Notes** button.

The **Display Properties** tab is used to control the display of the material definition's hatches and render material in different display representations. Material definitions include several General representations used in the different display configurations. Notice that there is not a separate Plan or Model representation as with other styles that have been discussed. Select the display representation to be modified, apply a style override, and pick the **Edit Display Properties** button. This opens the **Display Properties** dialog box for the selected representation. See **Figure 15-13**. The **Display Properties** dialog box for each of the material display representations includes **Layer/Color/Linetype**, **Hatching**, and **Other** tabs.

Figure 15-13.

The **Display Properties** dialog box is used to control the display of the material definition in a selected display representation.

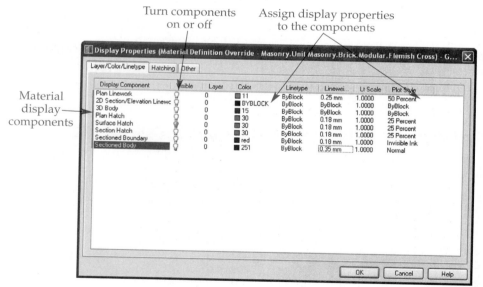

The **Layer/Color/Linetype** tab is similar to other **Display Properties** tabs. The **Display Component** column lists the available components for a material. See **Figure 15–13**. These components and what they reference in other AEC styles are listed below:

- **Plan Linework.** This component controls the display properties of Plan representation linework in an AEC style. When the object display for a Plan representation wall, door, window, or other AEC style has been set to use the **By Material** check box, the material definition's Plan Linework display component controls the display properties.
- **2D Section/Elevation Linework.** This component is used to specify the colors and linetypes for a 2D section and elevation object when its style is set to use the **By Material** check box. 2D section and elevation objects are discussed later in this text.
- **3D Body.** This component controls the linework display properties of a Model view object when viewed using a wireframe or hidden shademode. The AEC style's Model representation must be set to use the **By Materials** check box in order for this component to be displayed.
- **Plan Hatch.** This component is used to control the display of an object's Plan representation hatch pattern. In order for the material definition to control the color and hatch pattern visible in a Plan view, the AEC object's Plan representation Hatch component must be set to use the **By Material** check boxes.
- **Surface Hatch.** This component controls the display of a surface hatch applied to an object's Model or Elevation representation. In order to see the hatch pattern in a Model view or an Elevation view, the AEC object's Model or Elevation representation must be set to use the **By Material** check boxes.
- **Section Hatch.** This component is used when creating a 2D section. When a 2D section is cut, the AEC object's component that is being cut through can have a hatch pattern assigned that displays in the 2D section. The display controls for the section Hatch component set the color and linetype of the hatch assigned. In order for the hatched area to be displayed in a 2D section, the **By Material** check box must be turned on in the 2D section style.
- **Section Boundary.** This component controls the display of the sectioned boundary (or 3D components in an AEC object) of a live section. See **Figure 15-14**. A *live section* is a sectioned 3D model. Live sections are discussed in Chapter 20.

Figure 15-14.
Material definition display components control different parts of a model.

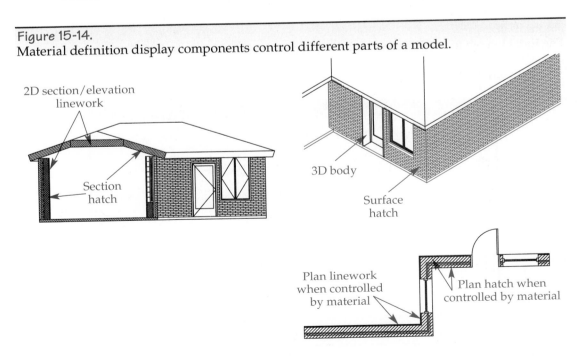

2D section/elevation linework

Section hatch

3D body

Surface hatch

Plan linework when controlled by material

Plan hatch when controlled by material

Figure 15-15.
The sectioned boundary and its display components are used in a live section. Courtesy 3D-DZYN.

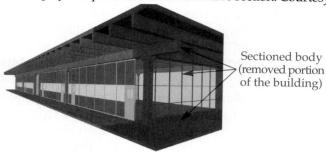

Sectioned body (removed portion of the building)

- **Section Body.** This component is used to control the display of a section body in a live section, as in **Figure 15-15**. The section body is the removed portion of the building in a live section.

As with other **Display Properties** dialog boxes, decide which components to turn on or off, and assign colors, linetypes, lineweights, and plot styles. When you are finished in the **Layer/Color/Linetype** tab, move to the **Hatching** tab.

The **Hatching** tab controls the hatch patterns assigned to the Hatch display components in the **Layer/Color/Linetype** tab. Three Hatch components are included in a material definition: Plan Hatch, Surface Hatch, and Section Hatch. See **Figure 15-16**. Pick the hatch swatch under the **Pattern** column to open the **Hatch Pattern** worksheet. See **Figure 15-17**. The four hatching options available in the **Type:** drop-down list are **Predefined**, **Custom**, **User-Defined**, and **Solid Fill**.

Selecting the **Predefined** option causes the **Pattern Name:** drop-down list and the **Browse...** button to become available. Select a hatch to use from the **Pattern Name:** drop-down list or select a pattern by picking the **Browse...** button. Picking the **Browse...** button displays the **Hatch Pattern Palette** dialog box. This dialog box includes four tabs containing hatch patterns. Select a hatch pattern from the list and pick the **OK** button to assign the hatch to the selected display component.

Figure 15-16.
The **Hatching** tab is used to control the hatch patterns for the hatch display components.

Hatch display components | Hatch pattern swatch | Hatch pattern scale | Hatch rotation angle | Hatch orientation | Hatch offsets

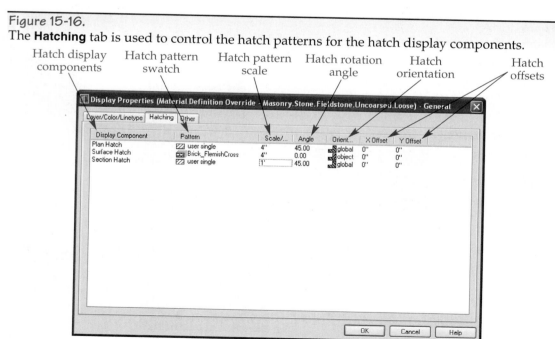

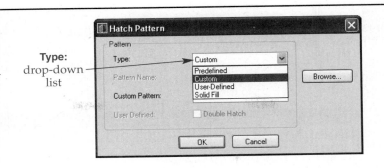

Figure 15-17.
The **Hatch Pattern** worksheet is used to assign a hatch pattern to a display component.

Type: drop-down list

The **Custom** option in the **Type:** drop-down list allows you to select a custom hatch pattern name. The **User-Defined** hatch type uses the current linetype as a repetitive pattern of single lines. If a crosshatch pattern is desired, select the **Double Hatch** check box. The last option is the **Solid Fill** option. This option uses a solid fill as a pattern. There is a **Solid** hatch pattern in the **Hatch Pattern Palette** dialog box that should not be used if a solid pattern is desired. In this case, select **Solid Fill** from the **Type:** drop-down list in the **Hatch Pattern** worksheet.

After the hatch pattern has been selected, the scale for the pattern can be controlled by picking on the scale number associated with the hatch pattern under the **Scale** column. The rotation angle of the hatch pattern is controlled by picking the number below the **Angle** column and entering a new rotation angle.

The **Orientation** column is used to set the orientation of the hatch pattern. Picking in this column changes the orientation, depending on whether the **Global** or **Object** option is used. The **Global** option causes the hatch pattern to remain in the same orientation throughout the drawing. The **Object** option orients the hatch to the angle of the object. See **Figure 15-18**.

When a hatch is created, it originates from the 0,0,0 point in the world coordinate system. If a hatch pattern needs to be shifted along the surface it is hatching, the **X Offset** and **Y Offset** columns can be used to set an offset distance for the hatch along the X and Y axes.

The **Other** tab is used to control the assignment of the hatch and render material to the material definition. See **Figure 15-19**. The tab is divided into four separate areas. Each area controls a different aspect of the hatch and render material in the material definition.

- **Surface Hatch Placement.** This area includes six check boxes. Picking one of the check boxes assigns the hatch pattern from the **Hatching** tab to an object's top, bottom, left, right, front, or back surface. Any combination of check boxes can be selected. By default, only the elevation surfaces are selected.

Figure 15-18.
The hatch pattern orientation can be set to follow the angle of the object or be set globally to the world coordinate system.

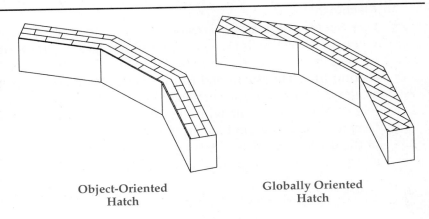

Object-Oriented
Hatch

Globally Oriented
Hatch

Figure 15-19.
The **Other** tab includes parameters for specifying how the hatch and the render material are applied to the surface of an AEC object.

Specify the faces to which the hatch pattern will be applied

Specify the render material to use when shading the model

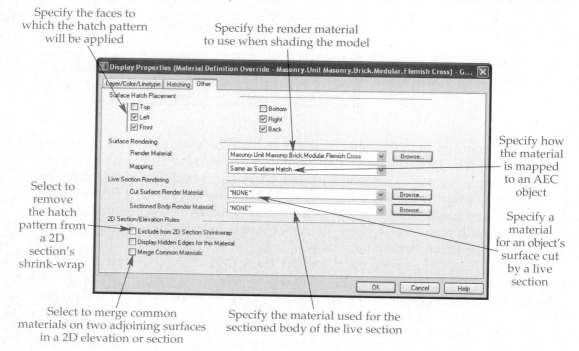

Specify how the material is mapped to an AEC object

Select to remove the hatch pattern from a 2D section's shrink-wrap

Specify a material for an object's surface cut by a live section

Select to merge common materials on two adjoining surfaces in a 2D elevation or section

Specify the material used for the sectioned body of the live section

- **Surface Rendering.** This area includes two drop-down lists. The **Render Material:** drop-down list includes a listing of render materials that have been added to the drawing from the **Content Browser** or from other AEC objects with materials. Choose a render material from the list or pick the **Browse...** button to choose the material from the **Select Rendering Material** dialog box.

    The **Mapping:** drop-down list controls how the render material is applied to an AEC object's surface. This list includes **Default Mapping**, **Face Mapping**, and **Same as Surface Hatch** options. The **Default Mapping** option maps the render material to all the faces of an object, without regard to any alignment of the material along the surface. The **Face Mapping** option is similar to the **Default Mapping** option, except the material is aligned with the orientation of the surface of the object. All faces of the AEC object are rendered when the drawing is shaded. The **Same as Surface Hatch** option aligns the render material in the same direction and orientation as the hatch pattern and places the render material on the surfaces of the object as specified in the **Surface Hatch Placement** area.

- **Live Section Rendering.** This area is used to control the display of materials when a live section is created. The **Cut Surface Render Material** drop-down list is used to assign a render material to an AEC object's surface that is cut by a section line. The **Sectioned Body Render Material:** drop-down list is used to assign a material to the sectioned body (removed portion of the building in a live section). By default, with the AEC object styles included with Architectural Desktop, a transparent blue material is assigned to this component. With either of the drop-down lists, the **Browse...** button can be selected to search through a list of loaded materials.

- **2D Section Rules.** This area includes check box options controlling the material in a 2D section or elevation. The **Exclude from 2D Section Shrinkwrap** option is used to exclude the render material hatch pattern from the Shrinkwrap component within a 2D section. The Shrinkwrap component in a 2D section is similar to the Shrinkwrap component for a Wall object. The shrink-wrap surrounds the area being cut by the section line. The **Merge Common Materials** check box is used to merge common materials of two adjacent surfaces in a 3D section or elevation, removing the line between the two surfaces.

When you are finished adjusting the properties for the display representation within the material definition, pick the **OK** button to return to the tabs containing properties for material definitions, so other display representations can be adjusted.

 **Exercise 15-3**   Complete the Exercise on the Student CD.

Creating Classification Definitions

A *classification definition* is a named property or characteristic that can be assigned to AEC object styles. Classification definitions are used to track AEC objects by construction status, project phase, building element, vendor, manufacturer, or any other criteria used to track information. Classifications can be assigned to different AEC styles and are used in conjunction with schedules, as a means to track and sort information. Examples of the use for classifications include the following:
- Multi-view blocks used to track interior furnishings and appliances.
- Attached to building styles such as walls, doors, and windows to track a project phase.
- Walls, doors, and windows to track new, existing, and demo construction.
- Doors and windows that indicate vendor information, such as the product number.

Classification definitions are created by picking **Format** > **Classification Definitions…** from the pull-down menu or typing CLASSIFICATIONDEFINITION. This displays the **Style Manager** opened to the Classification Definitions section, shown in **Figure 15-20**. Pick the **New Style** button to create a new classification or right-click over the Classification Definitions section icon. Type a name for the style, and then press the [Enter] key. After naming the style, pick the style in the tree view to display the tabs containing the definition's properties in the right pane.

The properties in the Classification Definition section include **General**, **Applies To**, and **Classifications** tabs. The **General** tab is used to rename or add a description to the classification definition. The **Applies To** tab is used to select where the AEC style's classification definition is applied. See **Figure 15-21**. Place a check in the box next to the desired styles to use the classification. This is particularly useful if you are creating a classification that is only used to track information in certain objects, such as multi-view blocks, as opposed to doors or windows.

After selecting the styles where the classification is applied, pick the **Classifications** tab. See **Figure 15-22**. Use the **Add** button to add a new classification name. Pick the **New Classification** name under the **Name** column to rename the classification. Pick the area beside the **Name** column under the **Description** column to add a description to the name. You can add as many classification names as needed under one definition. The **Property Sets…** button is used to attach additional scheduling information to the classification definition. The creation and use of property set definitions is discussed in Chapter 23.

Type
CLASSIFICATION DEFINITION

Pull-Down Menu
Format
> Classification Definitions…

CLASSIFICATIONDEFINITION

Figure 15-20.

The **Style Manager** is used to create classification definitions for AEC styles.

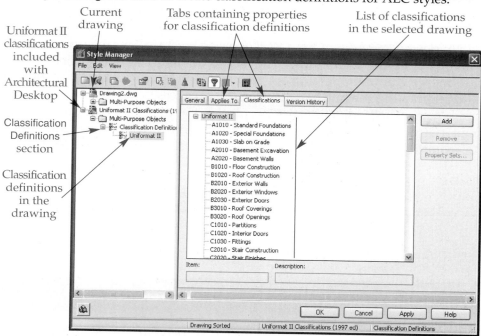

Current drawing

Uniformat II classifications included with Architectural Desktop

Tabs containing properties for classification definitions

List of classifications in the selected drawing

Classification Definitions section

Classification definitions in the drawing

Figure 15-21.

Use the **Applies To** tab to specify which AEC styles will be assigned the classification definition.

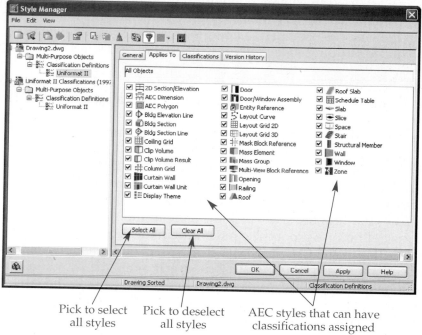

Pick to select all styles

Pick to deselect all styles

AEC styles that can have classifications assigned

A drawing and an AEC style can have as many classification definitions applied as needed. For example, you may create a Construction Status classification that includes the names New, Existing, Demo, and Phases classification, each of which includes the names Phase 1–Phase 9. Architectural Desktop also includes one sample classification definition in the Uniformat II Classifications (1997 ed).dwg found in the \\Styles\Imperial folder. This classification can be imported into your drawing for your own use.

Figure 15-22.
Add classification names for the classification definition in the **Classifications** tab.

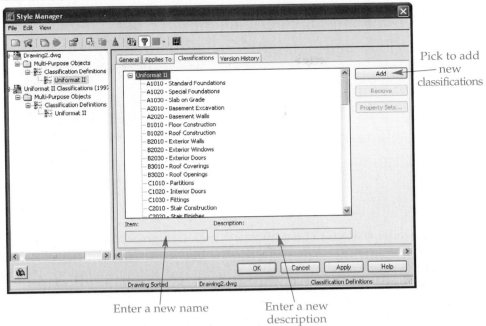

Enter a new name   Enter a new
                           description

Exercise
15-4   **Complete the Exercise on the Student CD.**

Using and Creating Wall Styles

In addition to using wall styles provided by Architectural Desktop, you can create custom wall styles to reflect your design needs. Many wall styles can be found in the **Walls** tool palette, and additional styles can be imported through the **Content Browser** or **Style Manager**.

Importing Additional Wall Styles

Architectural Desktop includes more than 150 different wall styles. These wall styles are divided into five types of walls: brick, casework, CMU, concrete, and stud. The **Walls** tool palette includes some of these wall styles, and the remaining styles are found in the **Content Browser** or the Styles directory under either the Imperial or Metric folder.

Wall styles can be used to model any type of horizontal object, such as casework. These types of walls represent cabinetry. They are considered a wall style because the wall style commands are used to create an object that looks like a cabinet with a countertop, as shown in **Figure 15-23**.

Additional wall styles can be imported into the current drawing through the **Style Manager**, the **WALLSTYLE** command, or the **Content Browser**.

NOTE   Keep in mind that if you access the **WALLSTYLE** command, the **Style Manager** is still being used, but the **Filter Style Type** button is on, which filters for wall styles.

Figure 15-23.
Wall styles can be used to create objects other than walls, such as casework.

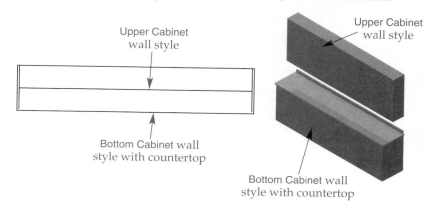

Upper Cabinet
wall style

Upper Cabinet
wall style

Bottom Cabinet wall
style with countertop

Bottom Cabinet wall
style with countertop

Type	
WALLSTYLE	
Pull-Down Menu	
Design	
> Walls	
> Wall Styles...	

To access the **WALLSTYLE** command, pick **Design** > **Walls** > **Wall Styles...** from the pull-down menu or type WALLSTYLE. The Wall Styles section can also be opened by right-clicking over an existing wall tool in the **Tool Palettes** window. This will display the **Style Manager** opened to the Wall Styles section. See **Figure 15-24**.

Use the **Open Drawing** button to open the drawings containing the additional wall styles. There are a few drawings that include additional wall styles, as shown in **Figure 15-24**. In the **Open drawing** dialog box, pick the **Content** button and browse to the \\Styles folder to open any of the wall styles drawings in the **Style Manager**. Drag and drop the desired wall styles from the wall style drawings into your current drawing folder icon.

Figure 15-24.
The **Style Manager** can be used to import and create new wall styles.

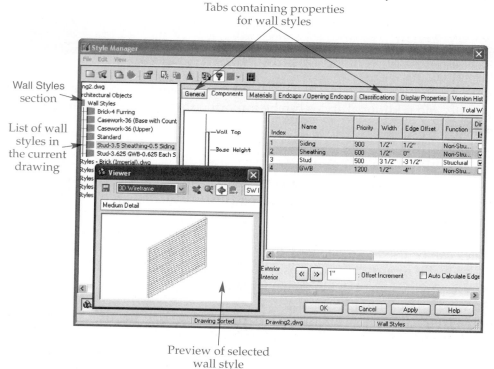

Tabs containing properties
for wall styles

Wall Styles
section

List of wall
styles in
the current
drawing

Preview of selected
wall style

Exercise
15-5   **Complete the Exercise on the Student CD.**

Creating Custom Wall Styles

In addition to using preestablished wall styles, you can create custom wall styles for use in your drawings. Custom wall styles can be as complex or as simple as needed.

To create a custom wall style, access the **WALLSTYLE** command. The **Style Manager** is displayed, filtered to the Wall Styles section. Select the **New Style** button to create a new custom wall style. A new wall style is created in the **Style Manager**. Enter a name for the new wall style, and then select the new wall style to display the wall style's tabs for properties in the right pane.

Wall style properties are divided into the following six tabs used to set the design parameters for the wall style:

- **General.** This tab is used to rename; provide a description for; add design notes, documents, and spreadsheets to; and attach property set definitions to the wall style. See **Figure 15-25**. Property set definitions are described in Chapter 23. Additionally, a keynote number may be added to the style by entering a value in the **Keynote:** text box. A keynote may also be chosen for the style by picking the **Select Keynote** button and browsing through the **Select Keynote** dialog box for a keynote to be assigned to the style.

Figure 15-25.
The **Wall Style Properties** dialog box is used to configure the parameters for the new custom wall style.

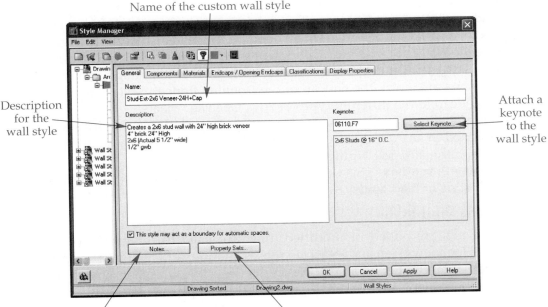

Name of the custom wall style

Description for the wall style

Attach a keynote to the wall style

Attach design notes, spreadsheets, and Web sites to the wall style

Attach property set definitions to the wall style

Figure 15-26.
The **Components** tab is used to assemble the wall style and to set any rules for the behavior of the components within the wall.

Pick the properties of a wall component to adjust the values

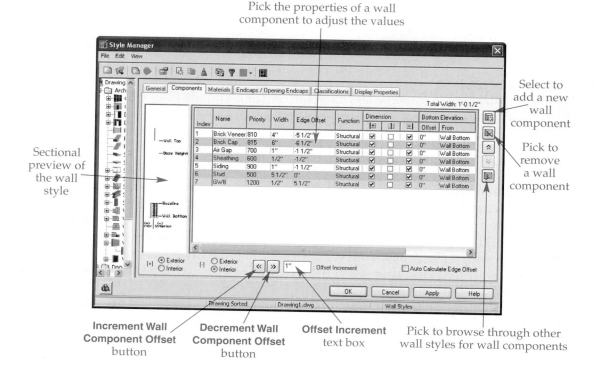

Sectional preview of the wall style

Select to add a new wall component

Pick to remove a wall component

Increment Wall Component Offset button

Decrement Wall Component Offset button

Offset Increment text box

Pick to browse through other wall styles for wall components

- **Components.** This tab is used to create the wall style by adding wall components to the style and setting parameters for the behavior of each component within a wall. See **Figure 15-26.** The **Components** tab is discussed in greater detail later in the next section.
- **Materials.** This tab lists the components within the wall style and assigns a material definition to each component, as shown in **Figure 15-27.** Pick the material from the **Material Definition** column to assign a material to the associated wall component. The **Add New Material** and the **Edit Material** buttons can be used to create and edit material definitions in the drawing.
- **Endcaps / Opening Endcaps.** This tab is used to place an endcap shape at the end of a wall or at the edges of an opening in the wall style, as in **Figure 15-28.** Use the **Wall Endcap Style** drop-down list to assign an endcap to the ends of the wall style. Wall endcap styles are discussed later in this chapter. In the **Opening Endcaps** area, pick the endcap in the **Opening Endcap Style** column to assign an endcap to the different types of AEC Opening objects.
- **Classifications.** As discussed in the last section, multiple classifications can be assigned to an AEC style. Choose the classifications to be assigned to the wall style in this tab. See **Figure 15-29.**
- **Display Properties.** This tab is used to configure the display properties of the wall style in Plan, Model, Reflected, and any other display representations.

Building the Wall Style

When walls are added or modified, they are used to represent how the wall appears in a Top view (Plan and Reflected representation) and an Elevation or isometric view (Model representation). Depending on the wall style, one component (boundary) or multiple components are used to represent different parts of the wall. For example, a simple wall style can include a single component representing a stud wall, and a complex wall style with a stud, gypsum board, airspace, brick veneer, and brick cap uses five components to represent each part of the wall. See **Figure 15-30.**

Figure 15-27.
Use the **Materials** tab to assign materials to wall components.

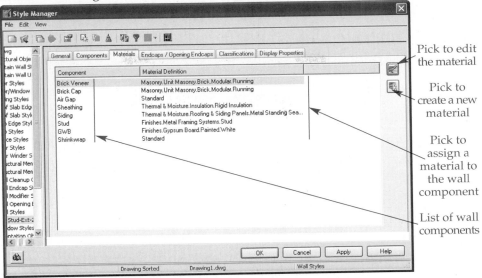

Pick to edit
the material

Pick to
create a new
material

Pick to
assign a
material to
the wall
component

List of wall
components

Figure 15-28.
The **Endcaps / Opening Endcaps** tab is used to assign an endcap to the edges of a wall or to
the ends of a wall when a wall opening is encountered.

Assign a wall endcap style
to the ends of the walls

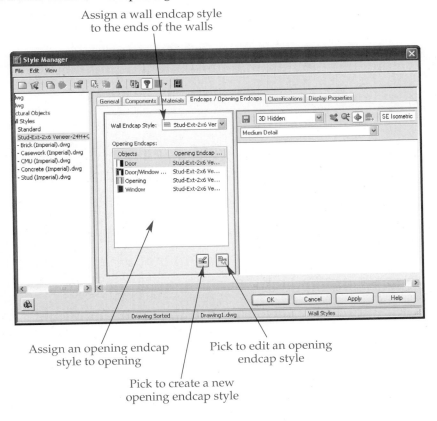

Assign an opening endcap
style to opening

Pick to edit an opening
endcap style

Pick to create a new
opening endcap style

Wall styles can use a total of 20 components. These components can be used to represent studs, brick, concrete, CMU block, siding, gypsum board, wainscot, baseboards, trim boards, countertops, casework, and many other construction materials. A wall component can be created only as a rectangular shape, but it can be modified using a wall sweep to represent a curved shape after the wall has been added to the drawing. See Chapter 12 on how to use wall sweeps.

Figure 15-29.
Use the **Classifications** tab to assign classifications to the wall style.

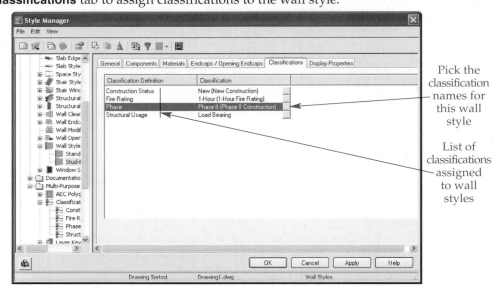

Pick the classification names for this wall style

List of classifications assigned to wall styles

Figure 15-30.
Wall styles are composed of wall components representing different construction materials.

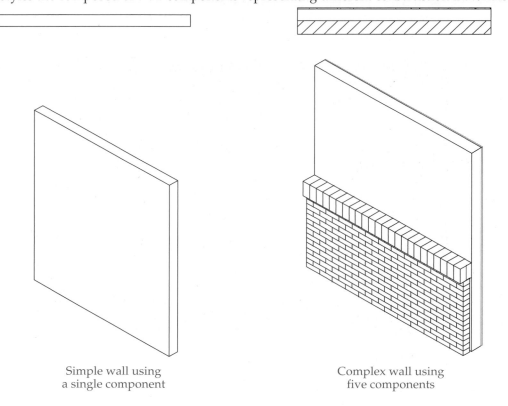

Simple wall using
a single component

Complex wall using
five components

Configuring Wall Components

Once a wall style has been created and the tabs containing properties for wall styles are displayed, the wall style can be configured. Select the **Components** tab to begin adding the wall components. See **Figure 15-26.** Initially, a new wall style includes one component with the name Unnamed. To rename the component, pick the name of the component, and then enter a new name in the text box under the **Name** column.

Beside the **Name** column is the **Priority** column. Pick the value to enter a new priority value. Each wall component is assigned a priority. Wall components with the same priority clean up with other wall components. A higher priority wall component cuts through a wall component of a lower priority, as in **Figure 15-31**. A value of 1 is the highest priority a wall component can be assigned. If a wall component is assigned a priority of 1, it can clean up with only another wall component with a value of 1 and cuts through all other priority wall components.

Appendix M provides a list of priorities that are assigned to different wall components within the default Architectural Desktop wall styles. For example, a Stud Wall component is assigned a priority of 500, and a Brick Veneer component is assigned a priority of 810, which indicates that a Stud Wall component can cut through a Brick Veneer component. The priorities established within the program vary, allowing you to use any priority value in between the Architectural Desktop priority values. For example, if you are creating a wall style that includes a stud and furring, you can assign the stud a priority of 500, and with the furring, it can be assigned a value of 510.

 NOTE Based on the type of wall component you are creating, assign a priority from the list in Appendix M. If a priority is not listed for the desired component, review the priority list and determine what the best priority would be. Keep in mind that higher priority components cut through lower priority wall components.

After determining the wall component name and priority, the width of the component can be entered. Beside the **Priority** column is the **Width** column. Selecting the area under the **Width** column displays a drop-down list arrow. Pick the arrow to specify the width of the wall component. See **Figure 15-32**. The first text box is known as the base value. The base value specifies the initial width of the wall component. A value of 0" allows the component to be a variable width, based on the width you enter when adding a wall to the drawing. The Standard wall style is an example of a component using a base value of 0".

If a value other than 0" is entered in the **Base Value** text box, the width is fixed for this component. For example, if you are creating an 8"-wide concrete component, enter 8" in the **Base Value** text box. The component now has a fixed width of 8" and cannot be changed when adding the wall to the drawing.

Beside the **Base Value** text box is a drop-down list to input the **Base Width**. If **0** is selected, the remaining text boxes are grayed out, and the width of the component is specified by the **Base Value** text box. The other option is the **Base Width** option. *Base*

Figure 15-31.
Wall components with the same priority will clean up with each other. Wall components with a higher priority cut through wall components with a lower priority.

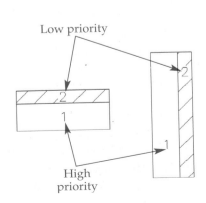
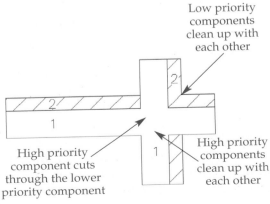

Figure 15-32.
Use the **Width** column to set the width of the wall component.

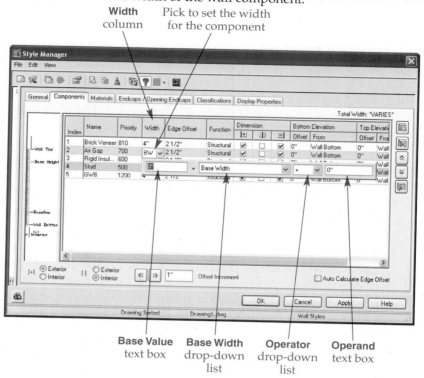

Width column

Pick to set the width for the component

Base Value text box

Base Width drop-down list

Operator drop-down list

Operand text box

width refers to the **Width** property of the wall when added to the drawing. When the **Base Width** option is specified, the base value and base width are added together to specify the total width for the wall component. For example, a 0″ Base Value + Base Width creates a wall component the width specified in the **Width** property, when adding a wall to the drawing; a 4″ Base Value + Base Width creates a wall the width specified in the **Width** property, plus 4″, when adding the wall.

When the **Base Width** option is selected, the last two text boxes are available. The drop-down list beside the **Base Width** drop-down list is known as the operator. The operator includes the **+, −, /,** and ***** symbols. Selecting an operator specifies a calculation to be performed on the width of the wall. Beside the **Operator** drop-down list is the **Operand** text box. Entering a value in this text box finishes the calculation for the total width of the wall component. For example, a wall component that specified a 2″ Base Value + Base Width / 2 creates a wall component half of the total value of the base value plus base width. In most situations, a wall component either has a set width in the Base Value + 0 Base Width or a 0 Base Value + Base Width.

After the width for the component has been determined, the placement of the component within the wall can be specified. The **Edge Offset** column is used to place the component in relation to the baseline of the wall. When walls are added to the drawing, one of the wall justifications is the **Baseline** option. This justification indicates that the wall is drawn from the baseline of the wall style. If you are looking at the wall from the left side, the wall components are added to the style by measuring a distance from the baseline to the right edge of the wall component. See **Figure 15-33.** A positive distance moves the component to the left, and a negative distance moves the wall component to the right.

Pick the value in the **Edge Offset** column for the wall component being adjusted. This displays a drop-down list. See **Figure 15-34.** Similar to the **Width** parameters, this drop-down list provides **Base Value, Base Width, Operator,** and **Operand** text boxes and drop-down lists. In the **Base Value** text box, enter the positive or negative distance

Figure 15-33.
The placement of a wall component is determined by the distance from the baseline to the right edge of the component.

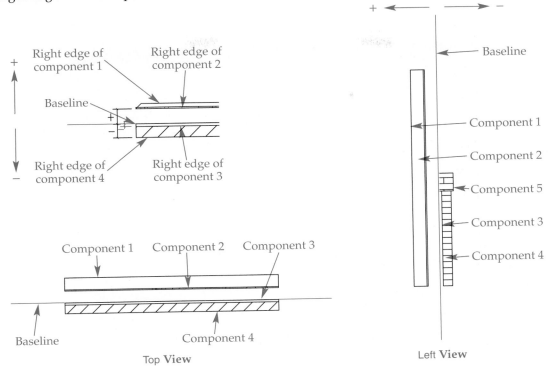

Top **View**

Left **View**

from the baseline to the right edge of the wall component. For example, a value of 6″ places the right edge of the component a positive 6″ from the baseline. A value of −6″ places the right edge of the component a negative 6″ from the baseline. The **Auto Calculate Edge Offset** check box is used to automatically place the new component to the right of the previous component in the list.

NOTE

In most cases, wall components are placed at a specific distance from the baseline, whether it is a positive or negative distance. Generally, the **Use Base Width** option is checked off for each of the components, unless the component is to vary in placement based on the width of the wall. This is a difficult process to master. Experiment with the operators. To make it easier to see how the components are placed in a wall style, use the **Viewer** to look at the Left view. You also may review an existing Architectural Desktop complex wall style that allows you to specify a wall width for ideas on how to use the operators and operands.

The **Base Width** drop-down list includes the **0** and **Base Width** options. If the **0** option is specified, the right edge of the component is always located at the base value location. If the **Base Width** option is specified, the value in the **Base Value** text box is added to the **Width** property specified when drawing a new wall. This sets the right edge of the component a total distance of the Base Value + Base Width from the baseline. Beside the **Base Width** drop-down list is the **Operator** drop-down list, which includes the **+**, **−**, **/**, and ***** operators, which can be used in an equation to specify the location of the wall component.

The last text box contains the operand. An equation for the location of the wall component can be constructed by specifying a base value, the base width, an operator, and an operand. For example, the right edge of a component next to a variable width

Figure 15-34.
The **Edge Offset** column is used to place the wall component in relation to the baseline of the wall.

Edge Offset
column

Pick to adjust the right
edge of the component in
relation to the baseline

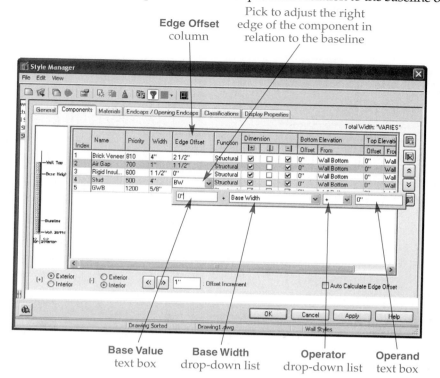

Base Value
text box

Base Width
drop-down list

Operator
drop-down list

Operand
text box

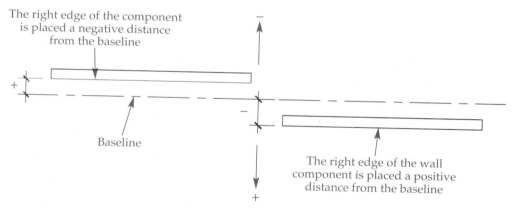

The right edge of the component
is placed a negative distance
from the baseline

Baseline

The right edge of the wall
component is placed a positive
distance from the baseline

component can be specified by entering a 0" Base Value + Base Width + 0". Another example is to create a wall component that is always centered on the baseline, no matter what the width of the wall property is. Use the equation of a 0" base value **+ Base Width * –1/2**. This indicates that the component looks to the **Width** property when adding a wall, and multiplies the width by a negative one-half. This repositions the component so the right edge is half the distance of the width from the baseline.

Wall components can be specified as Structural or Non-Structural components when dimensioning. Pick the drop-down list under the **Function** column to assign a function. When dimensioning with AEC dimensions, you can specify to dimension all components within a wall or only structural components.

The **Dimension** column is used to specify the side or center of a component to be dimensioned using AEC dimensions. If a wall component is to be dimensioned from the left side, select the **[+]** check box beside the component. If the AEC dimensions are to dimension to the center of the component, select the **[l]** check box beside the component. If the wall component will be dimensioned to the right side, select the **[–]** check box.

The final settings for the wall components include setting the vertical elevation offsets for the components. The right side of the **Components** tab includes **Bottom Elevation** and **Top Elevation** areas. Each of these areas sets the elevation for the wall component in relation to points on the wall.

The **Bottom Elevation** area sets the bottom of the wall component in relation to the four vertical locations described below. First, set an offset distance under the **Offset** column, and then select a vertical offset (**From**) location. For example, if the bottom of a wall component is to be located 3'-8" off the floor, enter a value of 3'-8" **From** the **Baseline**. The four location options are described next:

- **Wall Bottom.** This option is used when the wall component has the ability to be projected downward when the **FLOORLINE** command is used on the wall. This location specifies the lowest elevation of a wall. See Chapter 12 on how to use the **FLOORLINE** command.
- **Baseline.** This option generally represents the floor plate location. The baseline of a wall is always measured to the current Z axis location. Use this option if the wall component cannot be projected down with the **FLOORLINE** command.
- **Base Height.** This option represents the height of the wall, as specified in the **Properties** palette when adding the wall. The bottom of a wall can be specified in relation to the base height of the wall.
- **Wall Top.** This option is used if the wall component can be projected upward with the **ROOFLINE** command. See Chapter 12 on how to use the **ROOFLINE** command.

When placing the bottom of a wall component, you can place the component anywhere vertically in the wall by specifying a distance and a vertical offset location. The **Top Elevation** area is used to adjust the top of the wall component. As with the **Bottom Elevation** area, enter a vertical distance in relation to a vertical offset location.

Once you have configured the vertical elevation offsets for the wall component, you can add and configure additional wall components by picking the **Add Component** button. **Figure 15-35** displays a wall style that includes Stud, Airspace, Brick Veneer, Brick Veneer Cap, and Gypsum Board components. The settings for the wall components are listed in the figure.

In addition to configuring wall styles, tools within the **Components** tab can be helpful when creating a wall style. See **Figure 15-36**. The preview pane on the left side of the **Components** tab displays the wall components in a Left view. As a component is being modified, the component is surrounded by a green highlight, by default. The view can be adjusted by pressing down the pick button and moving the mouse, similar to when using the **Object Viewer** or **Viewer**. Right-clicking in the preview pane displays a shortcut menu of options to adjust the view.

Two arrow buttons are available below the preview pane to move the selected component from the table to the left or right of the entire wall assembly. The **Offset Increment** text box allows you to enter a value representing how far the component can be moved left or right with the increment and decrement buttons. Using these tools adjusts the **Edge Offset** for a component and updates the values in the **Components** tab.

On the right side of the tab are the **Add Component** and **Remove Component** buttons. The **Move Component Up** and **Move Component Down** buttons are used to move the component up and down the list. This has no impact on how the wall is assembled.

The last button on the right is the **Wall Style Browser** button. Picking this button opens the **Wall Style Components Browser**. See **Figure 15-36**. The **Wall Style Components Browser** allows you to open existing drawings containing wall styles, so wall components from other styles can be dragged into your custom style. Use the **Open Drawing** button to browse for a drawing with wall styles, and pick a wall style to list the wall components. Drag a component from the **Wall Style Components Browser** into the **Components** tab. The wall component and its settings are added to your wall style.

Figure 15-35.
A custom complex wall style can be created to represent any type of wall with up to 20 components.

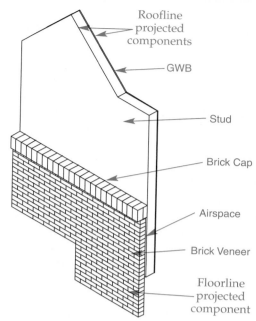

Index #	Name	Priority	Width	Edge Offset	Bottom Elevation	Top Elevation
1	GWB	1200	BV =5/8" + 0	BV= 0" + BW + 0"	0" from BL	0" from WT
2	Stud	500	BV =0" + BW + 0"	BV= 0" + 0	0" from BL	0" from WT
3	Airspace	700	BV = 1" + 0	BV= −1" + 0	0" from WB	3'-4" from BL
4	Brick Veneer	810	BV = 4" + 0	BV= −5" + 0	0" from WB	3'-4" from BL
5	Brick Cap	815	BV = 7" + 0	BV= −7" + 0	3'-4" from BL	4'-0" from BL

BL: Baseline
BV: Base Value
BW: Base Width
WB: Wall Bottom
WT: Wall Top

The wall style can be used to create many types of walls in detailed and schematic representation. Wall styles can be used to create walls with trim, veneer, casework, shelving, exterior corner quoins, custom railings, and anything you can imagine. See **Figure 15-37**. Remember that the components are rectangular and are represented horizontally. If you need shapes other than rectangules, apply wall sweeps to the wall components.

Exercise
15-6   **Complete the Exercise on the Student CD.**

Creating Wall Endcaps

Endcaps are another useful tool in creating a wall or wall style. *Endcaps* are graphics applied to the end of a wall or wall opening to provide a better representation of wall component construction. See **Figure 15-38**.

Figure 15-36.
Use the **Wall Style Components Browser** to drag and drop components from other wall styles.

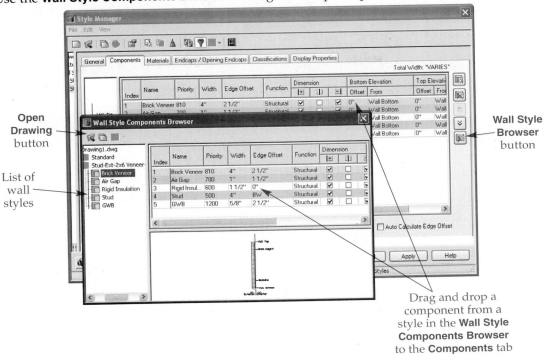

Open Drawing button

List of wall styles

Wall Style Browser button

Drag and drop a component from a style in the **Wall Style Components Browser** to the **Components** tab

Figure 15-37.
Some custom wall styles used for different purposes.

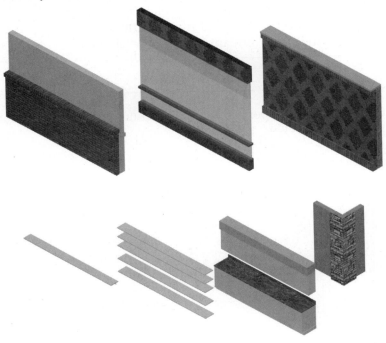

An endcap is created by drawing an open-ended polyline the shape desired at the end of the wall. A polyline should be drawn for each wall component within the wall style. The polylines are then assigned to the wall components through the **WALLENDCAPSTYLE** command.

Figure 15-38.
Endcaps are applied to the ends of walls and openings in a wall.

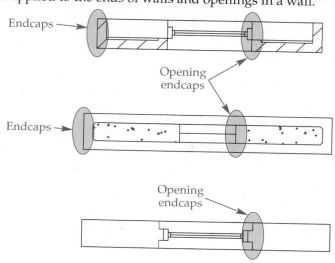

Creating Custom Endcap Styles

When a polyline is drawn for a wall component endcap, the start point and endpoint of the polyline must line up in the same plane. See **Figure 15-39.** The polyline shape can vary, depending on how the component should end.

NOTE

> The polylines for the endcaps do not have to be drawn separated, as shown in **Figure 15-39.** It is often easier to draw the polyline over the end of the wall where the endcap is to appear to better visualize where the components end in relation to the other wall component endcaps. Keep in mind that the starting and ending points of each of the polylines must line up in the same plane.

Figure 15-39.
Draw a polyline for each wall component, ensuring the start point and endpoint of the polyline line up in the same plane.

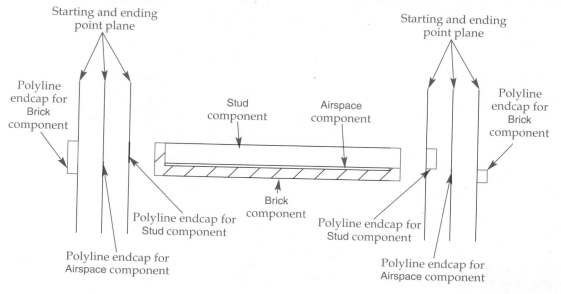

After drawing the polylines defining how the wall components end, you need to group the polylines together in a wall endcap style. To create the style, select **Design > Walls > Wall Endcap Styles...** from the pull-down menu or type WALLENDCAPSTYLE. This displays the **Style Manager** opened to the Wall Endcap Styles section.

Select the **New Style** button to create a new style and give it a name. Defining an endcap style is similar to defining a profile. First, select the style name from the **Style Manager**. Pick the **Set From** button, or right-click and pick **Set From...** from the shortcut menu. You are returned to the drawing screen, where you are prompted for a few settings.

During the process of defining the endcap, you must select each polyline and assign it to a wall component index number. These numbers correspond to the index numbers in the properties listed in the **Components** tab under the Wall Styles section. The last prompt allows you to specify a return offset. Entering a positive value offsets the endcap into the wall the specified distance. Entering a value of 0" places the outermost edge of the endcap at the endpoint of the wall, and entering a negative value places the start point and endpoint of the polyline endcap at the end of the wall. See **Figure 15-40.**

After the endcap style has been defined, the **Style Manager** is displayed again. Pick the **OK** button to save the style in the drawing. The endcap can now be assigned to a wall, wall style, or wall opening.

NOTE — Endcap polylines respect the direction in which the wall is drawn. Define an endcap, and then assign it to a wall. If the endcap appears reversed or mirrored, try redrawing the polyline in the opposite direction. For example, if the polyline is drawn clockwise and it appears mirrored, try drawing the polyline in a counterclockwise direction and redefining the endcap style.

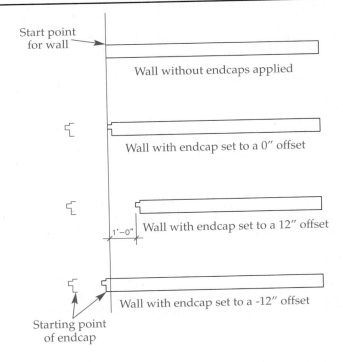

Figure 15-40. Different offset values place the endcap at different points within the wall.

An alternative way of adding a wall endcap style is to draw it directly over the wall, and then convert the polylines into an endcap. Draw a polyline for each component within the wall, ensure the start points and endpoints for the polylines line up in the correct plane, and draw the polylines where the wall components end. See **Figure 15-41.** After drawing the polylines, select the wall that will have the endcaps attached, right-click, and select **Endcaps** > **Calculate Automatically** from the shortcut menu. This initiates the **WALLAUTOENDCAP** command.

After entering the command, select the polylines to be used as the endcap. When you are finished selecting the polylines, press the [Enter] key. You are prompted to erase the polylines after converting or keeping them. The next prompt asks if the current endcap style will be modified by replacing the new polylines. The last prompt asks how the endcap will be applied. The endcap can be applied as the wall style default or as an override to that end of the wall. If the current endcap is not being modified, the **New Endcap Style** worksheet will appear, allowing you to name the new endcap style being created. After picking the **OK** button, the polylines are converted into an endcap.

Special Endcap Considerations

Special endcaps can be created with wide polylines. For example, these are used if your design requires a wall to be wrapped with gypsum wall board or a brick veneer. Another example is if you are remodeling a building that was originally drawn with 2D linework and you need the Architectural Desktop walls to be open-ended so they can tie into the 2D linework to make the walls appear to clean up. Draw the polyline endcap geometry as you would normally, except where two components' endcaps meet, and make that segment a wide polyline with a width greater than 0″. See **Figure 15-42.** In the case of an open-ended wall, create a single wide polyline. After drawing the components, create and apply the endcap as you would a standard endcap.

The open-ended endcap consists of a single wide polyline segment, added to 20 components (maximum number of wall components). This applies the wide polyline to 20 possible components in a wall style, leaving the endcap open.

Figure 15-41.
Polylines drawn directly over the wall can be converted into an endcap style.

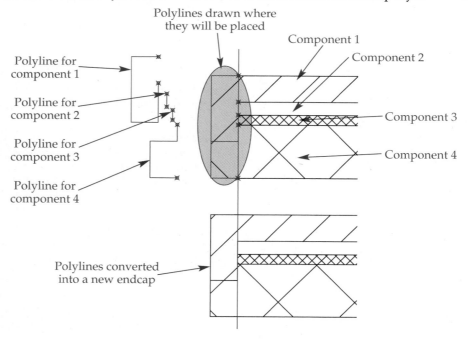

Architectural Desktop and Its Applications

Figure 15-42.
A wide polyline segment can be used when defining an endcap that is to be open on one end.

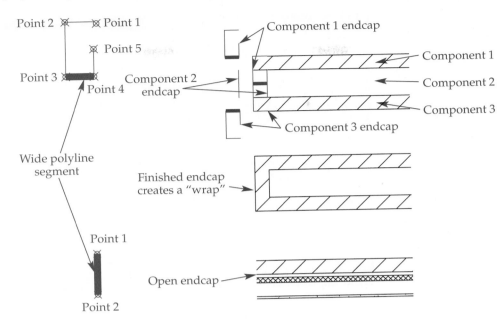

Creating Opening Endcap Styles

An *opening endcap style* is an endcap style applied to the edges of a Door, Door/ Window Assembly, Opening, or Window object within the wall. Opening endcap styles apply a wall endcap to the four edges: top, bottom, left, and right of an opening. To create an opening endcap style, select **Design** > **Walls** > **Wall Opening Endcap Styles...** from the pull-down menu or type OPENINGENDCAPSTYLE.

As with other styles, select the **New Style** button, or right-click over the Wall Opening Endcap Styles section and pick the **New** option to create a new style. Enter a name for the new style, and then pick the style in the tree view to display the tabs for the style properties. See **Figure 15-43**. Properties for these styles provide **General** and **Design Rules** tabs.

Use the **General** tab to rename the style and provide a description for the style. Pick the **Design Rules** tab to configure the settings for the opening endcap. The **Design Rules** include a list of four positions around an opening. Pick in the **Endcap Style** column beside the position to be modified, and select a wall endcap style to be used for that position. The jambs (sides of an opening) can have one type of endcap assigned, and the head (top) and sill (bottom) positions can have two different endcaps assigned.

After defining the endcap styles, wall endcaps and opening endcaps can be assigned to a wall style in the Wall Styles section under the **Endcaps / Open Endcaps** tab. In order for the opening endcaps to be displayed in a Model view and an Elevation view, the Model display representation for the wall style needs to be adjusted. In the wall style Model display representation **Other** tab, turn on the **Display Opening Endcaps** check box in the Model display representation.

Editing Endcaps in Place

Throughout this text, different objects have been introduced that can be edited in place. An endcap can also be edited in place, and its shape can be modified. To edit an endcap in place, select the wall to be modified, right-click, and pick **Endcaps** > **Edit In Place** from the shortcut menu. You are prompted to select a point near an endcap. Pick a point near the point of the endcap you want to modify. This displays the **In Place Edit** toolbar and highlights one of the wall components with its associated endcap.

Figure 15-43.
The tabs containing
properties for
opening endcap
styles are used to
configure endcaps
at an opening in a
wall.

Pick an endcap style to be assigned
to a position in the opening endcap

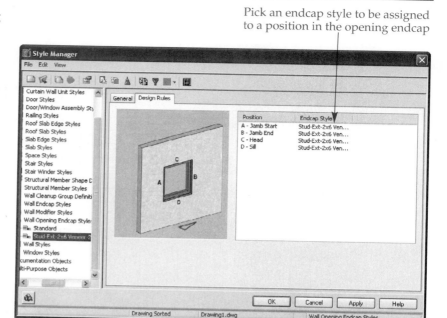

See **Figure 15-44.** Use the grips to modify the points for the endcap. If a different component's endcap is to be modified, select the component to display its endcap so editing can be accomplished.

Right-clicking while a component and endcap are highlighted displays a shortcut menu of options related to editing the endcap. Use the **Hide Edge** or **Show Edge** options to hide or display the edge of an endcap. Vertices can also be added or removed from the component endcap. When you are finished, pick **Save All Changes** to save the changes to the endcap style, which affects this endcap wherever it is used, or right-click and pick the **Save As New Endcap Style** to save what you have edited as a new endcap style. This new endcap style can then be applied as an override to different walls.

To override the endcap of a wall, pick the wall to highlight it, right-click, and select **Endcaps > Override Endcap Style** from the shortcut menu. If a wall or wall style includes an endcap style, you can override the style without having to use the **Properties** palette.

Figure 15-44.
Endcaps can be
edited in place.
Adjust the grips
or use the shortcut
menu for additional
editing options.

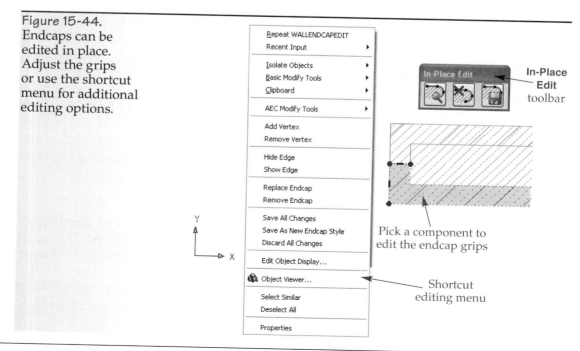

In-Place
Edit
toolbar

Pick a component to
edit the endcap grips

Shortcut
editing menu

On entering this command, you are prompted to select a point. Select the side of the wall that includes the endcap to be overridden. After the point is selected, the **Select an Endcap Style** dialog box is displayed, allowing you to select the endcap to use at the end of the selected wall.

You can also insert a wall endcap into the drawing as a polyline for any type of modification. Pick **Design** > **Walls** > **Insert Endcap Style as Polyline** from the pull-down menu.

Pull-Down Menu
Design
> Walls
> Insert Endcap
Style as
Polyline

The **Endcap Styles** dialog box is displayed with a list of endcaps in the drawing. Select the endcap you would like to insert into the drawing for modification. Pick the **OK** button, and then pick a location in the drawing to insert the polylines. Separate the polylines using the **MOVE** command and make any adjustments to the polylines. When you are finished, define the group of polylines as a new endcap or redefine an existing one.

Exercise
15-7   Complete the Exercise on the Student CD.

Using and Creating Door Styles

Architectural Desktop includes a number of door styles and the ability to create door styles. Many door styles can be found in the **Doors** tool palette, and additional styles can be imported through the **Content Browser** or **Style Manager**. Custom doors can also be created using standard shapes and door types or from a custom AEC profile.

Importing Additional Door Styles

The **Doors** tool palette contains many of the door styles needed to create a set of construction documents. Additional styles can be imported to the drawing through the use of the **Style Manager**. Door styles can also be i-dropped from the **Content Browser** into the drawing, loading the style for your use. To access the **DOORSTYLE** command, pick **Design** > **Doors** > **Door Styles…** from the pull-down menu or type DOORSTYLE. Right-clicking over a **Door** tool in the **Tool Palettes** window displays a shortcut menu with the **Door Styles…** command. This displays the **Style Manager** opened to the Door Styles section.

Type
DOORSTYLE
Pull-Down Menu
Design
> Doors
> Door Styles...

DOORSTYLE

To import door styles into your drawing, select the **Open Drawing** button. Pick the **Content** button to browse to the Styles folder, and open the Imperial or Metric folder. Select Door Styles.dwg, and then pick the **Open** button to open the drawing file within the **Style Manager**. Browse through the drawing's door styles by selecting a door style in the left tree view. Pick the **Floating Viewer** button to display the **Viewer** to review the door styles.

Drag the desired styles from the drawing into your current drawing folder icon in the tree view to import the styles into your drawing for use. More than 40 different door styles are available. The door styles range from simple door panel styles to door styles that have custom blocks and glazing applied. When you are finished importing door styles, right-click on Door Styles.dwg and select **Close** from the shortcut menu to close the drawing.

Door styles can also be found and imported from the **Content Browser**. Use the drag-and-drop procedure to import the styles from the **Content Browser** to the current drawing. Like wall styles, unused door styles take up space in the drawing. Use the **Purge Styles** button to purge any unwanted door styles from the drawing to reduce the size of the drawing.

Creating Custom Door Styles

Custom door styles can also be created through the **Style Manager**. A custom door can take on any default shape, such as a rectangle or an arched top, or it can use a custom AEC profile as its shape. In order for a custom door to be created, the definition must exist in the **Style Manager**. In the **Style Manager**, select the **New Style** button to create a new door style. Enter a name for the door style, and highlight the name to display the properties for the Door Styles section, as shown in **Figure 15-45**.

The properties for the Door Styles section include the following seven tabs for configuring the door style:

- **General.** This tab is used to rename and provide a description for the door style, attach design or specification notes, and assign property set definitions and keynotes to the door style.

- **Dimensions.** This tab is divided into three separate areas, as shown in **Figure 15-45**. The **Frame** area controls the size of the door frame. Enter a width and depth for the frame. Below the frame depth is a check box that adjusts the depth of the door to reflect the width of the wall where it is inserted. The **Stop** area is used to configure the size of the door stop. At the bottom of the tab are settings that control the thickness of the door panel and glazing within the door.

- **Design Rules.** This tab is used to configure the shape and type of door being created. See **Figure 15-46**. The left side of the tab is used to specify the shape of the door. The **Predefined:** radio button controls the predefined shapes for the door style. The drop-down list beside the **Predefined:** radio button includes several different types of shapes. As you select shapes from the drop-down list, use the **Floating Viewer** button to preview what the door will look like. The **Use**

Figure 15-45.
The tabs containing properties for door styles are used to create custom door styles.

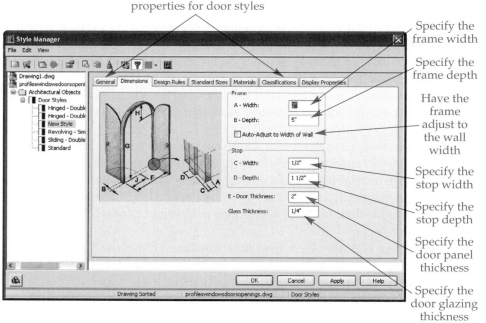

Figure 15-46.
The **Design Rules** tab is used to configure the shape and door type for the door style.

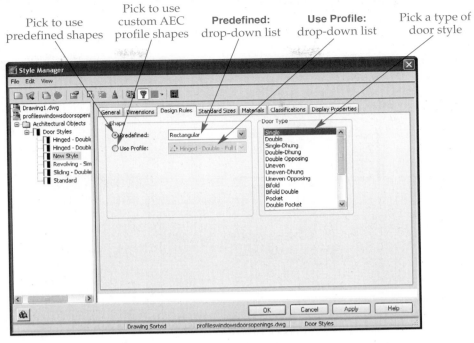

Pick to use predefined shapes · Pick to use custom AEC profile shapes · Predefined: drop-down list · Use Profile: drop-down list · Pick a type of door style

Profile: radio button is tied to the drop-down list to its right. This list includes all the AEC profiles in the current drawing. Any AEC profile can be used to create a custom door shape. If a profile includes void rings, the voided areas become Glass components in the door.

After you have selected the shape, select the type of door to use from the **Door Type** area on the right. As with the shape drop-down lists, use the **Floating Viewer** button to preview how the door will appear, using the different shapes in combination with the door type.

- **Standard Sizes.** This tab is used to specify predefined sizes for the door style. These sizes are then available when the door is added into the drawing through the **Properties** palette. See **Figure 15-47.** Select the **Add...** button to display the **Add Standard Sizes** dialog box. Enter sizes you need for this type of door.
- **Materials.** This tab is used to assign material definitions to the components of the door. See **Figure 15-48.** Pick in the **Material Definitions** column beside a door component to assign a material from a list of materials in the drawing. The **Add New Material** and the **Edit Material** buttons are also available.
- **Classifications.** This tab is used to assign predefined classifications to the style. Select any desired classifications for use in your style. See **Figure 15-49.**
- **Display Properties.** This tab controls the display of doors. The display for the doors can be controlled at the drawing default level or at the door style level. Remember to control the Plan, Reflected, Model, and Elevation representations for the door. Custom blocks can also be attached for most of the representations. See Chapter 13 for adding custom blocks to doors.

NOTE   It is generally a good idea to control the display of objects at the style level, especially when customizing your own styles.

Figure 15-47.
The **Standard Sizes** tab is used to define predefined sizes that are available in the **Properties** palette when the door is added to a wall.

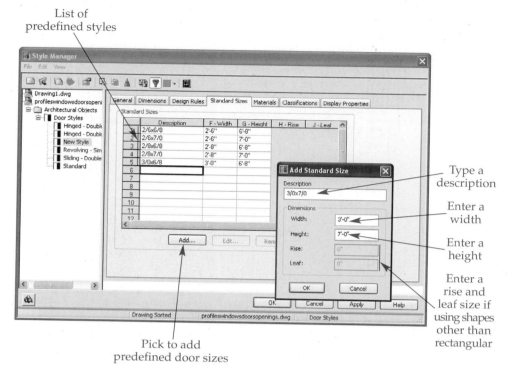

List of predefined styles

Type a description

Enter a width

Enter a height

Enter a rise and leaf size if using shapes other than rectangular

Pick to add predefined door sizes

Figure 15-48.
Use the **Materials** tab to assign materials to the door components.

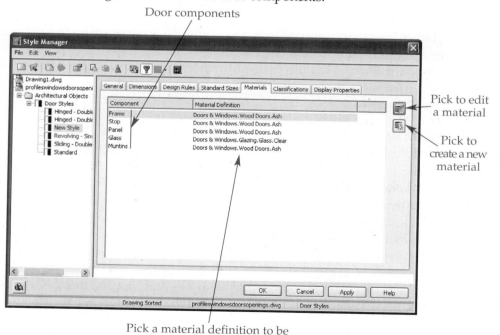

Door components

Pick to edit a material

Pick to create a new material

Pick a material definition to be assigned to the door component

Figure 15-49.
Assign classification definitions to the door style as needed.

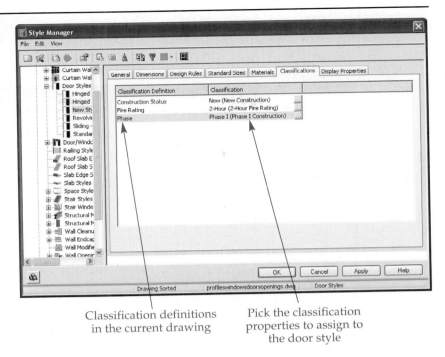

Classification definitions in the current drawing

Pick the classification properties to assign to the door style

Exercise 15-9   Complete the Exercise on the Student CD.

Using and Creating Window Styles

Window styles are very similar to door styles. Window styles can be imported from other drawings, or they can be customized. To access the Window Styles section of the **Style Manager**, select **Design > Windows > Window Styles...** from the pull-down menu or type WINDOWSTYLE. You can also access it by right-clicking over a window tool in the **Tool Palettes** window and picking the **Window Styles...** command.

Importing Additional Window Styles

To import window styles, select the **Open Drawing** button in the **Style Manager**. Any existing drawing can be used to select available window styles. Architectural Desktop includes additional window styles found in Window Styles.dwg. Pick the **Content** button to browse through the Styles folder and open Window Styles.dwg.

In the **Style Manager**, browse through the list of styles until you find the desired window styles. Drag and drop the styles from the open drawing in the **Style Manager** to another drawing icon in the **Style Manager**. Window Styles.dwg includes many window styles, such as Bow, Bay, and Shutter window styles.

When you have finished importing styles, select the drawing that was opened in the **Style Manager**, right-click, and select the **Close** option. This closes the drawing and helps keep the **Style Manager** from getting cluttered with open drawings. Like other styles, unused window styles take up room in the drawing. Use the **Purge Styles** button to purge any unwanted window styles from the drawing and reduce the size of the drawing file.

Figure 15-50.
The tabs containing properties for window styles are used to configure a window style.

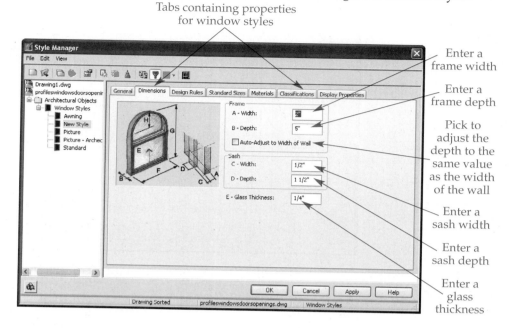

Creating Custom Window Styles

To create custom window styles, access the **WINDOWSTYLE** command, and then select the **New Style** button in the **Style Manager**. Enter a new name for the style, and then edit the style. The properties for the Window Styles section, shown in **Figure 15-50**, are displayed. The properties available in the Window Styles section are similar to those in the Door Styles section, except some of the options are different. When you have finished configuring the window style, the style is ready to be used.

The properties in the Window Styles section are divided into the same seven tabs available in the Door Styles section. The **General** tab, **Standard Sizes** tab, **Materials** tab, **Classifications** tab, and **Display Properties** tab offer the same options in both. The **Dimensions** tab controls the sizes of the frame sash and glass. See **Figure 15-50**. Use the **Auto-Adjust to Width of Wall** option to make the depth of the window the same as the width of the wall. The **Design Rules** tab is used to specify the shape and type of the window being created. See **Figure 15-51**. Unlike with door styles, the use of a custom profile shape with rings creates actual voids within the window. The edges of the inner rings become muntins within the window, and the void is an open hole in the window Glass component. If you create a window style using a profile with voids, fill the voids with a block representing glazing panels, and attach the block through the **Display Properties** tab for the appropriate display representation.

Exercise 15-11   Complete the Exercise on the Student CD.

Figure 15-51.
The **Design Rules** tab is used to specify a shape and type of window for the new window style.

Select to use
predefined shapes

Select to use
AEC profile
shapes

List of
predefined
window shapes

List of AEC
profiles in
the drawing

Select the type
of window to use

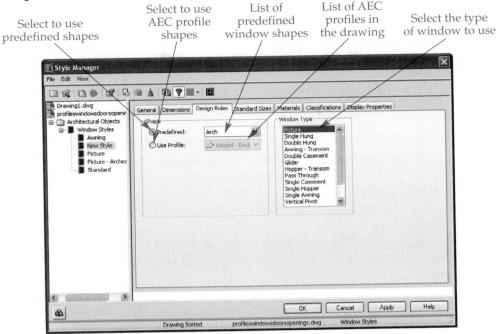

Chapter Test

Answer the following questions. Write your answers on a separate sheet of paper or complete the electronic chapter test on the Student CD.

1. Outline at least two uses for the **Style Manager**.
2. Identify two ways to open the **Style Manager**, and explain the difference in appearance between the methods.
3. What happens when you pick the + sign beside a folder in the **Style Manager**?
4. When new styles are defined, the styles are then placed under the appropriate styles section. What do you get when you select the + sign beside a style section icon?
5. Discuss how to import individual and multiple object styles.
6. Provide an advantage for purging unused styles from your drawing.
7. Briefly explain global and individual object styles.
8. Explain the function of the **Content Browser**.
9. Briefly explain how i-drop technology works.
10. What items are contained in the Design Tool catalog and the Documentation catalog?
11. Identify what is included in the Stock Tool catalog.
12. Define *render materials* and explain how they are added to the drawing.
13. Define and give the function of a *classification definition*.
14. How many components can you put in a custom wall style?
15. What can wall style components represent, and what shape(s) can they be?
16. Identify the highest priority a wall component can have and the wall component this priority can clean up.
17. Give a specific example of how assigning priority values affects wall cleanup.
18. What does the base value specify, and what does a 0″ value accomplish?
19. What happens if a value other than 0″ is entered as the base value?
20. Define *base width*, and give an example of a base width calculation.

Chapter Projects

Use the techniques covered in this chapter to create the following drawings.

1. Single-Level Residential Project
   A. Access the **Project Browser** and set Residential-Project-01 current.
   B. Access the **Constructs** tab of the **Project Navigator** and open the Main Floor construct.
   C. Import the following wall styles from the imperial or metric Casework.dwg:
      a. Imperial: Casework-36 (Base with Counter); Metric: Casework-900 (Base with Counter)
      b. Imperial: Casework-42 (Bar); Metric: Casework-1050 (Bar)
      c. Imperial: Casework-42 (Upper); Metric: Casework-1050 (Upper)
   D. Modify the Imperial: Casework-36 (Base with Counter) or Metric: Casework-900 (Base with Counter) wall style to use the Standard endcap style.
   E. Drag the Plumbing-Appliances construct into the Main Floor construct for use as a reference.
   F. Add the casework to the kitchen area, as shown in the diagram on the next page. Ensure you place the different types of casework on their own cleanup group.
   G. Create a wall style that looks like a closet shelf with a pole. Use the display properties to make the pole a Hidden linetype. Add the new style to the closets.
   H. Import the Hinged – Single – Exterior Panel door style from Door Style.dwg. Modify the front door to use this style.
   I. Modify the window styles to include muntin configurations.
   J. Purge any unused door, endcap, wall, and window styles from the drawing.
   K. Detach the Plumbing-Appliances construct.
   L. Save and close the drawing.

Note: You may need to adjust the appliance locations and elevations in the Plumbing-Appliances construct. To do this, open the Plumbing-Appliances construct, reference the Main Floor construct, and then adjust the appliances as needed. Detach the Main Floor construct when you are finished.

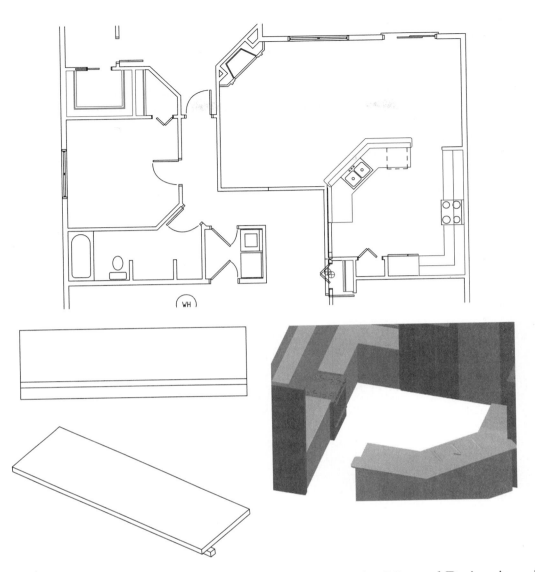

Design Courtesy Alan Mascord Design Associates

2. Single-Level Residential Project
   A. Access the **Project Browser** and set Residential-Project-02 current.
   B. Access the **Constructs** tab of the **Project Navigator** and open the Main Floor construct.
   C. Import the following wall styles from Casework.dwg:
      a. Imperial: Casework-36 (Base with Counter); Metric: Casework-900 (Base with Counter)
      b. Imperial: Casework-36 (Isle); Metric: Casework-900 (Isle)
      c. Imperial: Casework-42 (Upper); Metric: Casework-1050 (Upper)
      d. Imperial: Casework-60 (Tall); Casework-1500(Tall)
   D. Modify the Imperial: Casework-36 (Base with Counter) or Metric: Casework-900 (Base with Counter) wall style to use the Standard endcap style.
   E. Modify the Imperial: Casework-36 (Isle) or Metric: Casework-900 (Isle) wall style by adding an eating bar, similar to that in Exercise 15-6.
   F. Drag the Plumbing-Appliances construct into the Main Floor construct for use as a reference.
   G. Add the casework to the kitchen area, as shown in the diagram. Ensure you create wall cleanup groups and that the different types of casework are added to their own cleanup group.

H. Create a wall style that looks like a closet shelf with a pole. Use the display properties to make the pole a Hidden linetype. Add the new style to the closets.
I. Import the Hinged – Single – Exterior Panel door style from Door Style.dwg. Modify the front door to use this style.
J. Modify the window styles to include muntin configurations.
K. Purge any unused door, endcap, wall, and window styles from the drawing.
L. Detach the Plumbing-Appliances construct.
M. Save and close the drawing.

Note: You may need to adjust the appliance locations and elevations in the Plumbing-Appliances construct. To do this, open the Plumbing-Appliances construct, reference the Main Floor construct, and then adjust the appliances as needed. Detach the Main Floor construct when you are finished.

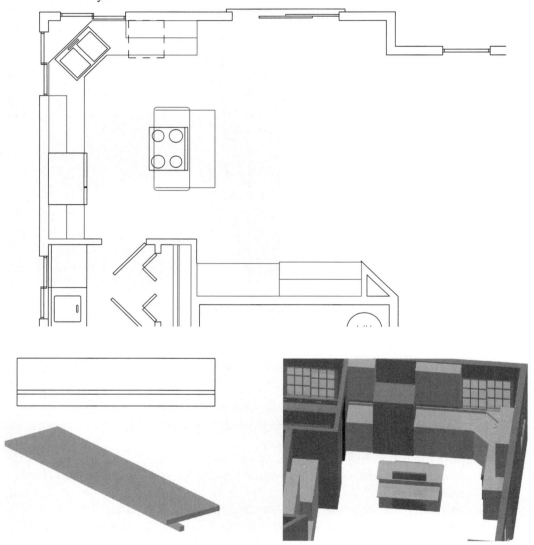

Design Courtesy Alan Mascord Design Associates

3. Two-Story Residential Project
   A. Access the **Project Browser** and set Residential-Project-03 current.
   B. Access the **Constructs** tab of the **Project Navigator** and open the Main Floor construct.
   C. Import the following wall styles from Casework (Imperial).dwg:
       a. Casework-36 (Base with Counter)
       b. Casework-36 (Isle)
       c. Casework-42 (Upper)
   D. Modify the Casework-36 (Base with Counter) wall style to use the Standard endcap style.
   E. Modify the Casework-36 (Isle) wall style by adding an eating bar similar to that in Exercise 15-6.
   F. Drag the Plumbing-Appliances construct into the Main Floor construct for use as a reference.
   G. Add casework to the kitchen area, as shown in the diagram. Ensure you create wall cleanup groups and that the different types of casework are added to their own cleanup groups.
   H. Create a wall style that looks like a closet shelf with a pole. Use the display properties to make the pole a Hidden linetype. Add the new style to the closets.
   I. Import the Hinged – Single – Exterior Panel door style from Door Styles.dwg. Modify the front door to use this style.
   J. Purge any unused door, endcap, wall, and window styles from the drawing.
   K. Detach the Plumbing-Appliances construct.
   L. Save and close the drawing.

Note: You may need to adjust the appliance locations and elevations in the Plumbing-Appliances construct. To do this, open the Plumbing-Appliances construct, reference the Main Floor construct, and then adjust the appliances as needed. Detach the Main Floor construct when you are finished.

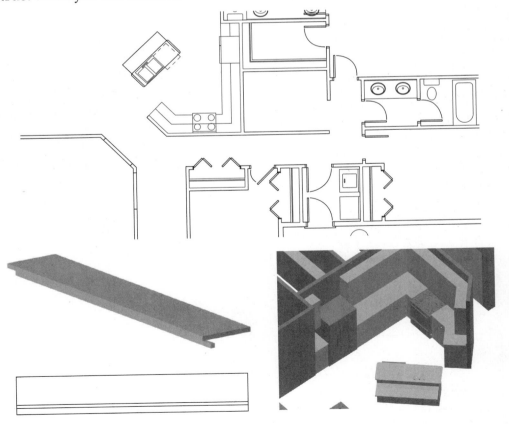

Drawing Courtesy 3D-DZYN

4. Two-Story Residential Project
  A. Access the **Project Browser** and set Residential-Project-04 current.
  B. Access the **Constructs** tab of the **Project Navigator** and open the Main Floor construct.
  C. Import the following wall styles from Casework (Imperial).dwg:
    a. Casework-36 (Base with Counter)
    b. Casework-36 (Isle)
    c. Casework-42 (Upper)
  D. Modify the Casework-36 (Base with Counter) wall style to use the Standard end-cap style.
  E. Modify the Casework-36 (Isle) wall style by adding an eating bar similar to that in Exercise 15-6.
  F. Drag the MainFlr-Plumbing-Appliances construct into the Main Floor construct for use as a reference.
  G. Add casework to the kitchen area, as shown in the diagram. Ensure you create wall cleanup groups and that the different types of casework are added to their own cleanup groups.
  H. Create a wall style that looks like a closet shelf with a pole. Use the display properties to make the pole a Hidden linetype. Add the new style to the closets.
  I. Import the Hinged – Single – Exterior Panel door style from Door Styles.dwg. Modify the front door to use this style.
  J. Purge any unused door, endcap, wall, and window styles from the drawing.
  K. Detach the MainFlr-Plumbing-Appliances construct.
  L. Save and close the drawing.
  M. Access the **Constructs** tab of the **Project Navigator** and open the Upper Floor construct.
  N. Import the closet wall style created for the main floor.
  O. Add the closet wall style to any closets on the upper floor.
  P. Purge any unused door, endcap, wall, and window styles from the drawing.
  Q. Save and close the drawing.

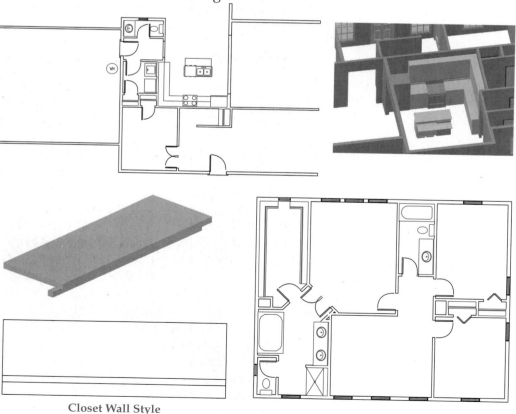

Closet Wall Style

Design Courtesy Alan Mascord Design Associates

5. Commercial Store Project
    A. Access the **Project Browser** and set Commercial-Project-05 current.
    B. Access the **Constructs** tab of the **Project Navigator** and open the Main Floor construct.
    C. Use the **Content Browser** to browse through the Metric or Imperial catalog of the Design Tool Catalog. Import the Hinged Double Center 3-0x6-8 + Sidelights 2-0 (R) + Transom door/window assembly style into the drawing.
    D. Use the **Properties** palette to change all the door/window assemblies to the Hinged Double Center 3-0x6-8 + Sidelights 2-0 (R) + Transom style
    E. Create the commercial doors shown in the diagram.
    F. Create a profile for each door with an interior ring for glazing.
    G. Create the door pull and push handles. Turn them into blocks.
    H. Create the two door styles using the profiles and attach the blocks.
    I. Use the **Properties** palette to change the doors in the door/window assemblies to the double commercial door.
    J. Modify the Masonry.Unit Masonry.Brick.Modular.Running material definition. Modify the General Medium Detail display representation. In the **Other** tab, under the **Surface Hatch Placement** area, turn on the **Top** and **Bottom** check boxes for each of the display representations.
    K. Save and close the drawing.

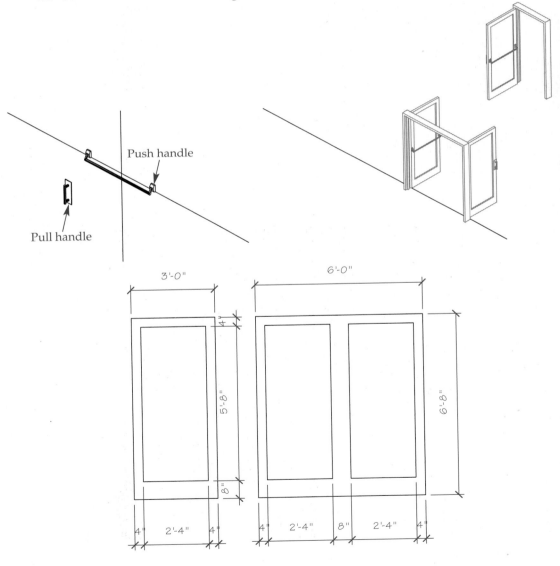

Drawing Courtesy 3D-DZYN

6. Commercial Car Maintenance Shop Project
   A. Access the **Project Browser** and set Commercial-Project-06 current.
   B. Access the **Constructs** tab of the **Project Navigator** and open the Main Floor construct.
   C. Use the **Content Browser** to browse through the Imperial or Metric catalog of the Design Tool Catalog. Import the Hinged Double Center 3-0x6-8 + Sidelights 2-0 (R) + Transom door/window assembly style into the drawing.
   D. Use the **Properties** palette to change all the front door/window assembly to the Hinged Double Center 3-0x6-8 + Sidelights 2-0 (R) + Transom style.
   E. Create the garage door profile. Modify the Overhead-Sectional door style to use the garage door profile.
   F. Create the commercial doors shown in the diagram.
   G. Create a profile for each door with an interior ring for glazing.
   H. Create the door pull and push handles. Turn them into blocks.
   I. Create the two door styles using the profiles and attach the blocks.
   J. Use the **Properties** palette to change the door in the front door/window assembly to the double commercial door.
   K. Modify the Masonry.Unit Masonry.Brick.Modular.Running material definition. In the **Other** tab, under the **Surface Hatch Placement** area, turn on the **Top** and **Bottom** check boxes for each of the display representations.
   L. Save and close the drawing.

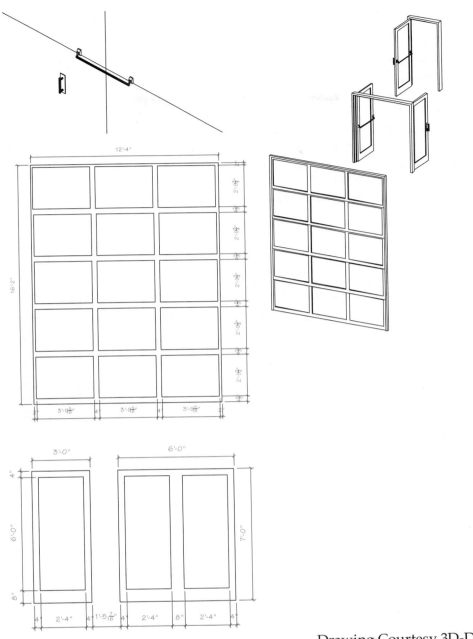

Drawing Courtesy 3D-DZYN

7. Governmental Fire Station
   A. Access the **Project Browser** and set Gvrmt-Project-07 current.
   B. Access the **Constructs** tab of the **Project Navigator** and open the Main Floor construct.
   C. Import the following wall styles from Casework (Imperial).dwg:
      a. Casework-36 (Base with Counter)
      b. Casework-42 (Upper)
   D. Modify the Casework-36 (Base with Counter) wall style to use the Standard end-cap style.
   E. Drag the Plumbing-Appliance construct into the Main Floor construct for use as a reference.
   F. Add the casework to the kitchen area and reception area, as shown in the diagram. Ensure you create wall cleanup groups and that the different types of casework are added to their own cleanup groups.

G. Access the **MATERIALDEFINE** command. Access Material Definitions.dwg, which is included with Architectural Desktop, and import the Doors & Windows. Glazing.Glass.Clear material definition.

H. Modify the Overhead-Sectional door style. In the **Materials** tab, assign the Doors & Windows.Glazing.Glass.Clear material definition to the Glass component.

I. Use the **Content Browser** to browse through the Imperial or Metric catalog of the Design Tool Catalog. Import the Hinged Double 6-8 + Transom door/window assembly style into the drawing.

J. Use the **Properties** palette to change the front door/window assembly at the entry to the Double 6-8 + Transom door/window assembly style.

K. Create the door pull and push handles. Turn them into blocks.

L. Edit the Hinged-Double-Full Lite-Frameless door style. Add the push and pull handles to the style.

M. Edit the Hinged-Single-Full Lite door style and add the push and pull door handles to the style.

N. Save and close the drawing.

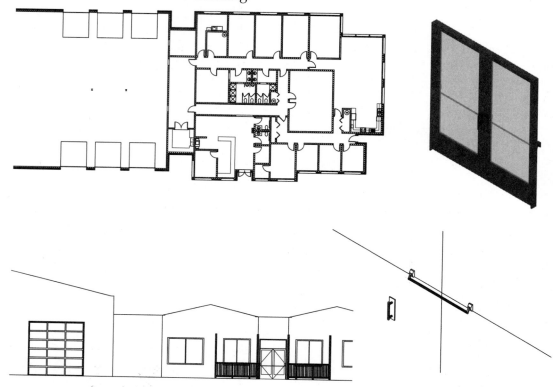

Drawing Courtesy 3D-DZYN

CHAPTER 16

Curtain Walls and Door and Window Assemblies

Learning Objectives

After completing this chapter, you will be able to do the following:

✓ Create and modify curtain walls and curtain wall units.
✓ Override curtain wall features.
✓ Use curtain wall tools and properties.
✓ Control curtain wall display.
✓ Create curtain wall unit styles.
✓ Create door/window assembly styles.
✓ Create curtain wall styles.

Curtain walls are an architectural feature typically used on commercial buildings. Similar to the door/window assemblies in Architectural Desktop, curtain walls work on a grander scale. Door/window assemblies are typically groups of windows used on a smaller commercial building or residential project and are inserted into a Wall object. The *Curtain Wall object* is usually the entire wall with glazing panels built in.

Curtain Wall objects provide a framework in which windows, doors, and door/window assemblies can be inserted. The framework, or grid, controls the spacing between infill panels with windows, doors, and door/window assemblies, as shown in **Figure 16-1.** Curtain walls are similar to standard AEC walls in that they include a baseline, roofline, and floor line and are drawn by specifying a start point and endpoint.

Curtain walls are different from standard AEC walls in that they are made up of a framework, or *grid.* The spaces between the grid lines are areas called infill panels. An infill panel can be "filled in" with other AEC objects, such as windows and doors. Grids contain rules that specify how infill panels are multiplied or divided as the curtain wall is made larger or smaller. A curtain wall grid is divided into a horizontal or vertical division. Divisions (grids) can be nested inside each other to create a variety of patterns for the curtain wall. *Divisions* determine how a curtain wall, curtain wall unit, or door/window assembly is divided into cells.

Figure 16-1.
Some examples
of curtain walls
included with
Architectural
Desktop.

Figure 16-1.
Some examples
of curtain walls
included with
Architectural
Desktop.

Infill panel
Frame
Infill panel
Frame
Framework (Grid)
Frame
Infill panel
Framework (Grid)
Mullion
Framework (Grid)
Mullion
Mullion

Creating Curtain Walls

CURTAINWALLADD

Type
CURTAINWALLADD
Pull-Down Menu
Design
> Curtain Walls
> Add Curtain
Wall...
Tool Palette
Design
Curtain Wall

Curtain walls can be added to the drawing by selecting **Design > Curtain Walls > Add Curtain Wall...** from the pull-down menu, typing CURTAINWALLADD, or picking the **Curtain Wall** tool on the **Design** palette. As with other AEC objects, the property settings for the new curtain wall can be specified in the **Properties** palette before the curtain wall is drawn.

The properties for curtain walls are displayed in **Figure 16-2.** Establish any properties such as the curtain wall style, height, and segment type before adding the curtain wall to the drawing. Many of the properties are similar to those of walls. See Chapter 4 and Chapter 12 for more on wall properties.

Use the **Base Height** property to enter an overall base height for the curtain wall. Generally, the full height curtain wall is established, and the different portions of the curtain wall at each floor level are established through **Display Configurations** by creating a construct that spans multiple levels.

Figure 16-2.
The **Properties** palette is used to configure the properties for the new curtain wall.

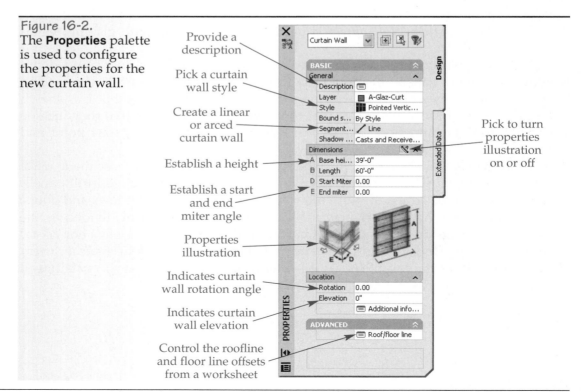

Provide a description
Pick a curtain wall style
Create a linear or arced curtain wall
Establish a height
Establish a start and end miter angle
Properties illustration
Indicates curtain wall rotation angle
Indicates curtain wall elevation
Control the roofline and floor line offsets from a worksheet

Curtain Wall

BASIC
General
Description
Layer   A-Glaz-Curt
Style   Pointed Vertic...
Bound s...   By Style
Segment...   Line
Shadow ...   Casts and Receive...
Dimensions
A Base hei... 39'-0"
B Length   60'-0"
D Start Miter 0.00
E End miter   0.00

Location
Rotation   0.00
Elevation   0"
Additional info...

ADVANCED
Roof/floor line

Pick to turn properties illustration on or off

The **Start Miter** and **End miter** properties allow you to enter a start mitering angle and an end mitering angle. Unlike walls, curtain walls do not clean up with each other. When two curtain walls meet at a corner, the ends need to be mitered. The miter angles are not displayed in the Plan view, but they will show in the Model views.

To draw a curtain wall, pick a point on the drawing screen for the start point, and then pick an endpoint. As curtain walls are drawn, they do not clean up with themselves as walls do. You can manually clean up the intersections of curtain walls with grip editing or the miter angle properties. When two or more curtain wall segments have been added during the same procedure, use the **ORtho close** or **PLINE Close** option to close the building. When you have finished adding curtain walls to the drawing, press the [Enter] key to exit the command.

Exercise 16-1   *Complete the Exercise on the Student CD.*

In addition to drawing curtain walls from scratch, you can convert standard Wall objects into Curtain Wall objects. This can be accomplished by right-clicking the **Curtain Wall** tool in the **Design** palette and picking **Apply Tool Properties to > Walls** from the shortcut menu or typing CURTAINWALLTOOLTOWALLS.

When walls are converted into curtain walls, the baseline (center) of the curtain wall is added to the left, right, center, or baseline of the wall being converted, as shown in **Figure 16-3**. Enter the appropriate location for the curtain wall at the Curtain wall baseline alignment [Left/Right/Center] <Baseline>: prompt.

Another tool that can be used to add curtain walls to a drawing is the **Referenced Base Curve** option. This option is similar to applying a wall style to linework because layout lines, arcs, polylines, circles, and splines are "referenced," and a curtain wall is added in their place. The layout geometry is also known as a *base curve*, whether the geometry is a straight or arced segment. The curtain wall references the curve, so any changes made to the shape of the base curve update the curtain wall to reflect the new shape.

To apply the curtain wall to a base curve (linework), right-click over the **Curtain Wall** tool in the **Design** palette and select **Apply Tool Properties to > Referenced Base Curve** from the shortcut menu.

When using the **Referenced Base Curve** option, you are prompted to select a curve. Pick one of the layout objects to reference. Once the object has been selected, a curtain wall is added over the linework. If the layout geometry is modified in any way, such as being stretched with grips, the curtain wall adjusts with the geometry.

Figure 16-3.
When walls are converted into curtain walls, the baseline alignment (center of curtain wall) can be placed along the converted wall's left, right, center, or baseline justification points.

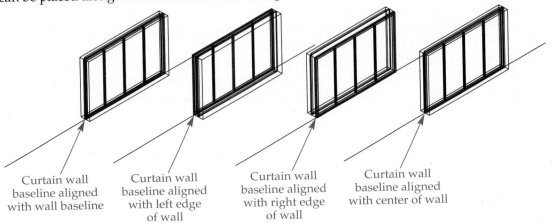

Curtain wall baseline aligned with wall baseline   Curtain wall baseline aligned with left edge of wall   Curtain wall baseline aligned with right edge of wall   Curtain wall baseline aligned with center of wall

Exercise 16-2 Complete the Exercise on the Student CD.

Modifying Curtain Walls

Most of the curtain wall styles found in the **Content Browser** are built with custom infill panels known as *curtain wall units*. When selecting a curtain wall for modification, you may find that the curtain wall unit is selected instead of the curtain wall framework. Selecting the actual frame edge of the curtain wall or a mullion grid selects the entire curtain wall so it can be modified.

The **Properties** palette is used to modify the different properties of an existing curtain wall, such as the height, style, miter angles, length, and elevation. Simply pick an existing curtain wall to be modified, and then adjust any of the properties in the **Properties** palette. In addition to the **Properties** palette, supplementary tools are available to further modify a curtain wall.

AutoCAD Review

Object Cycling

Some of the curtain walls include separate infill panels. When attempting to pick the curtain wall, the infill panels may be selected instead. If you have difficulty selecting the curtain wall grid, you can cycle through the objects using the [Shift]+[Spacebar] key combination.

Before selecting the object, press and hold the [Shift] key. Move the crosshairs over the area that includes two or more objects, and then press the [Spacebar] to highlight one of the objects. Let go of the [Shift] key and pick with the pick button on the mouse to select the object. This procedure is known as *object cycling*. You can use this method to cycle through the objects until the desired object is highlighted.

Modifying Elements within a Curtain Wall

The individual elements within a curtain wall (frame, mullions, and infills) can be changed for the individual wall selected. By using override options, infill cells can be merged together or assigned a different infill definition. Frame and mullion edges can be assigned to a custom profile or definition. Overrides do not affect the curtain wall style. They only affect the curtain wall being modified.

Before a cell (infill) can be merged or the cell assignment can be changed, the cell markers need to be turned on. To turn on the cell markers, select the curtain wall to be modified, right-click, and pick **Infill > Show Markers** from the shortcut menu.

Once the cell markers have been turned on, a cell marker is displayed in the center of each cell and is a selection point for the cell. The cell marker changes, depending on the direction of the grid and the cell assignment. For horizontal grids, the marker points up, indicating the cells are numbered from bottom to top beginning with cell number 1. See **Figure 16-4**. Markers displayed in vertical grids point to the right, indicating the cells are numbered from left to right beginning with cell number 1, as in **Figure 16-4**.

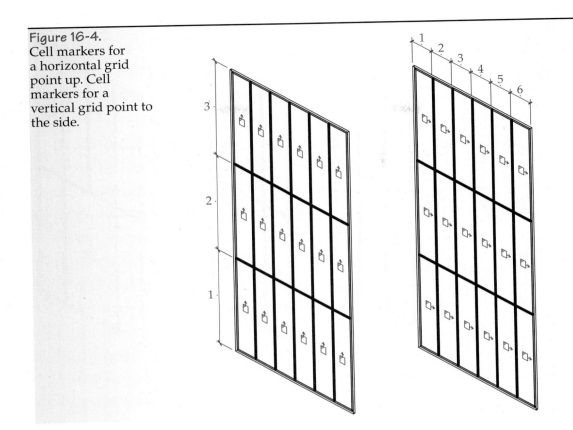

Figure 16-4.
Cell markers for
a horizontal grid
point up. Cell
markers for a
vertical grid point to
the side.

After the cell markers have been turned on, the individual cells can be overridden. The curtain wall overrides are available only from the shortcut menu, shown in **Figure 16-5.**

Merging Two Cells

Infill components include two types of overrides that can be applied: **Merge** and **Override Assignment**. The first override option is the **Merge Cells** command. This override merges two infill cells into one. When this command is used, you are prompted to select Cell A before Cell B, where Cell A is the first cell to be merged, and Cell B is the second cell merged. See **Figure 16-6.** Only cells that are next to one another (horizontally or vertically) can be merged.

Figure 16-5.
Each curtain wall
component includes
an **Override** option
that can be used to
modify the selected
curtain wall.

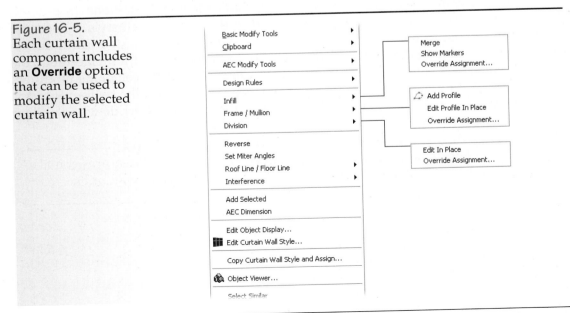

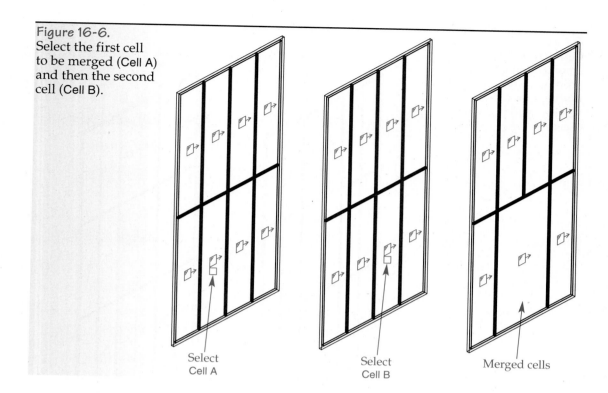

Figure 16-6.
Select the first cell to be merged (Cell A) and then the second cell (Cell B).

Select
Cell A

Select
Cell B

Merged cells

Overriding Cell Assignments

Each cell in a curtain wall is assigned an infill. The infill assigned to a cell can be overridden with a different infill element. Some of the curtain walls include multiple infill elements, whereas others include only one infill element. Additional infills can be created through the **Curtain Wall Style Properties** dialog box. The creation of additional infills will be discussed later in this chapter.

To change the infill assigned to a cell, select the curtain wall, right-click, and pick **Infill > Override Assignment...** from the shortcut menu. You are prompted to select an infill to override. Pick a cell marker that will have its infill replaced. The **Infill Assignment Override** worksheet is displayed after the cell marker is selected. See **Figure 16-7.** This worksheet is used to modify the infill selected or remove it from the curtain wall. Use the **Remove Infill and Frames** radio button to completely remove the selected infill and surrounding frames to create a hole in the curtain wall.

If the **Modify Infill** radio button is selected, the **Infill Element Definitions** drop-down list provides a list of infill definitions included in the curtain wall style. Choose an infill from the list to use as a replacement. **Figure 16-7** displays a door infill definition that was added to the curtain wall style. After selecting an infill replacement, the **Frame Removal** area allows you to remove the frames around the cell being modified. In **Figure 16-7,** as the door infill is being used as a replacement, the bottom frame is being removed from the cell. **Figure 16-8** displays the finished override with the door in place.

NOTE

The same procedures used to override curtain wall features can also be applied to door/window assemblies and curtain wall units.

Figure 16-7.
The **Infill Assignment Override** worksheet is used to assign an infill replacement (override) to a cell in the curtain wall or door/window assembly.

Pick to replace the selected infill with a different infill definition

Select an infill definition to use as an override

Select any frames around the infill to be removed

Pick to remove the infill and surrounding frames

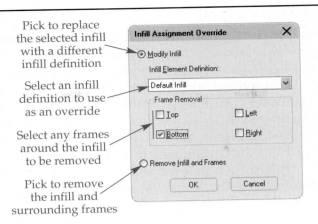

PROFESSIONAL TIP

In most of the curtain wall styles, only one or two infill elements are available. Additional infills can be created in a style for use as overrides. If a curtain wall has a list of infill elements, use the **Infill Element Definitions** drop-down list to view additional infill definitions.

Figure 16-8.
Overriding a cell infill assignment with another infill element.

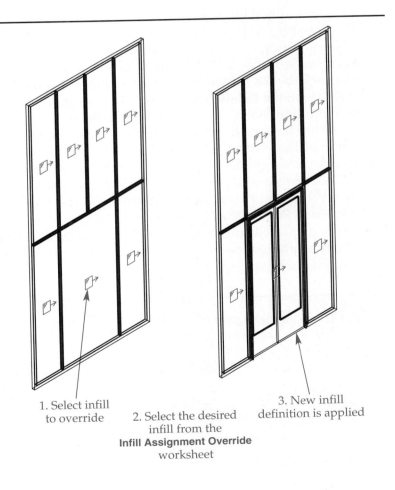

1. Select infill to override

2. Select the desired infill from the **Infill Assignment Override** worksheet

3. New infill definition is applied

Adding a Frame/Mullion Profile

By default, the Standard curtain wall and door/window assembly styles include frames and mullions that separate the infill components. These frames and mullions are initially created as a square shape. The shape of the frame and mullion may be determined by an AEC profile shape. To add a new shape to a frame or mullion, select the curtain wall, right-click, pick **Frame/Mullion > Add Profile** from the shortcut menu, and then pick the command. After accessing the command, you are prompted to select a frame or mullion to add a profile. Select a frame on the outside of the curtain wall or a mullion on the inside of the curtain wall to add a profile shape.

Depending on whether you pick a frame or a mullion, the **Add Frame Profile** or **Add Mullion Profile** worksheet will display. See **Figure 16-9**. These worksheets each contain the same information, except they apply to two different components.

The **Profile Definition** drop-down list is used to select an AEC profile for use as the profile shape for the frame or mullion. If there are no AEC profiles defined in the drawing, the **Start from scratch...** option can be used to add a new profile shape to the frame or mullion. When the **Start from scratch...** option has been selected, the **New Profile Name:** text box is available, allowing you to enter a new name for the profile shape. The **Apply Profile** area includes **To Shared Frame Element Definition** and **As Frame Profile Override** options. The first radio button applies the new profile shape to the curtain wall or door/window assembly style and any connected frames or mullions. Any curtain walls or door/window assemblies using this style are automatically updated with the profile changes. The second radio button option applies the profile changes as an override to the frame or mullion in the selected curtain wall or door/window assembly.

If an existing AEC profile is being used, the **Continue Editing** check box becomes available. Selecting this check box allows you to edit the AEC profile in place on the frame or mullion that was initially selected. When you are finished choosing your options, pick the **OK** button to continue editing. If you select the **Start from scratch...** option or **Continue Editing** check box, a shaded profile shape is displayed within the frame or mullion that is chosen. See **Figure 16-10**.

Grips are displayed surrounding the shaded profile. Use the grip boxes to adjust the shape of the profile. Additional vertices can be added to or removed from the profile shape by right-clicking and selecting the appropriate option from the shortcut menu. As changes are made to the profile, the shape of the frame and mullion is updated. When you are finished editing the profile, pick the **Save All Changes** button in the **In Place Edit** toolbar. If the profile is being applied as an override, the frame or mullion is displayed in the curtain wall. If the **To Shared Frame Element Definition** radio button option was selected, the profile is displayed in all curtain walls or door/window assemblies using this style.

Figure 16-9.
The **Add Frame Profile** and **Add Mullion Profile** worksheets are used to add a profile shape to a frame or mullion component.

Select an AEC profile or start from scratch

Type a name for the profile if starting from scratch

Apply the profile to the curtain wall style

Apply the profile as an override to the selected curtain wall

Select if an existing AEC profile will be used and needs further editing

Architectural Desktop and Its Applications

Editing a Frame/Mullion Profile in Place

After a profile shape has been added to a frame or mullion, it can be edited in place later. Select a curtain wall or door/window assembly, and then right-click and pick **Frame/Mullion > Edit Profile In Place** from the shortcut menu. Picking this option displays the profile as mentioned previously and allows you to grip edit the profiled shape. See **Figure 16-10**. Right-click to add or remove vertices, replace a profile ring, or save the changes as a new profile. Remember to save the changes when you are finished editing.

Overriding Frame/Mullion Assignments

When adding a profile, you have the option of attaching it to the style or using it as an override to the selected frame or mullion edge. If frame and mullion element definitions have been created for the curtain wall or door/window assembly style, the definitions can be applied as overrides to a frame or mullion.

To override a frame or mullion edge, select the curtain wall, and then right-click and pick **Frame/Mullion > Override Assignment...** from the shortcut menu. Depending on whether a frame or mullion is picked, the **Frame Assignment Override** or **Mullion Assignment Override** dialog box will be displayed. See **Figure 16-11**. Pick the **Modify Frame** or **Modify Mullion** radio button to override the selected frame or mullion with a frame or mullion element definition from the curtain wall style being modified.

The **Frame Element Definitions** and **Mullion Element Definitions** drop-down lists include element definitions that can be applied to the selected frame or mullion edge. If the frame or mullion edge is to be removed, pick the **Remove Frame** or **Remove Mullion** radio button. When you are finished, pick the **OK** button to apply the overrides to the curtain wall or door/window assembly. See **Figure 16-12**.

> NOTE By default, there are no additional frame or mullion element definitions in the curtain wall styles. You can custom create your own element definitions for frames and mullions. This process is discussed later in this chapter.

Exercise 16-3   Complete the Exercise on the Student CD.

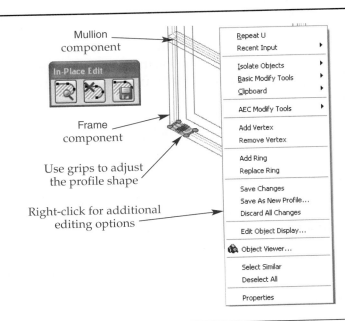

Figure 16-10.
When adding a profile or editing a profile in place, the profile shape is displayed as a shaded color with grips around the vertices.

Mullion component

Frame component

Use grips to adjust the profile shape

Right-click for additional editing options

Figure 16-11.
Use the **Frame Assignment Override** or **Mullion Assignment Override** dialog box to override a frame or mullion edge.

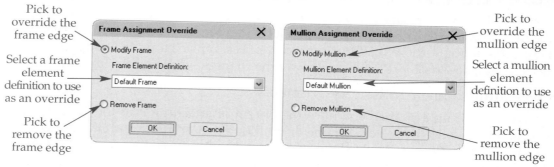

Pick to override the frame edge

Select a frame element definition to use as an override

Pick to remove the frame edge

Pick to override the mullion edge

Select a mullion element definition to use as an override

Pick to remove the mullion edge

Figure 16-12.
Overriding mullions within a curtain wall.

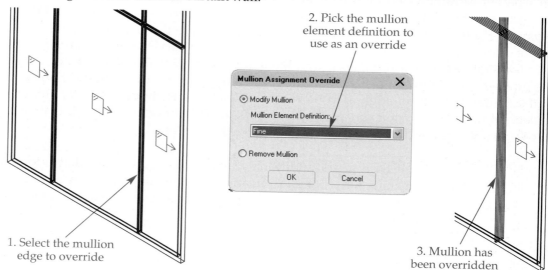

2. Pick the mullion element definition to use as an override

1. Select the mullion edge to override

3. Mullion has been overridden

Editing Divisions

In addition to overriding infill cells and frame/mullion edges, the curtain wall divisions can be overridden. The division in a curtain wall or door/window assembly is the mullion placements that partition the infill cells within the curtain wall. The divisions within the curtain wall can be edited in place to provide a variation of the division settings. To edit the divisions in place, select the curtain wall, and then right-click and pick **Division > Edit In Place** from the shortcut menu. You are prompted to select a grid division to edit.

As the crosshairs are moved around the curtain wall, a red diagonal hatch is displayed around the different grid divisions that can be edited, as shown in **Figure 16-13.** When the area you want to edit is highlighted with the hatch, press the left pick button. After picking the desired division area, the **In-Place Edit** toolbar is displayed. Grips are also located around the curtain wall at significant division editing points. See **Figure 16-14.**

Pick the **Auto Grid Bay Spacing** grip to adjust the infill cell divisions. Stretching the grip divides the cells into fewer or more cells, depending on the direction stretched. Picking the **Set Fixed Cell Dimension Rules** grip displays the **Set Fixed Cell Dimension Rules** worksheet. This worksheet is used to adjust the cell (infill) size of the curtain wall. The **Start Offset** and **End Offset** grips are used to adjust the offset of the division within the curtain wall and control where the **Auto Grid Spacing** begins measuring the divided grid.

Figure 16-13.
When editing divisions in place, different areas within the curtain wall will highlight, indicating the division to be edited.

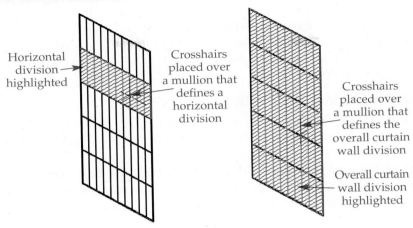

Horizontal division highlighted

Crosshairs placed over a mullion that defines a horizontal division

Crosshairs placed over a mullion that defines the overall curtain wall division

Overall curtain wall division highlighted

Figure 16-14.
The division assignments within a curtain wall can be edited in place.

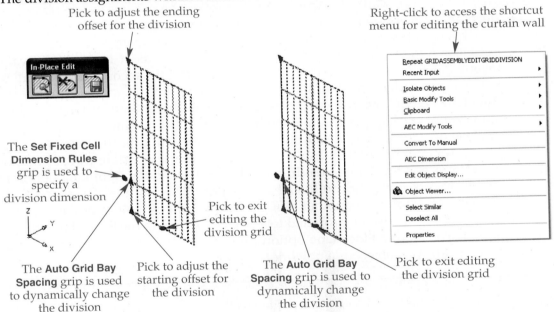

Pick to adjust the ending offset for the division

Right-click to access the shortcut menu for editing the curtain wall

The **Set Fixed Cell Dimension Rules** grip is used to specify a division dimension

Pick to exit editing the division grid

The **Auto Grid Bay Spacing** grip is used to dynamically change the division

Pick to adjust the starting offset for the division

The **Auto Grid Bay Spacing** grip is used to dynamically change the division

Pick to exit editing the division grid

When you are finished editing the division, pick the **Exit Editing Grid** grip. This displays the **Save Changes** dialog box. You can save the division changes back to the division being edited or pick the **New...** button to save the changes as a new division element that can be used in other curtain walls using this curtain wall style.

Overriding Divisions

Similar to overriding a frame or mullion assignment, a division assignment can be overridden with a different division element definition. To do this, select the curtain wall, and then right-click and pick **Division** > **Override Assignment...** from the shortcut menu. You are prompted to select an edge. Pick a frame or mullion edge to display the **Division Assignment Override** dialog box.

This dialog box includes a list of division element definitions belonging to the style. Choose a division element definition to use as an override. A *division element definition* is a definition that may divide the grid into equal spaces, grids that are always a specified cell width, or cells that adjust depending on the width and height of the curtain wall. By default, the Standard curtain wall style includes **Horizontal** and **Vertical** divisions. Additional divisions can be created. This is discussed later in this chapter. When you are finished assigning the override, pick the **OK** button to return to have the editing take effect.

Modifying the Curtain Wall with Grips

Similar to other AEC objects, curtain walls can be edited using grips. See **Figure 16-15**. Stretching the **Start**, **End**, or **Lengthen** grips will allow you to change the width of the curtain wall. Depending on the rules of the grid divisions, the mullions within the curtain wall increase or decrease. Picking the **Edit Grid** grip, which is the round gray grip, allows you to edit the grid divisions mentioned previously in place. Use the **Roof Line** and **Floor Line** grips to adjust the roofline or floor line of the curtain wall.

Using Curtain Wall Tools

In addition to being able to modify the individual components of a curtain wall, you can modify the appearance of curtain walls with some additional tools. To access these options, use the curtain wall's shortcut menu. The following options are displayed:

- **Reverse.** This option reverses the start point and endpoint of the curtain wall. Use this option when the curtain wall appears on the wrong side.
- **Set Miter Angles.** This option is used to miter the ends of two curtain walls meeting at a corner. After picking this option, select the second curtain wall to miter the two edges together.
- **Roof Line / Floor Line.** Selecting this option gives three more options. The **Edit In Place** option displays the **In-Place Edit** toolbar. This is similar to editing the roofline or floor lines of a Wall object in place. Any modifications made to the roofline or floor line of the curtain wall by projecting the curtain wall to another object or a polyline can be modified in place. The **Modify Roof Line** option is similar to projecting the roofline of a Wall object. The roofline of a curtain wall can be projected up to another AEC object by using the **Auto project** option. The roofline can also be projected to a polyline by using the **Project to polyline** option. The **Modify Floor Line** option projects the floor line of a curtain wall down to an AEC object or a polyline.

Figure 16-15.
Use grips to edit the length and height of a curtain wall.

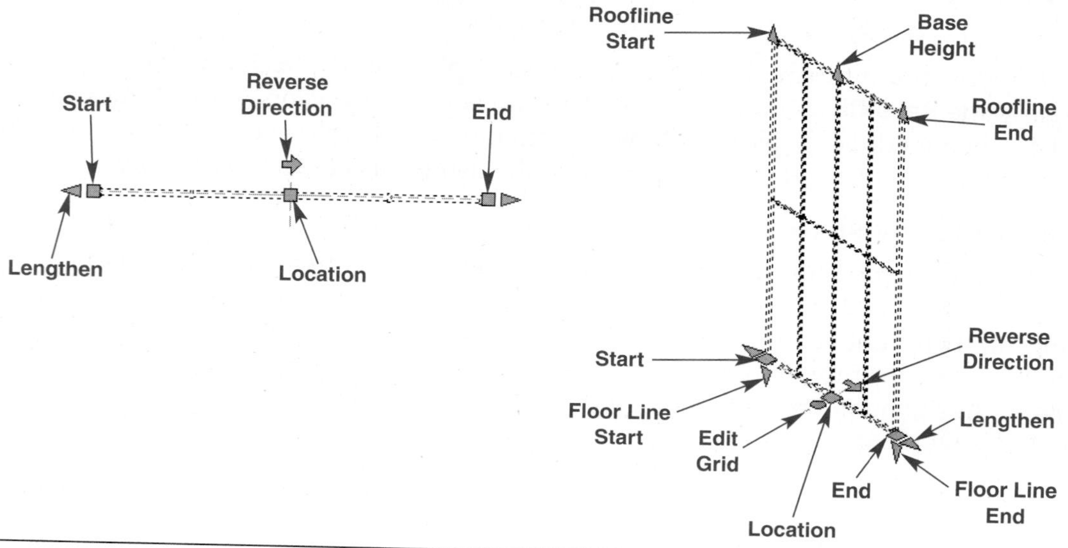

Architectural Desktop and Its Applications

- **Interference.** This option is used to apply an interference to a curtain wall. An interference can be a structural member, a mass element, a wall, or another AEC object that runs into the curtain wall. Use the **Add** option to add an interference and the **Remove** option to remove an interference.

NOTE   The mitering of two curtain walls applies to the walls' horizontal components only. If the corner of the wall is to have a special type of corner or, in a Plan view, if the walls need to appear as if they clean up, apply an interference condition to the walls at the corner.

Exercise
16-4   Complete the Exercise on the Student CD.

Using the Properties Palette

As mentioned at the beginning of this chapter, the **Properties** palette is used to adjust the settings of a curtain wall as it is being added to the drawing. After a curtain wall has been added, it can also be edited using the **Properties** palette.

Picking the **Overrides** property displays the **Overrides** worksheet shown in **Figure 16-16.** This worksheet is used to manage any overrides applied to the curtain wall. The overrides are listed in a table under the appropriate override heading. Picking an override value in the table provides you with a list of element definitions appropriate

Figure 16-16.
The **Overrides** worksheet is used to list and remove overrides applied to a curtain wall.

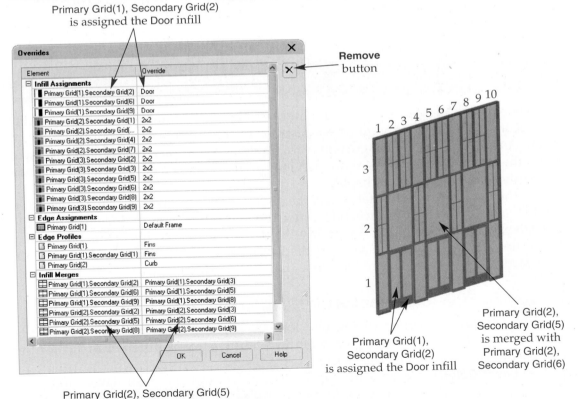

Figure 16-17.
The **Roof and Floor Line** worksheet is used to manage locations of vertices along the roofline or floor line of a curtain wall.

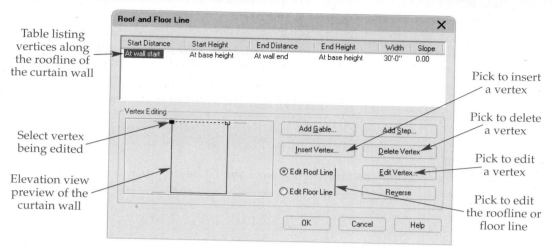

Table listing vertices along the roofline of the curtain wall

Select vertex being edited

Elevation view preview of the curtain wall

Pick to insert a vertex

Pick to delete a vertex

Pick to edit a vertex

Pick to edit the roofline or floor line

to the override type. An override can then be changed to use a different element definition. For example, an infill assignment with the Door override could be changed to the 2×2 element definition.

The overrides can be removed by highlighting an override, right-clicking, and selecting **Remove** from the shortcut menu or selecting the **Remove** button on the right of the worksheet. The table lists the cells and edges in relation to the grid divisions in the curtain wall, which aids in locating the appropriate cell or edge for modification.

When the **Roof/floor line** property is picked, the **Roof and Floor Line** worksheet is displayed, as shown in **Figure 16-17**. This worksheet is used to manage the roofline and floor lines of the curtain walls. Use the buttons in the lower-right corner of the worksheet to add, edit, and delete vertices in the curtain wall.

Controlling Curtain Wall Display

The display properties for individual curtain walls, much like for other AEC objects, are controlled through object display. To control the display properties of a single curtain wall, select the curtain wall, right-click, and pick **Edit Object Display...** from the shortcut menu. As with previously discussed objects, pick the **Display Properties** tab to modify the display.

In the **Display Properties** tab, select the display representation to be modified from the list, and then attach an override. After the override has been attached, pick the **Edit Display Properties** button to modify the display settings. This opens the **Display Properties** dialog box for the selected display representation. Curtain walls contain Plan, Model, and Reflected representations that can be edited.

Modifying Plan Representation Curtain Walls

The **Display Properties** dialog box for Plan representation Curtain Wall objects includes the following four tabs. Each of these tabs controls a different aspect for the display of Plan view Curtain Wall objects.

- **Layer/Color/Linetype.** This tab is used to control the color, layer, and linetype assigned to Plan view Curtain Wall objects. If the **By Material** check boxes are selected, the display properties for the components are controlled by the material that is assigned to the components. The curtain wall includes three main components: Default Infill, Default Mullion, and Default Frame. Each of these components also includes a hatching component. In addition to these components, Above Wall and Below Wall components are included to display curtain walls above or below the curtain wall cut plane. Select any of the symbols or text to modify the values assigned to the components.

- **Hatching.** This tab is used to assign the style of hatch pattern used for a component hatch.
- **Custom Plan Components.** This tab controls new components that can replace one of the three default components—Default Infill, Default Mullion, and Default Frame—similar to adding blocks to a door or window. When the **Add...** or **Edit...** button is selected, the **Custom Display Component** dialog box appears, as shown in **Figure 16-18.** To replace a default component, select the component that will be replaced in the **Component type:** drop-down list. Pick the **Select Element...** button to assign a new component element definition to the default component. The **Draw Custom Graphics** check box can be used to attach a custom block to the curtain wall, similar to the way you would attach a block to a door. When a new component type or block is added to the Plan representation Curtain Wall object, the component is added to the **Layer/Color/Linetype** tab.
- **Cut Plane.** This tab controls the cut plane for the selected curtain wall.

Modifying Model Representation Curtain Walls

The Model representation Curtain Wall object includes two tabs: **Layer/Color/Linetype** and **Other**. The **Layer/Color/Linetype** tab lists the three components of a Model view Curtain Wall object, plus the Cell Marker component. Adjust any of the properties for the Model view Curtain Wall objects.

The **Other** tab is used to assign a replacement component or block to the curtain wall, as with the Plan representation. This tab also includes a text box for controlling the size of the cell markers.

Figure 16-18.
The **Custom Display Component** dialog box is used to replace a Plan view component with another element definition or add a custom block to the curtain wall representation.

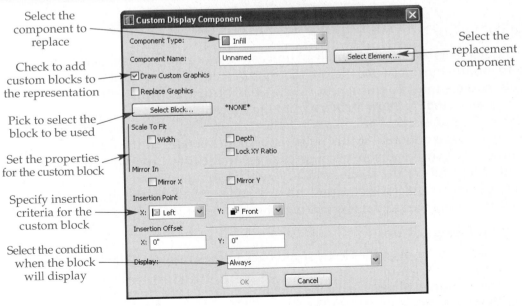

Select the component to replace

Check to add custom blocks to the representation

Pick to select the block to be used

Set the properties for the custom block

Specify insertion criteria for the custom block

Select the condition when the block will display

Select the replacement component

Curtain walls are a series of elements that work together to form a wall that is divided into a number of grid patterns. Each curtain wall includes an infill (cell), mullion, and frame. The frames and mullions are used to divide the wall into a series of divisions. Between each mullion and frame is an infill panel. Some of the curtain wall styles included with Architectural Desktop use an infill that is defined within the curtain wall style. Other curtain walls use curtain wall units as the infill between the frames and mullions.

The curtain wall unit is a separate object type whose only purpose is to be used as the infill within a curtain wall style. Curtain wall units can be used to create a complex series of divisions and grids without having to nest the complex divisions directly in the curtain wall. This allows more flexibility in overriding the infill panel of the curtain wall.

Adding Curtain Wall Units

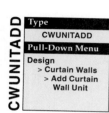

Curtain wall units can be added to the drawing for review and design purposes, but they cannot be added to a wall, as door/window assemblies can. Curtain wall units can be added to the drawing by selecting **Design > Curtain Walls > Add Curtain Wall Unit** from the pull-down menu or typing CWUNITADD. Curtain wall units can also be added from the **Content Browser** by accessing the Design Tool Catalog and browsing to the Curtain Walls > Curtain Wall Units section. Pick the desired curtain wall unit from the catalog, and then use i-drop to drag and drop the unit into your drawing.

Once the command has been accessed, pick a start point, an endpoint, and a height for the curtain wall unit. A curtain wall unit is added to the drawing. The benefit of adding the curtain wall unit to the drawing in this manner is it allows you to preview what the unit looks like within a curtain wall and allows you to edit the unit in place, in turn updating any other units in the drawing with the changes made.

Exercise 16-5 *Complete the Exercise on the Student CD.*

Modifying Curtain Wall Units

The elements within a curtain wall unit can be modified with the same commands used to modify curtain walls. Before the cells of a curtain wall unit can be modified, the cell markers must be turned on. First, select the curtain wall unit, and then right-click and select **Infill > Show Markers** from the shortcut menu.

After the cell markers are displayed, the curtain wall unit is ready to be modified with the override options. At this point, applying overrides to the individual curtain wall unit is not very valuable because changes made affect only the individual unit and not other units of the same style. If you want to modify the curtain wall unit so the changes made affect the curtain wall unit style globally in the drawing, you need to transfer the changes to the original object style.

Changing Design Rules

In order for your overrides to be saved back to the original curtain wall unit style, you need to be able to transfer the changes back to the object style. Before setting overrides to the curtain wall unit, select the curtain wall unit, and then right-click and pick **Design Rules > Transfer to Object** from the shortcut menu. This "opens" the style to any override editing you perform. Set any overrides as required, such as merging cells, overriding frame or mullion profiles, or overriding infill cells.

Figure 16-19.

The **Save Changes** dialog box is used to save any changes made to a curtain wall unit back to the unit style or into a new unit style.

Save changes to a curtain wall unit style in the drop-down list

Select the overrides applied to be saved to the curtain wall unit style

Pick to save the changes as a new curtain wall unit style

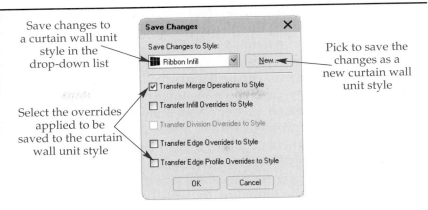

When you have finished making adjustments to the curtain wall unit, you can save the changes back to the unit style. Select the curtain wall unit, and then right-click and pick **Design Rules > Save to Style...** from the shortcut menu. This displays the **Save Changes** dialog box. See **Figure 16-19.**

The changes made to the unit style can be saved to a unit style found in the **Save Changes to Style:** drop-down list. New curtain wall unit styles can also be created from the changes by selecting the **New...** button. If the changes are to be saved in an existing style or a new style, select the appropriate check boxes at the bottom of the dialog box. As changes are made to the curtain wall unit, the different check boxes in the **Save Changes** dialog box become available.

NOTE

> The **Transfer to Object** option is a simple way of taking an existing curtain wall unit style, applying any overrides to the unit, and saving the changes as a new style. This process creates additional styles that can be used in a curtain wall style.

Exercise 16-6   **Complete the Exercise on the Student CD.**

Curtain Wall Unit Properties

Curtain wall unit properties can be adjusted and managed through the **Properties** palette. The properties for a curtain wall unit are similar to those for a curtain wall. When a curtain wall unit containing any overrides is selected, the **Overrides** property is displayed in the **Properties** palette. Pick the **Overrides** property to manage any overrides applied to the curtain wall unit.

Creating Curtain Wall Unit Styles

Curtain wall unit styles, curtain wall styles, and door/window assembly styles are all based on the same creation methods. These objects are based on four parts that, when assembled together, form the style. Divisions are rules that determine how a curtain wall, curtain wall unit, or door/window assembly is divided into cells. Infills are components that are placed within cells. The frame establishes the outer boundaries of the object, and the mullions are the boundaries within the frame that divide the infills.

CWUNITSTYLE

Type

CWUNITSTYLE

Pull-Down Menu

Design
> Curtain Walls
> Curtain Wall
Unit Styles...

As mentioned earlier, the curtain wall unit is an AEC object that is used as an infill within a curtain wall or door/window assembly. This allows you to create a curtain wall or door/window assembly with divisions separate from the details of the infill.

Curtain wall unit styles are created by accessing the Curtain Wall Unit Styles section of the **Style Manager**. This can be done by picking **Design > Curtain Walls > Curtain Wall Unit Styles...** from the pull-down menu or typing CWUNITSTYLE. See **Figure 16-20**.

In the **Style Manager**, pick the **New Style** button, or right-click the Curtain Wall Unit Styles section icon and select **New** to create a new curtain wall unit style. Enter a new name for the style to create a new style. Pick the new style in the tree view to begin editing the properties for the new style. See **Figure 16-21**.

The properties for curtain wall units are divided into six tabs. The **General** tab is used to rename the style and provide a description for the style. The **Design Rules** is the main tab and is used to define the rules for the curtain wall unit. The **Overrides** tab displays any overrides attached to the style when editing in place. The **Materials** tab is used to assign a material to the components within the curtain wall unit. Use the **Classifications** tab to assign any classification definitions to the style. The **Display Properties** tab is used to control the display of the elements within the curtain wall unit style.

Before configuring the style, you need to have an idea of how the curtain wall unit appears. Notice, in **Figure 16-21**, the icons in the **Element Definitions** area, in the left part of the tab. As mentioned earlier, curtain wall units are composed of divisions, infills, frames, and mullions. When creating the style, you must create element definitions for these definitions in order to assemble them together into one unit. Element definitions are also used when assigning overrides to the curtain wall, curtain wall unit, or door/window assembly.

Divisions establish how the cells within a unit are divided. There are two orientations for divisions: **Horizontal** and **Vertical**. Multiple divisions can be created and nested within one another to create a pattern of divisions. See **Figure 16-22**. A *primary grid* is always required and serves as the first level of division. As additional divisions are added, they become nested within the cells of the previous division.

Figure 16-20.

The **Style Manager** is used to organize styles in the drawing. Accessing the **CWUNITSTYLE** command displays the Curtain Wall Unit Styles section in the **Style Manager**.

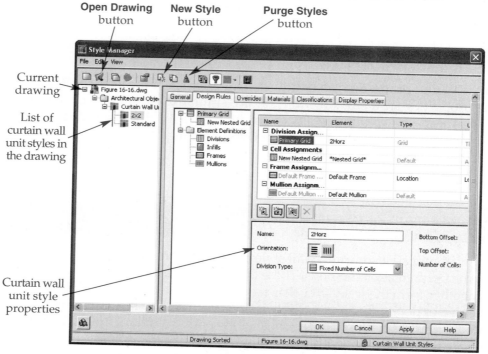

Figure 16-21.
The **Curtain Wall Unit Style Properties** dialog box is used to configure the appearance of the curtain wall unit.

Grid division design rules table

Grid division tree icons

Element definition icons

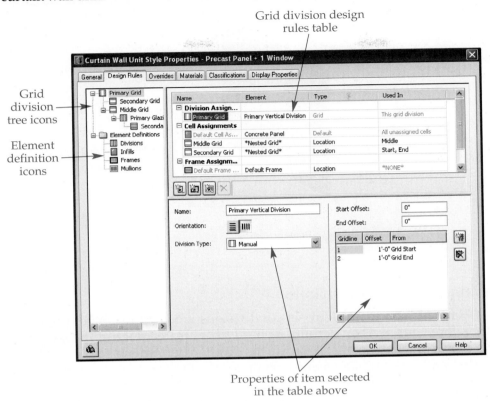

Properties of item selected in the table above

Figure 16-22.
Divisions establish how the cells within a curtain wall unit are created and organized.

Individual divisions are assembled to make one curtain wall unit

Nested secondary grid of four vertical divisions

Primary grid of three horizontal divisions

Nested tertiary grid of two horizontal divisions

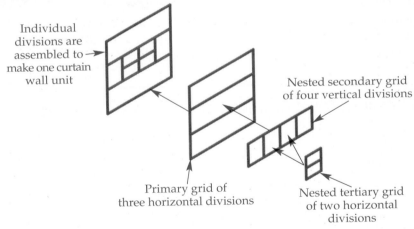

Infill definitions can be created from window, door, curtain wall unit, and AEC polygon styles. AEC polygons are a type of Hatch Pattern object. These are discussed in Chapter 19. Infills can also be created from a default element within the **Curtain Wall Unit Style Properties** dialog box. Frame and mullion definitions, by default, take on a rectangular shape, but they can be defined by using an AEC profile definition.

For the purposes of this discussion, the curtain wall unit to be created appears in **Figure 16-23.** The following section explains how to create the element definitions, and then finally how to assemble the pieces into one unit.

Figure 16-23.
The desired curtain wall unit.

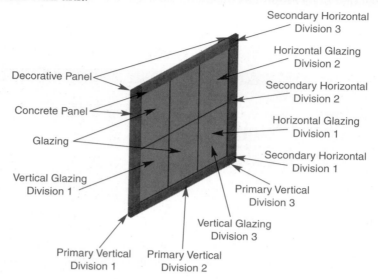

Establishing Division Definitions

Refer to **Figure 16-23**, where four sets of divisions are used to create the curtain wall unit; therefore, four division definitions need to be created. **Figure 16-24** displays the criteria for each of the divisions. To create the division definitions, make the **Design Rules** tab active, and select the **Divisions** icon under the Element Definitions folder icon. The table view changes to the division definition view. See **Figure 16-25**.

Select the **New Division** button to create a new definition. Highlight the new definition in the table to configure it. The definition properties at the bottom of this view allow you to name the definition and control the orientation and type of division used. In the **Name:** text box, type Primary Vertical Division. Select the **Vertical** orientation button. In the **Division Type:** drop-down list, select **Manual** to allow you to manually set the vertical divisions within the definition. This definition is to have two vertical grid lines 12″ from each edge, so use the table in the lower-right corner to specify the division settings.

Figure 16-24.
Four division definitions to be used in the creation of the curtain wall unit style.

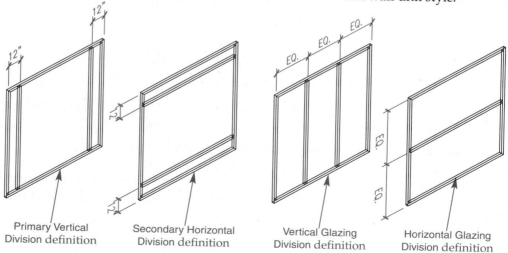

Figure 16-25.
Select the **Divisions** icon on the left to access the division definition view.

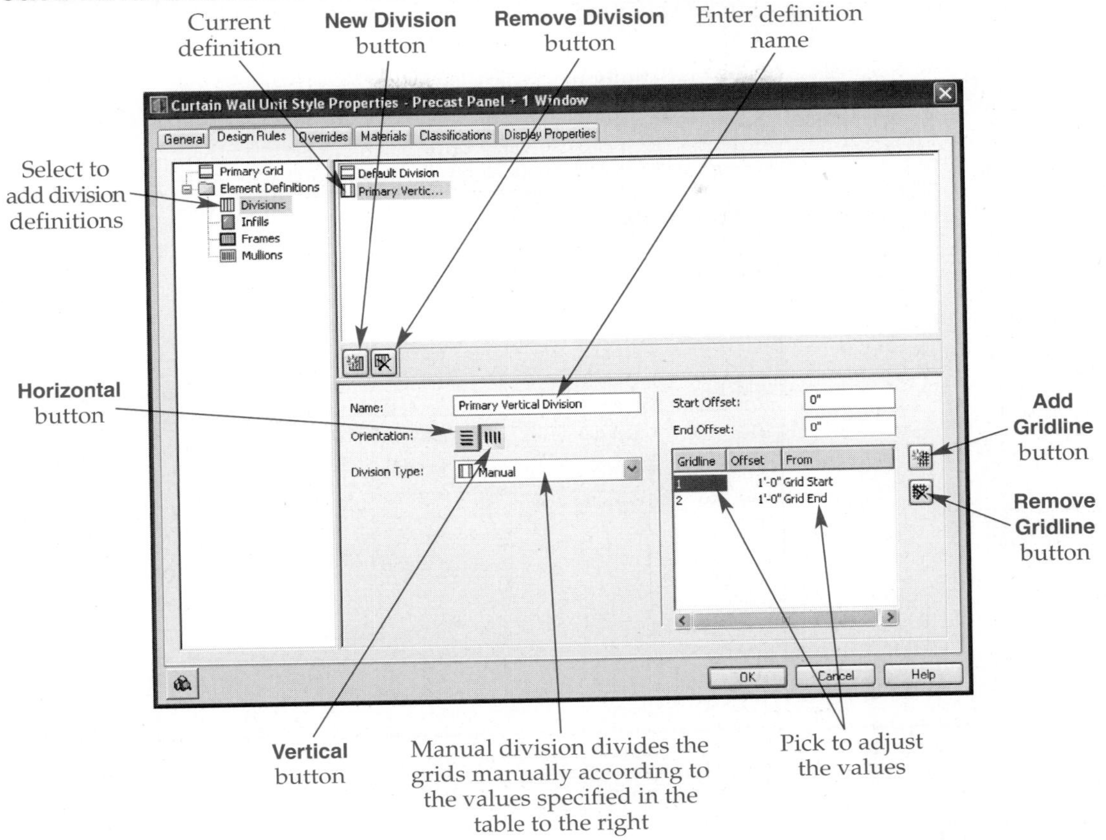

The table in the lower-right corner lists the number of gridlines used in the definition. The **Offset** column establishes the measured distance from a specified point. The **From** column establishes where the gridlines are being measured from. The division orientation is vertical, so the **From** column includes the **Grid Start**, **Grid Middle**, and **Grid End** options. Pick the values in the columns to make the modifications. You can add additional gridlines by picking the **Add Gridline** button.

The next definition is nested in each of the three cells of the primary vertical division. Create a new division definition named Secondary Horizontal Division. Set the orientation to **Horizontal** and the division type to **Manual**. Set the grid lines 12" from the grid bottom and 12" from the grid top. These are the two main divisions in the style.

The next two divisions are to be used for the glazing portion of the style. There are two definitions, one vertical and one horizontal. The divisions in each of these definitions are to have an equal spacing. Create another division definition named Vertical Glazing Division. Select the **Vertical** orientation button. In the **Division Type:** drop-down list, select the **Fixed Number of Cells** option to change the properties for this definition to reflect the settings made for this type of division. See **Figure 16-26.** Enter a value of 3 in the **Number of Cells:** text box. Add one final definition named Horizontal Glazing Division. Set the orientation to **Horizontal** and the fixed number of cells to 2.

Establishing Infill Definitions

The **Infills** definition icon is used to create infill definitions that are used within each cell of the curtain wall unit. **Figure 16-23** indicates that three separate infills are used: Decorative Panel, Concrete Panel, and Glazing. Select the **Infills** definition icon under the Element Definitions folder to create the infill definitions. The properties of infills are displayed as in **Figure 16-27**. Press the **New Infill** button to create a new definition.

Figure 16-26.
When **Division Type:** is set to **Fixed Number of Cells**, the bottom of the tab changes so a specific number of divisions can be specified.

Current definition

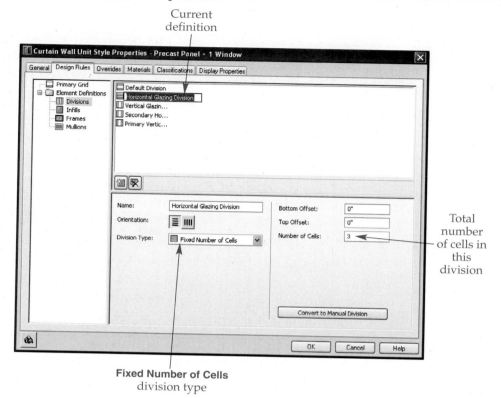

Total number of cells in this division

Fixed Number of Cells
division type

Figure 16-27.
Select the **Infills** icon to configure infill definitions.

New Infill button　Current definition　**Remove Infill** button　Type the name of the infill

Select to create new infill definitions

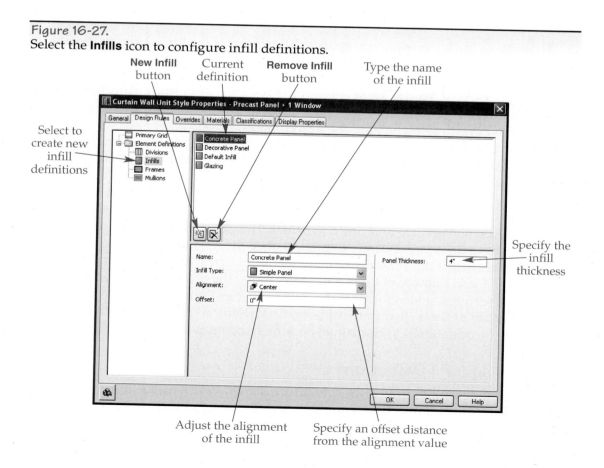

Specify the infill thickness

Adjust the alignment of the infill

Specify an offset distance from the alignment value

Architectural Desktop and Its Applications

Highlight the new definition, and enter the name Decorative Panel in the **Name:** text box. Enter a panel thickness of 4″. Create another infill named Concrete Panel, and set the thickness to 4″. Create the last panel, name it Glazing, and set the thickness to 1″. This creates the three infills required for the curtain wall unit.

Establishing Mullion Definitions

This curtain wall unit is used as an infill to a curtain wall, so a frame is not required; however, if you are creating a single panel of glazing as a curtain wall unit, you may want to create a frame around the panel. Two types of mullions are used in the style, one for the glazing divisions and one for the concrete panel divisions. Select the **Mullions** definition icon. Again, the tab view changes to reflect mullion definitions. See **Figure 16-28**.

Select the **New Mullion** button to create a new mullion definition. Highlight and name the new definition Concrete Mullion. Set the width to 1″ and the depth to 3″. You can use a custom profile as a special shape for the mullion by selecting the **Use Profile** check box and selecting an AEC profile from the list. Create a second mullion definition named Glazing Mullion, and set the width to 1″ and the depth to 2″. The two mullion definitions required for the style are created. You are now prepared to assemble the elements to create a custom curtain wall unit.

Assembling the Curtain Wall Unit Style

Now that the elements required for the style have been established and their properties set, the style can be created. In the tree view on the left edge of the **Design Rules** tab, select the **Primary Grid** icon. The tab view is changed to a table display. The table gives the settings used for the primary grid, also known as the *main division*.

Figure 16-28.
The mullion definition view is used to create custom mullion definitions.

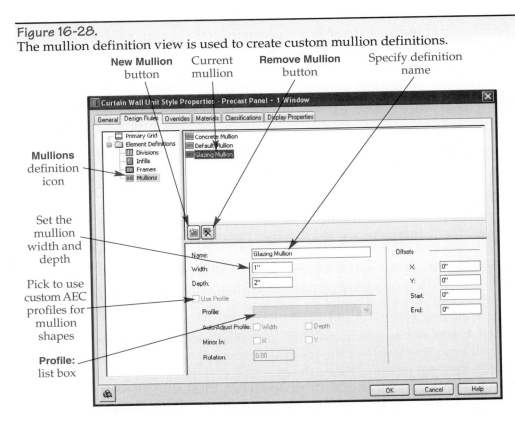

Figure 16-29.
Select the **Primary Grid** icon to view the table used to configure the style.

Select the **Primary Grid** icon to begin configuring the curtain wall unit style

Pick Default Division to select a new division definition

Default Infill definition

Default Frame definition

Default Mullion definition

New Cell Assignment button

New Frame Assignment button

New Mullion Assignment button

Remove Assignment button

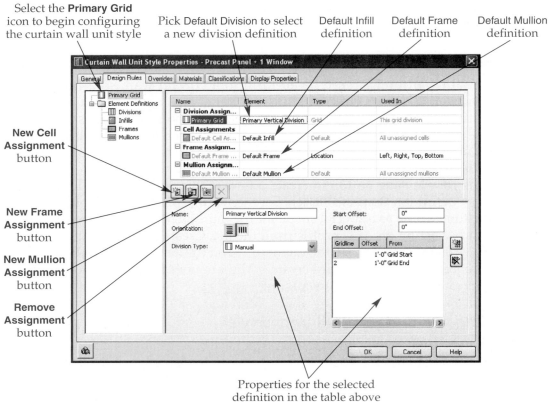

Properties for the selected definition in the table above

The primary grid includes division assignments, cell assignments, frame assignments, and mullion assignments. See **Figure 16-29**. Across the top of the table are four columns: **Name**, **Element**, **Type**, and **Used In**. At the top of the table, **Primary Grid** is the name of the division assignment. This grid is using the division element definition of Default Division. Pick the Default Division text under the **Element** column to display a drop-down list of division definitions you previously created. Select the Primary Vertical Division definition from the list.

The primary grid is then set to use your custom division that establishes grid lines 12″ from the start and end of the unit. The primary grid is now set with three separate cells. Moving down the table, note that **Cell Assignments** for the primary grid is set to use the Default Infill definition for all unassigned cells, as shown in **Figure 16-29**. Select the Default Infill text in the **Element** column, and select the Concrete Panel infill. The primary grid will, therefore, use the Concrete Panel infill definition for each of the three cells.

Referring to **Figure 16-23,** notice that the three vertical cells need to be subdivided into three horizontal divisions, totaling nine individual cells without the glazing divisions. In other words, three horizontal divisions need to be nested within each of the three vertical divisions.

In the **Cell Assignments** area of the table, pick the **New Cell Assignment** button to add another cell assignment to the primary grid. A new cell named New Cell Assignment is added. In the **Element** column beside the new cell, pick the text to produce a drop-down list. Pick *Nested Grid* from the drop-down list. The cell assignment's name is renamed to New Nested Grid. Pick the text in the **Name** column to change the name of New Nested Grid to Secondary Grid. The **Type** column should reflect the **Location** option. In the **Used In** column, pick the text to reveal an ellipsis button (**...**). Pick the ellipsis button to select the primary grid cells where the nested grid will be located. Make sure

Figure 16-30.
The primary grid is being configured to use the Concrete Panel infill definition for any unassigned cells. The starting and ending cells of the primary grid have been assigned a nested grid.

3. Pick to rename as Secondary Grid

2. Select to display a drop-down list to pick the *Nested Grid* option

4. The nested cells will be located in...

5. Pick to display the (...) button

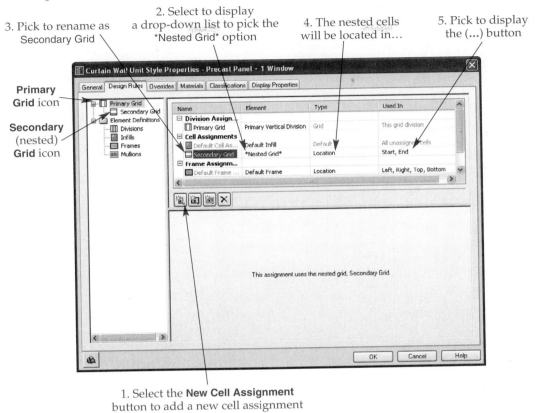

Primary Grid icon

Secondary (nested) Grid icon

1. Select the **New Cell Assignment** button to add a new cell assignment

that the **Start** and **End** check boxes have been selected, and clear the check mark in the **Middle** check box to specify that the starting and ending cells will be nested. Notice the tree to the left of the **Primary Grid** icon now includes a new icon below it named **Secondary Grid**, as shown in **Figure 16-30**.

The primary grid now includes two types of cell assignments: Concrete Panel and Secondary (nested) Grid. The primary grid's middle cell currently uses the Concrete Panel infill as the default infill, as it is considered an unassigned cell in the **Used In** column. Pick the **New Cell Assignment** button again to add another cell assignment. Set this cell assignment to *Nested Grid*, and set the nesting to be used in the middle primary grid cell only. Change the name of New Nested Grid to Middle Grid. The primary grid now uses a nested grid in the starting and ending cells and a separate nested grid in the middle cell.

Currently, the style uses the Default Frame definition around the curtain wall unit. A frame is not needed in this style, so you can turn this off. In the Default Frame Assignment element, move to the **Used In** column. Notice a frame is being used at the left, right, top, and bottom locations. These values reflect the four sides of the primary grid. Select the text **Left, Right, Top, Bottom** to reveal the ellipsis (...) button. Uncheck each of the values to turn off the frame around the primary grid.

The **Mullion Assignments** area is currently using the Default Mullion definition as the cell divider. Pick the Default Mullion text to display a drop-down list, and select the Concrete Mullions definition. This step completes the primary grid assignments, as shown in **Figure 16-31**.

Figure 16-31.
The primary grid assignments should appear as in the diagram. Two nested grid assignments, no framework, and concrete mullions define the primary grid.

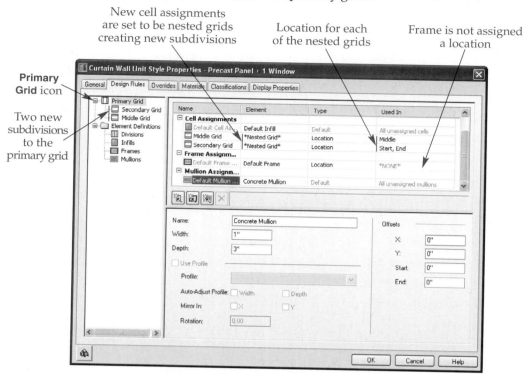

New cell assignments are set to be nested grids creating new subdivisions

Location for each of the nested grids

Frame is not assigned a location

Primary Grid icon

Two new subdivisions to the primary grid

Once you have configured the primary grid, begin making assignments for the nested grids. The secondary grid that controls the starting and ending cells of the primary grid will not be subdivided any further, but it does include two types of panels: Decorative Panel and Concrete Panel. Select the **Secondary Grid** icon in the tree view below the **Primary Grid** icon to assign definitions to the secondary grid level.

A horizontal grid division definition was created earlier, so you can assign this division definition to the secondary grid. In the **Division Assignment** area for the secondary grid, select the **Default Division** element, and pick the **Secondary Horizontal Division** definition from the list to divide the starting and ending cells of the primary grid into three horizontal cells with gridlines 12" from the top and bottom.

The secondary grid is now divided into three horizontal cells. The cell assignment is currently set to Default Infill. The top and bottom cells need to be assigned the Decorative Panel infill definition, and the middle cell needs to be assigned the Concrete Panel infill definition.

Pick the **New Cell Assignment** button to add a new cell assignment. In the **Element** column beside the new cell, select the Decorative Panel definition. Change the name of New Cell Assignment in the **Name** column to Top and Bottom Cells. In the **Used In** column, make sure the decorative panel is being used in the Top and Bottom Cells. Select the **New Cell Assignment** button again to add another new cell assignment. Change this assignment to the Concrete Panel definition, and use this definition in the middle cell location only. Rename this new cell assignment Middle Cell.

The final assignment to the secondary grid is the mullion assignment. Select the Default Mullion text in the **Element** column, and select the Concrete Mullions definition. The settings for the secondary grid are established. Use the **Viewer** to preview the results so far. **Figure 16-32** displays the settings for the secondary grid.

Figure 16-32.
The secondary grid uses the Secondary Horizontal Division definition to divide the starting and ending cells of the primary grid into three cells. The top and bottom cells are assigned the decorative panel infill definition, and the middle cell is assigned the concrete panel infill definition.

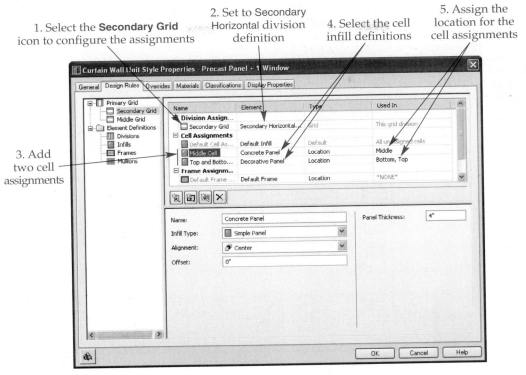

1. Select the **Secondary Grid** icon to configure the assignments

2. Set to Secondary Horizontal division definition

3. Add two cell assignments

4. Select the cell infill definitions

5. Assign the location for the cell assignments

Now that the primary and secondary grids have been defined, you can concentrate on the middle primary cell. Select the **Middle Grid** icon below the **Primary Grid** icon from the tree view. The middle grid also needs to be divided into three horizontal cells. The top and bottom cells use the Concrete Panel definition, and the middle cell becomes a nested grid for the glazing.

Select the Default Division element for the middle grid division assignment. Set this assignment to the Secondary Horizontal Division definition. In the **Cell Assignments** area, select the **New Cell Assignment** button to add a new cell assignment. Change the new cell assignment element to *Nested Grid*. Change the name of New Nested Grid to Primary Glazing. Set the location for the nested grid to the middle cell, which indicates that the middle cell of the Middle Grid division will be subdivided.

Change Default Cell Assignment to Concrete Panel, which indicates that any cells not defined (the top and bottom cells of the middle grid) will use the Concrete Panel infill definition. The last task is to set the mullion assignments. Change Default Mullion to the Glazing Mullions definition. The assignments for the **Middle Grid** level are displayed in **Figure 16-33.**

Now that the Middle Grid division has been defined, the Primary Glazing division needs to be defined. This division controls the middle cell of the Middle Grid division and needs to be broken down into three equal vertical glazing pieces. The three equal glazing pieces then need to be broken down further into two equal horizontal pieces.

Select the **Primary Glazing** icon from the left side of the tab in the tree view. Set the **Division Assignment** element to the Vertical Glazing Division. This division definition splits the middle cell of the Middle Grid division into three equal cells. In the **Cell Assignments** area, change the Default Infill to the Glazing definition. Create a new cell assignment and make the assignment a nested grid. Change the name of New Nested Grid to Secondary Glazing. In the **Used In** column for the Secondary Glazing cell assignment, set the location to Start, Middle, End. Finally, set the Default Mullion to the Glazing Mullion definition. **Figure 16-34** displays the settings for the Primary Glazing division.

Figure 16-33.
The Middle Grid division controls the middle cell of the primary grid. Assign the division element to use, followed by the cell assignments.

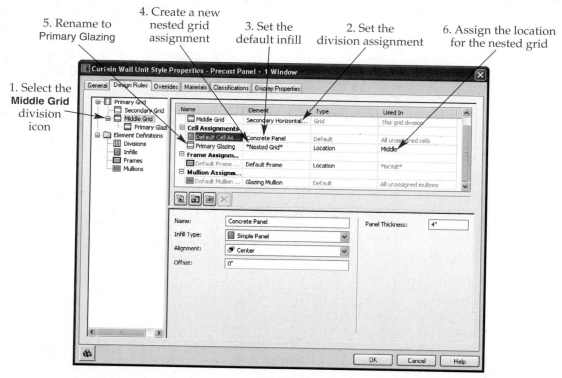

5. Rename to Primary Glazing

4. Create a new nested grid assignment

3. Set the default infill

2. Set the division assignment

6. Assign the location for the nested grid

1. Select the **Middle Grid** division icon

Figure 16-34.
The settings for the Primary Glazing division control the rules for the middle cell of the Middle Grid division.

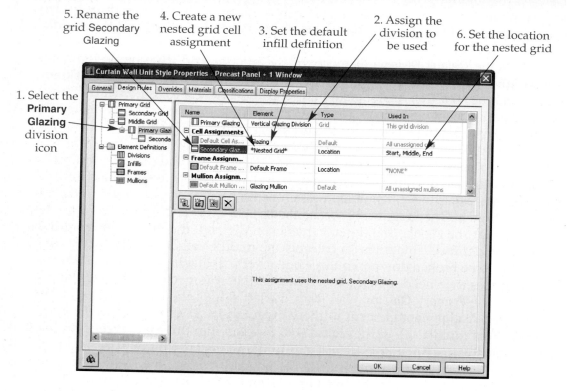

5. Rename the grid Secondary Glazing

4. Create a new nested grid cell assignment

3. Set the default infill definition

2. Assign the division to be used

6. Set the location for the nested grid

1. Select the **Primary Glazing** division icon

Architectural Desktop and Its Applications

Figure 16-35.
The Secondary Glazing division is the last division that needs to be configured.

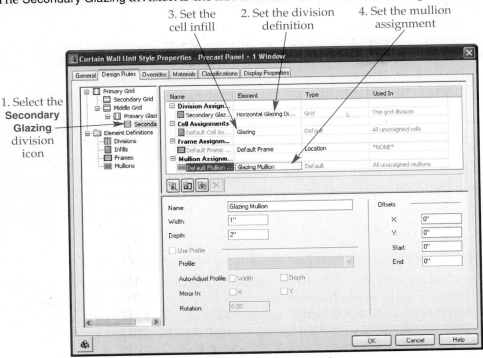

3. Set the cell infill

2. Set the division definition

4. Set the mullion assignment

1. Select the **Secondary Glazing** division icon

The final part that needs to be configured is the last division. Select the **Secondary Glazing** division icon from the tree view. Set the Division Assignment to use the Horizontal Glazing Division definition. Set the Default Infill to the Glazing definition and the Default Mullion to the Glazing Mullion definition. See **Figure 16-35.** The curtain wall unit rules are now complete. Use the **Viewer** to preview the new style.

The final step to creating the curtain wall unit style is to assign any material and classification assignments. In the **Materials** tab, the list of default components and custom components (element definitions) created are listed. Pick the text in the **Material Definition** column beside a component to assign a material. If no materials are present, use the **Add New Material** button to add a new material definition. If render materials need to be assigned to the material definition, you have to exit the **Style Manager** first. Then, use the **Content Browser** to import render materials and assign them to your material definitions.

If classifications are to be assigned to the style, pick the **Classifications** tab and select the classifications that are assigned to the style. If you need to make any adjustments to the display settings for the Model, Plan, or Reflective representations, pick the **Display Properties** tab and make the necessary adjustments. Pick the **OK** button when you are finished to return to the drawing.

Exercise 16-7 Complete the Exercise on the Student CD.

The addition of door/window assemblies was discussed in Chapter 5, and modification of the door/window assemblies was discussed in Chapter 13. Door/window assembly styles are discussed here, as they are similar to curtain wall units and curtain wall styles. The door/window assembly style section appears before the curtain wall styles discussion because curtain wall styles can use both curtain wall units and door/window assemblies as infill elements.

Door/window assembly styles are created using the same types of rules as used by curtain wall unit styles. A door/window assembly style is based on a series of divisions and nested grids. In addition to the standard infill panels that the curtain wall unit style uses, the door/window assembly style can use door and window styles as infill elements. Door/window assembly styles can be created by one of three methods: from scratch, converted from linework, or converted from a layout grid. The next section discusses how to create door/window assembly styles.

Creating a Door/Window Assembly Style from Scratch

The door/window assembly style to be created is a door with a sidelight containing muntins, as shown in **Figure 16-36.** To create the door/window assembly style, pick **Design > Door/Window Assemblies > Door/Window Assembly Styles...** from the pull-down menu, type DOORWINASSEMBLYSTYLE, or right-click over the **Door/Window Assembly** tool in the **Design** tool palette and pick the **Door/Window Assembly Styles** option.

The **Style Manager** is displayed, showing the Door/Window Assembly Styles section. Select the **New Style** button to create a new door/window assembly style. Name the style Hinged Single 3-0 × 7-0 Left + Sidelight with Grids. Select the new style to display the property tabs for the style in the right window pane. The **Door/Window Assembly Style** property tabs are shown in **Figure 16-37.** The style includes the following seven tabs:
- **General.** This tab is used to rename the style; provide a description; and add design notes, property set definitions, and keynotes.
- **Shape.** This tab is used to specify a shape for the door/window assembly style. Unlike the curtain wall unit style, the door/window assembly style can be created using different shapes, such as rectangular, oval, gothic, or a custom shape determined from an AEC profile. See **Figure 16-37.**

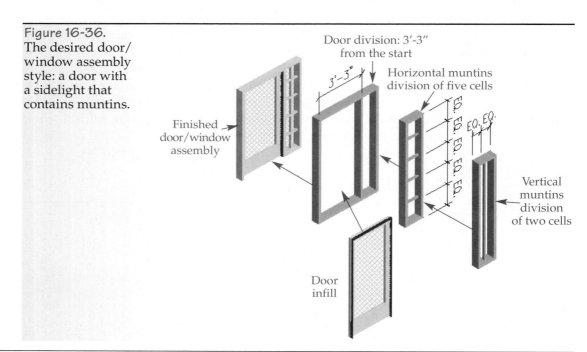

Figure 16-36.
The desired door/window assembly style: a door with a sidelight that contains muntins.

Figure 16-37.
The **Door/Window Assembly Style Properties** dialog box is used to configure a door/window assembly style.

Shape tab

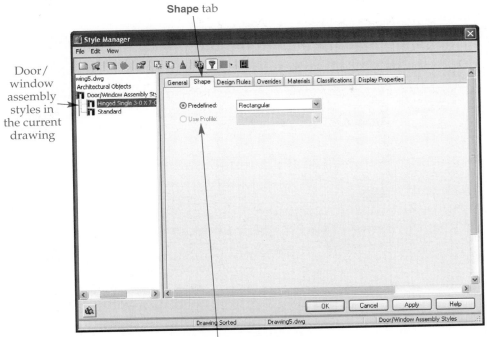

Door/window assembly styles in the current drawing

Use a predefined or profile shape for the door/window assembly style

- **Design Rules.** Similar to the tab for the curtain wall unit style, this tab is used to create the division, infill, frame, and mullion definitions and assemble them into a door/window assembly style.
- **Overrides.** This tab displays any overrides to a door/window assembly style when you edit the design rules in place.
- **Materials.** This tab is used to assign material definitions to the components used in the door/window assembly style.
- **Classifications.** Use this tab to assign any classification to the style.
- **Display Properties.** This tab controls the display of the door/window assembly style in different display representations.

Creating the Element Definitions

Access the **Design Rules** tab to begin assembling the style. A review of **Figure 16-36** reveals that three divisions need to be created: the primary grid places the door at the start of the grid (on the left), a horizontal muntins division is nested to the right of the primary grid, and a vertical muntins division is nested in the five horizontal sidelight cells.

First, create the Door Division definition. Create a new vertical division named Door Division. Use the **Manual** division type with a vertical orientation. Add a gridline 3'-3" from the grid start.

Next, create the horizontal division. Name the definition Horizontal Muntins. Set the division type to **Fixed Number of Cells**, with a total of five cells, and set the orientation to horizontal. Create one last division named Vertical Muntins. Set the **Division Type:** to **Fixed Cell Dimension**, with the cell dimension set to 12" using the vertical orientation. The **Fixed Cell Dimension** includes an option that allows cells to grow or shrink. See **Figure 16-38.** When you specify whether a cell is to grow or shrink and pick the appropriate button below the drop-down list, the door/window assembly continues to add 12" divisions until it stops at an odd dimension. Depending on whether the

Figure 16-38.

The **Fixed Cell Dimension** type allows you to specify if cells will get larger or smaller when an odd dimensional size is entered for the door/window assembly style.

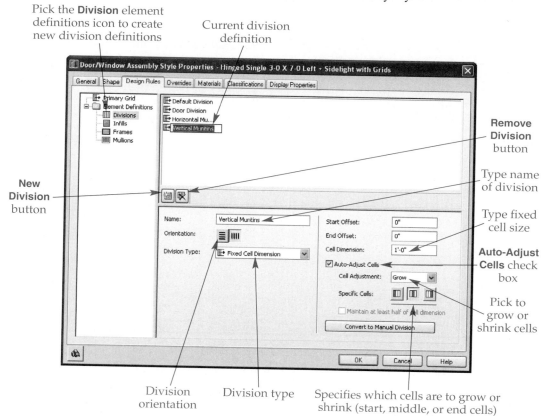

Pick the **Division** element definitions icon to create new division definitions

Current division definition

New **Division** button

Remove **Division** button

Type name of division

Type fixed cell size

Auto-Adjust Cells check box

Pick to grow or shrink cells

Division orientation

Division type

Specifies which cells are to grow or shrink (start, middle, or end cells)

starting, middle, or ending cell has been told to grow or shrink, that cell will become larger or smaller within the division. In this situation, you do not want the cells to grow or shrink, so uncheck the **Auto-Adjust Cells** check box.

After you have created the division definitions, create the infill definitions. Door and glazing infill definitions are required. Create a new infill named Glazing, using the Simple Panel infill type. Set the panel thickness to 1". The second infill will use a door style. Before you create the door infill, a door style for the door/window assembly style needs to be created. Pick the **OK** button to set the properties for the door/window assembly style properties and exit the **Style Manager**. On the **Doors** palette, locate the Hinged-Single-Full Lite door style. Right-click on the tool and pick the **Import 'Hinged-Single-Full Lite' Door Style** option. This imports the door style.

This door style has a frame already configured around the door panel, but you are creating a frame within the door/window assembly, so you want to modify the door style by setting its frame size to 0". Access the **DOORSTYLE** command, find the Hinged-Single-Full Lite door style, and edit the style. In the **General** tab, rename the door style to DW-Hinged-Single-Full Lite. This indicates that this door style is used in a door/window assembly. In the **Dimensions** tab, set the Frame width and depth to 0".

While still in the **Style Manager**, toggle the **Filter Style Type** button to see all of the AEC styles in the **Style Manager**. Locate the Door/Window Assembly Styles section, highlight it, and pick the **Filter Style Type** button again to return to filtering for door/window assembly styles. Find and edit the Hinged-Single 3-0 × 7-0 Left + Sidelight with Grids style.

Select the **Design Rules** tab and then the Infills element definition icon. Create a new infill type named Door. Pick the drop-down arrow under the **Infill Type:** property. Select the **Style** option. This displays a box containing styles on the right side of the tab. See **Figure 16-39**. Browse through the Door Styles folder to find and select the

Figure 16-39.
The **Style** infill type is an option that is available for door/window assembly styles and curtain wall styles. It allows you to use door, window, curtain wall unit, and AEC polygon styles as infills.

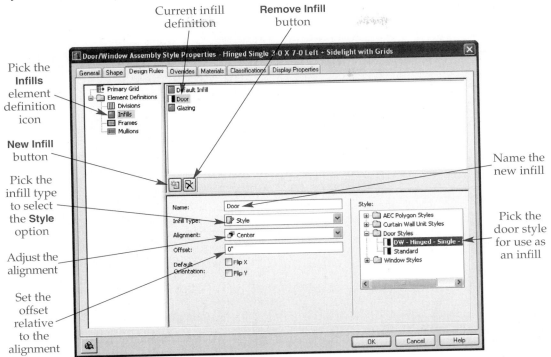

DW-Hinged-Single-Full Lite door style. Set the alignment to **center** and the offset to 2″. This completes the two infill definitions required for the style.

Create a frame definition named Assembly Frame. Set the width to 2″ and depth to 5″. Next, create two mullion definitions. One mullion definition is used between the door and the sidelight, and the other is used as the muntins in the sidelight. Create the first mullion definition, named Main Mullions, with a width of 2″ and depth of 5″. Create the second mullion definition, named Muntins, with a width of 1″ and depth of 2″. With the definitions created, the door/window assembly can be put together.

Creating the Rules for the Style

Select the **Primary Grid** icon in the **Design Rules** tab. Pick the Default Division text under the **Element** column. Change the division for the primary grid to the Door Division. Two vertical cells are created for the primary division. Move down to the **Cell Assignments** area, and select the Default Cell Assignment element. Change the default infill to the Door infill definition.

Next, add a New Cell Assignment, with the element type *Nested Grid*. The nested grid is used in the end location. Change the name of New Nested Grid to Horizontal Muntins. Change the default frame to the Assembly Frame definition. A frame is not needed below the door, so turn the frame off at the bottom of the primary grid. Select the **Used In** column for the frame definition, pick the (...) button, and uncheck the bottom check box.

The final step in the configuration of the primary grid is to assign the mullions dividing the door from the sidelight. Change the default mullions to the Main Mullions definition. Figure 16-40 displays the settings for the primary grid.

The next grid that needs to be configured is the Horizontal Muntins grid. Select the **Horizontal Muntins** icon from the tree on the left. Change the division type to the Horizontal Muntins definition, which divides the sidelight into five separate cells. In the **Cell Assignments** area, set the default cell assignment to use the Glazing infill definition.

Figure 16-40.
The rules for the primary grid separate the grid into two vertical cells, assigning the door infill and a nested infill for the sidelight.

6. Rename the nested grid Horizontal Muntins

3. Set the **Default Cell Assignment** to the Door infill definition

2. Change to the Door Division definition

4. Create a new cell assignment and set to *Nested Grid*

1. Pick the **Primary Grid** icon

5. Assign the *Nested Grid* infill to the End location

7. Set the **Frame Assignment** to the Assembly Frame definition

8. Set the frame location to the Left, Right, and Top parts of the door/window assembly

9. Set the **Mullion Assignment** to the Main Mullions definition

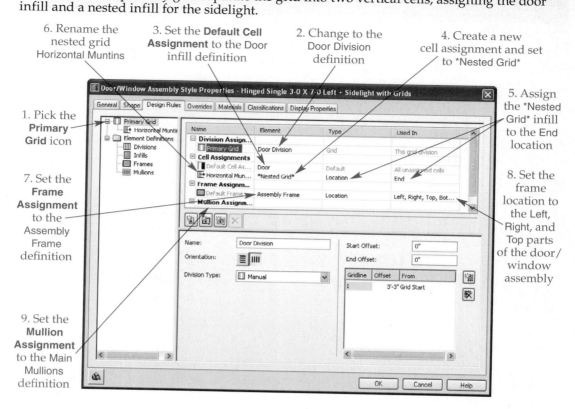

Create a new cell assignment. This cell assignment determines the vertical divisions within the Horizontal Muntins division. Set the New Cell Assignment to *Nested Grid*. Change the name of New Nested Grid to Vertical Muntins. This nested grid needs to be assigned to five cells. Select the Location text, and change it to Index. In the **Used In** column, type 1,2,3,4,5, which indicates that the vertical cells need to be added to the five horizontal cells, starting with cell number one on the bottom cell of the Horizontal Muntins division.

The frame was turned off at the bottom of the primary grid, so it is not turned on for the Horizontal Muntins division. Change the default frame to the Assembly Frame definition. In the **Used In** column, select the *NONE* text so you are able to place a check in the bottom check box. This turns the frame on for the bottom of the Horizontal Muntins division. Set the default mullions to the Muntins definition. **Figure 16-41** displays the settings for the Horizontal Muntins division.

The final step is to configure the Vertical Muntins division. Select the **Vertical Muntins** division icon from the tree view. Change the Default Division to the Vertical Muntins definition. Change the Default Infill to the Glazing definition and the Default Mullions to the Muntins definition. This step completes the configuration of the door/sidelight door/window assembly. **Figure 16-42** shows the settings for the Vertical Muntins division.

After the design rules have been set, you may decide to attach material definitions to the components. If the material definitions are not loaded, exit the Door/Window Assembly Style properties section, load any material definitions, edit the door/window assembly, and assign the materials to the components. If classifications are to be assigned, also ensure the classification styles are created in the drawing. Use the **Classifications** tab to assign any classification definitions to the style.

Figure 16-41.
The settings for the Horizontal Muntins division.

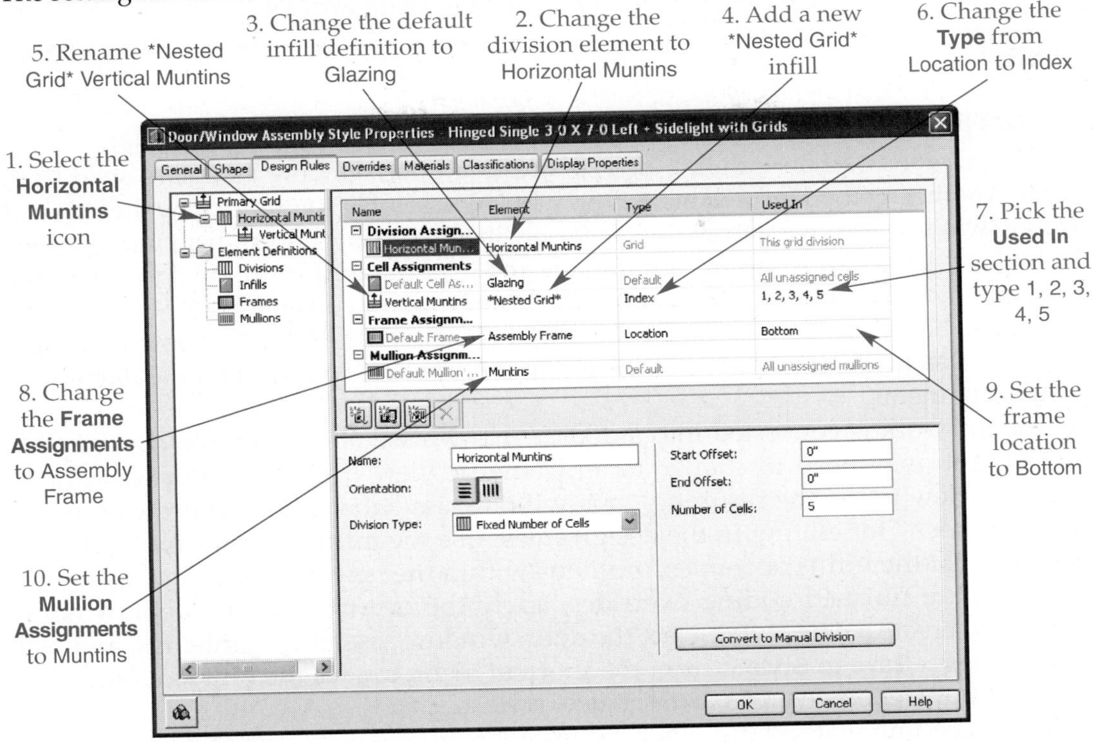

5. Rename *Nested Grid* Vertical Muntins
3. Change the default infill definition to Glazing
2. Change the division element to Horizontal Muntins
4. Add a new *Nested Grid* infill
6. Change the Type from Location to Index
1. Select the Horizontal Muntins icon
7. Pick the Used In section and type 1, 2, 3, 4, 5
8. Change the Frame Assignments to Assembly Frame
9. Set the frame location to Bottom
10. Set the Mullion Assignments to Muntins
Door/Window Assembly Style Properties - Hinged Single 3-0 X 7-0 Left + Sidelight with Grids
General
Shape
Design Rules
Overrides
Materials
Classifications
Display Properties
Name
Element
Type
Used In
Horizontal Muntins
Grid
This grid division
Glazing
Default
All unassigned cells
Nested Grid
Index
1, 2, 3, 4, 5
Assembly Frame
Location
Bottom
Muntins
Default
All unassigned mullions
Orientation:
Division Type:
Fixed Number of Cells
Start Offset:
End Offset:
Number of Cells:
Convert to Manual Division
OK
Cancel
Help

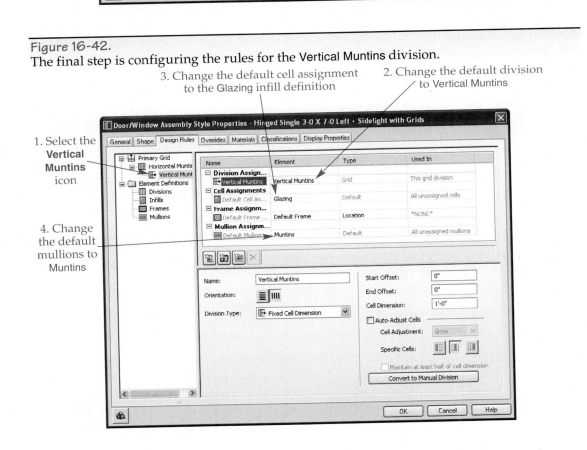

Figure 16-42.
The final step is configuring the rules for the Vertical Muntins division.

3. Change the default cell assignment to the Glazing infill definition
2. Change the default division to Vertical Muntins
1. Select the Vertical Muntins icon
4. Change the default mullions to Muntins
Door/Window Assembly Style Properties - Hinged Single 3-0 X 7-0 Left + Sidelight with Grids
General
Shape
Design Rules
Overrides
Materials
Classifications
Display Properties
Name
Element
Type
Used In
Vertical Muntins
Grid
This grid division
Glazing
Default
All unassigned cells
Default Frame
Location
NONE
Muntins
Default
All unassigned mullions
Orientation:
Division Type:
Fixed Cell Dimension
Start Offset:
End Offset:
Cell Dimension:
Auto-Adjust Cells
Cell Adjustment:
Specific Cells:
Maintain at least half of cell dimension
Convert to Manual Division
OK
Cancel
Help

Converting Linework to a Door/Window Assembly

The previous section outlined how to create a door/window assembly style from scratch. Another method for creating a door/window assembly style is to draw the layout of the door/window assembly using lines and polylines and then convert them into a style.

To do this, first draw the elevation shape and gridline configuration desired for the door/window assembly, and then apply the **Door/Window Assembly** tool to the elevation sketch. See **Figure 16-43**. To do this, right-click over the **Door/Window Assembly** tool in the **Design** palette, and select **Apply Tool Properties to** > **Elevation Sketch** from the shortcut menu.

The linework is converted into a door/window assembly when the command is finished. You may need to change to an isometric view if the linework was drawn in the Top view to see the resulting door/window assembly. The curtain wall unit is currently "open" for editing in the design rules. Use the infill or frame/mullion overrides to adjust the infills or frames/mullions within the new door/window assembly. When you are finished adding overrides, apply the overrides to the door/window assembly to create a new style. Select the door/window assembly, right-click, and pick **Design Rules** > **Save to Style...** from the shortcut menu to save the unit as a new style. Be sure to transfer any overrides to the new style.

The preceding method is a quick means of creating a door/window assembly for use in a wall; however, the drawn size of the door/window assembly is the size that is inserted into a wall. The door/window assembly cannot get larger or smaller within a wall as length changes are made to the door/window assembly.

PROFESSIONAL TIP

> Although the door/window assemblies converted from an elevation sketch cannot be resized, the style can be edited after saving the design rules by adding infill, frame, and mullion definitions. Infills including doors and windows can be added, and frame or mullion sizes can be adjusted. After defining the element definitions for the style, use overrides to apply the definitions to the door/window assembly. Apply the design rules as a new style.

Figure 16-43.
Draw the shape and gridlines for the door/window assembly style, and then apply the door/window assembly tool to the linework using the **Elevation Sketch** option.

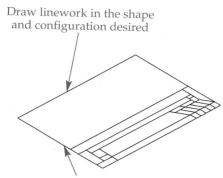
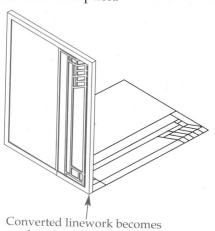

Draw linework in the shape and configuration desired

When converting a door/window assembly, pressing [Enter] for the baseline establishes the bottommost line as the baseline

Converted linework becomes a door/window assembly

Creating Additional Door/Window Assemblies

You also can create door/window assemblies from a layout grid, by using the **Layout Grid** command. This command is accessed by right-clicking over the **Door/Window Assembly** tool in the **Design** tool palette and selecting **Apply Tool Properties to** > **Layout Grid** from the shortcut menu. Answer the prompts to convert the layout grid into a door/window assembly.

Additional door/window assemblies are also included with Architectural Desktop. Use the **Style Manager** to open Door-Window Assembly Styles.dwg, found in the Styles folder. Drag and drop the styles from this drawing into your current drawing using the **Style Manager**. The **Content Browser** also includes a number of additional door/window assembly styles that can be added to tool palettes or imported into the drawing.

Creating Curtain Wall Styles

The previous discussions explained the process of creating a curtain wall unit style and a door/window assembly style. The techniques and dialog boxes are very similar for both types of objects. The process of creating the curtain wall style is the same. The only difference is that the curtain wall can use both the curtain wall unit and the door/window assembly style in its configuration as infills. The goal for this section is to create a curtain wall using the curtain wall unit created in Exercise 16-7 and the two door/window assemblies created in Exercise 16-9 as infills and combine them into one curtain wall. The curtain wall ends up looking like the diagram in Figure 16-44.

Creating the Curtain Wall Style

Referring to **Figure 16-45**, note that the curtain wall is broken into three separate divisions. The primary grid establishes divisions 12″ from the ends, with the middle being reserved for the curtain wall units and door/window assemblies. The vertical

Figure 16-44.
The curtain wall
style to be created.

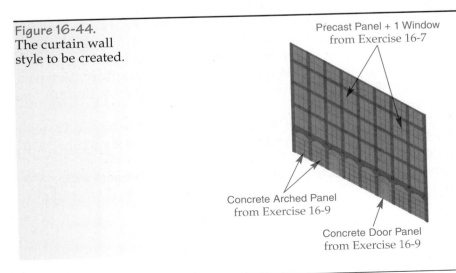

Precast Panel + 1 Window
from Exercise 16-7

Concrete Arched Panel
from Exercise 16-9

Concrete Door Panel
from Exercise 16-9

Figure 16-45.
The curtain wall style will be divided into three separate grids.

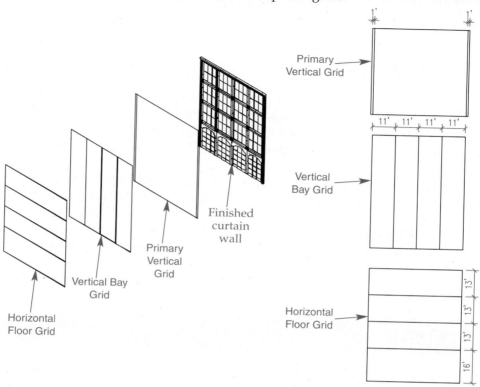

bay grid establishes the vertical divisions for the curtain wall units at 11'-0" apart. This number was established from the Concrete Panel door/window assemblies that were converted from 11'-wide linework in Exercise 16-9. The horizontal floor grid establishes the first gridline 16'-0" from the bottom, with subsequent gridlines 13' apart.

The infill definitions required are the Precast Panel + 1 Window (curtain wall unit), Concrete Door Panel (door/window assembly), Concrete Arched Panel (door/window assembly), and an 8"-thick infill for the ends of the wall. A mullion definition between the cells is also created 1" wide × 3" deep. With the parameters for the curtain wall calculated, the style can be created.

Curtain wall styles are created by picking **Design** > **Curtain Walls** > **Curtain Wall Styles...** from the pull-down menu, typing CURTAINWALLSTYLE, or right-clicking the **Curtain Wall** tool in the **Design** palette and picking the **Curtain Wall Styles...** option. This displays the **Style Manager** opened to the Curtain Wall Styles section.

Pick the **New Styles** button to create a new curtain wall style. Name the style Precast Concrete Panel. Highlight the new style in the tree view to display the property tabs in the right pane. The curtain wall property tabs include the following six tabs for the configuration of the curtain wall: **General**, **Design Rules**, **Overrides**, **Materials**, **Classifications**, and **Display Properties**, similar to the tabs for curtain wall units and door/window assemblies.

A single bay in the curtain wall is 11'-0" wide, and it is desired to have a 12"-wide brick panel at each end, so the minimum width for the curtain wall should be 13'-0". As new bays are added to the curtain wall, the curtain wall increases in size in 11'-0" increments. Enter the following description in the **General** tab: Minimum width 13'-0", increase size in 11'-0" increments.

Creating the Curtain Wall Definitions

Select the **Design Rules** tab to begin configuring the curtain wall. Begin by creating all the definitions required for the curtain wall. There are three divisions required, as noted in **Figure 16-45**. Select the **Divisions** element definition icon from the Element Definitions list on the left side of the tab. Add a new division named Primary Vertical Grid. Set the orientation to **vertical** and the division type to **Manual**. Add two gridlines, one 12″ from the grid start and the other 12″ from the grid end.

Create the next division definition, named Vertical Bay Grid. Set the orientation to **vertical** and the division type to **Fixed Cell Dimension**, with a cell dimension of 11′-0″. Uncheck the **Auto-Adjust Cells** check box. Create the last division, named Horizontal Floor Grid. Set the orientation to **horizontal** using a **Manual** division type. Add these four gridlines:

- 16′-0″ from the grid bottom
- 29′-0″ from the grid bottom
- 42′-0″ from the grid bottom
- 55′-0″ from the grid bottom

Next, create the four infill definitions. Select the **Infills** icon from the **Element Definitions** list. Add a new infill named Precast Window Panel. Set the **Infill Type:** drop-down list to **Style**, and then select the Precast Panel + 1 Window style from the Curtain Wall Unit Styles folder in the lower-right corner of the **Design Rules** tab. Add another new infill named Concrete Arched Panel. Set the infill type to **Style**, and select the Concrete Arched Panel door/window assembly style from the Door/Window Assembly Styles folder. Select the **New Infill** button again, and name the new style Concrete Door Panel. Use the Concrete Door Panel door/window assembly style. Create the last infill as a Simple Panel type. Name the new infill End Panels, and set the panel to be 8″ thick. This creates the four infill patterns that are used to make up the curtain wall style.

A cornice is to be added at the top of the curtain wall. This is the top frame member of the curtain wall. **Figure 16-46** displays the profile shape to be used at the top of the curtain wall. Before the frame element definition is created, the profile needs to be defined in the drawing. Pick the **OK** button to apply the settings to the curtain wall style and exit the **Style Manager**. Draw the shape shown in **Figure 16-46**. Convert the polyline into an AEC profile, with the insertion point as indicated in the figure. Name the profile Cornice.

After the profile is created, return to the Precast Concrete Panel curtain wall style. Pick the **Frame** element definition icon. Create a new frame member named Cornice. Select the **Use Profile** check box and **Cornice** profile. In the **Offsets** area, enter a value of -2″ for the **Start** and **End** properties. This causes the frame to extend 2″ past the edge of the curtain wall.

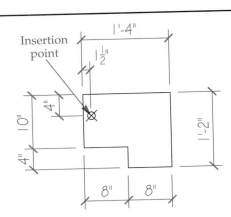

Figure 16-46.
An AEC profile will be used as a cornice for the curtain wall's top frame. Name the profile Cornice.

Finally, create the mullion definition. Select the **Mullions** icon from the **Element Definitions** list. Pick the **New Mullion** button. Name the new mullion Expansion Joint and set the width to 1″ and depth to 3″. With all the definitions created, the curtain wall can be assembled.

Assembling the Curtain Wall

Select the **Primary Grid** icon in the tree along the left of the **Design Rules** tab. Change the default division element to the Primary Vertical Grid definition to establish the first level of divisions for the curtain wall. Under the **Cell Assignments** area, select the *Nested Grid* text in the element column, and change the element type to the End Panels infill definition.

Select the **New Cell Assignment** button to add another cell to the Primary Vertical Grid division. Change the element of this new cell to *Nested Grid*, and rename the cell Vertical Bays. In the **Used In** column, select the Start, End text to display the ellipsis button (...). Select the button, uncheck the **Start** and **End** check boxes, and place a check mark in the **Middle** check box to place the nested Vertical Bay Grid in the middle primary grid cell.

The curtain wall has a cornice placed at the top of the wall. The left, right, and bottom edges of the curtain wall have the frame turned off. Select the Default Frame element and change to the Cornice frame. The location for the cornice is the top of the curtain wall. Select the Left, Right, Top, Bottom text in the **Used In** column beside the **Frame Assignments** section. Uncheck the **Left**, **Right**, and **Bottom** check boxes. In the **Mullion Assignments** area, set the default mullion to use the Expansion Joint definition to complete the configuration for the primary grid. **Figure 16-47** displays the settings for the first-level grid.

The next step is to configure the second grid, which is the first nested grid. Remember, this division is being placed in the middle cell of the Primary Vertical Grid division. Select the **Vertical Bays** icon under the **Primary Grid** icon in the tree along the left edge of the tab.

Figure 16-47.
The primary grid settings have been configured.

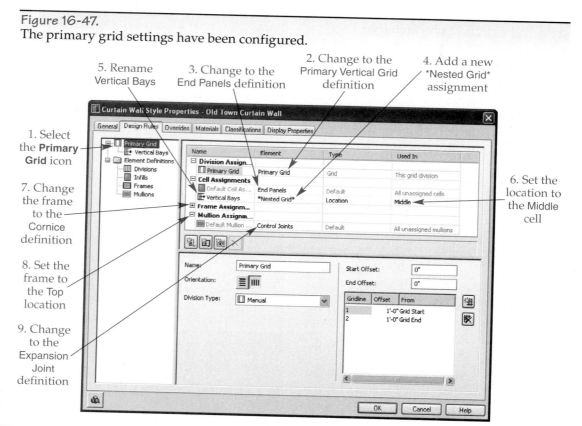

Architectural Desktop and Its Applications

Change the default division to the Vertical Bay Grid definition. Add a new cell assignment to the Vertical Bay Grid and set the element to *Nested Grid*. Change the name of the New Nested Grid to Horizontal Floors. Currently, the Vertical Bay Grid establishes 11′-0″ wide vertical bays. The Horizontal Floor nested grid needs to be told in which vertical bay cells it will be nested. In the **Type** column for the Horizontal Floors row, select the Location text. Change Location to Index. In the **Used In** column, type 1,2,3,4.5,6,7,8,9. This adds the Horizontal Floor nested grid to the first nine cells of the Vertical Bay division. Change the default mullion to the Expansion Joint definition to complete the configuration of the secondary grid (Vertical Bay Grid). See **Figure 16-48**.

The last step is to configure the horizontal floor cells. Select the **Horizontal Floors** icon from the tree list on the left. Change the default division to the Horizontal Floor Grid. Change the default infill to the Precast Window Panel definition. Add a new cell assignment. Change the new cell assignment to the Concrete Arched Panel definition. In the **Used In** column, set the panel to be placed in the bottom cell of the Horizontal Floor Grid. Finally, change the default mullions to the Expansion Joint definition to complete the curtain wall style, shown in **Figure 16-49**.

Exercise 16-10 Complete the Exercise on the Student CD.

Additional Methods of Creating Curtain Wall Styles

As with the door/window assemblies, linework can be converted into a curtain wall style. When linework is converted into a curtain wall style and then added to the drawing, the curtain wall is always drawn at the size established by the linework. There is not any flexibility in adjusting the size of the curtain wall. Another method of creating curtain walls is by converting a layout grid. A layout grid is an AEC object often used when creating column grids or layout bays. Unlike linework, layout grids converted to a curtain wall can be adjusted in width and height.

Figure 16-48.
The settings for the Vertical Bay grid are shown.

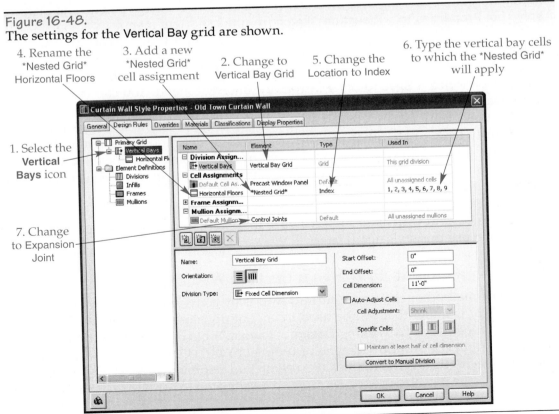

4. Rename the *Nested Grid* Horizontal Floors

3. Add a new *Nested Grid* cell assignment

2. Change to Vertical Bay Grid

5. Change the Location to Index

6. Type the vertical bay cells to which the *Nested Grid* will apply

1. Select the **Vertical Bays** icon

7. Change to Expansion Joint

Figure 16-49.
The settings for the Horizontal Floor grid are shown.

4. Add a new cell assignment and set to the Concrete Arched Panel definition

3. Change to the Precast Window Panel definition

2. Change the default division to the Horizontal floor grid

5. Use the Concrete Arched Panel in the bottom cell of the Horizontal Floor Grid

1. Pick the **Horizontal Floors** icon

6. Change to Expansion Joint

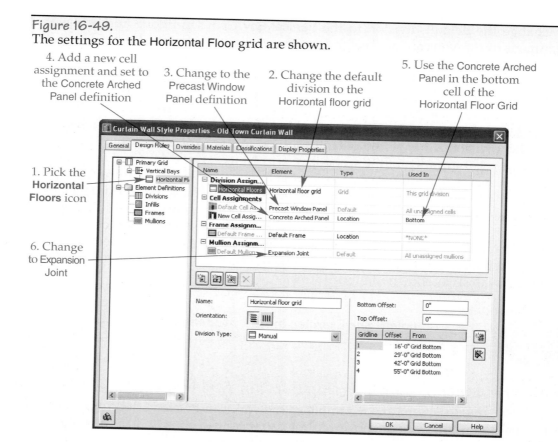

Converting Linework into a Curtain Wall Style

To convert linework into a curtain wall, draw the desired shape and configuration for the curtain wall style, and then use the **Elevation Sketch** command. Access this command by right-clicking over the **Curtain Wall** tool in the **Design** palette and picking **Apply Tool Properties to** > **Elevation Sketch** from the shortcut menu.

As with the door/window assembly command, select the linework that will be used to form the curtain wall. When you have finished answering the prompts, a new curtain wall is created. It is not a style until you select the curtain wall, right-click, and select **Design Rules** > **Save to Style...** from the shortcut menu. You can then save the curtain wall as a new style for use in your drawing.

After the curtain wall has been created as a new style, edit the style by adding any desired infill, frame, or mullion definitions. Division definitions are ignored, as the linework for the curtain wall is being derived from the converted linework. Once the linework has been converted, a new division named Custom Grid has been created and used as the primary grid.

After new infill, frame, and mullion definitions have been created, use overrides to adjust the curtain wall as desired. Be sure to save the overrides to the style if you would like to use this style again later.

Converting a Layout Grid into a Curtain Wall Style

The last method of creating a curtain wall is by converting it from a layout grid. A *layout grid* is a tool that can be used to lay out divisions along the X and Y axes. This tool can be found by picking **Design** > **Layout Tools and Anchors** > **Add Layout Grid (2D)...** from the pull-down menu or typing LAYOUTGRIDADD. Use the **Properties** palette to specify the overall dimensions (**Width** and **Depth** properties) of the grid. The X axis and Y axis **Bay size** properties can also be adjusted to configure the divisions of

Type
LAYOUTGRIDADD
Pull-Down Menu
Design
> Layout Tools and Anchors
> Add Layout Grid (2D)...

the grid. After configuring the properties for the layout grid, the grid can be added to the drawing. Select a point in the drawing for the first corner of the grid, and enter the rotation angle for the grid. A new layout grid is created in the drawing screen.

After the grid is drawn, it can be converted into a curtain wall unit. To do this, right-click over the **Curtain Wall Unit** tool in the **Design** tool palette, and select **Apply Tool Properties to** > **Layout Grid** from the shortcut menu.

When converting a layout grid into a curtain wall unit, you must specify a primary division. Select either horizontal or vertical. After you have specified what the primary division will be, the **Curtain Wall Unit Style Name** worksheet appears so you can give the new unit a name.

NOTE One additional tool to convert an object to a curtain wall is the **Face** option. Right-click over the **Curtain Wall** tool in the **Design** tool palette, and select **Apply Tool Properties to** > **Face** from the shortcut menu. This command will allow you to place a curtain wall style against the face of a mass element. Mass elements are discussed in Chapter 25.

Obtaining Additional Curtain Wall Styles

Architectural Desktop includes several additional curtain wall styles that can be used in other drawings. To use these styles, access the **CURTAINWALLSTYLE** command. Use the **Open Drawing** button, and then pick the **Content** button to browse through the Styles folder. Select Curtain Wall & Curtain Wall Unit Styles.dwg from the list of styles drawings to open the drawing in the **Style Manager**.

Select the Curtain Wall Styles section icon for the newly opened styles drawing. The styles are listed in the right pane. Drag and drop the styles from the right pane to the current drawing folder icon in the left pane. The additional styles are added into your current drawing for your use.

The **Content Browser** is another source for additional curtain wall styles. Browse through the Design Tool Catalog. Find the desired styles and use i-drop to drag and drop the content into your drawing. The Design Tool Catalog also includes additional curtain wall unit and door/window assembly styles that can be dragged and dropped into your drawing or onto a tool palette.

Chapter Test

Answer the following questions. Write your answers on a separate sheet of paper or complete the electronic chapter test on the Student CD.

1. Define and discuss the contents of a *curtain wall* and a *curtain wall unit*.
2. How are curtain walls similar to and different from standard AEC walls?
3. Describe an infill panel.
4. What are divisions?
5. Define *grids*.
6. When walls are converted into curtain walls, the center of the curtain wall is added to which optional locations on the wall being converted?
7. Explain the function of the **Reference Base Curve** option and describe the base curve.
8. Briefly define *curtain wall units*.
9. When modifying a curtain wall, how do you select the entire curtain wall, rather than just the curtain wall unit?
10. Explain how object cycling works.
11. Once the cell markers have been turned on, where are they displayed?
12. Identify the cells that can be merged.
13. As the crosshairs are moved around a curtain wall, what is displayed when editing grid divisions, and what is the process used to access the **In-Place Edit** toolbar?
14. When you pick the **Auto Grid Bay Spacing** grip to adjust the infill cell divisions, what does stretching the grip do?
15. What is a division element definition?
16. Explain the use of a curtain wall unit.
17. When is a primary grid required, and what is its function?
18. Give the function of the infill definition icon.
19. Give another name for the primary grid.
20. What is a layout grid?

Chapter Projects

Use the techniques covered in this chapter to create the following drawings.

1. Curtain Wall Styles
    A. Start a new drawing using one of the Aec Model templates.
    B. Access the **CURTAINWALLSTYLE** command.
    C. Select the **Open Drawing** button and use the **Content** button to browse through the Styles folder.
    D. Select and open Curtain Wall & Curtain Wall Unit Styles.dwg from the list of styles drawings.
    E. Drag and drop all of the styles into the current drawing.
    F. Add a curtain wall for each style in the drawing.
    G. Change to an isometric view.
    H. Use the **Properties** palette and grips as necessary to adjust the lengths and heights of the curtain walls.
    I. Save the drawing as P16-1.dwg.

2. Curtain Wall Building
   A. Start a new drawing using one of the Aec Model templates.
   B. Import the Hinged-Double-Full Lite door style from the **Doors** palette.
   C. Edit the door style by renaming the style CW-Hinged-Double-Full Lite. Set the door frames to a 0" width and 0" depth.
   D. Access the **CURTAINWALLSTYLE** command. Import the following two styles from Curtain Wall & Curtain Wall Unit Styles.dwg:
      • Square Grid 5'×5'
      • Ribbon
   E. Edit the Square Grid 5'×5' curtain wall style.
   F. In the **Design Rules** tab, select the **Infills** element definition icon.
   G. Create a new infill named Door. Use the **Style** infill type and set the infill definition to use the CW-Hinged-Double-Full Lite door style with a 2" offset from the **Center** alignment.
   H. Create another infill element definition named Spandrel. Use the Simple Panel infill type and set the panel thickness to 3".
   I. In the **Materials** tab, set the Default Infill to the Doors & Windows.Glazing.Glass. Clear material definition. Set the Spandrel infill to the Doors & Windows.Glazing. Glass.Mirrored material definition.
   J. Access the **CURTAINWALLUNITSTYLE** command.
   K. Pick the Ribbon infill curtain wall style.
   L. In the **Materials** tab, change the Glazing component to use the Doors & Windows. Glazing.Glass.Clear material definition.
   M. Create the building shown in the figure below. Use the Ribbon curtain wall style set to 50'-0" high for the straight segments. Use the Square Grid 5'×5' curtain wall style set to 50'-0" high for the curved segment.
   N. Select the Square Grid 5'×5', right-click, and pick **Design Rules > Transfer to Object** from the shortcut menu to "open" the style for editing.
   O. Use the **Merge** option to merge cells in the curved wall to make room for some door infills.
   P. Pick **Infill > Override Assignment...** from the shortcut menu to add the door infill to the merged cells.
   Q. Use the **Override Assignment** option to change some of the default infills to the Spandrel infill. See the figure for Spandrel patterns in the curved wall.
   R. Select the Square Grid 5'×5' curtain wall, right-click, and pick **Design Rules > Save to Style...** from the shortcut menu. Save the changes to the Square Grid 5'×5' curtain wall style.
   S. Save the drawing as P16-2.dwg.

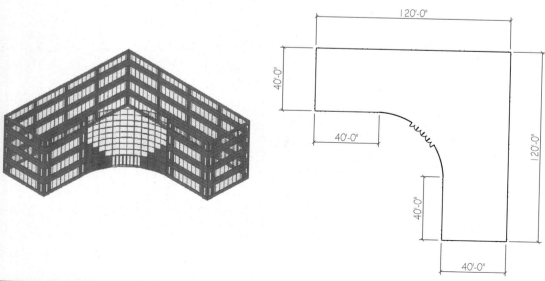

3. Curtain Wall Building
   A. Start a new drawing using one of the Aec Model templates.
   B. Access the **CURTAINWALLSTYLE** command. Import the following two styles from Curtain Wall & Curtain Wall Unit Styles.dwg:
      - Mass Base + 4×4 Grid Above
      - Stone Infill + Revolving Door
   C. Edit the Standard curtain wall style. In the **Materials** tab, assign the following material definitions to the default components:
      - **Default Infill:** Doors & Windows.Glazing.Glass.Clear
      - **Default Frame:** Doors & Windows.Metal Doors & Frames.Aluminum Frame. Anodized.Dark Bronze.Satin
      - **Default Mullion:** Doors & Windows.Metal Doors & Frames.Aluminum Frame. Anodized.Dark Bronze.Satin
   D. Draw the building shown in the figure. See the figure for the curtain wall styles to use in the building. Set the height to 62'-0".
   E. Miter the corners of the curtain walls as required.
   F. Save the drawing as P16-3.dwg.

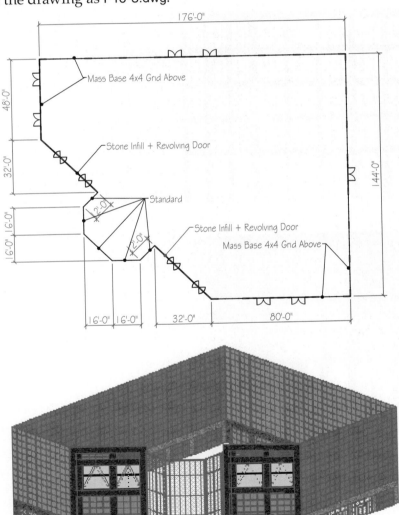

4. Curtain Wall Building
   A. Start a new drawing using one of the Aec Model templates.
   B. Create the two curtain wall unit styles shown in the figure below.
   C. Create the arched unit by using the **Curtain Wall Unit** tool's **Elevation Sketch** option.
   D. Create the window unit using nested grids and a bottom frame.
   E. Assign any material definitions to the components in the curtain wall unit styles as desired.
   F. Create a new curtain wall style using the two curtain wall unit styles. Refer to the figure for division spacing. Use 18"×18" mullions for the columns between the divisions.
   G. Use the new curtain wall style to create the building. Refer to the figure for building size. (Note: As the arched units were created from converted linework, the vertical bay sizes need to maintain a 12'-0" width).
   H. Miter the corners of the building.
   I. Save the drawing as P16-4.dwg.

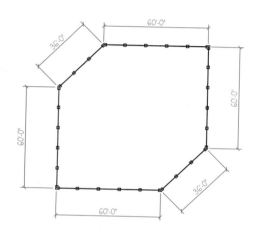

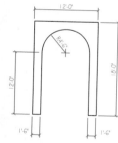
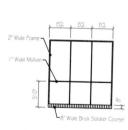

5. Commercial Store Project
   A. Access the **Project Browser** and set Commercial-Project-05 current.
   B. Access the **Constructs** tab of the **Project Navigator** and open the Main Floor construct.
   C. Access the **DOORWINASSEMBLYSTYLE** command. Import the Hinged Double 6-0x6-8 Ctr + Sidelights + Transom style from Door-Window Assembly Styles.dwg.
   D. Use the **Properties** palette to replace the existing door/window assemblies with the Hinged Double 6-0×6-8 Ctr + Sidelights + Transom style.
   E. Adjust the door/window assemblies to 32'-0" wide.
   F. Edit the Hinged Double 6-0×6-8 Ctr + Sidelights + Transom style.
   G. Create a new **Division** element definition named Vertical Sidelights. Set the orientation to **vertical** and the **Division Type:** to **Fixed Cell Dimension**. Set the **Cell Dimension** to 3'-0". Select **Auto-Adjust Cells**. In the **Cell Adjustment**, set the drop-down list to **Shrink**, and then select the **Start** and **End Specific Cells** buttons.
   H. Pick the New Nested Grid2 division in the primary grid tree. Add a New Cell Assignment and select the *Nested Grid* type in the **Element** column. Rename the **Cell Assignment** to Vertical Sidelights. Set the location to the Top.
   I. Pick the Vertical Sidelights division in the primary grid tree. Set the **Division Assignment** to the Vertical Sidelights division. Pick **OK** when you are finished.
   J. Access the **CURTAINWALLSTYLE** command. Import the Square Grid 5'×5' style from Curtain Wall & Curtain Wall Unit Styles.dwg.
   K. Convert the front wall of the front building to the Square Grid 5'×5' curtain wall style.
   L. Adjust the miter angle at the front of the left and right walls in the front building by picking the **Sweeps** worksheet property in the **Properties** palette. Depending on the direction of each wall, the start or end miter needs to be changed to 0.00.
   M. Save and close the drawing.

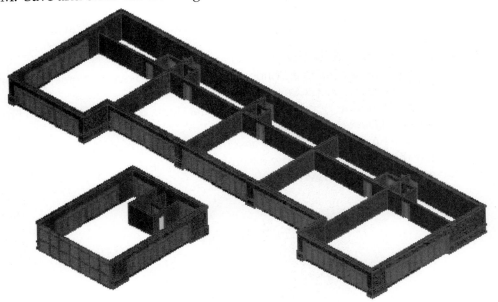

Drawing Courtesy 3D-DZYN

6. Commercial Car Maintenance Shop Project
   A. Access the **Project Browser** and set Commercial-Project-06 current.
   B. Access the **Constructs** tab of the **Project Navigator** and open the Main Floor construct.
   C. Access the **DOORWINASSEMBLYSTYLE** command. Import the Hinged Double Center 3-0×6-8 + Sidelights 2-0 (R) + Transom style from Door-Window Assembly Styles.dwg.
   D. Use the **Properties** palette to replace the existing door/window assembly at the front of the building with the Hinged Double Center 3-0×6-8 + Sidelights 2-0 (R) + Transom. Set the length to 26'-0", height to 9'-0", and head height to 9'-0".
   E. Edit the Hinged Double Center 3-0×6-8 + Sidelights 2-0 (R) + Transom style.
   F. Create a new **Infill** element definition named Double Door with Handles. Assign the Double Ext_Door style to the infill. Exit the door/window assembly style.
   G. Pick **Infill** > **Override Assignment...** from the shortcut menu to override the Door infill with the Double Door with Handles infill element.
   H. Edit the Standard door/window assembly. In the **Materials** tab, assign the following materials:
      • **Default Infill:** Doors & Windows.Glazing.Glass.Clear
      • **Default Frame:** Doors & Windows.Metal Doors & Frames.Aluminum Frame. Anodized.Dark Bronze.Satin
      • **Default Mullion:** Doors & Windows.Metal Doors & Frames.Aluminum Frame. Anodized.Dark Bronze.Satin
   I. Pick the door/window assembly in the left wall of the store. In the **Properties** palette, set the length to 14'-0", height to 9'-0", and head height to 9'-0".
   J. Pick the door/window assembly in the front wall of the car wash area. In the **Properties** palette, set the length to 24'-0", height to 8'-0", and head height to 9'-0".
   K. Add the Standard door/window assembly to the right wall in the garage area. Set the length to 18'-0", height to 10'-0", and head height to 11'-0".
   L. Save and close the drawing.
   M. Access the **Constructs** tab of the **Project Navigator** and open the Upper Floor construct.
   N. Edit the Standard door/window assembly. In the **Materials** tab, assign the following materials:
      • **Default Infill:** Doors & Windows.Glazing.Glass.Clear
      • **Default Frame:** Doors & Windows.Metal Doors & Frames.Aluminum Frame. Anodized.Dark Bronze.Satin
      • **Default Mullion:** Doors & Windows.Metal Doors & Frames.Aluminum Frame. Anodized.Dark Bronze.Satin
   O. Adjust the Front door/window assembly to a length of 24'-0".
   P. Adjust the Left door/window assembly to a length of 14'-0".
   Q. Save and close the drawing.

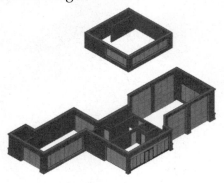

Drawing Courtesy 3D-DZYN

7. Governmental Fire Station
   A. Access the **Project Browser** and set Gvrmt-Project-07 current.
   B. Access the **Constructs** tab of the **Project Navigator** and open the Main Floor construct.
   C. Access the **DOORWINASSEMBLYSTYLE** command. Import the following styles from Door-Window Assembly Styles.dwg.
      - Hinged Double 6-8 + Transom
      - Hinged Single 6-8 + Transom
   D. Modify the Hinged Double 6-8 + Transom and Hinged Single 6-8 + Transom display properties. Assign a style override for the Sill Plan display representation and turn off the Sill A component.
   E. Edit the Standard door/window assembly. In the **Materials** tab, assign the following materials:
      - **Default Infill:** Doors & Windows.Glazing.Glass.Clear
      - **Default Frame:** Doors & Windows.Metal Doors & Frames.Aluminum Frame. Anodized.Dark Bronze.Satin
      - **Default Mullion:** Doors & Windows.Metal Doors & Frames.Aluminum Frame. Anodized.Dark Bronze.Satin
   F. Use the **Properties** palette to replace the door/window assembly at the front of the building in the reception area with the Double 6-8 + Transom style. See figure for location.
   G. Use the **Properties** palette to replace the middle door/window assembly at the back wall of the dayroom area with the Double 6-8 + Transom style. See figure for location.
   H. Erase the right exterior door in the hall between the office and kitchen areas. Add the Hinged Single 6-8 +Transom door/window assembly in the door's place. Specify a width of 3'-4", height of 9'-0", and head height of 9'-0". Use the **Reposition Within Wall** option to reposition the door/window assembly within the CMU component of the wall. See figure for location.
   I. Save and close the drawing.

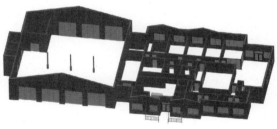

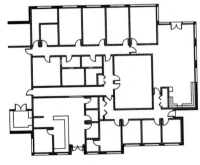

Dayroom Door

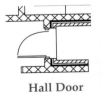

Hall Door

Reception Door

Drawing Courtesy 3D-DZYN.

The home page of the American Institute of Architects (AIA) Web site is www.aia.org. This Web site offers valuable information about news and upcoming events in the field of architecture. This site also provides resource centers, career information, and information about the impacts of architecture in our world.

CHAPTER 17

Using Slab Objects

Learning Objectives

After completing this chapter, you will be able to do the following:
- ✓ Add slabs to a drawing.
- ✓ Convert polylines and walls into slabs.
- ✓ Modify slabs.
- ✓ Modify the edges of slabs.
- ✓ Import slabs and slab edge styles.
- ✓ Create slabs and slab edge styles.
- ✓ Use slab tools.
- ✓ Extend slabs.
- ✓ Miter slabs.
- ✓ Cut slabs.
- ✓ Add and remove slab vertices.
- ✓ Add and remove holes in a slab.
- ✓ Add modifiers and interferences to a slab.

One of the key elements in any real building is a floor created before walls are added. Architectural Desktop includes a Slab object specifically for this purpose. A *slab* is an element that appears to have a thickness, similar to an AutoCAD solid, with an edge that can represent any shape.

Slab objects do not have to be used solely as floors; they can be used to represent driveways and sidewalks on a site plan, countertops, and ceilings. See Figure 17-1. Architectural Desktop also uses slab-type tools in commands designed specifically for the roof design. Roof designs are discussed in Chapter 18.

Slabs can be added by selecting vertex points, much like picking points for a polyline, or they can be converted from closed polylines or walls that form a closed room. These objects can also be carved, stretched, extended, and trimmed to form any desired shape. In addition to being able to be modified to any shape, Slab objects also can have holes cut into them.

Figure 17-1.
Slabs can be used
for concrete slabs,
walk paths, and
wood-framed floors.

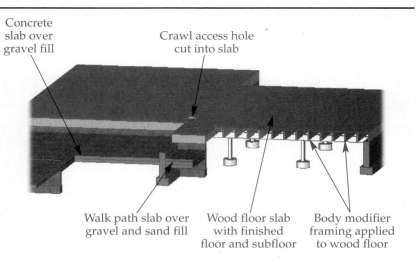

Concrete
slab over
gravel fill

Crawl access hole
cut into slab

Walk path slab over
gravel and sand fill

Wood floor slab
with finished
floor and subfloor

Body modifier
framing applied
to wood floor

Adding Slabs to a Drawing

Pull-Down Menu
Design
> Slabs
> Add Slab...
Tool Palette
Design
Slab

The **Add Slabs...** option adds slabs to a drawing. Slabs are added to the drawing by picking the **Slab** tool in the **Design** tool palette or **Design** > **Slabs** > **Add Slabs...** from the pull-down menu. After you enter the **Add Slab...** option, the **Properties** palette displays new properties that can be set for the slab being drawn. See **Figure 17-2.** The **BASIC** properties category includes three categories: **General**, **Dimensions**, and **Location**.

General Category

This category is used to specify the general properties of the slab being drawn. The following properties are available:

- **Description.** Picking this property displays the **Description** worksheet. Type a description for the Slab object being drawn.

Figure 17-2.
The **Properties**
palette is used to
add Slab objects to a
drawing.

General slab
properties

Dimensional slab
properties

Slab
properties

Slab
illustration

Location
properties

Pick to turn
on or off the
slab illustration

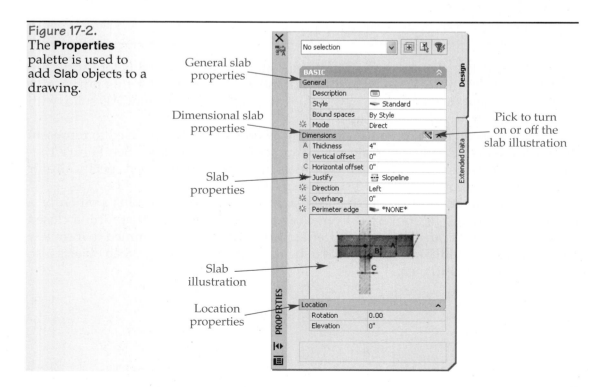

- **Style.** Select this property to display a list of slab styles available in the drawing. Additional slab styles are available through the **Slabs** tool palette, **Content Browser,** and **Style Manager.**
- **Bound spaces.** This drop-down list includes three options: **Yes, No,** and **By Style.** The **Bound spaces** property is used to specify whether the slab can be used as a bounding object for Space objects or it should defer to the slab style for the space-bounding properties.
- **Mode.** This drop-down list includes two options: **Direct** and **Projected.** The **Direct** mode creates a flat slab, and the **Projected** mode creates a slab that can be assigned a slope. See **Figure 17-3.** The **Projected** mode is called "projected" because the points picked for the vertices of the slab are picked in the current elevation, allowing the slab to be projected up along the slope of the slab. Depending on the option selected, different properties are displayed in the **Dimensions** subcategory.

Dimensions Category

The **Dimensions** category is used to specify the dimensional properties of the slab being drawn. The header bar includes the **Show/Hide the Illustration** button, which displays or hides an illustration of a slab with the dimensional properties pointed out. Picking the button turns on or off the illustration in the **Properties** palette. Depending on the **Mode** property selected, different properties are available for the slab being created. If the **Projected** mode is selected, an additional subcategory, named **Slope,** is displayed under the **Dimensions** category and controls the properties for the slope of the projected slab. The following properties are available in the **Dimensions** category:

- **Thickness.** This text box property allows you to enter a thickness for the slab. If the slab represents a 4"-thick concrete walk, type 4" in this box. Some slab styles might be configured to have a fixed thickness.
- **Vertical offset.** Picking this property allows you to enter a vertical offset value. The vertical offset value creates the slab a measured distance vertically off the 0" elevation plane. The points picked for the vertices of the slab are still picked in the current elevation, but the slab is created the vertical distance from the elevation, measured to the slab's justification. This property does not modify the existing elevation height.
- **Horizontal offset.** When a slab is created, points are picked in the current drawing plane to establish the edges of a slab. The first two points picked create the first edge of the slab. This edge is known as the *baseline* for a **Direct** mode slab. The first edge is known as the *slopeline* for a **Projected** mode slab. The **Horizontal offset** property offsets the slab the specified distance from the first point picked for the slab. This first point picked is known as the *pivot point.*

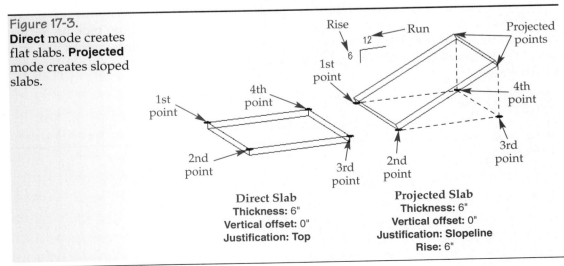

Figure 17-3.
Direct mode creates flat slabs. **Projected** mode creates sloped slabs.

Rise — Run
12
6
1st point
Projected points

1st point
4th point
2nd point
3rd point

2nd point
3rd point
4th point

Direct Slab
Thickness: 6"
Vertical offset: 0"
Justification: Top

Projected Slab
Thickness: 6"
Vertical offset: 0"
Justification: Slopeline
Rise: 6"

- **Justify.** Picking this property displays a drop-down list of four justifications: **Top**, **Center**, **Bottom**, and **Slopeline**. The justification used establishes how the slab is laid out when vertex points are selected. For example, if the slab is to be drawn by picking the top edge points, select the **Top** justification. The **Slopeline** justification aligns the baseline (the first edge) of the slab with the first point picked. It should be noted that the justification is used only when you are inserting a slab and is not retained information when you are editing a slab.
- **Base height.** This property is only available when the **Projected** mode is selected. The **Base height** property is similar to the **Vertical offset** property and controls the height, from the current elevation, at which the first edge of the slab is created.
- **Direction.** When this property is selected, two options are available: **Left** and **Right**. Either option creates the same slab orientation.
- **Overhang.** The slab edges are defined as vertex points picked in the drawing. If the slab is to have an overhang hanging past the edge of the vertices, enter a value in this text box. The **Overhang** value specifies the depth of the overhang from the vertex points to the edge of the slab.
- **Perimeter edge.** Picking this property displays a drop-down list of slab edge styles in the drawing. The edges of a slab can be assigned different edge styles that control their appearance. Slab edge styles are discussed later in this chapter.

The **Slope** subcategory of the **Dimensions** category is displayed if the **Projected** mode is selected. Three properties are available to control the slope of a projected slab.
- **Rise.** This text box property allows you to enter the **Rise** value of a sloping slab when specifying the rise over run of the slope.
- **Run.** This text box property controls the **Run** value of a sloping slab being specified using the rise over run of the slope.
- **Slope.** Pick this property to specify the sloping angle of the slab if the rise over run is not known for the slab.

Location Category

The **Location** category includes two read-only properties when you are creating a slab. These properties are used to display the current rotation and elevation in which the slab is being created:
- **Rotation.** This property is a read-only value indicating the rotation angle of the baseline or slopeline of the slab being created.
- **Elevation.** The **Elevation** property is a read-only value indicating the current elevation in which the points of the slab were picked.

After configuring the settings for the slab, pick a point in the drawing to establish the first vertex point. This point establishes the pivot point location. When the slope of a projected slab is changed, it adjusts from the pivot point. Continue picking vertex points to establish the slab. When you have finished selecting points, right-click and select the **Ortho close** or **Close** option to close the slab. Slabs must be closed in order to be created.

Exercise 17-1   Complete the Exercise on the Student CD.

Converting Polylines and Walls to Slabs

Another method of creating a slab is to convert closed polylines or walls that form a closed room into a slab. It is very important when polylines or walls are converted into slabs that the objects are closed, in order for the slab to be created correctly. To convert the polyline or walls into a slab, right-click on the **Slab** tool in the **Design** tool palette and pick **Apply Tool Properties to** > **Linework and Walls**.

To convert a closed polyline into a projected slab, right-click on the **Slab** tool in the **Design** tool palette and pick **Apply Tool Properties to** > **Linework and Walls**. When you are prompted, select the closed polyline. Decide whether or not you want to erase the layout geometry, and then choose the **Projected** creation mode. When you are prompted, type a base height for the projected slab, and then enter the justification for the new slab. To establish the pivot edge, move the crosshairs to highlight an edge and pick. When you are finished, select the style and thickness for the slab in the **Properties** palette.

Converting to a direct slab is very similar. Begin by right-clicking on the **Slab** tool in the **Design** tool palette and picking **Apply Tool Properties to** > **Linework and Walls**. Select the closed polyline. Decide whether or not you want to erase the layout geometry, and then choose the **Direct** creation mode. When you are prompted, enter the justification for the new slab. To establish the pivot edge, move the crosshairs to highlight an edge and pick. When you are finished, select the style and thickness for the slab in the **Properties** palette.

The **Linework and Walls** option allows you to choose between a **Direct** or **Projected** slab when a polyline is converted to a slab. When you choose a **Projected** slab, you can specify the base height, measured from the current 0" Z axis to the justification location. If you choose the **Direct** slab, the slab justification point is placed in the current 0" Z axis.

NOTE

> To create a slab with a curved edge, a closed polyline with a curved edge must first be drawn and then converted into a slab.

When walls are converted into a slab, the slab's **Projected** option is automatically used, and the slab is placed on the top of the walls using the specified justification. Just as when you are converting a closed polyline into a slab, when you are converting a series of walls that form a closed room into a slab, right-click on the **Slab** tool in the **Design** tool palette and pick **Apply Tool Properties to** > **Linework and Walls**. Select the walls that form a closed room. Decide whether or not you want to erase the layout geometry, and then enter the justification for the new slab, as it sits in relation to the top of the walls. When you are prompted, specify where the edges of the slab will be placed, in relation to the wall's justification. To establish the pivot edge, move the crosshairs to highlight an edge and pick. When you are finished, select the style and thickness for the slab in the **Properties** palette.

PROFESSIONAL TIP

> Be careful when converting walls into a slab. Each wall cannot go past the edge of another wall, without causing an undesired slab. If the walls extend past the enclosed area, the slab cannot be created. When you are converting walls into a slab, it is often best to convert the exterior shell of the building into a slab.

The **Properties** palette plays a major role in modifying the properties of an existing Slab object. When a Slab object is selected for modification, the **Properties** palette reflects the properties of the slab that can be edited. Many of the properties available when adding a slab are also available when modifying a slab. The following is a list of properties for a slab available only when modifying the slab:

- **Layer.** The **Layer** property displays the layer on which the slab is placed. Use the drop-down list property to change the assigned layer.
- **Shadow display.** This property includes four options for controlling how the selected slab will cast and receive shadows when shading or rendering the model. The options are **Casts and Receives shadows**, **Casts shadows**, **Receives shadows**, and **Ignore shadows**.
- **Edges.** Picking this property displays the **Slab Edges** worksheet. See **Figure 17-4.** This worksheet includes a table of slab edge values, preview illustration of what the values control in the slab, and preview pane of the selected slab. The edges of the slab are numbered in the table, in the **Edge** column. Picking an edge in the table displays a green line along the edge of the slab in the preview to indicate which edge is being modified. Picking additional values in the table allows you to modify different values, such as the edge **Overhang**, **Edge Style**, **Edge Cut**, and **Angle**. The **Slab Edges** worksheet will be discussed in greater detail later in this chapter.
- **Hold fascia elevation.** The *fascia* is the edge of the slab. Picking the **Hold fascia elevation** property provides a drop-down list of three options: **By adjusting overhang**, **By adjusting baseline height**, and **No**. When a fascia edge is applied to the slab, the fascia elevation can be held in its original orientation by modifying the overhang or baseline height.
- **Pivot Point X.** This property displays the pivot point's location (the location of the first point selected) in the X axis. Enter a new value to move the pivot point's X axis location. Picking the property also displays a pick point button that can be selected so a new point for the pivot point can be selected.

Figure 17-4.
The **Slab Edges** worksheet is used to modify the edges of a Slab object.

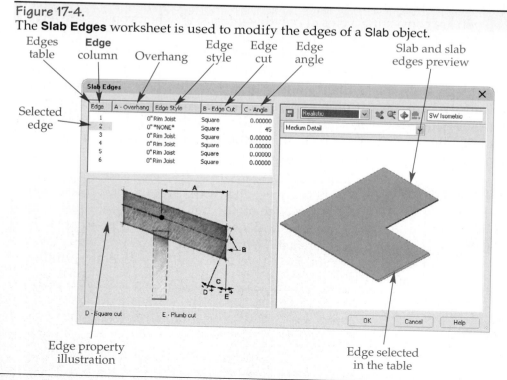

- **Pivot Point Y.** The **Pivot Point Y** property indicates the pivot point's location in the Y axis.
- **Pivot Point Z.** This property indicates the pivot point's location in the Z axis.
- **Elevation.** This property is displayed as a read-only value when you are creating a slab. When you are modifying a slab, pick this property to move the elevation of the slab. This is similar to the **Vertical offset** property, except the points picked for the vertices of the slab maintain their orientation in the Z axis, rather than referring to the 0" Z axis as the **Vertical offset** property does.
- **Additional information.** Picking this property displays the **Location** worksheet. This worksheet is used to specify a new elevation or enter a rotation angle for the slab.

Notice that the slab loses its justification property after it has been created. The vertices still maintain their justification on the slab, but the justification cannot be changed. Also, after a slab has been created as a direct or projected slab, it can still be given a sloping angle or modified to be a flat Slab object.

Modifying a slab is not solely limited to the **Properties** palette. As with other AEC objects, slabs can be edited using grips. After a slab has been created with either the **Direct** or **Projected** mode, it has the ability to be modified by being assigned a slope and vertical offset. When a Slab object is picked, grip boxes specifically for editing the slab are placed around the object. See **Figure 17-5.**

The first point picked for a slab or the first point of a polyline-converted slab becomes the pivot point. The pivot point is the point at which the slab is rotated when modifying the slope for the slab. Depending on the justification used, the **Pivot Point** grip is placed at the top, center, bottom, or slopeline of the slab. Occasionally, for graphical clarity, the pivot point is displayed away from, but next to, the first point picked. Pick the **Pivot Point** grip to move the location of the pivot point, in order to slope the slab from another location.

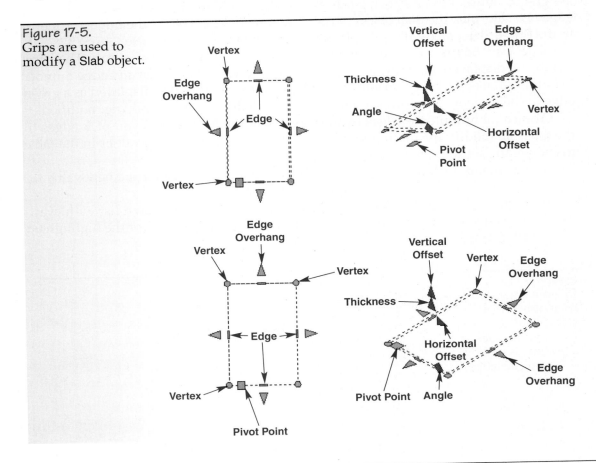

Figure 17-5.
Grips are used to modify a Slab object.

Move the crosshairs over the grips to display the name of the grips and, in some instances, additional functions that can be performed by pressing the [Ctrl] key when editing a grip. When a slab is selected in a Model view, additional grips for controlling the angle (slope), thickness, vertical offset, and horizontal offset of the slab are available. In some cases, when editing a dimensional value for a grip, pressing the [Tab] key toggles to different dimensions that can be entered. Pick a grip to modify its location or value to modify the slab. When you are finished editing with grips, press the [Esc] key to clear the grip boxes.

Exercise 17-2   Complete the Exercise on the Student CD.

Modifying the Edges of Slabs

Depending on the style of slab used, a custom edge can be added to the slab edges, as in **Figure 17-6**. When a drawing is initially started from one of the Aec Model templates, the only slab style available is the Standard style. The Standard style slab does not include custom edges. Custom slab edge styles can be assigned to any edge of a slab. Additional slab styles with edges can be imported through the **Style Manager** or **Content Browser**. In addition to these styles, custom slab edge styles can be created.

When you are using a slab tool from the **Slabs** tool palette or importing a slab style from the **Content Browser**, the slab edge styles used in the style are also imported into the drawing. Once the drawing includes slab edge styles, the edge style can be assigned to any edge of a slab, regardless of style. To assign a different edge style to the edge of a slab, pick the Slab object in the drawing, and then select the **Edges** property in the **Properties** palette. This displays the **Slab Edges** worksheet. See **Figure 17-7**.

The **Slab Edges** worksheet allows you to modify the edge of a slab. The edge number is displayed along the left side of the worksheet table. Select any edge number to modify that edge. When an edge is highlighted in the table, it is displayed as a green edge in the preview window, showing you which edge is currently being modified.

You can edit multiple edges by holding down the [Ctrl] key as you pick edges in the table. To modify the highlighted edges, pick any of the existing values in the table to change the setting. The following values can be changed:
- **Overhang.** Pick the existing value to reveal a text box. Enter the new value for the overhang, as shown in **Figure 17-8**.
- **Edge Style.** Selecting the existing value displays a drop-down list with available edge styles in the drawing. Select a different edge style for the highlighted edge. See **Figure 17-8**.

Figure 17-6.
Custom edges can be assigned to a slab. Architectural Desktop includes a few styles with different slab edge styles.

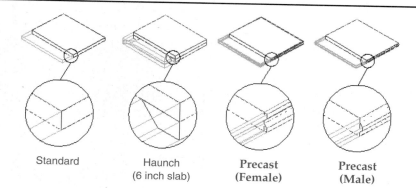

Standard   Haunch (6 inch slab)   Precast (Female)   Precast (Male)

Figure 17-7.
The **Slab Edges** worksheet allows you to modify the edges of a slab.

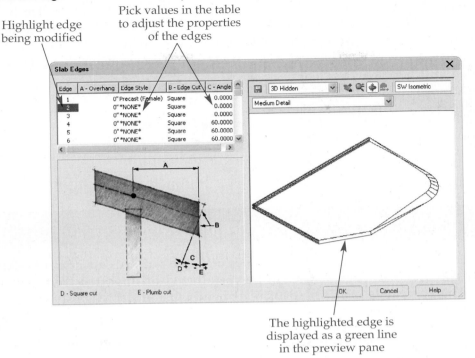

Highlight edge being modified

Pick values in the table to adjust the properties of the edges

The highlighted edge is displayed as a green line in the preview pane

Figure 17-8.
The different edge settings control how the edge of the slab will appear.

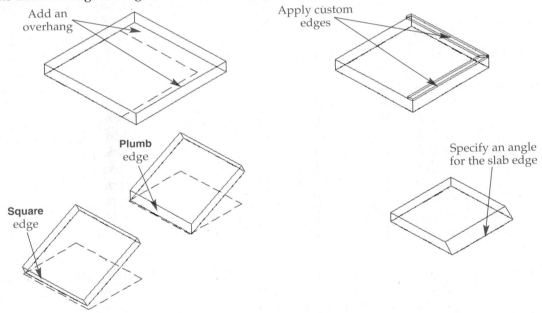

Add an overhang

Apply custom edges

Plumb edge

Specify an angle for the slab edge

Square edge

- **Edge Cut.** When the existing value is selected, a drop-down list including two options becomes available. The **Plumb** option always makes the edge of the slab perpendicular to the ground. The **Square** option squares the end of the slab between the top and bottom edge of the slab, as shown in **Figure 17-8.**
- **Angle.** Pick in this area to enter an angular value for the slab edge. See **Figure 17-8.**

In large slabs containing multiple edges, individual slab edges can be selected for modification. First select the slab that needs to be modified, right-click, and then pick the **Edit Slab Edges...** option. You are prompted to Select edges of one slab. Select any edges on a slab that will be modified, and then press the [Enter] key to begin editing. This will display the **Edit Slab Edges** worksheet, which looks like the **Slab Edges** worksheet, except the selected edges are the only edges available in the table. Make any modifications to the edges as needed.

Exercise 17-3

Complete the Exercise on the Student CD.

Slab and Slab Edge Styles

In addition to the slab and slab edge styles included with Architectural Desktop, additional slab and slab edge styles can be customized or imported from external drawings. This section describes how to create new slab and slab edge styles, as well as how to edit existing ones.

Importing Slab and Slab Edge Styles

Architectural Desktop includes additional slab styles in a master slab style drawing that are not included in the **Content Browser**. The **Style Manager** can be used to import additional slab styles and create new slab styles. Pick **Design > Slabs > Slab Styles...** from the pull-down menu. This displays the **Style Manager** opened to the Slab Styles section. See **Figure 17-9**.

Within the **Style Manager**, pick the **Open Drawing** button to display the **Open drawing** dialog box. Pick the Content shortcut icon to browse to the Styles folder. Within the Styles folder, the Imperial and Metric folders contain lists of drawings full of additional AEC content styles. Pick the Imperial or Metric folder to locate Slab & Slab Edge Styles (Imperial).dwg or Slab & Slab Edge Styles (Metric).dwg. Open the drawing to display its contents in the **Style Manager**. The drawing is opened as a drawing icon in the tree view pane of the **Style Manager**. Expand the drawing icon, the Architectural Objects folder, and then the Slab Styles section icon to display a list of slab styles.

Selecting a style from the left tree view displays the property tabs for the selected slab style, as shown in **Figure 17-9**. If the Slab Styles section icon is selected, the slab styles are listed in the right side of the window. Drag the desired styles from the right or left panes into the current drawing icon to import them.

In addition to importing slab styles, slab edge styles can also be imported. Pick **Design > Slabs > Slab Edge Styles...** from the pull-down menu. This will display the **Style Manager** opened to the Slab Edge Styles section. To import the slab edge styles, open the Slab & Slab Edge Styles (Imperial).dwg or Slab & Slab Edge Styles (Metric).dwg. Drag and drop any desired edge styles into the current drawing folder icon.

The **Content Browser** also includes slab styles, some of which include a few slab edge styles. Browse through the Design Tool Catalog - Imperial (or Design Tool Catalog - Metric) catalog to locate the slab styles. The tools can be dragged and dropped into the drawing for immediate use or added to a tool palette for future use.

Figure 17-9.
The **Style Manager** is used to import, export, create, and organize styles.

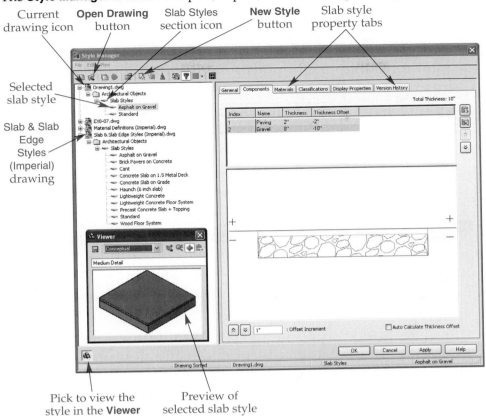

Current drawing icon · **Open Drawing** button · Slab Styles section icon · **New Style** button · Slab style property tabs

Selected slab style

Slab & Slab Edge Styles (Imperial) drawing

Pick to view the style in the **Viewer**

Preview of selected slab style

Creating Slab Styles

The **Slab Styles...** option previously discussed can also be used to create custom slab styles. Once the **Style Manager** has been opened, select the **New Style** button to create a new slab style. Enter a name for the new slab style. When the style is highlighted in the left tree view, its property tabs are displayed. The slab style includes the following five tabs used to configure the style:

- **General.** This tab is used to rename and provide a description of the slab style; attach documents, spreadsheets, and HTML documents; and assign property set definitions and keynotes to the style.
- **Components.** The **Components** tab is similar to the Wall Styles **Components** tab. This tab is used to create the slab style by adding horizontal slab components to the style and setting the thickness and location of each component within a slab. See **Figure 17-10.** The **Components** tab is discussed in greater detail later in this section.
- **Materials.** This tab is used to specify the material used for the Slab object. Slab styles can be created for different types of materials, such as brick or concrete pavers for a sidewalk, grass for site work, or tile or carpet for interior floors.
- **Classifications.** Use this tab to assign any classification definitions in the drawing to the slab style.

Figure 17-10.
The **Components** tab is used to add horizontal components to the slab style.

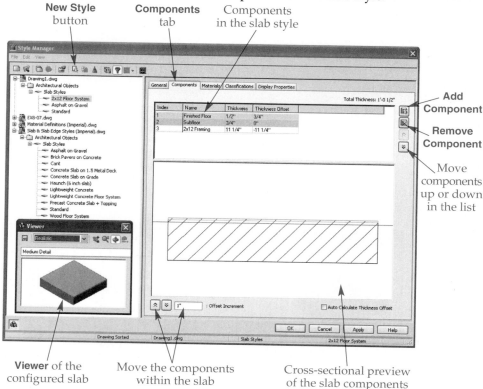

New Style button

Components tab

Components in the slab style

Add Component

Remove Component

Move components up or down in the list

Viewer of the configured slab

Move the components within the slab

Cross-sectional preview of the slab components

- **Display Properties.** This tab is used to control how the slab appears in Plan and Model representations. When modifying the display of Plan representation slab components, you can specify a cut plane to cut through the slab. The cut plane can display the cut line at the perimeter edges or in the body of the slab. In addition to the cut plane, a Hatch component can be turned on and configured for the slab. Both the Model and Plan display representations include Fascia and Soffit components. The *soffit* is a custom shape placed below the overhang. The Fascia and Soffit components control the display of a slab edge attached to the slab. These components can be turned on or off and assigned display properties by the material assigned to the slab edge style.

By default, a slab style is not assigned a specific slab edge style. Generally, when you are creating a slab, the edge style is assigned through the **Properties** palette when the slab is drawn or later, after the slab has been placed in the drawing. Slab tools in a tool palette can be assigned an edge style through the tool's properties. Modifying a tool's properties is discussed in Appendix B on the Student CD.

As mentioned previously, the **Components** tab of the **Style Manager** is used to add slab components to the slab style. This tab is similar to the **Components** tab used when creating a wall style. See Figure 17-10. The **Components** tab includes a table of components and a cross-sectional preview of the slab components. The table includes four columns: **Index**, **Name**, **Thickness**, and **Thickness Offset**. By default, a new slab style includes one component named Unnamed. Pick the component name in the **Name** column to rename the component.

Beside the **Name** column is the **Thickness** column. This column is similar to the Wall Styles **Width** column. Selecting the **Thickness** area for the component displays a drop-down list arrow. Pick the arrow to specify the thickness of the slab component. See Figure 17-11. The first text box is known as the base value. The base value specifies the thickness of the slab component. A value of 0" allows the component to be a

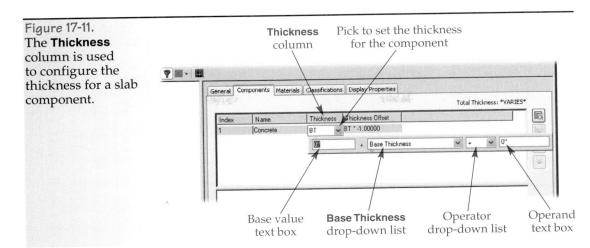

Figure 17-11.
The **Thickness** column is used to configure the thickness for a slab component.

Thickness column

Pick to set the thickness for the component

Base value text box

Base Thickness drop-down list

Operator drop-down list

Operand text box

variable thickness, based on the thickness you enter when adding a slab to the drawing. The Standard slab style is an example of a component using a base value of 0".

If a value other than 0" is entered in the base value text box, the thickness is fixed for this component. For example, if you are creating a 4"-thick concrete component, type 4" in the base value text box. The component now has a fixed thickness of 4" and cannot be changed when being added to the drawing.

Beside the base value text box is a drop-down list known as the **Base Thickness**. There are two options here. If **0** is selected, the remaining text boxes are grayed out, and the thickness of the component is specified by the base value text box. The other option is the **Base Thickness** option. Base thickness refers to the thickness property of the slab, when added to the drawing. When **Base Thickness** is specified, the base value and base thickness are added together to specify the total thickness for the slab component. For example, a 0" base value + **Base Thickness** creates a slab component the thickness specified in the **Thickness** property, when adding a slab to the drawing; a 4" base value + **Base Thickness** creates a slab the thickness specified in the **Thickness** property plus 4", when adding the slab.

When **Base Thickness** is selected, the last two text boxes are available. The drop-down list beside the **Base Thickness** is known as the operator. The operator includes **+, -, /,** and ***** symbols. Selecting an operator specifies a calculation to be performed on the thickness of the slab. Beside the operator drop-down list is the operand text box. Entering a value in this text box finishes the calculation for the total thickness of the slab component. For example, a slab component that specifies a 2" base value + **Base Thickness / 2** creates a slab component half the total value of the base value and the base thickness. In most situations, a slab component either has a set thickness in the base value text box + **0** for the base thickness or a 0" base value + a set base thickness.

After the thickness for the component has been determined, the placement of the component within the slab can be specified. The **Thickness Offset** column is used to place the component in relation to other components in the style. When slabs are added to the drawing, one of the slab justifications is the **Slopeline** option. This justification indicates that the slab is drawn from the slopeline, or baseline of the slab style. If you are looking at the slab in an elevation view, the slab components are added to the style by measuring a distance from the slopeline to the bottom edge of the slab component. See **Figure 17-12.** A positive distance moves the bottom of the component up, and a negative distance moves the bottom of the component down.

Pick the **Thickness Offset** area for the slab component being adjusted. This displays a drop-down arrow, similar to the **Thickness** column. See **Figure 17-13.** This drop-down list provides base value, **Base Thickness**, operator, and operand text boxes and drop-down lists. In the base value text box, enter the positive or negative distance from the slopeline to the bottom edge of the slab component. For example, a value of 6" places the bottom edge of the component 6" above the slopeline. A -6" places the bottom edge of the component 6" below the slopeline.

Figure 17-12.
The bottom of a slab component is placed an offset distance, measured from the bottom of the component to the slopeline.

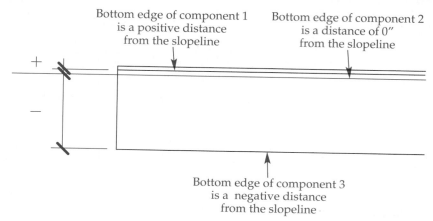

Bottom edge of component 1 is a positive distance from the slopeline

Bottom edge of component 2 is a distance of 0″ from the slopeline

Bottom edge of component 3 is a negative distance from the slopeline

Figure 17-13.
The **Thickness Offset** is used to place the slab component in relation to the slopeline of the slab.

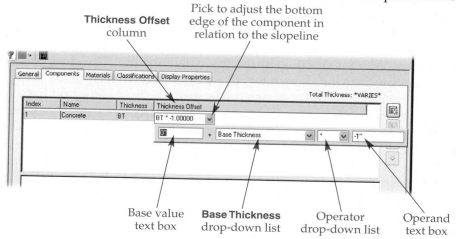

Thickness Offset column

Pick to adjust the bottom edge of the component in relation to the slopeline

Base value text box

Base Thickness drop-down list

Operator drop-down list

Operand text box

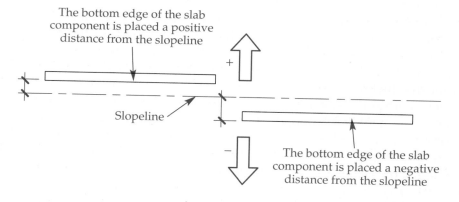

The bottom edge of the slab component is placed a positive distance from the slopeline

Slopeline

The bottom edge of the slab component is placed a negative distance from the slopeline

NOTE

In most cases, slab components are placed at a specific distance from the slopeline, whether it is a positive or negative distance. Experiment with the operators. Review an existing Architectural Desktop complex slab style that allows you to specify a slab thickness for ideas on how to use the operators and operands.

Architectural Desktop and Its Applications

The **Base Thickness** drop-down list includes two options: **0** and **Base Thickness**. If the **0** is specified, the bottom edge of the component is always located at the base value location. If the **Base Thickness** is specified, the base value is added to the **Thickness** property specified, when drawing a new slab. This sets the bottom edge of the component a total distance of the base value plus the base thickness from the slopeline. Beside the **Base Thickness** drop-down is the operator drop-down list, which includes the **+**, **-**, **/**, and ***** operators. These operators can be used in an equation to specify the location of the slab component.

The last text box is the operand. An equation for the location of the slab component can be constructed by specifying a base value, a base thickness, an operator, and an operand. For example, the bottom edge of a component next to a variable thickness component can be specified by entering a 0" base value **+ Base Thickness + 0**". Another example is to create a slab component that is always centered on the slopeline, no matter what the thickness of the slab. Use the equation of a 0" base value **+ Base Thickness * –1/2**. This indicates that the component looks to the **Thickness** property when adding a slab and multiplies the thickness by –1/2, repositioning the component so the bottom edge is half the distance of the thickness from the slopeline.

After the first component has been configured, additional slab components can be added to the style. Along the right side of the tab are four buttons: **Add Component**, **Remove Component**, **Move Component Up In List**, and **Move Component Down In List**. Use the **Add Component** button to add additional slab components. Along the bottom of the tab are the **Increment Slab Component Offset** and **Decrement Slab Component Offset** buttons and the **: Offset Increment** text box. Use these options to adjust where the bottom edge of a component is placed in the style. Adjusting a component's location using these tools automatically adjusts the **Thickness Offset** value for the selected component.

Creating Slab Edge Styles

Often, when a custom slab is created in the drawing, an edge is associated with it. Before a slab edge can be assigned to a new slab, the slab edge style must be defined in the drawing. Access the **Slab Edge Styles...** option, create a new style, and then select the style in the tree view to access the slab edge style's property tabs. The slab edge style includes the following tabs:

- **General.** This tab is used to rename and provide a description for the style and to attach design notes.
- **Defaults.** The **Defaults** tab is used to specify default values for the edge of the slab (see **Figure 17-14**). These settings control only the default values for the slab edge. The default values can be modified at the time the slab is added or modified. Specify a preset overhang value in the **Overhang:** text box. The **Edge Cut:** drop-down list can be used to specify a default **Square** or **Plumb** edge for the new slab being created. The **Angle:** text box is used to set a default angle for an edge when the slab using this slab edge style is created.
- **Design Rules.** This tab is used to add a custom shape for the edge style (see **Figure 17-15**). Initially, two check boxes are available for customizing the edge. The **Fascia** and **Soffit** check boxes, when selected, allow you to add a custom AEC profile shape for the fascia and soffit.

  When these check boxes are selected, an associated drop-down list becomes available. The items included in the list are AEC profiles defined in the drawing. See Chapter 9 for information on how to create a profile. When you are creating a profile for use as a fascia or soffit, specify the insertion points on the profile as indicated in **Figure 17-16**. Specify any other settings, including soffit location, in this tab. Refer to the diagram in this tab for value settings.
- **Materials.** Use this tab to assign a material to the Fascia and Soffit components defined for the slab edge style.

Figure 17-14.
Set any defaults for the slab edge in the **Defaults** tab.

Slab Edge Styles
section icon　　**New Style**
button　　　Enter an edge
overhang value　　Specify if the edge
will use a **Square** or
Plumb edge cut　　Enter an angle
for the edge

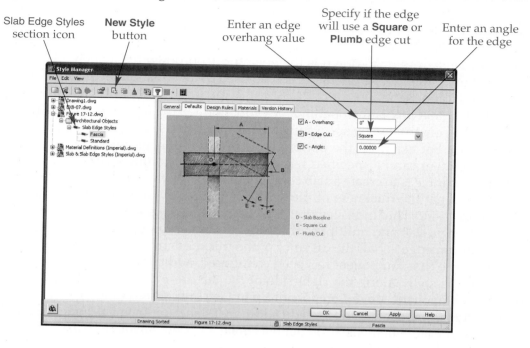

Figure 17-15.
The **Design Rules** tab is used to assign a fascia and soffit to the edge of a slab.

Fascia insertion
point on the profile　　Fascia　　Pick to add
a fascia　　Pick to add
a soffit

Select a
profile
for use as
a fascia

Select a
profile
for use as
a soffit

Enter an
angle for
the soffit

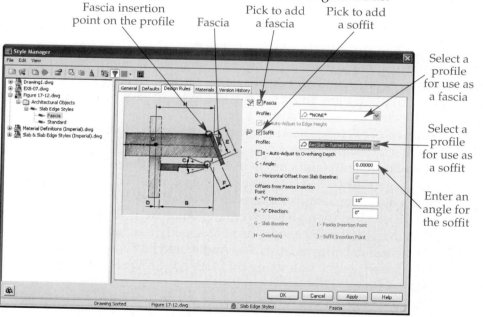

After a slab edge style has been defined, it can be assigned to a slab in the drawing. Pick the slab to have an edge style applied, and then in the **Properties** palette, select the **Edges** property to display the **Slab Edges** worksheet. Select any edges to have the edge style applied, and then select the edge style to be applied from the **Edge Style** drop-down list in the worksheet.

Figure 17-16.
When you are
creating a fascia
profile, the insertion
point is typically
set at the upper-
left corner of the
profile. When you
are creating a soffit,
the insertion point
is typically set to the
upper-right corner
of the profile.

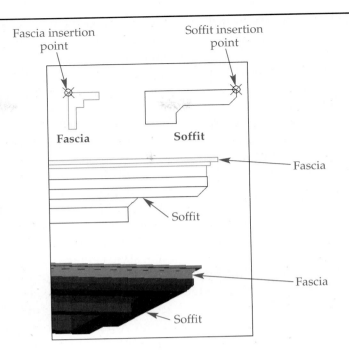

Fascia insertion
point

Soffit insertion
point

Fascia

Soffit

Fascia

Soffit

Fascia

Soffit

Exercise
17-4

Complete the Exercise on the Student CD.

Editing Edge Profiles in Place

Slab objects can have edge styles added and edited in place. If a slab edge style does not exist in a drawing, a new profile can be added to the slab in place. To do this, select the slab, right-click, and pick **Add Edge Profiles...** from the shortcut menu. You are prompted to Select an edge of the slab to add profile(s). Pick the edge of a slab. If the selected edge does not have an overhang value and edge style already assigned, an information box is displayed, allowing you to set these parameters. Pick **Yes** to continue.

This displays the **Edit Slab Edges** worksheet described earlier, allowing you to set an **Overhang** value and specify an **Edge Style**, which is modified in place. Pick **OK** to continue editing. The **Add Fascia / Soffit Profiles** worksheet is then displayed. This worksheet is similar to other profile worksheets. See **Figure 17-17**. The worksheet

Figure 17-17.
The **Add Fascia /
Soffit Profiles**
worksheet is used
to create new or
modify existing
profiles for a slab
edge style.

Pick to start
a fascia profile
from scratch

Provide a name
for the new
profile shape

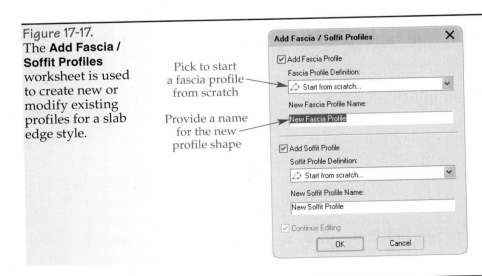

includes **Fascia Profile Definition:** and **Soffit Profile Definition:** drop-down lists and **New Fascia Profile Name:** and **New Soffit Profile Name:** text boxes.

The **Fascia Profile Definition:** drop-down list allows you to create a profile by picking the **Start from scratch...** option or using an existing profile in the drawing that can be edited. Below the **Fascia Profile Definition:** drop-down list is a **New Fascia Profile Name:** text box, where a name for a new profile can be added. When you are finished specifying the parameters, pick the **OK** button to begin editing. Additionally, a soffit profile definition can be edited and named by picking the appropriate options at the bottom of the worksheet.

The new fascia profile is displayed along the selected edge of the slab. See **Figure 17-18.** Pick the blue profile to begin editing. Using the grips, the profile shape can be changed. Right-clicking can also be used to add or remove vertices or replace the ring (polyline shape) with another closed polyline shape. When you are finished editing the profile, pick the **Save All Changes** button in the **In-Place Edit** toolbar.

Slabs that include a slab edge style can also be edited in place. Pick the slab, right-click, and select **Edit Edge Profile In Place**. You are prompted to Select an edge of the slab for editing. Pick an edge that includes an edge style needing to be edited. This will display the blue profile with grips, similar to **Figure 17-18.** Edit the profile using the grip boxes or shortcut menu. When you are finished, pick the **Save All Changes** button in the **In-Place Edit** toolbar to save the changes made to the existing profile shape.

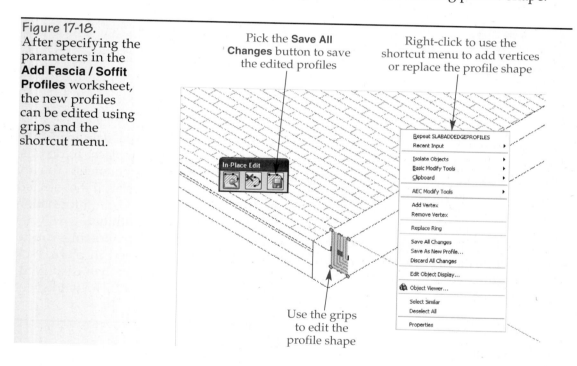

Figure 17-18.
After specifying the parameters in the **Add Fascia / Soffit Profiles** worksheet, the new profiles can be edited using grips and the shortcut menu.

Pick the **Save All Changes** button to save the edited profiles

Right-click to use the shortcut menu to add vertices or replace the profile shape

Use the grips to edit the profile shape

There are commands for performing advanced editing on slabs. These commands include tools similar to those used on polylines and walls. The available tools are described next.

Trimming Slabs

Slabs can be trimmed in much the same way as polylines, arcs, circles, and walls. When one of these objects is trimmed, you are able to determine the side of the cutting plane to be removed from the drawing. The process is similar for slabs: establish the trimming plane, and then trim the slab. When a slab is trimmed, part of the slab is removed from the drawing. Objects that can be used as trimming planes include slabs, walls, and polylines. If the slab being trimmed includes a custom edge, the fascia or soffit intersecting the trimming plane is trimmed at the same angle as the slab to which it is attached.

When the trimming plane is a polyline, the slab is trimmed to the edge of the polyline. If the trimming object is a wall or slab, the trimming plane is the closest surface to the part of the slab that will remain. The new edge of the slab is based on the angle of the wall or slab used as the trimming plane.

After a trimming object has been established, the slab can be trimmed. Select the Slab object, right-click, and select **Trim** from the shortcut menu. You are prompted to Select trimming object (a slab, wall, or polyline). Pick the trimming object. Next, select the slab on the side of the trimming object that will be trimmed. The slab will be trimmed against the edge of the trimming object.

To trim the slab away from a wall, type SLABTRIM. See **Figure 17-19**. When you are prompted, select the wall. Select the slab to trim, and then pick the side of the slab to be trimmed.

NOTE
> If a polyline with a mixture of arcs and straight segments is used as a trimming plane, the slab follows the contours of the polyline. If a curved wall is used as a trimming plane, the slab is trimmed along the straight-line angle between the start point and endpoint of the arced wall. It is not possible to trim only an overhang. The trimming plane must intersect the defined boundary of the slab at some location.

Extending Slabs

In addition to being trimmed, slabs can be extended. In order to extend a slab, the boundary being extended to must be a Slab or Wall object. When a slab is extended, one edge is actually moved to the boundary, with the two edges on either side being extended. Thus, you are prompted to select the adjacent edges that will be extended. Select the two edges adjacent to the edge of the slab to be extended, or moved, to the boundary. See **Figure 17-20**.

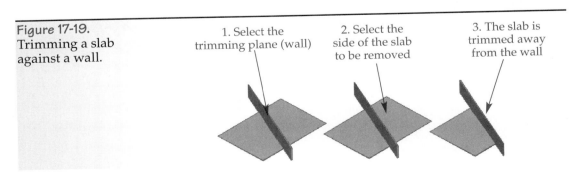

Figure 17-19.
Trimming a slab against a wall.

1. Select the trimming plane (wall)

2. Select the side of the slab to be removed

3. The slab is trimmed away from the wall

Figure 17-20.
When extending a slab to a wall or another slab, select the edges adjacent to the slab edge being extended, or moved.

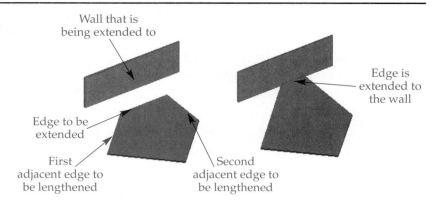

Wall that is being extended to

Edge is extended to the wall

Edge to be extended

First adjacent edge to be lengthened

Second adjacent edge to be lengthened

To extend a slab edge, pick a slab whose edge will be extended, right-click, and pick **Extend** in the shortcut menu; or type SLABEXTEND. See **Figure 17-18**. When you are prompted, select the wall or slab to extend to. Select the first edge to be lengthened to the wall and then the second edge.

Exercise 17-5   **Complete the Exercise on the Student CD.**

Mitering Slabs

A tool that is useful when working with slabs at different slopes is **Miter**. This tool allows you to miter two slabs together and join them at the points where the two slabs meet. To miter two edges together, select one of the slabs to be mitered, right-click, and pick **Miter** from the shortcut menu. When the **Miter** tool is used, two different methods of mitering the slab are available and are described next.

Mitering Intersecting Slabs

The **Intersection** option of the **Miter** tool is used when two slabs intersect each other. See **Figure 17-21**. When the two slabs are mitered using the **Intersection** option, they are trimmed along the intersection of their boundary lines. The new edges of the two slabs are set to an angle supporting a true miter cut between the slabs.

To miter three slabs, type SLABMITER, and choose the **Intersection** option. See **Figure 17-21**. When you are prompted, select the first slab on the side of the miter to be kept, and then select the second slab. Repeat this process with the remaining slab.

Figure 17-21.
The **Miter** tool using the **Intersection** option miters two slabs crossing through each other.

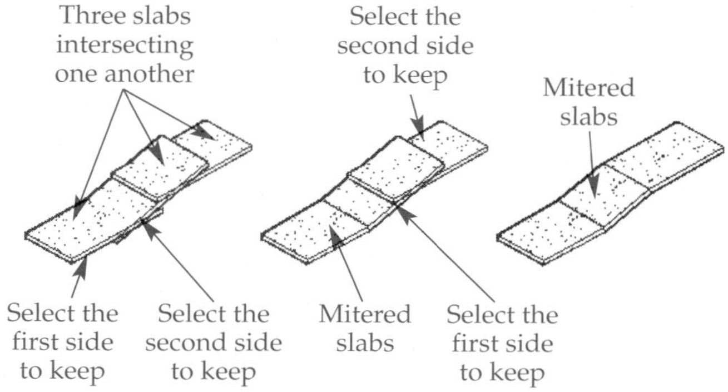

Three slabs intersecting one another

Select the second side to keep

Mitered slabs

Select the first side to keep

Select the second side to keep

Mitered slabs

Select the first side to keep

Architectural Desktop and Its Applications

Sometimes, multiple edges on a slab need to be mitered. Try stretching them, using the grip boxes to overlap the other slabs. Use the **Intersection** option of the **Miter** tool.

Mitering Slab Edges

The **Miter** tool with the **Edges** option provides more flexibility than the **Intersection** option of the **Miter** tool, because two particular edges are specified for mitering. This option allows you to miter the edges of two slabs without them having to intersect each other. See Figure 17-22. If the slabs do not intersect, the edges are extended to the point at which they meet. If the two slabs cross through each other, the slabs are trimmed, as with the **Intersection** option.

To miter slabs by edge, type SLABMITER, and choose the **Edges** option. See Figure 17-22. When you are prompted, select the first edge to miter, and then select the second edge. Repeat this process.

Exercise 17-6   *Complete the Exercise on the Student CD.*

Cutting Slabs

The **Cut** tool can be used to split a slab apart. This tool cuts the slab into two separate slabs by using a polyline or 3D object as the cutting line. If you are using a polyline, it can be a closed polyline or an open polyline crossing through the slab. If the open polyline crosses in and out of the slab, multiple slabs are created between the polyline cut lines.

A 3D object also can be used to cut a slab into two pieces. 3D objects include walls, slabs, mass elements, and AutoCAD solids. The only condition on using a 3D object as a cutting plane is that the object must cross through the slab being cut. When the slab is cut using a 3D object, it is cut along each surface of the 3D object.

A slab can be cut by picking the slab, right-clicking, and selecting **Cut** from the shortcut menu. After entering this option, you are prompted to select the cutting objects. Pick any polylines or 3D objects that will be used to cut the slab. After picking the cutting objects, you are asked if you want to erase the layout geometry or not. Decide whether or not to erase the cutting objects, and then press the [Enter] key to cut the slab.

Figure 17-22.
The **Miter** tool with the **Edges** option miters the edges of two slabs by allowing you to select the edges to be mitered.

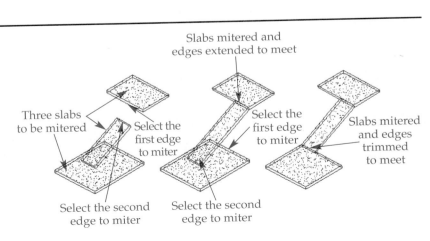

Slabs mitered and edges extended to meet

Three slabs to be mitered

Select the first edge to miter

Select the first edge to miter

Slabs mitered and edges trimmed to meet

Select the second edge to miter

Select the second edge to miter

Figure 17-23.
Use the **Cut** tool to cut the slab into two pieces. Both pieces are retained in the drawing.

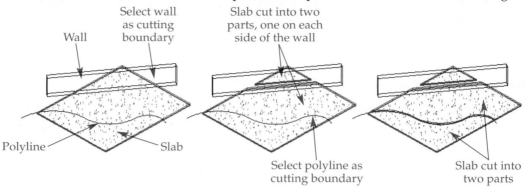

To cut a slab, type SLABCUT. See **Figure 17-23.** When you are prompted, select the wall that is the cutting object. The slab is cut to each side of the wall. Select the slab, right-click, and pick the **Cut** command. This begins the **SlabCut** command again. Select the polyline that is the cutting object. Decide whether or not to erase the cutting objects, and then press the [Enter] key to cut the slab.

 **Exercise 17-7**   *Complete the Exercise on the Student CD.*

Adding Slab Vertices

Occasionally, when a slab is modified, an additional edge needs to be added in order for the modifications to be correct, particularly when the slab is stretched with grips or the **Extend** command is used. To overcome this problem, the **Add Vertex** tool can be used to place a new vertex on the slab, which divides the existing edge into two edges. To add vertices to the edges of a slab so the edges can be stretched properly, select the slab, right-click, and pick **Add Vertex** from the shortcut menu; or type SLABADDVERTEX. See **Figure 17-24.** Type MID when you are prompted to specify a point for the new vertex. Select the midpoint of one of the slab edges. After a vertex has been added, select the object to display the grip boxes. A new grip box is located at the point you selected, and two grip boxes are located at the middle of the two edges created.

Figure 17-24.
Add vertices as required to make grip editing easier.

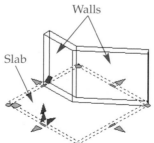 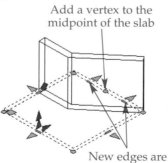 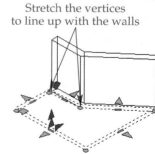

Architectural Desktop and Its Applications

Removing Slab Vertices

The slab tools also include an option for removing excess vertices. Access the **Remove Vertex** tool to remove any undesired vertices. Pick the slab, right-click, and select **Remove Vertex** from the shortcut menu.

Once the command has been entered, pick a point close to or on top of the vertex to be removed. The vertex is removed, and the two adjacent edges are joined together. See **Figure 17-25**.

Adding and Removing Holes in Slabs

A useful tool for cutting holes in slabs for elevator shafts, stairwells, and flues is the **Add Hole** tool. Holes can be added to a slab through the use of a polyline or 3D object. If a polyline is used, the polyline is projected through the thickness of the slab to create the hole. A 3D object is an object with mass, such as a wall, a mass element, or an AutoCAD solid. The 3D object must extend through both sides of the slab in order to cut the hole. If walls are used, the wall endpoints must touch, creating a closed boundary. After the hole is cut, new edges are created at the edge of the hole and can be modified using any of the commands discussed previously.

Adding Holes to Slabs

To add a hole to a slab, create the closed object to be used to create the hole. Pick the slab, right-click, and pick **Hole** > **Add**; or type SLABADDHOLE. See **Figure 17-26**. When you are prompted to select closed polylines or connected solid objects to define the holes, select the polyline and press [Enter]. Type Y when asked if you want to erase the layout geometry. Select the slab, right-click, and pick **Hole** > **Add**. This begins the **SlabAddHole** command again. When you are prompted to define the holes, select the four walls. Do not erase the layout geometry. Choose the **Outside** option.

Figure 17-25.
To remove a vertex, select the point or near the point to be removed.

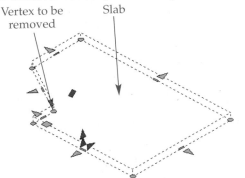

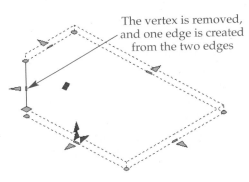

Figure 17-26.
Use the **SlabAddHole** command to add holes to a slab.

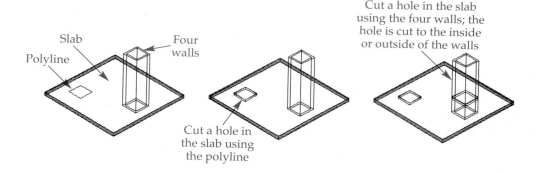

Slab

Polyline

Four walls

Cut a hole in the slab using the four walls; the hole is cut to the inside or outside of the walls

Cut a hole in the slab using the polyline

 NOTE

> When you use 3D objects that have an interior void, such as the walls around a room or a solid with a hole, you are prompted to cut to the inside or outside of the objects. If you select **Inside**, the hole edges are placed on the interior of the 3D object. If you select **Outside**, the hole is cut using the outer boundaries of the 3D object.

Removing Holes from Slabs

Holes can be removed from a slab with the **Remove** option of the **SLABHOLE** command. Select the slab with a hole to be removed, right-click, and pick **Hole** > **Remove** from the shortcut menu. You are prompted to Select an edge of hole to remove. Pick the edge of the hole. The hole is removed, and the void is filled.

 **Exercise 17-8**   *Complete the Exercise on the Student CD.*

Using Body Modifiers and Interference Conditions

There might be times when a slab requires 3D geometry to be added or removed that cannot be defined when the slab or edge styles are created. A pedestal in the middle of a slab and a pit that does not cut all the way through a slab are examples. Such geometry can be created using a body modifier or an interference condition applied to the slab. A body modifier is a 3D object used to adjust the shape of a slab. An *interference condition* is a 3D object that interferes, or collides, with a portion of the slab.

Using Body Modifiers in Slabs

Similar to Wall objects, Slab objects can have body modifiers applied. When you are using a body modifier, a 3D object can be added to, be subtracted from, or replace a slab component. Body modifiers can be applied as wood joists in a flooring system, sunken pits in a concrete slab, or raised equipment pads. See **Figure 17-27**.

To add a body modifier, first create the 3D geometry to be used as the body modifier and place it in the correct orientation on or in the slab. Next, pick the slab, right-click, and pick **Body Modifiers** > **Add...** from the shortcut menu. After entering the command, you are prompted to Select objects to apply as body modifiers. Select any objects that will be used as body modifiers. After selecting the objects, press the [Enter] key. This will display the **Add Body Modifier** dialog box. See **Figure 17-28**. Select the

Figure 17-27.
Body modifiers can be added to, be subtracted from, or replace a component within a slab.

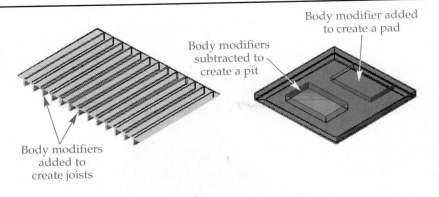

Body modifiers added to create joists

Body modifiers subtracted to create a pit

Body modifier added to create a pad

Figure 17-28.
The **Add Body Modifier** dialog box is used to add, subtract, or replace a body modifier with a slab component.

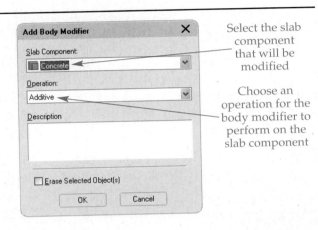

Select the slab component that will be modified

Choose an operation for the body modifier to perform on the slab component

Slab Component: to be affected by the body modifier. In the **Operation:** drop-down list, choose whether the body modifiers will be considered **Additive** to, be considered **Subtractive** from, or **Replace** the slab component. Pick the **OK** button to finish the operation.

After a body modifier has been added to a slab component, the area modified by the 3D object can be modified in place. To adjust a body modifier in place, pick the slab, right-click, and pick **Body Modifiers > Edit In Place**. This displays the **In-Place Edit** toolbar and an object where the body modifier was applied. See **Figure 17-29.** Use the grips to adjust the body modifier, or right-click to select different modifying tools from the shortcut menu. When you are finished making the change, pick the **Save All Changes** button in the **In-Place Edit** toolbar.

In addition to adding and modifying body modifiers, slabs can be restored by removing the body modifier from the slab. Pick the slab, right-click, and pick **Body Modifiers > Restore**. When this option is entered, you are prompted to Remove Body Modifiers? [Yes/No]: <No>. Typing NO restores an erased 3D object used to create the body modifier and keeps the body modifier applied to the slab, and typing YES removes the body modifier from the slab and restores the erased 3D object used as the body modifier.

Using Interference Conditions in Slabs

Interference conditions can be used where structural members cross through a slab, such as a column or post that must pass through a slab. Objects representing heating, ventilating, and air-conditioning (HVAC) or plumbing can also be used as interferences to a slab where they would pass through the Slab object. When an interference condition is created, the original geometry used to create the interference must remain in the drawing in order for the interference to be added or removed from the slab. See **Figure 17-30.**

Figure 17-29.
Body modifiers applied to a slab component can be edited in place.

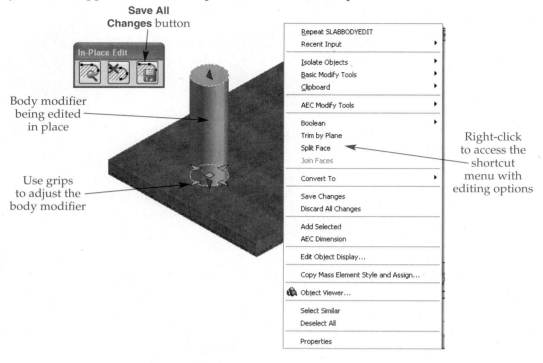

Save All Changes button

Body modifier being edited in place

Use grips to adjust the body modifier

Right-click to access the shortcut menu with editing options

Figure 17-30.
When an interference condition is applied to a slab, it can cause the slab's shrink-wrap to be additive or subtractive.

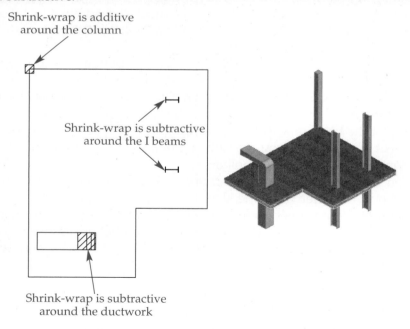

Shrink-wrap is additive around the column

Shrink-wrap is subtractive around the I beams

Shrink-wrap is subtractive around the ductwork

To add an interference condition to a slab, select the slab, right-click, and pick **Interference Condition** > **Add**. Upon entering this option, you are prompted to Select objects to add. Select any objects to be used as interference conditions to the slab. After selecting the items, press [Enter]. The next prompt asks you to Enter shrinkwrap effect [Additive/Subtractive]. The **Additive** effect causes the shrink-wrap for the slab to wrap around the interfering object. The **Subtractive** effect causes the shrink-wrap to be subtracted from the slab shrink-wrap.

Interferences can also be removed from a slab. Pick the Slab object with the interference condition, right-click, and pick **Interference Condition** > **Remove**. You are prompted to Select objects to remove. Select any desired interfering objects that will be removed from the slab.

Chapter Test

Answer the following questions. Write your answers on a separate sheet of paper or complete the electronic chapter test on the Student CD.

1. Define *slab*.
2. Identify the basic methods in which slabs are added to drawings.
3. What does the vertical offset value create?
4. Define *fascia* as related to slab terminology.
5. Define *pivot point* and identify where one would be placed.
6. Explain the function of the **Slab Edges** worksheet.
7. What do you get when you select any edge number along the left side of the **Slab Edges** worksheet table?
8. How do you edit multiple edges?
9. Define *soffit*.
10. What does the **Cut** tool do when used on a slab?
11. Give an example of where an interference condition can be used in a slab.
12. What must happen to the original geometry used to create the interference, when an interference condition is created in a slab?

Chapter Projects

Use the techniques covered in this chapter to create the following drawings.

1. Single-Level Residential Project
   A. Access the **Project Browser** and set Residential-Project-01 current.
   B. Access the **Constructs** tab of the **Project Navigator** and create a new construct named Main Floor Slab. Assign the level to the Main Floor level.
   C. Open the Main Floor Slab construct.
   D. Create a new slab style named Subfloor. Set a fixed thickness of 2" to the Unnamed component, with a 0" thickness offset. Assign a Wood material to the slab.
   E. Drag and drop the Main Floor construct into the Main Floor Slab construct for use as a reference file.
   F. Draw a slab, using the Subfloor slab style, at the exterior perimeter of all the walls of the building, including the exterior garage walls. Use a **Top** justification for the slab.
   G. Draw a polyline around the interior of the garage. At the garage door opening, jog the polyline to the exterior of the wall, and then jog it back inside.
   H. Use the **SlabCut** command to cut the subfloor into two pieces, using the polyline in the garage as the cutting line.
   I. Apply the Concrete Slab on Grade slab style found in the **Slabs** tool palette to the garage slab. Change the **Vertical offset** to -6".
   J. Adjust the display properties for each slab as desired.
   K. Save and close the drawing.

2. Single-Level Residential Project
   A. Access the **Project Browser** and set Residential-Project-02 current.
   B. Access the **Constructs** tab and create a new construct named Main Floor Slab. Assign the level to the Main Floor Framing level.
   C. Open the Main Floor Slab construct.
   D. Drag and drop the Main Floor construct into the Main Floor Slab construct for use as a reference file.
   E. Draw a 1" × 8" rectangle. Convert the rectangle into an AEC profile named Trim Board. Set the insertion point to the upper-left corner of the rectangle.
   F. Draw a 2" × 10" rectangle. Convert the rectangle into an AEC profile named Rim Joist. Set the insertion point to the upper-right corner of the rectangle.
   G. Create a new slab edge style named Rim and Trim Boards. In the **Design Rules** tab of the **Style Manager**, set the fascia to use the Trim Board profile. Uncheck the **Auto-Adjust to Edge Height** check box. Set the soffit to use the Rim Joist profile. Set the **"Y" Direction:** for the soffit to 1" and the **"X" Direction:** to 0". In the **Materials** tab, assign Wood materials to the Fascia and Soffit components.
   H. Create a new slab edge style named Rim Joist. In the **Design Rules** tab, set the soffit to use the Rim Joist profile. Set the **"Y" Direction:** for the soffit to 1" and the **"X" Direction:** to 0". In the **Materials** tab, assign Wood materials to the Fascia and Soffit components.
   I. Create a new slab style named Framing and Subfloor. Set a fixed thickness of 1" to the Unnamed component, with a 0" thickness offset. Assign a Wood material to the slab style.
   J. Adjust the display properties for the Plan representation Framing and Subfloor slab style to not display the Fascia and Soffit components.
   K. Draw a slab, using the Framing and Subfloor slab style, at the exterior of all walls of the building, including the exterior garage walls. Use a **Top** justification for the slab. Add the Rim and Trim Boards slab edge style to all the edges of the slab, except at the brick veneer locations. At the brick veneer edges, assign the Rim Joist slab edge style.

L. Draw a polyline around the interior of the garage. At the garage door opening, jog the polyline to the exterior of the wall to cut out a hole for the garage door, and then jog it back again.

M. Use the **Cut** tool to cut the Framing and Subfloor slab into two pieces, using the polyline at the garage as a cutting line.

N. Apply the Concrete Slab on Grade slab style in the **Slabs** tool palette to the garage slab created from cutting the main slab. Use the [Shift] + [Space] object cycling as needed to select the newly cut slab in the garage. Set the **Vertical offset** property to -7".

O. Add the Rim Joist slab edge style to the Framing and Subfloor slab's garage edges.

P. Save and close the drawing.

3. Two-Story Residential Project
   A. Access the **Project Browser** and set Residential-Project-03 current.
   B. Access the **Constructs** tab of the **Project Navigator** and create a new construct named Main Floor Slab. Assign the level to the Main Floor level.
   C. Open the Main Floor Slab construct.
   D. Drag and drop the Main Floor construct into the Main Floor Slab construct for use as a reference file.
   E. Create a new slab style named Subfloor. Assign a fixed thickness of 2" to the Unnamed component, with a 0" thickness offset. Assign a Wood material to the slab style.
   F. Right-click over the **Concrete Slab on Grade** tool in the **Slabs** tool palette and select **Import 'Concrete Slab on Grade' Slab Style**.
   G. Draw a slab, using the Subfloor style, around the perimeter of the exterior walls, including the garage walls. Use a **Top** justification.
   H. Draw a polyline around the interior of the garage walls. At the garage door locations, jog the polyline to the exterior wall, and then jog it back inside again.
   I. Use the **Cut** tool to cut the Subfloor slab into two pieces, using the garage polyline as a cutting line.
   J. Use the **Properties** palette to change the slab in the garage to the Concrete Slab on Grade slab style. Use the [Shift] + [Space] object cycling as needed to select the newly cut slab in the garage. Change the **Vertical offset** property to -6".
   K. Detach the Main Floor drawing.
   L. Save and close the drawing.
   M. Access the **Constructs** tab of the **Project Navigator** and create a new construct named Upper Floor Framing. Assign the level to the Upper Floor Framing level.
   N. Open the Upper Floor Framing construct.
   O. Drag and drop the Upper Floor construct into the Upper Floor Slab construct for use as a reference file.
   P. Create a new slab style named Floor with Framing. Add a slab component named Floor with a thickness of 3/4" and a -3/4" thickness offset. Add another component named Framing with a thickness of 11 1/4" and a -1'-0" thickness offset. Assign a Wood material to the components.
   Q. Add the slab at the perimeter of the external walls, using the new style and a justification set to **Top**.
   R. Drag and drop the Interior Stair construct into the Upper Floor Slab construct for use as a reference.
   S. Draw a polyline around the perimeter of the stair. Use the **SlabAddHole** command to add a hole in the slab for the stairwell.
   T. Detach the Upper Floor and Interior Stair references.
   U. Save and close the drawing.

4. Two-Story Residential Project
   A. Access the **Project Browser** and set Residential-Project-04 current.
   B. Access the **Constructs** tab of the **Project Navigator** and create a new construct named Main Floor Slab. Assign the level to the Main Floor level.
   C. Open the Main Floor Slab construct.
   D. Drag and drop the Main Floor construct into the Main Floor Slab construct for use as a reference file.
   E. Create a new slab style named Subfloor. Assign a fixed thickness of 2" to the Unnamed component, with a 0" thickness offset. Assign a Wood material to the slab style.
   F. Right-click over the **Concrete Slab on Grade** tool in the **Slabs** tool palette and select **Import 'Concrete Slab on Grade' Slab Style**.
   G. Draw a slab, using the Subfloor style, around the perimeter of the exterior walls, including the garage walls. Use a **Top** justification.
   H. Draw a polyline around the interior of the garage walls. At the garage door location, jog the polyline to the exterior wall, and then jog it back inside again.
   I. Use the **SlabCut** command to cut the Subfloor slab into two pieces, using the garage polyline as a cutting line.
   J. Use the **Properties** palette to change the slab in the garage to the Concrete Slab on Grade slab style. Change the **Vertical offset** property to -6".
   K. Detach the Main Floor drawing.
   L. Save and close the drawing.
   M. Access the **Constructs** tab of the **Project Navigator** and create a new construct named Upper Floor Framing. Assign the level to the Upper Floor Framing level.
   N. Open the Upper Floor Framing construct.
   O. Drag and drop the Upper Floor construct into the Upper Floor Slab construct for use as a reference file.
   P. Create a new slab style named Floor with Framing. Add a slab component named Floor with a thickness of 3/4" and a -3/4" thickness offset. Add another component named Framing with a thickness of 11 1/4" and a -1'-0" thickness offset. Assign a Wood material to the components.
   Q. Add the slab at the perimeter of the external walls, using the new style and a justification set to **Top**.
   R. Drag and drop the Interior Stair construct into the Upper Floor Slab construct for use as a reference.
   S. Draw a polyline around the foyer. See figure for placement. Use the **SlabAddHole** command to add a hole in the slab for the stairwell.
   T. Detach the Upper Floor and Interior Stair references.
   U. Save and close the drawing.

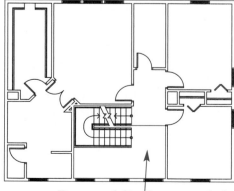

Draw a polyline for use as a hole

Design Courtesy Alan Mascord Design Associates

5. Commercial Store Project
   A. Access the **Project Browser** and set Commercial-Project-05 current.
   B. Access the **Constructs** tab of the **Project Navigator**. Open the Foundation construct.
   C. Right-click over the **Concrete Slab on Grade with turned down footing** tool in the **Slabs** tool palette and apply the tool properties to the two polylines in the Foundation construct.
   D. Drag and drop the Main Floor construct into the Foundation construct for use as a reference.
   E. Modify the **Vertical offset** property of the two slabs so the top of the slabs is flush with the bottom of the building walls.
   F. Drag and drop the Furniture construct for use as a reference.
   G. Use the Brick Pavers on Concrete slab style to add walkways between and around the buildings, in relation to the parking lot blocks. Refer to the figure for placement.
   H. Add a hole in the Brick Pavers on Concrete slab style, where the buildings sit over the slab.
   I. Use the **Vertical offset** property as needed for the Brick Pavers on Concrete slab style, to place the top of the slab flush with the bottom of the building walls.
   J. Detach all the reference files.
   K. Save and close the drawing.

Place the Concrete Slab on Grade with turned down footing slab style around each building

Draw the Brick Pavers on Concrete slab style around the building

Drawing Courtesy 3D-DZYN

6. Commercial Car Maintenance Shop Project
    A. Access the **Project Browser** and set Commercial-Project-06 current.
    B. Access the **Constructs** tab of the **Project Navigator**. Create a new construct named Main Floor Framing and assign it to the Main Floor Framing level.
    C. Open the Main Floor Framing construct.
    D. Drag and drop the Main Floor drawing into the construct for use as a reference.
    E. Use the **Concrete Slab on 1.5 Metal Deck** tool in the **Slabs** tool palette to add a 12"-thick concrete slab around the main portion of the building and the garage. Refer to the figure for location.
    F. Adjust the **Vertical offset** property as required to place the top of the slab flush with the bottom of the building walls.
    G. Drag and drop the Foundation construct into the drawing for use as a reference.
    H. Draw a polyline around each of the framed holes in the framing on the Foundation construct.
    I. Add two holes in the slab in the garage area. Refer to the figure for placement.
    J. Use the **Haunch (6 inch slab)** tool in the **Slabs** tool palette to add a slab around the car wash portion of the building. Refer to the figure for placement.
    K. Adjust the **Vertical offset** property as required to place the top of the slab flush with the bottom of the building walls.
    L. Detach any reference drawings.
    M. Save and close the drawing.
    N. Access the **Constructs** tab of the **Project Navigator**. Create a new construct named Upper Floor Framing and assign it to the Upper Floor Framing level.
    O. Open the Upper Floor Framing construct.
    P. Drag and drop the Upper Floor drawing into the construct for use as a reference.
    Q. Use the **Wood Floor System** tool in the **Slabs** tool palette to add a 12"-thick concrete slab around the upper floor. Refer to the figure for location.
    R. Adjust the vertical offset of the slab so the top of the Wood Floor System slab component is flush with the bottom of the walls.
    S. Edit the slab edge style in place by creating a custom edge to be used as a brick trim band between the floors of the building.
    T. Edit the slab edge style by assigning a Brick material.
    U. Detach any reference files.
    V. Save and close the drawing.

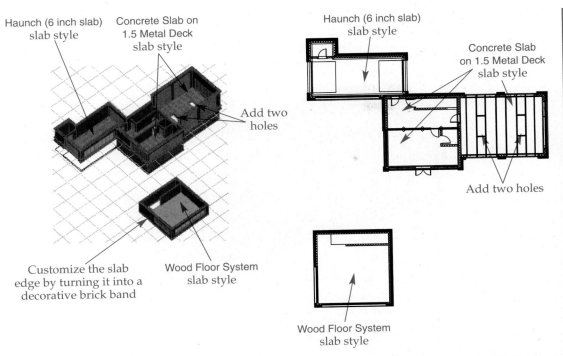

Haunch (6 inch slab) slab style

Concrete Slab on 1.5 Metal Deck slab style

Add two holes

Customize the slab edge by turning it into a decorative brick band

Wood Floor System slab style

Haunch (6 inch slab) slab style

Concrete Slab on 1.5 Metal Deck slab style

Add two holes

Wood Floor System slab style

Drawing Courtesy 3D-DZYN

7. Governmental Fire Station
   A. Access the **Project Browser** and set Gvrmt -Project-07 current.
   B. Access the **Constructs** tab of the **Project Navigator** and open the Foundation construct.
   C. Use the **Haunch (6 inch slab)** tool in the **Slabs** tool palette to apply the style to the polyline representing the outline of the building.
   D. Drag and drop the Main Floor construct into the drawing for use as a reference.
   E. Adjust the slab's **Vertical offset** property so the top of the slab is flush with the bottom of the building walls.
   F. Modify the Haunch (6 inch slab) style. Access the **Display Properties** tab of the **Style Manager** and modify the Plan display representation. Turn off the Below Cut Plane Body Shrink Wrap component and turn on the Below Cut Plane Outline component. Set the Soffit linetype to HIDDEN2.
   G. Use the **Brick Pavers on Concrete** tool in the **Slabs** tool palette to add a 20'-0" × 10'-0" patio slab behind the dayroom. Use a **Top** justification. Adjust the top of the slab to be flush with the bottom of the building walls.
   H. Add a walk at the front of the building, using a **Top** justification. Select the Brick Pavers on Concrete slab style. Adjust the top of the slab to be flush with the bottom of the building walls.
   I. Save and close the drawing.

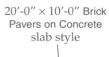

20'-0" × 10'-0" Brick
Pavers on Concrete
slab style

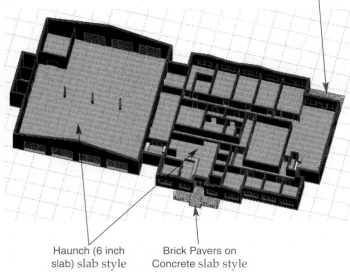

Haunch (6 inch
slab) slab style

Brick Pavers on
Concrete slab style

Drawing Courtesy 3D-DZYN

Chapter 17 Projects

CHAPTER 18

Creating Roofs

Learning Objectives

After completing this chapter, you will be able to do the following:

- ✓ Create a single- and double-sloped roof.
- ✓ Convert polylines and walls into roofs.
- ✓ Modify roofs.
- ✓ Use roof and roof slab properties.
- ✓ Use grips to modify roofs.
- ✓ Edit edges and faces.
- ✓ Adjust the roof display properties.
- ✓ Create roof slabs.
- ✓ Convert a roof into roof slabs.
- ✓ Modify roof slabs and roof slab edges.
- ✓ Create roof slabs and roof slab edge styles.
- ✓ Trim, extend, miter, and cut roof slabs.
- ✓ Add and remove roof slab vertices.
- ✓ Add and remove holes.
- ✓ Create a roof dormer.

Roofs can be created using Architectural Desktop. Two types of AEC objects can be used to draw a roof: AEC Roof objects and roof slabs. The AEC Roof object is used to model an entire roof of a building. Roofs can be created by selecting points, much like picking points for a slab, or converted from polylines or walls enclosing a room or area. The roof pitch (or slope), overhang, and roof plate height can be set and edited at any time. The ***roof pitch*** is the angle of the roof from horizontal, usually measured by height in inches per linear foot. For example, a 6:12 roof pitch indicates that the roof slopes up 6″ per 12″ of horizontal distance. The ***slope*** is the angle of the roof in elevation, measured up from horizontal.

The Roof object can be converted to Roof Slab objects for more modeling control over the appearance of a roof. Roof Slab objects are similar to Slab objects and provide control over the individual faces and edge style of a roof. Custom fascias and soffits can be added to the edge of a roof slab to control the detail.

Roof objects are created in one of two ways: by picking points in the drawing to establish vertex (corner) locations for the roof or by converting polylines or walls into roofs. When points are picked to draw a roof, the points are usually picked around the outside edges of the walls, to represent the truss locations, and the inside edges of walls, to represent rafter locations. As the corner points are picked, the Roof object begins taking shape. The points become hips and valleys for the roof, as shown in **Figure 18-1.**

Adding Roofs

Pull-Down Menu
Design
> Roofs
> Add Roof...

Tool Palette

Design

Roof

To start the **ROOF** command and create a standard Roof object, pick the **Roof** tool in the **Design** tool palette, or select **Design** > **Roofs** > **Add Roof...** from the pull-down menu. Before picking points in the drawing to establish the vertices or roof plate locations, adjust the roof settings in the **Properties** palette. When the **Roof** tool is picked, the **Properties** palette displays properties that control how the roof is created. See **Figure 18-2.** The properties are organized under the **BASIC** header. Under the **BASIC** header, four categories are available for controlling the properties for the new roof. These categories and their properties are described in the following sections.

General Category

The **General** category includes two properties: **Description** and **Bound spaces**. The **Bound spaces** property is used to bind Space objects to the Roof object when figuring out volumes of space. Use the **Description** property to enter a description for the roof being created.

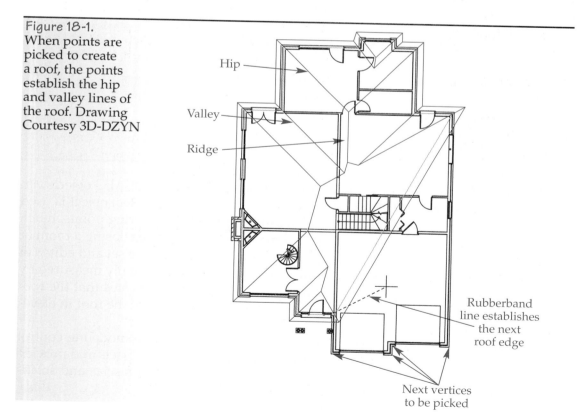

Figure 18-1.
When points are picked to create a roof, the points establish the hip and valley lines of the roof. Drawing Courtesy 3D-DZYN

Hip

Valley

Ridge

Rubberband line establishes the next roof edge

Next vertices to be picked

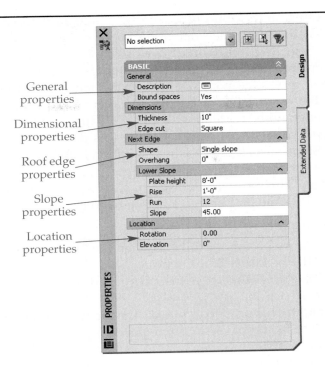

Figure 18-2.
The **Properties** palette is used to control the properties of new roofs.

General properties

Dimensional properties

Roof edge properties

Slope properties

Location properties

Dimensions Category

The **Dimensions** category includes two properties to control the dimensions of the Roof object. The **Thickness** property controls the overall thickness of the Roof object. This can be considered the roof sheathing plus the framing member underneath, for a total thickness, or the thickness of the framing member to be used in the design. Selecting the **Edge cut** property displays a drop-down list with two options: **Square** and **Plumb**. This property controls how the overhang edge is created. The **Square** edge cut squares the end of the roof between the top and bottom portions of the roof. The **Plumb** edge cut creates a vertical overhang edge that is plumb to the ground. See **Figure 18-3.**

Next Edge Category

The **Next Edge** category includes two properties that control how an edge along the roof is to be created. As new points are picked in the drawing to establish roof vertex points, an overhang edge is created between two points. This category controls the properties for the next edge to be created when the next point along the roof is

Figure 18-3.
The **Edge Cut** property controls how the overhang edge of the roof will be created.

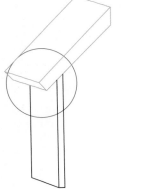

Square Edge Cut   Plumb Edge Cut

picked. Depending on the option chosen in the **Shape** property, additional subcategories are available to control the slope of the roof for the next edge to be created:

- **Shape.** Selecting this property value displays three options for the next edge being created: **Single slope**, **Double slope**, and **Gable**. The **Single slope** option creates a roof edge with one slope, or pitch. When this option is selected, a **Lower Slope** subcategory becomes available. The **Double slope** option creates a roof edge with two slopes, or pitches. This option is used to create gambrel or steeple-shaped roof edges. Picking this property displays **Lower Slope** and **Upper Slope** subcategories. The last option is **Gable**. This option creates a gable edge for the roof.
- **Overhang.** This property is used to set an overhang value for the edge being created. Pick the property to enter an overhang depth.

Lower Slope Subcategory

This subcategory becomes available when the **Single slope** or **Double slope** shape has been selected. The **Lower Slope** subcategory includes four properties: **Plate height**, **Rise**, **Run**, and **Slope**. **Figure 18-4** displays the properties in this subcategory for a single-slope roof:

- **Plate height.** This property controls the roof plate height for the roof edge being drawn. The next roof vertex point picked is placed at the Z axis height specified in this property.
- **Rise.** This text box property is used to set a rise height per 12″ (or 100 mm) of run. For example, a value of 6″ indicates that the roof rises 6″ for every 12″ of run. The rise entered automatically adjusts the **Slope** property. A rise of 6″ and run of 12″ create a sloping angle of 26.57°.
- **Run.** This property is a read-only value and indicates a constant run of **12″** or **100** mm.
- **Slope.** This property can be adjusted to establish a sloping angle for the edge being created. Entering a value for the slope of the roof adjusts the **Rise** property. For example, a value of 45 sets the **Rise** to 1′-0″.

Upper Slope Subcategory

This subcategory is displayed when the **Double slope** shape has been selected. Similar to the **Lower Slope** subcategory, the **Upper Slope** subcategory includes four properties: **Upper height**, **Rise**, **Run**, and **Slope**. **Figure 18-5** displays the properties for a double-slope roof:

- **Upper height.** This value is used to establish the upper slope of a double-slope roof. The **Upper height** value is measured from the 0″ Z axis to the point where the two slopes of a double roof meet at the underside of the roof. See **Figure 18-5**.

Figure 18-4.
The properties used to establish a single-slope roof.

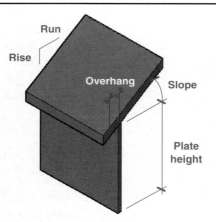

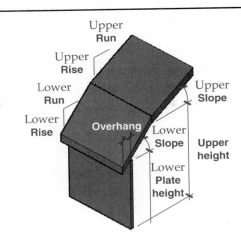

Figure 18-5.
The properties
used to establish a
double-slope roof.

- **Rise.** This property controls the rise of the upper portion of the roof.
- **Run.** This property is a read-only property, with a **12"** or **100** mm run.
- **Slope.** Enter a value in this property to control the slope of the upper portion of the double roof.

Location Category

The **Location** category includes two read-only options: **Rotation** and **Elevation**. These two properties initially do not display values. They are available later, however, after the Roof object has been created. These properties can be used to rotate the roof and change the elevation location of the entire Roof object.

Drawing Single-Sloped Roofs

The **Single slope** shape roof can be used to create a hip roof, gable roof, or combination of hip and gable roofs. After picking the **Roof** tool, select the **Single slope** shape and determine the plate height for the roof. The plate height is usually established by the height of the wall where the roof sits. If you are creating a roof with multiple plate heights, use the average or main plate height to draw the roof first, and then you can change the plate heights of the different edges later. Multiple-plate roofs are discussed later in this chapter.

Next, determine the rise or slope of the roof. Any rise height can be entered. If you are adjusting the **Slope** value, the maximum slope that can be used when initially creating a roof is 89.99°. Creating a roof with a slope of 0° establishes a flat roof. It is easiest to modify the slope edges of a roof after the initial shape has been drawn. Determine if the roof includes an overhang and, if so, specify the overhang depth in the **Overhang** property.

Once the parameters for the roof have been determined, the roof can be drawn. Pick the first point for the roof. Nothing appears until the second and third points of the roof have been picked. Use the **Endpoint** object snap to select exterior corners of the building or the **Node** object snap to snap to the baselines of walls. Begin selecting all the points of the building where the roof will be located. As the points are picked, the roof begins to appear. When you pick the last point, which is the point before the first point selected, press the [Enter] key to close and accept the new roof. **Figure 18-6** displays the points picked to create a roof.

Exercise
18-1   **Complete the Exercise on the Student CD.**

Figure 18-6.
Select all the exterior wall corners to use as the vertex locations for the roof.

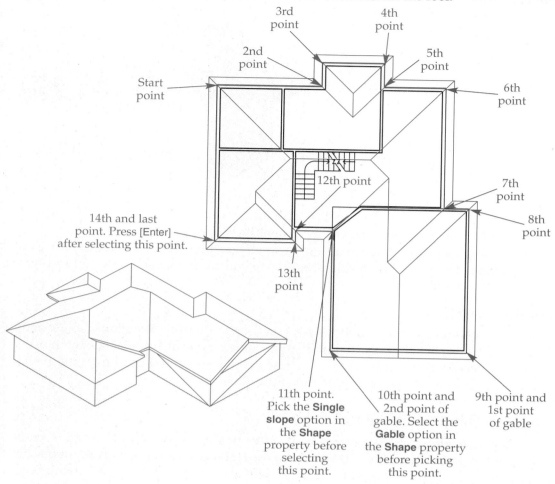

Drawing Double-Sloped Roofs

The **Double slope** shape is used to create a roof containing two roof slopes on each side of the ridge. In the **Properties** palette **Shape** property, select the **Double slope** shape. Determine the plate height for the roof, and then determine the upper height. The **Upper height** value specifies the point at which the lower roof slope meets the upper roof slope. See **Figure 18-5**. Next, specify the **Rise** values for each slope. If you use an overhang, specify the overhang depth. After determining the parameters for the double-sloped roof, begin picking the points for the roof. **Figure 18-7** shows the points picked to create a double-sloped roof.

PROFESSIONAL
TIP

You can create roofs in a separate drawing file by referencing the building floor that has a roof added above it. Using the reference, select the exterior points of the walls. After the roof is created, it can then be referenced into an assembly drawing for elevations and sections.

Exercise
18-2

Complete the Exercise on the Student CD.

Figure 18-7.
Picking points to create a double-sloped roof.

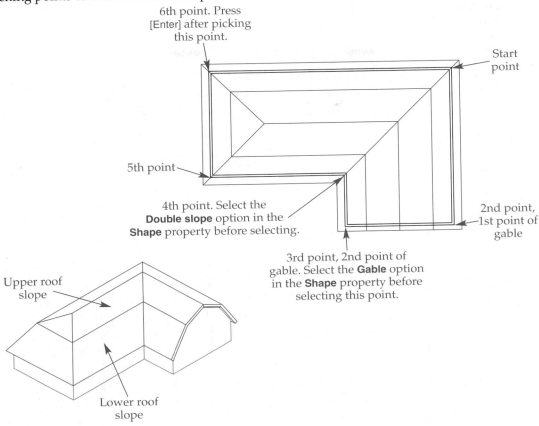

6th point. Press [Enter] after picking this point.

Start point

5th point

4th point. Select the **Double slope** option in the **Shape** property before selecting.

3rd point, 2nd point of gable. Select the **Gable** option in the **Shape** property before selecting this point.

2nd point, 1st point of gable

Upper roof slope

Lower roof slope

Converting Polylines and Walls into Roofs

In addition to drawing roofs manually, you can create roofs by converting polylines and walls into roofs. The ability to convert these objects into roofs provides the opportunity to create rounded edges for a roof. See **Figure 18-8**.

In order to convert polylines or a set of walls into a roof, the **Roof** tool must be applied to the polyline or Wall objects. To do this, right-click over the **Roof** tool in the **Design** tool palette, and select **Apply Tool Properties to** > **Linework and Walls**.

Converting Polylines into Roofs

Converting a polyline into a roof is the most flexible method of converting an object to a roof. The polyline can be any combination of straight and curved segments and does not have to be a closed polyline. If the polyline is not closed, the **Roof** tool closes the roof between the starting and ending points of the polyline, adding a sloped side between the two points. It is usually best to draw a polyline around the outer edges of your building model and then convert the polyline into a roof. To convert a polyline into a roof, right-click over the **Roof** tool in the **Design** tool palette, and select **Apply Tool Properties to** > **Linework and Walls**. When you are prompted, select the polyline. Press [Enter] to keep the layout geometry and end the command.

After you select the polyline to be converted and choose whether to erase the polyline, the roof is displayed in the drawing screen, with grip boxes around the vertices. Adjust any of the settings for the new roof through the **Properties** palette. When you have finished adjusting the roof, press [Esc] to finish the command.

Figure 18-8.
Walls and polylines with arc segments can be converted into rounded roofs.

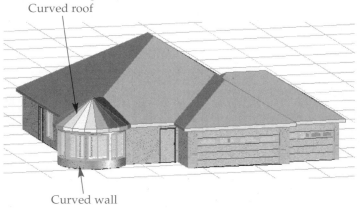

Curved roof

Curved wall

NOTE

If a polyline that includes curved segments is converted, the segments initially appear as a number of straight sloped segments, making the curved roof appear blocky. The appearance can be adjusted later by modifying the number of segments the curve uses. This technique is discussed later in this chapter.

Converting Walls into Roofs

Converting a series of walls is the same process as converting a polyline, however when walls are converted into a roof, the walls must form a closed building or room. If the walls being converted do not form a closed building, the roof is added on top of the walls to form a cap, as shown in **Figure 18-9.** The slightest opening between two walls forms a roof on top of the individual walls being converted.

Figure 18-9.
Walls forming an enclosed area can be converted into a roof, and walls that do not form an enclosed area are converted to a roof cap over the individual walls.

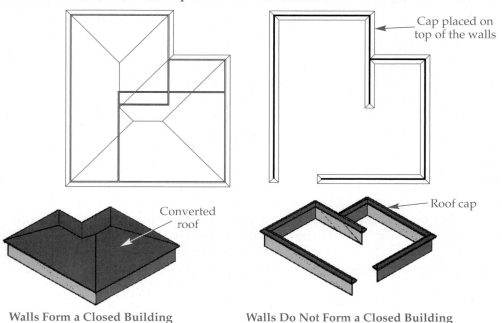

Cap placed on top of the walls

Converted roof

Roof cap

Walls Form a Closed Building   **Walls Do Not Form a Closed Building**

The prompt sequence for converting walls is the same as it is for converting polylines. Select the walls to be converted, ensuring that the walls selected form a closed building. If you have walls that enclose the entire building, you can use a crossing window to select all the walls, as Architectural Desktop only looks at the outer boundary of walls for the conversion process to a roof.

When the walls are converted, the **Plate height** property is automatically set in the **Properties** palette, based on the height of the walls. If the walls being converted include several different heights, the **Plate height** property is not displayed in the **Properties** palette. Converted polylines and walls create hip roofs only. If a gable is desired on an end or the entire roof needs to be composed of gables, you can make these changes later by modifying the roof edges.

NOTE If walls with multiple heights are converted, the Roof object is created using the different plates, properly adjusting the roof slopes and valley and hip intersections.

 Exercise 18-3   **Complete the Exercise on the Student CD.**

Using the Properties Palette to Modify Roofs

The **Properties** palette can be used to set properties for a roof when the roof is initially created. In addition to this functionality, it can be used to modify an existing Roof object. Many of the properties used to create a roof are also available when modifying the roof. To begin editing an existing roof, select the Roof object, and then access the **Properties** palette. **Figure 18-10** displays the **Properties** palette that appears when you are editing a Roof object. The **Properties** palette for roofs is made up of the following three categories:

Figure 18-10.
The properties available for modifying a roof are displayed in the **Properties** palette after a roof to be modified is selected.

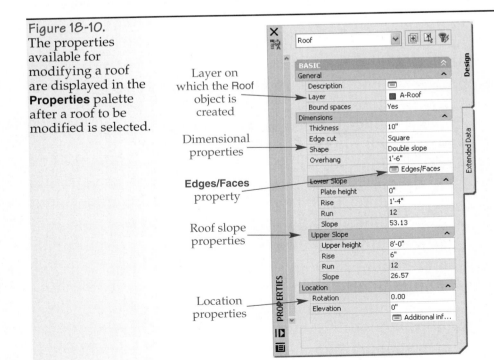

- **General.** This category is used to provide a description for the selected roof, bind Space objects to the roof, and assign a layer other than the default A-Roof layer to the Roof object.
- **Dimensions.** The **Dimensions** category is divided into two main sections: roof properties and slope properties. Directly below the **Dimensions** header are properties for the roof **Thickness, Edge cut, Shape, Overhang,** and **Edges/Faces.** Unlike the **Shape** property when you are first creating a roof, the **Shape** property for an existing roof includes two options: **Single slope** and **Double slope.** Depending on the type of shape selected, additional slope property subcategories become available.

  When the **Single slope** shape is selected, the **Lower Slope** subcategory becomes available for specifying the **Plate height, Rise,** and **Slope** of the entire roof. If the **Double slope** shape is selected, the **Lower Slope** and **Upper Slope** subcategories are displayed. The **Upper Slope** subcategory is used to set the **Upper height, Rise,** and **Slope** for the entire upper portion of the roof.

  A new property available in the **Dimensions** category is the **Edges/Faces** property. Picking this property displays the **Roof Edges and Faces** worksheet. See Figure 18-11. The worksheet is divided into two main areas: **Roof Edges** and **Roof Faces (by Edge).**

  The **Roof Edges** area includes a table of information for each edge of the selected roof. The **Edge** column lists each edge within the selected roof. For example, edge 0 is the edge between the first and second points picked when the roof was created. Most of the values within the table can be selected for modification. These values include the **Height, Overhang, Segments,** and **Radius,** if a curved roof exists. Picking a value in the table allows you to enter a new value for the associated edge.

  The **Roof Faces (by Edge)** table controls the face, or sloping side, of the roof belonging to the edge selected in the **Roof Edges** table below. For example, in Figure 18-11, edge 0 is highlighted in the **Roof Edges** table. The face information

Figure 18-11.
The **Roof Edges and Faces** worksheet allows you to control the parameters of each edge of the roof.

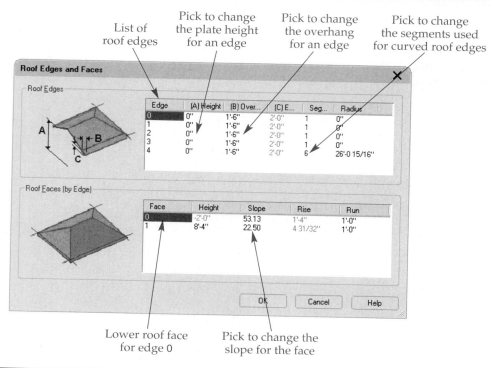

List of roof edges

Pick to change the plate height for an edge

Pick to change the overhang for an edge

Pick to change the segments used for curved roof edges

Roof Edges and Faces

Roof Edges

Edge	(A) Height	(B) Over...	(C) E...	Seg...	Radius
0	0"	1'-6"	2'-0"	1	0"
1	0"	1'-6"	2'-0"	1	0"
2	0"	1'-6"	2'-0"	1	0"
3	0"	1'-6"	2'-0"	1	0"
4	0"	1'-6"	2'-0"	6	26'-0 15/16"

Roof Faces (by Edge)

Face	Height	Slope	Rise	Run
0	-2'-0"	53.13	1'-4"	1'-0"
1	8'-4"	22.50	4 31/32"	1'-0"

OK   Cancel   Help

Lower roof face for edge 0

Pick to change the slope for the face

for edge 0 is displayed in the **Roof Faces (by Edge)** table. Each edge of a roof includes a face numbered 0. The information that can be adjusted for a face is found in the **Slope** column. To change the slope for a face, pick on the **Slope** value in the table and enter a new sloping angle. If a double-sloped face is selected, two faces are present in the table. Face 0 belongs to the lower portion of the roof, and face 1 belongs to the upper portion of the roof. Additional faces can be added to an edge by picking the **Face** column below the last face in the list. For example, a double-sloped roof could have three faces by picking the **Face** column below face 1. The slopes for each face can then have different values, creating a curved-slope roof.

- **Location.** This category includes information regarding the position of the Roof object in the drawing. The **Rotation** and **Elevation** properties are available to control the rotation angle and elevation of the selected roof. In addition to these properties, the **Additional information** property is available for additional control over the rotation angle and elevation of the roof.

 NOTE

Although the roof edges and face slopes can be adjusted in the **Roof Edges and Faces** worksheet, it is difficult to know which edge and face is actually being adjusted. To specify the edge and face being modified, use the **Edit Edges/Faces...** option. This option is discussed later in this chapter.

 Exercise 18-4   **Complete the Exercise on the Student CD.**

Using Grips to Modify Roofs

When a roof is selected, all the edges of the roof become highlighted. Grip boxes are also placed around the roof at all roof vertex corners, intersections of ridges, hips, and valleys. Picking a grip and stretching its location allows you to modify the roof in some way. Selecting a grip between two corner grips adjusts the roof plate location. Stretching a corner grip adjusts the two slopes on either side of the corner.

Gable end roofs can also be created with grips. To do this, select a grip at the intersection of two hips to highlight the grip. Stretch the grip point past the edge of the roof and pick with the left mouse button, as shown in Figure 18-12. The ridge is extended to the edge of the eave, and the sloping face is turned into a gable end. Using grips is often easier than manually creating a gable by selecting the **Gable** shape each time a gable is to be added when you are creating a roof. Use this method also after converting polylines or walls into a roof, because the roof is initially created as a hip roof.

Occasionally, stretching a grip to create a gable end produces undesired results. When the face of a roof being turned into a gable happens to be on the same plane as another face, stretching the grip causes both faces to be turned into gable roofs, as shown in Figure 18-13. In this situation, use the **Edit Edges/Faces...** option to edit the slope for the face that is to be turned into a gable. This procedure is discussed in the next section.

Grips can also be used on a double-sloped roof to create a Dutch-hip roof, as in Figure 18-14. If the Dutch hip is to have two different slopes, make the adjustments to the rise or slope as necessary. If the Dutch hip is to have the same slope, use the same rise and slope for the upper and lower roofs. In either case, a **Double slope** shape needs to be used. After the roof is drawn, select the grip where the two hips intersect, and pull the grip point past the edge between both sloped roofs.

Figure 18-12.
Use grips to create
gable ends in a roof.

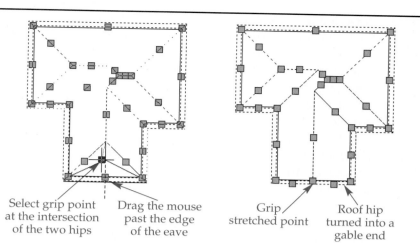

Select grip point
at the intersection
of the two hips

Drag the mouse
past the edge
of the eave

Grip
stretched point

Roof hip
turned into a
gable end

Figure 18-13.
Roof faces in the
same plane are
modified together if
one face is changed
to a gable.

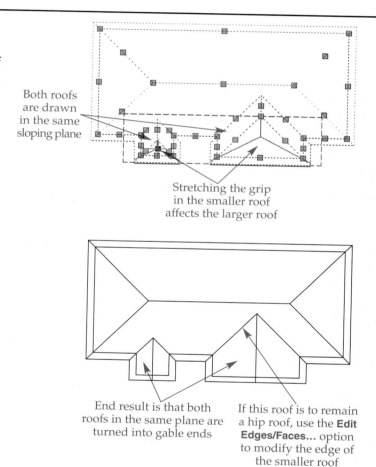

Both roofs
are drawn
in the same
sloping plane

Stretching the grip
in the smaller roof
affects the larger roof

End result is that both
roofs in the same plane are
turned into gable ends

If this roof is to remain
a hip roof, use the **Edit
Edges/Faces...** option
to modify the edge of
the smaller roof

NOTE

When gable-end roofs are created, an open hole is displayed between
the top of the wall and bottom of the roof. Use the wall's **ROOFLINE**
command with the **Auto project** option to automatically project the
walls up to the bottom of the roof. With the **Auto project** option, the
wall can be projected to any AEC object with an edge that can be
projected to. Walls can also be projected to roofs in an xref. To do this,
first select the walls to be projected, and then select the roof within the
xref. The walls are projected up to the roof.

Figure 18-14.
Creating a Dutch-hip roof.

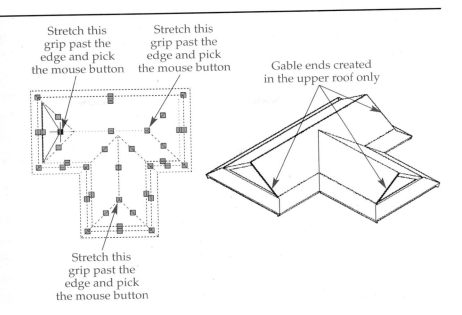

Stretch this grip past the edge and pick the mouse button

Stretch this grip past the edge and pick the mouse button

Gable ends created in the upper roof only

Stretch this grip past the edge and pick the mouse button

Exercise
18-5   Complete the Exercise on the Student CD.

Editing Edges and Faces

A problem with using the **Roof Edges and Faces** worksheet to modify edges is it is difficult to tell which edges are being modified. The **Edit Edges/Faces...** option makes this task simpler because you are able to select the edge needing to be modified. To access the option, select the roof to be modified, right-click, and pick **Edit Edges/ Faces...** from the shortcut menu.

Once the option has been accessed, you are prompted to Select a roofedge. Select any roof edge or eave to modify. When you finish selecting the edges you want to modify, press the [Enter] key. The **Roof Edges and Faces** worksheet, shown in **Figure 18-15**, is displayed. This worksheet looks similar to the **Roof Edges and Faces** worksheet you use when modifying an entire roof. The difference is only the edges selected are displayed in the **Roof Edges** area of the worksheet.

If you need to readjust the plate heights for different edges of the roof, select the edges needing to be modified, and then change the values in the **Height** column. As with editing all the edges discussed earlier, the only edge values that can be modified are the **Height**, **Overhang**, and **Segments**, if the edge is curved. If a curved roof edge is modified, the **Segments** column can be adjusted to add more segments, creating a smoother roof.

PROFESSIONAL
TIP

If you use the **Roof Edges and Faces** worksheet to edit a double-sloped roof, the selected edge displays two faces. Change both faces to reflect a 90° slope, to create a complete gable end.

Exercise
18-6   Complete the Exercise on the Student CD.

Figure 18-15.
The **Roof Edges and Faces** worksheet allows you to modify the selected edges of a roof.

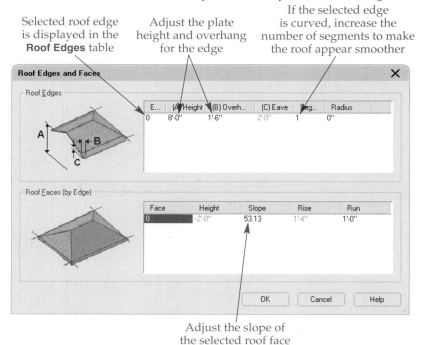

Selected roof edge is displayed in the **Roof Edges** table

Adjust the plate height and overhang for the edge

If the selected edge is curved, increase the number of segments to make the roof appear smoother

Adjust the slope of the selected roof face

A problem with grip editing was encountered in **Figure 18-13,** where both ends of the roof in the same plane were being modified into a gable end. With the **Edit Edges/Faces...** option, the one edge that needed to be turned into a gable end can be modified. To change a sloped roof into a gable end, adjust the slope to a 90° angle. This tips the slope straight up vertically, turning the slope into a gable end. The slope for an edge must be between 0° and 180°. See **Figure 18-16.**

Figure 18-16.
Changing the slope of a face to a 90° angle will tip the slope on end vertically, creating a gable end.

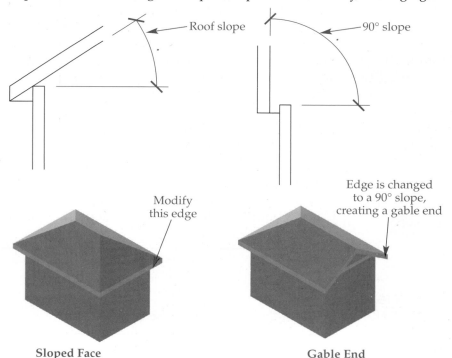

Roof slope

90° slope

Modify this edge

Edge is changed to a 90° slope, creating a gable end

Sloped Face

Gable End

NOTE The **Roof Edges and Faces** worksheet can also be used to create a shed roof. First, draw a rectangular roof. Use the **Edit Edges/Faces...** option to modify the slope of three sides of the roof to 90°.

Adjusting the Roof Object Display

The addition of AEC roofs produces a blue-colored roof in the Model and Plan representations. Like other objects, AEC roofs have the ability to appear differently, depending on the viewing direction. To modify the appearance of a roof in the different display representations, first select the roof, right-click, and select **Edit Object Display...** from the shortcut menu.

Select the **Display Properties** tab of the **Object Display** dialog box to modify the display of the Roof object. AEC roofs include Plan and Model representations. Select the representation to be modified, attach an override if required, and then edit the display properties. Both the Plan and Model representations for a Roof object include Roof and Eave components. These components can be turned on or off, have layers assigned, or have their colors adjusted. Make any display changes as needed and exit the **Object Display** dialog box.

In addition to modifying the display of Model or Plan representation roofs, materials can be added to the Roof object. In the **Object Display** dialog box, select the **Materials** tab, and then assign a material to the Roof component. Roof objects do not have a style, so the display properties for a Roof object are applied globally to all roofs or to individual roofs.

NOTE In many construction document sets that include roofs, the roof outline is shown in the upper floor as a dashed or dotted line. Use the object display to change the Plan view roofs so they use a DASHED or dotted linetype. You can create a custom display configuration including the dashed plan roof and another showing the roof as a solid line for a roof plan.

Creating Roof Slabs

As discussed in Chapter 17, Slab objects are used to create floors and solid shapes with mass. The Roof Slab object is a similar type of object, using the same techniques and type of commands as are available for the standard Slab objects. Roof slabs are used to model a single face, or side, of a roof. The roof slab is composed of components, surrounded by edges. Each edge can be assigned its own edge style to create fascia boards and soffits. As with the standard slabs, selecting several points to define the shape of the slab creates roofs slabs. The first two points selected establish the slope-line, or edge that determines the beginning of the slope, or angle, of the roof. Typically, the fascia and soffit are created along this first edge. See **Figure 18-17.**

The difference between a roof slab and an AEC Roof object is the roof slab is a separate part or side of a roof. Multiple roofs slabs placed together can be used to model an entire roof, but they remain a series of individual sides that can be edited separately. For this reason, roof editing tools are required to get the hip, valley, and ridge edges to miter and clean up properly.

Figure 18-17.
Roof slabs are single sides of a roof and defined by picking points in the current XY plane. The first two points selected define the slopeline of the roof slab.

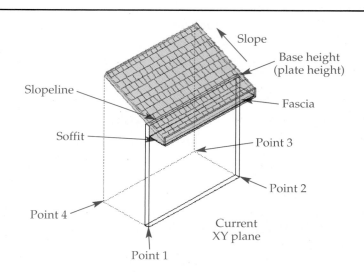

PROFESSIONAL TIP

It is suggested that you initially create a roof using the AEC Roof object to create as much of the roof as possible, when you are designing a complex roof with many hips and valleys. When the roof is significantly complete but needs further editing that cannot be accomplished through standard roof tools, convert the roof into roof slabs that can be edited individually.

In addition to manually drawing roof slabs, you can convert roof slabs from AEC roofs, walls, and polylines. Although the individual sides do not interact with each other as they do with an AEC roof, the roof edges can be trimmed, extended, and mitered the same as an AEC slab. Holes for skylights can be cut in a roof slab, and any type of edge style can be applied to the different edges of a roof slab.

Adding Roof Slabs

Pull-Down Menu
Design
> Roofs
> Add Roof
Slab...

Tool Palette
Design

Roof Slab

Roof slabs can be added to the drawing by picking the **Roof Slab** tool in the **Design** tool palette or **Design** > **Roofs** > **Add Roof Slab...** from the pull-down menu. Additional roof slab styles can be found in the **Slabs** palette of the **Tool Palettes** window or in the **Content Browser** catalogs. Use the **Properties** palette to set the properties for the new roof slab being drawn. See **Figure 18-18**.

The properties for roof slabs are considered basic properties and organized under the **BASIC** header. These properties are divided into three categories: **General**, **Dimensions**, and **Location**. The properties are discussed in the following sections.

General Category

This category includes properties that control the general parameters of the new roof slab. Picking the **Description** property displays the **Description** worksheet. A description for the roof slab can be entered in this worksheet. Use the **Style** property to pick a roof slab style to use. Initially, the only style available is the Standard style. Additional roof slab styles can be imported or created for use. Creating a roof slab style and importing additional styles are covered later in this chapter. Use the **Bound spaces** property to cause Space objects to be bound by the boundary of the Roof Slab object. When the **Mode** property is selected, a drop-down list with two options is present: **Direct** and **Projected**. The **Direct** mode creates a flat roof slab. The **Projected** mode creates sloped roof slabs. Depending on the option chosen in this property, different properties are available in the **Dimensions** category.

Figure 18-18.
The **Properties**
palette is used to set
the properties for a
new roof slab.

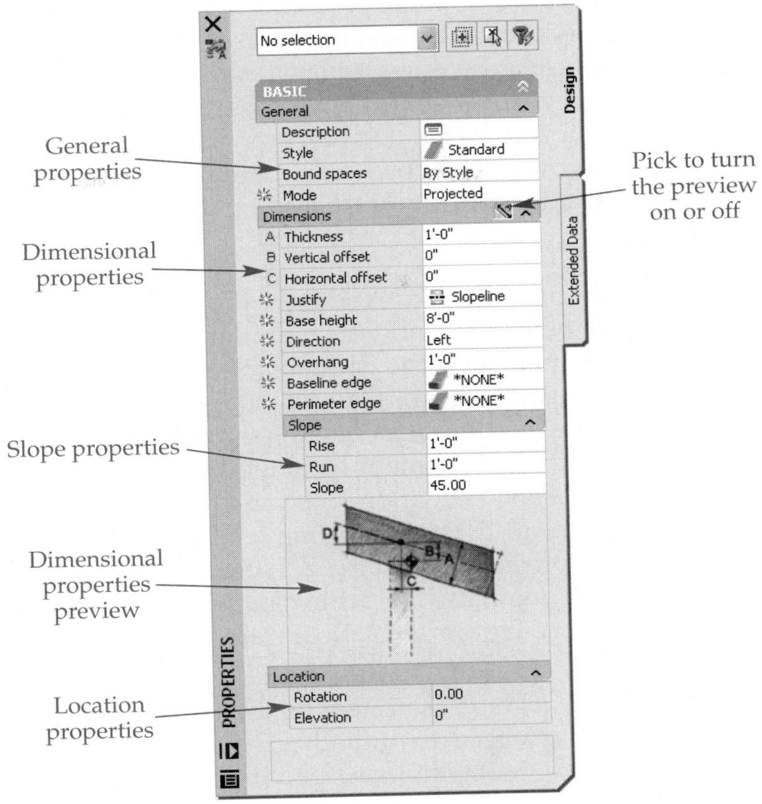

General
properties

Dimensional
properties

Slope properties

Dimensional
properties
preview

Location
properties

Pick to turn
the preview
on or off

Dimensions Category

The **Dimensions** category is used to control the dimensions for the roof slab being drawn. Direct and projected roof slabs share many properties and also include some unique ones. The following properties are available for both direct and projected roof slabs.

- **Thickness.** This text box property is used to specify a roof slab thickness. Depending on the slab style, components within the roof slab can be assigned a variable or specified thickness.
- **Vertical offset.** Enter a value in this text box property to set a vertical offset for the pivot point, measured from the top of the base height, or plate line, of the roof.
- **Horizontal offset.** This text box property controls the horizontal offset of the pivot point from the slopeline of the roof slab.
- **Justify.** Use this drop-down list property to set the justification for the Roof Slab object. The justifications available include **Top**, **Center**, **Bottom**, and **Slopeline**. By default, the **Slopeline** justification is selected and represents the sloping edge of the roof slab.
- **Base height.** This property is available if the **Projected** mode was selected for the roof slab. The base height represents the top plate of the walls on which the roof slab sits.
- **Direction.** This property is used to specify how the slab is drawn, relative to the baseline.
- **Overhang.** Enter a value in this text box property to set an overhang distance for the first two points specified, which create the slopeline edge of the roof slab.
- **Baseline edge.** This property includes a list of roof slab edge styles in the drawing that can be used for the overhang or slopeline edge of the roof slab. Initially, only the Standard style is available. Additional styles representing fascias and soffits can be created or imported to create a special overhang. The creation of roof slab edge styles is discussed later in this chapter.

- **Perimeter edge.** This property is similar to the **Baseline edge** property. Select a roof slab edge style to use around the edges of the roof slab, except the baseline edge.

The **Slope** subcategory is available when the **Projected** mode has been selected in the **General** category. The **Rise** text box property is used to set the rise for the roof slab slope. Enter a value in the **Run** text box property to set the run for the roof slab slope. The **Slope** text box property allows you to enter a sloping angle for the slope of the roof slab. This value is automatically set, based on the **Rise** and **Run** properties.

Location Category

This category includes two read-only properties: **Rotation** and **Elevation**. These properties display new information as points are picked in the drawing to establish the roof slab vertex points. Once the parameters for the roof slab have been determined, pick a point in the drawing to establish the first vertex point. This point also establishes the pivot point location. Selecting the second point of the roof slab determines the slopeline, which is the edge remaining along the roof plate. The remainder of the slab is sloped at the angle specified in the **Rise** and **Run** text boxes. Continue picking vertex points to establish the slab. The remaining selected points are picked in the current XY plane, but they are projected up in the Z axis to determine the proper slope. Once you have picked the last point, use the **Ortho close** or **Close** option on the shortcut menu to close the roof slab. See **Figure 18-19.** Roof slabs must be closed in order to be created.

PROFESSIONAL TIP

Points selected to establish roof slabs can be difficult to visualize initially. To make this process easier, sketch the roof plan using polylines to establish a 2D roof plan with hip, valley, and ridge lines. Use the **Roof Slab** tool to trace over the points of the 2D geometry, to place the roof slabs in the proper locations. Adjust the plate heights and slopes as necessary to create the 3D roof model.

Figure 18-19.
Selecting different combinations of points creates multisided roof slabs.

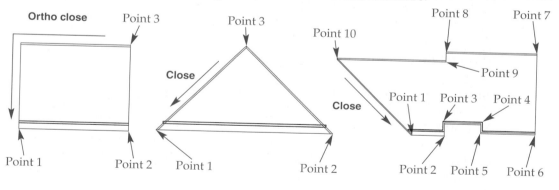

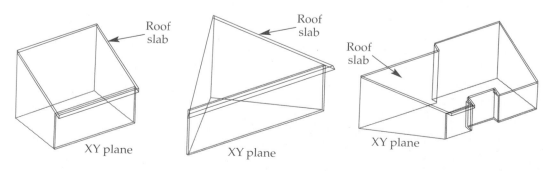

Exercise
18-7   Complete the Exercise on the Student CD.

Converting a Roof into Roof Slabs

The standard AEC Roof object is very good to use for laying out the basic shape of a roof. By modifying the plate heights and overhangs, you can utilize this type of roof to model many different roof situations. Sometimes, however, the Roof object is limited in its modeling abilities, especially when several different plate heights are used. Roofs at a lower plate height do not fill in under the eave of a roof at a higher plate height. Also, when a dormer or skylight is added, holes cannot be cut into a standard Roof object as they can be cut into a roof slab.

Both AEC Roof objects and roof slabs have positive and negative features. Roof objects can be quickly laid out, and the faces, or sides, of the roof can be generated automatically. Gable ends can quickly be modeled, and double-sloped roofs can be simply created. Advanced modeling techniques, however, such as adding fascias and soffits, adjusting roof edges, and cutting holes in a roof, cannot be used on the standard Roof object.

The use of roof slabs facilitates the addition of custom fascia and soffit edges, dormers, and holes for skylights. Each side of the roof needs to be added, however, and the sides do not automatically clean up or miter at the edges. Due to the advantages and disadvantages of Roof and Roof Slab objects, each type of object is used in certain situations to create a roof.

As indicated earlier in this chapter, it is highly recommended that you initially draw the basic roof shape with the standard Roof object. Make all adjustments to the overhangs and plate heights for the different edges, and then convert the Roof object into roof slabs to take advantage of all the advanced editing capabilities of the standard Roof Slab object. To convert a standard Roof object into roof slabs, right-click over the **Roof Slab** tool in the tool palette and select **Apply Tool Properties to > Linework, Walls and Roof**; or pick the standard Roof object, right-click, and pick **Convert to Roof Slabs...** from the shortcut menu. When you are prompted, pick the Roof object. Erase the layout geometry, and press [Enter] to finished the command. When the **Convert to Roof Slabs...** option is selected after picking an existing roof to be converted, the **Convert to Roof Slabs** worksheet is displayed, allowing you to select an existing roof style in the drawing to be used for the converted roof, as well as allowing you to choose whether or not to erase the layout geometry.

This process allows you to specify if you will erase the original Roof object or not and then converts each slope of the Roof object into a roof slab. If you think you might need to make adjustments to the original roof, you can choose not to erase the original object. The default roof slab style is the Standard style. Once this process has been completed, the Roof object is converted into individual roof slabs and can be modified with any of the roof slab editing tools or the **Properties** palette.

Exercise
18-8   Complete the Exercise on the Student CD.

The **Roof Slab** tool's **Apply Tool Properties to > Linework, Walls and Roof** option can also be used to convert walls and polylines into roof slabs. Converting these two types of objects can give unexpected results. When walls are converted into a roof slab, each wall is used to create an individual square-shaped slab. See Figure 18-20. The top of the wall is used as the slopeline, and the starting and ending points of the wall

Figure 18-20.
Conversion of walls
into roof slabs
converts each wall
into its own roof
slab. Additional
editing is required
to miter the edges
of each side of the roof.

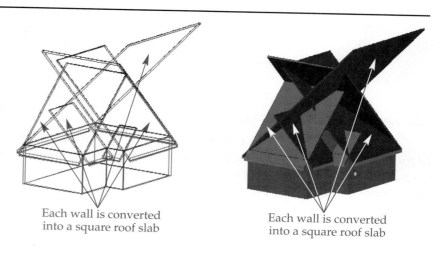

Each wall is converted
into a square roof slab

Each wall is converted
into a square roof slab

are used as the first and second points of the roof slab. This conversion does not miter the edges between two sides of the building, however, which must be done manually. Conversion of a polyline changes the shape of the polyline into one roof slab, as shown in **Figure 18-21.** The first and second points of the polyline are used as the first and second points for the roof slab and establish the slopeline.

Using the Properties Palette to Modify Roof Slabs

Existing roof slabs can also be modified through the **Properties** palette. When a Roof Slab object is selected in the drawing window, the properties for the selected roof slab appear in the **Properties** palette. Some of the properties are available when creating the roof slab and can be modified from their original settings. The following new properties are available when editing roof slabs through the **Properties** palette:

- **Layer.** This property lists the layer to which the roof slab is assigned. By default, new roof slabs are created on the A-Roof-Slab layer. If the roof slab is to be assigned to a different layer, select a different layer for the roof slab.
- **Shadow display.** This property controls how the roof slab casts or receives shadows.
- **Edges.** Pick this property to display the **Roof Slab Edges** worksheet. This worksheet is used to assign fascias and soffits to the edges of a roof slab. Modifying roof slab edges is discussed later in this chapter.

Figure 18-21.
Conversion of a
polyline converts
the entire polyline
into one Roof Slab
object.

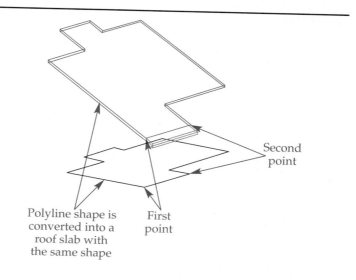

Second
point

Polyline shape is
converted into a
roof slab with
the same shape

First
point

- **Hold fascia elevation.** When roofs using different roof pitches are created, the fascia (edge of the overhang) adjusts, depending on the angle of the slope-line. Picking this property displays three options: **By adjusting overhang**, **By adjusting baseline height**, and **No**. The **By adjusting overhang** value maintains the fascia's elevation location of the overhang by changing the overhang value. This might cause overhang edges of varying widths. The **By adjusting baseline height** value maintains the fascia elevation location by moving the baseline (roof plate line) up or down. The **No** option maintains a consistent overhang edge and roof plate height for the slab. This causes roof slabs of varying pitches to have different fascia elevations.
- **Pivot Point X.** This property indicates the pivot point's X axis position.
- **Pivot Point Y.** This property indicates the pivot point's Y axis position.
- **Pivot Point Z.** This property indicates the pivot point's Z axis position.
- **Elevation.** This property indicates the roof slab's roof plate height. Change the value if the roof slab needs to be placed at a different elevation height.
- **Additional information.** Picking this property displays the **Location** worksheet. Use this worksheet to control the elevation and rotation angle of the selected roof slab.

When you are finished editing the roof slab properties, press the [Esc] key to clear the grip boxes from the roof slab.

Using Grips to Modify Roof Slabs

When a roof slab is picked, grip boxes are displayed around the object, as in **Figure 18-22.** Selecting the grips allows you to modify the overhang, slope, edge location, or pivot point location. Hover over each grip box to display a tooltip about the grip. Picking a **Vertex** grip allows you to modify the location of the vertex, maintaining the slope of the roof, no matter where the grip point is moved. When an **Edge Overhang** grip is picked, the overhang for the edge can be adjusted. If an overhang does not exist, stretching the grip adds an overhang to the edge.

When an **Edge** grip is hovered over, a tooltip with additional options is available. This tooltip allows you to access the different options by pressing the [Ctrl] key after

Figure 18-22.
Use grips to adjust vertices, edges, edge overhangs, and the slope of a roof slab.

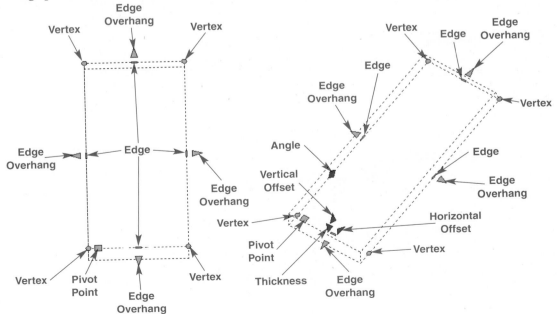

picking the **Edge** grip. The options include **Move edge - maintain slope, Move edge - change slope, Add new edges - maintain slope, Add new edges - change slope, Convert to Arc - maintain slope**, and **Offset all edges - maintain slope**.

The **Angle** grip is used to change the angle, or slope, of the roof slab. The **Thickness** grip is used to adjust the thickness of the roof slab. Pick the **Vertical Offset** and **Horizontal Offset** grips to adjust the offset location of the pivot point, in relation to the inserted point of the first vertex. The **Pivot Point** grip can also be moved to specify a new pivoting location when the roof slab's slope is adjusted.

Editing Roof Slab Edges

The edges of a roof slab can be assigned a fascia and soffit profile to enhance the overhang edge of a roof. Architectural Desktop includes several roof slab styles, found in the **Slabs** palette of the **Design** tool palette group, with roof slab edge styles already assigned. Roof slab edge styles can also be imported into the drawing through the **Style Manager**. To apply a **Roof Slab** tool with an edge to an existing roof slab, right-click on the tool, and pick **Apply Tool Properties to** > **Roof Slab**. The properties of the tool are then transferred to the roof slabs you select.

If only roof slab edge styles are to be imported into the drawing, pick **Design** > **Roofs** > **Roof Slab Edge Styles...** from the pull-down menu. This will open the **Style Manager** opened to the Roof Slab Edge Styles section. Use the **Open Drawing** button to browse for Roof Slab & Roof Slab Edge Styles (Imperial).dwg or Roof Slab & Roof Slab Edge Styles (Metric).dwg. As with other styles, drag and drop any desired roof slab edge styles into your drawing. This process is discussed in greater detail in the next section.

Once a few roof slab edge styles have been imported into your drawing, the styles can be assigned to any roof slab edge. Individual roof edges can use different combinations of roof slab edge styles. To assign a roof slab edge style to the edge of a roof slab, pick the roof slab, access the **Properties** palette, and pick the **Edges** property. This displays the **Roof Slab Edges** worksheet, which is shown in **Figure 18-23**. The worksheet includes a table of edges on the left side and a preview of the selected roof slab

Figure 18-23.
The **Roof Slab Edges** worksheet is used to modify the edges of a roof slab.

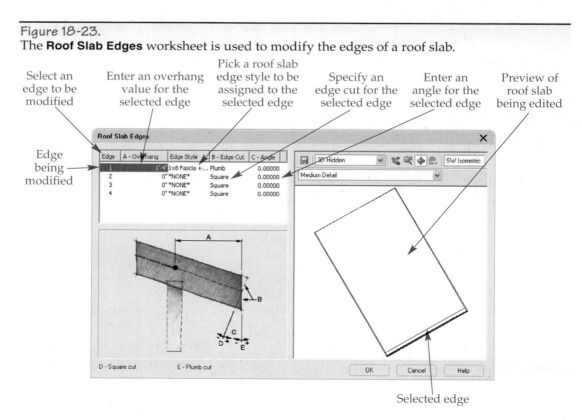

Architectural Desktop and Its Applications

on the right. Selecting an edge from the **Edge** column highlights the associated edge in the preview. The following values in the **Roof Slab Edges** worksheet can be modified by picking on top of their existing values:

- **Overhang.** This column is used to specify the overhang distance for the roof slab edge. Pick on top of the existing value to reveal a text box. Enter the new overhang distance in the text box.
- **Edge Style.** This column is used to assign a roof slab edge style to the selected edge. Picking on top of the existing value displays a drop-down list with the roof slab edge styles available in the drawing. Select a different edge style from the list to assign it to the highlighted roof edge.
- **Edge Cut.** This column controls whether the roof edge is cut at an angle (square) or plumb to the ground. Selecting the existing value provides a drop-down list with the **Plumb** and **Square** options. The **Plumb** option always makes the edge of the slab perpendicular to the ground. The **Square** option squares the end of the slab between the top and bottom edge of the slab.
- **Angle.** This column is used to specify a bevel angle for the roof edge. Pick in the area below the column to enter an angular value for the slab edge.

Individual edges of a roof slab can also be edited one at a time. To do this, pick the roof slab to be edited, right-click, and pick **Edit Roof Slab Edges...** from the shortcut menu. Once the option has been entered, you are prompted to Select edges of one roof slab. Select the edges of the roof slab to be modified. When you have finished selecting the roof edges, press the [Enter] key to display the **Edit Roof Slab Edges** worksheet. This worksheet is similar to the **Roof Slab Edges** worksheet. Instead of displaying all the edges in the selected roof slab, only edges that were selected are listed in the table. Use the **Overhang**, **Edge Style**, **Edge Cut**, and **Angle** columns to modify the edges of the roof slab.

Roof Slab and Roof Slab Edge Styles

A few roof slab and roof slab edge styles are available for use in the creation of your roofs. Custom roof slab styles with multiple components and roof slab edge styles can be created to reflect the design of your roof. Additionally, edge styles applied to the edge of a roof slab can have their shapes edited in place. Any modifications done in place are automatically updated within the edge style.

Creating Roof Slab Styles

Custom roof slab styles can be created by picking **Design** > **Roofs** > **Roof Slab Styles...** from the pull-down menu. Once the **Style Manager** is displayed, select the **New Style** button to create a new roof slab style, and then enter a name for the new roof slab style. See **Figure 18-24**. After naming the style, highlight it in the left tree view to display the properties for the new roof slab. Roof slab styles include the following five tabs used to configure the style:

- **General.** This tab is used to rename and provide a description for the roof slab style; attach documents, spreadsheets, and keynotes; and assign a property set definition to the style.
- **Components.** Similar to Slab objects, roof slabs can be composed of several individual components. Use this tab to add, modify, or delete roof slab components, such as rafters, sheathing, and roofing.
- **Materials.** Use this tab to assign materials, such as shake, shingle, tile, wood, insulation, and metal, to the slab components. If the desired materials are not available, import them by picking **Format** > **Material Definitions...** from the pull-down menu.

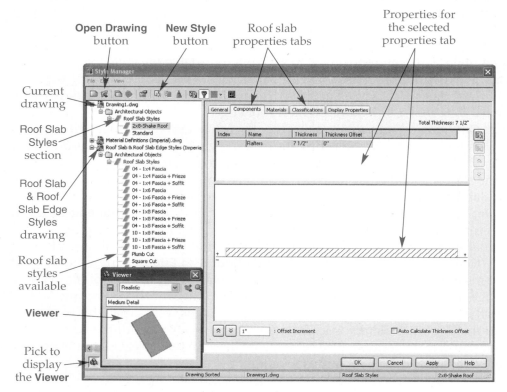

- **Classifications.** This tab is used to assign classification definitions to the roof slab style.
- **Display Properties.** This tab is used to control the appearance of the slab in Plan and Model representations. The Plan representation roof slab includes a cut plane height that can be specified to cut through the roof slab. In addition to the cut plane, Hatch components are assigned to each roof slab component and can be turned on or off for the different roof slab components. Both the Plan and Model representations include a Pivot Point component. You might decide to turn this component off or set it to a layer that will not plot, as the component will plot if turned on.

The **Components** tab is used to add roof slab components to the roof slab style, similar to the **Components** tab used when creating a slab style. See **Figure 18-25.** The **Components** tab includes a table of components and cross-sectional preview of the roof slab components. The table includes four columns: **Index**, **Name**, **Thickness**, and **Thickness Offset**. By default, a new roof slab style includes one component named Unnamed. Pick the component name in the **Name** column to rename the component.

Beside the **Name** component is the **Thickness** column. This column is similar to the slab's **Thickness** column. Selecting the **Thickness** area for the component displays a drop-down list arrow. Pick the arrow to specify the thickness of the roof slab component, as shown in **Figure 18-26.** The first text box is known as the base value. The base value specifies the base thickness of the roof slab component. A value of 0″ allows the component to be a variable thickness, based on the thickness you enter when adding a roof slab to the drawing. The Standard roof slab style is an example of a component using a base value of 0″.

If a value other than 0″ is entered in the base value text box, the thickness is fixed for this component. For example, if you are creating a 9 1/4″-thick rafter component, type 9 1/4″ in the base value text box. The component now has a fixed thickness of 9 1/4″ and cannot be changed when adding the roof slab to the drawing.

Figure 18-25.
The **Components** tab is used to add components for the roof slab style.

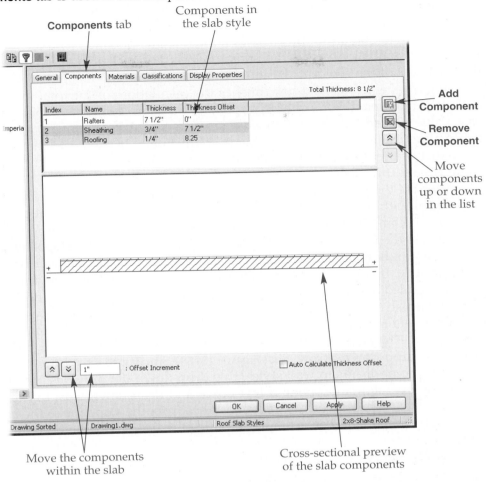

Figure 18-26.
The **Thickness** column is used to configure the thickness for a roof slab component.

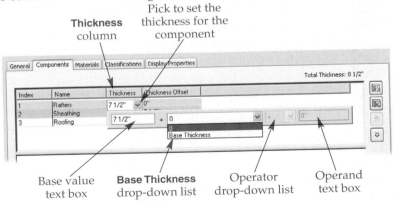

Beside the base value text box is a drop-down list known as the **Base Thickness**. There are two options here. If **0** is selected, the remaining text boxes are grayed out, and the thickness of the component is specified by the base value text box. The other option is the **Base Thickness** option. Base thickness refers to the **Thickness** property of the roof slab when the slab was added to the drawing. When **Base Thickness** is specified, the base value and base thickness are added together to specify the total thickness for the roof slab component. For example, a 0" base value **+ Base Thickness** creates a roof slab component the thickness specified in the **Thickness** property when adding a roof slab to the drawing; a 9 1/4" base value **+ Base Thickness** creates a roof slab the thickness specified in the **Thickness** property when adding the roof slab, plus 9 1/4".

When **Base Thickness** is selected, the last two text boxes are available. The drop-down list beside the base thickness is known as the operator. The operator includes **+, -, /,** and ***** symbols. Selecting an operator specifies a calculation to be performed on the thickness of the roof slab. Beside the operator drop-down is the operand text box. Entering a value in this text box finishes the calculation for the total thickness of the roof slab component. For example, a roof slab Insulation component that specified a 0" base value **+ Base Thickness / 4** would create a roof slab component a quarter of the total value of the base value plus the base thickness. In most situations, a roof slab component either has a set thickness in the base value **+ 0"** base thickness or a 0" base value **+ Base Thickness**.

After the thickness for the component has been determined, the placement of the component within the roof slab can be specified. The **Thickness Offset** column is used to place the component in relation to other components in the style. When roof slabs are added to the drawing, one of the roof slab justifications is the **Slopeline** option. This justification indicates that the roof slab is drawn from the slopeline or baseline of the roof slab style. If you are looking at the roof slab in an elevation view, the slab components are added to the style by measuring a distance from the slopeline to the bottom edge of the slab component. See **Figure 18-27**. A positive distance moves the bottom of the component up, and a negative distance moves the bottom of the component down.

Pick the **Thickness Offset** area for the roof slab component being adjusted. This displays a drop-down arrow. See **Figure 18-28**. Similar to the drop-down list used for adding components to wall styles, this drop-down list provides base value, **Base Thickness**, operator, and operand text boxes and drop-down lists. In the base value text box, enter the positive or negative distance from the slopeline to the bottom edge of the slab component. For example, a value of 8 1/4" places the bottom edge of the component a positive 8 1/4" from the slopeline. A -7 1/2" places the bottom edge of the component a negative 7 1/2" from the slopeline.

NOTE

> In most cases, roof slab components are placed at a specific distance from the slopeline, whether it is a positive or negative distance. Generally, the **Base Thickness** drop-down list is set to **0** for each of the components, unless the component is to vary in placement based on the thickness of the roof slab. This is a difficult process to master. Experiment with the operators. Review an existing Architectural Desktop complex roof slab style that allows you to specify a roof slab thickness for ideas on how to use the operators and operands.

Figure 18-27.
The bottom of a roof slab component is placed an offset distance, measured from the bottom of the component to the slopeline.

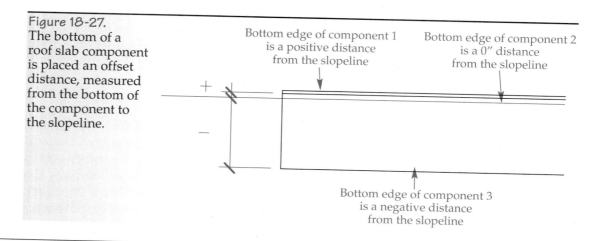

Bottom edge of component 1 is a positive distance from the slopeline

Bottom edge of component 2 is a 0" distance from the slopeline

Bottom edge of component 3 is a negative distance from the slopeline

Architectural Desktop and Its Applications

Figure 18-28.
The **Thickness Offset** is used to place the slab component in relation to the slopeline of the slab.

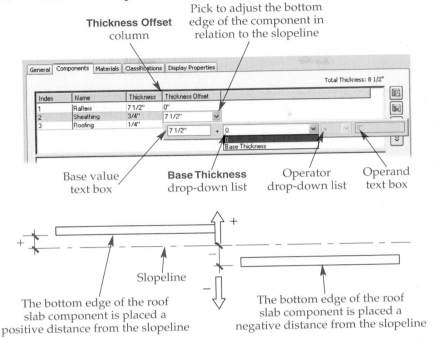

As with the thickness values, the **Base Thickness** drop-down list includes two options: **0** and **Base Thickness**. If **0** is specified, the bottom edge of the component will always be located at the base value location. If **Base Thickness** is specified, the base value is added to the **Thickness** property specified when drawing a new roof slab. This sets the bottom edge of the component a total distance of the base value plus the base thickness from the slopeline. Beside the **Base Thickness** drop-down list is the operator drop-down list. This drop-down list includes the **+, -, /,** and ***** operators, which can be used in an equation to specify the location of the slab component.

The last text box is the operand. An equation for the location of the slab component can be constructed by specifying a base value, a base thickness, an operator, and an operand. For example, the bottom edge of a component next to a variable thickness component can be specified by entering a 0" base value **+ Base Thickness +** 0". Another example is to create a roof slab component that is always centered on the slopeline, no matter what the thickness of the roof slab is. Use the equation 0" base value **+ Base Thickness * -1/2**. This indicates that the component looks to the **Thickness** property when adding a roof slab and multiplies the thickness by a negative one-half, repositioning the component so the bottom edge is half the distance of the thickness from the slopeline.

After the first component has been configured, additional roof slab components can be added to the style. Along the right side of the tab are four buttons: **Add Component, Remove Component, Move Component Up In List**, and **Move Component Down In List**. Use the **Add Component** button to add additional roof slab components. Along the bottom of the tab are the **Increment Slab Component Offset** and **Decrement Slab Component Offset** buttons and **: Offset Increment** text box. Use these buttons to adjust where the bottom edge of a component is placed in the style. Adjusting a component's location using these tools automatically adjusts the **Thickness Offset** value for the selected component.

NOTE

Additional roof slab styles can be imported into the current drawing through the **Style Manager**. Open Roof Slab & Roof Slab Edge Styles (Imperial).dwg or Roof Slab & Roof Slab Edge Styles (Metric).dwg. Drag and drop any desired roof slab styles onto the current drawing icon.

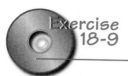

Exercise 18-9 **Complete the Exercise on the Student CD.**

Creating Roof Slab Edge Styles

Usually, when a roof slab is created from the **Slabs** tool palette, an edge is associated with it. To create a new roof slab edge style, pick **Design** > **Roofs** > **Roof Slab Edge Styles...** from the pull-down menu, create a new style, and then edit it. The Roof Slab Edge Styles section within the **Style Manager** includes the following four tabs:

- **General.** This tab is used to rename and enter a description for the style.
- **Defaults.** This tab specifies default values that control the edge of the roof slab. See Figure 18-29. As with the roof slab styles, these settings control only the default values for the slab edge. The values can be modified when the roof slab is added or modified.
- **Design Rules.** This tab is used to add a custom shape for the roof slab edge style. See Figure 18-30. Initially, two check boxes are available to customize the edge. The **Fascia** and **Soffit** check boxes allow you to add a custom shape for the fascia and soffit.

  A drop-down list is associated with each of these check boxes. The items included in the lists are AEC profiles defined in the drawing. Review Chapter 9 for information on how to create a profile. When you are creating a profile for use as a fascia or soffit, specify the insertion points on the profile as indicated in Figure 18-31.

Figure 18-29.
Set any defaults for the roof slab edge in the **Defaults** tab.

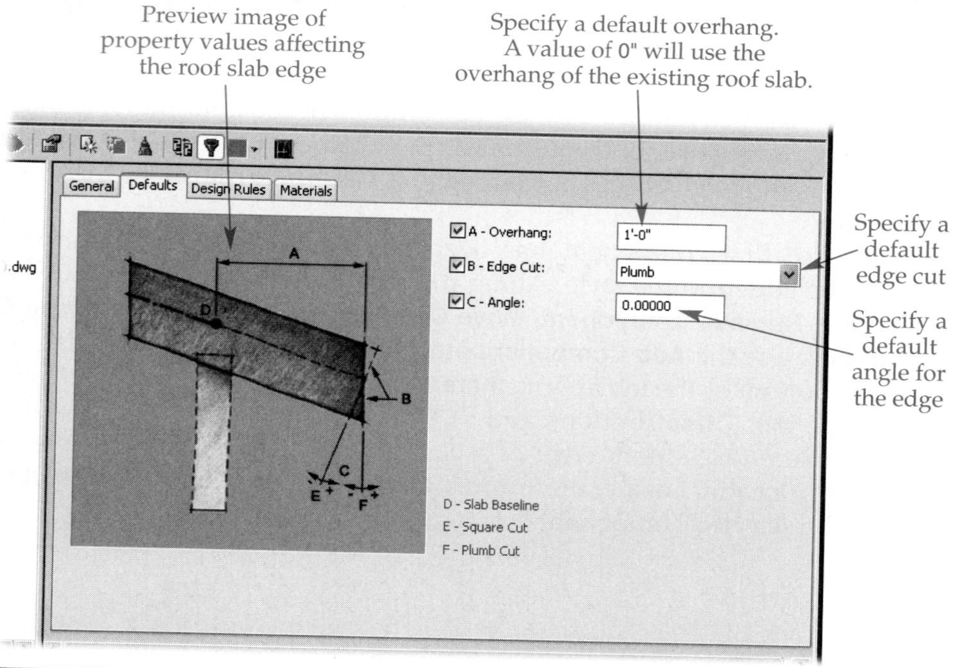
Preview image of property values affecting the roof slab edge
Specify a default overhang. A value of 0" will use the overhang of the existing roof slab.
General
Defaults
Design Rules
Materials
.dwg
A - Overhang:
1'-0"
B - Edge Cut:
Plumb
C - Angle:
0.00000
A
B
C
D
E
F
D - Slab Baseline
E - Square Cut
F - Plumb Cut
Specify a default edge cut
Specify a default angle for the edge

Figure 18-30.
The **Design Rules** tab is used to assign a fascia and soffit to the edge of a roof slab.

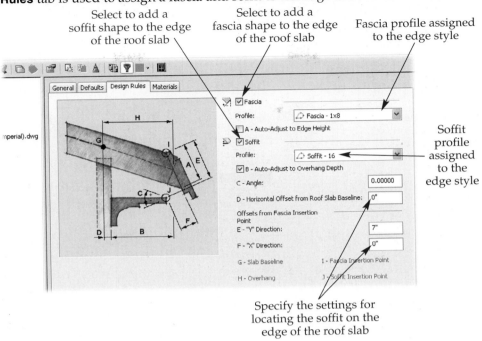

Select to add a soffit shape to the edge of the roof slab

Select to add a fascia shape to the edge of the roof slab

Fascia profile assigned to the edge style

Soffit profile assigned to the edge style

Specify the settings for locating the soffit on the edge of the roof slab

Figure 18-31.
Use the upper-left edge of the profile as the insertion point for the fascia profile. Use the upper-right edge of the profile as the insertion point for the soffit profile.

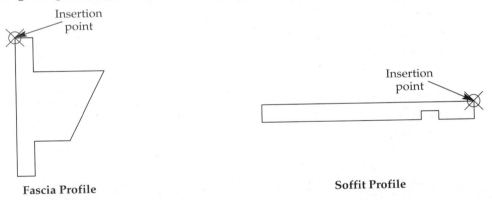

Insertion point

Fascia Profile

Insertion point

Soffit Profile

The **Fascia** area allows you to adjust the height of the profile to equal the height or thickness of the roof slab. Select the **Auto-Adjust to Edge Height** check box to automatically adjust the size of the fascia. The **Soffit** area also provides an option for adjusting the length to equal the width of the overhang by selecting the **Auto-Adjust to Overhang Depth** check box. Additionally, the **Soffit** area includes settings to locate the soffit in relation to the fascia profile.

- **Materials.** This tab is used to assign materials to the Fascia and Soffit components of a roof slab edge.

When you have finished specifying the roof slab edge style, the style is ready to be assigned to a roof slab style or placed on the edge of an existing roof slab.

Exercise
18-10   Complete the Exercise on the Student CD.

Figure 18-32.
When you are editing an edge profile in place, adjust the grips to create a new shape, or use the shortcut menu to add additional vertices or replace the profile ring.

Save All Changes button

Use grips to stretch the locations of the vertices

Use the shortcut menu to add vertices or replace the profile ring

After a roof slab has had an edge style assigned to one of its edges, the profile of the edge can be modified in place. Similar to other edit-in-place operations discussed throughout this text, the fascia and soffit profiles can be modified in place without re-creating a profile. To modify an edge in place, select a roof slab with an edge style assigned, right-click, and pick **Edit Edge Profile In Place**. After picking this option, you are prompted to Select an edge of the roofslab for editing. Pick the desired edge to be modified.

After picking the edge, the **In-Place Edit** toolbar is displayed. A cross section of the profile being edited is also displayed as a hatch pattern with grips. See **Figure 18-32.** Use the grips to stretch the profile into a new shape, or right-click to add new vertices to create a new shape. If a new closed polyline is drawn to be used as the edge shape, it can replace the existing edge profile by right-clicking and selecting **Replace Ring**. When you are finished making changes to the profile edge, pick the **Save All Changes** button in the **In-Place Edit** toolbar.

Using Roof Slab Tools to Modify Roof Slabs

Roof slabs are similar to standard Slab objects. They include several tools, which are discussed in the following sections. These tools can be used to modify the shapes of the slabs.

Trimming Roof Slabs

Roof Slab objects include a **Trim** tool that can be used to trim a roof slab against a trimming plane. The trimming plane can be a polyline, slab, or wall. If a polyline is used as a trimming plane, the polyline must extend to the edge or past the edge of the roof slab to be trimmed.

Once the trimming planes have been established in the drawing, the roof slab can be trimmed away from the trimming plane. When a roof slab is trimmed, part of the roof slab is removed from the drawing. If the part of the roof slab being trimmed includes a custom roof slab edge, that is also trimmed. The edge is trimmed at the point it intersects the trimming plane and cut at the same angle as the trimming plane.

To trim a roof slab, select the roof slab, right-click, and pick **Trim** from the shortcut menu. Once the command is entered, you are prompted to Select trimming object (a slab, wall, or polyline). Select the trimming object, and then pick the side to be trimmed, to trim the roof slab and finish the command.

To trim a slab away from a polyline, access the **ROOFSLABTRIM** command. When you are prompted, select the polyline, and then pick the side of the roof slab to be trimmed. See **Figure 18-33**.

NOTE It is not possible to trim only an overhang. The trimming plane must intersect the defined boundary of the slab at some location, in order to trim the overhang.

Extending Roof Slabs

Roof slabs' edges can be extended to a Wall, another Slab, or a Roof Slab object. When a roof slab is extended, the edge being extended is being moved to the face of the wall or other slab. The edges on either side of the edge being moved are the actual edges being extended. See **Figure 18-34**. To access the **ROOFSLABEXTEND** command, select the roof slab to be edited, right-click, and pick **Extend**.

After entering this option, you are prompted to Select an object to extend to (a slab or wall). Pick a Wall or Slab object to which the roof slab will be extended. This is known as the boundary object. Once the object has been picked, you are prompted to select the edges to be lengthened. Pick the edges on either side of the roof slab edge being moved. To extend an edge, access the **ROOFSLABEXTEND** command. See **Figure 18-34**. Referring to **Figure 18-34**, when you are prompted to select an object to extend to, select the dormer wall. Pick one edge of the roof slab to be extended, and then pick the second edge.

Mitering Roof Slabs

Occasionally, when roof slabs are modified, the edges of the roof slabs overlap or do not touch each other to form a clean edge. A clean edge can be attained by mitering the edges of the roof slabs. When two roof slabs are mitered, the edge of each roof slab is joined together, with a miter angle applied to each edge where the two slabs meet. The **ROOFSLABMITER** command can be accessed by selecting one of the roof slabs to be mitered, right-clicking, and then picking **Miter**. The **ROOFSLABMITER** command includes two methods of mitering the roof slab. These options are described in the next sections.

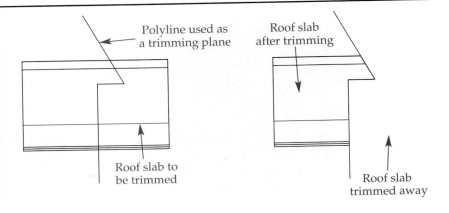

Figure 18-33.
Trimming a roof slab away from a polyline.

Polyline used as a trimming plane

Roof slab after trimming

Roof slab to be trimmed

Roof slab trimmed away

Figure 18-34.

The roof slab needs to be extended to the dormer wall. The side edge needs to be moved, and the top and bottom edges need to be extended. The roof slab is extended to the dormer wall.

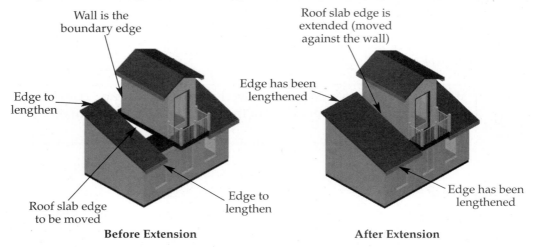

Wall is the boundary edge

Roof slab edge is extended (moved against the wall)

Edge to lengthen

Edge has been lengthened

Roof slab edge to be moved

Edge to lengthen

Edge has been lengthened

Before Extension

After Extension

Mitering by Intersection

The **Intersection** option of the **Miter** tool is used when two slabs intersect each other, as at the ridge, valley, or hip lines of the roof slabs being modified. See **Figure 18-35.** The **Intersection** option miters the two slabs at the intersection of the two edges. The new edges of the two slabs are then set to an angle that creates a true miter between the roof slabs. To miter two roof slabs, access the **ROOFSLABMITER** command. Select the **Intersection** option. When you are prompted, select an edge of a roof slab on the side of the roof slab that will be kept, and then select an edge of the other roof slab on the side that will be kept.

NOTE
> If you are mitering two slabs that include overhangs, ensure that the overhangs overlap each other before mitering, to cause the edges at the overhangs to be mitered as well. Use grips to stretch the edge of the roof slab past the overhang of the other slab to be mitered. Miter the two roof slabs.

Figure 18-35.

Two roof slabs cross through each other at the hip line. The two roof slabs are mitered.

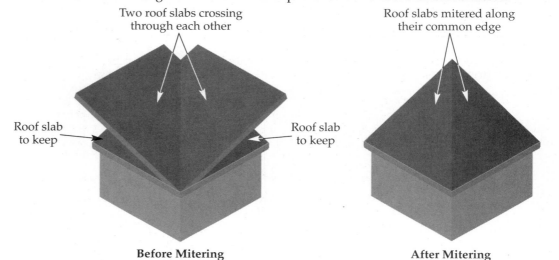

Two roof slabs crossing through each other

Roof slabs mitered along their common edge

Roof slab to keep

Roof slab to keep

Before Mitering

After Mitering

Mitering by Edge

Another way of mitering the edges of two roof slabs is by edge. This option allows you to miter the edges of two slabs even when they do not intersect each other, as in Figure 18-36. If the slabs do not intersect, the edges are extended to the point at which they meet. If the two slabs cross through each other, the slabs are trimmed, similar to the **Intersection** option. To miter slabs by edge, access the **ROOFSLABMITER** command. Type E to choose the **Edges** option. When you are prompted, select the edges of the first and second roof slabs to miter.

Cutting Roof Slabs

The **ROOFSLABCUT** command cuts the slab, but it retains both portions of the roof slab. A polyline or 3D object with mass can be used as a cutting tool to cut a roof slab. If a polyline is used as the cutting plane, it can be a closed polyline or an open polyline that crosses through the roof slab. If an open polyline crosses in and out of the roof slab, multiple roof slabs are created.

3D objects that can be used to cut a roof slab include walls, slabs, roof slabs, mass elements, and AutoCAD solids. When a 3D object is used as a cutting tool, the object must extend through the roof slab at both the top and bottom sides. If the objective is to create two individual roof slabs, the 3D object must also extend through the edges of the roof slab. If the 3D object does not extend through the edges of the roof slab, a hole is cut out of the roof slab.

To use the **ROOFSLABCUT** command, first select the desired roof slab, right-click, and pick **Cut**. After entering this option, you are prompted to Select cutting objects (a polyline or connected solid objects). Select the object to be used as the cutting plane or boundary. After picking the cutting object, press [Enter] to finish the command. If the cutting object is a polyline, you are prompted to Erase layout geometry [Yes/No] <No>. Type YES to erase the polyline or NO to retain the polyline. If the cutting object is a 3D object, the roof slab is immediately cut into two pieces on either side of the object.

To cut a slab, access the **ROOFSLABCUT** command. When you are prompted, select a cutting object (a polyline). Do not erase the layout geometry. See Figure 18-37.

Figure 18-36.
Two roof slabs do not meet at the hip line. Select the edge of one roof slab to use as the first edge to be mitered, and then pick the second edge to use as the second mitered edge. The finished roof has mitered edges.

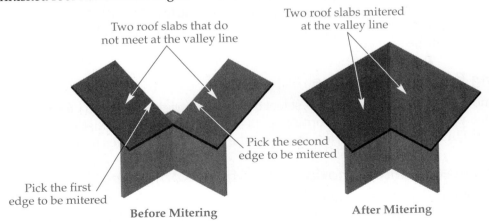

Two roof slabs that do not meet at the valley line

Two roof slabs mitered at the valley line

Pick the second edge to be mitered

Pick the first edge to be mitered

Before Mitering

After Mitering

Figure 18-37.
Use the roof slab's **Cut** command to cut the slab into two pieces. Both pieces are retained in the drawing.

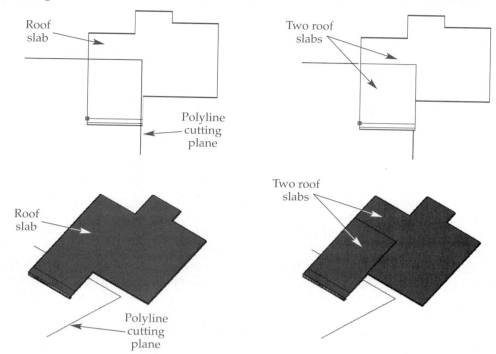

Adding Roof Slab Vertices

When roof slabs are initially created, the points selected become the vertex points for the roof slab. Occasionally, when a roof slab is modified, an additional edge or vertex needs to be added. Adding a vertex along the edge of a roof slab creates two new edges. Adding a new vertex is useful when an edge is not available to be used in the **ROOFSLABEXTEND** command.

To add vertices to a roof slab, pick the roof slab, right-click, and select **Add Vertex**. You are prompted to Specify point for new vertex. Pick a new location along a roof slab edge to add the new vertex point. After the vertex is added, a grip is placed at the new point. This grip can also have its position modified.

To add vertices to a slab edge, access the **ROOFSLABADDVERTEX** command. When you are prompted to specify the point for the new vertex, type MID. Select the midpoint of one of the slab edges.

Removing Roof Slab Vertices

To remove vertices from a roof slab, select the roof slab, right-click, and pick **Remove Vertex**. Once you have entered this option, pick a point on top of an existing vertex to be removed. This removes the vertex and joins the two adjacent edges together.

Adding Holes to and Removing Holes from Roof Slabs

The addition of skylights and dormers to a roof generally requires a hole to be placed in the roof. The **ROOFSLABHOLE** command can be used for this purpose. When a hole is added to a roof slab, the new vertices and edges are created at the perimeter of the hole.

Holes can be generated from a closed polyline or 3D object, such as a wall, a mass element, a slab, or an AutoCAD solid. When a polyline is used to create a hole, it must be within the boundary edge of the slab and projected through the roof slab. If a 3D

Figure 18-38.
Four walls are being used to create a chimney. The hole can be cut on the inside or outside of the four walls.

Add a hole in the roof slab for a chimney

Hole added and cut to the outside of the chimney walls

Four walls extending through the top and bottom of the roof slab will be used to add a hole

object is used, the object must physically extend through both the top and bottom faces of the roof slab. If the solid objects create a void in the slab, such as the four walls of a chimney, you are prompted to cut the hole on the inside or outside of the 3D objects. See **Figure 18-38.**

To add a hole, pick the roof slab, right-click, and pick **Hole** > **Add**. You are prompted to Select closed polylines or connected solid objects to define holes. Pick a closed polyline or 3D objects to be used as a hole. To cut a hole in a roof slab with four connected walls for a chimney and place the edges of the hole against the outside of the four walls, first access the **ROOFSLABADDHOLE** command. See **Figure 18-38.** When you are prompted, use a crossing window or window to select the four walls. Do not erase the layout geometry. Choose the **Outside** option.

To remove a hole, select the roof slab, right-click, and pick **Hole** > **Remove**. You are prompted to Select an edge of hole to remove. Pick an edge of the hole within the roof slab. The hole is filled, and the edges of the hole are removed from the slab.

Exercise 18-11 **Complete the Exercise on the Student CD.**

Using Body Modifiers and Interference Conditions

Occasionally, when creating a roof, you might need to add additional detail. For example, the addition of dentils and cornice details cannot be added to the roof through any of the roof commands. These types of details can be incorporated into the roof slab, however, after they have been created using a body modifier or an interference condition has been applied to the slab.

Using Body Modifiers in Roof Slabs

When using a body modifier, a 3D object can be added to, be subtracted from, or replace a roof slab component. Body modifiers can be applied as rafters in a framed roof system, as roof vents, or as gable end trim boards. See **Figure 18-39.**

To add a body modifier, first create the 3D geometry that will be used as the body modifier and place it in the correct orientation on or in the roof slab. Next, pick the roof slab, right-click, and pick **Body Modifiers** > **Add...** from the shortcut menu. After entering this option, you are prompted to Select objects to apply as body

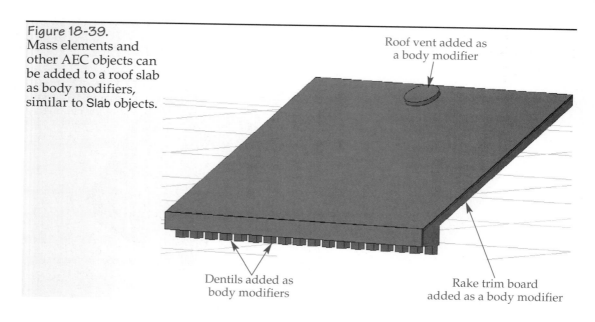

Figure 18-39.
Mass elements and other AEC objects can be added to a roof slab as body modifiers, similar to Slab objects.

Roof vent added as a body modifier

Dentils added as body modifiers

Rake trim board added as a body modifier

modifiers. Select any objects that will be used as body modifiers. After selecting the objects, press the [Enter] key. This displays the **Add Body Modifier** dialog box, which is shown in **Figure 18-40.** Select the component to be affected by the body modifier. In the **Operation:** drop-down list, choose whether the body modifiers are considered **Additive** to, are considered **Subtractive** from, or will **Replace** the roof slab component. When you are finished, pick the **OK** button to finish the operation.

After a body modifier has been added to a slab component, the area modified by the 3D object can be modified in place. To adjust a body modifier in place, pick the roof slab, right-click, and pick **Body Modifiers > Edit In Place**. This displays the **In-Place Edit** toolbar and an object where the body modifier was applied. Use the grips to adjust the body modifier, or right-click to select different modifying tools from the shortcut menu. When you are finished making the change, pick the **Save All Changes** button in the **In-Place Edit** toolbar.

In addition to adding and modifying body modifiers, roof slabs can be restored by removing the body modifier from the roof slab. Pick the roof slab, right-click, and pick **Body Modifiers > Restore**. When this command is entered, you are prompted to Remove Body Modifiers? [Yes/No]: <No>. Typing NO restores an erased 3D object used to create the body modifier and keeps the body modifier applied to the roof slab, and typing YES removes the body modifier from the slab and restores the erased 3D object used as the body modifier.

Figure 18-40.
The **Add Body Modifier** worksheet is used to add, subtract, or replace a body modifier with a slab component.

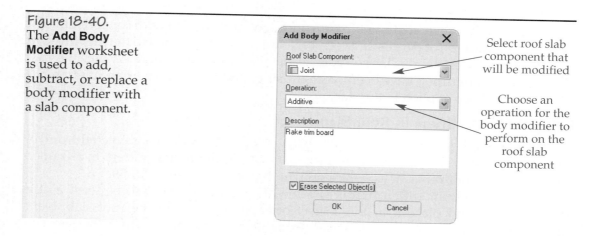

Select roof slab component that will be modified

Choose an operation for the body modifier to perform on the roof slab component

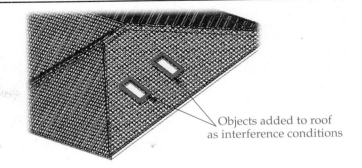

Figure 18-41.
A skylight created
from a window
style is added to
the roof slab as
an interference
condition.

Objects added to roof
as interference conditions

Using Interference Conditions in Roof Slabs

When an interference condition is used, the original geometry used to create the interference must remain in the drawing, in order for the interference to be added to or removed from the roof slab. Interferences can be used where structural members such as ceiling joists cross through a roof slab, such as a column or post that must pass through a slab. Objects representing HVAC venting or skylights can also be used as interferences to a roof slab where they pass through the Slab object, as in **Figure 18-41**.

To add an interference condition to a roof slab, select the roof slab, right-click, and pick **Interference Condition > Add**. On entering the command, you are prompted to Select objects to add. Select any objects to be used as interference conditions to the slab. After selecting the items, press the [Enter] key. The next prompt asks you to Enter shrinkwrap effect [Additive/Subtractive]. The **Additive** effect causes the shrink-wrap for the roof slab to wrap around the interfering object. The **Subtractive** effect causes the shrink-wrap to be subtracted from the roof slab shrink-wrap.

Interferences can also be removed from a slab. Pick the Slab object that includes the interference condition, right-click, and pick **Interference Condition > Remove**. You are prompted to Select object to remove. Select any desired interfering objects that will be removed from the slab.

Creating a Roof Dormer

The **Roof Dormer** command is used to cut a hole in a roof slab for a dormer and then miter the edges of the dormer roof with the face of the main roof slab. To create a roof dormer, you must create all the parts of the dormer first. Construct the dormer as a minihouse, with all the walls that create a room, plus the roof on top of the dormer walls. Include the back wall, because all the walls are used to cut a hole in the main roof slab. See **Figure 18-42**.

NOTE
In order for the dormer to be constructed properly, the walls must extend past the end (ridgeline) of the roof slab.

Once you have created the dormer, enter the **Roof Dormer** command. This command is accessed by picking the main roof slab to have a dormer added, right-clicking, and selecting the **Roof Dormer** command from the shortcut menu. After accessing the command, you are prompted to Select objects that form the dormer. Pick the four walls and the roof slabs creating the dormer. After the objects have been selected, the Slice wall with roof slab [Yes/No] <Yes> prompt is displayed. Press the [Enter] key to adjust the bottom of the walls of the dormer to sit on top of the main roof slab automatically.

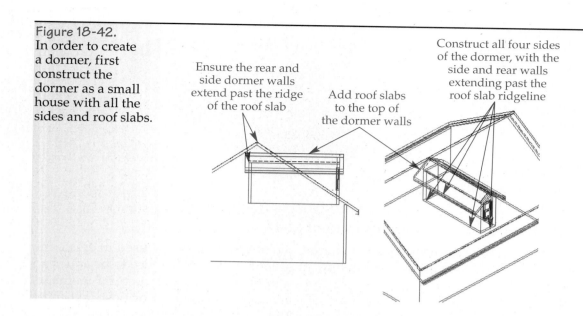

Figure 18-42.
In order to create a dormer, first construct the dormer as a small house with all the sides and roof slabs.

Ensure the rear and side dormer walls extend past the ridge of the roof slab

Add roof slabs to the top of the dormer walls

Construct all four sides of the dormer, with the side and rear walls extending past the roof slab ridgeline

To create a dormer, access the **ROOFSLABDORMER** command. When you are prompted, select the first, second, third, and fourth walls forming the dormer. After the rear wall is erased and the dormer is mitered correctly against the main roof slab, select the two dormer roof slabs. When you are asked if you want to its slice the wall with the roof slab, type Y to slice the walls against the top of the main roof slab. See **Figure 18-43.** After the dormer walls are sliced, the dormer and main roof slabs are mitered, the dormer walls are projected to the top face of the main roof slab, and a hole is cut in the main roof slab. The rear wall can now be erased, if it is no longer required.

NOTE

> The **Roof Dormer** command is good for creating standard roof dormers. You might run into situations, however, in which you have to use standard roof slab editing tools to cut the hole for the dormer and miter the edges of the dormer roof slabs with the main roof slab. Use the **Floor Line** command to project the walls to the main roof dormer.

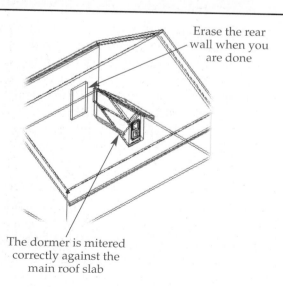

Figure 18-43.
The dormer has cut through the main slab, mitered the dormer roof, and sliced the dormer walls against the main roof slab.

Erase the rear wall when you are done

The dormer is mitered correctly against the main roof slab

Chapter Test

Answer the following questions. Write your answers on a separate sheet of paper or complete the electronic chapter test on the Student CD.

1. When creating the roof overhang, what does the **Plumb** edge cut perform?
2. What does a **Rise** value of 6″ indicate?
3. Identify how the normal plate height is established.
4. What does the **upper height** value specify?
5. What happens to the display when a roof is selected, and where are the grip boxes located?
6. What can you do when you select a grip between two corner grips?
7. Describe the result of stretching a corner grip.
8. Explain how to create a gable end roof with grips.
9. Why is it easier to use the **Edit Edges/Faces** command to modify roof edges than the **Roof Edges and Faces** worksheet?
10. What is the color of the AEC roof when added in the Model and Plan representations?
11. What do you get when you hover over a grip box when editing a roof slab?
12. Describe what you can do when you pick a vertex grip for editing a roof slab.
13. How do you adjust the overhang for the edge of a roof slab when grip editing?
14. Briefly explain how to add a roof slab overhang when grip editing.
15. When an **Edge** grip is hovered over, a tooltip with additional options is available. Identify how you access these options.

Use the techniques covered in this chapter to create the following drawings.

1. Single-Level Residential Project
   A. Access the **Project Browser** and set Residential-Project-01 current.
   B. Access the **Constructs** tab of the **Project Navigator** and create a new construct named Roof. Assign the level to the Roof level. Open the Roof construct.
   C. Drag and drop the Main Floor construct into the drawing for use as a reference.
   D. Use the standard **Roof** tool to add a roof with the following parameters:
      a. **Edge Cut**: Plumb
      b. **Shape**: Single slope
      c. **Overhang**: 1'-0"
      d. **Plate height**: 8'-0"
      e. **Rise**: 7"
   E. Use grips and the **Edit Edges/Faces** command to modify the hip roofs as necessary to create gable roofs. See the figure for the finished roof.
   F. Save and close the drawing.
   G. Access the **Constructs** tab of the **Project Navigator**. Open the Main Floor construct.
   H. Drag and drop the Roof construct into the drawing for use as a reference.
   I. Use the **Roofline** command to project gable walls to the roof.

Note: You will need to add two additional walls above the main floor walls for the front and rear gable ends. Create a wall cleanup group for these so they do not cleanup with your floor plan walls. Project the walls to the gable roof ends, and then use display properties to turn off the new walls' display in a Plan representation.

   J. Save and close the drawing.

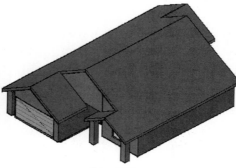

Front View

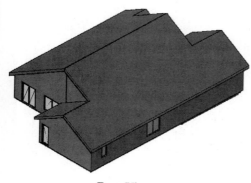

Rear View

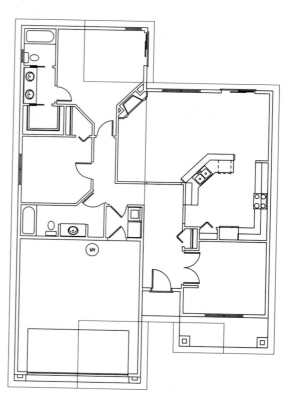

Design Courtesy Alan Mascord Design Associates

2. Single-Level Residential Project
   A. Access the **Project Browser** and set Residential-Project-02 current.
   B. Access the **Constructs** tab of the **Project Navigator** and create a new construct named Roof. Assign the level to the Roof level. Open the Roof construct.
   C. Drag and drop the Main Floor construct into the drawing for use as a reference.
   D. Use polylines to lay out the roof plan as diagrammed in the floor Plan view in the figure.
   E. Use the **10-1x8 Fascia** roof slab tool in the **Slabs** tool palette with the following properties to trace over the polyline points:
      a. **Base Height**: 8'-1"
      b. **Overhang**: 0"
      c. **Rise**: 8"
   F. Use the roof slab's **Miter** command as needed to miter any hips, valleys, and ridges. If you have difficulty mitering, use the **Roof Slab Edges** worksheet to modify the angle of different edges.
   G. Edit the 10-1x8 Fascia roof slab style's display properties at the style level. In the Plan representation, turn off the Below Cut Plane Body Shrink Wrap and Above Cut Plane Body Shrink Wrap components. Turn on Below Cut Plane Outline and Above Cut Plane Outline.
   H. Edit the edges of each roof slab as needed to provide a 1'-0" overhang at all sloping sides of the roof and a 6" overhang at any gable end roofs.
   I. Save and close the drawing.
   J. Access the **Constructs** tab of the **Project Navigator**. Open the Main Floor construct.
   K. Drag and drop the Roof construct into the drawing for use as a reference.
   L. Use the **Roofline** command to project gable walls to the roof.

Note: You will need to add an additional wall above the main floor walls for the front gable end. Create a wall cleanup group for this so it will not clean up with your floor plan walls. Project the wall to the gable roof ends, and then use display properties to turn off the new wall's display in a Plan representation.

   M. Save and close the drawing.

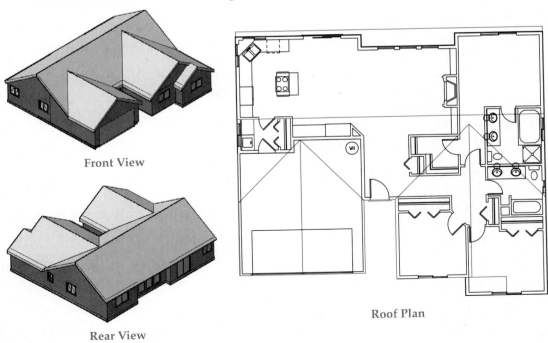

Front View

Rear View

Roof Plan

Design Courtesy Alan Mascord Design Associates

3. Two-Story Residential Project
   A. Access the **Project Browser** and set Residential-Project-03 current.
   B. Access the **Constructs** tab of the **Project Navigator** and open the Upper Floor construct.
   C. Change the walls to 8'-0".
   D. Change the window to 4'-0" high and head height to 6'-8".
   E. Stretch the dormer to be 2'-6" longer, toward the front of the house.
   F. Save and close the drawing.
   G. Access the **Constructs** tab of the **Project Navigator** and create a new construct named Roof. Assign the construct to the Roof level.
   H. Open the Roof construct.
   I. Drag and drop the Main Floor construct into the Roof construct for use as a reference file.
   J. Use the standard **Roof** tool to create a roof on top of the main floor walls with the following values, as indicated in the figure. Do not draw the dormer.
      a. **Thickness**: 8"
      b. **Edge Cut: Plumb**
      c. **Plate Height**: 9'-0"
      d. **Rise**: 9"
      e. **Overhang**: 1'-0"
   K. Drag and drop the Upper Floor construct into the Roof construct for use as a reference file. Change the view to an isometric view to view the upper floor location. Pick the Upper Floor xref and change its **Insertion point Z** property to a value of 0". Change back to a Top view.
   L. Use a polyline to draw a rectangle 10'-0" × 16'-0" over the dormer of the upper floor. Change the polyline's **Elevation** property to 18'-0".
   M. Convert the dormer rectangle to a standard Roof object with the following properties:
      a. **Thickness**: 4"
      b. **Edge Cut: Plumb**
      c. **Plate Height**: 18'-0"
      d. **Rise**: 9"
      e. **Overhang**: 1'-0"
   N. Convert the standard roofs to roof slabs using the standard **Roof slab** tool in the **Design** tool palette.
   O. Use the **Trim** command to clean up the dormer roofs with the main roof.
   P. Cut a hole in the main roof for the upper floor dormer.
   Q. Detach the Main and Upper floor constructs.
   R. Save and close the drawing.
   S. Access the **Constructs** tab of the **Project Navigator** and open the Upper Floor construct.
   T. Drag and drop the Roof construct into the Upper Floor construct for use as a reference file.
   U. Use the **Roof Line** command to project the upper floor walls to the Roof xref.
   V. Detach the Roof xref.
   W. Save and close the drawing.

Front View

Rear View

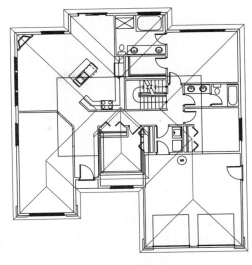

Roof Plan

Drawing Courtesy 3D-DZYN

4. Two-Story Residential Project
   A. Access the **Project Browser** and set Residential-Project-04 current.
   B. Access the **Constructs** tab of the **Project Navigator** and create a new construct named Roof. Assign the level to the Roof level.
   C. Open the Roof construct.
   D. Drag and drop the Main Floor and Upper Floor constructs into the Roof construct for use as a reference file.
   E. Use the standard **Roof** tool to create roofs over the garage, dining room bay, and fireplace with the following values. Refer to the figure for placement.
      a. **Thickness**: 8″
      b. **Edge Cut: Plumb**
      c. **Plate height for lower floor roofs**: 9′-0″
      d. **Plate height for upper floor roof**: 18′-0″
      e. **Rise**: 6″
      f. **Overhang**: 1′-0″
   F. Convert the roofs into roof slabs and assign any desired roof slab edge styles.
   G. Save and close the drawing.

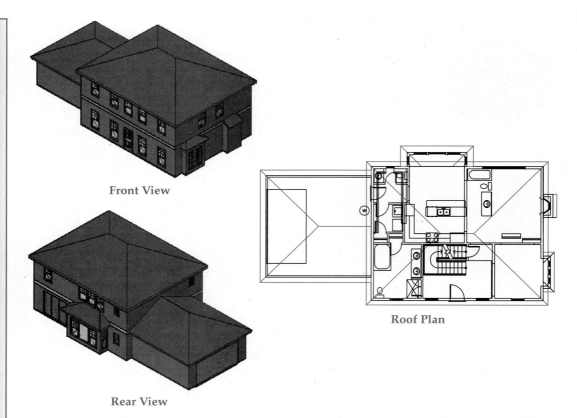

Front View

Rear View

Roof Plan

Design Courtesy Alan Mascord Design Associates

5. Commercial Store Project
   A. Access the **Project Browser** and set Commercial-Project-05 current.
   B. Access the **Constructs** tab of the **Project Navigator** and create a new construct named Roof. Assign the level to the Roof level.
   C. Open the Roof construct.
   D. Drag and drop the Main Floor construct into the Roof construct for use as a reference file.
   E. Create the fascia profile shown in the figure.
   F. Create a roof slab edge style named Parapet. Assign the following properties to the **Defaults** tab:
      a. **Overhang**: 0″
      b. **Edge Cut**: **Plumb**
      c. **Angle**: 0″
   G. In the **Design Rules** tab, select the **Fascia** check box and Parapet profile for the fascia. Uncheck the **Auto-Adjust to Edge Height** check box.
   H. Create a new roof slab style named Flat Roof with the following component properties:
      a. Metal Deck—**Thickness**: 1 1/2″, **Thickness offset**: 0″
      b. Roofing—**Thickness**: 1″, **Thickness offset**: 1 1/2″
   I. Add a roof slab to the top of the walls as indicated in the figure. Pick the vertex points at the outside of the brick walls. Set the following parameters for the roof slab:
      a. **Style: Flat Roof**
      b. **Mode: Direct**
      c. **Vertical Offset: 12′-0″**
      d. **Justification: Bottom**
      e. **Overhang: 0″**
      f. **Baseline Edge: Parapet**
      g. **Perimeter Edge: Parapet**

J. Use the standard **Roof** tool to create a roof over the central portion of the building, as in the figure. Use the following settings:
   a. **Thickness**: 10″
   b. **Edge Cut**: 10″
   c. **Shape: Single slope**
   d. **Overhang**: 0″
   e. **Plate height**: 12′-0″
   f. **Rise**: 4″
K. Add a stud wall to each gable end at an elevation of 12″. Use the **Roof Line** command to project the walls to the gable and use **Object Display** to turn off the Plan display representations.
L. Save and close the drawing.

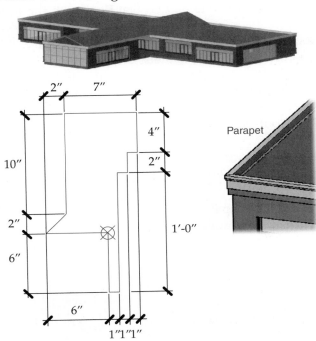

Drawing Courtesy 3D-DZYN

6. Commercial Car Maintenance Shop Project
   A. Access the **Project Browser** and set Commercial-Project-06 current.
   B. Access the **Constructs** tab of the **Project Navigator** and create a new construct named Roof. Assign the level to the Roof level.
   C. Open the Roof construct.
   D. Drag and drop the Main Floor and Upper Floor constructs into the Roof construct for use as a reference file.
   E. Use the standard **Roof** tool to create roofs over the garage and car wash with the following values. Refer to the figure for placement.
      a. **Thickness**: 10″
      b. **Edge cut: Plumb**
      c. **Plate height** for car wash roof: 12′-0″
      d. **Plate height** for garage roof: 18′-0″
      e. **Rise**: 1″
      f. **Overhang**: 1′-0″
   F. Convert the standard roofs into roof slabs using the 10-1x8 Fascia + Frieze roof slab style in the **Slabs** tool palette.
   G. Use the **Edit Roof Slab Edges** command to adjust any overhangs interfering with the upper floor walls.

H. Adjust the 10-1x8 Fascia + Frieze roof slab style's Plan display representation by turning off the Below Cut Plane Body Shrink Wrap and Above Cut Plane Body Shrink Wrap components and turning on Below Cut Plane Outline and Above Cut Plane Outline.

I. Create the polyline shape shown in the figure. Turn the shape into an AEC profile named Parapet.

J. Create a roof slab edge style named Parapet. Assign the following properties to the **Defaults** tab:
   a. **Overhang**: 0″
   b. **Edge Cut**: **Plumb**
   c. **Angle**: 0.00

K. In the **Design Rules** tab, select the **Fascia** check box and Parapet profile for the fascia. Uncheck the **Auto-Adjust to Edge Height** check box.

L. Create a new roof slab style named Flat Roof with the following component properties:
   a. Metal Deck—**Thickness**: 1 1/2″, **Thickness offset**: 0″
   b. Roofing—**Thickness**: 1″, **Thickness offset**: 1 1/2″

M. Add a roof slab to the top of the walls as indicated in the figure. Pick the vertex points at the outsides of the brick walls. Set the following parameters for the roof slab:
   a. **Style**: **Flat Roof**
   b. **Mode**: **Direct**
   c. **Vertical Offset**: 19′-0″
   d. **Justification**: **Bottom**
   e. **Overhang**: 0″
   f. **Baseline Edge**: **Parapet**
   g. **Perimeter Edge**: **Parapet**

N. Detach the Main Floor and Upper Floor xrefs.

O. Save and close the drawing.

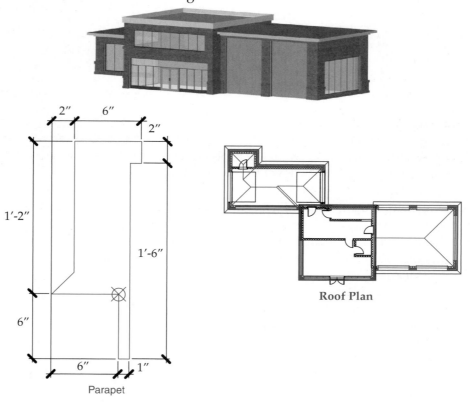

Parapet

Roof Plan

Drawing Courtesy 3D-DZYN

7. Governmental Fire Station
    A. Access the **Project Browser** and set Gvrmt-Project-07 current.
    B. Access the **Constructs** tab of the **Project Navigator** and create a new construct named Roof. Assign the level to the Roof level.
    C. Open the Roof construct.
    D. Drag and drop the Main Floor into the Roof construct for use as a reference file.
    E. Create the two profiles shown in the figure.
    F. Create a roof slab edge style named Parapet. Assign the following properties to the **Defaults** tab:
        a. **Overhang**: 0″
        b. **Edge Cut**: **Plumb**
        c. **Angle**: 0.00
    G. In the **Design Rules** tab, select the **Fascia** check box and Parapet profile for the fascia. Uncheck the **Auto-Adjust to Edge Height** check box.
    H. Create a roof slab edge style named Entrance Parapet. Assign the following properties to the **Defaults** tab:
        a. **Overhang**: 0″
        b. **Edge Cut**: **Plumb**
        c. **Angle**: 0.00
    I. In the **Design Rules** tab, select the **Fascia** check box and Entrance Parapet profile for the fascia. Uncheck the **Auto-Adjust to Edge Height** check box.
    J. Create a new roof slab style named Flat Roof with the following component properties:
        a. Roofing—**Thickness**: 1″, **Thickness offset**: 1 1/2″
        b. Metal Deck—**Thickness**: 1 1/2″, **Thickness offset**: 0″
        c. Insulation—**Thickness**: 3 1/2″, **Thickness offset**: -3 1/2″
    K. Add a roof slab to the top of the walls as displayed in the figure. Pick the vertex points at the insides of the exterior brick walls. Set the following parameters for the roof slab:
        a. **Style**: **Flat Roof**
        b. **Mode**: **Projected**
        c. **Vertical offset**: 0″
        d. **Horizontal offset**: 0″
        e. Justification: **Bottom**
        f. **Base height** at apparatus bay: 16′-0″
        g. **Base height** at main building: 12′-0″
        h. **Overhang**: 0″
        i. **Baseline edge**: **Parapet**
        j. **Perimeter edge**: **Parapet**
        k. **Rise**: 0″
    L. Adjust the roof slab edges as needed by turning off edges behind projected walls. Refer to the figure.
    M. Create a new roof slab style named Entablature with the following component properties for the Framing component:
        a. **Thickness**: 6″
        b. **Thickness offset**: 0″

N. Add a roof slab at the front of the building over the front porch area. Set the following parameters for the roof slab:
  a. **Style**: **Entablature**
  b. **Mode**: **Projected**
  c. **Vertical Offset**: 0″
  d. **Horizontal Offset**: 0″
  e. **Justification**: **Bottom**
  f. **Base Height**: 10′-0″
  g. **Overhang**: 0″
  h. **Baseline Edge**: **Entrance Parapet**
  i. **Perimeter Edge**: **Entrance Parapet**
  j. **Rise**: 0″
O. Adjust the roof slab edges as needed by turning off edges against brick walls. Refer to the figure.
P. Save and close the drawing.

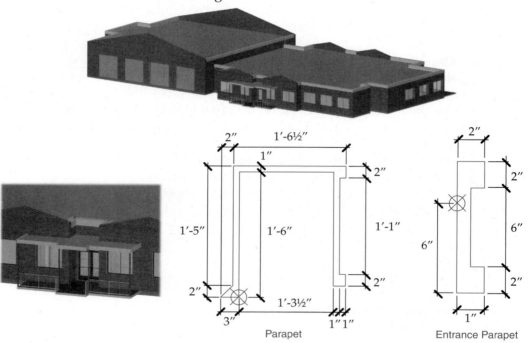

Drawing Courtesy 3D-DZYN

Creating Elevations

Learning Objectives

After completing this chapter, you will be able to do the following:

- ✓ Create exterior 2D elevations.
- ✓ Adjust elevation line properties.
- ✓ Create and use elevation styles.
- ✓ Establish rules for elevation styles.
- ✓ Set up the object display.
- ✓ Edit elevations.
- ✓ Edit and merge elevation linework.
- ✓ Generate interior elevations.
- ✓ Edit elevation marks.
- ✓ Create 3D elevations.
- ✓ Use the **Hidden Line Projection** command.
- ✓ Add AEC polygons.
- ✓ Create AEC polygon styles.
- ✓ Convert polylines to AEC polygons.
- ✓ Modify AEC polygons.

Elevations show how the vertical faces of a building appear. Through the use of exterior and interior elevations, information not found in plan sheets can be added and documented. Elevations include information, such as the building materials, distances between floors, and horizontal and vertical dimensions that cannot be found elsewhere. Elevations are 2D projections of the 3D model, as shown in **Figure 19-1**.

Figure 19-1.
Elevations are typically two-dimensional drawings of a three-dimensional building.

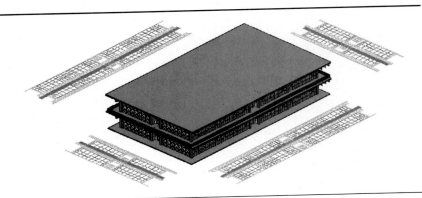

Once the building constructs/drawings have been created, elevations can be established from them. Architectural Desktop establishes elevations from the Model representation of the objects. You can create the elevations in the same drawing where you draw the walls, doors, and windows, or you can create the elevations from a view drawing with a series of xref drawings.

When you are using the **Project Navigator** for managing your drawings and the reference files used to create the building information model (BIM), a view drawing is created that assembles all of the reference files needed to create a model of the building. From this model, elevations can be generated.

If you are using the **Project Navigator**, a view drawing should be created before generating elevations. To do this, access the **Project Navigator**, and then pick the **Views** tab. In the **Views** tab, create a new view drawing by picking the **Add View** button at the bottom of the **Project Navigator** or by right-clicking under the Views folder and picking **New View Drawing** from the shortcut menu. Next, pick the **Section/Elevation** option for the view. This option uses the drawing template specified for the creation of sections and elevations. After choosing the **Section/Elevation** option, the **Add Section/Elevation View** worksheet is displayed. See **Figure 19-2**. Enter a name and description for the view drawing, verify the drawing template being used, and pick the **Next** button at the bottom of the worksheet.

The next page of the **Add Section/Elevation View** worksheet is the **Context** page. This page is used to select the levels and any combination of divisions used when assembling the project drawings for the elevation drawing. See **Figure 19-3**. Select any levels that will be used within the elevation drawing. When you are finished selecting the levels, pick the **Next** button to advance to the last page of the worksheet.

The last page of the **Add Section/Elevation View** worksheet is the **Content** page, which is shown in **Figure 19-4**. This page displays a list of drawings using the levels and divisions selected in the **Context** page. Place a check mark beside each of the drawings to be assembled into a model to generate an elevation from the model.

Figure 19-2.
When you are using the **Project Navigator** for managing your building information model (BIM) project, a view drawing is created for the elevations. The first page of the **Add Section/ Elevation View** worksheet is used to name the view drawing.

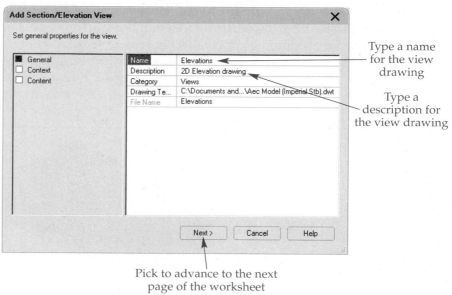

Type a name for the view drawing

Type a description for the view drawing

Pick to advance to the next page of the worksheet

Figure 19-3.
The **Context** page of the **Add Section/Elevation View** worksheet is used to select any levels that will be used in the view drawing.

Context page →

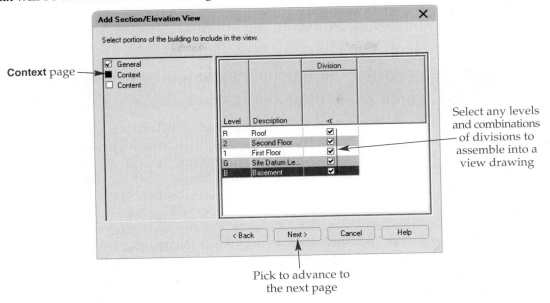

Select any levels and combinations of divisions to assemble into a view drawing

Pick to advance to the next page

Figure 19-4.
The **Content** page of the **Add Section/Elevation View** worksheet is used to select the drawings to be assembled into the view drawing for generating 2D elevations.

Content page →

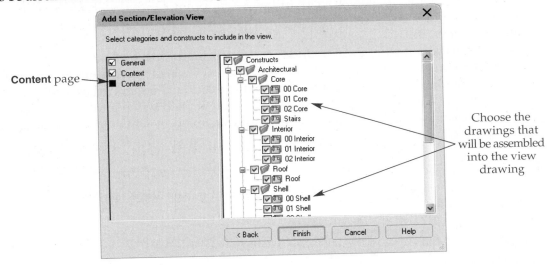

Choose the drawings that will be assembled into the view drawing

Creating Elevations

Once a section/elevation view has been created or a drawing with a completed model is available, 2D elevations can be generated. The tools for creating elevations can be found in the **Callouts** palette under the **Document** tool palette group. To access this group, pick the **Properties** button in the title bar of the **Tool Palettes** window, and then select **Document** from the bottom of the shortcut list. This changes the **Tool Palettes** window from the **Design** to **Document** tool palette group.

To create 2D elevations, select the **Callouts** palette, and select one of the three elevation mark tools. The **Elevation Mark A1** and **Elevation Mark A2** tools create a single elevation mark for the creation of one elevation. The **Exterior Elevation Mark A3** creates four elevation marks, one for each of the cardinal directions of the building, which establishes four separate elevations. *Cardinal directions* refer to the four principal directions: north, east, south, and west.

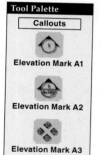

When using the **Elevation Mark A1** or **Elevation Mark A2** tool, pick a point in the drawing where you want the elevation mark located. After picking the location for the mark, use the mouse to rotate the arrow mark to point at the side of the building you would like to generate an elevation of and pick that point. Once the arrow is pointing in the direction of the desired elevation, the **Place Callout** worksheet is displayed, as shown in **Figure 19-5**.

The **Place Callout** worksheet includes the following properties:

- **Callout Only.** Pick this button to add only the callout, without generating an elevation.
- **New Model Space View Name.** When an elevation is generated, a model space view is created around the elevation, which is used when adding the view to a sheet drawing. The name you enter in this text box is the name of the model space view and the name entered in the title mark under the elevation.

Figure 19-5.
The **Place Callout** worksheet is used to generate an elevation and add a title mark and elevation scale callout.

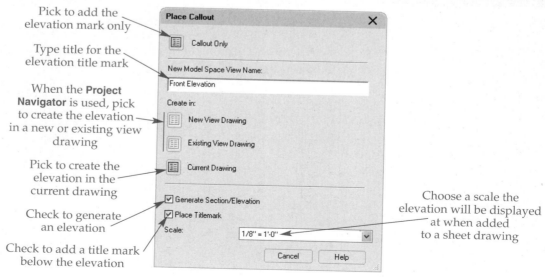

- **New View Drawing.** When you are using the **Project Navigator**, this button becomes available and is used to generate the elevation in a new section/elevation view drawing.
- **Existing View Drawing.** When the **Project Navigator** is used, this button is available to generate the elevation in an existing section/elevation view drawing.
- **Current Drawing.** Pick this button to generate the elevation in the current drawing.
- **Generate Section/Elevation.** Select this check box to create a 2D elevation.
- **Place Titlemark.** Select this check box to place a title mark below the elevation to name the elevation and specify the scale of the elevation when added to a sheet drawing.
- **Scale.** When an elevation is generated, a model space view is created around the elevation. The model space view is later added to a sheet drawing at the scale specified in this drop-down list.

If the elevation will be generated in the current drawing, pick the **Current Drawing** button. This returns the drawing screen. Pick a point outside of the building model to establish a box around the portions of the building that will be calculated into an elevation. Select around the portions of the building to be included in the elevation and pick the second point of the region. Finally, pick a location for the 2D elevation.

The 2D elevation is generated and placed at the location you specified. If a title mark is added, it is placed below the Elevation object. The elevation number, title, and scale are automatic fields and are updated after the elevation model space view is added to a sheet drawing. This is discussed in Chapter 24.

If you are using the **Exterior Elevation Mark A3** tool to generate the four cardinal elevations of the building, the command sequence is slightly different. When this tool is selected, you are prompted to select the two points of the region around the building.

The **Place Callout** worksheet is displayed after picking the region around the building. See **Figure 19-5**. Notice the **New Model Space View** name includes four names. This is because four separate elevations are created and a model space view for each is configured. Pick the **Current Drawing** button to generate the elevations. This returns the drawing window, where you are prompted to pick a location for the 2D elevation. Pick another point away from the insertion point to establish the spacing between each elevation and the direction in which the elevations will be generated. After picking the two points, the four elevations are generated, and title marks are placed below each elevation.

Manual Elevation Creation Method

In the previous discussion, the elevation marks from the **Callouts** palette were used to automatically generate 2D elevations. Another method of elevation creation involves creating an *elevation line*, which specifies a boundary around the building from which the elevations are generated. To add elevation lines into the drawing, type BLDGELEVATIONADD or pick **Document** > **Sections and Elevations** > **Add Elevation Line** from the pull-down menu.

After you have accessed the **BLDGELEVATIONLINEADD** command, you are prompted for a start point and an endpoint. These points specify the outer boundaries for the elevation.

When selecting points to establish an elevation line, pick the points in a counterclockwise direction around the building. See **Figure 19-6**. If you are creating multiple elevations, you need an elevation line for each elevation. Make sure the points you select are beyond the edge of the building being considered for the elevation.

When you finish creating the elevation line, an invisible box is added around the elevation. This box determines the parts of the building model available for the Elevation object. For a 2D elevation, the box needs to wrap only around the part of the building to be shown in the elevation. For a 3D elevation, the box should wrap around the entire building model. The box can be enlarged or shrunk by selecting the box to display the grips, picking a grip point, and respecifying the location of the point.

Type
BLDGELEVATION LINEADD
Pull-Down Menu
Document > Sections and Elevations > Add Elevation Line

BLDGELEVATIONLINEADD

Figure 19-6.
Pick a start point
and an endpoint
to establish an
elevation line.

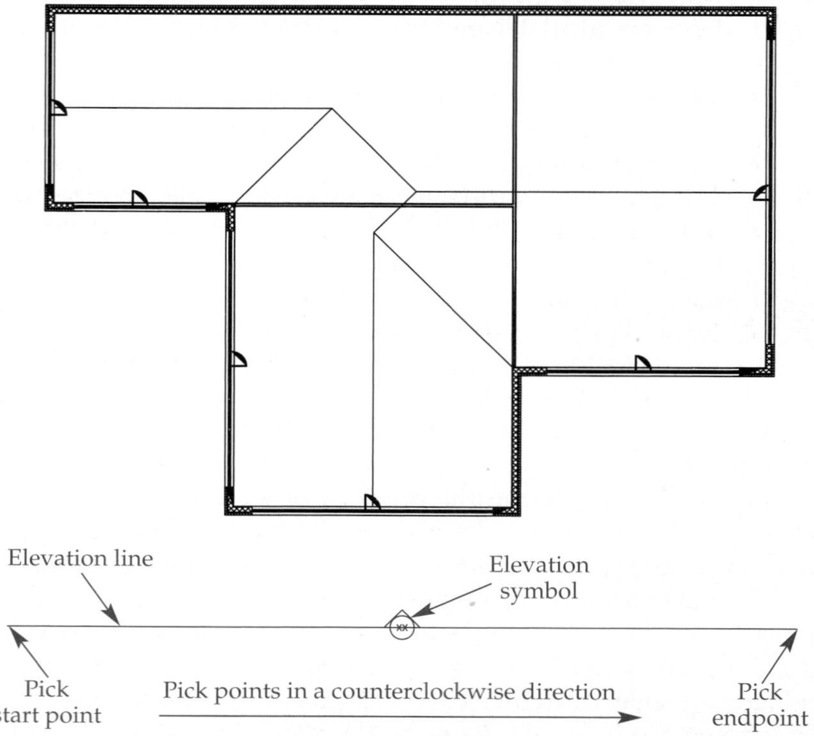

Elevation line

Elevation
symbol

Pick
start point

Pick points in a counterclockwise direction

Pick
endpoint

The elevation line is created on the A-Elev-Line layer, which is a nonplotting layer. This way, the line used to generate the elevation does not plot on the finished construction document set. Once an elevation line has been placed in the drawing, select the elevation line, right-click, and select the **Generate 2D Elevation...** option from the shortcut menu.

After accessing the option, the **Generate Section/Elevation** dialog box is displayed, as shown in **Figure 19-7**. The **Generate Section/Elevation** dialog box is divided into the following four areas:

- **Result Type.** This area is used to determine the type of elevation to be created. The default is the 2D elevation. The 2D elevation creates a two-dimensional elevation drawing, placing it in the current XY plane, similar to the automatic 2D elevations. The 3D elevation creates a three-dimensional elevation that is virtually a copy of the building model with a single color for plotting. The **Style to Generate** drop-down list includes a list of elevation and section styles that can be used to generate the elevation or section. The Standard elevation style generates the 2D and 3D elevations using one color for plotting purposes. Creating an elevation style is described later in this chapter.
- **Selection Set.** This area is used to select the objects to be added to the elevation. Pick the **Select Objects** button to return the drawing screen. Select any objects to be displayed in the elevation. If you select an object by accident, hold the [Shift] key and reselect the object to remove it from the selection set.
- **Placement.** This area is used to pick a location in the drawing to place the 2D or 3D elevation. Use the **Pick Point** button to pick a location on the drawing screen, or enter an absolute coordinate in the **X:**, **Y:**, and **Z:** text boxes.
- **Display Set.** This area includes a list of the available display sets in the drawing. Each display set displays the AEC objects in a different manner. Refer to Chapter 7. When a display set is selected for an elevation, the display properties controlled by the display set are used to generate the elevation. The new elevation is created based on the AEC object components displayed in the selected display set.

Figure 19-7.
The **Generate Section/Elevation** dialog box is used to create an elevation.

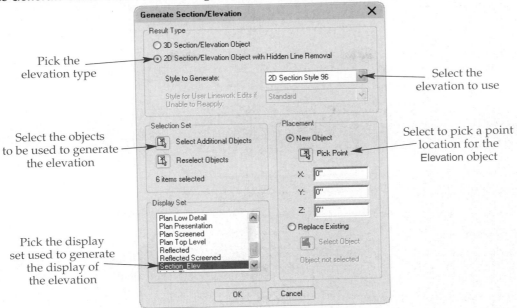

Pick the elevation type

Select the elevation to use

Select the objects to be used to generate the elevation

Select to pick a point location for the Elevation object

Pick the display set used to generate the display of the elevation

 NOTE It is recommended that the Section_Elev display set be used when creating an elevation. This displays the elevation correctly in the different default display configurations.

When you finish specifying elevation criteria, pick the **OK** button to create the elevation. Architectural Desktop generates the elevation at the point specified in the **Generate Section/Elevation** dialog box. See **Figure 19-8.**

The elevation is displayed on the drawing screen. If materials have been assigned to the objects in the building model, the elevation displays the surface hatches. The surface hatches display using the color designated by the material's Surface Hatch component in the material definition. All other linework representing the walls, roofs, doors, and windows in the elevation are assigned to a single color. Selecting the Elevation object highlights the entire elevation, as if it were a block. Selecting the elevation highlights all the objects. As long as the elevation remains in this state and is not exploded, it can be updated to reflect the latest changes to the plan drawings. Exploding the Elevation object breaks the link to the original building model.

 NOTE If an automatically generated elevation is selected, an invisible boundary is displayed with grips. This boundary specifies the model space view boundaries and represents the extents of view when it is added to a sheet drawing. The grips can be adjusted to increase or decrease the size of the model space view boundaries.

 **Exercise 19-2** Complete the Exercise on the Student CD.

Figure 19-8.
The new elevation is generated and placed at the specified point.

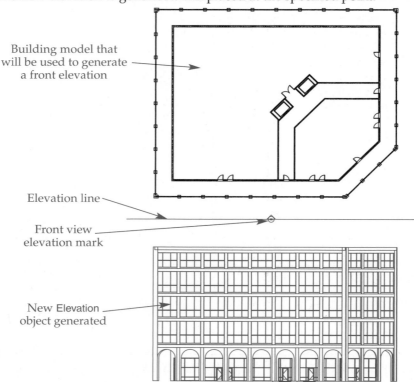

Building model that
will be used to generate
a front elevation

Elevation line

Front view
elevation mark

New Elevation
object generated

Adjusting the Elevation Line Properties

When an elevation is created, the elevation linework appears as a single color. This is the color designated for the elevation linework when the building model is completely inside the elevation line box. Some offices prefer to create elevations using different colors for the linework, representing the depth of the building. For example, if a building has several jogs in its outline, sides of the building farther away are plotted in gray tones to represent the depth or distance away from the closest side of the building.

When you are using CTB plot style tables, color in the drawing screen is used during plotting to interpret the plotted color, lineweight, and grayscale of the linework. For example, objects in an elevation closest to you can be plotted in a heavyweight black color to represent objects in front. As the building is stepped away from you, the linework can be plotted in a lightweight gray color. The colors used for the linework on the drawing screen can be any color desired. For example, you might decide that the heavyweight black line on the plotted paper is white on-screen, and the lightweight gray line on the plotted paper is cyan on the screen. When you are using STB plot style tables, plot style names are assigned to Elevation object components to assign the plotted color, lineweight, and grayscale. Plotting and the use of colors are discussed in Chapter 24.

Elevations can be adjusted to reflect coloring and plotting. When the elevation is first created, the box that wraps around the building model is considered to be one *subdivision*. Any object's linework within the box is generated into an elevation using the color assigned to the first subdivision. Additional subdivisions within the elevation line box can be created with their own colors, linetypes, lineweights, and plot styles assigned to each subdivision.

The **Properties** palette can be used to modify the parameters of the elevation line and elevation box and add more subdivisions, for greater elevation display control. To edit the properties of the elevation line, pick the elevation line and access the **Properties** palette.

Figure 19-9.
The **Properties** palette controls the properties of the elevation box.

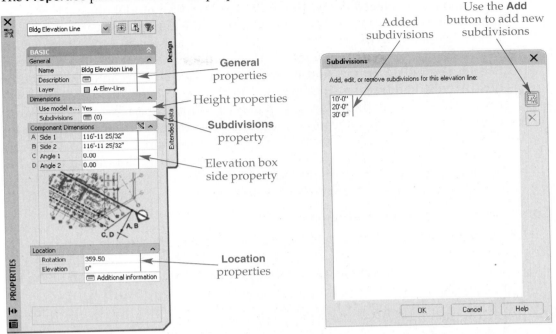

The properties for an elevation line are divided into four main categories under the **BASIC** header shown in **Figure 19-9.** These categories and their properties are described in the following sections.

General Category

The **General** category includes three properties: **Name**, **Description**, and **Layer**. The **Name** property indicates the name of the elevation line entered in the **Place Callout** worksheet when creating automatic elevations or the name of the elevation line when adding a single elevation mark or line. Pick the **Description** property to display the **Description** worksheet, where a description for the elevation line can be made. The **Layer** property indicates the layer on which the elevation line was created. Pick a new layer from the list to assign the elevation line to a different layer. By default, the elevation line is assigned to the A-Elev-Line layer, which is a nonplotting layer. This allows you to create elevations from the line, without having to plot the line.

Dimensions Category

The **Dimensions** category includes properties for controlling the height of the elevation box and subdivisions added within the box. These properties are described in the following:

- **Use model extents for height.** Picking this property displays a drop-down list with a **Yes** and **No** option. Picking the **Yes** option establishes the height of the elevation box based on the overall height of the building model. Any building model objects within the box are then calculated for inclusion in the Elevation object. If the **No** option is selected, the **Height** and **Lower extension** properties become available so a set elevation box height can be established. Setting specific heights for the elevation box gives you the capability of creating elevations with the top or bottom portions of the building model removed.
- **Height.** This property is available when the **Use model extents for height** property is set to **No**. Enter a value for the maximum height of the elevation box. Building model objects above the top of the elevation box are removed from the Elevation object.

- **Lower extension.** This property is also available when the **Use model extents for height** property is set to **No**. This property controls where the bottom of the elevation box is placed below the 0" Z axis. Building model objects below the bottom of the elevation box are removed from the Elevation object.
- **Subdivisions.** Pick this property to establish subdivisions within the elevation box. When this property is selected, the **Subdivisions** worksheet is displayed. See Figure 19-9. Use the **Add** button to add subdivisions into the elevation box. After a subdivision line is added to the worksheet, the location can be adjusted by picking the value in the table and entering a new distance, which is measured from the elevation line. When the Elevation object is created, the building model objects within each subdivision are then assigned to a different subdivision component that can be assigned to different colors and lineweights. See Figure 19-10. This is discussed further later in this chapter. A total of 10 subdivisions can be added to the elevation box.

Component Dimensions Category

The **Component Dimensions** category controls the size and angle of the sides of the elevation box.
- **Side 1.** Pick this property to enter a new value to control the length of the left side of the elevation box.
- **Side 2.** Pick this property to enter a new value to set the length of the right side of the elevation box.
- **Angle 1.** Pick this property to change the angle of the elevation box's left edge.
- **Angle 2.** Pick this property to change the angle of the elevation box's right edge.

Location Category

The **Location** category controls the rotation angle and elevation location of the elevation box. Use the **Rotation** property to rotate the box. By default, the bottom of the elevation box is placed at 0" on the Z axis. Enter a height to change the location of the bottom of the box.

After making any changes to the elevation line, the elevation box is updated. Any added subdivisions or adjustments made to the elevation line box are created. The subdivisions can be repositioned within the box using grips. Select the elevation line, and then select a grip on a subdivision line and reposition the line as desired. Any objects between the subdivision lines are assigned a different color for plotting.

Once a subdivision line or lines have been added and the position has been adjusted, the Elevation object needs to be assigned colors, linetypes, lineweights, and plot styles used between the subdivisions. To assign colors to the different subdivisions, select the Elevation object, right-click, and pick the **Entity Object Display** option. The **Object Display** dialog box is displayed. Attach any overrides as required, and then pick the **Edit Display Properties** button. In the **Layer/Color/Linetype** tab, assign a color to each subdivision used in the elevation line box shown in Figure 19-10.

After assigning the display properties to each subdivision, the elevation needs to be updated. Select the Elevation object, right-click, and pick the **Refresh** option. This updates the Elevation object with the new display properties assigned to the subdivisions. The portions of the building model within each subdivision are recalculated, and the linework within each subdivision is assigned the subdivision color.

After refreshing the elevation, the Elevation object is updated and displayed with the different colors, linetypes, and lineweights, based on the location of the objects between the subdivision lines.

Exercise
19-3

Complete the Exercise on the Student CD.

Figure 19-10.
Add subdivisions to the elevation box, assign colors to the subdivisions, and then update the Elevation object.

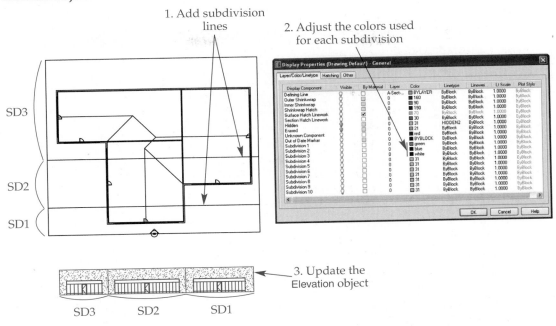

1. Add subdivision lines

2. Adjust the colors used for each subdivision

3. Update the Elevation object

Creating and Using Elevation Styles

When a 2D Elevation object is generated, a style is used to control the colors of the linework between the subdivision lines. New styles can be generated with rules that intercept the color of AEC objects used in the building model and assign them to a color to be used in the Elevation object. For example, a rule can be created to locate the window frame color in the Model display representation and assign the window frame a red color in the Elevation object.

To create an elevation style, type 2DSECTIONSTYLE or pick **Document** > **Sections and Elevations** > **Elevation Styles...** from the pull-down menu. This displays the **Style Manager** open to the 2D Section/Elevation Styles section, shown in **Figure 19-11**.

To create a new elevation style, pick the **New Style** button, or right-click over the **2D Section/Elevation** icon and select **New** from the shortcut menu. Enter a new name for the style in the text box provided to create a new elevation style. Highlight the new style in the tree view to display the section/elevation style's property tabs. A section/elevation style includes the following five property tabs:

- **General.** This tab is used to provide a description for the elevation style. Construction notes and documents can be attached to the style through the **Notes...** button.
- **Components.** This tab allows you to create components for the Elevation object that are used by the design rules. See **Figure 19-12**. For example, when subdivision lines are added in an elevation line box, the display components used are **Subdivision 1**, **Subdivision 2**, **Subdivision 3**, and so on. Custom components can be added here for the color rules section in the **Design Rules** tab. You might decide to create components that reflect the type of linework assigned to the component, as in **Figure 19-12**. Some examples of components are Walls, Glazing, Doors, Roofs, Light Lines, Medium Lines, and Heavy Lines.

Type
2DSECTIONSTYLE

Pull-Down Menu
Document > Sections and Elevations > Elevation Styles...

2DSECTIONSTYLE

Figure 19-11.
The **Style Manager** is used to create and edit elevation styles.

New Style button

Section/elevation style property tabs

2D Section/ Elevation Styles section

List of styles

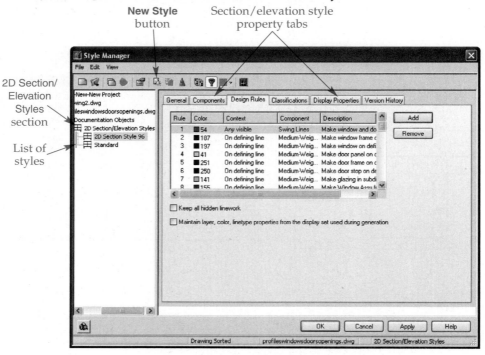

Figure 19-12.
Add custom components that the color rules in the **Design Rules** tab will use.

Use the **Components** tab to add custom components for the elevation style

List of custom components

Pick to create a custom component

Pick to delete a custom component

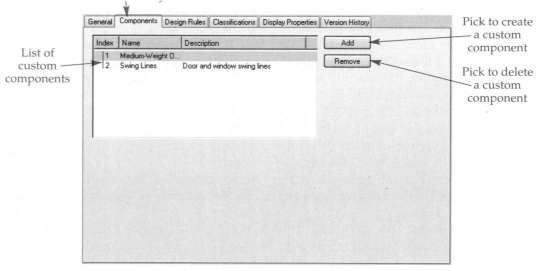

To add custom components, pick the **Add** button. A new custom component named Unnamed is created in the **Name** column. Pick the component to display a text box in which a new name can be entered. Add as many custom components as needed for the color rules. You can edit this tab as the style is developed by selecting a component and removing or renaming it.

NOTE Generally, when creating an elevation style, you should create custom components that reflect the lineweight used in the linework of the elevation. You can always edit these lists to reflect office standards or when a color rule is changed.

- **Design Rules.** This tab is used to create rules on how the Elevation object intercepts the colors of the building model and transfers them to a particular component within the elevation style. See **Figure 19-13.** Use the **Add** button to add a rule. Creating the rules is discussed in the next section.
- **Classifications.** This tab is used to assign a classification definition to the elevation style.
- **Display Properties.** This tab is used to configure the colors of the components (both default and custom) within the elevation style. This procedure is described in greater detail in the next section.

Exercise
19-4   **Complete the Exercise on the Student CD.**

Figure 19-13.
The **Design Rules** tab is used to create rules about how the building model colors are interpreted and sent to a display component within the Elevation object.

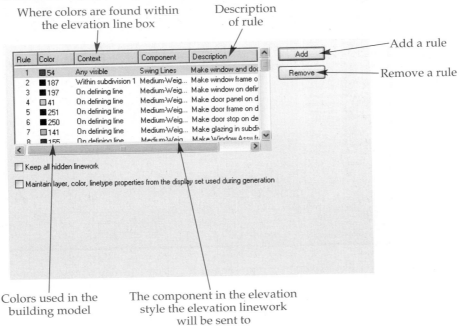

Where colors are found within the elevation line box

Description of rule

Add a rule

Remove a rule

Colors used in the building model

The component in the elevation style the elevation linework will be sent to

Creating Rules for the Elevation Style

Before creating a rule and a display set is referenced for the elevation geometry, it is necessary to understand what the elevation style looks for when the Elevation object is first created. In **Figure 19-14**, the Section_Elev display set is used. This display set groups together a series of display representations to be used when this set is viewed.

The Section_Elev display set looks to the Elevation display representation for windows and doors, General Medium Detail display representation for material definitions, Model display representation for the majority of the other AEC objects, and General display representations for AEC objects that do not have an Elevation or Model representation. The **Design Rules** tab in the elevation style looks to the colors used by AEC objects in these display representations for interpretation of how the rules will be applied to the end result 2D elevation. If another display set is used when the elevation is created, the rules interpret the representations differently.

Understanding that the elevation door and window are being interpreted by the elevation style rules, you can make rules to intercept these elevation representation colors and translate the colors to a different component within the elevation style. If a display representation's display component within an AEC object has a check mark in the **By Material** check box, the colors being used are set by the material definition. You might need to check the material definitions for the 3D Body display component for the color being used for the material. This color would then be the color used for the elevation design rule. To create the rules, access the elevation style and pick the **Design Rules** tab. Use the **Add** button to add a rule to the elevation style. See **Figure 19-15**.

Figure 19-14.
A display set is used when a new Elevation object is created. The Section_Elev display set uses elevation and Model display representations of different AEC objects.

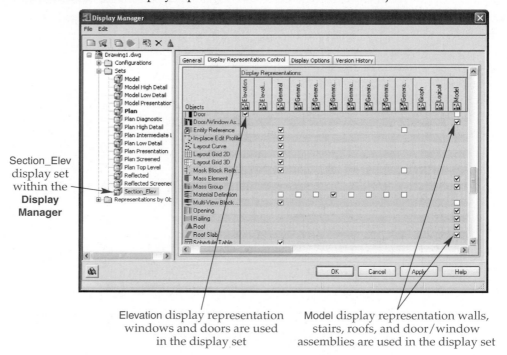

Section_Elev display set within the **Display Manager**

Elevation display representation windows and doors are used in the display set

Model display representation walls, stairs, roofs, and door/window assemblies are used in the display set

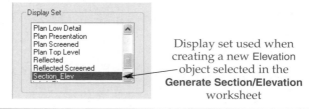

Display set used when creating a new Elevation object selected in the **Generate Section/Elevation** worksheet

Architectural Desktop and Its Applications

Figure 19-15.
This rule looks for a color within a subdivision and places it on a custom component.

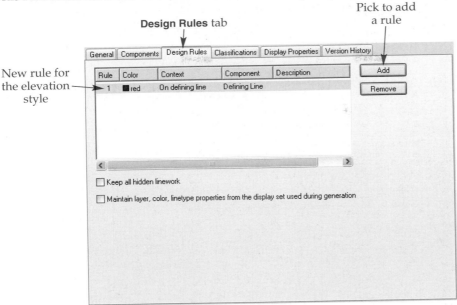

Once a new rule has been added, it can be configured. The **Color** column includes a color swatch representing the color of the display component the elevation style is looking for in the building model. Pick the swatch to select a color from the **Select Color** dialog box.

The **Context** column includes the first part of the rule defining where the color being looked for can be found within the elevation box. Selecting the text in this column displays a drop-down list of options. For example, in **Figure 19-15**, in the **Color** column, the color red is being looked for on the defining line (elevation line). If a red color is found in an AEC object's display component and it is on the elevation line, it is placed on the Defining Line elevation style component. Colors can be looked for in a particular subdivision within the elevation box, on any component visible in the drawing, or on the defining line.

The **Component** column is the second part of the rule defining to which elevation style component the color being looked for is to be assigned. Select the text under this column to see a list of components. The following default components are listed: Defining Line, Hidden Erased, and SubDiv 1–10. Any custom components added in the **Components** tab are also listed. **Figure 19-16** is an example of several rules in the elevation style. Rule 2 looks for Color 15 (the brick material's 3D Body color) within the first subdivision of the elevation line box and places it on a custom component named Heavy Lines.

The **Description** column is used to enter a description for the rule. This column does not need to be filled out. To add a description, pick in the table beside the rule.

Setting Up the Entity Display

Before the rule can be set into motion, the display properties for the elevation style need to be manipulated. In the 2D Section/Elevation Styles section, pick the **Display Properties** tab. Notice that the Elevation object only has one display representation—General. Attach a style override and select the **Edit Display Properties** button. The **Display Properties** dialog box is displayed.

Figure 19-16.
Rules have been added to the elevation style.

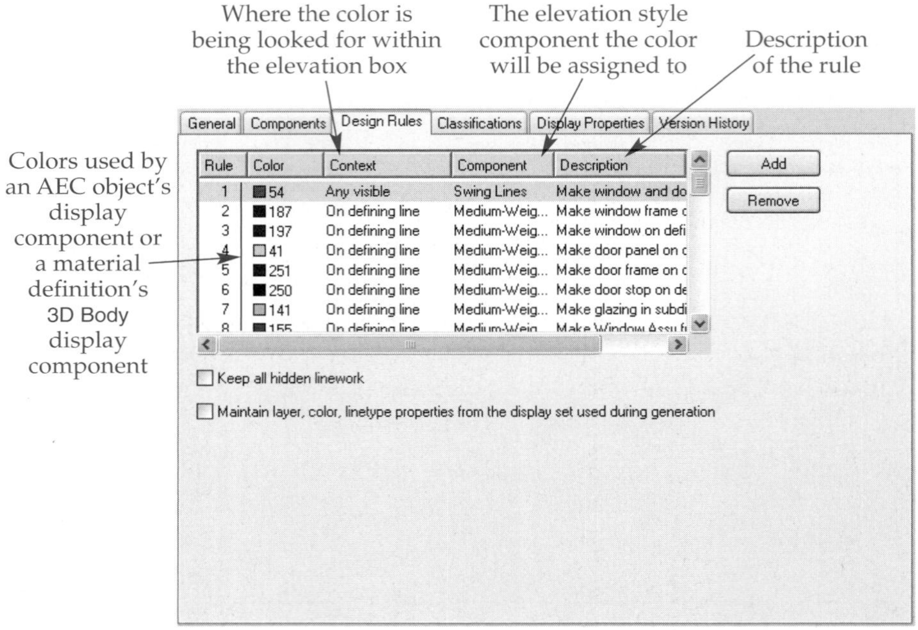

Where the color is being looked for within the elevation box

The elevation style component the color will be assigned to

Description of the rule

Colors used by an AEC object's display component or a material definition's 3D Body display component

Rule	Color	Context	Component	Description
1	■54	Any visible	Swing Lines	Make window and do
2	■187	On defining line	Medium-Weig...	Make window frame c
3	■197	On defining line	Medium-Weig...	Make window on defi
4	□41	On defining line	Medium-Weig...	Make door panel on c
5	■251	On defining line	Medium-Weig...	Make door frame on c
6	■250	On defining line	Medium-Weig...	Make door stop on de
7	□141	On defining line	Medium-Weig...	Make glazing in subdi
8	■155	On defining line	Medium-Weig...	Make Window Assu fi

General | Components | Design Rules | Classifications | Display Properties | Version History

Add
Remove

☐ Keep all hidden linework

☐ Maintain layer, color, linetype properties from the display set used during generation

This dialog box is divided into three tabs: **Layer/Color/Linetype**, **Hatching**, and **Other**. The **Layer/Color/Linetype** tab includes all the default display components within the Elevation object and the custom components added in the **Components** tab earlier. These components can be adjusted for visibility, layer, color, linetype, lineweight, and plot style. In addition to controlling the color, linetype, and lineweight of an elevation's display component, the **By Material** check box is available for most components. Selecting the check box for a display component causes the material assigned to an AEC object used in the elevation to use the display properties of the material.

The Shrinkwrap and Shrinkwrap Hatch display components, discussed in Chapter 20, are used when generating sections. The **Hatching** tab includes one component: Shrinkwrap Hatch. This controls the hatch type used for the Shrinkwrap Hatch component.

Use the **Other** tab to add additional custom components not defined in the **Components** tab of the elevation style. See **Figure 19-17**. In addition to adding custom display components to the display properties, two check boxes are available for further display control in the **Other** tab. If an Elevation object displays the linework using the subdivision color, linetype, and lineweight set, use the material's surface hatch display in the elevation, clear the **By Material** check box for the desired subdivision in the **Layer/Color/Linetype** tab, and then check **Use Subdivision properties for surface hatching** in the **Other** tab. This allows the linework in the elevation to look to the display component while using the hatching display properties specified by the material of the object.

If the display of the 2D elevation linework uses the display properties of the material assigned to an object, select the **Use 3D Body display component for By Material linework** check box. This will cause the linework of the 2D elevation to look to the material assigned to an object for its display properties.

When you finish adjusting the display properties, pick the **OK** button to return to the elevation style property tabs. **Figure 19-18** displays the **Layer/Color/Linetype** tab with the display settings for the Elevation object, the **Design Rules** tab, and how the rules move object colors to a specific elevation component. Exit the **Styles** dialog box when you are finished configuring the elevation style.

Figure 19-17.
The custom display components have been added to the display properties from the **Components** tab. Additional components not defined can be added here.

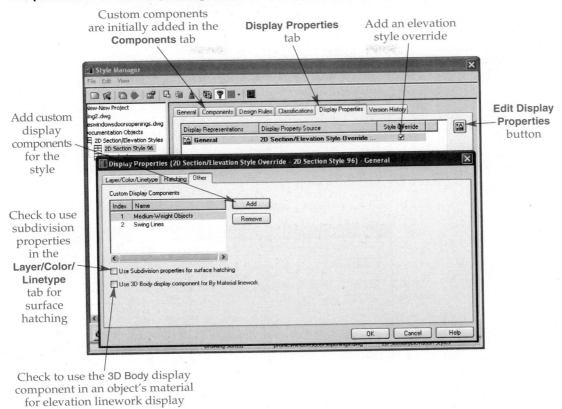

Custom components are initially added in the **Components** tab

Display Properties tab

Add an elevation style override

Add custom display components for the style

Edit Display Properties button

Check to use subdivision properties in the **Layer/Color/Linetype** tab for surface hatching

Check to use the 3D Body display component in an object's material for elevation linework display

The elevation style is now ready for use in new or updated Elevation objects. To update an existing Elevation object using the new style, select the Elevation object, right-click, and pick **Regenerate…** from the shortcut menu. This displays the **Generate Section/Elevation** dialog box discussed in the manual elevation section. Pick the style from the **Style to Generate** drop-down list in the **Generate Section/Elevation** dialog box, shown in **Figure 19-19.** Pick the **OK** button to regenerate the elevation. The elevation will be regenerated using the properties of the new elevation style. The design rules will interpret the colors of the building model, transferring the linework to the appropriate display components defined in the elevation style.

Exercise 19-5   **Complete the Exercise on the Student CD.**

Editing the Elevation Object

Occasionally when an Elevation object is created, linework appears on the wrong component or is displayed in a location that should not be seen. In most situations, these problems can be eliminated through the use of an elevation style and the elevation style design rules. When linework cannot be controlled through the design rules, it can be edited and placed on a particular elevation display component or removed from the elevation altogether.

Figure 19-18.
Once the display settings have been adjusted for the elevation style, the rules will be utilized when Elevation objects are created.

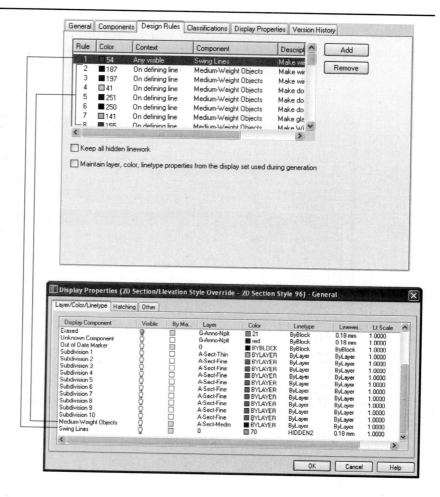

Figure 19-19.
Select the appropriate elevation style to use when creating a new Elevation object or updating an existing Elevation object.

Select the elevation style to use for new or updated Elevation objects

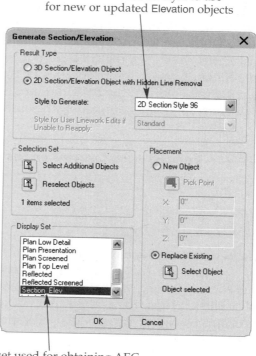

Display set used for obtaining AEC object colors for rule processing

In addition to editing the components to which the linework is assigned, you can merge new or existing geometry into an Elevation object. Geometry such as polylines representing trim work, signage, or hatches can all be merged into the Elevation object, forming one AEC object.

Editing Linework

To begin editing linework, select the Elevation object to be edited, right-click, and pick **Linework** > **Edit** from the shortcut menu. This "opens" the Elevation object so it can be edited in place.

After the **Edit** option has been accessed, pick the lines to be changed to a different elevation display component. When you are finished selecting the linework to be changed, right-click and pick the **Modify Component...** option from the shortcut menu. This displays the **Select Linework Component** worksheet. See **Figure 19-20**.

The **Select Linework Component** worksheet is used to move the selected linework in the Elevation object to a display component. Pick a display component from the **Linework Component** drop-down list. After the display component has been selected, pick the **OK** button. The selected linework is moved to the new display component.

The **Select Linework Component** worksheet also allows you to pick an existing line in the Elevation object that is on a display component and assign the display component to the linework being edited. First, pick the linework to be modified, right-click, and pick the **Modify Component...** option. Pick the **Match existing linework** button. You are prompted to select the linework. Select a line on the Elevation object that is using the desired display component. After picking the linework, the **Select Linework Component** worksheet is returned, displaying the name of the selected component. Pick the **OK** button to apply the modification of the linework being edited.

Linework can be assigned to any display component in the elevation style to include any Shrinkwrap, Subdivision, Hidden, Erased, or custom component. When linework is placed on the Hidden component, the linework appears as a hidden line. To erase geometry from the elevation, move the geometry to the Erased display component. If the **ERASE** command is used on the selected linework, the geometry is automatically placed on the Erased component.

After the linework within the elevation has been edited, the Elevation object needs to be closed so it can be updated if the building model changes. To close the editing in place and save your changes to the Elevation object, pick **Save All Changes** in the **In-Place Edit** toolbar or select any line in the Elevation object, right-click, and pick **Edit in Place** > **Save Changes** from the shortcut menu. This closes the edit in place session and saves the changes back to the Elevation object. If the building model is updated through the **Refresh** or **Regenerate...** shortcut menu option, the linework edits are saved in the elevation.

Figure 19-20. When you are editing elevation linework in place, the edited linework can be moved to a display component through the **Select Linework Component** worksheet.

Pick to move the selected linework to a component that is assigned to an existing line in the elevation

Pick a display component to move the selected linework to

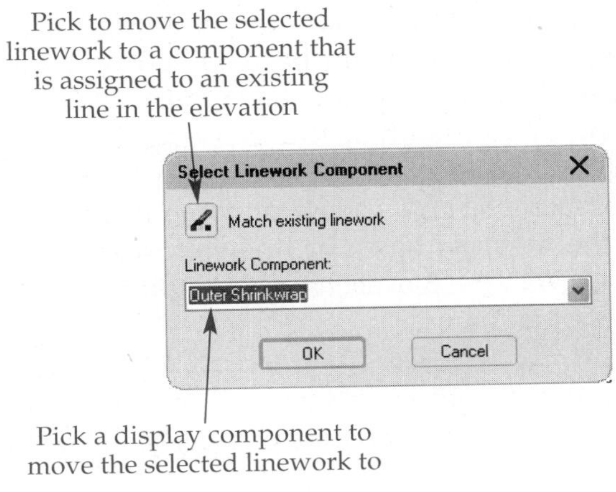

Exercise 19-6 Complete the Exercise on the Student CD.

Merging Linework

You can merge new geometry into the elevation and have it become a part of the Elevation object. First, draw any missing linework from the elevation or add new linework such as lines, polylines, arcs, or circles to the elevation. Next, pick the Elevation object, right-click, and pick **Linework > Merge...** from the shortcut menu.

Similar to using the **Edit** option, select the geometry to be merged into the Elevation object. When you have finished selecting the geometry, press [Enter] and select the linework component the merged objects will be placed on from the **Select Linework Component** worksheet.

> **NOTE** Most AutoCAD and Architectural Desktop objects can be merged into an elevation. Lines, polylines, arcs, blocks, and hatches are examples of entities that can be merged into an Elevation object.

> **PROFESSIONAL TIP** Linework should be edited and merged after the elevations have been decided on. Occasionally if the elevation is updated after editing, the original linework that was edited is displayed again in the Elevation object. The edited linework is also displayed as a separate group of lines. Use the **Merge** option after updating an elevation to group the edited linework back into the Elevation object.

Exercise 19-7 Complete the Exercise on the Student CD.

Adding Material Boundaries

Materials on AEC objects are processed during elevation creation, and their surface hatches are added to the Elevation object. Depending on the rules of the elevation style, the color of the material's Surface Hatch or Surface Hatch Linework display component in the elevation style is used. In addition to modifying the color of the elevation surface hatching, portions of the hatch can be removed or isolated on the Elevation object, through the **Material Boundary** option. See Figure 19-21.

A material boundary is similar to a masking block because it is used to mask out portions of a hatch or linework in an elevation. Before a material boundary can be applied to an Elevation object, a closed polyline must be drawn over the parts of the elevation where the material hatch or linework will be masked out. After the closed polyline is drawn, select the Elevation object, right-click, and pick **Material Boundary > Add...** from the shortcut menu.

> **NOTE** The **PLINE** command includes an **Arc** option to allow you to draw arc segments in the polyline to create a curved boundary.

Architectural Desktop and Its Applications

Figure 19-21.
The material hatches on an elevation can be removed or isolated on the Elevation object through the **Material Boundary** option.

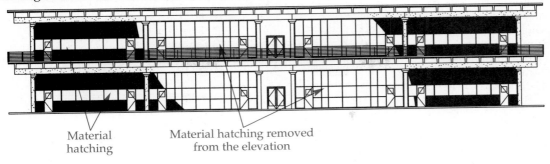

Material hatching

Material hatching removed from the elevation

After accessing the option, pick the closed polyline. After picking the polyline, decide whether to erase the selected linework (closed polyline) or not. The **2d Section/ Elevation Material Boundary** worksheet is then displayed. See **Figure 19-22.**

Once the **2d Section/Elevation Material Boundary** worksheet has been displayed, the material hatch and linework can be masked from the elevation. The **2d Section/ Elevation Material Boundary** worksheet includes three drop-down lists for applying the settings to the elevation. See **Figure 19-22.** A table of materials used in the drawing and two check boxes for controlling the material boundary in Section objects are available, with the following settings described:

- **Purpose.** This drop-down list includes two options to control how the mask is used. These options are **Limit** and **Erase**. The **Limit** option contains the hatch and linework within the boundaries of the closed polyline. Any hatches or lines outside of the polyline boundary are removed from the elevation. The **Erase** option removes the hatch and linework inside of the closed polyline boundary. See **Figure 19-23.**
- **Apply to.** This drop-down list controls how the material boundary mask will be applied. Five options are available. Picking the **Surface and Section Hatching** option masks out surface hatches on an elevation and section hatches on a Section object. Picking **Surface Hatching Only** masks out hatches on an elevation only. Picking the **Section Hatching Only** option masks out hatches in

Figure 19-22.
The **2d Section/Elevation Material Boundary** worksheet is used to mask out materials and linework in an Elevation object.

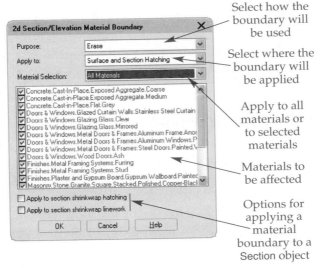

Select how the boundary will be used

Select where the boundary will be applied

Apply to all materials or to selected materials

Materials to be affected

Options for applying a material boundary to a Section object

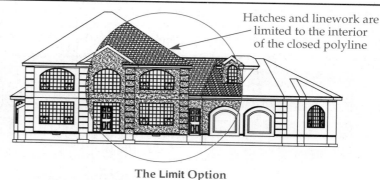

Figure 19-23.
Hatches and linework can be limited to the interior of a closed polyline or erased from the inside of a closed polyline. Drawing Courtesy 3D-DZYN.

Hatches and linework are limited to the interior of the closed polyline

The Limit Option

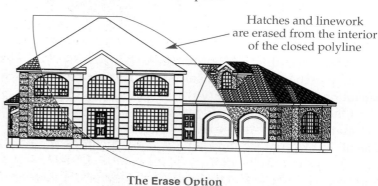

Hatches and linework are erased from the interior of the closed polyline

The Erase Option

a Section object. Section objects are discussed in Chapter 20. Picking the **Edge Linework Only** option masks out linework in an Elevation object or a Section object. Picking the **All Linework** option masks out all linework and hatching on an Elevation object or a Section object.

- **Material Selection.** This drop-down list controls whether all material hatches are masked or only specific material hatches are masked out. The **All Materials** option automatically masks out all materials in the Elevation or Section object. The **Specific Materials** option enables the table of materials, so specific hatches can be selected for masking. Place a check mark in any specific hatches in the **Material Selection** table to be affected.

The last two options apply specifically to Section objects. These are discussed in Chapter 20. When you are finished specifying how to apply the material boundary, pick the **OK** button. The elevations are updated to reflect the new masked out areas. See **Figure 19-24**.

NOTE

Multiple material boundaries can be added to a single Elevation object. When you are applying a material boundary to multiple closed polylines, the material boundary needs to be applied for each polyline. Use the **Erase purpose** option.

Editing Existing Material Boundaries

Similar to other options related to editing in place, the shape of the material boundary can be adjusted after the material boundary has been applied and erased. To adjust the shape of the material boundary or replace the boundary with a new closed polyline, pick the Elevation object, right-click, and pick **Material Boundary** > **Edit In Place** from the shortcut menu. This opens the **In-Place Edit** toolbar and displays a blue hatch over the areas of the material boundaries on the elevation. See **Figure 19-25**.

Figure 19-24.
Three separate material boundaries have been applied to the elevation with the surface hatching erased from the boundary. Note that the polyline boundaries have also been removed.

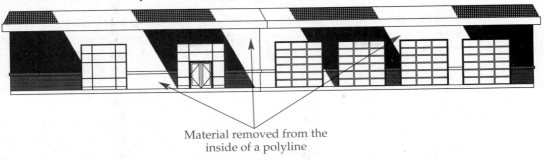

Material removed from the inside of a polyline

Figure 19-25.
Existing material boundaries can be edited through the **Edit in Place** option. Use the grips to change the shape of the boundary. The shortcut menu also includes options for modifying the boundary.

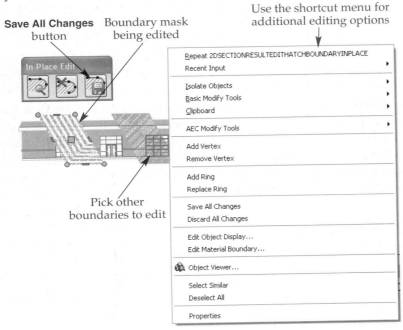

Save All Changes button

Boundary mask being edited

Use the shortcut menu for additional editing options

Pick other boundaries to edit

Pick the material boundary masking hatch to display grip boxes. Use the grips to edit the shape of the boundary. New vertices can be added to or removed from the boundary hatch by right-clicking and choosing the **Add Vertex** or **Remove Vertex** option. Pick a point on the masking hatch to add or remove vertices. If a new polyline is to be substituted, draw the closed polyline, and then right-click and choose the **Replace Ring** option from the shortcut menu.

When you are finished editing the shape of the material boundary, pick the **Save All Changes** button in the **In-Place Edit** toolbar. The new change is applied to the material boundary, and the surface hatches and linework on the elevation will be updated.

Exercise 19-8 Complete the Exercise on the Student CD.

Generating Interior Elevations

The **BLDGELEVATIONLINEADD** command or the interior elevation marks found in the **Callouts** palette can be used to create interior elevations for the set of construction documents. The **Interior Elevation Mark B1** and **Interior Elevation Mark B2** tools create four interior Elevation objects. The **Interior Elevation Mark C1** and **Interior Elevation Mark C2** tools create a single Elevation object.

When one of the interior elevation symbols is used from the **Callouts** palette, several prompts appear. First, pick a point for the insertion of the elevation mark. If you are using the **Interior Elevation Mark B1** or **Interior Elevation Mark B2** tool to generate four elevations, pick a point to determine the direction for the first elevation. If you are using the **Interior Elevation Mark C1** or **Interior Elevation Mark C2** tool to generate a single elevation, pick a point to determine the direction for the elevation. After you have picked the direction, the **Place Callout** worksheet is displayed.

The callout can be placed only in the plan, or elevations can be generated in a new drawing, an existing drawing, or the current drawing. A title mark and scale can also be added to the elevations being generated.

If generating the elevations, pick the appropriate **Create in** button. If a Space object or an Area object is being used, pick the object to indicate the region to be calculated in the elevations. Spaces and areas are discussed in Chapter 21. If you do not have spaces in the drawing, press the [Enter] key to window around the area of the room to have interior elevations generated.

After picking the region, specify the elevation line depth. The depth indicates how far into a room the elevation box looks to generate the elevation. Drag the crosshairs past the point where the elevation box will be created and use the pick button. Enter the height for the room or how tall the interior elevation will be drawn.

Once the depth and height have been specified for the elevation box, pick the location where the first Elevation object is to be drawn, and then pick a second point to specify the distance between interior elevations. Depending on the **Interior Elevation Mark** tool used, a single interior elevation is created, or multiple interior elevations are created, as in **Figure 19-26.**

Figure 19-26.
Interior elevations can be created if the elevation mark includes an elevation line.

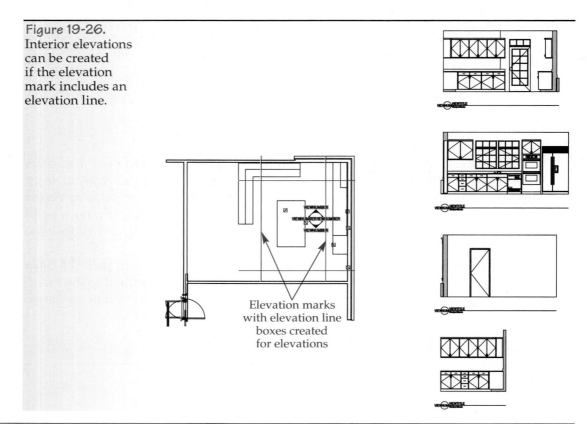

Elevation marks with elevation line boxes created for elevations

Once the interior elevations have been generated, use the **Edit**, **Merge**, and **Material Boundary** options as needed to adjust the appearance of the interior elevations. You might also decide to create a separate elevation style for use with interior elevations.

NOTE By default, the elevation boxes are placed on the A-Elev-Line layer. This layer is a nonplotting layer so you do not accidentally plot the elevation line/box.

Exercise 19-9   *Complete the Exercise on the Student CD.*

Creating a 3D Elevation

A 3D Elevation object can be used to create a perspective view of the building model using subdivisions of color. This object also uses an elevation mark and an elevation box to generate the Elevation object. It is useful to create the 3D Elevation object when you need an elevation with the same subdivision and color schemes as used by the 2D elevation. The difference is that a copy of all the geometry in the building model is made. See **Figure 19-27.**

To create a 3D elevation, first create an elevation line by picking **Document > Sections and Elevations** from the pull-down menu, and add any subdivision lines as required. Select the elevation line, right-click, and select the **Generate Elevation...** option from the shortcut menu. In the **Generate Section/Elevation** dialog box, select the **3D Section/Elevation Object** radio button in the **Result Type** area.

Note that selecting this option makes the elevation style to use unavailable because 3D elevations do not use an elevation style; they rely on entity display to show the subdivision colors. Complete the elevation process by selecting the objects to be included in the elevation and selecting a point for the new 3D Elevation object.

This process creates a new three-dimensional Elevation object, as shown in **Figure 19-27.** Like the 2D Elevation object, the 3D Elevation object maintains a link to the original building model. Any changes made to the building model can be updated in the 3D elevation. The drawback to the 3D elevation is that linework cannot be edited. What you see in the building model is duplicated in the 3D elevation.

NOTE The editing capabilities of 3D elevations are limited. The object can be updated to reflect changes made to the building model. Use 2D elevations to modify the elevation and set rules about how colors in the building model are interpreted and used in the elevation.

Figure 19-27.
The 3D Elevation
object is used when
a three-dimensional
object using the
same subdivided
color schemes as
the 2D elevation is
required.

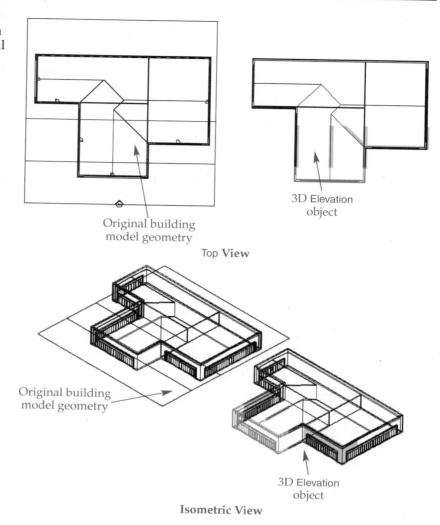

Original building
model geometry

Top **View**

Isometric View

Using the Hidden Line Projection Command

Another command that is useful for creating two-dimensional objects of a three-dimensional building is the **CREATEHLR** command. This command can be used to create 2D elevations from the building model or 2D perspectives from a perspective view. This command interprets a viewing direction of the building model and turns it into a 2D block. To access the command, pick **Document > Hidden Line Projection** from the pull-down menu or type CREATEHLR.

The best way to create the 2D block is to first obtain the desired viewing direction and then access the command. Use the **3D Orbit** or **Camera** tool to create a perspective viewing angle. Once the command is used, a series of prompts is issued to create the 2D block. See **Figure 19-28**.

When you enter the command initially, you are prompted to select objects. You can select any objects to be included in the two-dimensional block. After you finish selecting the geometry, the next prompt asks you to specify a block insertion point. You can enter an absolute coordinate, such as 0,0, or you can pick an insertion point in the drawing for the block. Finally, you are prompted to specify whether the block will be placed in a Plan view or the current view's XY plane. Generally, placing the hidden line projection at the 0,0 coordinates and in a Plan view makes it easy to locate the block when returning the drawing to a Plan view.

Figure 19-28.
The **CREATEHLR** command can be used to create a two-dimensional block of a view, whether it is an elevation view, a Top view, an isometric view, or a perspective view.

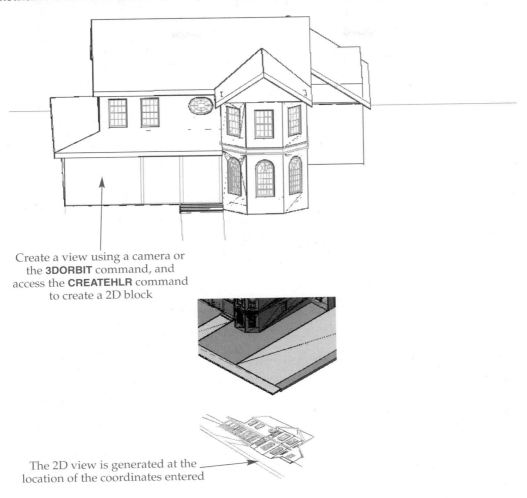

Create a view using a camera or the **3DORBIT** command, and access the **CREATEHLR** command to create a 2D block

The 2D view is generated at the location of the coordinates entered

Exercise 19-10   **Complete the Exercise on the Student CD.**

Using AEC Polygons

In many cases, elevations are detailed with patterns of lines to show the type of finish materials to be used. Many of the AEC styles included with Architectural Desktop already have materials with hatch patterns assigned. These material hatches will display in the elevations and sections when generated. The Standard AEC styles typically do not have materials assigned. When an elevation or section is created from a Standard style or a custom AEC style without a material, the elevation and section are displayed without the material hatches.

In cases where elevations and sections have been generated without hatches, a hatch pattern can be applied to the elevation or section through a tool known as an AEC polygon, shown in **Figure 19-29**. *AEC polygons* are two-dimensional objects that can be drawn over an object and fill the enclosed area with a hatch pattern.

Figure 19-29.
AEC polygons can be used to fill an area of the drawing with a hatch pattern.

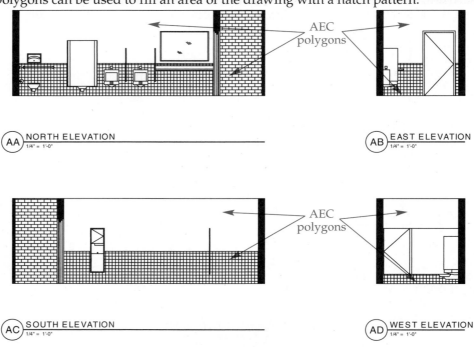

Creating AEC Polygon Styles

Before an AEC polygon can be used, a style representing the desired type of building material or hatch pattern needs to be created. To create an AEC polygon style, pick **Document** > **AEC Polygon** > **AEC Polygon Styles...** from the pull-down menu, or type AECPOLYGONSTYLE.

After entering the command, the **Style Manager** opens to the AEC Polygon Styles section. Pick the **New Style** button to create a new AEC polygon style. Enter a name, and then pick the style in the tree view to display the AEC polygon property tabs.

The **General** tab is used to rename the AEC polygon style; provide a description of the style; and attach any keynotes, design notes, or property set definitions. The **Dimensions** tab includes **Edge Width** and **Justify** options. The **Edge Width** text box controls the width of the exterior edge of the AEC polygon, as shown in **Figure 19-30**. The width can be set to 0″ if an edge is not desired. The **Justify** drop-down list controls the justification points for the AEC polygon. The **Other** tab includes a **Use Background Mask** check box. When this option is checked, the AEC polygon has masking capabilities similar to masking objects, except the AEC polygon will mask both AEC objects and standard AutoCAD linework, such as lines, arcs, and circles. The **Classifications** tab is used to assign classification definitions to the AEC polygon style.

The **Display Properties** tab controls the display of AEC polygons in the drawing. Three types of display representations are available: Model, Model Screened, and True Color.

The Model display representation is used in the default Plan and Model views. This representation allows you to display a hatch pattern on the interior and exterior of the AEC polygon. See **Figure 19-30**. This representation includes several components that can be turned on or off. Turn on the Interior Hatch and Edge Hatch display components to display a hatch pattern. In the **Hatching** tab, assign a hatch to the two Hatch components. Pick the swatch in the **Pattern** column to assign a predefined or user hatch to the Hatch components. Make any adjustment to scale and rotation by picking the values for the two components. The Interior Fill and Edge Fill components are used if the drawing is shaded, to display the AEC polygons in a shaded mode.

Figure 19-30.
AEC polygons can be created with or without an edge and with two different types of hatch patterns.

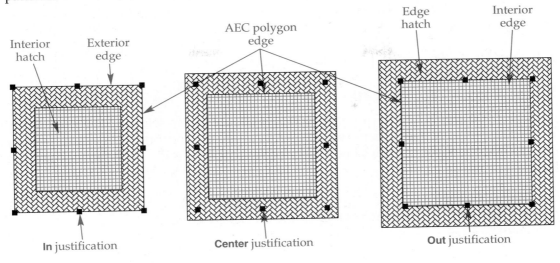

The Model Screened display representation is used in the Screened display configurations and displays the hatching in shades of gray. As with the Model display representation, if the hatch is to be displayed, turn on the Interior Hatch and Edge Hatch display components as appropriate.

The True Color representation is used in a Plan view with the Presentation display configuration to display interior and exterior solid fills. The True Color representations display a solid color using any true color available in addition to the AutoCAD standard 256 colors.

NOTE
AEC polygon styles can be incorporated as infill panels in a curtain wall style or in a door/window assembly style.

Adding AEC Polygons

To add an AEC polygon into the drawing, pick **Document** > **AEC Polygon** > **Add AEC Polygon...** from the pull-down menu, or type AECPOLYGONADD. This starts the process of adding an AEC polygon to the drawing.

The **Properties** palette is used to set the properties of the object being created before adding it to the drawing. Select the AEC polygon style to be used from the **Style** property. As with a polyline, begin picking vertex locations within the drawing for the AEC polygon. When you have finished selecting points, pick the **Close** option to close the AEC polygon. The AEC polygon is displayed in the shape drawn. AEC polygons are drawn in the current XY drawing plane or in any other plane by snapping the vertex point to a 3D point, such as the top of a wall.

Type
AECPOLYGONADD
Pull-Down Menu
Document
> AEC Polygon
> Add AEC
Polygon...

AECPOLYGONADD

Converting Polylines to AEC Polygons

There might be situations in which a curved area needs to have a hatch pattern applied. The **AECPOLYGONADD** command is limited to creating polygons as straight-line shapes. If a complex area or an area that includes curves needs to have the hatch pattern applied, an **AEC Polygon** tool can be applied to a closed polyline.

In order to apply the properties of an **AEC Polygon** tool to a closed polyline shape, a tool must be added to the **Tool Palettes** window. A generic **AEC Polygon** tool can be found in the Stock Tool Catalog in the **Content Browser**, under the Helper Tools section. Drag and drop the tool from the **Content Browser** to a tool palette so it can be used to convert polylines into AEC polygons.

To apply the **AEC Polygon** tool properties to a polyline, right-click over an **AEC Polygon** tool in the tool palettes, and pick **Apply Tool Properties to** > **Closed Polyline** from the shortcut menu. Select any polylines that will be converted into an AEC polygon. Use the **Properties** palette to change the style as needed.

Modifying an AEC Polygon

Once you create an AEC polygon, you can modify it by selecting the grip points along the polygon and specifying a new location for the point. In addition, you can change the style, description, and layer used by the AEC polygon through the **Properties** palette.

Exercise
19-11 **Complete the Exercise on the Student CD.**

Using Modifying Tools to Adjust AEC Polygons

AEC polygons include tools that can be used to change the shape and manner in which they are used. AEC polygons can be trimmed, divided, subtracted, merged, and cropped. The following sections describe these tools and how they can be used.

Trimming an AEC Polygon

When trimming an AEC polygon, a portion of the polygon is removed from the drawing. To trim an AEC polygon, pick the AEC polygon, right-click, and pick **AEC Modify Tools** > **Trim** from the shortcut menu. After accessing the option, pick a start point, and then pick the trim endpoint to establish the trimming plane. After picking the endpoint, pick a polygon on the side of the trim line that will be removed. This will remove the selected portion of the AEC polygon from the trimmed edge. See **Figure 19-31**.

Figure 19-31.
The **Trim** option removes a portion of the AEC polygon from a trim line.

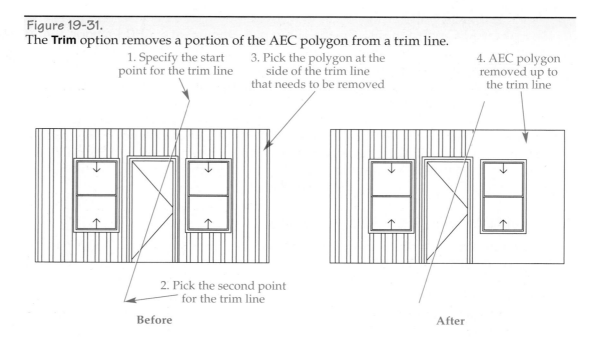

Architectural Desktop and Its Applications

Dividing an AEC Polygon

An AEC polygon can also be divided into two parts by specifying a dividing line. To divide an AEC polygon into two parts, select the AEC polygon, right-click, and pick **AEC Modify Tools** > **Divide** from the shortcut menu. Once the option has been accessed, pick the start point for the dividing line, and then pick the dividing endpoint. After picking the endpoint, the selected AEC polygon is divided into two pieces. See **Figure 19-32.**

Subtracting Polygons

AEC polygons can be subtracted from one another, to form holes in a polygon for windows or openings in an elevation, or used to take part of a polygon away from an edge. In order to use this option, the object being subtracted from the AEC polygon must form a closed boundary, such as another AEC polygon, a polyline, or a circle. See **Figure 19-33.** When you are subtracting an object from another AEC polygon, select the AEC polygon, right-click, and pick **AEC Modify Tools** > **Subtract** from the shortcut menu. Select the object to be subtracted. After picking the subtracting object, type Y to erase the subtracting object or N to retain the object. When you are finished, a hole is cut in the AEC polygon. See **Figure 19-33.**

Figure 19-32.
Use the **Divide** option to divide a polygon into two pieces.

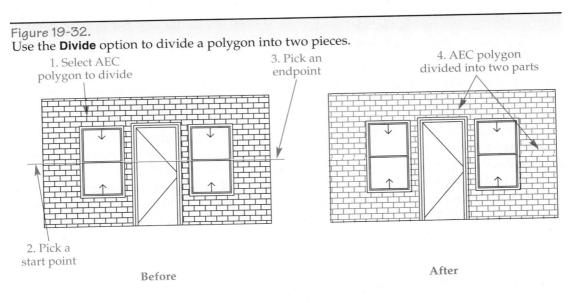

1. Select AEC polygon to divide

3. Pick an endpoint

4. AEC polygon divided into two parts

2. Pick a start point

Before

After

Figure 19-33.
Closed objects over an AEC polygon can be used to remove or subtract portions of an AEC polygon.

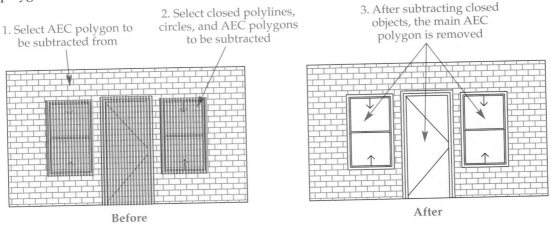

1. Select AEC polygon to be subtracted from

2. Select closed polylines, circles, and AEC polygons to be subtracted

3. After subtracting closed objects, the main AEC polygon is removed

Before

After

Merging Polygons

As AEC polygons are created, they might mistakenly get overlapped or need to be merged together to form a uniform pattern. The **Merge** option allows you to merge two AEC polygons together. To merge two AEC polygons together, pick one of the polygons, right-click, and select **AEC Modify Tools** > **Merge** from the shortcut menu. Pick an AEC polygon to be joined with the selected polygon. After picking additional AEC polygons to be merged together, type Y to erase the original AEC polygons or N to keep the original AEC polygons. The AEC polygons are joined using the first selected AEC polygon's hatch pattern. See **Figure 19-34.**

Cropping AEC Polygons

Occasionally after an AEC polygon has been created, you might need to crop the AEC polygon shape down to the boundaries of another closed object. The **Crop** option is used to crop the AEC polygon shape and hatch pattern down to a new shape. The shape representing the new cropped boundary can be within the AEC polygon or cross through the AEC polygon. To crop an AEC polygon, select the AEC polygon, right-click, and pick **AEC Modify Tools** > **Crop** from the shortcut menu.

After accessing the option, pick a closed object to be used to form the new AEC polygon boundary. After selecting the object to be used as the cropping boundary, type Y to erase the cropping boundary or N to keep the boundary. See **Figure 19-35.**

Adding and Removing Vertex Points

Like the Slab and Roof Slab objects, AEC polygons have the capability of having vertex points added or removed along the edge of the AEC polygon. To add vertices on an existing AEC polygon, select the polygon, right-click, and pick **Vertex** > **Add** from the shortcut menu. Pick a point in the drawing for the new vertex location. A new vertex is added, with the AEC polygon adjusting the shape to accommodate the new vertex. Additional vertex points can be added by picking multiple points. When you are finished adding vertices, press the [Enter] key to end the option.

To remove existing vertex points, pick the AEC polygon, right-click, and pick **Vertex** > **Remove** from the shortcut menu. After accessing the option, begin picking points in the drawing to remove vertices. Continue to remove vertices until you are finished. Press the [Enter] key to end the option.

Hiding and Displaying AEC Polygon Edges

There might be instances in which the side of an AEC polygon needs to be removed while maintaining the other edges of the shape. The **Hide Edge** option is used to hide different edges of an AEC polygon. To access this option, select the AEC polygon,

Figure 19-34.
Use the **Merge** option to join two AEC polygons together.

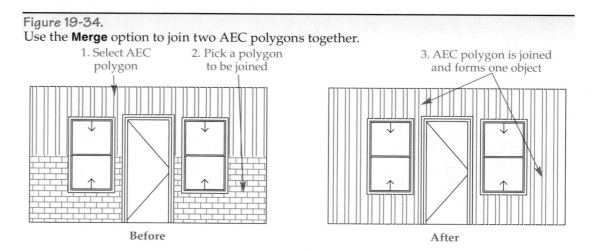

1. Select AEC polygon
2. Pick a polygon to be joined
3. AEC polygon is joined and forms one object

Before

After

Figure 19-35.
The **Crop** option is used to crop an AEC polygon down to a different cropping boundary.

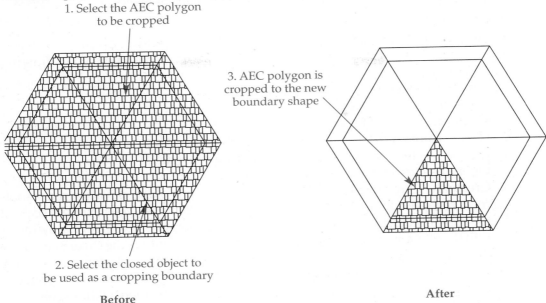

1. Select the AEC polygon to be cropped

3. AEC polygon is cropped to the new boundary shape

2. Select the closed object to be used as a cropping boundary

Before

After

right-click, and pick the **Hide Edge** option. Select any edges on the polygon to be hidden. As you pick edges, the edges change to a red color by default. Press the [Enter] key to exit the option and hide the edges.

If hidden edges on the AEC polygon need to be adjusted, select the AEC polygon and use the grip boxes to change the shape. The edges will maintain their hidden assignments.

Hidden edges on an AEC polygon can be made visible again by using the **Show Edge** option. To access this option, select the AEC polygon, right-click, and pick the **Show Edge** option. This displays the hidden edges of the polygon in red by default. You are prompted to select an edge to show. Select any of the hidden (red) edges to be redisplayed, and then press the [Enter] key. The hidden edges become visible again.

Chapter Test

Answer the following questions. Write your answers on a separate sheet of paper or complete the electronic chapter test on the Student CD.

1. Describe the information found in elevations.
2. What needs to be created before generating elevations when you are using the **Project Navigator**?
3. Define *cardinal direction*.
4. What is an *elevation line*?
5. Identify the direction used when selecting points to establish an elevation line.
6. Selecting the Elevation object highlights the entire elevation as if it were a block. Why is it important for the elevation to remain in this state and not be exploded?
7. Briefly discuss subdivisions related to elevations that can be adjusted to reflect coloring and plotting.
8. What do you have to do so linework can be updated if the building model changes after the linework within the elevation has been edited?
9. Give at least two drawbacks related to editing linework in the 3D elevation.
10. Define *AEC polygon*.

Chapter Projects

Use the techniques covered in this chapter to create the following drawings.

1. Single-Level Residential Project
   A. Access the **Project Browser** and set Residential-Project-01 current.
   B. Access the **Views** tab of the **Project Navigator** and create a new view drawing. Choose the **Section/Elevation** option.
   C. On the **General** page, enter the following:
      - **Name:** Exterior Elevations
      - **Description:** 2D Elevations
   D. On the **Context** page, select the four levels under Division 1.
   E. On the **Content** page, uncheck the Furniture construct.
   F. Open the Exterior Elevations view drawing.
   G. Create the four elevations of the building. Use one of the elevation mark tools from the **Callouts** tool palette. In the **Place Callout** worksheet, set the scale of the elevation to 1/4" = 1'-0". Generate the elevations in the current drawing.
   H. Edit the 2D Section Style 96 section/elevation style. Change the Outer Shrinkwrap display component's color to Green. Change the Inner Shrinkwrap color to Blue. Turn off the Surface Hatch Linework and Section Hatch Linework components. Change the linetype for the Hidden component to the Hidden2 linetype.
   I. Use **Linework** > **Edit** from the shortcut menu to change the foundation lines in each elevation to the Hidden Vectors component.
   J. Use editing options to edit or merge additional linework to the elevations as shown in the figures.
   K. Create AEC polygons for the material hatches and apply those to the elevations.
   L. Add documentation blocks, such as elevation labels and title marks, to the elevations. Add any additional blocks desired, such as trees and people.
   M. Save and close the drawing.

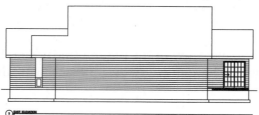

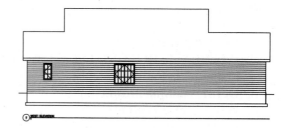

Design Courtesy Alan Mascord Design Associates

Chapter 19 Projects

2. Single-Level Residential Project
   A. Access the **Project Browser** and set Residential-Project-02 current.
   B. Access the **Constructs** tab of the **Project Navigator** and open the Main Floor construct.
   C. Adjust the floor line of the brick veneer walls at the front of the house to be –1'-0" from the baseline.
   D. Save and close the drawing.
   E. Access the **Views** tab of the **Project Navigator** and create a new view drawing. Choose the **Section/Elevation** option.
   F. On the **General** page, enter the following:
      • **Name:** Exterior Elevations
      • **Description:** 2D Elevations
   G. On the **Context** page, select the five levels under Division 1.
   H. On the **Content** page, uncheck the Furniture construct.
   I. Open the Exterior Elevations view drawing.
   J. Create the four elevations of the building. Use one of the elevation mark tools from the **Callouts** tool palette. In the **Place Callout** worksheet, set the scale of the elevation to 1/4" = 1'-0". Generate the elevations in the current drawing.
   K. Edit the 2D Section Style 96 section/elevation style. Change the Outer Shrinkwrap display component's color to Green. Change the Inner Shrinkwrap color to Blue. Change the linetype for the Hidden component to the Hidden2 linetype.
   L. Use **Linework** > **Edit** from the shortcut menu to change the foundation lines in each elevation to the Hidden Vectors component.
   M. Use editing options to edit or merge additional linework to the elevations as shown in the figures.
   N. Create AEC polygons for the material hatches and apply those to the elevations.
   O. Add documentation blocks, such as elevation labels and title marks, to the elevations. Add any additional blocks desired, such as trees and people.
   P. Save and close the drawing.

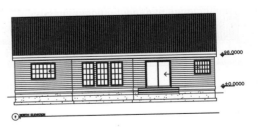

Design Courtesy Alan Mascord Design Associates

3. Two-Story Residential Project
   A. Access the **Project Browser** and set Residential-Project-03 current.
   B. Access the **Views** tab of the **Project Navigator** and create a new view drawing. Choose the **Section/Elevation** option.
   C. On the **General** page, enter the following:
      - **Name:** Exterior Elevations
      - **Description:** 2D Elevations
   D. On the **Context** page, select the six levels under Division 1.
   E. On the **Content** page, uncheck the Furniture construct.
   F. Open the Exterior Elevations view drawing.
   G. Create the four elevations of the building. Use one of the elevation mark tools from the **Callouts** tool palette. In the **Place Callout** worksheet, set the scale of the elevation to 1/4" = 1'-0". Generate the elevations in the current drawing.
   H. Edit the 2D Section Style 96 section/elevation style. Change the Outer Shrinkwrap display component's color to Green. Change the Inner Shrinkwrap color to Blue. Change the linetype for the Hidden component to the Hidden2 linetype.
   I. Use **Linework > Edit** from the shortcut menu to change the foundation lines in each elevation to the Hidden Vectors component.
   J. Use editing options to edit or merge additional linework to the elevations as shown in the figures.
   K. Create AEC polygons for the material hatches and apply those to the elevations.
   L. Add documentation blocks, such as elevation labels and title marks, to the elevations. Add any additional blocks desired, such as trees and people.
   M. Save and close the drawing.

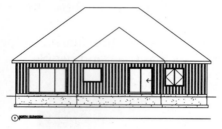

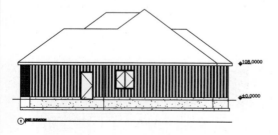

Drawing Courtesy 3D-DZYN

4. Two-Story Residential Project
   A. Access the **Project Browser** and set Residential-Project-04 current.
   B. Access the **Views** tab of the **Project Navigator** and create a new view drawing. Choose the **Section/Elevation** option.
   C. On the **General** page, enter the following:
      - **Name:** Exterior Elevations
      - **Description:** 2D Elevations
   D. On the **Context** page, select the six levels under Division 1.
   E. On the **Content** page, uncheck the MainFlr-Furniture and UpperFlr-Furniture constructs.
   F. Open the Exterior Elevations view drawing.
   G. Create the four elevations of the building. Use one of the elevation mark tools from the **Callouts** tool palette. In the **Place Callout** worksheet, set the scale of the elevation to 1/4" = 1'-0". Generate the elevations in the current drawing.
   H. Edit the 2D Section Style 96 section/elevation style. Change the Outer Shrinkwrap display component's color to Green. Change the Inner Shrinkwrap color to Blue. Change the linetype for the Hidden component to the Hidden2 linetype.
   I. Use **Linework** > **Edit** from the shortcut menu to change the foundation lines in each elevation to the Hidden Vectors component.
   J. Use editing options to edit or merge additional linework to the elevations as shown in the figures.
   K. Create AEC polygons for the material hatches and apply those to the elevations.
   L. Add documentation blocks, such as elevation labels and title marks, to the elevations. Add any additional blocks desired, such as trees and people.
   M. Save and close the drawing.

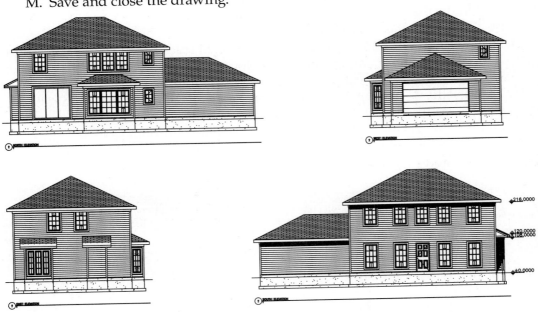

Design Courtesy Alan Mascord Design Associates

5. Commercial Store Project
   A. Access the **Project Browser** and set Commercial-Project-05 current.
   B. Access the **Views** tab of the **Project Navigator** and create a new view drawing. Choose the **Section/Elevation** option.
   C. On the **General** page, enter the following:
      - **Name:** Exterior Elevations
      - **Description:** 2D Elevations
   D. On the **Context** page, select the five levels under Division 1.
   E. On the **Content** page, uncheck the Furniture construct.
   F. Open the Exterior Elevations view drawing.
   G. Create an elevation style as desired. Create rules based on the colors of the display representation components found in the Section_Elev display set.
   H. Create a front elevation of the strip mall. Regenerate the elevation using the custom elevation style.
   I. Use editing options to edit or merge linework to the elevations as shown in the figures.
   J. Add any blocks as desired, such as people, trees, and vehicles in elevation, and elevation marks.
   K. Use the material boundary as needed to remove material hatches.
   L. Save and close the drawing.
   M. Access the **Views** tab of the **Project Navigator** and create a new view drawing. Choose the **Section/Elevation** option.
   N. On the **General** page, enter the following:
      - **Name:** Interior Elevations
      - **Description:** 2D Elevations
   O. On the **Context** page, select the five levels under Division 1.
   P. On the **Content** page, uncheck the Furniture construct.
   Q. Open the Interior Elevations view drawing.
   R. Create an elevation style as desired. Create rules based on the colors of the display representation components found in the Section_Elev display set.
   S. Regenerate the elevations using the custom interior elevation style.
   T. Use editing options to edit or merge linework to the elevations as shown in the figures.
   U. Add any blocks as desired, such as elevation bathroom blocks.
   V. Use the material boundary as needed to remove material hatches.
   W. Save and close the drawing.

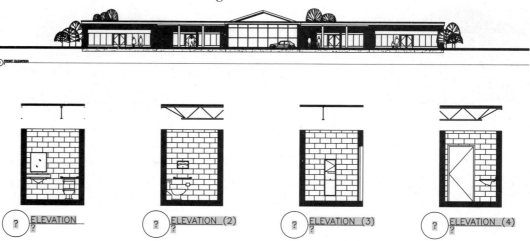

Drawing Courtesy 3D-DZYN

6. Commercial Car Maintenance Shop Project
   A. Access the **Project Browser** and set Commercial-Project-06 current.
   B. Access the **Views** tab of the **Project Navigator** and create a new view drawing. Choose the **Section/Elevation** option.
   C. On the **General** page, enter the following:
      - **Name:** Exterior Elevations
      - **Description:** 2D Elevations
   D. On the **Context** page, select the seven levels under Division 1.
   E. On the **Content** page, uncheck the MainFlr-Furniture and UpperFlr-Furniture constructs.
   F. Open the Exterior Elevations view drawing.
   G. Create an elevation style as desired. Create rules based on the colors of the display representation components found in the Section_Elev display set.
   H. Create a front elevation of the oil change and car wash building. Regenerate the elevation using the custom elevation style.
   I. Use editing options to edit or merge linework to the elevations as shown in the figures.
   J. Add any blocks as desired, such as people, trees, and vehicles in elevation, and elevation marks.
   K. Use the material boundary as needed to remove material hatches.
   L. Save and close the drawing.
   M. Access the **Views** tab of the **Project Navigator** and create a new view drawing. Choose the **Section/Elevation** option.
   N. On the **General** page, enter the following:
      - **Name:** Interior Elevations
      - **Description:** 2D Elevations
   O. On the **Context** page, select the following levels under Division 1:
      - Upper Floor Framing
      - Main Floor
      - Main Floor Framing
   P. On the **Content** page, uncheck the MainFlr-Furniture construct.
   Q. Open the Interior Elevations view drawing.
   R. Create an interior elevation style as desired. Create rules based on the colors of the display representation components found in the Section_Elev display set.
   S. Create interior elevations for one of the bathrooms. Regenerate the elevations using the custom interior elevation style.
   T. Use editing options to edit or merge linework to the elevations as shown in the figures.
   U. Add any blocks as desired, such as elevation bathroom blocks.
   V. Use material boundaries as needed to remove material hatches.
   W. Save and close the drawing.

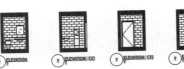

Drawing Courtesy 3D-DZYN

7. Governmental Fire Station
   A. Access the **Project Browser** and set Gvrmt-Project-07 current.
   B. Access the **Views** tab of the **Project Navigator** and create a new view drawing. Choose the **Section/Elevation** option.
   C. On the **General** page, enter the following:
      - **Name:** Exterior Elevations
      - **Description:** 2D Elevations
   D. On the **Context** page, select the five levels under Division 1.
   E. On the **Content** page, uncheck the Furniture construct.
   F. Open the Exterior Elevations view drawing.
   G. Create an elevation style as desired. Create rules based on the colors of the display representation components found in the Section_Elev display set.
   H. Create the four elevations of the fire station. Regenerate the elevation using the custom elevation style.
   I. Use editing options to edit or merge linework to the elevations as shown in the figures.
   J. Add material boundaries to the side and rear elevations.
   K. Use the **BHATCH** command to add gradient fills to the windows in the elevations.
   L. Add blocks and shadows as indicated in the figure.
   M. Save and close the drawing.

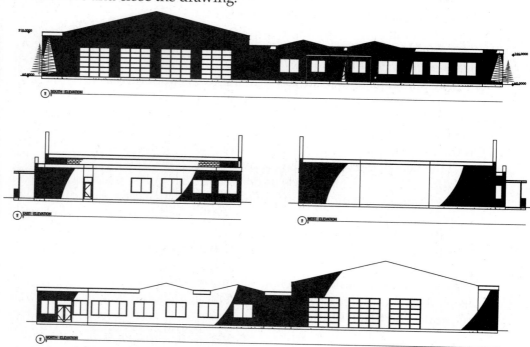

Drawing Courtesy 3D-DZYN

Creating Sections

Learning Objectives:

After completing this chapter, you will be able to do the following:
- ✓ Create a 2D section line.
- ✓ Draw a 2D section.
- ✓ Update the Section object.
- ✓ Edit and merge section linework.
- ✓ Use section line blocks and detail marks.
- ✓ Define section styles.
- ✓ Adjust section line properties.
- ✓ Create and modify a live section.

Architectural Desktop includes tools for generating Section objects. Sections are similar to elevations because they also provide information regarding the vertical aspects of the building. However, instead of displaying how the surface of the building or room appears on the surface, sections show how the building is assembled. A *section* is a drawing that displays part of the building as if it has been cut through and had a portion removed, showing the interior detail. Sections are typically created as two-dimensional drawings with additional information identifying construction techniques, as shown in **Figure 20-1**.

Architectural Desktop provides utilities for creating 2D and 3D sections. These are similar to Elevation objects, except they are created on their own section layer and provide a cutaway view of the interior of the BIM. 2D and 3D sections can be created from geometry within a drawing, xrefs attached to a drawing, or a section/elevation view drawing within the **Project Navigator**. In addition to these two utilities, a display known as a live section can be created that physically cuts the building model at the cut line and removes the portion of the building.

Figure 20-1.
A section is typically a two-dimensional drawing of the interior of a three-dimensional building.

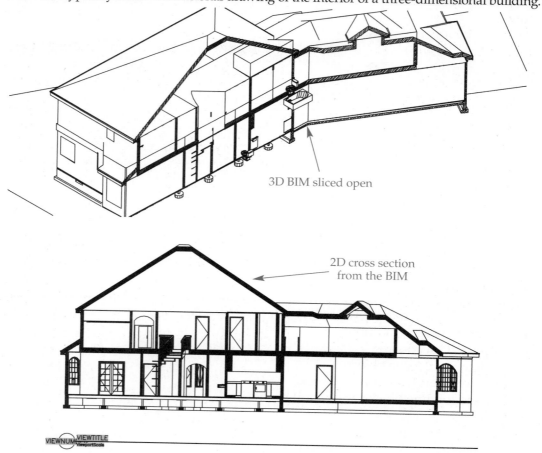

3D BIM sliced open

2D cross section
from the BIM

VIEWNUM VIEWTITLE
ViewportScale

Creating a Section View Drawing

After the building constructs/drawings have been created, sections can be established from the model. Architectural Desktop creates sections from the Model representation of the AEC objects. You can create the sections in the same drawing where the walls, doors, and windows are drawn, or you can create the sections from a view drawing with a series of xref drawings building the model.

When you are using the **Project Navigator** for managing your drawings and the reference files used to create the BIM, a view drawing is created that assembles all the reference files needed to create a model of the building. Similar to view drawings used to generate elevations, a view drawing is used to create sections.

If you are using the **Project Navigator**, a section/elevation view drawing should be created before generating sections. To do this, access the **Project Navigator**, and then pick the **Views** tab. In the **Views** tab, create a new view drawing by picking the **Add View** button at the bottom of the palette or by right-clicking under the Views folder and picking **New View Drawing** from the shortcut menu. Next, pick the **Section/Elevation** option for the view. This option uses the drawing template specified for the creation of sections and elevations in the project's properties. After choosing the **Section/Elevation** option, the **Add Section/Elevation View** worksheet is displayed. Next, enter a name and description for the view drawing, verify the drawing template being used, and then pick the **Next** button at the bottom of the worksheet. The next page of the **Add Section/ Elevation View** worksheet is the **Context** page. This page is used to select the levels and any combination of divisions that will be used when assembling the project drawings together for the view drawing. Select any levels to be used within the section drawing. When you are finished selecting the levels, pick the **Next** button to advance to the last page of the worksheet.

The last page of the **Add Section/Elevation View** worksheet is the **Content** page, which displays a list of drawings using the levels and divisions selected in the **Context** page. Place a check mark beside each of the drawings that will be assembled into a model so a section can be generated from the model.

Exercise
20-1   Complete the Exercise on the Student CD.

Creating Sections

Once a section/elevation view has been created or a drawing with a completed model is available, 2D sections can be generated. The tools for creating sections can be found in the **Callouts** palette in the **Document** tool palette group. To access this group, pick the **Properties** button in the title bar of the **Tool Palettes** window, and then select **Document** from the bottom of the shortcut list. This changes the tool palette group from **Design** to **Document**.

To create 2D sections, select the **Callouts** palette, and select one of the five section mark tools. The **Section Mark A1** and **Section Mark A1T** tools create a section mark with a section number in the bubble. The **Section Mark A1T** also includes a tail at the end of the section line, indicating the direction the section is cutting through. The **Section Mark A2** and **Section Mark A2T** tools are similar to the first two section marks, except the section bubble includes room for the section number and the sheet number where the section can be found. The **Section Mark A3T** tool includes section bubbles at each end of the section cut line, section number, and sheet number within the bubble.

When using any of the section mark tools, pick the start point for the section cut line that will be placed in the drawing. In this application, the section line or cut line is commonly referred to as a *cutting plane line* in drafting terminology. After picking the start point for the section cut line, pick the next point. A section cut line can be drawn as a straight line by picking a second point, drawn as a jogged line by picking multiple points, and broken to cut through specific objects. After picking the second point for the section cut line, you can pick the next point or use the **Break** option. These options are repeated while picking points, allowing you to pick additional points for the cut line. If the cut line is to be broken between long distances, type B to access the **Break** option. This allows you to break the cut line at the previous point selected and then start the cut line again by picking the next point.

When you are finished picking the points to define the section cut line, press the [Enter] key to exit the cut line point prompts. The last prompt is used to specify how deep into the model, away from the cut line, the section represents when it generates the section. Drag the crosshairs into the model to specify the depth for the section. Specifying the extents also sets the section arrow to point in the direction the section is cutting. This is the viewing direction. After the extents have been specified, the **Place Callout** worksheet is displayed. See **Figure 20-2**.

The **Place Callout** worksheet includes the following properties:
- **Callout Only.** Pick this button to add only the callout, without generating a section.

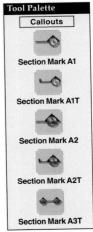

Tool Palette

Callouts

Section Mark A1

Section Mark A1T

Section Mark A2

Section Mark A2T

Section Mark A3T

Figure 20-2.
The **Place Callout** worksheet is used to generate a section and add a title mark and elevation scale callout.

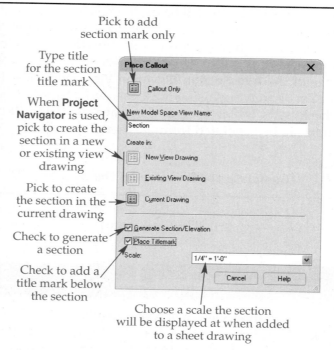

Pick to add section mark only

Type title for the section title mark

When **Project Navigator** is used, pick to create the section in a new or existing view drawing

Pick to create the section in the current drawing

Check to generate a section

Check to add a title mark below the section

Choose a scale the section will be displayed at when added to a sheet drawing

- **New Model Space View Name.** When a section is generated, a model space view is created around the section, which is used when adding the view to a sheet drawing. Refer to Chapter 3 for more information on model space views. The name you enter in this text box is the name of the model space view and the name entered in the title mark under the section.
- **New View Drawing.** When you are using the **Project Navigator**, this button becomes available and is used to generate the section in a new section/elevation view drawing.
- **Existing View Drawing.** When the **Project Navigator** is used, this button is available to generate the section in an existing section/elevation view drawing.
- **Current Drawing.** Pick this button to generate the section in the current drawing.
- **Generate Section/Elevation.** Select this check box to create a 2D section.
- **Place Titlemark.** Select this check box to place a title mark below the section to name the section and specify the scale of the section when added to a sheet drawing.
- **Scale.** When a section is generated, a model space view is created around the section. The model space view is later added to a sheet drawing at the scale specified in this drop-down list.

If the section is generated in the current drawing, pick the **Current Drawing** button. This returns the drawing screen, where you can pick a location in which the 2D Section object will be placed.

The 2D section is generated and placed at the location you specified. If a title mark was added, it is placed below the Section object. The section number, title, and scale are automatic fields and are updated after the section's model space view is added to a sheet drawing. This is discussed later in this text.

Manual Section Creation Method

Type
BLDGSECTION LINEADD
Pull-Down Menu
Document > Sections and Elevations > Add Section Line

BLDGSECTIONLINEADD

Another method of section creation involves creating a section line, which defines the section cut line and creates the section box for the depth of the section, which is similar to the function of section mark callout tools. After the section line is added, the section is generated by applying the **BLDGSECTIONLINEGENERATE** command. To add a section line to the drawing, pick **Document** > **Sections and Elevations** > **Add Section Line** from the pull-down menu or type BLDGSECTIONLINEADD.

After you access the **BLDGSECTIONLINEADD** command, you are prompted to select points to define the section line. After picking the points for the section cut, press the [Enter] key. Next, enter a numerical value specifying how far into the model the section will look to process the 2D section.

When you finish creating the section line, an invisible box is added around the model. This box determines the parts of the building model available for the Section object. For a 2D section, the box needs to wrap only around the part of the building that will be shown in the section. The box can be enlarged or shrunk by selecting the section line to display the grips, picking a grip point, and respecifying the location of the point.

The section line is created on the A-Sect-Line layer, which is a nonplotting layer. This way, the line used to generate the elevation does not plot on the finished construction document set, allowing you to add your own graphical section cut lines.

After the section line has been added, a 2D section can be created. The 2D section creates a two-dimensional section of anything visible within the section line box. Where the section line crosses through geometry, that geometry appears to be cut away in the section.

To create a 2D section, select the section line, right-click, and pick the **Generate 2D Section...** option. Once the option is entered, the **Generate Section/Elevation** dialog box is displayed, as in Figure 20-3. The options are similar to those given when generating elevations. See Chapter 19 for details.

NOTE

Although you can choose the display set to use for processing the Section object, it is recommended that you use the Section_Elevation display set until you fully understand how the Architectural Desktop display settings work. You can then begin experimenting with how other display sets control how the design rules are processed.

Figure 20-3.
The **Generate Section/Elevation** dialog box is used to manually create or regenerate a section.

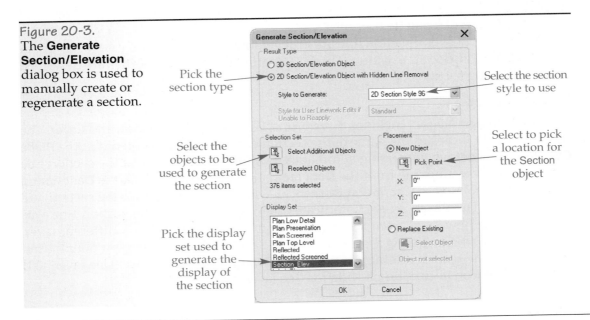

When you have finished specifying section criteria, pick the **OK** button to create the section. Architectural Desktop generates the section at the point specified in the **Generate Section/Elevation** dialog box.

If materials have been assigned to the objects in the building model, the section displays the surface and section hatches. The surface and section hatches display using the color designated by the material's Surface Hatch or Section Hatch component in the material definition. All other linework representing the walls, roofs, doors, and windows in the section are assigned to a single color. Selecting the Section object highlights the entire section as if it were a block. As long as the section remains in this state and is not exploded, it can be updated to reflect the latest changes to the plan drawings. Exploding the Section object breaks the link to the original building model.

NOTE

If an automatically generated section is selected, an invisible boundary is displayed with grips. This boundary specifies the model space view boundaries and represents the extents of the view when it is added to a sheet drawing. The grips can be adjusted to increase or decrease the size of the model space view boundaries.

Exercise
20-2   Complete the Exercise on the Student CD.

Adjusting Section Line Properties

Section cut lines can incorporate subdivision lines to place different objects within the model on different Section object components for display and plotting control. When the section is first created, the extents/depth box that extends forward of the section cut line is considered to be one subdivision. Any object's linework within the box is generated into a section using the color assigned to the first subdivision component within the section style. Additional subdivisions within the section cut line box can be created with their own colors, linetypes, lineweights, and plot styles assigned to each subdivision.

The **Properties** palette can be used to modify the parameters of the section cut line and section extents/depth box, as well as to add subdivisions for greater section display control. To edit the properties of the section cut line, pick the section line and access the **Properties** palette.

The properties for a section line are broken down into four main categories under the **BASIC** header. See Figure 20-4. These categories and their properties are described in the following sections.

General Category

The **General** category includes three properties: **Name**, **Description**, and **Layer**. The **Name** property indicates the name of the section cut line, which is entered in the **Place Callout** worksheet when creating automatic elevations, or the name of the section line when adding a section line from the **Document** pull-down menu. Pick the **Description** property to display the **Description** worksheet, where a description for the section line can be made. The **Layer** property indicates the layer on which the section line was created. Pick a new layer from the list to assign the section line to a different layer. By default, the section line is assigned to the A-Sect-Line layer, which is a nonplotting layer. To plot the section line, access the **Layer Manager**, find the A-Sect-Line layer, and select the **Plot** icon to turn on plotting for this layer.

Dimensions Category

The **Dimensions** category includes properties for controlling the height of the section extents/depth box and subdivisions added to the box. These properties are described below:

- **Use model extents for height.** Picking this property displays a drop-down list with a **Yes** and **No** option. Picking the **Yes** option establishes the height of the section box based on the overall height of the building model. Any building model objects within the box are then calculated for inclusion in the Section object. If the **No** option is selected, the **Height** and **Lower extension** properties become available so a set elevation height can be established. Setting specific heights for the section box gives you the capability of creating sections with the top or bottom portions of the building model removed.

- **Height.** This property is available when the **Use model extents for height** property is set to **No**. Enter a value for the maximum height of the section box. Building model objects above the top of the section box are removed from the Section object.

- **Lower extension.** This property is also available when the **Use model extents for height** property is set to **No**. This property controls where the bottom of the section box is placed below the 0" Z axis. Building model objects below the bottom of the section box are removed from the Section object.

- **Subdivisions.** Pick this property to establish subdivisions within the section box. When this property is selected, the **Subdivisions** worksheet is displayed. See **Figure 20-4**. Use the **Add** button to add subdivisions into the section box. After a subdivision line is added to the worksheet, the location can be adjusted by picking the value in the table and entering a new distance, which is measured from the section cut line. When the Section object is created, the building model objects within each subdivision are then assigned to a different subdivision component that can be assigned to different colors and lineweights. A total of 10 subdivisions can be added to the section box.

Figure 20-4.
The **Properties** palette controls the properties of the section extents/depth box.

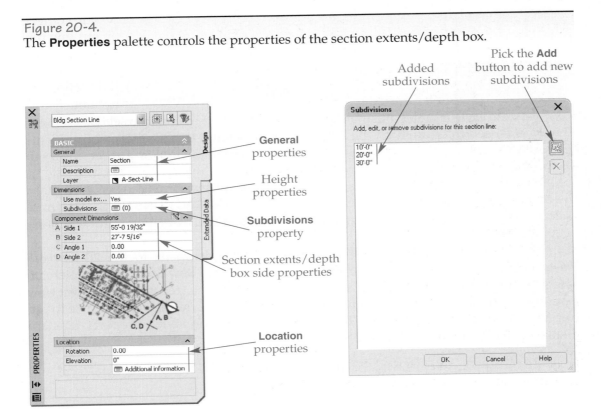

Component Dimensions Category

The **Component Dimensions** category controls the size and angle of the sides of the section box.

- **Side 1.** Pick this property to enter a new value to control the length of the left side of the secation box.
- **Side 2.** Pick this property to enter a new value to set the length of the right side of the section box.
- **Angle 1.** Pick this property to change the angle of the section box's left edge.
- **Angle 2.** Pick this property to change the angle of the section box's right edge.

Location Category

The **Location** category controls the rotation angle and elevation location of the section box. Use the **Rotation** property to rotate the box. By default, the bottom of the section box is placed at 0″ on the Z axis. Enter a height to change the location of the bottom of the box.

In addition to adjusting the section line box through this category, you can adjust it and the subdivisions with grips. Pick the section line to display the grip boxes. Pick a grip box to stretch its location, reshape the section line or the section box, or move a subdivision line.

After adding subdivision lines to the section, the 2D section needs to be updated. Select the Section object, right-click, and pick **Refresh**. The portions of the building model within each subdivision are recalculated, and the linework within each subdivision is assigned the subdivision color.

After refreshing the section, the 2D Section object is updated and displayed with the different colors, linetypes, and lineweights, based on the location of the objects between the subdivision lines.

Exercise 20-3   **Complete the Exercise on the Student CD.**

Defining the Section Style

A section style is created using the same process used to create an elevation style. The style is used to create both the 2D Elevation object and the 2D Section object. This discussion takes a brief look at the creation of a section style. For a more in-depth explanation, refer to Chapter 19.

To create or modify a section style, the 2D Section/Elevation Styles section within the **Style Manager** needs to be accessed. To access the **2DSECTIONSTYLE** command, pick **Document** > **Sections and Elevations** > **Section Styles...** from the pull-down menu or type 2DSECTIONSTYLE.

When the command is accessed, the **Style Manager** opens to the 2D Section/Elevation Styles section, as shown in **Figure 20-5**. Select the **New Style** button to create a new section style, or right-click over the style section in the tree view and select **New** from the shortcut menu. After typing a new name for the style, pick on the style in the tree view to begin configuring it. The 2D section/elevation style's property tabs are displayed, as shown in **Figure 20-5**.

Figure 20-5.
The **Style Manager** is used to configure the new section style. Once a new style has been created, pick the new style in the tree view to display the 2D section/elevation style's property tabs.

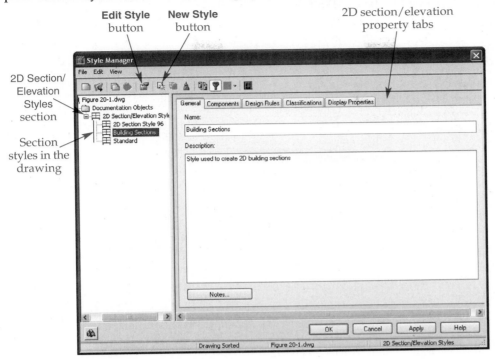

The 2D section/elevation style includes the following five tabs:

- **General.** This tab is used to rename the section/elevation style and to provide a description for its use. Because the style can be used for either 2D sections or 2D elevations, you may decide to create only one style for both, or you may decide to create one style for use with sections and another style for use with elevations. You can add any notes or additional information regarding the style of the section style by selecting the **Notes...** button.

- **Components.** This tab is used to create components used in the **Design Rules** tab. See **Figure 20-6.** The components created are then incorporated into a set of rules that determine how the geometry from the building model is to appear in the 2D Section object. You can create components that represent the types of objects in the building model, such as windows, walls, and doors, or components that represent how the components are displayed, such as lines beyond the section, hidden lines, heavy lines, and light lines.

  Use the **Add** button to create new components for the design rules. When a component is added, the name Unnamed is placed in the **Name** column. Pick on top of the name to rename the component. You can add a description for each component by picking in the description area and entering a description.

- **Design Rules.** This tab is used to establish rules covering how the colors of the objects used in the building model are to appear in the 2D section. See **Figure 20-7.**

  You can add a rule by picking the **Add** button. Pick the color swatch to choose a color to be looked for in the building model when the Section object is being processed. The color chosen should be a color the drawing uses in its Model or Elevation representation. For example, if you are looking for walls in the building model, pick color 113. The **Context** column specifies where in the building model the color is to be looked for. For example, for the color 113, a rule can be created that looks for color 113 (**Color** column) in the first subdivision

Figure 20-6.
The **Components** tab is used to create custom components that will be incorporated into a design rule. The design rules are then used to intercept color from the building model and process it into colors that will be used in the 2D Section object.

Components tab

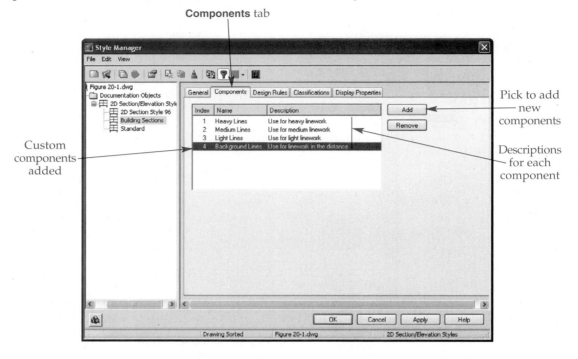

Custom components added

Pick to add new components

Descriptions for each component

Figure 20-7.
The **Design Rules** tab is used to set up rules to process the colors of AEC objects found in the building model and process them onto a component within the section style.

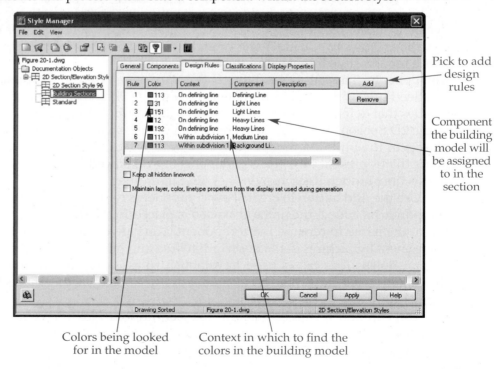

Pick to add design rules

Component the building model will be assigned to in the section

Colors being looked for in the model

Context in which to find the colors in the building model

(**Context** column) of the section line box. Finally, specify a component where the interpreted color will be placed in the Section object. The list of components includes default components for a Section object plus the components created in the **Components** tab.

You can establish as many rules as necessary to create the Section object. In Figure 20-7, several rules have been created. Some of the colors are repeated but are being looked for in a different context and sent to a different component.

- **Classifications.** This tab is used to assign classification definitions to the section style. If classification definitions are included in the drawing, choose the appropriate definition by picking in the **Classification** column.
- **Display Properties.** This tab is used to configure how the Section object is displayed. There is only a General display representation. Attach the style over-ride, and then pick the **Edit Display Properties** button. The **Display Properties** dialog box is displayed as shown in Figure 20-8. This dialog box includes three tabs: **Layer/Color/Linetype**, **Hatching**, and **Other**.

The **Layer/Color/Linetype** tab initially includes a list of default components for the Section object. See Figure 20-9. The first component is the defining line. AEC objects cut by the section line are placed on this component, unless a design rule specifies differently. The Hidden and Erased components are used when the linework is edited within the Section object. The Hidden component displays information using a hidden linetype.

Two shrink-wrap display components are available to provide shrink-wrap around objects cut by the section line. The Outer Shrinkwrap component controls the shrink-wrap applied to the outer portions of the building model linework, which is cut by the section line. The Inner Shrinkwrap component applies display properties to any linework cut by the section line that remains inside the outer boundaries of the section. The Shrinkwrap Hatch component applies a hatch

Figure 20-8.
The **Display Properties** tab is used to assign a style override to the 2D section/elevation style and edit the display properties for the style. Pick the **Edit Display Properties** button to access the **Display Properties** dialog box to configure the display settings for the style.

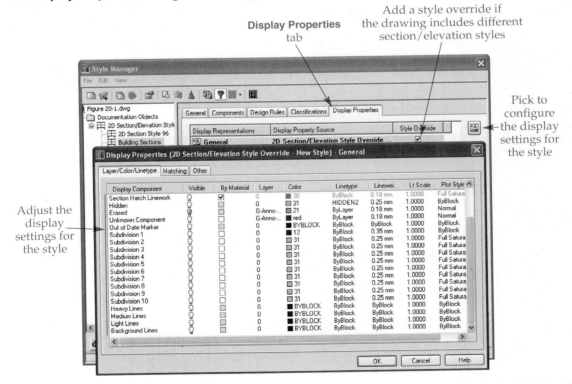

pattern between the Outer Shrinkwrap and Inner Shrinkwrap components to simulate the portions of the building being cut by the section line.

The **Hatching** tab is used to assign the hatch pattern for the Shrinkwrap Hatch display component. If the Shrinkwrap Hatch component is turned on, a hatch pattern can be assigned to the component. By default, ADT assigns a solid hatch pattern for cut portions of the building model.

The **Other** tab is used to add components to the **Layer/Color/Linetype** tab. If components were defined in the **Components** tab, they may also need to be added to this tab and spelled the same way in both tabs. Once a custom display component is added, it becomes a component in the **Layer/Color/Linetype** tab and has all the same display controls as the default components. See **Figure 20-9**.

Figure 20-9.
The **Layer/Color/Linetype** tab includes a list of display components within a 2D Section object. The **Other** tab is used to add custom display components listed in the **Components** tab and place them in the **Layer/Color/Linetype** list.

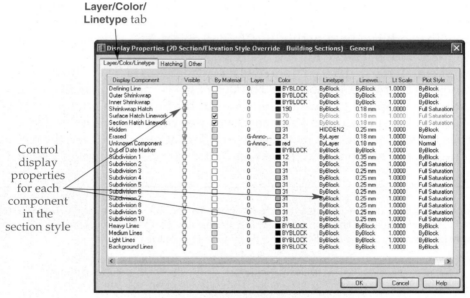

The Layer/Color/Linetype Tab

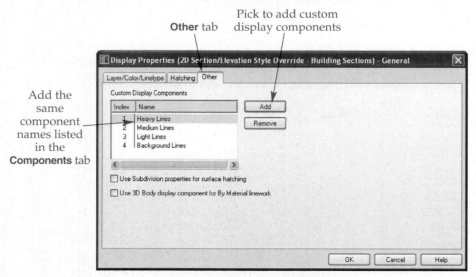

The Other Tab

Architectural Desktop and Its Applications

Once you have configured the 2D section/elevation style, pick the **OK** button to exit the **Style Manager**. The style can now be used when regenerating a section or creating a manual section.

**Exercise
20-4**   Complete the Exercise on the Student CD.

Updating the Section Object

A major benefit to using a 2D Section object is that it maintains a link to the original geometry that was used to create the section. Whenever a change is made to the building model, the section can be updated. This process works well for section/elevation view drawings in the **Project Navigator** or separately externally referenced drawings. Make the changes to the original constructs or reference drawings, reload the xref in the view drawing in which the sections are created, and then update the section.

To update the section, select the 2D Section object, right-click, and pick the **Refresh** option from the shortcut menu. The section is reprocessed and updated to reflect the latest changes to the building model.

Occasionally, new items are added to the building model, a revised portion of the building needs to be added to the Section object, or the section needs to use a different section/elevation style. In these cases, the Section object must be regenerated. To regenerate a section, select the Section object, right-click, and pick the **Regenerate...** option from the shortcut menu.

When a section is regenerated, the **Generate Section/Elevation** dialog box is displayed, as shown in **Figure 20-10.** If additional geometry has been created and needs to be added to the section, pick the **Select Additional Objects** button in the **Selection Set** area. You can also select a different section style, as well as a different display set. Pick the **OK** button to begin updating the section.

**Exercise
20-5**   Complete the Exercise on the Student CD.

Figure 20-10.
The **Generate Section/Elevation** dialog box is displayed when a Section object is regenerated.

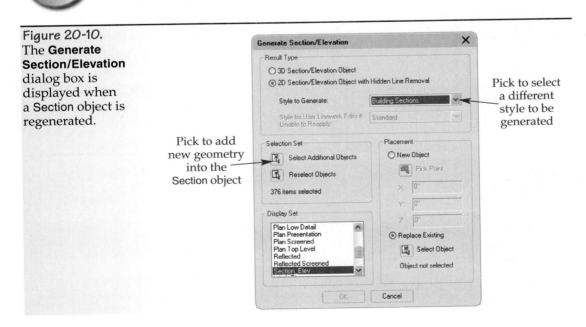

Editing the Section Object

The Section object is only as accurate as the building model. The more detailed the model, the more detailed the section. In many cases, it is not worthwhile to model everything in the building model. In these cases, the Section object can be edited to display a section with the information required to create the construction documents. Two different linework options can be used to edit the Section object: **Edit** and **Merge**.

Editing Linework

As the section is created from what the section line sees, some undesirable linework can get included in the Section object. For example, if a section line box includes part of the roof that should not be seen in the section, yet is displayed within the section, this becomes undesirable linework. Other linework can be placed on a color not desired because the design rules could not differentiate two objects using the same color. This also becomes undesirable linework.

Such lines within the section can be edited and placed on components within the section style for further display control. As long as the section remains one complete object (not exploded individual lines), the Section object maintains a link back to the original geometry. The linework cannot be edited through any conventional AutoCAD commands. The **Edit** option maintains the link while modifying how the lines appear in the section. To begin editing linework, select the Section object, right-click, and pick **Linework > Edit** from the shortcut menu. This opens the section for editing.

Begin selecting the linework to be changed to a different display component within the section style. For example, if several lines need to be placed on the Erased component, select the linework that will appear to be erased from the section.

When you are finished selecting the lines to be edited, right-click, and pick the **Modify Component...** command from the shortcut menu. The **Select Linework Component** worksheet is displayed, allowing you to select a different component for the selected geometry. See **Figure 20-11.** Pick the component from the drop-down list, and then pick the **OK** button. The edited linework is placed on the chosen component.

Continue to edit the linework until finished, repeating the process of placing the linework on any desired components. When you are finished, pick the **Save All Changes** button in the **In-Place Edit** toolbar, which is displayed when editing the linework. This closes the section to linework editing.

Merging Linework

In addition to editing existing linework, you can incorporate newly drawn lines into the Section object by using the **Merge** option. As mentioned earlier, the Section object is only as accurate as the building model. Unless structural framing has been incorporated into the building model, the section does not display framing.

In this case, structural framing can be added to the section through the use of polylines, lines, and rectangles. Once any linework has been drawn on the section, it can be merged into the Section object and placed on a component.

Figure 20-11.
After selecting linework to be edited, right-click, and pick the **Modify Component...** option to change the component assigned to the linework.

Choose a new component to which the edited linework will be assigned

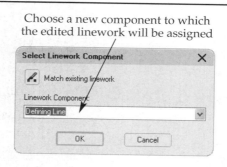

To merge new linework into the section, select the Section object, right-click, and pick **Linework > Merge...** from the shortcut menu. When this option is accessed, you are prompted to select objects to be merged. When you have finished selecting any new linework in the drawing to be merged, press the [Enter] key. The **Select Linework Component** worksheet is displayed, allowing you to select the Linework component where the merged linework is assigned. Select a component to assign the merged linework to, and pick the **OK** button. The merged linework becomes a part of the Section object and displays using the colors and linetypes specified by the display component.

Exercise
20-6   Complete the Exercise on the Student CD.

Using Material Boundaries

By default, AEC objects that include materials display a section hatch where the object has been cut by the section line. After editing linework, you may have unnecessary hatches that still appear in the section. These can be removed from the section by applying a material boundary to the section.

A material boundary is simply a closed polyline surrounding the hatched area of the section that needs to be removed. See **Figure 20-12**. After drawing the closed polyline, select the Section object, right-click, and pick **Material Boundary > Add...** from the shortcut menu.

After accessing the option, select the polyline, and determine if it will be erased. The **2d Section/Elevation Material Boundary** worksheet is displayed. See **Figure 20-13**.

The **2d Section/Elevation Material Boundary** worksheet includes three drop-down lists for applying the material boundary to the section. A table of materials used in the drawing is available, as well as two check boxes for controlling the material boundary in the section shrink-wrap hatch and shrink-wrap linework. The following settings in the worksheet are described:

- **Purpose.** This drop-down list includes two options to control how the mask is used. These options are **Limit** and **Erase**. The **Limit** option contains the hatch

Figure 20-12.
A closed polyline can be used as a material boundary to mask out hatches within the Section object.

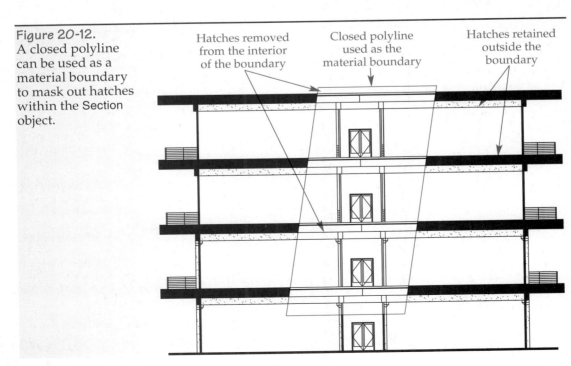

Hatches removed from the interior of the boundary

Closed polyline used as the material boundary

Hatches retained outside the boundary

and linework within the boundaries of the closed polyline. Any hatches or line-work outside the polyline boundary are removed from the elevation. The **Erase** option removes the hatch and linework inside the closed polyline boundary.

- **Apply to.** This drop-down list controls how the material boundary mask is applied. Five options are available. These are described below:
  - **Surface and Section Hatching.** Picking this option masks out surface and section hatches in a section.
  - **Surface Hatching Only.** This option masks out hatches on surfaces not cut by the section line.
  - **Section Hatching Only.** Pick this option to mask out hatches in a Section object. Section hatches are the hatches applied to a cut object.
  - **Edge Linework Only.** Pick this option to mask out linework in a section.
  - **All Linework.** This option will mask out all linework and hatching in a Section object.
- **Material Selection.** This drop-down list controls whether all material hatches are masked or only specific hatches are masked out. The **All Materials** option automatically masks out all materials in the section being masked by the material boundary. The **Specific Materials** option enables the table of materials so specific hatches can be selected for masking. Place a check mark in any specific hatches in the **Material Selection** table.
- **Apply to section shrinkwrap hatching.** When this check box is selected, the material boundary is applied to the Shrinkwrap Hatch component within the section. The Shrinkwrap Hatch component is the hatching placed between the Outer Shrinkwrap and Inner Shrinkwrap components.
- **Apply to section shrinkwrap linework.** When this check box is selected, the material boundary is applied to the Outer Shrinkwrap and Inner Shrinkwrap components of the Section object. The Outer Shrinkwrap is the outer outline of the building being cut by the section line. The Inner Shrinkwrap component is the inner outlines of rooms within the building being cut by the section line.

When you are finished specifying the parameters for the material boundary, pick the **OK** button to apply the material boundary.

Exercise
20-7   Complete the Exercise on the Student CD.

Figure 20-13.
The **2d Section/ Elevation Material Boundary** worksheet is used to apply a material boundary to the Section object.

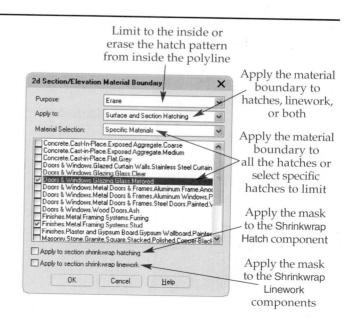

Limit to the inside or erase the hatch pattern from inside the polyline

Apply the material boundary to hatches, linework, or both

Apply the material boundary to all the hatches or select specific hatches to limit

Apply the mask to the Shrinkwrap Hatch component

Apply the mask to the Shrinkwrap Linework components

Architectural Desktop includes detail marks and detail boundaries that can be used to cut 2D and 3D section details and 2D plan details. The **Callouts** tool palette includes four detail mark tools and three detail boundary tools.

Using Detail Marks

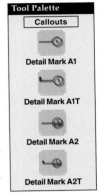

Tool Palette

Callouts

Detail Mark A1

Detail Mark A1T

Detail Mark A2

Detail Mark A2T

Four detail marks are available in the **Callouts** tool palette: **Detail Mark A1**, **Detail Mark A1T**, **Detail Mark A2**, and **Detail Mark A2T**. Similar to the section marks, the detail marks allow you to pick a start point and additional points to establish where the detail cut line cuts through your model. After picking the last point for the detail cut line, press [Enter] to display the **Place Callout** worksheet. See **Figure 20-14.**

Similar to the **Place Callout** worksheet used when adding section marks, the **Place Callout** worksheet for detail marks includes the same options. If the detail mark will be the only object generated in the drawing, select the **Callout Only** button. This adds the detail mark without placing a section box around the area being cut by the detail cut line.

By default, when a detail mark is placed in the drawing, the model space view around the 2D section detail and the title mark for the section detail is named Detail. Other detail marks added to the drawing are named Detail *n*, where *n* represents the next consecutive number. If you want to name the model space view and title mark before generating the section detail, enter a new name in the **New Model Space View Name:** text box.

If 2D section details will be generated, use the **New View Drawing**, **Existing View Drawing**, or **Current Drawing** button to create the detail in a new drawing, an existing drawing, or a current drawing. If the **New View** drawing option is selected, you are prompted to create the new view drawing, and then pick a location in the current drawing where the detail will be added in the new view drawing. If the **Existing View Drawing** button is selected, you are prompted to select an existing view drawing and then a location in the current drawing where the detail will be added in the existing drawing. When picking the location for the detail, model space views coordinated from

Figure 20-14.
Use the **Place Callout** worksheet to create a 2D section detail and detail title mark.

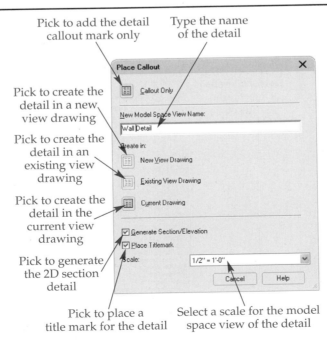

Pick to add the detail callout mark only

Type the name of the detail

Pick to create the detail in a new view drawing

Pick to create the detail in an existing view drawing

Pick to create the detail in the current view drawing

Pick to generate the 2D section detail

Pick to place a title mark for the detail

Select a scale for the model space view of the detail

the existing drawing appear, allowing you to place the detail in a location that does not interfere with the location of an existing 2D section detail. If the section detail will be added to the current drawing, select the **Current Drawing** button. After selecting the **New**, **Existing**, or **Current** button, the 2D section detail is generated in one of the view drawings.

Pick the **Generate Section/Elevation** check box to generate the section detail in a new drawing, an existing drawing, or a current drawing. If a title mark will be added below the section detail, select the **Place Titlemark** check box. Finally, select a scale for the model space view around the 2D section detail from the **Scale** drop-down list.

When section details are generated, the 2D section details use the 2D Section Style Background style. This style creates all the geometry on nonplotting layers. The purpose of this is to use the detail marks as layout tools for details. Actual detail components can be drawn over the 2D section details through the use of the **Detail Component Manager**. The **Detail Component Manager** is discussed in Appendix P on the Student CD. This allows you to use the 2D section details as a background for reference when adding detail components. If you want to use the 2D section details in the drawing, you need to regenerate the 2D section details using a section/elevation style that allows display components to be plotted.

Creating 3D Details

One of the benefits of modeling a building is that 3D details can be quickly created from the model. After a detail mark has been placed and a 2D section detail has been created, a 3D section detail can be generated. To do this, select the 2D Section Detail object, right-click, and select **Regenerate...** from the shortcut menu. The **Generate Section/Elevation** worksheet will be displayed. See **Figure 20-15**. In this worksheet, pick the **3D Section/Elevation Object** radio button at the top of the worksheet. Next, select the **New Object** radio button in the **Placement** area, and then select the **Pick Point** button to generate the 3D section detail at the location selected. This creates a 3D Section object in the drawing. Use an isometric view to display the 3D Section object. See **Figure 20-16**. Create a model space view around the 3D section detail so it can be added to a sheet when you are assembling sheets for printing.

NOTE   After creating 3D section details, use the **CREATEHLR** command to create a 2D block from an isometric view of the 3D section detail. Hidden line projection is discussed in Chapter 19.

Figure 20-15.
The **Generate Section/Elevation** worksheet can be used to create a 3D section detail from the 2D section detail.

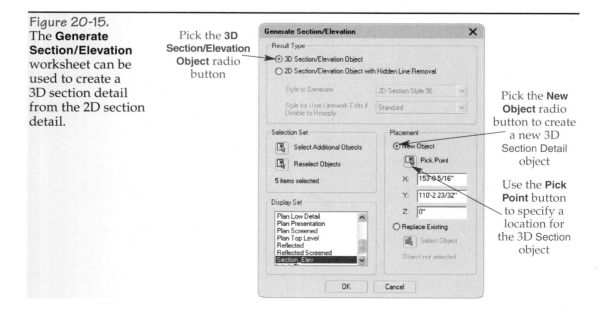

Pick the **3D Section/Elevation Object** radio button

Pick the **New Object** radio button to create a new 3D Section Detail object

Use the **Pick Point** button to specify a location for the 3D Section object

Architectural Desktop and Its Applications

Figure 20-16.
To create a 3D section detail, select an existing 2D section detail, right-click, and select the **Regenerate...** option. Change the result type to a **3D Section/Elevation Object**, create a new object, and pick the location for the new 3D Section Detail object.

Select an existing 2D section detail, right-click, and pick the **Regenerate** option

New 3D section detail from the same detail cut line used to generate the 2D Section object

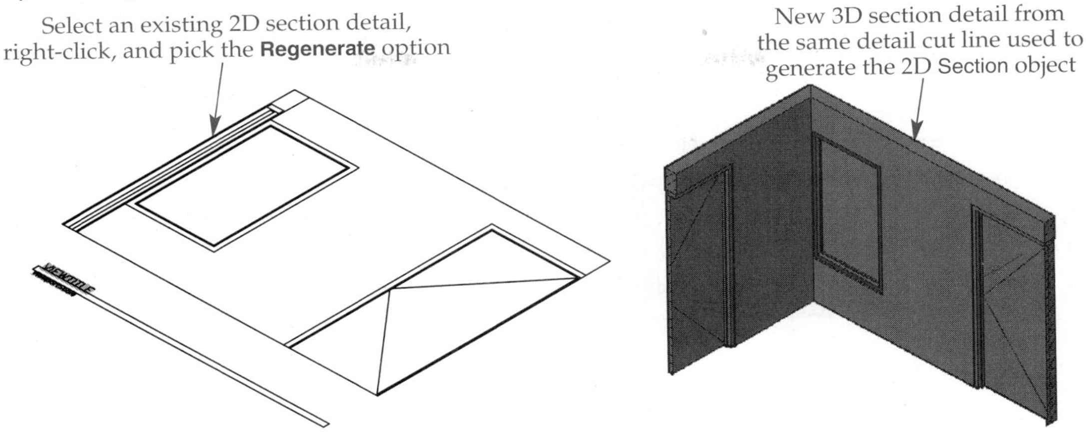

Using Detail Boundaries

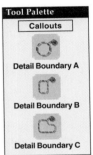

Another method of creating detail views from either Plan or Top view model geometry or from 2D Section or Elevation objects is by using a detail boundary. Three detail boundary tools are available in the **Callouts** tool palette: **Detail Boundary A**, **Detail Boundary B**, and **Detail Boundary C**. Depending on the type selected, you are prompted for different points to establish the detail boundary. Pick the points in a Plan or Top view around AEC objects that you want to use for a detail view, or pick boundary points around an area on a 2D Section or Elevation object. After establishing the boundary, you are prompted to specify a location for the detail boundary bubble.

Depending on whether you established the detail boundary around AEC objects or around a 2D Section or Elevation object, different prompts are displayed. If you created the boundary around AEC objects in a Top view, the **Place Callout** worksheet is displayed, allowing you to create a 2D Section Detail object of the Plan view within the boundary. Use the **New View Drawing**, **Existing View Drawing**, or **Current Drawing** button to place a new section detail in one of the view drawings. After picking the **New**, **Existing**, or **Current** button in the **Place Callout** worksheet, type the elevation at which the detail will cut horizontally through the model geometry. Next, type a distance from the elevation being cut by the section cut line down into the model to be included in the new detail view. Finally, pick a location for the new 2D Section Detail object. A new 2D Section object will be created displaying only the items that were within the detail boundary. These new detail views can be edited by providing additional detail to improve the detail view. See **Figure 20-17**.

When placing a detail boundary around an area within a 2D section/elevation, the **Place Callout** worksheet is also displayed. Choose the **New**, **Existing**, or **Current** button to create a new view detail from the items within the detail boundary. Pick a location where the section detail will be placed. A new section detail of the area around the 2D section detail within the detail boundary is created. See **Figure 20-18**.

Exercise 20-8 Complete the Exercise on the Student CD.

Figure 20-17.
When you are using a detail boundary in a Top view around AEC objects, a detail view of the floor plan within the boundary is generated.

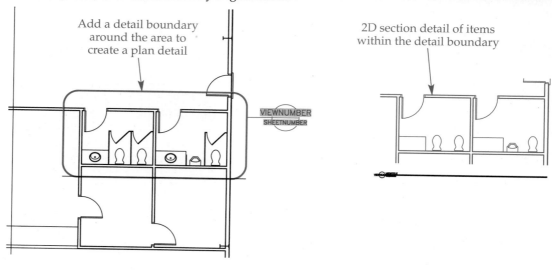

Add a detail boundary around the area to create a plan detail

2D section detail of items within the detail boundary

VIEWNUMBER
SHEETNUMBER

Figure 20-18.
A section detail can also be generated from a 2D section/elevation view.

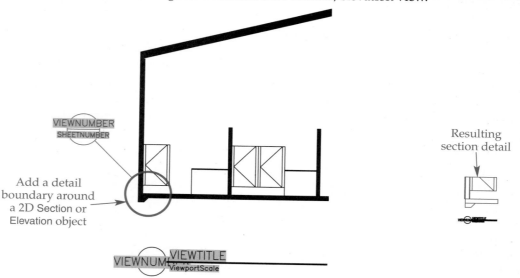

VIEWNUMBER
SHEETNUMBER

Add a detail boundary around a 2D Section or Elevation object

Resulting section detail

VIEWNUMBER VIEWTITLE
ViewportScale

Creating Live Sections

Live sections get their name from the fact that the building model is physically cut away, revealing the interior of the building, live. A live section is similar to a 3D section, with the exception that the live section is not a three-dimensional copy but the actual AEC objects being cut. When the live section is used, the building model is cut along the section line with the portion of the building within the section line box remaining. In a Top view, the entire building model is displayed without displaying the cut building. In Model, Elevation, or perspective views, the building model is displayed as if a portion of the building has been removed. Multiple section lines can be used at the same time, in order to cut away live sections at different portions of the building.

Figure 20-19.
The differences between the 2D, 3D, and live sections.

2D Section	3D Section	Live Section
Uses section style to control display settings	Uses the Bldg Sections Subdivisions display representation for display control	Uses the individual AEC object's display representations for display control
Cuts a separate 2D Plan view section	Cuts a separate 3D Model view section	Cuts the building model into a section
Cuts through all AEC objects, AutoCAD entities, and xrefs	Cuts through all AEC objects, AutoCAD entities, and xrefs	Cuts through all AEC objects, AutoCAD entities, and through xrefs
Creates one 2D object copied from building model	Creates one 3D object copied from building model	Cuts the actual building model, retaining the original objects
Linework can be edited and merged into 2D object	Linework cannot be edited or added	Original AEC objects can be modified
As building model is changed, the section can be refreshed or regenerated	As building model is changed, the section can be refreshed or regenerated	Changes made to the building model are automatically adjusted in the live section

The AEC objects within the live section can be modified using commands used to modify the building model in its uncut form. **Figure 20-19** tabulates the differences between standard 2D and 3D sections and live sections.

Like the standard sections, live sections use the section cut line to determine what will be cut away. Once the section line is created, the live section can be activated. To use the live section for a section line, select the section line box, right-click, and pick the **Enable Live Section** option from the shortcut menu. After enabling the live section to change to a Model view, this creates a live section through the building model, as shown in **Figure 20-20**.

If materials have been applied to the AEC objects within the building model, a Sectioned Boundary display component is used around the perimeter edges of the cut AEC object. This component can be turned on or off and assigned a color in the material definition's display properties to aid in defining the cut edges.

Exercise
20-9   Complete the Exercise on the Student CD.

Figure 20-20.
The finished building model after enabling a live section. Courtesy 3D-DZYN

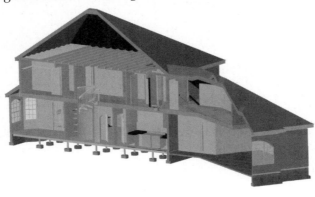

Chapter 20   Creating Sections

Modifying a Live Section

Any editing commands, such as **OBJECTDISPLAY**, the **Properties** palette, and AutoCAD commands can be used to modify the objects in a live section view. As the objects are modified, the live section is automatically updated to reflect the changes made to the drawing.

New objects can also be added to the building model. If you are working with a live section display, new objects are added and conform to the limits of the section line. When objects are moved, copied, or erased, the live section reflects the changes dynamically. If a window or door within a wall being cut by the live section is removed, the wall is filled back in up to the section cut line.

Sectioned Body Display

When a live section has been used, the portion of the building not within the section line box is removed to reveal the interior of the building model. The removed portion of the building can be displayed as a transparent building component to reveal the details of the interior of the building, allowing the viewer the opportunity to better understand the building as a whole. See **Figure 20-21**.

To turn on this transparent component, enable the live section, select the section line, right-click, and select the **Toggle Sectioned Body Display** option from the shortcut menu. Selecting this option displays the removed portions (sectioned body) of the building using a transparent material. The sectioned body material is assigned in the material definitions assigned to each AEC object. By default, the materials included with Architectural Desktop are assigned the Sectioned Body material.

Disabling a Live Section

At any time, the complete building model can be restored, and the live section can be turned off. To turn off the live section display, select the section line, right-click, and select **Disable Live Section** from the shortcut menu. The live section is turned off, and the sectioned body is restored to the building model.

Figure 20-21.
The sectioned body (removed portion of the building) can be displayed by toggling the sectioned body display. Courtesy 3D-DZYN

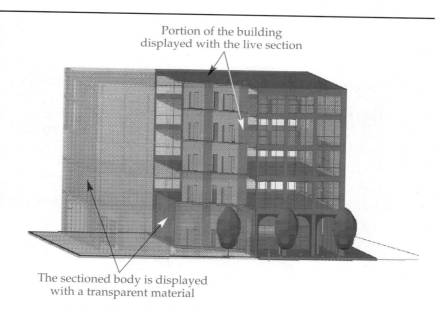

Portion of the building displayed with the live section

The sectioned body is displayed with a transparent material

Chapter Test

Answer the following questions. Write your answers on a separate sheet of paper or complete the electronic chapter test on the Student CD.

1. Define *section*.
2. Identify three ways a section cut line can be drawn.
3. What is displayed in a 2D section, in relationship to where the section line crosses through the geometry?
4. What happens to the link to the original building model when a Section object is exploded?
5. If an automatically generated section is selected, an invisible boundary is displayed with grips. Briefly discuss the function of this boundary and how it is increased or decreased in size.
6. How do you regenerate a section?
7. How does picking **Linework** > **Edit** from the shortcut menu differ from the use of conventional AutoCAD commands for editing a section?
8. By default, when a detail mark is placed in the drawing, the model space view around the 2D section detail and the title mark for the section detail is named Detail. Other detail marks added to the drawing are named Detail *n*. What does the *n* represent?
9. Define *live section*.
10. What happens as objects are modified in a live section?

Chapter Projects

Use the techniques covered in this chapter to create the following drawings.

1. Single-Level Residential Project
   A. Access the **Project Browser** and set Residential-Project-01 current.
   B. Access the **Views** tab of the **Project Navigator** and create a new section/elevation view drawing. Choose the **Section/Elevation** option.
   C. On the **General** page, enter the following:
      - **Name:** Building Sections
      - **Description:** 2D Sections
   D. On the **Context** page, select all the levels under Division 1.
   E. On the **Content** page, uncheck the Furniture construct.
   F. Open the Building Sections view drawing.
   G. Add two section lines as indicated in the figure. In the **Place Callout** worksheet, name one of the sections Building Section A and the other Building Section B. Assign a scale of 1/4" = 1'-0".
   H. Modify the 2D section/elevation style and turn off the Section Hatch Linework component.
   I. Use **Linework** > **Edit** and **Linework** > **Merge** as needed to adjust the 2D sections.
   J. Save and close the drawing.

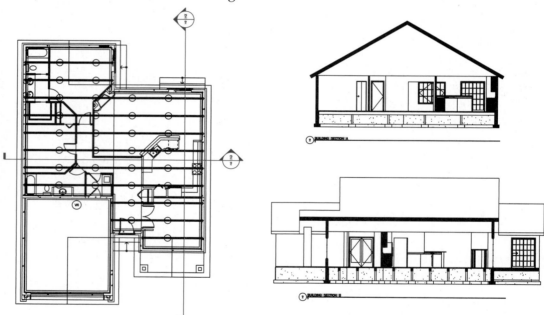

Design Courtesy Alan Mascord Design Associates

2. Single-Level Residential Project
   A. Access the **Project Browser** and set Residential-Project-02 current.
   B. Access the **Views** tab of the **Project Navigator** and create a new section/elevation view drawing. Choose the **Section/Elevation** option.
   C. On the **General** page, enter the following:
      - **Name:** Building Sections
      - **Description:** 2D Sections
   D. On the **Context** page, select all the levels under Division 1.
   E. On the **Content** page, uncheck the Furniture construct.
   F. Open the Building Sections view drawing.
   G. Add two section lines as indicated in the figure. In the **Place Callout** worksheet, name one of the sections Building Section A and the other Building Section B. Assign a scale of 1/4" = 1'-0".
   H. Modify the 2D section/elevation style and turn off the Section Hatch Linework component.
   I. Use **Linework** > **Edit** and **Linework** > **Merge** as needed to adjust the 2D sections.
   J. Create an AEC polygon style for the earth hatch, as shown in the figure. Add the earth AEC Polygon object around the sections as shown.
   K. Save and close the drawing.

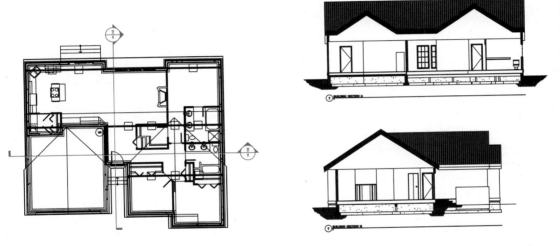

Design Courtesy Alan Mascord Design Associates

3. Two-Story Residential Project
   A. Access the **Project Browser** and set Residential-Project-03 current.
   B. Access the **Views** tab of the **Project Navigator** and create a new section/elevation view drawing. Choose the **Section/Elevation** option.
   C. On the **General** page, enter the following:
      • **Name:** Building Sections
      • **Description:** 2D Sections
   D. On the **Context** page, select all the levels under Division 1.
   E. On the **Content** page, uncheck the Furniture construct.
   F. Open the Building Sections view drawing.
   G. Add two section lines as indicated in the figure. In the **Place Callout** worksheet, name one of the sections Building Section A and the other Building Section B. Assign a scale of 1/4″ = 1′-0″.
   H. Modify the 2D section/elevation style and turn off the Section Hatch Linework component.
   I. Modify the two section line cuts and add a subdivision for each offset 2′-0″ from the defining line.
   J. Use **Linework** > **Edit** and **Linework** > **Merge** as needed to adjust the 2D sections.
   K. Create an AEC polygon style for the earth hatch, as shown in the figure. Add the earth AEC Polygon object around the sections as shown.
   L. Save and close the drawing.

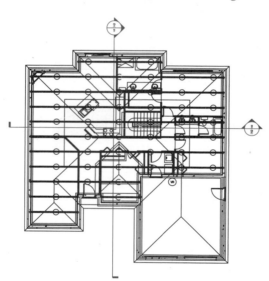

Drawing Courtesy 3D-DZYN

4. Two-Story Residential Project
   A. Access the **Project Browser** and set Residential-Project-04 current.
   B. Access the **Views** tab of the **Project Navigator** and create a new section/elevation view drawing. Choose the **Section/Elevation** option.
   C. On the **General** page, enter the following:
      - **Name:** Building Sections
      - **Description:** 2D Sections
   D. On the **Context** page, select all the levels under Division 1.
   E. On the **Content** page, uncheck the MainFlr-Furniture and UpperFlr-Furniture constructs.
   F. Open the Building Sections view drawing.
   G. Add two section lines as indicated in the figure. In the **Place Callout** worksheet, name one of the sections Building Section A and the other Building Section B. Assign a scale of 1/4" = 1'-0".
   H. Modify the 2D section/elevation style and turn off the Section Hatch Linework component.
   I. Modify the two section line cuts and add a subdivision for each offset 2'-0" from the defining line.
   J. Use **Linework** > **Edit** and **Linework** > **Merge** as needed to adjust the 2D sections.
   K. Create an AEC polygon style for the earth hatch, as shown in the figure. Add the earth AEC Polygon object around the sections as shown.
   L. Save and close the drawing.

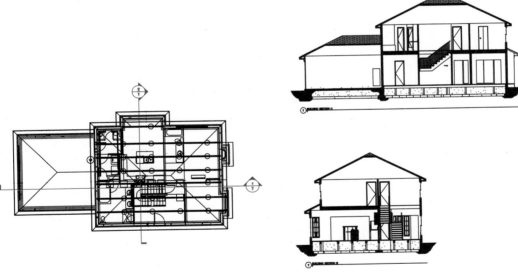

Design Courtesy Alan Mascord Design Associates

5. Commercial Store Project
   A. Access the **Project Browser** and set Commercial-Project-05 current.
   B. Access the **Views** tab of the **Project Navigator** and create a new section/elevation view drawing. Choose the **Section/Elevation** option.
   C. On the **General** page, enter the following:
      • **Name:** Building Sections
      • **Description:** 2D Sections
   D. On the **Context** page, select all the levels under Division 1.
   E. On the **Content** page, uncheck the Furniture construct.
   F. Open the Building Sections view drawing.
   G. Add two section lines as indicated in the figure. In the **Place Callout** worksheet, name one of the sections Building Section A and the other Building Section B. Assign a scale of 1/8″ = 1′-0″.
   H. Use **Linework > Edit** and **Linework > Merge** as needed to adjust the 2D sections.
   I. Create an AEC polygon style for the earth hatch, as shown in the figure. Add the earth AEC Polygon object around the sections as shown.
   J. Save and close the drawing.

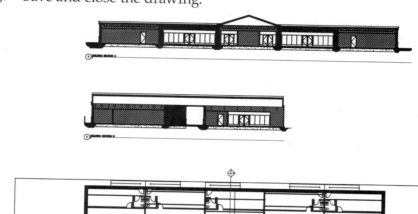

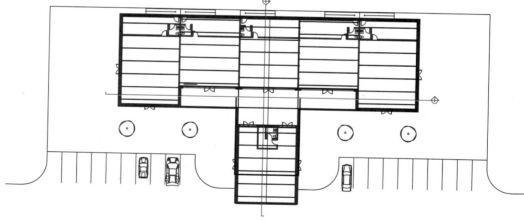

Drawing Courtesy 3D-DZYN

6. Commercial Car Maintenance Shop Project
   A. Access the **Project Browser** and set Commercial-Project-06 current.
   B. Access the **Views** tab of the **Project Navigator** and create a new section/elevation view drawing. Choose the **Section/Elevation** option.
   C. On the **General** page, enter the following:
      • **Name:** Live Building Section A
      • **Description:** Live Section
   D. On the **Context** page, select all the levels under Division 1.
   E. Open the Live Building Section A view drawing.
   F. Use the **BLDGSECTIONLINEADD** command to create a section line from the left side of the car wash area, crossing through the main building and to the right of the garage, as shown in the figure.

G. Enable the live section.

H. Select the Front view to change the UCS, and then change to a SW Isometric view.

I. Use the **3DORBIT** command to adjust the view as in shown in the figure.

J. Create a model space view around the live section named Building Section A, with a scale of 1/8" = 1'-0".

K. Save and close the drawing.

L. Access the **Views** tab of the **Project Navigator** and create a new section/elevation view drawing. Choose the **Section/Elevation** option.

M. On the **General** page, enter the following:
   - **Name:** Live Building Section B
   - **Description:** Live Section

N. On the **Context** page, select all the levels under Division 1.

O. Open the Live Building Section B view drawing.

P. Use the **BLDGSECTIONLINEADD** command to create a section line through the main building from top to bottom of the drawing, as shown in the figure.

Q. Enable the live section.

R. Select the Left view to change the UCS, and then change to a SW Isometric view.

S. Use the **3DORBIT** command to adjust the view as shown in the figure.

T. Create a model space view around the live section named Building Section B, with a scale of 1/8" = 1'-0".

U. Save and close the drawing.

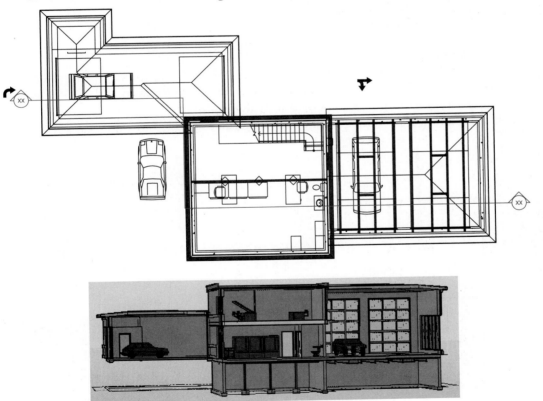

Drawing Courtesy 3D-DZYN

7. Governmental Fire Station
   A. Access the **Project Browser** and set Gvrmt-Project-07 current.
   B. Access the **Views** tab of the **Project Navigator** and create a new section/elevation view drawing. Choose the **Section/Elevation** option.
   C. On the **General** page, enter the following:
      - **Name:** Live Building Section A
      - **Description:** Live Section
   D. On the **Context** page, select all the levels under Division 1.
   E. Open the Live Building Section A view drawing.
   F. Use the **BLDGSECTIONLINEADD** command to create a section line from the left side of the building and to the right of the building, as shown in the figure.
   G. Enable the live section.
   H. Select the Front view to change the UCS, and then change to a SE Isometric view.
   I. Use the **3DORBIT** command to adjust the view as shown in the figure.
   J. Create a model space view around the live section named Building Section A, with a scale of 1/8″ = 1′-0″.
   K. Save and close the drawing.
   L. Access the **Views** tab of the **Project Navigator** and create a new detail view drawing. Choose the **Detail** option.
   M. On the **General** page, enter the following:
      - **Name:** Construction Details
      - **Description:** 2D Details
   N. On the **Context** page, select all the levels under Division 1.
   O. On the **Content** page, uncheck the Furniture construct.
   P. Open the Construction Details view drawing.
   Q. Add detail marks as indicated in the figure.
   R. In the **Place Callout** worksheet, create 2D detail sections, naming them Detail 1, Detail 2, Detail 3, and Detail 4, and assigning a scale of 1/2″ = 1′-0″ for each. Create the details in the current drawing.
   S. Use **Linework > Edit** and **Linework > Merge** as needed to adjust the 2D sections.
   T. Save and close the drawing.

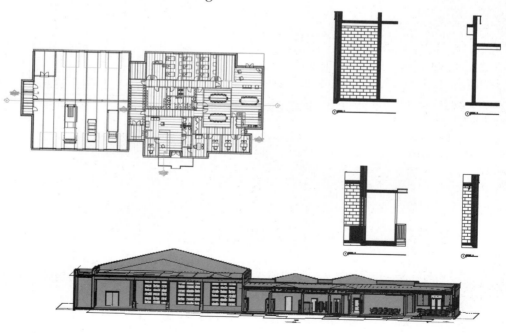

Drawing Courtesy 3D-DZYN

Space Planning

CHAPTER 21

Learning Objectives

After completing this chapter, you will be able to do the following:

- ✓ Create a space style.
- ✓ Design and modify spaces.
- ✓ Add spaces to your drawing.
- ✓ Generate space information.
- ✓ Modify spaces.
- ✓ Add and modify Zone markers in your space plan.
- ✓ Make space calculations.
- ✓ Assign calculation modifiers to your space plan.
- ✓ Create a space decomposition.
- ✓ Establish a zone template.
- ✓ Create a space evaluation report.

Space planning is a design process in which the interior spaces of a building are established and arranged to create a functional design. The creation of spaces allows you to define boundaries around the spaces to help identify the shape of the building around the space or the contained area of the space. Architectural Desktop provides **Space** tools specifically for this design process.

Space objects are 2D or 3D AEC objects that contain spatial information about a building, including floor area, wall area, and volume. Spaces can also be used to organize reports such as construction cost, energy requirements and analysis, and lists of furniture and equipment. The **Space** object represents the interior of a room or area, which can be contained by boundaries such as walls and slabs.

Working with Spaces

The **Space** object includes four different **Plan** view boundaries for calculating base, net, usable, and gross space areas. These boundaries display a different aspect of the space and can be scheduled and edited individually. **Figure 21-1** displays examples of each of the boundary types.

Figure 21-1.
Plan representation Space objects include different boundaries for calculating base, net, usable, and gross space.

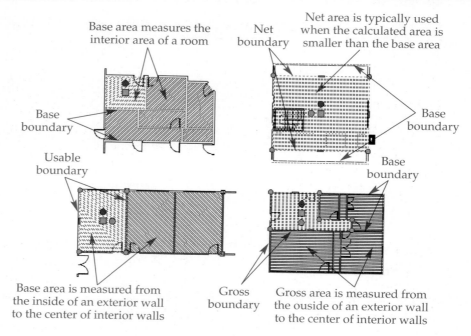

The *base boundary* typically represents the inner volume of a room. The boundaries for the base boundary are typically placed at the interior face of the walls. This boundary is often used for maintenance and operations in a building. For example, when determining the number of cleaning personnel needed for an office, the base boundary is used as the calculation basis.

The *net boundary* is typically used when the calculated area of a space is smaller than the base boundary. For example, many building codes calculate the area of an attic room by requiring only those areas of the space reaching a certain height to be counted as part of the space. In this example, the base space area may extend to the edges of the building, yet due to code requirements, the net boundary of the space can only be calculated where the net space boundary meets the specified height within the room. When adding a Space object, a calculation modifier can be used to adjust the area through the use of a calculation. This becomes the calculated area. Calculation modifiers are discussed later in this chapter.

The *usable boundary* is often used for renting calculations, tax calculations, maintenance, and pricing. This boundary generally extends from the inside of the exterior walls to the middle of interior walls or a specified distance inside of an interior wall.

The *gross boundary* is used for cost calculation and price estimation. This boundary is measured from the outside of the exterior walls to the middle of the interior walls.

In a Model view, the Space object includes a Floor and Ceiling component and a few volume and surface components. These components are controlled by the display system and can be turned on or off as desired. When a space is added, a style is used. The style for a space can be used to designate the room name and total square footage allotted to the space.

Figure 21-2.
Room name scheduling tags are attached to Space objects. The Space objects consist of a perimeter and hatched area in a Top view and a floor and ceiling in a Model view.

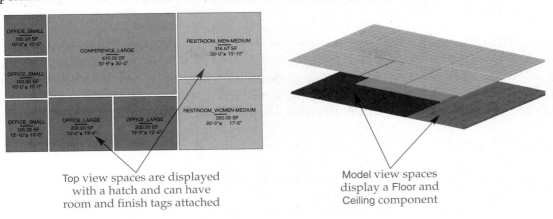

Top view spaces are displayed
with a hatch and can have
room and finish tags attached

Model view spaces
display a Floor and
Ceiling component

When spaces are added, they can be tagged using Room scheduling tags. See Figure 21-2. The space style can include a list of room names that are displayed when the space is tagged. The space name can also be used when room schedules and finish schedules are created. In addition to containing a list of room names, space styles can also include a different hatch pattern for each of the space areas (base, gross, net, and usable). The hatch pattern can be a series of lines or a solid hatch and can include materials that are assigned to the Floor and Ceiling components.

When you are adding spaces to the drawing, the objects can be associative or nonassociative. Nonassociative spaces are independent spaces with user-defined geometry. Nonassociative spaces can be drawn or converted from linework, mass elements, or slabs. A *nonassociative space* is not dependent on another object after it is created and does not update its shape if the original object is modified. *Associative spaces* are surrounded by objects that enclose the space. If the boundary objects change the shape containing the space, the space can be updated.

If you started designing with walls and have defined room areas with walls, you can generate associative Space objects from these enclosed areas and add name tags to help identify the different areas the spaces represent. This section discusses the tools and options available to you when working with spaces.

Creating a Space Style

Custom space styles can be created to suit your design needs. In addition, Architectural Desktop includes a few style drawings with space styles, and the Design Tool Catalog in the **Content Browser** includes four categories of space styles: Commercial, Educational, Medical, and Residential. By default, the **Spaces** tool palette in the **Design** tool palette group includes a sampling of the space styles included in Architectural Desktop. To create a new space style, pick **Design > Spaces > Space Styles...** from the pull-down menu, or type SPACESTYLE.

The **Style Manager** opens to the Space Styles section, as seen in Figure 21-3. To create a new space style, pick the **New Style** button in the **Style Manager**, or right-click on the space style text in the tree view and select **New**. A new space style is created in the tree view. Type a new name for the style.

After the space style has been created and named, it can be edited. Pick the style name in the tree view to display the space style property tabs in the right pane. Space styles include the following property tabs:

- **General.** This tab specifies the general properties of the space style. See Figure 21-3. The **Name:** text box displays the name of the style; rename the style as desired. Enter a description for the style in the **Description:** area. You can also attach external documents to the style, such as finish material specifications, by selecting the **Notes...** button. Property set definitions containing schedule information and keynotes can be assigned to the style by picking the **Property Sets...** or **Select Keynote...** buttons appropriately. Property set definitions will be discussed in Chapter 22 and Chapter 23.

- **Design Rules.** This tab is used to assign a list of names that can be applied to the space when adding the Space object and to specify the size parameters for the space style. See Figure 21-4. Use the **Space Names:** drop-down list to select a list definition containing a list of space names to be assigned to the style. List definitions are discussed later in this chapter. The **Area:** text boxes allow you to specify a target area, a minimum area, and a maximum area when adding spaces to the drawing. The **Length:** and **Width:** text boxes allow you to specify target sizes, minimum sizes, and maximum sizes when adding new spaces to the drawing.

   The **Net Offset:**, **Usable Offset:**, and **Gross Offset:** text boxes are used to set an offset distance for each type of area, measured from the base boundary of the space.

- **Materials.** This tab allows you to assign a material to the Model view Floor and Ceiling components of the space.

- **Classifications.** Use this tab to assign classification definitions to the space. Classifications can be used to sort different spaces in the drawing into different categories of a schedule.

Figure 21-3.
The **Style Manager**, opened to the Space Styles section, is used to create new space styles.

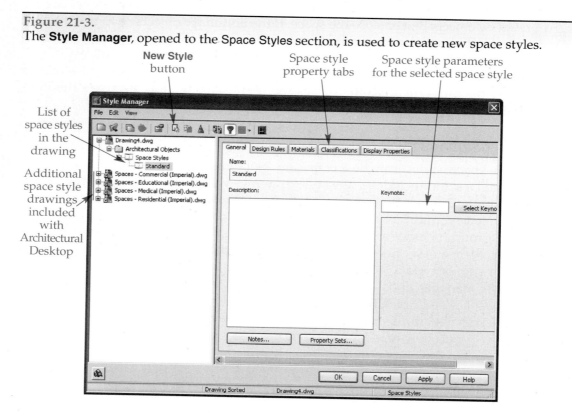

Figure 21-4.
The **Design Rules** tab controls size parameters for the space style and assigns a list definition containing a list of space names to the space style.

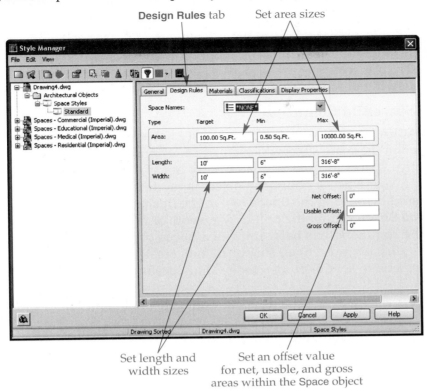

Set length and width sizes

Set an offset value for net, usable, and gross areas within the Space object

- **Display Properties.** This tab controls the appearance of the Space object in each display representation. The Model, Plan, and Reflected display representations are the most commonly adjusted display representations. The Model representation controls the display of the Floor and Ceiling components. The Plan representations control the display of the base, net, usable, and gross boundaries and their associated hatch patterns displayed when in a Top view. The Reflected representations are used when creating reflected ceiling plans and control the appearance of the space boundaries and hatch patterns displayed in a reflected Top view.

Once you have created the space style and set the parameters, pick the **OK** button to exit the **Style Manager**. Additional space styles are included in the Architectural Desktop Styles folder. Use the **Open Drawing** button in the **Style Manager** to open one of the style drawings. These styles can be found by browsing to the \\Styles folder. There are four drawings full of space styles for your use. Open these in **Style Manager**, and drag and drop the desired styles into your current drawing icon in the tree view. Additional space styles can also be found in the **Content Browser** under the Design Tool Catalog. To access these, drag the tools onto a tool palette for your use.

Exercise
21-1   Complete the Exercise on the Student CD.

Adding Spaces

Once a drawing includes a few space styles, spaces can be added to the drawing in a number of ways using the different styles. A space can be inserted into the drawing using the target area size specified in the space style. A rectangular shape can be created by picking points to define to opposite corners. A polygonal shape can be created by picking points defining the shape. Polylines, slabs, and mass elements can be converted into spaces. Spaces can also be generated from walls establishing a closed area. The following describes each method to add Space objects to your drawing.

Using the SpaceAdd Command

The **SPACEADD** command is used to insert a nonassociative space using the target area specified in the space style, which creates a rectangular or polygonal space shape. Nonassociative spaces are spaces that are not associated with a boundary and will not update in size when a boundary object is modified. The **SPACEADD** command can be accessed by picking the **Space** tool in the **Design** tool palette, picking **Design > Spaces > Add Space...** from the pull-down menu, or typing SPACEADD.

After the command has been entered, a Space object can be inserted or created as a rectangular or polygonal shape. Before creating the Space object, use the **Properties** palette to set the properties for the space being added to the drawing. See **Figure 21-5**.

When a space is being added to the drawing, the **Properties** palette includes a number of properties that are used to configure how the space is to be created. The space properties are divided into five categories under the **BASIC** header. See **Figure 21-5**.

General Category

The **General** category includes general space properties. The following are descriptions of the properties found in this category:

- **Description.** Pick this property to open the **Description** worksheet and enter a description for the space being added.
- **Style.** Picking this property provides a drop-down list of space styles available in the drawing. Pick the space style to be added to the drawing.

Figure 21-5.
The **Properties** palette is used to set any property parameters for the Space object before it is added to the drawing.

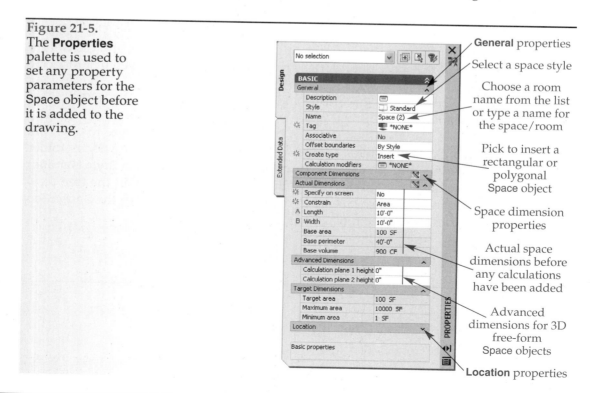

General properties
Select a space style
Choose a room name from the list or type a name for the space/room
Pick to insert a rectangular or polygonal Space object
Space dimension properties
Actual space dimensions before any calculations have been added
Advanced dimensions for 3D free-form Space objects
Location properties

- **Name.** This property lists possible room names for the space if the selected space style includes a list definition. Creating list definitions will be covered later in this chapter. If the selected style does not include a list of room names, a room name can be entered in the property text box. This assigns the room name to the space being created.
- **Tag.** This property is used to assign a tag to the space. A space tag can indicate the space name, room number, and size of the space. Space tag definitions must first exist in the drawing before they can be added to a Space object. The **Scheduling** tool palette in the **Document** tool palette group includes a few space tags. Additional space tags can be found in the Documentation Tool Catalog.
- **Associative.** This property is unavailable when using the **SPACEADD** command. Associative spaces can be created by picking interior areas surrounded by walls to create the space. This will be covered in the next section.
- **Offset boundaries.** This drop-down property includes two options: **By Style** and **Manual**. When the **By Style** option is selected, a Space object is created with the net, usable, and gross boundaries offset from the base boundary, based on the offset distances established in the space style. If the **Manual** option is selected, the base, net, usable, and gross boundaries overlap each other and can be modified using grips after the Space object is added to the drawing.
- **Create type.** This property is only available when using the **SPACEADD** command. This property allows you to choose from three different options: **Insert**, **Rectangle**, and **Polygon**. The **Insert** option inserts a square space with an area the size of the target values specified in the space style. The **Rectangle** option allows you to create a Space object by picking two opposite corners to establish the rectangular shape. The **Polygon** option allows you to pick points to establish the shape of the space. Picking the **Polygon** type will display the **Segment type** property.
- **Segment type.** This property is displayed when using the **Polygon** type. This option allows you to create straight line segments or curved arc segments as you pick points to establish the space shape.
- **Calculation modifiers.** This property displays a list of calculation modifiers that can be applied to the Space object. A calculation modifier applies a calculation to the actual area of a space to produce a revised area value, such as a 3% plaster deduction from an area.

Component Dimensions Category

The **Component Dimensions** category is used to control the properties of the Model view components. This category includes dimension properties and a diagram of what the settings control. The following properties are available when using the **SPACEADD** command:

- **Geometry type.** This drop-down list includes three space geometry types that can be created: **2D**, **Extrusion**, and **Freeform**. The **2D** type creates a two-dimensional only space with no model components. Picking this type removes the other **Component Dimension** properties. The **Extrusion** type creates a 3D space that includes a Floor and Ceiling component. The **Freeform** space is not an option when using the **SPACEADD** command, but it is available when establishing spaces from boundary objects such as walls and slabs. This type allows you to obtain volumetric space information.
- **Overall Space height.** This text box property designates the total height measured from the space below the floor component, the floor thickness, the space between the floor and ceiling, the ceiling thickness, and the space above the ceiling.
- **Ceiling Height.** This property specifies the height of the Ceiling component measured from the top of the floor to the bottom of the Ceiling component.

- **Floor thickness.** This property specifies the thickness of the Floor component. If the value is set to 0″, the Floor component is not created.
- **Ceiling thickness.** Similar to the floor thickness, this property controls the thickness of the Ceiling component. If you are using a dropped ceiling, as in commercial buildings, you may set this to the thickness of the ceiling panel. If using the space in a residential application, you may set the ceiling to the thickness of the gypsum board. If the value is set to 0″, the Ceiling component is not created.
- **Height above ceiling.** This property controls the space measured above the top of the Ceiling component, before the next floor. In commercial applications, this is called the interstitial space. Although there is not an actual component being created, a space schedule can be built to report on the available height above any given space.
- **Height below floor.** This property specifies the space measured from the bottom of the floor to the bottom of the Space object.
- **Default surface height.** This value specifies the total height of the **Ceiling height**, **Ceiling thickness**, and **Height above ceiling** properties.
- **Justification.** This property sets the vertical position of the space insertion point on the top of the floor, bottom of the floor, or bottom of the space below the floor.

Actual Dimensions Category

The **Actual Dimensions** category controls the actual area, width, and depth of the space being created. When the **Create type** property is set to **Insert**, this category will display different properties that can be used to reflect the size of the Space object being inserted. If the **Rectangle** or **Polygon** shapes are being added, the **Base Perimeter** and **Base Area** properties are only available as read-only values until the Space object has been added. The following **Actual Dimension** properties are available when using the **SPACEADD** command:

- **Specify On Screen.** This property is displayed when using the **Insert Create type** property. When **Yes** is selected, the space is created by using the target area specified in the space style, and the Space object sizes can be changed dynamically by moving the crosshairs to specify the width and depth of the space, yet maintaining the target size area. If **No** is selected in this property, the space must be created by entering a width or depth in the **Properties** palette.
- **Constrain.** This property is used to constrain the creation of the space. The space can be constrained by area, length, or width or have no constraint at all. When a constraint is selected, one of the properties (**Area**, **Length**, or **Width**) becomes locked and is dependent on the values entered for the other two properties. For example, if the **Area** property is constrained, the **Area** property is dependent on the length and width entered. The values for the length and width are based on the minimum and maximum values specified in the space style.
- **Length.** This text box property allows you to specify the space length, based on a value between the minimum and maximum size specified in the space style. If this value is constrained, it is not available and is dependent on the values specified for the area and width.
- **Width.** This text box property allows you to specify the space width, based on a value between the minimum and maximum size specified in the space style. If this value is constrained, it is not available and is dependent on the values specified for the area and length.
- **Base Area.** This property displays the base area of the space. When inserting the Space object based on the target size, you can enter a base area if the area is not constrained.

- **Base Perimeter.** This property displays the base perimeter of the Space object.
- **Base Volume.** This property displays the base volume for the Space object.

Target Dimensions Category

The **Target Dimensions** category includes a number of properties that indicate the target sizes specified in the space style. All of these properties are read-only values only displayed when you are using the **Insert Create type** property. If these values need to be modified, the space style must be edited.

- **Target area.** This property indicates the target area specified for the selected space style.
- **Maximum area.** This property indicates the maximum area for the style that can be entered for the **Base Area** property in the **Actual Dimensions** category.
- **Minimum area.** This property indicates the minimum area for the style that can be entered for the **Base Area** property in the **Actual Dimensions** category.

Location Category

The **Location** category includes two read-only properties. The **Rotation** property indicates the rotation angle of the space being created. The **Elevation** property indicates the elevation of the space being created.

Once you determine the parameters for the space, pick a point in the drawing screen to insert the space, or pick points to create the space if you are using the **Rectangle** or **Polygon Create type** property. A space is added with a diagonal hatch in the Top view. Add as many spaces as required for the design, and change the styles and names as you design.

Converting to Spaces

Spaces can also be converted from a closed polyline boundary or an AEC polygon. First, a polyline boundary or AEC polygon must exist in the drawing. Next, right-click over the **Space** tool in the **Design** tool palette or a space tool in the **Spaces** tool palette, and pick **Apply Tool Properties to > Linework and AEC Objects** from the shortcut menu.

 NOTE Slabs and mass elements can also be converted into Space objects. Right-click over the **Space** tool in the **Design** tool palette, pick the **Apply Tool Properties to** shortcut menu, and then select the **Slab** or **Mass Element** option. Mass elements are discussed in Chapter 25.

Select the polyline or AEC polygon defining the boundary for the space. Press [Enter] when you are finished selecting objects to be converted. The **Convert to Space** worksheet is displayed, allowing you to establish a cut plane height, establish the cut plane height on screen, and choose to erase the layout geometry or not.

Generating Spaces

Another method of creating spaces is by generating them from walls or linework. This method is similar to using the **BHATCH** command to hatch an internal area. When spaces are generated from a boundary object, the spaces are associated with the boundary. If the boundary objects are modified, the spaces can be updated to reflect the modified space size. In order to use the **SPACEAUTOGENERATE** command, you must have a closed area. The area does not have to be a closed polyline. The closed area can be a room made up of walls or lines and arcs that form a closed boundary. To access this tool, pick the **Space Auto Generate** tool in the **Design** tool palette, pick **Design > Spaces > Generate Spaces...** from the pull-down menu, or type SPACEAUTOGENERATE. After entering the command, the **Generate Spaces** dialog box is displayed. See **Figure 21-6.**

Type
SPACE AUTOGENERATE
Pull-Down Menu
Design > Spaces > Generate Spaces...
Tool Palette
Design
Space Auto Generate

SPACEAUTOGENERATE

Figure 21-6.
The **Generate Spaces** dialog box is used to create spaces from defined areas such as walls, lines, arcs, polylines, and circles.

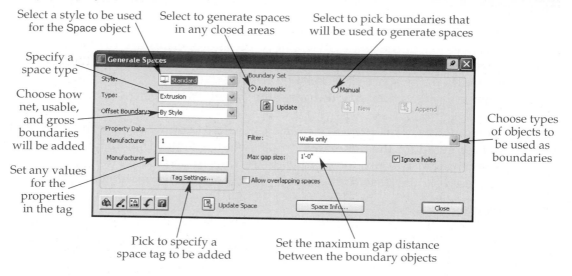

Select a style to be used for the Space object

Select to generate spaces in any closed areas

Select to pick boundaries that will be used to generate spaces

Specify a space type

Choose how net, usable, and gross boundaries will be added

Set any values for the properties in the tag

Choose types of objects to be used as boundaries

Pick to specify a space tag to be added

Set the maximum gap distance between the boundary objects

The **Generate Spaces** dialog box includes settings for style, type, and the offset boundary. The **Style:** drop-down list displays a list of space styles in the drawing from which to choose. Select the space style to be used for any new spaces selected. The **Type:** drop-down list allows you to create 2D, extrusion, or freeform spaces. The **2D** option only creates a 2D area of the room. The **Extrusion** option creates a floor and ceiling for the room. The **Freeform** option creates a volumetric space that conforms to the shape of the space boundaries. The **Offset Boundary:** drop-down list includes two options: **By Style** and **Manual**. The **By Style** option creates the spaces and establishes offset net, usable, and gross boundaries, offset the distance specified in the space style. The **Manual** option creates overlapping net, usable, and gross boundaries, allowing you to grip edit the boundaries after generating the spaces.

The **Property Data** area is used to assign a space tag and enter manual property set data for the space. Selecting the **Tag Settings…** button displays the **Tag Settings** dialog box. See **Figure 21-7.** This dialog box allows you to specify the room tag to be attached to the space, a property set definition to attach, and the properties within the property set definition to which you want to add information.

Figure 21-7.
The **Tag Settings** dialog box is used to specify a room tag and property set definition to attach to the space as it is generated.

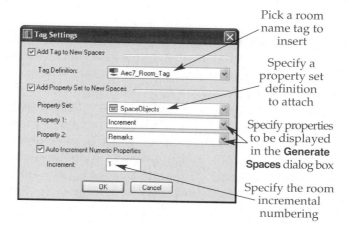

Pick a room name tag to insert

Specify a property set definition to attach

Specify properties to be displayed in the **Generate Spaces** dialog box

Specify the room incremental numbering

Architectural Desktop and Its Applications

Select the space tag from the **Tag Definition:** drop-down list to be added when a space is automatically generated. If you want to use a different tag, it must first be loaded in the drawing before it becomes available in the **Tag Definition:** drop-down list. The Documentation Tool Catalog includes additional space tags under the Schedule Tags section. Next, select a property set to be assigned to the Space object. *Property sets* are lists of information about the space that can be added to a schedule. Selecting two properties in the **Property 1:** and **Property 2:** drop-down lists displays properties that can be used as a default value that shows up in the **Generate Spaces** dialog box. These properties can be edited in the **Generate Spaces** dialog box, where the values become the default value assigned to the space. When you are finished specifying tag settings, pick the **OK** button to return to the **Generate Spaces** dialog box.

The **Boundary Set** area of the **Generate Spaces** dialog box is used to determine how spaces are generated and what types of objects are used to determine boundary areas that can contain the Space objects. The top of this area includes two radio buttons: **Automatic** and **Manual**.

Pick the **Automatic** radio button to have the **Space Auto Generate** tool automatically select boundary objects visible in the drawing. Any boundaries formed by objects in the **Filter:** drop-down list will be considered boundary objects for new spaces. When this option is selected, the **Update** button is available. This button is used to update the visible boundaries in the boundary set.

Pick the **Manual** radio button to manually select boundary objects in the drawing. Any objects selected that form a closed boundary are used to form the boundary for the Space objects. When this option is selected, the **New** and **Append** buttons become available. Select the **New** button to return to the drawing to select boundary objects to be considered when generating spaces. The **Append** button is used to add additional boundary objects to the boundary set.

After choosing either the **Automatic** or **Manual** radio button, a filter needs to be established to determine what types of objects may be used to determine space boundaries. Pick a selection filter from the **Filter:** drop-down list. The **Walls only** filter looks only to Wall objects to be used as boundaries for new spaces. The **Walls, lines, arcs, polylines, and circles** filter uses walls, lines, arcs, polylines, and circles as boundaries for a space. The **All linework** filter uses any type of object as a boundary, including all AEC objects, AutoCAD linework, and blocks.

Below the filter list is the **Max Gap size:** text box. The value entered in this text box allows a gap between two bounding objects and considers the gap as part of the boundary for the new space. When selected, the **Ignore holes** check box ignores holes in a boundary object. If you want to overlap Space objects, pick the **Allow overlapping spaces** check box.

After establishing all of the criteria to generate spaces, new spaces can be added to the interior of the boundary objects. When you are prompted to, move the crosshairs to the inside of a boundary area. The **Generate Spaces** dialog box will remain open while you pick points to establish the space locations. The pushpin button at the top-right corner of the dialog box can be picked to hide the dialog box, making picking space locations easier.

As internal space points are selected, valid areas are highlighted with a red outline, by default. Pick the internal point to generate the space. Continue picking internal points to add all of the Space objects. Alternatively, you can enter the **generate All** option by typing A. This automatically adds spaces to all valid boundaries. **Figure 21-8** displays spaces formed from boundaries. When you have finished selecting the objects for the selection filter, move the cursor over the **Generate Spaces** dialog box to make any additional changes to other new spaces.

The **Space Info...** button displays the **Space Information** dialog box. See **Figure 21-9.** This dialog box evaluates all the spaces in the drawing and provides you with information about the size and total square footage of each space or each type of space. This information can then be exported to a Microsoft Access database by selecting the **Create MDB** button.

Figure 21-8.
Pick a point inside the boundary that will generate the space. The space has been generated by using the walls as a selection filter and additional spaces added to the remaining boundaries.

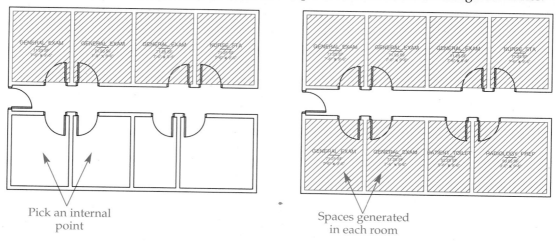

Pick an internal point

Spaces generated in each room

Figure 21-9.
The **Space Information** dialog box provides the total number of spaces and their square footages in the drawing.

Space information in the current drawing

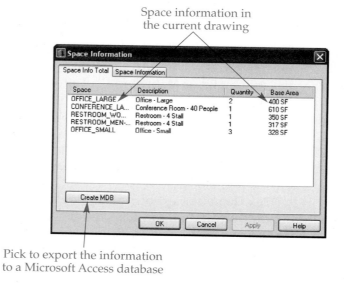

Pick to export the information to a Microsoft Access database

When you finish picking the points for the new spaces, pick the **Close** button to exit the command. Depending on the property set definition selected and the room name tag picked, the values of the room tag may not accurately reflect the name of the space. If the room names do not appear correctly, pick the Space objects, access the **Properties** palette, select the **Extended Data** tab, and add the **SpaceObjects** property set definition. Next, pick the **Regenerate model** button found in the **Standard** toolbar to update the display of the room name tags.

Exercise 21-2

Complete the Exercise on the Student CD.

Modifying Spaces

After spaces have been added to the drawing, the design may change, affecting the space plan, or the wrong space style may have been used when the space was initially inserted. There are a few commands that can be used to modify the Space objects in order to stay current with the design needs. The tools used to modify spaces are discussed in this section.

Modifying Spaces with the Properties Palette

After spaces have been added, the **Properties** palette can be used to modify the properties of a selected space. Most of the properties available when adding spaces can be modified to adjust the Space object.

Additionally, the **Layer** property found in the **General** category can be used to change the layer where the selected space is assigned. The **Rotation** and **Elevation** properties in the **Location** category are also available to modify the space. In addition to the physical properties of the space, property set definitions can be modified or added to the space for creating schedules by picking the **Extended Data** tab. Property set definitions will be discussed in Chapter 22 and Chapter 23.

Using Grips to Modify Spaces

Space objects, like other AEC objects, can be modified using standard AutoCAD commands. Spaces can be copied, moved, rotated, and stretched. In addition, grip editing can be used to modify a space. Depending on whether the space is selected in a Plan view or a Model view, different grips are located around the Space object, as in **Figure 21-10**.

Selecting a grip point and using the grip stretch mode allows you to relocate that point, and **Vertex**, **Edge**, and **Height** grips can all be stretched to adjust the size of the space. If a grip between two vertex points is selected, the entire edge is stretched. If a space is stretched using grips, its size parameters from the style are ignored. The **Vertex** and **Edge** grips also include options that can be accessed by pressing [Ctrl] to switch between the options after the grip has been selected. Hovering over these two grips displays a tooltip with the various options available for that grip. When you are selecting the **Edit Surfaces** grip displayed in a Model representation space, additional grip boxes become available for each surface of the 3D Space object.

AEC Modifying Tools

In addition to the tools previously mentioned, there are a few modifying tools specific to spaces available from the shortcut menu. These tools include: **Trim**, **Divide**, **Subtract**, **Merge**, and **Crop**. These tools are accessed by selecting a Space object, right-clicking, picking the **AEC Modify Tools** shortcut menu, and then selecting one of the options.

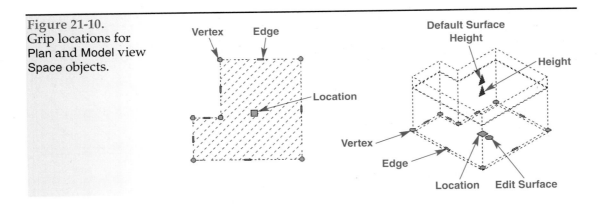

Figure 21-10.
Grip locations for Plan and Model view Space objects.

Trimming Spaces

The **Trim** option is used to trim a space and remove a portion of the space from the trimming line. This option is accessed by picking a space, right-clicking, and picking **AEC Modify Tools** > **Trim**. After accessing the option, pick two points to establish a trimming line. After you establish the trim line, move the mouse over the portion of the space to be trimmed. The space will be trimmed, with the trimmed portion removed. See **Figure 21-11**.

Dividing Spaces

A space can be divided into two separate space areas. To divide a space, select the space to be divided, right-click, and pick **AEC Modify Tools** > **Divide** from the shortcut menu. Pick a point that will designate the start point for the dividing line. Pick the second point to create the dividing line. Two spaces will be created from two points selected. See **Figure 21-12**.

Subtracting Spaces

Space objects can also be edited by subtracting an object such as a polyline, a circle, another space, or a wall occupying its area, thus removing the area occupied by the subtracted object. See **Figure 21-13**. To subtract objects from a space, first pick the Space object, right-click, and select **AEC Modify Tools** > **Subtract**. Select objects to be subtracted from the Space object's area. After selecting subtracting objects, type Y to erase the subtracting objects or N to retain the objects. The modified space is displayed when you are finished.

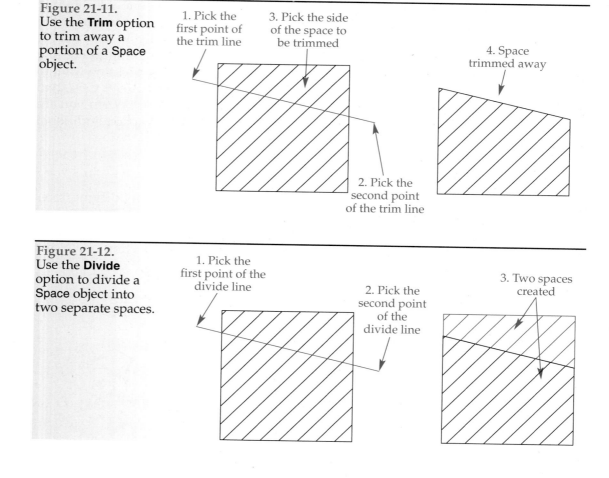

Figure 21-11.
Use the **Trim** option to trim away a portion of a Space object.

1. Pick the first point of the trim line

3. Pick the side of the space to be trimmed

4. Space trimmed away

2. Pick the second point of the trim line

Figure 21-12.
Use the **Divide** option to divide a Space object into two separate spaces.

1. Pick the first point of the divide line

2. Pick the second point of the divide line

3. Two spaces created

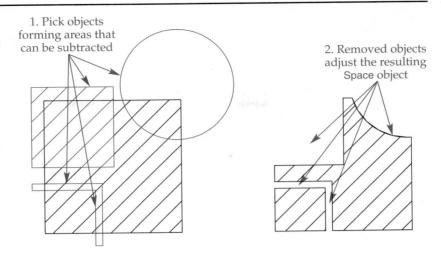

Figure 21-13.
Use the **Subtract** option to subtract objects occupying space area from the main space.

1. Pick objects forming areas that can be subtracted

2. Removed objects adjust the resulting Space object

Merging Spaces

Two spaces or closed objects such as polylines or circles can be joined together to form one Space object, which automatically updates the total area. The objects being merged do not have to be next to each other and can overlap. To merge two spaces together, select one of the spaces to be merged, right-click, and pick **AEC Modify Tools > Merge** from the shortcut menu. After accessing the option, pick a space beside, on, or away from the selected space.

Once the other space has been picked, type Y to remove the original space being merged, which replaces it with the updated merged space. Type N to keep the original spaces and add the newly merged space. Once the prompt is answered, the two spaces are merged together. If the spaces overlap each other, the boundaries around the intersecting space are removed, and the two spaces create a single space with a new area. If the two spaces do not overlap each other, the spaces are still joined together, adding to the total area. See **Figure 21-14.**

Cropping Spaces

The **Crop** tool allows you to crop a space against the edges of a cropping boundary, as in **Figure 21-15.** To access this option, select the space to be cropped, right-click, and pick **AEC Modify Tools > Crop.** Select the cropping boundary object. Type Y to remove the boundary and display the updated shape of the space. Note that, when a space is cropped, the space is merely trimmed away from the cropping boundary. The Space object does not fill the cropping boundary.

Figure 21-14.
The **Merge** option is used to merge spaces and closed objects with an existing space to modify and update the Space object.

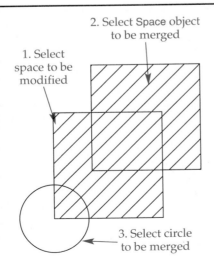

1. Select space to be modified

2. Select Space object to be merged

3. Select circle to be merged

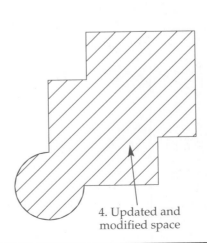

4. Updated and modified space

Figure 21-15.
The **Crop** option is used crop a space against a boundary object.

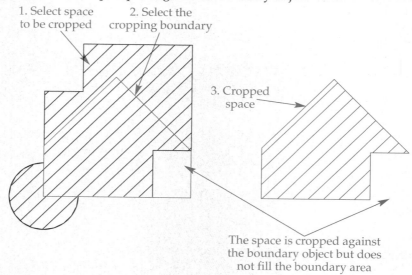

1. Select space to be cropped

2. Select the cropping boundary

3. Cropped space

The space is cropped against the boundary object but does not fill the boundary area

Applying an Interference

An interference object in a space is similar to an interference object in a wall. You may apply an interference within a space where a structural column appears in the middle of the space area or where a stair may interfere with the space as it goes to the next floor. The interference object can be a polyline or an AEC object. See **Figure 21-16**.

To add an interference to a space, select the Space object to include an interference, right-click, and pick **Interference Condition** > **Add**.

Once the objects are added as an interference, holes are cut into the space, removing any portion of the area occupied by the interfering objects. The total square footage amount is then updated.

Interferences can also be removed from a space by using the **Remove** option. Select the space containing an interference, right-click, and pick **Interference Condition** > **Remove**. After entering the command, pick any objects being used as an interference. When you are finished, the interferences are removed from the space.

Figure 21-16.
AEC objects and closed 2D objects can be used to create an interference within a Space object.

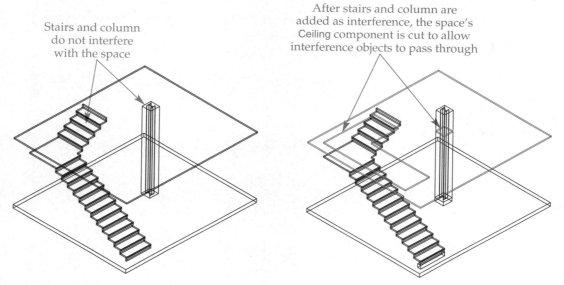

Stairs and column do not interfere with the space

After stairs and column are added as interference, the space's Ceiling component is cut to allow interference objects to pass through

Controlling Object Display

Space object display is controlled through the display system. Different components for the space can be controlled, such as a hatch pattern and color in the Plan views versus the appearance of the space in a Model view.

To control the display of an individual Space object, select the space, right-click, and pick **Edit Object Display...** from the shortcut menu. The **Object Display** dialog box is displayed, as shown in **Figure 21-17**. Select the appropriate display representation to control, and attach an object override. Pick the **Edit Display Properties** button to edit the display.

The Plan and Reflected representations include components for the base, net, usable, and gross boundaries and hatch patterns, as well as cut plane and calculation plane components. The Model representation includes a Floor and Ceiling component, and can have materials assigned to these components. The Volume representation controls the display of a 3D volumetric space in a Model view.

Exercise 21-3   Complete the Exercise on the Student CD.

Generating Space Information

After the spaces have been added to the drawing and modified as needed, the area information can be generated. The **Space Information** tool in Architectural Desktop evaluates all the spaces in the drawing and provides you with a detailed list of the space styles in the drawing. You can then export the list to a Microsoft Access database for further evaluation.

Figure 21-17.
The **Object Display** dialog box is used to assign an object display override to an individual object. Use the **Display Properties** dialog box to control how the components within the object will be displayed in the overridden display representation.

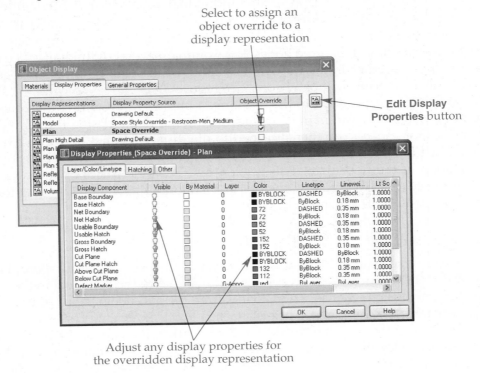

Select to assign an object override to a display representation

Edit Display Properties button

Adjust any display properties for the overridden display representation

Figure 21-18.
The **Space Information** dialog box organizes the space information in the drawing.

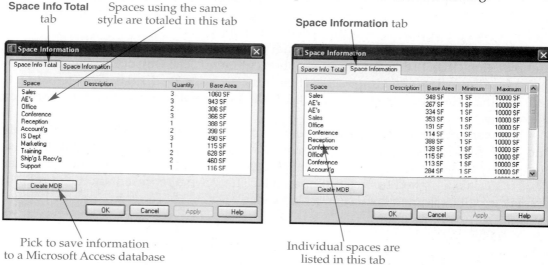

Space Info Total tab

Spaces using the same style are totaled in this tab

Space Information tab

Pick to save information to a Microsoft Access database

Individual spaces are listed in this tab

Type
SPACEINFO
Pull-Down Menu
Design
> Spaces
> Space
Information...

SPACEINFO

To evaluate spaces, pick **Design** > **Spaces** > **Space Information...** from the pull-down menu, or type SPACEINFO.

The **Space Information** dialog box includes the **Space Info Total** and **Space Information** tabs. See **Figure 21-18.** The **Space Info Total** tab provides the total square footage of all space styles used in the drawing. The **Space Information** tab lists each Space object in the drawing. At the bottom of the dialog box is the **Create MDB** button. Pick this button to save the space information as a Microsoft database MDB file.

Area Zone Basics

Spaces in a drawing represent an individual area, or part, of the building. Often these spaces are smaller parts of a larger organization, or zone. Spaces can be grouped together into a container known as a zone. Zones allow you to organize individual spaces into a set of structured zones. For example, several individual office spaces can be grouped together into a department zone, which may be grouped together with other zones to form a company zone. See **Figure 21-19.**

When a zone is added to the drawing, a marker representing the zone is drawn, as in **Figure 21-19.** The marker includes the zone name beside the marker for easy identification. Spaces are then attached to the different zones, forming a hierarchical structure for the total area. Later, these structured groups can be used to create a space evaluation of the floor plan. This section discusses the basics of adding a zone and attaching spaces to the zone. Other methods of organizing and adjusting the zone are discussed later in this chapter.

Adding a Zone

Type
ZONEADD
Pull-Down Menu
Design
> Zones
> Add Zone...
Tool Palette
Design
Zone

ZONEADD

Zone markers can be added at any time during the development of a space plan by using the **ZONEADD** command. To access this command, pick the **Zone** tool in the **Design** tool palette, pick **Design** > **Zones** > **Add Zone...** from the pull-down menu, or type ZONEADD. After entering the command, a box is attached to the crosshairs. This is the Zone marker. Pick a point in the drawing to add the Zone marker. By default, the marker includes a name that displays the name of Zone. If the zone is to include a name, such as department, building, or floor identification, the **Properties** palette can be used to name the group.

Figure 21-19.
Spaces can be added to space group containers (markers) known as zones, which in turn can be added to other zones.

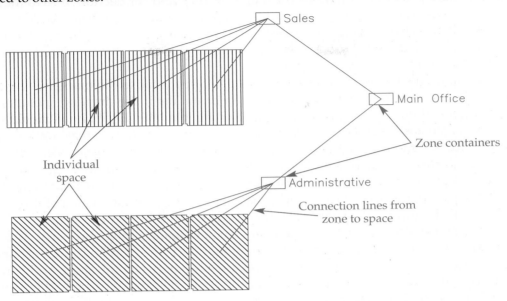

Before adding zones to the drawing, you may want to adjust the properties of the zone, such as the name, the style, and whether or not the zone can contain spaces or zones. After entering the command, access the **Properties** palette to establish the zone property parameters. See Figure 21-20. The following properties for area groups are available in the **Properties** palette.

Zone Properties

Before a zone is added to the drawing, the property settings for the zone should be set. When adding a zone, the **Properties** palette displays the properties used to control the zone. The **Properties** palette is divided into five categories under the **BASIC** header. See Figure 21-20.

The **General** category includes five properties that control the general parameters for the area group:

- **Description.** Pick this property to add a description to the zone being added. Picking the property displays the **Configuration** dialog box, where a description can be added.

Figure 21-20.
The **Properties** palette is used to set the parameters for a zone before it is added to the drawing.

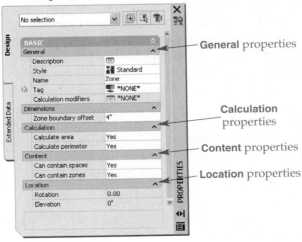

- **Style.** This drop-down list includes a list of zone styles that can be used to display the zone. Zone styles can be used to set the color and hatch for the Zone marker, as well as display the name, marker, and connection lines to the spaces assigned to the zone or other zones assigned to the zone being added.
- **Name.** This text box property is used to assign a name to the zone. The name entered in this property is the name of the zone that is placed beside the marker.
- **Tag.** This property allows you to assign a space tag to the marker being added. A list of tags is available in the drop-down list if the drawing includes space tags. If no tags are present in the drawing, the ***NONE*** option is displayed.
- **Calculation modifiers.** A calculation modifier is a definition that applies a mathematical modifier to the space being reported on. For example, a calculation modifier can be created to multiply the total area from all the individual Space objects assigned to the zone by a cost per square foot. When the calculation modifier is applied, the actual base area of the zone and the calculated area of the zone can be obtained. Calculation modifiers are discussed in the next section.

The **Dimensions** category includes the **Zone boundary offset** property. This property specifies an offset distance for a zone boundary that can be drawn around any space attached to the zone to show the relationship between the space and zone. The Zone Boundary is a display component for the zone style and is turned off by default.

The **Calculation** category includes two properties that establish whether or not the zone calculates the area of all grouped spaces and perimeters. The **Calculate area** property has a **Yes** or **No** value. Select **Yes** from the drop-down list to cause the zone to calculate the total area of all the individual Space objects grouped under this zone. The **Calculate perimeter** property has a **Yes** or **No** value. Select **Yes** to calculate the total perimeter of all Space objects grouped together.

The **Content** category is used to establish the types of area content that can be used by the area group. The **Can contain spaces** property allows the new zone to have Space objects attached if **Yes** is selected. The **Can contain zones** property allows other zones to be attached to this zone when **Yes** is selected.

The **Location** category initially is used to indicate the rotation and the elevation of the area group being added to the drawing. These properties are not available when you are adding a Zone marker, but they become available when you are editing a zone.

When you are finished specifying the zone settings, pick a point in the drawing to add the Zone marker. The marker and its name are added to the drawing and ready to have spaces attached and grouped under this marker and heading.

Attaching a Zone to a Space

Once you add a Zone marker to the drawing, you can attach individual spaces to the marker, which allows you to organize the individual spaces into groups of zones. One method of attaching a space to the zone is to select the space to be attached, right-click, and pick the **Attach to Zone** option. After entering the command, pick a Zone marker for attaching the Space object. Another method of attaching a space to a zone is to select the Zone marker, right-click, and pick the **Attach Spaces / Zones** option. After accessing the option, pick any Space object or other Zone marker you want attached to the zone.

In addition to using the shortcut menus to attach spaces and zones to a Zone marker, selecting a Zone marker will display a **+** grip, allowing you to attach spaces or zones to the selected Zone marker. See **Figure 21-21.** After picking the **+** grip, select any spaces or zones to be attached to the Zone marker.

Architectural Desktop and Its Applications

Figure 21-21.
Spaces and other zones can be attached to a zone marker by picking the **+** grip on the zone marker that will have spaces or zones attached.

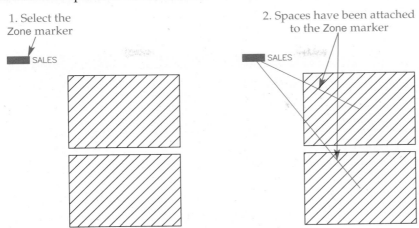

Detaching a Zone from a Space

In addition to attaching spaces to zones, you can detach spaces from a zone. Select the Zone marker, right-click, and pick the **Detach Spaces / Zones** option. After accessing the option, select the Space objects to be removed from the zone, and press [Enter]. Alternatively, you can pick an attached space or zone, right-click, and select the **Detach from Zone** option.

Another method is to select the zone to be removed. This displays grip boxes. See Figure 21-21. A **–** grip is displayed in the center of the space. Select the **–** to remove the space from the zone.

Exercise
21-4

Complete the Exercise on the Student CD.

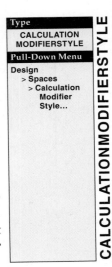

Space Calculations

Calculations are often used in conjunction with spaces. Often the purpose of obtaining the area of a space is to process it through a formula, in order to obtain a modified value. For example, suppose when a site plan is created, 10% of the total area needs to be landscaped. A calculation modifier can be applied to the site plan space to determine the value of 10% of the area.

As calculation formulas are developed, they can be applied to spaces or to zones. After the formulas are created and applied, a space evaluation report can be generated as part of the construction document set. Space evaluation reports are discussed later in this chapter.

Creating a Calculation Modifier Style

The calculation modifier formula can be applied to a Space object's total area, to the perimeter, or to both. The formula can be applied to an individual space or a zone. If the calculation modifier is applied to a zone, it affects all spaces attached to that zone. To create a calculation modifier, pick **Design** > **Spaces** > **Calculation Modifier Style...** from the pull-down menu, or type CALCULATIONMODIFIERSTYLE.

Type
CALCULATION MODIFIERSTYLE
Pull-Down Menu
Design
> **Spaces**
> **Calculation Modifier Style...**

CALCULATIONMODIFIERSTYLE

Figure 21-22.
The **Style Manager** is used to create calculation modifier styles that can be applied to spaces to obtain a modified area or perimeter value.

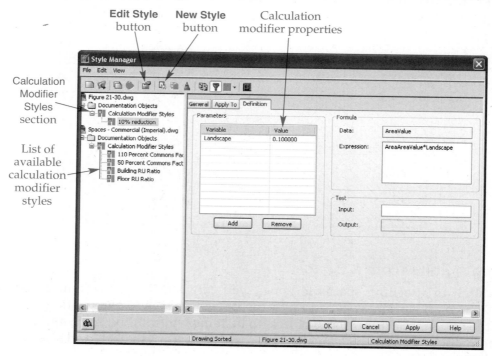

The **Style Manager** is displayed, opened to the Calculation Modifier Styles section, as in **Figure 21-22.** Pick the **New Style** button to create a new style. You can also right-click on the Calculation Modifier Styles section icon or in the right pane to display a shortcut menu and select **New** to create a new style. Enter a name for the calculation modifier style.

To edit the new style, highlight the style in the tree view to display the calculation modifier properties in the right pane. Calculation modifier styles include the following tabs:

- **General.** This tab allows you to rename the style, provide a description, and attach notes.
- **Apply To.** This tab is used to specify the part of the Space object to which the formula applies. See **Figure 21-23.** Two options are available: **Area** and **Perimeter**. Select the space component to be used in the calculation. Typically, one component is selected for the calculation. For example, if the space needed to be calculated to report on 10% of the total space area, the area component would be selected. If a room was to have an electrical receptacle placed every 6'-0", the perimeter component could be divided by 6'-0" to give you the total number of receptacles required.

  In most situations, the calculation modifier is applied to either the area or perimeter. However, both components can be selected, and the modifier can be applied to both values.
- **Definition.** This tab is used to enter a formula that modifies the component selected in the **Apply To** tab. See **Figure 21-24.** This tab has three main areas. The **Parameters** area allows you to set up variables that can be used in the formula. The **Formula** area is where the formula to be applied to the selected component is written. The **Test** area is where you can test the formula before applying it to an actual Area object.

Figure 21-23.
The **Apply To** tab is used to specify the space component that will be used in the calculation modifier formula.

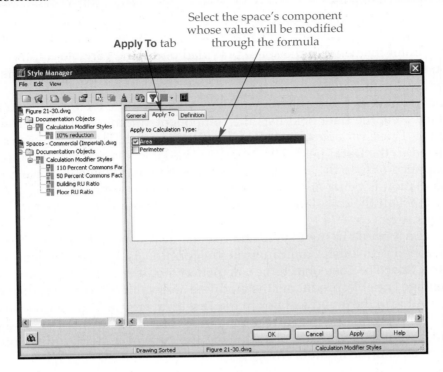

Apply To tab

Select the space's component whose value will be modified through the formula

Figure 21-24.
The **Definition** tab is used to write the formula that will be attached to a Space object and will modify the value of the area or perimeter component selected in the **Apply To** tab.

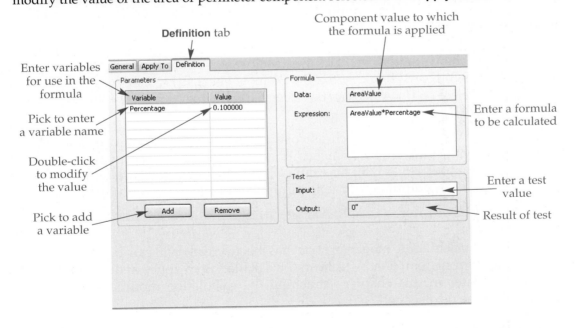

Definition tab

Component value to which the formula is applied

Enter variables for use in the formula

Pick to enter a variable name

Double-click to modify the value

Pick to add a variable

Enter a formula to be calculated

Enter a test value

Result of test

Creating a Formula

After you select the component for the modifier to apply, you can create the formula. In the **Definition** tab, you can create variables to be applied to the formula. For example, if you are going to multiply the space area by a percentage, you can create a percentage variable and assign it a value. See **Figure 21-24.** Use the **Add** button to add a variable. Enter the name in the space provided under the **Variable** column. To assign the value to the variable, double-click in the **Value** column beside the variable name and enter a value for the variable.

After you have defined all your variables, you can write the formula. At the top of the **Formula** area, the **Data** field lists the component variable that was selected in the **Apply To** tab. These variables must be a part of the formula. Three component variables can be listed in the **Data:** field. The **AreaValue** variable is displayed if the calculation is being applied only to the area component. The **PerimeterValue** variable is displayed if the calculation is being applied only to the perimeter component. The **Value** variable is available if the calculation is being applied to both the area and the perimeter components.

Write the formula in the **Expression** list box. If you are calculating the landscape area mentioned previously, you can write the formula as AreaValue*Percentage. When applied to a Space or Zone object, the calculation modifier multiplies the total area by the percentage variable, producing the modified area value. You can test the formula by entering a value in the **Input:** text box in the **Test** area. **Figure 21-24** shows this formula being used and producing the correct result: 10% of a 10′-0″ area is 1′-0″. Although the input and output values are displayed using the current drawing units notation, the idea is correct, and the formula works.

If you decide not to use variables, you can write actual values in the **Expression** area of the formula, and the variable must be entered as it is displayed. You can write complex formulas, but some characters are not allowed. Special characters, such as ?, $, ( ), and -, cannot be used, but the underscore can. Spaces are not allowed. Diacritical marks, such as è, â, ö, and æ, cannot be used. Some examples of calculation modifier styles are shown in **Figure 21-25.**

 NOTE

The value for one brick was established by multiplying the size of a 3-3/4″ × 8″ brick: $3.75 \times 8 = 30$ in$^2 \div 144$ (1 ft^2) $= .20833$. The area of a piece of 4″ × 4″ tile can be calculated the same way: $4 \times 4 = 16$ in$^2 \div 144 = .111$.

When variables such as cost and number totals are calculated, the values are output as inches (or millimeters if using decimal units). The output 148′ 6-1/8″, for example, in a cost output, translates to $148.50. If the output is for the total number of tiles, you round the value up to 149 tiles.

After the calculation modifier style has been created, it can be attached to a space, zone, or zone template. Attaching the calculation to zones and zone templates is discussed later in this chapter. Attaching the calculation modifier to a space is discussed in the next section.

 Exercise
21-5   *Complete the Exercise on the Student CD.*

Figure 21-25.
Examples of calculation modifier styles that can be used in the **Expression** area.

Calculation Modifier Name	Description	Applies To	Variables	Value	Formula
Number of Bricks	Calculates total number of bricks with 5% spoilage. Area of one brick = .2083	Area	OneBrick	.2083	AreaValue/ OneBrick*.05+ AreaValue
Landscape Area	Calculates 10% of an area	Area	Percentage	.10	AreaValue* Percentage
Baseboard Cost	Calculates the cost of baseboards applied to the perimeter of an area	Perimeter	Cost	2.47	Perimeter Value*Cost
Concrete Volume and Cost	Calculates the volume of an 8" high concrete area × $55.00 per cubic foot	Area	Cost
Height	55
8	AreaValue* Height*Cost
Plaster Deductions	Calculates a 3% plaster deduction along an area	Area	Plaster_Deduction	.97	AreaValue* Plaster_ Deduction
Building Cost	Calculates the area × $165.00 per square foot	Area	Cost	165	AreaValue* Cost

Assigning Calculation Modifiers to Spaces

In addition to the name and style of a space, the attachment of calculation modifier styles to spaces can be controlled through the **Properties** palette. To apply a calculation modifier to a space, select a Space object, and then pick the **Calculation modifiers** property in the **Properties** palette. This displays the **Calculation Modifiers** worksheet, which includes a list on the right of calculation modifiers available in the drawing. Pick any modifiers to be added to the area. After highlighting the desired modifiers, pick the **Attach calculation modifier** button to add the modifiers to the **Attached:** list box on the left. See **Figure 21-26.**

If a modifier in the **Attached:** list box is to be removed, highlight the modifier, and then pick the **Remove attached calculation modifier** button. This removes the modifier from the space only and not the drawing. The order in which the modifiers are added affects the outcome of the final calculation. Use the **Move up** and **Move down** buttons to reorder the modifiers in the **Attached:** list box.

When a calculation modifier is attached to a space, the modifier works through the formula, determining the modified space result. If another modifier has been attached, the modified space result of the first calculation is used in the next formula. For example, if two modifiers are applied to a space—style A calculates the 10% landscape area of a 500′ × 800′ building site, and style B calculates the cost at $45.00 per square foot for the landscaped area—the order in which the modifiers are applied affects the results of the calculation.

Figure 21-26.
The **Calculation Modifiers** worksheet is used to assign a calculation modifier to the selected Space object.

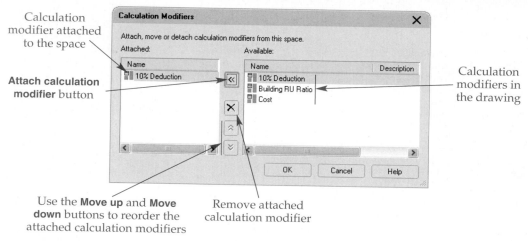

Calculation modifier attached to the space

Attach calculation modifier button

Use the **Move up** and **Move down** buttons to reorder the attached calculation modifiers

Remove attached calculation modifier

Calculation modifiers in the drawing

In addition to assigning calculation modifiers through the **Properties** palette, calculation modifiers can be assigned through the **Space/Zone Manager** worksheet. The **Space/Zone Manager** worksheet allows you to assign calculation modifiers to a space and assign the different spaces within the drawing to the different zones. See **Figure 21-27.**

To access the **Space/Zone Manager** worksheet, select a space to be modified, and then select the **Space/Zone Manager** property from the **Properties** palette. See **Figure 21-27.**

Figure 21-27.
The **Space/Zone Manager** worksheet is used to organize spaces under zones and attach calculation modifiers to the different Space objects.

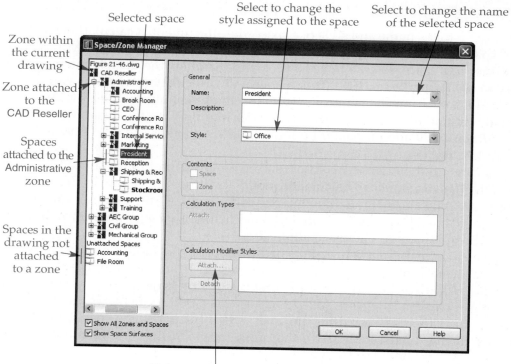

Selected space

Select to change the style assigned to the space

Select to change the name of the selected space

Zone within the current drawing

Zone attached to the CAD Reseller

Spaces attached to the Administrative zone

Spaces in the drawing not attached to a zone

Pick to assign calculation modifiers to the selected space

The left side of the worksheet displays a tree of zones and spaces within the current drawing. Depending on how spaces are assigned to zones and zones are assigned to other zones, the tree list displays the organization of the space plan. Spaces and zones can be reassigned to different spaces by dragging and dropping them onto a different zone within the tree view. The Unattached Spaces folder lists any spaces within the current drawing currently not assigned to a zone.

Picking a space from the list displays some of its properties in the right pane of the worksheet. For example, in **Figure 21-27**, the Men's Restroom has been selected in the tree view. The name and style of the space can be modified by choosing a different name and style from the properties in the right pane. At the bottom of the right pane, calculation modifiers within the drawing can be assigned to the selected Space object. When you are finished assigning information to the different spaces within the drawing, pick the **OK** button to exit the worksheet and return to the drawing.

Exercise 21-6   *Complete the Exercise on the Student CD.*

Space Decomposition

In some building jurisdictions, an important part of a space evaluation is a visual breakdown of the space area into subdivisions. This breakdown is also known as a *decomposed space*. In some cases, a diagram of the decomposition is required for building approval, as shown in **Figure 21-28**.

There are three types of decomposition available: **Trapezoid**, **Triangle (Overlap)**, and **Triangle**. You can adjust the display settings for each of these types by modifying the Decomposed display representation for the Space object. The decomposed space can be displayed by selecting the Diagnostic display configuration from the **Display Configuration** menu located in the drawing window status bar.

Editing the Decomposition Display

The display of the decomposed area is controlled through the Space objects' display properties. Display settings can be controlled at the style level by modifying the space style, accessing the **Display Properties** tab, attaching a style override to the Decomposition display representation, and then editing the display by picking the **Edit Display Properties** button in the **Display Properties** tab. Changes made here are applied to all spaces using this space style.

Figure 21-28.
Different space decomposition diagrams.

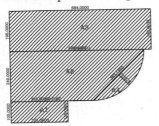
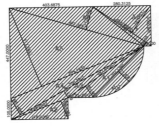
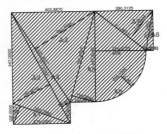

Trapezoid Decomposition   **Triangle (overlap) Decomposition**   **Triangle Decomposition**

If individual Space objects are to display different decomposed types, the display settings can be overridden for each individual Space object. Pick a Space object, right-click, and pick the **Edit Object Display...** option. This displays the **Object Display** dialog box. Pick the **Display Properties** tab, assign an object override, and then pick the **Edit Display Properties** button to begin editing the display of the single object.

This shows the **Display Properties** dialog box, shown in Figure 21-29. Three tabs are available for the Decomposed display representation: **Layer/Color/Linetype**, **Decomposition**, and **Proof**. Once these settings have been adjusted, the decomposed area will be displayed using the settings specified. The three tabs are described as follows:

- **Layer/Color/Linetype.** Use this tab to control the display of the different components within the decomposition.
- **Decomposition.** This tab is used to specify a decomposition type to be displayed. Refer to Figure 21-28. These types include the **Trapezoid**, **Triangle (overlap)**, and **Triangle** types. The **Explode Result** area specifies the type of objects the decomposition turns into if exploded.
- **Proof.** This tab is used to configure how the triangular or trapezoidal space tag and the dimension tags will be displayed. See Figure 21-30. When a space is broken up, it is decomposed into different subdivision areas. The subdivision is assigned a tag for easy identification of each decomposed subdivision area. The **A - Prefix:** text box allows you to specify a prefix for the decomposed space tag name. You can choose a text style for the tag and enter a text height in the **Tag Display** area. The **Display of Dimensions** area can be used to control the dimension tags along each edge of a decomposed area. The text style and the height values can be modified.

Figure 21-29

The display of the **Decomposition** area can be controlled through the space style or through individual Space objects in the drawing. If you are modifying the display of individual objects, the **Object Display** dialog box is used to assign an object override so the display can be modified. Once an override has been set, picking the **Edit Display Properties** button will open the **Display Properties** dialog box.

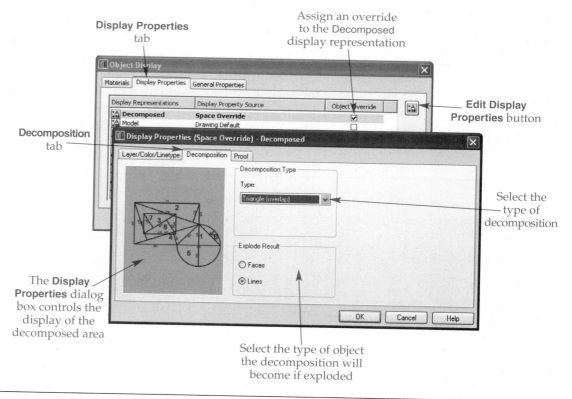

Display Properties tab

Assign an override to the Decomposed display representation

Edit Display Properties button

Decomposition tab

Select the type of decomposition

The **Display Properties** dialog box controls the display of the decomposed area

Select the type of object the decomposition will become if exploded

Architectural Desktop and Its Applications

Figure 21-30.
The **Proof** tab is used to control how the decomposed area tags and dimension tags will be displayed.

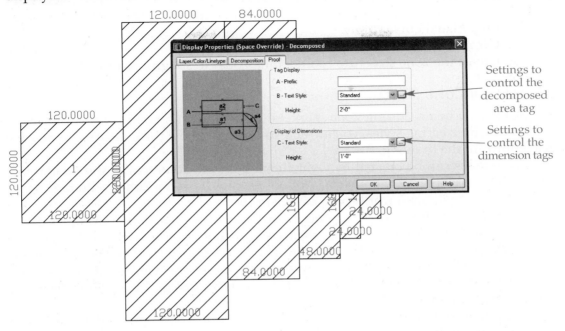

Settings to control the decomposed area tag

Settings to control the dimension tags

Advanced Zones

As defined earlier, a zone is a container for spaces and other zones that are grouped together in a hierarchical or zone structure, as in **Figure 21-31**. Generally, a space represents the lowest level of the zone structure, whereas zones organize different groups of spaces for an entire building or business.

Figure 21-31.
An example of a hierarchical zone structure for a business within a building.

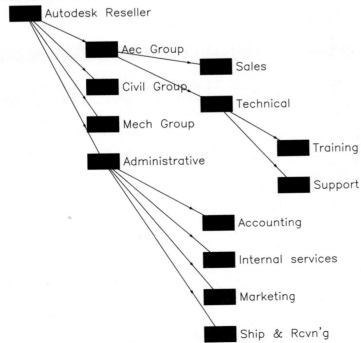

The following are a few basic steps in organizing a zone structure:

1. Decide on all the zones and subgroups of zones needed to complete the zone structure.
2. Decide how the zones and subgroups of zones are to relate to one another. Organize them logically.
3. Create the **Zone** markers.
4. Create the zone structure by attaching zones to subgroups of zones.

Creating a Zone Style

Before you begin adding **Zone** markers to the drawing, you may want to create zone styles. By creating styles, you are able to configure how the total area of the zone is to appear in the drawing.

Zone styles can be created by right-clicking on the **Zone** tool in the **Design** tool palette and picking the **Zone Styles...** option, picking **Design** > **Zones** > **Zone Styles...** from the pull-down menu, or typing ZONESTYLE.

The **Style Manager** is displayed, opened to the Zone Styles section, as in **Figure 21-32**. Create a new zone style by selecting the **New Style** button or by right-clicking on the **Zone Styles** icon and selecting the **New** command from the shortcut menu. Type a name for the zone style, and then pick the new zone style in the tree view to review its properties. Zone styles include four property tabs: **General**, **Design Rules**, **Classifications**, and **Display Properties**.

The **General** tab is used to rename the style, provide a description of the style, and add notes and property set definitions to the style.

The **Design Rules** tab is used to assign a list definition to the zone style through the **Zone Names:** drop-down list. A *list definition* is a definition of zone names that can be selected. The creation of list definitions will be discussed later in this chapter. The **Exclusivity** area is used to set content restrictions for zones based on the zone style. The **Space Exclusive** check box allows only one space to be assigned to a zone using this style. The **Zone Exclusive** check box allows zones of this style to only be grouped with other zones of this style.

Figure 21-32.
The Zone Styles section of the **Style Manager**. Create a new zone style, and then select the style in the tree view to display the style's properties.

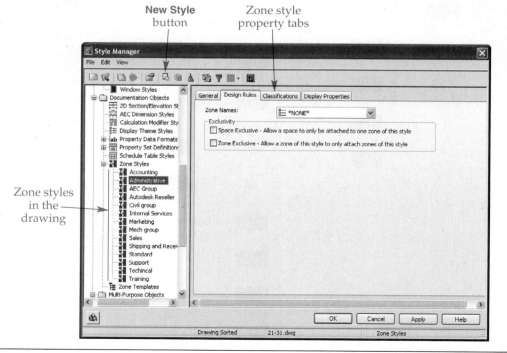

Architectural Desktop and Its Applications

The **Classifications** tab is used to assign any classification definitions that can be used to sort for specific groups within the building to create a schedule.

The **Display Properties** tab is used to configure the display properties for the zone. The display representations available are for Plan views. The Plan representation is typically used in the Medium display configuration. The Plan Low Detail display representation is typically used for small-scale drawings, and the Plan High Detail display representation is typically used in large-scale drawings.

After you select the display representation to be modified, attach a style override, and pick the **Edit Display Properties...** button. The **Display Properties** dialog box is displayed. See Figure 21-33.

The **Display Properties** dialog box includes the following three tabs:

- **Layer/Color/Linetype.** This tab includes a list of components for the Zone marker. Adjust the component's display, color, and linetype as desired. The following display components control the display of different parts of the Zone marker:
  - **Zone Boundary.** This component controls the display of an outline around the spaces that are attached to the zone.
  - **Hatch.** This component turns the hatch inside the Zone marker on or off. The hatch is also applied to the inside of the zone boundary.
  - **Name.** This component turns on the name assigned to the Zone marker.
  - **Marker.** This tab turns the Zone marker box on or off.
  - **Space Connection Line.** This component draws a line from the zone to the spaces that are attached.
  - **Zone Connection Line.** This component is a line that is drawn between Zone markers that are attached to one another.
  - **Zone Connection Error.** This component displays an error symbol for any errors within a zone structure.

Figure 21-33.
The zone style property tabs are used to configure settings for a zone style. The **Display Properties** dialog box is used to adjust the display for a zone's display representation.

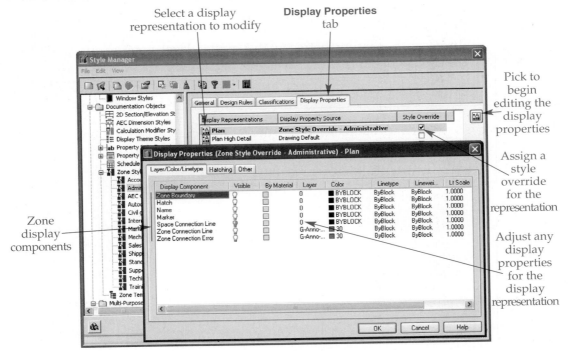

- **Hatching.** If the Hatch component has been turned on, this tab controls the display of the hatch pattern within the Zone marker and within the zone boundary. Assigning a different hatch to each zone style helps identify the individual spaces attached to each zone.
- **Other.** This tab controls additional properties for the Zone marker. See **Figure 21-34.** The **Name** area is used to assign a text style to the marker name. If a new text style is desired, pick the ellipsis (**...**) button to open the **Text Style** dialog box and create a new style. The **Height:** text box is used to enter a height for the marker name. To figure out the height, multiply the desired printed height times the scale factor of the drawing. For example, a 1/4″ high printed height × 96 scale factor = 24″ text.

The **User Defined Scaling** check box is used to determine the size of the marker. If the check box is not selected, the marker is scaled by the drawing scale. If the check box is selected, enter a width and height for the rectangular marker.

If the **Draw All** check box is selected, the hatch pattern for the zone is attached down through the zone structure to the space. Consequently, multiple hatch patterns can be created within one space, depending on how many levels of zones the space is attached to. If this check box is cleared, only the first zone level hatch is applied to the spaces that are attached.

When you have finished configuring the zone style, pick the **OK** button to exit all the dialog boxes. A new zone using this style is now available.

Attaching and Detaching Zone Groups

After a zone style has been created, it can be attached to Space objects and other Zone markers. The zone structure can be created by attaching zones to one another. **Figure 21-31** shows Zone markers attached to other Zone markers. A Zone marker can be attached to any number of spaces or other zones to form subgroups or be attached to other higher level zones.

To attach spaces or other Zone markers to a Zone marker, select the Zone marker, right-click, and pick the **Attach Space / Zones** option from the shortcut menu. Pick any Zone markers or spaces to be attached to the selected zone.

NOTE Depending on the display settings used in the zone style, connector lines can be drawn between the higher level zone group and the subgroups of zones and spaces that are attached to it.

Figure 21-34.
The **Other** tab is used to adjust additional properties for the Zone marker.

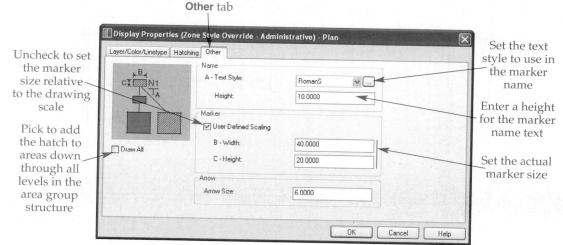

Architectural Desktop and Its Applications

As you develop and arrange the zone structure, you may decide that zones and spaces that were attached earlier no longer need to be attached to a particular zone. In this case, you can detach zones and Space objects from a higher level zone group. To detach spaces and zones from a Zone marker, select the Zone marker, right-click, and pick **Detach Spaces / Zones** from the shortcut menu.

Modifying Additional Properties

Properties, such as the attachment of calculation modifiers and the management of the zone structure, can be edited through the **Properties** palette. When a Zone marker has been selected, the **Properties** palette displays the available properties that can be modified. Five categories are included under the **BASIC** header that organize the different properties for the zone. These categories and their properties are described below.

General Category

The **General** category includes general properties for the selected zone. These properties include the following:

- **Description.** Picking this property displays the **Description** worksheet, where a description for the group can be entered.
- **Layer.** By default, zones are created on the A-Area-Zone layer. If the zone is to be placed on a different layer, select a new layer from the list.
- **Style.** This drop-down list property is used to assign a different style to the selected zone. Zone styles can have a different color, linetype, and hatch pattern displayed for easy recognition of the different zones in the drawing.
- **Name.** This text box property is used to name the Zone marker. The name entered here is displayed beside the marker.
- **Number of spaces.** This property lists the number of spaces directly attached to the zone.
- **Total number of spaces.** This property lists the total number of spaces attached to the zone to include spaces assigned to subgroups of zones, which are then attached to the selected zone.
- **Number of zones.** This property lists the number of zones directly attached to the selected zone.
- **Total number of zones.** This property lists the total number of zones attached to the selected zone to include zones attached to subgroups of zones within the structure.
- **Calculation modifiers.** Pick this property to display the **Calculation Modifiers** worksheet, where calculation modifiers can be added to the zone, which modifies the outcome of the total area or perimeter of all the spaces attached to the zone.
- **Space/Zone Manager.** Pick this property to display the **Space/Zone Manager** worksheet, where the different spaces in the drawing can be selected and attached to the zone selected for modification.

Dimensions Category

The **Dimensions** category displays the total and modified areas and perimeters of all spaces attached to the zone. Most of these properties are read-only values and cannot be modified without modifying the spaces being reported on within the zone.

- **Base area.** This read-only property displays the total area of all the Space objects attached to the selected zone.
- **Calculated area.** This property displays the modified area of all the spaces after they are evaluated through the calculation modifiers assigned to the zone.
- **Base perimeter.** This read-only property displays the total perimeter of all the spaces attached to the selected zone.
- **Calculated perimeter.** This read-only perimeter displays the modified perimeter of all the spaces attached to the selected zone after a calculation modifier has been applied.

- **Base volume.** This property displays the total volume of all the spaces attached to the selected zone.
- **Zone boundary offset.** This property controls the offset of the zone boundary component, measured from the outside edges of spaces to the edge of the boundary. The zone boundary is a display component that can be turned on or off in the current display representation.

Calculation Category

The **Calculation** category includes two properties. These properties are used to determine if the area and perimeter information from all of the spaces attached to the zone will be calculated. The **Calculate area** property is used to determine if the area is displayed in the **Calculated area** property in the **Dimensions** category. The **Calculate perimeter** property is used to determine if the perimeter of all the spaces attached to the zone is displayed.

Content Category

The **Content** category is used to determine whether or not spaces and zones can be attached to the selected zone. The **Can contain spaces** property is used to determine if spaces can be attached to the selected zone. The **Can contain zones** property is used to determine if zones can be attached to the selected Zone marker.

Location Properties

The **Location** category includes properties that control the elevation and rotation of the selected area group.
- **Rotation.** This property displays the rotation angle of the selected Zone marker. Entering a new angle rotates the marker and the text to the angle specified.
- **Elevation.** This value indicates the elevation at which the marker was placed in the Z axis. Enter a new value to adjust the elevation of the marker.
- **Additional information.** Pick this property to display the **Location** worksheet, where an elevation and rotation angle can be specified through a worksheet, rather than from the individual properties.

Exercise 21-7

Complete the Exercise on the Student CD.

Creating a Zone Layout

As Zone markers are added and arranged in the drawing, the hierarchical structure may become confusing. See **Figure 21-35.** The **ZONELAYOUT** command is used to sort the markers according to their logical and hierarchical positions. This command is accessed by typing ZONELAYOUT or by picking the Zone marker to be organized, right-clicking, and picking **Zone Layout** from the shortcut menu. Pick a point in the drawing to align the subgroups of zones under the selected zone. The **Distance, Row offset,** and **Column offset** options can also be used to align the area group markers. See **Figure 21-36.** When you are finished using these options, the Zone markers should be aligned to make the hierarchy easier to read.
- **Distance.** The **Distance** option is used to specify two opposite corners that determine both the row and column offsets establishing the distances between Zone markers. Type D, or right-click and pick the **Distance** option from the shortcut menu.
- **Row offset.** The **Row offset** option controls the vertical distance between Zone markers. Type R, or right-click and select **Row offset** from the shortcut menu. After the option has been accessed, enter a row offset value to space the Zone markers vertically.

Figure 21-35.
As zones are added, attached, and organized, the zone structure may become difficult to review. The same zone structure has been organized using the **ZONELAYOUT** command.

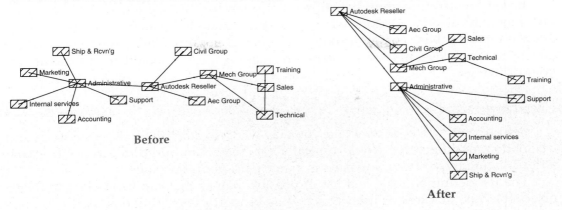

Before

After

Figure 21-36.
The **Area Group Layout** tool allows you to specify the distances between the zone markers.

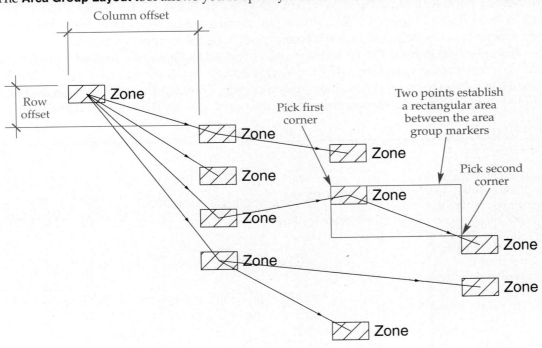

- **Column offset.** The **Column offset** option controls the horizontal distance between the Zone markers. Type C, or right-click and pick the **Column offset** option from the shortcut menu. After accessing this option, enter a distance value to space the Zone markers horizontally.

NOTE

When you are using the **ZONELAYOUT** command for a Zone marker that is a subgroup of a higher level zone, only the markers attached to the subgroup are aligned.

If you are creating zone structures that often use the same zone names, styles, and hierarchical organization, you can create a zone template. The zone template allows you to establish common zone names, styles, and calculation modifiers that are attached to each level in the zone structure, making it easier to add zone structures to your drawings.

Creating List Definitions

Before creating a zone template, you may want to establish all the zone styles and calculation modifiers that would typically get created and used in a zone structure. After creating these styles, you need to create a list definition style.

The list definition style is a list of possible names that can be applied to Space objects or Zone markers or used in schedule property set definitions. Within a zone structure, the list of names becomes available when a space is attached to a zone that is using the list definition style. The use of the **Properties** palette was discussed earlier. When creating a space or zone style, a list definition can be assigned to the **Space Names:** or **Zone Names:** drop-down list in the **Design Rules** tab for either a space style or a zone style. See **Figure 21-37.** Later, when adding a Space or Zone object, the name of the object can be selected in the **Name** property of the **Properties** palette.

To create your own list of names, access the **Style Manager.** Browse to the Multi-Purpose Objects folder, and then pick the List Definitions section. See **Figure 21-38.** Pick the **New Style** button to create a new list definition style. Enter a name for the style, and pick the new style in the tree view to review the property tabs for the new list definition.

Figure 21-37.
List definitions are assigned to space and zone styles, where the name of a space or zone can be selected from a list in the **Name** property of the **Properties** palette when adding a Space or Zone object.

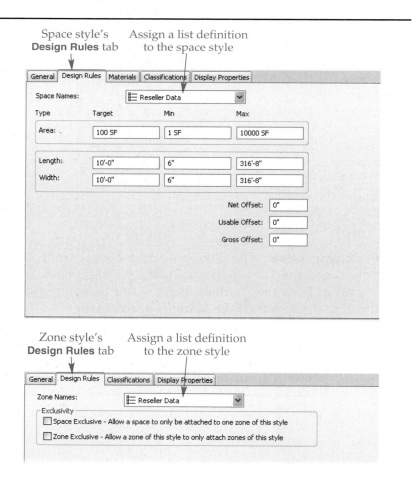

Figure 21-38.
The Multi-Purpose Objects folder includes the List Definitions section. Create a new list definition, and then edit the properties of the list.

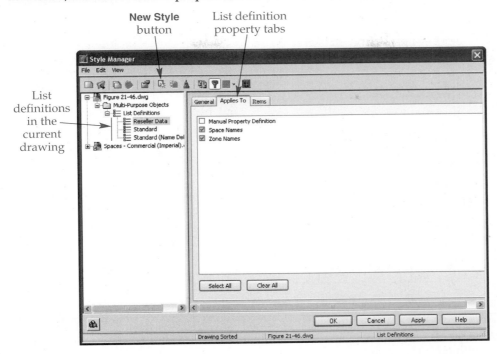

A list definition includes three property tabs: **General**, **Applies To**, and **Items**. See Figure 21-38. As with other styles, the **General** tab is used to name or rename the definition and to add notes regarding the list.

The **Applies To** tab is used to select the type of object the list can be applied to. Three options are available: **Manual Property Definition**, **Space Names**, and **Zone Names**. The **Manual Property Definition** check box allows a list of names to be available in a schedule's property set definition. Property set definitions and schedules are discussed in Chapter 22. The **Space Names** check box allows the list definition to be available for space styles. The **Zone Names** check box causes the list to be available within zone definitions. Select the desired check boxes to assign the list definition to the different styles. A list definition can be assigned to one, two, or all three types of objects.

The **Items** tab is used to create the list of names to be applied to the types of objects selected in the **Applies To** tab. See Figure 21-39. Use the **Add** button to add a name to the list, and then enter the name. Continue to pick the **Add** button to create names. You can also delete area names from the list by highlighting the desired name and picking the **Remove** button.

Creating a Zone Template

After you create the zone styles, calculation modifiers, and list definitions, you can assemble the zone template. The zone template can only be used to create a new zone structure and does not maintain any ties to a zone structure. If the zone structure is modified after it has been inserted, it does not affect the original template. Zone templates are created by picking **Design** > **Zones** > **Zone Templates...** from the pull-down menu or typing ZONETEMPLATE.

The **Style Manager** opens to the Zone Templates section. See Figure 21-40. Create a new style using the **New Style** button, or right-click on the section icon and select **New** to create a new section. Enter a new name for the template. This name can reflect the type of zone structure, such as Building Owners and Managers Association (BOMA), or the name of a company organization for easy identification of the style function.

Figure 21-39.
The **Items** tab is used to create the list of names within the list definition.

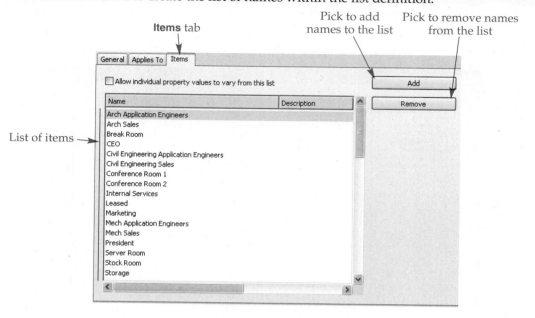

Figure 21-40.
The **Style Manager** is used to construct a zone template that is used to create a zone structure based on predefined information.

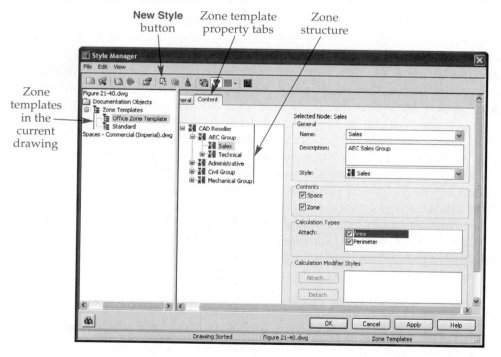

After creating the new style, pick the style in the tree view to begin editing the template. The property tabs for the style are displayed in the right pane. See **Figure 21-40**. Zone template styles include two tabs: **General** and **Content**. As with other styles, the **General** tab is used to rename the style, to enter a description for the template, and to attach notes to the template. The **Content** tab is used to configure the layout of the zone structure and to attach any properties to the different zone levels. See **Figure 21-40**.

The following are the different areas within the **Content** tab and the settings each controls:

- **Zone Template List Box.** This list box on the left side of the **Content** tab is used to create and organize the zone structure. Initially, this list box includes one zone level named Unnamed. Picking the Unnamed zone allows you to modify the properties assigned to the zone. Additional zones can be created by right-clicking over a Zone marker in the list box and selecting the **New** option. Enter a new name for the group level or select a name from the **Name:** list on the right, if the zone style has had a list definition assigned. Next, pick the zone to begin editing.

  The area group level you right-click over to create a new area group level determines the subgroups for the structure. As you create area group sublevels, you can drag them from one location in the structure to another to form the structure. You can also hold down [Ctrl] and drag an area group level marker to another part of the structure to copy it and its settings.

- **General.** This area includes three sections. The **Name:** text box allows you to enter or rename a zone level. If the zone style specified in the **Style:** drop-down has been assigned a list definition, a list of zone names is available in this drop-down list. The **Description** text box allows you to enter a description for your zone structure. The **Style:** drop-down list allows you to select a zone style from the styles available in the drawing to be assigned to the zone level being edited.

- **Contents.** This area specifies the types of objects that can be attached to the zone level being edited. The options include **Space** and **Zone**.

- **Calculation Types.** This area specifies that the area and perimeter components of a space assigned to the zone being edited can be assigned a calculation modifier.

- **Calculation Modifier Styles.** This area allows you to attach a calculation modifier to the zone being edited. Any spaces assigned to the zone inherits the calculation modifier style assigned to this zone.

NOTE   Calculation modifiers accumulate throughout the structure. For example, if a 50% modifier is applied to a lower level zone or space attached to a higher level zone with a 50% modifier, the end result is a total that is 25% of the actual space, instead of 50%.

When you have finished creating the structure and assigning the properties, you can add a new zone structure to the drawing using this template. **Figure 21-41** shows a finished zone structure that can be used in this drawing or in other drawings if it is imported through the **Style Manager**.

Creating a Zone Structure from a Template

Once the zone template has been created, it can be added to the drawing preassembled. When the zone structure is added to the drawing, zone connecting lines are drawn, and the Zone markers are ordered in the hierarchical order in which they appear in the zone template style.

To add a zone structure from a template, pick **Design > Zones > Create Zones from Template...** from the pull-down menu, or type ZONECREATEFROMTEMPLATE. Once the command has been entered, the **Properties** palette can be used to specify the zone template to be used. Pick an available template in the drawing from the **Zone Template** property. Next, enter a row offset and column offset value to space the zones within the structure. After the properties for the zone structure have been selected, pick a point in the drawing to place the zone structure.

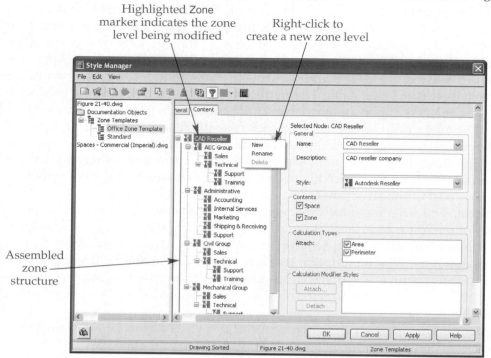

Highlighted Zone marker indicates the zone level being modified

Right-click to create a new zone level

Assembled zone structure

After you have inserted the group structure into the drawing, you can attach spaces to the zone structure. Use the **ZONELAYOUT** command to readjust the Zone marker spacing if necessary.

Exercise
21-8   *Complete the Exercise on the Student CD.*

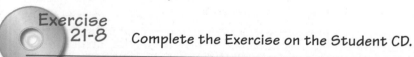

Space Evaluations

The final step when working with spaces is to create a space evaluation report. As defined previously, a *space evaluation* is a report that calculates the space and zone information in your drawing and exports the information into a Microsoft Excel spreadsheet or word processing document.

Space evaluation reports are often required when the construction documents are being evaluated for a building permit. These reports can also be used for cost estimating, assigning jobs to subcontractors, and management of the building by facilities personnel.

In order to create a space evaluation report, you need to include the spaces and to configure the output options. To access the **SPACEEVALUATION** command, pick the **Space Evaluation** tool in the **Scheduling** palette, pick **Design** > **Spaces** > **Space Evaluation...** from the pull-down menu, or type SPACEEVALUATION.

The **Space Evaluation** dialog box is displayed as shown in **Figure 21-42**. This dialog box includes a tree view along the left that lists the zone structures and Space objects in all drawings that are currently open in Architectural Desktop.

SPACEEVALUATION

Type
SPACEEVALUATION
Pull-Down Menu
Design
   > Spaces
   > Space
      Evaluation...
Tool Palette
Scheduling

Space Evaluation

Figure 21-42.
The **Space Evaluation** dialog box is used to display the total area of all the selected zones and spaces from the tree view and to set up the parameters for the exported evaluation report.

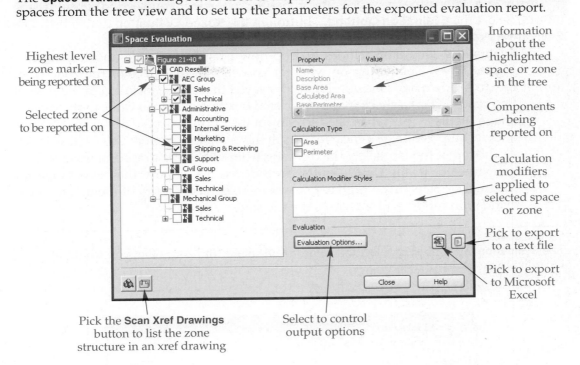

Highest level zone marker being reported on

Selected zone to be reported on

Information about the highlighted space or zone in the tree

Components being reported on

Calculation modifiers applied to selected space or zone

Pick to export to a text file

Pick to export to Microsoft Excel

Pick the **Scan Xref Drawings** button to list the zone structure in an xref drawing

Select to control output options

When a zone or space icon is selected in the tree view, information about the area is displayed in the upper-right corner of the dialog box. If there are reference drawings attached to one of the open drawings, you can pick the **Scan Xref Drawings** button to list zone structures in the references within the tree view.

From the tree view, place a check in the associated zone and space boxes you would like to report on. Spaces and zones to be excluded from the report can be removed by picking on the check marks to remove them.

When a check mark is placed in a box, it can be displayed in either gray, black, or blue. A black check mark indicates that the space or zone has been selected directly in the tree view for evaluation. Picking on top of a black check mark removes it from the evaluation. A blue check mark is placed in subgroups of and spaces attached to a zone, if a black check mark is placed in the zone above the subgroup. The blue check mark is automatically added because the space is part of a higher level zone that was selected. A gray check mark is displayed in higher level zones if the zones of a sublevel have been selected. Gray checked zones are not included in the evaluation report unless they are picked directly and the gray check mark is turned into a black check mark.

The **Calculation Type** area in the middle of the right side of the dialog box indicates the components of a space being reported. You cannot change this information. If you want to report on the area only and not on the perimeter, use the **Properties** palette to modify the reported components. The **Calculation Modifier Styles** area displays the calculation modifiers attached to a zone. The information in this area can be modified only from the **Properties** palette for a specific zone or space.

Setting Up Output Parameters

After you determine the spaces and zones for reporting, you need to configure the output. Select the **Evaluation Options...** button in the **Space Evaluation** dialog box. The **Evaluation Properties** dialog box is displayed, which includes four tabs.

- **Evaluation.** This tab includes a drop-down list for a space and a zone. See **Figure 21-43.** Depending on whether you choose the space or the zone from the drop-down list, a list of values is displayed that can be included in the evaluation report. Place a check in the associated box to include the value in the report.
- **Image Display.** This tab is used to control the output display of the space, zone, and decomposition graphical images in the evaluation report. See **Figure 21-44.** At the top of the tab, select the drawing from which the graphical images shall be extracted. In the **Color Depth:** drop-down list, choose the color range for the images. Selecting a high resolution increases the clarity of the image in the evaluation report and increases the file size.

Figure 21-43.

The **Evaluation** tab is used to select the values from spaces and zones that you would like included in an evaluation report.

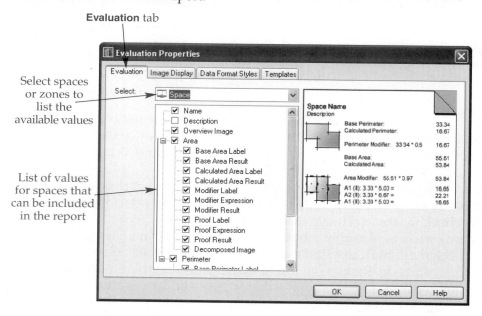

Evaluation tab

Select spaces or zones to list the available values

List of values for spaces that can be included in the report

Figure 21-44.

The **Image Display** tab is used to control how the graphical images of the spaces will appear in the final evaluation report.

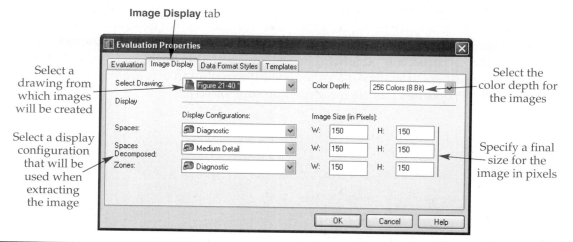

Image Display tab

Select a drawing from which images will be created

Select a display configuration that will be used when extracting the image

Select the color depth for the images

Specify a final size for the image in pixels

Spaces, **Spaces Decomposed**, and **Zones** are the three types of images that can be exported and are listed at the bottom of the dialog box. The **Display Configurations:** drop-down lists are assigned to each type of image. Select the display configuration that will be used to extract an image of the space, decomposed space, or zone. You can specify the image size to be displayed in the report in pixels beside each display configuration's drop-down list.

- **Data Format Styles.** This tab allows you to assign a data format style to the area and perimeter result values, to the area and perimeter modifier expression values, and to the area proof expression value. See **Figure 21-45**. The data format styles assigned designate how the final output for a value appears in the report. Data format styles are discussed later in this text and allow you to set textual formatting, including uppercase or lowercase, and unit data output, including decimal, architectural, or engineering.

    Select the values in the tree view, and then select the drawing being evaluated and the type of formatting to apply to each value. In some cases, a data format style can be set to round values to a whole number, to two decimal points, or to another value. If the report is to display the actual values of an area and not the rounded values, select the **Additional Exact Value** check box.

- **Templates.** When the space evaluation is exported to a Microsoft Excel spreadsheet or to a word processing text file, a template must be used. The template organizes the values being reported on in the exported files. This tab specifies both an Excel template and a text template to which the report can be exported. See **Figure 21-46**. The text boxes list the path and template name that the report uses for the final output. Additional templates can be used by selecting the ellipsis (...) button to browse for a different template to use.

NOTE

The Excel templates have an .xlt file extension. Additional Excel and text templates can be found by picking the ellipsis (...) button, which displays the **Open Template...** dialog box. Pick the **Content** button on the left side of the window, and then browse to the \\Template\Evaluation Templates folder. Two Excel templates are included with Architectural Desktop. The text templates have a .txt file extension and can be opened in any ASCII text editing software, such as Microsoft Notepad or Word. There is only one included .txt template.

Figure 21-45.
The **Data Format Styles** tab allows you to assign formatting to the values being reported on for the evaluation report.

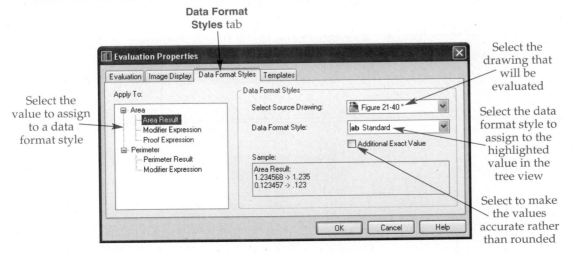

Figure 21-46.
The **Templates** tab is used to specify a template that the values will be exported to and organized into.

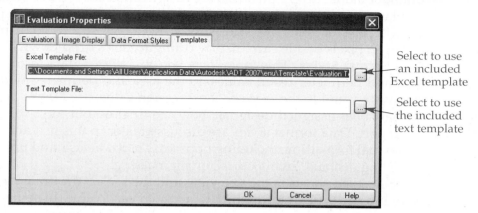

Select to use an included Excel template

Select to use the included text template

Creating the Space Evaluation

After selecting the spaces and zones to report and configuring the output settings, you can create the evaluation report. To create a Microsoft Excel spreadsheet report, pick the **Export Evaluation to Microsoft Excel** button. The **Save Excel Evaluation file...** dialog box is displayed. Browse to a folder in which to save the file, enter a name for the evaluation spreadsheet, and select the **Save** button. You are returned to the **Area Evaluation** dialog box, where Architectural Desktop processes the information and creates the evaluation report. See **Figure 21-47.**

Figure 21-47.
An example Excel area evaluation report from the building displayed.

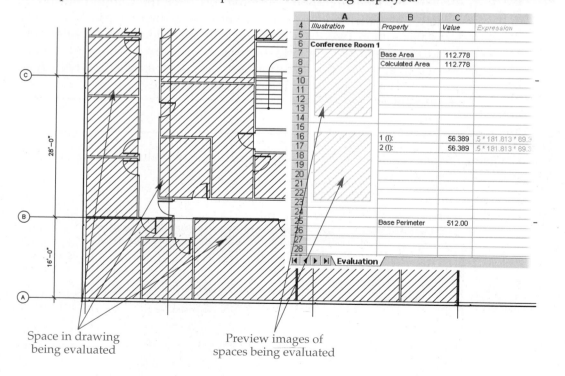

Space in drawing being evaluated

Preview images of spaces being evaluated

NOTE If the spreadsheet is to be added to the construction document set drawings, use object linking and embedding (OLE) to bring the Excel file into the drawing. For more information regarding OLE, look up the Link and Embed Data (OLE) section in the **Autodesk Architectural Desktop 2007 Help** window.

If the evaluation report is to be exported as a text document, pick **Export Evaluation to Text Format**. The **Save Text Evaluation file...** dialog box is then displayed. Select a folder into which to save the evaluation, enter a name for the evaluation, and pick the **Save** button. This file can be opened with the Windows Notepad program, Word, or any other software that recognizes ASCII text files.

NOTE If the text evaluation report is to be used in the construction documents, use the **MTEXT** command to import the TXT file as a piece of multiline text.

Exercise 21-9   Complete the Exercise on the Student CD.

Chapter Test

Answer the following questions. Write your answers on a separate sheet of paper or complete the electronic chapter test on the Student CD.

1. What is *space planning*?
2. What does the creation of spaces allow you to do?
3. Describe Space objects and identify at least three of their uses.
4. Define *base boundary* and give an example of its use.
5. Discuss the function of the net boundary.
6. What is the usable boundary?
7. Define *gross boundary*.
8. Describe nonassociative spaces.
9. Define *associative spaces*.
10. What does the **Space Information** tool provide?
11. Describe and give an example of zones.
12. Explain the purpose and give an example of how calculations are used.

Chapter Projects

Use the techniques covered in this chapter to create the following drawings.

1. Single-Level Residential Project
   A. Access the **Project Browser** and set Residential-Project-01 current.
   B. Access the **Views** tab of the **Project Navigator** and create a new general view drawing. Choose the **General View** option.
   C. On the **General** page, enter the following:
      - **Name:** Space Plan
      - **Description:** Room Spaces
   D. On the **Context** page, select the Main Floor Level under Division 1.
   E. On the **Content** page, uncheck the Furniture construct.
   F. Open the Space Plan view drawing. Set the drawing scale to 1/4″ = 1′-0″.
   G. Access the **SPACESTYLE** command. Open Spaces - Residential.dwg from the **Style Manager**.

Note: Pick the **Content** button in the **Open drawing** dialog box, and select the Styles folder and then either the Imperial or Metric folder to locate Spaces - Residential.dwg.

   H. Import the following space styles from Spaces - Residential.dwg into the current drawing: Bath_Small, Bedroom, Closet, Office, Dining_Room, Entry_Foyer, Garage_2-Car, Kitchen, Living-Room_Large, Hallway, Laundry, and Bedroom_Master.
   I. Access the Documentation Tool Catalog from the **Content Browser**. Browse to the Schedule Tags section and then the Room & Finish Tags section. I-drop the Room Tag (w/ Dimensions) tag into the drawing.
   J. Use the **Space Auto Generate** tool to add spaces into the drawing.
   K. In the **Generate Spaces** dialog box, select a style to be added into the drawing, the **Extrusion** type, and the **Walls only** filter. Pick the **Tag Settings** button to select the **Aec7_Space_Tag** tag definition.
   L. Begin adding spaces to each room, changing the style as necessary.
   M. After adding the spaces, use the **Divide** and **Merge** options to split the Living_Room space in the Dining_Room and Kitchen spaces.
   N. Use the **Properties** palette to change the space styles in the dining room and kitchen to the appropriate style.
   O. Copy one of the space tags and place it over each of the spaces in the living room, dining room, and kitchen. Anchor the copied space tags to the spaces for the living room, dining room, and kitchen.
   P. Save and close the drawing.

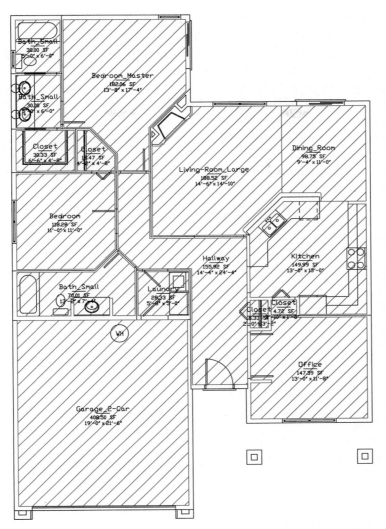

Design Courtesy Alan Mascord Design Associates

2. Single-Level Residential Project
   A. Access the **Project Browser** and set Residential-Project-02 current.
   B. Access the **Views** tab of the **Project Navigator** and create a new general view drawing. Choose the **General View** option.
   C. On the **General** page, enter the following:
      - **Name:** Space Plan
      - **Description:** Room Spaces
   D. On the **Context** page, select the Main Floor Level under Division 1.
   E. On the **Content** page, uncheck the Furniture construct.
   F. Open the Space Plan view drawing. Set the drawing scale to 1/4" = 1'-0".
   G. Access the **SPACESTYLE** command. Open Spaces - Residential.dwg from the **Style Manager**.

Note: Pick the **Content** button in the **Open drawing** dialog box, and select the Styles folder and then either the Imperial or Metric folder to locate Spaces - Residential.dwg.

   H. Import the following space styles from Spaces - Residential.dwg into the current drawing: Bath_Small, Bedroom, Closet, Office, Dining_Room, Entry_Foyer, Garage_2-Car, Kitchen, Living-Room_Large, Hallway, Laundry, and Bedroom_ Master.
   I. Access the Documentation Tool Catalog from the **Content Browser**. Browse to the Schedule Tags section and then the Room & Finish Tags section. I-drop the Room Tag (w/ Dimensions) tag into the drawing.

J. Use the **Space Auto Generate** tool to add spaces into the drawing.
K. In the **Generate Spaces** dialog box, select a style to be added into the drawing, the **Extrusion** type, and the **Walls only** filter. Pick the **Tag Settings** button to select the **Aec7_Space_Tag** tag definition.
L. Begin adding spaces to each room, changing the style as necessary.
M. After adding the spaces, use the **Divide** and **Merge** options as necessary. Use grips as needed to adjust the space boundaries.

Note: You may need to make the spaces nonassociative in order to modify them with grips.

N. Use the **Properties** palette to change the space styles in the living room, hallway, dining room, and kitchen to the appropriate style.
O. Copy one of the space tags and place it over each of the spaces in the living room, hallway, dining room, and kitchen. Anchor the copied space tags to the spaces.
P. Save and close the drawing.

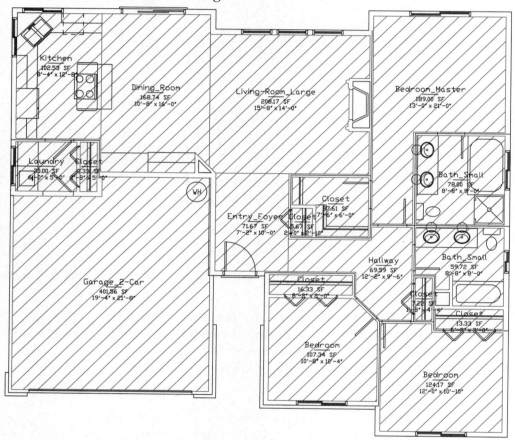

Design Courtesy Alan Mascord Design Associates

3. Two-Story Residential Project
   A. Access the **Project Browser** and set Residential-Project-03 current.
   B. Access the **Views** tab of the **Project Navigator** and create a new general view drawing. Choose the **General View** option.
   C. On the **General** page, enter the following:
      - **Name:** Main Floor Space Plan
      - **Description:** Main Floor Room Spaces
   D. On the **Context** page, select the Main Floor Level under Division 1.
   E. On the **Content** page, uncheck the Furniture construct.
   F. Open the Main Floor Space Plan view drawing. Set the drawing scale to 1/4" = 1'-0".
   G. Access the **SPACESTYLE** command. Open Spaces - Residential.dwg from the **Style Manager**.

Note: Pick the **Content** button in the **Open drawing** dialog box, and select the Styles folder and then either the Imperial or Metric folder to locate Spaces - Residential.dwg.

   H. Import the following space styles from Spaces - Residential.dwg into the current drawing: Bath_Small, Bedroom, Closet, Dining_Room, Entry_Foyer, Family_Room, Garage_2-Car, Kitchen, Living-Room, Hallway, Laundry, and Bedroom_Master.
   I. Access the Documentation Tool Catalog from the **Content Browser**. Browse to the Schedule Tags section and then the Room & Finish Tags section. I-drop the Room Tag (w/ Dimensions) tag into the drawing.
   J. Use the **Space Auto Generate** tool to add spaces into the drawing.
   K. In the **Generate Spaces** dialog box, select a style to be added into the drawing, the **Extrusion** type, and the **Walls only** filter. Pick the **Tag Settings** button to select the **Aec7_Space_Tag** tag definition.
   L. Begin adding spaces to each room, changing the style as necessary.
   M. After adding the spaces, use the **Divide** and **Merge** options as necessary. Use grips as needed to adjust the space boundaries.

Note: You may need to make the spaces nonassociative in order to modify them with grips.

   N. Use the **Properties** palette to change the divided spaces to the appropriate style.
   O. Copy one of the space tags and place it over each of the divided spaces. Anchor the copied space tags to the spaces.
   P. Save and close the drawing.
   Q. Access the **Views** tab of the **Project Navigator** and create a new general view drawing. Choose the **General View** option.
   R. On the **General** page, enter the following:
      - **Name:** Upper Floor Space Plan
      - **Description:** Upper Floor Room Spaces
   S. On the **Context** page, select the Upper Floor Level under Division 1.
   T. Open the Upper Floor Space Plan view drawing. Set the drawing scale to 1/4" = 1'-0".
   U. Import the Family_Room space style from Spaces - Residential.dwg into the current drawing.
   V. Use the **Space Auto Generate** tool to add the family room spaces into the drawing.
   W. Save and close the drawing.

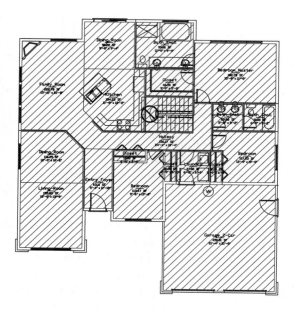

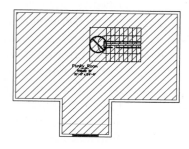

Drawing Courtesy 3D-DZYN

4. Two-Story Residential Project
   A. Access the **Project Browser** and set Residential-Project-04 current.
   B. Access the **Views** tab of the **Project Navigator** and create a new general view drawing. Choose the **General View** option.
   C. On the **General** page, enter the following:
      • **Name:** Main Floor Space Plan
      • **Description:** Main Floor Room Spaces
   D. On the **Context** page, select the Main Floor Level under Division 1.
   E. On the **Content** page, uncheck the MainFlr-Furniture construct.
   F. Open the Main Floor Space Plan view drawing. Set the drawing scale to 1/4" = 1'-0".
   G. Access the **SPACESTYLE** command. Open Spaces - Residential.dwg from the **Style Manager**.

Note: Pick the **Content** button in the **Open drawing** dialog box, and select the Styles folder and then either the Imperial or Metric folder to locate Spaces - Residential.dwg.

   H. Import the following space styles from Spaces - Residential.dwg into the current drawing: Bath_Small, Closet, Dining_Room, Entry_Foyer, Garage_2-Car, Kitchen, Laundry, Living-Room_Large, and Office.
   I. Access the Documentation Tool Catalog from the **Content Browser**. Browse to the Schedule Tags section and then the Room & Finish Tags section. I-drop the Room Tag (w/ Dimensions) tag into the drawing.
   J. Use the **Space Auto Generate** tool to add spaces into the drawing.
   K. In the **Generate Spaces** dialog box, select a style to be added into the drawing, the **Extrusion** type, and the **Walls only** filter. Pick the **Tag Settings** button to select the **Aec7_Space_Tag** tag definition.
   L. Begin adding spaces to each room, changing the style as necessary.
   M. After adding the spaces, use the **Divide** and **Merge** options as necessary. Use grips as needed to adjust the space boundaries.

Note: You may need to make the spaces nonassociative in order to modify them with grips.

   N. Use the **Properties** palette to change the divided spaces to the appropriate style.
   O. Copy one of the space tags and place it over each of the divided spaces. Anchor the copied space tags to the spaces.
   P. Save and close the drawing.

Q. Access the **Views** tab of the **Project Navigator** and create a new general view drawing. Choose the **General View** option.

R. On the **General** page, enter the following:
   - **Name:** Upper Floor Space Plan
   - **Description:** Upper Floor Room Spaces

S. On the **Context** page, select the Upper Floor Level under Division 1.

T. Open the Upper Floor Space Plan view drawing. Set the drawing scale to 1/4" = 1'-0".

U. Import the following space styles from Spaces - Residential.dwg into the current drawing: Bath_Medium, Bedroom, Bedroom_Master, Closet, and Closet_ Walk-in.

V. Access the Documentation Tool Catalog from the **Content Browser**. Browse to the Schedule Tags section and then the Room & Finish Tags section. I-drop the Room Tag (w/ Dimensions) tag into the drawing.

W. Use the **Space Auto Generate** tool to add spaces into the drawing.

X. In the **Generate Spaces** dialog box, select a style to be added into the drawing, the **Extrusion** type, and the **Walls only** filter. Pick the **Tag Settings** button to select the **Aec7_Space_Tag** tag definition.

Y. Begin adding spaces to each room, changing the style as necessary.

Z. Save and close the drawing.

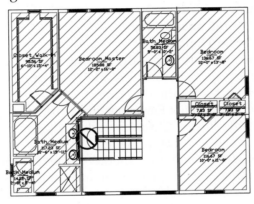

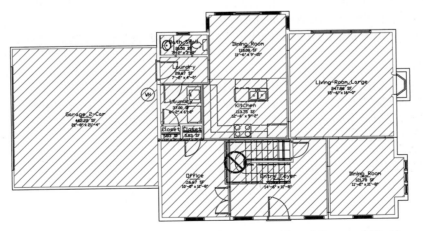

Design Courtesy Alan Mascord Design Associates

5. Commercial Store Project
    A. Access the **Project Browser** and set Commercial-Project-05 current.
    B. Access the **Views** tab of the **Project Navigator** and create a new general view drawing. Choose the **General View** option.
    C. On the **General** page, enter the following:
       • **Name:** Store Space Plan
       • **Description:** Store Spaces
    D. On the **Context** page, select the Main Floor Level under Division 1.
    E. On the **Content** page, uncheck the Furniture construct.
    F. Open the Store Space Plan view drawing. Set the drawing scale to 1/8" = 1'-0".
    G. Create space styles using the following names: Bookstore, Clothing Store, Electronics Store, Furniture Store, Restaurant, and Shoe Store.
    H. Assign a different color to the Plan representation's Base Hatch component for each style.
    I. Assign the solid fill hatch pattern to each Plan representation's Base Hatch component.
    J. Use the **SPACEADD** command to add spaces to the commercial building using the following property settings:
       • **Style:** (Make each store a different style)
       • **Create type:** Rectangle (or Polygon)
       • **Geometry type:** Extrusion
       • **Overall space height:** 12'-0"
       • **Ceiling height:** 9'-0"
    K. When you are manually adding the space, add the space to the entire store, including the bathrooms and stock and office areas, as shown in the figure.
    L. Save and close the drawing.
    M. Open the Interior Elevations view drawing.
    N. Edit the Interior Elevation style's display properties and turn off the Surface Hatch Linework component.
    O. Create a space style named Wall Tile. Turn the Base Hatch component on in the Plan display representation and set the hatch to a double user-defined hatch with a 4" spacing.
    P. Create a space style named Paint. Turn on the Base Hatch component in the Plan display representation and set the hatch to a sand hatch pattern.
    Q. For each interior elevation, add a space using the Wall Tile style between the floor and 4'-0" above the floor. Refer to the figure. When adding the wall tile space to the interior elevations, change the **Geometry type** space property to **2D**, to create a 2D space on the 2D elevations.
    R. Create a calculation modifier that estimates how much tile is required to fit against the walls, and attach it to the Wall Tile spaces.
    S. Add the Paint space style above the tile to the ceiling. Refer to the figure. Create the spaces as a **2D** geometry type.
    T. Save and close the drawing.

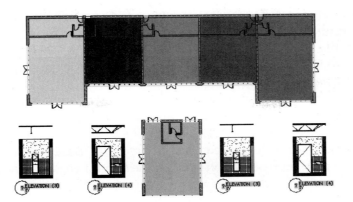

Drawing Courtesy 3D-DZYN

6. Commercial Car Maintenance Shop Project
   A. Access the **Project Browser** and set Commercial-Project-06 current.
   B. Access the **Views** tab of the **Project Navigator** and create a new general view drawing. Choose the **General View** option.
   C. On the **General** page, enter the following:
      - **Name:** Main Floor Space Plan
      - **Description:** Main Floor Room Spaces
   D. On the **Context** page, select the Main Floor Level under Division 1.
   E. On the **Content** page, uncheck the MainFlr-Furniture construct.
   F. Open the Main Floor Space Plan view drawing. Set the drawing scale to 1/4" = 1'-0".
   G. Create space styles using the following names: Bathroom, Car_Wash, Garage, Mini_Mart, Office, and Storage.
   H. Assign a different color to the Plan representation's Base Hatch component for each style.
   I. Access the Documentation Tool Catalog from the **Content Browser**. Browse to the Schedule Tags section and then the Room & Finish Tags section. I-drop the Room Tag (w/ Dimensions) tag into the drawing.
   J. Use the **Space Auto Generate** tool to add spaces into the drawing.
   K. In the **Generate Spaces** dialog box, select a style to be added into the drawing, the **Extrusion** type, and the **Walls only** filter. Pick the **Tag Settings** button to select the **Aec7_Space_Tag** tag definition.
   L. Begin adding spaces to each room, changing the style as necessary.
   M. Use the **SPACEADD** command to add spaces to the commercial building.
   N. Save and close the drawing.
   O. Access the **Views** tab of the **Project Navigator** and create a new general view drawing. Choose the **General View** option.
   P. On the **General** page, enter the following:
      - **Name:** Upper Floor Space Plan
      - **Description:** Upper Floor Room Spaces
   Q. On the **Context** page, select the Upper Floor Level under Division 1.
   R. On the **Content** page, uncheck the UpperFlr-Furniture construct.
   S. Open the Upper Floor Space Plan view drawing. Set the drawing scale to 1/4" = 1'-0".
   T. Create a space style named Office.
   U. Assign a different color to the Plan representation's Base Hatch component for the style.
   V. Access the Documentation Tool Catalog of the **Content Browser**. Browse to the Schedule Tags section and then the Room & Finish Tags section. I-drop the Room Tag (w/ Dimensions) tag into the drawing.

W.   Use the **Space Auto Generate** tool to add the space into the drawing.

X.   Save and close the drawing.

Y.   Open the Interior Elevations view drawing.

Z.   Edit the Interior Elevation style's display properties and turn off the Surface Hatch Linework component.

AA. Create a space style named Wall Tile. Turn the Base Hatch component on in the Plan display representation and set the hatch to a double user-defined hatch with a 4" spacing.

BB. Create a space style named Paint. Turn on the Base Hatch component in the Plan display representation and set the hatch to a sand hatch pattern.

CC. For each interior elevation, add a space using the Wall Tile style between the floor and 4'-0" above the floor, as shown in the figure. When you are adding the wall tile space to the interior elevations, change the **Geometry type** space property to **2D**, to create a 2D space on the 2D elevations.

DD. Create a calculation modifier that estimates how much tile is required to fit against the walls, and attach it to the Wall Tile spaces.

EE. Add the Paint space style above the tile to the ceiling. Refer to the figure. Create the spaces as a **2D** geometry type.

FF. Save and close the drawing.

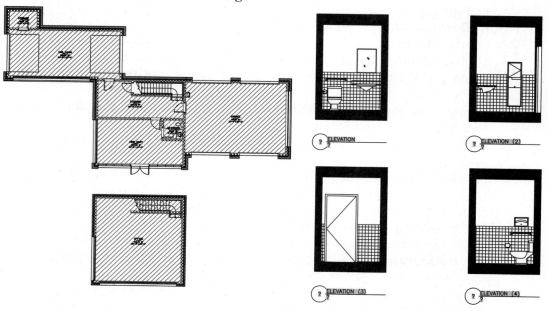

Drawing Courtesy 3D-DZYN

7. Governmental Fire Station
   A. Access the **Project Browser** and set Gvrmt-Project-07 current.
   B. Access the **Views** tab of the **Project Navigator** and create a new general view drawing. Choose the **General View** option.
   C. On the **General** page, enter the following:
      • **Name:** Space Plan
      • **Description:** Room Spaces
   D. On the **Context** page, select the Main Floor Level under Division 1.
   E. On the **Content** page, uncheck the Furniture and Plumbing-Appliance constructs.
   F. Open the Space Plan view drawing. Set the drawing scale to 1/8" = 1'-0".
   G. Create space styles for the following rooms: Apparatus Bay, Class Room, Compressor, Corridor, Dayroom, Dining Room, Dormitory, Electrical, EMT Room, Exercise Room, Generator, Hose Room, Kitchen, Laundry, Lobby, Locker Room, Men, Office, Reception, Shop, Storage, Turnouts, and Women.
   H. Assign a different color to the Plan representation's Base Hatch component for each style.
   I. Assign the solid fill hatch pattern to each Plan representation's Base Hatch component.
   J. Use the **Space Auto Generate** tool to add spaces into the drawing.
   K. In the **Generate Spaces** dialog box, select a style to be added into the drawing, the **Extrusion** type, and the **Walls only** filter. Pick the **Tag Settings** button to select the **Aec4_Room_Tag_Scale_Dependent** tag definition.
   L. Begin adding spaces to each room of the fire station, changing the style as necessary. Refer to the figure.
   M. In the reception and lobby area, split the space into two different space types: Lobby and Reception.
   N. In the classroom area, split the space into two classroom spaces.
   O. In the kitchen, dining, and dayroom space, split the area into a dayroom, dining room, kitchen, and corridor space. Refer to the figure for placement.
   P. Save and close the drawing.

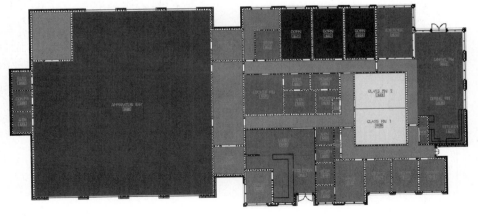

Drawing Courtesy 3D-DZYN

The home page of the e-Architect™ Web site is www.e-architect.com. This Web site offers valuable information about the architectural profession. This site allows architectural students to browse headlines about the architectural field and post their resumes. Architects can post job openings and browse project leads. Users of this site can also share information and their views on topics involving the architectural field.

CHAPTER 22

Using Schedules

Learning Objectives

After completing this chapter, you will be able to do the following:

✓ Add schedule tags to a drawing.
✓ Renumber schedule tags.
✓ Use property set definitions.
✓ Create a schedule.
✓ Update a schedule.
✓ Modify the properties of a schedule table.
✓ Export a schedule table.
✓ Access additional schedule table styles.
✓ Edit a schedule.

One of the key elements in producing a set of construction documents is the addition of schedules. *Schedules* provide information such as the types and sizes of doors and windows in a building, the finish materials used in different rooms, and equipment counts. The information found within a schedule is in a tabular format, which is referred to as the schedule table, as shown in **Figure 22-1.** Architectural Desktop includes several predefined schedules for use in your drawings and provides tools for customizing schedules to report on specific information the construction documents require.

The schedules maintain links back to the objects on which they are reporting. As new objects are added to the drawing or information about the objects changes, the schedule can automatically be updated. Schedules can also report on objects belonging to a reference drawing and maintain links to the referenced geometry.

Figure 22-1.
Examples of schedules included with Architectural Desktop.

DOOR AND FRAME SCHEDULE

| MARK | DOOR | | | | | LOUVER | | FRAME | | | | | FIRE RATING LABEL | HARDWARE | | NOTES |
| | SIZE | | | MATL | GLAZING | | | MATL | EL | DETAIL | | | | SET NO | KEYSIDE RM NO | |
	WD	HGT	THK			WD	HGT			HEAD	JAMB	SILL				
1	3'-0"	7'-0"	1"	WOOD	Y											
2	2'-6"	7'-0"	2"	WOOD	--	0	0"	WOOD	--	--	--	--	--	--	--	--
3	2'-4"	7'-0"	2"	WOOD	--	0	0"	WOOD	--	--	--	--	--	--	--	--
4	2'-8"	6'-8"	1"	WOOD	--	0	0"	WOOD	--	--	--	--	--	--	--	--
5	2'-8"	7'-0"	2"	WOOD	--	0	0"	WOOD	--	--	--	--	--	--	--	--
6	3'-0"	7'-0"	1"	WOOD	--	0	0"	WOOD	--	--	--	--	--	--	--	--
7	3'-0"	7'-0"	1"	WOOD	--	0	0"	WOOD	--	--	--	--	--	--	--	--
8	9'-0"	8'-0"	1 3/4"	WOOD	--	0	0"	WOOD	--	--	--	--	--	--	--	--
9	9'-0"	8'-0"	1 3/4"	WOOD	--	0	0"	WOOD	--	--	--	--	--	--	--	--

WINDOW SCHEDULE

MARK	TYPE	MATERIAL	NOTES
1	FXD	WOOD	TEMP
2	TRANS	WOOD	
3	FXD	WOOD	TEMP
4	SH	WOOD	
5	SH	WOOD	
6	SH	WOOD	
7	SH	WOOD	
8	SH	WOOD	
9	SH	WOOD	
10	SH	WOOD	
11	SH	WOOD	
12	SH	WOOD	
13	SH	WOOD	
14	SH	WOOD	
15	SH	WOOD	ARCHTOP
16	SH	WOOD	ARCHTOP
17	SH	WOOD	ARCHTOP

ROOM FINISH SCHEDULE

| ROOM NAME | FLOOR | WALLS | | | | CEILING | | NOTES |
		N	S	E	W	MATL	HEIGHT	
HALL	--	--	--	--	--	--	9'-0"	--
HALL	--	--	--	--	--	--	9'-0"	--
BATH	--	--	--	--	--	--	9'-0"	--
LAUNDRY	--	--	--	--	--	--	9'-0"	--
ENTRY	--	--	--	--	--	--	9'-0"	--
BEDROOM	--	--	--	--	--	--	9'-0"	--
KITCHEN	--	--	--	--	--	--	9'-0"	--
DINING ROOM	--	--	--	--	--	--	9'-0"	--
LIVING ROOM	--	--	--	--	--	--	9'-0"	--
FAMILY ROOM	--	--	--	--	--	--	9'-0"	--
GARAGE - DOUBLE	--	--	--	--	--	--	9'-0"	--

Schedule Tags

In addition to the predefined schedules, Architectural Desktop includes several notation blocks or symbols, known as schedule tags. *Schedule tags* are numbers or symbols pointing the person reviewing the drawing to a specific set of information within a schedule. The information found in the schedule is obtained from information attached to the object in the drawing or the schedule tag linked to the object. This information is known as a *property*. Entire sets of properties, called *property sets*, can be attached to an object. This chapter explains the tools used to attach schedule tags to objects, fill out property set information, and create a schedule.

Adding Schedule Tags to a Drawing

Schedule tags can be attached to AEC objects and standard AutoCAD entities. The symbol is typically a geometric shape containing a letter or number indicating its position within a schedule. Other schedule tags might include only text or a leader line pointing to the object. See **Figure 22-2**.

Architectural Desktop includes several different types of schedule tags for use. Some of the tags must be attached to specific types of AEC objects. For example, a door tag must be attached to a Door object.

The schedule tags are divided into five types: door and window tags, object tags, room and finish tags, structural member tags, and wall tags. Tags are applied to objects to identify the usage, identity, and function of each object. In the case of a *door and window tag*, a number or letter is added to a symbol to identify the door or window being marked. *Object tags* are tags attached to standard AutoCAD block references or multi-view blocks. *Room and finish tags* are tags added to a drawing to label a room name, number a room, provide a room size, perform BOMA calculations, or provide room finish information. *Structural member tags* are similar, but they can also identify the structural shape being identified. *Wall tags* are used to mark the

Figure 22-2.
Some examples of schedule tags included with Architectural Desktop.

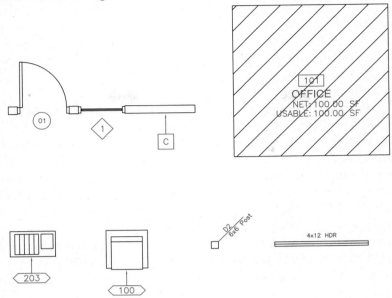

different types of walls in the drawing. All these schedule tags can be found in the Documentation Tool Catalog - Imperial or Documentation Tool Catalog - Metric catalog of the **Content Browser**, under the Schedule Tags section. A few of these tags can also be found in the **Scheduling** tool palette of the **Document** tool palette group.

Adding Door and Window Tags

Door and window tags can be added to the drawing by accessing the **Scheduling** palette in the **Document** tool palette group or accessing the **Content Browser**, selecting Documentation Tool Catalog - Imperial or Documentation Tool Catalog - Metric, picking the Schedule Tags section, and then selecting the Door & Window Tags section. See **Figure 22-3.** To insert a door or window tag into the drawing, i-drop (drag and drop) the symbol from the **Content Browser** catalog into the drawing screen, or pick the symbol in the tool palette. In either case, you are prompted to select the object to tag.

Figure 22-3.
Door and window schedule tags can be selected from the **Scheduling** tool palette or the **Content Browser**.

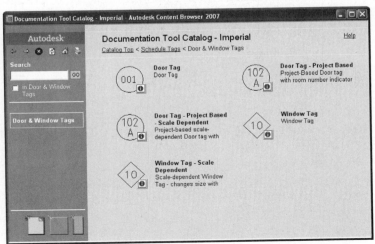

Depending on whether you have selected a door tag or window tag, pick a Door or Window object to link the tag with the AEC object. After selecting the door or window, pick a location for the tag block. The drawing scale selected in the **Drawing Setup** dialog box or from the **Scale** button at the bottom of the drawing screen determines the size of the tag block. The project-based door tags obtain their numbers from the room (space) the door opens into. For this reason, the project-based door tags require doors and Space objects to be used. Whichever space the door opens into determines the door tag number.

After a location for the tag is picked, the **Edit Property Set Data** worksheet is displayed. See **Figure 22-4**. Depending on the object (door or window), this worksheet contains property set definitions containing individual properties. *Property set definitions* are collections of properties assigned to an object and reported in a schedule. Most of the property values can be edited for the door or window selected by picking the property and entering a new value. When you have finished editing the properties, pick the **OK** button to close the worksheet. Property sets and properties are discussed in greater detail later in this chapter.

Once the first door or window tag is inserted, successive tags are sequentially numbered. In the **Edit Property Set Data** worksheet, the **Number** property can be used to adjust the door or window number, as shown in **Figure 22-4**. If the number value is changed, tag numbers following are sequenced from the new number. For example, if the door number is changed to 101, the next tags are numbered 102, 103, and so on.

NOTE
The tags included in Architectural Desktop are multi-view blocks. They can be displayed in the Top view using the Low Detail, Medium Detail, and High Detail display configurations. These blocks are not displayed in an isometric view or a Model view.

Figure 22-4.
The **Edit Property Set Data** worksheet contains property information that is assigned to the door or window. This information can then be assembled into a schedule.

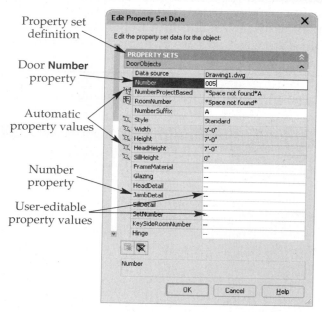

Architectural Desktop and Its Applications

PROFESSIONAL TIP

When you are working with the **Project Navigator**, scheduling tags are often placed in a view drawing that includes an externally referenced floor plan. The schedule tags are added to the view drawing, but the property set definitions are assigned to each individual object in the actual construct where the objects being tagged are located. If you are not working with the **Project Navigator** and adding all model and documentation items into the same drawing, tags can be added to the drawing, and the property set definitions are assigned to each individual object.

Exercise 22-1   Complete the Exercise on the Student CD.

Adding Object Tags

Object tags are typically used in schedules that must report on the types of equipment and furniture counts and that reflect the total number, type, and cost of a series of objects. The object tags can be found by accessing the **Content Browser**, picking Documentation Tool Catalog - Imperial or Documentation Tool Catalog - Metric, selecting the Schedule Tags section, and then browsing to the Object Tags section. The Object Tags section includes a number of tags that can be attached to different objects in the drawing. I-drop (drag and drop) the desired symbol from the catalog directly into the drawing or on top of a tool palette to access it. Once a tag has been selected, you are prompted to select an object to tag.

Select the block or multi-view block to which the tag is to be attached. If a multi-view block is selected, you are prompted to specify the location of the tag. If a standard AutoCAD block is selected, the prompts will allow you to assign the tag to the block or an object within the block at the point the block was picked. Pick a block reference when you are prompted to select an object to tag. When you are given selection options, enter the number of the object to assign the tag to. You will then be prompted to specify the location of the tag.

Pick a location in the drawing where the tag is to be inserted. After the tag location is selected, the **Edit Property Set Data** worksheet is displayed, allowing you to specify any data for the properties in the property set definition being attached to the object. Pick the **OK** button to complete the process. You can continue to select blocks or multi-view blocks to which to attach object tags. When you have finished, press the [Enter] key to complete the process.

Exercise 22-2   Complete the Exercise on the Student CD.

Adding Room and Finish Tags

Information can be attached to a room to indicate the square footage, length, width, and finish materials. Room and finish tags can be attached only to Space objects. Selecting a space and picking an insertion point location adds the room tag.

Tool Palette

Scheduling

Room Tag BOMA

OFFICE
100

Room Tag

Content Browser Catalog

Documentation Tool
Catalog - Imperial
> Schedule Tags
> Room &
Finish Tags

Documentation Tool
Catalog - Metric
> Schedule Tags
> Room &
Finish Tags

Room Tag BOMA

Documentation Tool
Catalog - Imperial
> Schedule Tags
> Room &
Finish Tags

Documentation Tool
Catalog - Metric
> Schedule Tags
> Room &
Finish Tags

OFFICE
100

Room Tag

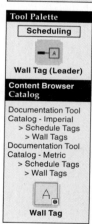

Tool Palette

Scheduling

Wall Tag (Leader)

Content Browser Catalog

Documentation Tool
Catalog - Imperial
> Schedule Tags
> Wall Tags
Documentation Tool
Catalog - Metric
> Schedule Tags
> Wall Tags

A

Wall Tag

Once Space objects have been added to the drawing, the objects can be tagged with room or finish tags. The **Scheduling** tool palette in the **Document** tool palette group includes three room tags that can be added to the drawing. Additional tags can be added by accessing the **Content Browser**, selecting the Documentation Tool Catalog - Imperial or Documentation Tool Catalog - Metric catalog, picking the Schedule Tags section, and then browsing through the Room & Finish Tags section. See **Figure 22-5**. I-drop (drag and drop) the tags from the **Content Browser** into the drawing and select a Space object to be tagged, or drag and drop the tool from the **Content Browser** onto a palette for your use.

Adding Structural Tags

Similar to other tags, structural tags are tags identifying a structural member type or style name. These tags can only be assigned to columns, braces, or beams. To add structural tags to the drawing, access the **Content Browser**, select Documentation Tool Catalog - Imperial or Documentation Tool Catalog - Metric, pick the Schedule Tags section, select the Structural Tags section, and choose a tag. Pick a beam, brace, or column tag and i-drop (drag and drop) it into the drawing to begin tagging different structural members. If you want to add the tags to a tool palette, drag and drop the tags from the **Content Browser** onto a tool palette. **Figure 22-6** displays the structural tags available.

Adding Wall Tags

Wall tags must be attached to Wall objects. The **Scheduling** tool palette in the **Document** tool palette group includes one wall tag. Additional wall tags can be found by opening the **Content Browser**, selecting Documentation Tool Catalog - Imperial or Documentation Tool Catalog - Metric, picking the Schedule Tags section, selecting the Wall Tags section, and then choosing a wall tag. See **Figure 22-7**.

Two types of tags are available. I-drop (drag and drop) the tag into the drawing from the **Content Browser** to insert the tag. Select a wall to attach the tag to, and then fill out the schedule information in the **Edit Property Set Data** worksheet.

Figure 22-5.

Room tags are assigned to Space objects and report the name, number, finish, and Building Owners and Managers Association (BOMA) calculations for the Space object.

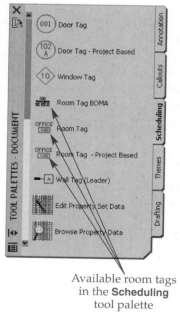

Available room tags
in the **Scheduling**
tool palette

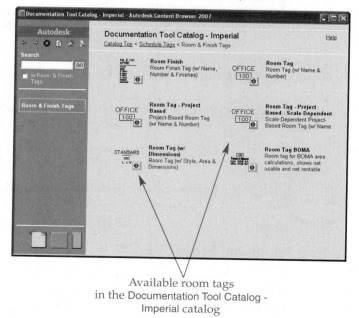

Available room tags
in the Documentation Tool Catalog -
Imperial catalog

Figure 22-6.
Architectural Desktop includes a few different beam, brace, and column tags that can be applied to structural members in the drawing.

Documentation Tool Catalog -
Imperial catalog

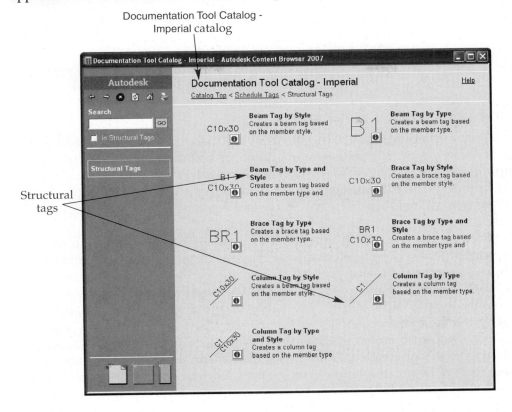

Figure 22-7.
Wall tags included in Architectural Desktop can be found in the Documentation Tool Catalog - Imperial and Documentation Tool Catalog - Metric catalogs.

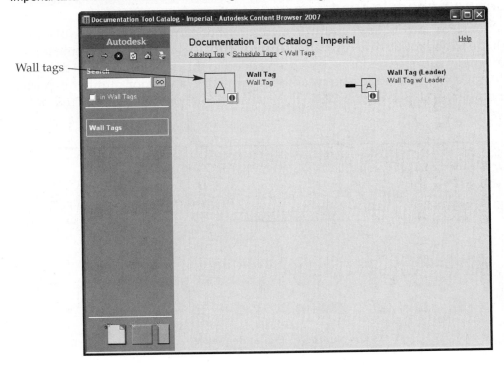

> All schedule tags can be tagged directly to objects in the drawing. Tags also can be added to objects within a reference file. In the host drawing, access the appropriate schedule tag, and pick the objects to be tagged in the reference drawing. The tag is placed in the host drawing, and the property set definition is assigned to the objects in the reference file.

Anchoring Tags to AEC Objects

You can copy schedule tags around the drawing so you do not have to add all the tags into the drawing during the same operation or continue i-dropping (dragging and dropping) the block icons from the **Content Browser**. When a tag is copied in the drawing, its property set information remains linked to the original object to which it was attached. Any changes made to a property value are reflected in the original and copied tags.

In these cases, the copied tag must be anchored to the new object. To attach a copied tag to a different object, select the tag, right-click, and pick **Tag Anchor** > **Set Object**. You are prompted to select the object to anchor to. Pick the object to which the new tag will be attached, or anchored. When you are asked whether or not you would like to constrain the tag to the object, type Y. Type Y again when you are asked if you want to rotate the tag to the object.

When you choose to constrain the tag to the object, if the object is moved or deleted, the tag moves or is deleted along with the object. The option to rotate the tag to the object rotates the tag in relation to the object's rotation angle. If the object the tag is being anchored to already includes property set information, the tag automatically updates with the property information, such as the number or name. If the object does not include property set information, a property set definition needs to be assigned to the object. This is discussed later in this chapter.

Renumbering Schedule Tags

As the construction documents are created, a new door, window, or piece of equipment might be added to the drawing, which can disrupt the numbering scheme for the tags. For example, suppose 10 doors have been added to the drawing, with 10 door tags attached. Another door is added between door number 5 and door number 6, with a door tag numbered 11. See **Figure 22-8**. This causes the doors to be numbered out of sequence.

Figure 22-8.
A new door is added to a wall, causing the door numbering to be out of sequence.

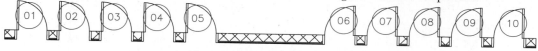

Doors Numbered in Sequence

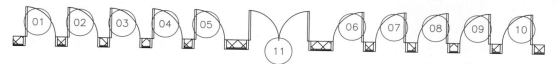

Doors Numbered Out of Sequence

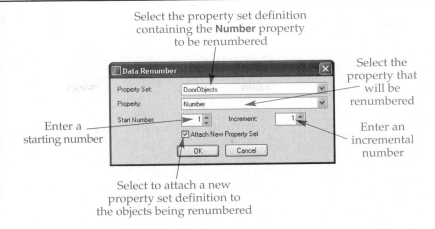

Figure 22-9.
The **Data Renumber**
dialog is used to
set up how the
schedule tags will
be renumbered.

Select the property set definition
containing the **Number** property
to be renumbered

Select the
property that
will be
renumbered

Enter a
starting number

Enter an
incremental
number

Select to attach a new
property set definition to
the objects being renumbered

Pull-Down Menu
Document
> Scheduling
> Renumber
Data...

Tool Palette
Scheduling

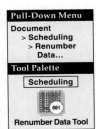

Renumber Data Tool

Fortunately, a command is available for renumbering schedule tags without having to individually modify each of the tags' schedule data. To renumber the tag numbers in the drawing, pick the **Renumber Data Tool** in the **Scheduling** tool palette of the **Document** tool palette group, or pick **Document** > **Scheduling** > **Renumber Data...** from the pull-down menu.

After entering the command, the **Data Renumber** dialog is displayed, as shown in **Figure 22-9**. First, select the property set definition containing the property that needs to be renumbered. Next, select the property to be renumbered. Enter a starting number to be used to start renumbering the schedule tags, and then enter a number for incrementing successive tag numbers. For example, if renumbering odd-numbered doors, you might begin the starting number at **5** and increment the numbers by **2**.

When you have finished setting the parameters for the renumbering of the tags, pick the **OK** button to begin renumbering. Select the schedule tag to be numbered with the start number specified. Continue to pick the tags needing to be renumbered in order. These tags are modified, based on the incremental number specified. When you finish, press the [Enter] key to exit the command. The schedule tags should be renumbered, and the property set definitions attached to the tags should be updated.

Understanding Property Set Definitions

Property set definitions are automatically assigned to AEC objects when tags are attached to objects. When a tag is inserted and the object to which it is attached is selected, the **Edit Property Set Data** worksheet appears, as in **Figure 22-10**. The properties available vary, depending on the type of tag being inserted and object selected. The schedule, in turn, queries the objects in the drawing, looking for properties and property set definitions to assemble the information into a logical table. The property set definitions available for use are those that can be assigned individually to AEC objects or to an object style.

Property Set Definitions by Object

Each tag inserted and attached to an object has its own property set definition assigned to the object. This ensures that each AEC object in the drawing contains unique information. For example, when door tags are attached to Door objects, each door has a unique number so you can keep track of the door.

Figure 22-10.
The **Edit Property Set Data** worksheet includes a list of properties available for the type of object selected. This worksheet displays the properties available for Door objects.

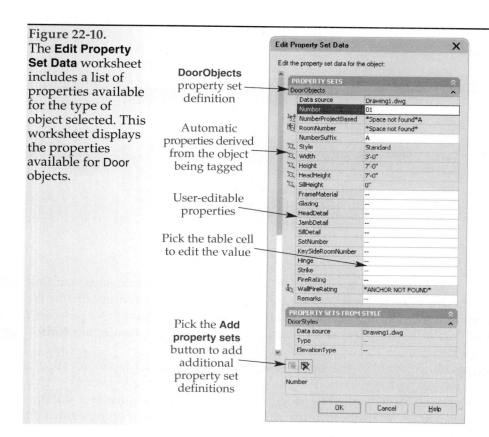

DoorObjects property set definition

Automatic properties derived from the object being tagged

User-editable properties

Pick the table cell to edit the value

Pick the **Add property sets** button to add additional property set definitions

When the **Edit Property Set Data** worksheet is displayed, the property set definition for that type of object appears. If additional property sets are available, the **Add property sets** button is highlighted, allowing you to attach additional property set definitions to the object. See **Figure 22-10.** Selecting the **Add property sets** button displays the **Add Property Sets** worksheet, shown in **Figure 22-11.** A list of available property set definitions that can be assigned to the object is displayed. Placing a check

Figure 22-11.
The **Add Property Sets** worksheet is displayed when the **Add property sets** button in the **Edit Property Set Data** worksheet is picked. A check next to the property set adds the definition to the object.

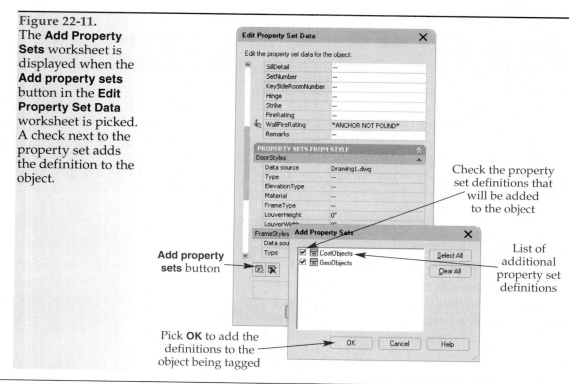

Check the property set definitions that will be added to the object

List of additional property set definitions

Add property sets button

Pick **OK** to add the definitions to the object being tagged

mark in the box beside the property set name adds the property set definition to the object. Pick the **OK** button to add the property set definition to the AEC object and the **Edit Property Set Data** worksheet.

If you need to change the property information within a property set definition or add additional property set definitions to an object after the object has been tagged, the **Properties** palette can be used to add or edit property set information. To add or edit property set definition information, select the object whose property values need to be updated, access the **Properties** palette, and then pick the **Extended Data** tab. See **Figure 22-12**. This tab includes three main sections: **DOCUMENTATION**, **PROPERTY SETS**, and **PROPERTY SETS FROM STYLE**. When an object's tag is selected, three sections similar to those mentioned above are available. These include **DOCUMENTATION**, **PROPERTY SETS FROM REFERENCED OBJECTS** (this is the equivalent of the **PROPERTY SETS** section for the selected object), and **PROPERTY SETS FROM REFERENCED STYLE** (this is the equivalent of the **PROPERTY SETS FROM STYLE** section for the selected object's style).

The **DOCUMENTATION** section includes properties attached to the selected object, such as hyperlinks, notes, and reference files. Pick one of the properties to add any of these features to the object. The **PROPERTY SETS** section (or the **PROPERTY SETS FROM REFERENCED OBJECTS** section, if the tag is selected) displays any property set definitions attached to the selected object. Within each of the property set definitions, user-editable and automatic properties are displayed for the object. *Automatic properties* are automatically filled out in a schedule, based on object information in the drawing. Pick any of the editable properties to change the value of the schedule property. If additional property set definitions are available, pick the **Add property sets** button to add them to the object. The **PROPERTY SETS FROM STYLE** section (or the **PROPERTY SETS FROM REFERENCED STYLE** section, if the tag is selected) displays the properties assigned to the selected object's style.

Figure 22-12.
The **Extended Data** tab in the **Properties** palette includes a listing of property set definitions assigned to the selected object.

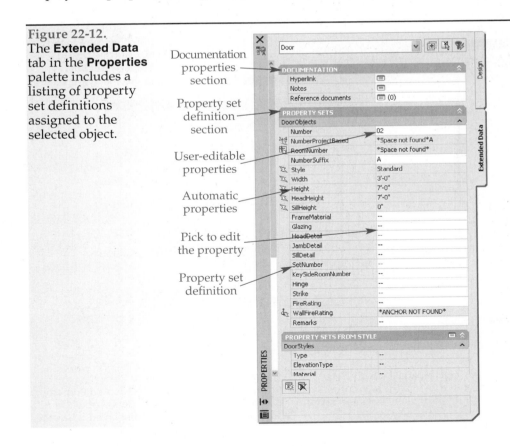

Documentation properties section

Property set definition section

User-editable properties

Automatic properties

Pick to edit the property

Property set definition

If several objects are selected that have differing property values, a ***VARIES*** value is displayed in the text box beside the property that is different for each object. Attach property set definitions individually to objects when the objects need to contain unique information, such as an itemized number, separate notes, or a specific description.

Property Set Definitions by Style

The creation of object styles was discussed in previous chapters. In the **Style Manager** for each of the object styles, the **General** tab includes a **Property Sets...** button. See **Figure 22-13**. This button allows you to assign property set definitions to the object style. When the **Property Sets...** button is selected in the **General** tab of the **Style Manager**, the **Edit Property Set Data** worksheet is displayed with the property set definitions assigned to that object style listed.

The object styles included in the tool palettes and **Content Browser** already have property set definitions assigned to them. See **Figure 22-14**. In many cases, these property set definitions include properties reporting on specific parts of the object. For example, the property set definition assigned to a door style includes properties reporting on the inserted door style material and hardware. Property set definitions assigned to a style contain properties common to objects of that type. For example, a

Figure 22-13.
The **Style Manager** for each AEC object style includes a **Property Sets...** button, found in the **General** tab, allowing you to assign property sets to the style.

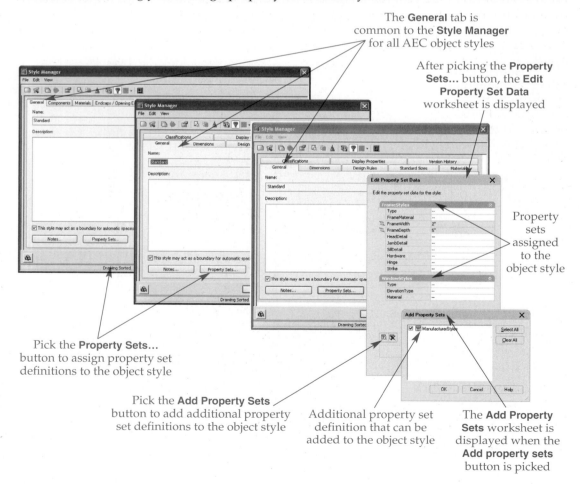

The **General** tab is common to the **Style Manager** for all AEC object styles

After picking the **Property Sets...** button, the **Edit Property Set Data** worksheet is displayed

Property sets assigned to the object style

Pick the **Property Sets...** button to assign property set definitions to the object style

Pick the **Add Property Sets** button to add additional property set definitions to the object style

Additional property set definition that can be added to the object style

The **Add Property Sets** worksheet is displayed when the **Add property sets** button is picked

Figure 22-14.
Property set definitions assigned to an AEC style contain general properties for the type of object, such as **Material**, **Type**, and **FrameWidth**.

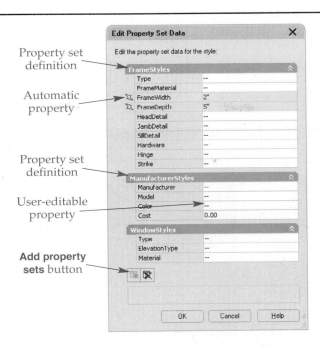

Property set definition

Automatic property

Property set definition

User-editable property

Add property sets button

property set definition assigned to an object style can contain a property for the type of window, material of door, or fire rating of a wall style.

One of the most helpful tools in the property set definitions for individual objects and assigned to a style is the addition of automatic properties. See **Figure 22-14**. A lightning bolt beside a property represents an automatic property. Automatic properties are automatically filled out in a schedule. For example, the width and height of a door is an automatic value, as a single door style can be inserted as a 3′-0″ × 7′-0″ or 2′-4″ × 6′-8″ door. Although the sizes vary when an individual door is created in the drawing, the automatic property looks to the inserted door size and reports that in the schedule.

Property set definitions assigned to a style include an **Add property sets** button. If additional property set definitions are available for the style being edited, the **Add property sets** button is available. If a property is edited for an object style, such as the material property, that property is assigned to each object using that style.

>
> **NOTE** Keep in mind that two separate property set definitions are assigned to objects: *individual object* and *object style* property set definitions. If the individual property set definitions need to be edited, use the **Extended Data** tab in the **Properties** palette. If the property set definition for a style needs to be modified, use the **General** tab of the **Style Manager**.

Accessing Additional Property Set Definitions

Initially, when an Architectural Desktop template is used, a few property set definitions are available. As new objects are drawn or schedule tags are added, additional property set definitions are added to the drawing. Architectural Desktop also includes additional property set definitions that can be added to the drawing.

Property set definitions are added to the drawing through the Property Set Definitions section in the **Style Manager**. To access this style section, pick **Document** > **Scheduling** > **Property Set Definitions...** from the pull-down menu. The **Style Manager** is displayed, opened to the Property Set Definitions section, as shown in **Figure 22-15**.

Pull-Down Menu
Document
> Scheduling
> Property Set
Definitions...

Figure 22-15.
The **Style Manager** opened to the Property Set Definitions section.

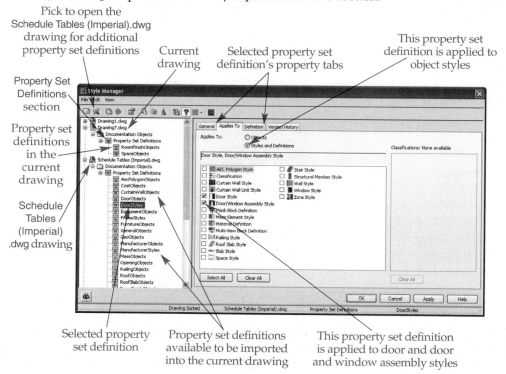

Pick to open the
Schedule Tables (Imperial).dwg
drawing for additional
property set definitions

Current
drawing

Selected property set
definition's property tabs

This property set
definition is applied to
object styles

Property Set
Definitions
section

Property set
definitions
in the
current
drawing

Schedule
Tables
(Imperial)
.dwg drawing

Selected property
set definition

Property set definitions
available to be imported
into the current drawing

This property set definition
is applied to door and door
and window assembly styles

Pick the **Open Drawing** button to open the Schedule Tables (Imperial).dwg or Schedule Tables (Metric).dwg drawing. In the **Open drawing** dialog box, pick the **Content** shortcut icon on the left side of the screen, and then browse to the \\Styles\Imperial\Schedule Tables (Imperial).dwg or \\Styles\Metric\Schedule Tables (Metric).dwg drawing. Select the Schedule Tables (Imperial).dwg or Schedule Tables (Metric).dwg file, and then pick the **Open** button. This drawing contains additional property set definitions that can be added to the current drawing.

A list of property set definitions is displayed below the Property Set Definitions section icon in the **Style Manager**. Property set definitions can be dragged from the list in the left tree view to the current drawing folder in the tree-view list. Selecting the Property Set Definitions section icon lists all the property set definitions in the right preview pane. The definitions can also be dragged from the right pane into the current drawing folder in the left tree pane.

Selecting a definition from the left tree view provides tabs for configuring the property set definition in the right pane. See **Figure 22-15**. The details of a property set indicate where the property set can be applied. For example, the property set definition selected in **Figure 22-15** is the DoorStyles property set definition. How the definition is applied is displayed in the right pane of the **Style Manager**. The **Applies To** tab indicates that this definition is a style-based definition and applies to Door and Door/Window Assembly object styles. Other property set definitions can be applied to entities, which are individual objects.

The property set definition naming conventions also indicate where the property set definitions are applied. If the property set definition name is the name of an AEC object followed by the word *Object*, the property set definition applies to individual objects. If the name begins with the type of object, followed by the word *Style*, the property set definition can be applied only to object styles. See **Figure 22-15**. After dragging and dropping additional property set definitions into the current drawing icon in the **Style Manager**, pick the **OK** button to exit the **Style Manager**.

Architectural Desktop and Its Applications

Exercise 22-3
Complete the Exercise on the Student CD.

Browsing through Property Data

Property set definitions can be browsed through, and properties can be modified quickly, through the **Browse Property Data** dialog box, which is shown in **Figure 22-16**. This dialog box is used to browse through property data on a grand scale and edit any properties available, whether they are assigned to individual objects or styles. To access the **Browse Property Data** dialog box, pick the **Browse Property Data** tool in the **Scheduling** tool palette of the **Documentation** tool palette group, or pick **Document > Scheduling > Browse Data...** from the pull-down menu. This displays the **Browse Property Data** dialog box, which is shown in **Figure 22-16**.

The **Browse Property Data** dialog box is divided into two main areas, two drop-down lists, and a few check boxes. The **Property Set Definitions:** drop-down list lists any property set definitions available in the current drawing. Select the property set definition to be reviewed. Below this drop-down list is the **Object Filter:** drop-down list. This list includes a listing of the object types in which the selected property set definition can be used. If a specific type of object is selected in this list, any objects in the drawing meeting the filter criteria are displayed in the list box on the left side of the dialog box. This drop-down list also includes an ***ALL*** option, which displays all the object types the property set definition in the list box can use.

Pull-Down Menu
Document
> Scheduling
> Browse
Data...

Tool Palette
Scheduling

Browse Property Data

Figure 22-16.
The **Browse Property Data** dialog box is used to browse through and edit property values on a global scale.

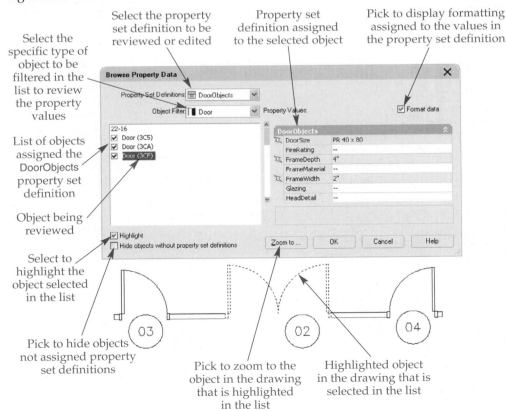

The list box lists any objects in the drawing meeting the criteria specified in the top two drop-down lists. **Figure 22-16** displays three Door objects displayed in the list box. A check mark in the box beside the object indicates that the property set definition listed in the **Property Set Definitions:** drop-down list has been assigned to the object. Clear the check mark to remove the property set definition from the object.

Below the list box are two check box options. The **Highlight** check box, when selected, highlights the object in the drawing selected in the list box. Use the **Zoom to...** button to zoom into the area where the highlighted object has been found. The **Hide objects without property set definitions** check box, when selected, hides any objects in the list box that do not have property set definitions assigned.

The right side of the **Browse Property Data** dialog box is where the property set definitions can be reviewed and edited. When an object has been selected from the list, the property set definition and its property values are displayed in the right side of the worksheet. Changes can be made to the user-editable properties by picking in the text box beside the property value and entering a new value.

The **Format data** check box in the upper-right corner of the worksheet displays property values as formatted or raw-data values. For example, the door number might be displayed in a formatted value of 07 or an unformatted value of 7. When you are finished browsing through the data, pick the **OK** button to close the worksheet.

The previous discussion outlined how to browse through property set data assigned directly to an object or object style in the current drawing. In addition to reviewing and editing property set information assigned directly to an object, the **Browse Property Data** worksheet can review the property set information in a reference drawing and assign an overriding property set definition in the host drawing. When the **Browse Property Data** worksheet has been accessed in a drawing containing reference drawings, the information in the list box might differ, depending on where the objects have been found. See **Figure 22-17**. Individual objects within a drawing can be assigned property set definitions. In addition to this, those same objects can be referenced into

Figure 22-17.
Property set definitions assigned to objects in a reference file or in the host drawing can be reviewed and edited.

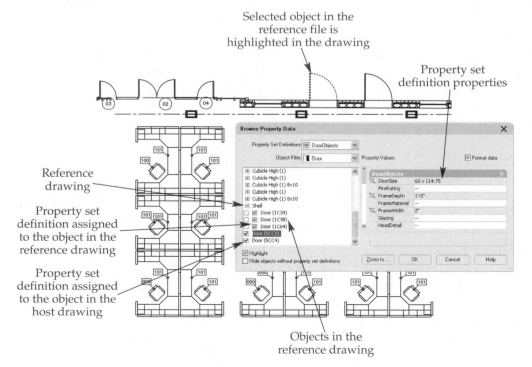

Architectural Desktop and Its Applications

another drawing and have overriding property set definitions assigned. When you are reviewing the list of objects in the **Browse Property Data** worksheet, select the desired property set definition to be browsed for from the **Property Set Definition** drop-down list. This will display the name of the current drawing with a list of the objects, with check boxes beside the objects that occur in the drawing and include the property set definition selected from the drop-down list.

The check boxes beside each object control the property set definition assigned to the object. Unchecking the check box removes the property set definition assigned to the object in the current drawing file. If the object listed is to use a property set definition in the current drawing, select the check box. Hovering over the check boxes displays a tip providing information about checking or unchecking the check boxes. When an object in the list is selected, the appropriate property set definition values are displayed on the right side of the worksheet.

Creating Schedules

Once schedule tags have been added and property values have been edited, a schedule can be created. Architectural Desktop includes a number of preconfigured schedule tables for your use. A few of these schedules can be found in the **Scheduling** tool palette, under the **Document** tool palette group. Additional schedule tables are available in the **Content Browser** catalogs and through the **Style Manager**. Access to these schedule tables is discussed later in the chapter.

To add a schedule table, select one of the schedule table tools from the **Scheduling** tool palette. You can also pick **Document** > **Scheduling** > **Add Schedule Table...** from the pull-down menu. Note that the pull-down option works only if the drawing includes a schedule table style.

Once the command to add a schedule table has been initiated, the **Properties** palette can be used to configure the properties of the schedule table. See **Figure 22-18**. The **Properties** palette includes the **BASIC** header, under which three categories are included: **General**, **Selection**, and **Location**. The categories and their properties available for the schedule table are discussed in the following sections.

Figure 22-18.
The **Properties** palette is used to set the properties for the schedule table.

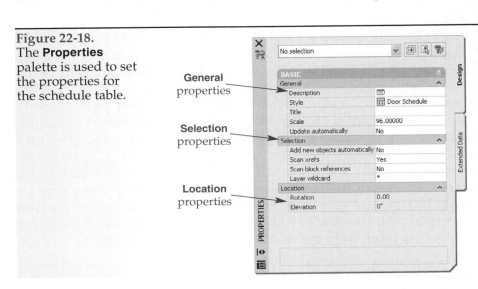

General Category

The **General** category includes general properties. These properties control the behavior of the schedule table. This category includes five properties:

- **Description.** Picking this property will display the **Description** worksheet, where a description for the schedule can be made.
- **Style.** When this property is selected, a list of schedule table styles loaded in the drawing is available. Choose the schedule table that will be created. The loading and creating of schedule styles in the current drawing are discussed later in this chapter.
- **Title.** This property is used to create the title for the schedule, which is displayed at the top of the schedule. The included schedules include a default name, but the name can be changed by entering a title in this text box.
- **Scale.** This property lists the scale factor of the schedule table, based on the drawing scale specified in the **Drawing Setup** dialog box. Picking the text box property allows you to enter a new scale factor for the schedule table. For example, a scale factor of 96 is used for 1/8″ = 1′-0″, and a scale factor of 48 is used for 1/4″ = 1′-0″.
- **Update automatically.** When this property is picked, a drop-down list with a **Yes** and **No** option is available. Selecting **Yes** will allow the schedule table to be updated automatically when a property set value is changed, such as the size or type of the door or window being reported. The schedule table is updated after the change has been made to reflect the most current properties of the object on which the schedule is reporting.

Selection Category

The **Selection** category includes properties to control how the schedule table finds and selects objects on which to report. This category includes four properties. These properties are described as follows:

- **Add new objects automatically.** This property drop-down list includes a **Yes** and **No** option. When the property is set to **Yes**, new objects added to the drawing on which the schedule is reporting are added automatically to the schedule. For example, a window schedule might include 12 different windows. As new windows are added to the drawing, the information about the windows is added to the schedule.
- **Scan xrefs.** Picking this property displays a drop-down list with a **Yes** and **No** value. Selecting **Yes** causes the schedule to scan through reference drawings for objects on which it can report. When an object is found in the reference file, it is added to the schedule.
- **Scan block references.** This property is similar to the **Scan xrefs** property. The property includes a **Yes** and **No** option. When the value is set to **Yes**, the schedule scans through standard blocks in the drawing for objects on which it can report in the schedule.
- **Layer wildcard.** This text box property initially includes an asterisk (*) in the text box area. The asterisk indicates that the schedule searches for objects on any layer, for inclusion into the table. The (*) represents any character in a layer name. If you want the schedule to look through objects only on specific layers, such as the A-Door layer, enter the layer names separated by commas.

 NOTE
The schedule style selected is set up to look for specific types of objects. For example, the Door Schedule looks only for doors in the drawing. If you are generating door schedules for each floor of a building from reference drawings, you might want to use a layer filter that filters for doors on the specific layer on which the reference drawing was inserted.

Architectural Desktop and Its Applications

Location Category

The **Location** category includes properties to control the placement of the schedule table. This category includes two read-only properties. These properties are described as follows:

- **Rotation.** This property indicates the rotation angle of the schedule table. After the schedule has been added to the drawing, picking the schedule and then accessing the **Properties** palette allows you to adjust the rotation of the schedule.
- **Elevation.** This property indicates the Z axis location of the schedule table. By default, the schedule is set at 0".

 NOTE If there are not any schedule table styles loaded in the drawing, you will receive an alert message when accessing **Add Schedule Table...** from the pull-down menu. In this case, a schedule table style must be present before using the pull-down option.

After configuring the properties for the schedule table, you are prompted to Select objects or ENTER to schedule external drawing. Select the objects to be used in the schedule or press [Enter] to add the schedule to the drawing, and then assign the reference file to be queried. If you select the objects, use crossing windows to select all the geometry, as the schedule table filters for the specific objects it is scheduling. For example, door schedules look for doors, and window schedules look for windows. If you accidentally select a wrong object, it is ignored. Additionally, the layer wild card filters for the specific type of objects on a specified layer.

When you have finished selecting the objects to be included in the schedule, press the [Enter] key. An outline of the schedule is attached to the crosshairs. Pick a location for the upper-left corner of the schedule. The schedule is inserted at that location. The next prompt asks you to specify the Lower right corner (or RETURN). If a lower-right corner of the schedule is picked, the schedule is not scaled correctly in the drawing. Pressing the [Enter] key at this prompt scales the schedule according to the drawing scale specified in the **Properties** palette. To place a schedule so it is scaled correctly in the drawing, pick a location for the upper-left corner of the schedule when you are prompted for the upper-left corner of the table. Press [Enter] when you are prompted for the lower-right corner. Architectural Desktop then inserts a schedule of information from the property values within the property set definitions attached to the objects in the drawing. See **Figure 22-19**.

If the schedule table is scheduling objects within an external drawing, the schedule needs to know where to find the drawing file. At the initial prompt of Select objects or ENTER to schedule external drawing:, press [Enter] to add the schedule table. The schedule table, with a title, headers, and column divisions, is displayed. Pick the schedule table, and then access the **Properties** palette. Scroll through the palette until you come to the **ADVANCED** header. See **Figure 22-20**.

Under the **External Source** category, pick the **Schedule external drawing** property and set the value to **Yes**. The **External drawing** property becomes available. Select the **External drawing** property, and then select the **Browse...** option. This opens the **Select a drawing file** dialog, where an external drawing can be selected for scheduling. The schedule is now tied to the external drawing file. A slash is displayed through the schedule table, indicating that the schedule needs to be updated. Select the schedule table, right-click, and pick **Update Schedule Table**. The schedule table will be updated with the property values of the objects in the external drawing file.

If the table includes question marks or incorrect information, open the external drawing file and go through the property set definitions assigned to the objects being reported on. Save the file. Update the schedule in the drawing containing the schedule table.

Figure 22-19.
A window schedule has been generated from the windows in a drawing. The property values within the windows' property set definition are displayed in the schedule.

WINDOW SCHEDULE

MARK	SIZE		TYPE	MATERIAL	NOTES
	WIDTH	HEIGHT			
1	3'-0"	5'-0"	SINGLE HUNG	WOOD	--
2	3'-0"	5'-0"	SINGLE HUNG	WOOD	--
3	1'-6"	5'-0"	SINGLE HUNG	WOOD	--
4	4'-0"	5'-0"	SINGLE HUNG	WOOD	--
5	1'-6"	5'-0"	SINGLE HUNG	WOOD	--
6	3'-0"	6'-0"	FIXED	WOOD	TEMPERED
7	3'-0"	6'-0"	FIXED	WOOD	TEMPERED
8	3'-0"	6'-0"	FIXED	WOOD	TEMPERED
9	3'-0"	6'-0"	FIXED	WOOD	TEMPERED
10	1'-6"	5'-0"	SINGLE HUNG	WOOD	--
11	4'-0"	5'-0"	SINGLE HUNG	WOOD	--
12	1'-6"	5'-0"	SINGLE HUNG	WOOD	--

Figure 22-20.
Schedule tables can schedule information in an external drawing.

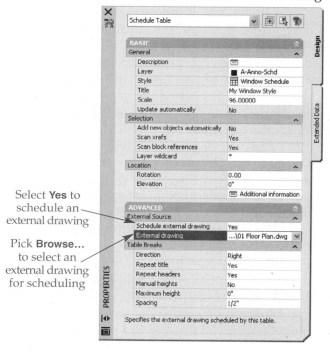

Select **Yes** to schedule an external drawing

Pick **Browse...** to select an external drawing for scheduling

Updating Schedules

When you start to create a schedule, you have the option of automatically updating the schedule as you make changes. If this option is not set to **Yes**, any changes to the objects being reported on do not accurately reflect information in the schedule. The schedule is no longer current if an object is deleted, an object changes size, or an object's property values are changed. This only applies to schedule tables in which the items being reported are in the same drawing file and are not being reported on through an external drawing.

Figure 22-21.
In most situations, if a schedule is out of date, a slash will run through the schedule, indicating that it needs to be updated.

WINDOW SCHEDULE

MARK	SIZE		TYPE	MATERIAL	NOTES
	WIDTH	HEIGHT			
1	3'-0"	5'-0"	SH	WOOD	--
2	3'-0"	5'-0"	SH	WOOD	--
3	1'-6"	5'-0"	SH	WOOD	--
4	4'-0"	5'-0"	SH	WOOD	--
5	1'-6"	5'-0"	SH	WOOD	--
6	3'-0"	6'-0"	FXD	WOOD	TEMPERED
7	3'-0"	6'-0"	FXD	WOOD	TEMPERED
8	3'-0"	6'-0"	FXD	WOOD	TEMPERED
9	3'-0"	6'-0"	FXD	WOOD	TEMPERED
10	1'-6"	5'-0"	SH	WOOD	--
11	4'-0"	5'-0"	SH	WOOD	--
12	1'-6"	5'-0"	SH	WOOD	--

If a schedule table is not up-to-date, a slash is displayed through the table to indicate that a change affecting the table has been made to the drawing. See **Figure 22-21.** To update the table, the **Update Schedule Table** option is used. To ensure that the schedule table is the most up-to-date schedule, select the schedule, right-click, and then pick **Update Schedule Table**. The schedule is updated, and the slash is removed to indicate the schedule is updated and current with the information assigned to the objects.

Exercise 22-4   Complete the Exercise on the Student CD.

Modifying the Properties of a Schedule Table

Each schedule remembers the properties that were set initially when the schedule was created. The schedule remembers the layer it is looking through for objects included in the schedule; whether it is looking through the drawing on which the schedule is located, an xref drawing, or xref blocks; and the schedule drawing scale. You can modify these values at any time after the schedule is generated by using the **Properties** palette. To modify the properties of an existing schedule table, select the table, and then access the **Properties** palette. The **Properties** palette is broken down into two main headers: **BASIC** and **ADVANCED**. See **Figure 22-22.** Under each of the headers are categories of properties. These are described in the following sections.

Basic Properties

The **BASIC** header includes three categories. These categories are the **General**, **Selection**, and **Location** categories. They and their properties are listed in the following sections.

Figure 22-22.
The **Properties** palette contains properties set up for the selected schedule table.

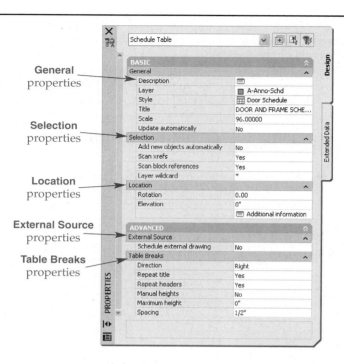

General Category

The **General** category contains similar properties to those that were available when initially creating the schedule table. This area focuses on the general properties of the schedule table. The properties are as follows:

- **Description.** Use this property to assign a description to the schedule table.
- **Layer.** This property displays the layer to which the schedule is assigned. Pick a different layer from the drop-down list to assign the schedule to a new layer.
- **Style.** This property displays the schedule style assigned to the selected schedule. Picking a different schedule from the list removes the selected schedule and adds a different one in its place.
- **Title.** Use this text box property to add a title name to the heading of the schedule table.
- **Scale.** This property displays the drawing scale of the schedule table.
- **Update automatically.** Use this property to make the schedule table update automatically when changes are made to the scheduled objects. Note that this applies only to schedules in which the objects being reported on are in the same drawing as the schedule table and is not available when scheduling external drawings.

Selection Category

The **Selection** category includes properties that were available when initially creating the schedule table. This area focuses on how the schedule table selects objects to be scheduled. The properties are as follows:

- **Add new objects automatically.** This property indicates whether or not new objects added to the drawing are also added to the schedule table automatically.
- **Scan xrefs.** Use this property to scan through reference drawings for objects to be reported on.
- **Scan block references.** Select this property to scan through block references containing objects to be reported on.

- **Layer wildcard.** This property indicates any layer wild cards used to filter for objects used in the schedule. For example, if you were creating two schedules—one for existing doors in the building and one for doors to be demolished—and the existing doors and doors to be demolished were on two different layers, a layer wild card, such as *-Door-Demo*, could be used to report on any doors on the -Door-Demo layer. Likewise, existing doors might be scheduled using the A-Door layer wild card.

Location Category

When you are initially creating a schedule, this area contains two read-only properties. After adding a schedule, the properties in this category become available for you to modify. The properties are as follows:

- **Rotation.** Enter a new value in this property to specify a new rotation angle for the schedule.
- **Elevation.** Enter a new value in this property to specify a new elevation height for the schedule.
- **Additional information.** Pick this property to specify a rotation value and an elevation value for the selected schedule.

Advanced Properties

When you are initially creating a schedule table, the **ADVANCED** header is not available. After a schedule table has been added to the drawing, advanced properties for the schedule are available. Two categories are available: **External Source** and **Table Breaks**. These are described in the following sections.

External Source Category

The **External Source** category is used when a schedule table schedules objects within an external drawing. Pick the **Yes** option of the **Schedule external drawing** property to have the schedule look to an external drawing file for items to be reported on. The **External drawing** property is used to pick the external drawing file the schedule searches for objects to be scheduled. Pick the **Browse...** option to browse for the location of the external drawing file.

Table Breaks Category

The **Table Breaks** category is used to assign the parameters to a large schedule needing to be split up into smaller schedules. See **Figure 22-23**. A large schedule table can be adjusted by selecting the schedule to display the grip boxes, picking the bottom grip labeled as the **Maximum Page Height** grip, and stretching the schedule table. Depending on the values of the schedule, additional overflow schedules are created to the right of or below the initially placed schedule table.

- **Direction.** This property controls whether the overflow schedule is created to the right of or below the original schedule table. See **Figure 22-23**.
- **Repeat title.** Setting this property to **Yes** adds a schedule table title to the top of the overflow schedule.
- **Repeat headers.** When this property is set to **Yes**, the headers of the schedule are repeated in the overflow schedule.
- **Manual heights.** This property allows the main and overflow schedule tables to have their heights manually set by stretching the grip boxes. When this value is set to **Yes**, an additional grip is placed at the bottom of each schedule.
- **Maximum height.** This property controls the maximum height of the schedule and overflow schedules. Specify a height value reflecting the maximum plotted height of the table.
- **Spacing.** This property controls the spacing between the main schedule and overflow schedules. The value is the distance between schedules when they are plotted.

Figure 22-23.
The **Table Breaks** category in the **Properties** palette controls the behavior of the schedule table when the height of the schedule is adjusted using the **Maximum Page Height** grip.

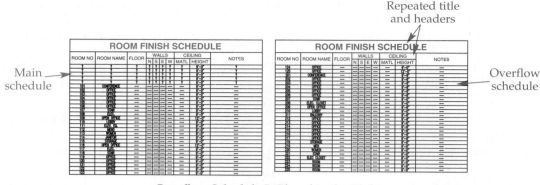

Overflow Schedule Is Placed to the Right
of the Main Schedule

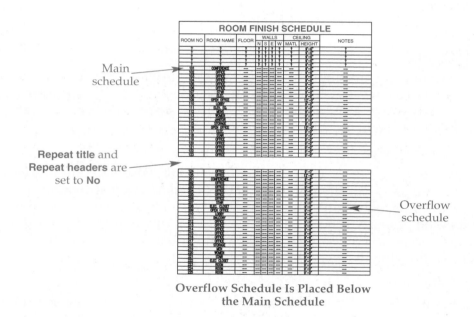

Overflow Schedule Is Placed Below
the Main Schedule

Exporting a Schedule Table

Some offices prefer to create schedules with other software, such as Microsoft Excel. To export schedule data, select the schedule, right-click, and pick **Export...** from the shortcut menu. This displays the **Export Schedule Table** dialog box. See **Figure 22-24**. The dialog box includes the following two areas:

- **Output.** This area includes a drop-down list and text box. The **Save As Type:** drop-down list allows you to pick the type of external file to be created. Options include **Microsoft Excel 97 (*.xls)**, **Microsoft Excel 2003 (*.xls)**, **Text (Tab delimited) (*.txt)**, and **CSV (Comma delimited) (*.csv)**. An example of the results for each type of file is displayed in **Figure 22-25**. The **File Name** text box is used to specify a name for the new file. Use the **Browse...** button to browse the folders for a location for the new file.

Figure 22-24.
The **Export Schedule Table** dialog box contains settings for exporting a schedule to an external file.

Pick to browse the hard drives and network drives for a location for the new file

Select to use an existing schedule in the drawing

Select to scan through reference files

Select to scan through blocks

Select the type of file to which to export the property values

Enter a name for the external file

If the **Use Existing Table** check box is cleared, select the type of schedule to use to obtain the proper property values

If the **Use Existing Table** check box is cleared, enter a layer filter to search for property information

Figure 22-25.
A schedule table can be exported out in three main data types: Microsoft Excel 97 (.xls), Microsoft Excel 2003 (.xls), Text (.txt), and Comma delimited (.csv).

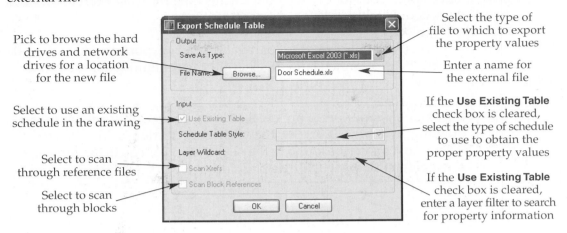

	A	B	C	D	E	F	G
1	WINDOW SCHEDULE						
2	MARK	WIDTH	HEIGHT	TYPE	MATERIAL	NOTES	
3	1	3'-0"	5'-0"	--	WOOD	--	
4	2	8'-0"	7'-0"	--	VINYL	Tempered	
5	3	5'-0"	5'-0"	--	ALUMINUM	--	
6	4	8'-0"	7'-0"	--	VINYL	Tempered	
7	6	8'-0"	7'-0"	--	VINYL	Tempered	
8	8	8'-0"	7'-0"	--	VINYL	Tempered	
9	9	3'-0"	5'-0"	--	WOOD		
10							
11							

Excel File

```
WINDOW SCHEDULE
MARK     WIDTH      HEIGHT     TYPE       MATERIAL        NOTES
1        3'-0"      5'-0"      --         WOOD            --
2        8'-0"      7'-0"      --         VINYL     Tempered
3        5'-0"      5'-0"      --         ALUMINUM         --
4        8'-0"      7'-0"      --         VINYL     Tempered
6        8'-0"      7'-0"      --         VINYL     Tempered
8        8'-0"      7'-0"      --         VINYL     Tempered
9        3'-0"      5'-0"      --         WOOD            --
```

Text File

```
WINDOW SCHEDULE
MARK,WIDTH,HEIGHT,TYPE,MATERIAL,NOTES
1,3'-0",5'-0",--,WOOD,--
2,8'-0",7'-0",--,VINYL,Tempered
3,5'-0",5'-0",--,ALUMINUM,--
4,8'-0",7'-0",--,VINYL,Tempered
6,8'-0",7'-0",--,VINYL,Tempered
8,8'-0",7'-0",--,VINYL,Tempered
9,3'-0",5'-0",--,WOOD,--
```

CSV File

- **Input.** This area includes several options for control. When the **Use Existing Table** check box is selected, an existing schedule in the drawing must be selected to be processed for exportation. Unchecking this check box allows you to select a schedule table style for processing, a layer wild card, and options to scan xrefs or blocks.

When you have finished selecting the parameters for exporting the schedule information, the objects are scanned, and an external file containing all the property values is created.

NOTE   Information exported to an Excel file can be brought back into your drawing by using OLE. See the OLELINKS section in the Command Reference. This can be found in the AutoCAD Help menu in the **Autodesk Architectural Desktop 2007 Help** window.

Accessing Additional Schedule Table Styles

Initially, when a new drawing is started from one of the model or sheet templates, no schedule table styles are loaded in the drawing. The **Scheduling** tool palette includes several schedule table tools that can be imported into the drawing. **Door Schedule**, **Window Schedule**, **Space Inventory Schedule**, and **Room Finish Schedule** are just a few. To import these schedule table styles into the drawing, right-click over the desired tool in the tool palette and pick **Import '***nnn***' Schedule Table Style**. This imports the desired style into the drawing, for your use through the **Properties** palette.

Additional schedule table tools are available through the **Content Browser** catalogs. The Architectural Desktop Documentation Tool Catalog - Imperial (or Documentation Tool Catalog - Metric) catalog includes several schedule table style tools that can be imported onto a tool palette, which in turn, can be imported into the drawing. In the catalogs, browse to the Schedule Tables section, and then i-drop (drag and drop) the desired schedule tables onto a tool palette or into the drawing.

In addition to using the **Content Browser** and tool palettes to access additional schedule styles, the **Style Manager** can be used to import schedule styles into the drawing. To access the **Style Manager**, pick **Document** > **Scheduling** > **Schedule Table Styles...** from the pull-down menu. This displays the **Style Manager**, opened to the Schedule Table Styles section. See **Figure 22-26.**

Use the **Open Drawing** button in the **Style Manager** to open the Schedule Tables (Imperial).dwg or Schedule Tables (Metric).dwg file. In the **Open drawing** dialog box, pick the **Content** shortcut in the upper-left corner of the dialog box, and then browse to the \\Styles\Imperial\Schedule Tables (Imperial) or \\Styles\Metric\Schedule Tables (Metric) drawing. Select the drawing and pick the **Open** button to open the drawing in the **Style Manager**.

Expand the Schedule Table Styles section of the Schedule Tables (Imperial).dwg or Schedule Tables (Metric).dwg drawing to list all the schedules available. Select any desired schedules, and then drag and drop them onto the current drawing icon to import additional schedules into the drawing. Close the **Style Manager**, and then add the new schedule to the drawing.

NOTE   Custom schedules can also be dragged into the current drawing using the same process. The creation of custom schedules is covered in Chapter 23.

Figure 22-26.
Use the **Open Drawing** button in the **Style Manager** to open Schedule Tables (Imperial).dwg or Schedule Tables (Metric).dwg. Drag any desired schedule table styles from Schedule Tables (Imperial).dwg or Schedule Tables (Metric).dwg into the current drawing icon in the tree view.

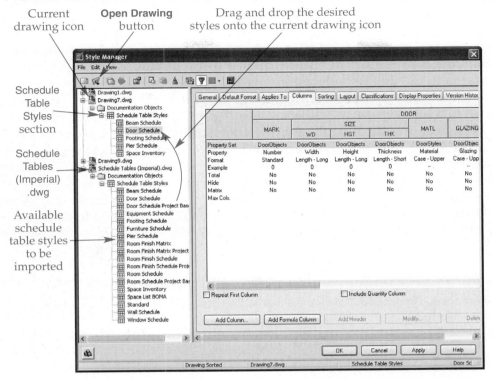

Editing Schedule Information

The information being reported in the schedule table contains property values that have been assigned to the objects the schedule is querying, whether they are in the same drawing or a referenced drawing. This information can be edited at any time, using the methods described earlier in this chapter or through other Architectural Desktop commands. This section describes additional tools that can be used to modify the information found in the schedule, when a schedule reports items in the same drawing in which the schedule table has been created. These procedures do not work on schedules referencing an external drawing.

Editing a Table Cell

Two types of property values are available within a property set definition: automatic properties and user-defined, editable properties. Within any given schedule, the information present might be data being retrieved directly from the actual object, such as width, height, or style, or data the user provides, such as material and remarks. Information within a cell of the schedule the user completes that is not automatic data can be edited from the schedule. The option to do this is **Edit Table Cell**. To access this option, select the schedule table, right-click, and pick **Edit Table Cell** from the shortcut menu. After picking this option, you are prompted to select the schedule table item or the border for all items, hover for information, or press [Ctrl] while selecting to zoom.

From this prompt, select text within a cell of the schedule to be edited, or select a column header to edit all the values within that column. After selecting the item to be edited, the **Edit Referenced Property Set Data** worksheet is displayed. See **Figure 22-27**. This worksheet displays the name of the property set to which the selected text belongs, the property name being modified, and the value of the property. Enter a new value for the property, and then pick the **OK** button to update the change in the schedule table.

If a column heading or border edge of a value is selected, the **Edit Referenced Property Set Data** worksheet is displayed, allowing you to modify the cell information. In addition to the **Edit Referenced Property Set Data** worksheet, some warning messages might be displayed. A warning is displayed if a cell value that is a property assigned to the object's style is selected. See **Figure 22-28**. Picking **Yes** closes the **AutoCAD** worksheet and displays the **Edit Referenced Property Set Data** worksheet. Changing the property value globally changes the values for other objects of the same style.

If an automatic value is selected in the table, another warning message is displayed, indicating that the selected data is derived from the actual object itself and cannot be edited from the table. See **Figure 22-29**. The actual item in the drawing is also highlighted, allowing you to see the object in question so it can be modified to change the automatic values. To edit the data, modify the actual object through the **Properties** palette.

Figure 22-27.
The **Edit Referenced Property Set Data** worksheet allows you to change the value of a single cell in the schedule table.

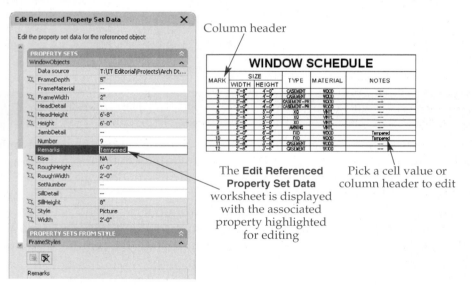

Figure 22-28.
When an object style value is selected in the schedule, a warning message is displayed, indicating that changing the value will globally change the values for other objects using the same style.

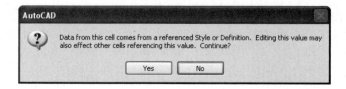

Figure 22-29.
When an automatic value is selected in a schedule, a warning message is displayed, indicating that the data cannot be edited directly and is derived from the actual object. Modifying the actual object will change the value in the schedule.

Adding Objects to and Removing Objects from a Schedule

When a new schedule is added to the drawing, one of the property options is **Add new objects automatically**. If this property is set to **Yes**, new objects being reported on are automatically added to the schedule. As objects are removed from the drawing, the schedule is also automatically updated, and the appropriate items are removed from the schedule.

If this property was set to **No** when the schedule was added, new objects can be added or removed from the schedule manually. To add new objects in the drawing to an existing schedule, select the schedule table, right-click, and pick **Selection** > **Add** from the shortcut menu. Select the new objects needing to be added to the schedule. When you have finished, press the [Enter] key to end the command and add the new objects to the schedule.

Objects can also be removed from a table schedule—for example, when you want to separate information into different tables, rather than keeping it all in one schedule. To remove an object from a schedule, pick the schedule table, right-click, and pick **Selection** > **Remove** from the shortcut menu. You are prompted to select objects. Begin selecting objects in the drawing that will be removed from the schedule. When you finish, press the [Enter] key to remove the items from the schedule.

Reselecting Objects for the Schedule

After a schedule table has been added to the drawing, the objects that used to be in the schedule can be reselected for placement in the schedule. When objects are reselected, only those objects selected are reentered into the schedule. For example, suppose a door schedule has already been created in the drawing, with doors numbered 1–10. If door numbers 1, 3, 5, 7, and 9 are reselected for placement in the schedule, the other doors are removed from the schedule, and only the selected doors remain in the schedule. To reselect items to be used in the schedule, select the schedule table, right-click, and pick **Selection** > **Reselect** from the shortcut menu. Select any objects in the drawing that will be kept in the schedule table. Press the [Enter] key when you are finished to update the schedule.

Locating an Object in the Schedule

When schedules are created, the property values within the schedule might need to be updated or filled in over time. In some cases, as objects are added to a drawing and the schedule is updated, you might see the schedule fill up with question marks, as shown in **Figure 22-30**. In these situations, property values need to be modified within the objects, or property set definitions need to be added to objects that have question marks in the schedule cells. If the drawing includes many objects being reported on, it might be difficult to locate the specific object in the drawing needing to be edited.

Figure 22-30.
As objects are added to the drawing and property values are filled in, the information within the schedule might not reflect a desired schedule output.

Objects being reported on do not have property set definitions assigned

Information needing to be filled out

WINDOW SCHEDULE

MARK	TYPE	MATERIAL	NOTES
?	?	?	?
?	?	?	?
?	?	?	?
?	?	?	?
1	--	WOOD	
3	--	ALUMINUM	
6	--	ALUMINUM	
9	--	WOOD	

The **Show** option can be used to locate the object in the drawing that is reporting erroneous information in the schedule. This command allows you to select a cell in the schedule, in order to locate the object reporting the wrong value. When the cell is picked, the object providing the information is highlighted. See **Figure 22-31.**

In order to show the objects that are generating question marks or need to have additional information filled out in the schedule, pick the schedule table, right-click, and pick **Selection** > **Show** from the shortcut menu. Pick the cell where the information needs to be modified. The object is highlighted in the drawing. After identifying the object, use the **Extended Data** tab of the **Properties** palette to modify the property values or add a property set to the object.

NOTE

If a schedule reports a number of question marks, use the **Extended Data** tab of the **Properties** palette to add the appropriate property set definitions. You might also need to add a property set definition to the object's style. If a schedule is reporting on objects in a reference file, the property data values must be edited in the original drawing where the objects are located. For example, suppose a schedule in a view drawing is reporting on Door objects from a construct drawing and the schedule is displaying question marks. You will need to access the construct drawing and then modify the property values for the Door objects reporting question marks. Select the Door objects and use the **Extended Data** tab of the **Properties** palette to modify the properties. Reload the construct in the view drawing and update the schedule.

After selecting the cell, the
object in question is highlighted

Select a cell
to show

WINDOW SCHEDULE			
MARK	TYPE	MATERIAL	NOTES
?	?	?	?
?	?	?	?
?	?	?	?
?	?	?	?
1	---	WOOD	
3	---	ALUMINUM	
6	---	ALUMINUM	
9	---	WOOD	

Chapter Test

Answer the following questions. Write your answers on a separate sheet of paper or complete the electronic chapter test on the Student CD.

1. Define *schedules*.
2. Identify the typical format used to create schedules.
3. What are schedule tags?
4. Briefly explain the terms *property* and *property set* as related to schedules.
5. Identify what a schedule tag looks like and the information contained on one.
6. Describe object tags and their use.
7. Explain the use of room and finish tags.
8. Identify the only feature to which room and finish tags can be attached.
9. What are wall tags used for, and where are they attached?
10. Describe property set definitions, explain their basic use, and give an example.
11. How are automatic properties represented, and how do they function?
12. Give an example of an automatic property.

Chapter Projects

Use the techniques covered in this chapter to create the following drawings.

1. Single-Level Residential Project
   A. Access the **Project Browser** and set Residential-Project-01 current.
   B. Access the **Views** tab of the **Project Navigator** and open the Main Floor Plan view drawing.
   C. Add door and window tags to the drawing. As the tags are added, fill out the property values in the **Edit Property Set Data** worksheet, as desired.
   D. Add a door and window schedule that will schedule the external drawing Main Floor construct, which can be found in the Constructs folder of Residential-Project-01.
   E. Update the schedule as needed.

   Note: If the schedule includes question marks, do not try to resolve the property sets. You will do this in the next chapter.
   F. Save and close the drawing.

2. Single-Level Residential Project
   A. Access the **Project Browser** and set Residential-Project-02 current.
   B. Access the **Views** tab of the **Project Navigator** and open the Main Floor Plan view drawing.
   C. Add door and window tags to the drawing. As the tags are added, fill out the property values in the **Edit Property Set Data** worksheet, as desired.
   D. Add a door and window schedule that will schedule the external drawing Main Floor construct, which can be found in the Constructs folder of Residential-Project-02.
   E. Update the schedule as needed.

   Note: If the schedule includes question marks, do not try to resolve the property sets. You will do this in the next chapter.
   F. Save and close the drawing.

3. Two-Story Residential Project
   A. Access the **Project Browser** and set Residential-Project-03 current.
   B. Access the **Views** tab of the **Project Navigator** and open the Upper Floor Plan view drawing.
   C. Add a window tag to the upstairs window, with a number of 201. As the tag is added, fill out the property values in the **Edit Property Set Data** worksheet, as desired.
   D. Save and close the drawing.
   E. Access the **Constructs** tab of the **Project Navigator** and open the Main Floor construct.
   F. Right-click over the Upper Floor construct and pick **Xref Overlay**.
   G. Save and close the drawing.
   H. Access the **Views** tab of the **Project Navigator** and open the Main Floor Plan view drawing.
   I. Add door and window tags to the main floor drawing, starting with door number 101 and window number 101. As the tags are added, fill out the property values in the **Edit Property Set Data** worksheet, as desired.
   J. Add a door and window schedule that will schedule the external drawing Main Floor construct, which can be found in Constructs folder of Residential-Project-03.
   K. Update the schedule as needed.

   Note: If the schedule includes question marks, do not try to resolve the property sets. You will do this in the next chapter.
   L. Save and close the drawing.

4. Two-Story Residential Project
   A. Access the **Project Browser** and set Residential-Project-04 current.
   B. Access the **Views** tab of the **Project Navigator** and open the Upper Floor Plan view drawing.
   C. Add door and window tags to the upper floor drawing, starting the door tags with number 201 and the window tags with number 201. As the tags are added, fill out the property values in the **Edit Property Set Data** worksheet, as desired.
   D. Save and close the drawing.
   E. Access the **Constructs** tab of the **Project Navigator** and open the Main Floor construct.
   F. Right-click over the Upper Floor construct and pick **Xref Overlay**.
   G. Save and close the drawing.
   H. Access the **Views** tab of the **Project Navigator** and open the Main Floor Plan view drawing.
   I. Add door and window tags to the main floor drawing, starting the door tags with number 101 and the window tags with number 101. As the tags are added, fill out the property values in the **Edit Property Set Data** worksheet, as desired.
   J. Add a door and window schedule that will schedule the external drawing Main Floor construct, which can be found in the Constructs folder of Residential-Project-04.
   K. Update the schedule as needed.
Note: If the schedule includes question marks, do not try to resolve the property sets. You will do this in the next chapter.
   L. Save and close the drawing.

5. Commercial Store Project
   A. Access the **Project Browser** and set Commercial-Project-05 current.
   B. Access the **Views** tab of the **Project Navigator** and open the Main Floor Plan view drawing.
   C. Add door and window tags to the drawing. As the tags are added, fill out the property values in the **Edit Property Set Data** worksheet, as desired.
   D. Add a door and window schedule that will schedule the external drawing Main Floor construct, which can be found in the Constructs folder of Commercial-Project-05.
   E. Update the schedule as needed.
Note: If the schedule includes question marks, do not try to resolve the property sets. You will do this in the next chapter.
   F. Save and close the drawing.

6. Commercial Car Maintenance Shop Project
   A. Access the **Project Browser** and set Commercial-Project-06 current.
   B. Access the **Views** tab of the **Project Navigator** and open the Upper Floor Plan view drawing.
   C. Add window tags to the upper floor drawing, starting the window tags with number 201. As the tags are added, fill out the property values in the **Edit Property Set Data** worksheet, as desired.
   D. Save and close the drawing.
   E. Access the **Constructs** tab of the **Project Navigator** and open the Main Floor construct.
   F. Right-click over the Upper Floor construct and pick **Xref Overlay**.
   G. Save and close the drawing.
   H. Access the **Views** tab of the **Project Navigator** and open the Main Floor Plan view drawing.
   I. Add door and window tags to the main floor drawing, starting the door tags with number 101 and the window tags with number 101. As the tags are added, fill out the property values in the **Edit Property Set Data** worksheet, as desired.
   J. Add a door and window schedule that will schedule the external drawing Main Floor construct, which can be found in the Constructs folder of Commercial-Project-06.
   K. Update the schedule as needed.
   Note: If the schedule includes question marks, do not try to resolve the property sets. You will do this in the next chapter.
   L. Save and close the drawing.

7. Governmental Fire Station
   A. Access the **Project Browser** and set Gvrmt -Project-07 current.
   B. Access the **Views** tab of the **Project Navigator** and open the Main Floor Plan view drawing.
   C. Add door and window tags to the drawing. As the tags are added, fill out the property values in the **Edit Property Set Data** worksheet, as desired.
   D. Add a door and window schedule that will schedule the external drawing Main Floor construct, which can be found in the Constructs folder of Gvrmt -Project-07.
   E. Update the schedule as needed.
   Note: If the schedule includes question marks, do not try to resolve the property sets. You will do this in the next chapter.
   F. Save and close the drawing.

Creating Custom Schedule Information

Learning Objectives

After completing this chapter, you will be able to do the following:
- ✓ Create custom property set definitions.
- ✓ Attach property set definitions to styles and definitions.
- ✓ Add properties to property set definitions.
- ✓ Add manual and automatic data properties.
- ✓ Create a data format style.
- ✓ Construct custom schedules.
- ✓ Create custom schedule tags.

An advantage of using Architectural Desktop is that default *schedule tags*, *property set definitions*, and *schedules* can be customized to look and provide information the way you desire. This chapter explains the procedures for creating custom property set definitions, schedules, and tags.

Custom Property Set Definitions

Architectural Desktop includes many property set definitions that can be assigned to individual objects or object styles. These default property set definitions can be found in Schedule Tables.dwg, located in the \\Styles folder.

In addition to these property set definitions, custom property set definitions can be created to reflect any type of property value desired. The first step in creating a custom property set definition is to access the **PROPERTYSETDEFINE** command. This command can be accessed by picking **Document** > **Scheduling** > **Property Set Definitions...** or by typing PROPERTYSETDEFINE. This opens the Property Set Definitions section of the **Style Manager**. See **Figure 23-1.**

To create a custom property set definition, pick the **New Style** button within the **Style Manager** or select the **Property Set Definitions** icon, right-click, and select **New** from the shortcut menu. A new property set definition is created. Type a new name for the property set definition and highlight the new style to begin editing it. This displays property tabs for the highlighted property set definition.

Type
PROPERTYSETDEFINE
Pull-Down Menu
Document > Scheduling   > Property Set   Definitions...

PROPERTYSETDEFINE

Figure 23-1.
The **Style Manager** is displayed when the **PROPERTYSETDEFINE** command is accessed.

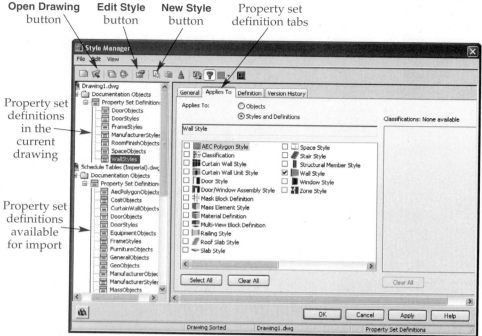

The **General** tab is used to rename the property set definition, provide a description for its use, or apply design notes to the definition. The **Applies To** tab is used to determine how the property set definition is applied in the drawing. See **Figure 23-1**. The property set definition can be applied either to objects (individual objects) or to styles and definitions (by object style). This tab is described in greater detail in the next section. The **Definition** tab is used to add and edit available properties within the property set definition. This tab is also described in the following section.

Applying Property Set Definitions

After a new property set definition has been created, it must be applied to an object. There are two types of property set definitions: definitions applied or attached to individual objects or entities and definitions attached to an object style. The **Applies To** tab is used to select the type of object to which the property set definition is assigned.

At the top of this tab are two radio button options: **Objects** and **Styles and Definitions**. See **Figure 23-2**. The **Objects** radio button sets up the property set definition so it can be attached to individual AEC objects or AutoCAD entities. The **Styles and Definitions** radio button is used to set up the property set definition for use with AEC object styles.

Attaching Property Set Definitions to Objects and Entities

To make the property set definition available only to individual objects and entities, select the **Objects** radio button. The **Applies To** tab lists the types of AEC and AutoCAD objects the property set definition can be applied to. See **Figure 23-2**. A check next to an object or entity name indicates that the property set definition can be attached only to that type of object. For example, in **Figure 23-2**, a check beside **Structural Member** indicates that the property set definition can be attached only to individual structural members in the drawing.

A property set definition can be applied to any or all of the items in the list or to only one item in the list. The **Select All** button below the list on the left places a check in all the boxes in the list. The **Clear All** button below the list on the left clears all the check marks.

Figure 23-2.
The **Applies To** tab for property set definitions is used to assign the property set definition to individual object types or object styles.

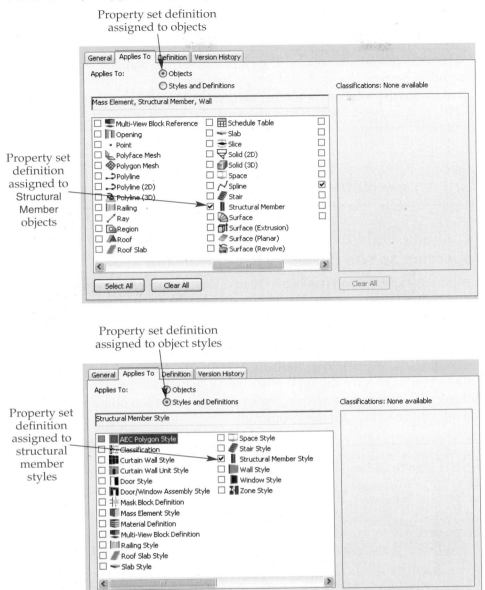

Property set definition assigned to objects

Property set definition assigned to Structural Member objects

Property set definition assigned to object styles

Property set definition assigned to structural member styles

Once this type of property set definition has been defined, it can be attached to individual AEC objects or to AutoCAD entities through the **Extended Data** tab in the **Properties** palette.

Attaching Property Set Definitions to Styles and Definitions

To make the property set definition available only to AEC object styles, select the **Styles and Definitions** radio button. When this option is selected, a list of AEC object styles becomes available, as shown in **Figure 23-2**.

The list includes the object styles and definitions in Architectural Desktop to which the property set definition can be attached. A check mark beside a style or definition name indicates that the property set definition can be assigned to that style or definition. The **Select All** button below the list places a check in all the style check boxes. The **Clear All** button removes all the check marks beside the style names.

A property set definition can be attached to one or more styles by selecting the appropriate boxes from the list. Once the property set definition has been defined, it can be attached to the style or definition by accessing the appropriate style or definition properties command. In the **General** tab for the style, pick the **Property Sets...** button to add the property set definition to the style.

NOTE

The **Classifications** area on the right side of the **Applies To** tab is not used in a property set definition. When creating a custom schedule, a list of classifications is available to filter for information to be included. This is discussed later in this chapter.

Exercise
23-1

Complete the Exercise on the Student CD.

Adding Properties to the Property Set Definition

Once a property set definition has been created and the objects or styles it will be assigned to have been selected, properties to be included in a schedule can be added. When editing a property set definition, the **Definition** tab is used to assign both *manual data* and *automatic data*. See **Figure 23-3**.

The **Definition** tab is a table of properties that can be reported on. The tab lists all properties assigned to the property set definition. It also includes property definition buttons that allow you to specify the type of property to be added to the property set definition. Picking different values within a property displays the ellipsis (...) button, where you can adjust the values for the properties.

Figure 23-3.
The **Definition** tab is used to add and configure properties for the property set definition.

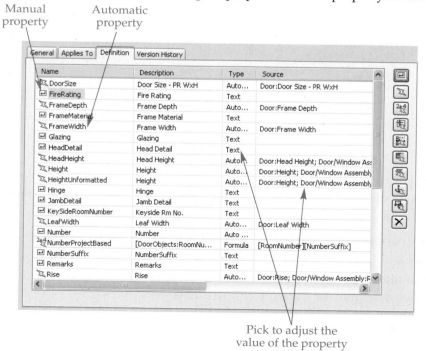

Architectural Desktop and Its Applications

Adding Manual Property Definitions

Before a manual property definition can be configured, it needs to be added to the **Definition** tab. Pick the **Add Manual Property Definition** button to the right of the property list to add a new user-defined property to the list. Picking this button displays the **New Property** dialog box. See **Figure 23-4.** Enter a name for the new property. Below the **Name:** text box is the **Start With:** drop-down list, which includes a list of all the properties currently defined in the drawing. Selecting one of these properties sets the parameters for the new property equal to the values for a previously defined property. Pick the **OK** button when you have finished.

A new property is added to the list area of the dialog box in **Figure 23-4.** In order to configure the values for the new property, select the property values for the property in the table. Depending on the type of value, a property can be renamed in a text box. An ellipsis (**...**) button may be displayed so a dialog box can be accessed, or a drop-down list of choices may be available. The following are value settings affecting the manual property definition:

- **Name.** Select this value to rename the property.
- **Description.** Pick this value to display the ellipsis (**...**) button so a description may be entered for the property.
- **Type.** Picking this value displays a drop-down list arrow. This drop-down list establishes the type of information the property is supposed to reflect. The following options are included in this list:
  - **Auto Increment - Character.** This setting sequentially alphabetizes the value as new property set definitions are added to objects in the drawing.
  - **Auto Increment - Integer.** This setting sequentially numbers the value as new property set definitions are added to objects in the drawing.

Figure 23-4.
A new manual property has been added to the property set definition, and its settings are being configured.

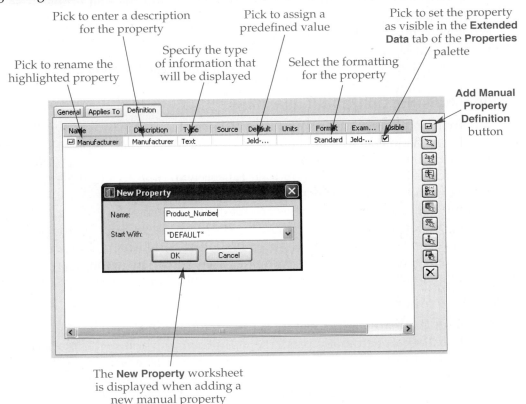

Pick to rename the highlighted property

Pick to enter a description for the property

Specify the type of information that will be displayed

Pick to assign a predefined value

Select the formatting for the property

Pick to set the property as visible in the **Extended Data** tab of the **Properties** palette

Add Manual Property Definition button

The **New Property** worksheet is displayed when adding a new manual property

- **Integer.** This type of formatting requires the input of a whole number. Examples include –3, 12, and 0.
- **List.** This option becomes available if a list definition is available in a drawing. A list definition is a list of information often repeatedly entered into a schedule, such as the color of the walls in different rooms or the manufacturer of different pieces of equipment or furniture. List definitions were discussed in Chapter 21.
- **Real.** This formatting requires the input of a real number. Examples include 1.25, 4.0, and .75.
- **Text.** This type indicates the property information is textual content instead of numerical content.
- **True/False.** This type indicates the property must be a true or false value.

- **Source.** This value indicates the source of the property. This column is used only in automatic value properties because the value may be derived from a style, definition, or symbol.
- **Default.** This text box value allows you to enter a default value for the property. A value entered in this text box becomes the default value for the property the next time the property set definition is attached to an AEC object.
- **Units.** This value displays the units applied to properties of measurement, such as the width or height of a door.
- **Format.** This drop-down list includes different formatting styles available for the property values. For example, a Case - Upper style makes any information in the property all uppercase in the **Edit Property Set Data** worksheet and within the schedule table. Creating custom data format styles is discussed later in this chapter.
- **Example.** This text box displays the default property value in its formatted form.
- **Visible.** This check box value determines whether the value is displayed in the schedule and **Extended Data** tab of the **Properties** palette.
- **Order.** This text box value is used to set the order the properties in the property set definition appear in the **Extended Data** tab and the **Edit Property Set Data** worksheet.

When you finish configuring the property, you can create additional manual data properties by picking the **Add Manual Property Definition** button and then formatting. If an automatic property is desired, select the **Add Automatic Property Definition** button.

Adding Automatic Data Properties

Automatic properties are properties with values derived directly from an object style or an individual object in the drawing. Unlike manual properties, where the value is set by the user, automatic properties query the style or object for a specific property, such as the door width, window style, or wall type, to add the information to the property set definition for inclusion in a schedule.

A number of automatic properties are available when creating a property set definition. Automatic properties are indicated by a lightning bolt symbol in the property set definition and on the button used to add them to the definition. There are eight types of automatic properties: automatic, formula, location, classification, material, project, anchor, and graphic. All of these properties are described in the following sections.

Automatic Property Definitions

Although there are eight separate types of automatic properties, one of them is specifically called an automatic property definition. The automatic property definition includes a list of properties specific to the type of object to which the property set definition is applied. To add an automatic property definition to the property set definition, pick the **Add Automatic Property Definition** button under the **Definition** tab for the property set definition.

When this button is selected, the **Automatic Property Source** worksheet is displayed, as shown in **Figure 23-5**. This worksheet lists the available automatic properties for the type of object to which the property set definition is being applied. Automatic properties for the Door/Window Assembly and Window objects are displayed in **Figure 23-5**. The property set definition is being applied to Door, Door/Window Assembly, and Window objects.

Scroll through the list until you find the type of automatic property you want to use in your property set definition. Place a check in the corresponding box. After selecting the type of property to be added to the property set definition, pick the **OK** button to add the property to the list. The new property can now be configured.

Many of the property values available for manual properties are also available for automatic properties. Pick any of the values to edit the default values to values of your choosing.

Formula Property Definitions

Another type of automatic property is the *formula property definition*. Formula property definitions can be used to compute a value based on the values of other property data. For example, to compute the area of the door, the width and height properties must be multiplied together. Before a formula using other properties can be created, the properties to be used in the formula must be present. Once these properties have been added to the property set definition, they can be used in the formula property.

To add a formula property definition, pick the **Add Formula Property Definition** button in the **Definition** tab. This opens the **Formula Property Definition** worksheet, shown in **Figure 23-6**. Begin the process of creating a formula by entering a name for the property in the **Name:** text box. The name entered is the name of the property displayed in the property set definition.

Below the **Name:** text box is a check box relating to the description of the formula property. If the box is checked, the formula created is used as the description. Below the **Description** check box is the **Formula** area.

Figure 23-5.
The **Automatic Property Source** worksheet displays the available properties for the type of object to which the property set definition is applied.

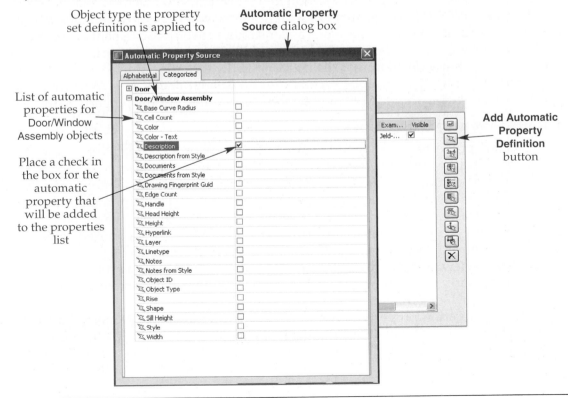

Object type the property set definition is applied to

Automatic Property Source dialog box

List of automatic properties for Door/Window Assembly objects

Place a check in the box for the automatic property that will be added to the properties list

Add Automatic Property Definition button

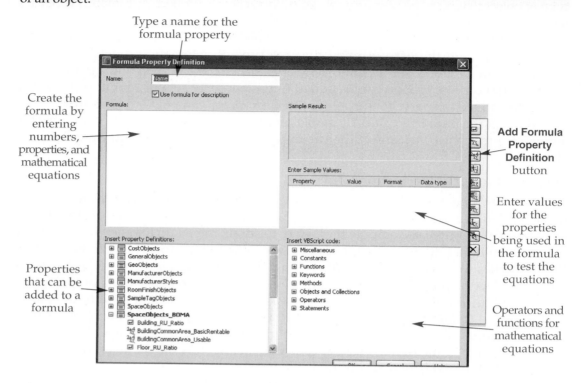

Type a name for the formula property

Create the formula by entering numbers, properties, and mathematical equations

Add Formula Property Definition button

Enter values for the properties being used in the formula to test the equations

Properties that can be added to a formula

Operators and functions for mathematical equations

The **Formula** area is used to create a formula for the property. Numbers, properties, operators, and other VBScript codes can be entered for the formula. Picking a property from the **Insert Property Definitions:** area at the bottom-left corner of the worksheet allows you to use the property value of an object in the equation. Picking the property adds it to the formula and displays it as text within brackets [ ]. If text or numbers are to be added, pick the location in the formula and enter the text.

The **Insert VBScript code:** area to the right of the **Insert Property Definitions:** area can be used to add VBScript codes, such as constants, functions, statements, and operators, to the formula. Examples include +, -, *, and /. If text or properties are to be included within a set of brackets, highlight the portions of the formula, and then double-click the () found in the **Miscellaneous** section of the **VBScript codes** area. When you are finished creating the formula, pick the **OK** button to add the formula property to the list.

Location Property Definitions

Location property values report on an AEC object's property data relating to any inclusive or nearby AEC polygons or spaces. When a selected object in the drawing, such as a door, includes a property set definition containing a location property, a **Data Location** grip is displayed along with its other grips, if the location property has been defined to retrieve property data from a Space object. For example, the property data comes from the space underneath the grip on the Door object being reported on. When the object is moved near a different Space object, the grip moves too.

If a multi-view block representing a piece of furniture includes a property set with a location property and is moved from one space to another, it has access to the space's property data, which might include the occupant of a room.

To add a location property definition, pick the **Add Location Property Definition** button. This displays the **Location Property Definition** dialog box, shown in **Figure 23-7.** Enter a name for the location property definition in the **Name:** text box at the top of the dialog box. In the property set definition list box at the bottom of the dialog box,

Figure 23-7.
The addition of a location property can keep track of where properties of an object are when they are located in or next to an AEC polygon or Space object.

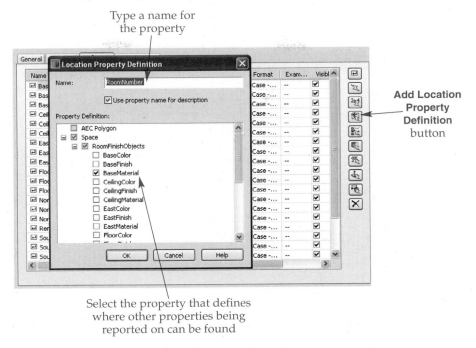

Type a name for the property

Add Location Property Definition button

Select the property that defines where other properties being reported on can be found

select a property from an AEC polygon or Space object to be used as the location property. If the description of the location property definition needs to match the selected property, select the **Description** check box. When you are finished adding the location property, pick the **OK** button to add the property to the property set definition list.

Classification Property Definitions

Property set definitions can be assigned to the individual classifications within a *classification definition* for additional reporting power. A property set definition being created for an object other than a classification definition can report on the value of a classification assigned to an object style or the properties of the classification assigned to a style.

To add a classification property definition to a property set, pick the **Add Classification Property Definition** button in the **Definition** tab of the **Property Set Definition Properties** dialog box. This displays the **Classification Property Definition** dialog. See **Figure 23-8.**

The dialog is split up into two list boxes. The **Classification Definition:** list box on the left side of the dialog lists all the classification definitions in the drawing that can be used on the type of object to which the property set definition is applied. Selecting a classification from this list will evaluate all the classifications assigned to each of the object styles being reported on.

The **Classification Property:** list box on the right is used to list specific properties assigned to a classification. If the property set definition is to report on a specific property assigned to a classification assigned to an object style, select the **Classification Property:** check box, and pick the property to be reported on. Enter a name for the new property in the **Name:** text box list and decide if the description is derived from the selected properties or not. When you are finished, pick the **OK** button to add the property to the property set.

Figure 23-8.
A classification property is used to report on the classification value or the classification value's property.

Type a name for the
property being added

Choose an
entire
classification
definition
to report on

Add
Classification
Property
Definition
button

Choose a
specific
classification
property to
report on

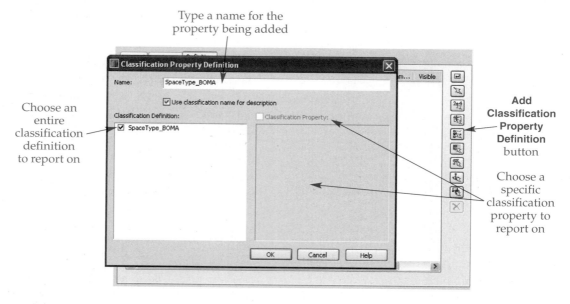

Material Property Definitions

If a material has been assigned to the different components in an object style, these properties can be extracted and placed in a schedule. The *material property definition* is used to report on the materials assigned to components within an object.

To add a material property to the property set, pick the **Add Material Property Definition** button in the **Definition** tab of the **Property Set Definition Properties** dialog box. See **Figure 23-9.** This displays the **Material Property Definition** dialog box.

The dialog box is split into two separate list boxes. The **Material:** list box lists the type of AEC objects and their components to which the property set definition is applied. If you want to report on the material assigned to a specific component, select the object's style and component to be reported on.

Figure 23-9.
The **Material Property Definition** dialog box is used to select a component in an AEC object style and report its material to the property set definition.

Type a name for
the property

Choose the
component
that contains a
material to be
reported

Pick if a
property
assigned to a
material is to
be reported

Add Material
Property
Definition
button

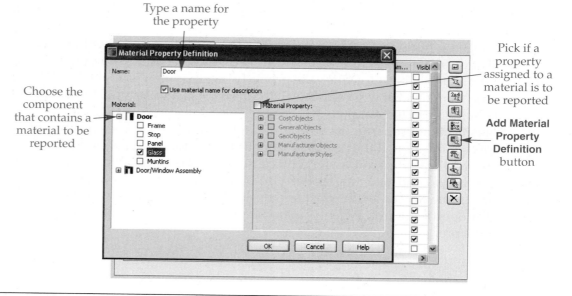

The **Material Property:** list box on the right side lists additional property set definitions that can be assigned to a material definition. The object style may be queried if it contains components that have materials assigned to them. These materials can have properties assigned to them, which are reported on by material properties. If this is the case, select the **Material Property:** check box, expand any of the desired property set definitions in the list, and select the properties to be reported on.

Enter a name for the material property being added to the property set definition. If the description for the material property is to use the material name being reported, select the **Description** check box under the **Name:** text box. When you are finished selecting the properties to be reported, pick the **OK** button to add the property to the property set definition.

Project Property Definitions

Project property definitions report on drawings within a drawing project managed by the **Project Navigator**. Drawing projects are linked together and remember information, such as the elevation of each floor, what is displayed, the sheet name, and project number. The **Project Browser** and **Project Navigator** are tools designed to help you manage a drawing project.

If you are working on a drawing tied to a project, you can create property set definitions that report on different properties within the project. To add a project property definition to the property set, pick the **Add Project Property Definition** button in the **Definition** tab of the **Property Set Definition Properties** dialog box. This displays the **Project Property Definition** dialog box. Project properties are displayed in the **Project Information:** list box. See **Figure 23-10**. Select one of the properties to be reported on, enter a name for the property, and then pick the **OK** button to add the property to the property set definition.

Anchor Property Definitions

Anchor properties allow an object being reported on to obtain information from another object to which it is anchored. For example, an anchor property for a door within a two-hour fire-rated wall could display the two-hour fire rating of the wall with an anchor property definition specified for the door.

Figure 23-10.
Project property definitions can report the values of drawing project values. Before a project property can be defined, the drawing must belong to a drawing project.

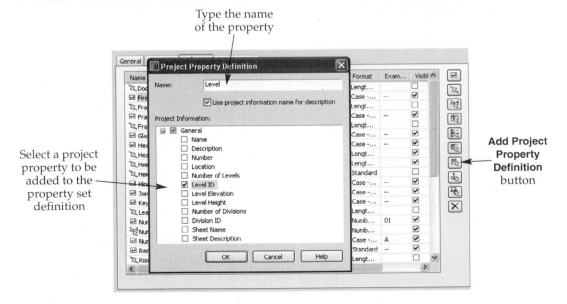

Type the name of the property

Select a project property to be added to the property set definition

Add Project Property Definition button

To add an anchor property to the property set definition, select the **Add Anchor Property Definition** button in the **Definition** tab. This displays the **Anchor Property Definition** dialog box. See **Figure 23-11**.

Enter a name for the new property in the **Name:** text box. Next, choose a property definition to be reported on when the object this property set definition is applied to is anchored to the object. For example, if a property set definition for a door is being created and you want to report on the name of the space the door is anchored to, select the **SpaceObjects Name** property.

Graphic Property Definitions

The *graphic property definition* is used to add a graphic property to a property set definition. Graphic property values can be blocks in the current drawing or image files, such as BMP, GIF, JPG, PNG, or TIF files. This property can be especially helpful when creating a schedule that reports on the object number, such as a door number, and includes the door tag symbol around the number property in the schedule.

Schedules display blocks as graphic properties only if the blocks exist in the current drawing. If you copy a schedule or a schedule table style to a new drawing, make sure you also copy all blocks. To create a graphic property definition, pick the **Add Graphic Property Definition** button in the **Definition** tab. **Figure 23-12** displays the **Graphic Property Definition** dialog box.

In this dialog box, type a name for the graphic property in the **Name:** text box. Under the **Source** area, choose whether to have the graphic property created by using a block or an image file. Depending on the type of source chosen, the **Block Name:** or **Image Name:** text boxes are available. The **Browse...** button can be used to browse for external drawings, blocks, or images to be used as the graphic. Use the **Rotation** area to set the rotation angle for the graphic property. At the bottom of the dialog box is the **Layer Key** area. Selecting a layer key for the graphic places the graphic on a specific layer when the graphic is added to a schedule.

Removing Properties from a Property Set Definition

As you are creating property set definitions, you may need to remove properties that are no longer required for scheduling. To remove a property from a property set definition, select the property to be removed, and then pick the **Remove** button under the **Definition** tab. This removes the property from the list.

Figure 23-11.
The **Anchor Property Definition** dialog box is used to select a property belonging to an object in which the object being reported on is anchored to it.

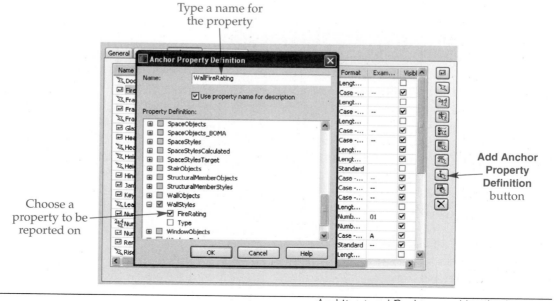

Type a name for the property

Choose a property to be reported on

Add Anchor Property Definition button

Figure 23-12.
Graphic property definitions are used to create a graphic from a block or an image, which in turn, is used within a schedule. When door numbers in the drawing are reported in a schedule, a graphic door tag symbol can be displayed in the schedule. This symbol is derived from the graphic property definition.

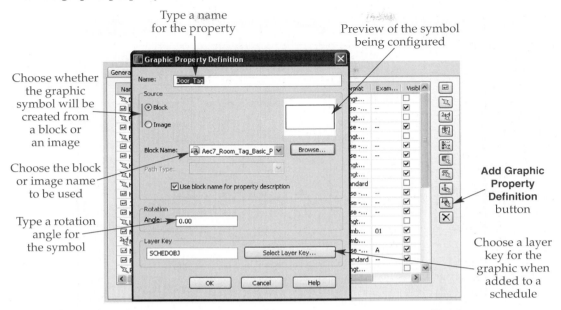

Exercise 23-2 Complete the Exercise on the Student CD.

Creating a Data Format Style

When configuring the properties in the property set definition, you have the option of choosing the type of formatting to apply to the data. The type of *data formatting* selected affects how information in the schedule tables, schedule tags, and the **Edit Property Set Data** worksheet appears. Architectural Desktop includes several different types of data formats and provides you with a tool to create your own types of formatting.

Data formats include one or two zeros in front of a number, uppercase or lowercase text, and a $ in front of a number for cost schedules. To create or modify a data format style, pick **Document** > **Scheduling** > **Data Format Styles...** or type PROPERTYFORMATDEFINE. This opens the **Style Manager** to the Property Data Formats section, as shown in Figure 23-13.

After the **Style Manager** has been opened, select the **New Style** button to create a new data format style. Enter a new name for the data format style. After the new data format style has been created, highlight the style in the tree view to display the style's property tabs in the right pane. See Figure 23-13.

The **Data Format Style** includes two tabs: **General** and **Formatting**. The **General** tab is used to name/rename the style and to add a description and notes. The **Formatting** tab is used to format the style. The **Formatting** tab is organized into the following six areas:

- **General.** This area is used to control the general settings for displaying property data and includes the following four text boxes:
  - **Prefix.** Enter a prefix for schedule property data. For example, if you are creating a format style that will be used in a pricing property, you may use $ as a prefix before a dollar amount or a set of letters before a manufacturer's model number.

Figure 23-13.
The Property Data Formats section of the **Style Manager** can be used to create and modify data format styles.

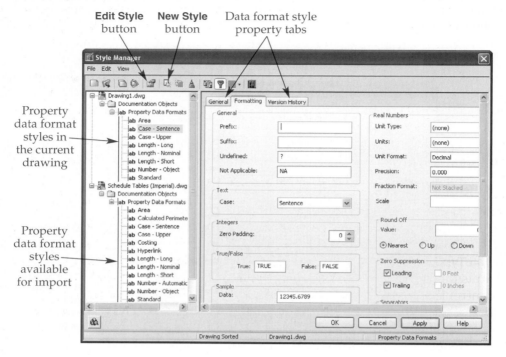

- **Suffix.** Enter a suffix for the schedule property data. For example, if you are using the format style for an area property, you may use the suffix SF to represent square feet.
- **Undefined.** This text box is used as a default property value for any value within a property that has not been defined in the property set definition. By default, the symbol ? is used, causing the schedule to produce question marks in the schedule for properties that have not been filled out. You may want to change this symbol to a hyphen or remove the value because the hyphen or an empty value may look better in a schedule when properties have not been specified.
- **Not Applicable.** This text box specifies text for a property that is not applicable in a schedule. Enter a text string in the text box to be displayed when the requested property does not apply to an object. For example, the rise property does not apply to a window with a rectangular opening, but it does apply to one with an arched top. The default setting of NA is then substituted in the schedule to indicate that the rise does not apply to the rectangular window.
- **Text.** This area includes options for controlling the appearance of text in a schedule property. There are five options available in the **Case:** drop-down list. The **As Is** option enters the data into the schedule and the property set definition as typed by the end user. The **Upper** option capitalizes all the letters of each word in a string of text entered in the property value, while the **Lower** option displays property text as all lowercase letters in the text string entered in the property value. The **Sentence** option capitalizes the first letter of the first word in a string of text entered in the property value. The **Title** option capitalizes the first letter of each word in a string of text entered in the property value.

- **Integers.** This area is used to specify the maximum length of a number after it has been "padded" with leading zeros before the number. This area is used when identity numbers are created, such as the numbers used for door and window tags. In the **Zero Padding:** list box, enter a number representing the total number of digits to be used for the number. For example, a padding value of 3 will cause the number 7 to appear as 007 or the value 21 to appear as 021.
- **True/False.** This area is used for property values using a true/false type value in the property. Type the text to appear in the schedule for a true statement in the **True:** text box and the text to appear in a false statement in the **False:** text box.
- **Sample.** This area is used to display an example of the settings specified in the **Real Numbers** area. Enter a value in the **Data:** text box to see the end result in the **Result:** field.
- **Set From Dimension Style.** Selecting this button provides you with a list of dimension styles in the drawing that can be used to format the values in this dialog box.
- **Real Numbers.** This area is used to configure numerical property values of the properties within a schedule or property set definition. The following settings are available:
  - **Unit Type.** Select the drop-down list to choose from several different types of units for formatting any numerical data in the property values. The options control the type of information provided in the **Units:** drop-down list.
  - **Units.** The available options are based on the type chosen in the **Unit Type:** drop-down list. More specific units may be chosen to format a property within a property set definition or schedule.
  - **Unit Format.** This drop-down list includes up to five different options: **Scientific**, **Decimal**, **Engineering**, **Architectural**, and **Fractional**. Depending on the unit type and units chosen in the previous two drop-down lists, one or more of these options may be available for formatting.
  - **Precision.** Enter a value for the precision level of the numerical unit formatting. This number directly corresponds to the unit type, units, and unit format selected. For example, a precision of .25 is used with decimal units, and a precision of 1/4" is used with architectural units.
  - **Fraction Format.** This area is available if the **Architectural** or **Fractional** unit formats have been selected. This option allows you to control how fractional values within a property are to appear.
  - **Scale.** This text box is used to enter a value by which a real number is scaled before it is added to the schedule. For example, if the current drawing units are inches, a scale of 25.4 converts the number to millimeters, and a scale of 2.54 converts the number to centimeters.
  - **Round Off.** This area rounds off the numerical value in the schedule or property set definition to the nearest value entered in this text box. For example, a value of .25 rounds the numerical value in the property to the nearest 1/4".
  - **Zero Suppression.** This area controls the visibility of zeroes before and after the numerical value. If a check is placed in the **Leading** (for decimal units) or **0 Feet** (for architectural units) box, zeros before the number are suppressed in the schedule. If a check is placed in the **Trailing** (for decimal units) or **0 Inches** (for architectural units) box, zeros after the number are suppressed.
  - **Separators.** This option controls how decimals and whole numbers are separated in a numerical property value. Both drop-down lists include a period, comma, and space as a separator.

After a new data format style has been created, it can be applied to the properties within a property set definition and a schedule table.

Exercise
23-3   *Complete the Exercise on the Student CD.*

Creating Custom Schedules

The schedules included with Architectural Desktop provide a basic set of information often required within a schedule. Often, offices use their own standards for schedule organization and the types of information that must be included in the schedule. The schedule styles included with Architectural Desktop can be modified to fit individual needs.

Custom schedule styles can also be created to report any type of information available in an AutoCAD or Architectural Desktop object. The only requirements for creating a custom schedule are as follows:

1. The data must be available for the object. These can be found by viewing the automatic properties of a particular object.
2. The properties desired in the schedule must be included in a property set definition.

Type
SCHEDULESTYLE
Pull-Down Menu
Document > Scheduling > Schedule Table Styles...

Once the appropriate property set definitions have been established, the custom schedule can be created, or an exiting schedule can be modified. To create a custom schedule, pick **Document** > **Scheduling** > **Schedule Table Styles...** or type SCHEDULESTYLE. The **Style Manager** opens to the Schedule Table Styles section. See **Figure 23-14.**

If you are going to edit a schedule style, select the desired schedule table from the tree view, and begin editing the properties of the schedule. If you are going to create a new style, select the **New Style** button, or right-click over the **Schedule Table Styles** icon or within the right pane and select **New** from the shortcut menu. After you have created a new style, name the style.

Once you have created the new style and entered the name, highlight the style in the tree view to edit it. Highlighting a schedule style displays the property tabs for the style, as in **Figure 23-14.** A schedule style includes the following property tabs:

*   **General.** This tab is used to rename the schedule table style and to provide a description for the schedule. Any additional notes or references can be added using the **Notes...** button in this tab.
*   **Default Format.** This tab controls the formatting applying to each cell within the schedule, unless the cell is overridden. See **Figure 23-15.** The following settings are available in this tab:
    *   **Style.** This drop-down list includes a list of text styles in the current drawing. Additional styles can be configured by using the **STYLE** command.
    *   **Alignment.** This drop-down list allows you to justify the text within a cell in the table. Options allow you to justify the text to the left or right or to center the text within the cell.

SCHEDULESTYLE

Architectural Desktop and Its Applications

Figure 23-14.
The Schedule Table Styles section of the **Style Manager** is used to create and edit schedule table styles.

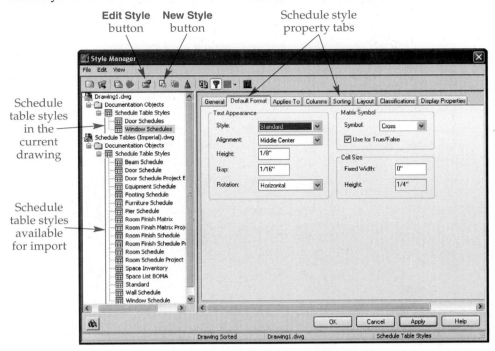

- **Height.** This text box is used to specify the height of the text within the schedule table as it should appear when plotted. Like documentation symbols, the schedule table is scaled by the drawing scale set up in the **Drawing Setup** dialog box.
- **Gap.** This text box allows you to specify the distance from the text to the cell border. This gap is applied all the way around the text.
- **Rotation.** This drop-down list allows you to set the schedule's text as horizontal or vertical.
- **Symbol.** This drop-down list is used to specify a symbol type when a schedule table is created displaying a matrix. See **Figure 23-15.** A matrix can be used when the value of a single property can have many different options. For example, the finish material property can be used in different rooms where different types of finishes are being applied.
- **Use for True/False.** This check box is used when a true/false property should be incorporated into a matrix schedule.
- **Fixed Width.** This text box allows you to set a fixed width for the cells in the schedule. If the value is set to 0″, the cells of the schedule are determined automatically based on the length of text in the property set definitions.
- **Height.** The height in the **Cell Size** area is a value automatically determined by the combination of the text height and the gap values.
- **Applies To.** Like property set definitions, the schedule table needs to be associated with an object reported within the schedule table. Select the type of object the schedule is used for by placing a check mark beside the object name from the list on the left, as shown in **Figure 23-16.**

The **Classifications:** list box on the right side of the tab lists any classifications defined in the drawing that can be applied to the same objects applied to the schedule. If the schedule is to report only on objects meeting a specific classification criteria, select the classification to be filtered from the list on the right. For example, if you wanted to add only furniture blocks being relocated in a building to the schedule, the

Figure 23-15.
The **Default Format** tab is used to set up default formatting for the information within the cells of a schedule. These settings can be overridden in the **Layout** tab.

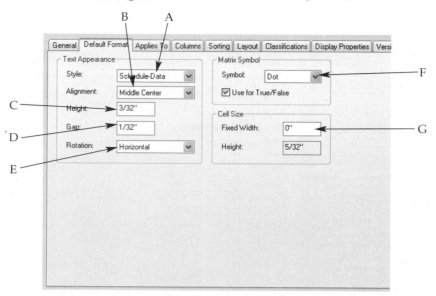

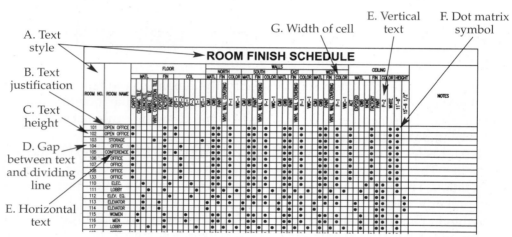

Relocate classification would be picked so the schedule would only filter for relocated furniture blocks. See **Figure 23-16.**

- **Columns.** This tab is used to configure the actual information to be reported. See **Figure 23-17.** The table area displays the properties from the property set definitions that will be reported on. The properties can be organized so the columns of information are arranged as desired. This tab includes several options for configuring the columns within the schedule.

  To begin adding columns of information, select the **Add Column...** button to display the **Add Column** worksheet, where properties can be selected and added to the schedule. See **Figure 23-18.** Select a property from one of the property set definition lists and pick the **OK** button to add the column to the schedule table. Continue pressing the **Add Column...** button to add columns to the schedule. Once you have added all the columns of information, you can move to the next tab. Adding and configuring the columns within the table is discussed in greater depth in the next section.

Figure 23-16.
The **Applies To** tab is used to apply the schedule to the objects that will be reported on in the schedule. Classifications can also be selected to be used as filters for the schedule information.

If the schedule will filter information about an object that is assigned a specific classification, select one or more classifications

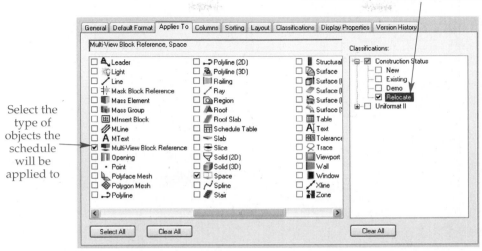

Select the type of objects the schedule will be applied to

Figure 23-17.
The **Columns** tab is used to add and configure columns for the schedule table.

Columns tab

First column in the table

Property set definition being referenced

Property from the property set that is being reported on

Pick to add a property to report on to the schedule

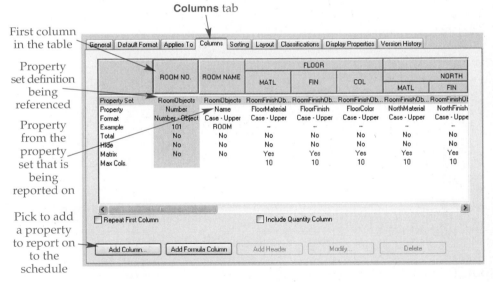

- **Sorting.** This tab is used to sort the property values from a property within the schedule. Information can be sorted in ascending or descending order. This feature may be used when numerical or alphabetic information such as door numbers or equipment numbers are sorted. Use the **Add...** button to add a column that will be sorted. Multiple columns can be sorted by picking the **Add...** button several times and selecting a new column each time. See **Figure 23-19.** You can remove columns being sorted and move them up or down the list by using the appropriate buttons at the top of the tab.

Figure 23-18.

Figure 23-18.
The **Add Column** worksheet is used to add properties that will be reported on in the schedule and form the columns of the schedule table.

Property set definitions available for the type of object being reported on

Select one property to add as a column to the schedule

Properties within each property set definition

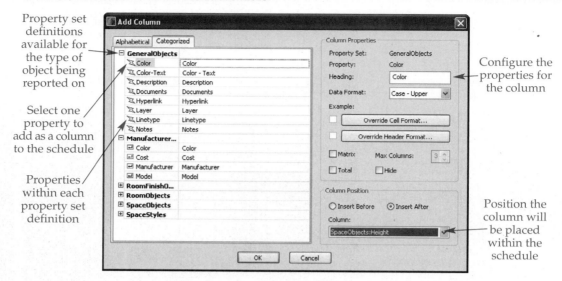

Configure the properties for the column

Position the column will be placed within the schedule

Figure 23-19.
The **Sorting** tab is used to sort property values alphabetically or numerically within a column.

Sorting tab

Pick to select a column to sort

Column/ property to be sorted

Select the type of sorting for the selected column

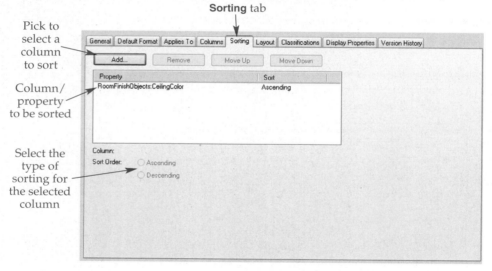

- **Layout.** This tab is used to configure how the title, header titles, and text information appear in the schedule table, which is shown in **Figure 23-20.** The text box at the top of this tab allows you to enter a title that appears at the top of the schedule table. Below the title text box are three buttons labeled **Override Cell Format**. Each of these buttons allows you to override how the schedule text is formatted in the **Default Format** tab.

  Picking one of the buttons displays the **Cell Format Override** dialog. This dialog contains the same information as found in the **Default Format** tab and allows you to format the title, column header titles, and matrix headers (information in the schedule).

- **Classifications.** This tab is used to specify a classification assigned to the schedule table.

Figure 23-20.
The **Layout** tab is used to override the settings found in the **Default Format** tab and to apply the overrides to the different text portions of the schedule table.

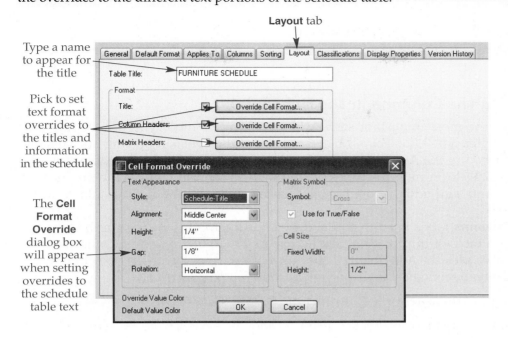

Type a name to appear for the title

Pick to set text format overrides to the titles and information in the schedule

The **Cell Format Override** dialog box will appear when setting overrides to the schedule table text

- **Display Properties.** This tab is used to configure the display settings for the Schedule object. See **Figure 23-21**. The General display representation is the only representation available. Attach a style override to configure the display of the schedule style. Once the override has been set, pick the **Edit Display Properties** button to configure the display of components, such as lines and text within the schedule.

Figure 23-21.
The **Display Properties** tab is used to configure the display properties for the schedule table.

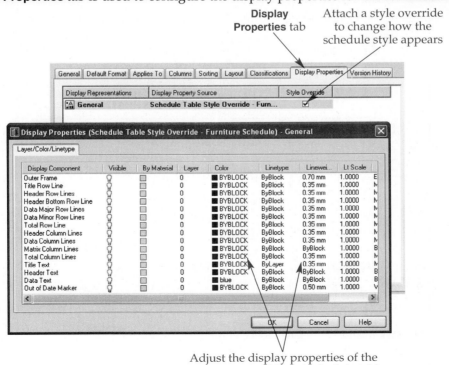

Adjust the display properties of the components within the schedule table

After you have configured the schedule table, pick the **OK** button to return to the drawing. The schedule table is now ready to be added to the drawing.

Exercise 23-4   *Complete the Exercise on the Student CD.*

Developing the Columns in the Schedule

One of the most important steps when creating or modifying a schedule is to determine what type of object or objects the schedule table is reporting on. This task is accomplished in the **Applies To** tab in the **Style Manager** for the schedule style. See **Figure 23-16.** Determining the types of objects to be reported makes the property set definitions and individual properties associated with those objects available in the **Columns** tab.

The **Columns** tab is used to add and configure the columns within the schedule to produce a table of information. See **Figure 23-22.** To begin adding columns to the schedule table, pick the **Add Column...** button located in the lower-left corner of the tab. The **Add Column** worksheet is displayed, as shown in **Figure 23-23.**

Adding and Configuring a Column

The **Add Column** worksheet is used to add the property to be reported on to the schedule and to configure how the information appears in the schedule. See **Figure 23-23.** The left side of the worksheet includes a list of property set definitions assigned to the same individual objects and object styles to which the schedule table is assigned. Select a property from the list to add to the schedule table.

Once a property has been selected, its name appears in the **Heading:** text box on the right. The text entered here is the text that appears as the header title in the schedule. Use the **Data Format:** drop-down list to select a type of formatting to apply to the information in this column that appears in the schedule.

Figure 23-22.
The **Columns** tab is used to add columns of information to the schedule table.

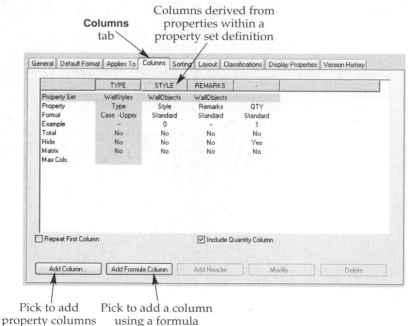

Pick to add property columns   Pick to add a column using a formula

---

Architectural Desktop and Its Applications

Figure 23-23.
The **Add Column** worksheet is used to add and configure a column for the schedule table.

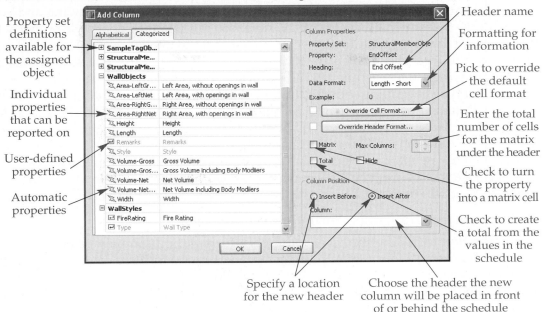

Property set definitions available for the assigned object

Individual properties that can be reported on

User-defined properties

Automatic properties

Header name

Formatting for information

Pick to override the default cell format

Enter the total number of cells for the matrix under the header

Check to turn the property into a matrix cell

Check to create a total from the values in the schedule

Specify a location for the new header

Choose the header the new column will be placed in front of or behind the schedule

The **Default Format** tab formats how all the data within the schedule appears. The **Override Cell Format...** button is used to control how the information within the cells below the header appears. Picking this button displays the **Cell Format Override** dialog. Make any adjustments to the text height, justification, and gap for the reported information. Below the **Override Cell Format...** button is the **Override Header Format...** button. As with the **Override Cell Format...** button, picking this button displays the **Cell Format Override** dialog. In this case, it controls the display of the header cell.

Below the **Override Header Format...** button is the **Matrix** check box. Selecting this box makes the **Max Columns:** list box available. Both of these options are used to turn the column into a matrix type of schedule. See **Figure 23-24.**

When the column is turned into a matrix, any values entered for the property in the **Edit Property Set Data** worksheet are sorted into separate columns under the heading title. The **Max Columns:** text box indicates the maximum number of values for the matrix column. For example, in **Figure 23-24**, the north wall finish property is being reported on. As the column is turned into a matrix, the maximum number of values that can be reported on is three. If other objects have four different values for the ceiling material, only the first three are displayed in the schedule.

Figure 23-24.
Example of a matrix schedule.

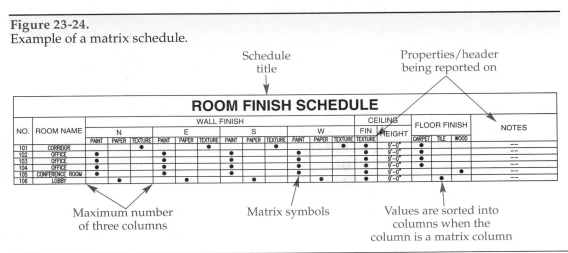

Schedule title

Properties/header being reported on

Maximum number of three columns

Matrix symbols

Values are sorted into columns when the column is a matrix column

Below the **Matrix** check box is the **Total** check box. This box is not available if the **Matrix** check box has been selected. Selecting this box provides a total at the bottom of the column. For example, suppose you are reporting on doors in the drawing and you need to know the total number of doors by style. You can select the door style property to report on and then select the **Total** check box to report the total number of door styles.

Beside the **Total** check box is the **Hide** check box. Selecting this check box includes the column within the schedule but hides it from being displayed in the schedule.

The last type of configuration for the new column is its position within the schedule table. The **Column Position** section at the bottom of the **Add Column** worksheet includes **Insert Before** and **Insert After** options. If this is the first column being added to the schedule, the column is placed at the beginning of the schedule. If this is an additional column, you have a choice of placing the column before or after a column currently in the schedule. Pick the **OK** button when you have finished, to add the column to the schedule. Repeat this process until all desired property columns have been added to the schedule.

Adding and Configuring a Formula Column

In addition to adding property columns, a formula column may be added to the schedule. Similar to a formula property in a property set, a formula column allows you to combine properties within a property set into the schedule. For example, a space room number and a door suffix property can be combined together within the same column. See **Figure 23-25.**

Figure 23-25.
The **Add Formula Column** button is used to combine properties together to form a value to be reported on in the schedule.

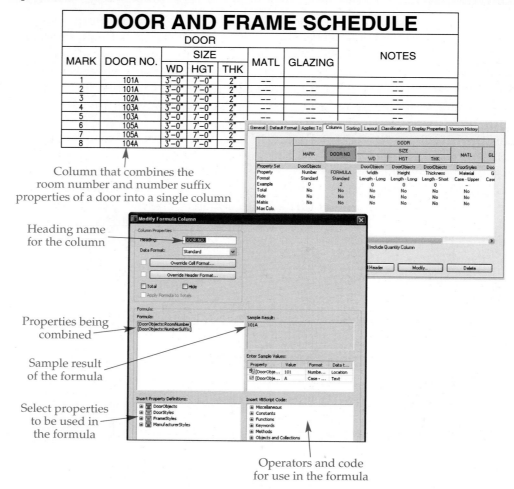

To add a formula column, pick the **Add Formula Column** button in the **Columns** tab for the schedule style. This displays the **Add Formula Column** worksheet, shown in **Figure 23-26.** This worksheet box is similar to the formula worksheet for property set definitions. This worksheet is comprised of three areas: **Column Properties**, **Column Position**, and **Formula**.

In the **Column Properties** area, enter a name for the column header in the **Heading:** text box. Assign a data format style to format the look of the column. If you need to override the cell or header format, pick the appropriate buttons and modify the cell properties. If the column has a total at the bottom, select the **Total** check box. When this is selected, the **Apply Formula to Totals** check box becomes available, which applies the formula written to the reported total.

The **Column Position** area is used to place the formula column within the schedule in relation to an existing column position.

The **Formula:** area is used to create the formula. Formulas can be as simple as combining property values or as complex as an algebraic formula to report a final value. This area is divided into four separate sections: **Formula:**, **Sample Result:**, **Insert Property Definitions:**, and **Insert VBScript Code:**. The **Formula:** section is used to assemble the formula. As property definitions and VBScript codes are added to the formula, they can be arranged in the **Formula:** section.

The **Insert Property Definitions:** section is used to select any properties used in the formula. Double-click a property to add it into the **Formula:** section. The **Insert VBScript Code:** section includes many codes and operators that can be used to combine the property definitions into a formula. Double-click any desired codes to add them to the **Formula:** section.

Finally, the **Sample Result:** section displays an example result of the formula to ensure the formula is written properly. When you are finished creating the formula column, pick the **OK** button to add the column to the schedule.

Figure 23-26.
The **Add Formula Column** worksheet is used to create a formula reported in a schedule.

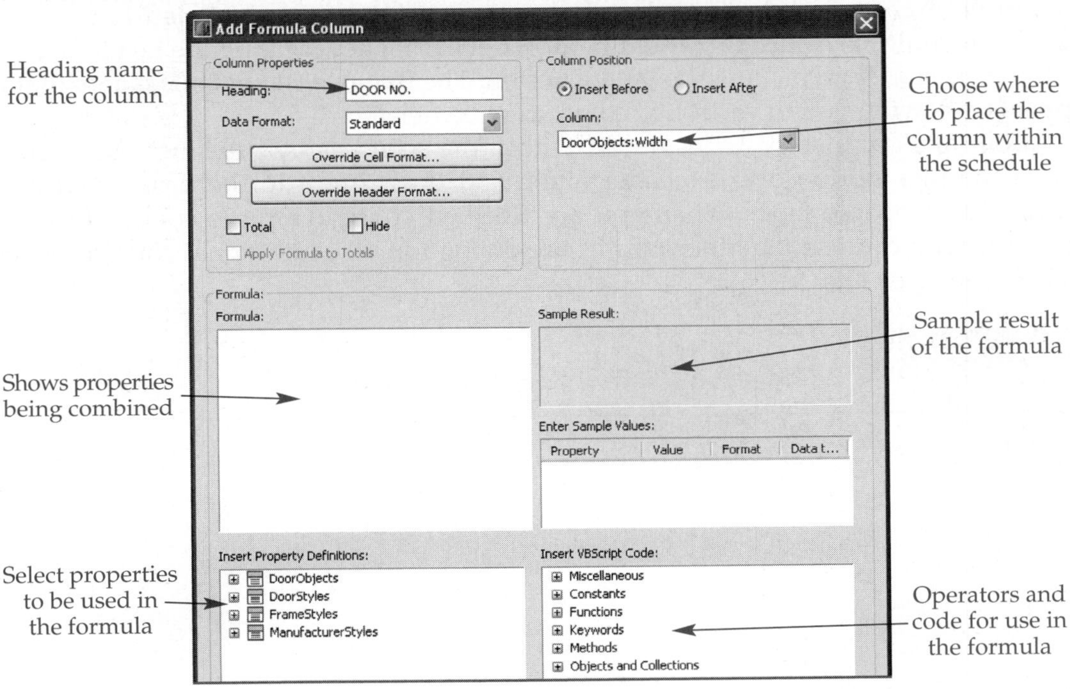

Adding Additional Columns

After you add property and formula columns to the schedule, additional built-in columns may be added to the schedule table. The **Columns** tab includes two additional check boxes that add columns to the schedule table. The **Repeat First Column** check box adds an additional column to the end of the schedule that is a duplicate of the first column in the schedule. This option can be used when a schedule is a long table and repeating the first column at the end of the schedule makes the schedule easier to read. The repeated column does not get added as a header in the **Columns** tab, but it is displayed at the end of the schedule in the drawing. The **Include Quantity Column** check box adds a column to the beginning of the schedule reporting the total quantity of an object within the schedule.

Finishing the Column Configurations

In addition to the **Add Column...** and the **Add Formula Column** buttons, three additional buttons are available in the configuration of the schedule columns: **Add Header**, **Modify**, and **Delete**.

The **Add Header** button is used to add a header above one or more headers derived from the selected properties to be reported on. Select one column, and then pick the **Add Header** button to add a new header over the selected header name. See **Figure 23-27**. If multiple property headers are to be placed under a single header, select the desired columns by holding down the [Ctrl] key, and then select the headers and pick the **Add Header** button, as shown in **Figure 23-27**. A new header is placed over the highlighted columns, and you have the opportunity to name the new header.

The **Modify...** button is used to modify any column in the schedule. First, select the column by picking on the header in the schedule or any text in the desired column, and then pick the **Modify...** button. The **Modify Column** dialog box is displayed, where you can rename the header name, apply overrides to the column formatting and the text information, or change the column to a matrix or to a totaled column.

The **Delete** button is used to delete a column from the schedule table. To remove a column from the schedule, first select the column, and then pick the **Delete** button. You can delete multiple columns by holding down the [Ctrl] key, picking the header names in the table, and then picking the **Delete** button. The **Remove Columns/Headers** dialog appears, allowing you to verify the columns to be deleted.

Columns can also be repositioned within the schedule by pressing and holding down the pick button over a header name and dragging it to the desired location within the schedule table. When you are finished configuring the columns for the schedule, you can use the other tabs in the dialog to make additional configurations in the schedule table.

Exercise
23-5   *Complete the Exercise on the Student CD.*

Architectural Desktop and Its Applications

Figure 23-27.
Example of a header added over a single column. Example of adding a header over multiple columns.

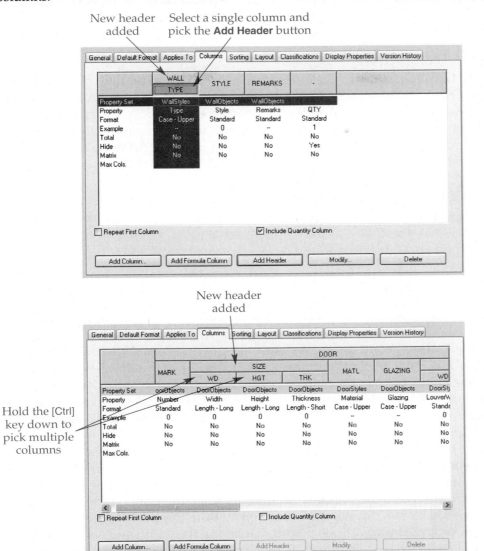

New header added — Select a single column and pick the **Add Header** button

New header added

Hold the [Ctrl] key down to pick multiple columns

Creating Custom Schedule Tags

Architectural Desktop includes a number of schedule tags that can be applied to different objects as documentation items and scheduling information. A few of these tags are available in the **Scheduling** tool palette under the **Document** tool palette group. Additional tags can be found in the Schedule Tags section of the Documentation Tool Catalog in the **Content Browser**.

Depending on the office standard or personal preference, these tags can be used as they are. Occasionally, some offices prefer to use a different size or type of symbol than those included with Architectural Desktop. In these situations, the custom tags can be created to meet office standards. This section explains how to create custom schedule tags for use in Architectural Desktop.

When you are creating a custom schedule tag, it is often helpful to begin a new drawing from scratch. This keeps the tag drawing from being cluttered with extra styles and layer names. To start a drawing from scratch, enter the **NEW** command. In the **Select Template** dialog box, pick the acad.dwt template, and then pick the **Open** button.

Drawing the Tag Block Geometry

Schedule tags are "smart" blocks, because they understand how to be scaled in the drawing, based on the chosen drawing scale and the type of units selected in the **Drawing Setup** dialog box. In order to replicate this process, the new tag geometry must be drawn eight times larger than the size it will be plotted. For example, a 1/4"-diameter circle with 1/8"-high text in a plotted drawing needs to be drawn as a 2"-diameter circle with 1"-high text (1/4" × 8 = 2" and 1/8" × 8 = 1").

NOTE

Chapter 9 discusses the creation of blocks. Remember that new geometry to be included into a block needs to be created on layer 0, using the ByBlock color, linetype, lineweight, and plot style.

For the purposes of this discussion, a custom window tag is created. Note that this process is similar for the creation of other custom schedule tags. Check with your instructor or manager before creating custom tags.

Create the desired geometric shape. The custom window tag will be a 3/8" × 3/8" square with a 1/8"-high window number within the box and a 3/32" window width and height text below the box on a plotted drawing. See **Figure 23-28**. Remember that the original geometry needs to be eight times its actual plotted size. This makes the square geometry 3" × 3" in the drawing. Use the **RECTANG** or **PLINE** command to create the shape.

Next, use the **TEXT** command to add the text within the block, representing the window number. It is desired to have this plot out as 1/8" high text. Therefore, when you are creating the geometry for the tag, it needs to be eight times its actual plotted size (1/8" × 8 = 1"). Make the window number text one inch high and use a middle-center justification to set the number centered within the box. Below the window number box, a Width X Height value is placed displaying the width and height of the tag. This text will be plotted as 3/32" high. Therefore, the tag geometry should be created as 3/4" high text (3/32" × 8 = 3/4"). Create three separate pieces of text, a middle-right justified, 3/4" high text for the window width; a middle-centered, 3/4" high text for the X; and a middle-left justified, 3/4" high text for the window height. See **Figure 23-29**. After the geometry has been drawn, select the rectangle and text, change it to layer 0, and change the color, linetype, and lineweight to ByBlock in the **Properties** palette.

Figure 23-28.
Desired end result custom window tag.

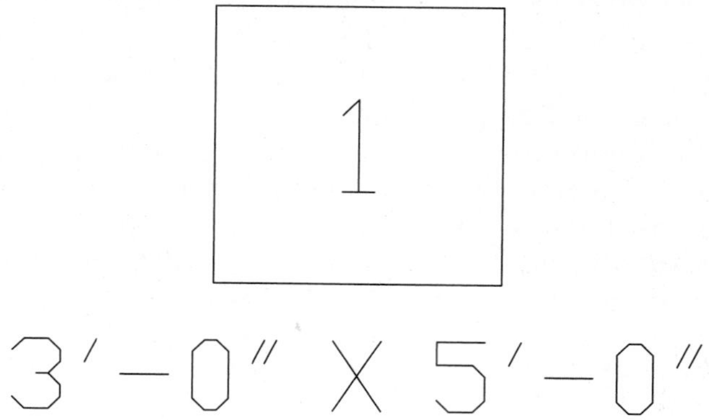

1

3′–0″ X 5′–0″

Figure 23-29.
The geometry
for the custom
window tag is laid
out, and the text is
configured.

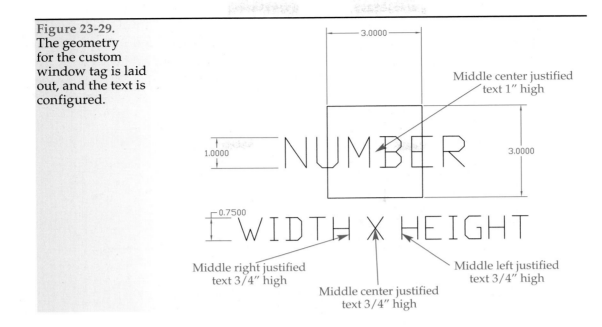

The text placed around the symbol is only a text placeholder for property data from a property data set. After the tag has been configured, the proper properties will be displayed in the tag when it has been assigned to a Window object.

The next step is to load any desired property set definitions into the drawing to which the custom tag refers. For example, in the above schedule tag, the window number, width, and height are reported on. These properties are found in the **WindowObjects** property set definition. Access the **PROPERTYSETDEFINE** command, and load or create the needed property set definitions into the drawing containing the tag geometry.

Once the tag geometry has been created and the property set definitions have been loaded, the tag can be created. Pick **Format** > **Define Schedule Tag...** or type DEFINETAG. Select all the geometry and text that will be used in the tag. When you are finished selecting the geometry, press [Enter]. This displays the **Define Schedule Tag** worksheet, as shown in **Figure 23-30**.

The **Define Schedule Tag** worksheet displays a preview of the selected geometry. If you missed something needing to be added to the tag, use the **Select Objects** button to return to the drawing window to select additional geometry. Enter a name for the custom tag in the name text box. At the bottom of the worksheet is a table of information. Any text placeholders added to the geometry are initially listed in this table. See **Figure 23-30**.

The text and property table includes four columns: **Label**, **Type**, **Property Set**, and **Property Definition**. The **Label** column initially displays the text string placeholder. The **Type** column is used to change the text placeholder to a property or leave the text as is. If the text placeholder will be a property displaying information from a property set, pick the space under the **Type** column associated with the text placeholder you are adjusting and select the **Property** option.

Beside the **Type** property, the **Property Set** column is used to specify the property set definition containing the property used in the schedule tag. A list of available property set definitions in the current drawing is displayed here. After specifying the property set definition, use the **Property Definition** column to select the actual property that will replace the original text placeholder and be displayed in the tag. Once the property set and the property definition have been selected, the name of the text placeholder under the **Label** column is changed to reflect the name of the property set and the property being reported, such as PropertySetDefinition:PropertyDefinition.

Figure 23-30.
The **Define Schedule Tag** worksheet is used to configure the text placeholders into properties from a property set definition.

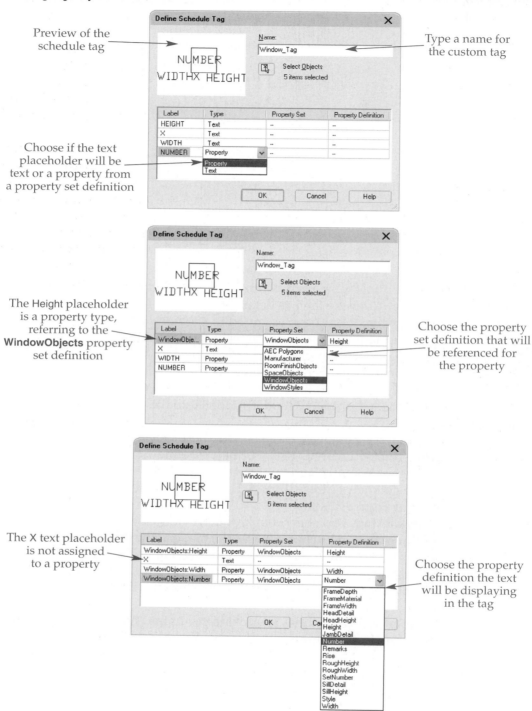

Preview of the schedule tag

Type a name for the custom tag

Choose if the text placeholder will be text or a property from a property set definition

The Height placeholder is a property type, referring to the **WindowObjects** property set definition

Choose the property set definition that will be referenced for the property

The X text placeholder is not assigned to a property

Choose the property definition the text will be displaying in the tag

Repeat the process for any text placeholders within the tag displaying property data. If text, such as the X between the width and height properties, will not be assigned a property, leave the **Type** as Text. Pick the **OK** button to finish the custom tag process. After exiting the worksheet, pick an insertion point for the new tag. Once the insertion point has been selected, the process is finished, and the geometry is turned into a multi-view block.

Before the tag can be used, two things need to occur. If this tag shall be used in future drawings, the drawing the tag was created in should be saved as a master drawing on your hard drive or a network drive, where the tag is always able to find the multi-view block definition. Second, a custom tool needs to be created on a tool palette so the tag may be utilized.

Once the drawing has been saved, select the multi-view block in the drawing, and drag the block onto an available tool palette, preferably an editable custom tool palette. Refer to Appendix B for information on creating custom tool palettes. Once the multi-view block has been added to the palette, right-click over the new tool and select the **Properties...** option. This displays the **Tool Properties** worksheet for the selected tool. See **Figure 23-31**.

In the **Tool Properties** worksheet, check that the **Property def location** has a path to the location where the master tag drawing has been saved. If the path is wrong, select the property and pick the **Browse...** option to browse for the correct location. Select the layer key property to choose a layer key for use with the tag. Choose a layer key that assigns the desired layer to the tag when it is added to a drawing. Finally check the **Tag location** property to ensure the path is pointing to the correct location where the tag can be found. This should be the same path as the **Property def location** property. Other properties may be adjusted as desired. When you are finished, pick the **OK** button to finish using the tool. The schedule tag tool is now ready for use in other drawings.

Exercise
23-6   Complete the Exercise on the Student CD.

Figure 23-31.
Add the multi-view block to a custom palette, and then modify the schedule tool's properties.

Drag the schedule tag from the drawing onto a tool palette

Verify the location path is correct

Assign a layer key to the tool

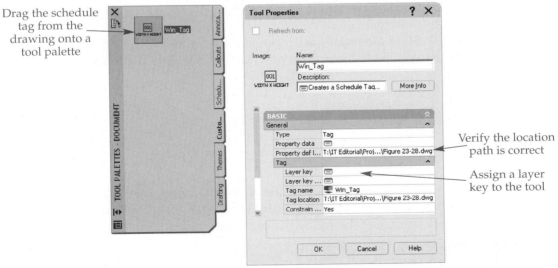

Chapter Test

Answer the following questions. Write your answers on a separate sheet of paper or complete the electronic chapter test on the Student CD.

1. Briefly explain the function of the formula property definition and give an example.
2. From where are location property values acquired?
3. Give the basic function of the material property definition.
4. Briefly describe project property definitions and their function.
5. Describe and give an example showing how anchor properties function.
6. Explain the graphic property definition and its use.
7. For a given AEC style or definition, where can property set definitions be assigned?
8. When creating or modifying a property set definition, where can new properties be added or existing properties be modified or deleted?
9. Describe the steps taken to create a data format style.
10. Define *zero padding* as used in a data format style.
11. When you are creating a custom schedule, what is the **Applies To** tab used for?
12. When you are adding columns to a schedule, the **Add Column...** button is selected in the schedule style's **Columns** tab. When this button is picked, what type of information is available for use as a column in a schedule?
13. What is the **Sorting** tab used for when customizing a schedule?
14. How can a custom schedule tag be created?

Chapter Projects

Use the techniques covered in this chapter to create the following drawings.

1. Single-Level Residential Project
   A. Access the **Project Browser** and set Residential-Project-01 current.
   B. Access the **Constructs** tab of the **Project Navigator** and open the Foundation construct drawing.
   C. Access the **Style Manager** and create a new list definition, named Structural Member List, applied to manual property definitions. Add the following to the list:
      - 2x4
      - 2x6
      - 2x8
      - 2x10
      - 2x12
      - 4x4
      - 4x8
   D. Create a new property set definition named Member_Styles. Apply the property set definition to styles and definitions, and select the **Structural Member Style** check box. Add the following automatic and manual data properties:

Name	Description	Type	Source	Default	Format	Example	Visible
Member_Type	Member_Type	List	Structural Member List	2x4	Standard	2x4	✓
Material	Material	Material	Structural Member Style: Member_Styles: Unnamed		Case-Upper		✓
Length	Length	Automatic	Structural Member:Length		Standard		✓
Style	Style	Automatic	Structural Member:Style		Standard		✓

E. Edit the 4×8 Girder member style. Select the **General** tab, and pick the **Property Sets...** button to add the Member_Styles property set definition. Set the **Member_Type** property to be 4x8.
F. Assign a wood material to the 4x8 Girder member style.
G. Assign the Member_Styles property set definition to the Post and Pier member style. Set the **Member_Type** property to be 4x4.
H. Assign a concrete material to the pier component and a wood material to the post component.
I. Save the drawing.
J. Access the **Views** tab of the **Project Navigator** and create a new general view named Foundation Plan. For the **Context**, select the Foundation level under Division 1. In the **Content** section, select the Foundation construct, and pick the **Finish** button. Open the Foundation Plan view drawing.
K. Drag and drop the Member_Styles property set definition from the Foundation construct into the Foundation Plan view drawing.
L. Save and close the Foundation construct.
M. In the Foundation Plan view drawing, create a new schedule table named Structural Schedule.
N. Apply the schedule to the structural members.
O. Configure the columns as shown in the figure.
P. Sort the information by style in ascending order and then by quantity in ascending order.
Q. Add the schedule to the drawing, reporting on the Foundation construct xref.
R. Add dimensions and notes to the plan as desired.
S. Save and close the drawing.

STRUCTURAL MEMBER SCHEDULE

MEMBER	QTY	SIZE	LENGTH
4X8 GIRDER	6	4X8	40'−0"
4X8 GIRDER	2	4X8	20'−8"
4X8 GIRDER	1	4X8	14'−0"
4X8 GIRDER	2	4X8	20'−0"
POST AND PIER	33	4X4	2'−10"

Design Courtesy Alan Mascord Design Associates

2. Single-Level Residential Project
   A. Access the **Project Browser** and set Residential-Project-02 current.
   B. Access the **Constructs** tab of the **Project Navigator** and open the Foundation construct drawing.
   C. Access the **Style Manager** and create a new list definition, named Structural Member List, applied to manual property definitions. Add the following to the list:
   - 2x4
   - 2x6
   - 2x8
   - 2x10
   - 2x12
   - 4x4
   - 4x8
   D. Create a new property set definition named Member_Styles. Apply the property set definition to styles and definitions, and select the **Structural Member Style** check box. Add the following automatic and manual data properties:

Name	Description	Type	Source	Default	Format	Example	Visible
Member_Type	Member_Type	List	Structural Member List	2x4	Standard	2x4	✓
Material	Material	Material	Structural Member Style: Member_Styles: Unnamed		Case-Upper		✓
Length	Length	Automatic	Structural Member:Length		Standard		✓
Style	Style	Automatic	Structural Member:Style		Standard		✓

   E. Edit the 4×8 Girder member style. Select the **General** tab, and pick the **Property Sets...** button to add the Member_Styles property set definition. Set the **Member_Type** property to be 4x8.
   F. Assign a wood material to the 4x8 Girder member style.
   G. Assign the Member_Styles property set definition to the Post and Pad member style. Set the **Member_Type** property to be 4x4.
   H. Assign a concrete material to the Pad component and a wood material to the Post component.
   I. Save the drawing.
   J. Access the **Views** tab of the **Project Navigator** and create a new general view named Foundation Plan. For the **Context**, select the Foundation level under Division 1. In the **Content** section, select the Foundation construct, and then pick the **Finish** button. Open the Foundation Plan view drawing.
   K. Drag and drop the Member_Styles property set definition from the Foundation construct into the Foundation Plan view drawing.
   L. Save and close the Foundation construct.
   M. In the Foundation Plan view drawing, create a new schedule table named Structural Schedule.
   N. Apply the schedule to the structural members.
   O. Configure the columns as shown in the figure.
   P. Sort the information by style in ascending order and then by quantity in ascending order.
   Q. Add the schedule to the drawing, reporting on the Foundation construct xref.

R. Add dimensions and notes to the plan as desired.

S. Save and close the drawing.

STRUCTURAL MEMBER SCHEDULE

MEMBER	QTY	SIZE	LENGTH
4X8 GIRDER	6	4X8	40'−0"
4X8 GIRDER	2	4X8	20'−8"
4X8 GIRDER	1	4X8	14'−0"
4X8 GIRDER	2	4X8	20'−0"
POST AND PIER	33	4X4	2'−10"

Design Courtesy Alan Mascord Design Associates

3. Two-Story Residential Project

A. Access the **Project Browser** and set Residential-Project-03 current.

B. Access the **Constructs** tab of the **Project Navigator** and open the Foundation construct drawing.

C. Create a property set definition for structural members named Member_Objects. Apply the property set definition to structural member objects.

D. Add and configure the following properties to the property set definition:

Name	Description	Type	Source	Format	Visible
Length	Length	Automatic	Structural Member:Length	Length-Nominal	✓
Style	Style	Automatic	Structural Member:Style	Case-Upper	✓
Size	Size	Text		Case-Upper	✓

E. In the **Properties** palette's **Extended Data** tab, attach the Member_Objects property set definition to each column and beam in the drawing. In the **Member_Size** property, enter a value of 4x4 for the Post and Pier and 4x8 for the beams.

F. Access the **PROPERTYSETDEFINE** command and import the StructuralMemberStyles property set definition from Schedule Tables.dwg. Edit the StructuralMemberStyles property set definition and add the **Style** automatic property for structural members.

G. Attach the StructuralMemberStyles property set definition to the 4x8 Girder and the Post and Pier structural styles.

H. Rename the Post and Pier style to 4x4-Post.

I. Access the **Views** tab of the **Project Navigator** and create a new general view named Foundation Plan. For the **Context**, select the Foundation level under Division 1. In the **Content** section, select the Foundation construct, and then pick the **Finish** button. Open the Foundation Plan view drawing. Set the scale to 1/4" = 1'-0".

J. Drag and drop the Member_Objects and the StructuralMemberStyles property set definitions from the Foundation construct into the Foundation Plan view drawing.

K. Save and close the Foundation construct.

L. Access the **Content Browser** and locate the Documentation Tool Catalog. Select the Structural Tags section from Schedule Tags, and add beam and column tags as indicated in the figure below.

M. Create a schedule table that looks similar to the figure below. Use the following table to lay out the schedule:

	TYPE	QTY	SIZE	LENGTH
Property Set	Member_Objects		Member_Objects	Member_Objects
Property	Style	QTY	Size	Length
Format	Case-Upper	Standard	Standard	Length-Nominal
Example	0	1		
Total	No	No	No	No
Hide	No	No	No	No
Matrix	No	No	Yes	No
Max Columns			3	

N. Sort the schedule based on the style property. Adjust the layout as desired.

O. Add the schedule to the drawing to report on the Foundation construct.

P. Add dimensions and notes to the plan as desired.

Q. Save and close the drawing.

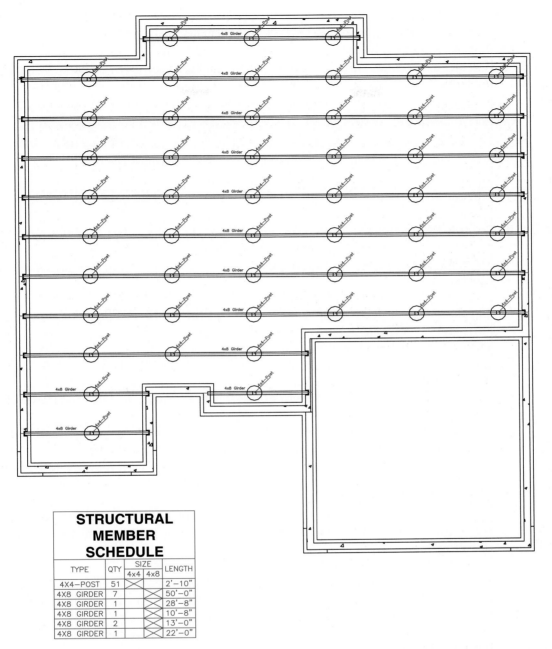

STRUCTURAL MEMBER SCHEDULE				
TYPE	QTY	SIZE		LENGTH
		4x4	4x8	
4X4—POST	51	✕		2'—10"
4X8 GIRDER	7		✕	50'—0"
4X8 GIRDER	1		✕	28'—8"
4X8 GIRDER	1		✕	10'—8"
4X8 GIRDER	2		✕	13'—0"
4X8 GIRDER	1		✕	22'—0"

Drawing Courtesy 3D-DZYN

4. Two-Story Residential Project
   A. Access the **Project Browser** and set Residential-Project-04 current.
   B. Access the **Constructs** tab and open the Foundation construct drawing.
   C. Create a property set definition for structural members named Member_ Objects. Apply the property set definition to structural member objects.
   D. Add and configure the following properties to the property set definition:

Name	Description	Type	Source	Format	Visible
Length	Length	Automatic	Structural Member:Length	Length-Nominal	✓
Style	Style	Automatic	Structural Member:Style	Case-Upper	✓
Size	Size	Text		Case-Upper	✓

   E. In the **Properties** palette's **Extended Data** tab, attach the Member_Objects property set definition to each column and beam in the drawing. In the **Member_Size** property, enter a value of 4x4 for the Post and Pier and 4x8 for the beams.
   F. Access the **PROPERTYSETDEFINE** command and import the StructuralMemberStyles property set definition from Schedule Tables.dwg. Edit the StructuralMemberStyles property set definition and add the **Style** automatic property for structural members.
   G. Attach the StructuralMemberStyles property set definition to the 4x8 Girder and the Post and Pier structural styles.
   H. Rename the Post and Pier style to 4x4 Post with Pier and the Post and Pad style to 4x4 Post with Pad.
   I. Access the **Views** tab of the **Project Navigator** and create a new general view named Foundation Plan. For the **Context**, select the Foundation level under Division 1. In the **Content** section, select the Foundation construct, and then pick the **Finish** button. Open the Foundation Plan view drawing. Set the scale to 1/4" = 1'-0".
   J. Drag and drop the Member_Objects and the StructuralMemberStyles property set definitions from the Foundation construct into the Foundation Plan view drawing.
   K. Save and close the Foundation construct.
   L. Access the **Content Browser** and locate the Documentation Tool Catalog. Select the Structural Tags section from Schedule Tags, and add beam and column tags as indicated in the figure on the next page.
   M. Create a schedule table that looks similar to the figure below. Use the following table to lay out the schedule:

	TYPE	QTY	SIZE	LENGTH
Property Set	Member_Objects		Member_Objects	Member_Objects
Property	Style	QTY	Size	Length
Format	Case-Upper	Standard	Standard	Length-Nominal
Example	0	1		
Total	No	No	No	No
Hide	No	No	No	No
Matrix	No	No	Yes	No
Max Columns			3	

   N. Sort the schedule based on the style property. Adjust the layout as desired.
   O. Add the schedule to the drawing to report on the Foundation construct.
   P. Add dimensions and notes to the plan as desired.
   Q. Save and close the drawing.

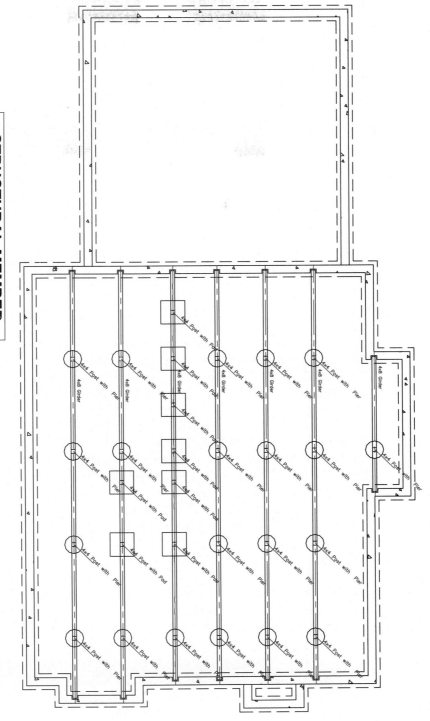

STRUCTURAL MEMBER SCHEDULE

TYPE	Quantity	SIZE 4x4	4x8	LENGTH
4X4 POST WITH PIER	21	4'4"		2'-10"
4X4 POST WITH PAD	8			2'-10"
4X8 GIRDER	4			36'-0"
4X8 GIRDER	2			37'-6"
4X8 GIRDER	1			12'-6"

Drawing Courtesy 3D-DZYN

Chapter 23 Projects

5. Commercial Store Project
   A. Access the **Project Browser** and set Commercial-Project-05 current.
   B. Access the **Constructs** tab of the **Project Navigator** and open the Ceiling Framing construct drawing.
   C. Create a property set definition for structural members named Member_Objects. Apply the property set definition to structural member objects.
   D. Add and configure the following properties to the property set definition:

Name	Description	Type	Source	Format	Visible
Length	Length	Automatic	Structural Member:Length	Length-Nominal	✓
Style	Style	Automatic	Structural Member:Style	Case-Upper	✓

   E. Attach the Member_Objects property set definition to each column and beam in the drawing.
   F. Access the **PROPERTYSETDEFINE** command and import the StructuralMemberStyles property set definition from Schedule Tables.dwg. Edit the StructuralMemberStyles property set definition and add the **Style** automatic property for structural members.
   G. Attach the StructuralMemberStyles property set definition to all the structural member styles in the drawing.
   H. Access the **Views** tab of the **Project Navigator** and create a new general view named Ceiling Framing Plan. For the **Context**, select the Ceiling Framing and the Main Floor levels under Division 1. In the **Content** section, select the Ceiling Framing and the Main Floor constructs, and then pick the **Finish** button. Open the Ceiling Framing Plan view drawing. Set the scale to 1/8" = 1'-0".
   I. Select the Main Floor construct xref, right-click, and select **Edit Object Display**. Pick the **Xref Display** tab, place a check in the **Override the display configuration set in the host drawing** check box, and then select the Reflected Screened display configuration. This will change the display of the Main Floor only in this view drawing.
   J. Drag and drop the Member_Objects and the StructuralMemberStyles property set definitions from the Ceiling Framing construct into the Ceiling Framing Plan view drawing.
   K. Save and close the Ceiling Framing construct.
   L. Access the **Content Browser** and locate the Documentation Tool Catalog. Select the Structural Tags section from Schedule Tags, and add beam and column tags as indicated in the figure below.
   M. Create a schedule table that looks similar to the figure below. Use the following table to lay out the schedule:

	TYPE	QTY	LENGTH
Property Set	Member_Objects		Member_Objects
Property	Style	QTY	Length
Format	Case-Upper	Standard	Length-Nominal
Example	0	1	
Total	No	No	No
Hide	No	No	No
Matrix	No	No	No
Max Columns			

   N. Sort the schedule based on the style property. Adjust the layout as desired.
   O. Add the schedule to the drawing to report on the Ceiling Framing construct.
   P. Add dimensions and notes to the plan as desired.
   Q. Save and close the drawing.

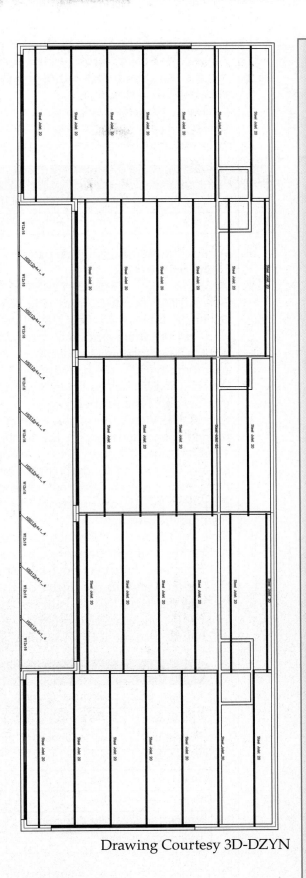

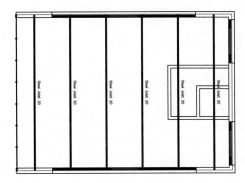

Drawing Courtesy 3D-DZYN

STRUCTURAL MEMBER SCHEDULE

TYPE	QTY	LENGTH
HSS12X4X1_4	08	11'-0"
STEEL JOIST 20	20	36'-0"
STEEL JOIST 20	17	36'-8"
W12X16	09	12'-0"

6. Commercial Car Maintenance Shop Project
    A. Access the **Project Browser** and set Commercial-Project-06 current.
    B. Access the **Constructs** tab of the **Project Navigator** and open the Foundation construct drawing.
    C. Create a property set definition for structural members named Member_Objects. Apply the property set definition to structural member objects.
    D. Add and configure the following properties to the property set definition:

Name	Description	Type	Source	Format	Visible
Length	Length	Automatic	Structural Member:Length	Length-Nominal	✓
Style	Style	Automatic	Structural Member:Style	Case-Upper	✓

    E. Attach the Member_Objects property set definition to each column and beam in the drawing.
    F. Access the **PROPERTYSETDEFINE** command and import the StructuralMemberStyles and the WallStyles property set definitions from Schedule Tables.dwg. Edit the StructuralMemberStyles property set definition and add the **Style** automatic property for structural members.
    G. Attach the StructuralMemberStyles property set definition to all the structural member styles in the drawing.
    H. Attach the WallStyles property set definition to all the wall styles in the drawing. Set the **Type** property to A.
    I. Access the **Views** tab of the **Project Navigator** and create a new general view named Foundation Plan. For the **Context**, select the Foundation level under Division 1. In the **Content** section, select the Foundation construct, and then pick the **Finish** button. Open the Foundation Plan view drawing. Set the scale to 1/8″ = 1′-0″.
    J. Drag and drop the Member_Objects, StructuralMemberStyles, and WallStyles property set definitions from the Foundation construct into the Foundation Plan view drawing.
    K. Save and close the Foundation construct.
    L. Access the **Content Browser** and locate the Documentation Tool Catalog. Select the Structural Tags section from Schedule Tags, and add beam and column tags as indicated in the figure on the next page. Access the Wall tags and add the Wall tag to all the walls in the drawing.
    M. Create a schedule table for structural members that looks similar to the figure below. Use the following table to lay out the schedule:

	TYPE	QTY	LENGTH
Property Set	Member_Objects		Member_Objects
Property	Style	QTY	Length
Format	Case-Upper	Standard	Length-Nominal
Example	0	1	
Total	No	No	No
Hide	No	No	No
Matrix	No	No	No
Max Columns			

    N. Sort the schedule based on the style property. Adjust the layout as desired.
    O. Add the schedule to the drawing to report on the Foundation construct.
    P. Create a schedule table for wall concrete volume that looks similar to the figure on the next page. Use the following table to lay out the schedule:

	TYPE	VOLUME	REMARKS
Property Set	WallStyles	WallObjects	WallObjects
Property	Type	Volume-Net	Remarks
Format	Case-Upper	Volume	Case-Upper
Example	--	0CF	--
Total	No	Yes	No
Hide	No	No	No
Matrix	No	No	No
Max Columns			

Q. Sort the schedule based on the **Volume** property. Adjust the layout as desired.
R. Add the schedule to the drawing to report on the Foundation construct.
S. Add dimensions and notes to the plan as desired.
T. Save and close the drawing.

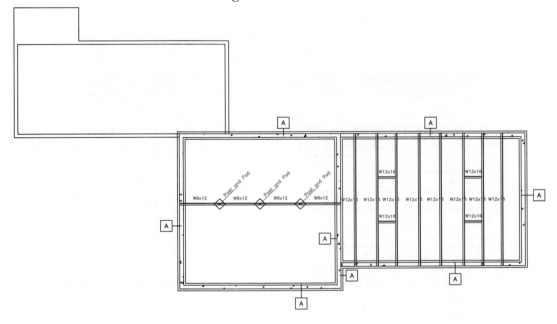

Structural Member Schedule

TYPE	QTY	LENGTH
POST AND PAD	3	8'-6"
W12X16	4	3'-4"
W12X16	8	24'-0"
W6X12	4	7'-0"

FND CONC. VOLUME

TYPE	VOLUME	Remarks
A	24.31 CF	PORTLAND CEMENT
A	149.40 CF	PORTLAND CEMENT
A	150.37 CF	PORTLAND CEMENT
A	176.15 CF	PORTLAND CEMENT
A	176.15 CF	PORTLAND CEMENT
A	177.01 CF	PORTLAND CEMENT
A	204.39 CF	PORTLAND CEMENT
A	204.75 CF	PORTLAND CEMENT
	1262.52 CF	

Drawing Courtesy 3D-DZYN

7. Governmental Fire Station
   A. Access the **Project Browser** and set Gvrmt-Project-07 current.
   B. Access the **Constructs** tab of the **Project Navigator** and open the Foundation construct drawing.
   C. Import the SlabObjects property set definition from Schedule Tables.dwg.
   D. Use the **Properties** palette's **Extended Data** tab to assign the SlabObjects property set to the slab objects under the building.
   E. Create a layer named A-Slab-Fnsh. Assign the Slab objects with the Brick Pavers on Concrete style to this layer.
   F. Access the **Views** tab of the **Project Navigator** and create a new general view named Foundation Plan. For the **Context**, select the Foundation level under Division 1. In the **Content** section, select the Foundation construct, and then pick the **Finish** button. Open the Foundation Plan view drawing. Set the scale to 1/8" = 1'-0".
   G. Copy the SlabObjects property set definition from the Foundation construct to the Foundation Plan view drawing.
   H. Save and close the Foundation construct drawing.
   I. Create a schedule table named Concrete Slab Foundation and apply it to Slab objects. Use the following table to lay out the schedule:

	THICKNESS	NET AREA	PERIMETER	VOLUME
Property Set	SlabObjects	SlabObjects	SlabObjects	SlabObjects
Property	Thickness	Area-Net	Perimeter	Volume
Format	Length-short	Area	Length-Long	Volume
Example	0	0SF	0	0CF
Total	No	Yes	No	Yes
Hide	No	No	No	No
Matrix	No	No	No	No
Max Columns				

   J. Sort the schedule based on the **Area** property.
   K. In the **Layout** tab, override the Title Cell format and assign the Schedule-Header text style with a height of 3/16".
   L. Add the schedule table to the main slab under the building, using a layer filter that looks for slabs on the A-Slab layer in the Foundation xref.
   M. Save and close the drawing.

CONC. SLAB FOUNDATION			
THICKNESS	NET AREA	PERIMETER	VOLUME

Drawing Courtesy 3D-DZYN

CHAPTER 24

Sheets and Plotting

Learning Objectives

After completing this chapter, you will be able to do the following:

✓ Manage your layout.
✓ Use the **Page Setup Manager**.
✓ Set up plot styles.
✓ Set up a sheet.
✓ Establish viewports.
✓ Control the viewport's layers, linetypes, and color display.
✓ Plot your drawings.
✓ Add a plot stamp.
✓ Plot to a Design Web Format (DWF) file.

Model geometry is created in the construct and element drawings, and view drawings are where the model geometry is annotated and model space views are created. These are drawn in the *model space* area of the drawing screen. Everything drawn in the model space area is always drawn full-scale. This helps in the development of a plan because you can create the building model accurately, without having to bother with a scale.

The model gets annotated with dimensions and notes in *view drawings*. This area is also used to create model space views of different portions of the drawing, including floor plans, elevations and sections, schedules, and specific areas on a floor plan, such as a conference room or kitchen. These model space views are assigned a plotting scale, named, and then added to sheets, where the construction document set can be printed.

The **Sheets** tab in the **Project Navigator** is used to create and manage printable sheet drawings within the project. These sheets are created in an area of the drawing called *layout space*. Layout space is also known as paper space because the sheet drawing is created and plotted on a sheet of paper. Sheet drawings may be of individual plans, elevations, sections, details, schedules, and even 3D views. This chapter explains how to create and use layouts and sheet drawings and how to plot your drawings.

Model space is the area in a drawing representing an unlimited drawing area, where model geometry, such as walls, floors, and roofs, is drawn full-scale (1:1). Model space is most easily identified by the appearance of the **UCS** icon in the lower-left corner of the drawing screen, as shown in **Figure 24-1.** The model space **UCS** icon is represented as two arrows pointing in the positive X and Y directions. Model space can also be identified by the **MODEL** button being depressed in the status bar at the bottom of the Architectural Desktop window.

Layout space is used to set up a sheet of paper for plotting/printing and is most commonly used in a sheet drawing. As with model space, everything drawn in this space is drawn at a 1:1 scale. The difference between layout space and model space is that layout space represents a real sheet of paper, such as a 36″ × 24″ sheet with a title block, while model space represents the real world. Therefore, a full-size sheet of paper with a title block is drawn at the correct size for final printing or plotting. When views such as floor plans, elevations, and sections are added to the sheets, the scales set in the model space views are used to fit the views onto the full-size sheets.

Layout space can also be identified with the appearance of the **UCS** icon. The layout space **UCS** icon is represented as a right triangle, with the letters X and Y indicating the positive axis directions, as in **Figure 24-1.** Additionally, the **LAYOUT** button in the status bar is depressed when layout space is active. There can be only one **Model** tab, but there can be multiple layout tabs in the drawing. Each layout tab uses a unique name and can represent different sizes of paper or use different plotters/printers.

Right-clicking over the **MODEL** or **LAYOUT** button in the status bar displays a command option allowing you to display the **Model** and layout tabs at the bottom of the drawing screen, as in **Figure 24-1.** If the tabs are displayed, selecting a tab sets that space as the active space for drawing. Right-clicking over the tabs and selecting the **Hide Layout and Model Tabs** option minimizes the tabs back to the default of using the **MODEL** and **LAYOUT** buttons in the status bar.

NOTE

When you are setting up the properties for a layout tab, such as the paper size, plotter, and pen settings to be used by the layout, it is common to have the layout tabs displayed so commands that modify the settings can easily be accessed.

Figure 24-1.
Model space is identified by the model space **UCS** icon and the depressed **MODEL** button. Layout space is identified by the layout space **UCS** icon and the depressed **LAYOUT** button. If the layout tabs are displayed, the active tab indicates which space is current.

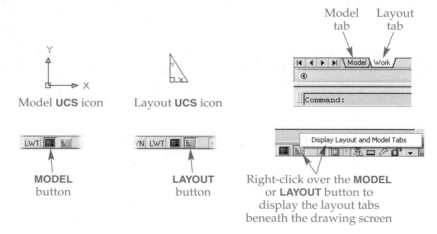

Architectural Desktop and Its Applications

Architectural Desktop includes four different plotting templates. These templates have multiple layout tabs for plotting different sheet sizes. Two of the templates use imperial units, and the other two use metric units. The two imperial and metric templates are divided into CTB and STB plot styles. CTB tables allow you to plot the drawing by assigning pen weights to colors. The STB tables allow you to assign a lineweight name to a layer or component within an AEC style. Plot style tables are discussed in detail later in this chapter. All four of the templates include multiple layout tabs and title blocks with attributes in the title block that can be edited. See Figure 24-2.

When you are using the **Project Navigator**, the creation of sheet drawings uses a template that includes multiple layout tabs with varying sheet sizes, such as the default sheet templates. Before sheets can be created with the desired paper size layout tabs, an understanding of layout space and how to set up a template with multiple layout sheet tabs of varying sizes must be accomplished.

Understanding Layout Space

Every component used to create the building model, floor plans, elevations, and sections should be drawn full-scale. The only exception to this should be annotation items such as text, dimension component sizes, and annotation blocks, such as detail bubbles, section arrows, revision clouds, and leader lines. These items are drawn according to the drawing scale determined in the **Drawing Setup** dialog box.

Annotation objects are created by multiplying the desired finished printed size by the drawing scale factor. For example, a 3/8"-diameter detail bubble scaled 1/4" = 1'-0" on a drawing is actually drawn as an 18"-diameter circle in model space. The drawing scale factor is automatically determined for dimension size and annotation blocks when the drawing scale is set up in the **Drawing Setup** dialog box.

Detail bubble: 1/4" = 1'-0" drawing scale

.25" = 12"

12" ÷ .25" = scale factor: 48

3/8" diameter (circle on paper) × 48 (scale factor) = 18" diameter (in model space)

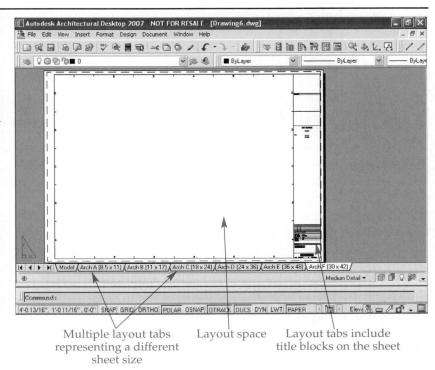

Figure 24-2.
The Aec Sheet templates included with ADT include multiple layout tabs for the different paper sheet sizes used in architectural drafting.

Multiple layout tabs representing a different sheet size

Layout space

Layout tabs include title blocks on the sheet

Figure 24-3.
Items drawn in layout space, such as the title block, title information, and text on the sheet, are drawn at a scale of 1:1. Model space viewports created in view drawings are added to sheets and scaled to fit on the paper.

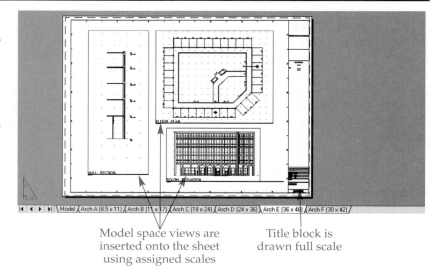

Model space views are inserted onto the sheet using assigned scales

Title block is drawn full scale

If you are creating text, multiply the plotted text height by the scale factor to get the model space text height. For example, text that is to appear 1/8″ high on the finished drawing at a scale of 1/8″ = 1′-0″ should be drawn 12″ high in model space.

Text height: 1/8″ = 1′-0″ drawing scale

.125″ = 12″

12″ ÷ .125″ = scale factor: 96

1/8″ (text height) × 96 (scale factor) = 12″ (text height in model space)

Layout space is where you set up a real-size sheet of paper in the drawing, draw a title block and notes, scale the model space drawing to fit on the paper, and arrange any views of the drawing on the sheet of paper. Geometry drawn directly in layout space is also drawn full-scale. For example, the layout is a full-size sheet of paper, so the text drawn directly on the layout sheet is drawn at the actual plotted height, such as 1/8″, and not the model space's scaled height of 12″.

The only thing scaled in a layout sheet is the view of the model within a floating viewport. These full-size views of the building are scaled to fit on the layout sheet. The building model is not actually scaled in model space, but the viewing distance is stepped away from the building, making it smaller, so it will fit on a piece of paper. See **Figure 24-3.**

Basic Layout Setup

By default, when a sheet is created, it imports a layout tab and title block from one of the included sheet templates. Title blocks with the Autodesk logo can be used; however, you will probably want to create your own template that includes a custom title block on a predetermined size of paper. Custom templates with paper sizes and title blocks can be created from scratch, or you can use one of the default templates and modify the paper sizes and title block to fit your needs.

Preconfigured layouts can be modified to use different paper sizes, assign a plotter, and assign plotted colors and lineweights to the model geometry. These settings are controlled by the **Page Setup Manager**. To access the **Page Setup Manager**, type PAGESETUP or pick **File** > **Page Setup Manager…** from the pull-down menu. The **Page Setup Manager** can also be accessed when the layout tabs are visible below the drawing sheet by right-clicking on the layout tab to be modified and then selecting **Page Setup…** from the shortcut menu. The **Page Setup Manager** is described in depth in the next section.

PAGESETUP

Type
PAGESETUP
Pull-Down Menu
File
> Page Setup Manager…

Additional layouts can be created and configured to plot on any size sheet of paper, with any scale, view, and arrangement desired. To create a new layout tab with the layout tabs visible at the bottom of the drawing sheet, right-click over a layout tab, and pick **New layout** from the shortcut menu. This creates a new layout tab named Layout 1, which is placed at the end of the existing layout tabs. Once a new layout has been added, you need to pick the layout tab to set it current, in order to adjust the setup for the layout sheet.

Setting Up a Layout Page

Once a layout tab has been created, it needs to be configured to display the desired paper size, plotter and pen settings to be used, and area to be plotted. A page setup is a group of settings controlling the parameters on how a sheet is to be plotted. A drawing can include a number of page setups. A layout tab can be assigned only one page setup. To control the settings within a page setup, right-click over the desired layout tab to be configured, and select the **Page Setup Manager...** option. This displays the **Page Setup Manager** for the current layout tab. See **Figure 24-4**. The **Page Setup Manager** is used to create, modify, and import page setups in the drawing and set a page setup current for the layout tab being modified.

To create a new page setup, select the **New...** button in the **Page Setup Manager**. This displays the **New Page Setup** dialog box, where the page setup can be named. Page names should reflect the page's use. For example, if you create an Architectural D-size sheet of paper, you can name it D-Size or 36X24. The **Page Setup** dialog box is displayed after naming the page setup and picking the **OK** button. See **Figure 24-5**.

The **Page Setup** dialog box includes many settings used to set up the layout sheet. Beginning at the top-left corner of the dialog box, the **Page setup** area lists the name of the page setup being configured. Below this area is the **Printer/plotter** area. The drop-down list in this area includes a list of plotters and printers configured in your computer. Choose the printer or plotter to be assigned to this page setup. The **Properties** button beside the plotter name can be selected to make any additional adjustments to the plotter. The preview window in this area displays the selected paper size assigned to the plotter and can be adjusted by choosing a different size of paper in the next section.

Figure 24-4.
The **Page Setup Manager** is used to create, modify, or import new page setups.

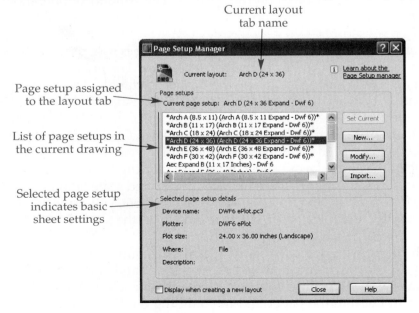

Current layout tab name

Page setup assigned to the layout tab

List of page setups in the current drawing

Selected page setup indicates basic sheet settings

Figure 24-5.
The **Page Setup** dialog box is used to set up plot settings that are assigned to a layout tab and used when plotting the drawing.

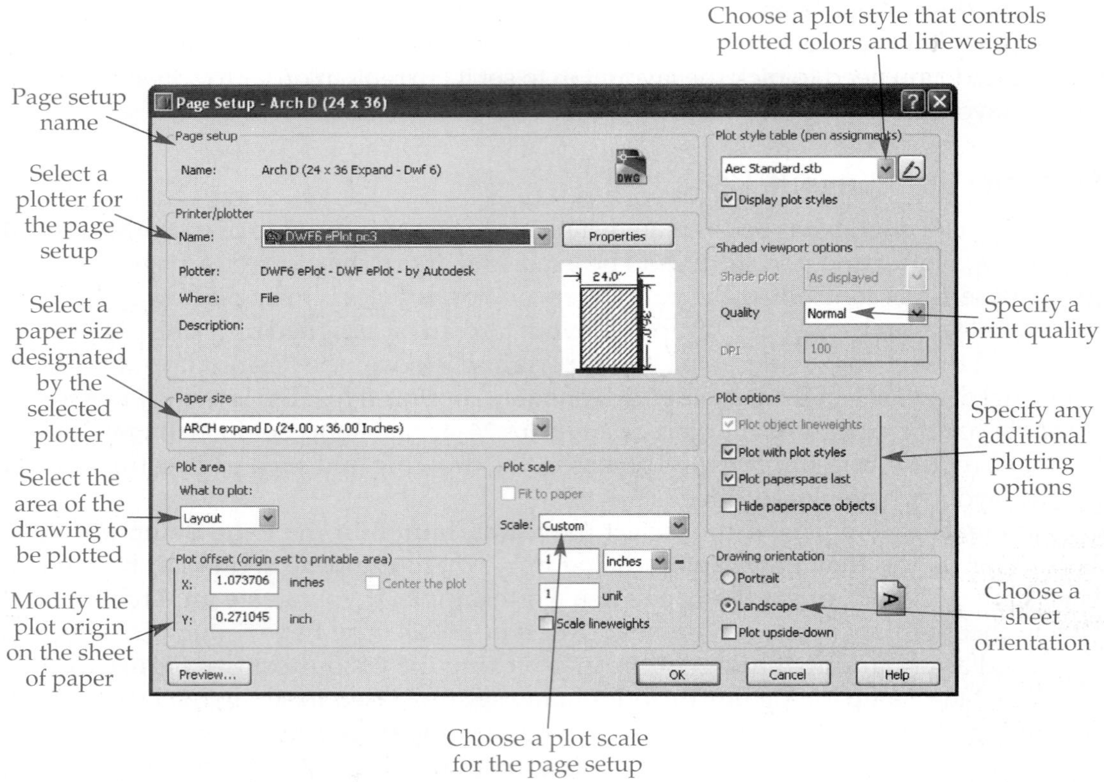

Choose a plot style that controls plotted colors and lineweights

Page setup name

Select a plotter for the page setup

Select a paper size designated by the selected plotter

Select the area of the drawing to be plotted

Modify the plot origin on the sheet of paper

Specify a print quality

Specify any additional plotting options

Choose a sheet orientation

Choose a plot scale for the page setup

The **Paper size** area is used to choose the paper size for the page setup. The paper sizes available in the list are based on the plotter selected in the **Printer/plotter** area. If a paper size is not available, try choosing a different plotter. The **Plot area** area below the **Paper size** area controls what is plotted in layout space. Options here are **Display**, **Extents**, **Layout**, and **Window**. The **Display** option prints the area currently visible in the drawing screen. The **Extents** option is used to plot everything up to the edges or extents of the geometry in layout space. The **Layout** option is the best option because it plots everything in layout space drawn on the "paper." The **Window** option allows you to window around an area in layout space to be plotted. In most cases, the **Layout** option is assigned to a page setup.

The **Plot offset** area at the bottom-left corner of the dialog box is used to offset the origin away from the lower-left corner of the printable area. The *printable area* is the area within the paper in layout space inside the dashed rectangle. This rectangle represents the locations of the margins for the selected paper size. Adjusting the X and Y values here will cause the printed sheet to be shifted left, right, up, or down on the paper.

The **Plot scale** area is used to assign a scale for the layout being plotted. This setting does not affect the scale of the building model within the model space view, but it designates the scale of the entire layout sheet. If you are plotting from model space, specifying a scale here scales the model space view to the selected scale on the printed sheet of paper. Because you are setting up a page for a layout sheet, you want the page setup to be plotted to a real-size sheet of paper, so you should select the scale of 1'-0" = 1'-0" (1:1 for metric).

When you finish configuring the page setup, pick the **OK** button to return to the layout. If this is an existing layout being modified, the paper size and any other settings are updated. If this is a new layout being configured, the paper size selected is displayed, with a floating viewport cut into the paper and the building model displayed inside the viewport, as in **Figure 24-3.** In addition to the paper size and floating viewport, a dashed line representing the margin area for the paper is displayed. Any geometry within the margin area is plotted. Anything outside the boundary is ignored and does not plot.

Moving to the top-right corner of the dialog box, the **Plot style table (pen assignments)** area is used to assign a plot style table. There are two types of plot style tables: color-dependent plot style tables (CTB) and named plot style tables (STB). Initially, when the drawing is created, the template contains either color-dependent or named plot styles. The CTB plot styles use the colors of the geometry to determine the final plotted color and lineweight. The STB plot styles assign names such as Medium Lines, Heavy Lines, and Dashed Lines to geometry. When choosing a plot style table from this area, either CTB or STB plot styles will be available. Choose a plot style table you want to use to print your drawing. Several preconfigured plot styles are available. Select one to assign to the page setup.

Below the **Plot style table** area is the **Shaded viewport options** area, which specifies a visual style to use in the **Shade plot** drop-down list when plotting a 3D view. This option is available if you are setting up the page for plotting in model space. The **Quality** drop-down list is used to assign a plot quality to the final output of the sheet. Below the **Shaded viewport options** area is the **Plot options** area, where check box options are available to control different plotting features for the final sheet.

The last area in the lower-right corner of the **Page Setup** dialog box is the **Drawing orientation** area. This area is used to orient the sheet of paper in layout space. Options include **Portrait** and **Landscape**. These options plot the layout space horizontally or vertically on the sheet. Use the **Plot upside-down** check box to plot either the **Portrait** or **Landscape** option upside-down.

When you are finished adjusting settings for the page setup, pick the **OK** button to return to the **Page Setup Manager**. If you need to, create additional page setups as previously outlined. When you are finished creating all the desired page setups, highlight the page setup to be assigned to the current layout tab, and then pick the **Set Current** button. This assigns the page setup to the layout. The next time this layout tab is selected for plotting, the page setup settings govern how the sheet plots. Pick **OK** to exit the **Page Setup Manager** and return to the drawing screen. If other layouts are created for the different sizes of paper, select the next layout tab, access the **Page Setup Manager**, and assign a page setup.

The final step in setting up the layout is to create a title block and border for the sheet. The paper size for the layout is determined in the page setup, so the correct paper size is displayed in the drawing window. Draw a title block full-scale, and add desired fields and text to finish the title block. Finally, to make this drawing with all the layout tabs available for other projects, the drawing needs to be saved as a template. Select **File** > **Save As...** to save the drawing as a template. In the **Save Drawing As** dialog box, select the **Files of type:** drop-down list at the bottom of the dialog box and choose the **AutoCAD Drawing Template (*.dwt)** option. This changes the **Save in:** directory to the Template folder in the default directories. Give the template a name and pick the **Save** button to save the drawing for future use in other projects.

NOTE In most situations, the default sheet templates are a good starting point for customizing your own layout template. These templates already include multiple layout tabs set to different sizes of paper. The only work that should have to be modified in these templates is setting the title block to meet your school or company standard and ensuring the page setups are set up correctly with the desired plotter. After making these changes, save the modified template as a new custom template.

The Sheets Tab

Now that you know how to create a template containing layout tabs, sheet drawings can be created and used in the **Project Navigator**. Chapter 3 provided an introduction to the **Project Navigator** and the different drawings created, managed, and used in a BIM project. Once the BIM modeling and elevation, plan, and section views have been annotated, sheet files can be created and plotted in hard copy form.

When the **Sheets** tab is first selected, a sheet set is listed at the top of the palette with the same name as the project. See **Figure 24-6.** The sheet set controls information about sheets, such as where the sheet files are saved, which template and plotting settings are used to create the sheet size, and the name of the project. Below the sheet set are subsets. *Subsets* are groups within the sheet set that organize sheets and have their own settings to control the creation of sheets stored under the subset. In **Figure 24-6,** the sheet set named New 2007 Project is listed with two subsets below it. The Architectural subset includes additional subsets for the different types of sheets that can be created for a construction document set. Each subset includes its own sheet settings, such as where the sheets are saved on the hard drive or network drives. Each subset also contains the template that includes layout tabs used to control the paper size and plot settings.

Before new sheets can be created, it is important to understand how the properties for sheet creation are set up. Right-clicking over the sheet set icon and selecting the **Properties...** option displays the **Sheet Set Properties** dialog box, shown in **Figure 24-7.** This dialog box is used to set the properties for the sheet set, such as the name of the sheet set, the project where the sheet set belongs, and the template file used to create the desired sheet sizes. Selecting a sheet creation template controls the paper size used when creating sheets filed under the sheet set icon. The settings assigned here control the properties for new sheets created under the sheet set icon.

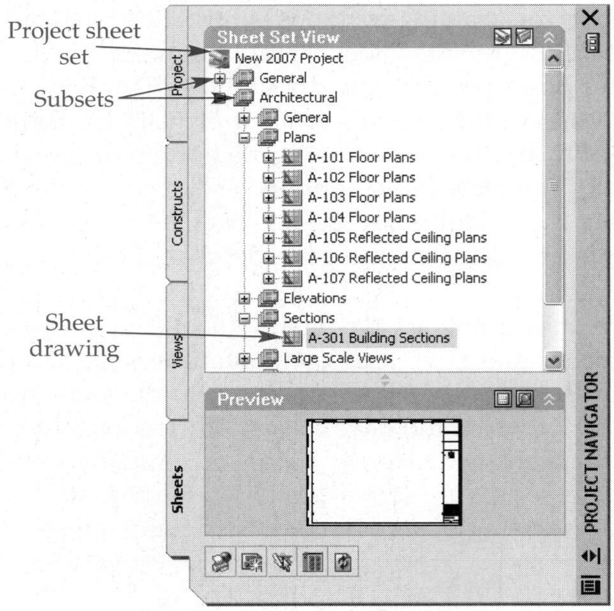

Figure 24-6.
The **Sheets** tab includes a sheet set that controls the properties for newly created sheets that will be used to print the construction document set of drawings.

Project sheet set

Subsets

Sheet drawing

Sheet Set View

New 2007 Project
General
Architectural
    General
    Plans
        A-101 Floor Plans
        A-102 Floor Plans
        A-103 Floor Plans
        A-104 Floor Plans
        A-105 Reflected Ceiling Plans
        A-106 Reflected Ceiling Plans
        A-107 Reflected Ceiling Plans
    Elevations
    Sections
        A-301 Building Sections
    Large Scale Views

Preview

PROJECT NAVIGATOR

Figure 24-7.
The **Sheet Set Properties** dialog box is used to set the properties for the sheet set. These properties are used as the default for new sheets created in the sheet set.

Sheet set name

Select to specify a template and sheet size to be used when creating new sheets

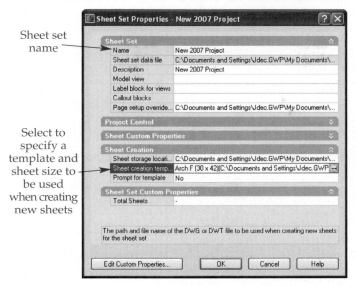

Right-clicking over the sheet set icon can also be used to create a new sheet organized under the sheet set icon or a new subset (a category under the sheet set), which can have its own properties controlling the creation of sheets organized under it. To create a new subset, right-click over the sheet set icon, and choose **New** > **Subset** from the shortcut menu. This creates a new subset. Subsets are similar to the root level sheet set, because they allow you to specify where the sheets categorized under this subset are stored and what template to use that governs the layout sheet size for any new sheets. Right-clicking over a subset and choosing the **Properties...** option displays the **Subset Properties** dialog box. See **Figure 24-8.** Notice that this dialog box only includes two options. Use the ellipsis (**...**) buttons to specify the storage location for the sheets or to select the template for sheet creation.

When choosing a template for sheet creation, choose a template that includes paper sizes you intend to use for any new sheets you create. When the ellipsis (**...**) button is chosen for the sheet creation template, the **Select Layout as Sheet Template** dialog box is displayed, as shown in **Figure 24-9.** This dialog box is used to specify the

Figure 24-8.
The **Subset Properties** dialog box is used to specify the storage location and the template to be used for sheet creation for any new sheets created under the subset.

Type a name for the subset

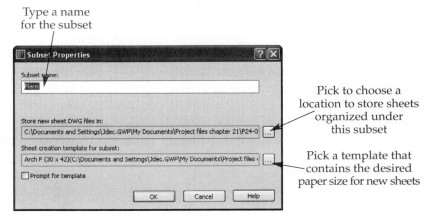

Pick to choose a location to store sheets organized under this subset

Pick a template that contains the desired paper size for new sheets

Figure 24-9.
The **Select Layout as Sheet Template** dialog box is used to specify the template and layout sheet size to be used for new sheets.

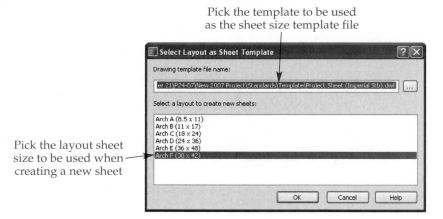

Pick the template to be used as the sheet size template file

Pick the layout sheet size to be used when creating a new sheet

path to the desired template. Once a template has been chosen, a list of layouts within the template is displayed in the list at the bottom of the dialog box. The layouts indicate the size of paper set up in the layout. Choose a layout tab to be the default paper size for the subset when new sheets are created.

Subsets can be created for each paper size you plan on using for plotting; building disciplines such as architectural, structural, mechanical, and electrical; or any other categories in which you want to organize the sheets. Subsets do not have to be used. The sheet set controls the same properties as the subset. If a subset is used, however, the properties for the subset override the settings in the sheet set for any drawings created under the subset.

Exercise
24-2   Complete the Exercise on the Student CD.

Creating a Sheet

To add a sheet to the project, right-click over a subset the sheet is organized under, or in the absence of a subset, right-click over the sheet set icon and select **New > Sheet...** from the shortcut menu. This displays the **New Sheet** dialog box, shown in **Figure 24-10.** Enter a number for the sheet number. This number is added to any detail or section tags referring to this sheet. Next, add a sheet title for the sheet drawing. While entering the number and sheet title fields, the sheet file name is automatically entered by combining the two fields.

The folder path displays where the sheet drawing is saved. By default, this location is specified in the project properties accessed from the **Project Browser**. The **Sheet template:** text box displays the layout tab name and the template from which it is being borrowed. If the **Subset Properties** dialog box had the **Prompt for template** check box selected, an ellipsis (...) button is located at the end of this path, allowing you to select a layout tab from the template file. When you are finished specifying the number and title name, pick the **OK** button to create the sheet drawing file.

A project can have as many sheets as needed for the construction documents. Appendix D provides some examples for sheet numbering and naming that can be applied to the sheet drawings in your Architectural Desktop projects.

Figure 24-10.
The **New Sheet** dialog box is used to name and number a new sheet drawing added to the project.

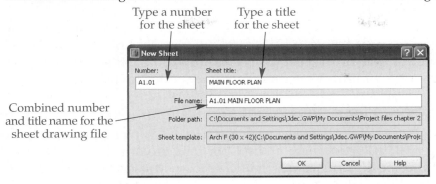

Type a number for the sheet

Type a title for the sheet

Combined number and title name for the sheet drawing file

Working with a Sheet

After a sheet has been created and added to the **Project Navigator**, the sheet can be opened for editing, and views can be added. Double-click the sheet in the **Project Navigator** to open the file. When a sheet is opened, the layout tab that was used to create the sheet is current in the drawing window, and the virtual sheet of paper is displayed in the window. See **Figure 24-11**.

If you are using the sheet templates or have created your own template based on the default sheet template, automatic text fields in the title block have been filled out based on the sheet number and sheet title entered when first creating the sheet. See **Figure 24-11**. Automatic fields are text values with a gray highlight by default.

Automatic values can be modified by double-clicking the text to open the **Text Formatting** tool. The automatic field is displayed in the window. If you want to overwrite the automatic value, highlight the value and enter a new value. If you want to

Figure 24-11.
When a sheet drawing is opened, the layout used to create the sheet is displayed. If the title block includes automatic text fields, some of the fields might already be filled out based on the sheet number and title.

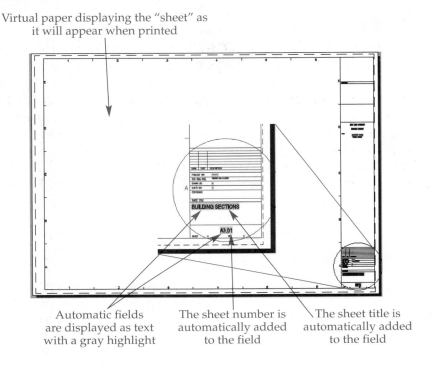

Virtual paper displaying the "sheet" as it will appear when printed

Automatic fields are displayed as text with a gray highlight

The sheet number is automatically added to the field

The sheet title is automatically added to the field

retain the automatic nature of the text, right-click over the automatic field and select the **Edit Field...** option from the shortcut menu. This displays the **Field** dialog box, where a different automatic field can be selected for use in the title block.

In addition to working with the text and automatic fields in layout space, geometry can be drawn on the paper, as in model space. Zooming and panning also work within the layout space area. Once a sheet has been set up and the title block has been edited, model space views within a view drawing can be added to the sheet.

Adding Model Space Views to the Sheet

Earlier in this text, model space views were discussed. Chapter 3 introduced the concept of creating a model space view around portions of your drawing. In later chapters, the creation of view drawings with model space views was discussed. Model space views are zoomed-in views of portions of your model. For example, in the case of a floor plan view drawing, a model space view can be created that surrounds the floor plan of the model and the dimensions around the floor plan. When the view is set current, the drawing window zooms in on the boundaries of the model space view.

In addition to using model space views to zoom around the model, the model space views are also the portions of the model added to a sheet drawing. When it is added to a sheet, the scale assigned to the model space view is applied as it is added to the sheet. This allows you to take a full-scale model drawing and have it display using a scale that allows it to fit on the sheet of paper. Multiple model space views can be added to a sheet. The only limitation is the amount of room you have on your sheet. Refer to **Figure 24-3.**

To add model space views to a sheet drawing, first open the sheet drawing from the **Sheets** tab in the **Project Navigator**. Next, access the **Views** tab in the **Project Navigator**, locate the view drawing containing the model space views you want to add to the sheet and expand the + sign beside the view drawing in the **Project Navigator**. This provides you with a list of model space views in the view drawing. See **Figure 24-12.**

With the view drawing expanded and displaying a list of model space views, select a model space view, and then drag the view from the **Project Navigator** onto the sheet of paper. Move the cursor onto the sheet of paper and release the pick button. This displays a viewport showing the model space view attached to the cursor. See **Figure 24-13.** A tooltip appears beside the cursor, indicating the current scale of the view. If this is the desired scale for the view, pick a point on the sheet to place the viewport. If you want to use a different scale, right-click to display a list of available scales that can be applied to the viewport. Choosing a different scale adjusts the size of the viewport automatically in the sheet drawing.

Figure 24-12.
Expanding a view drawing with model space views will display the model space views available for dragging and dropping onto the sheet layout.

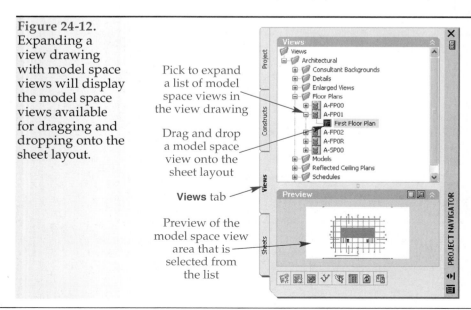

Pick to expand a list of model space views in the view drawing

Drag and drop a model space view onto the sheet layout

Views tab

Preview of the model space view area that is selected from the list

Figure 24-13.
Drag and drop a model space view from the **Project Navigator** onto the sheet layout. A viewport is displayed attached to the cursor, displaying the current scale for the view. Right-click to change the scale or pick a point to place the viewport.

When the view is dragged and dropped, it is placed in a viewport that is attached to the cursor

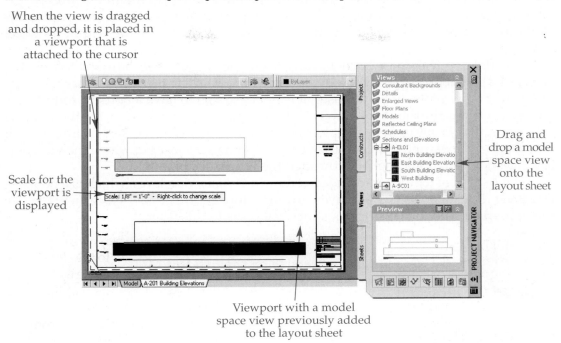

Scale for the viewport is displayed

Drag and drop a model space view onto the layout sheet

Viewport with a model space view previously added to the layout sheet

After adding a viewport, continue to drag and drop other model space views to add the viewports to the layout sheet. Views associated with a callout tag, such as details, elevations, and sections, are updated so the callout tag displays the detail/section number and the sheet number on which it is located.

NOTE
Floating viewports can overlap one another. Each viewport contains its own view to model space, so overlapping viewports do not interfere with one another.

Exercise
24-3   Complete the Exercise on the Student CD.

Working with Viewports

When a model space view is dragged and dropped onto a layout sheet, a *viewport* into "model space" is created containing the model space view. These viewports are known as floating viewports. *Floating viewports* are similar to holes cut into a sheet of paper so the model space building can be viewed under the paper. Floating viewports are separate objects that can be moved around and arranged, or floated, on the layout sheet. In addition to creating the viewport, the view drawing containing the model space view is externally referenced into the sheet drawing. Any changes made to the element, construct, or view drawings are updated in the sheet drawings.

Editing functions such as moving, copying, erasing, and stretching can be used on viewports when you are working in the layout space area to arrange and modify the floating viewports and their borders. Moving the viewport allows you to adjust where the viewport border is placed on the sheet. Moving a viewport maintains the current view and scale of the building within the viewport. Erasing a viewport removes the "hole" from the paper, but it maintains the referenced view drawing within the sheet drawing.

The floating viewport borders drawn on the layout sheet are created on the current layer. If a printable layer was current when dragging the model space view, the viewport border plots. In many cases, it is not desirable to have a border around each viewport on the finished plot. To avoid this situation, create a layer for the floating viewports that is set to be a nonplotting layer. Set this layer current before adding model space views, and then add the views or change the layer to which the viewport is assigned to a nonplotting layer through the **Properties** palette.

The Aec Sheet templates included contain a G-Anno-View layer, which is a nonplotting layer for viewports. Set this layer current before adding model space views, or use the **Properties** palette to change existing viewports to this layer.

Exercise
24-4   **Complete the Exercise on the Student CD.**

Modifying Viewport Properties

When viewports are first added to a layout sheet, the properties of the viewport are derived from the view drawing in which the model space view resides. Settings such as the current visual style and display configuration in the view drawing are applied to the viewport. Layer visibility and viewport scale are also set in the view drawing. The properties of the viewport can be adjusted after the viewport is added to the sheet.

The **Properties** palette can be used to make a number of adjustments to a viewport. To review the properties for a viewport, select the viewport border, and then access the **Properties** palette. See **Figure 24-14.** The properties for a viewport are divided into three separate categories: **General, Geometry,** and **Misc.** The following properties are available for modifying a viewport.

Figure 24-14.
Viewport properties in the **Properties** palette.

General viewport properties

Size and location properties

Viewport display settings

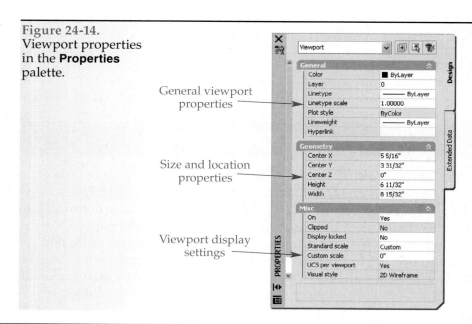

Architectural Desktop and Its Applications

The **General** category includes standard properties that all AutoCAD geometry share. These include the following:

- **Color.** This property controls the color of the viewport.
- **Layer.** This specifies the layer on which the viewport is drawn.
- **Linetype.** The **Linetype** property specifies the viewport border linetype.
- **Linetype scale.** This property specifies the visual scale of the viewport border's linetype.
- **Plot style.** This specifies a plot style name assigned to the viewport border if using STB pen tables.
- **Lineweight.** The **Lineweight** property sets a lineweight to the viewport border.
- **Hyperlink.** This property indicates a hyperlink assigned to the viewport border.

The **Geometry** category controls the location of the viewport on the layout sheet and the size of the viewport:

- **Center X**, **Y**, and **Z.** These three properties control the placement of the viewport onto the layout sheet in relation to the 0,0 point in the lower-left corner of the printable area of the sheet.
- **Height.** This specifies the height of the viewport in the Y axis.
- **Width.** This property specifies the width of the viewport in the Z axis.

The **Misc** category includes properties that control the display of the viewports contents:

- **On.** This property turns on or off the visibility of the contents within the viewport.
- **Clipped.** This property specifies whether the viewport has been clipped or is the standard viewport rectangular shape.
- **Display locked.** This property causes the scale of the viewport to be locked. If any zooming occurs within the viewport, this property will maintain the scale of the viewport.
- **Standard scale.** The **Standard scale** property specifies the scale of the viewport.
- **Custom scale.** This property displays a custom scale for the viewport if the viewport scale has been modified.
- **UCS per viewport.** This property controls the behavior of the UCS for the viewport.
- **Visual style.** This specifies the visual style used in the viewport.
- **Shade plot.** The **Shade plot** property specifies if the viewport is plotted hiding the lines behind other 3D faces, or if the viewport is using a visual style.
- **Linked to Sheet View.** This indicates if the viewport is linked between the sheet file and the view drawing.

In addition to using the **Properties** palette to adjust what is displayed within the borders of a viewport, a display configuration can be applied to viewport. To do this, first select a viewport to be assigned a display configuration, and then choose the desired display configuration to apply from the **Display Configuration** menu located in the drawing window status bar. This assigns the contents within the viewport the new display configuration. Display configurations are discussed in Chapter 7.

Alternatively, after picking the **Display Configuration** menu, you can pick any number of viewports in the layout sheet to which you want to apply a display configuration, and then press the [Enter] key. The **Display Configuration** menu appears, allowing you to select a display configuration that is applied to all the selected viewports.

Viewport Layer Display

As mentioned previously, whenever a viewport is added to the layout sheet, everything visible in the model space view is displayed in the layout sheet's viewport. Depending on how your drawings are organized and laid out, this can be a lot of geometry being sorted through in the viewport, possibly causing linework to overlap.

When a model space view is added to a layout sheet, the view drawing containing the model space view is externally referenced into the sheet drawing. When this happens, a layer is created with the same name as the view name, and the xref is placed on this layer. Freezing this layer freezes the entire contents of the xref. Additionally, any layers within the view drawing are named using the syntax of *drawingname|layername*. For example, the layer name MainFloor|A-Anno-Dims indicates the A-Anno-Dims layer is found in the MainFloor drawing. This syntax allows you to find layers based on the drawings where they are located.

There might be instances where a viewport displays geometry on a layer you want to freeze. This can be solved by freezing the layers that are not needed in this viewport, but this will also freeze the layers in other viewports on the same layout sheet. A better alternative is to freeze the layers within the viewports only.

Before any layers can be frozen, a viewport must be active. To make a viewport active, double-click within the border of the desired viewport. This makes the view within the viewport the current space. The active viewport is indicated by the viewport border becoming a bold outline. Notice also that all the viewports now display the UCS as the model space **UCS** icon in the lower-left corner of the viewport and not the layout space **UCS** icon located in the lower-left corner of the sheet. See **Figure 24-15.** Picking inside the border of another viewport sets that viewport as the active viewport. To make the layout space active again, double-click outside of the viewport border or outside of the layout sheet.

Once a viewport is active, layers within the viewport can be frozen or thawed. Layers inside floating viewports can be frozen by using the **Freeze** or **Thaw** option in the current viewport icon in the layer drop-down list on the **Layer Properties** toolbar, as in **Figure 24-16.** Locate the desired layer to be frozen, and then pick the icon. If the icon displays as a sun with a rectangle, the layer is thawed in the current viewport. If the icon is displayed as a snowflake with a rectangle, the layer is frozen in the current viewport.

Figure 24-15.
Double-click inside of a viewport to make it active. Pick inside of another viewport to make that viewport active. Double-click outside of a viewport to set the layout space current. Drawing courtesy 3D-DZYN.

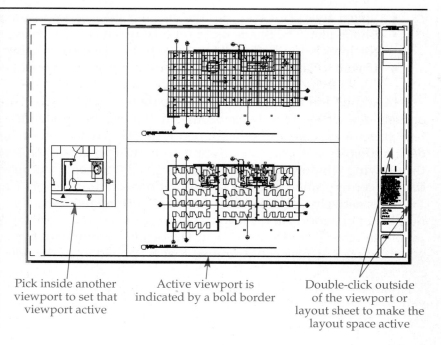

Pick inside another viewport to set that viewport active

Active viewport is indicated by a bold border

Double-click outside of the viewport or layout sheet to make the layout space active

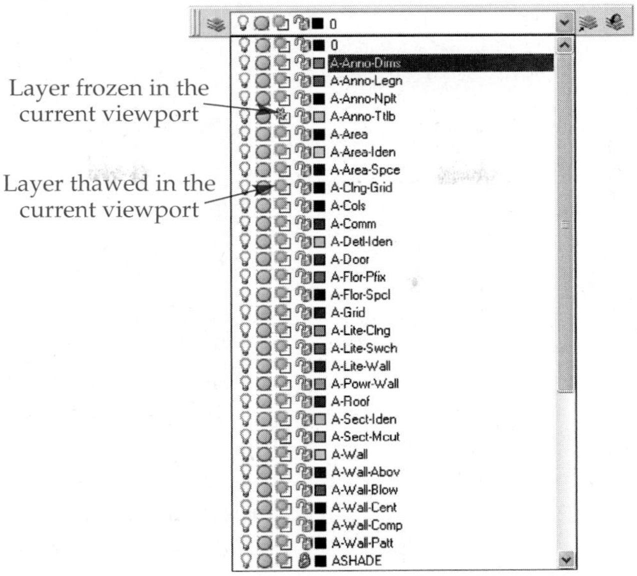

Figure 24-16.
Pick the snowflake or sun icon to freeze or thaw layers in the active viewport.

Layer frozen in the current viewport

Layer thawed in the current viewport

Freezing/thawing layers in the current viewport is different from the standard snowflake/sun icon because the layer is only frozen in the active viewport and not globally in the entire drawing. Freezing layers in a viewport also helps system performance. Layers beyond the viewport boundaries are still calculated by Architectural Desktop. Freezing these layers saves time regenerating the viewport because the layers are no longer being calculated.

When you are finished freezing or thawing layers in the current viewport, double-click outside of the viewport to set the layout space current.

NOTE

Do not freeze layer 0 in model space or in a viewport. Objects such as multi-view blocks are dependent on this layer. Freezing this layer affects objects on other layers.

Controlling Linetype Display

When a set of construction documents is produced, it is important to ensure the drawings look consistent, regardless of how many people have worked on them. When creating viewports that include different scales, however, the linetypes are scaled differently per the viewport's scale.

The **LTSCALE** system variable controls the scale of linetypes in a drawing. Typically, a **LTSCALE** value equals the drawing scale. For example, if you are working with a scale of 1/8″ = 1′-0″, the scale factor is 96. Thus, the **LTSCALE** value should be 96. This scale is good in most situations, especially when the drawing is being worked on in model space; however, when the drawing is taken to layout space and two viewports are assigned two different scales, the linetypes are also scaled differently. See **Figure 24-17.**

It is often desirable on the finished drawing to have the dashes and dots of the linetypes appear the same length. The variable known as **PSLTSCALE** is used to do this. **PSLTSCALE** stands for paper space linetype scale. Setting this value to 1 and the **LTSCALE** value to 1 makes the linetypes appear the same size in the two differently scaled viewports, as shown in **Figure 24-17.**

Figure 24-17.
Two floating
viewports with
different scales
and an **LTSCALE**
set to 48. The same
viewports with the
PSLTSCALE and
LTSCALE set to 1
display the linetypes
with the same length
dashes.

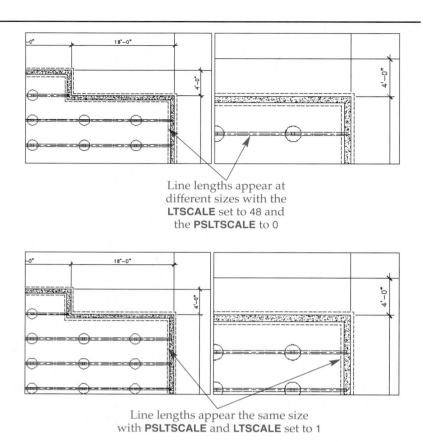

Line lengths appear at
different sizes with the
LTSCALE set to 48 and
the **PSLTSCALE** to 0

Line lengths appear the same size
with **PSLTSCALE** and **LTSCALE** set to 1

Once the viewports have been arranged on the layout sheet, desired layers have been frozen/thawed, and linetypes are displaying correctly, the sheet can be printed. The next section reviews plotting from within the **Project Navigator**.

Getting Ready to Plot

The final step in a building model project is to plot a hard copy set of drawings so the contractor, subcontractors, and building officials can refer to the drawings as the building is being constructed. Before plotting, you need to consider what type of final output is desired. For example, will the file be sent to a printer or plotter, or will it be a file that can be viewed over the Internet? This section discusses how to plot the layout sheet.

Plotting the Drawing

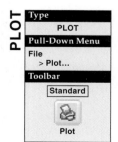

There are a couple of methods that can be used to plot the sheet drawings. The main method is to open the sheet drawing and use the **PLOT** command to plot the drawings. To access this command, pick **File > Plot...** from the pull-down menu, pick the **Plot** button in the **Standard** toolbar, type PLOT, or if the layout tabs are visible, right-click over the top of a layout tab and pick the **Plot...** option. This displays the **Plot** dialog box, shown in **Figure 24-18**. This dialog box is similar to the **Page Setup** dialog box, with a few additional settings. The **Plot** dialog box also displays the plot settings assigned to the layout through the page setup settings.

The new settings in the **Plot** dialog box not included in the **Page Setup** dialog box are found in the **Page setup** and **Plot options** areas of the **Plot** dialog box. These include the following:

Figure 24-18.
The **Plot** dialog box is used to verify the settings for the layout and plot the drawing.

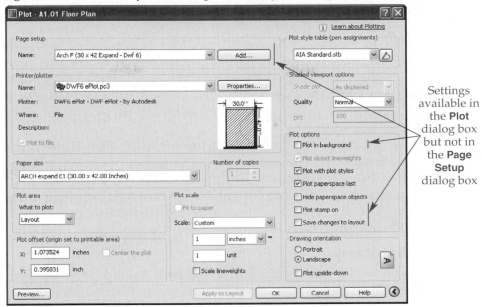

- **Name.** This drop-down list in the **Page setup** area includes a list of page setups available in the drawing. Choose a different page setup to use alternate plot settings. The **Add...** button is also available to create a new page setup. This will allow you to name a new setup and then make changes to the plot settings in the **Plot** dialog box.
- **Plot in background.** Choose this check box in the **Plot options** area to allow plotting of the drawing sheets while you continue to work within AutoCAD. Choosing this option slows performance of the AutoCAD program and can take longer than normal to plot the drawings.
- **Plot stamp on.** This option in the **Plot options** area is used to add a plot stamp to the drawing. Choosing this option displays the **Plot Stamp Settings...** button, where the plot stamp settings can be configured. Setting up a plot stamp is covered later in this chapter.
- **Save changes to layout.** Selecting this check box in the **Plot options** area allows you to save changes made in the **Plot** dialog box to the page setup name listed in the **Name:** drop-down list in the upper-left corner of the dialog box.

Once you have verified or modified the settings for the plot, pick the **OK** button. If the plot is sent to a plotter or printer, the hard copy will be available shortly. If the plot is going to the Design Web Format (DWF) plotter, an electronic file known as a DWF is created. A *DWF* is an electronic file of a printed drawing. This is similar to a PDF copy of the plan, but with interactive capabilities.

Publishing Drawings

Another method for plotting drawings is to use publishing tools. Within the publishing tools, there are three methods of publishing/plotting a drawing: **Publish to DWF**, **Publish to Plotter**, and **Publish to Alternate Page Setup**. These three publishing options can be accessed through the **Project Navigator** by right-clicking the sheet set icon, a sheet subset icon, or a sheet icon. Depending on the chosen option, the entire set of sheets, a subset of sheets, or an individual sheet is published/plotted.

If you want to publish a single-sheet file, right-click over a sheet in the **Sheets** tab, and select **Publish** from the shortcut menu. The three publishing methods and some publishing settings commands can be found within this shortcut menu. The following publishing options are included under the **Publish** shortcut menu:

- **Publish to DWF.** Choose this option to plot the sheet to a DWF file. This option overrides the plotter setting in the page setup and uses the default DWF plotter to create an electronic DWF file of the sheet. Depending on the sheet set settings, you might need to specify a name and location to which to save the DWF.
- **Publish to Plotter.** Choosing this option is similar to accessing the **PLOT** command. The differences here are that the **Plot** dialog box is not displayed and the sheet is published based on the settings in the page setup.
- **Publish to Alternate Page Setup.** This method allows you to choose a different page setup to use to plot the sheet. The settings previously set in the page setup are used to plot the drawing.

To publish all sheet drawings within the subset at once, right-click over a sheet subset, choose **Publish**, and then choose one of these options. Depending on the sheet set settings for DWF files, choosing the **Publish to DWF** option creates individual DWF files or one multipaged DWF file. To publish all the sheet drawings within the sheet set at once, right-click over the sheet set icon, choose **Publish**, and then choose one of the three publishing methods.

Adding a Plot Stamp

A *plot stamp* is a text tag applied to the final hard copy or DWF at the time of plotting. The plot stamp can include information, such as the drawing name, the date and time the drawing was plotted, and the plotter device to which the drawing was plotted. These settings can be configured while in the **Plot** dialog box by selecting the **Plot stamp on** check box and then picking the **Plot Stamp Settings...** button. You can also right-click over a sheet, subset, or the sheet set icon and pick the **Publish** > **Plot Stamp Settings...** option, which allows you to set up the plot stamp for inclusion on your prints. In either case, the **Plot Stamp** dialog box is displayed, as in **Figure 24-19**.

In the **Plot stamp fields** area, select the type of items you want to have included in the plot stamp. The **User defined fields** area allows you to define custom fields you would like to add to the plot stamp. Use the **Add/Edit** button to add custom fields to the **User defined fields** area. For example, the **Drafter** and **Student** custom fields have been added and then selected in the drop-down lists.

In order to add a plot stamp to the finished plot, you need to save the plot stamp as an external plot stamp settings file. Select the **Save As** button in the **Plot stamp parameter file** area and specify a location and name for the file. Selecting the **Advanced** button allows you to configure additional parameters for the plot stamp in the **Advanced Options** dialog box. See **Figure 24-20**.

Figure 24-19.
The **Plot Stamp** dialog box is used to configure the plot stamp to be added to the drawing.

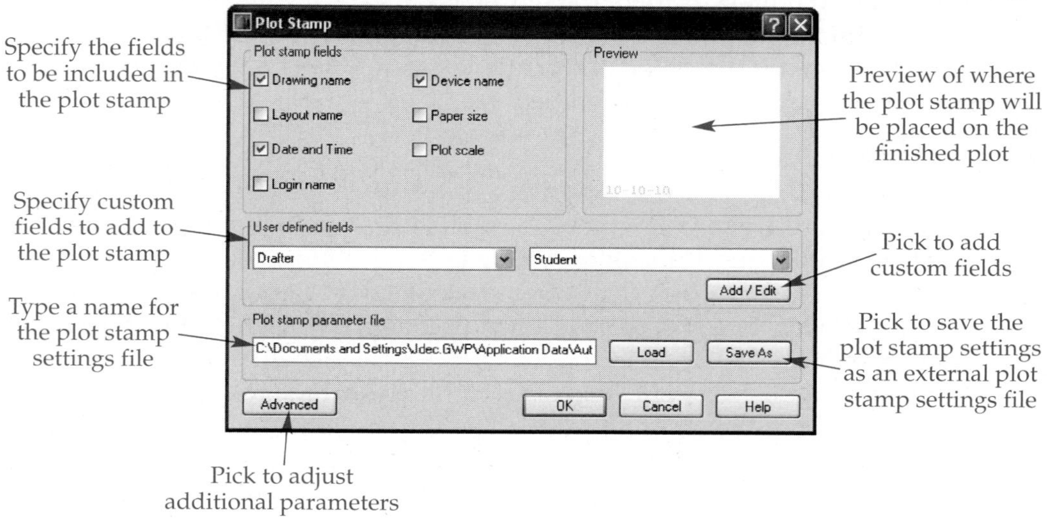

Specify the fields to be included in the plot stamp

Specify custom fields to add to the plot stamp

Type a name for the plot stamp settings file

Pick to adjust additional parameters

Preview of where the plot stamp will be placed on the finished plot

Pick to add custom fields

Pick to save the plot stamp settings as an external plot stamp settings file

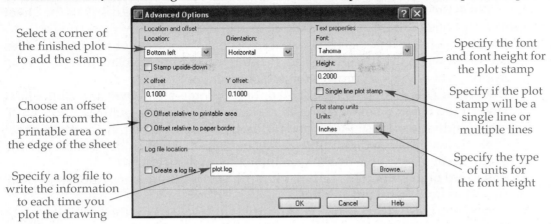

Select a corner of the finished plot to add the stamp

Choose an offset location from the printable area or the edge of the sheet

Specify a log file to write the information to each time you plot the drawing

Specify the font and font height for the plot stamp

Specify if the plot stamp will be a single line or multiple lines

Specify the type of units for the font height

The following options are included in the **Advanced Options** dialog box:

- **Location and offset.** This area is used to control where the plot stamp is located. This area includes a **Location:** drop-down list specifying a corner of the paper that includes the plot stamp. The **Orientation:** drop-down list specifies whether the plot stamp will be plotted horizontally or vertically. The **X offset:** and **Y offset:** text boxes offset the plot stamp from the corner of the plottable area or the corner of the layout sheet.
- **Text properties.** Use the **Font:** drop-down list to specify the font to use for the plot stamp. Specify a text height by entering a value in the **Height:** text box, and specify whether the plot stamp is printed as a single line or multiple lines in the **Single line plot stamp** check box.
- **Plot stamp units.** Select the type of units to use for the plot stamp text height. Values include inches, millimeters, and pixels.
- **Log file location.** Select the **Create a log file** check box to keep a log each time the layout is plotted. Use the **Browse...** button to determine a path and a name for the log file.

NOTE

A *log file* can be generated without generating a plot stamp. This file keeps track each time the layout is plotted and writes the information to a log file that can be opened in a text editor, such as the Windows Notepad program.

When you finish setting the parameters for the plot stamp, pick the **OK** button to return to the **Plot Stamp** dialog box. If you are generating a plot stamp, make sure the plot stamp parameters file has been specified, and then pick the **OK** button to return to the **Plot** dialog box.

The plot stamp is added to the final output if you selected the **Plot stamp on** check box in the **Plot** dialog box and picked the **OK** button. If you are publishing the drawings from the **Project Navigator**, the plot stamp is not added unless you right-click over the sheet, subset, or sheet set icon and pick **Publish** > **Include Plot Stamp**. This causes the published drawings to add a plot stamp to the final hard copies or the DWF files.

Sheet Set Publishing Options

Before publishing a set of sheets, you might want to review the publishing options for the sheet set. The sheet set controls the initial settings for publishing, and then any subsets below the sheet set inherit the same settings. You can make adjustments/overrides to the settings, and then the individual sheets also inherit the publishing settings from the subset where they belong. You can also set overrides to the settings. To check the settings at each level, right-click over the sheet set, subset, or sheet icons, and select **Publish > Sheet Set Publish Options...** from the shortcut menu. This displays the **Sheet Set Publish Options** dialog box. This dialog box includes the following settings:

- **Location.** This text box is used to specify the path location of where DWF files are saved when they are published. Picking the text box displays an ellipsis (...) button, where you can browse for a folder location.
- **DWF type.** This setting includes two options: **Single-sheet DWF** and **Multi-sheet DWF.** If the **Single-sheet DWF** option is selected, all sheets published to a DWF create individual DWF files—one for each sheet published. If the **Multi-sheet DWF** option is selected, multiple sheets being published under a subset or the entire sheet set is published into a single file multisheet DWF.
- **Password protection.** This setting allows you to determine if a published DWF file is password protected or not.
- **Password.** This setting is used to specify the password for the DWF file.
- **DWF naming.** This setting determines if a published DWF will be named from this dialog box or you are prompted to name the DWF at the time the DWF is published.
- **Name.** If the DWF name is specified in this dialog box, type the name for the DWF in this text box.

Depending on the options chosen, the DWF can include information about the drawing such as the layer names, property set information, and block information. By including this information in the DWF, you are making the electronic drawings very valuable to a contractor, building official, and owner. The following settings include information within the drawing that can be included in a published DWF file:

- **Layer information.** If this information is included, a reviewer of the DWF has the ability to turn layers on and off in the final DWF file. They do not have the ability to modify any part of the DWF, such as deleting a layer.
- **Sheet set information.** This setting allows you to include sheet set properties into the published DWF file.
- **Sheet information.** This setting is used to include sheet properties and attributes within the sheet in the published DWF file.
- **Block information.** Use this setting to include individual block properties and attributes in the published DWF file.
- **Block template file.** This setting becomes available when you are including block information and is used to specify a block template that defines the properties and attributes to publish from selected blocks.
- **AEC property set data.** This option is used to include property set data assigned to objects into the published DWF file. As BIM becomes the standard in the industry, more information about the objects within the drawing are required in the DWF file. Property set data assigned to an object could include specific information about the object specified in the drawings.
- **AEC DWF Options.** This text box indicates the path to the file containing the property set definitions that will be included in the published DWF file.

The final options are for use when publishing a 3D DWF file. A 3D DWF file is a file of the completed model from Architectural Desktop. The 3D DWF is a file a reviewer can look at, around, and through, without the ability to modify the original model geometry drawings. The following settings are used to control the 3D DWF:

- **Group by Xref hierarchy.** This setting arranges the objects in the 3D DWF by xref hierarchy in Autodesk's free application, the *DWF™ Viewer.*
- **Publish with materials.** This setting includes the materials specified in the model into the published 3D DWF file.
- **AEC Group Individual Objects By.** This setting groups the Architectural Desktop object found in the model into the 3D DWF file for easy recognition of the different model parts used in the model.

When you are finished specifying the settings for the sheet set, pick the **OK** button. It is recommended that you set the options at the sheet set level first to set the base settings for publishing. Next, adjust the subset and the individual sheet options as needed.

Exercise 24-5   *Complete the Exercise on the Student CD.*

2D DWF Files

DWF files give you the ability to plot a sheet or multiple sheets to an electronic file that can be viewed using the DWF Viewer. Architectural Desktop provides you with a DWF plotter configuration. Selecting this plotter plots the sheet to a DWF file instead of a hard copy. The file can later be printed to a plotter or printer; placed on a Web page; and e-mailed to clients, building jurisdictions, and contractors. When you are finished adjusting the parameters for the DWF file, pick the **Plot** button to plot the drawing as a DWF file.

The DWF file can be viewed through a Web page created with the **PUBLISHTOWEB** command. To access this command, pick **File** > **Publish to Web...** from the pull-down menu or type PUBLISHTOWEB. Another option is to use the DWF Viewer. For more information on how to create a Web page using the **PUBLISHTOWEB** command, look it up in the Command Reference section of the **Autodesk Architectural Desktop 2007 Help** window.

By default, the DWF Viewer is installed during the installation of Architectural Desktop. If you create DWF files that need to be sent to clients, vendors, or builders, the recipients need to have the DWF Viewer installed on their machines in order to review and print the drawings. **Figure 24-21** displays a DWF file opened in the DWF Viewer program. The DWF Viewer can be downloaded for free from the Autodesk Web site. Another free program from Autodesk called *Design Review* can be obtained from Autodesk and includes redline tools that can be used to mark up DWF files. The markups, in turn, can be inserted into the Architectural Desktop drawing by picking **Insert** > **Markup...** from the pull-down menu.

Figure 24-21.
The Design Web Format (DWF) Viewer included with Architectural Desktop is used to review DWF files.

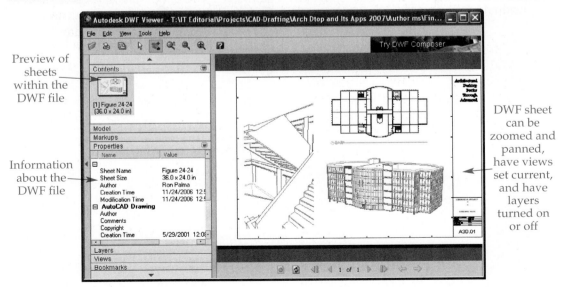

The advantage to plotting a drawing to a DWF file is that the drawings can be shared with another person without the other person actually having AutoCAD or Architectural Desktop. Another advantage is that the drawings cannot be edited. This provides a good means of sending a drawing file to consultants for review without them having the ability to edit the drawing. With both the DWF Viewer and Design Review, layers can be frozen, views can be restored, and zooming into or panning around the drawing can be accomplished. DWF files occupy very little memory in the actual electronic file and can, therefore, be sent through e-mail without much concern regarding file size.

Exercise 24-6 Complete the Exercise on the Student CD.

3D DWF Files

A 3D DWF file is three-dimensional model information published to a DWF file. Similar to the standard 2D DWF file, the model can be reviewed, be zoomed, be panned, have layers turned on and off, and be used by a consultant without AutoCAD or Architectural Desktop. To publish a model as a 3D DWF file, pick the **Open Drawing Menu** icon from the drawing window status bar. See **Figure 24-22**. Choose the **Publish to 3D DWF...** option.

This displays the **Export 3D DWF** dialog box. Choose a location and file name for the 3D DWF file. Pick the **Save** button to process the 3D DWF file. As with the 2D DWF files, use the Windows Explorer program to locate the DWF file and double-click the file to open the 3D DWF file in the DWF Viewer program. See **Figure 24-23**.

Exercise 24-7 Complete the Exercise on the Student CD.

Figure 24-22.
Pick the **Publish to 3D DWF...** option to create a three-dimensional DWF file.

Pick to publish a model as a 3D DWF file

Pick to access the **Open Drawing Menu**

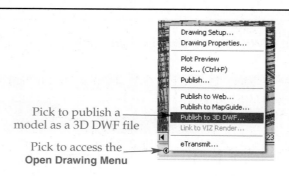

Architectural Desktop and Its Applications

Figure 24-23.
The 3D DWF file viewed in the DWF Viewer program. Notice the side bars are slightly different. The 3D DWF can be spun around and objects can be made transparent and turned on or off.

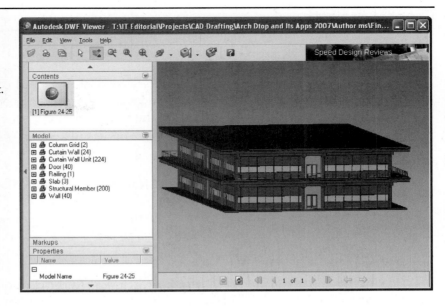

Chapter Test

Answer the following questions. Write your answers on a separate sheet of paper or complete the electronic chapter test on the Student CD.

1. Identify the area of the drawing screen where the construct and element drawings, the model geometry, and the view drawings are created.
2. Give the scale used when drawing in the model space area.
3. Describe and give an example of view drawings.
4. Explain where layout space is established and describe its function.
5. Give another name for layout space.
6. A 3/8"-diameter detail bubble scaled 1/4" = 1'-0" on a drawing is actually drawn as an 18"-diameter circle in model space. Give the formula and calculations for determining the scale factor.
7. Text that is to appear 1/8" high on the finished drawing at a scale of 1/8" = 1'-0" should be drawn 12" high in model space. Give the formula and calculations for determining the scale factor.
8. Where are preconfigured layouts modified to use different paper sizes, assign a plotter, and assign plotted colors and lineweights to the model geometry?
9. How many page setups can a layout tab be assigned?
10. Define *printable area* and identify its appearance.
11. Explain the basic difference between the CTB and STB plot styles.
12. Define *subsets*.
13. Describe floating viewports.
14. What happens when you erase a viewport?
15. Discuss the process used to make sure a viewport border does not plot.
16. How do you make a viewport active?
17. If a viewport is active, how do you make the layout space active?
18. Describe a plot stamp.
19. Explain the use of a log file.
20. What is a DWF file?

Use the techniques covered in this chapter to create the following drawings.

1. Single-Level Residential Project
   A. Access the **Project Browser** and set Residential-Project-01 current.
   B. Access the **Views** tab of the **Project Navigator**. Open the Main Floor Plan view drawing.
   C. Create model space views around the floor plan, door schedule, and window schedule. Set the scale for the views to 1/4" = 1'-0". Add any additional annotations as needed.
   D. Save and close the drawing.
   E. Access the **Views** tab of the **Project Navigator**. Open the Foundation Plan view drawing.
   F. Create model space views around the foundation plan and the structural schedule. Set the scale for the views to 1/4" = 1'-0". Add any additional annotations as needed.
   G. Save and close the drawing.
   H. Access the **Sheets** tab of the **Project Navigator**. Right-click over the Architectural subset and pick the **Properties...** option. In the **Subset Properties** dialog box, choose the Arch D (24x36) Sheet for the default sheet template. Apply the changes to the other nested subsets.
   I. Create the following sheets:

Number	Sheet Title	Sheet Subset
A1.01	Floor Plan	Plans
A1.02	Foundation Plan	Plans
A2.01	Elevations	Elevations
A2.02	Elevations	Elevations
A3.01	Sections	Sections

   J. Open the Floor Plan sheet and add the floor plan, door schedule, and window schedule model space views to the sheet. Make any additional changes as needed. Save and close the drawing.
   K. Open the Foundation Plan sheet and add the foundation and structural schedule model space views to the sheet. Make any additional changes as needed. Save and close the drawing.
   L. Open the elevation sheets and add the south and west model space views to the first sheet. Add the north and east model space views to the second sheet. Make any additional changes as needed. Save and close the drawing.
   M. Open the Section sheet and add the section model space views to the sheet. Make any additional changes as needed. Save and close the drawing.
   N. Right-click over the Residential-Project-01 sheet set icon and pick **Publish > Sheet Set Publish Options...** from the shortcut menu. Set the following settings:

Property	Setting
Location	Sheets folder of Residential-Project-01
DWF type	Multi-sheet DWF
DWF naming	Prompt for name
Layer information	Include
Sheet information	Include
AEC property set data	Include
Publish with materials	No
AEC Group Individual Objects By	Object Type and Style

O. Right-click over the Architectural subset and pick **Publish** > **Publish to DWF**.
P. Save and close any open drawings.
Q. In Windows Explorer, browse to the Sheets folder of Residential-Project-01 and open the DWF file.

2. Single-Level Residential Project
   A. Access the **Project Browser** and set Residential-Project-02 current.
   B. Access the **Views** tab of the **Project Navigator**. Open the Main Floor Plan view drawing.
   C. Create model space views around the floor plan, door schedule, and window schedule. Set the scale for the views to 1/4" = 1'-0". Add any additional annotations as needed.
   D. Save and close the drawing.
   E. Access the **Views** tab of the **Project Navigator**. Open the Foundation Plan view drawing.
   F. Create model space views around the foundation plan and the structural schedule. Set the scale for the views to 1/4" = 1'-0". Add any additional annotations as needed.
   G. Save and close the drawing.
   H. Access the **Sheets** tab of the **Project Navigator**. Right-click over the Architectural subset and pick the **Properties…** option. In the **Subset Properties** dialog box, choose the Arch D (24x36) Sheet for the default sheet template. Apply the changes to the other nested subsets.
   I. Create the following sheets:

Number	Sheet Title	Sheet Subset
A1.01	Floor Plan	Plans
A1.02	Foundation Plan	Plans
A2.01	Elevations	Elevations
A2.02	Elevations	Elevations
A3.01	Sections	Sections

   J. Open the Floor Plan sheet and add the floor plan, door schedule, and window schedule model space views to the sheet. Make any additional changes as needed. Save and close the drawing.
   K. Open the Foundation Plan sheet and add the foundation and structural schedule model space views to the sheet. Make any additional changes as needed. Save and close the drawing.
   L. Open the elevation sheets and add the south and west model space views to the first sheet. Add the north and east model space views to the second sheet. Make any additional changes as needed. Save and close the drawing.
   M. Open the Section sheet and add the section model space views to the sheet. Make any additional changes as needed. Save and close the drawing.
   N. Right-click over the Residential-Project-02 sheet set icon and pick **Publish** > **Sheet Set Publish Options…** from the shortcut menu. Set the following settings:

Property	Setting
Location	Sheets folder of Residential-Project-02
DWF type	Multi-sheet DWF
DWF naming	Prompt for name
Layer information	Include
Sheet information	Include
AEC property set data	Include
Publish with materials	No
AEC Group Individual Objects By	Object Type and Style

O. Right-click over the Architectural subset and pick **Publish** > **Publish to DWF**.
P. Save and close any open drawings.
Q. In Windows Explorer, browse to the Sheets folder of Residential-Project-02 and open the DWF file.

3. Two-Story Residential Project
   A. Access the **Project Browser** and set Residential-Project-03 current.
   B. Access the **Views** tab of the **Project Navigator**. Open the Main Floor Plan view drawing.
   C. Create model space views around the floor plan, door schedule, and window schedule. Set the scale for the views to 1/4″ = 1′-0″. Add any additional annotations as needed.
   D. Save and close the drawing.
   E. Access the **Views** tab of the **Project Navigator**. Open the Upper Floor Plan view drawing.
   F. Create a model space view around the floor plan. Set the scale for the view to 1/4″ = 1′-0″. Add any additional annotations as needed.
   G. Save and close the drawing.
   H. Access the **Views** tab of the **Project Navigator**. Open the Foundation Plan view drawing.
   I. Create model space views around the foundation plan and the structural schedule. Set the scale for the views to 1/4″ = 1′-0″. Add any additional annotations as needed.
   J. Save and close the drawing.
   K. Access the **Sheets** tab of the **Project Navigator**. Right-click over the Architectural subset and pick the **Properties...** option. In the **Subset Properties** dialog box, choose the Arch D (24x36) Sheet for the default sheet template. Apply the changes to the other nested subsets.
   L. Create the following sheets:

Number	Sheet Title	Sheet Subset
A1.01	Main Floor Plan	Plans
A1.02	Upper Floor Plan	Plans
A1.03	Foundation Plan	Plans
A2.01	Elevations	Elevations
A2.02	Elevations	Elevations
A3.01	Sections	Sections

   M. Open the Main Floor Plan sheet and add the floor plan, door schedule, and window schedule model space views to the sheet. Make any additional changes as needed. Save and close the drawing.

N. Open the Upper Floor Plan sheet and add the floor plan model space view to the sheet. Make any additional changes as needed. Save and close the drawing.

O. Open the Foundation Plan sheet and add the foundation and structural schedule model space views to the sheet. Make any additional changes as needed. Save and close the drawing.

P. Open the elevation sheets and add the south and west model space views to the first sheet. Add the north and east model space views to the second sheet. Make any additional changes as needed. Save and close the drawing.

Q. Open the Section sheet and add the section model space views to the sheet. Make any additional changes as needed. Save and close the drawing.

R. Right-click over the Residential-Project-03 sheet set icon and pick **Publish > Sheet Set Publish Options…** from the shortcut menu. Set the following settings:

Property	Setting
Location	Sheets folder of Residential-Project-03
DWF type	Multi-sheet DWF
DWF naming	Prompt for name
Layer information	Include
Sheet information	Include
AEC property set data	Include
Publish with materials	No
AEC Group Individual Objects By	Object Type and Style

S. Right-click over the Architectural subset and pick **Publish > Publish to DWF**.

T. Save and close any open drawings.

U. In Windows Explorer, browse to the Sheets folder of Residential-Project-03 and open the DWF file.

4. Two-Story Residential Project

A. Access the **Project Browser** and set Residential-Project-04 current.

B. Access the **Views** tab of the **Project Navigator**. Open the Main Floor Plan view drawing.

C. Create model space views around the floor plan, door schedule, and window schedule. Set the scale for the views to 1/4″ = 1′-0″. Add any additional annotations as needed.

D. Save and close the drawing.

E. Access the **Views** tab of the **Project Navigator**. Open the Upper Floor Plan view drawing.

F. Create a model space view around the floor plan. Set the scale for the view to 1/4″ = 1′-0″. Add any additional annotations as needed.

G. Save and close the drawing.

H. Access the **Views** tab of the **Project Navigator**. Open the Foundation Plan view drawing.

I. Create model space views around the foundation plan and the structural schedule. Set the scale for the views to 1/4″ = 1′-0″. Add any additional annotations as needed.

J. Save and close the drawing.

K. Access the **Sheets** tab of the **Project Navigator**. Right-click over the Architectural subset and pick the **Properties…** option. In the **Subset Properties** dialog box, choose the Arch D (24x36) Sheet for the default sheet template. Apply the changes to the other nested subsets.

L. Create the following sheets:

Number	Sheet Title	Sheet Subset
A1.01	Main Floor Plan	Plans
A1.02	Upper Floor Plan	Plans
A1.03	Foundation Plan	Plans
A2.01	Elevations	Elevations
A2.02	Elevations	Elevations
A3.01	Sections	Sections

M. Open the Main Floor Plan sheet and add the floor plan, door schedule, and window schedule model space views to the sheet. Make any additional changes as needed. Save and close the drawing.

N. Open the Upper Floor Plan sheet and add the floor plan model space view to the sheet. Make any additional changes as needed. Save and close the drawing.

O. Open the Foundation Plan sheet and add the foundation and structural schedule model space views to the sheet. Make any additional changes as needed. Save and close the drawing.

P. Open the elevation sheets and add the south and west model space views to the first sheet. Add the north and east model space views to the second sheet. Make any additional changes as needed. Save and close the drawing.

Q. Open the Section sheet and add the section model space views to the sheet. Make any additional changes as needed. Save and close the drawing.

R. Right-click over the Residential-Project-04 sheet set icon and pick **Publish** > **Sheet Set Publish Options...** from the shortcut menu. Set the following settings:

Property	Setting
Location	Sheets folder of Residential-Project-04
DWF type	Multi-sheet DWF
DWF naming	Prompt for name
Layer information	Include
Sheet information	Include
AEC property set data	Include
Publish with materials	No
AEC Group Individual Objects By	Object Type and Style

S. Right-click over the Architectural subset and pick **Publish** > **Publish to DWF**.

T. Save and close any open drawings.

U. In Windows Explorer, browse to the Sheets folder of Residential-Project-04 and open the DWF file.

5. Commercial Store Project
   A. Access the **Project Browser** and set Commercial-Project-05 current.
   B. Access the **Views** tab of the **Project Navigator**. Open the Main Floor Plan view drawing.
   C. Create model space views around the floor plan, door schedule, and window schedule. Set the scale for the views to 1/8" = 1'-0". Add any additional annotations as needed.
   D. Save and close the drawing.
   E. Access the **Views** tab of the **Project Navigator**. Open the Ceiling Framing Plan view drawing.
   F. Create a model space view around the floor plan and the structural schedule. Set the scale for the view to 1/8" = 1'-0". Add any additional annotations as needed.
   G. Save and close the drawing.
   H. Access the **Views** tab of the **Project Navigator**. Open the Store Space Plan view drawing.
   I. Create a model space view around the space plan. Set the scale for the views to 1/8" = 1'-0". Add any additional annotations as needed.
   J. Save and close the drawing.
   K. Create the following sheets:

Number	Sheet Title	Sheet Subset
A1.01	Floor Plan	Plans
A1.02	Space Plan	Plans
A1.03	Ceiling Framing Plan	Plans
A2.01	Elevations	Elevations
A3.01	Sections	Sections
A6.01	Schedules	Schedules and Diagrams

   L. Open the Floor Plan sheet and add the floor plan model space view to the sheet. Make any additional changes as needed. Save and close the drawing.
   M. Open the Space Plan sheet and add the space plan model space view to the sheet. Make any additional changes as needed. Save and close the drawing.
   N. Open the Ceiling Framing Plan sheet and add the ceiling frame floor plan model space view to the sheet. Make any additional changes as needed. Save and close the drawing.
   O. Open the elevation sheets and add the front model space view to the first sheet. Add the interior elevation model space views to the sheet. Make any additional changes as needed. Save and close the drawing.
   P. Open the Section sheet and add the section model space views to the sheet. Make any additional changes as needed. Save and close the drawing.
   Q. Open the Schedules sheet and add the door, window, and structural schedule model space views from the Main Floor Plan and the Ceiling Framing Plan view drawings to the sheet. Make any additional changes as needed. Save and close the drawing.
   R. Right-click over the Commercial-Project-05 sheet set icon and pick **Publish** > **Sheet Set Publish Options…** from the shortcut menu. Set the following settings:

Property	Setting
Location	Sheets folder of Commercial-Project-05
DWF type	Multi-sheet DWF
DWF naming	Prompt for name
Layer information	Include
Sheet information	Include
AEC property set data	Include
Publish with materials	No
AEC Group Individual Objects By	Object Type and Style

S. Right-click over the Architectural subset and pick **Publish** > **Publish to DWF**.
T. Save and close any open drawings.
U. In Windows Explorer, browse to the Sheets folder of Commercial-Project-05 and open the DWF file.

6. Commercial Car Maintenance Shop Project
   A. Access the **Project Browser** and set Commercial-Project-06 current.
   B. Access the **Views** tab of the **Project Navigator**. Open the Main Floor Plan view drawing.
   C. Create model space views around the floor plan, door schedule, and window schedule. Set the scale for the views to 1/8″ = 1′-0″. Add any additional annotations as needed.
   D. Save and close the drawing.
   E. Access the **Views** tab of the **Project Navigator**. Open the Main Floor Space Plan view drawing.
   F. Create model space views around the floor plan. Set the scale for the view to 1/8″ = 1′-0″. Add any additional annotations as needed.
   G. Save and close the drawing.
   H. Access the **Views** tab of the **Project Navigator**. Open the Upper Floor Plan view drawing.
   I. Create a model space view around the floor plan. Set the scale for the view to 1/8″ = 1′-0″. Add any additional annotations as needed.
   J. Save and close the drawing.
   K. Access the **Views** tab of the **Project Navigator**. Open the Upper Floor Space Plan view drawing.
   L. Create model space views around the floor plan. Set the scale for the views to 1/8″ = 1′-0″. Add any additional annotations as needed.
   M. Save and close the drawing.
   N. Access the **Views** tab of the **Project Navigator**. Open the Foundation Plan view drawing.
   O. Create model space views around the foundation plan, structural schedule, and concrete volume schedule. Set the scale for the views to 1/8″ = 1′-0″. Add any additional annotations as needed.
   P. Save and close the drawing.
   Q. Create the following sheets:

Number	Sheet Title	Sheet Subset
A1.01	Floor Plans	Plans
A1.02	Foundation Plan	Plans
A1.03	Space Plans	Plans
A2.01	Elevations	Elevations

   R. Open the Floor Plans sheet and add the main and upper floor plans, door schedule, and window schedule model space views to the sheet. Make any additional changes as needed. Save and close the drawing.
   S. Open the Foundation Plan sheet and add the foundation, structural schedule, and concrete volume schedule model space views to the sheet. Make any additional changes as needed. Save and close the drawing.
   T. Open the Space Plans sheet and add the main floor and upper floor space plan model space views to the sheet. Make any additional changes as needed. Save and close the drawing.
   U. Open the Elevations sheet and add the front model space view. Add the interior elevation model space views to the sheet. Make any additional changes as needed. Save and close the drawing.

V. Right-click over the Commercial-Project-06 sheet set icon and pick **Publish** > **Sheet Set Publish Options...** from the shortcut menu. Set the following settings:

Property	Setting
Location	Sheets folder of Commercial-Project-06
DWF type	Multi-sheet DWF
DWF naming	Prompt for name
Layer information	Include
Sheet information	Include
AEC property set data	Include
Publish with materials	No
AEC Group Individual Objects By	Object Type and Style

W. Right-click over the Architectural subset and pick **Publish** > **Publish to DWF**.
X. Save and close any open drawings.
Y. In Windows Explorer, browse to the Sheets folder of Commercial-Project-06 and open the DWF file.

7. Governmental Fire Station
    A. Access the **Project Browser** and set Gvrmt-Project-07 current.
    B. Access the **Views** tab of the **Project Navigator**. Open the Main Floor Plan view drawing.
    C. Create model space views around the floor plan, door schedule, and window schedule. Set the scale for the views to 1/8" = 1'-0". Add any additional annotations as needed.
    D. Save and close the drawing.
    E. Access the **Views** tab of the **Project Navigator**. Open the Foundation Plan view drawing.
    F. Create a model space view around the foundation plan. Set the scale for the view to 1/8" = 1'-0". Add any additional annotations as needed.
    G. Save and close the drawing.
    H. Access the **Views** tab of the **Project Navigator**. Open the Space Plan view drawing.
    I. Create a model space view around the space plan. Set the scale for the views to 1/8" = 1'-0". Add any additional annotations as needed.
    J. Save and close the drawing.
    K. Create the following sheets:

Number	Sheet Title	Sheet Subset
A1.01	Floor Plan	Plans
A1.02	Space Plan	Plans
A1.03	Foundation Plan	Plans
A2.01	Elevations	Elevations
A5.01	Details	Details
A6.01	Schedules	Schedules and Diagrams

    L. Open the Floor Plan sheet and add the floor plan model space view to the sheet. Make any additional changes as needed. Save and close the drawing.
    M. Open the Space Plan sheet and add the space plan model space view to the sheet. Make any additional changes as needed. Save and close the drawing.

N. Open the Foundation Plan sheet and add the foundation plan model space view to the sheet. Make any additional changes as needed. Save and close the drawing.

O. Open the Elevations sheet and add the front model space view to the first sheet. Add the interior elevation model space views to the sheet. Make any additional changes as needed. Save and close the drawing.

P. Open the Details sheet and add the detail model space views from the Construction Details view drawing. Make any additional changes as needed. Save and close the drawing.

Q. Open the Schedules sheet and add the door and window schedule model space views from the Main Floor Plan view drawings to the sheet. Make any additional changes as needed. Save and close the drawing.

R. Right-click over the Gvrmt-Project-07 sheet set icon and pick **Publish** > **Sheet Set Publish Options…** from the shortcut menu. Set the following settings:

Property	Setting
Location	Sheets folder of Gvrmt-Project-07
DWF type	Multi-sheet DWF
DWF naming	Prompt for name
Layer information	Include
Sheet information	Include
AEC property set data	Include
Publish with materials	No
AEC Group Individual Objects By	Object Type and Style

S. Right-click over the Architectural subset and pick **Publish** > **Publish to DWF**.

T. Save and close any open drawings.

U. In Windows Explorer, browse to the Sheets folder of Gvrmt-Project-07 and open the DWF file.

CHAPTER 25

Conceptual Design

Learning Objectives

After completing this chapter, you will be able to do the following:

✓ Build a mass model.
✓ Add custom shapes to the mass model.
✓ Convert AutoCAD solids to mass elements.
✓ Create mass element styles.
✓ Modify mass elements.
✓ Group the mass objects.
✓ Add AEC objects to a mass group.
✓ Use the **Model Explorer**.
✓ Create floor plates.
✓ Create polylines from slices.
✓ Export slices to another drawing.

Until now, you have been working with objects and geometry used in the design, design development, and documentation phases of the architectural work flow. In most cases, a new building begins with an idea. This idea can consist of sketches, preliminary drawings, and models. Architectural Desktop adds to these tools by providing the architect and designer with a series of options that can be used to create a conceptual, three-dimensional model. The conceptual model can be used for design analyses, massing studies, sun studies, site studies, and approvals. When mass elements are placed together to form a design, the result is called a *massing study*. The 3D shapes included with Architectural Desktop are known as *mass elements*. See **Figure 25-1**. Once the conceptual model has been approved, it can be moved forward to the design and design development phases. From the conceptual model, walls and spaces can be generated to create the construction documents.

Although Architectural Desktop provides you with many tools for all phases of work, construction documents do not have to begin with a conceptual model. The conceptual model can be used as a starting point in the development of a building, however, and carried all the way through to the final plotted documents. This chapter explains the tools included to create a conceptual model and prepare it for the design phase.

Figure 25-1.
A shaded view of a conceptual model. Drawing courtesy SERA Architects Inc., Portland, OR.

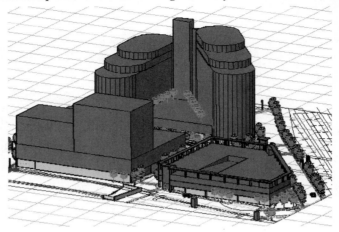

Building a Mass Model

When the conceptual model is created, 3D shapes are used to mass together a building idea. The 3D shapes included with Architectural Desktop have volume or mass. Mass elements come in an assorted number of 3D shapes and give you the ability to create custom shapes.

Using Mass Elements

Many of the mass element shapes can be found on the **Massing** tool palette, shown in **Figure 25-2.** This palette includes many mass element tools for use in your designs. Pick on one of the tools to begin adding the shape to the drawing. Mass elements can also be added by picking **Design** > **Massing** and then picking one of the mass element options from the menu.

Once a mass element has been selected, you can add the element by dynamically picking an insertion point and stretching the size of the object or by setting specific element properties through the **Properties** palette, shown in **Figure 25-3.** The properties for mass elements are divided into three categories: **General**, **Dimensions**, and **Location**. These categories are all found under the **BASIC** header. Some properties are available only for certain mass element shapes. The following properties are available in the **Properties** palette when you are adding mass elements to the drawing.

The **General** category includes properties controlling the general parameters of a mass element. These properties include the following:

- **Description.** The **Description** property allows you to assign a description to the mass element. Picking this property displays the **Description** worksheet, where a description or name can be entered for the mass element. As you are developing a design, you might want to assign descriptions to mass elements so you can reference different areas of your design later.
- **Style.** This drop-down list allows you to select a mass element style to use for the mass shape being created. Mass element styles allow the assignment of materials, classifications, and display settings that can be applied to any of the shapes. The creation of a mass element style is discussed later in this chapter.
- **Bound spaces.** This drop-down list property is used to specify if the mass element can be used as a space boundary when you are creating Space objects.

Architectural Desktop and Its Applications

Figure 25-2.
The **Design** pull-down menu and the **Massing** tool palette include mass element tools to begin creating a massing study.

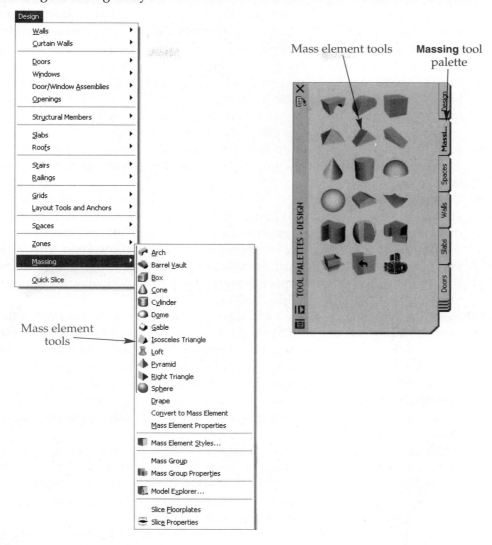

Mass element tools

Massing tool palette

Mass element tools

Figure 25-3.
The **Properties** palette is used to configure mass element settings.

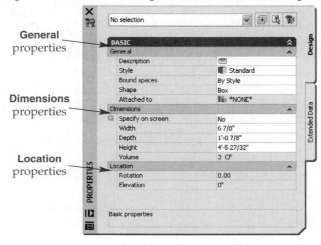

General properties

Dimensions properties

Location properties

- **Shape.** Picking this property displays a drop-down list of mass element shapes that can be created. Even if a mass element shape has been selected from the tool palette or pull-down menu, the shape can be changed by choosing a different shape here. The different shapes available include **Arch**, **Barrel Vault**, **Box**, **Cone**, **Cylinder**, **Dome**, **Doric**, **Gable**, **Pyramid**, **Sphere**, **Isosceles Triangle**, **Right Triangle**, **Extrusion**, **Revolution**, and **Free Form**. The different mass element shapes are discussed in greater detail in the next section.
- **Profile.** This property is available only when the **Extrusion** or **Revolution** shape has been selected. The **Profile** property includes a list of AEC profiles defined in the drawing that can be used to create a custom mass element shape. The creation of custom shapes is discussed later in this chapter.
- **Attached to.** This drop-down list displays a list of mass groups defined in the drawing to which the mass element can be assigned. Mass groups are discussed later in this chapter.
- **Operation.** This property is available only when a mass element is being attached to a mass group. When a mass element is a part of a mass group, the mass element can be given one of three operations: **Add**, **Subtract**, or **Intersect**. Adding joins mass elements together, subtracting allows you to subtract one mass from another mass, and intersecting creates a mass group shape from the shared or intersecting space between two mass elements. Assigning operations is discussed later in this chapter.

The **Dimensions** category includes a list of properties controlling the size of the mass element shape being created. Depending on the shape selected, different properties are available for the different shapes. These properties are listed as follows:

- **Specify on screen.** Picking this property yields a **Yes** or **No** option. When **Yes** is selected, the size of the mass element can be determined by picking an insertion point for the mass and stretching the size of the shape dynamically. If **No** is selected, the size of the shape is set by the **Width**, **Depth**, **Height**, **Radius**, and **Rise** properties.
- **Width.** This property is available when the **Specify on screen** property is set to **No**. Enter a width value for the shape. This option is available for the **Arch**, **Barrel Vault**, **Box**, **Gable**, **Pyramid**, **Isosceles Triangle**, **Right Triangle**, **Extrusion**, and **Free Form** mass element shapes. *Free form mass elements* are massing elements that can be edited through the use of grips.
- **Depth.** This property is available when the **Specify on screen** property is set to **No**. Enter a depth value for the shape. This option is available for the **Arch**, **Box**, **Gable**, **Pyramid**, **Isosceles Triangle**, **Right Triangle**, **Extrusion**, and **Free Form** mass element shapes.
- **Height.** This property is available when the **Specify on screen** property is set to **No**. Enter a height value for the shape. This option is available for the **Arch**, **Box**, **Cone**, **Cylinder**, **Doric**, **Gable**, **Pyramid**, **Isosceles Triangle**, **Right Triangle**, **Extrusion**, **Revolution**, and **Free Form** mass element shapes.
- **Radius.** This property is available when the **Specify on screen** property is set to **No**. Enter a radius value for the shape. This option is available for the **Arch**, **Barrel Vault**, **Cone**, **Cylinder**, **Dome**, **Doric**, **Sphere**, and **Revolution** mass element shapes.
- **Rise.** This property is available when the **Specify on screen** property is set to **No**. Enter a rise value for the shape. This option is available only for the **Gable** shape.
- **Volume.** This property displays the total volume for the mass element being added to the drawing.

The **Location** category includes two read-only values: **Rotation** and **Elevation**. These properties indicate the rotation of the mass element as it is created and the elevation in the Z axis in which it is created. Later, when you are modifying mass elements, these properties become available for modification of the mass element.

Adding Mass Elements to Conceptual Plans

After selecting the desired shape and setting any size parameters, you can add the mass element to the drawing. If you are inserting a shape with its size values entered in the **Properties** palette, a mass element representation of the shape is attached to the crosshairs. Picking a point in the drawing establishes the location for the shape. After the insertion point has been located, you are prompted to enter a rotation angle for the shape. After the rotation angle has been entered, another shape is attached to the crosshairs for continued addition of mass elements. Continue to add new mass elements, making changes in the **Properties** palette as required. When you finish adding mass elements, press the [Enter] key to end the command.

If you set the **Specify on screen** property to **Yes** when adding shapes, you are prompted with a few questions at the Command: prompt. Each shape requires a different set of techniques in order to be added. For example, the **Box** requires you to select two opposite diagonal corners for the width and depth, a height, and a rotation angle. The **Cylinder** requires a center point, radius, height, and rotation angle. When you are working in a Top view, specifying the height value on screen can be difficult, because the shape is being extended perpendicularly to your line of sight. It is often easier to add mass elements in an isometric view when you are specifying their sizes on screen.

NOTE

When the mass element is added in a Top view, the shape appears as a 2D shape with a light green color. If the mass element crosses through the default cutting plane, a hatch is displayed through the mass. Mass elements, like other AEC objects, can be controlled through object display.

As mass elements are added, they are placed on the A-Area-Mass layer. The shapes can overlap one another, be separated, and be placed inside one another. The different visual styles such as **3D Hidden**, **Realistic**, and **Conceptual** can give you a general idea of the shape of your design.

Using Mass Elements with Other Geometry

Mass elements are not limited to conceptual design. Like other AEC objects, mass elements can be integrated into the construction documents. For example, mass elements can be used as interference conditions within a wall, incorporated into a block for use in a window or door style as trim, or used to create a fireplace and mantle, as in **Figure 25-4.** Be creative when using mass elements. Use them to develop a conceptual plan or to enhance the design of a building.

Figure 25-4.
Mass elements are not only used for conceptual design, but they can be used to create parts of a building that cannot be built with other ADT tools.

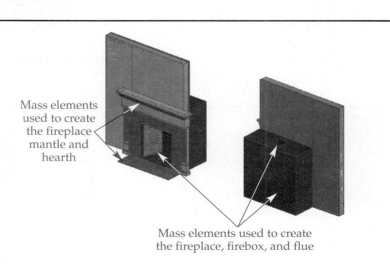

Mass elements used to create the fireplace mantle and hearth

Mass elements used to create the fireplace, firebox, and flue

The **Curtain Wall** tool can also be applied to faces of mass elements. Curtain walls were discussed in Chapter 16. To apply the **Curtain Wall** tool to a mass element face, right-click over the **Curtain Wall** tool in the **Design** tool palette, and pick **Apply Tool Properties to > Faces**. You are prompted to select the surface of an object. As the cursor is moved over different faces of the mass element, the face is highlighted, indicating to which face the curtain wall is applied. After selecting the face, the **Convert to Curtain Walls** worksheet is displayed. Choose a curtain wall style from the drop-down list to apply to the mass element face, and then pick the **OK** button. **Figure 25-5** displays a mass element with curtain walls applied to different faces.

Working with Primitive Mass Element Shapes

Architectural Desktop includes several primitive shapes. These shapes can be combined to form more complex shapes, helping you build a design. The following section describes each of the primitive shapes available for your design needs.

The Arch Shape

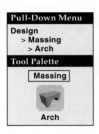

Pull-Down Menu
Design
 > Massing
 > Arch
Tool Palette
Massing
Arch

The **Arch** mass element creates a box-shaped mass element with an arch cut through the box. See **Figure 25-6**. To create this shape, pick the **Arch** tool in the **Massing** tool palette or **Design > Massing > Arch**. After accessing the tool, choose to create the shape dynamically by picking points on the screen or enter dimensional values in the **Properties** palette. The **Arch** shape uses the **Width**, **Depth**, **Height**, and **Radius** dimension properties. If you are creating the arch by specifying points on the drawing screen, access the **MASSELEMENTADD** command. When prompted, pick the first and second corners for the **Arch** shape. Enter a height value or pick a point to set the height. Specify the rotation angle, and press [Enter] to end the command. Use the **Properties** palette to modify the radius of the arch and the height, depth, and width of the arch mass after the shape has been created.

Figure 25-5.
The **Curtain Wall** tool can be used to apply a curtain wall style to the faces of a mass element for conceptual design purposes.

After entering the **Faces** option, move the cursor around to highlight a face to which to apply the curtain wall

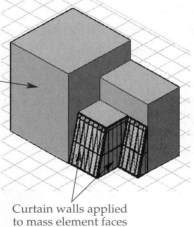

Curtain walls applied to mass element faces

Figure 25-6.
The **Arch** shape mass element.

Pick the second point

Pick the first point

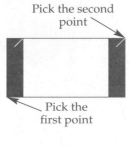

Plan **View**   **Isometric View**

The Barrel Vault Shape

The **Barrel Vault** mass element creates a half-barrel shape. See **Figure 25-7**. Pick the **Barrel Vault** tool in the **Massing** tool palette or **Design > Massing > Barrel Vault**. After accessing the tool, choose to create the shape dynamically by picking points on the screen or enter dimensional values in the **Properties** palette. The **Barrel Vault** shape uses the **Width** and **Radius** dimension properties. If you are creating the barrel vault by specifying points on the drawing screen, access the **MASSELEMENTADD** command. When prompted, pick the first and second corners for the **Barrel Vault** shape. Specify the rotation angle when you are prompted to do so, and press [Enter] to end the command.

| Pull-Down Menu |
| Design |
| > Massing |
| > Barrel Vault |
| Tool Palette |
| Massing |

Barrel Vault

The Box Shape

The **Box** mass element creates a box shape. See **Figure 25-8**. Select the **Box** tool in the **Massing** tool palette or pick **Design > Massing > Box**. After accessing the tool, choose to create the shape dynamically by picking points on the screen or enter dimensional values in the **Properties** palette. The **Box** shape uses the **Width**, **Depth**, and **Height** dimension properties. If you are creating the box by specifying points on the drawing screen, access the **MASSELEMENTADD** command. When prompted, pick the first and second corners for the **Box** shape. Enter a height value or pick a point to set the height. Specify the rotation angle, and press [Enter] to end the command.

| Pull-Down Menu |
| Design |
| > Massing |
| > Box |
| Tool Palette |
| Massing |

Box

The Cone Shape

The **Cone** mass element creates a cone shape. See **Figure 25-9**. Select the **Cone** tool in the **Massing** tool palette or pick **Design > Massing > Cone**. After accessing the tool, choose to create the shape dynamically by picking points on the screen or enter dimensional values in the **Properties** palette. The **Cone** shape uses the **Height** and **Radius** dimension properties. If you are creating the cone by specifying points on the drawing screen, access the **MASSELEMENTADD** command. When prompted, pick an insertion point for the cone. Specify the radius, height, and rotation angle when you are prompted to do so, and press [Enter] to end the command.

| Pull-Down Menu |
| Design |
| > Massing |
| > Cone |
| Tool Palette |
| Massing |

Cone

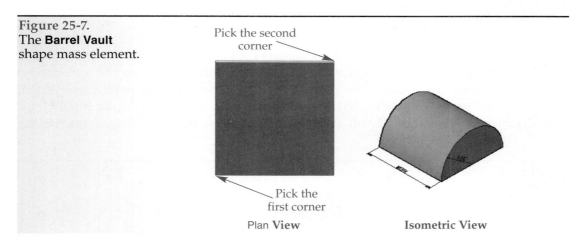

Figure 25-7.
The **Barrel Vault** shape mass element.

Pick the second corner

Pick the first corner

Plan **View**   **Isometric View**

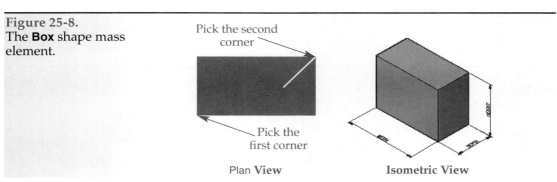

Figure 25-8.
The **Box** shape mass element.

Pick the second corner

Pick the first corner

Plan **View**   **Isometric View**

Figure 25-9.
The **Cone** shape
mass element.

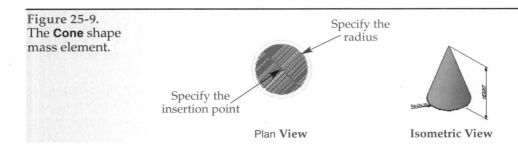

Specify the
radius

Specify the
insertion point

Plan **View**

Isometric View

The Cylinder Shape

The **Cylinder** mass element creates a cylinder shape. See **Figure 25-10**. Select the **Cylinder** tool in the **Massing** tool palette or pick **Design** > **Massing** > **Cylinder**. After accessing the tool, choose to create the shape dynamically by picking points on the screen or enter dimensional values in the **Properties** palette. The **Cylinder** shape uses the **Height** and **Radius** dimension properties. If you are creating the cylinder by specifying points on the drawing screen, access the **MASSELEMENTADD** command. When prompted, pick an insertion point for the cylinder. Specify the radius, height, and rotation angle when you are prompted to do so, and press [Enter] to end the command.

The Dome Shape

The **Dome** mass element creates a dome shape. See **Figure 25-11**. Select the **Dome** tool in the **Massing** tool palette or pick **Design** > **Massing** > **Dome**. After accessing the tool, choose to create the shape dynamically by picking points on the screen or enter dimensional values in the **Properties** palette. The **Dome** shape uses the **Radius** dimension property. If you are creating the dome by specifying points on the drawing screen, access the **MASSELEMENTADD** command. When prompted, pick an insertion point for the dome. Specify the radius and rotation angle when you are prompted to do so, and press [Enter] to end the command.

The Gable Shape

The **Gable** mass element creates a box-shaped mass element with a gabled-roof shape above the box. See **Figure 25-12**. To create the gable shape, pick the **Gable** tool in the **Massing** tool palette or **Design** > **Massing** > **Gable**. After accessing the tool, choose to create the shape dynamically by picking points on the screen or enter dimensional values in the **Properties** palette. The **Gable** shape uses the **Width**, **Depth**, **Height**, and **Rise** dimension properties. If you are creating the gable by specifying points on the

Figure 25-10.
The **Cylinder** shape
mass element.

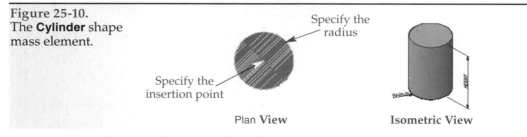

Specify the
radius

Specify the
insertion point

Plan **View**

Isometric View

Figure 25-11.
The **Dome** shape
mass element.

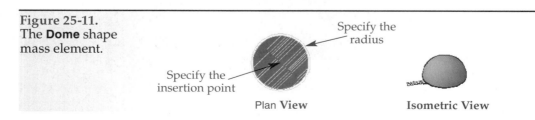

Specify the
radius

Specify the
insertion point

Plan **View**

Isometric View

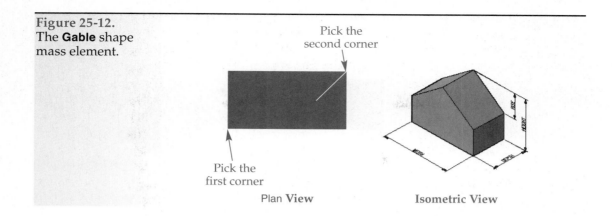

Figure 25-12.
The **Gable** shape mass element.

Pick the second corner

Pick the first corner

Plan **View**

Isometric View

drawing screen, access the **MASSELEMENTADD** command. When prompted, pick the first and second corners for the **Gable** shape. Enter a height value or pick a point to set the height. Specify the rotation angle, and press [Enter] to end the command.

The Isosceles Triangle Shape

The **Isosceles Triangle** mass element creates an isosceles-triangle shape. See **Figure 25-13.** Select the **Isosceles Triangle** tool in the **Massing** tool palette or pick **Design** > **Massing** > **Isosceles Triangle**. After accessing the tool, choose to create the shape dynamically by picking points on the screen or enter dimensional values in the **Properties** palette. The **Isosceles Triangle** shape uses the **Width**, **Depth**, and **Height** dimension properties. If you are creating the isosceles triangle by specifying points on the drawing screen, access the **MASSELEMENTADD** command. When prompted, pick the first and second corners for the **Isosceles Triangle** shape. Enter a height value or pick a point to set the height. Specify the rotation angle, and press [Enter] to end the command.

Pull-Down Menu
Design
  > Massing
    > Isosceles
      Triangle
Tool Palette
Massing

Isosceles Triangle

The Pyramid Shape

The **Pyramid** mass element creates a pyramid shape. See **Figure 25-14.** Select the **Pyramid** tool in the **Massing** tool palette or pick **Design** > **Massing** > **Pyramid**. After accessing the tool, choose to create the shape dynamically by picking points on the screen or enter dimensional values in the **Properties** palette. The **Pyramid** shape uses the **Width**, **Depth**, and **Height** dimension properties. If you are creating the pyramid by specifying points on the drawing screen, access the **MASSELEMENTADD** command. When prompted, pick the first and second corners for the **Pyramid** shape. Enter a height value or pick a point to set the height. Specify the rotation angle, and press [Enter] to end the command.

Pull-Down Menu
Design
  > Massing
    > Pyramid
Tool Palette
Massing

Pyramid

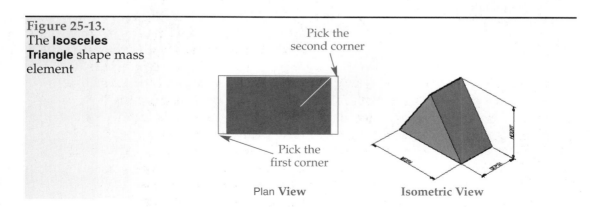

Figure 25-13.
The **Isosceles Triangle** shape mass element

Pick the second corner

Pick the first corner

Plan **View**

Isometric View

Figure 25-14.
The **Pyramid** shape
mass element.

Pick the
second corner

Pick the
first corner

Plan **View**

Isometric View

The Right Triangle Shape

Pull-Down Menu
Design
> Massing
> Right Triangle
Tool Palette
[Massing]

Right Triangle

The **Right Triangle** mass element creates a right-triangle shape. See **Figure 25-15.** Select the **Right Triangle** tool in the **Massing** tool palette or pick **Design** > **Massing** > **Right Triangle**. After accessing the tool, choose to create the shape dynamically by picking points on the screen or enter dimensional values in the **Properties** palette. The **Right Triangle** shape uses the **Width**, **Depth**, and **Height** dimension properties. If you are creating the right triangle by specifying points on the drawing screen, access the **MASSELEMENTADD** command. When prompted, pick the first and second corners for the **Right Triangle** shape. Enter a height value or pick a point to set the height. Specify the rotation angle, and press [Enter] to end the command.

The Sphere Shape

Pull-Down Menu
Design
> Massing
> Sphere
Tool Palette
[Massing]

Sphere

The **Sphere** mass element creates a spherical shape. See **Figure 25-16.** Select the **Sphere** tool in the **Massing** tool palette or pick **Design** > **Massing** > **Sphere**. After accessing the tool, choose to create the shape dynamically by picking points on the screen or enter dimensional values in the **Properties** palette. The **Sphere** shape uses the **Radius** dimension property. If you are creating the sphere by specifying points on the drawing screen, access the **MASSELEMENTADD** command. When prompted, pick an insertion point for the sphere. Specify the radius and rotation angle when you are prompted to do so. Press [Enter] to end the command.

Exercise
25-1   **Complete the Exercise on the Student CD.**

Figure 25-15.
The **Right Triangle**
shape mass element.

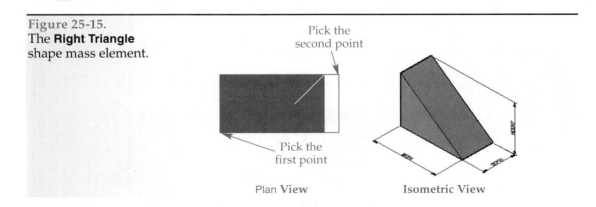

Pick the
second point

Pick the
first point

Plan **View**

Isometric View

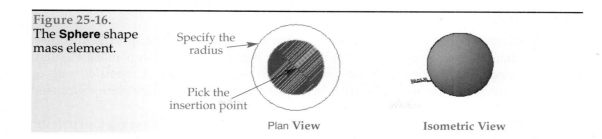

Figure 25-16.
The **Sphere** shape mass element.

Specify the radius

Pick the insertion point

Plan **View**

Isometric View

Creating Custom Shapes

Five types of mass element shapes can be used to create custom shapes. These mass element shapes are **Extrusion**, **Revolution**, **Drape**, **Free Form**, and **Loft**. These tools are described in the following sections.

The Drape Shape

The **Drape** mass element shape is used to create a 3D topographic mass of a site. Before this shape can be created, polylines representing land contours need to be drawn and placed at the appropriate heights. To place the polyline contours at the correct heights, select a polyline, access the **Properties** palette, and adjust the **Elevation** property. See **Figure 25-17.**

Once the polyline contours have been created, the **Drape** tool can be used to convert the polylines into a massed site. Select the **Drape** tool from the **Massing** tool palette, or pick **Design > Massing > Drape**. Once the **_AECDRAPE** command is accessed, you are prompted to select the objects representing contours. Pick the first and second corners of a crossing window to select the polyline contours. After picking the polyline contour lines, you are prompted to erase the contours. Type Y to erase the contours or N to keep the contours. The next prompt asks if you will create a regular mesh or not. A regular mesh is used to create a drape mass element with rectangular boundaries. Typing Y here will allow you to pick two corners to create a rectangular boundary. Typing N will use the contour extents to create the boundary for the drape.

When creating a regular mesh, you are prompted to select a rectangular mesh corner and then its opposite corner. After establishing the mesh corners, you are prompted to enter a mesh subdivision along the X and Y directions. The mesh size establishes how smooth the drape appears. The default size is **30** for the X and Y directions of the mesh. A higher mesh size produces a smoother site massing, but it can affect the computer performance. Finally, enter a base thickness. This is the thickness of the mass, measured from the lowest polyline contour down to the bottom of the mass element.

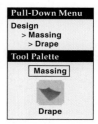

Pull-Down Menu
Design
  > Massing
  > Drape
Tool Palette
  Massing

Drape

Figure 25-17.
Use the **Drape** mass element to create a 3D modeled site.

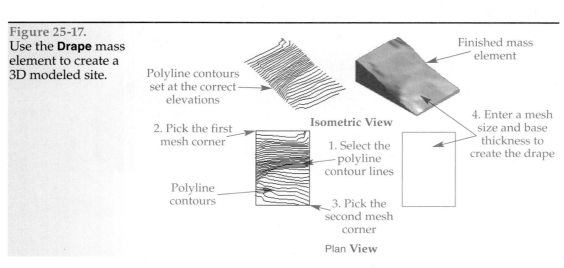

Polyline contours set at the correct elevations

Finished mass element

Isometric View

2. Pick the first mesh corner

1. Select the polyline contour lines

4. Enter a mesh size and base thickness to create the drape

Polyline contours

3. Pick the second mesh corner

Plan **View**

The Extrusion Shape

The **Extrusion** mass element creates a mass shape from an AEC profile and then assigns a height to the mass. See **Figure 25-18.** Before the **Extrusion** mass element can be created, an AEC profile must be defined in the drawing. AEC profiles with or without voids can be created and used in the extrusion. AEC profiles were discussed in Chapter 9 of this text.

After a profile has been created, pick the **Extrusion** tool in the **Massing** tool palette. In the **Properties** palette, pick the **Profile** property and select a profile shape from the list. Choose whether to create the shape dynamically in the drawing or to specify dimensional properties in the **Properties** palette by choosing the appropriate option in the **Specify on screen** property. After specifying any property information, pick an insertion point in the drawing to create the shape. The **Extrusion** shape uses the **Width**, **Depth**, and **Height** dimensional properties.

Closed polyline shapes can also be converted into extrusion shapes. To do this, first draw the desired shape using a polyline, and then close it. Next, select the polyline, right-click, and pick **Convert To** > **Mass Element** from the shortcut menu. You are prompted to erase the linework or not and then to enter an extrusion height. This converts the closed polyline into an **Extrusion** shape mass element.

The Revolution Shape

The **Revolution** mass element creates a revolved custom shape around an axis of revolution from an AEC profile. As with the **Extrusion** shape, an AEC profile must be defined in the drawing before a revolution shape can be created. See **Figure 25-19.**

After a profile has been created, pick the **Revolution** tool in the **Massing** tool palette. In the **Properties** palette, pick the **Profile** property and select a profile shape from the list. Choose whether to create the shape dynamically in the drawing or to specify dimensional properties in the **Properties** palette by choosing **Yes** or **No** in the **Specify on screen** property. After specifying any additional property information, pick an insertion point in the drawing to create the shape.

The AEC profile shape is revolved around an axis of revolution determined by a horizontal plane at the bottommost extents of the profile. See **Figure 25-19.** The **Revolution** shape uses the **Height** and **Radius** dimensional properties.

The Free Form Shape

Another type of custom shape that can be created is the **Free Form** mass. When a **Drape** mass has been created, it is turned into a free form mass that can be edited. Any existing mass element shape can be turned from its native shape into a **Free**

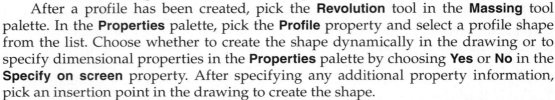

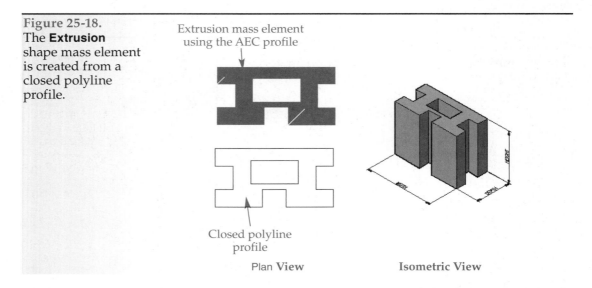

Figure 25-18.
The **Extrusion** shape mass element is created from a closed polyline profile.

Extrusion mass element using the AEC profile

Closed polyline profile

Plan **View**   **Isometric View**

Figure 25-19.
The **Revolution** shape mass element revolves an AEC profile to create a rounded shape.

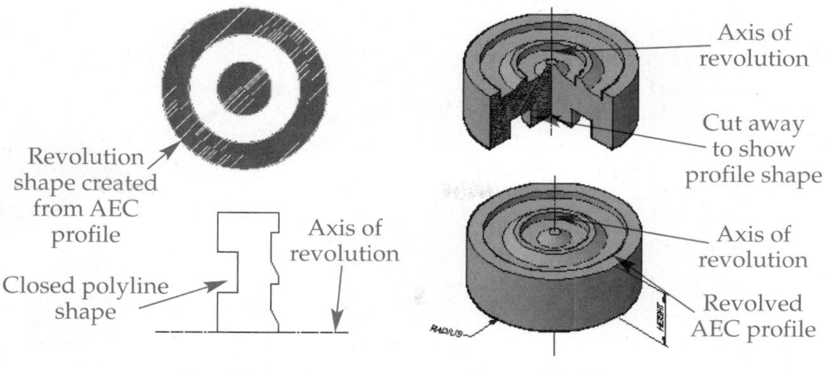

Revolution shape created from AEC profile

Closed polyline shape

Axis of revolution

Plan **View**

Axis of revolution

Cut away to show profile shape

Axis of revolution

Revolved AEC profile

Isometric View

Form element by changing the **Shape** property in the **Properties** palette. In addition to changing an existing shape into a **Free Form** mass element, new **Free Form** elements can be added to the drawing.

To add a new **Free Form** element, pick any of the mass element tools, and then change the **Shape** property to **Free Form**. When you are adding a **Free Form** mass, the basic shape initially selected is the shape inserted into the drawing. This type of mass element uses the **Width**, **Depth**, and **Height** dimensional properties, however, even if the initial mass element shape does not. The only difference between a new **Free Form** mass element and one of the mass element shapes is that they use different types of grips for editing. The editing of mass elements is discussed later in this chapter.

The Loft Shape

Pull-Down Menu
Design
> Massing
> Loft

The **LOFT** command is used to create an AutoCAD solid object by selecting a series of cross sections. The cross sections define the shape of the resulting solid. Cross sections are generally polylines, curves, or lines that can be open, such as an arc, or closed, such as a polyline. The **LOFT** command is used to fill in the space between the cross sections to create the solid material. At least two cross sections must be used to create a lofted object. Enter this command by picking **Design** > **Massing** > **Loft**.

When first entering the command, you are prompted to Select cross-sections in lofting order:. Begin selecting open or closed cross-section objects in order, from first to last. The loft is filled between the cross sections selected. When finished, you are prompted to Enter an option [Guides/Path/Cross-sections only] <*current option*>:.

The **Cross-sections only** option uses the cross-sectional profiles to determine how the loft is created. Loft material is added between the cross-sectional profiles. See Figure 25-20. After selecting this option, the **Loft Settings** dialog box is displayed, allowing you to choose different options to smooth the **Loft** shape.

The **Guides** option uses cross-sectional profiles to create the general shape for the loft and then uses guides the lofted material follows for refining the shape. In Figure 25-20, 3D polylines define the initial cross-sectional shape of the loft, and the circles define the rounded shape between the cross-sectional profiles. Finally, the **Path** option uses cross-sectional profiles to create the basic shape for the loft, and a path is used for the loft material to follow between the cross-sectional profiles.

Although the **LOFT** command is found in the **Design** > **Massing** menu, the **LOFT** command does not create an AEC mass element. Instead, the type of object created is an AutoCAD solid object. AutoCAD solid objects can be converted into mass element shapes for easier implementation into your Architectural Desktop model.

Figure 25-20.
Cross-sectional
profiles, guides, and
a path are used to
create a loft.

Polyline cross-sectional
profiles

3D polyline
cross-sectional
profiles

Circles
used as
guides

Circle
cross-sectional
profiles

Path

Converting AutoCAD Solids into Mass Elements

Standard AutoCAD solids can also be created and converted into mass elements. The **3D Solids** pull-down menu includes a number of predefined solid shapes and solid-editing tools. Initially, this pull-down menu is not available. To add the **3D Solids** pull-down menu to the pull-down menu bar, pick **Window > Pulldowns > 3D Solids Pulldown**. This adds the **3D Solids** pull-down menu to your Architectural Desktop.

Many of the shapes act similar to the mass element shapes. Solid objects can be joined (glued) together, subtracted from one another, and intersected to create new solid object shapes by using the AutoCAD **UNION**, **SUBTRACT**, and **INTERSECT** commands, respectively. Additionally, these commands can be accessed by picking the appropriate command from the **3D Solids** pull-down menu, which can be loaded by picking **Window > Pulldowns > 3D Solids Pulldown**. The modified solid shapes can then, in turn, be converted into a **Free Form** mass element. See the online help for more information on working with AutoCAD solids.

Once a solid object has been created and you want to convert it into a mass element, pick the solid, right-click, and pick **Convert to > Mass Element**. You can also pick **Design > Massing > Convert to Mass Element**. After the **MASSELEMENTCONVERT** command is accessed, you are asked if you want to erase the layout geometry. Type Y or N. When you are prompted for the mass element, press [Enter]. This converts the solid into a mass element shape for incorporation into your models.

Exercise
25-2   *Complete the Exercise on the Student CD.*

Mass Element Styles

Like most AEC objects, mass elements are created using a style. The Standard mass element style controls the display settings for the mass elements using the style. New mass element styles can be created to control different display settings, such as material and object display.

To create a mass element style, pick **Design > Massing > Mass Element Styles...** from the pull-down menu. This displays the **Style Manager** opened to the Mass Element Styles section, shown in **Figure 25-21**. Pick the **New Style** button to create a new style, and enter a name for the style. Oftentimes, the style name represents the material assigned or an area of the building the mass element represents.

Figure 25-21.
The **Style Manager** is used to create mass element styles.

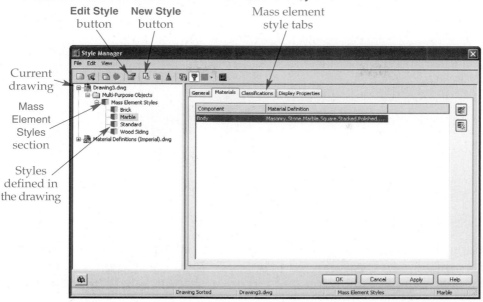

After creating a new style, pick the style in the left tree view pane to begin editing the style in the right pane. The mass element style properties are divided into four tabs: **General**, **Materials**, **Classifications**, and **Display Properties**. These tabs are described below.

- **General.** Use this tab to rename and provide a description for the style. Xref documents can be added by picking the **Notes...** button. Property set definitions can also be added to the style by picking the **Property Sets...** button.
- **Materials.** The **Materials** tab is used to assign a material to the mass element style. Pick a material definition from the **Material Definition** drop-down list. Material definitions can also be edited from this tab.
- **Classifications.** If the drawing includes classification definitions, they can be assigned to the mass element style.
- **Display Properties.** This tab is used to assign a display override to the mass element style and set any display settings to the different display representations for the style. The display representations include Model, Plan, Reflected, and Sketch. The Plan display representations include settings to control the cut plane and hatch displayed in a Plan view.

Modifying Mass Elements

The mass element tools, when initially created, form basic shapes, such as boxes, cylinders, pyramids, and cones. Often, these shapes are combined to create a design idea or something greater than the simple shapes they represent. These individual shapes can be modified and changed to create new geometric shapes or individual parts of a greater whole.

Using AutoCAD Commands to Modify Mass Elements

Common AutoCAD commands such as **MOVE**, **COPY**, **ROTATE**, **MIRROR**, and **STRETCH** can be used on mass elements. When you are using these commands, it is helpful to use the osnaps to snap to specific points on the mass elements. For example, if you are moving a pyramid shape from the midpoint of one side to a corner of a box, use the **Midpoint** and **Endpoint** osnaps accordingly.

Figure 25-22.

Mass elements include **Node** osnap locations at the bottom and top of the mass element shape.

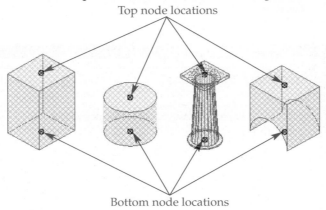

In addition to having the standard osnap points, mass elements include some specific node osnap locations, as shown in **Figure 25-22.** There is a node located at the bottom of the shape and one at the top centroid of the shape. Using the **Node** osnap on a mass element selects one of these points.

Using Grips to Modify Mass Elements

Mass elements can also be modified through the use of grips. Picking a mass element displays a series of grip boxes at vertices, insertion points, nodes, and center points. See **Figure 25-23.** As with other objects, picking a grip box enters the grip editing mode. The grip points selected can be stretched or used as base points for the grip edit **MOVE**, **SCALE**, **ROTATE**, and **MIRROR** commands.

Selecting a grip along the perimeter of a mass element and using the grip stretch mode adjusts the width or depth of the mass element. Selecting a **Height** grip at the top or bottom of the mass changes the height of the mass, and picking the **Location** grip

Figure 25-23.
Stretching the width, depth, and height of a mass element and moving the mass element location.

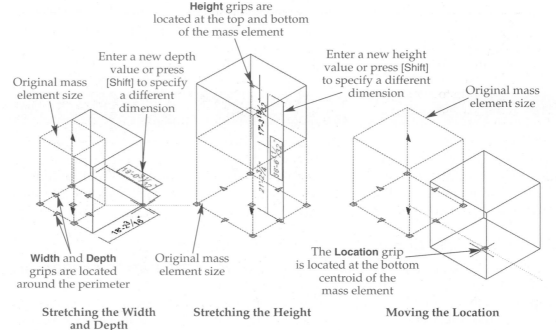

adjusts the location of the mass element. If the grip stretch dimensions are displayed, a new value can be entered for the highlighted dimension. Use the [Tab] key to toggle to a different dimension to enter a new value.

The standard grips mentioned above are available on all the mass element shapes, except the **Drape** and **Free Form** shapes. The **Drape** and **Free Form** mass element shapes include additional grips known as **Face** grips, which allow you to modify the faces, or surface locations, of the mass element. See **Figure 25-24.**

When a **Face** grip is selected to be modified, a tooltip is displayed indicating to press the [Ctrl] key to cycle through different grip editing modes for **Face** grips. These different modes allow you to move, push, and pull the face location selected. As the different modes are cycled through, the UCS changes to indicate the drawing plane within which the face can be moved. To cycle through the different face-editing options, select the **Face** grip to be modified once to display the tooltip and highlight the grip, and then pick the grip a second time to modify the face. As the face is being edited, press the [Ctrl] key to cycle through the different face-editing options.

Mass Element Modifying Tools

In addition to the standard AutoCAD and grip editing commands, mass elements include some mass element–specific tools. These tools can be accessed by selecting a mass element, right-clicking, and then selecting an option from the shortcut menu. The following section describes the tools specific to editing mass elements.

Using Boolean Commands

Similar to Slab objects, mass element shapes can be modified through the use of Boolean **MASSELEMENTUNION**, **MASSELEMENTSUBTRACT**, and **MASSELEMENTINTERSECT** commands. To join one or more mass elements together, the Boolean **MASSELEMENTUNION** command is used. To access this command, select a mass element to be joined, right-click, and pick **Boolean > Union**. When mass elements are joined, the mass element becomes a **Free Form** shape. To create the **Free Form** mass element in **Figure 25-25**, access the **MASSELEMENTUNION** command. When you are prompted, select the mass elements to be unioned. Press [Enter] when you are done. When you are asked if you want to erase the layout geometry, type Y, and press [Enter] to end the command.

Figure 25-24.
Picking a **Free Form** or **Drape** mass element will display **Face** grip boxes. Pick a **Face** grip to modify the surface face of the mass element.

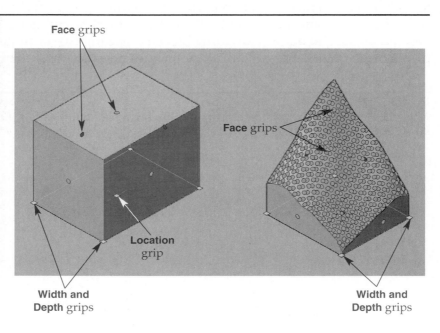

Face grips

Face grips

Location grip

Width and Depth grips

Width and Depth grips

Figure 25-25.
Mass elements can be joined together through the Boolean **MASSELEMENTUNION** command.

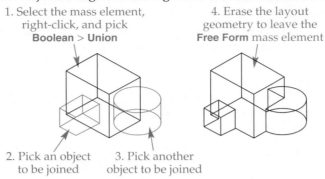

1. Select the mass element, right-click, and pick **Boolean > Union**

4. Erase the layout geometry to leave the **Free Form** mass element

2. Pick an object to be joined

3. Pick another object to be joined

Mass elements can also be subtracted from one another to create voids in different mass elements, creating complex shapes. To subtract one mass element from another, select the mass element to be subtracted from, right-click, and pick **Boolean > Subtract**. You are prompted to select objects to be subtracted. Pick any mass elements to be subtracted from the main mass element. To subtract the mass elements in Figure 25-26, access the **MASSELEMENTSUBTRACT** command. When you are prompted, select the mass elements to be subtracted. Press [Enter] when you are done. When you are asked if you want to erase the layout geometry, type Y, and press [Enter] to end the command.

The last type of Boolean operation available is the **MASSELEMENTINTERSECT** command. When two or more mass elements occupy the same common space, a new mass element can be created from the shared, or intersected, space. To intersect a mass element between two or more mass elements, select a mass element to be intersected with another mass element, right-click, and pick **Boolean > Intersect**. You are prompted to select objects to be intersected. To intersect the mass elements in Figure 25-27, access the **MASSELEMENTINTERSECT** command. When you are prompted, select the mass elements to be intersected. Press [Enter] when you are done. When you are asked if you want to erase the layout geometry, type Y, and press [Enter] to end the command.

Splitting Mass Elements

Another tool specific to mass elements is the **Split by Plane** tool. This tool is used to split a mass element into two parts. To use this tool, select the mass element to be split, right-click, and pick **Split by Plane** from the shortcut menu. The **Split by Plane** tool can be used to define a dividing plane by picking two or three points. By default, picking two points along the mass element divides the mass element into two parts

Figure 25-26.
Mass elements can be subtracted from another mass element through the Boolean **MASSELEMENTSUBTRACT** command.

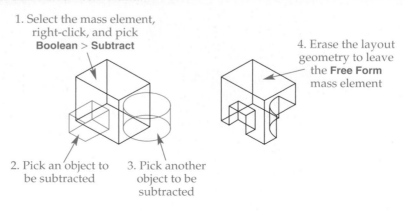

1. Select the mass element, right-click, and pick **Boolean > Subtract**

4. Erase the layout geometry to leave the **Free Form** mass element

2. Pick an object to be subtracted

3. Pick another object to be subtracted

Figure 25-27.
Mass elements can be created from the intersected, or shared, space between two or more mass elements by using the Boolean **MASSELEMENTINTERSECT** command.

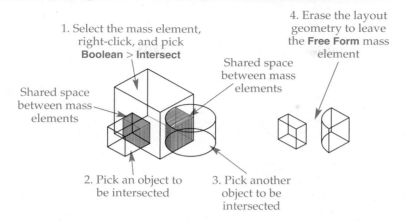

1. Select the mass element, right-click, and pick **Boolean > Intersect**

4. Erase the layout geometry to leave the **Free Form** mass element

Shared space between mass elements

Shared space between mass elements

2. Pick an object to be intersected

3. Pick another object to be intersected

and creates two extruded mass elements. A dividing plane can also be established by picking three points along the mass element to create a dividing plane. When the three-points option is used, two **Free Form** mass elements are created. To split the mass element in **Figure 25-28**, access the **MASSELEMENTDIVIDE** command. When you are prompted, pick a starting point and an ending point for the dividing plane.

Trimming Mass Elements

Mass elements can be trimmed, similar to carving away a slice from a cube of butter, to form complex mass elements. Similar to the **Split by Plane** tool, the mass element **Trim by Plane** tool uses two or three points to establish a trimming plane. Once the trim plane has been determined, you are prompted to pick the side of the mass element to be removed. After you pick the side to remove, the portion of the mass picked is removed, leaving the remaining mass element. This tool can be accessed by picking the mass element to be trimmed, right-clicking, and selecting **Trim by Plane**. To trim a portion of a mass element away using the three-point method of establishing a trimming plane, as shown in **Figure 25-29**, access the **MASSELEMENTTRIM** command. When you are prompted to specify the trim plane start point, type 3. Pick the first, second, and third points of the trimming plane. Pick the side of the mass element to remove when you are prompted to do so.

Figure 25-28.
The **Split by Plane** tool can be used to split a mass element into two parts.

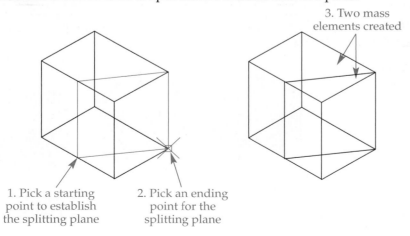

3. Two mass elements created

1. Pick a starting point to establish the splitting plane

2. Pick an ending point for the splitting plane

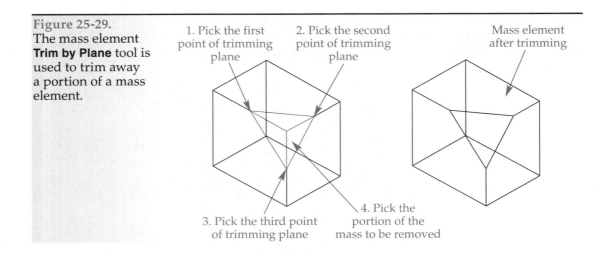

Figure 25-29.
The mass element **Trim by Plane** tool is used to trim away a portion of a mass element.

1. Pick the first point of trimming plane

2. Pick the second point of trimming plane

Mass element after trimming

3. Pick the third point of trimming plane

4. Pick the portion of the mass to be removed

Splitting Mass Element Faces

Occasionally, you might want to divide a face of a mass element in order to push or pull the face of the massing. Mass element faces can be divided into two separate faces so the free-form grips can be used to push or pull the faces into place. When a mass element face is divided, the mass element is automatically changed to a **Free Form** mass. To divide the faces of a mass element, pick the mass element to be modified, right-click, and then select **Split Face** from the shortcut menu. Once the option is entered, you are prompted to pick two points to split a face. To split the face shown in Figure 25-30, access the **MASSELEMENTFACEDIVIDE** command. When you are prompted, pick an edge or point on the face to be divided, and then pick another edge or point on the face to establish the dividing line. The mass element is converted to a **Free Form** mass. When you are prompted to select the first point on a face again, pick another point to divide another face or press [Enter] to end the command.

Joining Mass Element Faces

In addition to splitting faces, free-form faces can be joined together to form a single face. In order to use the **Join Faces** tool, the mass element being edited must be a **Free Form** shape. Select the **Free Form** mass element, right-click, and pick **Join Faces**. The valid edges between faces that can be joined are displayed in red. Pick the edges between the faces to be joined and press [Enter]. To join the faces in Figure 25-31, access the **MASSELEMENTFACEJOIN** command. When you are prompted, pick the edges of coplanar faces. After all the edges are found, pick another edge between two coplanar faces or press [Enter] to end the command.

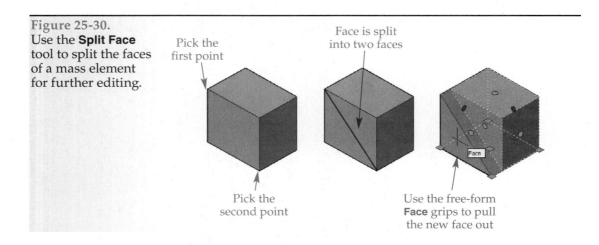

Figure 25-30.
Use the **Split Face** tool to split the faces of a mass element for further editing.

Pick the first point

Face is split into two faces

Pick the second point

Use the free-form **Face** grips to pull the new face out

Architectural Desktop and Its Applications

Figure 25-31.
The **Join Faces** tool is used to pick an edge between two faces that will be removed to join the faces together.

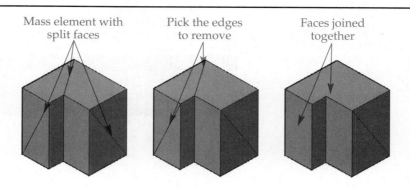

Mass element with split faces

Pick the edges to remove

Faces joined together

Using the Properties Palette to Modify Mass Elements

As mass elements are created, their properties can be adjusted before they are placed in the drawing. After mass elements have been placed into the drawing, they can be edited with AutoCAD commands, grip editing, and special mass element–editing tools. In addition to these tools, the **Properties** palette can be used to modify an existing mass element. See Figure 25-32.

General properties such as the description, layer, style, and shape can be modified. The **Description** property can be important when working with masses to help distinguish different portions of the building design. Type simple descriptions describing the elements' use—for example, Main Building, West Wing, Foyer, and Roof.

The **Dimensions** properties allow you to change the size of the elements by entering new values for the **Width**, **Depth**, **Height**, **Radius**, and **Rise** properties. The **Location** properties are also available for modification. An existing mass element can be given a new rotation angle or elevation location.

Editing Object Display

Like other AEC objects, mass elements include their own display system. By default, mass elements appear as 2D shapes in a Top view and as 3D shapes in an isometric view, an elevation view, or a perspective view. If mass elements have been created using the Standard style, a basic display configuration is set up that sets a cut plane in the Plan display representations, sets display components on and off, assigns colors, and sets other display properties. The individual display of a mass element can be overridden and assigned its own display properties, similar to other AEC objects.

Figure 25-32.
The **Properties** palette can be used to modify the properties of a mass element.

General properties

Dimensions properties

Location properties

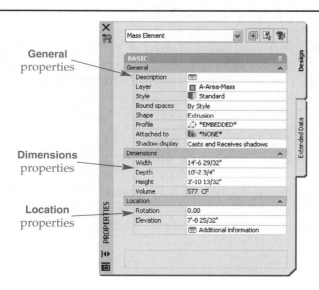

Figure 25-33.
The **Object Display** dialog box is used to edit the individual display of mass elements.

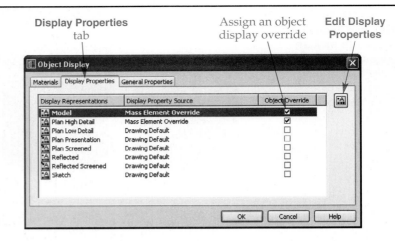

Display Properties tab — Assign an object display override — Edit Display Properties

To override the individual display for a mass element, select the mass element to modify, right-click, and pick **Edit Object Display...** from the shortcut menu. This displays the **Object Display** dialog box, shown in Figure 25-33. In the **Display Properties** tab, assign an object override for the display representation to be modified, and then pick the **Edit Display Properties** button to begin editing.

Exercise 25-3

Complete the Exercise on the Student CD.

Grouping the Mass Objects

The mass elements in a massing study are evaluated together as a group, which represents the building as a whole. During the development of the conceptual design, there might be areas needing to have holes or voids in the sides or top of the building. When the **HIDE** command is performed on the building, intersections between mass elements do not show up properly. Some of these issues can be addressed by using the Boolean commands on the mass elements, but then the mass elements are no longer individual pieces that can be modified during the schematic design phase. In this situation, the mass elements can be grouped together to form one object while maintaining their individuality.

The **MASSGROUP** command is used to group individual mass elements or other AEC objects together to form one object. Operations such as subtractions, additions, and intersections can then be performed on this one object, similar to Boolean operations, yet the individual objects will still be grouped together. Later, floors can be cut from the perimeter of the group of objects, and complex shapes can be formed in the development of the design.

Adding Mass Elements to a Mass Group

When a mass group is added to the drawing, you are prompted to select objects to be attached. Selecting any AEC object groups the objects together into a single object. The original objects are retained and can be edited at any time.

To add the mass group, pick the **Mass Group** tool in the **Massing** tool palette or **Design** > **Massing** > **Mass Group**. You are prompted to Select elements to attach:. Select any AEC objects that will be grouped together to form a single mass group. After selecting the objects to be grouped, you are prompted with Location:. The location is the placeholder location for the mass group. This placeholder contains grips when the mass group is selected, allowing you to add or detach objects to or from the mass group. Pick a location near the mass group so the grips can be accessed quickly later.

Pull-Down Menu
Design
  > Massing
    > Mass Group
Tool Palette
Massing

Mass Group

After picking the location point, the selected objects are grouped together to form a single mass group object. This object creates a "shrink-wrap" around all the objects added to the mass group. The individual objects appear to be removed from the drawing, but they are simply hidden as long as the objects are attached to the mass group. Picking the mass group will highlight the entire group and display a set of grips at the location point for the placeholder. See **Figure 25-34.**

Editing Mass Groups

The location grips include four different grips, as indicated in **Figure 25-34.** Pick the **Attach Elements** grip to add new objects to the mass group. Once this option is entered, you are prompted to Select elements to attach:. Select any additional mass elements or other AEC objects to be grouped into the mass group. Adding elements to a mass group can also be accomplished by selecting the mass group, right-clicking, and picking the **Attach Elements** option.

As the design progresses, you might find you no longer want or need a mass element within the mass group. This item can be detached from the mass group. To do this, select the mass group, and then pick the **Detach Elements** grip. This temporarily disables the mass group, displaying the original objects attached to the mass group. You are prompted to Select elements to detach:. Select any objects to be removed from the mass group. Press the [Enter] key when you are finished to hide the original objects and redisplay the mass group with the items detached. Detaching elements can also be accomplished by selecting the mass group, right-clicking, and picking the **Detach Elements** option.

The **Edit In Place** grip is used similar to other edit-in-place operations discussed throughout the book. Once the **Edit In Place** grip has been selected, the mass group is temporarily hidden, and all the individual elements attached to the group are displayed. The **In-Place Edit** toolbar is also displayed while you are editing the individual objects within the mass group. Make any changes to the objects attached to

Figure 25-34.
Once a mass group has been added, all the objects grouped together are grouped into a single object, which applies a "shrink-wrap" around the objects. Selecting the mass group displays the location placeholder grips.

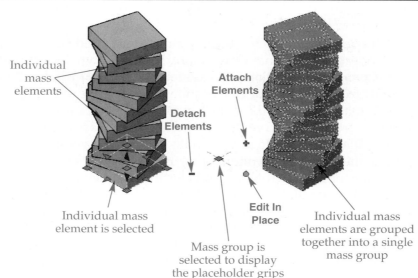

Individual mass elements

Attach Elements

Detach Elements

Edit In Place

Individual mass element is selected

Mass group is selected to display the placeholder grips

Individual mass elements are grouped together into a single mass group

the mass group, such as changing the size, changing the shape of a mass element, or moving the object to a new location. When you are finished, pick the **Save All Changes** button in the **In-Place Edit** toolbar, which was displayed when the grip was selected. This toolbar can also be accessed by picking the mass group, right-clicking, and then selecting the **Edit In Place** option.

In addition to the grip editing commands used to attach, detach, and edit in place, new mass elements can be added to the mass group without having to edit the mass group. When a new mass element is added, the **Attached to** property in the **Properties** palette becomes available, allowing you to attach the new mass element to a mass group in the list. When initially created, the mass group is arbitrarily assigned a name, which might consist of a series of letters and numbers. Select the group to which to attach the mass element, and the mass element is automatically added to the group. If a new mass element is being attached to a mass group, the **Operation** property becomes available and allows you to set one of the following operators: **Add**, **Subtract**, or **Intersect**. These affect how the new mass element will interact with other elements within the group. The **Add**, **Subtract**, and **Intersect** operators are discussed in greater depth later in this chapter.

NOTE | If multiple mass groups are added to the drawing, it might be difficult to determine to which group new elements should be attached. In this situation, selecting the **Pick mass group on screen** option in the **Attached to** property allows you to pick a mass group to which to add your new mass element. Additionally, mass groups, like mass elements, can be given a description. Select the mass group, and then enter a description for the mass group in the **Description** property in the **Properties** palette. When a new mass element is added, the **Attached to** property lists the mass groups with their descriptions. You can add as many mass groups into a drawing as required. You might want to enter descriptions when a design requires multiple mass groups that can be used independently.

Exercise
25-4   *Complete the Exercise on the Student CD.*

Mass Group Properties

Mass groups, like other objects, can be modified through the **Properties** palette. The properties for a mass group are broken down into three categories: **General**, **Dimensions**, and **Location**. The **General** category includes **Description**, **Layer**, and **Attached to** properties. For clarification with multiple mass groups, enter a description for each mass group in the drawing. Mass groups can also be attached to other mass groups to create other complex assemblies from mass group subassemblies.

The **Dimensions** category includes a read-only **Volume** property, so you can keep track of the amount of volume your conceptual design is occupying. The **Location** properties control the rotation and elevation of the mass group placeholder only. The **Additional information** property provides a worksheet of values for changing the insertion point location and rotation of the mass group placeholder instead of changing the text box entries in the **Properties** palette. Because the mass group is made up of individual elements, the elements control the rotation and elevation placement. Moving or rotating the mass group does not adjust the elements attached to it.

Mass Group Object Display

Because a mass group is an AEC object, it has the ability to be displayed differently, depending on your viewing direction. Mass groups do not include styles, so the display of the mass group cannot be controlled through a **Styles** dialog box. Instead, the mass group can be controlled by selecting the mass group, right-clicking, and selecting **Edit Object Display...** from the shortcut menu.

When the **Object Display** dialog box is displayed, select the display representation you want to modify. The common display representations are Plan and Model. Next, attach an object override to begin editing the display of the mass group.

When the display properties are adjusted, the mass group includes the entity and marker. The entity controls the display of the grouped masses, and the marker controls the display of the mass group placeholder. When you have finished adjusting the display properties for the mass group in the display representation you want to control, pick the **OK** button to return to the drawing screen.

Using the Model Explorer

When an idea is being conceptualized, masses and mass groups are used to create the massing study. Along with these tools, another tool known as the **Model Explorer** can be used to manipulate the way the objects interact with one another. The **MODELEXPLORER** command opens a separate window in Architectural Desktop, where the elements within a mass group can be adjusted, new elements can be added, and operators on the elements can be controlled.

After adding a mass group to the drawing and attaching elements, the **Model Explorer** can be used for fine-tuning your idea. The **Model Explorer** can be opened by picking **Design** > **Massing** > **Model Explorer...** from the pull-down menu. The **Model Explorer** window can also be accessed by selecting the mass group, right-clicking, and picking **Show Model Explorer...** from the shortcut menu. Once the option has been selected, the **Model Explorer** window is displayed in the drawing screen. See **Figure 25-35**. The **Model Explorer** displays a tree along the left side, listing the open drawings in Architectural Desktop, the mass groups in each drawing, and the objects attached to the mass group. The right side of the window displays the selected object from the tree list.

Pull-Down Menu
Design
> Massing
> Model
Explorer...

Model Explorer Menus

Initially, two toolbars and a series of pull-down menus are displayed in the **Model Explorer** window. The top toolbar is the **Model Explorer Object Viewer Toolbar**. This toolbar controls how the object selected in the tree view is displayed in the preview pane. The first drop-down list in the toolbar allows you to control whether the preview is displayed in a **3D Hidden**, **3D Wireframe**, **Conceptual**, or **Realistic** visual style. The buttons control zooming and panning. The drop-down list at the end of the toolbar includes predefined viewing directions, which can be set for the preview pane. See **Figure 25-36**.

The **Model Explorer Toolbar** allows you to modify the elements within the tree structure and add new mass elements or mass groups. Additional tools can be used to make copies of mass elements within a group and paste them into a different mass group. See **Figure 25-37**.

Figure 25-35.
The **Model Explorer** is a separate window allowing you to manipulate the elements within a mass group.

The **Model Explorer Toolbar** includes tools to manipulate the mass group

The **Model Explorer Object Viewer Toolbar** controls the display in the preview pane

Open drawing in Architectural Desktop

Mass group icon in the drawing

Mass group description

List of elements attached to the mass group

Mass element description

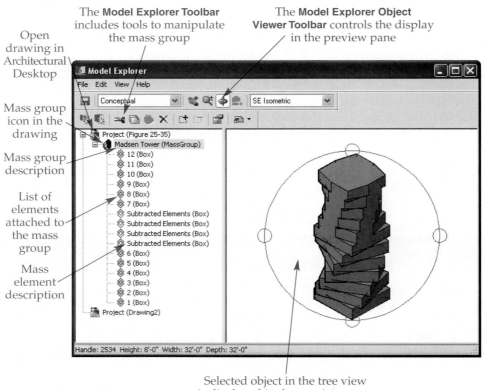

Selected object in the tree view is displayed in the preview pane; in this case, the mass group is selected, so the entire group is displayed

Figure 25-36.
The buttons in the **Model Explorer Object Viewer Toolbar** control the display of the preview pane.

This drop-down list includes options for displaying your model in the preview pane

Allows you to zoom closer to or away from the objects in the preview pane

Adjusts the perspective distance in the preview pane

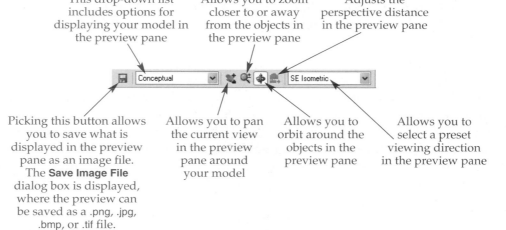

Picking this button allows you to save what is displayed in the preview pane as an image file. The **Save Image File** dialog box is displayed, where the preview can be saved as a .png, .jpg, .bmp, or .tif file.

Allows you to pan the current view in the preview pane around your model

Allows you to orbit around the objects in the preview pane

Allows you to select a preset viewing direction in the preview pane

The pull-down menus duplicate the tools found in the toolbars and allow you to control all the parameters of the elements within a mass group. Additionally, right-clicking over an object in the tree view list displays a shortcut menu specific to the object. See **Figure 25-38.** Right-clicking in the preview pane provides a shortcut menu controlling the display in the preview pane.

Figure 25-37.

The **Model Explorer Toolbar** includes tools for modifying elements in a mass group and adding new mass elements or groups to the drawing.

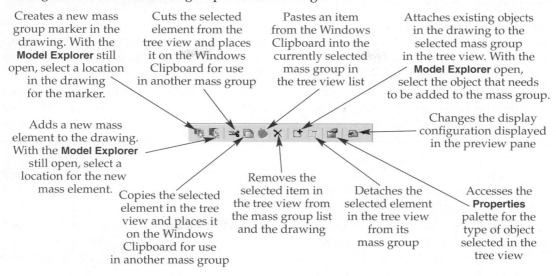

Creates a new mass group marker in the drawing. With the **Model Explorer** still open, select a location in the drawing for the marker.

Cuts the selected element from the tree view and places it on the Windows Clipboard for use in another mass group

Pastes an item from the Windows Clipboard into the currently selected mass group in the tree view list

Attaches existing objects in the drawing to the selected mass group in the tree view. With the **Model Explorer** open, select the object that needs to be added to the mass group.

Adds a new mass element to the drawing. With the **Model Explorer** still open, select a location for the new mass element.

Copies the selected element in the tree view and places it on the Windows Clipboard for use in another mass group

Removes the selected item in the tree view from the mass group list and the drawing

Detaches the selected element in the tree view from its mass group

Changes the display configuration displayed in the preview pane

Accesses the **Properties** palette for the type of object selected in the tree view

Figure 25-38.
Right-clicking on top of an object in the tree view list displays a menu specific to the selected object. Right-clicking in the preview pane provides a menu list of items to control the display.

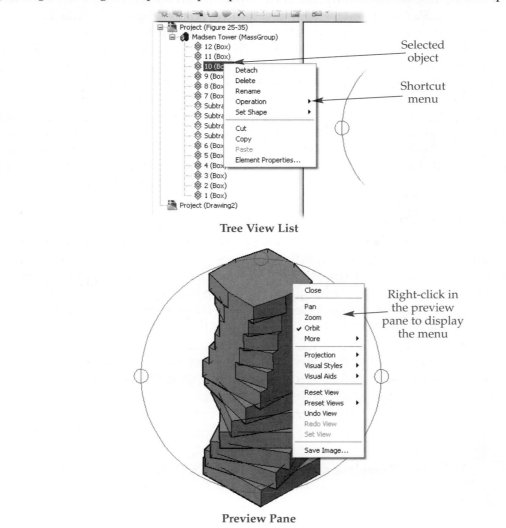

Selected object

Shortcut menu

Tree View List

Right-click in the preview pane to display the menu

Preview Pane

Working with the Tree View

The tree view is the most important part of the **Model Explorer** window, because this is the area where the elements are arranged and modified to create a conceptual design. The tree view list displays an icon representing each drawing open in Architectural Desktop. See **Figure 25-35**. Below each drawing icon is a mass group icon, if the drawing includes a mass group. If the mass group was given a description in the **Properties** palette, the description appears beside the icon.

Below each mass group icon is a list of the objects grouped within the mass group. As with the mass groups, if the object has a description, it appears beside the icon. The objects in the tree view are placed in a hierarchical list. The element listed above another element is generated first in the drawing. This becomes important as operators are configured for the elements.

Beside each object is an icon representing its operational status. The icons represent additive, subtractive, and intersection operators. Each of these operators is described as follows:

- **Additive.** This icon indicates that the element is an additive object and is added to the object listed above it in the tree view list. See **Figure 25-39**.
- **Subtractive.** This icon indicates that the element is a subtractive object and subtracts itself from the element listed above it in the tree view list.
- **Intersect.** This icon indicates that the element is an intersection object. This type of operator creates a new object, based on the geometric space this element and the element above it in the tree view list share.

Dragging one element in the list above another can reorganize the order in which elements appear and interact with one another. For example, suppose you have a subtracting element listed first in the tree view. This element is created before the additive elements. Therefore, it subtracts itself out of the mass group before the additive elements create the group, as in **Figure 25-40**. To overcome this problem, drag an element in the list above the subtraction element. Thus, the additive element is created first, and then the subtractive element subtracts itself from this additive element.

To drag an element in the list, press and hold the left mouse button on the desired element. Drag the mouse until the element is above or on top of the element in the list needing to be created after the element being dragged. This allows you to reorganize the hierarchical list to create a list of element operators that work with one another to form a new design.

Changing the Element Operator

The operator used on an element can be changed at any time during the process of designing, either from the **Properties** palette when editing the mass group in place or from within the **Model Explorer**. Changing the operator will affect how the mass group is created. In the tree view, right-click on top of the element in the tree view list whose operator is to be changed. See **Figure 25-41**. The shortcut menu is displayed. Move to the **Operation** shortcut menu and change the operator being used.

NOTE Additionally, the operation of a mass element can be modified by selecting the mass element when in **Edit In Place** mode and changing the operation to the desired operator.

Exercise
25-5   *Complete the Exercise on the Student CD.*

Figure 25-39.
The **Additive** operator joins two objects together. The **Subtractive** operator subtracts one element from another. The **Intersect** operator produces an object from the intersection of two elements.

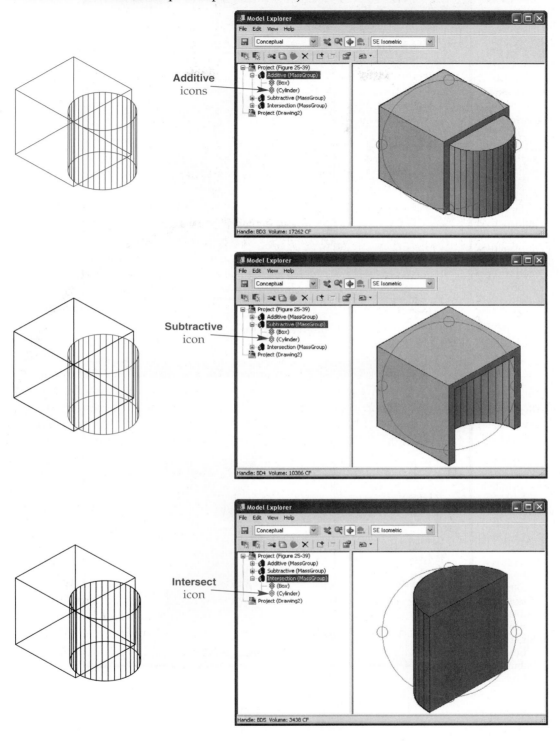

Once the mass model has been completed, it can be used in conjunction with other mass models referenced together for design studies and approvals. For example, see the model displayed in **Figure 25-42.** A conceptual design of a proposed building in Portland, Oregon is placed with other mass models of the city to form a design study drawing.

Figure 25-40.
Rearranging the elements in the tree view list can result in different designs.

Order in
which the
elements
were created

1. Additive
 box
2. Additive
 box
3. Subtractive
 box
4. Subtractive
 box
5. Subtractive
 box
6. Subtractive
 box
7. Additive
 box
8. Additive
 box...

The four subtractive boxes subtract
themselves from the 1 and 2 boxes only

Order in
which the
elements
were
rearranged

10. ...Additive
 box
11. Additive
 box
12. Additive
 box
13. Additive
 box
14. Subtractive
 box
15. Subtractive
 box
16. Subtractive
 box
17. Subtractive
 box

The four subtractive boxes now subtract
the edges of each of the additive boxes

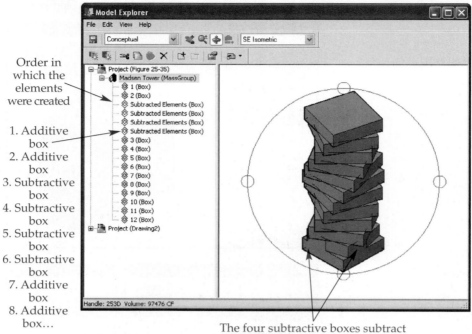

Figure 25-41.
The shortcut menu in the tree view allows you to change the operator of a selected object.

Right-click over an object

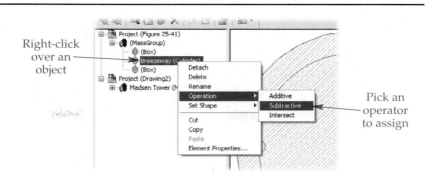

Pick an operator to assign

Figure 25-42.
Groups of mass models are placed together to form a larger study of a proposed building. Drawing Courtesy SERA Architects Inc., Portland, OR.

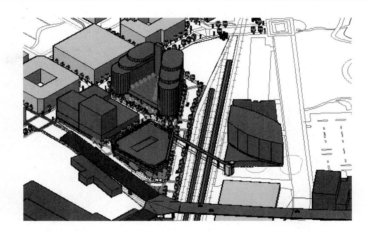

Creating Floor Plates

After the conceptual design has been completed, the massing drawing can be moved forward toward the design development phase. Before this can be done, the mass model (either mass groups or Booleaned mass elements) needs to be sliced into *floor plates* representing each floor of the building. The **Slice** tool found in the **Massing** tool palette is used to generate floor slices from the edges of the mass model. Before slicing the floors, you need to determine how many floors to cut into the mass model and the distance between floors.

Generating Slices

To add floor slices to the drawing, pick the **Slice** tool in the **Massing** tool palette or **Design > Massing > Slice Floorplates**. When a slice is added to the drawing, a slice marker is drawn, representing each elevation of the floor, as shown in **Figure 25-43**. During the process of adding a slice marker, you are prompted for the first and second corners. These are the corners of the slice marker. You do not need to wrap the slice marker around the mass model. Instead, pick two corner points off to the side of the mass model. This marker is then used as a placeholder for slices applied to the mass model and represent the actual elevation height where floors will be added into the building. The slices can be initially started at the 0'-0" elevation or any other desired elevation height in either a positive or negative direction from 0'-0". To add a slice and set the distance in elevation between slices and floors for the drawing in **Figure 25-44**, access the **AECSLICECREATE** command. When you are prompted, enter the total

Pull-Down Menu
Design
 > Massing
  > Slice
   Floorplates

Tool Palette
Massing

Slice

Figure 25-43.
The slice marker is similar to the mass group marker. When the **AECSLICECREATE** command is run, the marker is placed by picking two corners of a box and determining the number of and distance between floors.

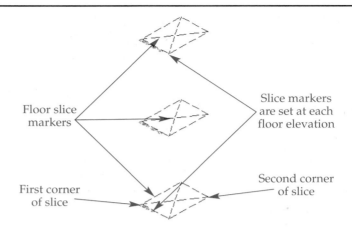

Floor slice markers

Slice markers are set at each floor elevation

First corner of slice

Second corner of slice

Figure 25-44.
Slice markers have been added to the drawing with a spacing of 12'-0" between slices and floors.

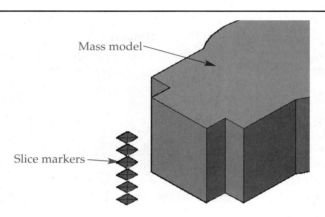

Mass model

Slice markers

number of floors, or slices, desired. Select a point for the first corner of the marker when you are prompted to do so. Select a point for the second corner of the marker. Do not wrap the marker around the mass model. When you are prompted for the rotation, press [Enter] to accept the default value of 0.00. Enter the first floor elevation and the distance between floors when you are prompted to do so. Press [Enter] to end the command.

NOTE

When you are placing the slice markers, it is a good idea to place these away from the model so they do not interfere with the model slice that will be attached to the mass model. Placing them away from the model also makes it easier to select them when modifying them.

PROFESSIONAL TIP

The slice markers are placed in the current XY drawing plane. In order to properly represent floors of a building, the slice markers need to be oriented horizontally in your model. Use the **UCS** command and reset the **World** UCS, or change to a Top view before changing to an isometric view to set the UCS to the top UCS plane.

Architectural Desktop and Its Applications

Attaching the Slices to the Mass Group

After adding the slice markers to the drawing, the slices need to be attached to the mass model in order to cut the floor plates. Select the slice markers, right-click, and pick **Attach Objects** from the shortcut menu. After entering the **AECSLICEATTACH** command, you are prompted to Select elements to attach:. Select the mass group or element objects.

When an object is selected, the slice draws a perimeter around each object it finds. Attaching the slice to a mass group causes the perimeter of the building to be generated at each floor level. If you attach the slice to individual mass elements, a perimeter is drawn around each mass element. If the mass element has had other mass elements Booleaned to it, however, the slice follows the perimeter of the mass element. When you have finished selecting the mass groups and elements to which the slice is attached, press the [Enter] key to end the command. The slices draw a perimeter outline around the mass group. See **Figure 25-45**.

If a slice is not supposed to have cut through the mass group, it can be removed or detached from the massing with the **Detach Objects** option. Select the slice to be removed from the mass group, right-click, and pick **Detach Objects**. You are prompted to Select elements to detach:. Pick the mass group or element the slice is attached to in order to detach the slice from the mass model.

Adjusting the Slice Elevation

The elevations of individual floor plates can be adjusted after the slices have been placed. For example, suppose a series of slices is added to a mass group. The majority of the slices maintain a distance of 12'-0", but a few slices have a distance of 14'-0" between the floors. To adjust the slice elevation, select the slice marker, right-click, and pick **Set Elevation**.

After selecting this option, type a new elevation at the New elevation: prompt. The slice is repositioned in elevation, and the perimeter is adjusted as the mass model designates. If multiple slices are selected to adjust their elevations, entering a new elevation places all the selected slices at the same elevation. At this point, design changes can still be made to the mass elements and group. As long as the slices are still attached to the mass group, they are updated as the perimeter of the building changes.

Exercise 25-6   **Complete the Exercise on the Student CD.**

Figure 25-45.
The slice markers have been attached to the mass group, generating the perimeter floor levels.

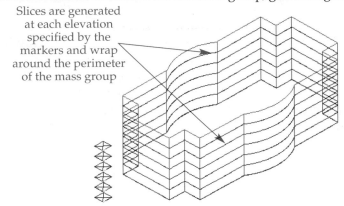

Slices are generated at each elevation specified by the markers and wrap around the perimeter of the mass group

Creating Polylines from Slices

Slices can be converted into polylines, which in turn, can be converted into walls, curtain walls, floor slabs, and roofs for the floor plans. To convert a slice into a polyline, select the slice, right-click, and pick **Convert To Polyline** in the shortcut menu. The slice around the mass group is converted into a polyline representing the perimeter of the building. This polyline can now be converted to walls, slabs, curtain walls, and roofs. As the slice is no longer needed, the A-Area-Mass-Slce layer can be frozen to freeze the display of the slice marker and perimeter slice.

Exporting the Slices to Separate Drawings

After the floor slices have been converted to polylines, they can be used to generate walls, curtain walls, floor slabs, and roofs. Once the polylines have been generated, it is best to move the polylines and slices to individual constructs or drawings representing each floor of the building. The best method of exporting each polyline slice to a different drawing file is to use **Copy** and **Paste** tools. These tools allow you to copy a single slice to the Windows Clipboard so it can be pasted into a new template drawing or construct, where the floor plans can be developed.

To create the slices as individual drawing files, select the first-floor polyline slice, right-click, and pick **Clipboard > Copy with Base Point**. You are prompted to Specify base point:. Use the **Insertion** osnap to snap to the insertion point of the first-floor slice marker. This copies the polyline slice to the Windows Clipboard.

Start a new drawing using a template or open the construct drawing for the desired floor, right-click, and pick **Clipboard > Paste**. You are prompted to Specify insertion point:. Type the coordinates 0,0,0. The polyline slice is copied from the massing drawing and pasted to the new drawing. Save the file.

Repeat the same process for each polyline slice in the massing drawing, and paste the subsequent polyline slices into new template drawings or construct drawings (one per slice), using the same 0,0,0 coordinates. This process creates individual drawings with polyline slices reflecting the shape of the building at each floor level. The slices can now be converted into walls, curtain walls, floor slabs, and roofs.

 Exercise 25-7   **Complete the Exercise on the Student CD.**

Chapter Test

Answer the following questions. Write your answers on a separate sheet of paper or complete the electronic chapter test on the Student CD.

1. Define *massing study*.
2. Define and describe *mass elements*.
3. Define *free form mass element*.
4. What does the **Arch** mass element create?
5. Describe the shape of the **Barrel Vault** mass element.
6. Identify the shape the **Box** mass element creates.
7. What shape do you get from the **Cone** mass element?
8. Describe the shape of the **Dome** mass element.
9. Identify the shape the **Gable** mass element creates.
10. What does the **Isosceles Triangle** mass element create?
11. Describe the shape of the **Pyramid** mass element.
12. What shape do you get from the **Right Triangle** mass element?
13. Identify the shape the **Sphere** mass element creates.
14. Explain the basic function of the **Extrusion** mass element.
15. Briefly discuss the shape the **Revolution** mass element creates.
16. Explain the function of the **LOFT** command.
17. With regard to grips, what happens when you select a mass element?
18. Explain how to cycle through different grip editing modes.
19. What are floor plates?
20. Explain the function and use of a slice marker.

Chapter Projects

Use the techniques covered in this chapter to create the following drawings.

1. Draw the figure below, given the following criteria:
   A. Start a new drawing using one of the Aec Model templates.
   B. Create the following objects using mass elements. Use your own dimensional sizes.
   C. Combine the elements into a mass group.
   D. Use the **Model Explorer** as needed to adjust the mass element operators and reorder the elements within the mass group.
   E. Save the drawing as P25-1-Mass.dwg.

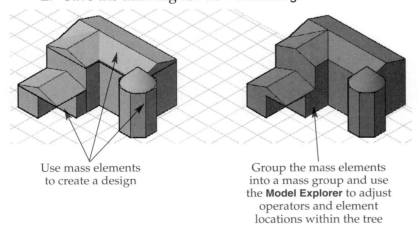

Use mass elements to create a design

Group the mass elements into a mass group and use the **Model Explorer** to adjust operators and element locations within the tree

2. Draw the figure below, given the following criteria:
   A. Start a new drawing using one of the Aec Model templates.
   B. Create the following objects using mass elements. Use your own dimensional sizes.
   C. Combine the elements into a mass group.
   D. Use the **Model Explorer** as needed to adjust the mass element operators and reorder the elements within the mass group.
   E. Save the drawing as P25-2-Mass.dwg.

Create Mass Elements **Add Mass Elements into a Mass Group**

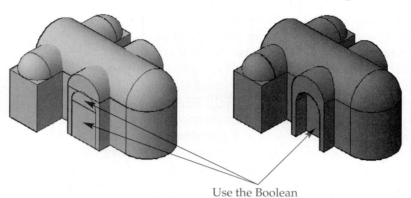

Use the Boolean
MASSELEMENTSUBTRACT
command to subtract the barrel
vault and box from the main mass

Architectural Desktop and Its Applications

3. Draw the figure below, given the following criteria:
   A. Start a new drawing using one of the Aec Model templates.
   B. Create the following objects using mass elements.
   C. Use the **Doric** mass element shape found in the **Shape** drop-down list in the **Properties** palette when you are adding mass elements to create the columns. Use your own dimensional sizes.
   D. Use the Boolean **MASSELEMENTUNION** command to join the parts together as indicated and the Boolean **MASSELEMENTSUBTRACT** command to subtract the barrel vaults from the overall masses.
   E. Copy the mass with the railing and place it around the mass without a railing.
   F. Combine the elements into a mass group.
   G. Create a new marble material.
   H. Use the **Edit Object Display...** option to assign the material to the mass group.
   I. Save the drawing as P25-3-Mass.dwg.

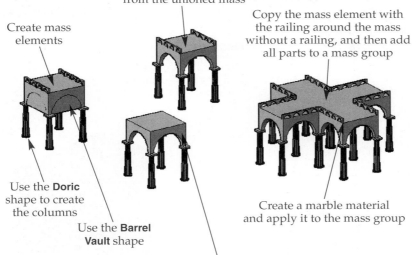

Use the Boolean **MASSELEMENTUNION** command to join the mass elements together and the Boolean **MASSELEMENTSUBTRACT** command to subtract the barrel vaults from the unioned mass

Create mass elements

Copy the mass element with the railing around the mass without a railing, and then add all parts to a mass group

Use the **Doric** shape to create the columns

Use the **Barrel Vault** shape

Create a marble material and apply it to the mass group

Use the Boolean **MASSELEMENTUNION** command to join the mass elements together and the Boolean **MASSELEMENTSUBTRACT** command to subtract the barrel vaults from the unioned mass

Chapter 25 Projects

4. Draw the figure below, given the following criteria:
   A. Start a new drawing using one of the Aec Model templates.
   B. Create a mass element style named Brick. Assign the Masonry.Unit Masonry. Brick.Modular material to the style.
   C. Create a mass element style named Firebrick. Assign the Masonry.Unit Masonry. Brick.Modular.Stacked.Grey material to the style.
   D. Add a **Box** mass element, 5'-0" × 2'-10" × 8'-0" high, to represent the overall shape of the fireplace. Use the Brick style.
   E. Draw a polyline for the firebox opening in the fireplace.
   F. Convert the polyline into a mass element with a height of 2'-0".
   G. Use the **Properties** palette to adjust the **Elevation** of the opening mass to be 18".
   H. Use the Boolean **Subtract** function to subtract the opening from the fireplace.
   I. Draw a polyline around the firebrick on the inside of the fireplace.
   J. Convert the polyline to a 2'-0"–tall mass element. Change the style to Firebrick, and adjust the **Elevation** to be 18".
   K. Use mass element–modifying tools, such as Boolean commands, **Split by Plane**, **Trim by Plane**, **Split Face**, and **Join Faces**, to edit the fireplace mass to create a hearth and shelf.
   L. Use the **Face** grips to push and pull the faces of the free-form fireplace mass element into shape.
   M. Save the drawing as P25-4-Mass.dwg.

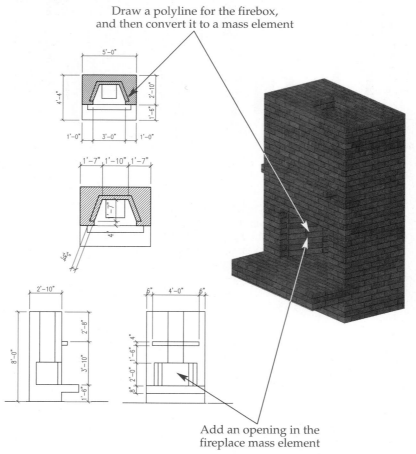

Draw a polyline for the firebox, and then convert it to a mass element

Add an opening in the fireplace mass element

Architectural Desktop and Its Applications

5. Draw the figure below, given the following criteria:
   A. Start a new drawing using one of the Aec Model templates.
   B. Create the following figure using mass elements. Use any mass element shapes to create the model. Use the basic dimensions provided for an idea of the width, depth, and height of the overall building. Use your own dimensional values for other sizes.
   C. Combine the elements into a mass group.
   D. Add four slices spaced 10'-0" apart.
   E. Save the drawing as P25-5-Mass.dwg.

Create individual mass elements to form the design idea, and then mass them together using a mass group

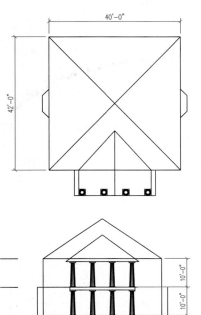

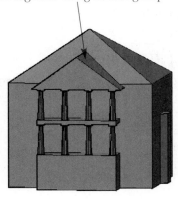

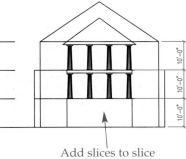

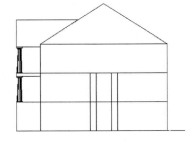

Add slices to slice the mass group

6. Draw the figure below, given the following criteria:
   A. Start a new drawing using one of the Aec Model templates.
   B. Create the following figure using mass elements. Use any mass element shapes to create the model. Use the basic dimensions provided for an idea of the width, depth, and height of the overall building. Use your own dimensional values for other sizes.
   C. Combine the elements into a mass group.
   D. Add thirteen slices spaced 13'-0" apart.
   E. Save the drawing as P25-6-Mass.dwg.

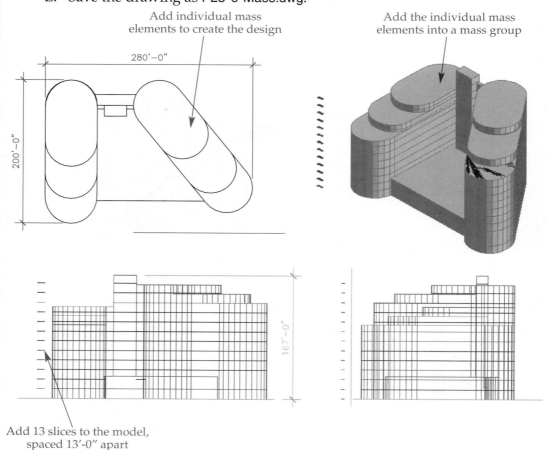

Add individual mass elements to create the design

Add the individual mass elements into a mass group

280'-0"

200'-0"

167'-0"

Add 13 slices to the model, spaced 13'-0" apart

Drawing Courtesy SERA Architects Inc., Portland, OR

7. Draw the figure below, given the following criteria:
    A. Start a new drawing using one of the Aec Model templates.
    B. Create the following figure using mass elements. Use any mass element shapes to create the model. Use the basic dimensions provided for an idea of the width, depth, and height of the overall building. Use your own dimensional values for other sizes.
    C. Use mass element–modifying tools, such as Boolean commands, **Split by Plane**, **Trim by Plane**, **Split Face**, and **Join Faces**, as needed to create custom shapes.
    F. Save the drawing as P25-7-Mass.dwg.

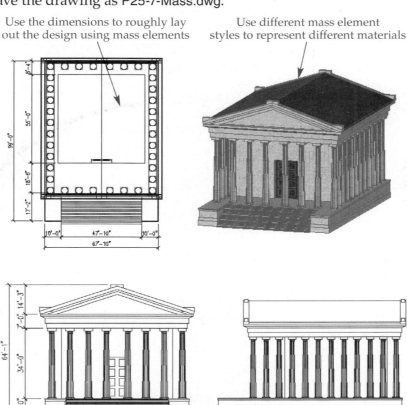

Use the dimensions to roughly lay out the design using mass elements

Use different mass element styles to represent different materials

The home page of the AECCafé Web site is www.aeccafe.com. This Web site offers AEC product news, job listings, company presentations, technical papers, case studies, downloads, book reviews, and newsgroups.

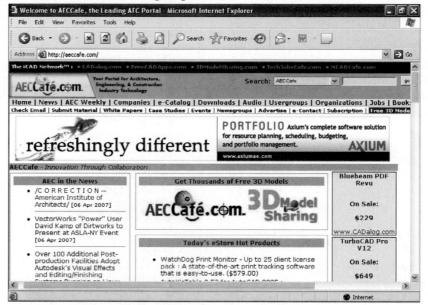

Architectural Desktop and Its Applications

Index

Architectural Desktop and Its Applications